1992

This book belongs to:

_____

_____

If found, please return to, or notify, the above.

CONSTITUTIONAL
RIGHTS
OF
PRISONERS

FOURTH EDITION

JOHN W. PALMER, J.D.
PROFESSOR OF LAW
CAPITAL UNIVERSITY LAW CENTER

anderson publishing co.
2035 reading road
cincinnati, ohio 45202
(513) 421-4142

This book is dedicated to my wife, Caryl, sons, Scott and Stephen,
and daughter, Cristy Ann.

CONSTITUTIONAL RIGHTS OF PRISONERS, Fourth Edition

Copyright © 1973 by The W.H. Anderson Company
Copyright © 1977, 1985, 1991 by Anderson Publishing Co./Cincinnati, OH

ISBN 0-87084-692-2

Library of Congress Catalog Number 90-82311

Kelly Humble *Managing Editor*   *Project Editor* Elisabeth Roszmann

PREFACE TO THE FIRST EDITION

Never before in the history of corrections have correctional staffs and administrators faced legal challenges to their actions as they do today. The number of suits filed in both state and federal courts seeking monetary damages and equitable relief will soon number in the thousands. Some wardens have claims amounting to millions of dollars filed in court against them.

There are many reasons for the deluge of legal actions. Filing fees, court costs, fear of malicious prosecution actions and cost of legal counsel do not act as a deterrent to inmates, the vast majority of whom are indigent. In effect, the taxpayers subsidize these legal actions.

Further, increasing numbers of activist lawyers are turning to corrections and the courts as vehicles to institute their concepts of social reform now that the Vietnam war is in its terminal stage. Some would use the courts as the vehicle to destroy the existing social order. Only too often these lawyers seek out clients and issues rather than observing the traditional legal ethic of lawyers only representing clients in litigation after a dispute has arisen.

Can correctional staffs and administrators withstand the pressure? There are many reasons why protracted litigation can be counterproductive to the correctional process. First, due to liberalized rules of discovery in both state and federal courts, correctional staff can find themselves inundated with depositions, interrogatories, motions to produce, and other fact-finding methods. Overworked staff can find themselves spending the bulk of their time preparing for litigation rather than working with inmates toward their rehabilitation. Morale suffers when inmates file spurious claims, asking for millions of dollars in damages for alleged injuries suffered. It becomes a game with some inmates as to who can add more zero's to the damage figure. Many states do not provide free counsel to their employees, except for those executives at the cabinet level and above. Further, when provided, the attorneys are on the state payroll. A warden, or his family who looks to him for financial security, does not feel too confident when represented by a young assistant Attorney General one year out of law school. Also, the interests of state political leaders in settling a law suit can conflict with the interests of an individual defendant.

Meaningful reform in a correctional system is brought about as a result of legislation and administrative rule-making, *i.e.*, the political process. Judicial decisions themselves may lead to administrative changes, but they do not themselves result in broad-based reform. One can only speculate as to whether correctional litigation in the past decade has encouraged, or retarded administrative reform. Since so much time and energy is devoted toward litigation within correctional systems, one can again only speculate as to what could have been accomplished if that effort had been directed toward more direct rehabilitative ends.

Speculation aside, litigation is here to stay. This book is an attempt to provide the people who are involved or will become involved in the correctional process with a basic introduction into this emerging field of law, the rights of prisoners. It is not intended to be a scholarly analysis of the many cases in this field. It is not aimed at the law student. Rather it is hoped that the book will serve as a useful guide and reference manual for those actively involved in the correctional process.

The author serves as a consultant to the Ohio Department of Rehabilitation and Correction, and has during the past two years, used the substance of the book in seminar discussions with various members of the Ohio correctional system, from correctional officers to the Director. Staff personnel have found it to be useful and comprehendible.

We must realize that the Supreme Court of the United States is the final interpreter of the Federal Constitution. Unfortunately, there are few Supreme Court decisions in the field of correctional law. Consequently, new law will constantly emerge as cases work their way up through the judicial system.

The judicial cases cited in this book tell only a small part of the correctional story. Statutes and administrative rules often far exceed constitutional minimums. As an example, in the summer of 1971, Ohio adopted an administrative policy which abolished mail censorship of first class letters. This decision was made by an enlightened administration, not because it was legally required, but because the administration felt it to be right, and to be a useful tool in the rehabilitative process. Ohio is again currently issuing sweeping administrative rules which should far exceed constitutional minimums.

The role of legislative and administrative rule-making must be left to another book. The reader is only cautioned here that the cases and decisions used in this book reflect, primarily, past history —past practices which have either been constitutionally approved or rejected by the courts.

Part I, Chapter 1, of the book gives the reader a basic introduction into the legal system—hopefully, a perspective through which the individual cases, and their effect on local practices, can be measured. Chapters 2 through 8 deal with the substantive law in several critical areas. Chapter 9 outlines the remedies available to a successful plaintiff or the liabilities to which an unsuccessful defendant may be subjected. It, perhaps, should be the most interesting chapter for the correctional worker.

Part II of the book contains leading decisions decided by the courts. Cases were selected not only for their importance, but also for the policies or judicial thinking that is represented. In any case, the facts are of critical importance. "Bad facts make bad law." If the facts are exceptionally bad—often worse than appears in print—a judge will stretch and strain precedent in order to grant appropriate relief. Again, the facts of a case are critical in understanding why the court reached the decision it did. For this reason, the facts of the cases are included in depth.

Appreciation is extended to Deborah Edmonston, Bill Eachus, Michael Velotta, Tom Young, research assistants; Miss Marie Deweese, typist; and above all to members of the Ohio Department of Rehabilitations and Corrections, Director Bennet J. Cooper, former Assistant Commissioner, M. J. Koloski, Martha Wheeler, Suprintendent of the Women's Reformatory and President of the American Correctional Association, and the Committee on Correctional Law composed of Warden Harold Cardwell and Superintendents E.B. Haskins and P. Perini in particular, without whose support and encouragement this book could not have been possible.

December 1, 1972   JOHN W. PALMER
Columbus, Ohio

PREFACE TO THE FOURTH EDITION

The Fourth Edition contains all of the significant United States Supreme Court cases involving prisoners' rights through January, 1990.

The past five years have been significantly affected by the conservative nature of the United States Supreme Court, and its policy of returning the running of America's jails and prisons from the federal courts to the administrators.

The Third Edition left off with *Procunier v. Martinez*, which described the principles that framed judicial analysis of prisoners' constitutional claims.

The first of these principles is that federal courts must recognize the valid constitutional claims of prison inmates. Prison walls do not form a barrier separating prison inmates from the protections of the Constitution.

A second principle was the recognition that courts are ill-equipped to deal with the increasingly urgent problems of prison administration and reform. The Court acknowledged that the problems of prisons in America are complex and intractable, and, more to the point, they are not readily susceptible of resolution by judicial decree. It was further recognized that the running of a prison is an inordinately difficult undertaking that requires expertise, planning, and the commitment of resources, all of which are peculiarly within the province of the legislative and executive branches of government. It became obvious to a majority of the Justices that prison administration was a task that has been committed to the responsibility of those branches, and separation of powers concerns counselled a policy of judicial restraint. Where a state penal system is involved, federal courts have additional reason to accord deference to the appropriate prison authorities.

The Supreme Court's task was to formulate a standard of review for prisoners' constitutional claims that was resposive both to the policy of judicial regarding prisoner complaints and to the need to protect the constitutional rights of prisoners.

In the cases following *Martinez*, the Supreme Court addressed many questions of prisoners rights. *Pell v. Procunier* involved a constitutional challenge to a prison regulation prohibiting face-to-face media interviews with individual inmates. The Court rejected the inmate's First Amendment challenge to the ban on media interviews, noting that judgments regarding prison security were peculiarly within the province and professional expertise of corrections officials, and, in the absence of substantial evidence to indicate that the officials have exaggerated their response to these considerations, courts should ordinarily defer to their expert judgment in such matters.

In *Jones v. North Carolina Prisoners' Union*, the prisoners' constitutional challenge was rejected, because the administrative action was rationally related to the reasonable, indeed to the central, objectives of prison administration.

Bell v. Wolfish upheld restrictions on pre-trial detainees, because the restrictions were a rational response to a clear security problem. Because there was no evidence that officials had exaggerated their response to the security problem, the Court held that the considered judgment of these experts must control.

In *Block v. Rutherford*, a ban on contact visits was upheld on the ground that responsible, experienced administrators had determined, in their sound discretion, that such visits would jeopardize the security of the facility, and the regulation was reasonably related to these security concerns.

Finally, in *Thornburgh v. Abbott*, the Court held that regulations that affect First Amendment rights are valid if they are reasonably related to legitimate penological interests. Prison officials are given due considerable deference in regulating the delicate balance between prison order and security and the legitimate demands of "outsiders" who seek to enter the prison environment. The less deferential standard articulated in *Martinez* was overruled in this regard.

In these five "prisoners' rights" cases the Court inquired whether a prison regulation that burdens fundamental rights is "reasonably related" to legitimate penological objective, or whether it represents an "exaggerated response" to those concerns. The present state of the law is that when a prison regulation impinges on inmates' constitutional rights, the regulation is valid if it is reasonably related to legitimate penological interests.

Such a standard became necessary, in the view of the Court, if prison administrators, and not the courts, are to make the difficult judgments concerning institutional operations. Subjecting the day-to-day judgments of prison officials to an inflexible judicial review would seriously hamper their ability to anticipate security problems and to adopt innovative solutions to the intractable problems of prison administration. Judicial interference would also distort the decision making process, for every administrative judgment would be subject to the restrictive way of solving the problem at hand. Courts inevitably would become the primary arbiters of what constitutes the best solution to every administrative problem, thereby unnecessarily perpetuating the involvement of the federal courts in affairs of prison administration. This the Supreme Court refused to permit the federal judiciary to do.

Columbus, Ohio 　　　　　　　　　　　　　　　　　JOHN W. PALMER

TABLE OF CONTENTS

Chapter 1

AN OVERVIEW OF THE JUDICIAL SYSTEM

§1.1   Introduction

Law is the set of rules that governs the conduct of individuals or entities in our society. The rules are applied in cases or controversies by the judicial branch of government in the United States. There are three principal sources of laws: federal and state constitutions, federal and state statutes, and the common law, or judge-made law. Taken collectively, these sources establish what is known as "the law."

The federal Constitution is the product of a balance of power between the sovereign states in the late eighteenth century. It established the basic form of the federal government of the United States as we know it today.

It divided federal power among three branches of government: the legislative, the executive, and the judicial. Only limited power is granted by the sovereign states to the federal government. All power not expressly or implicitly granted to the federal government is reserved to the states. Congress is given the duty of legislating in areas of national interest, the executive branch is to carry out the execution of federal laws, and the judicial branch is entrusted with the administration of federal justice and laws. Each branch of government has specifically enumerated functions and powers under the federal Constitution. Thus, the federal Constitution is law, as it provides the basic rules for the functioning of the national government. It also governs the relationships between the states and the federal government, between the sovereign states themselves, and between states and foreign governments. *The federal Constitution, then, is the Supreme Law of the Land.*

State constitutions, on the other hand, are limitations on the power of the states. Whereas the federal government can act only in those areas where the federal Constitution specifically or implicitly so provides, state governments can legislate in any area, except where state or federal constitutions limit their power. State consti-

1

tutions also provide for the organization of the state government and for the duties and powers of the members of government that they create.

Federal and state statutes are other sources of law. Congress is entrusted with enacting law for the national good, while state legislatures provide for the welfare of the citizens of their respective states. The statutes enacted for these purposes become the law, subject only to the limitations of the state and federal constitutions. Statutory laws are enacted to specifically guide the conduct of affected individuals or entities. The courts, both federal and state, apply the rules thus established, which are then enforced by the executive branch of government.

The other major source of law in the United States is a body of rules called the *common law.* Common law, in the sense used here,[1] is the rule of law which has its origins in the courts rather than in the legislatures.

§ 1.2   The American Common Law

The "common law" is called such because originally it was the law common to all of England. It was the law that the English courts used in deciding cases where there was no legislative enactment.

The common law has never been regarded as static. It is "the wisdom, counsel, experience, and observation of many ages of wise and observing men."[2]

The common law for many centuries was oral and there were in olden times no reports of the judicial decisions. Thus, it was often known as the "unwritten law." With the practice of reporting decisions,[3] the written opinions of the judges in deciding actual cases provided a starting point in determining the legal principles applicable to new factual situations which faced the courts. The "old" law was applied when the facts of a "new" case were the same as they were in the "old" case. If the facts were different, a new rule often developed.

The English common law was transplanted to America through English colonization. The charters of colonies provided for the protection of the rights of free men according to the laws of England.[4] Several state constitutions such as Massachusetts, New York, New Jersey and Maryland, specifically adopted the English com-

---

[1] The term *common law* has many meanings, dependent usually upon context. In its very broadest sense, "common law" refers to the entire Anglo-American system of law, contrasted with the civil law (entirely code-based) systems of most non-English speaking nations. It also can refer to the body of law originating in the courts of common law rather than the courts of equity.

[2] 1 KENT'S COMMENTARIES 472 (12th ed. 1873).

[3] Some of the first reports were made during the reign of Henry III (1216-1272) with the first volume of reports, called the Year Books, which began in the latter part of the reign of Edward II (1307-1326) and continued until Henry VIII (1509-1547). However, the Year Books were first printed during the reign of James I (1603-1625) and reprinted in 1679. Parts of the Year Books were incorporated in the treatises of the legal scholars of the times, such as Statham, Fitzherbert and Brooke. When the practice of reporting cases for the Year Books was discontinued by the Crown, English lawyers made reports for their own uses. Legal scholars then began to make their commentaries serve the function of the reporter of the common law.

[4] *The law in the Massachusetts Bay Colony,* READINGS IN AMERICAN LEGAL HISTORY 101-102 (M. Howe, ed. 1949).

mon law as the law in that state except as changed by the state statutes.[5] Other state statutes and court decisions adopted the English common law as the law of the land.[6] Once transplanted, however, American common law was adapted to meet the needs of the American economic and social system.

§ 1.2.1   —Equity as Part of the Common Law

At the end of the thirteenth century in England, there were three main court systems: The King's courts (including King's Bench, Common Pleas, and Exchequer), the communal courts of the counties and hundreds, and the ecclesiastical courts. The King's courts administered the King's justice common to all of England (common law); the communal courts and ecclesiastical courts administered specialized justice which was not within the jurisdiction of the King's courts.

To secure access to the King's courts, a person had to procure a "writ" from the King's Chancellor, who was the "King's Secretary of State for all departments whose office was responsible for any writing done in the King's name."[7] A writ was a command from the King to a named person to appear in one of the King's courts to answer a claim. There were certain standardized claims, or forms of action, which could be issued by the Chancellor, although the Chancellor had authority to frame new writs where the case was similar to cases in which existing writs were issued as a matter of right. For a writ to be valid, it had to follow the rigid patterns set by the common law principles which the King's courts administered. As a result of the rigid rules applied by the King's judges in the common law courts, which had to conform to the writ issued, many people who were wronged were denied adequate relief. No writ, no remedy.

The King, as the source of all justice in England, naturally could fill the void left by the rigidity of the common law. Thus, people could petition the King and his council for redress as a matter of favor, if no relief was available in the common law courts.

The Chancellor, as the King's chief minister and secretary, and keeper of the Great Seal, was delegated the power and authority to grant redress in such cases in the King's name. The Chancellor was generally a cleric, often a bishop. He dispensed the King's justice, or equity, and was strongly influenced by moral and ethical considerations and the justice of the conflict rather than by past decisions of courts. He became the conscience of the legal system.

The granting of a special favor in a particular case where no adequate remedy existed in the common law became a practice. The relief granted by the Chancellor was popular and much sought after. Once established, relief given by the Chancellor, known as equitable relief, became an integral part of the law, standing side by side with the common law, rather than something granted as a favor of the King. It

---

[5] 1 KENT'S COMMENTARIES 472-473 (12th ed. 1873).

[6] *Id.*

[7] W. GELDART, ELEMENTS OF ENGLISH LAW 23 (6th ed. 1959).

became more than one man could manage, and this led to the establishment of a Court of Chancery (or court of equity). The body of principles of moral justice applied to individual cases developed into rules of equity by subsequent repetition. Thus, a body of court-made law separate from the traditional common law developed, administered by a separate court of equity. The separation of common law courts and courts of equity remained until recent times, e.g., 1848 in New York, 1873-1875 in Great Britain. Now, in most states, a single court administers both "law" in the sense of common law and "equity."

Distinctions still remain, however, dependent upon whether the relief sought was traditionally administered by the common law courts or the courts of equity. For example, the right to a jury trial attaches only where the claim was recognized by the "law" courts, since a claim in the court of equity was decided by the Chancellor without the aid of a jury. Also, the traditional remedy granted by equity was an order against a person (*i.e.*, an injunction) while the traditional remedy of the common law courts was an order involving property (*i.e.*, damages).

Equity has the power of contempt of court to enforce its orders, as equity relief is directed against the person and not against the person's property. Contempt of court is an act when a person willfully disobeys an order of the court of equity, either in the presence of the court (direct contempt) or when a person obstructs the justice of the court out of the presence of the court (indirect contempt). Thus one cannot be held in contempt of court for the failure to pay a money judgment, since that is a judgment in "law." The court can only execute judgment and levy on the property of the defendant.

Equitable relief is discretionary and can only be granted where the remedy of law, or in damages, is inadequate. If monetary damages will adequately compensate a wrong, equitable relief, such as an injunction against future conduct, cannot be obtained.

§ 1.2.2   —The Role of Case Law

As the previous sections indicated, the legal principles applied in a particular case before a court become part of the "common law." It takes its place as a part of the body of court-made rules that will form the basis of future decisions.

With publication of reports of cases contemporaneous with the decision in England, published cases were at first merely instructive and informative. However, courts began to cite previously decided cases to support their own conclusions, and ever-increasing weight was placed on reported cases. For the past three centuries *the decisions of judges of higher courts are precedent for later cases.*[8] A *precedent* is a decision of a court which furnishes authority for an identical or similar case which arises subsequently. The practice of using past case law as the basis for current decisions is called *stare decisis,* which means to let the decision stand. The use of a case as subsequent precedent or authority requires that the exact rule

[8] *Id.* at 6-7.

or principle of law, known as the *holding,* be determined from the language of the reported decision. Any reasoning or principle of law in a decision which is not part of the holding, or not essential to the determination of the case, is termed *obiter dictum,* or simply, *dictum,* meaning words "spoken by the way."

The precise effect of precedent, or the doctrine of *stare decisis,* depends upon the factual similarity between a prior case and a subsequent controversy. The principle of *stare decisis* rests upon the presumption that a previous court determined "the law" applicable to a factual situation after reasonable consideration and that it is the best evidence of the law.

The reasons for applying the doctrine of *stare decisis* include: 1) certainty and predictability of the law, which is necessary for the regulation of personal conduct and commerce; 2) growth where new issues arise; 3) equality of application; and 4) respect for the prior judgments of an esteemed legal mind.

As an exposition of the applicable law, the prior decision of a court is *binding* on that court and the inferior courts (courts lower in the hierarchical judicial structure) of that judicial system. Thus a decision of the Supreme Court of the United States on questions of federal law is binding on all lower courts (courts of appeals and district courts) when a particular rule of law is established by the Supreme Court. Likewise, the decisions of the highest court of each state are binding on inferior state courts of each respective state. However, a decision of the Supreme Court of Ohio is not precedent for a New York court. The New York court may follow the Ohio precedent voluntarily, due to its persuasiveness, but it is not bound to do so. No state is so bound.

However, certain handicaps are present in the doctrine of *stare decisis,* such as hardships resulting from rigidity, illogical distinctions on the facts of a case, and the sheer numbers of reported cases which establish law. Also, the American social and economic system changes with the passage of time. As has been said:

> The life of the law has not been logic: it has been experience. The felt necessities of the time, the prevalent moral and political theories, institutions of public policy, avowed or unconscious, even the prejudices which judges share with their fellow-men, have had a good deal more to do than the syllogism in determining the rules by which men should be governed.[9]

The methods for changing case-made law to meet new demands on the law are *distinguishing* or *overruling* precedent cases.

Distinguishing precedent cases occurs when subsequent courts confine precedents strictly to their facts, and apply a new rule to the facts of the controversy at issue. The effect is to give an earlier case a very limited application.

---

[9] O. HOLMES, THE COMMON LAW 1 (1881).

A court *overrules* a prior rule of law by finding that it was improperly decided or that the social and economic conditions have changed from the time when the decision was previously made. Hence, a new rule of law should apply.

§1.3　The American Court Structure

The court system of the United States is composed of 51 independent court systems. The federal court system and each of the 50 state systems operate within their respective judicial spheres.

The states operate their court systems as one of the powers reserved to them by the Tenth Amendment of the United States Constitution. Each state has its own peculiar system, with the structure and jurisdiction of the courts established by the state constitution and state statutes. However, all court structures include two types of courts: *trial courts* and *appellate courts*.

The state trial courts generally include courts of limited jurisdiction and those of general jurisdiction. The limited jurisdictional courts are the numerous local courts which have power to hear civil cases involving limited monetary amounts and minor criminal offenses, such as traffic violations. Above the limited jurisdictional courts in the hierarchical structure of the state courts are the trial courts of general jurisdiction. They generally have power to hear all civil cases involving any monetary amount greater than that handled by the limited jurisdictional courts.

The functions of the trial court are the reception of proper evidence, the compilation of a record of the evidence introduced, the finding of disputed facts from the evidence introduced, the application of appropriate law to the facts, and, then, granting appropriate relief. The fact-finding function of a trial can be exercised either by the jury, if the right to jury trial exists and is exercised; *or,* by the judge who then has two separate and distinct duties: fact-finding and application of the proper law.

Every state has at least one level of appellate courts. The highest appellate court is generally called the *supreme court,* with some states calling it the *court of appeals* (e.g., New York and Kentucky). The supreme court of a state is the court of last resort, as it is the final, authoritative source of judicial relief in the state court system. In the more populous states, such as California, Illinois, New York, or Ohio, there is an intermediate appellate court in the state court system, generally called a *court of appeals.* These courts handle appeals from the trial courts and are in turn reviewable by the supreme court of the state. The function of the appellate courts is to review the decisions of trial courts, or lower-level appellate courts, for errors which might have prejudiced the rights of a party, such as errors in procedure or errors in applying the proper rule of law to the facts established by the evidence. The factual findings of the trial court are generally final and, therefore, the appellate courts do not receive any evidence in reviewing a case, but use the record of the trial court. Whenever there was a dispute at the trial level as to the existence of a particular fact, the finding of the trier of fact (either the judge or jury) is binding upon the appellate court and the appellate court cannot overturn the trial court's factual findings unless they are clearly erroneous.

The federal court system was created by the Constitution, which expressly provided for the Supreme Court and authorized Congress to create inferior federal courts. As a result of this latter grant of power to Congress, federal statutes provide for 91 federal trial courts (district courts) and thirteen intermediate appellate courts (courts of appeals).

The types of cases that a federal court can adjudicate are limited: that is, the federal courts have only limited jurisdiction. The limited jurisdiction of the federal courts is a result of our federal structure of government. The sovereign states have granted (to the federal government through the Constitution) certain powers to be exercised for the common good, among them the judicial power as specified. The federal judicial power extends to cases arising under the Constitution, federal laws or treaties, all cases affecting ambassadors, public ministers and consuls, admiralty and maritime cases, controversies where the United States is a party, controversies between states, between a state and a citizen of another state, between citizens of the same state claiming lands under grants from different states, and in cases between a state or citizens of a state and foreign states, citizens or subjects.[10]

In order for a case to be heard in a federal court, it must come within one of the enumerated categories. The greatest number of federal cases involved cases arising under the Constitution, cases based upon federal statutory rights and cases between citizens of different states, referred to as "diversity of citizenship" cases. Cases arising under the Constitution are those which enforce the provisions of the Constitution; that is, a right created by the Constitution itself, such as the First Amendment right of freedom of speech. Controversies arising under federal laws are those cases in which a federal statute has specifically provided a procedure for judicial relief such as the various Civil Rights Acts. Diversity of citizenship cases are those where the cause of action, or right to seek judicial relief, arises under a state's law, either statutory or common, but is between citizens of different states. In a diversity case, the federal court applies state law. The federal court merely provides a neutral forum for resolving a dispute. Congress has placed a statutory limit on diversity cases by requiring that the controversy involve an amount in excess of $10,000. This was done to limit the number of cases utilizing the federal court system at the expense of the state court systems.

The federal district courts' jurisdictional areas (in a geographical sense) are the result of a division of the nation into judicial districts by population. For example, New York is divided into four districts while in less populated states, like Maine or Arizona, the district encompasses the entire state.

The federal district court is a trial court for federal criminal prosecutions and civil actions with its function being the same as a state trial court. It also has the

---

[10] U.S. CONST. art. III, § 2.

power to review (appellate jurisdiction) the decisions of certain federal administrative agencies.

Federal statutes have also created several specialty courts which have the same functions as a district court, but limit the type of cases entertained to one subject, such as tax, patents or military appeals. The specialty courts are created to handle a highly specialized subject so that the judges of the courts will have exceptional knowledge of the complex subject involved.

The federal courts of appeals are the intermediate appellate courts. There are thirteen circuits, dividing the country geographically according to the volume of judicial case work. One circuit is provided exclusively for the District of Columbia, due to the heavy volume of appeals from federal administrative agencies. The function of the federal court of appeals is similar to that of a state court of appeals. It reviews the decisions of the federal district courts and some federal administrative agencies.

The United States Supreme Court serves as the court of last resort for cases from the federal system. The Supreme Court is the ultimate interpreter of the Constitution and federal statutes. It reviews the decisions of the courts of appeals, and some direct appeals from district courts. The Supreme Court also reviews the decisions of state courts involving matters of federal constitutional rights where the case has been finally adjudicated in the state court system. Besides its appellate function, the court has original jurisdiction in suits where a state is a party and in controversies involving ambassadors, ministers and consuls.[11]

Cases are brought to the Supreme Court for consideration by two methods: (1) appeal as of right, and (2) discretion of the court. The appeals of right are those appeals which are expressly provided for by statute. The court grants discretionary review by issuing a *writ of certiorari*, which is an order to review the action of an inferior court. The court grants few petitions for the writ of certiorari. Less than five percent of the petitions submitted are granted.[12]

§ 1.4   Anatomy of a Case

Case law is a major source of law in a common law system of jurisprudence. A great amount of a common law lawyer's time is spent reading and studying cases to determine the rule of law on a particular point. It is appropriate, then, to briefly describe the anatomy of a decision.

A *case* is a published report of an opinion indicating the decision of a court on a controversy heard by the reporting court. Generally, only appellate court decisions are published on a national basis, except for decisions of the federal district courts. The report contains at least the *opinion of the court* which is the decision of the court as decided by a numerical majority of the tribunal (court) making the decision. The report is written by a judge of the court who is expressing the opinion for

---

[11] *Id.*

[12] D. KARLEN, THE CITIZEN IN COURT 23 (1964).

the court. If any judge of the court (where more than one judge hears the controversy) disagrees with the majority decision, he may write a separate opinion, termed a *dissenting opinion,* explaining his reasons for holding a view that is different from the majority opinion of the court. A judge may also agree with the results of the decision of the court, but for different or additional reasons not shared by the opinion of the court. This opinion is termed a *concurring opinion.*

When the opinion, or opinions, are made public, they are kept by the clerk of the court and accumulated along with other opinions until published in a volume. The volumes are numbered consecutively by the clerk; they are termed *"state reports"* when they involve state court decisions. The West Publishing Company also publishes the appellate decisions in a series of reports (called the National Reporter System) which contain the decisions of all state and federal courts. West groups the state jurisdictions geographically.

§ 1.4.1 —Citations

In order to find a particular opinion among the staggering number of reported decisions, a system of reference has developed, termed *citations.* The following is an example of a citation to a state court opinion or "cite": *Ford Motor Co. v. London,* 217 Tenn. 400, 398 S.W.2d 240 (1966). The citation indicates the following information: (1) The names of the parties, generally the plaintiff first (***Ford Motor Co.***) and the defendant second (***London***); (2) the volume of the state reporter where the opinion is found (**217**); (3) the state reporter system (**Tenn.**); (4) the page in the state reporter system volume where the opinion begins (**400**). Then listed is the exact same case in the West Reporter system: (5) the volume of the West Reporter system (**398**); (6) the West Reporter where the opinion is found (**S.W.2d**); (7) the page in the West Reporter where the opinion begins (**240**); and (8) the date that the court decided the case (**1966**). In California and New York, the decisions of those state courts may appear in two West Reporter systems, the regional reporter (Pacific and North Eastern, respectively) and a special supplement reporter which deals exclusively with the cases of that particular state (California Reporter and New York Supplement). An example of a citation of a case from New York is: *Greenburg v. Lorenz,* 9 N.Y.2d 195, 196 N.E.2d 430, 213 N.Y.S.2d 39 (1966).

A citation to a case from a federal district court appears as: *Landman v. Royster,* 333 F. Supp. 621 (E.D.Va. 1971). The citation gives the following information about a federal case: (1) The parties, plaintiff first and defendant second (***Landman v. Royster***); (2) the volume of the West Federal Reporter where the opinion appears (**333**); (3) the West Reporter system which publishes the case (**F. Supp.**); (4) the page in the reporter where the opinion begins (**621**); (5) the court that decided the case (**E.D.Va.**), the federal district court for Eastern District of Virginia; and (6) the date of the decision (**1971**). A citation to a federal court of appeals for example, *Jackson v. Bishop,* 404 F.2d 571 (8th Cir. 1968), gives the same information; that is, parties, volume, reporter, page, court and date.

The symbol "2d" appearing in many citations indicates that the reporter system has begun a second series of the reporter.

The citation may also give a history of the case. Such history is only included in the citation if it is significant to the point of law for which the case is cited. The signals of citation used to indicate history are:

aff'd—the decision of the court was upheld on appeal.

rev'd—the decision of the court was overruled on appeal.

aff'd (or rev'd) on other grounds—the rule of law cited from the case was unaffected by a subsequent affirmation (or overruling) of the court's decision.

cert. denied (or granted)—petition for writ of certiorari or, grant of discretionary review of an inferior court's decision, was denied (or granted).

modified—the decision of a case was modified by a reviewing court.

sub nom.—the names of the parties of the appellate decision differ from the names of the lower court decisions.

The reader will also find several citations which read [44 U.S.L.W. 1000] or [19 Cr. L. 2133]. Both of those represent publications which provide judicial decisions to the public before they are printed in the publications mentioned earlier. These publications serve to keep the public current on the most recent decisions from the judiciary. U.S.L.W. stands for United States Law Week and Cr. L. represents an abbreviation for Criminal Law Reporter.

§ 1.5 Conclusion

The first chapter has provided an overview of the American judicial system, including "common law," equity, the role of case law, the American court structure, and an illustrative case anatomy. To derive the most benefit from this chapter, the reader should review key concepts herein, giving special attention, too, to significant terms such as those on page 6. All are essential to understanding the legal system in which we function.

LIST OF THE WEST REPORTERS AND RESPECTIVE JURISDICTIONS

Atlantic (A)

Connecticut	New Jersey
Delaware	Pennsylvania
Maine	Rhode Island
Maryland	Vermont
New Hampshire	
District of Columbia	
(Municipal Court of Appeals)	

North Eastern (N.E.)

Illinois	New York
Indiana	Ohio
Massachusetts	

Southern (So.)

Alabama	Louisiana
Florida	Mississippi

West's California Reporter (Cal.)

California Supreme Court
District Courts of Appeal
Superior Court, Appellate Department

Pacific (P.)

Alaska	Montana
Arizona	Nevada
California	New Mexico
(Sup. Ct. only)	Oklahoma
Colorado	Oregon
Hawaii	Utah
Idaho	Washington
Kansas	Wyoming

South Eastern (S.E.)

Georgia	Virginia
North Carolina	West Virginia
South Carolina	

New York Supplement (N.Y.S.)

Court of Appeals
Appellate Division
Miscellaneous

North Western (N.W.)

Iowa	Nebraska	Wisconsin
Michigan	North Dakota	
Minnesota	South Dakota	

Federal Supplement (F. Supp.)

U.S. District Courts
U.S. Customs Courts

Federal Rules Decisions (F.R.D.)

U.S. District Courts

Federal (F.)

U.S. Court of Appeals
U.S. Court of Claims
U.S. Court of Customs and Patent Appeals

U.S. Supreme Court* (S.Ct.)

---

*Supreme Court decisions are also reported by the government, cited as U.S., and reported by Lawyers Co-Operative Publishing Co., cited as L. Ed.

The Federal Judicial Circuits

Chapter 2

USE OF FORCE; USE OF CORPORAL PUNISHMENT TO ENFORCE PRISON DISCIPLINE

§ 2.1 Introduction

As the legal custodians of large numbers of men, including many who are being confined for crimes of violence, prison staffs are often confronted with situations in which it is necessary to use force against an inmate or group of inmates. Force, in this connection, means any physical force directed toward another, either by direct physical contact or by the use of a weapon such as tear gas, chemical mace, a billy club, or a firearm.

Every person, including an incarcerated felon, has the right to be free from the *fear* of offensive bodily contact and to be free from *actual* offensive bodily contact. Any person who violates either of these rights can be held liable, both civilly and criminally, unless such conduct is privileged.

It has generally been recognized that prison officials have a privilege to use force against inmates in five fact situations. These areas are: (1) self-defense; (2) defense of third persons; (3) enforcement of prison rules and regulations; (4) prevention of escape; and (5) prevention of crime.

13

## § 2.2	Degree of Force Permitted

The above situations in which a prison official is justified in using force are relatively easy to recognize. However, the *degree* of force which may be used in any one of the situations listed is not so clear. The courts speak of the justification of using "reasonable" force in any given situation to control the inmate. The factual elements in each case determine whether or not the force used was excessive and, hence, not privileged.

The controlling factual elements are the degree of force used by the inmate, the inmate's possession or nonpossession of a deadly weapon, the reasonable perception on the part of the guard that he or a third person is in danger of death or serious bodily harm, and the means of force available to the guard.

When discussing the amount of force that is legally permissible, it is helpful to distinguish between deadly force and less-than-deadly force. "Deadly force" may be defined as force which will likely cause death or serious bodily harm. Knives and firearms are always considered instruments of deadly force. "Less-than-deadly" force is force which will normally cause neither death nor serious bodily harm. The use of fists, judo holds, chemical mace, and tear gas are examples of less-than-deadly force.

The employment of certain methods of applying force cannot, in the abstract, be categorized as either the use of deadly or less-than-deadly force. Certain factual elements of the case, primarily the area of the body struck, must be considered. For example, a blow to the head from a billy club is likely to cause death or serious bodily harm, and hence must be regarded as use of deadly force. However, a blow to the knees would probably constitute the use of less-than-deadly force.

Our society places great emphasis on the value of human life and on the right of every person to be free from offensive physical contact by another. Consequently, the use of force by one individual against another is frowned upon. For this reason, force is permissible only when all non-forceful alternatives have failed.

## § 2.3	Self-Defense

Every person has the right to protect himself against an assault by another. Prison staffs may use force against an inmate in their own self-defense.[1] Prison staffs may use that degree of force reasonably necessary under the circumstances to protect themselves from the assault and to subdue the inmates.[2] While prison officials are afforded broad discretion in maintaining order, they are not justified in using any amount of force when the threat of disorder has subsided.[3] The extent of such force is dependent upon the degree of force being used by the inmate, the staffs' reasonable perception of injury, and the means of resisting the assault. The test of reasonable force is whether the degree of force used is necessary under the

---

[1] *Butler v. Bensinger,* 377 F. Supp. 409 F. Supp. 651 (W.D. Ky. 1976). 870 (N.D.Ill. 1974); *Tate v. Kassulke,* 409 F. Supp. 651 (W.D.Ky. 1976).

[2] *Suits v. Lynch,* 437 F. Supp. 38 (D. Kan. 1977).

[3] *Ridley v. Leavitt,* 631 F.2d 358 (4th Cir. 1980); *Spain v. Procunier,* 600 F.2d 189 (9th Cir. 1979).

facts and circumstances of the particular case,[4] as illustrated by the two following cases.

In a Maryland case, a fight erupted between five inmates and a number of correctional officers. The inmates received numerous injuries, including severe cuts and bruises and broken bones. One of the officers was hurt so severely that he had to be taken to intensive care. After hearing the evidence, the court found that the inmates were resisting prison authority and that the force used was reasonable and necessary under the circumstances.[5]

The use of excessive force by correctional officers is again illustrated in the case of *Inmates of Attica Correctional Facility v. Rockefeller.*[6] The case arose out of the bloody rioting that occurred at the Attica Correctional Facility in September of 1971. The inmates alleged that after the prison was retaken by force on September 13, state officials constantly subjected the inmates to unprovoked acts of brutality, including the following:

> Injured prisoners, some on stretchers, were struck, prodded or beaten with sticks, belts, bats or other weapons. Others were forced to strip and run naked through gauntlets of guards armed with clubs which they used to strike the bodies of the inmates as they passed. Some were dragged on the ground, some marked with an "X" on their backs, some spat upon or burned with matches, and others poked in the genitals or arms with sticks. According to the testimony of the inmates, bloody or wounded inmates were apparently not spared in this orgy of brutality.[7]

The federal appellate court enjoined state officials from future acts of brutality and torture, and authorized the district court to station federal monitors in the institution if necessary.

Deadly force as a means of self-defense is never justified unless the prison official is in reasonable apprehension of death or serious injury and the use of deadly force is his last resort.

It is obduracy and wantonness, not inadvertence or error in good faith, that characterize the conduct prohibited by the Cruel and Unusual Punishments Clause, whether that conduct occurs in connection with establishing conditions of confinement, supplying medical needs, or restoring control over a tumultuous cell block.

The infliction of pain in the course of a prison security measure does not amount to cruel and unusual punishment simply because it may appear in retrospect that the degree of force authorized or applied for security purposes was unreasonable,

---

[4] *Jackson v. Allen,* 376 F. Supp. 1393 (E.D. Ark. 1974).

[5] *Green v. Hawkins,* U.S. Dist. Ct. (Md. 1977).

[6] *Inmates of Attica Correctional Facility v. Rockefeller,* 453 F.2d 12 (2d Cir. 1971); *see also George v. Evans,* 633 F.2d 413 (5th Cir. 1980) (use of undue force by a prison guard against a prisoner is actionable as a deprivation of due process).

[7] *Inmates of Attica Correctional Facility v. Rockefeller, supra,* at 18-19.

and unnecessary in the strict sense. The general requirement that an Eighth Amendment claimant establish the unnecessary and wanton infliction of pain should also be applied with due regard for differences in the kind of conduct involved. Consequently, where a prison security measure is undertaken to resolve a disturbance that poses significant risks to the safety of inmates and prison staff, the question whether the measure taken inflicted unnecessary and wanton pain and suffering ultimately turns on whether force was applied in a good-faith effort to maintain or restore discipline, or maliciously and sadistically for the purpose of causing harm.

An error in judgment when prison officials decide on a plan that employed potentially deadly force falls far short of a showing that there was no plausible basis for their belief that this degree of force was necessary. Shooting may be part and parcel of a good-faith effort to restore prison security. Further, the Due Process Clause of the Fourteenth Amendment is not an alternative basis for finding prison officials culpable of using excess force, independently of the Eighth Amendment. In the prison security context, the Due Process Clause affords a prisoner no greater protection than does the Cruel and Unusual Punishments Clause.[8]

§ 2.4   Defense of Third Persons

Force may be used against an inmate[9] in defense of third persons, such as another inmate, prison staff or visitors. The law regarding the use of force to prevent injury to third persons is similar to the rules regarding self-defense. A person is justified in using that degree of force reasonably necessary under the circumstances to protect the third party and to control the attacker. Prison officials may find themselves under a duty to provide inmates reasonable protection from constant threats of violence.[10] What is reasonable under the circumstances is again dependent upon the degree of force being used by the attacker, the person's reasonable estimate of injury to the third party and the means available to the person to control the attacker. Deadly force may be used against the attacker only if the third party reasonably appears to be in danger of death or serious injury and the use of deadly force is the last resort.

§ 2.5   Enforcement of Prison Rules and Regulations

Courts have long recognized that penal authorities have the right and duty to prescribe rules and regulations for the internal discipline and control of inmates. The necessary corollary to this authority is the privilege of using reasonable force to see that the rules are enforced. A distinction must be drawn between the use of force as punishment for the violation of a prison rule and the use of force as a means

---

[8] *Whitley v. Albers*, 475 U.S. 312 (1986).

[9] *Harrah v. Leverette*, 271 S.W.2d 322 (W.Va. 1980).

[10] *O'Neal v. Evans*, 496 F. Supp. 867 (S.D. Ga. 1980); *Barnard v. State*, 265 N.W.2d 620 (Iowa 1978); *Woodhous v. Virginia*, 487 F.2d 889 (4th Cir. 1973); *Wilson v. City of Kotzebue*, 627 P.2d 623 (Alaska 1981); *Leonardo v. Moran*, 611 F.2d 397 (1st Cir. 1979).

of insuring that the inmate is brought under control. For example, in the case of *Johnson v. Glick,*[11] the court stated, "the management by a few guards of large numbers of prisoners, not usually the most gentle or tractable of men and women, may require and justify the use of a degree of intentional force."[12]

If the prisoner resists an officer's reasonable order, additional officers should be summoned to control him. Even where the order is based upon a prison rule later found to be unconstitutional, guards may use reasonable force to obtain inmate compliance.[13] It is difficult to imagine any justification for using force sufficient to kill or maim in order to compel compliance to a disciplinary rule. If the inmate's resistance amounts to an assault upon an officer, that officer has the privilege of self-defense and other officers have the privilege of defending third persons. The rules pertaining to self-defense and defense of third persons would then be controlling, as the situation would no longer be one of using force solely to maintain discipline.

§ 2.6   Prevention of Crime

Prison officials have the duty, sometimes imposed by statute,[14] to prevent inmates from committing crimes within a detention facility. Therefore, such officials have the privilege of using reasonable force to prevent either a misdemeanor or a felony. However, the degree of force permissible will depend upon whether the attempted crime is a misdemeanor or a felony. Generally, deadly force can be employed to prevent the commission of a felony,[15] but only after all other means reasonably available have failed.[16] Common examples of felonies committed within a prison are rioting and assault with a weapon upon another inmate.

Deadly force is never justified to prevent the commission of a misdemeanor.[17] If, however, an inmate physically resists less-than-deadly force employed by a correctional officer to prevent the commission of a misdemeanor and becomes an aggressor, the rules pertaining to self-defense are applicable.

---

[11] *Johnson v. Glick,* 481 F.2d 1028 (2d Cir. 1973).

[12] *Id.* at 1033.

[13] *Jackson v. Allen,* 376 F. Supp. 1393 (E.D.Ark. 1974).

[14] *See* OHIO REV. CODE §5145.04.

[15] *See State v. Taylor,* 9 Ariz. App. 290, 451 P.2d 648 (1969). The use of deadly force to prevent the escape of all felony suspects, whatever the circumstances, is constitutionally unreasonable. The broad common law rule has been rejected. Where a law enforcement officer has probable cause to believe that the suspect poses a threat of serious physical harm, either to the officer or to others, it is not constitutionally unreasonable to prevent an escape by the use of deadly force. If the suspect threatens the officer with a weapon or there is probable cause to believe that the suspect has committed a crime involving the infliction or threatened infliction of serious physical harm, deadly force may be used if necessary to prevent escape, and where feasible, some warning has been given. As this case involved a fleeing burglary suspect, it is not directly applicable to prisoners going "over the wall." The law remains unclear. *Tennessee v. Garner,* 471 U.S. 1, 37 Cr. L. 3233 (1985).

[16] 6 C.J.S., *Arrest,* 13b (1937).

[17] *See State v. Jones,* 211 S.C. 300, 44 S.E.2d 841 (1947)

§ 2.7   Prevention of Escape

Practically every state has, by statute, made escape or attempted escape by a convicted felon a felony.[18] Hence, the rules regarding use of force to prevent a felony apply to preventing an escape; that is, force, including deadly force as a last resort, may be employed. However, at least one court has held that the use of deadly force to stop an escaping prisoner violates constitutional rights unless there is good reason to believe that the use of such force is necessary to prevent death or great bodily harm.[19]

§ 2.8   The Use of Corporal Punishment to Enforce Prison Discipline

The term "corporal punishment" as used herein means the infliction of physical pain upon an inmate as a punishment for the violation of a prison rule or regulation. Such forms of conduct include, but are not limited to, whipping, use of cold showers, electrical shocking devices and suspension from cell bars by handcuffing. The use of solitary confinement as a method for punishing violations of prison discipline is not included within the definition of corporal punishment. Many states have no statutes specifically forbidding the use of corporal punishment. Other states, however, by statute, prohibit corporal punishment in detention facilities.[20]

§ 2.8.1 —Brief History of Corporal Punishment

Corporal punishment has a long history of use in prisons, as was stated in *United States v. Jones*:[21]

> From time immemorial prison officials were vested with the power and authority of imposing corporal punishment upon prisoners as a part of the discipline and restraint . . . [F]or centuries whipping or corporal punishment has been a recognized method of discipline of convicts.

The use of corporal punishment to enforce prison discipline has continued into the early parts of the twentieth century. In 1927, a North Carolina statute authorizing the use of whipping of convicts was upheld.[22] In 1963, in *State v. Cannon*,[23] the Delaware Supreme Court held that the use of whipping to punish certain crimes did not violate either the state or federal constitutional bans on cruel and unusual pun-

---

[18] *See* PA. STATE ANN. tit. 18 § 4309 (Supp. 1972); WASH. REV. CODE § 9.31.010 (1961); MODEL PENAL CODE § 242.6 (Proposed Official Draft, 1962).

[19] *Ayler v. Hopper*, 532 F. Supp. 198 (M.D. Ala. 1981).

[20] *See e.g.*, CAL. PENAL CODE § 673.

[21] *United States v. Jones*, 108 F. Supp. 266, 270 (S.D. Fla. 1952), *rev'd on other grounds*, 207 F.2d 785 (5th Cir. 1953).

[22] *State v. Revis*, 193 N.C. 192, 136 S.E. 346 (1927). In 1955, however, North Carolina enacted a statute forbidding the use of corporal punishment on any prisoner. N.C. GEN. STAT. § 148-20 (1964).

[23] *State v. Cannon*, 55 Del. 587, 190 A.2d 514 (1963).

ishment. In *Talley v. Stevens,*[24] the court refused to declare whipping unconstitutional as such, but held that whipping must not be excessive and must be inflicted as dispassionately as possible. A 1949 case[25] involving handcuffing a prisoner to a cell door for sixty hours without food also discusses the use and misuse of corporal punishment. Corporal punishment, including the use of electrical shocking devices, was openly utilized by the state of Arkansas until the 1960s. Electric shock treatments that served a legitimate purpose were not considered cruel and unusual punishment in a Minnesota case in 1976.[26]

§ 2.8.2 —Is Corporal Punishment Rational?

Advocates of corporal punishment maintain that to enforce prison discipline it is necessary to punish past offenders, hopefully deterring future infractions of the rules. However, the harmful effects of such treatment may well outweigh any of its supposed benefits. The possible psychological effects of inhumane punishment have been described as follows:[27]

> [M]ethods of discipline have a profound effect on the offender in regard to his mental and social attitudes both within the prison and after release. This is particularly evident in the case of first offenders, in whom permanent attitudes are often established which make for later social success or for a continued life of crime. The consequences of discipline are also grave in their effect on the mental conditions of offenders, leading them often into the so-called "prison neurosis" if unfavorable, or leading to constructive modification of personality if constructively administered.

Prison authorities have also recognized the futility of corporal punishment. The American Correctional Association has stated unequivocally that "corporal punishment should never be used under any circumstances."[28] In justifying this position the Association commented:

> Punishments out of all proportion to the offense, employing inhumane and archaic methods and dictated by brutality coupled with ignorance, incompetence, fear and weakness, are demoralizing both to inmates and staff. Staff punishments substantially increase the chances that the inmates will continue to be disciplinary problems in the institution and will return to crime after release.[29]

---

[24] *Talley v. Stevens,* 247 F. Supp. 683 (E.D. Ark. 1965).

[25] *State v. Carpenter,* 231 N.C. 229, 56 S.E.2d 713 (1949).

[26] *Price v. Sheppard,* 239 N.W.2d 905 (Minn. 1976).

[27] J. WILSON AND M. PESCOR, PROBLEMS IN PRISON PSYCHIATRY 226 (1939).

[28] AMERICAN CORRECTIONAL ASSOCIATION, A MANUAL OF CORRECTIONAL STANDARDS 417 (3d ed. 1966). *See also* NATIONAL ADVISORY COMMISSION ON CRIMINAL JUSTICE STANDARDS AND GOALS, STANDARD 2.4 (1973), in Appendix.

[29] *Id.*

James V. Bennett, Director of Federal Prisons from 1937 to 1964, testified during the trial of *Jackson v. Bishop* that whipping and other forms of corporal punishment were "brutal and medieval and did no real good."[30]

§ 2.8.3   —Judicial Treatment of Corporal Punishment

Until the late 1960s, cases could be found which held that corporal punishment was not cruel and unusual punishment. In *United States v. Jones,*[31] the director of a Florida convict camp was charged with deprivation of the civil rights of several inmates whom he allegedly assaulted and whipped. The district court, relying strongly on the proposition that the administration of state penal institutions was a matter of exclusive state jurisdiction, held that an inmate has no constitutional right to be free from corporal punishment. The court further stated that although Florida had a law prohibiting the use of corporal punishment, the law was based "on principles of Christianity and humanity" and not upon the federal Constitution, thereby intimating that the use of corporal punishment could be reestablished by the Florida legislature at any time.

State v. Cannon[32] involved the constitutionality of a Delaware law that prescribed whipping as a form of punishment for specified crimes. Discussing the validity of whipping in light of the state constitution's ban on cruel and unusual punishment, the court reasoned that since whipping had been permitted in the state since 1719, while other forms of punishment that had formerly been utilized, such as burning at the stake, had been eliminated by the state legislature, it must be presumed that whipping was not considered cruel by the people of Delaware. Any change, the court declared, must come from the state legislature. As for the Eighth Amendment to the United States Constitution, the court said it could not find a single case as of that time in which a court had held, as a matter of federal constitutional law, that whipping violates the Eighth Amendment.

State v. Cannon was decided in 1963; in 1968, however, the United States Court of Appeals for the Eight Circuit held, in the case of *Jackson v. Bishop,*[33] that whipping as a means of enforcing prison discipline *did* violate the Eighth and Fourteenth Amendments. The court stated that the prohibition against cruel and unusual punishment could not be defined exactly, but that "the applicable standards are flexible…and that broad and idealistic concepts of dignity, civilized standards, humanity, and decency are useful and usable."[34] Using these criteria, the court held whipping to be cruel and unusual punishment for the following reasons:[35]

---

[30] *Jackson v. Bishop,* 268 F. Supp. 804, 813 (E.D. Ark. 1967), *aff'd,* 404 F.2d 571 (8th Cir. 1968).

[31] *United States v. Jones,* 108 F. Supp. 266 (S.D. Fla. 1952), *rev'd on other grounds,* 207 F.2d 785 (5th Cir. 1953).

[32] *State v. Cannon,* 55 Del. 587, 190 A.2d 514 (1963).

[33] *Jackson v. Bishop,* 404 F.2d 571 (8th Cir. 1968).

[34] *Id.* at 579.

[35] *Id.* at 579-580.

(1) We are not convinced that any rule or regulation as to the use of the strap, however seriously or sincerely conceived and drawn, will successfully prevent abuse . . . (2) Rules in this area often seem to go unobserved . . . (3) Regulations are easily circumvented . . .(4) Corporal punishment is easily subject to abuse in the hands of the sadistic and unscrupulous. (5) Where power to punish is granted to persons in lower levels of administrative authority, there is an inherent and natural difficulty in enforcing the limitations of that power. (6) There can be no argument that excessive whipping or an inappropriate manner of whipping or too great frequency of whipping or the use of studded or overlong straps all constitute cruel and unusual punishment. But if whipping were to be authorized, how does one, or any court, ascertain the point which would distinguish the permissible from that which is cruel and unusual? (7) Corporal punishment generates hate toward the keepers who punish and toward the system which permits it. It is degrading to the punisher and to the punished alike. It frustrates correctional and rehabilitative goals . . . (8) Whipping creates other penological problems and makes adjustment to society more difficult. (9) Public opinion is obviously adverse. Counsel concede that only two states still permit the use of the strap.

The reasoning of *Jackson v. Bishop* in eliminating corporal punishment has been consistently followed in judicial decisions, statutes and administrative rulings in this country. Any attempt to revive the practice, at this time, would face serious, if not insurmountable, constitutional challenge. Also significant is the fact that the opinion in *Jackson v. Bishop* was written by then Judge Blackmun, now a member of the United States Supreme Court.

§ 2.8.4 —Alternatives to Corporal Punishment

The fact that prison officials must have methods of punishing violations of prison rules and regulations is obvious. As previously stated, some prison administrators wish to include the use of corporal punishment among their possible methods of enforcing discipline. However, there are numerous other punishments which may be employed, none of which involve the infliction of physical pain, and hence these punishments may be more effective both in maintaining discipline and in rehabilitating the inmate. For example, in fiscal year 1968-1969, the Chillicothe Correctional Institution, one of Ohio's adult detention facilities, conducted a total of 271 disciplinary hearings. The dispositions that were made are as follows:[36]

Total Court Cases	271
Total Inmates to Segregated Confinement	183
Total Lost Time Recommendation (Held in Escrow)	20

---

[36] OHIO LEGISLATIVE SERVICE COMMISSION, STAFF RESEARCH REPORT NO. 105, OHIO'S ADULT CORRECTIONS SYSTEM 41 (1971).

Total Days in Segregated Confinement	744
Total Lost Time Recommendations	15
Total Extra Duty Hours	331
Total Days Television Privileges Suspended	6
Total Honor Status Removals	15
Total Loss of Movie Privileges	11
Total Dormitory Transfers	25
Total Job Changes	34
Total Confiscated Contraband	14
Total Recommendations for Transfer to Ohio Penitentiary (the maximum security prison in the state) (Held in Escrow)	19
Total Recommendations for Return to Ohio Penitentiary	9
Total Radios Temporarily Confiscated	1
Total Loss of Pay	3
Total Apologies to Officer	10
Total Medical Referrals	6
Total Psychological Referrals	8
Total Segregated Confinement; Probation	68
Total Recommendations for Parole Board Review	4
Total Transfer to CPU (psychiatric unit)	2
Total Removed from Industrial Arts	6

This list is by no means exhaustive of all possible non-corporal punishments that could be used, but it does demonstrate that reasonable alternatives to corporal punishment do exist, and that these alternatives allow the prison administrator to better fit the punishment to the infraction.

§ 2.9   Conclusion

In recognizing that prisons do not house the most docile or easily governed persons, courts will allow the use of reasonable force by prison officials in five fact situations: self-defense, defense of third persons, enforcement of prison rules and regulations, prevention of escape, and prevention of crime. The test of reasonableness is whether the force is reasonable and necessary under the facts and circumstances of the particular case.

Unreasonable corporal punishment to enforce prison discipline is considered cruel and unusual punishment prohibited by the Eighth Amendment. Prison officials who attempt to revive the use of corporal punishment may find themselves facing criminal and civil actions. To avoid criminal and civil liability, prison officials should refrain from corporal punishment and seek alternative methods of inmate control.

Chapter 3

PRISONERS' RIGHTS TO VISITATION/ASSOCIATION

Section

§ 3.1   Introduction

Traditionally, the right of inmates to have visitors while incarcerated has been severely limited by prison officials. Many states permit an inmate to see only those persons who have previously been approved by the prison administrators. Cases concerning the inmates' rights to have visitors generally hold that control of such activity is within the prison officials' discretion and that such control is not subject to judicial reversal unless a clear abuse of discretion is shown.[1] Further, any restrictions imposed by prison visitation policies must merely be reasonably related to a legitimate governmental interest.[2]

Although visitation privileges are considered matters within the scope of internal prison administration, this fact does not permit discriminatory application of visiting regulations.[3] For example, refusal to permit visitation privileges because the visitor and inmate are of different races constitutes racial discrimination under the Fourteenth Amendment.[4]

Visiting regulations that set forth procedures where visitors "may" be refused admittance and have visitation privileges suspended does not give state inmates a liberty interest in receiving visitors that is entitled to the protections of the Due Process Clause. In order to create a protected liberty interest in the prison context, state regulations must use "explicitly mandatory language," in connection with the establishment of "specific substantive predicates" to limit official discretion, and

---

[1] *Walker v. Pate*, 356 F.2d 502 (7th Cir. 1966), *cert. denied*, 384 U.S. 966 (1966).

[2] *James v. Wallace*, 406 F. Supp. 318 (M.D. Ala. 1976).

[3] *Underwood v. Loving*, 391 F. Supp. 1214 (W.D. Va. 1975) was reversed in part on appeal with no published opinion. *Underwood v. Loving*, 538 F.2d 325 (4th Cir. 1976).

[4] *Martin v. Wainwright*, 525 F.2d 983 (5th Cir. 1976).

23

thereby require that a particular outcome be reached upon a finding that the relevant criteria have been met.

Although regulations provide certain "substantive predicates" to guide prison decisionmakers in determining whether to allow visitation, regulations have no protected federal constitutional interest unless they are worded in such a way that an inmate could reasonably form an objective expectation that a visit would necessarily be allowed absent the occurrence of one of the listed conditions or could reasonably expect to enforce the regulations against prison officials should that visit not be allowed.[5]

The question has been raised whether the right to visitation may be restricted for disciplinary reasons. In *Agron v. Montanye*,[6] inmates challenged the practice of barring visits from family and friends to inmates refusing to shave. The Court granted a preliminary injunction since New York's policy was not to bar visitation to inmates as punishment. The Court, in its analysis, drew attention to the constitutional dimensions of an inmate's right to visitation with reference to rights of association as well as the interests of family members who need and want to visit with the inmate, citing *Pell v. Procunier*.[7] Since most courts defer to the authority of prison officials, it is doubtful that the case would have been decided similarly absent the pre-existing state policy.

The court in *Ribideau v. Stoneman*[8] held that the transfer of inmates and its effects on visitation rights did not raise a federal constitutional issue.

§ 3.2   Pretrial Detainees

Pretrial detainees constitute a special category of inmates. It has been generally held that pretrial detainees are entitled to the rights of other citizens except to the extent necessary to assure their appearance at trial and the security of the institution.[9] Although a pretrial detainee may be subject to some of the same restrictions as convicted prisoners, the restrictions are not unconstitutional unless they amount to punishment.[10] Some courts have held that for pretrial detainees, restrictions on access by visitors must be justified by a compelling interest.[11]

There have been a number of cases that have dealt with delineating the particular rights of visitation for pretrial detainees. One such case is *Rhem v. Malcom*,[12] in which pretrial detainees made demands for a minimum number of visitors per visit (three), as well as a minimum number and length of visits per week (two hours

[5] *Kentucky Department of Corrections v. Thompson*, ___ U.S. ___, 109 S. Ct. 1904 (1989).

[6] *Agron v. Montanye*, 392 F. Supp. 454 (W.D. N.Y. 1975).

[7] *Pell v. Procunier*, 417 U.S. 817, 71 Ohio Op. 2d 195 (1974).

[8] *Ribideau v. Stoneman*, 398 F. Supp. 805 (D. Vt. 1975).

[9] *Bell v. Wolfish*, 441 U.S. 520 (1979); *Rhem v. Malcolm*, 396 F. Supp. 1195 (S.D.N.Y. 1975), *aff'd*, 527 F.2d 1041 (2d Cir. 1975).

[10] *Occhino v. United States*, 686 F.2d 1302 (8th Cir. 1982).

[11] *Inmates of Allegheny County Jail v. Pierce*, 612 F.2d 754 (3d Cir. 1979); *Cooper v. Morin*, 49 N.Y.2d 69, 399 N.E.2d 1188, (1979), *cert. denied*, 466 U.S. 983; *Epps v. Levine*, 480 F. Supp. 50 (D. Md. 1979).

[12] *Rhem v. Malcolm, supra*, n.8.

daily). The court reasoned that the detainees did not have a constitutional right to receive a minimum number of visitors at any one time. Another is *Jordan v. Wolke*,[13] in which the Federal Seventh Circuit Court of Appeals ruled that if jail officials' blanket refusal to allow contact visits for pretrial detainees is not intended as punishment, is rationally related to the goal of maintaining order and security in the jail, and is not excessive in relation to that goal, it does not constitute "punishment" forbidden by the Fourteenth Amendment's Due Process Clause. Further, under a standard of reasonableness, the number of visitors allowed at any one time was a function of the capacity of the facility. The court also ruled that the pretrial detainees had no constitutional right to the minimum number and length of visits.

The matter of physical contact visits for pretrial detainees has been another issue discussed by the courts. The general thinking appears to be that the detainees should be afforded at least reasonably controlled contact visits.[14]

Even the use of telephones for such inmates has been litigated. In *Feeley v. Sampson*,[15] the court held that inmates need not be allowed a reasonable number of calls per day, but the court further held that a total ban on social calls was unreasonable. The court suggested that some social calls could be allowed if they were monitored by a guard.

§ 3.3 Communication Among Prisoners and Union Formation

In terms of "visitation" or communication among prisoners, it has been held that rules against communication at certain times and places between prisoners is not unreasonable. This view was explained in *United States v. Dawson*,[16] where the court reasoned that increased prison violence makes the need to regulate prison life more compelling.

Jail officials may have a blanket prohibition on any pretrial detainee's contact visits with outsiders. This includes even low-risk detainees. The prohibition is a reasonable, nonpunitive response to legitimate security concerns. The dispositive inquiry is whether the challenged practice or policy constitutes punishment or is reasonably related to a legitimate governmental objective. Courts should play a very limited role in this inquiry. Such considerations are peculiarly within the province and professional expertise of corrections officials. Here, contact visits invite a host of security problems. They open a detention facility to the introduction of drugs, weapons and other contraband. Also, to expose to others those detainees who are awaiting trial for serious, violent offenses or have prior convictions carries with it the risk that the safety of innocent individuals will be jeopardized. There-

---

[13] *Jordan v. Wolke*, 615 F.2d 749 (7th Cir. 1980); *In re Smith*, 169 Cal. Rptr. 564 (Cal. App. 1980) (a jail policy which prohibited the visitation of minor children with their incarcerated parents was a denial of the incarcerated parents' rights); *Valentine v. Englehardt*, 492 F. Supp. 1039 (D. N.J. 1980).

[14] *Dillard v. Pitchess*, 399 F. Supp. 1225 (C.D. Cal. 1975); *McNulty v. Chinlund*, 438 N.Y.S.2d 734 (N.Y. 1981); cf. *Cooper v. Morin*, 399 N.E.2d 1188, 49 N.Y.2d 69 (N.Y. 1979), *cert. denied*, 466 U.S. 983; *Valentine v. Englehardt*, 492 F. Supp. 1039 (D. N.J. 1980)

[15] *Feeley v. Sampson*, 570 F.2d 364 (1st Cir. 1978).

[16] *United States v. Dawson*, 516 F.2d 796 (9th Cir. 1975).

fore, totally disallowing contact visits is not excessive in relation to the security and other interests at stake.[17]

In *Brooks v. Wainwright*,[18] the court dismissed an inmate's complaint that he was deprived of his First Amendment freedoms and his right to Equal Protection when his custody classification was changed after he had attempted to organize a prisoner's union. The court felt that the opposition by prison officials to the formation of this union was not a deprivation of the inmate's constitutional rights. The court stated:

> Prisons are not motels or resorts where inmates can check in or out at their liberty. Neither is a prison a public forum providing open access to citizens to freely express their beliefs. The full range of constitutional freedoms that ordinary members of society enjoy must be curtailed in order to achieve the legitimate purposes of imprisonment. So long as the restrictions and limitations are not patently unreasonable, the discretionary decisions of prison officials will be given deference by the courts.[19]

In this case the court found that the prison officials' argument that the organizing of a prisoners' union carried with it inherent dangers and threats to the security of the prison and was not unreasonable.

The California courts, however, have not gone so far in some respects. They have held that while inmates have no constitutional right to participate in a prisoners' union meeting,[20] their right to liberty of speech was unlawfully restricted by prison officials' denial of permission for the prisoners to wear prisoner union lapel buttons.[21]

The Supreme Court has denied the rights of inmates to solicit membership for a "union." In *North Carolina Prisoners' Union v. Jones*,[22] the prison administration permitted membership in a "union" which was actually a prison reform organization. At issue was the prison rule forbidding members from soliciting other inmates to join the organization. The lower court saw little sense and even less legality in this rule and held that since membership was already permitted, solicitation for membership was to be permitted. The Supreme Court disagreed. The lower court also held that although outsiders may urge prisoners to join the union, the prison administrator may prohibit entry of those whose proposed mission is one of union proselytism. The Supreme Court, however, reversed the District Court and held that prisoners do not have the right to organize prison unions. The Supreme

---

[17] *Block v. Rutherford*, 468 U.S. 576, 35 Cr.L. 3221 (1984).
[18] *Brooks v. Wainwright*, 439 F. Supp. 1335 (M.D. Fla. 1977).
[19] *Id.* at 1340.
[20] *In re Price*, 158 Cal. Rptr. 873, 600 P.2d 1330 (Cal. 1979).
[21] *In re Reynolds*, 157 Cal. Rptr. 892 (Cal. 1979).
[22] *North Carolina Prisoners' Union v. Jones*, 433 U.S. 119 (1977).

Court also held that prison regulations prohibiting unions did not violate the First Amendment.

§ 3.4   Conjugal Visitation

Many foreign countries and at least two states — Mississippi and California — have provided facilities in their penal institutions for "conjugal" visits; that is, visits by an inmate's spouse with an opportunity for intimate sexual relations.[23] However, a federal appellate court has held, in *Payne v. District of Columbia*,[24] that such visits are not constitutionally required. The holding in *Payne* was buttressed in the case of *Tarlton v. Clark*,[25] where a different federal appellate court said that an inmate's claim to a right to conjugal visitation "would not come up to the level of a federal constitutional right so as to be cognizable as a basis for relief in the federal court."[26] The cases of *Polakoff v. Henderson,*[27] and *Lyons v. Gilligan*,[28] indicate the continuing refusal of the federal courts to recognize conjugal visitation as a constitutional right of prison inmates. The former case declared that the denial of conjugal visitation did not constitute cruel and unusual punishment prohibited by the Eighth Amendment. In the *Lyons* case the court denied the inmate's assertion that failure to provide conjugal visits violated a married couple's right to privacy. Even assuming that such a right of privacy could be implied from the Supreme Court's decision in *Griswold v. Connecticut*[29] to apply to a prison setting, the Court explained: "The rub of *Griswold* was restraint on governmental intrusion. It cannot be extended to impose an affirmative duty on the government."[30]

The same federal appellate court which decided *Tarlton* indicated the firmness of its position in a subsequent case, *McCray v. Sullivan*,[31] when it said: "Failure to permit conjugal visits does not deny an inmate a federal constitutional right."[32] However, the visiting rights of a wife cannot be summarily suspended after she and her prisoner husband were caught together in an unauthorized area of the prison during visiting hours.[33]

---

[23] *See* Kent, *The Legal and Sociological Dimensions of Conjugal Visitations in Prisons*, 2 NEW ENG. J. ON PRISON L. 47 (1975).

[24] *Payne v. District of Columbia*, 253 F.2d 867 (D.C. Cir. 1958).

[25] *Tarlton v. Clark*, 441 F.2d 384 (5th Cir.), *cert. denied*, 403 U.S. 934 (1971).

[26] *Id.* at 385.

[27] *Polakoff v. Henderson*, 71 Ohio Op. 2d 106, 370 F. Supp. 690 (N.D. Ga. 1973), *aff'd*, 488 F.2d 977 (5th Cir. 1974).

[28] *Lyons v. Gilligan*, 382 F. Supp. 198 (N.D. Ohio 1974).

[29] *Griswold v. Connecticut*, 381 U.S. 479 (1965).

[30] *Lyons v. Gilligan*, 382 F. Supp. 198, 200.

[31] *McCray v. Sullivan*, 509 F.2d 1332 (5th Cir.), *cert. denied*, 423 U.S. 859 (1975).

[32] *Id.* at 1334.

[33] *McKinnis v. Mosley*, 693 F.2d 1054 (11th Cir. 1982).

§ 3.5   News Media Interviews

In *Seattle-Tacoma Newspaper Guild v. Parker*[34] a federal appellate court held that a regulation of the Federal Bureau of Prisons which completely denied press interviews with individual inmates did not violate the inmates' First Amendment freedom of speech. The regulation was also seen as not unduly restricting the flow of information to the public through the news media. Recognizing that the Director of the Bureau of Prisons and the warden at the federal prison must be given wide discretion in formulating rules to govern prison life, the court observed that there were sufficient alternative means of communication which would insure that "any real complaint about the treatment of the inmate or the administration of the prison"[35] would not go unredressed. The court noted that the challenged regulation would not affect an inmate's right to confer freely with his counsel, to conduct unlimited confidential correspondence, to visit with the relatives and friends, to counsel with the clergymen of his faith, and to have free access to the courts. In view of the damaging consequences of a policy permitting press-inmate interviews, such as increased disciplinary problems and the creation of "big wheel" status for certain inmates, who often became less subject to constructive rehabilitation, the court said it was convinced that any burden imposed on the media's ability to report occasioned by the interview ban was more than justified.[36]

The companion cases of *Pell v. Procunier,*[37] and *Saxbe v. Washington Post Company,*[38] presented the United States Supreme Court with the question of the constitutionality of the same federal regulation at issue in *Seattle-Tacoma,* along with a similar provision from the California Department of Corrections Manual. In *Pell* the court answered the claim of four inmates and three professional journalists that the state prison regulation violated their First Amendment freedom of speech by declaring that neither the prisoners nor the press had a freedom of speech right to specific personal interviews. Alternative channels of communication were seen to be open to inmates, and would be protected by the court's ruling in *Procunier v. Martinez,*[39] which established standards for the review of inmate correspondence by prison officials.[40] So long as the restriction on interviews operated in a neutral fashion, without regard to the content of expression, it was seen as falling within the appropriate rules and regulations to which inmates are necessarily subject.[41] As to members of the press, the courts said that since such interviews were not available to members of the general public, they need not be made available to the media on a privileged basis.

---

[34] *Seattle-Tacoma Newspaper Guild v. Parker,* 480 F.2d 1062 (9th Cir. 1973).
[35] *Id.* at 1066.
[36] *Id.* at 1067.
[37] *Pell v. Procunier,* 417 U.S. 817, 71 Ohio Op. 2d 195 (1974).
[38] *Saxbe v. Washington Post Company,* 417 U.S. 843 (1974).
[39] *Procunier v. Martinez,* 416 U.S. 396, 71 Ohio Op. 2d 139 (1974).
[40] *Pell v. Procunier,* 417 U.S. 817, 824, 71 Ohio Op. 2d 195 (1974).
[41] *Id.* at 828.

In the *Saxbe* case, the challenge to the federal prison regulation prohibiting personal interviews by the news media and individually designated inmates was made only by news media representatives. Referring to its decision in *Pell*, the court declared that the regulation did not violate any First Amendment guarantees, since it "does not deny the press access to sources of information available to members of the general public," but is merely a particularized application of the general rule that nobody may enter the prison and designate an inmate whom he would like to visit, unless the prospective visitor is a lawyer, clergyman, relative, or friend of that inmate.[42]

In the case of *Main Road v. Aytch*,[43] a federal district court and federal appellate court had occasion to apply the holdings of *Pell* and *Saxbe* in a suit brought by pretrial detainees of the Philadelphia prison system. Inmates of the Philadelphia prisons had on two separate occasions sought permission from the superintendent to hold press conferences in which they desired to express to the public their concern over problems encountered by them in dealings with a defenders association which represented many of the inmates in their criminal cases, and to allege improprieties in probation procedures. Both requests were denied, although the district court found that the superintendent had authorized other large gatherings of inmates and outsiders, particularly other group press conferences.[44] The decisions in *Pell* and *Saxbe* were announced while *Main Road* was under consideration by the district court, and although the evidence presented indicated that permission to hold the press conferences had been denied on the basis of their expected content, contrary to the neutral approach mandated by *Pell*, the trial judge denied injunctive or declaratory relief, on the ground that he believed such censorship was unlikely to recur.[45]

On appeal, the appellate court also observed that the ban had not been applied in a neutral fashion without regard to the content of the expression, and declared that the criteria which the superintendent applied in determining whether to permit a news conference provided too much occasion for subjective evaluation, thus enabling him to act as a censor.[46] Whether subjects were "explosive" or "sensitive" were said to be standards lacking the constitutionally indispensable "narrowly drawn limitations" on administrative discretion, which therefore ran afoul of the tests of valid prison regulations prescribed in *Procunier v. Martinez*.[47] The case was remanded, and the district court was directed to determine whether the superintendent intended to continue to grant some but not all prisoner requests for interviews and press conferences. If such were the case, the superintendent was to

---

[42] *Saxbe v. Washington Post Co.*, 417 U.S. 843, 849 (1974).

[43] *Main Road v. Aytch*, 385 F. Supp. 105 (E.D. Pa. 1974), *vacated and remanded*, 522 F.2d 1080 (3d Cir. 1975).

[44] *Main Road v. Aytch*, 522 F.2d 1080 (3d Cir. 1975) at 1084.

[45] *Id.* at 1088.

[46] *Id.* at 1089.

[47] *Id.* at 1090.

develop proposed regulations governing the issuance of such permission, which delineated precise and objective tests on the basis of which permission may be denied. Additionally, the district court was directed to implement a review process which would assure a fair determination of the facts upon which a prison adminis-trator denied permission to hold a news conference.[48]

The case of *KQED v. Houchins*[49] dealt further with the issue of the standards followed by prison authorities in denying media access to prisons and prisoners. A sheriff refused to allow the anchorpersons of an educational radio-TV station to inspect the grounds of a county jail after a program by the station reported the suicide of an inmate there, together with certain allegations made by a staff psychi-atrist as to jail conditions. The exclusion was justified as a matter of "policy," but subsequently a limited program of monthly public tours of the facility was imple-mented. The federal district court read *Pell* as standing for the proposition that a prison or jail administrator may curtail media access upon a showing of past resul-tant disruption or present institutional tension, but found that the sheriff had not made such a showing in this case.[50] The inadequacy of the policy in question was more apparent in view of the fact that officials at two neighboring facilities testified that media interviews of inmates had proved neither unduly disruptive nor danger-ous to prison security. A preliminary injunction was issued prohibiting the sheriff from excluding from the jail facilities, as a matter of general policy, responsible representatives of the news media.

The decision was appealed to the United States Supreme Court in *Houchins v. KQED.* The Court reversed the lower court's decision and held that the news media has no constitutional right of access to a county jail, over and above that of other persons, to interview inmates and make sound recordings, films, and photographs for publication and broadcasting by newspapers, radio, and television. There is no requirement that prison officials provide the press with information. The Supreme Court saw the issue as involving the question of whether the news media has a constitutional right of access to a county jail, over and above that of other persons, to interview inmates and gather other information. It held that the degree of open-ness of a penal institution is a question of policy which a legislature, and not a court, must resolve.[51]

§ 3.6 Attorney Representatives

In light of recent case law it is impermissible for prison officials to arbitrarily limit an inmate's right to an attorney's assistance in perfecting appeals of conviction or protesting prison conditions. However, what about the legal paraprofessional, investigator, or law student working for an attorney or legal clinic? Does the inmate have a constitutional right to meet with these persons?

---

[48] *Id.*
[49] *Houchins v. KQED,* 438 U.S. 1 (1978).
[50] *Id.*
[51] *Id.* at 12.

In *Souza v. Travisono*[52] the court recognized that a corollary to the right of access to the courts was the right of access to reasonably available, competent legal assistance. The warden's arbitrary decision to exclude a student legal assistant was held to be unconstitutional. Although prison officials may not arbitrarily limit access to non-attorney legal assistance, they may place reasonable regulations on such visitations. The time, place, and manner of visits may be regulated to further the governmental interest of security, order, or rehabilitation.[53]

The Court of Appeals affirmed the District Court ruling but refused to decide whether inmates must be given reasonable access to law students for the resolution of such issues as divorce, bankruptcy, or probate. Resolution of these issues lies in future litigation.[54]

§ 3.7   Searches of Visitors

Visits may be conditioned on the willingness of the visitors to submit to reasonable searches of their property and person. Visiting pursuant to reasonable regulations would trigger the "consent" exception to the search warrant requirement. However, without an adequate basis to believe contraband is being smuggled into the facility, no forcible search may be made. The sanction would be to immediately terminate visiting rights, subject to appropriate due process hearings.[55]

Strip searches raise different issues.[56] Strip searches of prison visitors were considered unreasonable where they were based solely on anonymous tips that were not investigated to confirm their validity. To justify a strip search of the visitor, prison officials must point to specific objective facts, and rational inferences drawn therefrom, that indicate that the visitor will attempt to smuggle contraband into the prison on his person. Individualized suspicion is essential.[57]

Searches of prisoners following visits are more easily justified. Strip searches, including visual rectal searches, of segregation unit inmates following interviews with visitors, including attorneys, and after visits to the prison law library, do not violate the Fourth and Eighth Amendments, any right of privacy, or any denial of free access to the courts.[58]

---

[52] *Souza v. Travisono*, 368 F. Supp. 459 (D. R.I. 1973), *aff'd*, 498 F.2d 1120 (1st Cir. 1974); *see also Dreher v. Sieloff*, 636 F.2d 1141 (7th Cir. 1980); *United States v. Blue Thunder*, 604 F.2d 550 (8th Cir. 1979).

[53] *See Shakur v. Malcolm*, 525 F.2d 1144 (2d Cir. 1975); *Reed v. Evans*, 455 F. Supp. 1339 (S.D. Ga. 1978), *aff'd*, 592 F.2d 1189 (5th Cir. 1979).

[54] *See* § 7.8

[55] *See* § 12.4 concerning searches of prisoners.

[56] *Cf. Bell v. Wolfish*, 441 U.S. 520 (1979).

[57] *Hunter v. Auger*, 672 F.2d 668 (8th Cir. 1982).

[58] *Arruda v. Fair*, 547 F. Supp. 1324 (D. Mass. 1982).

Chapter 4

PRISONERS' RIGHTS TO USE OF THE MAIL

§ 4.1   Introduction

Detention in a penal institution necessitates a withdrawal of full enjoyment of constitutional rights. But exactly which rights are terminated completely and which are retained is usually unclear. Even those rights not forfeited by incarceration are often retained in a diminished form. These general statements are illustrated by an analysis of the inmate's specific right to use the mail system to send and receive various items such as letters, legal materials, books and magazines.

Article I, § 8 of the Constitution vests power in Congress to establish post offices; this power has been interpreted by the Supreme Court as granting to Congress and the U.S. Postal Service the exclusive right to regulate the postal system of the country.[1] That an inmate has at least a qualified federal right to use the mail system would thus seem clear. However, a long line of cases has established the

---

[1] *Public Clearing House v. Coyne*, 194 U.S. 497 (1904).

33

principle that prison officials may place reasonable restrictions on this right.[2] Restrictions include limiting the number of persons with whom an inmate can correspond, opening and reading incoming and outgoing material, deleting sections from both incoming and outgoing mail, and refusing to mail material for an inmate or to forward correspondence to an inmate subject to important exceptions discussed below. For purposes of this chapter, the phrase "mail censorship" will be used to denote deletion of material from inmate mail.

Two general reasons have been advanced by both prison administrators and the judiciary to justify placing restrictions on an inmate's right to use the mail system.

First, prison security requires such restrictions. Contraband must be kept out of the prisons; escape plans must be detected; material which might incite the prison population must be excluded.

The second rationale for mail restrictions, that the orderly administration of a prison requires them, is closely related to the first. The correctional systems do not have unlimited funds which can be utilized to hire employees to enforce the restrictions placed on sending and receipt of mail. However, because prison security may reasonably demand that inmate mail be opened, inspected for contraband, read, and some sections deleted, some limit on the amount of mail to be checked must be established. Hence, prison officials have justified rules limiting the quantity of mail that an individual can send and receive.

A third reason, rehabilitation of inmates, is infrequently either implicitly or explicitly used to justify mail restrictions. Thus, although the twin requirements of security and administration may justify limiting the amount of mail each inmate may send or receive, neither requirement will justify the establishment of a mail list whereby an inmate can send or receive mail only from sources approved by the prison authorities. However, the goal of rehabilitation has been advanced by penal administrators to justify such action.[3]

Several topics which could logically have been included in this chapter are covered elsewhere. They are: the right to buy and receive legal material;[4] the right to correspond with religious leaders;[5] and the right to receive religious literature.[6]

§ 4.2   The General Right to Control an Inmate's Use of The Mail System—The Traditional Approach

This section, together with the following sections, will discuss the general right of prison authorities to regulate inmate mail, and several of the specific procedures they utilize to accomplish this regulation.

---

[2] *Adams v. Ellis*, 197 F.2d 483 (5th Cir. 1952); *Numer v. Miller*, 165 F.2d 986 (9th Cir. 1948); *Medlock v. Burke*, 285 F. Supp. 67 (E.D. Wis. 1968); *Sherman v. MacDougatt*, 656 F.2d 527 (9th Cir. 1981); *Parnell v. Waldrep*, 511 F. Supp. 764 (D.N.C. 1981).

[3] *Carothers v. Follette*, 314 F. Supp. 1014 (S.D. N.Y. 1970); *Milburn v. McNiff*, 437 N.Y.S.2d 445 (N.Y. App. Div. 1981).

[4] *See* Ch. 7.

[5] *See* Ch. 6.

[6] *See* Ch. 6.

As a starting point, it may be stated that a myriad of past cases had established and maintained the proposition that control of inmate mail is an administrative matter in which the courts will not interfere, unless it is shown that some independent constitutional right is being infringed in that control.[7] This may, for lack of a better phrase, be termed the "traditional view" of the courts on inmate mail regulation. The reason most often advanced to support the traditional view is that courts will not become involved in the normal management of a prison system.

In retrospect, we can see that in all of the areas in the preceding sections in which the courts *did* interfere with prison mail rules, another constitutional right was involved. Thus, communication between an inmate and a court involved in the right of access to the court system. Communication between an inmate and his attorney involved both the right of access to courts and the Sixth Amendment's guarantee of counsel for criminals. The First Amendment right to petition government for redress of grievances justified court intervention in correspondence to and from non-judicial public officials and agencies. The cherished American freedoms of speech and press were involved in regulations concerning access to news media. These rights also were involved in attempts by prison officials to exclude newspapers, magazines, and books from an institution. Inclusion of white-oriented periodicals on approved mailing lists which excluded black-oriented material raised an equal protection argument.

If, however, an inmate could not couple his complaint of undue restriction on his use of the mail with an allegation that a separate constitutional right was thereby infringed, he was, under the "traditional view," doomed to failure in the courts. Thus, in *Dayton v. McGranery*,[8] an inmate's allegation that he was prevented from writing a young woman was dismissed because he did not state a cause of action. *Stroud v. Swope*[9] affirmed the dismissal of an inmate's complaint which sought to restrain a federal prison warden from refusing to mail the inmate's manuscript to a publisher. Such allegations, the court held, did not constitute a deprivation of any of the petitioner's rights. Several federal appellate courts also refused to inquire into the reasons for not allowing an inmate to take a correspondence course. Such decisions are "simply an exercise of administrative discretion."[10]

§ 4.2.1   —The New Approach

Reading and inspection of inmate mail does serve a two-fold purpose: 1) it prevents contraband from being smuggled in or out of an institution; and, 2) it enables

---

[7] *E.g.*, *Brown v. Wainwright*, 419 F.2d 1308 (5th Cir. 1969); *Ortega v. Ragen*, 216 F.2d 561 (7th Cir. 1954); *Medlock v. Burke*, 285 F. Supp. 67 (E.D. Wis. 1968); *Zaczek v. Hutto*, 642 F.2d 74 (4th Cir. 1981); *McBride v. Martin*, No. 77-301 (D. Ore. 1978).

[8] *Dayton v. McGranery*, 201 F.2d 711 (D.C. Cir. 1953); *Carwile v. Ray*, 481 F. Supp. 33 (E.D. Wa. 1979).

[9] *Stroud v. Swope*, 187 F.2d 850 (9th Cir. 1951), *cert. denied*, 342 U.S. 829 (1951).

[10] *Diehl v. Wainwright*, 419 F.2d 1309 (5th Cir. 1970); *Carey v. Settle*, 351 F.2d 483 (8th Cir. 1965); *Numer v. Miller*, 165 F.2d 986 (9th Cir. 1948); *Cook v. Brockway*, 424 F. Supp. 1046 (N.D. Tex. 1977), *aff'd*, 559 F.2d 1214 (5th Cir. 1977).

the prison authorities to detect plans for illegal activity, namely escape. Hence, such action, as least for incoming mail, has uniformly been upheld by the courts.[11] However, the administrators' refusal to mail correspondence which does not contain contraband or details of illegal schemes has been subject to judicial criticism. Under the traditional view, described in the preceding section, such a refusal is normally held as unreviewable. Under what we call the "new approach," prison officials are being judicially required to justify such actions. Thus, in *McNamara v. Moody*,[12] prison officials were held to have violated a prisoner's constitutional rights by refusing to mail a letter to the inmate's girlfriend. The court held that censorship must be limited to concrete violations such as escape plans, plans for disruption of the prison system or work routine, or plans for importing contraband.[13]

The "new approach" to regulation of inmate mail is best illustrated by contrasting *Procunier v. Martinez*[14] with *Turner v. Safley*[15] and *Thornburgh v. Abbott*.[16] The inmate-plaintiffs attacked the validity of a California prison mail regulation which authorized prison officials to refuse to send inmate mail, and to refuse to distribute mail to inmates. The United States Supreme Court held the regulation void for vagueness and overbreadth. In doing so the Court recognized that the First Amendment rights of the "free world" correspondent were at issue. Guidelines for regulating prison mail were established.

Censorship of prison mail is justified if the following criteria are met. First, the regulation must further a substantial governmental interest unrelated to the suppression of expression. Prison officials may not censor inmate correspondence simply to eliminate unflattering or unwelcome opinions of factually inaccurate statements. Rather, they must show that a regulation authorizing mail censorship furthers one or more of the substantial government interests of security, order, and rehabilitation. Second, the limitation of the First Amendment freedoms must be no greater than is necessary or incidental to the protection of the particular government interest involved.[17]

In addition to providing the criteria for censorship, *Procunier* enunciated the minimum procedure that must be followed when prison officials censor or with-

---

[11] *Sostre v. McGinnis*, 442 F.2d 178 (2d Cir. 1971), *cert. denied*, 405 U.S. 978 (1972); *Jones v. Wittenberg*, 58 Ohio Op. 2d 47, 330 F. Supp. 707 (N.D. Ohio 1971) (incoming parcels or letters addressed to inmates awaiting trial can be inspected for contraband, but letters cannot be read); *Palmigiano v. Travisono*, 317 F. Supp. 776 (D.R.I. 1970) (all incoming mail may be read and inspected, but no outgoing mail may be read without a search warrant); *Smith v. Shimp*, 562 F.2d 423 (7th Cir. 1977).

[12] *McNamara v. Moody*, 606 F.2d 621 (5th Cir. 1979); *Carothers v. Follette*, 314 F. Supp. 1014 (S.D. N.Y. 1970).

[13] *McNamara v. Moody, supra* n. 12.

[14] *Procunier v. Martinez*, 416 U.S. 396 (1974).

[15] *Turner v. Safley*, 482 U.S. 78 (1987).

[16] *Thornburgh v. Abbott*, ___ U.S. ___, 109 S. Ct. 1874 (1989).

[17] *Id.* at 413.

hold mail. The inmate must be notified of the rejection of his letter, the letter's author must be allowed to protest the refusal and the complaint must be decided by an official other than the one who made the original decision to refuse delivery.[18]

Thirteen years later, in *Turner v. Safley,* a different standard was used. The United States Supreme Court held that lower courts had been in error in holding that *Martinez* required the application of a strict scrutiny standard of review for resolving prisoners' constitutional complaints. Rather, a lesser standard is appropriate when inquiry is made into whether a prison regulation that impinges on inmates' constitutional rights is "reasonably related" to legitimate penological interests. In determining reasonableness, relevant factors include (a) whether there is a "valid, rational connection" between the regulation and a legitimate and neutral governmental interest put forward to justify it, which connection cannot be so remote as to render the regulation arbitrary or irrational; (b) whether there are alternative means of exercising the asserted constitutional rights that remain open to inmates, which alternatives, if they exist, will require a measure of judicial deference to the corrections officials' expertise; (c) whether and the extent to which accommodation of the asserted right will have an impact on prison staff, on inmates' liberty, and on the allocation of limited prison resources, which impact, if substantial, will require particular deference to corrections officials; and (d) whether the regulation represents an "exaggerated response" to prison concerns, the existence of a ready alternative that fully accommodates the prisoner's rights at *de minimis* costs to valid penological interests being evidence of unreasonableness.

Inmate correspondence regulations that permitted correspondence between immediate family members who were inmates at different institutions within the State Division's jurisdiction, and between inmates "concerning legal matters," but allowed other inmate correspondence only if each inmate's classification was reasonable and facially valid, passed constitutional review. The regulations were logically related to the legitimate security concerns of prison officials. It was felt that mail between prisons could be used to communicate escape plans, to arrange violent acts, and to foster prison gang activity. The regulation did not deprive prisoners of all means of expression, but simply barred communication with a limited class of people — other inmates — with whom authorities have particular cause to be concerned. The regulation was entitled to deference on the basis of the significant impact of prison correspondence on the liberty and safety of other prisoners and prison personnel. Such correspondence facilitates the development of informal organizations that threaten safety and security at penal institutions. Nor was there an obvious, easy alternative to the regulation, since monitoring inmate correspondence imposed more than a *de minimis* cost in terms of the burden on staff resources required to conduct item-by-item censorship. It also created an appreciable risk of missing dangerous communications. The regulation was content-neutral

---

[18] *See Padgett v. Stein,* 406 F. Supp. 287 (M.D. Pa. 1975); *Gates v. Collier,* 525 F.2d 965 (5th Cir. 1976).

and did not unconstitutionally abridge the First Amendment rights of prison inmates.

Two years later, in *Thornburgh v. Abbott*, the Supreme Court reviewed Federal Bureau of Prisons regulations that generally permitted prisoners to receive publications from the "outside," but authorized wardens, pursuant to specified criteria, to reject an incoming publication if it is found "to be detrimental to the security, good order, or discipline of the institution or if it might facilitate criminal activity." Wardens could not reject a publication solely because of its religious, philosophical, political, social, sexual, unpopular or repugnant content, or establish an excluded list of publications, but were required to review each issue of a subscription separately.

The Court held that mail regulations that affect the sending of publications to prisoners must be analyzed under the standard set forth in *Turner v. Safley* and are valid if they are reasonably related to legitimate penological interests. Prison officials are due considerable deference in regulating the delicate balance between prison order and security and the legitimate demands of "outsiders" who seek to enter the prison environment. The less deferential standard of *Martinez* — whereby prison regulations authorizing mail censorship must be "generally necessary" to protect one or more legitimate government interests — was limited to regulations concerning outgoing personal correspondence from prisoners, regulations which are not centrally concerned with the maintenance of prison order and security. In addition, *Martinez* was overruled to the extent that it might support the drawing of a categorical distinction between incoming correspondence from prisoners (to which *Turner* applied its reasonableness standard) and incoming correspondence from nonprisoners.

The regulations under review were facially valid under the *Turner* standard. Their underlying objective of protecting prison security was legitimate and was neutral with regard to the content of the expression regulated. The broad discretion the regulations accorded wardens was rationally related to security interests. Further, alternative means of expression remained open to the inmates, since the regulations permitted a broad range of publications to be sent, received, and read, even though specific publications were prohibited. Lastly, the prisoners established no alternative to the regulations that would accommodate their constitutional rights at a *de minimis* cost to valid penological interests.

The "new approach" to inmate mail advanced by *Martinez, Turner,* and *Abbott,* does not eliminate mail censorship, but only regulates it. When the screening of mail is done pursuant to regulations reasonably related to legitimate government interests, the prison official's right to read, inspect, and stop inmate correspondence remains intact.

§ 4.3   Communication with the Courts

It has been the law of the land since 1941 that a state and its officers may not abridge or impair an inmate's right to apply to a federal court for a writ of habeas corpus. In *Ex parte Hull*,[19] the inmate-plaintiff was confined in the Michigan State Prison. He had prepared a petition for a writ of habeas corpus to be filed in the United States Supreme Court, but a prison official refused to mail it, pursuant to a prison regulation requiring legal papers to go through the institutional welfare officer. The regulation provided that if the writ were favorably acted upon, it would be referred to the legal section of the parole board, and then if found to be properly drawn, it would be directed to the appropriate court. The Supreme Court of the United States held this regulation as invalid, declaring that a state and its officers may not abridge or impair an inmate's right to apply to a federal court for a writ of habeas corpus. Whether the writ is properly drawn is a question for the court to determine, not prison officials.

Since the decision in *Ex parte Hull*, federal courts have closely scrutinized any prison regulation which allows the prison administrators to refuse to forward inmate mail. For example, in *Bryan v. Werner*[20] a federal court struck down a prison regulation which permitted officials to refuse to mail legal matters for inmates if the officials felt the form used was improper.

Although there would seem to be no rational basis for distinguishing between legal material which pertains to the inmate's conviction and legal material which involves other matters, at least one federal appellate court has sustained such a distinction. *Kirby v. Thomas*[21] involved a regulation of the Kentucky Department of Corrections which forbade mailing of legal papers unless they pertained to the validity of the inmate's conviction. The court stated only one reason for upholding the regulation: the state prison administrator's need for discretion in maintaining discipline.

However, the vast majority of courts now recognize that an inmate has the right to petition the courts concerning not only his conviction, but also the constitutionality of the conditions of his confinement. Access to the courts is a fundamental right and "all other rights of an inmate are illusory without it . . ."[22]

§ 4.3.1   —Censorship of Communication with the Courts

Several decisions have dealt with the right of prison officials to censor mail sent to and received from a court by an inmate. In *Smith v. Shimp*[23] the court stated that privileged mail, i.e., mail between the inmate and attorneys, government officials, or news media personnel, can be opened only in the presence of the inmate and only to verify the addressee. Emphasizing the inmate's right of access to the courts, the Eighth Circuit Court of Appeals held that legal mail which is identified as

---

[19] *Ex parte Hull*, 316 U.S. 546 (1961).

[20] *Bryan v. Werner*, 516 F.2d 233 (3d Cir. 1975).

[21] *Kirby v. Thomas*, 336 F.2d 462 (6th Cir. 1964).

[22] *McCray v. Sullivan*, 509 F.2d 1332, 1337 (5th Cir. 1975), *cert. denied*, 423 U.S. 859 (1975); *cf.*, *Coleman v. Crisp*, 444 F. Supp. 31 (W.D. Okla. 1977).

[23] *Smith v. Shimp*, 562 F.2d 423 (7th Cir. 1977); *Frazier v. Donelon*, 381 F. Supp. 911 (E.D. La. 1974), *aff'd*, 520 F.2d 941 (5th Cir. 1975).

such cannot be opened for inspection for contraband except in the presence of the prisoner.[24]

The clear trend of the case law is to allow incoming mail from the courts to be inspected for contraband, but with prohibitions against reading the correspondence.

§ 4.4 Communication with Attorneys

A basic corollary to the right of access to the courts is the inmate's right to communicate with an attorney concerning the validity of his conviction or the constitutionality of conditions within the detention facility.[25] If the inmate is not represented by counsel, he has the right to correspond with an attorney in an attempt to secure legal representation, and this communication may set forth factual elements of his claim, even though critical of the prison administration.[26] The right to seek legal representation extends not only to the right to communicate with individual members of the bar, but also to the right to seek advice and possible representation from legal organizations such as the American Civil Liberties Union.[27]

The right to communicate with an attorney has been limited to communication involving legal matters. In *Rhinehart v. Rhay,*[28] for example, Washington state prison officials refused to mail several letters from the plaintiff to his attorney. The officials claimed, and the court agreed, that the purpose of the letters in question was to express the plaintiff's belief that homosexual acts among consenting prisoners ought to be legalized. There was no evidence that the plaintiff was denied access to his attorney for the purpose of perfecting an appeal of his conviction.

§ 4.4.1 —Censorship of Communication with Attorneys

The right of an inmate to communicate with his attorney concerning pending or contemplated legal action is recognized by all courts today. Of more importance, however, is the right of prison authorities to open, read, and censor such communications. Inmates often complain that such conduct interferes with their right to counsel as guaranteed by the Sixth Amendment.

Generally, the cases concerning censorship of inmate letters to their attorneys fall into three groups. In the first group are cases which recognize that the censoring of inmate mail, including correspondence to attorneys, is a matter of internal

---

[24] *Jensen v. Klecker,* 648 F.2d 1179 (8th Cir. 1981); *Ramos v. Lamm,* 639 F.2d 559 (10th Cir. 1980); *Jones v. Diamond,* 594 F.2d 997 (5th Cir. 1979); *Taylor v. Sterrett,* 532 F.2d 462 (5th Cir. 1976).

[25] *Sostre v. McGinnis,* 442 F.2d 178 (2d Cir. 1971), *cert. denied,* 405 U.S. 978 (1972); *Blanks v. Cunningham,* 409 F.2d 220 (4th Cir. 1969); *Marsh v. Moore,* 325 F. Supp. 392 (D. Mass. 1971); *Thibadoux v. LaVallee,* 411 F. Supp. 862 (W.D. N.Y. 1976).

[26] *Bounds v. Smith,* 430 U.S. 817 (1977).

[27] *Burns v. Swenson,* 430 F.2d 771 (8th Cir. 1970), *cert. denied,* 404 U.S. 1062 (1971), *reh. denied,* 405 U.S. 969 (1971); *Nolan v. Scafati,* 430 F.2d 548 (1st Cir. 1970).

[28] *Rhinehart v. Rhay,* 314 F. Supp. 81 (W.D. Wash. 1970).

prison administration with which the courts hesitate to interfere.[29] These cases state that inspection of inmate mail is necessary to detect contraband or to discover escape plans, and as long as the contents of the communications are not disclosed to the prosecuting attorney, and the inmate is afforded ample time to confer privately with his attorney in the institution, there is no infringement on the inmate's Sixth Amendment right to counsel.[30] An extreme application of this reasoning is found in the case of *Cox v. Crouse*.[31] There, while a criminal charge was being tried against the inmate, the warden systematically opened and read the inmate's correspondence with his attorney, and then communicated the contents to the state attorney general. The inmate argued that prejudice could be presumed from such disclosure; the court rejected this claim, stating that the inmate must show actual prejudice to be entitled to relief.

In the second group, the case of *Sostre v. McGinnis*[32] represents a compromise between the position of no censorship of correspondence between an inmate and an attorney and the position of treating such correspondence like any other type of mail, and hence allowing it to be censored. In *Sostre,* the court held that officials could open and read such letters, but could not delete anything from them or refuse to forward them unless the inmate was clearly abusing the privilege. Two examples of clear abuse of the privilege, the court stated, would be mailing or receipt of contraband and mailing of plans for an illegal activity.

Smith v. Robbins,[33] another federal appellate decision, sought to give even more protection to inmate-attorney correspondence than did *Sostre.* In the *Smith* case, the warden was enjoined from reading the correspondence, and he could open such material to inspect for contraband only in the presence of the inmate involved.

The third group of cases represents the current view, which is a significant break with the past. These cases hold that prison officials are permitted to open attorney correspondence in the presence of the inmate to check for contraband, but the contents may not be read. This procedure of checking for contraband neither constitutes censorship, nor does it place a chilling effect on the correspondence.[34] However, reasonable regulations of the correspondence are permitted. Such regulations may require that the attorney first identify himself in a signed letter or that the inmate supply prison officials with the name and business address of his attorney.[35]

---

[29] *Brabson v. Wilkins,* 19 N.Y.2d 433, 227 N.E.2d 383, 280 N.Y.S.2d 561 (1967); *Frazier v. Donelon,* 381 F. Supp. 911 (E.D. La. 1974), *aff'd,* 520 F.2d 941 (5th Cir. 1975).

[30] *Ramer v. United States,* 411 F.2d 30 (9th Cir. 1969), *cert. denied,* 396 U.S. 965 (1969); *Haas v. United States,* 344 F.2d 56 (8th Cir. 1965).

[31] *Cox v. Crouse,* 367 F.2d 824 (10th Cir. 1967).

[32] *Sostre v. McGinnis,* 442 F.2d 178 (2d Cir. 1971), *cert. denied,* 405 U.S. 978 (1972).

[33] *Smith v. Robbins,* 454 F.2d 696 (1st Cir. 1972).

[34] *Wolff v. McDonnell,* 418 U.S. 539, 71 Ohio Op. 2d 336 (1974); *Jensen v. Klecker,* 648 F.2d 1179 (8th Cir. 1981).

[35] *Taylor v. Sterrett,* 532 F.2d 462 (5th Cir. 1976).

Inmates who are serving sentences need the assistance of counsel to perfect appeals of their convictions and to initiate and litigate civil actions. Many inmates of detention facilities, however, do not stand convicted of any crime, but are being held pending trial on charges lodged against them. The need of the pretrial detainee for counsel is obviously crucial. Therefore, it is not surprising that cases, relying on the *Wolff* rationale, recognize the right to uncensored correspondence between pretrial detainees and their legal counsel.[36]

§ 4.5 Communication with Non-Judicial Public Officials and Agencies

One of the rights specified in the First Amendment is the right to petition the government for the redress of alleged grievances. This right is especially important to prisoners when they seek to complain of conditions of confinement. Quite often, however, an administrative complaint to the department of government ultimately responsible for the management of the prison is both quicker and more effective than seeking judicial review. Hence, the courts have generally protected the right of inmates to utilize the mail system to communicate with nonjudicial public officials and agencies. *LeVier v. Woodson*[37] prevented state prison officials from stopping letters (complaining of prison conditions) to the state governor, attorney general, and the attorney attached to the state's pardon agency.

Reading and censoring inmate correspondence became more restricted after the decisions of *Procunier* and *Wolff.* The rationale of these two cases was relied upon in *Taylor v. Sterrett,*[38] and applied to inmate correspondence with government agencies. Emphasizing the inmate's First Amendment right to petition the government for redress of grievances, and finding the reading of government agency correspondence not substantially related to jail security, the court enjoined prison officials from reading the correspondence. The decision, however, allowed prison officials to continue opening incoming mail to check for contraband.

Punishing an inmate for communicating his complaints to higher administrative levels is as much a denial of the right to petition government as is outright refusal to mail such letters. This principle is exemplified by *Cavey v. Williams,*[39] in which a warden was ordered to pay compensatory and punitive damages to the inmate-plaintiff because the warden violated his First Amendment rights by punishing him for a letter he wrote criticizing prison policies.

The few cases which are cited in support of the proposition (that inmates do not have the right to use the mails to voice complaints to government officials) either are void of legal reasoning or simply do not involve a petition seeking redress of

---

[36] *Id.*

[37] *LeVier v. Woodson,* 443 F.2d 360 (10th Cir. 1971).

[38] *Taylor v. Sterrett,* 532 F.2d 462 (5th Cir. 1976).

[39] *Cavey v. Williams,* 435 F. Supp. 475 (D. Md. 1977), *aff'd,* 580 F.2d 1047 (4th Cir. 1978); *Fulwood v. Clemmer,* 206 F. Supp. 370 (D.C. Cir. 1962).

prison grievances. For example, the inmate-plaintiff in *McCloskey v. Maryland*[40] sought to enjoin state penal officials from refusing to mail letters from him to his elected state and federal legislators. However, the letters did not complain of conditions of confinement, but were expressions of the inmate's anti-Semitic views. In such a case, the court held, refusal to mail the letters was not an abuse of the prison officials' control over inmates' mailing privilege. *McCloskey,* therefore, is not authority for the view that prison administrators may arbitrarily refuse to forward a letter from an inmate to the state director of corrections, complaining of conditions within the prison, even though it has been cited as such.[41] A case similar to *McCloskey* is *United States ex rel. Thompson v. Fay,*[42] in which the court held that a state prisoner had no right to mail a letter that sought legal advice to a federal committee which was investigating the problems of indigent defendants accused of federal crimes. The committee was not rendering legal aid to indigents and furthermore, the inmate had not been charged or convicted of a federal crime. Thus, not only did the correspondence fail to complain of conditions of confinement, but it was entirely frivolous.

Prison rules for mailing non-privileged matter required the mailing of a form to the addressee with whom the prisoner wanted to correspond. The form had to be mailed back by the addressee. The prisoner then requested permission to mail his "correspondence request" mail sealed. The rules did not permit the prisoner to state on the form his reasons for requesting permission to correspond. The rule was held to be irrational and unconstitutional as applied to three letters to public officials or agencies and one to the ACLU.[43]

§ 4.6   Communication with News Media—Inmates' Right to Use the Mail to Contact News Media

The First Amendment prohibits governmental interference with freedom of speech and freedom of the press. Although the judiciary has construed the amendment so as to allow reasonable restraints on these freedoms, it is still true that these rights occupy a preferred position in the American system of government. Hence, the courts generally require that any restriction on First Amendment rights be based upon a "substantial and controlling" state interest which requires such restriction,[44] and requires that the restriction be the least drastic method of accomplishing the state goal.[45]

A prison ban on an inmate sending letters which complain of internal conditions in the institution to the news media—radio, television, and the press—restricts First Amendment freedoms in two ways. First, the inmate's right to free speech is

---

[40] *McCloskey v. Maryland,* 337 F.2d 72 (4th Cir. 1964).
[41] *Belk v. Mitchell,* 294 F. Supp. 800 (W.D. N.C. 1968).
[42] *United States ex rel. Thompson v. Fay,* 197 F. Supp. 855 (S.D. N.Y. 1961).
[43] *Davidson v. Skully,* 694 F.2d 50 (2d Cir. 1982).
[44] *Jackson v. Godwin,* 400 F.2d 529, 541 (5th Cir. 1968).
[45] *Shelton v. Tucker,* 364 U.S. 479 (1960); *Vienneau v. Shanks,* 425 F. Supp. 676 (W.D. Wis. 1977).

curtailed. Second, the public's right to know what is happening within the prison system, a right which can only be fulfilled through an informed press, is restricted.

Regardless of the degree of restriction on the actual flow of information between inmate and reporter, however, prisoners would seem to have an interest in communication with the public through press that is distinctive from and additional to their interest in simply communicating with newsmen.[46]

In *Nolan v. Fitzpatrick*,[47] the inmates contested the legality of a Massachusetts state prison regulation which totally banned letters from inmates to the news media. The right of prison officials to read such letters and to inspect them for contraband or for escape plans was not challenged. The prison officials advanced various reasons in support of the rule: that such communications would inflame the inmates and, hence, endanger prison security; that complaint letters would create administrative problems because they would encourage the news media to seek personal interviews with inmates; and that complaint letters would retard the rehabilitation of both the writer and other inmates. The district court found these reasons to be either unsupported by evidence or insufficient to require a total ban on letters to the press.

The rationale of *Procunier v. Martinez* and its applicability to all classes of inmate correspondence becomes evident. Applying the *Procunier* rationale to inmate contact with the media, a federal court invalidated prison regulations on the grounds that they ". . . provide too much occasion for subjective evaluation, thus enabling the licensing official to act as a censor."[48] Similarly, in *Taylor v. Sterrett*,[49] the court recognized the inmate's right to communicate with the press under *Procunier* guidelines:

. . . the interest of jail security necessitates that incoming mail from the press be inspected for contraband . . . And the distinctive ethical standards attorneys are held to cannot apply to the press. We cannot say, therefore, that the reading of outgoing inmate correspondence to the press does not further a substantial governmental interest. Transmitting unread mail to supposed members of the press could be used as subterfuge for discussing illegal activities.

. . . Since the free expression and petition interests of the inmate-plaintiffs are operative in this case, the practice of reading this mail must be essential to jail security.

---

[46] The Supreme Court, 1973 Term, 88 HARV. L. REV. 165-73 (1974).

[47] *Nolan v. Fitzpatrick*, 451 F.2d 545 (1st Cir. 1971), *rev'g*, 326 F. Supp. 209 (D. Mass. 1971).

[48] *Main Road v. Aytch*, 522 F.2d 1080 (3d Cir. 1975).

[49] *Taylor v. Sterrett*, 532 F.2d 462 (5th Cir. 1976).

The decision further stated that the inmate-press correspondence should be treated under procedures similar to those applying to inmate-attorney mail.[51]

§ 4.7　Communication with Inmates in Other Institutions

The courts have generally given prison administrators unfettered discretion in refusing to allow one inmate to correspond with another inmate. The reason most often given to justify such action is that the control of inmate mail is an administrative function in which the courts refuse to intervene. Thus, in *Scholbohm v. U.S. Attorney General*,[52] a federal district court held that a prison policy of prohibiting correspondence between inmates of different institutions was permissible. The court stated that indefinite mail restriction imposed as a punishment was a legitimate exercise of disciplinary power where a prisoner had violated existing prison mail regulations.[53]

Johnson v. Avery[54] held that prison officials who fail to provide adequate legal assistance cannot forbid a jailhouse lawyer from rendering legal assistance to a fellow inmate. The case left open the interesting question concerning correspondence between inmates. Even though prison officials might have the general power to prevent such correspondence, would the *Johnson* rationale prevent the refusal to allow an inmate to engage in legal correspondence with an inmate in another institution? The Ninth Circuit Court of Appeals held that the complete prohibition of an inmate's correspondence with his jailhouse lawyer in another institution was a violation of that inmate's rights.[55]

§ 4.8　Receipt of Inflammatory Material

The Supreme Court has held that the First Amendment freedoms of speech and press encompass the "right to receive information and ideas."[56] These rights are not, however, absolute, but are subject to two important qualifications: 1) pornographic material is not protected by the First Amendment, and 2) the First Amendment does not protect activity which involves a clear and present danger of inciting or producing imminent lawless action.[57] This section will discuss the authority of prison administrators to exclude material, mainly magazines and books, from the institution because they constitute a clear and present danger of disrupting prison security.

Although the "clear and present danger" test did not originate in prison litigation, it is applicable as a general principle of law to that specific environment. In

---

[51] *See* § 4.4.1

[52] *Scholbohm v. U.S. Attorney General*, 479 F. Supp. 401 (M.D. Pa. 1979); *Lawrence v. Davis*, 401 F. Supp. 1203 (W.D. Pa. 1979).

[53] *Ibid.*

[54] *Johnson v. Avery*, 393 U.S. 483 (1969).

[55] *Storseth v. Spellman*, 654 F.2d 1349 (9th Cir. 1981).

[56] *Stanley v. Georgia*, 394 U.S. 557, 564 (1969).

[57] *Brandenburg v. Ohio*, 395 U.S. 444, 48 Ohio Op. 2d 320 (1969).

fact, due to the tense atmosphere that often exists in such institutions, prison officials may be able to exclude material using this test, even though such material is clearly protected by the First Amendment outside of the prison walls. The application of the clear and present danger test in a prison setting was explained in the case of *Sostre v. Otis*:

> We accept the premise that certain literature may pose such a clear and present danger to the security of a prison, or to the rehabilitation of prisoners, that it should be censored. To take an extreme example, if there were mailed to a prisoner a brochure demonstrating in detail how to saw prison bars with utensils used in the mess hall, or how to provoke a prison riot, it would properly be screened. A magazine detailing for incarcerated drug addicts how they might obtain an euphoric "high," comparable to that experienced from heroin, by sniffing aerosol or glue available for other purposes within the prison walls, would likewise be censorable as restraining effective rehabilitation. Furthermore, it is undoubtedly true that in the volatile atmosphere of a prison, where a large number of men, many with criminal tendencies, live in close proximity to each other, violence can be fomented by the printed word much more easily than in the outside world. Some censorship or prior restraint on inflammatory literature sent into prisons is, therefore, necessary to prevent such literature from being used to cause disruption or violence within the prison. It may well be that in some prisons where the prisoners' flash-point is low, articles regarding bombing, prison riots, or the like, which would be harmless when sold on the corner newsstand would be too dangerous for release to the prison population.[58]

Even though all courts formerly accepted the proposition that prison officials can exclude literature which presents a clear and present danger to prison security, the judiciary was often called upon to review the procedure that administrators utilize to make the determination that a certain book or newspaper is a clear and present danger to the institution's security. This aspect of judicial review is crucial; if the courts routinely sanction the officials' decision, with little or no analysis of the process and standards used to reach that decision, the First Amendment rights of the inmates are likely to be lost. This loss can be illustrated by two cases decided by the federal courts. In the first case, *Abernathy v. Cunningham*,[59] the prisoner-plaintiff sought court permission to obtain a book entitled *The Message of the Black Man in America* and to subscribe to the newspaper, *Elijah Muhammad Speaks*. Both publications pertained to the Black Muslim religion. The appellate court upheld the prison officials' refusal to comply with the requests, stating that the

[58] *Sostre v. Otis*, 330 F. Supp. 941, 944-945 (S.D.N.Y. 1971).
[59] *Abernathy v. Cunningham*, 393 F.2d 775 (4th Cir. 1968).

evaluation of the literature by the officials as to its probable effects on the prison population must be given great weight.

In the later case of *Battle v. Anderson*[60] the court recognized that an inmate retains some of his First Amendment rights even while incarcerated, and the prison officials had the burden of proving to the court that the publications, *Elijah Muhammad Speaks* and *The Message to the Black Man in America*, present a threat to security, discipline, and order within the institution.

Battle was written to conform to *Procunier* standards for protecting the inmate's right to receive literature, delineating the restrictions and procedures under which mail may be censored. Accordingly, "censorship of these publications is permissible only if it furthers the prison's substantial interest in security, order, or rehabilitation, and no less restrictive means would suffice to protect the prison's interest."[61] Recognizing the significant contributions of *Procunier* to prison mail regulation, later decisions have refined the holding to fashion the law concerning inflammatory material.[62] Publications containing enlarged views of the inner mechanisms of guns may be withheld.[63]

§ 4.9   Receipt of Obscene Material

In 1957, the United States Supreme Court held that obscene literature is not within the ambit of constitutionally-protected freedoms of speech or press.[64] Therefore, obscene material can be regulated by both the federal and state governments. Federal regulation is usually effected by prohibiting the mailing of obscene material. State regulation is accomplished by confiscating such material and by criminally punishing those who sell it. In a prison environment, however, pornography is controlled by refusing to forward such literature to the inmate. Because pornographic material is not protected by the First Amendment, such refusal by prison administrators is not unconstitutional.[65] At least one case has stated that obscene material can also be excluded from a prison because of its tendency to incite homosexual activity, which in turn often leads to violence.[66]

Sexually explicit material may be kept from inmates on the grounds that the material is detrimental to rehabilitation and leads to deviate sexual behavior by some inmates.[67] Regulations excluding such material must not be overbroad so that

---

[60] *Battle v. Anderson*, 376 F. Supp. 402 (E.D. Okla. 1974).

[61] *Carpenter v. South Dakota*, 536 F.2d 759 (8th Cir. 1976).

[62] *E.g.*, *Chiarello v. Bohlinger*, 391 F. Supp. 1153 (S.D.N.Y. 1975) (refusal to mail inmate's manuscript); *Morgan v. LaVallee*, 526 F.2d 221 (2d Cir. 1975) (refusal to allow inmate to receive specific publication); *Aikens v. Jenkins*, 534 F.2d 751 (7th Cir. 1976) (regulations concerning publications must not be overbroad); *Blue v. Hogan*, 553 F.2d 960 (5th Cir. 1977) (regulations must be governed by the test in *Procunier*).

[63] *Sherman v. MacDougatt*, 656 F.2d 527 (9th Cir. 1981).

[64] *Roth v. United States*, 354 U.S. 476, 14 Ohio Op. 2d 331 (1957).

[65] *In re Van Geldern*, 14 Cal. App. 3d 838, 92 Cal. Rptr. 592 (1971).

[66] *Id.*

[67] *Carpenter v. South Dakota*, 536 F.2d 759 (8th Cir. 1976).

"nudes" not designed primarily to arouse sexual desires are unconstitutionally excluded.[68]

The problem in excluding pornography from the prisons is similar to the problem encountered in excluding allegedly inflammatory literature: Is the decision to exclude made under safeguards which protect the inmates' rights to receive constitutionally protected material? If the decision to exclude literature as obscene is left to a prison censor, without meaningful administrative or judicial review, the inmates' rights will often be dependent upon highly subjective decisions. This is not necessarily the fault of the censor; although he may be judicially ordered to exclude only those "books or periodicals which would come clearly within the definition of pornography established by the decisions of the Supreme Court . . . ."[69] The definition of "pornographic" is nebulous at best.

The Supreme Court first sanctioned the following test: material is obscene if "to the average person, applying contemporary community standards, the dominant theme of the material taken as a whole appeals to prurient interest."[70] Subsequent cases, however, led to various interpretations of this definition by different members of the Court. Two justices believed "community standards" meant varying local standards[71]; others felt it meant a uniform national standard.[72] Another justice found it impossible to define obscenity, but stated "I know it when I see it . . . ."[73]

In 1973 the Supreme Court of the United States decided *Miller v. California*[74] and held contemporary community standards were not necessarily a national standard. However, no case has held, or could reasonably be expected to hold, that the "community" is the prison itself!

With this variety of definitions, a prison censor must be fully informed as to the current legal definition of pornography. Memoranda from the institution's legal advisor could accomplish this need. One court, however, decided to relieve the censor of such worries by allowing him to use the *Roth* guidelines, without regard to post-*Roth* decisions.[75] In any event, minimum due process and opportunity to appeal the censor's decision would seem to be required.

§ 4.10   Receipt of Racially-Oriented Newspapers and Magazines

The Fourteenth Amendment to the Constitution forbids the states to deny any person "equal protection of the law;" that is, the state must treat all similarly situated persons in an identical manner. Black inmates at several institutions have suc-

---

[68] *Aikens v. Jenkins*, 534 F.2d 751 (7th Cir. 1976).

[69] *Jones v. Wittenberg*, 58 Ohio Op. 2d 47, 330 F. Supp. 707, 720 (N.D. Ohio 1971), *aff'd*, 456 F.2d 854 (6th Cir. 1972).

[70] *Roth v. United States*, 354 U.S. 476, 489, 14 Ohio Op. 2d 331 (1957).

[71] *Jacobellis v. Ohio*, 378 U.S. 184, 200, 28 Ohio Op. 2d 101 (1964) (Warren, C.J., and Clark, J., dissenting).

[72] *Id.* at 192-195 (Brennan and Goldberg, JJ.).

[73] *Id.* at 197 (Stewart, J., concurring).

[74] *Miller v. California*, 413 U.S. 15 (1973).

[75] *Palmigiano v. Travisono*, 317 F. Supp. 776, 790 (D.R.I. 1970).

cessfully used the equal protection clause to contest the refusal of prison officials to allow them to subscribe to non-subversive periodicals published primarily for blacks (for example, national magazines such as *Ebony* and *Sepia*). *Jackson v. Godwin*[76] is illustrative of such cases. Petitioner Jackson, an inmate in the Florida State Prison, alleged that although one-half of the institution's population was black, non-subversive newspapers and magazines written primarily for blacks were systematically kept off the approved list of periodicals, while numerous white-oriented publications were approved for receipt. The administrators claimed the establishment of an approved periodicals list was a function of prison management which was not reviewable by the courts, and that the literature in question would harm prison security.

The court held that an inmate retains his Fourteenth Amendment right to equal protection even while he is incarcerated, and that the exclusion of all black-oriented periodicals from a prison in which the receipt of many white-oriented publications is permitted, violated the equal protection clause. The penal officials were ordered to allow blacks to subscribe to non-subversive black newspapers and magazines.

The case of *Aikens v. Lash*,[77] relying on *Procunier* standards, held that prison officials must afford inmates minimal due process when publications are prohibited. The "liberty interest" required the following form of review: 1) written notice to the inmate of the denial and reason for denial of the publication; 2) opportunity to object to the denial; and 3) prompt review by a prison official other than one who made the original denial to forward the publication.

§ 4.11   Use of Mail Lists

One method commonly used by prison authorities to control correspondence between an inmate and the outside world is the requirement that an inmate can send mail to and receive correspondence from only those persons approved by the prison authorities. Names can be added to and deleted from the mail list at any time. The administrators justify the use of mail lists on two grounds: 1) that the time-consuming task of reading and inspecting inmate mail required a limit on the number of persons with whom an inmate can correspond; and 2) that the rehabilitation of inmates demands controls upon the people with whom an inmate corresponds.

Generally, the few cases which have considered the legality of mail lists have held that the establishment and maintenance of such lists is a necessary incident of

---

[76] *Jackson v. Godwin*, 400 F.2d 529 (5th Cir. 1968); *accord, Owens v. Brierley*, 452 F.2d 640 (3d Cir. 1971); *see also Martin v. Wainwright*, 525 F.2d 983 (5th Cir. 1976).

[77] *Aikens v. Lash*, 390 F. Supp. 663 (N.D. Ind. 1975), *modified in*, 514 F.2d 55 (7th Cir. 1975); *Hopkins v. Collins*, 548 F.2d 503 (4th Cir. 1977).

prison administration which does not violate any federal right.[78] *Jones v. Witten-berg*[79] prohibited county jail officials from placing limitations on the persons to whom inmates awaiting trial could write. However, in another case involving inmates who were awaiting trial, a federal district court sanctioned the use of an approved addressee list of seven persons to whom an inmate could write.[80] Such a regulation, the court stated, "is a reasonable method of maintaining prison secu-rity without undue restriction on the First Amendment rights of prisoners . . . ."[81]

The use of mail lists has been closely scrutinized by the courts. Prison officials have been required to justify mail list regulations with evidence that such rules are "necessary to protect a substantial government interest unrelated to the suppres-sion of expression and the limitations imposed were no greater than necessary to accomplish that objective."[82]   Hence, *Finney v. Arkansas Board of Corrections*[83] enjoined prison officials from enforcing a broad regulation concerning mail lists until the tests of *Procunier* had been met. Prohibiting prisoners from correspond-ing with minors to whom they were not related by blood or marriage, without the prior consent of the minor's parents, violates the First Amendment.[84]

§ 4.12   Receipt of Books and Packages From Outside Sources

The United States Supreme Court approved special institutional regulations regarding the receipt of books and packages in *Bell v. Wolfish.*[85] The Court recog-nized that prisons have a legitimate governmental purpose to provide security and order. This permits placing restrictions on an inmate's receipt of books and pack-ages. The institution's regulations prohibited the inmates and pretrial detainees from receiving any books that did not come directly from a publisher. The Court held that the regulation was a rational response by officials to the obvious security problem of preventing the smuggling of contraband.[86]

Likewise, the Court upheld a regulation prohibiting the receipt of packages from the outside. The fact that packages are easily used for the smuggling of contraband justified the prohibition and served the governmental interest of maintaining insti-tutional security and order. Therefore, under this decision, prisoners, including pretrial detainees, have no constitutional right to receive packages from outside sources. Institutions may restrict or completely prohibit the flow of incoming pack-

---

[78] *Lee v. Tahash*, 352 F.2d 970 (8th Cir. 1965) (number of persons with whom inmate could correspond limited to 12); *Labat v. McKeithen*, 243 F. Supp. 662 (E.D. La. 1965) (Louisiana statute limiting death row inmate's correspondence to specific persons).

[79] *Jones v. Wittenberg*, 59 Ohio Op. 2d 47, 330 F. Supp. 707 (N.D. Ohio 1971).

[80] *Palmigiano v. Travisono*, 317 F. Supp. 776 (D. R.I. 1970).

[81] *Id.* at 791.

[82] *Finney v. Arkansas Board of Corrections*, 505 F.2d 194 at 210-211 (8th Cir. 1974).

[83] *Id.*

[84] *Hearn v. Morris*, 526 F. Supp. 267 (E.D. Cal. 1981).

[85] *Bell v. Wolfish*, 441 U.S. 520 (1979).

[86] *Id.* at 550, 551; *Rich v. Luther*, 514 F. Supp. 481 (W.D.N.C. 1981).

ages to prisoners because of their overriding interest in protecting the security and order of the institution.[87]

In *Parratt v. Taylor,*[88] mailed materials were lost when the normal procedure for receipt of mail packages was not followed. It was held that there was no deprivation of a right, privilege, or immunity secured by the Constitution or laws of the United States. The case for relief under the Civil Rights Act, 42 U.S.C. § 1983, was dismissed.

§ 4.13   Conclusion

Prison administrators may place reasonable restrictions on mail, subject to the inmate's qualified right to use the mail system. Formerly many federal courts refused to intervene in inmate suits that alleged undue restriction on mail rights unless the inmate alleged that restrictions infringed upon another federal right, such as the rights of free speech and press, the right to petition the government for the redress of grievances, the right to communicate with an attorney and the right to receive information.

Following *Turner* and *Abbott,* prison officials have great discretion in allowing inmates to send and receive mail and publications. As long as they act "reasonable," their actions will not be reviewed by the federal courts. The standards to determine "reasonableness" include: whether there is a "valid, rational connection" between the regulation and a legitimate and neutral governmental interest put forward to justify it, the existence of alternative means of exercising the asserted constitutional rights that remain open to inmates, the extent to which accommodation of the asserted right will have an impact on prison staff, on inmates' liberty, and on the allocation of limited prison resources, and whether the regulation represents an "exaggerated response" to prison concerns.

---

[87] *Id.* at 554, 555; *Jones v. Diamond,* 594 F.2d 997 (5th Cir. 1979).
[88] *Parratt v. Taylor,* 451 U.S. 527 (1981).

Chapter 5

ISOLATED CONFINEMENT — "THE HOLE"

§ 5.1   Introduction

Prison administrators have always faced the task of maintaining order and discipline in a prison. Some means of dealing with inmates who violate instructional rules and regulations are required.

One such means is the use of punitive isolation, which is isolation from the general prison population imposed as a penalty for violation of institutional rules.

> Almost every correctional institution includes a special confinement unit for those who misbehave seriously after they are incarcerated. This "prison within a prison" usually is a place of solitary confinement . . . accompanied by a reduced diet and limited access to reading materials and other diversions, and occasionally without any kind of light.[1]

Another means is administrative isolation, which is isolation from the general population for any reason other than punitive, such as protective isolation or isolation during investigation of an alleged institutional rule violation or of a felony.

§ 5.2   Intervention by the Courts

Prior to the mid-1960s, the federal courts applied the traditional "hands-off" doctrine and failed to grant any relief to state prisoners who challenged the use or conditions of isolated confinement. The rule of law applied to cases of prison policies or affairs was that these were matters of internal prison concern beyond the power of the courts to supervise. This doctrine, as to the federal prisons, was based on the separation of powers, as federal prisons were part of the executive

---

[1] President's Commission on Law Enforcement and Administration of Justice. Task Force Report: Corrections, 50-51 (1967).

branch of government. As to state prisons, the courts held that the administration of these state prisons was within the power reserved to the states under the Tenth Amendment to the United States Constitution and that any federal judicial review would interfere with prison administrators' performance of their duties. The courts also held that they, the courts, had only limited power to supervise the rules and regulations of prisons.

§ 5.3   Application of the Eighth Amendment

Even where a federal court is willing to review an inmate's complaint concerning isolated confinement, some federally protected right must be involved. The right involved is created by the Eighth Amendment of the United States Constitution which prohibits "cruel and unusual punishments inflicted." The Supreme Court has interpreted this clause to prohibit punishments which indicate torture, unnecessary cruelty or something inhuman and barbarous,[2] where the punishment is disproportionate to the offense,[3] and when a punishment is unnecessarily cruel in view of the purpose for which it is used.[4]

In order for the Eighth Amendment's prohibition to apply, a punishment must be involved. In a criminal law sense, punishment is "Any pain, penalty, suffering, or confinement inflicted upon a person by the authority of the law and the judgment and sentence of a court, for some crime . . . or for his omission of a duty enjoined by law."[5]

As applied to correctional law, a punishment consists of four elements: 1) Action by an administrative body, 2) which constitutes the imposition of a sanction, 3) for the purpose of penalizing the affected person, and 4) as the result of the commission of an offense.

One court has suggested that "any treatment to which a prisoner is exposed is a form of punishment . . ."[6] as it is an additional punishment above that imposed by the sentencing criminal court. As the result of being a punishment, it is subject to the Eighth Amendment standards.

§ 5.3.1   —Constitutionality of the Use of Isolated Confinement

During the past twenty years, many actions by state and federal inmates have challenged the validity of the use of isolated confinement itself, claiming that the practice is *per se* unconstitutional; that is, unconstitutional without the need of any proof other than the fact that the petitioner (inmate) is held in an isolated confine-

---

[2] *In re Kemmler,* 136 U.S. 436 (1890); *Wilkerson v. Utah,* 99 U.S. 130 (1878).

[3] *Trop v. Dulles,* 356 U.S. 86 (1958); *Weems v. United States,* 217 U.S. 349 (1910).

[4] *Robinson v. California,* 370 U.S. 660 (1962) (Douglas, J., Concurring Opinion); *Weems v. United States,* 217 U.S. 349 (1910).

[5] BLACK'S LAW DICTIONARY 1398 (4th ed. 1968).

[6] *Landman v. Royster,* 333 F. Supp. 621, 645 (E.D. Va. 1971).

ment area. This contention has been rejected by the federal courts.[7] The use of isolated confinement is seen as a valid means of protecting the general prison population and for preventing disobedience, disorders or escapes. However, the conditions of isolated confinement can be disproportionate to the offense involved or used for an improper means and thus run afoul of the Eighth Amendment. Furthermore, the procedure by which isolation is enforced can be unfair, thus violating "due process of law."[8]

§ 5.3.2 —Constitutionality of the Conditions of Isolated Confinement

A federal remedy exists when the conditions of isolated confinement violate the Eighth Amendment's ban on cruel and unusual punishments. Proof of the existence of the unconstitutional conditions is the initial burden on the inmate bringing an action. Failure to sufficiently establish as a fact the existence of the alleged conditions is a major basis for denying relief in complaints involving isolated confinement.[9] When the facts of the allegation are established, it is then a matter of law (as opposed to fact) as to whether the factual conditions are such that a violation of the prohibition on cruel and unusual punishments exists. At this stage, it is then a matter for the court, not a jury, to decide if the Eighth Amendment has been violated. Each court must look at the facts as proved and determine in its judgment whether the conditions amount to the infliction of cruel and unusual punishment.

The conditions that have been scrutinized include the personal hygienic conditions of the inmate, the physical conditions of the cell, the exercise allowed, the diet and the duration of the isolated confinement.

Where an inmate is deprived of means of maintaining personal hygiene, such as soap, water, towel, toilet paper, toothbrush, and clothing, the conditions become constitutionally intolerable.[10] However, where the inmate is provided with water, soap, towel and periodic bathing, the conditions have been held to be constitution-

---

[7] *Sostre v. McGinnis*, 442 F.2d 178 (2d Cir. 1971), *cert. denied*, 405 U.S. 978 (1972); *Burns v. Swenson*, 430 F.2d 771 (8th Cir. 1970); *Ford v. Board of Managers*, 407 F.2d 937 (3d Cir. 1969); *Graham v. Willingham*, 384 F.2d 367 (10th Cir. 1967); *Krist v. Smith*, 309 F. Supp. 497 (S.D. Ga. 1970), *aff'd*, 439 F.2d 146 (5th Cir. 1971); *Roberts v. Barbosa*, 227 F. Supp. 20 (S.D. Cal. 1964); *Bauer v. Sielaff*, 372 F. Supp. 1104 (E.D. Pa. 1974); *Villanueva v. George*, 632 F.2d 707 (8th Cir. 1980); *Nadeau v. Helgemoe*, 423 F. Supp. 1250 (D.N.H. 1976), *modified in*, 561 F.2d 411 (1st Cir. 1977); 581 F.2d 275 (1st Cir. 1978); *Morris v. Travisono*, 549 F. Supp. 291 (D.D.C. 1982), *aff'd*, 707 F.2d 28 (1st Cir. 1983) (segregated confinement for 8½ years was unjustified and violates the Eighth Amendment); *Gibson v. Lynch*, 652 F.2d 348 (3d Cir. 1981) (there is no state created "liberty interest" that entitles a prisoner to get out of solitary confinement and enter the general population after his first thirty days in prison).

[8] *See* Chapter 8 *infra* for a discussion on procedures for disciplining inmates.

[9] *Courtney v. Bishop*, 409 F.2d 1185 (8th Cir.), *cert. denied*, 396 U.S. 915 (1969); *Landman v. Peyton*, 370 F.2d 135 (4th Cir. 1966), *cert. denied*, 388 U.S. 920 (1967).

[10] *Wright v. McMann*, 387 F. 2d 519 (2d Cir. 1967); *Knuckles v. Prasse*, 302 F. Supp. 1036 (E.D. Pa. 1969), *aff'd*, 435 F.2d 1255 (3d Cir. 1970); *Hancock v. Avery*, 301 F. Supp. 786 (M.D. Tenn. 1969); *Jordan v. Fitzharris*, 257 F. Supp. 674 (N.D. Cal. 1966); *Kimbrough v. O'Neil*, 523 F.2d 1057 (7th Cir. 1975); *Brown v. State*, 391 So. 2d 113 (La. App. 1980).

ally acceptable.[11] One court has found that lack of water and a shower provided every fifth day did not constitute unhygienic conditions.[12] Yet, another court[13] held that the deprivation of a comb, pillow, toothbrush and toothpaste for 7-10 days in a maximum security cell with continuous lights, a few roaches and mice in the cell, and no reading material, did not constitute cruel and unusual punishment where the inmate was not denied the minimum necessities of food, water, sleep, exercise, toilet facilities and human contact. Contrast that to *Griffin v. Smith*,[14] where the court held that conditions which might constitute infringements of civil rights of prisoners in a special housing unit included excessive and unnecessary use of force by guards, grossly inadequate provision for exercise, denial of access to psychological specialists, unsanitary food utensils, including cigarette burns and hair on food trays, portions smaller than those provided to the general inmate population, and/or loss of mail sent to the superintendent.

The physical state of the cell is another aspect of the condition of isolated confinement. The existence of certain conditions in cells has led to varying results. Confinement of more than two men in a single cell in punitive isolation or administrative segregation is not unconstitutional *per se*.

In *Hutto v. Finney,* the Supreme Court refused to overturn the district court's series of detailed remedial orders holding that punitive isolation in sections of the Arkansas penal system violated the Eighth Amendment. These orders included limits placed on the number of men that could be confined to one cell, required that each man have a bunk, discontinued the "gruel" diet, and set 30 days as the maximum isolation sentence.[15]

The rationale the Court expressed in *Hutto* was that if the state had fully complied with the district court's earlier orders, the present limits may not have been necessary. However, when a system refuses to comply with orders to remedy cruel and unusual conditions in isolation cells, a federal court is fully justified in substituting its judgment by entering a comprehensive order to insure against the risk of inadequate compliance.

From this decision it is clear that there is not yet a minimum set standard on the number of days or other conditions that will constitute cruel and unusual punishment in punitive isolation in every situation. The Supreme Court stated that the length of confinement was only one factor in the decision, and short durations of oppressive conditions may not rise to the level of a constitutional deprivation.

---

[11] *Sostre v. McGinnis*, 442 F.2d 178 (2d Cir. 1971), *cert. denied*, 405 U.S. 978 (1972); *Gibson v. Lynch*, 652 F.2d 348 (3d Cir. 1981).

[12] *Ford v. Board of Managers of New Jersey State Prison*, 407 F.2d 937 (3d Cir. 1969).

[13] *Bauer v. Sielaff*, 372 F. Supp. 1104 (E.D. Pa. 1974).

[14] *Griffin v. Smith*, 493 F. Supp. 129 (W.D. N.Y. 1980).

[15] *Hutto v. Finney*, 437 U.S. 678 (1978); cf. *Rhodes v. Chapman*, 452 U.S. 337 (1981).

Courts have found that the lack of lighting or windows in the cells, and lack of mattresses are not impermissible.[16] These same conditions, however, when coupled with overcrowding in the cells, unclean cells, or lack of heat have been held to be violative of the Eighth Amendment.[17]

The personal hygiene of the inmate, the physical condition of the inmate and the physical condition of the isolation cell have been the focal point of most judicial attention in the area of isolated confinement. However, other aspects have received judicial consideration as well. The exercise outside the cell that an inmate is allowed during isolated confinement has been noted by several courts. Conditions have been upheld where there is an opportunity for exercise[18] even though it is for only an hour every eleven days[19] or where the allotted exercise time does not meet the requirements of the Bureau of Prisons policy.[20] It has been held that inmates on death row may not be confined in their cells for long periods of time without outdoor exercise.[21] This same reasoning applies to isolated confinement. The prisoner could also be deprived of contact visits, library privileges, and radio and television, so long as his nutritional and hygienic needs are met.[22]

The diet that an inmate receives while in isolated confinement has been a factor in several cases. Where the diet is basically the same as the general prison population, obviously no problem is presented.[23] A "reduced" diet has been approved, [24] and so has a diet of bread and water supplemented with a full meal every third day.[25] However, a bread and water diet has been termed "generally disapproved and obsolescent"[26] and has been strongly disapproved by the American Correctional Association as constituting the imposition of physical (corporal) punishment.[27] Similarly, at least one court has ruled that the broad prohibition against prisoners in

---

[16] *Novak v. Beto*, 453 F.2d 661 (5th Cir. 1971); *Ford v. Board of Managers of New Jersey State Prison*, 407 F.2d 937 (3d Cir. 1969); *Knuckles v. Prasse*, 302 F. Supp. 1036 (E.D. Pa. 1969), *aff'd*, 435 F.2d 1255 (3d Cir. 1970).

[17] *Anderson v. Nosser*, 438 F.2d 183 (5th Cir. 1971); *Wright v. McMann*, 387 F.2d 519 (2d Cir. 1967); *Landman v. Royster*, 333 F. Supp. 621 (E.D. Va. 1971); *Hancock v. Avery*, 301 F. Supp. 786 (M.D. Tenn. 1969); *Knuckles v. Prasse*, 302 F. Supp. 1036 (E.D. Pa. 1969), *aff'd*, 435 F.2d 1255 (3d Cir. 1979); *Holt v. Sarver*, 300 F. Supp. 825 (E.D. Ark. 1969); *Jordan v. Fitzharris*, 257 F. Supp. 674 (N.D. Cal. 1966); *Newson v. Sielaff*, 375 F. Supp. 1189 (E.D. Pa. 1974).

[18] *Sostre v. McGinnis*, 442 F.2d 178 (2d Cir. 1971), *cert. denied*, 405 U.S. 978 (1972); *Knuckles v. Prasse*, 302 F. Supp. 1036 (E.D. Pa. 1969), *aff'd*, 435 F.2d 1255 (3d Cir. 1970).

[19] *Lake v. Lee*, 329 F. Supp. 196 (S.D. Ala. 1971).

[20] *Jordan v. Arnold*, 408 F. Supp. 869 (M.D. Pa. 1976).

[21] *Sinclair v. Henderson*, 331 F. Supp. 1123 (E.D. La. 1971).

[22] *Gibson v. Lynch*, 652 F.2d 348 (3d Cir. 1981).

[23] *Sostre v. McGinnis*, 442 F.2d 178 (2d Cir. 1971), *cert. denied*, 405 U.S. 978 (1972); *Royal v. Clark*, 447 F.2d 501 (5th Cir. 1971).

[24] *Knuckles v. Prasse*, 302 F. Supp. 1036 (E.D. Pa. 1969), *aff'd*, 435 F.2d 1255 (3d Cir. 1970).

[25] *Novak v. Beto*, 453 F.2d 661 (5th Cir. 1972); *Ford v. Board of Managers of New Jersey State Prison*, 407 F.2d 937 (3d Cir. 1969).

[26] *Landman v. Royster*, 333 F. Supp. 621, 647 (E.D. Va. 1971).

[27] American Correctional Association, A Manual of Correctional Standards 417 (1966).

isolation or segregated confinement attending prison chapel was unconstitutional.[28]

The length of isolated confinement has been considered by several courts. A distinction exists between administrative and punitive isolation, in that the reasons for isolating inmates is either for punishment for specific actions (punitive isolation) or for more severe behavioral problems for longer periods (administrative isolation). It is a distinction of form rather than of substance, as the basic difference is the length of time. One court held that punitive isolation for a period of more than 15 days was cruel and unusual punishment;[29] but this judgment was subsequently overturned.[30] While periods of 36 days[31] and 15 days[32] have been held by some courts to be constitutionally permissible, other courts have found shorter periods, for example 48 hours, to violate an inmate's right to be free from cruel and unusual punishment.[33] Administrative isolation lasting 12 months[34] and 187 consecutive days[35] has been upheld. Placement in disciplinary segregation for an indeterminate amount of time did not violate the inmate's rights so long as the inmate was given a hearing to comply with due process safeguards at the earliest reasonable time.[36]

Confinement for five years in a maximum security section of a prison where an inmate is allowed out of his cell for one hour daily to exercise, and is not permitted any outdoor exercise, does not violate the Eighth Amendment's prohibition against cruel and unusual punishment. The court found that where the prisoner had participated in a riot, assaulted correctional officers, and was convicted of murdering another inmate while in the maximum security section of the prison, this past prison conduct justified the reclassification board's decision to keep the prisoner in maximum security.[37]

An inmate's claim that he had been placed in solitary confinement without any notice of charges or any hearing, that he was threatened with violence when he asked what the charges were, and that he was still in the hole a week later, states a cause of action. The claim may not be dismissed summarily on the ground that the case was moot because the prisoner had been transferred to another facility. Further, the inmate's inartful pleading must be construed liberally.[38]

As a general rule, state prisoners have no liberty interest protected by the United States Constitution in continued confinement in the general prison population.

---

[28] *St. Claire v. Cuyler*, 634 F.2d 109 (3d Cir. 1980).

[29] *Sostre v. Rockefeller*, 312 F. Supp. 863 (S.D. N.Y. 1970), *aff'd, rev'd*, and *modified sub nom.*, *Sostre v. McGinnis*, 442 F.2d 178 (2d Cir. 1971), *cert. denied*, 405 U.S. 978 (1972).

[30] *Sostre v. McGinnis*, 442 F.2d 178 (2d Cir. 1971), *cert. denied*, 405 U.S. 978 (1972).

[31] *Stiltner v. Rhay*, 322 F.2d 314 (9th Cir. 1963), *cert. denied*, 376 U.S. 920 (1964). *See also Bloeth v. Montanye*, 514 F.2d 1192 (2d Cir. 1975).

[32] *Novak v. Beto*, 453 F.2d 661 (5th Cir. 1971); *Jackson v. Werner*, 394 F. Supp. 805 (W.D. Pa. 1975).

[33] *O'Conner v. Keller*, 510 F. Supp. 1359 (D. Md. 1981).

[34] *Sostre v. McGinnis*, 442 F.2d 178 (2d Cir. 1971), *cert. denied*, 405 U.S. 978 (1972).

[35] *Knuckles v. Prasse*, 302 F. Supp. 1036 (E.D. Pa. 1969), *aff'd*, 435 F.2d 1255 (3d Cir. 1970).

[36] *Adams v. Carlson*, 376 F. Supp. 1228 (E.D. Ill. 1974).

[37] *Wilkerson v. Maggio*, 703 F.2d 909 (5th Cir. 1983).

[38] *Boag v. MacDougall*, 454 U.S. 364 (1982).

However, states may create such interests by the repeated use, in the state prison regulations governing administrative segregation, of explicit mandatory language about procedures and by requirements that administrative segregation not occur absent specified substantive predicates. When such interests are created, a Due Process hearing is required. The hearing should be an informal, nonadversary evidentiary review that is preceded by notice to the prisoner that offers the prisoner an opportunity to submit his views in writing, and that occurs within a reasonable time after the prisoner's transfer to administrative segregation. The prison officials must then decide whether the prisoner represents a security threat requiring confinement in administrative segregation pending completion of an investigation into misconduct charges against him. Here, the inmate was placed in segregation pending an investigation into his role in a riot. The next day he received notice of a misconduct charge against him. Five days after his transfer a Hearing Committee reviewed the evidence. The inmate acknowledged that he had an opportunity to have his version of the events reported, but no finding of guilt was made. Criminal charges were filed, but later dropped. A Review Committee concluded that the inmate should remain in administrative segregation as he posed a threat to the safety of other inmates, prison officials, and the security of the prison. Ultimately, the Hearing Committee, based on a second misconduct report, found the inmate guilty of the second charge and ordered him confined in disciplinary segregation for six months, while dropping the first charge. This procedure satisfied due process.[39]

Appointed counsel must be provided to inmates who are in administrative detention pending investigation and trial on felonies committed in prison. The counsel must be appointed prior to indictment. Solitary confinement effectively curtails an inmate's ability to investigate evidence and interview witnesses. This is particularly meaningful considering the transient nature of prison society. For the right to counsel to attach, the inmate must ask for an attorney, establish indigency, and make a prima facie showing that the reason for his continued detention is the investigation of a felony. Once this is done, the prison administration must either refute the showing, appoint counsel, or return the prisoner to the general population. When these steps are not followed, there is a presumption of prejudice, necessitating the dismissal of the indictment.[40] An inmate in maximum security has no right to unlimited use of the telephone.[41]

§ 5.3.3   —The Purpose of Isolated Confinement

In addition to granting relief on the basis of isolated confinement conditions, federal courts have also found a violation of the Eighth Amendment when the punishment is imposed for an improper purpose. The courts view the proper purpose

---

[39] *Hewitt v. Helms*, _____ U.S. _____, 103 S. Ct. 864, 74 L. Ed. 2d 675 (1983).
[40] *United States v. Gouveia*, 704 F.2d 1116 (9th Cir. 1983).
[41] *Lopez v. Reyes*, 692 F.2d 15 (5th Cir. 1982).

of isolated confinement to be the maintenance of order within the institution.[42] Therefore, any punishment inflicted which is *not necessary to maintain order* is cruel and unusual and prohibited by the Eighth Amendment. Thus, unsanitary conditions in confinement are unnecessarily punitive in nature and thus violate the Eighth Amendment.[43]

An inmate cannot be placed in isolated confinement because of his militant political ideas or his past or threatened litigation.[44] Nor can he be denied access to paper for use in petitioning courts or communicating with his attorney.[45] Also, denying of food for a fifty-hour period was held to go beyond what was necessary to achieve a legitimate penal aim.[46] A trial court's order that prison officials place a defendant in solitary confinement and feed him only bread and water on the anniversary of his offense was impermissible.[47]

§ 5.3.4   —Punishment Proportionate to the Offense

A further basis for granting relief is where the punishment is disproportionate to the rule infraction committed by the inmate. Thus, again, the unsanitary conditions of a cell can make the punishment disproportionate to the offense.[48] Another example of a disproportionate punishment was found when isolation was imposed for five months for failure to sign a safety sheet.[49] The unconstitutionality of disproportionate punishment applies to other areas of correctional law. It was the basis for one court to prohibit whipping[50] and for another court to find that the entire prison system as administered in Arkansas was disproportionate punishment for any offense,[51] and, hence, unconstitutional.

§ 5.4   Conclusion

The courts have found that the use of isolated confinement is a valid method of penal administration. However, federal courts will provide relief for deprivation of an inmate's constitutional right to be free of cruel and unusual punishment during

---

[42] *River v. Fogg,* 371 F. Supp. 938 (W.D.N.Y. 1974); *Kelly v. Brewer,* 239 N.W.2d 109 (Iowa Sup. Ct.); *Daughtery v. Carlson,* 372 F. Supp. 1320 (E.D. Ill. 1974); *Clifton v. Robinson,* 500 F. Supp. 30 (E.D. Pa. 1980).

[43] *Hancock v. Avery,* 301 F. Supp. 786 (M.D. Tenn. 1969); *Jordan v. Fitzharris,* 257 F. Supp. 674 (N.D. Cal. 1966); *Attorney General v. Sheriff of Worcester Cty.,* 413 N.E.2d 772 (Mass. 1980); *West v. Lamb,* 497 F. Supp. 989 (D. Nev. 1980); *Milhouse v. Carlson,* 652 F.2d 371 (3d Cir. 1981).

[44] *Wojtczak v. Cuyler,* 480 F. Supp. 1288 (E.D. Pa. 1979); *Morgan v. LaVallee,* 526 F.2d 221 (2d Cir. 1975).

[45] *Dearman v. Woods,* 429 F.2d 1288 (10th Cir. 1970); *McCray v. Sullivan,* 399 F. Supp. 271 (S.D. Ala. 1975).

[46] *Dearman v. Woods,* 429 F.2d 1288 (10th Cir. 1970).

[47] *People v. Joseph,* 434 N.E.2d 453 (Ill. App. 1982).

[48] *Jordan v. Fitzharris,* 257 F. Supp. 674, 679 (N.D. Cal. 1966).

[49] *Wright v. McMann,* 321 F. Supp. 127 (N.D.N.Y. 1970).

[50] *Jackson v. Bishop,* 404 F.2d 571 (8th Cir. 1968).

[51] *Holt v. Sarver,* 309 F. Supp. 362 (E.D. Ark. 1970), *aff'd,* 442 F.2d 304 (8th Cir. 1971).

his stay in isolated confinement. When the conditions of the confinement become such that an inmate is deprived of personal hygiene and the facility or his diet are inadequate, the Eighth Amendment has been violated. Also, punishment that is imposed for an improper purpose or is disproportionate to the offense the inmate committed can be violative of the Eighth Amendment.

Chapter 6

RELIGION IN PRISON

§ 6.1 Introduction: Effect of Imprisonment on Religious Rights

The First Amendment to the United States Constitution states in part that "Congress shall make no law respecting an establishment of religion, or prohibiting the free exercise thereof . . . ."[1] An obvious contradiction exists within the two clauses of this Amendment. This contradiction is particularly apparent when the amendment is applied to the inmates of correctional systems. In *Gittlemacker v. Prasse*[2] the inherent difficulty in the application of First Amendment religious freedom to inmates is pointed out:

> The requirement that a state interpose no unreasonable barriers to the free exercise of an inmate's religion cannot be equated with the suggestion that the state has an affirmative duty to provide, furnish, or supply every inmate with a clergyman or religious services of his choice. It is one thing to provide facilities for worship and the opportunity for any clergy to visit the institution. This

---

[1] U.S. Const. amend. I; *see* Appendix III.
[2] *Gittlemacker v. Prasse*, 428 F.2d 1 (3d Cir. 1970).

may be rationalized on the basis that since society has removed the prisoner from the community where he could freely exercise his religion, it has an obligation to furnish or supply him with the opportunity to practice his faith during confinement. Thus, the Free Exercise Clause is satisfied.

But, to go further and suggest that the Free Exercise Clause demands that the state not only furnish the opportunity to practice, but also *supply* the clergyman, is a concept that dangerously approaches the jealousy guarded frontiers of the Establishment Clause.

The existence of this conflict between the *Free Exercise Clause* and the *Establishment Clause* provides one explanation for the recognition by the courts of a need to balance the interests of the state with the interests of the inmate. Although the state interest in avoiding the establishment of religion is a problem of constitutional proportions, this interest has not negated the equally significant right of the inmate to the free exercise of his religious beliefs.

In spite of the difficulty in balancing these two fundamental and conflicting rights, courts in the past fifteen years have given increasing attention to the needs of inmates in this area. The traditional reluctance of the judiciary to interfere in the management of the prison[4] is no longer apparent. Rather than simply dismissing an action, as in the past, the courts are now giving recognition to the existence of First Amendment rights behind prison walls. Furthermore, they have required prison officials to provide a reasonable explanation for any attempt to limit such rights.

The requirement for prison officials to explain their rationale for impeding the free exercise of religion was pointed out in *Barnett v. Rodgers*[5] where the court stated:

To say that religious freedom may undergo modification in a prison environment is not to say that it can be suppressed or ignored without adequate reason. And although "within the prison society as well as without, the practice of religious beliefs is subject to reasonable regulation necessary for the protection and welfare of the community involved," the mere fact that government, as a practical matter, stands a better chance of justifying curtailment of fundamental liberties where prisoners are involved does not eliminate the need for reasons imperatively justifying the particular retraction of rights challenged at bar. Nor does it lessen governmental responsibility to reduce the resulting impact upon those rights to the fullest extent consistent with the justified objective.[6]

---

[4] *Wright v. McMann,* 257 F. Supp. 739 (N.D. N.Y. 1966), *rev'd on other grounds,* 387 F.2d 519 (2d Cir. 1967).

[5] *Barnett v. Rodgers,* 410 F.2d 995 (D.C. Cir. 1969).

[6] *Id.* at 1000-1001.

§ 6.2   Restrictions on the Free Exercise of Religion

In response to the demands of the courts, prison officials have provided a number of explanations for the restrictions they have placed upon the inmate's free exercise of religion. Among these are the maintenance of discipline or security, proper exercise of authority and official discretion, the fact that the regulation is reasonable, and economic considerations. Frequently, these explanations are used interchangeably by the courts, and it is sometimes difficult to determine which justification was the basis of the decision. However, in most cases, if prison officials are able to show that restrictions on religious practices are actually based upon one or more of these enumerated reasons, the courts will allow the restrictions to continue. In addition to providing explanations for the restrictions they have placed upon the inmate's free exercise of religion, prison officials, and the courts, have had to attempt to define what a "religion" is, and what "religious practices" are, for purposes of First Amendment protection. Unfortunately, few precise guidelines have emerged from these cases.[7]

§ 6.2.1   —Restrictions Based on the Maintenance of Discipline or Security

The duty of prison officials to maintain security within an institution is the most frequently cited justification for limiting an inmate's religious freedom. In *Jones v. Willingham*,[8] the court, concerned with 1) the trouble allegedly caused by Black Muslims in the early 1960s, and 2) the fact that the petitioner was confined at Leavenworth, Kansas, a maximum security institution, held that the warden had a duty to prevent disruptions and thus concluded that there was no religious discrimi-

---

[7] *Theriault v. Sibler*, 391 F. Supp. 578 (W.D. Tex. 1975), was vacated on appeal. *Theriault v. Sibler*, 547 F.2d 1279 (5th Cir. 1977). The court of appeals held that the requirement of a belief in a supreme being as a criterion to determine whether a practice constitutes a religion within the protection of the first amendment is too narrow. The court stated that,

When reconsidering what constitutes a religion, a thorough study of the existing case law should be accompanied by appropriate evidentiary exploration of philosophical, theological, and other related literature and resources on this issue. *Id.* at 1281.

In a subsequent case, *Theriault v. Sibler*, 453 F. Supp. 254 (W.D. Tex. 1978) (a Texas federal district court ruled that an inmate-created religion was not entitled to First Amendment protection, since it was not a true "religion" for purposes of federal law. After reviewing the facts in the case the court concluded:

The professed views of Mr. Theriault that he 'would have established a New World order' with Harry W. Theriault as the head of the Order . . . are, in the opinion of the Court more closely akin to the megalomania of Adolph Hitler and the Nazis or Charles Manson and his 'family' than any 'belief . . . that occupies a place parallel to that filled by the orthodox belief in God.'); *Remmers v. Brewer*, 396 F. Supp. 145 (S.D. Iowa 1975), *rev'd on other grounds*, 529 F.2d 656 (8th Cir. 1976); *cf. Ron v. Lennane*, 445 F. Supp. 98 (D. Conn. 1977); *cf. Loney v. Scurr*, 474 F. Supp. 1186 (S.D. Iowa 1979) (the Church of the New Song was a religion entitled to the protection of the First Amendment); *Africa v. Comm. of Pennsylvania*, 662 F.2d 1025 (3d Cir. 1981). (On the facts of the case, an inmate's belief was not a religion within the purview of the First Amendment. His organization did not address fundamental and ultimate questions. It was not comprehensive in nature and did not have the defining structural characteristics of a traditional religion.)

[8] *Jones v. Willingham*, 248 F. Supp. 791 (D. Kan. 1965).

nation under the facts of that case. In *St. Claire v. Cuyler et al.*,[9] the court held that a reasonable relation to security interests justified the denial of a prisoner's request to attend religious services. The prisoner had the burden to prove by substantial evidence that the security concerns were unreasonable or exaggerated. In *Wojtczak v. Cuyler*,[10] a Pennsylvania court held that inmates confined in segregation for their own safety may not unduly be restricted in the rights held by prisoners in the general population; however, the inmate bears a heavy burden to disprove a claim that different treatment is based upon genuine security considerations.

This rationale likewise was applied in *McDonald v. Hall*.[10a] The appellate court took notice of an affidavit, filed by prison officials, that indicated that allowing segregated inmates to attend services outside of their unit would pose a safety threat. The court upheld the officials' decision because it was neither arbitrary nor capricious.

In *Cooper v. Pate*,[11] the court allowed prison officials to restrict the religious freedom of certain individuals where they showed that such free exercise had been abused at some prior time. It held that, although a complete ban on religious services was discrimination, such precautions as were necessary for security would be sanctioned. Inmates with records of prior misconduct "which reasonably demonstrates a high degree of probability that the individual would seriously misuse the opportunity for participation with the group"[12] could be excluded from religious services at the authorities' discretion.

The use of the "clear and present danger" test enunciated by the United States Supreme Court[13] as a valid reason for limiting First Amendment freedoms on speech was utilized by analogy by the court in *Knuckles v. Prasse*.[14] The court permitted certain infringements of religious freedoms on the basis that they presented a "*clear and present danger* of a breach of prison security or discipline or some other substantial interference with the orderly functioning of the institution."[15] The court further stated that prison officials had the right to be present and to monitor religious services and if the services became nonreligious the authorities could cancel them. Prisons must not be forced to experience a catastrophic riot . . ."[16] The court further found that its ". . . task is not to evaluate plaintiffs' religious wisdom but rather to determine whether regulations of that religion in a prison context are reasonable."[17]

---

[9] *St. Claire v. Cuyler et al.*, 634 F.2d 109 (3d Cir. 1980); *Montoya v. Tanksley*, 446 F. Supp. 226 (D. Colo. 1978).

[10] *Wojtczak v. Cuyler*, 480 F. Supp. 1288 (E.D. Pa. 1979).

[10a] *Walker v. Blackwell*, 411 F.2d 23 (5th Cir. 1969).

[11] *Cooper v. Pate*, 382 F.2d 518 (7th Cir. 1967).

[12] *Id.* at 523.

[13] *Brandenburg v. Ohio*, 395 U.S. 444, 48 Ohio Op. 2d 320 (1969).

[14] *Knuckles v. Prasse*, 302 F. Supp. 1036 (E.D. Pa. 1969), *aff'd*, 435 F.2d 1255 (3d Cir. 1970).

[15] *Id.* at 1049 citing *Long v. Parker*, 390 F.2d 816, 822 (3d Cir. 1968).

[16] *Id.* at 1058.

[17] *Id.*

Prison officials are under an obligation to maintain security and discipline within the institution. For this reason, the courts analyze restrictions of religious freedom within the prison setting in the framework of that obligation. A proper justification by prison officials of the need for such restrictions will frequently result in its approval by the courts.

§ 6.2.2   —Restrictions Based on the Exercise of Authority and Official Discretion

The argument that control over religious freedom in prison is a proper subject for the exercise of authority and official discretion is a carryover from the historical approach of *non-interference* by the judiciary. Although this argument is now subject to closer court scrutiny, it has not been altogether abandoned. *Knuckles v. Prasse* again pointed out that constitutional standards for the practice of religion in prison must be analyzed in the realistic context of the prison situation. The process requires a balancing of broad discretionary powers vested in prison officials with the right of inmates to practice religion in a prison.[18]

The non-interference approach was further evidenced in *Kennedy v. Meacham*,[19] a case involving the free exercise of the "satanic religion." The court recognized that matters of inmate regulation and discipline are to be left to the discretion of prison authorities as long as the officials' conduct does not involve the deprivation of constitutional rights and is not clearly capricious or arbitrary.

Assuming for the sake of argument that "Satanism" is a religion, the state's interest in the proper administration of its penal system outweighs a prisoner's right to organize a branch of his sect within the prison. The prisoner's request to hold meetings was properly denied in view of his inability to provide the name of a sponsor or information relating to the proposed activities of the group. Safety considerations also justified the denial of the use of candles or incense in a cell. Denial of the right to borrow library books for group use was consistent with general prison policies, and in any event the prisoner was not prejudiced since he owned many of the books himself.[20]

Another case wherein the significance of unlimited discretion exercised by prison officials was reviewed is *Belk v. Mitchell*.[21] The prisoner was put in solitary confinement for thirty days, and his request to attend Sunday services was denied. The court held:

---

[18] *Id.* at 1048.

[19] *Kennedy v. Meacham*, 382 F. Supp. 996 (D. Wyo. 1974), was vacated and remanded on appeal. *Kennedy v. Meacham*, 540 F.2d 1057 (10th Cir. 1976). The court of appeals ruled that the district court improperly dismissed the complaint and the case would be remanded to determine whether the practice of a religious belief was involved, whether there were restrictions imposed upon it, and whether such restrictions were justified.

[20] *Childs v. Duckworth*, 705 F.2d 915 (7th Cir. 1983).

[21] *Belk v. Mitchell*, 294 F. Supp. 800 (W.D. N.C. 1968).

If the solitary confinement itself is justifiable, then it would seem entirely reasonable to allow some discretion to the prison authorities whether to allow or not allow the Sunday morning commingling of solitary prisoners with the others. Prison authorities of course have no right to restrict the prisoner's freedom of religious beliefs and convictions. However, absent a showing of prolonged and unjustifiable discrimination, his "public" exercise of his religious beliefs and his access to publicly provided chaplains during temporary punitive solitary confinement would seem to be matters within the reasonable discretion of the prison authorities.[22]

In *Mims v. Shapp*,[23] the denial of congregational prayer to inmates (thus, in 399 F. Supp.) in a segregation unit was held not to have been an improper denial of the right to practice religion, but rather a proper exercise of official discretion.

In this connection, contrast the case of *Collins v. Vitek*[24] in which the court held that all inmates, regardless of status, were entitled to attend religious services of their choice, with the *Mims* case. Although this case reflects a departure from the holdings in the *Belk* and *Mims* decisions, it does not necessarily reflect a basic change in the courts' traditional view of approving broad official discretion.

The court in *Sweet v. Department of Corrections*[25] recognized the need for broad official discretion in light of the peculiar problems necessary to the maintenance of a prison. Because prison society is both sensitive and explosive, it is necessary for those with experience to make decisions in light of their particular knowledge. For this reason, prison authorities may adopt any regulation dealing with the exercise by an inmate of his religion that may be reasonable and substantially justified by consideration of prison administrative requirements. The court's rationale in the *Sweet* decision is significant in that, like most courts, it demonstrates a certain hesitancy to interfere with the internal management of a prison.

Another case wherein the significance of unlimited discretion exercised by prison officials was reviewed was *Wojtczak v. Cuyler.*[26] The court held:

> Prisoners confined for their own safety in segregation may not be unduly restricted in the rights held by prisoners in the general population. However, the prisoner bears a heavy burden to disprove a claim that different treatment is based upon genuine security considerations . . . The state must permit the

---

[22] *Id.* at 802.

[23] *Mims v. Shapp*, 399 F. Supp. 818 (W.D. Pa. 1975), was vacated and remanded on appeal. *Mims v. Shapp*, 541 F.2d 415 (2d Cir. 1976). The court of appeals held that the inmates' affidavits sufficiently alleged personal bias of the judge and that the district judge erred in denying the inmates' refusal motion.

[24] *Collins v. Vitek*, 375 F. Supp. 856 (D. N.H. 1974).

[25] *Sweet v. Department of Corrections*, 529 F.2d 854 (4th Cir. 1974).

[26] *Wojtczak v. Cuyler*, 480 F. Supp. 1288 (E.D. Pa. 1979); *Nadeau v. Helgemoe*, 423 F. Supp. 1250 (D. N.H. 1976), *modified*, 561 F.2d 411 (1st Cir. 1977); 581 F.2d 275 (1st Cir. 1978).

prisoner in segregation to receive both a chaplain and communion in his cell . . . but need not escort him to the prison chapel . . ..[27]

In *Jones v. Bradley*,[28] the Ninth Circuit Court of Appeals held that the right to the free exercise of religion was not absolute, but could be restricted by the legitimate policies of correctional institutions. In this connection, contrast the case of *Montoya v. Tanksley*[29] in which the court held that religious freedom was of such importance that it could only be overridden by compelling state interests of the highest order.

The court in *McDonald v. Hall*[30] recognized the need for broad official discretion in light of the peculiar problems necessary to the maintenance of a prison. Because prison society is both sensitive and explosive, it is necessary for those with experience to make decisions in light of their particular knowledge. For this reason, prison authorities may adopt any regulation dealing with the exercise by an inmate of his religion that may be reasonable and substantially justified by consideration of prison administrative requirements. The court's rationale in the *McDonald* decision is significant in that, like most courts, it demonstrates a certain hesitancy to interfere with the internal management of a prison.

Another relevant and closely related issue in discussing official discretion arises when arguments are made that prison rules and regulations are capricious and arbitrary. This was pointed out in *In re Ferguson*[31] wherein the court discussed the reasonableness of a regulation restricting the activities of Black Muslims. The court stated:

> [I]n the instant circumstances, the refusal to allow these petitioners to pursue their requested religious [activities] does not appear to amount to such extreme mistreatment, so as to warrant the application of whatever federal constitutional guarantees which may exist for the protection of inmates in state prisons. * * * We are . . . reluctant to apply federal constitutional doctrines to state prison rules reasonably necessary to the orderly conduct of the state institution.
>
> * * *
>
> Even conceding the Muslims to be a religious group it cannot be said under the circumstances here presented that the Director of Corrections has made an unreasonable determination in refusing to allow petitioners the opportunity to pursue their claimed religious activities while in prison.[32]

---

[27] *Wojtczak v. Cuyler*, 480 F. Supp. 1288 (E.D. Pa. 1979).

[28] *Jones v. Bradley*, 590 F.2d 294 (9th Cir. 1979).

[29] *Montoya v. Tanksley*, 446 F. Supp. 226 (D. Colo. 1978).

[30] *McDonald v. Hall*, 576 F.2d 120 (1st Cir. 1978) citing *Sweet v. Department of Corrections*, 529 F.2d 854 (4th Cir. 1974).

[31] *In re Ferguson*, 361 P.2d 417 (Cal. 1961).

[32] *Id.* at 421.

The court then determined that in view of the inflammatory nature of the *Koran* the officials were under no obligation to retract a restriction on its use.

While the courts have upheld the suppression of inflammatory religious litera- ture, in at least one case, *Mukmuk v. Commissioner,*[33] it was held that an inmate cannot be punished for the mere possession of religious literature.

§ 6.2.3   —Restrictions Based on Economic Considerations

Although carefully circumscribed, economic considerations are another factor cited by prison administrators as a justification for controlling the inmate's free exercise of religion. In *Gittlemacker v. Prasse,*[34] a Jewish prisoner alleged a viola- tion of the First Amendment because the state did not provide him with a rabbi. The court stated that the requirement that a state interpose no unreasonable barriers to the free exercise of a prisoner's religion could not be equated with the suggestion that the state had the affirmative duty to provide, furnish or supply every prisoner with a clergyman or with religious services of his choice. The court pointed out that it was no great burden on the institution or on prison officials to provide facili- ties of worship and the opportunity for clergy to visit the institution. This require- ment could be rationalized on the basis that, since society had removed the prisoner from the community where he could freely exercise his religion, the state had an obligation to furnish or supply the prisoner with the opportunity to practice his faith.

> But, to go further and suggest that the Free Exercise Clause demands that the state not only furnish the opportunity to practice, but also [to] *supply* the clergyman, is a concept that dangerously approaches the jealousy guarded frontiers of the Establishment Clause.[35]

The court pointed out that the sheer number of religious sects was a practical consideration. It suggested that there were perhaps 120 distinctive, established reli- gious denominations in the state. To the court, it became readily apparent that to accept the inmate's contention was to suggest that each state prison have an extrava- gant number of clergyman available. Although the court did not reach this ques- tion, it did recognize that explicit in the First Amendment were two separate and distinct concepts designed to guarantee religious liberties: 1) the Establishment Clause and 2) the Free Exercise Clause. The court also recognized that under the circumstances of the case, a slavish insistence upon a maximum interpretation of rights vested in one clause would collide with the restrictions of the other clause. Using the analogy of the school prayer cases, the court approved the language:

---

[33] *Mukmuk v. Commissioner,* 529 F.2d 272 (2d Cir. 1976).
[34] *Gittlemacker v. Prasse,* 428 F.2d 1 (3d Cir. 1970).
[35] *Id.* at 4.

It is no defense to urge that the religious practices here may be relatively minor encroachments on the First Amendment. The breach of neutrality that is today a trickling stream may all too soon become a raging torrent, and, in the words of Madison, "it is proper to take alarm at the first experiment on our liberties."[36]

In *Gittlemacker*, the inmate alleged that the officials denied Jewish inmates a rabbi in regular attendance, although they provided Catholic and Protestant chaplains. The response of the prison superintendent was: "The small number of Jewish inmates at Dallas, usually two or three, makes the use of a full-time rabbi economically unfeasible and unwarranted."[37] The court also found that the superintendent had, on numerous occasions, attempted to secure the services of a rabbi for Jewish inmates. It was asserted that the official intended to have him come to the institution on a fee basis. The court concluded that the inmate's claim of religious discrimination was effectively and conclusively refuted.

In *Walker v. Blackwell*[38] Muslim inmates proposed that they be provided with a special meal during Ramaden, their religious period, and that it be served after the normal dinner time, but at a time which would not interfere with their work schedules. Inmates asserted that the cost of purchasing the special foods would not be prohibitive, and that, under present conditions, they could not make adequate selections from the menus prepared because pork was included. The prison officials' argument was that they could not afford to buy the various special items within the limits of the existing budget. They further pointed out that while once-a-year special purchases were made for Passover, the Muslims were requesting thirty days of special menus.

With respect to the after-sunset meals, the court felt that supplying such meals could only be done at a prohibitive cost. It held further that there were problems of security and additional staff involved in serving Muslims after all other prisoners had eaten. In the court's opinion, considerations of expense and security outweighed "whatever constitutional deprivation petitioners may claim. In this regard . . . the government has demonstrated a substantial compelling interest . . . ."[39]

The same analysis has been applied to the Jewish Kosher food cases. Represented by the holding in *Kahane v. Carlson*,[40] the attitude of the courts appears to be that there is no obligation to provide *all* Jewish inmates with Kosher food on a full-time basis.[41]

In the only significant United States Supreme Court case concerning prison inmates who were members of the Islamic faith, it was contended that prison poli-

---

[36] *Id.* at 5.
[37] *Id.*
[38] *Walker v. Blackwell*, 411 F.2d 23 (5th Cir. 1969).
[39] *Id.* at 26.
[40] *Kahane v. Carlson*, 527 F.2d 492 (2d Cir. 1975).
[41] *See* § 6.4.6 *infra.*

cies prevented them form attending Jumu'ah, a congregational service held on Friday afternoons, and thereby violated their rights under the Free Exercise Clause of the First Amendment. The first policy required inmates in the plaintiff's custody classifications to work outside the buildings in which they were housed and in which Jumu'ah was held, while the second prohibited inmates assigned to outside work from returning to those buildings during the day.

The United States Supreme Court held that there was no burden on prison officials to disprove the availability of alternative methods of accommodating prisoners' religious rights. The Constitution allows respect for and deference to the judgment of prison administrators. The policies were reasonably related to legitimate penological interests, and therefore did not offend the Free Exercise Clause of the First Amendment. Both policies had a rational connection to the legitimate governmental interests in institutional order and security invoked to justify them. One was a response to critical overcrowding and was designed to ease tension and drain on the facilities during that part of the day when the inmates were outside. The policy was necessary since returns from outside work details generated congestion and delays at the main gate, a high-risk area. The need to decide return requests placed pressure on guards supervising outside work details. Rehabilitative concerns also supported the policy as corrections officials sought to simulate working conditions and responsibilities in society. Although the policies may have prevented some Muslim prisoners from attending Jumu'ah, they did not deprive the Muslims of all forms of religious exercise but instead allowed participation in a number of Muslim religious ceremonies. There were no obvious, easy alternatives to the policies since both of the suggested accommodations would, in the judgment of prison officials, have adverse effects on the prison institution. Placing all Muslim inmates in inside work details would be inconsistent with the legitimate prison concerns while providing weekend labor for Muslims would require extra supervision that would be a drain on scarce human resources. Both proposed accommodations would also threaten prison security by fostering "affinity groups" likely to challenge institutional authority, while any special arrangements for one group would create a perception of favoritism on the part of other inmates.

Even where claims are made under the First Amendment, the Supreme Court will not substitute its judgment on difficult and sensitive matters of institutional administration for the determinations of those charged with the formidable task of running a prison.[42]

§ 6.3 Religious Discrimination: The Equal Protection Clause

The cases dealing with religious freedom frequently refer to the Equal Protection Clause of the Fourteenth Amendment. Section 1 of that amendment provides,

---

[42] *O'Lone v. Estate of Shabazz*, 482 U.S. 342 (1987).

in part, that "Nor shall any state . . . deny to any person within its jurisdiction the equal protection of the laws."[43]

The application of the Equal Protection Clause is particularly relevant in cases dealing with minority religions. This was apparent in *Newton v. Cupp*[44] where the court stated: "If members of one faith can practice their religious beliefs and possess religious materials, equivalent opportunity must be available to members of another faith."[45]

The soundness of this decision is apparent from the Supreme Court's subsequent decision in *Cruz v. Beto*,[46] holding that Texas prison officials had discriminated against an inmate by denying him a reasonable opportunity to pursue his Buddhist faith comparable to that offered other inmates adhering to conventional religious precepts. Similarly in *People ex rel. Rockey v. Krueger*,[47] the court found that since an orthodox Jew would be allowed to retain his beard without being placed in solitary confinement, a Muslim who had been placed in solitary confinement for not shaving his beard was entitled to be released. Thus, since prison policy permitted orthodox Jews to wear beards, other religious beliefs requiring beards could not be suppressed even in the face of a Commissioner of Correction's Regulation which required that prisoners be "clean-shaven."

In *Konigsberg v. Ciccone*,[48] an inmate alleged denial of exercise of his religious rights. He claimed that while he was confined in close custodial supervision, he was not permitted to attend any religious services. Further, when he was transferred from such custody, his attendance at Jewish religious services was conditioned upon a pass, issued specifically for that purpose. On the other hand, Protestant and Catholic prisoners in close custody confinement were allowed to attend services. The prison officials established that the Protestants and Catholics did not need passes to attend services because those services were held at a time when no other activity was in progress. Thus, the destination of people moving through the corridors could be easily identified. Also it was proved that sufficient staff was available to guarantee security at that time. However, prison officials stated that inmates who attended services at times other than Sunday needed passes to move through the corridors just as any other inmate would at the same time.

The court would not accept as reasonable the prison officials' basis for denying minority religions the right to attend services while at the same time permitting Protestants and Catholics to do so. The court said that it was unrealistic to take the position that sufficient escorts were not available to conduct them to services "in view of the high importance the law places on the right to worship and [on] the

---

[43] U.S. Const. amend. XIV, §1. *See* Appendix III.

[44] *Newton v. Cupp*, 474 P.2d 532 (Or. App. 1970).

[45] *Id.* at 536.

[46] *Cruz v. Beto*, 405 U.S. 319 (1972). *See* § 6.4.1, *infra*.

[47] *People ex rel. Rockey v. Krueger*, 306 N.Y.S.2d 359 (Sup. Ct. 1969); *see also, Maguire v. Wilkinson*, 405 F. Supp. 637 (D. Conn. 1975).

[48] *Konigsberg v. Ciccone*, 285 F. Supp. 585 (W.D. Mo. 1968), *aff'd*, 417 F.2d 161 (8th Cir. 1969), *cert. denied*, 397 U.S. 963 (1970).

right to be free of religious discrimination."[49] The court then directed that such an inmate be allowed to attend religious services unless: 1) his physician certified medical reasons; 2) there was proof that the inmate was a dangerous security risk; or 3) his attendance would substantially and adversely affect security.

In *Cooper v. Pate,*[50] the court stopped prison officials from preventing an inmate's communication (by mail and visitation) with ministers of his faith, subject to usual prison regulations. The court felt that such communication did not present a clear and present danger to prison security, and to grant it to one faith, but deny it to another, was religious discrimination. However, note in this case that the inmate also wished to purchase Swahili grammar books. He pointed out that prisoners were allowed to purchase foreign language books. The lower court held that these books were not necessary for the practice of the prisoner's religion and that the denial was based on staff and facility limitations. The court of appeals affirmed the holding that this involved no impairment of a constitutional right.

The case of *State v. Cubbage* [51] also expressed the importance of equal protection of minority religions. Of primary concern to the petitioning inmates were the general discriminatory practices against the Black Muslim religion. The court concluded that in fact there had been no discrimination as to religious beliefs, but that the inmates had been denied equal protection of the law because they were not given an opportunity to practice their beliefs or to wear religious symbols. The state asserted that this denial of equal protection should be weighed against the "clear and present danger" test. The court, however, held that this test was inapplicable when it stated that "the right to equal protection of law is almost an absolute right, always to be respected . . ."[52] Furthermore, the court found, "no reason to deny the relators the equal protection of the laws, even if it is feared they might hereafter abuse the rights herein recognized."[53]

§ 6.4 Specific Areas of Constitutional Concern

While the right of Black Muslims to practice their religious beliefs has dominated the case law during the past decade, the controversy over this right has declined. Issues such as the right to attend services, to obtain literature, and to wear religious medals were usually raised by Black Muslims because, unlike Protestant or Catholic inmates, the Black Muslims had been denied the right to engage in such practices. The threshold question was the recognition of the Muslim faith as a "religion." It has been recognized as a religion in several cases[54] and, for this

---

[49] *Id.* at 595.
[50] *Cooper v. Pate,* 382 F.2d 518 (7th Cir. 1967).
[51] *State v. Cubbage,* 210 A.2d 555 (Del. Super. Ct. 1965).
[52] *Id.* at 567.
[53] *Id.* at 568.
[54] *See Howard v. Smyth,* 365 F.2d 28 (4th Cir. 1966); *Lee v. Crouse,* 284 F. Supp. 541 (D. Kan. 1968), *aff'd,* 396 F.2d 952 (10th Cir. 1968); *Fulwood v. Clemmer,* 206 F. Supp. 370 (D.C. Cir. 1962); *State v. Cubbage,* 210 A.2d 555 (Del. Super. Ct. 1965).

reason, it can now be asserted, in theory at least, that a Black Muslim retains the same constitutional protection offered to other members of recognized religions.

In spite of the general recognition of the Black Muslim faith as a religion, certain specific problems remain relative to the total free exercise of its beliefs. Those problems, although usually presented by Black Muslim petitioners, are often common among all inmates seeking to exercise religious freedoms. For this reason, it must be assumed that the rights accorded by the judiciary to the Black Muslim inmate must also be rendered to all recognized religions. The general applicability of these decisions to all recognized religions practiced within penal institutions is consistent with the constitutional mandate of the First Amendment and the Equal Protection Clause.

§ 6.4.1 —The Right to Hold Religious Services

Numerous cases have recognized the Black Muslims' right to hold some sort of religious services.[55] However, the cases wherein such right was not extended were usually based upon the belief that a congregation of Black Muslim inmates would result in some security risk. This was apparent in the decisions of *Jones v. Willingham*[56] and of *Cooke v. Tramburg.*[57] In the first of these decisions, *Jones,* the court refused to grant the Black Muslims the right to assemble for worship. The court based its decision upon the duty of the warden to prevent breaches of security. It asserted that, in view of the possibility of disruptions resulting from a congregation of Black Muslims, the contested restriction was a valid exercise of the warden's duty. In the *Cooke* case, the court also denied the right to hold religious services because of the danger it believed was inherent in such assemblage. It was found that freedom to exercise religious beliefs is not absolute, but is subject to restriction for the protection of the society as a whole.

However, *Banks v. Havener*[58] held that a prison could not prohibit the practice of an established religion unless it could prove (by satisfactory evidence) that the teaching and practice of the act created a clear and present danger to the orderly functioning of the institution. Absent such evidence, the court in *Battle v. Anderson*[59] found that the policy of prison officials of denying to all inmates, including Muslims, the opportunity to gather together for corporate religious services, was unjustified.

---

[55] *See Knuckles v. Prasse,* 435 F.2d 1255 (3d Cir. 1970); *Sewell v. Pegelow,* 304 F.2d 670 (4th Cir. 1962); *Banks v. Havener,* 234 F. Supp. 27 (E.D. Va. 1964).

[56] *Jones v. Willingham,* 248 F. Supp. 791 (D. Kan. 1965).

[57] *Cooke v. Tramburg,* 43 N.J. 514, 205 A.2d 889 (1964).

[58] *Banks v. Havener,* 234 F. Supp. 27 (E.D. Va. 1964).

[59] *Battle v. Anderson,* 376 F. Supp. 402 (E.D. Okla. 1974).

The most significant cases concerning the right of non-traditional religious groups to hold services are *Theriault v. Carlson*[60] and *Remmers v. Brewer,* [61] both dealing with an inmate-devised religion based on the Eclatarian faith and organized around The Church of the New Song of Universal Life. In *Theriault,* the inmate who devised the religion and who was head of the newly-developed church was confined in punitive segregation for attempting to hold religious services to promote the new belief. Although the district court ordered his restoration to the general prison population and directed prison officials to permit the inmate to hold religious services, this ruling was overturned on appeal and remanded for an evidentiary hearing.[62] On remand, a different district court concluded that the Eclatarian faith was not a "religion" entitled to First Amendment protection, but was rather "a masquerade designed to obtain protection for acts which otherwise would have been unlawful and /or reasonably disallowed by various prison authorities."[63]

While failing to provide a precise definition of what a "religion" is for purposes of First Amendment protection, the court declared that such protection does not extend to so-called religions "which tend to mock established institutions and are obviously shams and absurdities and whose members are patently devoid of religious sincerity."[64]

Essentially the same issue was present in *Remmers,* but the court in that case, while aware of the holdings in the *Theriault* case, nevertheless decided that the Eclatarian faith was a "religion" and that members of such religion were entitled to protection under the Free Exercise Clause. However, the court declared that if it were subsequently proved that the Eclatarian faith, as practiced at the prison, was in fact a sham, then the prison administrators and the court could deal with the eventuality. The two decisions, *Theriault* and *Remmers,* highlight the continuing legal problem facing prison administrators when apparently inconsistent decisions are rendered by different federal courts, and the United States Supreme Court is either unwilling or unable to resolve the conflict.

A number of courts have adjudicated petitions which have alleged that religious liberties were denied when authorities prohibited attendance at general services while the petitioner was confined in a correctional cell.[65] A majority of these courts dismissed the complaint and distinguished between one's freedom to believe and one's freedom to *exercise* his belief. Such a restriction on the free exercise of belief

[60] *Theriault v. Carlson,* 339 F. Supp. 375 (N.D. Ga. 1972), *vacated and remanded,* 495 F.2d 390 (5th Cir. 1974), *cert. denied,* 419 U.S. 1003 (1974).

[61] *Remmers v. Brewer,* 361 F. Supp. 537 (S.D. Iowa 1973), *aff'd,* 494 F.2d 1277 (8th Cir. 1974), *cert. denied,* 419 U.S. 1012 (1974).

[62] *Theriault v. Carlson,* 495 F.2d 390 (5th Cir. 1974).

[63] *Theriault v. Silber,* 391 F. Supp. 578 (W.D. Tex. 1975), *vacated and remanded,* 547 F.2d 1279 (5th Cir. 1977).

[64] *Id.*

[65] *See Sharp v. Sigler,* 408 F.2d 966 (8th Cir. 1969); *Belk v. Mitchell,* 294 F. Supp. 800 (W.C. N.C. 1968); *Konigsberg v. Ciccone,* 285 F. Supp. 585 (W.D. Mo. 1968), *aff'd,* 417 F.2d 161 (8th Cir. 1969), *cert. denied,* 397 U.S. 963 (1970); *Morgan v. Cook,* 236 So. 2d 749 (Miss. 1970).

is justified on the basis of maintaining both security and institutional internal correctional discipline. [66] However, in *Konigsberg v. Ciccone*, [67] the Jewish petitioner established that Protestant and Catholic inmates confined in close custodial supervision were permitted to attend services while he was not. The court refused to accept as reasonable the administration's contention that they could not find sufficient escorts to conduct him to services. The court held that he should be allowed to attend services unless: 1) a physician certified medical reasons; 2) an officer certified that the prisoner was a dangerous security risk; or 3) his attendance would substantially and adversely affect security.

A Mississippi court[68] indicated that full access to a minister of one's denomination while confined in maximum security units (correctional cells) satisfies the constitutional right to free exercise of religion. This case could be cited for two propositions: 1) that it is not necessary to release prisoners from maximum security cells to attend services with the general population, or 2) that it is not necessary to conduct formal services for prisoners confined in correctional custody. Note, however, that this court held that full access to a minister of *one's denomination* satisfied the constitutional requirements. Another court[69] ruled, however, that the petitioner who was being held on death row be permitted to attend midweek services in the chapel instead of having to receive communion and services in a shower room.

§ 6.4.2 —The Wearing of Religious Medals

In general, the courts have recognized that the Black Muslims have a right to possess and wear religious medals.[70] This recognition has, in at least two cases, [71] been based upon the fact that inmates practicing other religions had been given such a right by prison officials. However, the issue of internal security has been asserted in this area as well as in the other areas concerning religious freedoms. In *Rowland v. Sigler,*[72] the court felt that, in view of the possibility of a prisoner's using a medallion as a weapon, prison officials could justifiably prohibit the prisoner from wearing the medallion. Any possible infringement of First Amendment rights was justified by the state interest in regulating the non-speech aspect, i.e., the use of a medallion as a weapon. This case would not support, of course, the denial (by prison officials) of medallions to Black Muslims where officials permitted medallions to be worn by Catholics.

---

[66] *See Sharp v. Sigler,* 408 F.2d 966 (8th Cir. 1969); *Belk v. Mitchell,* 294 F. Supp. 800 (W.D. N.C. 1968); *McBride v. McCorkle,* 44 N.J. Super. 468, 130 A.2d 881 (App. Div. 1957).

[67] *Konigsberg v. Ciccone,* 285 F. Supp. 585 (W.D. Mo. 1968), *aff'd,* 417 F.2d 161 (8th Cir. 1969), *cert. denied,* 397 U.S. 963 (1970).

[68] *Morgan v. Cook,* 236 So. 2d 749 (Miss. 1970).

[69] *Gunn v. Wilkinson,* 309 F. Supp. 411 (W.D. Mo. 1970).

[70] *See Knuckles v. Prasse,* 302 F. Supp. 1036 (E.D. Pa. 1969), *aff'd,* 435 F.2d 1255 (3d Cir. 1970).

[71] *See Coleman v. District of Columbia Commissioners,* 234 F. Supp. 408 (E.D. Va. 1964) and *State v. Cubbage,* 210 A.2d 555 (Del. Super. Ct. 1965).

[72] *Rowland v. Sigler,* 327 F. Supp. 821 (D.C. Neb. 1971).

§ 6.4.3 —The Right to Correspond with Religious Leaders

Numerous prisoners have petitioned the court for the right to correspond with Elijah Muhammad, a Black Muslim leader. Some institutions have a general restriction pertaining to correspondence with heads of religious groups. This regulation is based on the theory that such communications are not meaningful contacts.[73] Occasionally, courts have accepted this rationale and have held that because the policy is applicable to all religions it does not result in religious discrimination. However, in *Walker v. Blackwell*,[74] when prison officials gave as their reasons for not allowing such correspondence the fact that Elijah Muhammad had a prison record, and that the prison had a general policy not to allow Catholics to correspond with the Pope, the court held that Elijah Muhammad's confinement had occurred more than 25 years ago, that a criminal record was only one factor to be considered in approving a correspondence according to the Bureau of Prisons, and, that "[T]he prohibition against Catholics' correspondence with the Pope is of questionable constitutional merit."[75] Nevertheless, both the *Theriault* and *Remmers* decisions expressly declare that prison authorities may ascertain the contents of such correspondence with religious leaders in order to make certain that what is sought is spiritual guidance and advice, and that such correspondence is not used for other than religious purposes.[76]

§ 6.4.4 —The Right to Proselytize

Although there is no case which recognized an absolute right of a prisoner to proselytize, we could say that Black Muslims have the same right to proselytize in the prison as do other prisoners. This right does not extend, however, to such activity as would create a disturbance or interfere with the right of privacy of the other inmates.[77] Furthermore, when the purpose of proselytizing is "to cause or encourage disruption of established prison discipline for the sake of disruption," such activity enjoys no First Amendment protection since it is not based on an underly-

---

[73] *See Knuckles v. Prasse*, 302 F. Supp. 1036 (E.D. Pa. 1969), *aff'd*, 435 F.2d 1255 (3d Cir. 1970); *Long v. Katzenbach*, 258 F. Supp. 89 (M.D. Pa. 1966); *Desmond v. Blackwell*, 235 F. Supp. 246 (M.D. Pa. 1964).

[74] 411 F.2d 23 (5th Cir. 1969).

[75] *Id.* at 29.

[76] *Theriault v. Carlson*, 339 F. Supp. 375 (N.D. Ga. 1972), *vacated and remanded*, 495 F.2d 390 (5th Cir. 1974), *cert. denied*, 419 U.S. 1003 (1974); *Remmers v. Brewer*, 361 F. Supp. 537 (S.D. Iowa 1973), *aff'd*, 494 F.2d 1277 (8th Cir. 1974), *cert. denied*, 419 U.S. 1012 (1974).

[77] *See Evans v. Ciccone*, 377 F.2d 4 (8th Cir. 1967); *Sewell v. Pegelow*, 304 F.2d 670 (4th Cir. 1962); *Long v. Katzenbach*, 258 F. Supp. 89 (M.D. Pa. 1966).

ing "religion."[78] In *Fulwood v. Clemmer*,[79] prison authorities presented evidence to show that the prisoner's "field preaching" had resulted in a disturbance among the other prisoners. As a result, he had been placed in solitary for six months, excluded from the prison population for two years, and denied the use of rehabilitation and recreational facilities. The court held that this punishment was not reasonably related to the infraction.

§ 6.4.5 —Free Access to Ministers

The cases dealing with the right of an inmate, particularly a Black Muslim, to have access to a minister have been inconsistent. In two of these cases, *Jones v. Willingham*[80] and *Coleman v. Commissioner,* [81] the courts held that the prison officials could exclude Muslim ministers for the protection or for security in the institution. In *Cooper v. Pate,*[82] however, the court enjoined the administration from refusing to permit an inmate to communicate through the mail or personal visitation with the ministers of their faith. It was found that because such communication did not constitute a clear and present danger to prison security and because such communication was permitted for other religious denominations, the restriction against the Black Muslims was discriminatory.

There can be little doubt, irrespective of the controversy dealing with security within the institution, that Black Muslim ministers, once admitted to the institution, must be permitted to wear such religious robes and raiment as they desire.[83] Furthermore, they must be paid at an hourly rate comparable to that paid to chaplains of other faiths.[84]

§ 6.4.6 —Restrictions of Diet

As a general rule, the courts have refused to order prisons to provide Black Muslims with pork-free meals in spite of the fact that such dietary restraint is an essential doctrine found in that faith. The rationale for such refusal has been diverse. For example, in *Northern v. Nelson,*[85] where the petitioner sought special meals during the period of Ramadan, the court asserted that budgetary restrictions constituted a

---

[78] *Theriault v. Sibler,* 391 F. Supp. 578 (W.D. Tex. 1975), *vacated on appeal,* 547 F.2d 1279 (5th Cir. 1977). The court of appeals held that the requirement of a belief in a supreme being as a criterion to determine whether a practice constitutes a religion within the protection of the First Amendment is too narrow. The court stated that,

    When reconsidering what constitutes a religion, a thorough study of the existing case law should be accompanied by appropriate evidentiary exploration of philosophical, theological, and other related literature and resources on this issue. *Id.* at 1281.

[79] *Fulwood v. Clemmer,* 206 F. Supp. 370 (D. D.C. 1962).

[80] *Jones v. Willingham,* 248 F. Supp. 791 (D. Kan. 1965).

[81] *Coleman v. Commissioner,* 234 F. Supp. 408 (E.D. Va. 1964).

[82] *Cooper v. Pate,* 382 F.2d 518 (7th Cir. 1967).

[83] *See Samarion v. McGinnis,* 314 N.Y.S.2d 715 (N.Y. A.D. 1970).

[84] *See Northern v. Nelson,* 315 F. Supp. 687 (N.D. Cal. 1970).

[85] *See also Young v. Robinson,* 29 Cr. L. 2587 (M.D. Pa. 1981). (Muslim inmates are not required to be furnished diets that conform to their religious beliefs.)

justifiable reason for refusing to serve pork-free meals. The court found that, despite the constitutional deprivations claimed, the government had demonstrated a substantial compelling interest and, for that reason, dismissed relief.

Another court[86] justified the failure to provide pork-free meals by finding that a prisoner could acquire adequate nourishment by avoiding pork foods. In view of this fact, the prison was under no obligation to provide specified meals. In a third case, *Childs v. Pegelow,*[87] the court simply found that there was no constitutional issue involved and that, essentially, the Muslims were demanding special privileges rather than constitutional rights.

A unique approach to the issue of pork-free meals is found in *Barnett v. Rodgers.*[88] The District of Columbia Circuit Court held that the lower court erred in dismissing the inmate's complaint without determining whether the government had compelling justification and purposes for denying their request. The court felt that the prison officials had not adequately demonstrated a budgetary constraint which would prevent the use of pork, and had not shown why they could not post a menu or why they could not distribute pork meals more evenly throughout the week. "To say that religious freedom may undergo modification in a prison environment is not to say that it can be suppressed or ignored without adequate reason."[89] Upon remand, judgment was entered in favor of the prison superintendent.[90]

A District Court injunction obtained by Muslim inmates in Iowa was reversed. Several parts of the injunction dealing with congregational prayer sessions, pork-free diets, and prayer classes were not based on findings of constitutional or statutory violations. Also reversed were requirements that Muslim inmates be allowed to wear prayer caps and robes outside their prayer services, and that Muslim religious leaders be allowed to visit with Muslim inmates after the initial five-day period of an emergency lock down. The Appeals Court held that prison officials had cited security reasons for opposing these measures, and the District Court should have deferred to their judgment.

Generally, the analysis employed in the Black Muslim food cases had been echoed in the Jewish Kosher food cases. Cases out of New York have added much to the discussion of the Kosher food question. Within two days of one another, two federal district courts in New York came to apparently opposite conclusions. Both cases involved Jewish prisoners who had applied to the court for orders directing the Bureau of Prisons to make Kosher foods, meeting the requirements of Jewish orthodox dietary laws, available to them during their incarceration.

---

[86] *Abernathy v. Cunningham,* 393 F.2d 775 (4th Cir. 1968).

[87] *Childs v. Pegelow,* 321 F.2d 487 (4th Cir. 1963), *cert. denied,* 376 U.S. 932 (1964); *cf. Muhammad-D.C.C. v. Keve,* 479 F. Supp. 1311 (D. Del. 1979). (Muslim inmates have a constitutional right to a pork-free diet.)

[88] *Barnett v. Rodgers,* 410 F.2d 995 (D.C. Cir. 1969).

[89] *Id.* at 1000.

[90] Unreported decisions HC 174-66 and HC 66-66 (S.D. N.Y. 1975).

In the first case, *United States v. Huss,*[91] the court ruled that the prison was not obligated to provide Kosher food. In arriving at this conclusion, the court relied on four primary considerations: 1) the extra cost of providing Kosher foods to Jewish prisoners on a regular basis; 2) the obvious problems that would arise from special treatment given to such prisoners; 3) the security risk involved, given the relative ease of smuggling contraband to a prisoner when it is known that the food is for a designated prisoner; and 4) the availability of substitute foods to insure a sufficient diet. On appeal, this judgment was vacated on procedural grounds.[92]

The second case, *United States v. Kahane,*[93] involved the Kosher food requests of an orthodox rabbi. Here, the court decided that the inmate was entitled to receive Kosher meals. It was reasoned that comparatively simple administrative procedures, i.e., a combination of pre-prepared frozen Kosher meals and suitable dietary alternatives, would result in a nutritionally sound diet consistent with Kosher requirements. In the court's opinion, the government had shown no serious reasons why provision of a Kosher diet for the prisoner would affect prison security or discipline.

The conflict arising from these two cases is somewhat settled by *Kahane v. Carlson.*[94] In this decision, the Second Circuit Court of Appeals affirmed and modified *United States v. Kahane.* The court agreed that the finding of deep religious significance for a practicing orthodox Jew was justified and was entitled to constitutional protection. It was explained that the difficulties encountered by the prisons were surmountable in view of the small number of practicing orthodox Jews in federal prisons (approximately twelve).[95] The court clarified and modified the district court's decision by explaining that the use of frozen prepared Kosher foods, while helpful, was not constitutionally required. Rather, the prison was required to provide the incarcerated orthodox rabbi with a diet sufficient to sustain his good health without violating Jewish dietary laws. However, the court did not mandate specific items of diet.

While the court ordered the provision of a Kosher diet in this instance, it should be noted that this does not necessarily apply to *all* Jewish inmates. The application of this decision seems to require at least a situation involving a practicing orthodox Jew before a prison is required to provide a Kosher diet.

Where the Jewish prison population was small, it was within the official's discretion whether or not to provide a rabbi and other Jewish services upon request.[96]

Finally, with respect to dietary restrictions and isolated confinement, it was held in *Jones v. Gallahan*[97] that prison officials must provide an inmate in isolation a

---

[91] *Rogers v. Scurr,* 676 F.2d 1211 (8th Cir. 1982).

[92] *United States v. Huss,* 394 F. Supp. 752 (S.D.N.Y. 1975), *vacated,* 520 F.2d 598 (2d Cir. 1975).

[93] *United States v. Huss,* 520 F.2d 598 (2d Cir. 1975).

[94] *United States v. Kahane,* 396 F. Supp. 687 (E.D.N.Y. 1975), *modified sub nom., Kahane v. Carlson,* 527 F.2d 492 (2d Cir. 1975).

[95] *Kahane v. Carlson,* 527 F.2d 492 (2d Cir. 1975).

[96] *Id.* at 495.

[97] *Garza v. Miller,* 688 F.2d 480 (7th Cir. 1982).

diet with a daily minimum caloric requirement that will not be rejected on religious grounds. The Court noted that this requirement may be met by providing acceptable food alternatives.

§ 6.4.7 — Access to Religious Literature

Access to religious literature by inmates is one of the most controversial areas now confronting the courts. The justification for suppressing religious literature that the prison administrators frequently advance is that the material is inflammatory and will cause disruptions and breaches in security. Consequently, the decisions usually turn on when the court believes that the material requested is of a nature tending to incite disruptions or security problems. A case finding no such tendency is *Northern v. Nelson.*[98] Here, the court held that the prison library was under an obligation to make available copies of the holy Qu-ran. Further, the court ordered that prisoners be allowed to receive the publication *Muhammad Speaks* unless it could be clearly demonstrated that a specific issue would substantially disrupt prison discipline.

In *Walker v. Blackwell,* [99] although the district court held that issues of *Muhammad Speaks* were inflammatory, the Fifth Circuit Court reached a conclusion similar to *Northern,* and reversed the district court. The basis of its decision is found in the following:

First, taken as a whole, the newspapers are filled with news and editorial comment, a substantial portion of which generally encourages the Black Muslim to improve his material and spiritual condition of life by labor and study. Nowhere, including the supposedly inflammatory portions described by the court below, does there appear any direct incitement to the Black Muslims to engage in any physical violence.[100]

This court thus concluded that *Muhammad Speaks* was not inflammatory and ordered that Black Muslims be allowed to receive the newspaper. The court qualified this, however, by saying that they were not holding that exclusion of the newspaper could not take place, if it became inflammatory. The order was merely to direct that the warden not *arbitrarily* deny Black Muslims the right to read *Muhammad Speaks.*

While *Northern* and *Walker* have found that, taken as a whole, the Muslim publications presented no threat to prison security, other courts have come to the opposite conclusion. In *Knuckles v. Prasse,*[101] the district court found that it was not mandatory that prison officials make available Muslim books and periodicals. The court found that, without proper guidance and interpretation by trained Muslim

[98] *Jones v. Gallahan,* 370 F. Supp. 488 (W.D. Va. 1974).
[99] *Northern v. Nelson,* 315 F. Supp. 687 (N.D. Cal. 1970).
[100] *Walker v. Blackwell,* 411 F.2d 23 (5th Cir. 1969).
[101] *Id.* at 28-29.

ministers, these materials might be misinterpreted by an inmate. An uninformed inmate could read the material as an encouragement to defy whites generally and prison authorities specifically. Thus, the literature could constitute "*a clear and present danger* of a branch of prison security or discipline or some other substantial interference with the orderly functioning of the institution."[102] Another decision following this basic rationale is *Abernathy v. Cunningham*.[103] There, an inmate desired to obtain a copy of "Muhammad's Message to the Black Man in America," and to subscribe to *Muhammad Speaks*. The Fourth Circuit held that the prison's decision denying access to this literature, so far as the record disclosed, was not motivated by religious prejudice, and that the particular materials under question contained recurring themes of Negro superiority and hatred for the white race. It was the prison authorities' opinion that such materials would be inflammatory and subversive to discipline. And, the court felt it should not attempt to substitute its judgment on the nature of the publication for that of the prison authorities. For this reason, the court denied relief. In his dissent, Judge Craven stated that he failed to understand why the prisoner could not be granted access to the materials on the condition that he could not circulate them throughout the prison. Since this alternative was available, exclusion was not the only remedy to prevent danger to internal discipline.

In spite of the courts' determination as to whether material is inflammatory or not, most courts place upon the prison the burden of proving that the deprivation of constitutional rights is justified. In *Burns v. Swenson*,[104] prison officials were ordered to return plaintiff's *Koran*. The court felt that deprivation of his holy book would interfere with his right to freely practice his religion, particularly since the prison officials had given no explanation of why this book should not be returned to the prisoner. Similarly in *Long v. Parker*,[105] the Third Circuit placed the burden on prison authorities who wished to suppress *Muhammad Speaks*. The court found that the administration must show that "[T]he literature creates a clear and present danger of a breach of prison security or discipline or some other substantial interference with the orderly functioning of the institution."[106] However, it also required the Muslims to establish that it was basic religious literature essential to their belief and understanding of their religion.

As indicated above, the courts have been fairly uniform in supporting administrative decisions to exclude various Black Muslim publications. With the primary emphasis being placed on maintenance of security, the courts have given the following reasons for excluding such publications: 1) Without proper guidance by trained Muslims, the reader could interpret them as condoning disruption within institutions; 2) Such publications may advocate and encourage conduct which the

---

[102] *Knuckles v. Prasse*, 302 F. Supp. 1036 (E.D. Pa. 1969).
[103] *Id.* at 1049.
[104] *Abernathy v. Cunningham*, 393 F.2d 775 (4th Cir. 1968).
[105] *Burns v. Swenson*, 288 F. Supp. 4 (W.D. Mo. 1968), *modified*, 300 F. Supp. 759 (W.D. Mo. 1969).
[106] *Long v. Parker*, 390 F.2d 816 (3d Cir. 1968).

officials may lawfully suppress; 3) They advocate themes of Negro superiority and hatred of the white race and are thus inflammatory and subversive to discipline; and 4) Publications that are not necessary to the practice of religion may be excluded.

It must be noted that although inflammatory religious material may be suppressed, at least one case, *Mukmuk v. Commissioner*,[107] has held that an inmate may not be punished for possession of the religious literature.

§ 6.4.8   —Classification on Religious Grounds

It is a frequent practice in various correctional institutions to require that an inmate specify his religious preference upon entering the prison. The inmate is then forbidden to alter this choice during his period of confinement. For the most part, such practices have been upheld by courts.

In *Long v. Katzenbach*,[108] the court sustained the classification procedure as a valid means of controlling the proselytizing which had been a source of disruption within the institution. A similar finding was handed down in *Peek v. Ciccone*[109] wherein prison officials had refused to permit a non-Jewish inmate to attend Jewish services. The prison allowed inmates to attend any service connected with their specified religious affiliation. The court found that such a restriction was not unreasonable in that it did not curtail religious belief. This was especially true in light of the fact that the Jewish rabbi in the institution had a policy of refusing conversion of inmates to the Jewish faith. The court found religious practices, as distinguished from religious beliefs, may properly be the subject of administrative regulation control.

A law which stated that legal recognition of religious names adopted by prisoners could be withheld was held to be unconstitutional. Further, correction officials may maintain inmate records in the names that inmates used when convicted. There is no right to force prison officials to put inmate-adopted religious names on their official records.[110]

A prisoner commenced suit against the superintendent of the institution alleging that the superintendent had violated his statutory and constitutional rights to freely exercise his religion. Where the prisoner could not state specifically how the restrictive institutional policies were violating his rights, and which of his religious rights were specifically being violated, the superintendent had qualified immunity from a Section 1983 civil suit.[111]

---

[107] *Id.* at 822.

[108] *Mukmuk v. Commissioner,* 529 F.2d 272 (2d Cir. 1976).

[109] *Long v. Katzenbach,* 258 F. Supp. 89 (M.D. Pa. 1966).

[110] *Peek v. Ciccone,* 288 F. Supp. 329 (W.D. Mo. 1968).

[111] *Barrett v. Commonwealth of Virginia,* 689 F.2d 498 (4th Cir. 1982).

A patdown search of a prisoner conducted by a female guard does not violate the constitutional right to free exercise of religion of a prisoner whose faith teaches that a man is forbidden to be touched by a woman not of his family.[112]

Although the issue is not entirely clear, religious classification would appear to be supportable so long as equal treatment is afforded to all religious groups and there is a rational basis for such classification.

§ 6.4.9   —Beards and Haircuts

Both *Brown v. Wainwright* [113] and *Brooks v. Wainwright*[114] held that regulations requiring shaves and haircuts were proper and were not a source of religious discrimination. However, the court in *People ex rel. Rockey v. Krueger*[115] heard evidence from the prisoner that he was being held in solitary because he had refused to shave his beard. The prison administration justified the regulation as one for the protection of health. The jail supervisor also testified that there was no formal regulation about hair, but that the order to the staff was that inmates were only permitted to wear neatly trimmed mustaches. He said that an orthodox Jew would not be required to shave his beard. The court held that, on the basis of the treatment afforded orthodox Jews, the prisoner was the subject of religious discrimination.

In cases concerning prison haircut regulations as applied to American Indians, at least three courts have held that where a long hairstyle is motivated by indisputably sincere religious beliefs, then such regulations impermissibly infringe on the inmate's right under the First Amendment to the free exercise of his religion.[116] However, in *Proffitt v. Ciccone,*[117] the court upheld prison haircut regulations despite the inmate's contention that he was thereby forced to violate religious vows he had taken. In this area, in order to restrict inmate conduct based upon religious motivations, prison authorities face a heavy burden.

A one-half blooded Cherokee Indian may not be required to cut his hair if the prison regulation infringes on his religious beliefs.[118]

§ 6.5   Conclusion

The primary emphasis of decisions concerning an inmate's religious freedom has been upon the fact that the prison is a closed environment. It is because of this fact that the court frequently invokes the "non-interference" logic so prevalent in early cases dealing with prisons. The state interest in maintaining security within the institution, together with the need for administrative discretion in handling dis-

---

[112] *Green v. White*, 693 F.2d 45 (8th Cir. 1982).

[113] *Sam'l v. Mintzes*, 554 F. Supp. 416 (E.D. Mich. 1983).

[114] *Brown v. Wainwright*, 419 F.2d 1376 (5th Cir. 1970).

[115] *Brooks v. Wainwright*, 428 F.2d 652 (5th Cir. 1970).

[116] *People ex rel. Rockey v. Krueger*, 306 N.Y.S.2d 359 (Sup. Ct. 1969).

[117] *Teterud v. Gillman*, 385 F. Supp. 153 (S.D. Iowa 1974), *aff'd*, 522 F.2d 357 (8th Cir. 1975), and *Crowe v. Erickson*, 17 Cr. L. 2093 (D.S.D. 1975); *Gallahan v. Hollyfield*, 516 F. Supp. 1004 (E.D. Va. 1981), *aff'd*, 670 F.2d 1345 (4th Cir. 1982).

[118] *Proffitt v. Ciccone*, 371 F. Supp. 282 (W.D. Mo. 1973), *aff'd*, 506 F.2d 1020 (8th Cir. 1974).

ciplinary problems, has been held sufficient reason for limiting an inmate's First Amendment rights.

One of the few restrictions placed upon the prison administrator in his dealings with First Amendment rights of inmates has been that of equal protection, that is, treating all classes of inmates equally. Courts have consistently held that where one religious group is permitted to engage in a particular activity, the same right must be accorded all other religious groups within the institution. Thus, it would appear that although prison officials have a right to regulate religious activity in order to promote valid institutional interests, the regulation must, in all cases, be equally applied to all groups. Likewise, where one group is permitted to manifest its religious beliefs in a certain manner, all other religious groups must be accorded the same privilege.

Chapter 7

LEGAL SERVICES

§ 7.1   Introduction: Access to the Courts as a Constitutional Right

The United States Supreme Court has repeatedly affirmed that one of the fundamental rights within the due process clause of the Fourteenth Amendment includes the right of access to the courts. Essential to the concept of due process of law is the right of an individual to have "an opportunity . . . granted at a meaningful time and in a meaningful manner,"[1] "for [a] hearing appropriate to the nature of the case."[2]

The right of an inmate to exercise this basic constitutional right was established in the 1940 case of *Ex parte Hull*.[3] In *Hull*, a state prison regulation required that all legal documents in an inmate's court proceedings must be submitted to a prison official for examination and censorship before they are filed with the court. The United States Supreme Court found this regulation invalid on the ground that "the state and its officers may not abridge or impair petitioner's right to apply to a federal court for a writ of habeas corpus."[4]

---

[1] *Armstrong v. Manzo*, 380 U.S. 545, 552 (1965).
[2] *Mullane v. Central Hanover Tr. Co.*, 339 U.S. 306, 313 (1950).
[3] *Ex parte Hull*, 312 U.S. 546 (1941); *See also, Webb v. State*, 412 N.E.2d 790 (Ind. 1980).
[4] *Ex parte Hull*, 312 U.S. 549 (1941).

In spite of the rule of law established in *Hull,* courts have been hesitant to interfere with the exercise of discretion by prison administrators in matters concerning institutional control. The courts have frequently stated that prison administration was a function relegated to the executive branch of government, and that for this reason, the judiciary would interfere only where the wrongs committed by institution officials were of monumental proportions.[5] This judicial reluctance offers insight as to why various prison practices (although they may be violations of the inmates' constitutional rights), have gone uncontested for the past several decades.

Neither the Eighth Amendment nor the Due Process Clause requires states to appoint counsel for indigent death-row inmates seeking state post-conviction relief. State collateral proceedings are not constitutionally required as an adjunct to the state criminal proceeding and serve a different and more limited purpose than either the trial or appeal. Eighth Amendment safeguards imposed at the trial stage—where the court and jury hear testimony, receive evidence, and decide the questions of guilt and punishment—are sufficient to assure the reliability of the process by which the death penalty is imposed.

The meaningful access requirement of *Bounds v. Smith*[6] can be satisfied in various ways, and state legislatures and prison administrators must be given "wide discretion" to select appropriate solutions from a range of complex options.[7]

§ 7.2   The Nature of Legal Services in Prison—Prevailing Practices

Many of the practices which have prevailed in prisons throughout the country have amounted to impairments of the inmates' right of access to the courts. Disciplinary actions for inmates' pursuing legal remedies, censorship or wholesale confiscation of a prisoner's legal documents, and other such practices have been common in many of America's prison systems.

Further restriction on access to the courts is seen in the fact that prison officials seldom provide inmates with any services related to legal needs. In most cases, only a few outdated law books and, occasionally, the services of a notary public are supplied. As a result of this lack of legal assistance, inmates were frequently forced to accept the aid of a self-proclaimed "jailhouse lawyer." A *jailhouse lawyer* is an inmate who, through self-education, has acquired minimum legal skills and, notwithstanding prison restriction, offers legal advice and counseling to fellow inmates, either with or without compensation. These individuals have been subject to a great deal of restriction and regulation by prison officials. It is on the restriction of the jailhouse lawyer and alternatives to him that judicial concern has focused in the modern cases.

---

[5] *See Lee v. Tahash,* 352 F.2d 970 (8th Cir. 1965); *United States v. Marchese,* 341 F.2d 782 (9th Cir. 1965); *See also, Webb v. State,* 412 N.E.2d 790 (Ind. 1980); *Johnson v. Teasdale,* 456 F. Supp. 1083 (W.D. Mo. 1978); *Miller v. Stanmore,* 636 F.2d 986 (5th Cir. 1981).

[6] *Bounds v. Smith,* 430 U.S. 817 (1977).

[7] *Murray v. Giarratano,* _____ U.S. _____, 109 S. Ct. 2765 (1989).

Restriction on the legal practice of jailhouse lawyers, in light of the unique position of an incarcerated individual, places an impossible burden upon the inmate seeking legal relief. These restrictions, coupled with the unavailability of legal assistance in the outside world, have resulted in the complete loss of a basic constitutional right. This loss and difficulty was finally acknowledged and partially resolved by the United States Supreme Court in 1969.

§ 7.3   The Rule of *Johnson v. Avery*

The United States Supreme Court case of *Johnson v. Avery*[8] has had a profound effect upon the power of prison officials to regulate or prohibit an inmate's right of access to the courts. The case involved the constitutionality of a Tennessee prison regulation which provided: "No inmate will advise, assist or otherwise contract to aid another, either with or without a fee, to prepare Writs or other legal matters . . . Inmates are forbidden to set themselves up as practitioners for the purpose of promoting a business of writing Writs."[9]

In analyzing this prison rule, the court emphasized the fact that inmates, a great percentage of whom are illiterate, are frequently not able to obtain assistance in preparing requests for post-conviction relief from any source other than one available within the prison walls. Therefore, since the necessary legal assistance is usually available only in the form of a jailhouse lawyer or inmate writ-writer, the Supreme Court reasoned that a regulation which effectively cuts off this assistance amounts to a denial of access to the courts. For this reason, together with the "fundamental importance of the writ of habeas corpus in our constitutional scheme . . . ,"[10] the Supreme Court declared the Tennessee regulation invalid.

Although *Johnson v. Avery* has played a prominent role in bringing about prison reform, the ruling itself was very narrow in scope. Essentially, the only "right" guaranteed by this decision is that of an illiterate prisoner to receive legal aid from a fellow prisoner in preparation of petitions for writs of habeas corpus. This right was not absolute, but was restricted to those inmates incarcerated in a prison system that had failed to provide a "reasonable alternative" by which access to the courts (*i.e.*, competent legal assistance) could be gained. The Supreme Court further limited this right by allowing prison authorities to: 1) place reasonable restrictions upon the time and place where the inmates' legal counseling could be given, and 2) impose punishment or discipline for any exchange of consideration or payment for the services rendered. Thus, a prison rule which provides for the discipline of a jailhouse lawyer who charges for his services or receives anything of value in return for such services is authorized under the rule of *Johnson v. Avery*.

---

[8] *Johnson v. Avery*, 393 U.S. 483 (1969).
[9] *Johnson v. Avery*, 393 U.S. 483, 484 (1969).
[10] *Id.* at 485.

§ 7.3.1 —Judicial Interpretation of *Johnson v. Avery*

Johnson v. Avery recognized the existence of two competing interests in the area of corrections: 1) the legitimate exercise of control by prison officials, and 2) the constitutionally protected rights retained by its incarcerated individuals. As a result of this dual concern, the lower courts applying the rule of *Johnson v. Avery* have attempted to balance the proper state concern with the concern of the inmate in obtaining the legal assistance necessary to gain access to the courts. The state has the choice of providing inmates with access to the courts by making available either adequate law libraries or persons trained in the law.[11] A clear test is found in a decision of the Supreme Court of California,[12] wherein the court established three governing principles to guide future decisions. First, the court must determine the extent to which the institutional regulations impede or discourage mutual inmate legal assistance. Second, the court is to decide, from the standpoint of legitimate custodial objectives, how undesirable the conduct is that the particular regulation sought to avoid. Third, the court must determine whether there are alternative means of dealing with the undesirable conduct, means which do not result in significant restriction on mutual inmate aid.[13] It should be noted, however, that, consistent with the ruling of *Johnson,* emphasis is placed upon the needs of the inmate rather than on those of the institution. In effect, the court is stating that where an irreconcilable conflict exists, the prison officials, rather than the inmate, must alter their practices.

Although other courts have not enumerated so specific a test as California, they have nevertheless maintained the same theoretical approach in dealing with the conflict existing in a prison setting.[14] There is a tendency for the courts to retain the same non-interference rhetoric used by the pre-*Johnson* cases, but an obvious change in attitude has occurred.

In *Cruz v. Hauck*[15] the court held that a broad rule which prohibited inmates from giving or receiving legal assistance on habeas corpus or other general civil legal matters in jail was invalid. It approved, however, reasonable rules governing the time and place where inmates could get legal assistance. The court said that the officials have a duty to maintain security in the jail cell block and can restrict the storage of law books in inmates' cells for security purposes. If inmates cannot safely store legal materials in their cells, arrangements for storage of these materials in a readily available area with reasonable procedures for their use are required. To maintain a proper balance between competing interests of prison control and prisoner rights, the court held that an inmate should be permitted to obtain legal

[11] *Carter v. Kamka,* 515 F. Supp. 825 (D. Md. 1980), *aff'd,* 573 F.2d 172 (4th Cir. 1978).
[12] *In re Harrell,* 470 P.2d 640 (Cal. 1970).
[13] *Id.*
[14] *See Gittlemacker v. Prasse,* 428 F.2d 1 (3d Cir. 1970); *Gilmore v. Lynch,* 319 F. Supp. 105 (N.D. Cal. 1970), *aff'd sub nom.,* *Younger v. Gilmore,* 404 U.S. 15 (1971); *Jordan v. Johnson,* 381 F. Supp. 600 (E.D. Mich. 1974), *aff'd,* 513 F.2d 631, *cert. denied,* 423 U.S. 851 (1975); *McKinney v. DeBord,* 507 F.2d 501 (9th Cir. 1974).
[15] *Cruz v. Hauck,* 515 F.2d 322 (5th Cir. 1975).

materials from sources other than attorneys or publishing houses, subject to screening only for security purposes. It appears that the courts will no longer defer to administrative discretion, but will more closely scrutinize the fact situation in order to prevent possible violation of constitutional rights.

The *Johnson* case opened a new area of concern for the judiciary in its recognition of the necessity for mutual inmate legal assistance in the preparation of writs. Five primary concerns of the courts deal with the issue of mutual inmate legal assistance:

1. Which inmates are permitted to receive legal assistance from a jailhouse lawyer?
2. Who may act as a jailhouse lawyer?
3. How prison authorities may reasonably restrict the jailhouse lawyer?
4. What type of legal assistance may be received from the jailhouse lawyer?
5. What is a reasonable alternative is to the jailhouse lawyer?

§ 7.4   Which Inmates Are Permitted to Receive Legal Assistance from the Jailhouse Lawyer?

The emphasis in *Johnson* was on recognition of the need for an illiterate or functionally illiterate inmate to receive legal assistance in the preparation of legal documents to be filed with the courts. The lower federal courts that have dealt with this issue, however, have refused to restrict the *Johnson* doctrine to its narrow confines.

Jailhouse lawyers may also play a role in internal prison matters. In *Kirby v. Blackledge*[16] prison officials had to allow the assistance of a fellow inmate, or some designated staff member, to be part of proceedings to transfer an illiterate and disadvantaged inmate to maximum security. The reason for counsel-substitute was that the inmate might not have the capacity to collect and present necessary evidence for an adequate presentation of the case.

In *Clutchette v. Enomoto*[17] the court held that prison discipline procedures must permit an inmate who is illiterate or who faces complex issues adequate assistance in lieu of counsel. The reason for counsel substitute was that the inmate might not have the capacity to collect and present necessary evidence for an adequate presentation of the case.

Restrictions which forbid the receipt of legal assistance by any but illiterate prisoners have been invalidated as contrary to the Supreme Court ruling. Where there is no "reasonable alternative," all inmates in the institution must be permitted to seek legal counseling from the jailhouse lawyer.[18] However, a state inmate already

---

[16] *Kirby v. Blackledge*, 530 F.2d 583 (4th Cir. 1976).

[17] *Clutchette v. Enomoto*, 471 F. Supp. 1113 (N.D. Cal. 1979); *Moore v. Smith*, 390 N.E.2d 1052 (Ind. App. 1979); *cf. Lamb v. Hutto*, 467 F. Supp. 562 (E.D. Va. 1979) (a prisoner does not have a right to counsel at a prison transfer hearing).

[18] *Wolff v. McDonnell*, 418 U.S. 539, 71 Ohio Op. 2d 336 (1974); *See Wainwright v. Coonts*, 409 F.2d 1337 (5th Cir. 1969); *United States ex rel. Stevenson v. Mancusi*, 325 F. Supp. 1028 (W.D. N.Y. 1971); *State v. Williams*, 595 P.2d 1104 (Kan. 1979); *Carter v. Kamka*, 515 F. Supp. 825 (D.C. Md. 1980); *Storseth v. Spellman*, 654 F.2d 1349 (9th Cir. 1981).

paroled was found to be in the same situation as any other *pro se* plaintiff who had the choice of representing himself or finding an attorney. The parolee was not entitled to be represented by the jailhouse lawyer who had initially prepared the pleadings in the inmate's civil rights action against a prison physician.[19] The uncontrolled discretion of a prison official as to who may or may not receive legal counseling has been invalidated where official approval is not subject to established standards.[20]

An exception to the broad statement that all inmates must be permitted assistance from the jailhouse lawyer occurs when inmates have been temporarily confined in isolation. So long as the confinement is not for an extended period, thereby hindering access to the courts, isolated inmates need not be afforded assistance from the jailhouse lawyer.[21]

§ 7.5 Who May Act as the Jailhouse Lawyer?

Related to the issue of who may receive legal assistance from a jailhouse lawyer is the problem of who among the inmate population may function as the jailhouse lawyer. The courts have stressed that the right asserted in *Johnson* was not the privilege of the jailhouse lawyer to practice law. Rather, it was the right of an inmate to receive legal assistance from a fellow inmate.[22] This principle is most clearly expressed in cases where jailhouse lawyers have attempted to send legal material to an inmate in another prison and, as a result, have been subjected to disciplinary action. The rule which has emerged from these cases has been that the "client" inmate could receive legal assistance from inmates of *his own* prison. Since his rights could be protected there, there was no necessity that legal assistance be furnished to him by an inmate confined in another prison. Therefore, because no inmate needed legal assistance from a particular inmate in another prison, the jailhouse lawyer could be restricted accordingly,[23] in the absence of evidence that alternative ways of obtaining legal assistance were unavailable.[24]

§ 7.6 How May Prison Officials Restrict the Jailhouse Lawyer?

In *Johnson v. Avery,* the Supreme Court stated that the activities of the jailhouse lawyer could be restricted as to time and place. Furthermore, an absolute prohibition against the jailhouse lawyer receiving fees was also sanctioned. As a result of

---

[19] *Rizzo v. Zubrik,* 391 F. Supp. 1058 (S.D. N.Y. 1975).

[20] *See Sostre v. McGinnis,* 442 F.2d 178 (2d Cir. 1971), *cert. denied,* 405 U.S. 978 (1972); *Williams v. Department of Justice,* 443 F.2d 958 (5th Cir. 1970); *Carothers v. Follette,* 314 F. Supp. 1014 (S.D. N.Y. 1970); *Prewitt v. State ex rel. Eyman,* 315 F. Supp. 793 (D. Ariz. 1969).

[21] *See In re Harrell,* 470 P.2d 640 (Cal. 1970).

[22] *See Guajardo v. Luna,* 432 F.2d 1324 (5th Cir. 1970); *In re Harrell,* 470 P.2d 640 (Cal. 1970); *Bounds v. Smith,* 430 U.S. 817 (1977); *Delgado v. Sheriff of Milwaukee County,* 487 F. Supp. 649 (E.D. Wis. 1980); *Rhodes v. Robinson,* 612 F.2d 766 (3d Cir. 1979); *State v. Williams,* 595 P.2d 1104 (Kan. 1979).

[23] *See McKinney v. DeBord,* 324 F. Supp. 928 (E.D. Cal. 1970); *Putt v. Clark,* 297 F. Supp. 27 (N.D. Ga. 1969); *In re Harrell,* 470 P.2d 640 (Cal. 1970); *Storseth v. Spellman,* 654 F.2d 1349 (9th Cir. 1981).

[24] *Boehme v. Smith,* 378 N.Y.S.2d 170 (N.Y. App. Div. 1976); *Webb v. State,* 412 N.E.2d 790 (Ind. 1980).

the "reasonableness" requirement, the interpretation given this rule by the lower courts has generally been varied.

One of the most litigated issues involving restrictions placed upon mutual inmate legal assistance has concerned the proper exercise of discretion by prison officials. Courts have asserted that the uncontrolled discretion of prison officials in their restricting the practice of the jailhouse lawyer is unconstitutional under *Johnson*. This discretion, according to these courts, must be subject to established guidelines or standards in order to assure that they are reasonable.[25]

Another related issue is the validity of a rule that required all legal work to be conducted in a special writ room. The courts, both before and after the *Johnson* ruling, have approved such a rule so long as prison officials were not unduly restrictive[26] in the hours of use they permitted.

The right of a jailhouse lawyer to have legal papers of another inmate in his possession is unclear. In one case, in order for jailhouse lawyers to function effectively, the court held that they must be able to have in their possession papers that pertain to their client's case.[27]

Another court interpreted a prison regulation as authorizing the papers to be kept by the jailhouse lawyer only until such time as the petition was complete, after which the papers had to be returned to the "client."[28]

At a minimum, it would appear that a prison regulation could not forbid the jailhouse lawyer from having papers of another inmate in his possession on that ground alone.

The Supreme Court of California, in the case of *In re Harrell*,[29] dealt extensively with the type of restrictions permissible under the *Johnson* ruling. The regulations discussed were typical of many institutions and, for that reason, are relevant to our present discussion.

One regulation invalidated by the court forbade the jailhouse lawyer to file with a court an application for relief on behalf of, or as "next friend" of his client. The court held that the *Johnson* rule authorized legal assistance in writ writing, not in representation before the courts. Although an application submitted by a "next friend" will not generally be accepted by a court unless there are exceptional circumstances, this judicial policy did not, according to *Harrell*, give prison officials the right to examine such applications to determine whether the request for relief

---

[25] *See Sostre v. McGinnis*, 442 F.2d 178 (2d Cir. 1971), *cert. denied*, 405 U.S. 978 (1972); *Carothers v. Follette*, 314 F. Supp. 1014 (S.D. N.Y. 1970); *Prewitt v. State ex rel. Eyman*, 315 F. Supp. 793 (D. Ariz. 1969); *Wolff v. McDonnell*, 418 U.S. 539, 71 Ohio Op. 2d 336 (1974).

[26] *See Novak v. Beto*, 320 F. Supp. 1206 (S.D. Tex. 1970), *rev'd on other grounds*, 453 F.2d 661 (5th Cir. 1972); *Brown v. South Carolina*, 286 F. Supp. 998 (D. S.C. 1968); *Ex parte Wilson*, 235 F. Supp. 988 (E.D. S.C. 1964); *Corpus v. Estelle*, 409 F. Supp. 1090 (S.D. Tex. 1975); *Ford v. LaVallee*, 390 N.Y.S.2d 269 (1976); *Cruz v. Androd*, 15998B Opinion (5th Cir. 1980); *cf. Jensena v. Satran*, 303 N.W.2d 568 (N.D. 1981).

[27] *See In re Harrell*, 470 P.2d 640 (Cal. 1970).

[28] *Gilmore v. Lynch*, 319 F. Supp. 105 (N.D. Cal. 1970), *aff'd sub nom.*, *Younger v. Gilmore*, 404 U.S. 15 (1971).

[29] *In re Harrell*, 470 P.2d 640 (Cal. 1970).

had merit. This determination is a decision for the courts, not prison officials. Therefore, prison officials may not refuse to forward a document to the courts on the grounds that it is improperly prepared.[30]

Another disputed restriction dealt with the right of an inmate to correspond on legal matters with inmates in other institutions. The petitioner in *Harrell* sought to give legal advice through use of the mails. The court found that the prison rule restricting this practice was valid under *Johnson*. The *Johnson* rule, stated the court, guaranteed the right to be assisted, but did not give the "client" the right to be assisted by a particular jailhouse lawyer. No infringement upon that right necessarily resulted from a restriction upon the activities of a particular inmate "lawyer." The restriction placed on the jailhouse lawyer in this area is valid because the inmates of another prison can seek assistance from jailhouse lawyers at their own prison.[31]

A third regulation attacked by the petitioner involved the number of books which could be retained by the jailhouse lawyer in his own cell. The court found that such restrictions on the jailhouse lawyer,

> [I]mpinge upon the rights enumerated in *Johnson* only to the extent it is shown that the ability of other inmates seeking legal assistance to gain such assistance is affected. Unless and until it is demonstrated that other sources of legal assistance—*e.g.*, other inmates who use the library—cannot provide assistance to disadvantaged inmates, the state of any inmate's personal library is of no significance.[32]

Under the facts, the regulation was upheld.

§ 7.7 What Type of Legal Assistance May an Inmate Receive from the Jailhouse Lawyer?

The issue before the United States Supreme Court in *Johnson v. Avery* was concerned with habeas corpus petitions. It was because of the vital necessity to protect the right of an inmate to file this writ that the Supreme Court heard the case. The lower federal courts, however, have again refused to restrict themselves to such narrow applications of constitutional rights. They have, on the contrary, expanded the right to include other legal petitions besides habeas corpus petitions. Two cases have held that the theoretical basis of *Johnson* was protection of the inmate's right of access to the courts and, for this reason, the *Johnson* ruling must be extended beyond habeas corpus petitions. Similarly protected, the court said, was the right of a jailhouse lawyer to aid in preparing a specific type of petition outside of habeas corpus, such as a civil rights action under §1983 of Title 42 of the United States

---

[30] *In re Harrell*, 470 P.2d 640, 649.
[31] *Id.; Boehme v. Smith*, 378 N.Y.S.2d 170 (N.Y. App. Div. 1976).
[32] *Id.; See Storseth v. Spellman*, 654 F.2d 1349 (9th Cir. 1981).

Code.[33] In *Nolan v. Scafati*,[34] a prisoner alleged that his constitutional rights of access to the courts were violated when prison officials refused to mail his letter to the American Civil Liberties Union. This letter sought advice and assistance on his constitutional rights in a prison disciplinary hearing. The court found that the rule of *Johnson v. Avery* stood for "the general proposition that an inmate's right of access to the court involves a corollary right to obtain some assistance in preparing his communication with the court."[35] In view of this "general proposition," the court refused to confine the *Johnson* rule exclusively to inmates seeking post-conviction relief. The court felt that to so limit that rule would allow prison officials to silence—and perhaps to punish—inmates seeking vindication of those constitutional rights clearly held by prison inmates.[36] The findings of the *Nolan* case were cited with approval by the court in *Cross v. Powers*.[37] The result of these two cases was to extend to all inmates the right to assistance in their preparation of civil rights actions against their prison officials.

Subsequent cases have expanded the type of aid to be given. In *Williams v. Department of Justice*,[38] the court went one step beyond the *Nolan* and *Cross* cases. *Williams* held that *Johnson* stood for the proposition that a prison regulation prohibiting inmate assistance in the drafting of *pro se* legal papers constituted a "deprivation of due process of law, where no 'reasonable alternative' was available to furnish legal advice."[39] This would appear to be an assertion that, at least to this court, inmates must be permitted the assistance of a jailhouse lawyer in the preparation of all of their legal petitions.

In *Wolff v. McDonnell*,[40] the Supreme Court held that the doctrine of *Johnson v. Avery* was not limited to cases involving the preparation of habeas corpus petitions and applied equally well to civil rights actions.

Therefore, unless the state provides a reasonable alternative to the "jailhouse lawyer" in the preparation of civil rights actions, prisoners cannot be barred from furnishing such assistance to one another. In compliance with *Wolff v. McDonnell*, *Graham v. State Dept. of Corrections*[41] held that a counsel substitute must be available whenever the inmate is unable to competently handle his case in a prison reclassification proceeding. If a counsel substitute is requested by an inmate on such grounds, and the request is denied, the record of the reclassification proceeding should contain findings to support the denial.

---

[33] *See Nolan v. Scafati*, 430 F.2d 548 (1st Cir. 1970); *Cross v. Powers*, 328 F. Supp. 899 (W.D. Wis. 1971).

[34] *Nolan v. Scafati*, 430 F.2d 548 (1st Cir. 1970).

[35] *Id.* at 551.

[36] *Id.*

[37] *Cross v. Powers*, 328 F. Supp. 899 (W.D. Wis. 1971).

[38] *Williams v. Department of Justice*, 433 F.2d 958 (5th Cir. 1970).

[39] *Id.* at 959. The term *pro se* is used to mean any petition filed by an individual for himself; *Corpus v. Estelle*, 409 F. Supp. 1090 (S.D. Tex. 1975).

[40] *Wolff v. McDonnell*, 418 U.S. 539, 71 Ohio Op. 2d 336 (1974).

[41] *Graham v. State Dept. of Corrections*, 392 F. Supp. 1262 (W.D. N.C. 1975).

§ 7.8   What is the Reasonable Alternative to the Jailhouse Lawyer?

The main thrust of *Johnson v. Avery* was that a state may not restrict the practices of the jailhouse lawyer unless a "reasonable alternative" to legal services is available to the inmates.

In the cases relating to this issue, it is clear that some measure of professional assistance must be made available if prison officials desire to suppress the activities of the jailhouse lawyer. In reality, this "professional assistance" means the services of an attorney or a law school assistance program. It should be noted, however, that the courts have differed as to the adequacy of legal assistance programs. Courts dealing in this issue have expressed little concern over the adequacy of the reasonable alternative provided by a prison.[42]

In *Ayers v. Ciccone*,[43] a single attorney working for twelve hours a week was held to be a reasonable alternative to the jailhouse lawyer. It should be apparent, however, that an attorney working for such a limited period of time could not effectively meet the legal needs of many inmates. A similar decision was *Novak v. Beto*.[44] In that case, a Texas district court upheld an absolute restriction against a jailhouse lawyer because the state had provided the services of two full-time attorneys to assist the 13,000 inmates in the Texas correctional system. The failure of the district court to question the effectiveness of such a program in assuring the availability of assistance resulted in a reversal on appeal.[45] That this court found it necessary to inquire into the adequacy of the existing program is not unusual. This is evidenced by other cases dealing with the issue.

Beard v. Alabama[46] held that an absolute restriction against jailhouse lawyers "might well be sustained if the state were to make available a sufficient number of qualified attorneys or other persons capable and willing to render voluntary assistance in the preparation of petitions for habeas corpus relief."[47] This court asserted that the state must provide a "sufficient" legal services system, implying that the courts have the obligation to inquire into the effectiveness of the legal services provided.

In *Noorlander v. Ciccone*[48] the court of appeals remanded the case to the trial court to determine the adequacy of the prison law library and to see if adequate alternatives to legal publications for inmates existed. The court rejected the inmate's claim that his right to self-representation required a law library at the institution. The reasoning of the court was that the public defender program was

---

[42] *See Novak v. Beto*, 320 F. Supp. 1206 (S.D. Tex. 1970); *Ayers v. Ciccone*, 303 F. Supp. 637 (W.D. Mo. 1969); *Collins v. Haga*, 373 F. Supp. 923 (W.D. Va. 1974). *But see Bounds v. Smith*, 21 Cr. L. 3017 (U.S. S. Ct. 1977).

[43] *Ayers v. Ciccone*, 303 F. Supp. 637 (W.D. Mo. 1969).

[44] *Novak v. Beto*, 320 F. Supp. 1206 (S.D. Tex. 1970).

[45] *Novak v. Beto*, 453 F.2d 661 (5th Cir. 1971).

[46] *Beard v. Alabama*, 413 F.2d 455 (5th Cir. 1969).

[47] *Id.* at 457.

[48] *Noorlander v. Ciccone*, 489 F.2d 642 (8th Cir. 1973).

sufficient, and the inmate was provided reasonable opportunity for access to the courts. However, he was not entitled to access by all available means.

Two other cases which have given careful scrutiny to the legal services provided to inmates are *Williams v. Department of Justice*[49] and *Cross v. Powers.*[50] Both cases dealt with the use of a law school clinic program in prisons. It should also be noted that, as mentioned above, both cases expanded *Johnson* to legal actions beyond habeas corpus petitions. *Williams* included all *pro se* petitions and *Cross* allowed inmates filing civil rights actions to receive the assistance of a jailhouse lawyer. The crucial similarity between these cases is the fact that both courts found the clinic programs inadequate to meet the reasonable alternative requirements of *Johnson v. Avery.* The petitioner in *Williams* claimed that there was an 18-month delay between the time an inmate requested aid and the time he received it from the student clinic.[51] The court held that such a delay was inconsistent with the goals of the Supreme Court ruling.

Cross v. Powers[52] invalidated an absolute restriction against jailhouse lawyers because the law school clinic did not assist inmates who wished to file civil rights actions against prison officials. The effect of this decision is to require legal services programs to provide inmates with assistance not only in habeas corpus actions but also in those cases wherein an inmate seeks civil rights relief, if the prison officials desire to suppress jailhouse lawyers.

Prison officials act on questionable grounds if they attempt to restrict a law clinic from conducting full legal services. In *Bryan v. Werner*[53] the court held that restrictions preventing a law clinic from assisting inmates in suits against the prison were valid only if there were reasonable alternatives to the clinic for obtaining assistance in such suits. The prison could prohibit the clinic from using its title in suits which were not authorized under clinic rules, but it could not prevent the clinic from notarizing or mailing legal papers relevant to such suits. Such practice would be invalid as impeding access to the courts.

A prison policy denying inmates access to law students who assisted attorneys in post-conviction or civil rights hearings was held invalid, although the court found that inmate access to law students as such is not always a matter of constitutional right.[54]

Although few prison officials will voluntarily open their prisons to law school clinics so that legal services will be provided to inmates suing them for monetary damages, it seems clear that such legal services must be provided if the jailhouse lawyer is prohibited. To not provide these legal services has been held as a violation

[49] *Williams v. Department of Justice,* 433 F.2d 958 (5th Cir. 1970).

[50] *Cross v. Powers,* 328 F. Supp. 899 (W.D. Wis. 1971).

[51] *But see Ramsey v. Ciccone,* 310 F. Supp. 600 (W.D. Mo. 1970) where the court asserted that some delay must necessarily accompany any new program and for this reason found a three-month delay acceptable.

[52] *Cross v. Powers,* 328 F. Supp. 899 (W.D. Wis. 1971).

[53] *Bryan v. Werner,* 516 F.2d 233 (3d Cir. 1975).

[54] *Souza v. Travisono,* 498 F.2d 1120 (1st Cir. 1974).

of the prisoner's rights to legal representation and access to the courts. In *Cruz v. Beto*[55] the former director of the Texas Department of Corrections was held personally liable in money damages to a group of indigent prisoners for depriving them of the opportunity to continue consultations with their attorney. The director alleged that the attorney was causing trouble and consequently prohibited her from visiting the state prisons. At trial the allegations were never substantiated. The court noted that no criminal charges were ever filed against the attorney, nor was any complaint ever made to the state bar association.

In *Procunier v. Martinez*,[56] the United States Supreme Court considered a California prison regulation which provided in part:

> Investigators for an attorney-of-record will be confined to not more than two. Such investigators must be licensed by the State or must be members of the State Bar. Designation must be made in writing by the Attorney.[57]

This regulation restricted access by the prisoners, to members of the bar and licensed private investigators, and imposed an absolute ban on the use of law students and legal paraprofessionals by attorneys to interview prisoner clients. Attorneys were also prohibited from delegating to such persons the task of obtaining prisoners' signatures on legal documents. However, law school clinical programs were permitted in the prison.

Citing *Johnson v. Avery,* the Court held the regulation void because it created an artificial distinction between law students employed by practicing attorneys and those associated with law school programs providing legal assistance to the prisoners. Further, the regulation was overbroad.

> Its prohibition was not limited to prospective interviewers who posed some colorable threat to security or to those inmates thought to be especially dangerous. Nor was it shown that a less restrictive regulation would unduly burden the administrative task of screening and monitoring visitors.[58]

Thus, it is clear that carefully drawn regulations placing reasonable limitations on lawyers' helpers will be held valid, and yet will not deny the prisoners' "access to the courts."

§ 7.9　Access to Legal Materials

Prior to *Johnson v. Avery,* the courts, with few exceptions, staunchly deferred to official discretion as to what legal materials could be kept by an inmate in his own cell. Their rationale was the right of a state to impose reasonable restrictions upon

---

[55] *Cruz v. Beto*, 19 Cr. L. 2094 (S.D. Tex. 1976).
[56] *Procunier v. Martinez*, 416 U.S. 396, 71 Ohio Op. 2d 139 (1974).
[57] *Id.* at 419.
[58] *Id.* at 420.

the times and places where an inmate could engage in legal work.[59] It was felt that there was in fact no interference with access to the courts as a result of these types of reasonable restrictions.[60] Restrictions as to the possession of any law books or limitations on numbers were treated in much the same manner. It was felt that the inmate had no constitutional right to possess law books where no one had alleged a lack of access to the courts.[61] Therefore, where a limitation upon the number of books prisoners could possess was found not to be arbitrary, unreasonable, or discriminatory, discretion of the officials was valid and controlling.[62]

Although a majority of the courts take the conservative approach, recent decisions have taken a contrary view. For example, a California court concluded that the constitutional right of an inmate of access to the courts:

> [I]ncludes not only the right to place a petition for relief in the mails, *** but also the right to possess in his cell the legal materials which the inmate desires to include in such a document while they are being collated into mailable form.[63]

This right, however, was not interpreted to mean that inmates could collect in their cells all-purpose compendiums which could substitute for law books from the library. This decision did not prevent prison officials from restricting legal research to an area, and from forbidding the storage of legal notes in a prisoner's cell.

A county jail rule prohibiting storage of hard cover law books in inmates' cells and restricting storage of non-hard cover materials so as not to limit the "floor or wall space dimensional of the jail cell block" was held to be reasonable, in light of the duty of jail authorities to maintain security and to protect against dangers of fire.[64]

In the *United States ex rel. Mayberry v. Prasse*,[65] the court found that the right of access to the courts included "the right of a prisoner to prepare, serve, and file legal papers and prosecute legal actions affecting his personal liberty."[66] The court held that, although there was no constitutional right to be supplied with a law library, the inmate could not be restrained from effectively prosecuting his appeal. Based upon the facts of that case, and in view of the absence of effective counsel to

---

[59] *See Hatfield v. Bailleaux*, 290 F.2d 632 (9th Cir. 1961); *Edmundson v. Harris*, 239 F. Supp. 359 (W.D. Mo. 1965); *Austin v. Harris*, 226 F. Supp. 304 (W.D. Mo. 1964).

[60] *See Taylor v. Burke*, 278 F. Supp. 868 (E.D. Wis. 1968).

[61] *Williams v. Wilkins*, 315 F.2d 396 (2d Cir. 1963), *cert. denied*, 375 U.S. 852 (1963); *See Roberts v. Pepersack*, 256 F. Supp. 415 (D. Md. 1966), *cert. denied*, 389 U.S. 877 (1967).

[62] *See Walker v. Pate*, 356 F.2d 502 (7th Cir. 1966), *cert. denied*, 384 U.S. 966 (1966); *People v. Mathewes*, 46 Misc. 2d 1054, 261 N.Y.S.2d 654 (Sup. Ct. Crim. Term, 1965); *Cruz v. Hauck*, 515 F.2d 322 (5th Cir. 1975).

[63] *In re Schoingarth*, 425 P.2d 200, 207 (Cal. 1967).

[64] *Cruz v. Hauck*, 515 F.2d 322 (5th Cir. 1975).

[65] *United States ex rel. Mayberry v. Prasse*, 225 F. Supp. 752 (E.D. Pa. 1963).

[66] *Id.* at 754.

assist him in prosecuting his legal action, the inmate was permitted, through court order, to acquire the rules of procedure of Pennsylvania. Without these rules, access to the courts would be unconstitutionally restrained.

Another court ruled that, although prison officials may regulate the manner in which an inmate conducts his research, they may not engage in wholesale confiscation of significant legal documents. The court further suggested that the prison officials should consult the inmate about the relevance of legal materials in his possession before any action is taken to remove them.[67]

Johnson v. Avery did not substantially affect the law in this area. Courts have permitted prison officials to restrict the number of books kept by an inmate. Regulations forbidding the accumulation of a law library within the confines of an inmate's cell have been held valid on the basis of two reasons. One, that the state has the right to reasonably restrict the time and manner in which legal research may be done as long as no unconstitutional impediment of access to the courts arises,[68] and two, the condition of an inmate's personal law library carries no constitutional significance so long as the inmates of the prison have available other sources of assistance, such as other jailhouse lawyers who use the prison law library. A prison regulation which does not impede access to the courts will be held valid.[69]

Thus, an inmate was not prejudiced by the inability to do his own research to supplement that of his legal counsel. A warden's policy of returning ordered law books to the publisher was upheld under such circumstances. The prison had a procedure for receiving books by mail, and the inmate failed to follow the procedure.[70]

On the other hand in *Sigafus v. Brown*,[71] the court held that confiscation of materials necessary to afford reasonable access to the courts resulted in a denial of constitutional rights. Prison officials may not prevent an inmate from possessing his own legal material while permitting him to possess other articles, on the grounds that the legal material might serve as incendiary matter during future, although unanticipated, disturbances.[72]

---

[67] *See Konigsburg v. Ciccone,* 285 F. Supp. 585, *aff'd,* 417 F.2d 161 (8th Cir. 1969), *cert. denied,* 397 U.S. 963 (1970); *See Hiney v. Wilson,* 520 F.2d 589 (2d Cir. 1975) where the confiscation of inmates' legal papers may constitute a denial of access to the courts.

[68] *See Gittlemacker v. Prasse,* 428 F.2d 1 (3d Cir. 1970); *McKinney v. DeBord,* 324 F. Supp. 928 (E.D. Cal. 1970).

[69] *See In re Harrell,* 470 P.2d 640 (Cal. 1970). *But see Sigafus v. Brown,* 416 F.2d 105 (7th Cir. 1969) where the court found that confiscation of legal materials necessary to afford reasonable access to the courts results in a denial of due process for which damages may be claimed.

[70] *Russell v. Hendrick,* 376 F. Supp. 158 (E.D. Pa. 1974); *United States v. Wilson,* 690 F.2d 1267 (9th Cir. 1982). There is no absolute right for an inmate to conduct his own legal research when he has appointed counsel to assist in preparing his defense. The services of a lawyer cannot be rejected as a means of achieving access to a law library.

[71] *Sigafus v. Brown,* 416 F.2d 105 (7th Cir. 1969).

[72] *Adams v. Carlson,* 352 F. Supp. 882 (E.D. Ill. 1973), *rev'd and rem'd on other grounds,* 488 F.2d 619 (7th Cir. 1973).

It would thus appear that in cases both before and after *Johnson* the majority of courts have allowed the state to have the discretion of determining where legal research may be carried on. As a result, prison officials may enforce a rule forbidding the possession of personal legal materials and books in an inmate's cell.

The application of this rule, however, leads to inconsistent results. The confusion arises in those cases where a jailhouse lawyer has, in his possession, papers pertaining to another inmate's case. *In re Harrell*[73] held that a rule permitting confiscation of those papers prevented meaningful aid in the preparation of legal documents by the jailhouse lawyer. It was there asserted that the chief purpose of the rule of *Johnson v. Avery* was to permit inmates to assist each other in the drafting of legal documents. In view of this purpose, the court felt that prison officials were forbidden to impose a rule which prohibited inmates from possessing legal documents which pertained to another inmate's case. Similarly, *Gilmore v. Lynch*,[74] considered the identical prison regulation found in the *Harrell* case. It stated: "One inmate may assist another inmate in the preparation of legal documents, but . . . all briefs, petitions, and other legal papers must be and remain in the possession of the inmate to whom they pertain."[75] This court applied a somewhat different rule to this regulation than that found in the *Harrell* decision. The court held that if the rules were applied only to completed documents, that application would be valid. Thus, the jailhouse lawyer may retain possession of another inmate's papers while preparing a brief or petition. But, upon their completion, he must deliver them to his client without accepting payment.

The inconsistent results of these cases leave a double standard. An inmate may be restricted from having in his own possession legal documents pertaining to his own case, while at the same time, an inmate doing legal work for a fellow prisoner may keep with him legal materials pertaining to the other inmate's case.

Fortunately, the source from which personal legal materials may be obtained is better defined. Prison officials may restrict an inmate from ordering law books from any source other than that which is approved by them,[76] so long as this does not amount to a restriction of the *type* of book that may be ordered.[77]

A delay in delivery of books to an inmate does not necessarily infringe upon his access to the courts.[78] Requiring an inmate to wait on one occasion for ten days to have a document notarized does not unconstitutionally deprive the inmate of access to the courts.[79] The justification for such decision has been that prison officials

---

[73] *In re Harrell*, 470 P.2d 640 (Cal. 1970).

[74] *Gilmore v. Lynch*, 319 F. Supp. 105 (N.D. Ca. 1970), *aff'd sub nom.*, *Younger v. Gilmore*, 404 U.S. 15 (1971).

[75] *Id.* at 112.

[76] *See McKinney v. DeBord*, 324 F. Supp. 928 (E.D. Cal. 1970); *Wakely v. Pennsylvania*, 247 F. Supp. 7 (E.D. Pa. 1965).

[77] *See In re Harrell*, 470 P.2d 640 (Cal. 1970).

[78] *Russell v. Hendrick*, 376 F. Supp. 158 (E.D. Pa. 1974).

[79] *Hudson v. Robinson*, 678 F.2d 462 (3d Cir. 1982).

have a legitimate right to prevent introduction of contraband through the prisoners' mail.[80]

§ 7.10   Legal Material That Must Be Supplied by Prison Officials

The traditional view as to what legal materials prison officials must supply inmates was expressed in the 1961 case of *Hatfield v. Bailleaux,*[81] where the court stated:

> State authorities have no obligation under the federal Constitution to provide library facilities and an opportunity for their use to enable an inmate to search for legal loopholes in the judgment and sentence under which he is held, or to perform services which only a lawyer is trained to perform. All inmates are presumed to be confined under valid judgments and sentences. If an inmate believes he has a meritorious reason for attacking his, he must be given an opportunity to do so. But he has no due process right to spend his prison time or utilize prison facilities in an effort to discover a ground for overturning a presumptively valid judgment.

> Inmates have the constitutional right to waive counsel and act as their own lawyers, but this does not mean that a non-lawyer must be given the opportunity to acquire a legal education.[82]

The view expressed by the *Hatfield* decision, however, was repudiated by the United States Supreme Court in the 1971 case of *Gilmore v. Lynch.*[83] *Gilmore* was decided by a three-judge panel in California and subsequently affirmed by the United States Supreme Court.[84] The district court stated that access to the courts is a right which encompasses "all the means a defendant or petitioner might require to get a fair hearing from the judiciary on all charges brought against him or grievances alleged by him."[85] In affirming, the Supreme Court, citing *Johnson v. Avery,* approved the invalidation of a regulation which had established, as a standard for prison libraries, a highly restrictive list of law books. The decision has set a new precedent by asserting that prison officials have a duty to take affirmative action in assuring inmates the right of access to the courts. The state must make available, notwithstanding economic difficulties, sufficient legal materials to assure that the prisoner is able to file petitions which contain at least some legal proficiency.

---

[80] *See Lockhart v. Prasse,* 250 F. Supp. 529 (E.D. Pa. 1965).
[81] *Hatfield v. Bailleaux,* 290 F.2d 632 (9th Cir. 1961).
[82] *Id.* at 640-641.
[83] *Gilmore v. Lynch,* 319 F. Supp. 105 (N.D. Cal. 1970), *aff'd,* 404 U.S. 15 (1971).
[84] *Gilmore v. Lynch,* 404 U.S. 15 (1971).
[85] *Gilmore v. Lynch,* 319 F. Supp. 105, 110 (N.D. Cal. 1970).

In *Bounds v. Smith,*[86] the Supreme Court took an affirmative view toward the responsibility of prison authorities to provide prisoners with adequate law libraries or some other viable source of legal knowledge. The Court did not mandate the use of law libraries if a sufficient alternative program for legal services is in operation. Law libraries were held to be one constitutionally acceptable method to insure meaningful access to the courts for prisoners. Other alternatives mentioned in the decision included the training of inmates as paralegal assistants to work under lawyers' supervision, the use of paraprofessionals and law students either as volunteers or in formal clinical programs, the organization of volunteer attorneys through bar associations or other groups, the hiring of lawyers on a part-time consultant basis, and the use of full-time staff attorneys working either in new prison legal assistance programs or as a part of a public defender or legal services office.

Several decisions have stressed the necessity of supplying inmates with sufficient material for legal research by listing exactly what state statutes and volumes of the court reporters the prison law library must contain.[87]

A plan for Georgia prison law libraries was approved, with the following mandatory revisions: The library must be kept open for 9 hours a week at a minimum, and for such additional hours as may be needed to afford each inmate wishing to use the facility the equivalent of one full day (eight hours) of research time every three weeks; the library must contain *Constitutional Rights of Prisoners* and certain other reference material; prisoners must be permitted to receive and use appropriate volumes from the county library, subject only to a requirement that these materials be returned in good order within reasonable time periods. The use of paralegals was not required.[88]

The limited resources of a law library do not violate the prisoner's right when he could obtain the materials needed by directing his appointed counsel to obtain such material from a more complete law library.[89]

A state prisoner maintained that the denial of his request for free photocopies of legal precedents to use in preparation for hearing on his motion for post-conviction relief, had deprived him of his right to free access to the courts. The court held that since he had access to the law library at the county jail and had made no allegations of inadequacy of the facility, his complaint failed to state a cause of action.[90]

---

[86] *Bounds v. Smith,* 430 U.S. 817 (1977); *See Morales v. Schmidt,* 340 F. Supp. 544, 548 (W.D. Wis. 1972) where Judge Doyle recognized that access by inmates "to a certain minimum of legal books and materials" was a constitutionally protected right; *United States v. West,* 557 F.2d 151 (8th Cir. 1977); *Dreher v. Sielaff,* 636 F.2d 1141 (7th Cir. 1980); *State v. Simon,* 297 N.W.2d 206 (Iowa 1980); *State v. Ahearn,* 403 A.2d 696 (Vt. 1979); *Wojtczak v. Cuyler,* 480 F. Supp. 1288 (E.D. Pa. 1979).

[87] *See Gaglie v. Ulibarri,* 507 F.2d 721 (9th Cir. 1974); *White v. Sullivan,* 368 F. Supp. 292 (S.D. Ala. 1973); *Craig v. Hocker,* 405 F. Supp. 656 (D. Nev. 1975).

[88] *Mercer v. Griffin,* 29 Cr. L. 2058 (D.C. Ga. 1981).

[89] *United States v. Garza,* 664 F.2d 135 (7th Cir. 1981).

[90] *Wanninger v. Davenport,* 697 F.2d 992 (11th Cir. 1983); *Johnson v. Parke,* 642 F.2d 337 (10th Cir. 1981).

§ 7.11   Inmate's Right to Counsel

An individual accused of a crime has a fundamental right to counsel and the right to be represented by an attorney of his choice, if the attorney indicates a willingness to represent him. If the individual is indigent and unable to afford counsel when he has a right to counsel, the state must appoint it.[91] This right is protected by the Fifth and Sixth Amendments and may not be limited unreasonably by state officials.[92] This right is not altered when the individual is incarcerated. Prison officials may not unreasonably prevent legal counsel from meeting with their prisoner clients as long as the attorney observes all of the rules of the institution.[93] Nor may officials infringe upon an inmate's right to communicate with his attorney by placing undue restrictions on his correspondence[94] or his visitation rights.[95] However, a prisoner who has exercised his right to proceed without counsel in pursuing his appeal does not have the right to receive for his use an adequate law library where the state has offered to appoint counsel.[96]

Inmates in a federal prison were placed in administrative detention in individual cells during the investigation of a murder of a fellow inmate. They were held in administrative detention for 19 months before they were indicted and counsel appointed for them. The inmates had no constitutional right to counsel while in administrative segregation and before any adversary proceedings had been initiated against them. The right to counsel attaches only at or after the initiation of adversary judicial proceedings. Further, providing a defendant with a pre-indictment private investigator is not a purpose of the right to counsel.[97]

§ 7.12   Conclusion

In view of the very liberal interpretation given the *Johnson* decision by many lower courts, the prison administration is confronted with an extremely difficult task.

In order to comply with constitutional standards and to avoid possible court action, prison officials must either allow the jailhouse lawyer to practice or to implement an effective legal services program. Whichever alternative is selected will inevitably result in numerous difficulties. To allow the virtually unrestricted practice of inmate writ-writers would result in the continuation of long-recognized abuses. The alternative, to provide a judicially acceptable legal service program, presents equally difficult problems. The program must provide professional assistance sufficient to meet the needs of the inmate population without undue delay. Furthermore, it must provide assistance to any inmate wishing to file habeas cor-

---

[91] *Argersinger v. Hamlin*, 407 U.S. 25 (1972).
[92] *Sander v. Russell*, 401 F.2d 241, 247 (5th Cir. 1968); *State ex rel. McCamie v. McCoy*, 276 S.E.2d 534 (W. Va. 1981).
[93] *Lynott v. Henderson*, 610 F.2d 340 (5th Cir. 1980).
[94] *Jones v. Diamond*, 594 F.2d 997 (5th Cir. 1979); *See* § 4.5, *supra*.
[95] *See* § 3.6, *supra*.
[96] *Bell v. Hooper*, 511 F. Supp. 452 (S.D. Ga. 1981).
[97] *United States v. Gouveia*, 467 U.S. 180, 35 Cr. L. 3091 (1984).

pus, civil rights or *pro se* petitions. Only by providing such complete legal services can the prison administration insure itself against court action. The fact that this burden could be overwhelming in most states is irrelevant to the courts.

The effect of *Younger v. Gilmore,* wherein the Supreme Court assured inmates a supply of adequate legal material in order to give them access to the courts, is yet to be determined. If, however, the lower courts interpret this decision in the same liberal manner accorded *Johnson,* prison officials will be confronted with even greater responsibilities.

The determination of what constitutes "adequate" legal materials has been left to the lower courts. Because the present approach of these courts is to scrutinize the actual legal needs of the inmate population, it would appear that the state could be held responsible for the failure to furnish complete law libraries for each institution. The economic burdens tied to this responsibility have already been discounted as irrelevant. The obligation to supply legal materials has been established and prisons must comply with that order. If they do not, they face judicial consequences.

Chapter 8

PRISON DISCIPLINARY PROCEEDINGS

§ 8.1   Introduction

Discipline, order, and control of correctional institutions are major concerns of the administrative staffs of penal institutions. These issues relate to the security of the institution, to the safety of institutional staff and inmates, and to rehabilitation of the inmates.

The body or individual generally responsible for administering discipline for the violation of institutional rules and regulations has varying names in correctional institutions, ranging from a rules infraction board or committee, behavior committee, summary court or simply "court." In recent years, great emphasis has been given by the courts to the procedures and practices of disciplinary action taken by prison administrators on inmates in their custody.

§ 8.2   Due Process of Law

The phrase "due process of law" is found in both the Fifth[1] and Fourteenth[2] Amendments to the Constitution. The Fifth Amendment applies to federal action; the Fourteenth Amendment to state action. The phrase means little on its own; it is completely dependent on court interpretations to give it relevant meaning. The Supreme Court has indicated that "due process" has two aspects: 1) substantive, and 2) procedural.

The substantive aspect involves the "fundamental" rights of the individual (such as life, liberty and property) which are protected from government action. It is a question of whether an individual's interest can be protected by the federal courts as a constitutional right. The individual rights or interests protected by substantive due process vary, depending on whether a particular court regards the interest as "fundamental." The first eight amendments specifically enumerate fundamental rights of citizens that are protected from federal government action, such as freedom of religion, speech, press, right of assembly. The same fundamental rights are protected against state action through the Fourteenth Amendment. Substantive due process requires that government treat the people with "fundamental fairness."

The procedural aspect of due process deals with the procedures or means by which government action can affect the fundamental rights of the individual; it is the guarantee that only after certain fair procedures are followed can the government affect an individual's fundamental rights. The exact procedural rights guaranteed depend upon what procedural rights a particular court regards as required by "justice and liberty."[3]

A consideration of what procedures due process may require varies with the circumstances. The precise nature of the governmental function involved must be ascertained, as well as the private interest that has been affected by the governmental action.[4]

A planned series of disciplinary actions as retaliation for initiating a civil rights suit against prison officials violated the prisoner's rights.[5]

An inmate's allegation that he had been placed in solitary confinement without any notice of charges or any hearing for one week and that he was threatened with violence when he asked what the charges were, stated a cause of action under the Civil Rights Act.[6]

---

[1] U.S. Const. Amend. V states in part, "no person shall . . . be deprived of life, liberty, or property, without due process of law . . . ." This amendment is a prohibition on the federal government, and not the states. *Barron v. Baltimore,* 32 U.S. (7 Pet.) 243 (1833).

[2] U.S. Const. Amend. XIV states in part, "(N)or shall any state deprive any person of life, liberty, or property, without due process of law . . . ." The language in the amendment indicates a specific prohibition on the states.

[3] *Palko v. Connecticut,* 302 U.S. 319 (1937); *Synder v. Massachusetts,* 291 U.S. 97 (1934); *Hurtado v. California,* 110 U.S. 516 (1884).

[4] *Cafeteria & Restaurant Workers Union v. McElroy,* 367 U.S. 886 (1961).

[5] *Milhouse v. Carlson,* 652 F.2d 371 (3d Cir. 1981).

[6] *Boag v. McDougall,* 454 U.S. 364 (1982).

§ 8.3   Due Process Requirements in a Prison Disciplinary Hearing

The "due process of law" involved in prison disciplinary proceedings is the procedural aspect of the due process requirement of the Fifth and Fourteenth Amendments. When federal courts initially considered inmates' due process rights, the courts which were willing to grant relief held that due process prevented only "capricious" or "arbitrary" actions by prison administrators. One court found that placing an inmate in solitary confinement, without a hearing, for activities associated with requests for Black Muslim services, was a violation of due process.[7] The same court in another opinion noted:

> Where the lack of effective supervisory procedures exposes men to the capricious imposition of added punishment, due process and Eighth Amendment questions inevitably arise.[8]

Another court found that reclassification which resulted in a loss of "merit" or "good" time was arbitrary action.[9] The court found that the reclassification was unreasonable due to lack of factual basis for the classification.

In the early 1970s, the federal courts began to focus their attention on the specific procedures used in prison disciplinary proceedings. The courts have provided a forum for the protection of the right of an inmate to procedural due process. They have sought to balance the interest of the institution in maintaining order, discipline and control and a recognition of the need for prompt and individual treatment with the knowledge that the process can add a further burden to an inmate's sentence or that the disciplinary action noted on his institutional record may affect his parole eligibility.

In deciding what procedures are constitutionally required by due process at prison disciplinary hearings, the federal courts have been influenced by the due process requirements of administrative law. Administrative agencies, as a branch of government whose actions directly affect individuals, must insure that an affected individual's procedural due process rights are guaranteed. In general terms, administrative agencies are required by due process to act only after adequate notice and only after an opportunity for a fair hearing.[10] In a case involving a state welfare department's procedure for terminating welfare benefits,[11] the

---

[7] *Howard v. Smyth*, 365 F.2d 428 (4th Cir. 1966); *See also, Drayton v. Robinson*, 519 F. Supp. 545 (M.D. Pa. 1981); *In re Davis*, 599 P.2d 690, 158 Cal. Rptr. 384 (Cal. 1979); *McAlister v. Robinson*, 488 F. Supp. 545 (D.C. Conn. 1978), aff'd, 607 F.2d 1058 (2d Cir. 1979).

[8] *Landman v. Peyton*, 370 F.2d 135, 141 (4th Cir. 1966), *cert. denied*, 388 U.S. 920 (1967).

[9] *United States ex rel. Campbell v. Pate*, 401 F.2d 55 (7th Cir. 1968); *In re Westfall*, 162 Cal. Rptr. 462 (Cal. App. 1980); *South v. Franzen*, 413 N.E.2d 523 (Ill. App. 1980); *Bartholomew v. Reed*, 477 F. Supp. 223 (D.C. Or. 1979); *Taylor v. Franzen*, 417 N.E.2d 242 (Ill. App. 1981); *cf. People ex rel. Stringer v. Rowe*, 414 N.E.2d 466 (Ill. App. 1980); *McGhee v. Belisle*, 501 F. Supp. 189 (E.D. La. 1980).

[10] W. Gellhorn and C. Byse, ADMINISTRATIVE LAW 486 (3d ed. 1970).

[11] *Goldberg v. Kelly*, 397 U.S. 254 (1970).

Supreme Court found that: . . . adequate notice and an opportunity to be heard required: 1) the affected welfare recipient receive timely and adequate notice of the proposed action including the reasons for termination, 2) an opportunity to defend, which also meant (a) right to confront adverse witnesses, (b) right to present arguments and evidence orally, and (c) right to be represented at the hearing by retained counsel, and 3) an impartial decisionmaker who must state his reasons and indicate the evidence relied on, if welfare is terminated.[12]

Wolff v. McDonnell

Federal courts had taken all or part of these requirements imposed on administrative agencies and had held that due process in the prison disciplinary setting required basically the same safeguards.[13] On June 26, 1974, the United States Supreme Court decided *Wolff v. McDonnell*,[14] which involved a state prisoner in Nebraska who had filed a Civil Rights Action (42 U.S.C. § 1983) in federal court alleging that he had been denied due process during a prison disciplinary proceeding.

Considering the nature of prison disciplinary proceedings, the Court held that the full range of procedures mandated by *Morrissey*[15] and *Scarpelli*[16] for parole revocation was inapplicable. The Court felt that the unique environment of a prison demanded a more flexible approach in accommodating the interests of the prisoners and the needs of the prison. Specifically, the Court held that due process in a prison disciplinary setting requires:

1. Advance written notice of the charges against the prisoner must be given to him at least 24 hours before his appearance before the prison disciplinary board;
2. There must be a written statement by the factfinders as to the evidence relied upon and reasons for the disciplinary action;
3. The prisoner should be allowed to call witnesses and present documentary evidence in his defense providing there is no undue hazard to institutional safety or correctional goals.
4. Counsel substitute (either a fellow prisoner, if permitted, or staff) should be allowed where the prisoner is illiterate or where the complexity of the issues makes it unlikely that the prisoner will be able to collect and present the evidence necessary for an adequate comprehension of the case.

---

[12] *Id.* at 267-268, 270, 271.
[13] *Landman v. Royster*, 333 F. Supp. 621 (E.D. Va. 1971); *Clutchette v. Procunier*, 328 F. Supp. 767 (N.D. Cal. 1971); *Clutchette v. Enomoto*, 471 F. Supp. 1113 (N.D. Cal. 1979); *Chavis v. Rowe*, 643 F.2d 1281 (7th Cir. 1981); *Wright v. Enomoto*, 462 F. Supp. 397 (N.D. Cal. 1980), *summary aff'd*, 434 U.S. 1052 (1978); *Powell v. Ward*, 487 F. Supp. 917 (S.D. N.Y. 1980).
[14] *Wolff v. McDonnell*, 418 U.S. 539, 71 Ohio Op. 2d 336 (1974).
[15] *Morrissey v. Brewer*, 408 U.S. 471 (1972).
[16] *Gagnon v. Scarpelli*, 411 U.S. 778, 71 Ohio Op. 2d 279 (1973).

5. The prison disciplinary board must be impartial.

Equally important is what the Court held was *not* constitutionally required:

1. The prisoner has no constitutional right to confrontation and cross-examination. The permitting of confrontation and cross-examination are left to the discretion of the prison disciplinary board.
2. The prisoner has no constitutional right to *retained* or *appointed* counsel.

Further, the *Wolff* decision is not to be applied retroactively; there is no right of a prisoner to have his prison record of prior disciplinary proceedings expunged.

It should also be noted that *Wolff* arose in the context of discipline for "serious misconduct." The Court stated: "We do not suggest, however, that the procedures required by today's decision for the deprivation of good-time would also be required for the imposition of lesser penalties such as the loss of privileges."[17]

Therefore, the Supreme Court has severely restricted the law that had been emerging from the Circuit Courts of Appeals, and recognizes that more flexibility and experimentation in the prison setting is needed before further review by the Court. As Mr. Justice White stated:

> Our conclusion that some, but not all, of the procedures specified in *Morrissey* and *Scarpelli* must accompany the deprivation of good-time by state prison authorities is not graven in stone. As the nature of the prison disciplinary process changes in future years, circumstances may then exist which will require further consideration and reflection of this Court.[18]

The decision in *Wolff* laid down constitutional guidelines, but left flexibility in the conduct of disciplinary hearings. This aspect of the case has been severely criticized. One court expressed regret that the Supreme Court failed to deal more precisely with the "profound federal constitutional issues implicated in the prison system." It was noted that *Wolff* "failed to make the constitution a living document for many human beings,"[19] by not requiring additional procedural rights in the prison context.

Baxter v. Palmigiano

After the decision in *Wolff,* the federal courts filled in some of the gaps, a task which *Wolff* expressly left to the discretion of prison officials, not federal courts. One Circuit Court of Appeals held that:

---

[17] *Wolff v. McDonnell,* 418 U.S. at 571, 71 Ohio Op. 2d 336 at 350.
[18] *Wolff v. McDonnell,* 418 U.S. at 571, 71 Ohio Op. 2d 336 at 350.
[19] *Taylor v. Schmidt,* 380 F. Supp. 1222 (W.D. Wis. 1974).

1. Minimum notice and a right to respond are due an inmate faced even with a temporary suspension of privileges;
2. An inmate at a disciplinary hearing who is denied the privilege of confronting and cross-examining witnesses must receive written reasons or the denial will be deemed "prima facie" evidence of an abuse of discretion;
3. An inmate facing prison discipline for a violation that might also be punishable in state criminal proceedings has a right to legal counsel (not just counsel substitute) at the prison hearing.[20]

Another Circuit Court of Appeals held that where an inmate brought before a prison disciplinary committee faces possible prosecution for a violation of state law:

1. He must be advised of his right to remain silent and must not be questioned further once he exercises that right;
2. Such silence may not be used against him at that time or in future proceedings;
3. Where criminal charges are a realistic possibility, prison authorities should consider whether legal counsel (not just counsel substitute), if requested, should be permitted at the proceeding.[21]

On April 20, 1976, the United States Supreme Court reversed both decisions. It held in *Baxter v. Palmigiano*[22] that the procedures set forth above were inconsistent with the "reasonable accommodation" reached in *Wolff v. McDonnell* between institutional needs and objectives and the constitutional provisions of general application.

Specifically, the Court held that:

1. Prison inmates do not "have a right to either retained or appointed legal counsel in disciplinary hearings;" (citing *Wolff*)
2. An adverse inference may be drawn from an inmate's silence at his disciplinary proceeding;
3. Federal courts have no authority to expand the *Wolff* requirements which leave the extent of cross-examination and confrontation of witnesses to the sound discretion of prison officials;
4. The Court of Appeals acted prematurely when it required procedures such as notice and an opportunity to respond even when an inmate is faced with

[20] *Clutchette v. Procunier,* 497 F.2d 809 (9th Cir. 1974), *reh'g,* 510 F.2d 613 (9th Cir. 1975) in light of *Wolff.*
[21] *Palmigiano v. Baxter,* 510 F.2d 534 (1st Cir. 1974).
[22] *Baxter v. Palmigiano,* 96 S. Ct. 1551 (1976); *Enomoto v. Clutchette,* 96 S. Ct. 1551 (1976).

a temporary suspension of privileges, as distinguished from a serious penalty.

Thus, the Supreme Court severely restricted the judicially imposed procedural requirements that had been emerging in the wake of *Wolff*, and added no new constitutional requirements to those set forth in *Wolff*. Thus, *Wolff* established maximum constitutional requirements, and not bare minimum requirements.

§ 8.3.1 —Notice of the Hearing

A prison disciplinary proceeding in which the inmate is not informed of the nature of the accusation against him, nor of the evidence to be used against him, does not comply with due process requirements.

Notice is required because it enables the inmate to prepare information to explain the alleged offense or defend himself against it. It gives the inmate information about the nature of the proceeding. The notice must adequately inform the inmate of what he is accused.[23]

Wolff requires that there must be a minimum of 24 hours between receipt by the inmate of written notice of the charges and the inmate's appearance before the prison disciplinary board. However, where an inmate may desire to expedite his hearing, he may waive his right to 24-hour notice, thereby appearing at the earliest hearing scheduled after he receives a conduct ticket or "write-up." The use of waivers may create legal difficulties due to the inherent coercive atmosphere of a prison. If waivers are used, it is submitted that the waiver should be in writing and signed by the inmate under such circumstances that the inmate is made fully aware of his right to the 24-hour notice and voluntarily waives it. However, the Supreme Court has said that a "knowing and intelligent" waiver is not demanded in every situation where a person has relinquished a constitutional protection. Generally, the requirement of a "knowing and intelligent" waiver has been applied only to those rights which the constitution guarantees to a criminal defendant in order to preserve a fair trial.[24] Wherever waivers are used, the written waiver should be witnessed. Oral waivers may also be used, but care should be taken to document the waiver, as a question of proof may arise at a later date.

Inmates in disciplinary hearings are entitled to disclosure of the details concerning the charges against them except where prison officials have made a specific and independent finding that: 1) retaliation against an informant will result from his identification; 2) disclosure of the information will identify the informant; and 3) the identity of the informant would not otherwise be known to the accused. Further,

---

[23] *Landman v. Royster,* 333 F. Supp. 621 (E.D. Va. 1971); *Clutchette v. Procunier,* 328 F. Supp. 767 (N.D. Cal. 1971); *Bundy v. Cannon,* 328 F. Supp. 165 (D. Md. 1971); *Carter v. McGinnis,* 320 F. Supp. 1092 (W.D.N.Y. 1970); *Nolan v. Scafati,* 306 F. Supp. 1 (D. Mass. 1969), (dictum) *rev'd on other grounds,* 430 F.2d 548 (1st Cir. 1970); *Chavis v. Rowe,* 643 F.2d 1281 (7th Cir. 1981); *Rinehard v. Brewer,* 483 F. Supp. 165 (S.D. Iowa 1980); *Flaherty v. Fogg,* 421 N.Y.S.2d 736 (N.Y. App. Div. 1979).

[24] *Schneckloth v. Bustamonte,* 412 U.S. 218 (1973).

the accused must be notified that he has not been provided with the specific details of the incidents charged because the prison officials have determined that the information would reveal the identify of informants and present a serious risk to their safety.[25]

§ 8.3.2   —An Opportunity To Be Heard

The right to notice and an opportunity to be heard are a part of the basic concept of procedural due process of law. As such, a hearing is required in the disciplinary process.

A hearing, in administrative law, is an oral proceeding before a tribunal.[26] Professor Kenneth C. Davis, a leading authority in administrative law, points out two forms of hearings, trial and argument. The trial is a proceeding for presenting evidence, with cross-examination and rebuttal, and ends with a decision based on the record made at the proceeding. The trial is designed to resolve disputes of fact. Argument, on the other hand, is a process for the presentation of *ideas,* as distinguished from evidence. It is the process for resolving non-factual issues, such as policy or discretion.

The courts have generally recognized that a hearing is fundamental to the concept of due process, and thus have required a hearing in some form. It is one of the procedural safeguards to which an inmate is entitled when action is taken against him.[27] As one court has said, "The right to be heard before being condemned to suffer grievous loss of any kind is a principle basic to our society."[28]

The Supreme Court in *Wolff* did not attempt to set forth comprehensive guidelines for the conduct of disciplinary hearings, but only those elements that are constitutionally required. The national body of prison administrators, the American Correctional Association, recognized that a hearing is a "common . . . concept" of the disciplinary procedure.[29] The Association's manual describes the function of the hearing as "an orderly attempt to arrive at the truth and is not a formal court proceeding."[30] The problem in defining the exact procedures required of the disciplinary hearing is that it combines two functions in the proceeding: 1) the fact-finding process, and 2) the correctional process.

The fact-finding process involves a determination of the truth of the allegation that a specified institutional rule has been violated; that is, did the inmate in fact

[25] *Franklin v. Israel,* 537 F. Supp. 1112 (W.D. Wis. 1982).

[26] Kenneth C. Davis, ADMINISTRATIVE LAW TEXT 157 (3d ed. 1972).

[27] *Meola v. Fitzpatrick,* 322 F. Supp. 878 (D. Mass. 1971); *Tyree v. Fitzpatrick,* 325 F. Supp. 554 (D. Mass. 1971); *Carothers v. Follette,* 314 F. Supp. 1014 (S.D.N.Y. 1970), *appeal dismissed,* 631 F.2d 725 (3d Cir. 1980); *Jordan v. Arnold,* 472 F. Supp. 265 (M.D. Pa. 1979); *Deane v. Coughlin,* 439 N.Y.S.2d 792 (N.Y. App. Div. 1981); *Hayes v. Walker,* 555 F.2d 625 (7th Cir. 1977).

[28] *Kristsky v. McGinnis,* 313 F. Supp. 1247, 1250 (N.D.N.Y. 1970); *See also, Mack v. Johnson,* 430 F. Supp. 1139 (E.D. Pa. 1977) ($765.00 awarded to inmate placed in punitive segregation without opportunity to present evidence at disciplinary hearing), *aff'd,* 582 F.2d 1275 (3d Cir. 1978).

[29] AMERICAN CORRECTIONAL ASSOCIATION, MANUAL OF CORRECTIONAL STANDARDS 408 (1966).

[30] *Id.* at 410.

violate the rule? This type of function, under administrative law, has traditionally been handled in a *trial-type hearing*. The correctional process is a policy or judgment decision by a prison administrator or board of administrators who view every action taken in terms of its correctional or rehabilitative effects on the individual involved, on the inmates, and on the staff of the institution as a whole. The correctional process must be concerned with the *best interest of the inmate* involved (as determined by the prison administrators) and not be solely geared to the facts of a particular incident.

The result of the combination of these two functions in a single proceeding had caused the courts to require, prior to *Wolff,* varying and often inconsistent procedures in the hearing itself. Some courts found that certain aspects of a trial-type hearing, such as the right to call witnesses and to have counsel, were required by due process in prison disciplinary hearings. Other courts found that the same features were not required for a "fair hearing" in accordance with due process. The precise features required of the hearing depended upon the definition of a "fair" hearing as interpreted by the individual court involved.

The procedures required by *Wolff* center around the effectiveness of an inmate's opportunity to be heard. However, a disciplinary board might be faced with an inmate who chooses not to take advantage of that opportunity and does not speak in his own defense. The Supreme Court in *Baxter*[31] held that the board was permitted to draw an "adverse inference" from such silence. Thus, it would be proper for the board to consider the fact that an inmate chose not to defend himself in deciding whether he was guilty of the conduct charged. An inmate may be advised, in effect: "You have the right to remain silent. However, if you choose to remain silent, your silence can and will be used against you."

Care should be taken, however, to use silence to corroborate other evidence presented at the hearing. If the silence of the inmate is the only evidence presented, a finding of guilt would constitute constitutional error.

In *Baxter* the Supreme Court was very careful to point out that a disciplinary proceeding was *not* a criminal proceeding, but a civil proceeding. Perhaps an analogy could be to a revocation of welfare benefits, even if the grounds for revocation would constitute criminal fraud.

§ 8.3.3   —Right to Counsel

In *Wolff* the Supreme Court held that an inmate had no constitutional right to either retained or appointed legal counsel at the disciplinary proceeding. In *Baxter* this was reiterated as "the law" even in the situation where an inmate may be subject to outside criminal prosecution for the misconduct which is the subject of the prison proceeding.

However, *Wolff* does require "counsel substitute" (either a fellow prisoner, if permitted, or a staff member) where the prisoner is illiterate or where the complex-

---

[31] *Supra*, note 18.

ity of the issues makes it unlikely that the prisoner will be able to collect and present the evidence necessary for an adequate comprehension of the case.

In cases where inmates have complained that they were denied the right to "counsel substitute," the courts have relied on the record of the disciplinary proceeding to determine the literacy of the inmate, or whether the factual issues involved were complex.[32] The counsel substitute should be someone who is capable of offering helpful advice, but does not have to be a witness or someone connected with the incident in question.[33] It is essential for prison officials to carefully make inquiry, and place such inquiries in the record, in order to avoid a later legal attack based on the failure to appoint counsel substitute.

§ 8.3.4   —Witnesses; Confrontation; Cross-Examination

Wolff v. McDonnell provided that the inmate should be allowed to call witnesses and present documentary evidence in his defense when there was no undue hazard to institutional safety or correctional goals. The right to call witnesses and present documentary evidence, thought advisable in *Wolff,* has been required by lower courts.[34] Under the *Wolff* standard, prison officials are permitted some discretion based on the "undue hazard" criterion. Care must be taken to avoid a later judicial finding of an "abuse of discretion." The disciplinary committee, or some official prior to the hearing, should review the inmate's requests for witnesses and act on each one using the "undue hazard" standard. It is also implicit in *Wolff* that discretion may also be used to avoid redundant and irrelevant testimony. Thus, where an inmate requests one hundred fellow inmates as witnesses to an incident in a dining hall, to allow all those inmates to appear, one by one, before the disciplinary board could create a major security problem, as well as being unduly repetitive. It is submitted that calling one or a representative number of the one hundred would be sufficient, if it was determined that all the inmates would be offering identical testimony. To this end, it is suggested that the charged inmate be required to state, in a written request for witnesses, prior to the hearing, what he expects them to say if they are called. The importance and relevance of their testimony can then be better balanced against the problems which may result if they are called as witnesses.

If the requested witness is in another institution, it is also submitted that a written statement can be taken, and that "live" testimony of the inmate's witnesses is

---

[32] *Daigle v. Helgemoe*, 399 F. Supp. 416 (D.N.H. 1975); *Grever v. Oregon State Correctional Institution, Corrections Division*, 561 P.2d 669 (Or. App. 1977).

[33] *Mills v. Oliver*, 367 F. Supp. 77 (E.D. Va. 1973); *Clutchette v. Enomoto*, 471 F. Supp. 1113 (N.D. Ca. 1979).

[34] *United States ex rel. Miller v. Twomey*, 479 F.2d 701 (7th Cir. 1973), *cert. denied*, 414 U.S. 1146 (1974); *Workman v. Mitchell*, 502 F.2d 1201 (9th Cir. 1974); *Murphy v. Wheaton*, 318 F. Supp. 1252 (N.D. Ill. 1974); *Adargo v. Barr*, 482 F. Supp. 283 (D. Colo. 1980); *Pollard v. Baskerville*, 481 F. Supp. 1157 (E.D. Va. 1979), *aff'd*, 620 F.2d 294 (4th Cir. 1980); *Pace v. Oliver*, 634 F.2d 302 (5th Cir. 1981); *Bekins v. Oregon State Penitentiary*, 617 P.2d 653 (Or. App. 1980); *Cruz v. Oregon State Penitentiary*, 617 P.2d 650 (Or. App. 1980).

not constitutionally required. It should be recognized, however, that if written statements of a witness against the inmate are used, the issue of confrontation and cross-examination will arise.

The decision to grant or not grant a witness request should be made in the record, and should be supported by an explanation if the request was denied. The lack of such an explanation has led one court to label the refusal to call witnesses an "arbitrary" decision,[35] a label which can lead to civil liability.

Wolff left the issues of confrontation and cross-examination to the sound discretion of prison officials. By not requiring confrontation, disciplinary boards are often left to rely on written conduct reports as the only evidence on which to base a decision. The inmate may, of course, deny the allegations of such reports and call witnesses or present documents to dispute them, but may not directly face and question his accuser, except as prison officials deem wise. This exercise of discretion was reinforced by the decision in *Baxter*. It is not required that the board state reasons for denying cross-examination or confrontation. If the inmate pleads "guilty" and thereby waives his rights under *Wolff*, prison officials should carefully document the factual basis for the plea, and make certain that the plea was knowingly made.[36]

A state prisoner was charged with violating a prison regulation as a result of a fight that occurred in the prison office. At the disciplinary board hearing, the prisoner requested that certain witnesses be called, but the board refused to call the

---

[35] *Murphy v. Wheaton, supra,* note 34; *Devaney v. Hall,* 509 F. Supp. 497 (D.C. Mass. 1981).

[36] Cases deal with such diverse topics as: *Smith v. Rabalais,* 659 F.2d 539 (5th Cir. 1981). (In a disciplinary proceeding, it was not an abuse of discretion in refusing to provide an inmate with the identification of a confidential informant where there were possible fatal consequences to the informant and where the inmate would be given an opportunity to establish an alibi for the time, place, and date of the alleged sale of narcotics.); *Kyle v. Hanberry,* 677 F.2d 1386 (11th Cir. 1982). (A prison disciplinary finding based upon the affidavit of a prison chaplain who was merely passing on the statements of a "reliable inmate source," was reversed. Minimum due process requires that the disciplinary committee undertake in good faith to establish the informant's reliability. There must be some information on the record from which a court can reasonably concluded that the committee undertook such an inquiry, and upon such inquiry, concluded that the informant was reliable. The committee should describe the nature of its inquiry to the extent that the committee is satisfied that such disclosure would not identify an informant.); *Chavis v. Rowe,* 643 F.2d 1281 (7th Cir. 1981). (A disciplinary committee must disclose to an inmate any exculpatory report as well as a written statement as to the evidence relied upon and reasons for the disciplinary action taken. It must also provide him with a written statement as to the evidence relied upon and reasons for the disciplinary action taken against him.); *Bartholomew v. Watson,* 665 F.2d 915 (9th Cir. 1981). (A prison procedure that prevented an inmate from calling an inmate or a staff member as a witness in a disciplinary hearing violated due process.); *Langton v. Berman,* 667 F.2d 231 (1st Cir. 1981). (A state prisoner in a disciplinary hearing had no right to cross-examine witnesses. His right to confront his accusers and to have full access to all evidence should be left to the discretion of state prison officials.); *Ward v. Johnson,* 667 F.2d 1126 (4th Cir. 1981). (An inmate was denied due process when he was not permitted to call witnesses at a disciplinary hearing. Due process was involved even though the punishment was the loss of recreational time.); *Segarra v. McDade,* 706 F.2d 1301 (4th Cir. 1981). (Due process is not violated by a prison official's decision to prohibit an inmate from calling witnesses at a prison disciplinary hearing concerning the loss of good time. Such is not required by *Wolff v. McDonnell.* Here, the request was denied when he made his request during the hearing, after earlier refusing to compile a witness list or to allow statements to be taken.)

witnesses. No explanation was given at the time nor as part of the written record of the disciplinary hearing. The prisoner was found guilty and 150 days of "good-time" were forfeited. Due process does not require that the disciplinary board's reasons for denying the prisoner's witness request appear as part of the administrative record of the disciplinary hearing. Due process does require that the board, at some time, state its reason for refusing to call witnesses, but may do so either by making the explanations a part of the administrative record or by later presenting evidence in court if the deprivation of a "liberty" interest, such as that afforded by "good-time" credits, is challenged because of the refusal to call the requested witnesses. The arguments that the burden of proving noncompliance with *Wolff v. McDonnell* was on the prisoner, and that a prisoner may not challenge disciplinary procedures unless a "pattern of practice" was shown, was rejected. The Supreme Court stressed that explaining the decision at the disciplinary hearing will not immunize prison officials from later court challenge to their decision. However, so long as the reason for denying prisoner witness requests are logically related to preventing undue hazards to institutional safety or correctional goals, the explanation should satisfy due process. It was also suggested that if prison security or similar paramount interests appear to require it, a court should allow at least in the first instance a prison official's justification for refusal to call witnesses to be presented to the court *in camera,* or outside the presence of the prisoner.[37]

§ 8.3.5   —Administrative Review

Administrative review of the decision resulting from a prison disciplinary hearing is *wise administrative policy* although it is not constitutionally required. A suggested procedure recommends that an inmate "shall be provided and advised of a regular channel of appeal from the finding made or the penalty assessed at any disciplinary hearing."[38] The right to review of a disciplinary decision has not been interpreted as a requirement under constitutional procedural due process, but the presence of an appellate procedure has been an element encouraged by the courts.[39] However, if a statute or prison regulation provides for an appeal, the Equal Protection Clause of the Fourteenth Amendment requires that all those affected be treated alike.

The review must be restricted to the charge made and to the evidence presented. The practice of reviewing the decision based on evidence that is not in the record is not permitted. If an appeal is granted, notice of the right to appeal must be distributed to all inmates. Word-of-mouth to notify inmates of their right to appeal or the procedures for such an appeal cannot be permitted. Since the Equal Protection

---

[37] *Ponte v. Real,* 471 U.S. 491, 37 Cr. L. 3051 (1985).

[38] AMERICAN CORRECTIONAL ASSOCIATION, MANUAL OF CORRECTIONAL STANDARDS 410 (1966).

[39] *Beishir v. Swenson,* 331 F. Supp. 1227 (W.D. Mo. 1971); *Morris v. Travisono,* 310 F. Supp. 857 (D.R.I. 1970); *Burns v. Swenson,* 300 F. Supp. 759 (W.D. Mo. 1969); *Riner v. Raines,* 409 N.E.2d 575 (Ind. 1980); *Scott v. DeJarnette,* 470 F. Supp. 766 (E.D. Ark. 1979); *Adams v. Duckworth,* 412 N.E.2d 789 (Ind. 1980); *Dawson v. Hearing Committee,* 597 P.2d 1353 (Wash. 1979).

Clause of the Fourteenth Amendment contemplates uniform treatment of all procedures, failure to notify inmates at the conclusion of the disciplinary procedure of their right to appeal when others are told is a violation of the inmate's constitutional rights.

Administrative review by a warden, or even an official of the state corrections department, also provides the opportunity to set forth policy to be followed in certain situations. For example, standards can be established for the exercise of discretion in calling witnesses or allowing cross-examination. It should be noted that state statutes dealing with administrative procedures may foreclose "rule-making" in this manner; nevertheless, the use of administrative review as a check on arbitrary action of subordinates is a wise policy. Furthermore, judges then feel free to require inmates to follow the administrative appeal process to its end. A system of administrative appeals may keep many cases out of the federal courts so long as the administrative review process is not a rubber stamp for arbitrary decisions made at the institutional level.

There is no requirement of a "stay" pending appeal. However, if the finding of guilt is set aside, the inmate's record should be expunged, and his prior status restored.

§ 8.3.6 —The Record

Wolff v. McDonnell requires that a written statement be made by the factfinders as to the evidence relied upon and reasons for the disciplinary action. This requirement is consistent with the earlier decision in *Morrissey v. Brewer* dealing with parole revocation.[40] *Wolff* does not require that the inmate receive a copy of the written statement, but this is essential if there is an available means of administrative appeal. No appeal procedure is meaningful if the inmate is not made fully aware of the basis of the original decision. It is also good policy to expand the scope of the written record to include the reasons underlying *any* exercise of discretion concerning the disciplinary proceeding. This may include reasons why witnesses were denied, why an inmate's request for "counsel substitute" was not granted, or why a more stringent sanction was imposed than is usually imposed for a given offense. Having these reasons organized in a written record of the proceeding will help assure that decisions are not made arbitrarily, and it can be shown that discretion was not abused. Such a record may be used not only to state the evidence relied upon (which will often be the allegations in a conduct report), but also to summarize the evidence which was rejected. Tape-recording all hearings is expensive, but may prove invaluable for countering inmate allegations of unfairness, to document inmate literacy, or to obtain oral waivers.

---

[40] *Morrissey v. Brewer*, 408 U.S. 471 (1972); *Hayes v. Thompson*, 637 F.2d 483 (7th Cir. 1980); *Rinehard v. Brewer*, 483 F. Supp. 165 (S.D. Iowa 1980); *State ex rel. Meeks v. Gagnon*, 289 N.W.2d 357 (Wis. App. 1980); *Jerry v. Wainwright*, 383 So. 2d 1110 (Fla. App. 1980); *Craig v. Franke*, 478 F. Supp. 19 (E.D. Wis. 1979); *Jensen v. Satran*, 651 F.2d 605 (8th Cir. 1981).

Inmates receive disciplinary reports charging them with assaulting another inmate. At separate hearings, the disciplinary hearing board heard testimony from a prison guard and received his written report. The guard testified that he heard some commotion in the prison walkway and upon investigation discovered an inmate who had been assaulted. He saw three other inmates fleeing down the walkway. The inmates were found guilty before the hearing board, which revoked their good-time credits. The decision will be upheld if there is any evidence in the record that could support the conclusions reached by the disciplinary board.[41]

§ 8.3.7 —Impartiality

Wolff v. McDonnell requires that the prison disciplinary board be impartial. This is one of the traditional aspects of a "fair hearing" and generally requires that the decisionmaker is not directly involved in the incident in question or the investigation of it. This helps assure that the decision will be based strictly on the facts adduced at the hearing, and not on personal knowledge or impressions which a decisionmaker brings with him to the hearing.[42] One court specifically held that a disciplinary committee which included as one of its members a correctional officer involved in the incidents leading to the disciplinary hearing was not sufficiently impartial to satisfy the Due Process Clause.[43] The court felt that the presence of the "charging party" prevented the board from rationally determining the facts.

The requirement that the decision should be based strictly on facts adduced at the hearing also involves the concept of "command influence." This results when a warden or other official in effect dictates what the decision of the disciplinary committee should be. One court analyzed "command influence" as follows:

It is not improper for a member of the adjustment committee to discuss with the warden the procedures which should be followed, although it would clearly be improper for the warden to tell a member of the adjustment committee what the decision of the adjustment committee should be or for them to discuss what the decision should be. Nor is it improper for the members of the adjustment committee to discuss among themselves the procedure to be followed, although it would be improper for them to decide the proper disposition of the case before the hearing.[44]

If the prison system has an appellate procedure, it is not necessary to have a different disciplinary board hear the case if the prior decision is reversed and sent back for a "new hearing." In criminal cases, the judge who pronounced sentence,

---

[41] *Superintendent, Mass. Corr. Inst., Walpole v. Hill*, 472 U.S. 445, 37 Cr. L. 3107 (1985).
[42] *Landman v. Royster*, 333 F. Supp. 621 (E.D. Va. 1971); *Langley v. Scurr*, 305 N.W.2d 418 (Iowa 1981).
[43] *Fife v. Crist*, 380 F. Supp. 901 (D. Mont. 1974); *Bartholomew v. Reed*, 477 F. Supp. 223 (D. Or. 1979).
[44] *Crooks v. Warne*, 516 F.2d 837 (2d Cir. 1975); *See also Commonwealth v. Manlin*, 441 A.2d 532 (Pa. Super. 1979). (Conviction of deputy warden was upheld for "official oppression" by Superior Court.)

or determined guilt after a non-jury trial, may be the judge at the new trial. Similarly, the judge who presides over a preliminary hearing is not barred from being the judge at the later hearing.

§ 8.3.8 —Pre-hearing Detention and Emergencies

Where an inmate has committed a physical assault, or in other cases where his conduct poses an immediate threat to the security of the institution, pre-hearing detention may be justified, so long as a hearing complying with the requirements of *Wolff v. McDonnell* is held within a reasonable time after the detention begins. Whether to place an inmate in pre-hearing detention is another area where the discretion of prison officials comes into play. It is good administrative policy to assure that the exercise of such discretion is not abused. Thus, standards should be developed by which a hearing officer or some other official can determine what factual circumstances trigger pre-hearing detention under administrative guidelines. The practice of imposing prolonged detention prior to disciplinary hearings should be avoided.

One court approved a policy requiring immediate removal from a minimum security honor farm of any inmate charged by a formal conduct report pending a prompt hearing, even though such inmate must spend a brief period in isolated confinement.[45] This is an example of a court balancing the requirement of *Wolff* against the practical realities of the institutional setting—the honor farm was not equipped to handle disciplinary hearings.

A few courts have also recognized the overriding concerns for security in emergency situations, and have allowed greater flexibility in administering disciplinary cases than would be permissible under normal conditions.[46]

So long as the conditions of confinement do not constitute "punishment," or there is no undue delay, there would appear to be no sound reason to deny prison officials the authority to hold an inmate in isolation for "investigation" prior to formal charges being made. As in pre-hearing detention after charges have been made, *Wolff* does not specify the maximum delay; *Wolff* requires only a minimum of 24 hours. In any event, the hearing should be held, or the inmate returned to his former status, as soon as practicable.

---

[45] *Bickham v. Cannon*, 516 F.2d 885 (7th Cir. 1975); *See also, Helms v. Hewitt*, 29 Cr. L. 2429 (3d Cir. 1981); *Deane v. Coughlin*, 439 N.Y.S.2d 792 (N.Y. App. Div. 1981); *Collins v. Coughlin*, 442 N.Y.S.2d 191 (N.Y. App. Div. 1981); *cf. United States ex rel. Smith v. Robinson*, 495 F. Supp. 696 (E.D. Pa. 1980). (An inmate has a right to freedom from disciplinary sanctions until proven guilty of a rule violation. An inmate has a constitutional liberty interest in freedom from segregated confinement.)

[46] *Morris v. Travisono*, 509 F.2d 1358 (1st Cir. 1975); *La Batt v. Twomey*, 513 F.2d 641 (7th Cir. 1975); *Aikens v. Lash*, 371 F. Supp. 482 (N.D. Ind. 1974), *modified in*, 514 F.2d 55 (7th Cir. 1975); *Hayward v. Procunier*, 629 F.2d 599 (9th Cir. 1981); *Gray v. Levine*, 455 F. Supp. 267 (D. Mo. 1978), *aff'd*, 605 F.2d 1202 (4th Cir. 1979); *Clifton v. Robinson*, 500 F. Supp. 30 (D.C. Pa. 1980).

§ 8.3.9 —Double Jeopardy

Frequently, the argument is made that it is double jeopardy for an inmate to receive administrative punishment for conduct which is subject to a criminal prosecution. This argument was rejected in *United States v. Hedges.* "Five hundred and forty-three days of good behavior time were administratively forfeited . . . because of an attempted escape."[47] In affirming the conviction in the subsequent criminal trial, a federal court of appeals stated: "It is established . . . that administrative punishment does not render a subsequent judicial prosecution violative of the Fifth Amendment prohibition of double jeopardy."[48] The same reasoning is applicable to proceedings in state prisons.

However, criticism of this view is widespread. The rationale of *Hedges* was rejected in considering a disciplinary proceeding held after an inmate was acquitted of criminal charges arising out of the same conduct in *Barrows v. Hogan* where the court said:

> The question here is not one of double jeopardy, for the [inmate] does not allege that he has been charged twice for the same offense. The holding of a jury of twelve men and women is a final determination against the government on the question of whether [the inmate] assaulted the officer. In view of the judicial determination that this prisoner is not guilty of the offense charged, it is impermissible for the prison administration to determine otherwise and punish the prisoner for an offense as to which he has been acquitted.[49]

Since *Baxter* carefully distinguished criminal proceedings to which the Double Jeopardy Clause applies, from disciplinary proceedings which are "civil," the authority of prison officials to proceed independently of the criminal courts should be recognized and approved.

§ 8.3.10 —Evidence

The evidence relied upon in many prison disciplinary proceedings may be limited to the written conduct report of a guard or other staff member. It may include the oral testimony of witnesses for both side or documents such as letters. It is impossible to quantify the amount of evidence required to make a decision, but it is clear that the criminal trial standard of proof "beyond a reasonable doubt" is inapplicable to prison disciplinary proceedings. A popular standard is that borrowed from administrative law for purposes of judicial review: substantial evidence considering the record as a whole.[50] Thus, after considering the evidence on both sides of the case, if the members of the board feel there is substantial evidence in light of

---

[47] *United States v. Hedges,* 458 F.2d 188, 190 (10th Cir. 1972).
[48] *Id.*
[49] *Barrows v. Hogan,* 379 F. Supp. 314 (M.D. Pa. 1974); *cf. Rusher v. Arnold,* 550 F.2d 896 (3d Cir. 1977).
[50] *Universal Camera Corp. v. NLRB,* 340 U.S. 474 (1951).

the evidence offered by the inmate, they may validly find an inmate guilty of the offense charged.

A conviction on a disciplinary charge cannot rest solely upon a hearsay report of an unidentified informant whose credibility was unsubstantiated.[51]

Although polygraph examinations are looked upon with disfavor by the courts, the results of a polygraph may be considered as evidence in a prison disciplinary proceeding. However, there must be evidence aside from the polygraph report on which a decision is based. The polygraph may be used as corroborative evidence on the issue of guilt.

A difficult problem arises where the traditional criminal law defenses are raised. For example, a guard might come upon a "fight" in progress and charge the two inmates with "fighting." At the disciplinary hearing, one inmate might assert "self-defense." The general rule of criminal law is that one who is himself free from fault is privileged to use reasonable and necessary force to defend himself against personal harm threatened by the unlawful act of another. The force he uses for this purpose must be reasonable under all the circumstances. Thus, this defense would raise a number of questions, all of which should be dealt with by the disciplinary board: Which party was the aggressor? Was the inmate claiming self-defense free from fault? Was the force he used reasonable under the circumstances? Did the "defendant" become the aggressor by the use of excessive force in self-defense?

An inmate may assert his ignorance of a rule of conduct. However, in response, the familiar phrase "ignorance of the law is no excuse" may be applied. This is, however, applicable only to those offenses which would be crimes outside of the penal setting. Due process requires that inmates be given notice of what rules of conduct govern prison life and it further requires that those rules clearly define what conduct is violative of those rules. Due process is violated if an inmate is punished for violating a rule which is so vague as to make it impossible to conform his conduct to the rule.[52]

§ 8.4   Inmate's Legal Remedies

A violation of rights afforded inmates either under state or federal law will give rise to a number of remedial actions. Although they are fully discussed in Chapter 11, it should be noted that the remedies in the federal courts are usually limited to injunctive relief, civil suit under 42 U.S.C. § 1983, and habeas corpus under 28 U.S.C. § 2241.

---

[51] *Helms v. Hewitt*, 655 F.2d 487 (3d Cir. 1981), *rev'd on other grounds*, 459 U.S. 460, 103 S. Ct. 864, 74 L. Ed. 2d. 675 (1983); *See* § 8.3.4.

[52] *Meyers v. Alldredge*, 492 F.2d 296 (3d Cir. 1974); *Sagerser v. Oregon State Penitentiary, Corrections Division*, 597 P.2d 1257 (Or. App. 1979); *Haller v. Oregon State Penitentiary, Corr. Div.*, 570 P.2d 983 (Or. App. 1977).

Recently, state courts have shown interest in the conduct of prison disciplinary proceedings. This has ranged from hearing complaints concerning conditions and practices,[53] to detailed judicial review of disciplinary board findings.[54]

Whether pursued in state or federal court, one of the results of a reversal of a disciplinary board's action will probably be an order requiring the expungement of any records dealing with or relying on the disciplinary action which is found to have been invalid. One court deemed expungement appropriate to protect the inmate "from future prejudice in obtaining parole, work assignments, and the transfer to a prison nearer his home."[55]

§ 8.5 Conclusion

Federal courts have indicated a willingness to inquire into all aspects of prison administration to insure that the constitutional rights of inmates are observed. Although the courts have traditionally been extremely hesitant to place restraints on prison authorities in matters of internal prison administration, one court noted that:

This simple hands-off attitude has been complexified by recent Supreme Court cases which have held that prisoners are not stripped of their constitutional rights, including the right to due process, when the prison gate slams shut behind them. Rather, prisoners continue to enjoy the protections of the Due Process Clause subject to restrictions imposed by the practical necessities of prison life and the legitimate aims of the correctional process.[56]

In the context of "due process" it is important to note that long before the requirements of *procedural* due process were imposed on prison disciplinary proceedings, it was recognized that such proceedings must at least afford *substantive* due process[57] in that they must be fair.

Clearly, the courts have gone beyond the era when inmates' constitutional claims were disregarded out of hand by statements such as: "A convicted felon . . . has, as a consequence of his crime, not only forfeited his liberty, but all of his personal rights except those which the law in its humanity accords to him. He is for the time being the slave of the State."[58] The contemporary view in the federal courts is that if

[53] *People ex rel. Bright v. Warden,* 361 N.Y.S.2d 809 (Trial term SC Bronx County, 1975); *McGinnis v. Stevens,* 543 P.2d 1221 (Sup. Ct. Alaska 1975); *Wilkerson v. Oregon,* 544 P.2d 198 (Or. App. 1976); *Steele v. Gray,* 223 N.W.2d 614 (Wis. Sup. Ct. 1974).
[54] *Palmer v. Oregon State Penitentiary,* 545 P.2d 141 (Or. App. 1976); *Dawson v. Hearing Committee,* 597 P.2d 1353 (Wash. 1979); *Sandlin v. Oregon Women's Correctional Center, Corrections Division,* 559 P.2d 1308 (Or. App. 1977); *Riner v. Raines,* 409 N.E.2d 575 (Ind. 1980); *Reed v. Parratt,* 301 N.W.2d 343 (Neb. 1981).
[55] *Chapman v. Kleindienst,* 517 F.2d 1246 (7th Cir. 1974); *Powell v. Ward,* 487 F. Supp. 917 (S.D. N.Y. 1980); *Hurley v. Ward,* 402 N.Y.S.2d 870 (N.Y. App. Div. 1976).
[56] *United States ex rel. Gereau v. Henderson,* 526 F.2d 889 (5th Cir. 1976).
[57] *Wilwording v. Swenson,* 502 F.2d 844 (8th Cir. 1974).
[58] *Ruffin v. Commonwealth,* 62 Va. (21 Gratt.) 790, 796 (1871).

a constitutionally protected interest can be made out, and if some harm thereto can be shown that is sufficiently grievous and that cannot be justified by the exigencies of incarceration, then a proper case for relief exists.[59] However, *Baxter* makes it clear that the days of federal court tinkering with prison internal management are over. Prison disciplinarians who follow the clear teachings of *Wolff,* and who initiate procedures to prevent the abuse of administrative discretion need not fear legal liability.

---

[59] *Shimabuku v. Britton,* 503 F.2d 38 (10th Cir. 1974); *Haines v. Kerner,* 404 U.S. 519 (1972).

Chapter 9

PAROLE

§ 9.1 Introduction

The term, "parole," means a procedure by which a duly convicted defendant who has been sentenced to a term of imprisonment is allowed to serve the last portion of his sentence outside the prison walls, though he remains under supervision. The essence of parolee is release from prison before the completion of his sentence, on the condition that the parolee abide by certain rules during the balance of his sentence. It is applicable only to cases in which the convicted and sentenced defendant has served part of the imposed sentence. It is a conditional release from confinement, contingent upon future conduct as set forth in the terms of the parole. The parolee is subject to future confinement for the unserved portion of his sentence in the event he violates the provisions of parole.[1]

---

[1] *Nibert v. Carroll Trucking Co.*, 82 S.E.2d 445 (W.Va. 1954); *Richmond v. Commonwealth*, 402 A.2d 1134 (Pa. Commw., 1979).

§ 9.2   Parole Is Not a Right

One of the primary purposes of parole is to aid inmates in being reintegrated into society as constructive individuals as soon as they are able, without their being confined for the full term of the court-imposed sentence. Another purpose is to alleviate the costs to society of keeping inmates in prison.

In some states, parole is granted automatically after inmates serve an established minimum prison term. In others, parole is granted or withheld by the discretionary action of a parole authority which bases its decision on information about an inmate. In essence, the parole authority makes a prediction as to whether or not the inmate is ready to return to the free society.

In *Greenholtz v. Inmates of the Nebraska Penal and Correctional Complex,*[2] the Supreme Court held that there is no protected liberty interest in the possibility of parole before the termination of the sentence. Since there is no entitlement, due process hearings are not required by the state's system of parole. States are not constitutionally required to establish a parole system; it is instead a discretionary decision of the state to determine when an inmate is ready for release. The Court explained that the reason for not requiring due process standards is simply that a decision for the granting of parole is not the equivalent of a guilt determination as in a criminal proceeding or as in the revocation of parole.

In *Martinez v. California,*[3] a fifteen-year-old girl was murdered by a parolee with a history of being a sex offender, five months after he had been released from prison. The Supreme Court held that since the parolee was not an agent of the parole board, and the parole board was unaware of the decedent, as distinguished from her as a member of the public at large, the death was too remote a consequence of the decision to parole to hold the board responsible under 42 U.S.C. § 1983.

In *Connecticut Board of Pardons v. Dumschat,*[4] a prisoner applied for commutation of his life sentence. He was rejected without any explanation being given. Relying upon *Greenholtz v. Inmates of the Nebraska Penal and Correctional Complex,* the Supreme Court held that an inmate has no constitutionally inherent right to commutation of his life sentence. The inmate has nothing more than an expectation, as, for example, the expectation that he will not be transferred to another prison within the system. It is not a constitutional right, but a unilateral hope. It was pointed out that the Connecticut statute in issue referred to the mere existence of a power to commute. There was no limit on what procedure was to be followed, what evidence could be considered, nor what criteria were to be applied, all in

---

[2] *Greenholtz v. Inmates of the Nebraska Penal and Correctional Complex,* 442 U.S. 1 (1979); *Board of Pardons v. Allen,* 482 U.S. 369 (1987) (A Montana statute provided that a prisoner eligible for parole "shall" be released when there is a reasonable probability that no detriment will result to him or the community, and specified that parole shall be ordered for the best interests of society, and when the State Board of Pardons (Board) believed that the prisoner is able and willing to assume the obligations of a law-abiding citizen. This statute created the same liberty interest that was protected in *Greenholtz.*)

[3] *Martinez v. California,* 444 U.S. 227 (1980).

[4] *Connecticut Board of Pardons v. Dumschat,* 449 U.S. 898 (1981).

contrast to the statute in *Greenholz,* which created a right to parole under state law. However, this does not mean that the inmate has no constitutional rights in the procedure used in granting or denying him parole.

Statutes usually control the time at which specific groups of inmates will become eligible for parole. The right to be considered at a parole hearing and the timing of the parole hearing are frequently within the sole discretion of the parole authority. However, in *Grasso v. Norton*[5] the court held that a federal prisoner who is sentenced under a statute which permits parole eligibility consideration at any time is entitled to "effective and meaningful" parole consideration at or before the one-third point of the maximum sentence. This was required even though the prisoner was given an initial parole hearing when entering the prison. "Meaningful" consideration for parole was satisfied by a "file review" and did not require a personal interview. However, *Garafola v. Benson*[6] held that a "file review" was not "meaningful" and a full-scale institutional hearing was required. In *Franklin v. Shields,*[7] the Fourth Circuit Court of Appeals held that there is no constitutional requirement that each prisoner receive a personal hearing, have access to his files, or be entitled to call witnesses in his behalf to appear before a parole board. The court believed that such matters were better left to the discretion of the parole authorities. As a general rule, the courts will not interfere with the exercise of discretion in granting or refusing parole to an inmate. This rule of noninterference was used in *Tarlton v. Clark.*[8] An inmate sought an order reviewing the action of the United States Board of Parole in not granting him parole at the time he first became eligible. The petitioner claimed that Sections 4202 and 4203 of Title 18 of the United States Code gave him the right to parole after completing one-third of his total sentence, provided that he had obeyed all the rules of the institution wherein he was confined. The court held that:

> By the language of Title 18 U.S.C.A. 4203, the Board of Parole is given absolute discretion in matters of parole. The courts are without power to grant a parole or to determine judicially eligibility for parole. ... Furthermore, it is not the function of the courts to review the discretion of the Board in the denial of application

[5] *Grasso v. Norton,* 520 F.2d 27 (2d Cir. 1975); *Didousis v. New York State Board of Parole,* 391 N.Y.S.2d 222 (1977).

[6] *Garafola v. Benson,* 505 F.2d 1212 (7th Cir. 1974); *Walker v. Prisoner Review Board,* 694 F.2d 499 (7th Cir. 1982). (The Rules governing parole have no exception for withholding documents that are considered by the Parole Board from a candidate for parole. This created a justified expectation of access to his file. A prisoner's Civil Rights case was remanded to the District Court to determine whether the Board considered papers which it did not permit the prisoner to see.); *Dixon v. Hadden,* 550 F. Supp. 157 (D.Colo. 1982). (The use of a letter that makes serious accusations without indicating the reliability of sources in making a parole decision violates Due Process.)

[7] *Franklin v. Shields,* 569 F.2d 784 (4th Cir. 1977); *see also Garafola v. Benson,* 505 F.2d 1212 (7th Cir. 1974).

[8] *Tarlton v. Clark,* 441 F.2d 384 (5th Cir. 1971); *cert. denied,* 403 U.S. 934 (1971); *Schlobohm v. U.S. Parole Commission,* 479 F. Supp. 474 (M.D. Pa. 1979).

for parole or to review the credibility of reports and information received by the Board in making its determination.[9]

There is, in light of this and several other cases,[10] no right to be paroled at any specified time, although there may be a "right" to be considered for parole eligibility."[11] Under present case law, the determination as to eligibility for release is vested entirely in the paroling authority.

Similarly, the paroling authority is given wide discretion in determining how the interview or hearing with the inmate will be conducted. *Menechino v. Oswald*[12] summarized the rights of an inmate at a parole hearing.

The petitioner alleged that due process rights had been violated at his parole hearing. He claimed that the Constitution required that he be given 1) notice; 2) a fair hearing with right to counsel, cross-examination and presentation of witnesses, and 3) specification of the reasons used by the parole authority in its determination. The court denied that the inmate had any due process rights at his parole hearing. It asserted that many of the essential conditions necessary for the application of due process standards are absent in the context of a parole hearing.

First, the proceeding is non-adversary in nature. Both parties, the parole authority and the inmate, have the same concern—rehabilitation.

Second, the primary function of the hearing is not in a fact-finding determination. On the contrary, the parole authority is making a determination based upon numerous tangible and intangible factors.

Third, the inmate has no present private interest to be protected, as is required before the due process clause is applicable.

This wide discretion given the paroling authority is limited however. Written reasons for the denial of parole must be given to the inmate. In *United States ex rel. Johnson v. Chairman, New York State Board of Parole*[13] the court stated that the Due Process Clause of the Fourteenth Amendment requires the Parole Board to provide a written statement of reasons to the inmate when parole is denied. This conclusion is consistent with *Menechino,* which held only that an inmate was not entitled to a specification of charges, counsel and cross-examination.

In federal courts, the requirement to provide an inmate with written reasons for the denial of parole has been based on either statutory or constitutional grounds. First, it is argued that the parole board is an *agency* under the Federal Administrative Procedure Act, Section 555(e) which provides generally for notice of denial in whole or in part of a written application made in connection with any agency pro-

---

[9] *Id.* at 385.

[10] *See United States v. Frederick*, 405 F.2d 129 (3d Cir. 1968); *State v. Freitas*, 602 P.2d 914 (Haw. 1979); *Boothe v. Hammock*, 605 F.2d 661 (2d Cir. 1979); *Smith v. Marchewka*, 519 F. Supp. 897 (D.C. N.Y. 1981).

[11] *See Stroud v. Weger*, 380 F. Supp. 897 (M.D. Pa. 1974); *Matter of Bonds*, 613 P.2d 1196 (Wash. App. 1980).

[12] *Menechino v. Oswald*, 430 F.2d 403 (2d Cir. 1970).

[13] *Johnson, U.S. ex rel. v. Chairman, New York State Board of Parole*, 363 F. Supp. 416, *aff'd*, 500 F.2d 925 (2d Cir. 1971), *vacated as moot, Regan v. Johnson*, 419 U.S. 1015 (1971).

ceeding.[14] Second, it is argued that the parole granting decision results in a "grievious loss" of conditional liberty to the inmate and therefore *due process* requires that written reasons for denial be provided.[15] The U.S. Parole Commission and Reorganization Act[16] states that a prisoner must be provided with written notice of the Parole Commission's decision after the parole determination proceeding. If parole is denied, the notice must state with particularity the reasons for such denial.[17]

In *Rowe v. Whyte*[18] the court held that release on parole is a substantial liberty interest and that the procedures by which it is granted or denied must satisfy Due Process standards. Compare this to the position taken by the Sixth Circuit Court of Appeals which has stated that a prisoner does not have a sufficient liberty interest in his future parole release to be entitled to due process in his parole release proceedings.[19]

In *Franklin v. Shields*[20] it was held that certain other minimum procedures are required at the parole granting hearing. The statute in effect in Virginia, as interpreted by the court, extended an "expectation of liberty" to its prisoners. Therefore the procedure to determine eligibility for parole had to be "fundamentally fair," including:

1. Published standards and criteria governing parole determinations which must be made available to the inmates.
2. A personal hearing.
3. Access by the inmate to the information which the Parole Board relies upon in making its decision. Although most of the information in the prisoner's files is harmless, certain information may be removed and some reports

[14] *King v. United States*, 492 F.2d 1337 (7th Cir. 1974).

[15] *Childs v. United States Board of Parole*, 511 F.2d 1270 (D.C.C. 1974); *United States ex rel. Harrison v. Pace*, 357 F. Supp. 354 (E.D. Pa. 1973); *United States ex rel. Richerson v. Wolff*, 525 F.2d 797 (7th Cir. 1975), *cert. denied*, 425 U.S. 914 (1976).

[16] Public Law 94-233, March 15, 1976. *See* Appendix I (includes only portions relevant to this section). §§ 4206, 4218.

[17] *Ronning v. United States*, 547 F. Supp. 301 (M.D. Pa. 1982). (In order for a District Court to overturn the U.S. Parole Commission's parole determination, a court must find that there was no rational basis in the record for the Commission's decisions); *Campbell v. U.S. Parole Commission*, 704 F.2d 106 (3d Cir. 1983), (a prisoner, with intent to rob a bank, participated in a murder, although his two confederates actually did the killing. This fact was properly considered by the U.S. Parole Commission as an aggravating factor to keep him in prison six years longer than recommended by the guidelines. A District Court's decision to require the Commission to reconsider the prisoner's parole eligibility without reference to the murder was an "unjustified interference" with the Commission's discretion, and was reversed); *Artez v. Mulcrone*, 673 F.2d 1169 (10th Cir. 1982). (A prisoner's parole category in the most severe category was not denying him any fundamental right. An administrative classification is permissible if it has some rational basis or advances a legitimate governmental interest.)

[18] *Rowe v. Whyte*, 280 S.E.2d 301 (W.Va. 1981); *Williams v. Missouri Bd. of Probation and Parole*, 661 F.2d 697 (8th Cir. 1981); *Bradford v. Weinstein*, 519 F.2d 728 (4th Cir. 1976), *vacated as moot*, 423 U.S. 147 (1976). (The prisoner had obtained a full release by that time.)

[19] *Wagner v. Gilligan*, 609 F.2d 866 (6th Cir. 1979); *Sharp v. Leonard*, 611 F.2d 136 (6th Cir. 1979).

[20] *Franklin v. Shields*, 399 F. Supp. 309 (W.D. Va. 1975).

may be rewritten to protect the author's identity. Reports considered potentially harmful include psychiatric and psychological reports on the inmate and reports by informers or others who made statements in confidence. The Board must provide an inmate access to the information in his file for a reasonable period prior to the parole hearing. Access may be denied to information which would threaten prison security or present a substantial likelihood of harm to the inmate or others.

4. A statement of the reasons for denial. Such reasons are to be as clear and precise as possible but they need only be substantially related to the criteria adopted by the Board.

No right exists to call witnesses in the prisoner's behalf or to call and cross-examine persons who have provided adverse information to the Board. There is no right of the inmate to legal counsel.

In addition to case law, the new Federal Parole Commission and Reorganization Act should be consulted for the procedure required in the federal system of corrections.[21]

"The Parole Commission and Reorganization Act is repealed as of 1992 by the Sentencing Reform Act of 1984,[22] which, *inter alia,* created the United States Sentencing Commission[23] as an independent body in the Judicial Branch with power to promulgate binding Sentencing Guidelines establishing a range of determinate sentences for all categories of federal offenses and defendants according to specific and detailed factors. The Sentencing Reform Act was held to be constitutional in *Mistretta v. United States.*[23a]

The purpose of requiring written reasons for the denial of parole is to provide the courts with a record upon which to evaluate whether the actions of the Parole Board have been "arbitrary and capricious," a standard of judicial review of administrative acts. The reason for denial which has been attacked most often is "release at this time would depreciate the seriousness of the offense." Although many courts still recognize the broad discretion vested in the paroling authority,[24] courts have held that something more than a general reason for the denial of parole is required.[25] Denial of parole based in general language and not specifically addressed to the inmate's personal situation may amount to no reason at all and does not protect the inmate from arbitrary and capricious action by the Parole Board.

---

[21] Appendix I §§ 4206, 4207, and 4208.

[22] 28 U.S.C. §§ 991, 994, and 995(a)(1).

[23] 18 U.S.C. § 3551 *et seq.* (1982 ed., Supp. IV), and 28 U.S.C. §§ 991-998 (1982) ed., Supp. IV.)

[24] *Wiley v. United States Board of Parole,* 380 F.Supp. 1194 (M.D. Pa. 1974); *Roach v. Board of Pardons and Paroles, Arkansas,* 503 F.2d 1367 (8th Cir. 1974); *Calabro v. United States Board of Parole,* 525 F.2d 660 (5th Cir. 1975); *Zannino v. Arnold,* 531 F.2d 687 (3d Cir. 1976); *Lott v. Dalsheim,* 474 F.Supp. 897 (N.Y. 1979); *Campbell v. Montana State Board of Pardons,* 470 F. Supp. 1301 (D. Mont. 1979).

[25] *Soloway v. Weger,* 389 F. Supp. 409 (M.D. Pa. 1974); *Candarini v. United States Attorney General,* 369 F. Supp. 1132 (E.D. N.Y. 1974); *Craft v. United States Attorney General,* 379 F. Supp. 538 (M.D. Pa. 1974); *cf. Young v. Duckworth,* 394 N.E.2d 123 (Ind. 1979); *Bowles v. Tennant,* 613 F.2d 776 (9th Cir. 1980).

Another limitation was recognized in *Palermo v. Rockefeller,*[26] in which an early release was guaranteed for the petitioners in exchange for a guilty plea and was reneged. The court held the board had abused its discretionary powers.

Similarly, the courts will not permit a parole authority to exercise power allocated exclusively to the courts. In *Johnson v. Haskins,*[27] the court released an inmate from custody because the parole authority had deliberately circumvented the obvious intent of the sentencing court that the inmate's sentences run concurrently. The court admonished the parole authority by reminding it that the court's judgment as to whether sentences are to be concurrent or consecutive is not subject to modification, directly or indirectly, by them.

In discussing limitations on the discretion of the parole authority to grant or refuse release, we should note that the above cases are *exceptional.* The prevailing view is that the discretion of the parole authority in release hearings is broad.

§ 9.3   Parole Revocation

Three theories have been advanced in the past to justify the unlimited discretion of a parole authority in revoking the parole once it is granted: The Privilege Theory; The Contract Theory; and The Continuing Custody Theory. The present judicial treatment of parole revocation modifies these theories by subjecting parole authorities to the requirements of due process in revoking parole.

§ 9.3.1   —The Privilege Theory

Most frequently argued is the privilege theory. This theory holds that parole is an act of grace by the state. Since the release on parole is granted to the inmate as a matter of privilege, no right attaches to it even after it is given. The release may be given, conditioned, or terminated, according to the theory, at the whim of the granting authority.

There are weaknesses to the use of this particular theory of parole. The system of parole is an integral part of the American criminal justice process. Prison administrators use it as a rehabilitative tool as well as a stimulus for good behavior of inmates. Furthermore, it is relied upon by the inmates and is frequently the reason why inmates behave properly while incarcerated. To allow parole authorities an unlimited control over the parolee would appear, in light of the above, to be unwise and unjust. Further, courts have expressed their displeasure with the whole concept of "privilege" as opposed to "right." The Supreme Court in cases concerning students, welfare recipients and security clearances, has reviewed the privilege theory and has rejected it as improper in these cases. Most recently, the "privilege" theory of parole was repudiated by the United States Supreme Court in *Morrissey v. Brewer.*[28]

---

[26] *Palermo v. Rockefeller,* 323 F. Supp. 478 (S.D. N.Y. 1971).

[27] *Johnson v. Haskins,* 20 Ohio St.2d 156, 49 Ohio Op. 481, 254 N.E.2d 362 (Ohio 1969); *Wilkerson v. United States Board of Parole,* 606 F.2d 750 (7th Cir. 1979).

[28] *Morrissey v. Brewer,* 408 U.S. 471 (1972).

§ 9.3.2 —The Contract Theory

A second theory used as a reason for allowing unreviewable revocation of parole is the contract theory. It is argued that the release by the parole authority is contingent upon the parolee's acceptance of the conditions of such release. The acceptance constitutes a contractual obligation on the part of the inmate to live up to the conditions specified. If the conditions are violated, there is a "breach of contract" which justifies revocation. An obvious difficulty in the contract theory is that the parolee has no bargaining power in determining the terms of the contract. Furthermore, any "consent" to the terms of his contractual release is coerced by virtue of the fact that no alternative means of obtaining release is available.

§ 9.3.3 —The Continuing Custody Theory

A third theory used in conjunction with parole is that of "continuing custody." It is argued that because the parolee remains in the custody of the granting authority, he is still subject to the same restrictions as he was prior to his release on parole. However, the avowed purpose of the parole system is rehabilitation. An inmate is released so that he may be readjusted to the conditions of society, under supervision. It cannot be denied that his situation is substantially distinct from that of an inmate. To attempt to apply the standards used in dealing with an inmate to that of a parolee is inherently irrational, so the theory contends.

§ 9.3.4 —The Due Process Theory

The present approach to parole revocation modifies, if not rejects, these three theories. This approach recognizes that one of the chief goals of the correctional system is to impress upon those within the system the belief that the criminal justice process operates fairly for the protection of all society. It is recognized that the arbitrary operation of the parole system can only result in the parolees' loss of respect for a system which claims to encourage responsible action in accordance with established law. Furthermore, it is acknowledged that the interests of the people are best served by a proper treatment of the parolee in order to prevent recidivism. If revocation is accomplished through an arbitrary procedure, respect for society will be further diminished. Finally, although it cannot be asserted that the parolee maintains the same rights as does a free man, it is recognized that basic constitutionally protected rights are applicable to the parolee. Consequently, the requirements of due process should be applicable to parole revocation.

§ 9.4 Parole Revocation Proceedings

In *Morrissey v. Brewer*,[29] the United States Supreme Court mandated that due process applies to parole revocation proceedings.

---

[29] *Ibid.*

Prior to *Morrissey,* the leading case dealing with the rights associated with revocation proceedings was *Mempa v. Rhay.*[30] However, *Mempa v. Rhay* dealt with revocation of probation. In *Mempa,* two defendants had each been convicted of felonies and had been placed on probation. Both had violated the conditions of their probation and were consequently given the maximum sentence at a deferred sentencing or probation hearing. The petitioners had not been represented by counsel at these proceedings nor were they offered court appointed counsel at these proceedings. The Supreme Court held that the "right to counsel is not a right confined to representation during the trial on the merits."[31] On the contrary, "appointment of counsel for an indigent is required at every stage of a criminal proceeding where substantial rights of a criminal accused may be affected."[32] For this reason, the Court found that the failure to provide such representation at the probation revocation was reversible error.

As noted, the decision rendered in *Mempa* specifically dealt with probation rather than with parole. Furthermore, it was limited to the right to counsel rather than to the full panoply of procedural due process rights.

In *Morrissey,* the Supreme Court distinguished parole from probation. Unlike probation, parole only arises at the end of a criminal prosecution, including the imposition of sentence. Further, in parole, supervision is not directed by the courts, but by an administrative agency. Most significantly, parole revocation deprives an individual, not of the absolute liberty to which every citizen is entitled, but only of the conditional liberty which depends on compliance with special parole restrictions.

Nevertheless, the requirements of due process are applicable to parole revocations. The Supreme Court completely rejected the theory that constitutional rights turn upon whether the government benefit is characterized as a "right" or a "privilege." Rather, the crucial issue is the extent to which the individual will be condemned to suffer "grievous loss."

In *Morrissey,* the Supreme Court held that revocation of parole was a "grievous loss" to the parolee.

The liberty of a parolee enables him to do a wide range of things open to persons who have never been convicted of any crime. The parolee has been released from prison based on an evaluation that he shows reasonable promise of being able to return to society and function as a responsible, self-reliant person. Subject to the conditions of his parole, he can be gainfully employed and is free to be with family and friends and to form the other enduring attachments of normal life. Though the state properly subjects him to many restrictions not applicable to other citizens, his conditions are very different from that of confinement in a prison. He may have been on parole for a num-

---

[30] *Mempa v. Rhay,* 398 U.S. 128 (1967).
[31] *Id.* at 133.
[32] *Id.* at 134.

ber of years and may be living a relatively normal life at the time he is faced with revocation. The parolee has relied on at least an implicit promise that parole will be revoked only if he fails to live up to the parole conditions. In many cases, the parolee faces lengthy incarceration if his parole is revoked.

We see, therefore, that the liberty of a parolee, although indeterminate, includes many of the core values of unqualified liberty and its termination inflicts a "grievous loss" on the parolee and often on others. It is hardly useful any longer to try to deal with this problem in terms of whether the parolee's liberty is a "right" or a "privilege." By whatever name, the liberty is valuable and must be seen as within the protection of the Fourteenth Amendment. Its termination calls for some orderly process, however informal.[33]

The remaining issue is the extent of the "orderly process." The Supreme Court in *Morrissey* recognized that given the previous criminal conviction and the proper imposition of parole conditions, the state has an interest in being able to return the parolee to imprisonment without the burden of a new criminal trial on the merits if in fact the parolee has failed to live up to the conditions of his parole. However, the summary treatment that may be necessary in controlling a large group of potentially disruptive inmates in actual custody, and the argument that revocation is so totally a discretionary matter that some form of hearing would be administratively intolerable, was rejected.

The parolee is not the only one who has a stake in his conditional liberty. Society has a stake in whatever may be the chance of restoring him to normal and useful life within the law. Society thus has an interest in not having parole revoked because of erroneous information or because of an erroneous evaluation of the need to revoke parole, given the breach of parole conditions. ... And society has a further interest in treating the parolee with basic fairness: fair treatment in parole revocations will enhance the chance of rehabilitation by avoiding reactions to arbitrariness.[34]

Therefore, what the Supreme Court felt was needed was an informal hearing structured to assure that the findings of a parole violation would be based on verified facts and that the exercise of discretion would be based on accurate knowledge of the parolee's behavior.

Pro forma language and routine phrases will not satisfy the requirement of a written statement of evidence and reasons relied upon.[35]

Article III of the Interstate Agreement on Detainers applies only to criminal charges. A probation violation charge which does not accuse an individual with having committed a criminal offense in the sense of initiating a prosecution does

---

[33] *Morrissey v. Brewer,* 408 U.S. 471 (1972).

[34] *Id.* at 484.

[35] *United States v. Martinez,* 650 F.2d 744 (5th Cir. 1981).

not come within Article III. Here, a probationer from New Jersey was arrested and convicted on burglary, involuntary deviate sexual intercourse, and loitering in Pennsylvania. New Jersey sought to revoke the defendant's probation based upon the criminal conduct in Pennsylvania, and placed a detainer on the prisoner in Pennsylvania.[36]

§ 9.4.1 —Arrest and Preliminary Hearing

The first step in the parole revocation process is the arrest of the parolee. This can occur either by his arrest on new criminal charges, or at the direction of a parole officer for a breach of the terms of parole. There is usually a substantial period of time between arrest and the eventual determination by the parole authority that parole should be revoked. Further, often the parolee is arrested at a place far distant from the prison to which he may be returned prior to the formal action of the parole authority.

Given these circumstances, the United States Supreme Court held in *Morrissey v. Brewer* that

> due process would seem to require that some minimal inquiry be conducted at or reasonably near the place of the alleged parole violation or arrest and as promptly as convenient after arrest while information is fresh and sources are available.[37]

The inquiry required is in the nature of a "preliminary hearing" in which it must be determined that there is probable cause or reasonable grounds to believe that the arrested parolee has committed acts which would constitute a violation of the conditions of parole.

Therefore, *Morrissey* deals with both the "place" and the "promptness" of the initial inquiry. Of these two the "promptness" issue has triggered considerable litigation. In addition, questions have arisen as to what proceedings may serve as a "substitute" for the *Morrissey* preliminary hearing. "Promptness" has been determined by statute in some jurisdictions.[38] Other parole authorities have had "promptness" defined for them by the courts.[39] Nevertheless, the entire revocation process should ideally be completed within two months since *Morrissey* stated that this was not an unreasonable time.

Another problem which has arisen concerning the timing of both the preliminary and the final *Morrissey* revocation hearing occurs when a parolee is held in a different jurisdiction for criminal acts committed while on parole and the paroling authority has issued a detainer against the parolee. The issue is whether the issu-

---

[36] *Carchman v. Nash*, 473 U.S. 716, 37 Cr. L. 3198 (1985).
[37] *Id.* at 485. *But see Moody v. Daggett*, 429 U.S. 78 (1976).
[38] *Michigan*, M.S.A. § 28.2310 (1).
[39] *Thompson v. McEvoy*, 337 N.Y.S. 2d 83 (1972); *State v. Sylvester*, 401 So. 2d 1123 (Fla. App. 1981); *Commonwealth v. Boykin*, 411 A.2d 1244 (Pa. Super. 1979).

ance of the detainer triggers the requirement for a "prompt" revocation hearing. *Moody v. Daggett*[40] has solved the dilemma by holding that there is no requirement for an immediate hearing. The loss of liberty stems from the new conviction and thus the detainer has no immediate effect. Parole authorities may therefore hold the warrant for either execution or dismissal at the completion of the term of the new sentence. It is at that time that the *Morrissey* standard applies.[41]

The United States Parole Commission and Reorganization Act[42] states that imprisonment in an institution cannot be used as an excuse for not issuing a detainer against a parole violator, but when new criminal charges are pending, the issuance may be delayed until disposition of the new charge. When a parolee has been convicted of a crime committed while on parole and is serving a new sentence and a detainer has been placed against him, a revocation hearing must be held within 180 days of the placement of the detainer, or upon his release, whichever occurs first.

Some courts have determined that preliminary hearings on new criminal charges may serve as the *Morrissey* preliminary hearing.[43] The parolee must, however, receive prior notification that the criminal hearing will serve as a substitute. Other situations have been held sufficient to substitute for the *Morrissey* preliminary hearing. Foremost among these is when the parolee is convicted of a new crime. In *United States v. Tucker*[44] the court stated that where a probationer was incarcerated pursuant to a final conviction at the time of the attempted probation revocation, there was no requirement that there be a preliminary as well as a final probation revocation hearing. This has been held to apply even though the conviction is under appeal. However, if the conviction is reversed, logic would suggest that a prompt hearing be held at that time. In *Wells v. Wise*,[45] however, the court held that even though the fact of a violation has already been conclusively determined either by a conviction or an admission, a hearing must be held.

Where a parole board has relied on criminal proceedings as a substitute for the *Morrissey* preliminary hearing, and the parolee was acquitted of the charge, at least one court[46] has held that the parole board was "collaterally estopped" from revoking parole based on the same set of facts. The court held that such a revocation violated the doctrine of collateral estoppel as contained in the Double Jeopardy

---

[40] *Moody v. Daggett*, 429 U.S. 78 (1976).

[41] *Reese v. United States Board of Parole*, 530 F.2d 231 (9th Cir. 1976); *Gaddy v. Michael*, 519 F.2d 669 (4th Cir. 1975); *Small v. Britton*, 500 F.2d 299 (10th Cir. 1974); *Moody v. Daggett*, 429 U.S. 78 (1976).

[42] Appendix I §§ 4213 and 4214.

[43] *Inmates' Councilmatic Voice v. Rogers*, 541 F.2d 633 (6th Cir. 1976); *In re Law*, 513 P.2d 621 (Cal. Sup. Ct. 1973); *Battle v. Commonwealth, Pennsylvania Board of Probation and Parole*, 403 A.2d 1063 (Pa. Cmwlth. 1979); *Commonwealth v. Del Conte*, 419 A.2d 780 (Pa. Super. 1980).

[44] *United States v. Tucker*, 524 F.2d 77 (5th Cir. 1975).

[45] *Wells v. Wise*, 390 F. Supp. 229 (C.D. Cal. 1975).

[46] *Standlee v. Rhay*, 403 F. Supp. 1247 (E.D. Wash. 1975).

Clause of the Fifth Amendment.[47] The court rejected the state's argument that the lesser burden of proof (preponderance of evidence) at the revocation hearing permitted the parole board to revoke parole based on the same facts presented at the criminal trial where the burden of proof was "beyond a reasonable doubt."

In contrast, the court in *In re Coughlin*[48] held that a court, at a probation revocation hearing, or the Adult Authority, at a parole revocation hearing, may properly consider evidence indicating that a probationer or parolee has committed another criminal offense during the period of his probation or parole, despite the fact that he was acquitted of the criminal charge at trial.[49] Further, in *Standlee v. Rhay*[50] the court of appeals held that the doctrine of collateral estoppel did not prohibit the parole board from finding the parolee guilty of a parole violation even after the accused had been acquitted in a criminal trial on the same charges. Parole revocation proceedings require a lower standard of proof than criminal adjudicatory proceedings. This may result in a revocation of parole even though the accused is found not guilty of the charges at the trial level.

The split in opinion centers around the different burden of proof requirements for a criminal trial and a revocation proceeding, and the nature of the proceeding itself. It has been stated that proof beyond a reasonable doubt of the violation of a condition of probation is not required by statute or the Constitution in a revocation proceeding.[51] In spite of this recognized difference in the burden of proof some courts have imposed the criminal acquittal as a final decision for the parole board. This appears to be too broad since a technical violation of parole which occurred in the same factual setting as the criminal charge would be precluded from consideration by the parole board in the revocation hearing. In addition, the United States Supreme Court suggested in *Baxter v. Palmigiano*[52] that a prison disciplinary hearing was not a criminal proceeding, but a civil proceeding, and authorized a prison court to hold a disciplinary hearing while state criminal charges were pending, where both involved the same facts. Although the law is not clear, it can be argued that the revocation of parole is not a criminal proceeding, that the civil standards for burden of proof (preponderance of the evidence) should apply at the revocation hearing, and the doctrine of Double Jeopardy should not apply.

---

[47] *See also, Barrows v. Hogan*, 379 F. Supp. 314 (M.D. Pa. 1974); *People v. Grayson*, 319 N.E. 2d 43 (Ill. 1974), *cert. denied*, 421 U.S. 994 (1975); *cf. People ex rel. Murray v. New York State Board of Parole*, 417 N.Y.S.2d 286 (N.Y. App. Div. 1979) and *People ex rel. Froats v. Hammock*, 443 N.Y.S.2d 500 (N.Y.A.D. 1981).

[48] *In re Coughlin*, 545 P.2d 249 (Cal. Sup. Ct. 1976).

[49] *United States ex rel. Carrasquillo v. Thomas*, 527 F. Supp. 1105 (S.D. N.Y. 1981). (The fact that an idictment was dismissed with prejudice did not preclude a parole revocation proceeding resting upon the same allegations as contained in the indictment); *See also, In re Dunham*, 545 P.2d 255 (Cal. Sup. Ct. 1976); *Standlee v. Smith*, 518 P.2d 721 (Wash. 1974).

[50] *Standlee v. Rhay*, 557 F.2d 1303 (9th Cir. 1977).

[51] *State v. Rasler*, 532 P.2d 1077 (Kan. Sup. Ct. 1975); *People ex rel. Walker v. Hammock*, 435 N.Y.S.2d 410 (N.Y. App. Div. 1981); *Avery v. State*, 616 P.2d 872 (Alaska 1980).

[52] *Baxter v. Palmigiano*, 425 U.S. 308 (1976).

The United States Parole Commission and Reorganization Act states in Section 4214(b)(1) that conviction for a Federal, State or local crime committed subsequent to release on parole shall constitute probable cause for the purposes of a preliminary hearing. Furthermore, if a full revocation hearing is held on-site "promptly" after the detainer is filed, there would appear to be no justifiable reason for requiring two hearings.[53] At least one court has held that where a probationer is not "in custody" there is no requirement for preliminary hearing.[54] Further, pending criminal proceedings justify a delay.[55]

Federal authorities may, pursuant to a general policy, wait until after state sentencing proceedings are completed before instituting federal probation revocation proceedings. Further, a plea agreement between the defendant and state prosecutors, contemplating that the state sentence would run concurrently with the federal sentence for probation violation, was not binding on the federal court.[56]

Subsequent to the arrest, due process now requires that the determination that reasonable grounds exist for parole revocation be made by someone not directly involved in the case. Although it is recognized that a conscientious supervising parole officer will interview the parolee, confront him with the reasons for revocation, and bears no personal hostility towards the parolee, the officer directly involved in making recommendations cannot always have completely objectivity in evaluating the status of the parolee. This contention is not to attribute bad motivation to the officer. "Parole agents are human, and it is possible that friction between the agent and parolee may have influenced the agent's judgment."[57]

Since the granting and revoking of parole are decisions traditionally made by administrative personnel, the reviewing officer need not be a judicial officer, nor a lawyer. The only requirement is that the reviewing officer must be some person other than the one who initially supervised the parolee or caused his arrest.

It will be sufficient, therefore, in the parole revocation context, if an evaluation of whether reasonable cause exists to believe that conditions of parole have been violated is made by someone such as a parole officer other than the one who has made the report of parole violations or has recommended revocation.[58]

At the preliminary hearing the parolee must be given notice that the hearing will take place and that its purpose is to determine whether there is probable cause to

---

[53] *People v. Gulley,* 238 N.W.2d 421 (Mich. Ct. App. 1975).

[54] *United States v. Scuito,* 531 F.2d 842 (7th Cir. 1976); *See also Pearson v. State,* 241 N.W.2d 490 (Minn. Sup. Ct. 1976); *People ex rel. Spinks v. Dillon,* 416 N.Y.S. 2d 942 (1979) and *Board of Trustees of Youth Correctional Institution Complex v. Smalls,* 410 A.2d 691 (N.J. Super. A.D. 1979).

[55] *Hall v. State of Ohio,* 535 F. Supp. 1121 (S.D. Ohio 1982). (An indictment returned by a Grand Jury eliminated the necessity of conducting a preliminary parole violation hearing until such time as the parolee was acquitted on the criminal charges.); *United States v. Bazzano,* 712 F.2d 826 (3rd Cir. 1982). (Probation proceedings in federal court should await completion of the criminal trial resolving the underlying substantive charges, unless the probationer requests otherwise, or the government shows a compelling contrary need.)

[56] *United States v. Sackinger,* 704 F.2d 29 (2d Cir. 1983).

[57] *Morrissey v. Brewer,* 408 U.S. at 486.

[58] *Id.* at 486.

believe that he has committed a parole violation. The parole conditions alleged to have been violated must be stated in the notice. At the hearing, the parolee has the right to appear and to speak in his own behalf. Further, he may bring letters, documents, or witnesses who are able to give relevant information to the hearing officer. If the parolee requests to question in his presence persons who have given adverse information upon which his parole revocation is to be based, the request must be granted, unless the hearing officer determines that the adverse witness, or informant, would risk harm if his identity were disclosed.

Finally, the hearing officer must make a summary of the proceedings, including the responses of the parolee, the substance of the documents or evidence given in support of revocation, and the parolee's position. Based upon such information, the hearing officer must then determine whether there is probable cause to hold the parolee for the parole authority's final decision on revocation. Thereafter, the parolee may lawfully be continued in detention and returned to prison pending the final decision of the parole authority.

§ 9.4.2 —The Revocation Hearing

The *Morrissey* holding requires that the parolee be given the opportunity for a hearing, if he so desires, prior to the final decision or revocation by the parole authority.

The revocation hearing must lead to a final evaluation of any contested relevant facts, and must consider whether the facts, as determined, warrant parole revocation.

Minimum due process at the parole revocation hearing now requires that the parolee be given an opportunity to be heard and to show, if he is able to, that he did not violate the conditions of his parole, or, if he did, the mitigating circumstances that might suggest the violation does not warrant revocation.

Although the Supreme Court requires the revocation hearing to be made within a reasonable period of time after the parolee is taken into custody, two months was not deemed unreasonable.

§ 9.4.3 —Procedural Due Process at the Revocation Hearing

At the present time, and in the foreseeable future, the following procedure must be followed in a parole revocation hearing to conform with the requirements of due process:

1. There must be written notice of the claimed violations of parole;
2. The evidence against the parolee must be disclosed to him;
3. The parolee must be given the opportunity to be heard in person and to present witnesses and documentary evidence;
4. The parolee has the right to confront and cross-examine adverse witnesses, unless the parole authority specifically finds good cause for not allowing

confrontation, such as a risk of harm to the informant if his identity were disclosed;

5. The hearing body, such as a traditional parole board, must be neutral and detached, but need not be judicial officers or lawyers;

6. The parole authority must compose a written statement as to the evidence it relied on and the reasons for revoking the parole.[59]

There was no intent by the Supreme Court to equate the revocation hearing to a formal criminal prosecution. Further, a process flexible enough to consider material that would not be admissible in an adversary criminal trial, such as letters and affidavits, was sanctioned. Also, the power of the parole authorities over the proceedings was authorized to assure that the delaying tactics and other abuses often present in the traditional criminal trial do not occur. In any case, a parolee cannot use the revocation hearing to relitigate issues determined against him in other forums, such as when the revocation is based on conviction of another crime.

The above Supreme Court mandates are applicable to revocation proceedings which are held after the date of *Morrissey,* or June 29, 1972. The due process requirements of *Morrissey* were not made retroactive.

§ 9.4.4   —The Revocation Hearing—Right to Counsel

In *Morrissey* the Supreme Court stated: "We do not reach or decide the question whether the parolee is entitled to the assistance of retained counsel or to appointed counsel if he is indigent."[60] The Supreme Court did answer that question in *Gagnon v. Scarpelli.*[61]

In *Scarpelli* the United States Supreme Court dealt with the question of whether a previously sentenced probationer was entitled to be represented by state-appointed counsel at a probation revocation hearing. As to parole revocation, the Court relied heavily on *Morrissey v. Brewer,* and stated that it could not perceive any relevant difference between the revocation of parole and the revocation of probation.

The court recognized that despite the informal nature of the proceedings and the absence of technical rules of procedure or evidence, an unskilled or uneducated probationer or parolee might have difficulty in presenting his version of a disputed set of facts without the aid of a lawyer. This was recognized to be particularly true in cases where the proceedings required the examining or cross-examining of witnesses, or the offering or dissecting of complex documentary evidence. However,

---

[59] *Atkins v. Marshall,* 533 F. Supp. 1324 (S.D. Ohio 1982). (A parolee's rights at a revocation hearing were violated when there was a disparity in the notice of reasons for revocation and the parole board's asserted grounds for revocation.); *Morishita v. Morris,* 702 F.2d 207 (10th Cir. 1983). (Written findings in a probation revocation hearing are constitutionally required only when the record is such that a reviewing court is unable to determine the reasons for revocation. Failure to make written findings do not violate a probationer's due process rights when the revocation is based upon a single ground.)

[60] *Morrissey v. Brewer,* 408 U.S. at 389.

[61] *Gagnon v. Scarpelli,* 411 U.S. 778, 71 Ohio Op. 2d 279 (1973).

the Court did not mandate that counsel be appointed for every parolee in all cases, but held that "the need for counsel must be made on a case-by-case basis in the exercise of a sound discretion by the state authority charged with responsibility for administering the probation and parole system."[62]

The Court set no firm guidelines as to when counsel *must* be provided, but said that the state should do so where the indigent probationer or parolee may have difficulty in presenting his version of disputed facts or, if the violation is not disputed, there are substantial reasons in justification or mitigation that make revocation inappropriate. The Court did hold that "in every case in which a request for counsel at a preliminary or final hearing is refused, the grounds for refusal should be stated succinctly in the record."[63]

Courts dealing with the issue of counsel at revocation proceedings have not found *Scarpelli* helpful. The Supreme Court of Indiana, in *Russell v. Douthitt,*[64] stated that the suggestion that the appointment of counsel be made on a case-by-case basis serves to "delude and only becloud the issue and create uncertainty as to what the law is."[65] The court finally threw up its hands, and held:

In our opinion, "on a case-by-case basis" means that those involved in parole revocation can take no other course than to appoint counsel in all cases and to have a full-blown trial for every alleged charge of parole violation.[66]

§ 9.4.5 —The Revocation Hearing—Right to Appointed Counsel

Related to the issue of a right to counsel is the right to appointed counsel for the parolee if he cannot afford to hire one with private funds. It is arguable that counsel must be provided in all cases where retained counsel is permitted. In other words, if the state permits counsel to participate at parole revocation hearings for those who can afford to have one, it should provide counsel at state expense for those who cannot afford one.

The majority of cases still find that the question of whether a revocation proceeding involving a particular parolee is one requiring counsel, is to be determined in the first instance by the paroling authority. The decision is to be made on a case-by-case basis in the exercise of sound discretion and on the guidelines set forth in *Scarpelli.*[67] In contrast, where a revocation proceeding amounts to a resentencing, appointment of counsel for an indigent is required under *Mempa v. Rhay,* and not under the discretionary standards of *Scarpelli.*[68]

Where the facts show that counsel is required, it has been held that lack of authority or funds by a state parole commission to appoint counsel is not a legally

[62] *Id.* at 790.
[63] *Id.* at 791.
[64] *Russell v. Douthitt,* 304 N.E.2d 793 (1973).
[65] *Id.* at 794.
[66] *Id.* at 794.
[67] *Cottle v. Wainwright,* 493 F.2d 397 (5th Cir. 1974).
[68] *United States v. Ross,* 503 F.2d 940 (5th Cir. 1974).

sufficient reason for refusing to appoint counsel for a parolee.[69] Some states have provided for counsel under the guidelines of *Scarpelli* by regulation or statute. The right to counsel at the preliminary hearing in New York is the same test as *Scarpelli*, a case-by-case approach, but the New York rule on final revocation proceedings guarantees the right to counsel.[70] In Indiana the Supreme Court has declared that counsel will be required in all cases.[71]

Scarpelli states that access to counsel is a presumptive right only, but *Preston v. Piggman*[72] held that the burden is on the paroling authority to overcome that presumption. A silent record containing no reasons for denying counsel, or not providing counsel, would open the possibility for a reversal of the proceedings. It would appear that the presumptive right to counsel could be overcome when the parolee is made aware of the charges against him, and the record shows that he understands the nature of the proceedings and is capable of adequately expressing himself and explaining the circumstances. Under *Scarpelli* it is also clear that the presumptive right to counsel applies to both the preliminary and the final revocation hearings.

§ 9.4.6 —Evidence at Revocation Hearing

Morrissey provides that at the preliminary hearing "a parolee may appear and speak in his own behalf; he may bring letters, documents, or individuals who can give relevant information to the hearing officer." The court pointed out that the hearing officer should state the reasons for his decision and the evidence he relied on. Since the preliminary hearing is not a final determination, there is no requirement of "formal findings of fact and conclusions of law" at that stage.

As to the final hearing, *Morrissey* states that the inquiry involved is a narrow one. "The process should be flexible enough to consider evidence including letters, affidavits, and other material that would not be admissible in an adversary criminal trial."[73]

In *Scarpelli* the court makes a distinction between a criminal trial and the revocation hearing.

In a criminal trial, the State is represented by a prosecutor; formal rules of evidence are in force; a defendant enjoys a number of procedural rights which may be lost if not timely raised; and, in a jury trial, a defendant must make a presentation understandable to untrained jurors. In short, a criminal trial under our system is an adversary proceeding with its own unique characteristics. In a revocation hearing, on the other hand, the State is represented not by

---

[69] *Rhodes v. Wainwright*, 378 F. Supp. 329 (M.D. Fla. 1974).

[70] *Donohoe, People ex rel. v. Montanye*, 318 N.E.2d 781 (N.Y. Ct. App. 1974).

[71] *Supra* at nn. 41 and 42; *cf. Passaro v. Commonwealth, Pennsylvania Board of Probation and Parole,* 424 A.2d 561 (Pa. Commw. 1981). (The Board has no duty or responsibility to appoint counsel for an indigent appearing before it.); *Gates v. DeLorenzo,* (2d Cir. 1976), *cert. denied,* 20 Cr. L. 4195 (March 23, 1977), (Due process does not require the participation of counsel in parole release hearings.)

[72] *Preston v. Piggman,* 496 F.2d 270 (6th Cir. Ky. 1974).

[73] *Morrissey v. Brewer,* 408 U.S. at 489.

a prosecutor, but by a parole officer . . .; formal procedures and rules of evidence are not employed; and the members of the hearing body are familiar with the problems and practice of probation or parole.[74]

The reference in *Morrissey* and *Scarpelli* to a revocation hearing as a proceeding not subject to the formal rules of evidence applicable to a criminal trial has raised the question of whether "hearsay" will be permitted in evidence at the revocation hearing. In simple terms, "hearsay" is a statement made by someone outside of the hearing, offered at the hearing to prove the truth of the statement. The main objection to "hearsay" is that the person who made the original statement is not available at the hearing to be questioned or cross-examined. "Hearsay" may be a statement, conduct, or a writing. Therefore, "hearsay" evidence may not be tested for its truthfulness. However, the courts have recognized that "hearsay" can be made under circumstances which assure truthfulness. There are therefore many "exceptions" to the hearsay rule.[75] Although courts have permitted "hearsay" to be considered at the revocation hearings,[76] there is judicial reluctance to accept "hearsay" at the revocation hearings[77] as the sole basis of the final decision.

In the Fourth Circuit, federal probation officers may not use unconstitutionally obtained evidence in federal probation revocation proceedings. In other words, the exclusionary rule applies in that circuit. Nevertheless, the exclusionary rule is *not* required to be followed in *state* revocation proceedings. Consequently, so long as an inmate had the opportunity to litigate the matter in the state court, federal habeas corpus will not be granted.[78]

In the Second Circuit, probation officers, like police officers, need a search warrant to search a probationer's home, or some recognized exception. (The Ninth Circuit is contrary.) Evidence seized without a warrant must be excluded at a subsequent revocation proceeding. However, there is no Fifth or Sixth Amendment right to have counsel present during questioning by a probation officer.[79]

It is becoming increasingly apparent that the record of the hearing is of the utmost importance. If the record clearly shows what evidence was relied on and that the evidence is reasonably related to the decision of a finding of probable cause, or the revocation of parole, then the decision has a much higher chance of survival. When the record does not disclose the reasons and evidence upon which

---

[74] *Gagnon v. Scarpelli*, 411 U.S. 778 at 789, 71 Ohio Op. 2d 279 at 284.

[75] Federal Rules of Evidence, Appendix II.

[76] *Commonwealth v. Kates*, 305 A.2d 701 (1973); *Ward v. Parole Board*, 192 N.W.2d 537 (Mich. App. 1971); *Zizzo v. United States*, 470 F.2d 105 (7th Cir. 1972); *United States v. Miller*, 514 F.2d 41 (9th Cir. 1975); *State v. Marrapese*, 409 A.2d 544 (R.I. 1979); *cf. In re Diane B.*, (D.C. Super. Ct. 1981) 29 Cr. L. 2040. (Hearsay evidence may not be used in the D.C. court to revoke a juvenile's probation.)

[77] *State v. Miller*, 42 Ohio St.2d 102, 71 Ohio Op. 2d 74, 326 N.E.2d 259 (1975); *Birzon v. King*, 469 F.2d 1241 (2d Cir. 1972); *People v. Lewis*, 329 N.E.2d 390 (Ill. App. Ct. 1975); *People ex rel. Wallace v. State*, 417 N.Y.S.2d 531 (N.Y. App. Div. 1979); *Anaya v. State*, 606 P.2d 156 (Nev. 1980).

[78] *Grimsley v. Dodson*, 696 F.2d 303 (4th Cir. 1982).

[79] *United States v. Rea*, 678 F.2d 382 (2d Cir. 1982).

the decision is based, or why "hearsay" was used and not "live" testimony, the courts are more likely to reverse the decision.

It should be noted that rights are subject to waiver. However, courts will not approve a waiver unless it has been a voluntary and knowing waiver of a known right. It is important that the record reflect that the person waiving the right understood what he was doing.

The Fifth and Fourteenth Amendments do not prohibit the introduction of the admissions by a probationer to his probation officer into evidence in a criminal trial. After being convicted of a felony, the defendant was placed on probation. The terms of probation required him to participate in a treatment program, to report to his probation officer periodically, and to be truthful with the officer in all matters. While being interviewed by his probation officer concerning a prior rape and murder, the defendant confessed and was subsequently convicted. The conviction was affirmed. The general obligation to appear before the probation officer and answer questions truthfully did not in itself convert the defendant's otherwise voluntary statements into compelled ones. There was no duty to give *Miranda* warnings. When confronted with questions that the probation officer should reasonably expect to elicit incriminating evidence, the probationer must assert the Fifth Amendment privilege rather than answer if he desires not to incriminate himself. If he chose to answer rather than to assert the privilege, his choice is considered to be voluntary. He was free to claim the privilege and suffers no penalty as a result of his decision to do so. As there was no formal arrest or restraint on his freedom of movement associated with formal arrest, the probationer was not "in custody." The probationer's failure to claim the privilege in a timely manner is not excused by the fact that the probation officer could compel the probationer's attendance and truthful answers, and consciously sought incriminating evidence, that the probationer did not expect questions about his prior criminal conduct, could not seek counsel before attending the meeting, and that there were no observers to guard against abuse or trickery. Further, the reasonably perceived threat of revocation of his probation does not deter the probationer from claiming the privilege. The legal compulsion to attend the meeting with the probation officer and to answer truthfully the questions of the officer who anticipated incriminating answers was held to be indistinguishable from that felt by any witness who is required to appear and to give testimony. Fear of revocation is not an impermissible penalty so as to trigger *Miranda*.

The fact that the statements made by a probationer to his probation officer could well lead to revocation of probation does not make the statements "compelled." Although it is recognized that a state may not impose substantial penalties because a witness elects to exercise his Fifth Amendment rights, the rule does not apply in probation cases where the questioning concerns violations of the terms and conditions of release. A state may require a probationer to appear and discuss matters that affect his probationary status. Such a request alone does not give right to a self-executing privilege. An example would be when a residential restriction is imposed as a condition of probation. As this would not be a criminal act, a claim of refusal to answer on Fifth Amendment grounds would be improper. "Just as there is no right to a jury trial before probation may be revoked, neither is the privilege against compelled self-incrimination available to a probationer. ... [A] state may validly insist on answers to even incriminating questions and hence sensibly administer its probation system, as long as it recognizes that the required answers may not be used in a criminal proceeding. ... [N]othing in the Federal Constitution would prevent a State from revoking probation for a refusal to answer that violated an express condition of probation or from using the probationer's silence as 'one of a number of factors to be considered by a finder of fact' in deciding whether other conditions of probation have been violated." The result would have been opposite had the questioning related solely to new criminal charges not concerning the terms and conditions of probation, or had the probationer been told that his probation would be revoked if he exercised his valid Fifth Amendment rights concerning the new crimes.[80]

Although as an aside and in the context of a confession case, the United States Supreme Court suggested that drug treatment centers receiving federal funds are covered by federal statues that provide for the confidentiality of patient records.[80a] A counselor may inform a patient's probation officer of incriminating statements made by the patient, but may not relate such statements to the police. It was also suggested that the probation officer could not have made the counselor's information available for use in a criminal prosecution.

The voiding of parole because of the failure of the parolee to voluntarily disclose information regarding a pre-parole conspiracy for which he was convicted, violated his Fifth Amendment right against self-incrimination.[81]

If the District Court decides, or the government insists that probation revocation proceedings be held first, the defendant should be given use immunity to testify in the revocation proceedings. The decision was based on the court's supervisory powers and not on constitutional grounds. The exclusionary rules of evidence are not to be applied to probation revocation proceedings since the application of the exclusionary rule would do little to deter constitutional violations.[82]

§ 9.4.7 —Rescission of Parole

"Rescission" of parole raises the question of what Due Process rights an inmate has who has been given a "future parole date" but subsequently has that date changed or withdrawn. There would appear to be three alternatives. First, to consider the "loss" as a revocation, and apply the standards of *Morrissey-Scarpelli.*

---

[80] *Minnesota v. Murphy,* 465 U.S. 420, 34 Cr. L. 3057 (1984).

[81] *Tortora v. Petrovsky,* 545 F. Supp. 569 (W.D. Mo. 1982).

[82] *United States v. Bazzano,* 712 F.2d 826 (3d Cir. 1982). The *Bazzano* decision was not followed in *United States v. Dozier,* 707 F.2d 862 (5th Cir. 1982). (Specifically, the probationer had no constitutional right to be granted judicial immunity for any testimony that he might be wiling to give at the probation revocation hearing.)

Second, to equate the "loss" to a prison disciplinary finding, and apply the standards of *Wolff v. McDonnell*.[83] Third, to treat the "loss" as a denial of parole, and apply the same standards as those applicable to parole hearings in general.

At one time the grant of parole could be summarily rescinded without notice or a hearing prior to final physical release, unless a statute or regulation provided otherwise. The courts, however, have recognized that although the loss of liberty is more grievous to a parolee out on the street, the taking away of a future parole date seems clearly to be a grievous loss subject to some minimal due process protections.[84]

In *Jackson v. Wise*[85] the court analogized the rescission of parole to a prison hearing subject to the requirements of *Wolff v. McDonnell,* and determined that the following were the minimum due process requirements for rescission:

1. advance written notice of the charge
2. written statement by factfinders of the evidence relied on and the reasons for their decision
3. right of prisoner to be present
4. right of prisoner to present witnesses and documentary evidence on his behalf, if so doing would not be unduly hazardous to institutional safety or correctional goals
5. the right, if the prisoner is found illiterate or otherwise incompetent to protect his own interests, to have an attorney-substitute and
6. adjudication of the charges by a panel sufficiently impartial to satisfy due process requirements. Other decisions have also found that minimum due process must accompany the rescission of parole.[86]

However, in *Williams v. United States Bd. of Parole*[87] the court required the full procedural requirements of *Morrissey* and *Scarpelli.*

Decisions can also be found which follow the earlier view that a future date of parole may be rescinded summarily without notice, or a hearing, until the time that the inmate has been physically released from custody of the institution.[88] And, where a prisoner had escaped and was not returned until after his parole release date, a state court held that he was not entitled to a full-scale hearing.[89]

---

[83] *Wolff v. McDonnell,* 418 U.S. 539, 71 Ohio Op. 2d 336 (1974).

[84] *Lepre v. Butler,* 394 F. Supp. 185 (E.D. Pa. 1975).

[85] *Jackson v. Wise,* 390 F. Supp. 19 (C.D. Cal. 1974).

[86] *Id.* at 21. *See also Karger v. Sigler,* 384 F. Supp. 10 (D. Mass. 1974); *Batchelder v. Kenton,* 383 F. Supp. 299 (C.D. Cal. 1974).

[87] *Williams v. United States Bd. of Parole,* 383 F. Supp. 402 (D. Conn. 1974).

[88] *Sexton v. Wise,* 494 F.2d 1176 (5th Cir. 1974); *McIntosh v. Woodward,* 514 F.2d 95 (5th Cir. 1975); *State ex rel. Van Curen v. Ohio Adult Parole Authority,* 45 Ohio St.2d 298, 74 Ohio Op.2d 465, 345 N.E.2d 75 (1976); *Van Curen v. Jago,* 454 U.S. 14 (1981). (When a state does not make parole a "right," the rescission of parole without a hearing violates no constitutional rights of the prisoner.)

[89] *Temple v. Smith,* 548 P.2d 1274 (Utah Sup. Ct. 1976).

§ 9.5 Conditions of Parole

One of the more difficult issues regarding the legal status of parolees is the rights of the individual while on parole. The conditions attached to the issuance of parole frequently conflict with the retained constitutional rights of the parolee.

The "contract" rationale is frequently used as a justification for revocation of the parole after a violation of a particular condition. The acceptance of conditional release is said to prevent the parolee from later claiming that one of the conditions imposed was invalid. This contract theory may be discredited, recognizing that the consent is coerced consent. However, most challenges to the legality of conditions continue to be dismissed by the courts by virtue of the contract theory.

It would appear that the only conditions which courts are likely to invalidate are those that require illegal, immoral, or impossible actions by the parolee. For example, if the pathological nature of one's alcoholism made it impossible for him to abstain from alcohol completely, a condition requiring complete abstention from alcohol would be invalidated as unreasonable.[90] Another condition which would usually be invalidated as unreasonable, even though possible of performance, is a condition of banishment.[91]

Requiring participation in psychological counseling as a condition of probation does not violate any rights of privacy.[92]

Due Process is violated by the automatic revocation of probation because of an indigent probationer's failure to meet a condition of probation requiring him to pay a fine or make restitution. Absent findings that the probationer willfully refused to make bona fide efforts to pay or that alternate forms of punishment, other than imprisonment, are inadequate to meet the state's interests in punishment and deterrence, imprisonment violates the Fourteenth Amendment.[93]

§ 9.5.1 —Free Speech of a Parolee

It is more difficult to predict the validity of conditions which limit the parolee in areas in which free men enjoy broad constitutional rights. These rights, particularly First Amendment freedoms, are respected above other personal rights and thus, the courts generally subject to more intensive review conditions which diminish these freedoms. For example, *Hyland v. Procunier*[94] held that a condition requiring a parolee to secure permission before making any public speech is

---

[90] *Sweeney v. United States,* 353 F.2d 10 (7th Cir. 1965); *See also, cf. State v. Cooper* (N.C. Ct. App. 1981), 29 Cr. L. 2125. (A credit card defendant's condition of probation that he be forbidden to drive a car between midnight and 5:30 a.m. was held to be reasonably related to his offense and valid.)

[91] *Bird v. State,* 190 A.2d 804 (Ct. App. Md. 1963); *But cf. State v. Morgan* (La. Sup. Ct. 1980), 28 Cr. L. 2260. (A probation condition that required a woman convicted of attempted prostitution to stay out of the French Quarter was valid.)

[92] *United States v. Stine,* 675 F.2d 69 (3d Cir. 1982), 31 Cr. L. 2081.

[93] *Bearden v. Georgia,* 461 U.S. 660, 103 S. Ct. 2064, 76 L.Ed.2d 221 (1983).

[94] *Hyland v. Procunier,* 311 F. Supp. 749 (N.D. Cal. 1970).

invalid. Such a condition would have "an unwarranted chilling effect on the exercise by plaintiff of his undisputed rights."[95]

A similar decision was handed down in *Sobell v. Reed*[96] where the parolee was denied the right to give an anti-war speech. The court found that this denial of First Amendment freedoms was beyond the parole authority. Such freedoms may be restricted only "upon a showing that such prevention or withholding of permission is necessary to safeguard against specific, concretely described and highly likely dangers of misconduct by plaintiff himself."[97]

In re Mannino[98] upheld a condition prohibiting speaking at and participating in public demonstrations because the probationer's offense (kicking a policeman) had occurred during the heat of such events. The reason for the condition was the explosive temperament of the defendant. However, a ban against writing and distributing written materials was held invalid because of a lack of relation to the underlying offense.

Similarly, a condition of probation which stipulated that the defendant not communicate with any of his children, except through the State Department of Welfare, and not have any of his children live with him until they reach eighteen years of age, was not violative of due process. The defendant had been convicted of aggravated crimes against nature, directed at his children.[99]

§ 9.5.2 —Search of a Parolee

A difficult question is presented when the parolee's Fourth Amendment rights are questioned. That amendment protects the citizen from unreasonable interference with his privacy by the government and generally requires that a warrant be obtained before an official may undertake a search. However, exceptions to the rule exist. The Fourth Amendment prohibits only *unreasonable* searches. When one is arrested, a search incident to that arrest may be lawfully made. A search may also be undertaken when reasonable cause exists to believe that the law has been or is being broken and a search warrant cannot be obtained without unreasonable delay. Even without a warrant, a search may be made if one waives his Fourth Amendment protection by consenting to the search. All other searches have been held to be unconstitutional. The argument is, of course, made that the parolee, as a condition of parole, consents to a search by the parole authorities.

In searches of parolees and probationers the courts have focused on the "reasonableness" of the search, and the admissibility of any evidence found while conducting the search in later criminal or revocation proceedings. In *Latta v. Fitzharris*[100] the court held that where a parolee was arrested by his parole officer with a pipe

---

[95] *Id.* at 750; *See also, Barton v. Malley,* 626 F.2d 151 (10th Cir. 1980).
[96] *Sobell v. Reed,* 327 F. Supp. 1294 (S.D. N.Y. 1971).
[97] *Id.* at 1306.
[98] *In re Mannino,* 92 Cal. Rptr. 880 (Ct. App. Cal. 1971).
[99] *State v. Credeur,* 328 So. 2d 59 (La. Sup. Ct. 1976).
[100] *Latta v. Fitzharris,* 521 F.2d 246 (9th Cir. 1975).

full of marijuana in his hand, a warrantless search of that parolee's home by the parole officer and accompanying police officers was reasonable. The use of evidence obtained by such a search was not limited to parole revocation.

A parole officer's searches and seizures are subject to a less stringent standard than the probable cause required for searches of ordinary citizens. In relationships with their parole officers, parolees are not entitled to the full protection of the Fourth Amendment. Searches and seizures should be subject to the "reasonable suspicion" standard. The parole officer must only be able to point to specific and articulable facts that, taken together with rational inferences, reasonably warrant belief that a condition of parole is being violated. With respect to police, however, the parolee is on the same footing as an ordinary citizen.[101]

The traditional view on searches of parolees is set forth in *People v. Hernandez,*[102] which states that a search by a parole officer of the person, residence, or effects of a parolee is not a violation of the Fourth Amendment, because it is done without a warrant, without consent, and without probable cause. However, other courts have determined that a condition which requires a parolee to submit to searches at any time is too broad, and that a restriction on Fourth Amendment rights cannot exceed the legitimate needs of the probation or parole process.[103]

A condition of probation, allowing for the warrantless search of a probationer's person and property by both his probation supervisors and law enforcement officers, does not violate the probationer's Fourth Amendment rights. Using a three-part analysis, the court determined that the condition would: 1) dissuade the probationer from again possessing illegal drugs, 2) promote his rehabilitation, and 3) further the legitimate needs of law enforcement. Even though they do have some Fourth Amendment rights, probationers are subject to special limitations and have a diminished expectation of privacy.[104]

However, if the police attempt to avoid the Fourth Amendment by using the parole officer as their agent in making a search when otherwise a warrant would be required, the search becomes unreasonable.[105] The Court in *United States v. Winsett*[106] held that evidence obtained in violation of the Fourth Amendment is admissible in revocation proceedings if, at the time of the search, the law enforcement

---

[101] *United States v. Scott,* 678 F.2d 32 (5th Cir. 1982).

[102] *People v. Hernandez,* 40 Cal. Rptr. 100 (1964); *State v. Bollinger,* (N.J. 1979), 25 Cr. L. 2447; *State v. Coahran,* 620 P.2d 116 (Wash. App. 1980).

[103] *United States v. Consuelo-Gonzales,* 521 F.2d 259 (9th Cir. 1975); *Tamez v. State,* 534 S. W.2d 686 (1976); *United States v. Dally,* 606 F.2d 861 (9th Cir. 1979); *Gomez v. Superior Ct.,* 132 Cal. App.3d 947 (Cal. App. 1982). (A parolee may not be required as a condition of his parole to completely waive his Fourth Amendment protection against warrantless searches by police officers. A warrantless search by police officers without the knowledge of the parolee's supervisor and for purposes other than the administration of his parole cannot be justified by such a waiver.)

[104] *Owens v. Kelley,* 681 F.2d 1362 (11th Cir. 1982).

[105] *See People v. Kanos,* 14 Cal. App. 3d 642 (1971); *But cf. Quigg v. France,* 502 F. Supp. 516 (D.C. Mont. 1980). (A parolee may be searched by a parole officer assisted by sheriff's deputies if the search is for a parole purpose.)

[106] *United States v. Winsett,* 518 F.2d 51 (9th Cir. 1975).

officers did not know or have reason to believe that the suspect was on probation. This follows the almost unanimous view that the exclusionary rule does not usually apply in probation revocation proceedings.[107]

As pointed out by the court in *United States v. Vandemark*,[108] "the prime purpose of the exclusionary rule is to deter unlawful police conduct." The court held that the illegally seized evidence could be considered in imposing sentence on the probationer.

A reasonable warrantless search of the personal belongings of a half-way house resident has also been upheld.[109]

The most recent case involving search of a probationer's home by a probation officer is *Griffin v. Wisconsin*.[110] Wisconsin law places probationers in the legal custody of the State Department of Health and Social Services and renders them subject to conditions set by the rules and regulations established by the department. One such regulation permitted any probation officer to search a probationer's home without a warrant as long as his supervisor approved and as long as there were "reasonable grounds" to believe the presence of contraband. In determining whether "reasonable grounds" exist, an officer was required to consider a variety of factors, including information provided by an informant, the reliability and specificity of that information, the informant's reliability, the officer's experience with the probationer, and the need to verify compliance with the rules of probation and with the law. Another Wisconsin regulation forbade a probationer to possess a firearm without a probation officer's advance approval.

Upon information received from a police detective that there were or might be guns in a probationer's apartment, probation officers searched the apartment and found a handgun. The probationer was tried and convicted of the felony of possession of a firearm by a convicted felon. The trial court denied his motion to suppress the evidence seized during the search. It concluded that no warrant was necessary and that the search was reasonable.

The United States Supreme Court held that the warrantless search of the probationer's residence was "reasonable" within the meaning of the Fourth Amendment because it was conducted pursuant to a regulation that is itself a reasonable response to the "special needs" of a probation system.

The Court recognized that supervision of probationers was a "special need" of the State that justified departures from the usual warrant and probable-cause requirements of the Fourth Amendment. Supervision was necessary to ensure that probation restrictions were in fact observed, that the probation served a genuine

---

[107] *United States v. Brown*, 488 F.2d 94 (5th Cir. 1973); *United States v. Farmer*, 512 F.2d 160 (6th Cir. 1975); *United States v. Hill*, 447 F.2d 817 (7th Cir. 1971); *State v. Alfaro*, 678 F.2d 382 (2d Cir. 1982); *But see, United States v. Rea*, 678 F.2d 826 (3d Cir. 1982). (Probation officers, like police officers, need a search warrant to search a probationer's home, or some recognized exception. Evidence seized without a warrant must be excluded at a subsequent revocation proceeding.)

[108] *United States v. Vandemark*, 522 F.2d 1019 (9th Cir. 1975).

[109] *United States v. Lewis*, 400 F. Supp. 1046 (S.D. N.Y. 1975).

[110] *Griffin v. Wisconsin*, 483 U.S. 868 (1987).

rehabilitation period, and that the community was not harmed by the probationer's being at large.

Here, the search regulation was valid because the "special needs" of Wisconsin's probation system made the warrant requirement impracticable and justified replacement of the probable-cause standard with the regulation's "reasonable grounds" standard. It was reasonable to dispense with the warrant requirement here, since such a requirement would interfere to an appreciable degree with the probation system by setting up a magistrate rather than the probation officer as the determiner of how closely the probationer must be supervised. It would also make it more difficult for probation officials to respond quickly to evidence of misconduct. It would reduce the deterrent effect that the possibility of expeditious searches would otherwise create. Moreover, unlike a police officer who conducts an ordinary search, a probation officer is required to have the probationer's welfare particularly in mind.

It was felt by the Court that a probable-cause requirement would unduly disrupt the probation system by reducing the deterrent effect of the supervisory arrangement and by lessening the range of information the probation officer could consider in deciding whether to search. A probation agency must be able to act based upon a lesser degree of certainty in order to intervene before the probationer damages himself or society. It must be able to proceed on the basis of its entire experience with the probationer and to assess probabilities in the light of its knowledge of his life, character, and circumstances. Thus, the Supreme Court held that it was reasonable to permit information provided by a police officer, whether or not on the basis of firsthand knowledge, to support a probationary search. All that was required was that the information provided indicated, as it did here, the likelihood of facts justifying the search.

The conclusion that the regulation in question was constitutional made it unnecessary to consider whether any search of a probationer's home is lawful when there are "reasonable grounds" to believe contraband is present. The Supreme Court deferred this issue to another day.

§ 9.6   Conclusion

The decisions of *Morrissey v. Brewer* and *Gagnon v. Scarpelli* have defined the center limits of procedural Due Process with respect to parole revocation. The requirements for granting and rescission of parole have yet to be fully developed. Another confused area is the status of inmates on furlough or other work release programs. Calling them "inmates" or "parolees" does not answer the question of what process is due if their status is changed. Hopefully, the courts will not require the full procedural Due Process requirements of *Morrissey*. If so, the result could well be a reduction of such release programs, and fewer inmates released into viable community activities.

The administrative decisions of granting, rescinding, revoking, and continuing of parole will always be subject to judicial attack by those adversely affected. Disenchantment with the parole process has led to movements to abolish indeterminate sentencing, upon which parole is based. Whether or not the proponents of determinate or indeterminate sentencing ultimately win out, the majority of jurisdictions in the foreseeable future will be faced with complying with procedural due process requirements necessary for a "fundamentally fair" parole system.

The federal system of parole will be abolished in 1992, and is replaced by the United States Sentencing Commission. Although the new scheme was held to be constitutional in *Mistretta,* only time will tell how the relationship between sentencing and release decisions will develop.

Chapter 10

RIGHT TO REHABILITATION PROGRAMS, RIGHT TO MEDICAL AID, AND RIGHT TO LIFE

§ 10.1   Introduction

The eight areas of inmate complaints which have been most frequently litigated by the courts in recent years—use of force, visitation and association rights, mail, isolated confinement, religious rights, legal services, disciplinary proceedings and parole—have been analyzed in Chapters 2 through 9. This chapter will discuss four fact situations which are faced less frequently by the judiciary, but which are nevertheless of importance to both inmates and prison administrators. The four areas to be discussed are an inmate's right to rehabilitation programs, an inmate's right to medical aid, the death-row inmate's right to life as enunciated by recent Supreme Court cases concerning the use of death as a criminal penalty, and an inmate's civil disabilities.

§ 10.2   Right to Rehabilitation Programs

Many state constitutions and statutes encourage rehabilitation of inmates.[1] Such programs are considered essential by virtually all penologists if incarceration is to reduce the incidence of crime. For example, the American Correctional Association has stated that "prison serves most effectively for the protection of society against crime when its major emphasis is on rehabilitation."[2] A commission appointed by President Lyndon Johnson to study the crime problem in the United

---

[1] *E.g., see,* R.I. Gen. Laws Ann. 13-3-1 (1956).

[2] The American Correctional Association, Manual of Correctional Standards 10 (3d ed. 1966).

155

States concluded that "rehabilitation of offenders to prevent their return to crime is, in general, the most promising way to achieve this end (reduction of crime)."[3]

§ 10.2.1   —Judicial Decisions

Despite the view that rehabilitative programs should be the core of any correctional system, the courts have refused to hold that there is an absolute right to rehabilitation during incarceration.

In *Padgett v. Stein*[4] inmates of a county prison sought enforcement of a consent decree entered into with prison authorities to remedy allegedly unconstitutional conditions of confinement. The inmates contended that convicted inmates have a constitutional right to receive meaningful rehabilitative treatment, and that the failure of the prison authorities to afford inmates rehabilitative programs constituted cruel and unusual punishment. The court rejected the inmates' contentions on the ground that there is no constitutional duty imposed on a governmental entity to rehabilitate prisoners. The court went on to state that

> . . . whether penal institutions should undertake to rehabilitate prisoners at all—in view of the serious questions which exist with respect to the effectiveness of rehabilitation programs—is a social policy question which should be resolved by the representative branches of government—i.e., the legislative and executive branches—and not by the courts.[5]

Courts have repeatedly stated that inmates possess no constitutional right to rehabilitative treatment.[6] One court has characterized the duty owed to an inmate by prison officials as the duty "to exercise ordinary care for his protection and to keep him safe and free from harm."[7]

In *Holt v. Sarver,*[8] however, a district court did state that when examining the totality of conditions within a penal institution, a federal court should consider the lack of any meaningful rehabilitation programs as a factor "in the overall constitutional equation before the Court."[9] But since that court had previously stated that lack of rehabilitative opportunities was not, by itself, a defect of constitutional mag-

---

[3] The President's Commission on Law Enforcement and Administration of Justice, Task Force Report: Corrections 16 (1967).

[4] *Padgett v. Stein,* 406 F. Supp. 287 (M.D. Pa. 1976).

[5] *Id.* at 296; *Pace v. Fauver,* 479 F. Supp. 456 (D.N.J. 1979), *aff'd,* 694 F.2d 860 (4th Cir. 1981); *Bresolin v. Morris,* 558 P.2d 1350 (Wash. Sup. Ct. 1977); *State v. Damon,* 20 Cr. L. 2530 (Wash. Ct. App. Jan. 31, 1977).

[6] *Russell v. Oliver,* 392 F. Supp. 470 (W.D. Va. 1975); *Lunsford v. Reynolds,* 376 F. Supp. 526 (W.D. Va. 1974); *Wright v. Rushen,* 642 F.2d 1129 (9th Cir. 1981); *Rucker v. Meachum,* 513 F. Supp. 32 (W.D. Okla. 1980).

[7] *Wilson v. Kelley,* 294 F. Supp. 1005 (N.D. Ga. 1968), *aff'd per curiam,* 393 U.S. 266 (1969); *Graham v. Vann,* 394 So. 2d 180 (Fla. App. 1981); *Layne v. Vinzant,* 657 F.2d 468 (1st Cir. 1981); *Leonardo v. Moran,* 611 F.2d 397 (1st Cir. 1979).

[8] *Holt v. Sarver,* 309 F. Supp. 362 (E.D. Ark. 1970), *aff'd,* 442 F.2d 304 (8th Cir. 1971).

[9] *Id.* at 379.

nitude, it was evident that the prison administrators could remove the absence of rehabilitative programs from federal judicial consideration. They could do so by rectifying the other major deficiencies in the institution. The court tacitly recognized this by omitting lack of rehabilitative services from its list of defects that had to be corrected. The court which decided *Holt v. Sarver* has since required that an overall program for treatment and rehabilitation of the inmates be submitted to the court.[10]

Lack of meaningful rehabilitative opportunities is one of the grounds upon which several state prison systems have been declared to be unconstitutional.[11] In *James v. Wallace*[12] it was noted that courts have not made a positive rehabilitative program a constitutional right. It is clear, however, that a penal system cannot be operated in such a manner that it impedes the ability of inmates to attempt their own rehabilitation, or simply to avoid physical, mental, or social deterioration. The court's opinion in *Alberti v. Sheriff of Harris Co., Tex.*[13] was more specific when it ordered officials who were responsible for the operation and maintenance of a county jail to provide adequate vocational and educational programs to foster the inmates' rehabilitation. However, an inmate has no constitutional right to participate in community programs, to enroll and attend classes in college outside the prison, nor to visit with relatives outside the prison.[14]

Another aspect of the rehabilitation program is the extent of a state's right to rehabilitate its inmates without the consent of the inmates. Aversion therapy—the so-called "Clockwork Orange" technique—has been held to be cruel and unusual punishment, not rehabilitative treatment, and is thus unconstitutional. In *Knecht v. Gillman*[15] severely nauseating injections were used to produce what the officials called a "Pavlovian" aversion to minor infractions of prison rules. The court prohibited the treatment program, holding such sanctions to be cruel and unusual punishment, violating the Eighth Amendment, and not treatment. In such cases the courts look to the substance of a program, not its name or label. Labeling a program as "treatment," rather than "punishment," makes no difference in terms of the constitutional requirements which must be met.[16]

Short of aversion therapy, courts have been sympathetic toward state requirements that inmates be enrolled, either voluntarily or involuntarily, in educationally oriented rehabilitative programs. In *Rutherford v. Hutto*[17] a state was held to have a

---

[10] *Finney v. Arkansas Board of Corrections*, 505 F.2d 194, 209 (8th Cir. 1974).

[11] *Miller v. Carson*, 401 F. Supp. 835, 900 (M.D. Fla. 1975); *Battle v. Anderson*, 376 F. Supp. 402 (E.D. Okla. 1974); *Inmates v. Allegheny County Jail v. Pierce*, 612 F.2d 754 (3d Cir. 1979).

[12] *James v. Wallace*, 406 F. Supp. 318 (M.D. Ala. 1976); *Morris v. Travisono*, 499 F. Supp. 149 (D. R.I. 1980).

[13] *Alberti v. Sheriff of Harris Co., Tex.*, 406 F. Supp. 649 (S.D. Tex. 1975); *Ohlinger v. Watson*, 652 F.2d 775, 28 Cr. L. 2321 (9th Cir. 1980).

[14] *Breedlove v. Cripe*, 511 F. Supp. 467 (N.D. Tex. 1981).

[15] *Knecht v. Gillman*, 488 F.2d 1136 (8th Cir. 1973).

[16] *Clonce v. Richardson*, 379 F. Supp. 338 (W.D. Mo. 1974).

[17] *Rutherford v. Hutto*, 377 F. Supp. 268 (E.D. Ark. 1974).

sufficient interest in the elimination of illiteracy among its convicts, including adults, to justify its requirement that illiterate convicts attend classes which were designed to bring them up to at least a fourth grade reading level. More than mere attendance at such classes can be required; meaningful participation can be encouraged by sanctions for non-participation. In *Jackson v. McLemore*[18] a disciplinary action which arose from an inmate's refusal to comply with a prison teacher's instruction to spell in a class attended by the inmate under a compulsory educational program was held not to violate the inmate's constitutional right to be let alone.

In conjunction with the discussion of involuntary rehabilitative programs, it should be noted that the basically coercive nature of prison life severely undercuts any notion that an inmate's consent to treatment is motivated primarily by the inmate's desire to be rehabilitated, i.e., is not coerced. In *McGee v. Aaron*[19] the court recognized implicitly that consent may not always be genuine, but merely the least of several evils. That case involved the sufficiency of the reasons given for denial of parole. One of the reasons given was the parole board's estimation of the need for the inmate to complete his high school equivalency and to complete a training program which would provide him with a salable skill. The court upheld the decision, thus giving the inmate a concrete goal to train toward; not some ideal form of rehabilitation, but freedom in the form of early parole.

The voluntariness of an inmate's consent to participation in therapeutic medical experimentation and research is also suspect. Modern medical research and drug testing techniques require the participation of large numbers of subjects for substantial periods of time. Prisons provide an excellent source for such volunteers. However, due to the indigency of most inmates and the emphasis which parole boards place upon cooperative activity by inmates, there is a real question as to whether true consent is ever obtainable from inmates for their participation in sometimes painful or dangerous medical experimentation.[20]

A patient has a right to refuse drug treatment. The right is adequately protected by hospital regulations that provide a series of informal consultations and interviews to determine, from a medical standpoint, whether compelled administration of drugs is necessary. It is not necessary to provide the patient with a due process hearing, a system of "patient advocates," or an independent decisionmaker.[21]

---

[18] *Jackson v. McLemore*, 523 F.2d 838 (8th Cir. 1975); *Mukmuk v. Comm'r Dept. of Corr. Ser.*, 529 F.2d 272 (2d Cir. 1976).

[19] *McGee v. Aaron*, 523 F.2d 825 (7th Cir. 1975).

[20] Comment, NON-THERAPEUTIC PRISON REARCH: AN ANALYSIS OF POTENTIAL LEGAL REMEDIES, 39 Alb. L. Rev. 799 (1975); *Bailey v. Talley*, 481 F. Supp. 203 (D. Md. 1979).

[21] *Rennie v. Klein*, 653 F.2d 836 (3d Cir. 1981), *vacated and remanded* in light of *Youngberg v. Romeo*, 457 U.S. 307 (1982).

The scope and nature of rehabilitation are left largely to the discretion of prison authorities. In *Sellers v. Ciccone*,[22] which involved rejection of long-term inmates for admission to an X-ray technician training program, the court stated that, absent arbitrariness or caprice, the balance between individual benefit and institutional benefit is for prison officials to determine. The court declined to intervene in order to meet the desires of the individual inmate. However, in certain situations courts will order specific rehabilitative opportunities to be made available prior to specific individual inmates or classes of inmates. In *Cudnik v. Kreiger*[23] pretrial detainees were held to be entitled to continue with the methadone treatment program in which they had been involved prior to their detention.

There is no requirement that a specialized treatment program be available prior to a transfer of a state prisoner to a federal institution under 18 U.S.C. § 5003(a).[24]

§ 10.2.2   —Analogy of Right to Treatment in Other Areas

In the past few years, several courts have recognized that certain groups of persons who have been deprived of their liberty have a right to treatment. These cases were based, however, on statutory interpretation and not on any constitutional right. Thus, in *Rouse v. Cameron*[25] a federal appellate court held that the District of Columbia['s] Hospitalization of the Mentally Ill Act required treatment programs for persons who were involuntarily committed to a mental health facility after their acquittal by reason of insanity. Minnesota's Hospitalization and Commitment Act has been interpreted to confer a statutory right upon persons who are involuntarily civilly committed to state institutions to receive minimally adequate treatment while so institutionalized.[26] In *New York State Assn. for Retard. Ch., Inc. v. Carey*[27] an expansion of current notions of the right to treatment of involuntarily civilly committed mental patients occurred when inmates of state mental facilities were held to have a constitutional right to some treatment regardless of whether their confinement was voluntary or involuntary.

---

[22] *Sellers v. Ciccone*, 530 F.2d 199 (8th Cir. 1976); *Yusaf Asad Madyun v. Thompson*, 657 F.2d 868 (7th Cir. 1981). (In order to maintain an action based upon insufficient opportunities for vocational and educational training, it is necessary to show that prison environment threatens a prisoner's mental and physical well-being.)

[23] *Cudnik v. Kreiger*, 392 F. Supp. 305 (N.D. Ohio 1974); *Gawreys v. D.C. General Hospital*, 480 F. Supp. 853 (D.D.C. 1979); *cf. Holly v. Rapone*, 476 F. Supp. 226 (E.D. Pa. 1979). (There is no constitutional right to receive methadone.); *United States ex rel. Walker v. Fayette County, Pennsylvania*, 599 F.2d 573 (3d Cir. 1979). (State law did not require the establishment of methadone maintenance facilities at corrective institutions, therefore, the county was not obligated to provide methadone to its prisoners.)

[24] *Howe v. Smith*, 452 U.S. 473 (1981).

[25] *Rouse v. Cameron*, 373 F.2d 451 (D.C. Cir. 1966).

[26] *Welsch v. Likins*, 373 F. Supp. 487 (D. Minn. 1974).

[27] *New York State Assn. for Retard. Ch., Inc. v. Carey*, 393 F. Supp. 715 (E.D. N.Y. 1975).

In *O'Connor v. Donaldson*[28] the United States Supreme Court made specific note of its refusal to decide whether mental patients have a constitutional right to treatment as a consequence of their detention by the state. The Fifth Circuit Court of Appeals had concluded[29] that where a non-dangerous patient was involuntarily committed to a state mental hospital under a civil commitment procedure, the only constitutionally permissible purpose of such confinement was to provide treatment, and that such confinement must involve rehabilitative treatment, or minimally adequate habilitation and care where rehabilitation was impossible, in order to justify the confinement. The Court of Appeals made a careful distinction between the rights of those who are civilly committed for an indefinite term and those who are adjudged guilty of a specific offense and who are sentenced for a fixed term. The Supreme Court's refusal to affirm even this relatively simple distinction suggests that the Court will not require, at least upon a constitutional basis, rehabilitative treatment for ordinary prisoners in the near future.

The United States Supreme Court held that involuntarily committed mentally retarded persons have, under the Fourteenth Amendment Due Process Clause, constitutionally protected liberty interests in reasonably safe conditions of confinement, freedom from unreasonable bodily restraints, and such minimally adequate training as reasonably may be required by such interests. The proper standard for determining whether the state has adequately protected such rights is whether professional judgment has been exercised. The judgment of a qualified professional is entitled to a presumption of correctness. Liability may only be imposed when the decision is such a substantial departure from accepted professional judgment as to demonstrate that the decision was not based on professional judgment.[30]

Certain trends in Juvenile Law may eventually affect the right to rehabilitative treatment in prison. The Juvenile Court Act for the District of Columbia mandates treatment services for juvenile pretrial detainees[31] and for juveniles adjudicated to be delinquent.[32] In *Morales v. Turman*[33] it was held that an incarcerated juvenile must be involved in a cohesive treatment strategy which has been professionally designed to suit his individual needs and to achieve his rehabilitation and return to the community. Without such a program the involuntary commitment of the juvenile would amount to an arbitrary exercise of governmental power in violation of

---

[28] *O'Connor v. Donaldson*, 422 U.S. 563 (1975); *See Mills v. Rogers*, 457 U.S. 291 (1982). (The United States Supreme Court reversed a lower court decision that mental patients who are involuntarily committed have a federal constitutional right to refuse treatment with antipsychotic drugs. The decision must be reexamined by the lower court in light of an intervening state supreme court decision concerning noninstutionalized mental patients.)

[29] *Donaldson v. O'Connor*, 493 F.2d 507 (5th Cir. 1974), *vacated and remanded*, 422 U.S. 563 (1975).

[30] *Youngberg v. Romeo*, 457 U.S. 307 (1982).

[31] *Creek v. Stone*, 379 F.2d 106 (D.C. Cir. 1967).

[32] *In re Elmore*, 382 F.2d 125 (D.C. Cir. 1967).

[33] *Morales v. Turman*, 383 F. Supp. 53 (E.D. Tex. 1974), was reversed. *Morales v. Turman*, 535 F.2d 864 (5th Cir. 1976). The court of appeals held that the case be remanded back to the district court because it was reversible error for the district court not to empanel a three-judge court to hear the case as required by 28 U.S.C. Sec. 2281.

due process. In *Long v. Powell*[34] the United States Supreme Court ruled that a juvenile who has been adjudged not amenable to rehabilitation within the programs regularly conducted by his state for that purpose cannot be committed to such programs without provision for greater protection, security, and rehabilitative treatment.

One of the consequences of conviction under a habitual sex offender statute, which usually carries a sentence of from one day to life, seems to be a right to rehabilitative treatment. In *People v. Feagley*[35] the California Supreme Court ruled that a statutory scheme which provides for confinement of mentally disordered sex offenders for an indefinite period in prison without treatment violates the cruel and unusual punishment clauses of the state and federal constitutions. However, judicial expansion of the indefinitely sentenced inmate's right to treatment[36] has motivated the New York legislature to alter its habitual sex offender statute so as to eliminate such a right.[37]

In *Ohlinger v. Watson*[38] the court held that the goal of the Oregon statutory scheme for sex offenders is rehabilitation. Consequently, sex offenders in Oregon have a right to individual treatment that will afford them a reasonable opportunity to be cured or to improve their mental conditions. Further, such treatment is also required by Due Process.

As noted, many state statutes and constitutions say that rehabilitation is an objective of their correctional systems.[39] It is, therefore, possible that courts in the future will demand that prison administrators implement, with specific programs, the state's statutory and constitutional requirement of rehabilitation programs. Judge David Bazelon, the author of several right-to-treatment decisions from the Federal Circuit Court of Appeals for the District of Columbia, has written that:

> The rationale for the right to treatment is clear. If society confines a man for the benevolent purpose of helping him . . . then its right to so withhold his freedom depends entirely upon whether help is in fact provided. . . . When the legislature justifies confinement by a promise of treatment, it thereby commits the community to provide the resources necessary to fulfill the promise.[40]

§ 10.3   Right to Medical Aid

Inmates in state and federal institutions have sought redress in the federal court system for the medical treatment they have received or failed to receive. The com-

---

[34] *Long v. Powell*, 388 F. Supp. 422 (N.D. Ga. 1975), *jud. vac.*, 423 U.S. 808 (1975) (*dismissed as moot*).

[35] *People v. Feagley*, 14 Cal. App. 3d 338, 535 P.2d 373 (Cal. Sup. Ct. 1975).

[36] *People v. Wilkins*, 23 App. Div. 2d 178, 259 N.Y.S.2d 462 (N.Y. App. Div. 1965).

[37] *People v. Hutchings*, 74 Misc.2d 15, 343 N.Y.S.2d 845 (Cortland County Court 1973).

[38] *Ohlinger v. Watson*, 652 F.2d 775 (9th Cir. 1980) 28 Cr. L. 2321.

[39] *See* n. 1 *supra*.

[40] Bazelon, IMPLEMENTING THE RIGHT TO TREATMENT, 36 U.Chi.L. Rev. 742, 748-49 (1969).

plaints about medical treatment have included claims about the adequacy and nature of the medical care that inmates have received, allegations of a total denial of medical care, improper medical care, inadequate care and conduct of prison officials attendant to the medical care.

The power of the federal courts to adjudicate an inmate's complaint about medical treatment requires that a federal right be involved in the medical treatment.[41] The inmate must allege the presence of a federally protected right. Several federally protected rights have been enunciated by the federal courts in medical treatment cases:

1. Right to due process of law under the Fifth or Fourteenth Amendments.[42] The due process right has been couched in terms of the inmate's right to be free from an abuse of discretion on the part of prison administrators;[43] protection from unconstitutional administrative action;[44] protection of an inmate's life and health from administrative action.[45]
2. Right to be free from the infliction of cruel and unusual punishments guaranteed by the Eighth Amendment.[46] The Eighth Amendment right has been found when there is an intentional denial of needed medical care, or when a prison official's conduct indicates deliberate indifference to medical needs of inmates.

Despite the willingness of federal courts to hear cases which involve the federally protected rights of inmates to medical aid, there are limits to what inmates can expect to accomplish through the courts. In *Priest v. Cupp*[47] the court explained that neither federal nor state constitutional prohibitions of cruel and unusual punishment guarantee any inmate that he will be free from or cured of all real or imagined medical disabilities while he is in custody. What is required is that he be afforded such medical care, in the form of diagnosis and treatment, as is reasonably available under the circumstances of his confinement and medical condition.

---

[41] A federal inmate complaining about medical treatment in the institution utilizes the federal habeas corpus procedure. A state inmate may use a Civil Rights Action (42 U.S.C. 1983) or the federal habeas corpus procedure. *See* Chapter 11, *infra*, for a discussion of prisoner's remedies.

[42] *See* Chapters 8, 9, *supra*, for a discussion of due process of law.

[43] *Shannon v. Lester*, 519 F.2d 76 (6th Cir. 1975); *Derrickson v. Keve*, 390 F. Supp. 905 (D. Del. 1975); *Nickolson v. Choctaw County, Alabama*, 498 F. Supp. 295 (S.D. Ala. 1980); *Lareau v. Manson*, 507 F. Supp. 1177 (D. Conn. 1980), *modified in* 651 F.2d 96 (2d Cir. 1981).

[44] *Clements v. Turner*, 364 F. Supp. 270 (D. Utah 1973).

[45] *Hoitt v. Vitek*, 497 F.2d 598 (1st Cir. 1974); *Runnels v. Rosendale*, 499 F.2d 733 (9th Cir. 1974); *Johnson v. Harris*, 479 F. Supp. 333 (S.D. N.Y. 1979).

[46] *Bishop v. Stoneman*, 508 F.2d 1224 (2d Cir. 1974); *Russell v. Sheffer*, 528 F.2d 318 (4th Cir. 1975). See Comment, THE EIGHTH AMENDMENT: MEDICAL TREATMENT OF PRISONERS AS CRUEL AND UNUSUAL PUNISHMENT, 1 Cap.U.L. Rev. 83 (1972). *Estelle v. Gamble*, 429 U.S. 97 (1976); *Burks v. Teasdale*, 492 F. Supp. 650 (W.D. Mo. 1980); *Hampton v. Holmesburg Prison Officials*, 546 F.2d 1077 (3d Cir. 1976); *Kelsey v. Ewing*, 652 F.2d 4 (8th Cir. 1981); *Inmates of Allegheny County Jail v. Pierce*, 612 F.2d 754 (3d Cir. 1979); *Duncan v. Duckworth*, 644 F.2d 653 (7th Cir. 1981).

[47] *Priest v. Cupp*, 545 P.2d 917 (Or. Ct. App. 1976).

Just as prison officials cannot deny all medical aid, inmates cannot expect a flawless medical services system. Consequently, litigation involving the medical rights of inmates has now focused upon the nature of so-called adequate or reasonable medical care.

What amount of medical aid is adequate is largely dependent upon the facts of each case. In *Gates v. Collier*[48] the Fifth Circuit Court of Appeals reviewed the medical treatment which was available at the Mississippi State Penitentiary. With over 1800 inmates, the prison administration relied upon one full-time physician, several inmate assistants, and a substandard hospital to provide medical care. The court ruled that the services and facilities were inadequate and ordered the prison administration: (1) to employ such additional medical personnel as necessary so that the prison's medical staff would consist of at least three full-time physicians, one of which must be a psychiatrist and another the prison's chief medical officer,[49] two full-time dentists, two full-time trained physicians' assistants, six full-time registered or licensed practical nurses, one medical records librarian, and two medical clerical personnel, and to obtain the consultant services of a radiologist and a pharmacist; (2) to comply with the general standards of the American Correctional Association relating to medical services for prisoners; (3) to have the prison hospital and equipment brought into compliance with state licensing requirements for a hospital and infirmary, including adequate treatment for the chronically ill; (4) to refrain from punishment of inmates who seek medical aid unless the superintendent makes an express finding that the inmate sought medical care unnecessarily and for malingering purposes; and (5) to refrain from the use of inmates to fill any of the above described civilian medical staff, but to encourage utilization of trained and competent inmates to supplement the above minimal civilian medical staff.[50] As in most "treatment" cases, the lack of funds has not been recognized as a defense or excuse. However, in *Miller v. Carson*,[51] a federal court approved a Florida county prison's medical services staff which included one full-time physician, a licensed physician's assistant and thirteen nurses, because their work schedule allowed a crisis intervention desk to be staffed twenty-four hours per day, with the physician or the licensed physician's assistant on call at the jail twenty-four hours a day as well. The proximity to the jail of a university hospital for emergency treatment made such a minimal staff feasible. This Florida county prison had a maximum capacity of four hundred and thirty-two inmates.[52] Other states have also grappled with this personnel problem. In *Craig v. Hocker*[53] the court found that medical care was adequate and reasonable based on the presence

[48] *Gates v. Collier*, 501 F.2d 1291 (5th Cir. 1974).
[49] *Gates v. Collier*, 390 F. Supp. 482, 488 (N.D. Miss. 1975).
[50] *Gates v. Collier*, 501 F.2d 1291, 1303 (5th Cir. 1974).
[51] *Miller v. Carson*, 401 F. Supp. 835 (M.D. Fla. 1975).
[52] *Id.* at 898; *see also Brown v. Beck*, 481 F. Supp. 723 (S.D. Ga. 1980).
[53] *Craig v. Hocker*, 405 F. Supp. 656 (D. Nev. 1975); *see also Jackson v. State of Mississippi*, 644 F.2d 1142 (5th Cir. 1981).

of a full-time physician and a full-time dentist in the prison, as well as two registered nurses, a psychiatrist, a part-time pharmacist who gave reasonably prompt
attention to genuine complaints from inmates, a prison hospital ward to which sick
inmates could be removed when so directed by a doctor, and provisions for taking
inmates under guard to local hospitals for diagnostic or treatment procedures not
available in the prison. The prison contained eight hundred and fifty-four inmates
prior to trial.

Once the courts have assured themselves that adequate or reasonable medical
care is available to an inmate, the courts' historic "hands off" doctrine is again
evident. What constitutes necessary and proper medical care of an inmate, in the
absence of allegations of intentional negligence or mistreatment, must be left to the
medical judgment of the prison physician, and cannot form the basis for a civil
rights complaint.[54] Inmates cannot be the ultimate judges of what medical treatment is necessary or proper, and courts must place their confidence in the reports
of reputable prison physicians.[55] The allegations by inmates that they have received
inadequate medical care can be disproved by prison medical records.[56]

An apparent difference of opinion between an inmate and his physicians as to
what treatment is necessary and proper does not give rise to a legal cause of action
against the physician.[57] Medical mistreatment or non-treatment must be capable of
characterization as cruel and unusual punishment in order to present a claim under
a civil rights statute.[58] The standard for what treatment rises to cruel and unusual
punishment was set forth in *Estelle v. Gamble*.[59] In that case the Supreme Court
reasoned that there must be facts and evidence to show a deliberate indifference to
serious medical needs. Thus, simple negligence will not be sufficient to obtain a
judgment against prison medical or security staff for inadequate treatment as a
constitutional violation. The lack of medical treatment must be intentional; an accident or inadvertent failure to provide proper medical care is not sufficient to meet
the Supreme Court's standard of deliberate indifference to serious medical needs.
It should be noted, however, that negligence may be actionable in state courts under
state law.

In *Ricketts v. Ciccone*[60] the court held that where a federal inmate was in need of
medical treatment due to chronic rhinitis caused by allergic sensitivity of an identified mold, the director of the prison and the Bureau of Prisons were legally

---

[54] *United States ex rel. Hyde v. McGinnis*, 429 F.2d 864 (2d Cir. 1970).

[55] *Fore v. Godwin*, 407 F. Supp. 1145 (E.D. Va. 1976).

[56] *Ross v. Bounds*, 373 F. Supp. 450 (E.D. N.C. 1974); *Estelle v. Gamble*, 429 U.S. 97 (1976).

[57] *Ray v. Parrish*, 399 F. Supp. 775 (E.D. Va. 1975); *Jackson v. Moore*, 471 F. Supp. 1068 (D.C. Colo. 1979).

[58] *Boyce v. Alizadun*, 595 F.2d 948 (4th Cir. 1979); *Shepard v. Stidham*, 502 F. Supp. 1275 (M.D. Ala. 1980); *DiLorenze v. United States*, 496 F. Supp. 79 (S.D. N.Y. 1980); *Campbell v. Sacred Heart Hospital*, 496 F. Supp. 692 (E.D. Pa. 1980); *Estelle v. Gamble*, 429 U.S. 97 (1976).

[59] *Estelle v. Gamble*, 429 U.S. 97 (1976).

[60] *Ricketts v. Ciccone*, 371 F. Supp. 1249 (W.D. Mo. 1974); *Commissioner of Corrections v. Meyers*, 399 N.E.2d 452 (Mass. 1979).

required to provide the most suitable medical treatment reasonably available. In determining a claim for lack of medical treatment, the standard is whether needed or essential, as opposed to desirable, medical treatment is being denied. The court held that denial of the request by the inmate, suffering from chronic rhinitis, to be transferred to a federal prison in a relatively dry climate as treatment for his illness, was arbitrary and unreasonable. Such action was held to be a denial to the prisoner of the best reasonable available medical treatment, when there was available at least one federal prison in a climate beneficial to the prisoner's illness.

§ 10.4   Right to Life

The United States Supreme Court in its landmark five-to-four decision of *Furman v. Georgia*[61] held, in the cases under review, that the death penalty amounted to cruel and unusual punishment because it was imposed in an arbitrary manner. Only two justices held that the death penalty amounts to cruel and unusual punishment in all cases. Because each member of the Court wrote a separate opinion, the exact effect of the *Furman* decision upon the constitutionality of the death penalty as such was uncertain. The focus of the opinions holding the statute in question unconstitutional was that standardless capital-sentencing discretion, whether vested in a judge or a jury, allowed the imposition of this most irrevocable of all legal sanctions to be freakish or discriminatory.

In apparent response to the *Furman* decision, thirty-five states enacted modified death penalty statutes. Some of the new statutes attempted to comply with *Furman* by complete elimination of capital-sentencing discretion. These statutes specified mandatory death sentences for certain crimes. Other new statutes sought to fulfill *Furman's* requirement of non-discriminatory, reasoned capital-sentencing by stringent specification of standards within which capital-sentencing discretion must be exercised. Appeals by convicts who had been sentenced to death under various statutes began to reach the United States Supreme Court late in 1973 and by March, 1976 over four hundred and thirty inmates were awaiting execution in state prisons.

After careful selection of representative capital-sentencing statutes, the Supreme Court decided five death penalty cases on July 2, 1976. In *Gregg v. Georgia*,[62] the Court analyzed the perennial argument that the death penalty amounts to cruel and unusual punishment in all cases. Rejecting this argument, Justice Stewart stated that the existence of capital punishment was accepted by the Framers of the Constitution, and that the Supreme Court has recognized for nearly two centuries that capital punishment for the crime of murder is not invalid per se. The *Gregg* case involved a double murder during an armed robbery. The Georgia capital-sentencing statute requires a two-part trial: a guilt stage and a penalty stage. The Georgia statute provides for jury sentencing, with instructions from the judge. Jury

---

[61] *Furman v. Georgia*, 408 U.S. 238 (1972).
[62] *Gregg v. Georgia*, 428 U.S. 153 (1976).

sentencing is considered desirable in capital cases in order to maintain a link between contemporary community values and the penal system—a link without which the determination of punishment could hardly reflect the evolving standards of decency that mark the progress of a maturing society. When it is considering whether to sentence an inmate to life imprisonment or to death, a Georgia jury must consider mitigating or aggravating circumstances of the crime and the criminal. The jury's attention is directed to the specific circumstances of the crime.

Was it committed in the course of another capital felony? Was it committed for money? Was it committed upon a peace officer or judicial officer? Was it committed in a particularly heinous way or in a manner that endangered the lives of many persons? In addition, the jury's attention is focused on the characteristics of the person who committed the crime: Does he have a record of prior convictions for capital offenses? Are there any special facts about this defendant that mitigate against imposing capital punishment (*e.g.*, his youth, the extent of his cooperation with the police, his emotional state at the time of the crime.)?[63]

An automatic review of each death sentence by the Georgia Supreme Court is provided to standardize capital-sentencing statewide. Such standardization is to be achieved by a comparison, on a case-by-case basis by the Georgia Supreme Court, of each new death sentence with sentences imposed on similarly situated defendants. The Georgia Supreme Court can reduce such sentences. In the *Gregg* case, for example, the court vacated a death sentence imposed for the armed robbery alone because the death penalty had rarely been imposed in Georgia for that offense. It should be noted that *Zant v. Stephens*[64] indicates that the state of Georgia may be relaxing the standards used for the imposition of capital punishment as espoused in *Gregg v. Georgia*. In *Zant*, the state court explained that statutory aggravating factors were used in Georgia as merely a threshold to determine the class of cases in which those defendants who are convicted of murder may be eligible for the death penalty. Further case law amplification may indicate that such a posture does not satisfy the *Furman v. Georgia* prohibition against standardless sentencing.

The other four death sentence cases which the U.S. Supreme Court decided in July, 1976, were *Proffitt v. Florida*,[65] *Jurek v. Texas*,[66] *Woodson v. North Carolina*,[67] and *Roberts v. Louisiana*.[68] These cases presented statutory variations upon the theme of the Georgia statute, i.e., elimination of standardless capital-sentenc-

---

[63] *Id.*

[64] *Zant v. Stephens*, 462 U.S. 862, 103 S. Ct 2733., 77 L.Ed.2d 235 (1983).

[65] *Proffitt v. Florida*, 428 U.S. 242 (1976).

[66] *Jurek v. Texas*, 428 U.S. 262 (1976).

[67] *Woodson v. North Carolina*, 428 U.S. 280 (1976).

[68] *Roberts v. Louisiana*, 428 U.S. 325 (1976).

ing discretion. The Supreme Court affirmed the Florida and Texas cases, and reversed the North Carolina and Louisiana cases.

The Florida capital-sentencing statute vests capital-sentencing discretion in its trial judges who are given specific and detailed guidance to assist them in deciding whether to impose a death penalty or life imprisonment.[69] Capital cases are also two-part proceedings in Florida. Juries make advisory sentence recommendations by majority vote in the penalty stage. The trial judge must justify the imposition of the death penalty with written findings. Such written findings encourage the meaningful appellate review mandated by the statute. Trial judges are directed to weigh eight specified aggravating factors against seven justified mitigating factors to determine whether the death penalty shall be imposed. This determination requires the trial judge to focus on the circumstances of the crime and the character of the convict.

In *Jurek v. Texas,* a statutory scheme which is somewhat more mechanical than those upheld in *Gregg* and *Proffitt* was also upheld. Texas mandates two-part proceedings, and its juries are the actual sentencing authorities because, dependent upon the jury's response to specific statutorily mandated questions, the trial judge imposes the single statutory sanction available. As Texas narrows its capital offense category, it implicitly requires its juries to find the existence of a statutory aggravating circumstance before the death penalty can be imposed.[70] Although mitigating circumstances are not explicitly mentioned in the statute, Texas courts have construed the statute to allow juries to consider such evidence.[71] The Texas capital-sentencing statute guides and focuses the jury's objective consideration of the specific circumstances of the individual offender and offense. Thus, it fulfills *Furman's* requirement for guided discretion.

In *Woodson v. North Carolina* and *Roberts v. Louisiana,* North Carolina's and Louisiana's death statutes were declared unconstitutional. Rather than establishing specific standards as Georgia, Florida, and Texas had, North Carolina and Louisiana tried to eliminate completely all capital-sentencing discretion. To this end they adopted mandatory capital-sentencing. Historically, they were on firm ground as all the states had mandatory death sentences for specified offenses at the time of the adoption of the Eighth Amendment in 1791. However, the Supreme Court concluded that the two crucial indicators of evolving standards of decency with respect to the imposition of punishment in our society—jury determinations and legislative enactments—conclusively point to present-day repudiation of automatic death sentences. Additionally, both the North Carolina and the Louisiana statutes fall within *Furman's* prohibition against standardless discretion in that each merely pushes unfettered sentencing discretion into the ostensible guilt-determination stage of the proceeding. The difference between the North Carolina and the Louisiana statutes

---

[69] *Proffitt v. Florida,* 428 U.S. 242 (1976).
[70] *Jurek v. Texas,* 428 U.S. 262 (1976).
[71] *Id.* at 265.

lies in the somewhat narrower definition of capital murder under Louisiana law.[72] In addition, Louisiana's subsequent attempt to cure the defects found in *Roberts* by narrowing the scope of mandatory capital punishment to include only cases in which the victim is a murdered policeman, was similarly rejected by the Supreme Court.[73]

In *Gregg,* the United States Supreme Court specifically noted that it was not deciding whether states could or could not allow or provide for death sentences in cases which do not involve murder of the victim, i.e., rape, kidnapping, armed robbery, etc. However, since 1976 the Court has begun to address this issue and has demonstrated a general reluctance to uphold the imposition of capital punishment when, although convicted of a serious crime, the defendant has not taken the life of another. By way of example, in *Coker v. Georgia*[74] the Court held that Georgia's death penalty statute was unconstitutional as applied to a defendant who, although guilty of rape, had not killed the victim. This position was modified somewhat in *Enmund v. Florida.*[75] In *Enmund,* the Court refused to permit the death penalty to be imposed upon a so-called nontriggerman in a felony-murder conviction. However, the Supreme Court carefully noted that its decision was not establishing a requirement that imposition of the death penalty mandates that the defendant be the actual killer; rather the trial court's reversible error was its refusal during sentencing to consider the defendant's lack of intent that the killings occur.

In 1987, the United States Supreme Court held that although two brothers neither intended to kill the victims nor inflicted the fatal wounds, the record supported a finding that they had the culpable mental state of reckless indifference to human life. Consequently, the Eighth Amendment did not prohibit the death penalty as disproportionate in the case of a defendant whose participation in a felony that results in murder is major and whose mental state is one of reckless indifference. A survey of state felony-murder laws and judicial decisions after *Enmund* indicated societal consensus that a combination of factors may justify the death penalty even without a specific "intent to kill." Reckless disregard for human life also represents a highly culpable mental state that may support a capital sentencing judgment in combination with major participation in the felony resulting in death.[76]

Since 1976, the Supreme Court has spent considerable time attempting to determine the constitutional parameters of mitigating and aggravating circumstances as utilized by the various states in the determination of whether to impose capital punishment in a particular case. In *Lockett v. Ohio,*[77] the Supreme Court held that a statute which provided too limited a range of mitigating circumstances is unconstitutional. The Court established in *Lockett* that only rarely should the sentencing

---

[72] *Roberts v. Louisiana,* 428 U.S. 325 (1976).
[73] *Roberts v. Louisiana,* 431 U.S. 633 (1977).
[74] *Coker v. Georgia,* 433 U.S. 584 (1977).
[75] *Enmund v. Florida,* 458 U.S. 782 (1982).
[76] *Tison v. Arizona,* 481 U.S. 137 (1987).
[77] *Lockett v. Ohio,* 438 U.S. 586 (1978).

authority be precluded from considering "any" mitigating factors relative to the defendant's character or the circumstances of the offense. In *Eddings v. Oklahoma*,[78] the Supreme Court vacated the death sentence of a convicted murderer by applying the rule established in *Lockett*. In *Eddings*, the Court explicitly noted that a state may not by statute preclude the sentencer from considering any mitigating factor.

The United States Supreme Court continues to define "mitigating evidence."

In a capital murder case, the defendant presented as mitigating evidence his own testimony and that of his former wife, his mother, his sister, and his grandmother. He then sought to introduce testimony of two jailers and a "regular visitor" to the effect that he had "made a good adjustment" during the 7½ months he had spent in jail between his arrest and trial. The trial court ruled such evidence irrelevant and inadmissible, and the defendant was sentenced to death. The United States Supreme Court reversed, and held that the trial court's exclusion from the sentencing hearing of the testimony of the jailers and the visitor denied the defendant his right to place before the sentencing jury all relevant evidence in mitigation of punishment.[79]

In another capital murder case, the trial judge instructed the advisory jury not to consider, and himself refused to consider, evidence of mitigating circumstances not specifically enumerated in the state's death penalty statute. The United States Supreme Court reversed and held that this procedure was not consistent with the requirement that the sentencer may neither refuse to consider nor be precluded from considering any relevant mitigating evidence.[80]

While serving a life sentence without possibility of parole upon a first-degree murder conviction, an inmate was sentenced to death for the murder of a fellow prisoner. Under a Nevada statute the death penalty was mandated in these circumstances. The United States Supreme Court held that under the individualized capital-sentencing doctrine, it is constitutionally required that the sentencing authority consider, as a mitigating factor, any aspect of the defendant's character or record and any of the circumstances of the particular offense. Consequently, a statute that mandates the death penalty for a prison inmate who is convicted of murder while serving a life sentence without possibility of parole violates the Eighth and Fourteenth Amendments.[81]

Decisions related to aggravating factors tend to focus upon the content rather than the presence or absence of statutory provisions. In *Godfrey v. Georgia*,[82] the Supreme Court held that aggravating factors may be found to be so vague that a sentencing authority may have so much discretion as to give rise to a standardless

---

[78] *Eddings v. Oklahoma*, 455 U.S. 104 (1982).
[79] *Skipper v. South Carolina*, 476 U.S. 1 (1986).
[80] *Hitchcock v. Dugger*, 481 U.S. 393 (1987).
[81] *Sumner v. Nevada*, 483 U.S. 66 (1987).
[82] *Godfrey v. Georgia*, 446 U.S. 420 (1980).

imposition of the death penalty such as the United States Supreme Court specifically rejected as unconstitutional in *Furman v. Georgia.*

Affirmation of the constitutionality of capital punishment by the U.S. Supreme Court in *Gregg* and its related cases does not, however, resolve this issue. Two other considerations must be noted. One is the status of the capital punishment under state constitutions, and the other is the effect of future community values toward the constitutionality of capital punishment in a federal constitutional sense.

In *Commonwealth v. O'Neal,*[83] the Massachusetts Supreme Judicial Court concluded that a Massachusetts statute which prescribed the death penalty of a convicted rapist-murderer was unconstitutional under the Massachusetts state constitution. The major focus of this decision was that the state's imposition of capital punishment is the least compelling means available to attain its legitimate goal of public safety. This argument was specifically rejected by the United States Supreme Court in *Gregg v. Georgia,* but because of the vagaries of our federal system of government it is not binding upon a state's interpretation of its own constitution. This case points out the basically minimal nature of United States Supreme Court decisions—in many areas the minimum a state must do is mandated through the federal courts. A state is free to adopt standards higher than the federal standard if it wishes. As a result of the *O'Neal* decision, Massachusetts has ended capital punishment regardless of the latitude which was bestowed upon all the states in the *Gregg* decision.

Another example of higher state standards is *People v. Anderson.*[84] In that case the California Supreme Court declared its state's capital punishment statute to be unconstitutional. The basis of that decision was the existence of the disjunctive "or" rather than the conjunctive "and" in the California constitution's equivalent of the Federal Constitution's Eighth Amendment prohibition against "cruel and unusual punishment." California's phrase reads "cruel *or* unusual punishment." The California Supreme Court concluded that infrequent imposition of the death penalty equals unusual punishment, and struck down its use completely. The opinion noted that public acceptance of capital punishment is a relevant, but not controlling, factor in any assessment of whether it is consonant with contemporary standards of decency. However, the California court readily acknowledged the distribution of political clout when it enforced the new capital punishment statute enacted in California following a statewide referendum on whether or not the death penalty should be used in California.[85]

The other consideration which should enter into any discussion of capital punishment after *Gregg* is the effect of ethical evolution. One of the primary supports for the *Gregg* decision is the United States Supreme Court's assessment of the level of decency in the states. Several states do not authorize capital punishment under

[83] *Commonwealth v. O'Neal,* 339 N.E.2d 676 (Mass. Sup. Jud. Ct. 1975).
[84] *People v. Anderson,* 6 Cal. 3d 628, 493 P.2d 880, *cert. denied,* 406 U.S. 958 (1976).
[85] *See, Gregg v. Georgia,* 428 U.S. 153 (1976).

their internal laws. If these states ever become the majority, the U.S. Supreme Court may reconsider the holding of *Gregg* so as to better reflect the needs of a maturing society.

Other issues continue to plague the Court. The jury's imposition of a death sentence after considering a presentence report which included a victim impact statement violated the Eighth Amendment. The information contained in the victim impact statement was irrelevant to a capital sentencing decision, and its admission creates a constitutionally unacceptable risk that the jury may impose the death penalty in an arbitrary and capricious manner.[86]

The prosecutor's closing argument at the sentencing phase in a death penalty case included his reading to the jury at length from a religious tract the victim was carrying and commenting on the personal qualities that the prosecutor inferred from the victim's possession of the religious tract and a voter registration card. The United States Supreme Court held that for purposes of imposing the death penalty the defendant's punishment must be tailored to his personal responsibility and moral guilt. The prosecutor's comments concerned the victim's personal characteristics, and allowing the jury to rely on this information could result in imposing the death sentence because of factors about which the defendant was unaware, and that were irrelevant to the decision to kill. The content of the religious tract and the voter registration card could not possibly have been relevant to the "circumstances of the crime." Where there was no evidence that the defendant read either the tract or the voter card, the content of the papers the victim was carrying was purely fortuitous and could not provide any information relevant to respondent's moral culpability, notwithstanding that the papers had been admitted in evidence for other purposes. The death penalty was set aside.[87]

Although the Eighth Amendment prohibits a state from inflicting the death penalty upon a prisoner who is insane,[88] the Eighth Amendment does not categorically prohibit the execution of mentally retarded capital murderers of diminished reasoning ability nor the execution of youth.[89] The imposition of capital punishment on an individual for a crime committed at 16 or 17 years of age does not constitute cruel and unusual punishment under the Eight Amendment.[90] However, when a fifteen-year-old youth actively participated in a brutal murder and was sentenced to death, a plurality of the United States Supreme Court reversed the death penalty.[91] Four members of the Supreme Court, Justices Stevens, Brennan, Marshall, and Blackmun concluded that the "cruel and unusual punishment" prohibition of the Eighth Amendment, made applicable to the States by the Fourteenth Amendment, prohibits the execution of a person who was under sixteen years of age at the time of his

---

[86] *Booth v. Maryland*, 482 U.S. 496 (1987).
[87] *South Carolina v. Gathers*, ___ U.S. ___, 109 S. Ct. 2207 (1989).
[88] *Ford v. Wainwright*, 477 U.S. 399 (1986).
[89] *Penry v. Lynaugh*, ___ U.S. ___, 109 S. Ct. 2934 (1989).
[90] *Stanford v. Kentucky*, ___ U.S. ___, 109 S. Ct. 2969 (1989).
[91] *Thompson v. Oklahoma*, 487 U.S. 815, 108 S. Ct. 2687 (1988).

or her offense. To establish the plurality in setting aside the death sentence, Justice O'Connor held that because the available evidence suggested a national consensus forbidding the imposition of capital punishment for crimes committed before the age of sixteen, the youth and others whose crimes were committed before that age may not be executed pursuant to a capital punishment statute that specifies no minimum age. Thus, the issue on whether a fifteen-year-old may be executed remains open.

§ 10.5   Civil Disabilities

Occasionally a case reaches the courts which involves the extent to which a prisoner is "civilly dead" or suffers loss of his civil rights upon conviction of a felony. Historically, convicted felons were held to have forfeited all their civil rights; they were mere slaves of the state.[92] This extreme view has been modified in recent years.[93]

In *Richardson v. Ramirez*[94] the United States Supreme Court considered a provision of the California constitution which disenfranchised convicted felons. The Court held that this provision did not violate the Equal Protection Clause of the Fourteenth Amendment, without reaching the general constitutional issue of "civil death."

In *In re Goalen*,[95] Easthope, an inmate in the Utah State Prison, and Goalen desired to marry. Both were of legal age and were competent to enter into marriage under state law. However, a section of the Utah Code provided:

A sentence of imprisonment in the state prison for any term less than for life suspends all civil rights of the person so sentenced during such imprisonment, and forfeits all private trusts and public offices, authority or power.[96]

In implementation of this statute, the Utah Board of Corrections issued a policy statement that, "It shall be the policy that the Warden may, upon recommendation of the treatment team, authorize inmates nearing their release dates to marry."[97] This policy had been interpreted and applied by the state corrections officials to permit marriage by an inmate only when he was within six months of release, if the marriage was recommended by the treatment team. Upon the application by Easthope, the Warden determined that he was not within the terms of the policy and denied permission for the marriage to take place. Easthope contended that the freedom to marry was constitutionally protected and that the State could not prohibit

---

[92] *Ruffin v. Commonwealth*, 62 Va. (21 Gratt.) 790, 796 (1871).

[93] *Wolff v. McDonnell*, 418 U.S. 539, 555-556 (1974); *Chesapeake Utilities Corp. v. Hopkins*, 340 A.2d 154 (Del. Sup. Ct. 1975).

[94] *Richardson v. Ramirez*, 418 U.S. 24, 72 Ohio Op.2d 232 (1974).

[95] *In re Goalen*, 30 Utah 2d 27, 512 P.2d 1028 (1973), *cert. denied*, 414 U.S. 1148 (1974). *See also*, *Holden v. Florida Dept. of Corr.*, 400 So. 2d 142 (Fla. App. 1981); *Dept. of Corrections v. Roseman*, 390 So. 2d 394 (Fla. App. 1980); *cf. Salisbury v. List*, 501 F. Supp. 105 (D. Nev. 1980). (A state prison regulation severely restricting an inmate's right to marry was declared unconstitutional.)

[96] *In re Goalen*, 414 U.S. at 1149 (dissenting opinion).

[97] *Id.*

the marriage in the absence of some compelling state interest. The interest that the State asserted in support of its policy was that the denial of such civil rights, in conjunction with their gradual return to the convict, "acts as an incentive for the convict to aid in his own rehabilitation."[98] Judicial relief to Easthope and Goalen was denied.

A prison rule which prohibited prisoners from marrying while incarcerated was a lawful exercise of the prison's administrative power.[99]

Prison restrictions on the right to marry are now questionable. Inmates in Missouri challenged a regulation permitting an inmate to marry only with the prison superintendent's permission, which could be given only when there were "compelling reasons" to do so. Only a pregnancy or the birth of an illegitimate child would be considered "compelling." This regulation was declared unconstitutional and the United States Supreme Court held that prisoners have a constitutionally protected right to marry.[100]

Although marriages are subject to substantial restrictions as a result of incarceration, sufficient important attributes of marriage remain to form a constitutionally protected relationship. The Missouri regulation was facially invalid under the reasonable relationship test. Although prison officials may regulate the time and circumstances under which a marriage takes place, and may require prior approval by the warden, an almost complete ban on marriages is not reasonably related to legitimate penological objectives. The contention that the regulation served security concerns by preventing "love triangles" that may lead to violent inmate confrontations was held to be without merit, since inmate rivalries were likely to develop with or without a formal marriage ceremony. Moreover, the regulation's broad prohibition was not justified by the security of fellow inmates and prison staff, who were not affected where the inmate made the private decision to marry a civilian. Rather, the regulation represented an exaggerated response to the claimed security objectives, since allowing marriages unless the warden found a threat to security, order, or the public safety represented an obvious, easy alternative that would accommodate the right to marry while imposing a *de minimis* burden. Nor was the regulation reasonably related to the articulated rehabilitation goal of fostering self-reliance by female prisoners. In requiring refusal of permission to marry to all inmates absent a compelling reason, the regulation swept much more broadly than was necessary. Male inmates' marriages had generally caused prison officials no problems and that they had no objections to prisoners marrying civilians.

In *Bush v. Reid*,[101] the Alaska Supreme Court held that an Alaskan "civil death" statute which barred prisoners and parolees from bringing a civil lawsuit which was unrelated to conviction or confinement was unconstitutional. According to this

---

[98] *Id.*

[99] *Bradbury v. Wainwright*, 538 F. Supp. 377 (M.D. Fla. 1982).

[100] *Turner v. Safley*, 482 U.S. 78 (1987).

[101] *Bush v. Reid*, 516 P.2d 1215 (Alaska Sup. Ct. 1973); *Thompson v. Bond*, 421 F. Supp. 878 (W.D. Mo. 1976).

court, the right to bring a civil suit for damages is a form of property. In this case denying a parolee the opportunity to convert his claim to a far more valuable money judgment was held to be "taking of property" without due process.

The extent of a convicted felon's civil disability is now the focus of substantial litigation. For example, the issue of the liability of ex-felons for possession of firearms was in such confusion that in *Barrett v. United States,*[102] the United States Supreme Court held that the Gun Control Act (18 U.S.C. § 922h), which forbids a convicted felon to receive any firearm which has been shipped or transported in interstate commerce, applied to a felon's isolated intrastate purchase of a firearm which had previously traveled in interstate commerce. This is also true where the firearm is issued by a state to a rehabilitated felon for use within the scope of his employment as a *state corrections officer.*[103]

Convicted felons have unsuccessfully litigated their purported rights to use checking accounts while incarcerated,[104] to rear their children in prison,[105] and to exercise fully their First Amendment guarantees.[106]

The Supremacy Clause of the Federal Constitution prevents a state from attaching Social Security benefits as well as other types of pension or retirement benefits in order to help defray the costs of maintaining its prison system.[107]

The state has a compelling interest in maintaining security and order in its prisons, and, to the extent that it furthers that interest in reasonable and nonarbitrary ways, property claims by inmates must give way. A prison's restrictions on possessing currency amounts to reasonable attempts to guarantee the individual safety of the prisoner and the security of the prison and therefore the confiscation of the inmate's money did not violate his civil rights.[108]

§ 10.6 Conclusion

Penologists argue that effective rehabilitation programs are the key to success from any correctional system.[109] Judicial concern for penal reform, coupled with the fact that many state statutes and constitutions specifically make rehabilitation an objective of incarceration, raise the probability that treatment programs may soon be judicially required in penal facilities, though *O'Connor v. Donaldson* may slow this trend.

---

[102] *Barrett v. United States,* 423 U.S. 212 (1976).

[103] *Hyland v. Fukuda,* 580 F.2d 1977 (9th Cir. 1978).

[104] *Nix v. Paderick,* 407 F. Supp. 844 (E.D. Va. 1976).

[105] *Pendergrass v. Toombs,* 546 P.2d 1103 (Or. Ct. App. 1976); *Wainwright v. Moore,* 374 So. 2d 586 (Fla. App. 1979); *Delaney v. Booth,* 400 So. 2d 1268 (Fla. App. 1981).

[106] *United States v. Huss,* 394 F. Supp. 752 (S.D. N.Y. 1975); *Secretary, Department of Public Safety and Correctional Services v. Allen,* 406 A.2d 104 (Md. 1979); *French v. Butterworth,* 614 F.2d 23 (1st Cir. 1980); *Garland v. Polley,* 594 F.2d 1220 (8th Cir. 1979); *People v. Coleman,* 174 Cal. Rptr. 756 (Cal. App. 1981).

[107] *Bennett v. Arkansas,* 485 U.S. 395 (1988).

[108] *Harris v. Forsyth,* 735 F.2d 1235 (11th Cir. 1984).

[109] *See* footnotes 2 and 3, *supra,* and accompanying textual material.

It should be recognized that the main objective to "treatment" or "medical experimentation" is the reality that no "voluntary" program in prison is truly free from coercion. Perhaps innovative techniques, such as the appointment of legal guardians for the inmates concerned, or prior judicial review or approval may answer the problem of "free and voluntary consent" within the prison context.

Judicial intervention in medical treatment cases has markedly increased in recent years. Unfortunately, however, federal courts are divided as to when a complaint alleging inadequate medical treatment is sufficient to state a cause of action for deprivation of a federal right. The Supreme Court has not yet rendered a decision clarifying the law in this area.

The constitutionality of capital punishment for the crime of murder has been firmly underscored. Certain types of capital-sentencing statutes are necessary to constitutionally impose the death penalty, but the death penalty is not unconstitutional per se. The furor over death as a sanction will abate for some time, but the problem will not be permanently solved because of continual changes in community and ethical values.

Litigation in the area of the civil disabilities of convicted felons, both incarcerated and released, will continue to increase as the revolution in prison law follows the inmate beyond the prison wall.

Chapter 11

CIVIL AND CRIMINAL LIABILITIES OF PRISON OFFICIALS

§ 11.1   Introduction

The preceding chapters have described various rights which inmates retain while they are incarcerated. This chapter will set forth, in general terms, the judicial remedies that exist to vindicate past violations and to prevent future deprivations of those rights. Several frequently encountered obstacles to inmate suits will also be discussed.

It is important to note that this chapter will discuss only *judicial* remedies. Not included in this chapter, therefore, is a discussion of possible "administrative remedies;" that is, methods that have been established within the correctional system itself to investigate, punish and prevent deprivations of inmate rights.

177

Two reasons can be given for this exclusion: 1) many correctional systems simply do not have formal administrative remedies; and 2) among the states that do have administrative methods to investigate inmate complaints, there is a lack of uniformity, and, hence, general statements would be misleading at best. Nevertheless, prison officials should seriously consider development of administrative remedies as a faster and more effective method of dealing with inmate complaints.

§ 11.2   Jurisdiction of Federal Courts

With some exceptions not relevant here, the subject matter jurisdiction of federal courts is limited to cases arising under the Constitution or laws of the United States.[1] Hence, before a federal court can render a valid decision in a case, the plaintiff must show that he is being denied a right secured to him by either the Constitution or by a specific federal statute. If the inmate-plaintiff's allegations do not constitute a violation of a federal right, the case must be dismissed if it is instituted in a federal court.[2] Since the judicial power of federal courts is defined and limited by the Constitution, federal courts are commonly referred to as courts of *limited* jurisdiction.

§ 11.3   Jurisdiction of State Courts

In contrast to federal courts, state courts are courts of *general* jurisdiction. That is, there is a presumption that they have jurisdiction over a particular controversy unless a contrary showing is made. Hence, the subject matter jurisdiction of state courts is much broader than that of federal courts. In addition to being the exclusive means of judicially enforcing rights created by the state's constitution, statutes and common law, a *state* court has concurrent jurisdiction with the federal courts to decide cases based entirely on a federal claim,[3] provided that Congress has not given the federal judiciary exclusive jurisdiction in the matter. Therefore, an inmate who alleges a violation of his federal constitutional rights may have a choice of forums in which he may bring the action; that is, either state or federal court, at his option.

§ 11.4   Barriers to Inmates' Suits—
Doctrine of Sovereign Immunity

An inmate attempting to sue his keepers faces several serious obstacles, one of which is the doctrine of sovereign immunity. According to this doctrine, a private citizen may not sue a governmental unit or its agent without its consent. Various reasons advanced in support of the doctrine are: the idea that "the King can do no wrong;" that public funds should not be dissipated to compensate private injuries; and that governmental officials need to be free from the threat of suit to function

---

[1] U.S. Const. art. III, 2.
[2] *United States ex rel. Atterbury v. Ragen,* 237 F.2d 953 (7th Cir. 1956).
[3] *Claflin v. Houseman,* 93 U.S. 130 (1876).

most effectively for the common good. Hence, in a state where sovereign immunity is recognized, the state prison system is immune from a private suit for damages.[4] Similarly, California has held that the operation of a jail by a municipality or a county is a governmental function and therefore an inmate may not sue the political subdivision for injuries received while he is incarcerated.[5]

Many states have either totally or partially abrogated the doctrine of sovereign immunity by judicial decision or by constitutional or statutory amendment.[6] Hence, the defense of sovereign immunity in an inmate's suit depends on the law in each state.

Even in states which retain the doctrine of sovereign immunity, an inmate who has been denied constitutional rights may obtain an injunction against the allegedly wrongful conduct of an official in his individual capacity. In *Alabama v. Pugh*,[7] the Supreme Court dismissed an injunction sought by inmates of the Alabama prison system as against the State and the Alabama Board of Corrections because the Eleventh Amendment prohibits federal courts from entertaining suits against states and their agencies without its consent. The case, which alleged that conditions of the Alabama prisons constituted cruel and unusual punishment, had to proceed against the individual officials responsible for the administration of the prisons instead of the State government itself. Even though it is a legal fiction, the courts treat such a suit as one against the defendant personally, and not against the state. Hence, the defense of sovereign immunity is not available. The courts reason that a governmental official acting unconstitutionally is not acting as an agent of the government.[8]

The liability of governmental officials in monetary damage suits presents a confusing picture. Federal employees on practically every level are given immunity from suit, even if they act maliciously.[9] The rationale of these decisions is that federal officers must be free from fear of monetary liability for their acts in order to accomplish their public duties. However, in many states, governmental employees can be sued as individuals for committing intentional wrongs. Thus, in *Gullatte v. Potts*,[10] the court held that the state classification officer may be sued for the death

---

[4] *Moody v. State's Prison*, 128 N.C. 12, 38 S.E. 131 (1901); *Pharr v. Garibaldi*, 252 N.C. 803, 115 S.E.2d 18 (1960); *Staley v. Commonwealth*, 380 A.2d 515 (Pa. Commw. 1977); *McKnight v. Civiletti*, 497 F. Supp. 657 (E.D. Pa. 1980); *City of Newport v. Facts Concerts*, 453 U.S. 247 (1981).

[5] *Grove v. County of San Joaquin*, 156 Cal. App. 2d 808, 320 P.2d 161 (1958); *Bruce v. Riddle*, (4th Cir. 1980); *cf. Meyer v. City of Oakland*, 166 Cal. Rptr. 79 (Cal. App. 1980). (The City of Oakland was held liable in the amount of $35,000 for an assault on an inmate by fellow inmates. The court, while recognizing the doctrine of sovereign immunity, did not apply it to the facts of this case. The court held that a detainee in a drunk tank is not a "prisoner" for purposes of this statute.)

[6] *Van Alstyne*, GOVERNMENTAL TORT LIABILITY: A DECADE OF CHANGE, 1966 U.Ill.L.F. 919.

[7] *Alabama v. Pugh*, 438 U.S. 781 (1978).

[8] *Ex parte Young*, 209 U.S. 123 (1908).

[9] *Barr v. Matteo*, 360 U.S. 564 (1959) (acting director of Office of Rent Stabilization); *Norton v. McShane*, 332 F.2d 855 (5th Cir. 1964) (deputy United States marshal); *Eide v. Timberlake*, 497 F. Supp. 1272 (D. Kan. 1980); *cf. Procunier v. Navarette*, 434 U.S. 555 (1978).

[10] *Gullatte v. Potts*, 630 F.2d 322 (5th Cir. 1980); *Bogard v. Cook*, 586 F.2d 399 (5th Cir. 1978); *Fitchette v. Collins*, 402 F. Supp. 147 (D. Md. 1975); *see also, Carder v. Steiner*, 170 A.2d 220 (1961).

of an inmate where the officer could reasonably have expected his action to result in harm to the inmate. The court stated that the action involved in this case was precisely the sort of abuse of governmental power that is necessary to raise an ordinary tort by a government agent to the stature of a constitutional violation. In those states adhering to sovereign immunity, the liability of officers for negligence will often depend upon the discretionary or non-discretionary nature of their acts, as will be more fully discussed below.[11] In a recent case from the Fourth Circuit Court of Appeals[12] the question of the liability of a probation officer for negligent supervision of a probationer was litigated. The Court held that there is a duty to protect the public from the reasonably foreseeable risk of harm at the hands of a person on probation. The facts giving rise to this suit involved an individual who had been indicted for abducting a young girl. Before his trial he was placed in an institute for psychiatric treatment. The judge, after conferring with the doctor responsible for his evaluation, sentenced the prisoner, based on his guilty plea, to twenty years imprisonment but suspended the sentence based on further treatment and commitment to the psychiatric facility.

When the doctor and probation officer requested the judge to permit the probationer to visit his family the judge approved. When the probationer informed his probation officer of possible job opportunities out of state the probation officer granted passes to the probationer to travel to the location to make the necessary arrangements. The probation officer had discussed these trips with the doctor prior to approving the passes. None of the passes were submitted to the judge for approval. Subsequently the out-of-state probation officer refused to accept the probationer's transfer and the doctor discharged the probationer from the facility. The doctor, after the probation officer instructed the probationer to return, placed the probationer in therapy sessions which met two nights a week. The probationer obtained a job and lived outside the facility to which he had been committed by the judge in the original sentence. The judge was never informed of these changes surrounding the probationer. Subsequently the probation officer was promoted and a new probation officer took over; the probationer then killed the plaintiff's daughter.

The court, in finding the doctor and probation officer liable, stated that the decision to release the probationer from a mental facility was not simply a medical judgment. That decision also involved the question of whether release would be in the best interests of the community. The court found liability for negligent supervision in large part because the probation officer and doctor had substituted their judgment for that of the court. Had the court been kept informed, and approved the actions taken, the doctor and probation officer would not have been liable.

It is clear that the defense of sovereign immunity will often deny relief to innocent citizens injured by governmental officers. On the other hand, it is also clear

---

[11] See § 11.11.1 infra.

[12] Semler v. Psychiatric Institute of Washington, D.C., 588 F.2d 121 (4th Cir. 1976); Martinez v. California, 444 U.S. 277 (1980).

that immunity for such officers will encourage them to work vigorously for the public good without fear of nuisance lawsuits. One possible solution to this paradox is suggested by Professor Kenneth C. Davis, a leading authority in America on administrative law.

What the law of tort liability of public officers and employees most needs is an expansion of tort liability of governmental units. If the particular governmental unit is liable for the tort, so that the loss will thus be properly spread, then the courts will be relieved from the need for choosing between leaving a deserving plaintiff without remedy and imposing liability upon the individual officer or employee, who is usually either ill-equipped to bear the loss or is performing the type of function that can be properly performed only if the officer is free from the need considering his own pocketbook. The public interest in fearless administration usually should come first, so that officers must be immune from liability even when the plaintiff asserts that the officers have acted maliciously; when this is so, the only proper way to compensate deserving plaintiffs is to impose liability on the governmental unit. When the public gets the benefit of a program, the public should pay for the torts that may be expected, to carry out the program. The only satisfactory solution of many problems about liability of officers and employees is to compensate the plaintiff but to hold the officer or employee immune.[13]

A distinction must be made between a public official being sued in his official capacity where the "real" defendant is a governmental unit, and when the public official is sued for his individual conduct. Personal capacity suits seek to impose personal liability upon a governmental official for actions he takes under color of state law. In official capacity suits, as long as the governmental entity receives notice and an opportunity to respond, the suit is, in all respects other than the name, a suit against the entity. It is not a suit against the official personally, for the real party in interest is the entity. An award of damages against an official in his personal capacity can be enforced only against the official's personal assets. A plaintiff seeking to recover on a damages judgment in an official capacity suit must look to the governmental entity itself. To establish liability in a § 1983 suit, it must be shown that the official, acting under color of law, caused the deprivation of a federal right. More is required in an official capacity suit. It must be shown that the governmental entity was a "moving force" behind the deprivations. In an official capacity suit, the entity's "policy or custom" must have played a part in the violation of federal law. As to defenses of liability, an official in a personal capacity suit may, depending on his position, be able to assert personal immunity defenses, such as objectively reasonable reliance on existing law. The only immunities that can be claimed in an official capacity action are forms of sovereign immunity that the entity may possess, such as the Eleventh Amendment. There is no longer any need to bring official capacity suits against officials of local government, as local government may be sued directly for damages and injunctive or declaratory relief.

---

[13] K. Davis, ADMINISTRATIVE LAW TEXT 26.07 (1959).

Absent waiver, however, under the Eleventh Amendment, a state cannot be sued directly in its own name, regardless of the relief sought. In this regard, a civil rights suit against a government official in his personal capacity cannot lead to imposition of attorney fee liability upon the governmental entity. A victory of a plaintiff against a governmental official being sued in his individual capacity is a victory against the individual defendant, not against the governmental entity that employs him. However, although a state in a § 1983 action may be found liable either because the state was a proper party defendant or because state officials were sued in their official capacity, attorney fees may be awarded to a state under § 1983. Only in an official capacity action is a plaintiff who wins entitled to look for relief, both on the merits and for attorney fees, to the governmental entity.[14]

Neither a State nor State officials acting in their official capacities are "persons" within meaning of § 1983. A State is not a person under § 1983. This is supported by the statute's language, congressional purpose, and legislative history. In common usage, the term "person" does not include a State. This usage is particularly applicable where it is claimed that Congress has subjected the States to liability to which they had not been subject before. Reading § 1983 to include States would be a decidedly awkward way of expressing such a congressional intent. The statute's language also falls short of satisfying the ordinary rule of statutory construction that Congress must make its intention to alter the constitutional balance between the States and the Federal Government unmistakably clear in a statute's language. Moreover, the doctrine of sovereign immunity was one of the well-established common-law immunities and defenses that Congress did not intend to override in enacting § 1983. The ruling in *Monell* —which held that a municipality is a person under § 1983—is not to the contrary, since States are protected by the Eleventh Amendment while municipalities are not. Further, a suit against state officials in their official capacities is not a suit against the officials but rather is a suit against the officials' offices and, thus, is no different from a suit against the State itself. Such a suit cannot be predicated on § 1983.[15]

§ 11.4.1　—The "Hands-Off" Doctrine

Courts have traditionally abstained from hearing suits brought by inmates against their keepers. This practice became so prevalent that it acquired its own name—the "hands-off doctrine." Some courts have explained the doctrine in terms of a lack of subject matter jurisdiction over claims of inmates.[16] An article discussing inmates' complaints recognized three separate reasons relied on by courts to support the doctrine:[17] 1) separation of powers (administration of prisons is an executive function); 2) lack of judicial expertise in penology; and 3) fear that judicial intervention will subvert prison discipline.

---

[14] *Kentucky v. Graham,* 473 U.S. 159 (1985).
[15] *Will v. Michigan Department of State Police,* ___ U.S. ___, 109 S.Ct. 2304 (1989).
[16] *Garcia v. Steele,* 193 F.2d 276 (8th Cir. 1951).
[17] *Goldfarb and Singer,* REDRESSING PRISONERS' GRIEVANCES, 39 GEO. WASH. L. REV. 175,181 (1970).

The hands-off doctrine has subsided in importance, at least in federal courts. One extremely important step in the doctrine's decline was *Cooper v. Pate*,[18] in which the United States Supreme Court expressly held that a state inmate could bring suit against his keepers under the Civil Rights Act.[19] The hands-off doctrine in federal courts today can probably best be described as a reluctance on the part of the judiciary to interfere in prison administration, but a reluctance which it will quickly shed upon allegations of denials of important federal constitutional or statutory rights.[20] The increasing number of inmate suits being heard in federal courts tends to indicate that many courts today will liberally construe inmate complaints as alleging denials of important federal rights.[21]

However, it is important to note that the flood of inmate suits which has ended up in federal courts has created great concern for the federal judiciary system. As stated by Chief Justice Burger of the United States Supreme Court:

> Fully a sixth of the 117,000 cases of the civil docket of federal courts (19,000) are petitions from prisoners, most of which could be handled effectively and fairly within the prison systems. ... Federal judges should not be dealing with prisoner complaints which, although important to a prisoner, are so minor that any well-run institution should be able to resolve them fairly without resorting to federal judges.[22]

This would indicate that the courts may not be willing to liberally construe inmate complaints unless it appears that there have been denials of important federally protected rights.

§ 11.5   Federal Remedies—Civil Suits Against Federal Prison Officials

A federal inmate who claims that he suffered injuries as a result of negligent conduct by federal prison officials should theoretically be able to sue for damages. However, the doctrine of sovereign immunity[23] precluded such suits until Congress, in 1946, passed the Federal Tort Claims Act,[24] in which the federal government consented to be sued in certain situations. In 1963 the Supreme Court held that federal inmates could maintain an action under the Federal Tort Claims Act.[25]

---

[18] *Cooper v. Pate*, 378 U.S. 546 (1964).
[19] 42 U.S. C. § 1983 (1970).
[20] *Johnson v. Avery*, 393 U.S. 483 (1969); *Wright v. McMann*, 387 F.2d 519 (2d Cir. 1967).
[21] For an exhaustive study of judicial treatment of inmate suits, *see Goldfarb and Singer*, REDRESSING PRISONERS' GRIEVANCES, 39 GEO. WASH. L. REV. 175 (1970).
[22] 62 American Bar Association Journal 189 (Feb. 1976).
[23] *See* § 11.4 *supra*.
[24] *See* 28 U.S.C. § 2674 (1964).
[25] *United States v. Muniz*, 374 U.S. 150 (1963).

Claims arising from certain specific fact situations are expressly excepted from the act.[26] The most important exception in a prison setting exempts:

Any claim arising out of assault, battery, false imprisonment, false arrest, malicious prosecution, abuse of process, libel, slander, misrepresentation, deceit, or interference with contract rights.[27]

However, subject to the immunity doctrine,[28] federal officers are now liable for "constitutional torts" to the same extent as state officials under 42 U.S.C. § 1983.[29]

In addition, the Federal Bureau of Prisons has put into effect an internal "administrative remedy procedure" which has helped to keep federal inmate complaints out of the federal courts. As pointed out by Chief Justice Burger:

Rather than litigate complaints in overburdened federal courts, inmates may now file them with prison officials. To date, 17 percent of those complaints have been resolved in the inmate's favor by prison wardens. An additional 27 percent of complaints appealed to a regional director were resolved favorably to the inmate. Many of these complaints would otherwise have been presented to federal courts as civil rights or habeas corpus suits.[30]

§ 11.6   Federal Remedies—Civil Rights Act

The federal remedy most frequently used today by state inmates in § 1983 of the Civil Rights Act, which provides:

Every person who, under color of any statute, ordinance, regulation, custom, or usage, of any State or Territory, subjects, or causes to be subjected, any citizen of the United States or other person within the jurisdiction thereof to the deprivation of any rights, privileges, or immunities secured by the Constitution and laws, shall be liable to the party injured in an action at law, suit in equity, or other proper proceeding for redress.[31]

---

[26] 28 U.S.C. § 2680 (1964).

[27] 28 U.S.C. § 2680 (h) (1964).

[28] *See* § 11.6.2.

[29] *Bivens v. Six Unknown FBI Agents*, 403 U.S. 387 (1971); *Butz v. Economou*, 438 U.S. 478, 98 S.Ct. 2954, 57 L.Ed.2d 895, (1978).

A plaintiff may maintain a *Bivens* action, with trial by jury, even though he also has a remedy under the Federal Tort Claims Act. Further, when a defendant's unconstitutional act leads to death, federal common law permits survival of the *Bivens* claim, even though state law would not permit survival. *Carlson v. Green*, 446 U.S. 14, 100 S.Ct. 1468, 64 L.Ed.2d 15, (1980).

[30] 61 American Bar Association Journal 303 (March 1975).

[31] 42 U.S.C. § 1983 (1970).

In 1964, the United States Supreme Court held that state inmates can bring suit against their keepers under the Civil Rights Act.[32]

In 1973, the United States Supreme Court held that a § 1983 action was a proper remedy for a state inmate to make a constitutional challenge to the *conditions* of his prison life, but not to the *fact* or *length* of his custody.[33] If the fact or length of custody is being challenged, habeas corpus must be used.

To be liable under § 1983, a defendant must be acting under "color of law." Not every injury is a "federal case." Questions often arise as to whether private parties who are in contract with state agencies act under "color of law" in dealing with prisoners.

A private physician was under contract with North Carolina to provide orthopedic services at a state-prison hospital on a part-time basis. He treated a prisoner for a leg injury sustained in prison. The prisoner was barred by state law from employing or electing to see a physician of his own choosing. The doctor's conduct in treating the prisoner was fairly attributable to the State. The State has an obligation, under the Eighth Amendment and state law, to provide adequate medical care to those whom it has incarcerated. The State had delegated that function to physicians and deferred to their professional judgment. This result was not altered by the fact that the doctor was paid by contract and was not on the state payroll nor by the fact that he was not required to work exclusively for the prison. It is the physician's function within the state system, not the precise terms of his employment, that was determinative.[34]

The liability of a defendant in a civil rights case must be personal. In civil rights litigation, there is no basis for *respondeat superior* liability.[35] The master-servant or employer-employee basis for liability is not applicable in these federal lawsuits. To

---

[32] *Cooper v. Pate,* 378 U.S. 546 (1964); Even though the state is exempt from damages under a U.S.C. § 1983 action, cities do not have a similar immunity. In *Monell v. Department of Social Services of the City of New York,* 436 U.S. 658, 98 S.Ct. 2018, 56 L.Ed.2d 611, (1978), the Supreme Court held that cities are not immune from civil rights suits. Under this holding, municipalities can now be directly liable for their constitutional deprivations as long as the violation stems from official policy and not simply from the actions of an employee or agent. In the latter instance, a complaining party would have to seek relief from the individual official and not the city itself.

Monell left open the issue of whether a municipality could cloak itself with the good faith immunity defense available to its public officers. This issue was decided in the negative in *Owen v. City of Independence,* 445 U.S. 622, 100 S.Ct. 1398, 63 L.Ed.2d 673, 27 Cr. L. 3047 (1980). Municipalities are not subject to immunity from liability in Sec. 1983 actions, even though the unconstitutional conduct was undertaken in good faith.

[33] *Preiser v. Rodriguez,* 411 U.S. 475 (1973).

[34] *West v. Atkins,* 487 U.S. 42, 108 S.Ct. 2250 (1988).

[35] *City of Los Angeles v. Heller,* 475 U.S. 796 (1986).

be liable under the federal civil rights act, the action of the defendant must have directly caused the injury. Mere negligence is not enough.[36]

The Due Process Clause was not implicated by a state official's negligent act causing unintended loss of or injury to life, liberty, or property. The Due Process Clause was intended to secure an individual from an abuse of power by government officials. Far from an abuse of power, lack of due care, such as from alleged negligence, suggests no more than a failure to measure up to the conduct of a reasonable person. To hold that injury caused by such conduct is a deprivation within the meaning of the Due Process Clause would trivialize the centuries-old principle of due process of law. *Parratt v. Taylor*[37] was overruled to the extent that it stated otherwise.

The Constitution does not purport to supplant traditional tort law in laying down rules of conduct to regulate liability for injuries that attend living together in society. While the Due Process Clause speaks to some facets of the relationship between jailers and inmates, its protections are not triggered by lack of due care by the jailers. Jailers may owe a special duty of care under state tort law to those in their custody, but the Due Process Clause does not embrace such a tort law concept.[38]

In a police brutality case, it was a jury question as to whether police officers used excessive and unreasonable force against a suspect that resulted in severe injury. As regarding personal liability, it was held that the mere presence of an office at the beating is sufficient to make him liable under 42 U.S.C. § 1983, *when he made no effort to intervene and stop the beating.* Under these circumstances, the involvement was personal.

A city may only be held accountable if the deprivation was the result of a municipal "custom or policy." A city cannot be held liable solely on the basis of the acts of its officers and agents. As a general rule, a city is not responsible for the unauthorized and unlawful acts of its officers, even though done under color of law. It must further appear that the officers were expressly authorized to do the acts by the city government, or that the acts were done legitimately pursuant to a general authority to act for the city on the subject to which they related; or that, in either case, the act was adopted and ratified by the city. The word "policy" generally implies a course of action consciously chosen from among various alternatives. The "official policy" requirement of *Monell*[39] intended to distinguish acts of the municipality from acts of the municipality's employees. Municipal liability is limited to actions for which the municipality is actually responsible. *Monell* held that recovery from a

---

[36] *Estelle v. Gamble*, 429 U.S. 97 (1976); *see* § 10.3 *supra; Stewart v. Love*, 696 F.2d 43 (6th Cir. 1982). (An inmate was injured by an assault by another prisoner. As the conduct of the prison officials did not constitute gross negligence or deliberate indifference to the inmate's risk of injury, there was no violation of the Eighth Amendment. In the context of prison cases involving assaults on inmates by inmates, mere negligence on the part of prison officials is not sufficient to give rise to liability.)

[37] *Parratt v. Taylor*, 451 U.S. 527 (1981).

[38] *Daniels v. Williams*, 474 U.S. 327 (1985).

[39] *Monell v. Department of Social Services of the City of New York*, 436 U.S. 658 (1978).

municipality is limited to acts that are, properly speaking, "of the municipality," that is, acts that the municipality has officially sanctioned or ordered. Municipal liability may be imposed for a single decision by municipal policymakers under appropriate circumstances. If the decision to adopt a particular course of action is directed by those who establish governmental policy, the municipality is equally responsible whether that action is to be taken only once or to be taken repeatedly.[40]

As to municipal liability for a failure to train its officers, the United States Supreme Court held that a municipality may, in certain circumstances, be held liable under § 1983 for constitutional violations resulting from its failure to train its employees. The contention that § 1983 liability can be imposed only where the municipal policy in question is itself unconstitutional was rejected. There are circumstances in which a "failure to train" allegation can be the basis for liability.

The inadequacy of training may serve as the basis for § 1983 liability only where the failure to train in a relevant respect amounts to deliberate indifference to the constitutional rights of persons with whom the officials come into contact. This "deliberate indifference" standard is most consistent with the rule of *Monell,* that a city is not liable under § 1983 unless a municipal "policy" or "custom" is the moving force behind the constitutional violation. Only where a failure to train reflects a "deliberate" or "conscious" choice by the municipality can the failure be properly thought of as an actionable city "policy." *Monell* cannot be satisfied by a mere allegation that a training program represents a policy for which the city is responsible. Rather, the focus must be on whether the program is adequate to the tasks the particular employees must perform, and if it is not, on whether such inadequate training can justifiably be said to represent "city policy." Moreover, the identified deficiency in the training program must be closely related to the ultimate injury. Thus, the plaintiff must still prove that the deficiency in training actually caused the constitutional violation. To adopt lesser standards of fault and causation would open municipalities to unprecedented liability under § 1983, would result in *de facto respondeat superior* liability, a result rejected in *Monell,* would engage federal courts in an endless exercise of second-guessing municipal employee-training programs, a task that they are ill suited to undertake, and would implicate serious questions of federalism.[41]

When there is a basis for § 1983 liability against a municipality, the city is not entitled to a defense of "good faith" as is an individual.[42]

Settlement agreements may be enforced in certain situations. An agreement was negotiated whereby the prosecutor would dismiss the charges against the defendant if he would agree to release any claims he might have against the town, its officials, or the victim for any harm caused by his arrest. The agreement was enforced when ten months later, he filed an action under 42 U.S.C. § 1983 alleging that the town

---

[40] *Pembaur v. City of Cincinnati,* 475 U.S. 469 (1986).
[41] *City of Canton , Ohio v. Harris,* ___ U.S. ___, 109 S.Ct. 1197 (1989); *See also, Oklahoma City v. Tuttle,* 471 U.S. 808 (1985).
[42] *Brandon v. Holt,* 469 U.S. 464 (1984).

and its officers had violated his constitutional rights by arresting him, defaming him, and imprisoning him falsely. The suit was dismissed on the basis of the assertion by the defendant's of the release-dismissal agreement as an affirmative defense. The United States Supreme Court held that such agreements are not *per se* invalid. The question whether the policies underlying § 1983 may in some circumstances render a waiver of the right to sue thereunder unenforceable is one of federal law, to be resolved by reference to traditional common-law principles. The relevant principle is that a promise is unenforceable if the interest in its enforcement is outweighed in the circumstances by a public policy harmed by enforcement of the agreement.[43]

§ 11.6.1   —Civil Rights Act—Exhaustion of Remedies

Whether exhaustion of available state judicial and administrative remedies is a prerequisite to bring suit in federal court under the Civil Rights Act is frequently discussed by lower level federal courts. Although the Supreme Court has stated that exhaustion of state remedies is not required,[44] it has confused the question by stressing that futility or unavailability of state remedies in a particular case will not require an inmate to perform the act of processing his claim through state agencies. However, several factors indicate that exhaustion is not required if the suit seeks to redress past deprivations of constitutional rights by prison administrators. First, the statute itself does not require such exhaustion. Second, there is no reason to believe that federal courts are any less competent than are state courts to punish violations of the federal constitution. Hence, the Supreme Court has held that a state inmate complaining of living conditions at the Missouri State Penitentiary need not exhaust state judicial or administrative remedies.[45] As the great bulk of inmate complaints under the Civil Rights Act complain of past deprivations of constitutional rights, no exhaustion is required.[46]

As emphasized by the Second Circuit Court of Appeals in *Morgan v. LaVallee:* "This court has flatly held that exhaustion of state judicial remedies is unnecessary in a § 1983 prisoner's suit."[47]

However, the constitutional provision that federal courts can adjudicate only actual "cases or controversies" may, in some situations, force a party to exhaust available state administrative remedies before he brings suit in federal court alleging deprivations of constitutional rights. This is because many administrative orders made by lower-echelon officers are subject to review and modification by

[43] *Town of Newton v. Rumery,* 480 U.S. 386 (1986).

[44] *McNeese v. Bd. of Educ.,* 373 U.S. 668 (1963); *Monroe v. Pape,* 365 U.S. 167 (1961); *Steffel v. Thompson,* 415 U.S. 452 (1974); *Preiser v. Rodriguez,* 411 U.S. 475 (1973); *Huffman v. Pursue, Ltd.,* 420 U.S. 592 (1975).

[45] *Wilwording v. Swenson,* 404 U.S. 249 (1971); *see also, United States v. Mogavero,* 521 F.2d 625 (4th Cir. 1975). *See also, Dickerson v. Warden, Marquette Prison,* 298 N.W.2d 841 (Mich. App. 1980).

[46] *See, e.g., Sostre v. McGinnis,* 442 F.2d 178 (2d Cir. 1971), *cert. denied,* 405 U.S. 978 (1972); *Clutchette v. Procunier,* 328 F. Supp. 767 (N.D. Cal. 1971).

[47] *Morgan v. LaVallee,* 526 F.2d 221 (2d Cir. 1975) at 223.

higher-level officials. Hence, the first order is not a "final" one. For example, a federal appellate court held that if the state provides for a speedy appeal to a higher administrative officer, a landlord must utilize the review procedure before he can maintain an action under the Civil Rights Act against a regional officer of the rent control agency.[48] The court stressed that the plaintiff faced only monetary loss, not deprivation of personal liberty. However, another federal court required several college professors who had been denied reappointment for the following academic year to exhaust what the court held to be an adequate administrative remedy, even though the professors sued under the Civil Rights Act, claiming they were being dismissed merely because they had exercised their First Amendment rights.[49] The decision was rendered several months *before* the plaintiffs' current appointments were to expire. The court stated that although exhaustion of administrative remedies is not required if the alleged constitutional deprivation has already taken place, it could be required if designed to prevent *threatened* deprivations of civil rights.

In the prison setting a federal court held that inmates are required to exhaust their state remedies under the Maryland Inmate Grievance Commission Act prior to initiating civil rights actions against prison officials. However, on appeal, the United States Court of Appeals for the Fourth Circuit reversed the decision. Feeling itself bound by prior decisions and interpreting the decisions handed down by the United States Supreme Court, the court stated that exhaustion of state remedies is not required in a § 1983 action but also recommended that the case be appealed to the United States Supreme Court.[50] In a curious display of judicial discretionary decision-making the United States Supreme Court first granted certiorari,[51] then reversed itself, and held that its decision to grant certiorari was "improvidently granted."[52] Thus, the issue is again left open.

Although the United States Supreme Court has not directly decided this issue, in *Procunier v. Martinez*[53] the Court recognized that:

> The problems of prisons in America are complex and intractable, and, more to the point, they are not readily susceptible of resolution by decree. Most require expertise, comprehensive planning, and the commitment of resources, all of which are peculiarly within the province of the legislative and executive branches of government. For all of those reasons, courts are ill-equipped to deal with the increasingly urgent problems of prison administra-

---

[48] *Eisen v. Eastman*, 421 F.2d 560 (2d Cir. 1969), *cert. denied*, 400 U.S. 841 (1970).

[49] *Toney v. Reagan*, 326 F. Supp. 1093 (N.D. Cal. 1971).

[50] *McCray v. Burrell*, 516 F.2d 357 (4th Cir. 1975); *See also Fontaine v. Walls*, 515 F.2d 884 (5th Cir. 1975).

[51] *Burrell v. McCray*, 423 U.S. 923, 46 L.Ed.2d 249, 96 S.Ct. 264 (1975).

[52] *Burrell v. McCray*, 426 U.S. 471 (1976).

[53] *Procunier v. Martinez*, 416 U.S. 396, 71 Ohio Op.2d 139 (1974).

tors and reform. Judicial recognition of that fact reflects no more than a healthy sense of realism.[54]

Of particular significance, in a footnote, Mr. Justice Powell, who wrote the decision for the Court stated:

As one means of alleviating this problem, THE CHIEF JUSTICE has suggested that federal and state authorities explore the possibility of instituting internal administrative procedures for disposition of inmate grievances.[55]

Although "failure to exhaust" may not be a basis upon which an inmate's civil rights action is summarily dismissed by a federal court, in practice, federal judges will permit the case to be docketed, and then delayed until after the prison grievance procedure has been used. Many of these cases will ultimately be dismissed when the underlying issue has been resolved internally. Correctional administrators should recognize, however, that in order for this emerging doctrine to apply, the administrative procedure must be meaningful and not a sham.

Exhaustion of state administrative remedies is not a prerequisite to an action under the Civil Rights Act, 42 U.S.C. § 1983. The only exception is for adult prisoners, due to 42 U.S.C. § 1997(e), provided that the administrative procedures satisfy certain minimum standards. The minimum standards must provide: (A) for an advisory role for employees and inmates of any jail, prison, or other correctional institution (at the most decentralized level as is reasonably possible), in the formulation, implementation, and operation of the system; (B) specific maximum time limits for written replies to grievances with reasons thereto at each decision level within the system; (C) for priority processing of grievances which are of an emergency nature, including matters in which delay would subject the grievant to substantial risk of personal injury or other damage; (D) for safeguards to avoid reprisals against any grievant or participant in the resolution of a grievance; and (E) for independent review of the disposition of grievances, including alleged reprisals, by a person or other entity not under the direct supervision or direct control of the institution.[56]

Although *Patsy v. Board of Regents of Florida* held that plaintiffs need not exhaust state administrative remedies before instituting § 1983 suits in federal court, the doctrine is not inapplicable to state "notice of claims" statutes on the theory that States retain the authority to prescribe the rules and procedures governing suits in their courts. That authority does not extend so far as to permit States to place conditions on the vindication of a *federal* right. Congress meant to provide individuals immediate access to the federal courts and did not contemplate that

---

[54] *Procunier v. Martinez*, 416 U.S. at 405, 71 Ohio Op.2d at 142.

[55] *Procunier v. Martinez*, 416 U.S. at 405 n. 9, 71 Ohio Op.2d at 142; *see also, Parratt v. Taylor*, 451 U.S. 527 (1981); *Miller v. Stanmore*, 636 F.2d 986 (5th Cir. 1981).

[56] *Patsy v. Florida Board of Regents*, 457 U.S. 496 (1982).

those who sought to vindicate their federal rights in state courts could be required to seek redress in the first instance from the very state officials whose hostility to those rights precipitated their injuries. There is no merit to the contention that the exhaustion requirement imposed by the "notice of claims" statutes are essentially *de minimis* because the statutory settlement period entails none of the additional expense or undue delay typically associated with administrative remedies, and does not alter a claimant's right to seek full compensation through suit. Moreover, to the extent the exhaustion requirement is designed to sift out "specious claims" from the stream of complaints that can inundate local governments in the absence of immunity, such a policy is inconsistent with the aims of the federal legislation.[57]

In summary, the current state of the law would seem to require exhaustion of state administrative remedies before suing under the Civil Rights Act only if the alleged unconstitutional action will not be effective until some future date (as, for example, a set of rules and regulations promulaged by the prison administrators) and if a speedy and effective procedure for administrative review exists. If, on the other hand, the suit complains of either a past deprivation of a federal right or a threatened deprivation for which there is no adequate administrative review procedure, no exhaustion of state remedies, either judicial or administrative, will be required.

§ 11.6.2   —The Immunity Defenses

Sovereign Immunity

It is evident that if sovereign immunity could be asserted by state officials as a defense to a suit based on the Civil Rights Act, the statute would be stripped of its vitality, as it literally applies to persons acting under state law. Hence it is not surprising to find that the Civil Rights Act has been successfully used against prison wardens[58] and prison guards.[59]

There are no reported cases in which money damages have been recovered from a state's chief executive under the Civil Rights Act. However, the Supreme Court has stated that Congress did not intend "to abolish wholesale all common-law immunities"[60] when it passed the Civil Rights Act. Hence, the Court has approved

---

[57] *Felder v. Casey,* 487 U.S. 131, 108 S.Ct. 2302 (1988).

[58] *Sostre v. McGinnis,* 442 F.2d 178 (2d Cir. 1971), *cert. denied,* 405 U.S. 978 (1972); *Withers v. Levine,* 615 F.2d 158 (4th Cir. 1980); *Estelle v. Gamble,* 429 U.S. 97 (1976).

[59] *Wiltsie v. California Department of Corrections,* 406 F.2d 515 (9th Cir. 1968). *See also, Meredith v. State of Arizona,* 523 F.2d 481 (9th Cir. 1975); *Harris v. Chancellor,* 537 F.2d 204 (5th Cir. 1976); *Collins v. Cundy,* 603 F.2d 824 (10th Cir. 1979).

[60] *Pierson v. Ray,* 386 U.S. 547, 554 (1967).

the immunity of state legislators[61] and state judges.[62] In 1909, the Supreme Court had an opportunity to give state governors an absolute immunity, but it refused to do so, apparently satisfied to give governors a qualified immunity when they act in good faith.[63]

In *Scheuer v. Rhodes*[64] the United States Supreme Court stated: ". . . the Eleventh Amendment[65] provides no shield for a state official confronted by a claim he had deprived another of a federal right under the color of state law."[66] The Court cited the case of *Ex parte Young*,[67] stating that a state official acting under state law in a manner which violates the Federal Constitution is ". . . stripped of his official or representative character and is subjected in his person to the consequences of his individual conduct."[68]

Executive Immunity—Absolute Immunity

The idea that government officials are immune from personal liability follows the same rationale that brought us the doctrine of sovereign immunity. The general proposition which has supported this immunity has been that the public has an interest in having public officials making decisions and taking action to enforce the laws for the protection of the public, without worrying about facing numerous lawsuits for their actions. This immunity has been the product of constitutional and legislative provisions as well as judicial determination, as pointed out above.

Whenever the issue of official immunity is discussed, a distinction must be made between *absolute* immunity and *qualified* immunity. Absolute immunity means just that. If the doctrine applies, it is not possible to maintain a civil action for personal damages against the individual no matter how extensive the injuries, or malicious the intent. If such injury occurs, the remedy is injunctive relief, impeachment, or criminal prosecution. The class of persons protected by absolute immunity is basically limited to judges,[69] prosecutors,[70] and legislators.[71] The United States Supreme Court has held that federal executive officials exercising

---

[61] *Tenny v. Brandhove*, 341 U.S. 367 (1951).

[62] *Pierson v. Ray*, 386 U.S. 547 (1967); *Briscoe v. LaHue*, 460 U.S. 325, (1983). (Even though a testifying police officer allegedly committed perjury at a criminal trial, he is immune from a suite for damages under the Civil Rights Act [42 USC 1983] brought by the former defendant. The common law provides absolute immunity from subsequent damages liability for all persons, governmental or private, who are integral parts of the judicial process.)

[63] *Moyer v. Peabody*, 212 U.S. 78 (1909) (state governor not liable for ordering arrest of plaintiff when governor acted in good faith belief that such arrest was necessary to prevent insurrection).

[64] *Scheuer v. Rhodes*, 416 U.S. 232 (1974).

[65] Appendix III.

[66] *Scheuer v. Rhodes*, 416 U.S. at 237.

[67] *Ex parte Young*, 209 U.S. 123 (1908).

[68] *Id.* at 159-160.

[69] *Pierson v. Ray*, 386 U.S. 547, 554 (1967).

[70] *Id.*

[71] *Tenny v. Brandhove*, 341 U.S. 367 (1951).

discretion are entitled to the qualified immunity specified in *Scheuer v. Rhodes,*[72] subject to those situations where the official is performing judicial acts, such as an agency attorney. In those cases the official is entitled to absolute immunity because it is deemed essential for the conduct of the public business. However, even though there may be no absolute immunity, the government official may still be protected by a qualified immunity.

Qualified Immunity

Whether an official has a qualified immunity will depend on the functions and responsibilities of the official claiming the immunity as well as the purposes behind 42 U.S.C. § 1983. Section 1983 includes "misuse of power, possessed by virtue of state law and made possible only because the wrongdoer is clothed with the authority of state law."

The Court in *Scheuer* stated:

In varying scope, a qualified immunity is available to officers of the executive branch of government, the violation being dependent upon the scope of discretion and responsibilities of the office and all the circumstances as they reasonably appeared at the time of the action on which liability is sought to be based. It is the existence of reasonable grounds for the belief formed at the time and in light of all the circumstances, coupled with good-faith belief, that affords a basis for qualified immunity of executive officers for acts performed in the course of official conduct.[74]

The issue of qualified immunity arose in the "school" setting with respect to a working definition of "good-faith." The case was *Wood v. Strickland,*[75] and the United States Supreme Court established a two-prong test, based on "subjective" and "objective" good-faith determinations. The Court held:

Therefore, in the specific context of school discipline, we hold that a school board member is not immune from liability for damages under § 1983 if he knew or reasonably should have known that the action he took within his sphere of official responsibility would violate the constitutional rights of the student affected, or if he took the action with the malicious intention to cause a deprivation of constitutional rights or other injury to the student. That is not to say that school board members are "charged with predicting the future course of constitutional law." A compensatory award will be appropriate only if the school board member has acted with such an impermissible motivation or

---

[72] *Scheuer v. Rhodes,* 416 U.S. 232 (1974).
[74] *Scheuer v. Rhodes,* 416 U.S. at 247.
[75] *Wood v. Strickland,* 420 U.S. 308 (1975).

with such disregard of the student's clearly established constitutional rights that his action cannot reasonably be characterized as being in good-faith.[76]

Under the *Wood* test, the official involved must himself be acting sincerely, *and* with a belief that he is doing right. However, an act violating a constitutional right cannot be justified by ignorance or disregard of settled law. In other words, an executive official is held to a standard of conduct based not only on permissible *intentions,* but also on knowledge of the *basic, unquestioned constitutional rights* of the individuals for whom the official is responsible.

Therefore, there is no immunity from civil damages if the official *knows,* or *reasonably should have known* that the action taken, within the sphere of his official responsibility, would violate the constitutional rights of the person affected, *or* if the official took the action with malicious intent to cause a deprivation of constitutional rights of injury.

Wood was a five-to-four decision. The dissenting Justices argued, in effect, that it is unsound to hold public officials liable for actions taken, without malice, which violated "unquestioned constitutional rights," when the Supreme Court itself cannot determine unanimously what those rights are. Justice Powell writing for the dissent stated:

> The Court states the standard of required knowledge in two cryptic phrases: "settled, indisputable law" and "unquestioned constitutional rights." Presumably these are intended to mean the same thing, although the meaning of neither phrase is likely to be self-evident to constitutional law scholars—much less the average school board member. One need only look to the decisions of this Court—to our reversals, our recognition of evolving concepts, and our five-four splits—to recognize the hazard of even informed prophecy as to what are "unquestioned constitutional rights."[77]

The dilemma facing public officials is highlighted by *O'Connor v. Donaldson.*[78] In *O'Connor,* a mental patient sued the superintendent of the mental institution for depriving him of his liberty. The judge and jury agreed, and the mental patient recovered a judgment of $38,500 against the superintendent personally. The superintendent argued on appeal that he was merely acting pursuant to an Alabama statute, and that he could not reasonably have been expected to know that the state law, as he understood it, was constitutionally invalid. The Court of Appeals was not sympathetic, and affirmed the money judgment. On appeal to the United States Supreme Court the case was reversed and remanded to the lower courts for reconsideration in light of *Wood v. Strickland.*

---

[76] *Id.* at 322.
[77] *Id.* at 329.
[78] *O'Connor v. Donaldson,* 422 U.S. 563 (1975).

A subsequent decision of a federal Court of Appeals found "bad faith" along more traditional lines. The court found that the state officials had maintained a defense stratagem of delay for delay's sake, as well as an unconscionable—and continued—denial of facts that were well documented and known to all parties interested in the subject. An award of $52,000 was made.[79]

In *Procunier v. Navarette*,[80] the *Wood* standard was applied to prison officials. The court ruled that as prison officials, the defendants were not absolutely immune from liability in the § 1983 damages suit and could only rely on qualified immunity as described in *Scheuer* and *Wood*. Using the first standard put forth in *Wood*, the court stated ". . . the immunity defense would be unavailing to [the prison officials] if the constitutional right allegedly infringed by them was clearly established at the time of their challenged conduct, if they knew or should have known of that right, and if they knew or should have known that their conduct violated the constitutional norm."

Also, in *Knell v. Bensinger*,[81] the *Wood* standard was applied to prison officials. In discussing *Wood's* two-pronged test for qualified immunity the court defined the subjective good-faith requirement as, whether, in enforcing the challenged regulation against the plaintiff, the defendant "sincerely and with a belief that he was doing right" carried out the regulation. In defining the objective good-faith requirement the court stated that the prison official would not be immune if he acted "with such disregard of the plaintiff's clearly established constitutional rights that his action cannot reasonably be characterized as being in good-faith."

The court then held that in the field of prison administration, officials must be aware of the protections given inmates through the judicial process. Imposition of personal liability is a shorthand method of informing prison officials that they must be concerned with and informed of legal developments in the rights of the confined, as set forth by the courts, the legislature and the agency for which the officials work. At the same time the court recognized the importance of experimentation and discretion in developing correctional policies and disciplinary procedures.

Another case imposing the *Wood* standard on prison officials is *Cruz v. Beto*,[82] where the former Director of the Texas Department of Corrections was held liable in the amount of approximately $10,000 for violating inmate's rights. The violations which were actionable for money damages included: (1) wrongful segregation, humiliation, denial of access to the courts and to the attorney of the inmate's choice, and improper censorship of mail between attorney and client; (2) denial of access to educational materials with a corresponding interference in inmates' efforts to rehabilitate themselves; (3) wrongful deprivation of the opportunity to earn Point Incentive Program merit points solely because of inmate's choice of counsel, and;

---

[79] *Gates v. Collier*, 70 F.R.D. 341 [18 Cr. L. 2471] (N.D. Miss. 1976).
[80] *Procunier v. Navarette*, 434 U.S. 555 (1978).
[81] *Knell v. Bensinger*, 522 F2d 720 (7th Cir. 1975).
[82] *Cruz v. Beto*, 405 U.S. 319 (1972).

(4) imposition of excessive demands of physical labor upon those inmates who were duly categorized by corrections officials as medically unfit to perform such tasks.

Cruz is an example of facts alleged by prison officials to justify their decisions and actions which were not proved in court. The court took note that the witnesses which were to testify as to the danger to security failed to appear, that no complaints were ever made to the Texas Bar Association about the conduct of the attorney, nor were any criminal charges ever filed. Prison officials must realize that naked allegations are not a sufficient defense. The burden of proving justification for interfering with fundamental constitutional rights is on the prison officials— and they must be *proved in court.*

In *Harlow v. Fitzgerald,*[83] the Supreme Court felt that too many cases were going to the jury or leading to too-extensive pretrial discovery. The Supreme Court also felt that more cases should be disposed of on summary judgment. The Court stated: ". . . [B]are allegations of malice should not suffice to subject government officials either to the costs of trial or to the burdens of broad-reaching discovery . . . [G]overnment officials performing discretionary functions generally are shielded from liability for civil damages insofar as their conduct does not violate clearly established statutory or constitutional rights of which a reasonable person would have known. ... On summary judgment, the judge appropriately may determine, not only the currently applicable law, but whether that law was clearly established at the time the action occurred. If the law at that time was not clearly established, an official could not reasonably be expected to anticipate subsequent legal developments, nor could he fairly be said to 'know' that the law forbade conduct not previously identified as unlawful. Until this threshold immunity question is resolved, discovery should not be allowed. If the law was clearly established, the immunity defense ordinarily should fail, since a reasonably competent public official should know the law governing his conduct. Nevertheless, if the official pleading the defense claims extraordinary circumstances and can prove that he neither knew nor should have known the relevant legal standard, the defense should be sustained." Other examples of bad faith include *Williams v. Treen*[84] and *Bennett v. Williams.*[85]

In *Williams,* it was held that where state prison officials violated clearly established state law, their belief in the lawfulness of their actions was *per se* unreasonable. They were not entitled to claim immunity based upon the defense of good faith. In other words, a good faith immunity from liability in a Civil Rights action cannot

---

[83] *Harlow v. Fitzgerald,* 457 U.S. 800 (1982); *Alexander v. Alexander,* 706 F.2d 751 (6th Cir. 1983). (The defendant in a civil rights action retains the burden of pleading the qualified immunity defense, and proving either the law was not clearly established at the time of the plaintiff's alleged injury or, if the law was clearly established, that he neither knew nor should have known of the relevant legal standard due to extraordinary circumstances.)

[84] *Williams v. Treen,* 671 F.2d 892 (5th Cir. 1982).

[85] *Bennett v. Williams,* 689 F.2d 1370 (11th Cir. 1983).

be asserted by officials whose actions clearly violate established state law. Here, applicable state fire, safety, and health regulations were violated. Further, state officials are charged with knowledge of their state's own explicit and clearly established regulations.

In *Bennett,* in light of a determination that living conditions in Alabama prisons constituted cruel and unusual punishment in violation of the Eighth Amendment in a prior § 1983 case, prison officials were precluded from invoking qualified immunity as the prior litigation put them on notice of the continuing violations of the prisoner's constitutional rights. A jury instruction suggesting that the state could not be required to pay any part of the judgment against the officials and employees was sufficiently prejudicial to the prisoner that reversal of the favorable judgment for the prison officials was reversed.

Lack of "standing" may also be asserted as a defense. In *Leeke v. Timmerman,* a lower court decision awarding damages against the South Carolina legal advisor to the Department of Corrections and the Director, of $3,000 compensatory damages, $1,000 punitive damages, and attorney fees was reversed. The allegation was that the two defendants had attempted to prevent criminal charges being filed by an inmate against correctional guards after an alleged beating within the prison by intervening with the local prosecutor. The Supreme Court held that a private citizen (here the inmate) had no "standing" in federal court to challenge the discretion of a prosecutor in his determination that criminal charges should or should not be filed. Since a complaining witness has the right to try to persuade a prosecutor to file charges, potential targets also have the right to try to persuade a prosecutor to not file charges.[86]

However, the defense that the public official acted in reliance upon state policy still retains some force. In *Milton v. Nelson*[87] the court stated:

> Once it is established that a defendant was acting pursuant to official regulations, the burden shifts to the plaintiff to assert that the defendant was not acting in good faith. . . . Even if the regulations are subsequently found to be invalid a defendant's good faith enforcement of these regulations can still be a defense to a section 1983 suit.[88]

---

[86] *Leeke v. Timmerman,* 457 U.S. 496 (1981).

[87] *Milton v. Nelson,* 527 F.2d 1158 (9th Cir. 1976); *See also, Nix v. Paderick,* 407 F. Supp. (844 E.D. Va. 1976).

[88] *Milton v. Nelson,* 527 F.2d at 1160; *Salinas v. Brier,* 695 F.2d 1073 (7th Cir. 1982). (In a Civil Rights Act suit against a city police chief alleging an illegal body search of a suspect, the court held that the requirement that the search be conducted pursuant to established police department policy was satisfied when the policies were embodied in a police academy manual used in training recruits for three years prior to the search.)

In *James v. Wallace*,[89] the court held that a public official may be held liable under the civil rights statute where he, in subjective good faith, acts in disregard of a person's clearly established constitutional rights.

In *Procunier v. Navarette*,[90] the Court held that a prison official was eligible for qualified immunity because his interference with an inmate's mail was not a firmly established constitutionally protected right at the time that the alleged interference occurred. Thus, unless the constitutional protection of some right is firmly established at the time of the action, the official cannot be held to the knowledge that he has invaded a constitutional right of an inmate.

The defense of qualified immunity is available so long as the official's actions do not violate clearly established statutory or constitutional rights of which a reasonable person would have known. This standard permits an official to carry out his duties wholly free from concern for his personal liability. On the other hand, he may on occasion have to pause to consider whether a proposed course of action can be squared with the Constitution and laws of the United States. Where an official could be expected to know that his conduct would violate statutory or constitutional rights, he should be made to hesitate. The essential issue, and problem, of the qualified immunity defense is timing. If the best that a public official-defendant can expect is a favorable jury instruction at the termination of a case, the defense is really unsatisfactory. What is needed is a summary procedure to avoid long and costly pretrial discovery proceedings, and the trial itself.

Harlow v. Fitzgerald refashioned the qualified immunity doctrine in such a way to permit the resolution of may insubstantial claims on summary judgment and to avoid subjecting government officials either to the costs of trial or to the burdens of broad-reaching discovery in cases where the legal norms the officials were alleged to have violated were not clearly established at the time. Unless a plaintiff's allegations state a claim of the violation of clearly established law, a defendant pleading qualified immunity is entitled to dismissal before the commencement of discovery. Further, even if the plaintiff's complaint adequately alleges the commission of acts that violate clearly established law, the defendant is entitled to summary judgment if discovery fails to uncover evidence sufficient to create a genuine issue as to whether the defendant in fact committed those acts. There is an entitlement not to stand trial or face the other burdens of litigation, conditioned on the resolution of the essentially legal question whether the conduct of which the plaintiff complains violated clearly established law. The entitlement is an immunity from suit rather than a mere defense to liability. Consequently, an order denying qualified immunity is an appealable "final decision." An appellate court reviewing the denial of a defendant's claim of immunity need not consider the correctness of the plaintiff's version of the facts, nor even determine whether the plaintiff's version of the facts,

---

[89] *James v. Wallace*, 406 F. Supp. 318 (M.D. Ala. 1976); *See also, Bogard v. Cook*, 405 F. Supp. 1202 (N.D. Miss. 1975).

[90] *Procunier v. Navarette*, 434 U.S. 555 (1978).

nor even determine whether the plaintiff's allegations actually state a claim. All that is needed is for the appellate court to determine a question of law; whether the legal norms established at the time of the challenged actions or, in cases where the trial court has denied summary judgment for the defendant on the ground that even under the defendant's version of the facts the defendant's conduct violated clearly established law, whether the law clearly forbade the actions the defendant claims he took.[91]

Applying the immunity tests to a Parole Board in *Bricker v. Michigan Parole Board*,[92] the court held that the qualified immunity described in *Scheuer* and *Wood* does not apply to Parole Board members. Instead the court characterized the position of Parole Board members as an "arm of the sentencing judge" and when making decisions on the grant, denial or revocation of parole, the Parole Board members are acting in a quasi-judicial capacity and entitled to an immunity similar to the absolute immunity granted judges. This same rationale, giving members of Parole Boards a "quasi-judicial" immunity has been followed in other cases.[93] However, most members of the corrections department will be clothed only with a qualified immunity and subject to the two-prong good faith test in *Wood v. Strickland*.

Martinez v. California[94] came to the Supreme Court involving, among other issues, whether parole officials enjoyed quasi-judicial immunity under the Civil Rights Act, 42 U.S.C. § 1983, in parole-release decisions. In affirming the decision below on other grounds, it was said in a footnote: "We reserve the question of what immunity, if any, a state parole officer has in a Sec. 1983 action, where a constitutional violation is made out by the violations."[95]

In *Payton v. United States*, the federal government was not liable for the allegedly negligent parole of a dangerously psychotic prisoner who later killed a woman. The actual decision to grant or deny parole is within the complete discretion of the parole board, and therefore falls under the "discretionary function" exemption of the Federal Tort Claims Act. However, the Bureau of Prisons may be held liable for their failure to supply the parole board with records that would show an inmate to be dangerously psychotic and a menace to society when that inmate later kills a woman after his parole. Further, the law places an affirmative undiscretionary mandate upon the federal government to examine inmates who may be insane. Any

---

[91] *Mitchell v. Forsyth*, 472 U.S. 511 (1985).

[92] *Bricker v. Michigan Parole Board*, 405 F. Supp. 1340 (E.D. Mich. 1975). (The authority of the *Bricker* case is lessened by the fact that a district court in the same federal judicial circuit held the Ohio Parole Board clothed with a qualified immunity, which was affirmed by the Sixth Circuit, *Joyce v. Gilligan*, 510 F.2d 973 (6th Cir. 1975.); the federal district court sitting in Detroit was apparently unaware of the earlier Sixth Circuit case; *see also*, *Neely v. Eshelman*, 507 F. Supp. 78 (D. Pa. 1981). (Where employees of the Parole Board engage in duties which are administrative rather than adjudicative in nature, they are entitled to a qualified good-faith immunity from suit for their actions.)

[93] *Pope v. Chew*, 521 F.2d 400 (4th Cir. 1975); *Freach v. Commonwealth*, 354 A.2d 908 (Pa. 1976); *Reiff v. Commonwealth*, 397 F. Supp. 345 (E.D. Pa. 1975).

[94] *Martinez v. California*, 444 U.S. 227 (1980).

[95] *Id.* at 285, n. 11.

negligence on the part of the federal government for failure to examine an inmate and later report their findings to the Attorney General or his designee is actionable.[96]

Members of a disciplinary committee are entitled only to qualified immunity, and not absolute immunity.[97]

§ 11.6.3 —Monetary Damages

A plaintiff who brings an action under the Civil Rights Act is entitled to an award of monetary damages in order to redress deprivations of his constitutional rights. A federal court listed three distinct classes of damages that an inmate might recover from prison officials who have violated his constitutional rights:[98] 1) actual damages to compensate the inmate for his out-of-pocket expenses and mental suffering; 2) nominal damages to vindicate the inmate's rights, if no actual damages were sustained; and 3) punitive damages if the wrongful act was done intentionally and maliciously.

In the case of *Sostre v. McGinnis*[99] a federal appellate court upheld an award of $9300 in compensatory damages rendered against a prison warden and state commissioner of corrections. The damages were based upon the rate of $25 per day for the 372 days which plaintiff spent in isolated confinement with deplorable conditions.[100] However, the appellate court reversed an additional award of $3720 in punitive damages, as it found no malice exercised on the part of defendants.

In *Cruz v. Beto*,[101] the following formula was used by the court in determining monetary damages to the inmates:

1. $1.00 to each inmate-plaintiff for each day the segregation policy was imposed upon him . . .;

---

[96] *Payton v. United States*, 679 F.2d 475 (5th Cir. 1982); *see also, Bowers v. Devito*, 686 F.2d 616 (7th Cir. 1982). (The dismissal of a § 1983 action against Illinois state health officials for the release of an allegedly dangerous mental patient who later stabbed a woman to death was upheld. Members of the general public do not have a constitutional right to be protected by the state from attacks by convicts and madmen.)

[97] *Cleavinger v. Saxner*, 474 U.S. 193 (1985).

[98] *Wilson v. Prasse*, 325 F. Supp. 9 (W.D. Pa. 1971).

[99] *Sostre v. McGinnis*, 442 F.2d 178 (2d Cir. 1971), *rev'g in part*, 312 F. Supp. 863 (S.D. N.Y. 1970), *cert. denied*, 405 U.S. 978 (1972).

[100] The district court expressly held that the conditions of confinement, such as lack of exercise, restricted diet, sensory deprivation, and deprivation of intellectual stimulation, constituted cruel and unusual punishment, and bases its award of compensatory damages on this finding. *Sostre v. Rockefeller*, 312 F. Supp. 863, 885 (S.D. N.Y. 1970). However, the appellate court overrruled this finding, stating that the conditions of segregated confinement did not amount to cruel and unusual punishment. *Sostre v. McGinnis*, 442 F.2d 178, 190-94 (2d Cir. 1971), *cert. denied*, 405 U.S. 978 (1972). Nevertheless, the appellate court bases its affirmation of the compensatory damages upon "the conditions . . . of segregation." *Id.* at 205, n. 52. Hence, exactly what the plaintiff was being compensated for is somewhat unclear, but since the appellate court held that the prison officials placed Sostre in segregated confinement for invalid reasons, it may be presumed that damages were upheld merely because Sostre had been placed in isolation.

[101] *Cruz v. Beto*, 453 F. Supp. 905 (S.D. Texas 1976), *aff'd*, 603 F.2d 1178 (5th Cir. 1979). *See also*, discussion of this case in § 11.6.2.

2. $25.00 to each inmate-plaintiff for being deprived of (merit) PIP points while segregated;

3. $250.00 to each inmate-plaintiff who was classified as medically unfit and who should not have been required, but was so required, to perform field labor while segregated;

4. $250.00 to each inmate-plaintiff who was prohibited from continuing college level or secondary level education while segregated. In addition, the court found that the attorney involved in the *Cruz* case was entitled to damages of $1000.00 for "embarassment, humiliation, and improper deprivation . . . of the right to practice law through representation of . . . inmates."

Another court held that where an inmate was punished for possession of inflammatory papers, the prison officials were liable, the commissioner and the warden were each personally liable, and a verdict of $1000.00 was not excessive.[102]

Punitive damages may be recovered for reckless or callously indifferent deprivations of federal statutory or constitutional rights as well as for deprivations motivated by actual malicious intent. Punitive damages may be recovered for reckless or callous indifference to federally protected rights even when the standard of liability for compensatory damages is also one of recklessness. Here, the respondent, while an inmate in a Missouri reformatory for youthful first offenders, was harassed, beaten and sexually assaulted by his cellmates. He sued a guard at the reformatory, and others, alleging that his Eighth Amendment rights had been violated. Damages affirmed were $25,000 compensatory and $5,000 punitive. Smith, the guard, placed the inmate in administrative segregation. He was placed in a cell with another inmate. Smith later placed a third inmate in the cell. The cellmates harassed, beat, and sexually assaulted the inmate-plaintiff. Evidence at trial showed that the inmate-plaintiff had placed himself in protective custody because of prior incidents of violence against him by other inmates. The third prisoner that Smith placed in the cell had been placed in administrative segregation for fighting. Smith made no effort to find out whether another cell was available. In fact there was another cell in the same dormitory with only one occupant. Further, only a few weeks earlier, another inmate had been beaten to death in the same dormitory during the same shift, while Smith had been on duty. It was held that Smith knew or should have known that an assault against the inmate-plaintiff was likely under the circumstances.[103] However, municipalities are immune from punitive damages in civil rights suits under 42 U.S.C. § 1983.[104]

Damages based on the abstract "value" or "importance" of constitutional rights are not a permissible element of compensatory damages in § 1983 cases. The basic purpose of a damage award in a § 1983 case is to compensate persons for injuries

---

[102] *United States ex rel. Larkins v. Oswald,* 510 F.2d 583 (2d Cir. 1975).
[103] *Smith v. Wade,* 461 U.S. 30, 103 S.Ct. 1625, 75 L.Ed.2d 632 (1983).
[104] *City of Newport v. Facts Concerts,* 453 U.S. 247 (1981).

that are caused by the deprivation of constitutional rights. Damages measured by a jury's perception of the abstract "importance" of a constitutional right are not necessary to vindicate the constitutional rights that § 1983 protects, and moreover are an unwieldy tool for ensuring compliance with the Constitution. As such damages are wholly divorced from any compensatory purpose, they cannot be justified as presumed damages, which are a substitute for ordinary compensatory damages, not a supplement for an award that fully compensates the alleged injury.[105]

§ 11.6.4 —Injunctive Relief

In addition to monetary damages, the Civil Rights Act authorizes equitable remedies, such as issuing an injunction. An injunction is a judicial order that requires the person to whom it is directed to do a particular thing or to refrain from doing it. Injunctive relief is extremely useful in prison litigation, as the successful inmate-plaintiff will usually remain in custody and thus will wish to prevent future deprivations of his constitutional rights.

A trend in prison litigation is a judicial examination of the totality of internal conditions at specific detention facilities. In a number of cases, federal courts have declared such conditions to be so intolerable as to amount to the imposition of cruel and unusual punishment.[106] Although some courts in such cases have allowed the prison administrators to submit plans to the court for rectification of the facility's deficiencies,[107] several courts have judicially detailed the changes that must be made,[108] and other courts have offered the state legislature the opportunity to solve the problem before intervening.[109] In the case of *Jones v. Wittenberg*,[110] several months after declaring that the totality of conditions within the Lucas County (Toledo, Ohio) Jail rendered incarceration therein cruel and unusual punishment,[111] the federal court issued a lengthy relief decree mandating many specific changes.[112] This remedial relief covered all aspects of operating the institution, from the required wattage of light bulbs to work-release programs, and in effect made the federal judge the *jailer for Lucas County*.

---

[105] *Memphis Community School District v. Stachura*, 477 U.S. 299 (1986).

[106] *Jones v. Wittenberg*, 57 Ohio Op. 2d 109, 328 F. Supp. 93 (N.D. Ohio 1971), *aff'd sub nom.*, *Jones v. Metzger*, 456 F.2d 854 (6th Cir. 1972); *Hamilton v. Schiro*, 338 F. Supp. 1016 (E.D. La. 1970); *Holt v. Sarver*, 309 F.Supp. 362 (E.D. Ark. 1970), *aff'd*, 442 F.2d 304 (8th Cir. 1971); *Felciano v. Barcelo*, 497 F. Supp. 14 (D. Puerto Rico 1979); *Ramos v. Lamm*, 520 F. Supp. 1059 (D. Colo. 1981).

[107] *See, e.g.*, *Holt v. Sarver*, 309 F. Supp. 362 (E.D. Ark. 1970), *aff'd*, 442 F.2d 304 (8th Cir. 1971).

[108] *Costello v. Wainwright*, 397 F. Supp. 20 (M.D. Fla. 1975); *Gates v. Collier*, 390 F. Supp. 482 (N.D. Miss. 1975; *James v. Wallace*, 406 F. Supp. 318 (M.D. Ala. 1976).

[109] *McCray v. Sullivan*, 399 F. Supp. 271 (S.D. Ala. 1975).

[110] *Jones v. Wittenberg*, 57 Ohio Op. 2d 109, 323 F. Supp. 93 (N.D. Ohio 1971), *aff'd sub nom.*, *Jones v. Metzger*, 456 F.2d 854 (6th Cir. 1972); *Jones v. Wittenberg*, 509 F. Supp. 653 (N.D. Ohio 1980). (In the federal supervision of the Lucas County Jail, the court held that the sheriff had complied with most of the rules adopted by the state court, but had not complied with others).

[111] The declaratory judgment opinion, which sets forth in detail the deplorable conditions of the jail, can be found in *Jones v. Wittenberg*, 57 Ohio Op. 2d 109, 323 F. Supp. 93 (N.D. Ohio 1971).

[112] The relief decree in *Jones v. Wittenberg* is set out in 58 Ohio Op. 2d 47, 330 F. Supp. 707 (N.D. Ohio 1971).

The substandard conditions that exist in many American detention facilities, and the court's awareness that needed changes are not being initiated by prison administrators or legislators has, and will continue to result in judicial orders specifying the required changes to bring the facilities up to constitutional standards. The constant complaint that money is not available to make the required changes will not be an acceptable excuse for maintaining unconstitutional confinement facilities.[113]

In most instances, judges are immune from liability under the Civil Rights Act. However, immunity from damages does not prevent an injunction from being issued against a judicial officer under some circumstances. In such case, the judge may be liable for costs and attorney fees, even though the result may eviscerate the doctrine of judicial immunity. Suit was filed against a magistrate by former county jail inmates, alleging that the practice of imposing bail on persons arrested for nonjailable offenses and incarcerating them if they could not make bail violated the Constitution. The practice was enjoined by a federal judge. Attorneys' fees and court costs in the amount of $7,691 were awarded.[114]

An item of monetary expense which a defendant prison official may be required to pay is the cost of attorney fees to the inmate-plaintiff. The United States Supreme Court in *Alyeska Pipeline Service Co. v. Wilderness Society*[115] reaffirmed the general rule that, absent statute or enforceable contract, litigants must pay their own attorney fees. The Court pointed out, however, that there are recognized exceptions to this general rule. One exception is that a court may assess attorneys' fees for the willful disobedience of a court order, or when the losing party has acted in bad faith, "vexatiously, wantonly, or for oppressive reasons." However, in response to the *Alyeska* decision, on October 19, 1976 Congress passed a statute which grants attorney's fees in various civil rights actions, including suits against prison officials.[116]

An example where the court awarded attorney fees is *Gates v. Collier.*[117] The court stated that under 42 U.S.C. § 1988, the Civil Rights Attorney's Fees Award Act, the court may order that fees be paid out of the state treasury, and to effectuate this, may join the state auditor and treasurer as defendants. The court also held that interest may be awarded on attorney fees but not on out-of-pocket costs which are reimbursed under the Act. *Hutto v. Finney*[118] also held that the award of attorney fees to be paid out of Department of Correction funds is adequately supported by the court's finding that state officials acted in bad faith, and does not violate the Eleventh Amendment. The court further held that 42 U.S.C. § 1988 supports the

---

[113] *Alberti v. Sheriff of Harris Co. Tex.*, 406 F. Supp. 649 (S.D. Tex. 1975); *Costello v. Wainwright*, 525 F.2d 1239 (5th Cir. 1976); *Miller v. Carson*, 401 F. Supp. 835 (M.D. Fla. 1975); *Gates v. Collier*, 501 F.2d 1291 (5th Cir. 1974); *Smith v. Sullivan*, 553 F.2d 373 (5th Cir. 1977); *Mitchell v. Untreiner*, 421 F. Supp. 886 (N.D. Fla. 1976); *Martinez Rodriguez v. Jiminez*, 409 F. Supp. 582 (D.P.R. 1976).
[114] *Pulliam v. Allen*, 466 U.S. 522 (1984).
[115] *Alyeska Pipeline Service Co. v. Wilderness Society*, 421 U.S. 240 (1975).
[116] 42 U.S.C. § 1988 (1976).
[117] *Gates v. Collier*, 616 F.2d 1268 (5th Cir. 1980).
[118] *Hutto v. Finney*, 437 U.S. 678 (1978).

court's award of additional attorney fees to offset the cost of appeal.[119] Attorney fees under 42 U.S.C. § 1988 may be awarded to the appropriate prevailing party in any § 1983 action, even though the action was brought in state rather than federal court.[120]

In a civil rights suit, the District Court granted summary judgment for the parole board on the basis of qualified immunity. While the appeal was pending, the State Corrections Bureau revised its regulations to include procedures for the use of confidential source information in inmate disciplinary proceedings. The District Court then denied a prisoner's claim for attorney's fees on the ground that he was not a "prevailing party" as required by 42 U.S.C. § 1988. A plaintiff must receive at least some relief on the merits of his claim before he can be said to "prevail." The prisoner obtained neither a damages award, injunction, or declaratory judgment, nor a consent decree, settlement, or other relief without benefit of a formal judgment.

A favorable judicial statement of law in the course of litigation that results in a judgment against the plaintiff in civil rights cases is not sufficient to render a plaintiff a "prevailing party." Even if the prisoner's non-monetary claims were not rendered moot by his release from prison, and it could be said that those claims were kept alive by his interest in expunging his misconduct conviction from his prison record, his counsel never took the steps necessary to have a declaratory judgment or expungement order properly entered. The argument that the initial holding of the District Court was a "vindication of rights" that is at least the equivalent of declaratory relief ignored the fact that a judicial decree is not the end of the judicial process but is rather the means of prompting some action (or cessation of action) by the defendant. Here, the prisoner obtained nothing from the State. Moreover, equating statements of law (even legal holdings enroute to a final judgment for the defendant) with declaratory judgments has the practical effect of depriving a defendant of any valid defenses that a court might take into account in deciding whether to enter a declaratory judgment. Furthermore, the same considerations that influence courts to issue declaratory judgments may not enter into the decision whether to include statements of law in opinions. However, if they do, the court's decision is not appealable in the same manner as is its entry of a declaratory judgment.[121]

There is no entitlement to attorney's fees unless the requesting party prevailed. By the time a District Court entered its judgment in the underlying suit one of the plaintiffs had died and the other was no longer in custody. Under the circumstances, the plaintiffs were not "prevailing parties" under *Hewitt v. Helms* and the plaintiffs were not entitled to attorney fees.[122]

A prevailing party must be one who has succeeded on any significant claim affording it some of the relief sought, either *pendente lite* or at the conclusion of the

---

[119] *Id.* at 689.
[120] *Maine v. Thiboutot*, 448 U.S. 1 (1980).
[121] *Hewitt v. Helms*, 482 U.S. 755 (1987).
[122] *Rhodes v. Stewart*, 488 U.S. 1, 109 S.Ct. 202 (1988).

litigation. A plaintiff has crossed the threshold to a fee award of some kind if he or she satisfies the "significant issue"—"some benefit" standard. Under that standard, at a minimum, the plaintiff must be able to point to a resolution of the dispute which materially alters the parties' legal relationship in a manner which Congress sought to promote in the fee statute.[122a] Where the plaintiff's success on a legal claim can be characterized as purely technical or *de minimis,* a district court would be justified in concluding that it is so insignificant as to be insufficient to support prevailing party status. However, where the parties' relationship has been materially changed, the degree of the plaintiff's overall success goes to the reasonableness of the award under *Hensley,* not to the availability of the fee award.[123]

Who is the "prevailing party" was the issue in *Hanrahan v. Hampton*[124] and *Maher v. Gagne.*[125] In *Hanrahan,* the court held that a party does not "prevail" merely by obtaining an appellate court order for a new trial. In *Maher,* the court held that fees may be awarded in a consent decree, even though there was no judicial determination that federal rights had been violated.

The extent of a plaintiff's success is a crucial factor in determining the proper amount of such fees. The time spent on unsuccessful claims that are completely distinct from successful claims should be excluded in determining a reasonable fee. However, the fee should not be reduced simply because the court did not adopt each of several related claims. A plaintiff who achieves only limited success with a group of related claims should be awarded only that amount of fees that is reasonably related to the results obtained. In order to recover, the plaintiff must be a "prevailing party." Plaintiffs may be considered "prevailing parties" for attorney's fees purposes if they succeed on any significant issue in litigation which achieves some of the benefit the parties sought in bringing suit. The starting point is the number of hours reasonably expended on the litigation multiplied by a reasonable hourly rate. The fee may then be adjusted up or down depending upon the "results obtained." The burden is on the fee applicant to establish entitlement to an award and to document the appropriate hours expended and hourly rates. For appellate review, if a district court has articulated a fair explanation for its fee award in a given case, the court of appeals should not reverse or remand the judgment unless the award is so low as to provide clearly inadequate compensation to the attorneys in the case or so high as to constitute an unmistakable windfall. However, here, the decision of the district court was reversed as the opinion did not properly consider the relationship between the extent of success and the amount of the fee award. The fee award against Missouri hospital officials at the forensic unit of a Missouri state hospital was in excess of $133,000.[126]

Attorney fees awarded under 42 U.S.C. § 1988 are to be calculated according to the prevailing market rates in the relevant community. Fees are not to be calculated

---

[123] *Texas State Teachers Association v. Garland,* ___U.S.___, 109 S.Ct. 1486 (1989).
[124] *Hanrahan v. Hampton,* 446 U.S. 754 (1980).
[125] *Maher v. Gagne,* 448 U.S. 122 (1980).
[126] *Hensley v. Eckerhart,* 457 U.S. 496 (1983).

according to the actual cost of providing legal services. Policy arguments based on a cost-based standard should be made to Congress and not to the courts. The rule applies to both private and non-profit counsel. An upward adjustment in determining attorney fees in civil rights cases is permissible. This is calculated by multiplying the reasonable number of hours expended by a reasonable hourly rate. However, in some cases of exceptional success, an enhanced award may be justified. In seeking an enhanced award, the burden is on the attorney. However, once the attorney has carried his burden of showing that the claimed rate and number of hours are reasonable, the resulting product is presumed to be the reasonable fee contemplated by 42 U.S.C. §1988. The record must show the complexity of the litigation, the novelty of the issues, the high representation and the great benefit to the class represented by the attorney. There is no basis for an award on "riskiness" of the lawsuit.[127]

However, an important factor, among others, for consideration in adjusting the "lodestar" figure upward or downward is the "results obtained." Where a plaintiff has obtained excellent results, his attorney should recover a fully compensatory fee, and the fee award should not be reduced simply because the plaintiff failed to prevail on every contention raised in the lawsuit.

The lodestar approach is appropriate in civil rights cases where a plaintiff recovers only monetary damages. Fees in excess of the amount of damages recovered are not necessarily unreasonable. Although the amount of damages recovered is relevant to the amount of attorney's fees to be awarded under § 1988, it is only one of many factors that a court should consider in calculating an award of attorney's fees.

A civil rights action for damages is not merely a private tort suit benefiting only the individual plaintiffs whose rights were violated. Unlike most private tort litigants, a civil rights plaintiff seeks to vindicate important civil and constitutional rights that cannot be valued solely in monetary terms. Because damages awards do not reflect fully the public benefit advanced by civil rights litigation, Congress did not intend for fees in civil rights cases, unlike most private law cases, to depend on obtaining substantial monetary relief, but instead recognized that reasonable attorney's fees under § 1988 are not conditioned upon and need not be proportionate to an award of money damages. Consequently, a rule limiting attorney's fees in civil rights cases to a proportion of the damages awarded would seriously undermine Congress' purpose in enacting § 1988. Congress enacted § 1988 specifically because it found that the private market for legal services failed to provide many victims of civil rights violations with effective access to the judicial process. A rule of proportionality would make it difficult, if not impossible, for individuals with meritorious civil rights claims but relatively small potential damages to obtain redress from the courts, and would be totally inconsistent with Congress' purpose of ensuring sufficiently vigorous enforcement of civil rights. In order to ensure that lawyers would be willing to represent persons with legitimate civil rights griev-

---

[127] *Blum v. Stetson*, 465 U.S. 886 (1984).

ances, Congress determined that it would be necessary to compensate lawyers for all time reasonably expended on a case.[128]

Later during the same Term of Court, the Supreme Court held that a trial court erred in increasing the attorney's fee award based on the "superior quality" of counsel's performance. The lodestar figure includes most, if not all, of the relevant factors constituting a "reasonable" attorney's fee, and it is unnecessary to enhance the fee for superior performance in order to serve the statutory purpose of enabling plaintiffs to receive legal assistance.[129]

An attorney's fee allowed under § 1988 is not limited to the amount provided in an plaintiff's contingent-fee arrangement with his counsel. To hold otherwise would be inconsistent with the statute, which broadly requires all defendants to pay a reasonable fee to all prevailing plaintiffs if ordered to do so by the court acting in its sound judgment and in light of all the circumstances of the case.[130]

Immunity from damages does not prevent an injunction from being issued. In such case, the defendant may be liable for costs and attorney fees.[131]

Attorney fees are payable for work done in optional administrative proceedings involving the prevailing party in a § 1983 action only when a "discrete portion" of the attorney's work in the state proceeding was "useful and of a type ordinarily necessary" to advance the § 1983 litigation.[132] However, they are not awarded *solely* for legal services performed before state administrative agencies.[133]

The settlement of a § 1983 may be made contingent upon the waiver of attorney fees under § 1988. Neither the statute nor the legislative history suggests that Congress intended to forbid all waivers of attorney's fees. Congress neither bestowed fee awards upon attorneys nor rendered them nonwaivable or nonnegotiable. It added them to the remedies available to combat civil rights violations, a goal not invariably inconsistent with conditioning settlement on the merits on a waiver of statutory attorney's fees.

A general prohibition against waiver of attorney's fees in exchange for a settlement on the merits would itself impede vindication of civil rights by reducing the attractiveness of settlement. It is reasonable to assume that parties to a significant number of civil rights cases would refuse to settle if liability for attorney's fees remained open, thereby forcing more cases to trial, unnecessarily burdening the judicial system, and disserving civil rights litigants.[134]

A distinction must be made between a public official being sued in his official capacity where the "real" defendant is a governmental unit, and when the public official is sued for his individual conduct. In official capacity suits, as long as the

[128] *City of Riverside v. Rivera*, 477 U.S. 561 (1986).
[129] *Pennsylvania v. Delaware Valley Citizens' Council for Clean Air*, 478 U.S. 546 (1986).
[130] *Blanchard v. Bergeron*, ___U.S.___ 109 S.Ct. 939 (1989).
[131] *Pulliam v. Allen*, 466 U.S. 522 (1984).
[132] *Webb v. Board of Educ. of Dyer City, Tenn.*, 471 U.S. 234 (1975).
[133] *North Carolina Department of Transportation v. Crest Street Community Council*, 479 U.S. 6 (1986).
[134] *Evans v. Jeff D.*, 475 U.S. 717 (1986).

governmental entity receives notice and an opportunity to respond, the suit is, in all respects other than the name, a suit against the entity. When a state in a § 1983 action may be found liable either because the state was a proper party defendant or because state officials were sued in their official capacity, attorney fees may be awarded to a state under § 1988. Only in an official capacity action is a plaintiff who wins entitled to look for relief, both on the merits and for attorney fees, to the governmental entity.[135]

A civil rights plaintiff runs the risk of refusing an officer to settle a § 1983 case. If the eventual judgment is less than the amount proposed by the defense, the plaintiff must pay all "costs" incurred after the offer.[136] "Costs" include attorney fees.[137]

§ 11.6.5   —Statute of Limitations

A statute of limitations prevents the litigation of "stale" claims. Section 1983 does not specify the appropriate statute of limitations for civil rights actions. Federal rather than state law governs the characterization of a § 1983 claim for statute of limitations purposes. However, the length of the limitations period, and related questions of tolling and application, are to be governed by state law. In such cases, the claims are to be treated as personal injury actions under state law.[138]

A state "notice of claim" statute has the same effect as an abbreviated statute of limitations. These are unconstitutional when applied to 42 U.S.C. § 1983 when litigated in a state court. Application of "notice of claims" statutes to state-court § 1983 actions cannot be approved as a matter of equitable federalism. Just as federal courts are constitutionally obligated to apply state law to state claims, the Supremacy Clause imposes on state courts a constitutional duty to proceed in such manner that all the substantial rights of the parties under controlling federal law are protected. A state law that predictably alters the outcome of § 1983 claims depending solely on whether they are brought in state or federal court within the State is obviously inconsistent with the federal interest in intrastate uniformity.[139]

A District Court's rejected the contention that § 1983 actions were governed by the state's one-year statute of limitations covering assault, battery, false imprisonment, and five other intentional torts, and applied the state's three-year residual statute of limitations for personal injury claims not embraced by specific statutes of limitations. The United States Supreme Court held that where state law provides multiple statutes of limitations for personal injury actions, courts considering § 1983 claims should borrow the state's general or residual personal injury statute of limitations. Although *Wilson v. Garcia* ruled that 42 U.S.C. § 1983 required courts to borrow and apply to all § 1983 claims a state's personal injury statute of limitations, *Wilson* did not indicate which statute of limitations applies in states

---

[135] *Kentucky v. Graham,* 473 U.S. 159 (1985).
[136] Fed. R. Civ. Pro. 68.
[137] *Marek v. Chesny,* 473 U.S. 1 (1985).
[138] *Wilson v. Garcia,* 471 U.S. 261 (1985).
[139] *Felder v. Casey,* 487 U.S. 131, 108 S.Ct. 2302 (1988).

with multiple personal injury statutes. In light of *Wilson's* practical approach of eliminating uncertainty by providing one simple broad characterization of all § 1983 actions, a rule endorsing the choice of the state statute of limitations for intentional torts would be manifestly inappropriate. Every state has multiple intentional tort limitations provisions. In contrast, every state has one general or residual personal injury statute of limitations, which is easily identifiable by language or application. The argument that intentional tort limitations periods should be borrowed because such torts are most analogous to § 1983 claims failed to recognize the enormous practical disadvantages of such a selection in terms of the confusion and unpredictability the selection would cause for potential § 1983 plaintiffs and defendants. Moreover, the analogy between § 1983 claims and state causes of action was felt to be too imprecise to justify such a result, in light of the wide spectrum of claims which § 1983 has come to span, many of which bear little if any resemblance to a common-law intentional tort.[140]

A tolling statute stops, or "tolls," the running of a statute of limitations. A federal court applying a state statute of limitations to an inmate's federal civil rights action should give effect to the State's provision tolling the limitations period for prisoners. Limitations periods in § 1983 suits are to be determined by reference to the appropriate state statute of limitations and the coordinate tolling rules, as long as the state law would not defeat the goals of the federal law at issue. The state tolling statute here was consistent with § 1983's remedial purpose, since some inmates may be loathe to sue adversaries to whose daily supervision and control they remain subject, and even those who do file suit may not have a fair opportunity to establish the validity of their allegations while they are confined.[141]

§ 11.7   Federal Remedies—Declaratory Judgments

In the Anglo-American judicial system, court action is normally predicted upon past actions of two or more adverse parties. However, it is plain that many situations could arise in which two or more parties are uncertain of their legal relationship and desire a judicial determination of their respective rights and responsibilities prior to committing some act which might result in legal lability. In order to provide such a remedy, Congress passed the Declaratory Judgment Act, which provides in part:

> In a case of actual controversy within its jurisdiction . . . any court of the United States, upon the filing of an appropriate pleading, may declare the rights and other legal relations of any interested party seeking such declaration. . . .[142]

The federal law further authorizes federal courts to grant "necessary or proper relief based on a declaratory judgment. . . ."[143] This power to grant relief beyond the declaratory judgment is discretionary with the court. Hence, a court which is

---

[140] *Owens v. Okure,* ___U.S.___, 109 S.Ct. 573 (1989).
[141] *Hardin v. Straub,* ___U.S.___, 109 S.Ct. 1998 (1989).
[142] 28 U.S.C. § 2201 (1970).
[143] 28 U.S.C. § 2202 (1970).

wary of interfering with internal management of a prison,[144] but which has found a certain rule or regulation or course of conduct by the prison officials to be unconstitutional, may partially avoid interference by issuing a judgment declaring the alleged practice to be unconstitutional, but allowing the administrators to submit to the court plans for remedying the problem.

Thus, in *Holt v. Sarver*[145] a federal district court, after examining the totality of conditions at Arkansas' two state prison farms, declared incarceration therein to be cruel and unusual punishment. The burden of eliminating these constitutional defects, however, was placed upon the state prison administration, whose progress (or lack thereof) would be monitored by the court through submission of reports by the defendants.

§ 11.8   Federal Remedies—Habeas Corpus

Traditionally, the writ of habeas corpus has been used to contest the legality of confinement itself.[146] However, in a 1944 case, a federal appellate court expanded the scope of federal habeas corpus to include suits which contest the conditions of confinement, and not merely the legality of the confinement itself.[147] The court reasoned that:

> A prisoner is entitled to the writ of habeas corpus when, though lawfully in custody, he is deprived of some right to which he is lawfully entitled even in his confinement, the deprivation of which serves to make his imprisonment more burdensome than the law allows or curtails his liberty to a greater extent than the law permits.[148]

The Supreme Court has expressly approved the expanded use of habeas corpus.[149]

Federal habeas corpus action to rectify an allegedly unconstitutional condition of incarceration presents one serious procedural problem to state inmates. The statute requires them to exhaust state judicial and administrative remedies before they apply for the writ in federal court.[150] In *Preiser v. Rodriguez*,[151] the United States Supreme Court held that federal habeas corpus must be used by an inmate in a state institution to obtain release by challenging the fact or duration of his physical imprisonment, and that he could not avoid the "exhaustion of state remedies" doc-

---

[144] *See* § 11.4.1 *supra.*

[145] *Holt v. Sarver,* 309 F. Supp. 362 (E.D. Ark. 1970), *aff'd,* 442 F.2d 304 (8th Cir. 1971).

[146] U.S.C. § 2254 (1970) authorizes federal courts to hear applications for writs of habeas corpus from persons who allege that their detention by the state violates a federal right.

[147] *Coffin v. Reichard,* 143 F.2d 443 (6th Cir. 1944).

[148] *Id.* at 445.

[149] *Jones v. Cunningham,* 371 U.S. 236 (1963).

[150] 28 U.S.C. § 2254(b) (1970).

[151] *Preiser v. Rodriguez,* 411 U.S. 475 (1973).

trine[152] by using 42 U.S.C. § 1983. Thus, even though § 1983 on its face gives a remedy for every deprivation of federal rights by state law, the Writ of Habeas Corpus is the exclusive federal remedy for state inmates who, on the grounds that they were unconstitutionally deprived of good-time credit under prison disciplinary rules, challenge the fact or duration of their confinement, and seek immediate release.

Wolff v. McDonnell[153] considered whether *Preiser* applied to a § 1983 action involving the validity of the procedures for denying good-time credits. The Court held that although *Preiser* prevented the restoration of good-time credits under § 1983, damage claims were properly before the Court. Consequently the District Court was held to have jurisdiction under the Civil Rights Act to determine the validity of the procedures employed for imposing punishment, including loss of good-time, for flagrant or serious misconduct. However, exhaustion of state remedies will not be required if resort to them would obviously be futile.[154] Probably the best example of a futile state remedy which would not have to be pursued by the inmate is a prior adverse decision by the state's highest court on the identical federal question which the inmate seeks to raise.[155]

§ 11.9 Federal Remedies—Criminal Prosecution

The criminal counterpart of the Civil Rights Act provides in part:

> Whoever, under color of any law, statue, ordinance, regulation, or custom, willfully subjects any inhabitant of any State, Territory, or District to the deprivation of any rights, privileges, or immunities secured or protected by the Constitution or laws of the United States shall be fined not more than $1,000 or imprisoned not more than one year, or both; and if death results, shall be subject to imprisonment for any term of years or for life.[156]

The elements that must be present for a conviction under this statute, and the interpretation given these elements by the Supreme Court, are as follows:

(1) There must be a deprivation of a right, privilege, or immunity secured by the Constitution or by federal law. In refuting the contention that inclusion of Fourteenth Amendment rights of "due process" and "equal protection" in the criminal statute would make it void because of vagueness, the Supreme Court has stated that the deprivation must be "of a right which

---

[152] *See* § 11.6.1.
[153] *Wolff v. McDonnell,* 418 U.S. 539, 71 Ohio Op. 2d 336 (1974).
[154] *Patton v. North Carolina,* 381 F.2d 636 (4th Cir. 1967), *cert. denied,* 390 U.S. 905 (1968).
[155] *See e.g., Davis v. Sigler,* 415 F.2d 1159 (8th Cir. 1969).
[156] 18 U.S.C. § 242 (1970).

has been made specific, either by the express terms of the Constitution or laws of the United States or by decisions interpreting them."[157]

(2) The deprivation must be "wilful." That is, there must be a specific intent to deprive the person of his constitutional rights.

(3) The deprivation must be "under color of state law." This phrase has been interpreted as meaning, "Misuse of power, possessed by virtue of state law and made possible only because the wrongdoer is clothed with the authority of state law. . . ."[158]

In *United States v. Jackson*[159] an Arkansas prison guard was indicted under this statute for allegedly beating an inmate with a club. The district court dismissed the indictment for failure to state an offense against the United States. In reversing the lower court and in reinstating the indictment, the court of appeals held that:

A convicted prisoner remains under the protection of the Fourteenth Amendment except as to those rights expressly or by necessary implication taken from him by law. He still has his right to be secure in his person against unlawful beating done under color of law willfully to deprive him of the right.[160]

§ 11.10   Federal Remedies—Contempt

Contempt of court has been defined as "disobedience to the court, by acting in opposition to the authority, justice, and dignity thereof."[161] Because they are responsible for executing sentences imposed by the courts, prison officials are regarded as officers of the courts. Moreover, a state official who is holding an inmate sentenced by a federal court has been judged to be an official of the sentencing federal court, in relation to his treatment of the federal inmate.[162] In the case of *In re Birdsong*,[163] a federal judge held a county jailer liable in contempt for mistreating a federal inmate who was being detained in the local jail.

§ 11.11   State Remedies—Civil Suits

Prison officials have the duty, often imposed by statute,[164] to provide their inmates with the basic necessities of life, such as clothing, food, shelter, and medical care. Failure to provide these items will render the official liable to the inmate

---

[157] *Screws v. United States*, 325 U.S. 91, 104 (1945); *See also United States v. Senak*, 477 F.2d 304 (7th Cir. 1973).

[158] *United States v. Classic*, 313 U.S. 299, 326 (1941).

[159] *United States v. Jackson*, 235 F.2d 925 (8th Cir. 1956).

[160] *Id.* at 929. *See also United States v. Walker*, 216 F.2d 683 (5th Cir. 1954); *United States v. Jones*, 207 F.2d 785 (5th Cir. 1953).

[161] 17 C.J.S. *Contempt* § 2 (1963).

[162] *Randolph v. Donaldson*, 13 U.S. (9 Cranch) 76 (1815).

[163] *In re Birdsong*, 39 F. 599 (S.D. Ga. 1889); *See also United States v. Shipp*, 203 U.S. 563 (1906); *McCall v. Swain*, 510 F.2d 167 (D.C. Cir. 1975).

[164] *See e.g.*, Mass. Gen. Laws, Ann. 16, 28, 34 (1958) (county detention facilities); N.Y. Correctional Laws 137 (Supp. 1971) (state penal institutions).

in a civil action. Hence, prison officials have been held liable in state courts for failure to provide needed medical services,[165] food[166] and other necessities such as bedding, clothing and sanitary conditions.[167]

In addition to their duties to provide the necessities of life, prison officials have a general duty to use reasonable care to prevent injuries to their inmates. Failure to exercise such care is negligence, and a prison official will be liable in damages for the injuries caused by his negligence. Thus, a complaint which alleged that the superintendent of a camp for delinquent juveniles used one of his charges to fight a forest fire, without warning the youth of the danger was held to state a cause of action for the boy's wrongful death.[168] Similarly, a petition which alleged that a sheriff forced an inmate to use a wobbly ladder when painting, knowing it to be defective, was sufficient to state a cause of action for negligence.[169]

A prison official who intentionally injures an inmate will be liable to him in a tort action for damages. Assault and battery is the most common intentional tort situation in a prison environment. An inmate, like any other person, has the right to be free from offensive bodily contact that is intentionally inflicted upon him.[170]

§ 11.11.1 —Effect of Sovereign Immunity

An inmate seeking to recover damages against prison officials for neglect, negligence, or intentional injury will often be faced with the defense of sovereign immunity.[171] The courts generally split upon the question of liability depending upon whether the officials' actions are labeled "ministerial" or "discretionary." A ministerial duty is one that is absolute and certain. It is a duty that involves no freedom of choice on the part of the actor. Several states have held that the duty of prison officials to provide their inmates with necessities is ministerial, and so the official is liable to the inmates for failure to fulfill the duty.[172] Other states, however, interpret the officials' duties as "discretionary." That is, the official has a certain freedom of choice in providing necessities to his prisoners. He is thus free from liability for his acts, as he should not be discouraged by fear of lawsuit from freely

---

[165] *Farmer v. State*, 224 Miss. 96, 79 So. 2d 528 (1955); *State ex rel. Morris v. National Surety Co.*, 162 Tenn. 547, 39 S.W.2d 581 (1931); *State ex rel. Williams v. Davis*, 219 S.E.2d 198 (Sup. Ct. N.C. 1975).

[166] *Smith v. Slack*, 125 W. Va. 812, 26 S.E.2d 387 (1943); *Richardson v. Capwell*, 63 Utah 616, 176 P. 205 (1918).

[167] *Clark v. Kelly*, 101 W.Va. 650, 133 S.E. 365 (1926); *Roberts v. Williams*, 456 F.2d 819 (5th Cir. 1972).

[168] *Collenburg v. County of Los Angeles*, 150 Cal. App. 2d 795, 310 P.2d 989 (1957) (sovereign immunity protects the county, but not the individual official).

[169] *Moore v. Murphy*, 254 Iowa 969, 119 N.W.2d 759 (1963).

[170] *Fernelius v. Pierce*, 22 Cal. 2d 226, 138 P.2d 12 (1943); *Farmer v. Rutherford*, 136 Kan. 298, 15 P.2d 474 (1932); *Bowman v. Hayward*, 1 Utah 2d 131, 262 P.2d 957 (1953).

[171] *See* § 11.4 supra.

[172] *Kusah v. McCorkle*, 100 Wash. 318, 170 P. 1023 (1918); *Smith v. Slack*, 125 W.Va. 812, 26 S.E.2d 307 (1943).

exercising this discretion.[173] However, if the discretion is grossly abused, the result is liability.

In *Martinez v. California*,[174] the Supreme Court considered the constitutionality of a California statute that gave public employees absolute immunity from liability for any injury resulting from parole-release determinations. The statute was upheld as applied to defeat a state tort claim arising from California law.

§ 11.12 State Remedies—Declaratory Judgments

Many states[175] have enacted declaratory judgment acts similar in scope to the federal act previously discussed.[176] Although a state declaratory judgment action would be an excellent method of testing the legality of conditions of confinement in state institutions, this state remedy has been totally ignored by inmates and prison officials in the past.

§ 11.13 State Remedies—Habeas Corpus

The availability of state habeas corpus proceedings to contest conditions of state confinement depends on the wording of the state statute and the judicial interpretation thereof. For example, Ohio's habeas corpus statute has a section which provides:

> If it appears that a person alleged to be restrained of his liberty is in the custody of an officer under process issued by a court or magistrate, or by virtue of the judgment or order of a court of record, and that the court or magistrate had jurisdiction to issue the process, rendered the judgment, or make the order, the writ of habeas corpus shall not be allowed.[177]

Thus, habeas corpus relief is not available in Ohio unless the court ordering confinement lacked jurisdiction.[178] In other words, Ohio has limited habeas corpus to those cases which would result in release from confinement for the petitioner if he were successful in his action.[179] Hence, state habeas corpus is not a proper method of contesting conditions of confinement in Ohio.

Other states have, however, extended the scope of habeas corpus to include cases of alleged unlawful treatment of an inmate lawfully in custody,[180] and follow the federal analogy.

---

[173] *Bush v. Babb*, 23 Ill. App. 2d 285, 162 N.E.2d 594 (1959); *St. Louis ex rel. Forest v. Nickolas*, 374 S.W.2d 547 (Mo. App. 1964); *Rose v. Toledo*, 1 Ohio C.C.R. (N.S.) 321, 14 Ohio C. Dec. 540 (1903).

[174] *Martinez v. California*, 444 U.S. 227 (1980).

[175] *See e.g.*, N.Y. Civil Prac. Law and Rules 3001 (McKinney 1963); Ohio Rev. Code Ann. § 2721.02.

[176] *See* § 11.7 supra.

[177] Ohio Rev. Code Ann. § 2725.05 (1976).

[178] *In re Edsall*, 26 Ohio St. 2d 145, 55 Ohio Op. 2d 276, 269 N.E.2d 848 (1971).

[179] *Ball v. Maxwell*, 177 Ohio St. 39, 29 Ohio Op. 2d 1, 201 N.E.2d 786 (1964).

[180] *See In re Riddle*, 57 Cal. 2d 848, 372 P.2d 304, 22 Cal. Rptr. 472 (1962). *See generally* 155 A.L.R. 145 (1945).

§ 11.14   State Remedies—Criminal Prosecution

Some states have criminal statutes which are specifically aimed at mistreatment of inmates by their keepers. For example, an Arizona law provides that:

A public officer who is guilty of willful inhumanity or oppression toward a prisoner under his care or in his custody shall be punished by a fine not exceeding one thousand dollars, by imprisonment in the county jail for not to exceed six months, or both.[181]

In the absence of any specific criminal statute directed solely at them, correctional officials are subject to the general criminal statutes of the state, such as assault and battery and the homicide laws. Thus, in *State v. Mincher,*[182] the North Carolina Supreme Court upheld an assault and battery conviction against an inmate guard who had administered excessive corporal punishment to another inmate.

§ 11.15   State Remedies—Contempt

As stated above,[183] prison officials are officers of the sentencing court, and can be held in contempt by such a court for mistreating an inmate sentenced to the institution by the court. At least two states have sanctioned the use of contempt to punish mistreatment of inmates. In *Howard v. State,*[184] the Arizona Supreme Court upheld a contempt citation against the superintendent of an adult prison who allegedly mistreated inmates. However, in 1952, the same court dismissed a contempt proceedings against the director of a boys' training school[185] expressly overruling any holding of the *Howard* case which might lead to an opposite result. Another case seemed to reaffirm the *Howard* decision as it pertained to adult correctional officials. *Dutton v. Eyman*[186] held that state habeas corpus is not a valid method of contesting the conditions of confinement. However, the court cited the *Howard* case with approval as a possible remedy in such a situation.

The Supreme Court of Rhode Island has also held that contempt is a proper method of punishing abuse of prisoners.[187]

§ 11.16   Conclusion

An inmate has a wide variety of remedies to rectify past denials of constitutional rights and to insure future respect of these rights by prison administrators. The inmate often has a choice of going to either federal or state courts. However, many obstacles, most notably "the hands-off" doctrine, blocked judicial redress of constitutional deprivations in the past. With the decline of this doctrine in recent years, courts are hearing and deciding a greatly increasing number of inmate complaints.

---

[181] Ariz. Rev. Stat. Ann. § 31-127 (1956). *See also* Cal. Penal Code 2650 (West 1970).
[182] *State v. Mincher,* 172 N.C. 895, 90 S.E. 429 (1916).
[183] *See* § 11.10 supra.
[184] *Howard v. State,* 28 Ariz. 433, 237 P. 203 (1925).
[185] *Ridgway v. Superior Court,* 74 Ariz. 117, 245 P.2d 268 (1952).
[186] *Dutton v. Eyman,* 95 Ariz. 95, 387 P.2d 799 (1963).
[187] *State v. Brant,* 99 R.I. 583, 209 A.2d 455 (1965).

With the current concern for penal reform, judicial intervention in prison administration will probably continue to grow. Federal and state correctional officials should therefore initiate administrative reforms before the courts are called upon to do it for them.

In addition, prison officials must become increasingly aware of the potential for liability when conducting the operations and forming the policies for the prison system. The recent Supreme Court decisions make it clear that prison officials will be expected to know what the constitutional rights of inmates are, and this places the burden on prison officials to keep themselves apprised of the current state of the law. Ignorance will not be a defense when confronted with a lawsuit for monetary damages.

Chapter 12

ADDITIONAL LITIGATION

Section

§ 12.1 Introduction

There are numerous different legal issues of constitutional magnitude affecting inmates which do not readily fit into any of the preceding chapters. The topics noted here do not, of course, exhaust the differences between free people and inmates. They do, however, point up the fact that incarceration is much more than merely a change in location. It is a change in constitutional status.

§ 12.2 Classification

Classification is the assessment, for rehabilitative and security purposes, of an inmate's personality, background, and potential, and the assignment of the inmate to a specific status or setting which is commensurate with these findings. Classification occurs at numerous times while an inmate is involved in the criminal justice system; but this section is concerned only with the narrow area of classification by prison authorities, that is, administrative classification. That prison authorities have the right and duty to classify inmates has been clearly determined by the courts.[1] The assessment aspect of administrative classification is usually fulfilled by committees of prison officials.[2] Such bodies are frequently labeled adjustment committees because their initial goal is to enable new inmates to adjust to the rigors of incarceration. Administrative classification committees, however, have a continual mission beyond intake assessment and assignment. Behavioral changes in

---

[1] *Marchesani v. McCune*, 531 F.2d 459 (10th Cir. 1976); *McGruder v. Phelps*, 608 F.2d 1023 (5th Cir. 1979); *Jones v. Diamond*, 594 F.2d 997 (5th Cir. 1979); *Jennings v. State*, 389 N.E.2d 283 (Ind. 1979). (State only needs to show a reasonable basis for the classification.)

[2] *James v. Wallace*, 406 F. Supp. 318 (M.D. Ala. 1976); *Zaczet v. Hutto*, 642 F.2d 74 (4th Cir. 1981); *French v. Hevne*, 547 F.2d 994 (7th Cir. 1976).

inmates, for better or for worse, that occur as time is served, demand constant reassessment and reassignment.[3]

In *Meachum v. Fano*,[4] the United States Supreme Court held that a transfer of an inmate from one prison to another, although arguably a "grievous loss," did not require a due process hearing. This decision, by analogy, may also apply to the classification of inmates. However, lower federal courts that have considered the classification issue have determined that some degree of procedural due process is applicable to prison classification hearings. In *Kirby v. Blackledge*[5] an informal hearing procedure which was used to assign inmates to maximum security cell-blocks was found to violate due process. Illiterate or otherwise disadvantaged inmates, for whom the complexity of issues may foreclose the needed capacity to collect and present the evidence necessary for an adequate comprehension of the case, were allowed the assistance of fellow inmates or some designated staff member. Other courts have specified the form of intake classification to be undertaken. In *Alberti v. Sheriff of Harris Co., Tex.*[6] The court held that a sufficient number of classification officers should be employed so that at least one is on duty at all times to interview incoming inmates. Inmates are to be classified and segregated on the basis of the danger which they pose to others, based on their prior criminal record, the danger posed to the new inmate by the existing prison population, and the likelihood of successful rehabilitation by proper placement.

The proposed imposition or assignment of certain classifications can trigger a need for more substantial due process safeguards. In *Cardopoli v. Norton*,[7] the court held that inasmuch as classification of an inmate as a special offender hinders or precludes eligibility for social furloughs, work release, transfer to community treatment centers, and the opportunity for early parole, changes in an inmate's status which accompany the designation create a "grievous loss" and may not be imposed in the absence of basic elements of rudimentary due process. When a special offender classification is contemplated, the inmate must be given at least ten days' notice in writing specifying the reason or reasons for the proposed designation and provided a description of the evidence to be relied on. The inmate must be afforded a personal appearance before a disinterested decisionmaker and must be permitted to call witnesses and present documentary evidence. If the hearing officer determines that the classification is warranted, he must support that decision with written findings submitted within a reasonable time after the hearing.

---

[3] *Fitzgerald v. Procunier*, 393 F. Supp. 335 (N.D. Cal. 1975).

[4] *Meachum v. Fano*, 427 U.S. 215 (1976); *cf. Cuyler v. Adams*, 449 U.S. 433 (1981); *Vitek v. Jones*, 445 U.S. 480 (1980).

[5] *Kirby v. Blackledge*, 530 F.2d 583 (4th Cir. 1976); *In re Westfall*, 162 Cal. Rptr. 462 (Cal. App. 1980); *Cobb v. Aytch*, 643 F.2d 946 (3d Cir. 1981), (wherein the court distinguishes between the transfer rights of sentenced and pre-trial prisoners).

[6] *Alberti v. Sheriff of Harris Co., Tex.*, 406 F. Supp. 649 (S.D. Tex. 1975).

[7] *Cardopoli v. Norton*, 523 F.2d 990 (2d Cir. 1975); *see also Raia v. Arnold*, 405 F. Supp. 766 (M.D. Pa. 1975); *People ex rel. Williams v. Ward*, 423 N.Y.S.2d 692 (N.Y. App. Div. 1980); *Makris v. United States Bureau of Prisons*, 606 F.2d 575 (5th Cir. 1979).

Beyond the procedural considerations of classification hearings, there exists the problem of the permissibility of certain types of classifications or statuses. In *McDonald v. McCracken*[8] a court held that if an inmate is placed in lockup status, for the protection of other prisoners and prison employees rather than for the imposition of punishment, in this case for thirteen months, and such classification is not arbitrary, abusive, or capricious, the hearing requirements of *Wolff v. McDonnell*[9] for rule infraction board proceedings are not applicable. Classification based upon a discriminatory basis such as race or religion will usually be held to be unconstitutional. However, classification on the basis of sex or age is permissible.

Under Indiana law, inmates have no right to be assigned to a particular security class. The decision to alter security classifications is solely within the discretion of the Department of Corrections.[10]

The use of the "level system," a mandatory behavior modification system employed by the Kentucky Correctional Institute for Women to govern the access of female prisoners to certain inmate privileges, was declared unconstitutional. The system resulted in grossly unequal treatment of female as opposed to male prisoners in the availability of inmate privileges. In addition, the imposition of the system on the prison population as a whole violates the inmates' substantive due process rights. Behavior modification was found to have a unique effect upon each individual. Officials of the Kentucky Correctional Institute for Women were cited by the district court for failing to fulfill their obligation to provide equal programs and facilities for women, especially in the areas of prison industries, institutional jobs, vocational education and training, and community release programs.[11]

§ 12.3 Transfer

Incident to all classifications, whether initial or review, is transfer. This topic has generated much litigation. Federal District Courts and Courts of Appeals that have dealt with the need for due process safeguards in conjunction with intraprison and interprison transfers of inmates have specified substantial safeguards. A typical case is *Fano v. Meachum*,[12] in which the First Circuit Court of Appeals held that whether an inmate's transfer is thought of as punishment or as a way of preserving institutional order its effect upon the inmate is the same. The appropriateness of the transfer depends upon the accuracy of the official allegation of misconduct. Under normal circumstances, notice and a hearing must be afforded to an inmate prior to a transfer from a medium to a maximum security prison and, at the very least, must state the time and place of the alleged offense with reasonable accuracy. How-

[8] *McDonald v. McCracken*, 399 F. Supp. 869 (E.D. Okla. 1975); *Wojtczak v. Cuyler*, 480 F. Supp. 1288 (E.D. Pa. 1979).

[9] *Wolff v. McDonnell*, 418 U.S. 539, 71 Ohio Op. 2d 336 (1974).

[10] *Kincaid v. Duckworth*, 689 F.2d 702 (7th Cir. 1982); *Hoptowit v. Ray*, 682 F.2d 1237 (9th Cir. 1982). (The misclassification of prisoners is not a violation of the 8th Amendment.)

[11] *Carterino v. Wilson*, 546 F. Supp. 174 (W.D. Ky. 1982), 562 F. Supp. 106 (W.D. Ky. 1983).

[12] *Fano v. Meachum*, 520 F.2d 374 (1st Cir. 1975).

ever, the decision was reversed by the United States Supreme Court. In *Meachum v. Fano*[13] the Court held that, absent a state law or practice which conditions the transfer of inmates between institutions upon proof of serious misconduct or the occurrence of other specified events, the Fourteenth Amendment's due process clause in and of itself does not entitle an inmate to a fact-finding hearing prior to his transfer from one penal institution to another, even if the conditions of the recipient institution are substantially less favorable to him than those existing in the institution from which he was transferred, provided that such conditions area within the sentence imposed upon him and do not otherwise violate the Constitution. The Supreme Court further considered inmates' transfer rights in *Montanye v. Haymes*,[14] a companion case to *Meachum,* and held that the Fourteenth Amendment's Due Process Clause does not, on its face, require a hearing prior to the transfer, *for whatever reason,* of an inmate from one institution to another in the same penal system, provided that the conditions or degree of the confinement to which the inmate is thus subjected are within the sentence imposed upon him and do not otherwise violate the Constitution.

A state prisoner has no justifiable expectation that he will not be transferred to a prison in another state, where state prison regulations create no constitutionally protected liberty interest against such a transfer. The regulation under review provided for a pretransfer hearing but left prison administrators with unfettered discretion over transfers. Confinement in another state is within the normal limits or range of custody which the conviction has authorized the transferring state to impose.[15]

Taken together, *Meachum* and *Montanye* eliminate the constitutional underpinnings of the argument that minimal procedural due process must be accorded to inmates before they are transferred. As mentioned in the preceding section, beyond the narrow scope of the inmate transfer issue, these decisions suggest a possible reexamination by the Supreme Court of the constitutional validity of the "grievous loss" argument which has required minimal procedural due process requirements for administrative classification hearings in general.

The statutory right of a prisoner to a hearing under Article IV(d) of the Interstate Agreement on Detainers before he is transferred to another jurisdiction, was upheld in *Cuyler v. Adams.*[16] However, an involuntary transfer of a convicted felon from a state prison to a mental hospital violates a liberty interest that is protected by the Due Process Clause of the Fourteenth Amendment.[17] The stigmatizing consequences of a transfer to a mental institution for involuntary psychiatric treatment,

---

[13] *Meachum v. Fano,* 427 U.S. 215 (1976).

[14] *Montanye v. Haymes,* 427 U.S. 236 (1976).

[15] *Olim v. Wakinekona,* 456 U.S. 1005, 33 Cr. L. 3051 (1983); *Shango v. Jurich,* 681 F.2d. 1091 (7th Cir. 1982). (A state prison inmate has no liberty interest in remaining in any particular prison that is protected by the United States Constitution.)

[16] *Cuyler v. Adams,* 449 U.S. 433 (1981).

[17] *Vitek v. Jones,* 445 U.S. 480 (1980).

including mandatory behavior modification, require that the procedure to be used includes:

1. A written notice to the prisoner that a transfer to a mental institution is being considered;
2. A hearing, sufficiently after the notice to permit the prisoner to prepare, at which disclosure to the prisoner is made of the evidence being relied upon for the transfer and at which an opportunity to be heard in person and to present documentary evidence is given;
3. An opportunity at the hearing to present testimony of witnesses by the defense and to confront and cross-examine witnesses called by the state, except upon a finding, not arbitrarily made, of good cause for not permitting such presentation, confrontation, or cross-examination;
4. An independent decisionmaker;
5. A written statement by the fact finder as to the evidence relied on and the reasons for transferring the inmate;
6. Availability of legal counsel, furnished by the state, if the inmate is financially unable to furnish his own; and
7. Effective and timely notice of all the foregoing rights.

With respect to the appointment of legal counsel, the decision was indecisive. Four of the nine Justices believed:

The District Court did go beyond the requirements imposed by prior cases by holding that counsel must be made available to inmates facing transfer hearings if they are financially unable to furnish their own. We have not required the automatic appointment of counsel for indigent prisoners facing other deprivations of liberty. *Gagnon v. Scarpelli; Wolff v. McDonnell;* but we have recognized that prisoners who are illiterate and uneducated have a greater need for assistance in exercising their rights. *Gagnon v. Scarpelli; Wolff v. McDonnell.* A prisoner thought to be suffering from a mental disease or defect requiring involuntary treatment probably has an even greater need for legal assistance, for such a prisoner is more likely to be unable to understand or exercise his rights. In these circumstances, it is appropriate that counsel be provided to indigent prisoners whom the State seeks to treat as mentally ill.

Mr. Justice Powell concurred in the decision,[18] except for the provision for legal counsel. He agreed that qualified and independent assistance must be provided, but stated that an inmate need not always be provided with a licensed attorney.

The issue of transferring prisoners from state custody to the federal system for service of sentence arose in *Howe v. Smith.*[19] A high-risk Vermont prisoner was transferred to a federal prison because Vermont had closed its only maximum security prison. It was held that the transfer was authorized and proper, even though no particularized, specialized treatment program was available in the fed-

---

[18] *Id.* at 496, 497.
[19] *Howe v. Smith,* 452 U.S. 473 (1981).

eral system to meet the needs of the prisoner. The plain wording of the statute, 18 U.S.C. § 5003(a), authorizes transfers not simply for treatment, but also for the custody, care, subsistence, education, and training of state prisoners in federal institutions. However, a prisoner was deprived of an independent decisionmaker guaranteed by Hawaii regulations. The same committee that recommended his transfer to a California prison also initiated the transfer. A valid claim under 42 U.S.C. § 1983 was stated.[20]

§ 12.4   Search and Seizure

A prison inmate has no reasonable expectation of privacy in his prison cell entitling him to any Fourth Amendment protection against unreasonable searches and seizures. It would be impossible for prison officials to accomplish the objective of preventing the introduction of weapons, drugs and other contraband into the prison if inmates retained a right of privacy in their cells. The unpredictability that attends random searches of cells renders such searches the most effective weapon of the prison official in the fight against contraband. Further, prison officials must be free to seize from cells any articles which, in their view, disserve legitimate institutional interests.[21]

Pretrial detainees have no due process rights to observe jail officials' random shakedown searches of their cells.[22]

A state's right to incarcerate inmates includes the right to limit or extinguish inmates' constitutional rights which are inconsistent with incarceration. In *Olsen v. Klecker*,[23] the Federal Constitution's Fourth Amendment prohibition against unreasonable searches and seizures was held not to restrict warrantless searches of prison cells. The basic point of this case is not that the Fourth Amendment does not apply to inmates, but that the reasonability of prison searches and seizures is to be assessed in light of the institutional needs of security, order, and rehabilitation. An example of this special measure of reasonability is evident in the cases which involve body cavity searches. In *Hodges v. Klein*,[24] it was stated that a prison policy which requires inmates to submit to anal searches not only upon leaving or entering the institution, but following personal contact visits with other prisoners or friends

---

[20] *Wakinekona v. Olim*, 664 F.2d 708 (9th Cir. 1981), *rev'd on other grounds*, 456 U.S. 1005, 33 Cr. L. 3051 (1983).

[21] *Hudson v. Palmer*, 468 U.S. 517, 35 Cr. L. 3230 (1984).

[22] *Block v. Rutherford*, 468 U.S. 571, 35 Cr. L. 3221 (1984).

[23] *Olsen v. Klecker*, 642 F.2d 1115 (8th Cir. 1981); *Clifton v. Robinson*, 500 F. Supp. 30 (E.D. Pa. 1980); *Beckett v. Powers*, 494 F. Supp. 364 (W.D. Wis. 1980); *Brown v. Hilton*, 492 F. Supp. 771 (D.N.J. 1980); *State v. Pietraszewski*, 283 N.W.2d 887 (Minn. 1979); *Butler v. Bensinger*, 377 F. Supp. 870 (N.D. Ill. 1974).

[24] *Hodges v. Klein*, 412 F. Supp. 896 (D.N.J. 1976); *see also, United States v. Lilly*, 599 F.2d 619 (5th Cir. 1979); *Coleman v. Hutto*, 500 F. Supp 586 (D.C. Va. 1980); *Vera v. State*, 29 Cr. L. 2409 (Fla. Ct. App., 3d Cir. 1981); *Williams v. State*, 400 So.2d 988 (Fla. App. 1981); *but cf. Sims v. Brierton*, 500 F. Supp. 813 (N.D. Ill. 1980); *Arruda v. Berman*, 522 F. Supp. 766 (D. Mass. 1981). (Repeated rectal cavity searches accompanied by abusive and insulting comments and beatings stated a cause of action under the Civil Rights Act.)

and relatives as well, is constitutional. The state's interest in the prevention of contraband from transmission into and within the prison is very strong, and private contact with an individual from outside of the prison presents an excellent opportunity for the introduction of all types of contraband into the prison community. Prison officials must be able to shut off completely this port of entry for contraband. To do so, an anal examination, degrading though it is, as part of a strip search, is not, in view of the state's compelling interest, an unreasonable requirement. However, the court held that mandatory anal searches were not permissible as applied to inmates who are entering or leaving solitary confinement. There is no compelling state interest which can justify anal examinations prior to or following a segregated inmate is moved within the segregation area or anywhere in the prison while under escort or observation. The court felt that metal detectors provide the security which is necessary.[25]

The Supreme Court approved both body cavity searches and room searches. In *Bell v. Wolfish*,[26] the Court held that body cavity searches are not unreasonable and do not violate the Constitution. Prison officials may conduct them on less than probable cause as long as they are not conducted in an abusive manner. Also, room searches are a reasonable security measure and do not infringe upon a detainee's or prisoner's right to privacy. Further, inmates do not have any protected right to be present or watch room searches.

There are, however, certain factors which can counterbalance the institutional needs of security, order, and rehabilitation, and which can make the search or seizure unreasonable, and therefore unconstitutional. Clearly established inmate rights, such as the right to possess legal and religious material, can clash with the state's right to search and seize inmates' property. For example, in *Bonner v. Coughlin*,[27] an inmate was awarded damages for the seizure by prison guards of his copy of his trial transcript. Also, in *O'Connor v. Keller*,[28] an inmate was awarded punitive damages from a prison official who made an unreasonable seizure of personal property from the inmate's cell. In such cases it is not an inherent right to be free from searches and seizures which allows recovery, but the constitutional protection which surrounds and flows from the property seized.

In a jail setting, a prisoner's personal effects may be "inventoried" without violating the Fourth Amendment. It is reasonable for police to search the personal effects of a person under lawful arrest as part of the routine administrative procedure at a police station incident to booking and jailing of persons arrested. It is entirely proper for police to remove and list or inventory property found on the

[25] Cf. Lee v. Downs, 641 F.2d 1117 (4th Cir. 1981). (Where a female prisoner was possibly suicidal, it was proper for prison guards to forcibly remove her clothes in the presence of male guards.)
[26] Bell v. Wolfish, 441 U.S. 520 (1979).
[27] Bonner v. Coughlin, 517 F.2d 1311 (7th Cir. 1975).
[28] O'Connor v. Keller, 510 F. Supp. 1359 (D. Md. 1981); Steinburg v. Taylor, 500 F. Supp. 477 (D. Conn. 1980); Diguiseppe v. Ward, 514 F. Supp. 503 (S.D. N.Y. 1981); cf. Roque v. Warden, Conn. Corrections, 434 A.2d 348 (Conn. 1980).

person or in the possession of an arrested person who is to be jailed. The justification of the search is not based on probable cause. The absence of a warrant is immaterial to the reasonableness of the search. Reasons justifying the search are considerations of orderly police administration, protection of a suspect's property, deterrence of false claims of theft against the police, security, and identification of the suspect. The fact that the bag could have been otherwise secured did not make the search unreasonable. Even if some less intrusive means existed, it would be unreasonable to expect police officers in the everyday course of business to make fine and subtle distinctions in deciding which containers or items may be searched, and which must be sealed without examination as a unit. As a caution, the Court stresses that it is important as to whether the suspect was to be incarcerated or released after being booked. If the suspect was to be released, there is arguably no reason to inventory his property.[29] For searches of parolees and probationers, see § 9.5.2.

§ 12.5   Conditions of Confinement

Courts have a duty to protect inmates from unlawful and onerous treatment of a nature that, of itself, adds punitive measures to those legally meted out by a court.[30] While the federal courts continue to recognize the broad discretion which state prison officials require in order to maintain orderly and secure institutions, constitutional deprivations of such a magnitude as to allow the maintenance of facilities which are wholly unfit for human habitation cannot be countenanced. The courts are under a duty to, and will, intervene to protect incarcerated persons from such infringements of their constitutional rights.[31] However, federal courts are limited in their intervention into the operations of institutions to the issue of whether there are constitutional violations. In *Bell v. Wolfish,* [32] the Supreme Court said:

> . . . There was a time not too long ago when the federal judiciary took a completely "hands-off" approach to the problem of prison administration. In recent years, however, these courts largely have discarded this "hands-off" attitude and have waded into this complex arena. The deplorable conditions and draconian restrictions of some of our Nation's prisons are too well known to require recounting here, and the federal courts rightly have condemned these sordid aspects of our prison systems. But many of these same courts have, in the name of the Constitution, become increasingly enmeshed in the minutiae of prison operations. Judges, after all, are human. They, no less than others in our society, have a natural tendency to believe that their individual solutions to often intractable problems are better and more workable than

---

[29] *Illinois v. Lafayette,* 462 U.S. 640, 103 S.Ct. 2605, 77 L.Ed.2d 65 (1983).

[30] *Stickney v. List,* 519 F.Supp 617 (D. Nev. 1981).

[31] *Jordan v. Arnold,* 472 F. Supp. 265 (M.D. Pa. 1979); *Taylor v. Sterrett,* 600 F.2d 1135 (5th Cir. 1979); *Robson v. Biester,* 420 A.2d 9 (Pa. Commw. Ct. 1980); *James v. Wallace,* 406 F. Supp. 318 (M.D. Ala. 1976).

[32] *Bell v. Wolfish,* 441 U.S. 520 (1979).

those of the persons who are actually charged with and trained in the running of the particular institution under examination. But under the Constitution, the first question to be answered is not whose plan is best, but in what branch of the Government is lodged the authority to initially devise the plan. This does not mean that constitutional rights are not to be scrupulously observed. It does mean, however, that the inquiry of federal courts into prison management must be limited to the issue of whether a particular system violates any prohibition of the Constitution, or in the case of a federal prison, a statute. The wide range of "judgment calls" that meet constitutional and statutory requirement[s] are confided to officials outside of the Judicial Branch of Government.

Similarly, in *Rhodes v. Chapman,*[33] the Supreme Court reinforced its holding in *Bell v. Wolfish,* and admonished the lower federal courts that in their oversight responsibilities to determine whether prison conditions constitute cruel and unusual punishment under federal standards, the federal courts cannot assume that the state legislatures and prison officials are insensitive to the requirements of the Constitution, or to the sociological problems of how best to achieve the goals of the prison function in the criminal justice system.

For a variety of reasons, overcrowding is a major problem at almost all penal institutions. Overcrowding has not, in itself, been declared unconstitutional. However, overcrowding has been viewed as a causal factor, which, when other conditions are present, may be enough to declare a prison's conditions to be unconstitutional.[34]

---

[33] *Rhodes v. Chapman,* 452 U.S. 337 (1981).

[34] *Wichman v. Fisher,* 629 P.2d 896 (Utah 1981); *Benjamin v. Malcolm,* 495 F. Supp. 1357 (S.D. N.Y. 1980).

In *Bell v. Wolfish,* the Court held that double bunking does not deprive pretrial detainees of liberty without due process and that a particular restriction is valid if it is reasonably related to a legitimate nonpunitive governmental objective. The Court emphasized that regulations or practices must be rationally related to a legitimate non-punitive governmental purpose and must not appear excessive in relation to that purpose. Security and order is a non-punitive objective which may necessarily infringe upon or cause many restrictions to the rights of inmates or pretrial detainees. *Bell v. Wolfish,* 441 U.S. 520 (1979).

In *Rhodes v. Chapman,* the Supreme Court held that double-celling at Ohio's maximum security prison did not amount to cruel and unusual punishment prohibited by the Eight and Fourteenth Amendments. In order for conditions of confinement to constitute punishment, they must involve the wanton and unnecessary infliction of pain or be grossly disproportionate to the severity of the crime warranting imprisonment. The fact that overcrowding falls below contemporary standards does not make the overcrowding unconstitutional. The Supreme Court recognizes that to the extent that such conditions are restrictive, and even harsh, they are part of the price that criminals must pay for their offenses against society. *Ruiz v. Estelle,* 679 F.2d 1115 (5th Cir. 1982). (A district court decree requiring single-celling in Texas prisons and at least 60 square feet per inmate in dormitories was set aside. The district court's requirements go beyond that which is necessary for the elimination of unconstitutional prison conditions. The constitutional mandate against cruel and unusual punishment is not a warranty of pleasant prison conditions. Also, the district court acted properly within its discretion in prescribing certain exercise requirements for the Texas Department of Corrections. Although the deprivation of exercise is not per se cruel and unusual punishment, in certain circumstances such a denial may constitute an impairment of health forbidden under the 8th Amendment); *Smith v. Fairman,* 690 F.2d 122 (7th Cir. 1982). (A prison practice of housing two inmates in a single cell did not violate the 8th Amendment prohibiting cruel and unusual punishment. The lower court's ruling was reversed.)

Constitutional treatment of human beings who are confined to penal institutions is not dependent upon the willingness or the financial ability of the state to provide decent penitentiaries,[35] especially where the legislature has had ample opportunity to make provision for the state to meet its constitutional responsibilities.[36] Although federal courts may lack the power to order public or governmental entities, which represent the public, to expend funds to build new facilities, they do have the power to order the release of persons who are being held under conditions which deprive them of rights guaranteed to them by the Federal Constitution, unless such conditions are corrected within a reasonable time.[37] Some courts have gone so far with the conditions-of-confinement argument that they have allowed escapee defendants to raise the criminal defenses of necessity and duress to criminal charges of prison escape.[38] Such cases usually involve threats of homosexual rape as the mitigating condition of confinement.

Most aspects of prison life are dictated by the needs of institutionalization. Prison authorities have wide discretion to regulate or prohibit inmates' comforts, including the keeping of pets,[39] permissible clothing,[40] plumbing,[41] and checking accounts.[42]

Inmates who complain of their conditions of confinement, but who are transferred to other facilities before their complaints are adjudicated, may have their complaints dismissed as moot.[43]

§ 12.6　Corrections Personnel

There are several unique problems which affect correctional personnel. As free people they are entitled, of course, to full measure of liberty accorded to all other persons. However, two counterforces may circumscribe the exercise of such liberty. First, those prison employees who are also police officers are subject to the same occupationally generated need for uniformity and discipline as regular civil police forces. There is a paramilitary aspect to prison employment, and certain

---

[35] *Smith v. Sullivan*, 611 F.2d 1039 (5th Cir. 1980); *Williams v. Edwards*, 547 F.2d 1209 (5th Cir. 1977); *Gates v. Collier*, 407 F. Supp. 1117 (N.D. Miss. 1975).

[36] *Clay v. Miller*, 626 F.2d 345 (4th Cir. 1980); *Battle v. Anderson*, 594 F.2d 786 (10th Cir. 1979); *James v. Wallace*, 406 F. Supp. 318 (M.D. Ala. 1976).

[37] *Padgett v. Stein*, 406 F. Supp. 287 (M.D. Pa. 1975).

[38] *United States v. Bailey*, 23 Cr. L. 2373 (D.C. Cir. 1978); *State v. Reese*, 24 Cr. L. 2331 (Iowa 1978); *People v. Lovercamp*, 43 Cal. App. 2d 823, 118 Cal. Rptr. 110 (1974); *People v. Harmon*, 53 Mich. App. 482, 220 N.W.2d 212 (1974).

[39] *Sparks v. Fuller*, 506 F.2d 1238 (1st Cir. 1974).

[40] *Id.* at 1239; *See also, State v. Rouse*, 629 P.2d 167 (Kansas 1981).

[41] *Mims v. Shapp*, 399 F. Supp. 818 (W.D. Pa. 1975), was vacated and remanded on appeal. *Mims v. Shapp*, 541 F.2d 415 (2d Cir. 1976). The court of appeals held that the inmates' affidavits sufficiently alleged personal bias of the judge and that the district judge erred in denying the inmates' recusal motion; *See also, Freeman v. Trudell*, 497 F. Supp. 481 (E.D. Mich. 1980) and *Jefferson v. Douglas*, 493 F. Supp. 13 (D. Okla. 1979). (Whether a prisoner has a proper diet is a question wholly within the discretion of the prison administration.); *Herring v. Superintendent, Danville City Jail*, 387 F. Supp. 410 (W.D. Va. 1974).

[42] *Nix v. Paderick*, 407 F. Supp. 844 (E.D. Va. 1976).

[43] *Strader v. Blalock*, 405 F. Supp. 1155 (W.D. Va. 1975).

sacrifices must be made by the employees so that the police power of the states may be most efficiently used and effectively displayed. In *Kelley v. Johnson*,[44] the United States Supreme Court upheld a county regulation which specified its policemen's hair length. The Court concluded that whether a state or local government's choice to have its police in uniform reflects a desire to make police officers readily recognizable to the public or to foster the *esprit de corps* which similarity of garb and appearance may inculcate within the police force itself, the justification for the hair length regulation is sufficiently rational to defeat a claim based upon the liberty guarantee of the Fourteenth Amendment.[45] Likewise, the court in *Lucas County Sheriff's Department v. Mixon*,[46] held that a public agency may compel its employees to participate in internal affairs investigations, upon penalty of removal. The court went on to say that although an employee may not be faced with the issue of relinquishing his constitutional rights, he may be disciplined for refusal to participate in the investigation.

The second counterforce to the untrammeled exercise of the constitutional liberties of correctional personnel is applicable equally to uniformed and non-uniformed employees. The institutional needs of security, order, and rehabilitation provide the basis for certain limitations upon such employees' liberties. Limitations upon the right to be free from search and seizure and upon the exercise of the rights to free association are examples of the numerous daily adjustments which correctional personnel must make when they physically cross the barriers between prison society and free society. The smuggling of contraband into prisons is so dangerous to institutional order that its prevention outweighs the probable cause requirement which normally limits searches and seizures in free society. Rehabilitative considerations can dictate that correctional personnel limit or minimize their personal associations with inmates.

Another aspect of corrections work is the standard prohibition against the use of armed trusties, or inmate assistants, as prison guards. Once quite prevalent, this practice is now limited[47] to areas such as medical services. Medically trained inmate assistants are encouraged in addition to, though not as total fulfillment of, the prison's medical services staff.[48] Some prison systems, however, still use unarmed trusties as corridor bosses.[49]

In *Armstrong v. New York State Comm. of Corrections*, it was held that there was no justification in subjecting a correctional officer to a body cavity search where there was only a bare assertion that officials had received information that the offi-

---

[44] *Kelley v. Johnson*, 425 U.S. 238 (1976).

[45] *Id.*

[46] *Lucas County Sheriff's Department v. Mixon*, No. L-80-098 (C.A. Lucas Cty., Ohio 1981).

[47] *Finney v. Arkansas Bd. of Corr.*, 505 F.2d 194 (8th Cir. 1974); *Alberti v. Sheriff of Harris Co., Tex.*, 406 F. Supp. 649 (S.D. Tex. 1975).

[48] *Gates v. Collier*, 501 F.2d 1291 (5th Cir. 1974).

[49] *Taylor v. Sterrett*, 499 F.2d 367 (5th Cir. 1974).

cer was involved in smuggling contraband, and there were no other articulable facts to support the allegation.[50]

§ 12.7   Rights of Privacy

The right of privacy of female prisoners customarily housed inside cells in a county jail was infringed by the failure to provide toilets sheltered from general vision. Consequently, the failure to provide prisoners with clean bedding, towels, clothing, sanitary mattresses, toilet articles and sanitary napkins for female prisoners violate constitutional rights.[51] However, female guards may perform frisk searches of male prison inmates. Although it may be humiliating and degrading, it is not offensive to the Constitution.[52]

§ 12.8   Conclusion

As this chapter, and indeed the entire book has attempted to demonstrate, incarceration is much more than merely a change in location or an obstacle to physical mobility. It is a fundamental change in one's constitutional status. There is one final consideration which is relevant in this regard. There is a grain of truth to the oft-repeated aphorism that a society is best judged by its prisons, and its treatment of its outcasts. Certainly the accomplishments of Science and the Arts are a correct measure of the character of a people. However, a society's ethics, as manifested by its treatment of those who have offended it, may be a more telling characteristic. Beyond considerations such as "there but for the grace of God go I," a society's treatment of its prison inmates can be viewed as the constitutional floor below which society will tolerate no variations in condition. The treatment of prison inmates may be characterized as a society's moral lowest common denominator.

In a pluralistic society, as America is, there can be no moral ceiling. This is the essence of our theory and practice—people are and of right ought to be free to realize their potential, to reach their own level. However, given our society's relatively haphazard processes of socialization and values internalization, failure, though somewhat less prevalent than success, is still rather commonplace. Thus, the need for some externally dictated minimal standard is felt. Our criminal codes fill this need, but create the problem of what is the constitutional status of the resultant inmates. The evolving solution to this problem is that prison inmates retain all the rights of free people except those which are inconsistent with the institutional needs of security, order, and rehabilitation, and of necessity must be withdrawn during incarceration. The determination of which rights are restricted and which are guaranteed is at the root of the explosive increase and frenzied pace of prison-related litigation today. As our society evidences the evolving standards of decency which mark the progress of a maturing society, reassessment of prior determinations will be necessary, and thus, the need for prison-related litigation will be constant.

---

[50] *Armstrong v. New York State Comm. of Corrections,* 545 F. Supp. 728 (N.D. N.Y. 1982).
[51] *Dawson v. Kendrick,* 527 F. Supp. 1252 (S.D. W. Va. 1982).
[52] *Smith v. Fairman,* 678 F.2d 52 (7th Cir. 1982).

PART II:

JUDICIAL DECISIONS RELATING TO PART I

Included in this section of the book are the court decisions and cases to which the text discussion refers.

Note that the cases are grouped acccording to the text chapter to which they relate. A table of cases for Part II begins on page 231.

TABLE OF CASES FOR PART II

USE OF FORCE; USE OF CORPORAL PUNISHMENT TO ENFORCE PRISON DISCIPLINE

WHITLEY v. ALBERS

475 U.S. 312, 106 S. Ct. 1078, 89 L. Ed. 2d. 251 (1986)

[Citations and Footnotes Omitted]

JUSTICE O'CONNOR delivered the opinion of the Court.

This case requires us to decide what standard governs a prison inmate's claim that prison officials subjected him to cruel and unusual punishment by shooting him during the course of their attempt to quell a prison riot.

I

At the time he was injured, respondent Gerald Albers was confined in cell-block "A" of the Oregon State Penitentiary. Cell-block "A" consists of two tiers of barred cells housing some 200 inmates. The two tiers are connected by a stairway that offers the only practical way to move from one tier to another.

At about 8:30 on the evening of June 27, 1980, several inmates were found intoxicated at the prison annex. Prison guards attempted to move the intoxicated prisoners, some of whom resisted, to the penitentiary's isolation and segregation facility. This incident could be seen from the cell windows in cellbock "A," and some of the onlookers became agitated because they thought that the guards were using unnecessary force. Acting on instructions from their superiors, Officers Kemper and Fitts, who were on duty in cell-block "A," ordered the prisoners to return to their cells. The order was not obeyed. Several inmates confronted the two officers, who were standing in the open area of the lower tier. One inmate, Richard Klenk, jumped from the second tier and assaulted Officer Kemper. Kemper escaped but Officer Fitts were taken hostage. Klenk and other inmates then began breaking furniture and milling about.

Upon being informed of the disturbance, petitioner Harol Whitley, the prison security manager, entered cell-block "A" and spoke to Klenk. Captain Whitley agreed to permit four residents of cell-block "A" to view the inmates who had been taken to segregation earlier. These emissaries reported back that the prisoners in segregation were intoxicated but unharmed. Nonetheless, the disturbance in cell-block "A" continued.

Whitley returned to the cell-block and confirmed that Fitts was not harmed. Shortly thereafter, Fitts was moved from an office on the lower tier to cell 201 on the upper tier, and Klenk demanded that media representatives be brought into the cell-block. In the course of the negotiations, Klenk, who was armed with a homemade knife, informed Whitley that one inmate had been beaten but not killed by other prisoners.

Captain Whitley left the cell-block to organize an assault squad. When Whitley returned to cell-block "A," he was taken to see Fitts in cell 201. Several inmates assured Whitley that they would protect Fitts from harm, but Klenk threatened to kill the hostage if an attempt was made to lead an assault. Klenk and at least some other inmates were aware that guards had assembled outside the cell-block and that shotguns had been issued. Meanwhile, respondent had left his cell on the upper tier to see if elderly prisoners housed on the lower tier could be moved out of harm's way in the event that tear gas was used. Respondent testified that he asked Whitley for the key to the row of cells housing the elderly prisoners, and Whitley indicated that he would

return with the key. Whitley denied that he spoke to respondent at any time during the disturbance.

Whitley next consulted with his superiors, petitioners Cupp, the prison Superintendent, and Kenney, the Assistant Superintendent. They agreed that forceful intervention was necessary to protect the life of the hostage and the safety of the inmates who were not rioting, and ruled out tear gas as an unworkable alternative. Cupp ordered Whitley to take a special squad armed with shotguns into cell-block "A."

Whitley gave the final orders to the assault team, which was assembled in the area outside cell-block "A." Petitioner Kennicott and two other officers armed with shotguns were to follow Whitley, who was unarmed, over the barricade the inmates had constructed at the cell-block entrance. A second group of officers, without firearms, would be behind them. Whitley ordered Kennicott to fire a warning shot as he crossed the barricade. He also ordered Kennicott to shoot low at any prisoners climbing the stairs toward cell 201, since they could pose a threat to the safety of the hostage or to Whitley himself, who would be climbing the stairs in an attempt to free the hostage in cell 201.

At about 10:30 p.m., Whitley reappeared just outside the barricade. By this time, about a half hour had elapsed since the earlier breaking of furniture, and the noise level in the cell-block had noticeably diminished. Respondent, who was standing at the bottom of the stairway, asked about the key. Whitley replied "No," clambered over the barricade, yelled "shoot the bastards," and ran toward the stairs after Klenk, who had been standing in the open areaway with a number of other inmates. Kennicott fired a warning shot into the wall opposite the cell-block entrance as he followed Whitley over the barricade. He then fired a second shot that struck a post near the stairway. Meanwhile, Whitley chased Klenk up the stairs, and shortly thereafter respondent started up the stairs. Kennicott fired a third shot that struck respondent in the left knee. Another inmate was shot on the stairs and several others on the lower tier were wounded by gunshot. The inmates in cell 201 prevented Klenk from entering, and Whitley subdued Klenk at the cell door, freeing the hostage.

As a result of the incident, respondent sustained severe damage to his left leg and mental and emotional distress. He subsequently commenced this action pursuant to 42 U.S.C. § 1983, alleging that petitioners deprived him of his rights under the Eighth and Fourteenth Amendments and raising pendent state law claims for assault and battery and negligence. Many of the facts were stipulated, but both sides also presented testimony from witnesses to the disturbance and the rescue attempt, as well as from expert witnesses with backgrounds in prison discipline and security. At the conclusion of trial, the District Judge directed a verdict for petitioners. He understood respondent's claim to be based solely on the Eighth Amendment as made applicable to the States by the Fourteenth Amendment.

The District Judge held:

"[D]efendents' use of deadly force was justified under the unique circumstances of this case. Possible alternatives were considered and reasonably rejected by prison officers. The use of shotguns and specifically the order to shoot low anyone following the unarmed Whitley up the stairs were necessary to protect Whitley, secure the safe release of the hostage and to restore order and discipline. Even in hindsight, it cannot be said that defendants' actions were not reasonably necessary." In the alternative, he held that petitioners were immune from damages liability because the constitutional constraints on the use of force in a prison riot were not clearly established. Finally, the District Judge held that respondent was barred from recovery on his pendent state law claims by virtue of an immunity conferred on public officers by the Oregon Tort Claims Act as to claims arising out of riots or mob actions.

A panel of the Court of Appeals for Ninth Circuit reversed in part and affirmed in part, with one judge dissenting. The court held that an Eighth Amendment violation would be established "if a prison official deliberately shot Albers under the circumstances where the official, with due allowance for the exigency, knew or should have known that it was unnecessary," or "if the emergency plan was adopted or carried out with 'deliberate indifference' to the right of Albers to be free of cruel unusual punishment." The Court of Appeals pointed to evidence that the general disturbance in cell-block "A" was subsiding and to respondent's experts' testimony that the use of deadly force was excessive under the circumstances and should have been preceded by a verbal warning, and concluded that the jury could have found an Eighth Amendment violation.

***

II

The language of the Eighth Amendment, "[e]xcessive bail shall not be required, nor excessive fines imposed, nor cruel and unusual punishments inflicted," manifests "an intention to limit the power of those entrusted with the criminal-law function of government." The Cruel and Unusual Punishments Clause "was designed to protect those convicted of crimes," and consequently the Clause applies "only after the State has complied with the constitutional guarantees traditionally associated with criminal prosecutions." An express intent to inflict unnecessary pain is not required, *Estelle v. Gamble*, ("deliberate indifference" to a prisoner's serious medical needs is cruel and unusual punishment), and "conditions of confinement" may constitute cruel and unusual punishment unless such conditions "are part of the penalty that criminal offenders pay for their offenses against society." *Rhodes v. Chapman.*

Not every governmental action affecting the interests or well-being of a prisoner is subject to Eighth Amendment scrutiny, however. "After incarceration, only the ' "unnecessary and wanton infliction of pain" ' ... constitutes cruel and unusual punishment forbidden by the Eighth Amendment." To be cruel and unusual punishment, conduct that does not purport to be punishment at all must involve more than ordinary lack of due care for the prisoner's interests or safety. This reading of the Clause underlies our decision in *Estelle v. Gamble*, which held that a prison physician's "negligen[ce] in diagnosing or treating a medical condition" did not suffice to make out a claim of cruel and unusual punishment. It is obduracy and wantonness, not inadvertence or error in good faith, that characterize the conduct prohibited by the Cruel and Unusual Punishments Clause, whether that conduct occurs in connection with establishing conditions of confinement, supplying medical needs, or restoring official control over a tumultuous cell-block. The infliction of pain in the course of a prison security measure, therefore, does not amount to cruel and unusual punishment simply because it may appear in retrospect that the degree of force authorized or applied for security purposes was unreasonable, and hence unnecessary in the strict sense.

The general requirement that an Eighth Amendment claimant allege and prove the unnecessary and wanton infliction of pain should also be applied with due regard for differences in the kind of conduct against which an Eighth Amendment objection is lodged. The deliberate indifference standard articulated in *Estelle* was appropriate in the context presented in that case because the State's responsibility to attend to the medical needs of prisoners does not ordinarily clash with other equally important government responsibilities. Consequently, "deliberate indifference to a prisoner's serious illness or injury," *Estelle*, *supra*, can typically be established or disproved without the necessity of balancing competing institutional concerns for the safety of prison staff or other inmates. But, in making and carrying out decisions involving the use of force to restore order in the face of a prison disturbance, prison officials undoubtedly must take into account the very real threats the unrest presents to inmates and prison officials alike, in addition to the possible harms to inmates against whom force might be used. As we said in *Hudson v. Palmer*, prison administrators are charged with the responsibility of ensuring the safety of the prison staff, administrative personnel, and visitors, as well as the "obligation to take reasonable measures to guarantee the safety of the inmates themselves." In this setting, a deliberate indifference standard does not adequately capture the importance of such competing obligations, or convey the appropriate hesitancy to critique in hindsight decisions necessarily made in haste, under pressure, and frequently without the luxury of a second chance.

Where a prison security measure is undertaken to resolve a disturbance, such as occurred in this case, that indisputably poses significant risks to the safety of inmates and prison staff, we think the question whether the measure taken inflicted unnecessary and wanton pain and suffering ultimately turns on "whether force was applied in a good faith effort to maintain or restore discipline or maliciously and sadistically for the very purpose of causing harm." As the District Judge correctly perceived, "such factors as the need for the application of force, the relationship between the need and the amount of force that was used, [and] the extent of injury inflicted," are relevant to that ultimate determination. From such considerations inferences may be drawn as to whether the use of force could plausibly have been thought necessary, or instead evinced such wantonness with respect to the unjustified infliction of harm as is tantamount to a knowing willingness that it occur. But equally relevant are such factors as the extent of the threat to the safety of staff and inmates, as reasonably perceived by the responsible officials on the basis of the facts known to them, and any efforts made to temper the severity of a forceful response.

When the "ever-present potential for violent confrontation and conflagration," ripens into actual unrest and conflict, the admonition that "a prison's internal security is peculiarly a matter normally left to the administrators ... should be accorded wide-ranging deference in the adoption and execution of policies and practices that in their judgment are needed to preserve internal order and discipline and to maintain institutional security." That deference extends to a prison security measure taken in response to an actual confrontation with riotous inmates, just as it does to prophylactic or preventive measures intended to reduce the incidence of these or any other breaches of prison discipline. It does not insulate from review actions taken in bad faith and for no legitimate purpose, but it requires that neither judge nor jury freely substitute their judgment for that of officials who have made a considered choice. Accordingly, in ruling on a motion for a directed verdict in a case such as this, courts must determine whether the evidence goes beyond a mere dispute over the reasonableness of a particular use of force or the existence of arguably superior alternatives. Unless it appears that the evidence, viewed in the light most favorable to the plaintiff, will support a reliable inference of wantonness in the infliction of pain under the standard we have described, the case should not go to the jury.

III

***

The Court of Appeals believed that testimony that the disturbance was subsiding at the time the assault was made, and the conflicting expert testimony as to whether the force used was excessive, were enough to allow a jury to find that respondent's Eighth Amendment rights were violated. We think the Court of Appeals effectively collapsed the distinction between mere negligence and wanton conduct that we find implicit in the Eighth Amendment. Only if ordinary errors of judgment could make out an Eighth Amendment claim would this evidence create a jury question.

To begin with, although the evidence could be taken to show that the general disturbance had quieted down, a guard was still held hostage, Klenk was armed and threatening, several other inmates were armed with homemade clubs, numerous inmates remained outside their cells, and the cell-block remained in the control of the inmates. The situation remained dangerous and volatile. As respondent concedes, at the time he was shot "an officer's safety was in question and ... an inmate was armed and dangerous." Prison officials had no way of knowing what direction matters would take if they continued to negotiate or did nothing, but they had ample reason to believe that these options presented unacceptable risks.

Respondent's expert testimony is likewise unavailing. One of respondent's experts opined that petitioners gave inadequate consideration to less forceful means of intervention, and that use of deadly force under the circumstances was not necessary to "prevent imminent danger" to the hostage guard or other inmates. Respondent's second expert testified that prison officials were "possibly a little hasty in using the firepower" on the inmates. At most, this evidence, which was controverted by petitioners' experts, establishes that prison officials arguably erred in judgment when they decided on a plan that employed potentially deadly force. It falls far short of a showing that there was no plausible basis for the officials' belief that this degree of force was necessary. Indeed, any such conclusion would run counter to common sense, in light of the risks to the life of the hostage and the safety of inmates that demonstrably persisted notwithstanding repeated attempts to defuse the situation. An expert's after-the-fact opinion that danger was not "imminent" in no way establishes that there was no danger, or that a conclusion by the officers that it was imminent would have been wholly unreasonable.

Once the basic design of the plan was in place, moreover, it is apparent why any inmate running up the stairs after Captain Whitley, or interfering with his progress towards the hostage, could reasonably be thought to present a threat to the success of the rescue attempt and to Whitley—particularly after a warning shot was fired. A sizable group of inmates, in defiance of the cell—in order and in apparent support of Klenk, continued to stand in the open area on the lower tier. Respondent testified that this was not "an organized group," and that he saw no way of knowing which members of that group of inmates had joined with Klenk in destroying furniture, breaking glass,

seizing the hostage, and setting up the barricade, and they certainly had reason to believe that some members of this group might intervene in support of Klenk. It was perhaps also foreseeable that one or more of these inmates would run up the stairs after the shooting started in order to return to their cells. But there would be neither means nor time to inquire into the reasons why each inmate acted as he did. Consequently, the order to shoot, qualified as it was by an instruction to shoot low, falls short of commanding the infliction of pain in a wanton and unnecessary fashion.

As petitioners' own experts conceded, a verbal warning would have been desirable, in addition to a warning shot, if circumstances permitted it to be given without undue risk. While a jury might conclude that this omission was unreasonable, we think that an inference of wantonness could not be properly be drawn. First, some warning was given in the form of the first shot fired by Officer Kennicott. Second, the prison officials could have believed in good faith that such a warning might endanger the success of the security measure because of the risk that it would have allowed one or more inmates to climb the stairs before they could be stopped. The failure to provide for verbal warnings is thus not so insupportable as to be wanton. Accordingly, a jury could not properly find that this omission, coupled with the order to shoot, offended the Eighth Amendment.

To be sure, the plan was not adapted to take into account the appearance of respondent on the scene, and, on the facts as we must taken them, Whitley was aware that respondent was present on the first tier for benign reasons. Conceivably, Whitley could have added a proviso exempting respondent from his order to shoot any prisoner climbing the stairs. But such an oversight simply does not rise to the level of an Eighth Amendment violation. Officials cannot realistically be expected to consider every contingency or minimize every risk, and it was far from inevitable that respondent would react as he did. Whitley was about to risk his life in an effort to rescue the hostage, and he was understandably focusing on the orders essential to the success of the plan. His failure to make special provision for respondent may have been unfortunate, but is hardly behavior from which a wanton willingness to inflict unjustified suffering on respondent can be inferred.

Once it is established that the order to shoot low at anyone climbing the stairs after a warning shot was not wanton, respondent's burden in showing that the actual shooting constituted of the wanton and unnecessary infliction of pain is an extremely heavy one. Accepting that respondent could have sought safety in a cell on the lower tier, the fact remains that had respondent thrown himself to the floor he would not have been shot at. Instead, after the warning shot was fired, he attempted to return to his cell by running up the stairs behind Whitley. That is equivocal conduct. While respondent had not been actively involved in the riot and indeed had attempted to help matters, there is no indication that Officer Kennicott knew this, nor any claim that he acted vindictively or in retaliation. Respondent testified that as he started to run up the stairs he "froze" when he looked to his left and saw Kennicott, and that "we locked eyes." Kennicott testified that he saw several inmates running up the stairs, that he thought they were pursuing Whitley, and that he fired at their legs. To the extent that this testimony is conflicting, we resolve the conflict in respondent's favor by assuming that Kennicott shot at respondent rather than at the inmates as a group. But this does not establish that Kennicott shot respondent knowing it was unnecessary to do so. Kennicott had some basis for believing that respondent constituted a threat to the hostage and to Whitley, and had at most a few seconds in which to react. He was also under orders to respond to such a perceived threat in precisely the manner he did. Under these circumstances, the actual shooting was part and parcel of a good-faith effort to restore prison security. As such, it did not violate respondent's Eighth Amendment right to be free from cruel and unusual punishments.

IV

As an alternative ground for affirmance, respondent contends that, independently of the Eighth Amendment, the shooting deprived him of a protected liberty interest without due process of law, in violation of the Fourteenth Amendment. Respondent ... argues that he has maintained throughout this litigation that his "constitutional protection against the use of excessive and unnecessary force, as well as the deadly force without meaningful warning," derives from the Due Process Clause as well as the Eighth Amendment. ***

We need say little on this score. We think the Eighth Amendment, which is specifically concerned with the unnecessary and wanton infliction of pain in penal institutions, serves as the primary source of substantive protection to convicted prisoners in cases such as this one, where the deliberate use of force is challenged as excessive and unjustified. It would indeed be surprising if, in the context of forceful prison security measures, "conduct that shocks the conscience," or "afford[s] brutality the cloak of law," and so violates the Fourteenth Amendment, were not also punishment "inconsistent with contemporary standards of decency" and " 'repugnant to the conscience of mankind,' " in violation of the Eighth. We only recently reserved the general question "whether something less than intentional conduct, such as recklessness or 'gross negligence,' is enough to trigger the protections of the Due Process Clause." Because this case involves prison inmates rather than pretrial detainees or persons enjoying unrestricted liberty we imply nothing as to the proper answer to that question outside the prison security context by holding, as we do, that in these circumstances the Due Process Clause affords respondent no greater protection than does the Cruel and Unusual Punishments Clause.***

The judgement of the Court of Appeals is

Reversed.

JUSTICE MARSHALL, with whom JUSTICE BRENNAN, JUSTICE BLACKMUN, and JUSTICE STEVENS join, dissenting.

I share the majority's concern that prison officials be permitted to respond reasonably to inmate disturbances without unwarranted fear of liability. I agree that the threshold for establishing a constitutional violation under these circumstances is high. I do not agree, however, that the contested existence of a "riot" in the prison lessens the constraints imposed on prison authorities by the Eighth Amendment.

The majority has erred, I believe, both in developing its legal analysis and in employing it. First, the especially onerous standard the Court has devised for determining whether a prisoner injured during a prison disturbance has been subjected to cruel and unusual punishment is incorrect and not justified by precedent. That standard is particularly inappropriate because courts deciding whether to apply it must resolve a preliminary issue of fact that will often be disputed and properly left to the jury. Finally, the Court has applied its test improperly to the facts of this case. For these reasons, I must respectfully dissent.

I

The Court properly begins by acknowledging that, for a prisoner attempting to prove a violation of the Eighth Amendment, "[a]n express intent to inflict unnecessary pain is not required. Rather, our cases have established that the "unnecessary and wanton" infliction of pain on prisoners constitutes cruel and unusual punishment prohibited by the Eighth Amendment, even in the absence of intent to harm. Having correctly articulated the teaching of our cases on this issue, however, the majority inexplicably arrives at the conclusion that a constitutional violation in the context of a prison uprising can be established only if force was used "maliciously and sadistically for the very purpose of causing harm,"—thus requiring the very "express intent to inflict unnecessary pain" that it had properly disavowed.

The Court imposes its heightened version of the "unnecessary and wanton" standard only when the injury occurred in the course of a "disturbance" that "poses significant risks." But those very questions—whether a disturbance existed and whether it posed a risk—are likely to be hotly contested. It is inappropriate, to say the least, to condition the choice of a legal standard, the purpose of which is to determine whether to send a constitutional claim to the jury, upon the court's resolution of factual disputes that in many cases should themselves be resolved by jury.

The correct standard for identifying a violation of the Eighth Amendment under our cases is clearly the "unnecessary and wanton" standard, which establishes a high hurdle to be overcome by a prisoner seeking relief for a constitutional violation. The full circumstances of the plaintiff's injury, including whether it was inflicted during an attempt to quell a riot and whether there was a reasonable apprehension of danger, should be considered by the factfinder in determining whether that standard is satisfied in a particular case. There is simply no justification for creating a distinct and more onerous burden for the plaintiff to meet merely because the judge believes that the injury at issue was caused during a disturbance that "pose[d] significant risks to the safety of inmates and prison staff." Determination of whether there was such a disturbance or risk, when disputed, should be made by the jury when it resolves disputed facts, not by the court in its role as arbiter of law.

II

The Court properly begins its application of the law by reciting the principle that the facts must be viewed in the light most favorable to respondent, who won a reversal of a directed verdict below. If, under any reasonable interpretation of the facts, a jury could have found the "unnecessary and wanton" standard to be met, then the directed verdict was improper. The majority opinion, however, resolves factual disputes in the record in petitioners' favor and discounts much of the respondent's theory of the case. This it is not entitled to do.

The majority pays short shrift to respondent's significant contention that the disturbance had quieted down by the time the lethal force was employed. Respondent presented substantial testimony to show that the disturbance had subsided, that only one prisoner, Klenk, remained in any way disruptive, and that even Klenk had calmed down enough at that point to admit that he had " 'gone too far.' " The majority asserts that "a guard was still held hostage. Klenk was armed and threatening, several other inmates were armed with homemade clubs, numerous inmates remained outside their cells, and ... [t]he situation remained dangerous and volatile." Respondent's evidence, however, indicated that the guard was not, in fact, in danger. He had been put into a cell by several inmates to prevent Klenk from harming him. Captain Whitley had been to see the guard, and had observed that the inmates protecting him from Klenk were not armed and promised to keep Klenk out. According to respondent's evidence, moreover, no other inmates were assisting Klenk in any way when the riot squad was called in; they were simply "milling around," waiting for Klenk to be taken into custody, or for orders to return to

their cells. Respondent's evidence tended to show not that the "situation remained dangerous and volatile," but, on the contrary, that it was calm. Although the Court sees fit to emphasize repeatedly that "the risks to the life of the hostage and the safety of inmates that demonstrably persisted notwithstanding repeated attempts to defuse the situation," I can only point out that respondent bitterly disputed that any such risk to guards or inmates had persisted. The Court just does not believe his story.

The Court's treatment of the expert testimony is equally insensitive to its obligation to resolve all disputes in favor of respondent. Respondent's experts testified that the use of deadly force under these circumstances was not justified by any necessity to prevent imminent danger to the officers or the inmates, that the force used was excessive, and that even if deadly force had been justified, it would have been unreasonable to unleash such force without a clear warning to allow nonparticipating inmates to return to their cells. Insofar as expert testimony can ever be useful to show that prison authorities engaged in the "unnecessary and wanton" infliction of pain, even thought it will always amount to "after-the-fact opinion" regarding the circumstances of the injury, respondent's expert evidence contributed to the creation of a factual issue.

The majority characterizes the petitioners' error in using deadly force where it was not justified as an "oversight." This is an endorsement of petitioners' rendition of the facts. As portrayed by respondent's evidence, the "error" was made in cold blood. Respondent's involvement started when, at the request of one of the inmates, he approached petitioner Whitley, who was talking to Klenk, to ask if Whitley would supply a key to a gate so that the elderly and sick patients could be removed before any tear gas was used. Captain Whitley said that he would go and get the key, and left the cell-block. In two or three minutes, Whitley returned. Respondent went to the door of the cell-block, and asked Whitley if he had brought the key. Whitley responded " 'No,' " turned his head back and yelled: " 'Let's go, let's go. Shoot the bastards!' "

Respondent, afraid, ran from his position by the door and headed for the stairs, the only route back to his cell. He caught some movement out of the corner of his eye, looked in its direction, and saw petitioner Kennicott. According to respondent: " 'I froze. I looked at him; we locked eyes, then I looked down and seen the shotgun in his hand, then I seen the flash, and the next thing I know I was sitting down, grabbing my leg.' " Losing a great deal of blood, respondent crawled up the stairs and fell on his face, trying to get out of range of the shotguns. After about 10 minutes, an officer grabbed respondent by the hair and dragged him downstairs. As he lay there, another officer came and stood over respondent's face. Respondent was left lying and bleeding profusely for approximately 10 or 15 more minutes, and was taken to the prison hospital. He suffered very severe injury. Meanwhile, Klenk had been subdued with no resistance by Whitley, who was unarmed.

Other testimony showed that, although most of the inmates assembled in the area were clearly not participating in the misconduct, they received no warning, instructions, or opportunity to leave the area and return to their cells before the officers started shooting. Neither respondent nor any other inmate attempted to impede the officers as they entered the cell-block. The officers were described as "wild, " "agitated, excited," not in full control of their emotions. One officer, prior to entering cell-block "A," told the officer to " 'shoot their asses off, and if Klenk gets in the way, kill him.' " At the time of this assault, the cell-block was described as "quiet."

If a jury credited respondent's testimony and that one of his witnesses, it would have believed that there was only one inmate who was temporarily out of control, Klenk—"scared," and "high,"—and ready to give up. The disturbance in the block had lasted only 15 or 20 minutes when it was subsided, and there appeared to be no lasting danger to anyone. Respondent was shot while he stood motionless on the stairs, and was left to bleed for a perilously long time before receiving any assistance.

III

***

The majority suggests that the existence of more appropriate alternative measures for controlling prison disturbance is irrelevant to the constitutional inquiry, but surely it cannot mean what it appears to say. For if prison officials were to drop a bomb on a cell-block in order to halt a fistfight between two inmates, for example, I feel confident that the Court would have difficult concluding, as a matter of law, that such an action was not sufficiently wanton to present a jury question, even though concededly taken in an effort to restore order in the prison. Thus, the question of wantonness in the context of prison disorder, as with other claims of mistreatment under the Eighth Amendment, is a matter of degree. And it is precisely in cases like this one, when shading the facts one way or the other can result in different legal conclusions, that a jury would take into account the petitioners' legitimate need to protect security, the extent of the danger presented, and the reasonableness of force used, in assessing liability. Moreover, the jury would know that a prisoner's burden is a heavy one, if he is to establish an Eighth Amendment violation under these circumstances. Whether respondent was able to meet that burden here is a question for the jury. From the Court's usurpation of the jury's function, I dissent. I would affirm the judgment of the Court of Appeals.

PRISONERS' RIGHTS TO VISITATION/ASSOCIATION

PELL v. PROCUNIER
417 U.S. 817, 94 S. Ct. 2800, 41 L. Ed. 2d 495 (1974)

Mr. Justice Stewart delivered the opinion of the Court.

I

In No. 73-754, the inmate plaintiffs claim that § 415.071, by prohibiting their participation in face-to-face communication with newsmen and other members of the general public, violates their right of free speech under the First and Fourteenth Amendments. Although the constitutional right of free speech has never been thought to embrace a right to require a journalist or any other citizen to listen to a person's views, let alone a right to require a publisher to publish those views in his newspaper, see Avins v. Rutgers, State University of New Jersey, 385 F.2d 151 (CA 3 1967); Chicago Joint Board, Amal. Cloth. Workers v. Chicago Tribune Co., 435 F.2d 470 (CA 7 1970); Associates & Aldrich Co. v. Times Mirror Co., 440 F.2d 133 (CA 9 1971), we proceed upon the hypothesis that under some circumstances the right of free speech includes a right to communicate a person's views to any willing listener, including a willing representative of the press for the pur-

pose of publication by a willing publisher.

We start with the familiar proposition that "[l]awful incarceration brings about the necessary withdrawal or limitation of many privileges and rights, a retraction justified by the considerations underlying our penal system." Price v. Johnston, 334 U.S. 266, 285 (1948). See also Cruz v. Beto, 405 U.S. 319, 321 (1972). In the First Amendment context a corollary of this principle is that a prison inmate retains those First Amendment rights that are not inconsistent with his status as a prisoner or with the legitimate penological objectives of the corrections system. Thus, challenges to prison restrictions that are asserted to inhibit First Amendment interests must be analyzed in terms of the legitimate policies and goals of the corrections system, to whose custody and care the prisoner has been committed in accordance with due process of law.

An important function of the corrections systems is the deterrence of crime. The premise is that by confining criminal offenders in a facility where they are isolated from the rest of society, a

249

condition that most people presumably find undesirable, they and others will be deterred from committing additional criminal offenses. This isolation, of course, also serves a protective function by quarantining criminal offenders for a given period of time while, it is hoped, the rehabilitation process of the corrections system work to correct the offender's demonstrated criminal proclivity. Thus, since most offenders will eventually return to society, another paramount objective of the corrections system is the rehabilitation of those committed to its custody. Finally, central to all other corrections goals is the institutional consideration of internal security within the corrections facilities themselves. It is in the light of these legitimate penal objectives that a court must assess challenges to prison regulations based on asserted constitutional rights of prisoners.

The regulation challenged here clearly restricts one manner of communication between prison inmates and members of the general public beyond the prison walls. But this is merely to state the problem, not to resolve it. For the same could be said of a refusal by corrections authorities to permit an inmate temporarily to leave the prison in order to communicate with persons outside. Yet no one could sensibly contend that the Constitution requires the authorities to give even individualized consideration to such requests. Cf. Zemel v. Rusk, 381 U.S. 1, 16-17 (1965). In order properly to evaluate the constitutionality of § 415.071, we think that the regulation cannot be considered in isolation but must be viewed in the light of the alternative means of communication permitted under the regulations with persons outside the prison. We recognize that there "may be particular qualities inherent

in sustained, face-to-face debate, discussion and questioning," and "that [the] existence of other alternatives [does not] extinguis[h] altogether any constitutional interest on the part of appellees in this particular form of access." Kleindienst v. Mandel, 408 U.S. 753, 765 (1972). But we regard the available "alternative means of [communication] * * * [as] a relevant factor" in a case such as this where "we [are] called upon to balance First Amendment rights against [legitimate] governmental * * * interests." Ibid.

One such alternative available to California prison inmates is communication by mail. Although prison regulations until recently called for the censorship of state, inter alia, that "unduly complain" or "magnify grievances," that express "inflammatory political, racial, or religious, or other views," or that were deemed "defamatory" or "otherwise inappropriate," we recently held that "the Department's regulations authorized censorship of prisoner mail far broader than any legitimate interest of penal administration demands," and accordingly affirmed a district court judgment invalidating the regulations. Procunier v. Martinez, 416 U.S. 396, 416, 71 Ohio Op.2d 139, 147 (1974) * * *. In addition, we held that "[t]he interests of prisoners and their correspondents in uncensored communication by letter, grounded as it is in the First Amendment, is plainly a 'liberty' interest within the meaning of the Fourteenth Amendment even though qualified of necessity by the circumstances of imprisonment." Accordingly, we concluded that any "decision to censor or withhold delivery of a particular letter must be accompanied by minimal procedural safeguards." * * * Thus, it is clear that the medium of written correspondence affords inmates an open and substantially unimpeded channel for communication with persons outside the prison, including representatives of the news media.

Moreover, the visitation policy of the California Corrections Department does not seal the inmate off from personal contact with those outside the prison. Inmates are permitted to receive limited visits from members of their families, the clergy, their attorneys, and friends of prior acquaintance.[4] The selection of these categories of visitors is based on the Director's professional judgment that such visits will aid in the rehabilitation of the inmate while not compromising the other legitimate objectives of the corrections system. This is not a case in which the selection is based on the anticipated content of the communication between the inmate and the prospective visitor. If a member of the press fell within any of these categories, there is no suggestion that he would not be permitted to visit with the inmate. More importantly, however, inmates have an unrestricted opportunity to communicate with the press or any other member of the public through their families, friends, clergy, or attorneys who are permitted to visit

[4] This policy does not appear to be codified or otherwise expressly articulated in any generally applicable rule or regulation. The statement of visiting privileges for San Quentin State Prison indicates that all visitors must be approved by the corrections officials and must be either "members of the family or friends of long standing." It also permits visits by attorneys to their clients. Although nothing is said in this statement about visits by members of the clergy, there is no dispute among the parties that the practice of the Department of Corrections is to permit such visits. There is also no disagreement among the parties that this visitation policy is generally applied by the Department throughout the state corrections system.

them at the prison. Thus, this provides another alternative avenue of communication between prison inmates and persons outside the prison.

We would find the availability of such alternatives unimpressive if they were submitted as justification for governmental restriction of personal communication among members of the general public. We have recognized, however, that "[t]he relationship of state prisoners and the state officers who supervise their confinement is far more intimate than that of a State and a private citizen," and that the "internal problems of state prisons involve issues * * * peculiarly within state authority and expertise." Preiser v. Rodriguez, 411 U.S. 475, 492 (1973).

In Procunier v. Martinez, *supra*, we could find no legitimate governmental interest to justify the substantial restrictions that had there been imposed on written communication by inmates. When, however, the question involves the entry of people into the prison for face-to-face communication with inmates, it is obvious that institutional considerations, such as security and related administrative problems, as well as the accepted and legitimate policy objectives of the corrections system itself, require that some limitation be placed on such visitations. So long as reasonable and effective means of communication remain open and no discrimination in terms of content is involved, we believe that, in drawing such lines, "prison officials must be accorded great latitude." Cruz v. Beto, *supra*, at 321.

In a number of contexts, we have held "that reasonable 'time, place, and manner' regulations [of communicative activity] may be necessary to further significant governmental interests, and are permitted." Grayned v. City of

Rockford, 408 U.S. 104, 115 (1972); Cox v. New Hampshire, 312 U.S. 569, 575-576 (1941); Poulos v. New Hampshire, 345 U.S. 395, 398 (1953); Cox. v. Louisiana, 379 U.S. 536, 554-555 (1965); Adderley v. Florida, 385 U.S. 39, 46-48 (1968). "The nature of a place, the pattern of its normal activities, dictate the kinds of regulations of time, place, and manner that are reasonable." Grayned, *supra*, at 116 (internal quotations omitted). The "normal activity" to which a prison is committed—the involuntary confinement and isolation of large numbers of people, some of whom have demonstrated a capacity for violence—necessarily requires that considerable attention be devoted to the maintenance of security. Although they would not permit prison officials to prohibit all expression or communication by prison inmates, security considerations are sufficiently paramount in the administration of the prison to justify the imposition of some restrictions on the entry of outsiders into the prison for face-to-face contact with inmates.

In this case the restriction takes the form of limiting visitations to individuals who have either a personal or professional relationship to the inmate— family, friends of prior acquaintance, legal counsel, and clergy. In the judgment of the state corrections officials, this visitation policy will permit inmates to have personal contact with those persons who will aid in their rehabilitation, while keeping visitations at a manageable level that will not compromise institutional security. Such considerations are peculiarly within the province and professional expertise of corrections officials, and, in the absence of substantial evidence in the record to indicate that the officials have exaggerated their response to these considerations, courts should ordinarily

defer to their expert judgment in such matters. Courts cannot, of course, abdicate their constitutional responsibility to delineate and protect fundamental liberties. But when the issue involves a regulation limiting one of several means of communication by an inmate, the institutional objectives furthered by that regulation and the measure of judicial deference owed to corrections officials in their attempt to serve those interests are relevant in gauging the validity of the regulation.

Accordingly, in light of the alternative channels of communication that are open to prison inmates,[5] we cannot say on the record in this case that this

---

[5] It is suggested by the inmate-appellees that the use of the mails as an alternative means of communication may not be effective in the case of prisoners who are inarticulate or even illiterate. There is no indication, however, that any of the four inmates before the Court suffer from either of these disabilities. Indeed, the record affirmatively shows that two of the inmates are published writers. Although the complaint was filed as a class action, the plaintiffs never moved the District Court to certify the case as a class action as required by F.R.C.P. 23 (b) (3) and (c). Thus, the short answer to the inmates' contention is that there is neither a finding by the District Court nor support in the record for a finding that the alternative channels of communication are not an effective means for the inmates-appellees to express themselves to persons outside the prison.

Even with respect to inmates who may not be literate or articulate, however, there is no suggestion that the corrections officials would not permit such inmates to seek the aid of fellow inmates or of family and friends who visit them to commit their thoughts to writing for communication to individuals in the general public. Cf. JOHNSON v. AVERY, 393 U.S. 483 (1969). Merely because such inmates may need assistance to utilize one of the alternative channels does not make it an ineffective alternative, unless, of course, the State prohibits the inmate from receiving such assistance.

restriction on one manner in which prisoners can communicate with persons outside of prison is unconstitutional. So long as this restriction operates in a neutral fashion, without regard to the content of the expression, it falls within the "appropriate rules and regulations" to which "prisoners necessarily are subject," Cruz v. Beto, *supra,* at 321, and does not abridge any First Amendment freedoms retained by prison inmates.[6]

---

6 The inmates argue that restricting their access to press representatives unconstitutionally burdens their First and Fourteenth Amendment right to petition the government for the redress of grievances. Communication with the press, the inmates contend, provides them with their only effective opportunity to communicate their grievances, through the channel of public opinion, to the legislative and executive branches of the government. We think, however, that the alternative means of communication with the press that are available to prisoners, together with the substantial access to prisons that California accords the press and other members of the public, see infra, at 12-13, satisfies whatever right the inmates may have to petition the government through the press.

We also note that California accords prison inmates substantial opportunities to petition the executive, legislative, and judicial branches of government directly. Section 2600 of the California Penal Code permits an inmate to correspond confidentially with any public office holder. And various rules promulgated by the Department of Corrections explicitly permit an inmate to correspond with the Governor, any other elected state or federal official, and any appointed head of a state or federal agency. Similarly, California has acted to assure prisoners the right to petition for judicial relief. See, e.g., IN RE JORDAN, 7 Cal.3d 930 (1972); IN RE VAN GELDERN, 5 Cal.3d 832 (1971); IN RE HARRELL, 2 Cal.3d 675 (1970). Section 845.4 of the California Government Code also makes prison officials liable for intentional interference with the right of a prisoner to obtain judicial relief from his confinement.

II

In No. 73-918, the media plaintiffs ask us to hold that the limitation on press interviews imposed by § 415.071 violates the freedom of the press guaranteed by the First and Fourteenth Amendments. They contend·that, irrespective of what First Amendment liberties may or may not be retained by prison inmates, members of the press have a constitutional right to interview any inmate who is willing to speak with them, in the absence of an individualized determination that the particular interview might create a clear and present danger to prison security or to some other substantial interest served by the corrections system. In this regard, the media plaintiffs do not claim any impairment of their freedom to publish, for California imposes no restrictions on what may be published about its prisons, the prison inmates, or the officers who administer the prisons. Instead, they rely on their right to gather news without governmental interference, which the media plaintiffs assert includes a right of access to the sources of what is regarded as newsworthy information.

We note at the outset that this regulation is not part of an attempt by the State to conceal the conditions in its prisons or to frustrate the press' investigation and reporting of those conditions. Indeed, the record demonstrates that, under current corrections policy, both the press and the general public are accorded full opportunities to observe prison conditions.[7] The De-

---

7 This policy reflects a recognition that the conditions in this Nation's prisons are a matter that is both newsworthy and of great public importance. As THE CHIEF JUSTICE has commented, we cannot "continue

partment of Corrections regularly conducts public tours through the prisons for the benefit of interested citizens. In addition, newsmen are permitted to visit both the maximum and minimum security sections of the institutions and to stop and speak about any subject to any inmates whom they might encounter. If security considerations permit, corrections personnel will step aside to permit such interviews to be confidential. Apart from general access to all parts of the institutions, newsmen are also permitted to enter the prisons to interview inmates selected at random by the corrections officials from the prison population. By the same token, if a newsman wishes to write a story on a particular prison program, he is permitted to sit in on group meetings and to interview the inmate participants. In short, members of the press enjoy access to California prisons that is not available to other members of the public.

The sole limitation on newsgathering in California prisons is the prohibition in § 415.071 of interviews with individual inmates specifically designated by

representatives of the press. This restriction is of recent vintage, having been imposed in 1971 in response to a violent episode that the Department of Corrections felt was at least partially attributable to the former policy with respect to face-to-face prisoner-press interviews. Prior to the promulgation of § 415.071, every journalist had virtually free access to interview any individual inmate whom he might wish. Only members of the press were accorded this privilege; other members of the general public did not have the benefit of such an unrestricted visitation policy. Thus, the promulgation of § 415.071 did not impose a discrimination against press access, but merely eliminated a special privilege formerly given to representatives of the press vis-a-vis members of the public generally.[8]

In practice, it was found that the policy in effect prior to the promulgation of § 415.071 had resulted in press attention being concentrated on a relatively small number of inmates who, as a result, became virtual "public figures" within the prison society and gained a disproportionate degree of notoriety and influence among their fellow inmates. Because of this notoriety and in-

---

* * * to brush under the rug the problems of those who are found guilty and subject to criminal sentence * * * It is a melancholy truth that it has taken the tragic prison outbreaks of the past three years to focus widespread public attention on this problem." W. Burger, "Our Options are Limited," pp. 4-5 (Remarks before the 1972 Annual Dinner of the National Conference on Christians and Jews, Phil., Pa., Nov. 16, 1972). Along the same lines, THE CHIEF JUSTICE has correctly observed that "[i]f we want prisoners to change, public attitudes towards prisoners and ex-prisoners must change * * * A visit to most prisons will make you a zealot for prison reform." W. Burger. "For Whom the Bell Tolls," pp. 9-11 (Remarks before the Assn. of the Bar of the City of New York, N. Y., Feb. 17, 1970).

---

8 It cannot be contended that because California permits family, friends, attorneys, and clergy to visit inmates, it cannot limit visitations by the press. No member of the general public who does not have a personal or professional relationship to the inmate is permitted to enter the prison and name an inmate with whom he would like to engage in face-to-face discourse. Thus, the press is granted the same access in this respect to prison inmates as is accorded any member of the general public. Indeed, as is noted in the text, the aggregate access that the press has to California prisons and their inmates is substantially greater than that of the general public.

fluence, these inmates often became the source of severe disciplinary problems. For example, extensive press attention to an inmate who espoused a practice of non-cooperation with prison regulations encouraged other inmates to follow suit, thus eroding the institutions' ability to deal effectively with the inmates generally. Finally, in the words of the District Court, on August 21, 1971, "[d]uring an escape attempt at San Quentin three staff members and two inmates were killed. This was viewed by the officials as the climax of mounting disciplinary problems caused, in part, by its liberal posture with regard to press interviews, and on August 23, § 415.071 was adopted to mitigate the problem." 364 F.Supp., at 198. It is against this background that we consider the media plaintiffs claims under the First and Fourteenth Amendments.

The constitutional guarantee of a free press "assures the maintenance of our political system and an open society," Time, Inc. v. Hill, 385 U.S. 374, 389 (1967), and secures "the paramount public interest in a free flow of information to the people concerning public officials," Garrison v. Louisiana, 379 U.S. 74, 77 (1964). See also New York Times v. Sullivan, 376 U.S. 254 (1964). By the same token, "[a]ny system of prior restraints of expression comes to this Court bearing a heavy presumption against its constitutional validity." New York Times v. United States, 403 U.S. 713, 714 (1971); Organization for a Better Austin v. Keefe, 402 U.S. 415 (1971); Bantam Books, Inc. v. Sullivan, 372 U.S. 58, 70 (1963); Near v. Minnesota, 283 U.S. 697 (1931). Correlatively, the First and Fourteenth Amendments also protect the right of the public to receive such information and ideas as are published. Kleindienst v. Mandel,

supra, at 762-763; Stanley v. Georgia, 394 U.S. 557, 564 (1969).

In Branzburg v. Hayes, 408 U.S. 665 (1972), the Court went further and acknowledged that "newsgathering is not without some First Amendment protection," at 707, for "without some protection for seeking out the news, freedom of the press could be eviscerated," at 681. In Branzburg the Court held that the First and Fourteenth Amendments were not abridged by requiring reporters to disclose the identity of their confidential sources to a grand jury when that information was needed in the course of a good-faith criminal investigation. The Court there could "perceive no basis for holding that the public interest in law enforcement and in insuring effective grand jury proceedings [was] insufficient to override the consequential, but uncertain, burden on news gathering that is said to result from insisting that reporters, like other citizens, respond to relevant questions put to them in the course of a valid grand jury investigation or criminal trial," at 690-691.

In this case, the media plaintiffs contend that § 415.071 constitutes governmental interference with their newsgathering activities that is neither consequential nor uncertain, and that no substantial governmental interest can be shown to justify the denial of press access to specifically designated prison inmates. More particularly, the media plaintiffs assert that, despite the substantial access to California prisons and their inmates accorded representatives of the press—access broader than is accorded members of the public generally—face-to-face interviews with specifically designated inmates is such an effective and superior method of newsgathering that its curtailment amounts to unconstitutional state interference with a free press. We do not agree.

"It has generally been held that the First Amendment does not guarantee the press a constitutional right of special access to information not available to the public generally * * *. Despite the fact that newsgathering may be hampered, the press is regularly excluded from grand jury proceedings, our own conferences, the meetings of other official bodies in executive session, and the meetings of private organizations. Newsmen have no constitutional right of access to the scenes of crime or disaster when the general public is excluded." Branzburg v. Hayes, *supra*, at 684-685. Similarly, newsmen have no constitutional right of access to prisons or their inmates beyond that afforded the general public.

The First and Fourteenth Amendments bar government from interfering in any way with a free press. The Constitution does not, however, require government to accord the press special access to information not shared by members of the public generally.[9] It is

one thing to say that a journalist is free to seek out sources of information not available to members of the general public, that he is entitled to some constitutional protection of the confidentiality of such sources, cf. Branzburg v. Hayes, *supra*, and that government cannot restrain the publication of news emanating from such sources. Cf. N. Y. Times v. United States, *supra*. It is quite another thing to suggest that the Constitution imposes upon government the affirmative duty to make available to journalists sources of information not available to members of the public generally. That proposition finds no support in the words of the Constitution or in any decision of this Court. Accordingly, since § 415.071 does not deny the press access to sources of information available to members of the general public, we hold that it does not abridge the protections that the First and Fourteenth Amendments guarantee.

For the reasons stated, we reverse the District Court's judgment that § 415.071 infringes the freedom of speech of the prison inmates and affirm its judgment that that regulation does not abridge the constitutional right of a free press. Accordingly, the judgment is vacated, and the case is remanded to the District Court for further proceedings consistent with this opinion.

It is so ordered.

---

[9] As Chief Justice Warren put the matter in writing for the Court in ZEMEL v. RUSK, 381 U.S. 1, 16-17 (1965), "[t]here are few restrictions on action which could not be clothed by ingenious argument in the garb of decreased data flow. For example, the prohibition of unauthorized entry into the White House diminishes the citizen's opportunities to gather information he might find relevant to his opinion of the way the country is being run, but that does not make entry into the White House a First Amendment right. The right to speak and publish does not carry with it the unrestricted right to gather information."

PART II: CASES RELATING TO CHAPTER 3
Saxbe v. Washington Post Co.

257

SAXBE v. WASHINGTON POST CO.
417 U.S. 843, 94 S. Ct. 2811, 41 L. Ed. 2d 514 (1974)

MR. JUSTICE STEWART delivered the opinion of the Court.

The respondents, a major metropolitan newspaper and one of its reporters, initiated this litigation to challenge the constitutionality of ¶ 4b (6) of Policy Statement 1220.1A of the Federal Bureau of Prisons.[1] At the time that the case was in the District Court and the Court of Appeals, this regulation prohibited any personal interviews between newsmen and individually designated federal prison inmates. The Solicitor General has informed the Court that the regulation was recently amended "to permit press interviews at federal prison institutions that can be characterized as minimum security."[2] The general prohibition of press interviews with inmates remains in effect, however, in three-quarters of the federal prisons, i.e., in all medium security and maximum security institutions, including the two institutions involved in this case.

In March 1972, the respondents requested permission from the petitioners, the officials responsible for administering federal prisons, to conduct several interviews with specific inmates in the prisons at Lewisburg, Pennsylvania, and Danbury, Connecticut. The petitioners denied permission

for such interviews on the authority of Policy Statement 1220.1A. The respondents thereupon commenced this suit to challenge these denials and the regulation on which they were predicated. Their essential contention was that the prohibition of all press interviews with prison inmates abridges the protection that the First Amendment accords the newsgathering activity of a free press. The District Court agreed with this contention and held that the Policy Statement, insofar as it totally prohibited all press interviews at the institutions involved, violated the First Amendment. Although the court acknowledged that institutional considerations could justify the prohibition of some press-inmate interviews, the District Court ordered the petitioners to cease enforcing the blanket prohibition of all such interviews and, pending modification of the Policy Statement, to consider interview requests on an individual basis and "to withhold permission to interview . . . only where demonstrable administrative or disciplinary considerations dominate." 357 F.Supp. 770, 775 (D.C. 1972).

The petitioners appealed the District Court's judgment to the Court of Appeals for the District of Columbia Circuit. We stayed the District Court's order pending the completion of that appeal, sub. nom. Kleindienst v. Washington Post Co., 406 U.S. 912 (1972). The first time this case was before it, the Court of Appeals remanded it to the District Court for additional findings of fact and particularly for reconsideration in light of this Court's intervening decision in Branzburg v. Hayes, 408 U.S. 665 (1972). 155 U.S. App. D.C. 283, 477 F.2d 1168 (1972).

---

[1] "Press representatives will not be permitted to interview individual inmates. This rule shall apply even where the inmate requests or seeks an interview. However, conversation may be permitted with inmates whose identity is not to be made public, if it is limited to the discussion of institutional facilities, programs and activities."

[2] Letter of Apr. 16, 1974, to Clerk, Supreme Court of the United States, presently on file with the Clerk.

On remand, the District Court conducted further evidentiary hearings, supplemented its findings of fact, and reconsidered its conclusions of law in light of Branzburg and other recent decisions that were urged upon it. In due course, the court reaffirmed its original decision, 357 F.Supp. 779 (D.C. 1972), and the petitioners again appealed to the Court of Appeals.

The Court of Appeals affirmed the judgment of the District Court. It held that press interviews with prison inmates could not be totally prohibited as the Policy Statement purported to do, but may "be denied only where it is the judgment of the administrator directly concerned, based on either the demonstrated behavior of the inmate, or special conditions existing at the institution at the time the interview is requested, or both, that the interview presents a serious risk of administrative or disciplinary problems." 161 U.S. App. D.C. 75, 87-88, 494 F.2d 994, 1006-1007 (1974). Any blanket prohibition of such face-to-face interviews was held to abridge the First Amendment's protection of press freedom. Because of the important constitutional question involved, and because of an apparent conflict in approach to the question between the District of Columbia Circuit and the Ninth Circuit,[3] we granted certiorari. 415 U.S. 956 (1974).

The policies of the Federal Bureau of Prisons regarding visitations to prison inmates do not differ significantly from the California policies considered in Pell v. Procunier, ante. As the Court of Appeals noted, "inmates' families, their attorneys, and religious counsel are accorded liberal visitation privileges. Even friends of inmates are allowed to visit, although their privileges appear to be somewhat more limited." 161 U.S. App. D.C., at 78, 494 F.2d, at 997. Other than members of these limited groups with personal and professional ties to the inmates, members of the general public are not permitted under the Bureau's policy to enter the prisons and interview consenting inmates. This policy is applied with an even hand to all prospective visitors, including newsmen, who, like other members of the public, may enter the prisons to visit friends or family members. But, again like members of the general public, they may not enter the prison and insist on visiting an inmate with whom they have no such relationship. There is no indication on this record that Policy Statement 1220.1A has been interpreted or applied to prohibit a person, who is otherwise eligible to visit and interview an inmate, from doing so merely because he is a member of the press.[4]

Except for the limitation in Policy Statement 1220.1A on face-to-face press-inmate interviews, members of the press are accorded substantial access to the federal prisons in order to observe and report the conditions they find there. Indeed, journalists are given access to the prisons and to prison inmates that in significant respects exceeds that afforded to members of the general public. For example, Policy Statement 1220.1A permits press representatives to tour the prisons and to

---

3 See Seattle-Tacoma Newspaper Guild v. Parker, 480 F.2d 1062, 1066-1067 (1973). See also Hillery v. Procunier, 364 F.Supp. 196, 199-200 (N.D. Cal. 1973).

4 The Solicitor General's brief represents that "[m]embers of the press, like the public generally, may visit the prison to see friends there." Presumably, the same is true with respect to family members. The respondents have not disputed this representation.

photograph any prison facilities.[5] During such tours a newsman is permitted to conduct brief interviews with any inmates he might encounter.[6] In addition, newsmen and inmates are permitted virtually unlimited written correspondence with each other.[7] Outgoing correspondence from inmates to press representatives is neither censored or inspected. Incoming mail from press representatives is inspected only for contraband or statements inciting illegal action. Moreover, prison officials are available to the press and are required by Policy Statement 1220.1A to "give all possible assistance" to press representatives in providing background and a specific report" concerning any inmate complaints.[8]

The respondents have also conceded in their brief that Policy Statement 1220.1A "has been interpreted by the Bureau to permit a newsman to interview a randomly selected group of inmates." As a result, the reporter respondent in this case was permitted to interview a randomly selected group of inmates at the Lewisburg prison. Finally, in light of the constant turnover in the prison population, it is clear that there is always a large group of recently released prisoners who are available to both the press and the general public as a source of information about conditions in the federal prisons.[9]

Thus, it is clear that Policy Statement 1220.1A is not part of any attempt by the Federal Bureau of Prisons to conceal from the public the conditions prevailing in federal prisons. This limitation on prearranged press interviews with individually designated inmates was motivated by the same disciplinary and administrative considerations that underlie § 115.071 of the California Department of Corrections Manual, which we considered in Pell v. Procunier and Procunier v. Hillery, *ante*. The experience of the Bureau accords with that of the California Department of Corrections and suggests that the interest of the press is often "concentrated on a relatively small number of inmates who, as a result, [become] virtual 'public figures' within the prison society and gai[n] a disproportionate degree of notoriety and influence among their fellow inmates." Pell, *ante*. As a result those inmates who are conspicuously publicized because of their repeated contacts with the press tend to become the source of substantial disciplinary problems that can engulf a large portion of the population at a prison.

The District Court and the Court of Appeals sought to meet this problem by decreeing a selective policy whereby prison officials could deny interviews likely to lead to disciplinary problems. In the expert judgment of the petitioners, however, such a selective policy would spawn serious discipline and morale problems of its own by engendering hostility and resentment among inmates who were refused interview privileges granted to their fellows. The Director of the Bureau testified that "one of the very basic

[5] Policy Statement 1220.1A ¶¶ 4b (5) and (7).
[6] See *id.*, ¶ 4b (6) set out in n. 1, *supra*. The newsman is requested not to reveal the identity of the inmate, and the conversation is to be limited to institutional facilities, programs, and activities.
[7] *Id.*, ¶¶ 4b (1) and (2).
[8] *Id.*, ¶ 4b (12).
[9] The Solicitor General's brief informs us that "approximately one-half of the prison population on any one day will be released within the following 12 months. The average population is 23,000, of whom approximately 12,000 are released each year."

tenets of sound correctional administration" is "to treat all inmates incarcerated in [the] institutions, as far as possible, equally." This expert and professional judgment is, of course, entitled to great deference.

In this case, however, it is unnecessary to engage in any delicate balancing of such penal considerations against the legitimate demands of the First Amendment. For it is apparent that the sole limitation imposed on newsgathering by Policy Statement 1220.1A is no more than a particularized application of the general rule that nobody may enter the prison and designate an inmate whom he would like to visit, unless the prospective visitor is a lawyer, clergyman, relative, or friend of that inmate. This limitation on visitations is justified by what the Court of Appeals acknowledged as "the truism that prisons are institutions where public access is generally limited." 161 U.S. App. D.C., at 80, 494 F.2d, at 999. See Adderley v. Florida, 385 U.S. 39, 41 (1966). In this regard, the Bureau of Prisons visitation policy does not place the press in any less advantageous position than the public generally. Indeed, the total access to federal prisons and prison inmates that the Bureau of Prisons accords to the press far surpasses that available to other members of the public.

We find this case constitutionally indistinguishable from Pell v. Procunier, ante, and thus fully controlled by the holding in that case. "[N]ewsmen have no constitutional right of access to prisons or their inmates beyond that afforded the general public." Id., at 834. The proposition "that the Constitution imposes upon government the affirmative duty to make available to journalists sources of information not available to members of the public generally . . . finds no support in the words of the Constitution or in any decision of this Court." Id., at 834-835. Thus, since Policy Statement 1220.1A "does not deny the press access to sources of information available to members of the general public," id., at 835, we hold that it does not abridge the freedom that the First Amendment guarantees. Accordingly, the judgment of the Court of Appeals is reversed and the case is remanded to the District Court for further proceedings consistent with this opinion.

It is so ordered.

JONES v. NORTH CAROLINA PRISONERS' LABOR UNION, INC.
433 U.S. 119, 97 S. Ct. 2532, 53 L. Ed. 2d 629 (1977)

. . .

I

Appellee, an organization self-denominated as a Prisoners' Labor Union, was incorporated in late 1974, with a stated goal of "the promotion of charitable labor union purposes' and the formation of a "prisoners' labor union at every prison and jail in North Carolina to seek through collective bargaining...to improve... working...conditions...." It also proposed to work towards the alteration or elimination of practices and policies of the Department of Correction which it did not approve of, and to serve as a vehicle for the presentation and resolution of inmate grievances. By early 1975, the Union had attracted some 2,000 inmate "members" in 40 different prison units throughout North Carolina. The State of North Carolina, unhappy with these developments, set out to prevent inmates from forming or operating a "union." While the State tolerated individual "membership," or belief, in the Union, it sought to prohibit inmate solicitation of other inmates, meetings between members of the Union, and bulk mailings concerning the Union from outside sources. Pursuant to a regulation promulgated by the Department of Correction on March 26, 1975, such solicitation and group activity was proscribed.

Suit was filed by the Union in the United States District Court for the Eastern District of North Carolina on March 18, 1975, approximately a week before the date upon which the regulation was to take effect. The Union claimed that its rights, and the rights of its members, to engage in protected free speech, association, and assembly activities were being infringed by the no-solicitation and no-meeting rules. It also alleged a deprivation of equal protection of the laws in that the Jaycees and Alcoholics Anonymous were permitted to have meetings and other organizational rights, such as the distribution of bulk mailing material, that the Union was being denied. A declaratory judgment and injunction against continuation of these restrictive policies was sought, as were substantial damages.

A three-judge District Court, convened pursuant to 28 U.S.C. §§ 2281 and 2284, while dismissing the Union's prayers for damages and attorneys' fees, granted it substantial injunctive relief. The court found that appellants "permitted" inmates to join the Union, but "oppose[d] the solicitation of other inmates to join," either by inmate-to-inmate solicitation or by correspondence. The court noted that appellants

> "sincerely believe that the very existence of the Union will increase the burdens of administration and constitute a threat of essential discipline and control. They are apprehensive that inmates may use the Union to establish a power block within the inmate population which could be utilized to cause work slowdowns or stoppages or other undesirable concerted activity."

The District Court concluded, however, that there "was no consensus" among experts on these matters, and that it was "left with no firm conviction that an association of inmates is necessarily good or bad...." The court felt that since appellants countenanced the bare fact of Union membership, it had to allow solicitation activity, whether by inmates or by outsiders:

"We are unable to perceive why it is necessary or essential to security and order in the prisons to forbid solicitation of membership in a union permitted by the authorities. This is not a case of riot. There is not one scintilla of evidence to suggest that the Union has been utilized to disrupt the operation of the penal institutions."

The other questions, respecting the bulk mailing by the Union of literature into the prisons for distribution and the question of meetings of inmate members, the District Court resolved against appellants "by application of the equal protection clause of the fourteenth amendment." Finding that such meetings and bulk mailing privileges had been permitted the Jaycees, Alcoholics Anonymous, and, in one institution, the Boy Scouts, the District Court concluded that appellants "may not pick and choose depending on [their] approval or disapproval of the message or purpose of the group" unless "the activity proscribed is shown to be detrimental to proper penological objectives, subversive to good discipline, or otherwise harmful." The Court concluded that appellants had failed to meet this burden. Appropriate injunctive relief was thereby ordered.

II

A

The District Court, we believe, got off on the wrong foot in this case by not giving appropriate deference to the decisions of prison administrators and appropriate recognition to the peculiar and restrictive circumstances of penal confinement. While litigation by prison inmates concerning conditions of confinement, challenged other than under the Eighth Amendment, is of recent vintage, this Court has long recognized that "[l]awful incarceration brings about the necessary withdrawal or limitation of many privileges and rights, a retraction justified by the considerations underlying our penal system." *Price* v. *Johnston*, 334 U.S. 266, 285 (1948). The fact of confinement and the needs of the penal institution impose limitations on constitutional rights, including those derived from the First Amendment, which are implicit in incarceration. We noted in *Pell* v. *Procunier*, that

"[a] prison inmate retains those First Amendment rights that are not inconsistent with his status as a prisoner or with the legitimate penological objectives of the corrections system. Thus, challenges to prison restrictions that are asserted to inhibit First Amendment interests must be analyzed in terms of the legitimate policies and goals of the corrections system, to whose custody and care the prisoner has been committed in accordance with due process of law."

Perhaps the most obvious of the First Amendment rights that are necessarily curtailed by confinement are those associational rights that the First Amendment protects outside of prison walls. The concept of incarceration itself entails a restriction on the freedom of inmates to associate with those outside of the penal institution. Equally as obviously, the inmate's "status as a prisoner" and the operational realities of a prison dictate restrictions on the associational rights among inmates.

Because the realities of running a penal institution are complex and difficult, we have also recognized the wide-ranging deference to be accorded the decisions of prison administrators. We noted in *Procunier* v. *Martinez,* that

"courts are ill equipped to deal with the increasingly urgent problems of prison administration and reform. Judicial recognition of that fact reflects no more than a healthy sense of realism. Moreover, where state penal institutions are involved, federal courts have a further reason for deference to the appropriate prison authorities."

It is in this context that the claims of the Union must be examined.

B

State correctional officials uniformly testified that the concept of a prisoners' labor union was itself fraught with potential dangers, whether or not such a union intended, illegally, to press for collective-bargaining recognition. Appellant Ralph Edwards, the Commissioner of the Department of Correction, stated in his affidavit that

"The creation of an inmate union will naturally result in increasing the existing friction between inmates and prison personnel. It can also create friction between union inmates and non-union inmates."

Appellant David Jones, Secretary of the Department of Correction, stated that

"The existence of a union of inmates can create a divisive element within the inmate population. In a time when the units are already seriously over-crowded, such an element could aggravate already tense conditions. The purpose of the Union may well be worthwhile projects. But it is evident that the inmate organizers could, if recognized as spokesmen for all inmates, make themselves to be powerful figures among the inmates. If the Union is successful, these inmates would be in a position to misuse their influence. After the inmate Union has become established, there would probably be nothing this Department could do to terminate its existence, even if its activities became overtly subversive to the functioning of the Department. Work stoppages and routines are easily foreseeable. Riots and chaos would almost inevitably result. Thus, even if the purposes of the Union are as stated in this Complaint, the potential for a dangerous situation exists, a situation which would not be brought under control."

The District Court did not reject these beliefs as fanciful or erroneous. It, instead, noted that they were held "sincerely," and were arguably correct. Without a showing that these beliefs were unreasonable, it was error for the District Court to conclude that appellants needed to show more. In particular, the burden was not on appellants to show affirmatively that the Union would be "detrimental to proper penological objectives" or would constitute a "present danger to security and order." Rather "[s]uch considerations are peculiarly within the province and professional expertise of corrections officials, and, in the absence of substantial evidence in the record to indicate that the officials have exaggerated their response to these considerations, courts should ordinarily defer to their expert judgment in such matters." *Pell* v. *Procunier.* The necessary and correct result of our deference to the informed discretion of prison administrators permits them, and not the courts, to make the difficult judgments concerning institutional operations in situations such as this.

The District Court, however, gave particular emphasis to what it viewed as appellants' tolerance of membership by inmates in the Union as undermining appellants' position. It viewed a system which permitted inmate "membership" but prohibited inmate-to-inmate solicitation (as well, it should be noted, as meetings, or other group activities) as bordering "on the irrational," and felt that "[t]he defendants' own hypothesis in this case is that the existence of the Union and membership in it are not dangerous, for otherwise they would surely have undertaken to forbid membership." This, however, considerably overstates what appellants' concession as to pure membership entails. Appellants permitted membership because of the reasonable assumption that each individual prisoner could believe what he chose to believe, and that outside individuals should be able to communicate ideas and beliefs to individual inmates. Since a member *qua* member incurs no dues or obligations— a prisoner apparently may become a member simply by considering himself a member—this position simply reflects the concept that thought control, by means of prohibiting

beliefs, would not only be undesirable but impossible.

But appellants never acquiesced in, or permitted, group activity of the Union in the nature of a functioning organization of the inmates within the prison, nor did the District Court find that they had. It is clearly not irrational to conclude that individuals may believe what they want, but that concerted group activity, or solicitation therefor, would pose additional and unwarranted problems and frictions in the operation of the State's penal institutions. The ban on inmate solicitation and group meetings, therefore, was rationally related to the reasonable, indeed to the central, objectives of prison administration.

C

The invocation of the First Amendment, whether the asserted rights are speech or associational, does not change this analysis. In a prison context, an inmate does not retain those First Amendment rights that are "inconsistent with his status as a prisoner or with the legitimate penological objectives of the corrections system." *Pell* v. *Procunier.* Prisons, it is obvious, differ in numerous respects from free society. They, to begin with, are populated, involuntarily, by people who have been found to have violated one or more of the criminal laws established by society for its orderly governance. In seeking a "mutual accommodation between institutional needs and objectives [of prisons] and the provisions of the Constitution that are of general application," *Wolff* v. *McDonnell,* this Court has repeatedly recognized the need for major restrictions on a prisoner's rights. These restrictions have applied as well where First Amendment values were implicated.

An examination of the potential restrictions on speech or association that have been imposed by the regulations under challenge, demonstrate that the restrictions imposed are reasonable, and are consistent with the inmates' status as prisoners and with the legitimate operational considerations of the institution. To begin with, First Amendment speech rights are barely implicated in this case. Mail rights are not themselves implicated; the only question respecting the mail is that of *bulk* mailings. The advantages of bulk mailings to inmates by the Union are those of cheaper rates and convenience. While the District Court relied on the cheaper bulk mailing rates in finding an equal protection violation, it is clear that losing these cost advantages does not fundamentally implicate *free speech* values. Since other avenues of outside informational flow by the Union remain available, the prohibition on bulk mailing, reasonable in the absence of First Amendment consideration, remain reasonable.

Nor does the prohibition on inmate-to-inmate solicitation of membership trench untowardly on the inmates' First Amendment speech rights. Solicitation of membership itself involves a good deal more than the simple expression of individual views as to the advantages or disadvantages of a Union or its views; it is an invitation to collectively engage in a legitimately prohibited activity. If the prison officials are otherwise entitled to control organized union activity within the prison walls, the prohibition on solicitation for such activity is no then made impermissible on account of First Amendment considerations, for such a prohibition is then not only reasonable but necessary.

First Amendment associational rights, while perhaps more directly implicated by the regulatory prohibitions, likewise must give way to the reasonable considerations of penal management. As already noted, numerous associational rights are necessarily curtailed by the realities of confinement. They may be curtailed whenever the institution's officials, in the exercise of their informed discretion, reasonably conclude that such associations, whether through group meetings or otherwise, possess the likelihood of disruption to prison order or stability, or otherwise interfere with the legitimate penological objectives of the prison environment. As we noted in *Pell* v. *Procunier*, "central to all other correctional goals is the institutional consideration of internal security within the correctional facilities themselves."

Appellant prison officials concluded that the presence, perhaps even the objectives, of a prisoners' labor union would be detrimental to order and security in the prisons.... It is enough to say that they have not been conclusively shown to be wrong in this view. The interest in preserving order and authority in the prisons is self-evident. Prison life, and relations between the inmates themselves and between the inmates and prison officials or staff, contain the ever-present potential for violent confrontation and conflagration. Responsible prison officials must be permitted to take reasonable steps to forestall such a threat, and they must be permitted to act before the time when they can compile a dossier on the eve of a riot. The case of a prisoners' union, where the focus is on the presentation of grievances to, and encouragement of adversary relations with, institution officials surely would rank high on anyone's list of potential trouble spots. If the appellants' views as to the possible detrimental effects of the organizational activities of the Union are reasonable, as we conclude they are, then the regulations are drafted no more broadly than they need be to meet the perceived threat—which stems directly from group meetings and group organizational activities of the Union. When weighed against the First Amendment rights asserted, these institutional reasons are sufficiently weighty to prevail.

D

The District Court rested on the Equal Protection Clause of the Fourteenth Amendment to strike down appellants' prohibition against the receipt and distribution of bulk mail from the Union as well as the prohibition of Union meetings among the inmates. It felt that this was a denial of equal protection because bulk mailing and meeting rights had been extended to the Jaycees, Alcoholics Anonymous, and the Boy Scouts. The court felt that just as outside the prison, a "government may not pick and choose depending on its approval or disapproval of the message or purpose of the group," so, too, appellants could not choose among groups without first demonstrating that the activity proscribed is "detrimental to proper penological objectives, subversive to good discipline, or otherwise harmful."

This analysis is faulty for two reasons. The District Court erroneously treated this case as if the prison environment was essentially a "public forum." We observed last Term in upholding a ban on political meetings at Fort Dix that a government enclave such as a military base was not a

public forum. *Greer* v. *Spock,* 424 U.S. 828 (1976). We stated:

"The fact that other civilian speakers and entertainers had sometimes been invited to appear at Fort Dix did not of itself serve to convert Fort Dix into a public forum or to confer upon political candidates a First or Fifth Amendment right to conduct their campaigns there. The decision of the military authorities that a civilian lecture on drug abuse, a religious service by a visiting preacher at the base chapel, or a rock musical concert would be supportive of the military mission of Fort Dix surely did not leave the authorities powerless thereafter to prevent any civilian from entering Fort Dix to speak on any subject whatever."

A prison may be no more easily converted into a public forum than a military base. Thus appellants need only demonstrate a rational basis for their distinctions between organizational groups. Here, appellants' affidavits indicate exactly why Alcoholics Anonymous and the Jaycees have been allowed to operate within the prison. Both were seen as serving a rehabilitative purpose, working in harmony with the goals and desires of the prison administrators, and both had been determined not to pose any threat to the order or security of the institution. The affidavits indicate that the administrators' view of the Union differed critically in both these respects.

Those conclusions are not unreasonable. Prison administrators may surely conclude that the Jaycees and Alcoholics Anonymous differ in fundamental respects from appellee Union, a group with no past to speak of, and the avowed intent to pursue an adversary relationship with the prison officials. Indeed, it would be enough to distinguish the Union from Alcoholics Anonymous to note that the chartered purpose of the Union, apparently pursued in the prison, was illegal under North Carolina law.

Since a prison is most emphatically not a "public forum," these reasonable beliefs of appellants are sufficient. . . . The District Court's further requirement of a demonstrable showing that the Union was in fact harmful is inconsistent with the deference federal courts should pay to the informed discretion of prison officials. It is precisely in matters such as this, the decision as to which of many groups should be allowed to operate within the prison walls, where, confronted with claims based on the Equal Protection Clause, the courts should allow the prison administrators the full latitude of discretion, unless it can be firmly stated that the two groups are so similar that discretion has been abused. That is surely not the case here. There is nothing in the Constitution which requires prison officials to treat all inmate groups alike unless differentiation is necessary to avoid an imminent threat of institutional disruption or violence. The regulations of appellants challenged in the District Court offended neither the First nor the Fourteenth Amendments, and the judgment of that Court holding to the contrary is

Reversed.

MR. JUSTICE MARSHALL, with whom MR. JUSTICE BRENNAN joins, dissenting.

There was a time, not so very long ago, when prisoners were regarded as "slave[s] of the State," having "not only forfeited [their] liberty, but all [their] personal rights. . ." *Ruffin* v. *Commonwealth*, 62 Va. 790, 792 (1871). In recent years, however, the courts increasingly have rejected this view, and with it the corollary which holds that courts should keep their "hands off" penal institutions. Today, however, the Court, in apparent fear of a prison reform organization that has the temerity to call itself a "union," takes a giant step backwards towards that discredited conception of prisoners' rights and the role of the courts. I decline to join in what I hope will prove to be a temporary retreat.

I

In *Procunier* v. *Martinez*, I set forth at some length my understanding of the First Amendment rights of prison inmates. The fundamental tenet I advanced is simply stated: "A prisoner does not shed. . .basic First Amendment rights at the prison gate. Rather, he 'retains all the rights of an ordinary citizen except those expressly, or by necessary implication, taken from him by law.' *Coffin* v. *Reichard*, 143 F.2d 443, 445 (CA6 1944)." It follows from this tenet that a restriction on the First Amendment rights of prisoners, like a restriction on the rights of nonprisoners, "can only be justified by a substantial government interest and a showing that the means chosen to effectuate the State's purpose are not unnecessarily restrictive of personal freedoms." This does not mean that any expressive conduct that would be constitutionally protected outside a prison is necessarily protected inside; as I also stated in *Martinez*, "[t]he First Amendment must in each context 'be applied "in light of the special characteristics of the... environment... " ' and the exigencies of governing persons in prison are different from and greater than those in governing persons without." But the basic mode of First Amendment analysis—the requirement that restrictions on speech be supported by "reasons imperatively justifying the particular deprivation." *ibid.*—should not be altered simply because the First Amendment claimants are incarcerated.

The Court today rejects this analytic framework, at least as it applies to the right of prisoners to associate in something called a prison "union." In testing restrictions on the exercise of that right the Court asks only whether the restrictions are "rationally related to the... objectives of prison administration," and whether the reasons offered in defense of the restrictions have been "conclusively shown to be wrong." While proclaiming faithfulness to the teaching of *Pell* v. *Procunier*, that "[a] prison inmate retains those First Amendment rights that are not inconsistent with his status as a prisoner," the Court ultimately upholds the challenged regulations on a ground that would apply to any restriction on inmate freedom: they "are consistent with the inmates' status as prisoners."

Nothing in the Court's opinion justifies its wholesale abandonment of traditional principles of First Amendment analysis. I realize, of course, that "the realities of running a penal institution are complex and difficult," and that correctional officers possess considerably more "professional expertise" in prison management than do judges. I do not in any way minimize either the seriousness of the problems or the significance of the

expertise. But it does seem to me that "the realities of running" a school or a city are also "complex and difficult," and that those charged with these tasks—principals, college presidents, mayors, councilmen, and law enforcement personnel—also possess special "professional expertise." Yet in no First Amendment case of which I am aware has the Court deferred to the judgment of such officials simply because their judgment was "rational." I do not understand why a different rule should apply simply because prisons are involved.

The reason courts cannot blindly defer to the judgment of prison administrators—or any other officials for that matter—is easily understood. Because the prisons administrator's business is to maintain order, "there inheres the danger that he may well be less responsive than a court—part of an independent branch of government—to the constitutionally protected interests in free expression." *Freedman* v. *Maryland*, 380 U.S. 51, 57-58 (1965). A warden seldom will find himself subject to public criticism or dismissal because he needlessly repressed free speech; indeed, neither the public nor the warden will have any way of knowing when repression was unnecessary. But a warden's job can be jeopardized and public criticism is sure to come should disorder occur. Consequently, prison officials inevitably will err on the side of too little freedom. That this has occurred in the past is made clear by the recent report of the American Bar Association Joint Committee on the Legal Status of Prisoners:

> "All organizations including correctional organizations overreact to suggested changes, whether sweeping or merely incre-

mental.... [M]any of the fears voiced by prison officials in the 1960s to the growing tide of court determinations invalidating prison regulations have simply not come to pass; indeed, in several instances...those groups feared in prisons in the 1960s have become stabilizing influences in the 1970s."

I do not mean to suggest that the views of correctional officials should be cavalierly disregarded by courts called upon to adjudicate constitutional claims of prisoners. Far from it. The officials' view "constitute a body of experience and informed judgment to which courts...may properly resort for guidance. The weight of such a judgment in a particular case will depend upon the thoroughness evident in its consideration, the validity of its reasoning...and all those factors which give it power to persuade...." My point is simply that the ultimate responsibility for evaluating the prison officials' testimony, as well as any other expert testimony, must rest with the courts, which are required to reach an independent judgment concerning the constitutionality of any restriction on expressive activity.

The approach I advocate is precisely the one this Court has followed in other cases involving the rights of prisoners. In *Johnson* v. *Avery*, for example, the Court expressly acknowledged the rationality of the rule at issue which prohibited inmate writ writers from aiding fellow prisoners in preparing legal papers. We nevertheless concluded that the rule was unconstitutional because of its impact on prisoners' right of access to the courts. In *Lee* v. *Washington*, we did not even inquire whether segregating prisoners by race was

rational, although it could be argued that integration in a southern prison would lead to disorder among inmates; we held that in any event segregation was prohibited by the Fourteenth Amendment. And in *Bounds* v. *Smith*, *Wolff* v. *McDonnell*, and *Cruz* v. *Beto*, we followed the approach of *Lee*. By word and deed, then, we have repeatedly reaffirmed that "a policy of judicial restraint cannot encompass any failure to take cognizance of valid constitutional claims.... When a prison regulation or practice offends a fundamental constitutional guarantee, federal courts will discharge their duty to protect constitutional rights."

II

Once it is established that traditional First Amendment principles are applicable in prisoners rights cases, the dispute here is easily resolved. The three-judge court not only found that there was "not one scintilla of evidence to suggest that the Union had been utilized to disrupt the operation of the penal institutions," *North Carolina Prisoners' Labor Union, Inc.* v. *Jones*, 409 F. Supp. 937, 944 (EDNC 1976), as the Court acknowledges, it also found no evidence "that the inmates intend to operate [the union] to hamper and interfere with proper interests of government," 409 F. Supp., at 944, or that the union posed a "present danger to security and order." In the face of these findings, it cannot be argued that the restrictions on the union are "imperatively justif[ied]."

The regulation barring inmates from soliciting fellow prisoners to join the union is particularly vulnerable to attack. As the late Judge Craven stated for the court below, "To permit an inmate to join a union and forbid his inviting others to join borders on the irrational." The irrationality of the regulation is perhaps best demonstrated by the fact that the Court does not defend it; rather, as my Brother STEVENS suggests, the Court defends some hypothetical regulation banning "an invitation to collectively engage in a legitimately prohibited activity." Because the actual regulation at issue here needlessly bars solicitation for an activity—joining the union—which is not and presumably could not be prohibited. I would hold it unconstitutional.

Once the rule outlawing solicitation is invalidated, the prohibition on bulk mailing by the Union must fall with it. Since North Carolina allows the Union to mail its newsletters to prisoners individually, the State cannot claim that the bulk mail rule serves to keep "subversive material" out of the prison. Rather, the primary purpose of the rule must be to supplement the ban on solicitation; overturning that ban would sap all force from the rationale for excluding bulk mailings. The exclusion would then be left as one that unnecessarily increases the cost to the Union of exercising its First Amendment rights while allowing other inmate groups such as the Jaycees to exercise their rights at a lower price. It would, therefore, be plainly unconstitutional.

The regulation prohibiting the Union from holding meetings within the prison is somewhat more justifiable than the regulations previously considered. Once the Union is permitted to hold meetings it will become operational within the prisons. Appellants' fears that the leaders of an operating Union "would be in a position to misuse their influence" and

that the Union itself could engage in disruptive, concerted activities or increase tension within the prisons, are not entirely fanciful. It is important to note, however, that appellee's two expert witnesses, both correctional officers who had dealt with inmate reform organizations, testified that such groups actually play a constructive role in their prisons. The weight of professional opinion seems to favor recognizing such groups. Moreover, the risks appellant fears are inherent in any inmate organization, no matter how innocuous its stated goals; indeed, even without any organizations some inmates inevitably will become leaders capable of "misus[ing] their influence," and some concerted activity can still occur.

But even if the risks posed by the Union were unique to it, and even if appellants' fear of the Union were more widely shared by other professionals, the prohibition on Union meetings still could not survive constitutional attack. The central lesson of over a half-century of First Amendment adjudication is that freedom is sometimes a hazardous enterprise, and that the Constitution requires the State to bear certain risks to preserve our liberty. As the ABA Joint Committee put it, "[t]he doubts and risks raised by creating a humane and open prison must be accepted as a cost of our society; democracy is self-definitionally a risk taking form of government." To my mind, therefore, the fact that appellants have not acted wholly irrationally in banning union meetings is not dispositive. Rather, I believe that where, as here, meetings would not pose an immediate and substantial threat to the security or rehabilitative functions of the prisons, the First Amendment guarantees Union members the right to associate freely, and the Fourteenth Amendment guarantees them the right to be treated as favorably as members of other inmate organizations. The State can surely regulate the time, place, and manner of the meetings, and perhaps can monitor them to assure that disruptions are not planned, but the State cannot outlaw such assemblies altogether.

III

If the mode of analysis adopted in today's decision were to be generally followed, prisoners eventually would be stripped of all constitutional rights, and would retain only those privileges that prison officials, in their informed discretion," designed to recognize. The sole constitutional constraint on prison officials would be a requirement that they act rationnally. Ironically, prisoners would be left with a right of access to the courts, see *Bounds* v. *Smith; Johnson* v. *Avery,* but no substantive rights to assert once they get there. I cannot believe that the Court that decided *Bounds* and *Johnson*—the Court that has stated that "[t]here is no iron curtain drawn between the Constitution and the prisoners of this country." *Wolff* v. *McDonnell,* and that "[a] prison inmate retains those First Amendment rights not inconsistent with his status as a prisoner," *Pell* v. *Procunier,* intends to allow this to happen. I therefore believe that the tension between today's decision and our prior cases ultimately will be resolved not by the demise of the earlier cases, but by the recognition that the decision today is an aberration, a manifestation of the extent to which the very phrase "prisoner union" is threatening to those holding traditional conceptions of the nature of penal institutions.

I respectfully dissent.

KENTUCKY v. THOMPSON

___ U.S. ___, 109 S.Ct. 1904, 104 L. Ed. 2d 506 (1989)

[Citations and Footnotes Omitted]

JUSTICE BLACKMUN delivered the opinion of the Court.

In this case we consider whether Kentucky prison regulations give state inmates, for purposes of the Fourteenth Amendment, a liberty interest in receiving certain visitors.

I

In September 1976, Kentucky inmates brought a federal class action under 42 U.S.C. § 1983 challenging conditions of confinement in the Kentucky State Penitentiary at Eddyville. *** The litigation was settled by a consent decree dated 28 May 1980, and supplemented 22 July 1980, containing provisions governing a broad range of prison conditions. Of sole relevance here, the consent decree provides: "The Bureau of Corrections encourages and agrees to maintain visitation at least at the current level, with minimal restrictions," and to "continue their open visiting policy."

The Commonwealth in 1981 issued "Corrections Policies and Procedures" governing general prison visitation, including a nonexhaustive list of visitors who may be excluded. Four years later, the Reformatory issued its own more detailed "Procedures Memorandum" on the subject of "Visiting Regulations." The Memorandum begins with a Statement of Policy and Purpose: "Although administrative staff reserves the right to allow or disallow visits, it is the policy of the Kentucky State Reformatory to respect the rights of inmates to have visits in the spirit of the Court decisions and the Consent Decree, while insuring the safety and security of the institution." The Memorandum then goes on to state that a visitor may be denied entry if his or her presence would constitute a "clear and probable danger to the safety and security of the institution or would interfere with the orderly operation of the institution." A nonexhaustive list of nine specific reasons for excluding visitors is set forth. The Memorandum also states that the decision whether to exclude a visitor rests with the Duty Officer, who is to be consulted by any staff member who "feels a visitor should not be allowed admittance."

This particular litigation was prompted in large part by two incidents when applicants were denied the opportunity to visit an inmate at the Reformatory. The mother of one inmate was denied visitation for six months because she brought to the Reformatory a person who had been barred for smuggling contraband. Another inmate's mother and woman friend were denied visitation for a limited time when the inmate was found with contraband after a visit by the two women. In both instances the visitation privileges were suspended without a hearing. The inmates were not prevented from receiving other visitors.

The representatives of the Kendrick-inmate class filed a motion with the United States District Court *** claiming that the suspension of visitation privileges without a hearing in these two instances violated the decree and the Due Process Clause of the Fourteenth Amendment. By a Memorandum dated June 26, 1986, the District Court found that the prison policies did not violate the decree, but concluded that the language of the decree was "mandatory in character," and that, under the standards articulated by this Court in *Hewitt v. Helms*, the respondents "possess a liberty interest in open visitation." The District Court directed petitioners to develop "minimal due process procedures," including "an informal, nonadversary review in which a prisoner receives notice of and reasons for" any decision to exclude a visitor, as well as an opportunity to respond. A formal order was issued accordingly. ***

II

***

Respondents do not argue—nor can it seriously be contended, in light of our prior cases—that an inmate's interest in unfettered visitation is guaranteed directly by the Due Process Clause. We have rejected the notion "that any change in the conditions of confinement having a substantial adverse impact on the prisoner involved is sufficient to invoke the protections of the Due Process Clause." This is not to say that a valid conviction extinguishes every direct due process protection; "consequences visited on the prisoner that are qualitatively different from the punishment characteristically suffered by a person convicted of crime" may invoke the protections of the Due Process Clause even in the absence of a state-created right. However, "[a]s long as the conditions or degree of confinement to which the prisoner is subjected is within the sentence imposed upon him and is not otherwise violative of the Constitution, the Due Process Clause does not in itself subject an inmate's treatment by prison authorities to judicial oversight." The denial of prison access to a particular visitor "is well within the terms of confinement ordinarily contemplated by a prison sentence," and

therefore is not independently protected by the Due Process Clause.

We have held, however, that state law may create enforceable liberty interests in the prison setting. We have found, for example, that certain regulations granted inmates a protected interest in parole, *Board of Pardons v. Allen, Greenholtz v. Nebraska Penal Inmates*, in good time credits, *Wolff v. McDonnell*, in freedom from involuntary transfer to a mental hospital, *Vitsk v. Jones*, and in freedom from more restrictive forms of confinement within the prison, *Hewitt v. Helms*. In contrast, we have found that certain state statutes and regulations did not create a protected liberty interest in transfer to another prison. *Meachum v. Fano*, (intrastate transfer); *Olim v. Wakinekona*, (interstate transfer). The fact that certain state-created liberty interests have been found to be entitled to due process protection, while others have not, is not the result of this Court's judgment as to what interests are more significant than others; rather, our method of inquiry in these cases always have been to examine more closely the language of the relevant statutes and regulations. Most of our procedural due process cases in the prison context have turned on the presence or absence of language creating "substantive predicates" to guide discretion. For example, the failure of a Connecticut statute governing commutation of sentences to provide "particularized standards of criteria [to] guide the State's decisionmakers," *Connecticut Board of*

Pardons v. Dumschat, defeated an inmate's claim that the State had created a liberty interest. In other instances, we have found that prison regulations or statutes do provide decisionmaking criteria which serve to limit discretion. See also *Olim v. Wakinekona*, (interstate prison transfer left to "completely unfettered" discretion of administrator); *Meachum v. Fano*, (intrastate prison transfer at discretion of officials); *Montanye v. Haymes*, (same). In other instances, we have found that prison regulations or statutes do provide decisionmaking criteria which serve to limit discretion. See, e.g., *Hewitt v. Helms*, (administrative segregation not proper absent particular substantive predicates); *Board of Pardons v. Allen*, (parole granted unless certain standards met, even though the decision is " 'necessarily subjective ... and predictive' "). ***

We have also articulated a requirement, implicit in our earlier decisions, that the regulations contain "explicitly mandatory language," i.e., specific directives to the decisionmaker that if the regulations' substantive predicates are present, a particular outcome must follow, in order to create a liberty interest. The regulations at issue in *Hewitt* mandated that certain procedures be followed, and "that administrative segregation will not occur absent specified substantive predicates." In *Board of Pardons v. Allen*, the relevant statute "use[d] mandatory language ['shall'] to 'creat[e] a presumption that parole release will be granted' when the

designated findings are made." In sum, the use of "explicitly mandatory language," in connection with the establishment of "specific substantive predicates" to limit discretion, forces a conclusion that the State has created a liberty interest.

III

The regulations and procedures at issue in this case do provide certain "substantive predicates" to guide the decisionmaker. The state procedures provide that a visitor "may be excluded" when, inter alia, officials find reasonable grounds to believe that the "visitor's presence in the institution would constitute a clear and probable danger to the institution's security or interfere with [its] orderly operation." Among the more specific reasons listed for denying visitation are the visitor's connection to the inmate's criminal behavior, the visitor's past disruptive behavior or refusal to submit to a search or show proper identification, and the visitor's being under the influence of alcohol or drugs. The Reformatory Procedures are nearly identical, and include a prohibition on a visit from a former reformatory inmate, without the prior approval of the warden. These regulations and procedures contain standards to be applied by a staff member in determining whether to refer a situation to the Duty Officer for resolution, and require the staff member to notify the Duty Officer if the staff member feels that a visitor should not be allowed admittance. The same "substantive predicates" undoubtedly are intended to guide the Duty Officer's discretion in making the ultimate decision.

The regulations at issue here, however, lack the requisite relevant mandatory language. They stop short of requiring that a particular result is to be reached upon a finding that the substantive predicates are met. The Reformatory Procedures Memorandum begin with the caveat that "administrative staff reserves the right to allow or disallow visits," and goes on to note that "it is the policy" of Reformatory "to respect the rights of inmates to have visits." This language is not mandatory. Visitors may be excluded if they fall within one of the described categories, but they need not be. Nor need visitors fall within one of the described categories in order to be excluded. The overall effect of the regulations is not such that an inmate can reasonably form an objective expectation that a visit would necessarily be allowed absent the occurrence of one of the listed conditions. Or, to state it differently, the regulations are not worded in such a way that an inmate could reasonably expect to enforce them against the prison officials.

***[T]he regulations at issue here do not establish a liberty interest entitled to the protections of the Due Process Clause.....

JUSTICE KENNEDY, concurring.

I concur fully in the opinion and judgment of the Court. I write separately to note that this case involves a denial of prison access to particular visitors, not a general ban of all prison visitation. Nothing in the Court's opinion forecloses the claim that a prison regulation permanently forbidding all visits to some or all prisoners implicates the protections of the Due Process Clause in a way that the precise and individualized restrictions at issue here do not.

JUSTICE MARSHALL, with whom JUSTICE BRENNAN and JUSTICE STEVENS join, dissenting.

As a result of today's decision, correctional authorities at the Kentucky State Reformatory are free to deny prisoners visits from parents, spouses, children, clergy members, and close friends for any reason whatsoever, or for no reason at all. Prisoners will not even be entitled to learn the reason, if any, why a visitor has been turned away. In my view, the exercise of such unbridled governmental power over the basic human need to see family members and friends strike at the heart of the liberty protected by the Due Process Clause of the Fourteenth Amendment. Recognizing a liberty interest in this case would not create a right to "unfettered visitation," but would merely afford prisoners rudimentary procedural safeguards against retaliatory or arbitrary denials of visits. Because the majority refuses to take this small step, I dissent.

I

The majority begins its analysis by conceding, as it must under our precedents, that prisoners do not shed their constitutional rights at the prison gate, but instead retain a residuum of constitutionally protected liberty independent of any state laws or regulations. In the balance of its opinion, however, the majority proceeds to prove the emptiness of this initial gesture. In concluding that prison visits implicate no retained liberty interest, the majority applies the following oft-cited test: " '[a]s long as the conditions or degree of confinement to which the prisoner is subjected is within the sentence imposed upon him and is not otherwise violative of the Constitution, the Due Process Clause does not in itself subject an inmate's treatment by prison authorities to judicial oversight.' " On its face, the "within the sentence" test knows few rivals for vagueness and pliability, not the least because a typical prison sentence says little more than that the defendant must spend a specified period of time behind bars. As applied, this test offers prisoners scant more protection, for the Justices employing it have rarely scrutinized the actual conditions of confinement faced by the prisoners in the correctional institutions at issue. Under this approach, therefore, "a prisoner crosses into limbo when he enters into penal confinement." In theory he retains some minimal interest in liberty protected by the Due Process Clause, but in practice this interest crystallizes only on those infrequent occasions when a majority of the Court happens to say so.

Prison visits have long been recognized as critically important to inmates as well as to the communities to which the inmates ultimately will return. Without visits, a prisoner "may be entirely cut off from his only contacts with the outside world." Confinement without visitation brings alienation and the longer the confinement the greater the alienation. There is little, if any, disagreement that the opportunity to be visited by friends and relatives is more beneficial to the confined person than any other form of communication.***

The majority intimates that the actions taken against prisoners Bobbitt and Black were based on good cause, but the very essence of these prisoners' factual allegations is that no such cause existed. If Bobbitt and Black are correct, they may well have suffered a "grievous loss" by being singled out arbitrarily for unjustifiably harsh treatment. No evidence whatsoever indicates that visitors to the Reformatory have ever been barred for any reason except those enumerated as legitimate in the Commonwealth Procedures and the institution-specific Reformatory Procedures Memorandum (Reformatory Memorandum). It is nowhere suggested, furthermore, that these prisoners' sentences contemplated denials of visits for nonenumerated reasons, or that such denials are " 'well within the terms of confinement ordinarily contemplated' " in the Reformatory. Under the majority's disposition, neither prisoner will ever have a right to contest the prison authorities' account. One need hardly be cynical about prison administrators to recognize that the distinct possibility of retaliatory or otherwise groundless deprivations of visits calls for a modicum of procedural protections to guard against such behavior.

II

Even if I believed that visit denials did not implicate a prisoner's retained liberty interest, I would nonetheless find that a liberty interest has been "created" by the Commonwealth's visitation regulations and policies. As the majority notes, " 'a State creates a protected liberty interest by placing substantive limitations on official discretion.' " I fully agree with the majority that "[t]he regulations and procedures at issue in this case do provide certain 'substantive predicates' to guide the decisionmaker." But I cannot agree that Kentucky's prison regulations do not create a liberty interest because they "lack the requisite relevant mandatory language."

As an initial matter, I fail to see why mandatory language always is an essential element of a state-created liberty interest. Once it is clear that a State has imposed substantive criteria in statutes or regulations to guide or limit official discretion, there is no reason to assume—as the majority does—that officials applying the statutes or regulations are likely to ignore the criteria if there is not some undefined quantity of the words "shall" or "must." Drafters of statutes or regulations do not ordinarily view the criteria they establish as mere surplusage. Absent concrete evidence

that state officials routinely ignore substantive criteria set forth in statutes or regulations (and there is no such evidence here), it is only proper to assume that the criteria are regularly employed in practice, thereby creating legitimate expectations worthy of protection by the Due Process Clause. Common sense suggests that expectations stem from practice as well as from the language of statutes or regulations. This point escapes the majority, which apparently harbors the "unrealistic [belief] that variations such as the use of 'may' rather than 'shall' could negate the expectations derived from experience with a [prison] system and ... enumerated criteria...."

Even if I thought it proper to rely on the presence or absence of mandatory language, I would still disagree with the majority's determination that the regulations here lack such language. The majority relies primarily on a statement in the Reformatory Memorandum that "administrative staff reserves the right to allow or disallow visits." It is important, however, to put this "caveat," in proper context. The Reformatory Memorandum's section on visitation occupies 33 pages of the Joint Appendix. The caveat appears just once in a general, introductory paragraph which also includes the statement that "it is the policy of the Kentucky State Reformatory to respect the right of inmates to have visits." Over the next 20 pages, the Reformatory Memorandum lays out in great detail the mandatory "procedures to be enforced in regard to all types of visits." It states, for example, that "[v]isits will be conducted seven (7) days a week," that "[a]n inmate is allowed three (3) separate visits ... per week," that "[t]here will be no visit list maintained which specifies who may visit an inmate," that "[a]n inmate is allowed to have ... three (3) adult visitors ... per visit," that visits "will be one and one-half hours," and that "[e]ach inmate will be allowed one (1) outdoor visit per week."

Only then does the Reformatory Memorandum enumerate the very specific reasons for which a visitor may be excluded. The duty officer does not have unfettered discretion with respect to visitors. Rather, he "has the responsibility of denying a visit for the above [enumerated] reasons." When a visit is denied, the reasons "will be documented." Presumably this means that the duty officer must keep a record of which of "the above reasons" caused him to exclude the visitor. The Reformatory Memorandum also expressly references the American Correctional Association's visitation standards, which provide that "visits may be limited only by the institution's schedule, space, and personnel constraints, or when there are substantial reasons to justify such limitations." Nothing in these standards even remotely contemplates the arbitrary exclusion of visitors.

When these mandatory commands are read in conjunction with the detailed rules set forth in the Commonwealth Procedures, it is inconceivable that prisoners in the Reformatory would not "reasonably form an objective expectation that a visit would necessarily be allowed absent the occurrence of one of the listed conditions." The majority inexplicably ignores nearly all of these commands, despite claiming to have considered the "overall effect of the regulations, " and despite the Commonwealth's striking concession that the regulations "repeated use 'will', 'shall', and similar directive or mandatory language" in an effort "to advise inmates and potential visitors what is expected." In light of these mandatory commands, the caveat, as well as any other language that could be taken to suggest that visitors need not "fall within one of the described categories in order to be excluded," amount to nothing more than mere boilerplate. The Court should reject the view "that state laws which impose substantive limitations and elaborate procedural requirements on official conduct create no liberty interest solely because there remains the possibility that an official will act in an arbitrary manner at the end of the process."

Finally, the majority's reliance on the fact that both the Commonwealth Procedures and the Reformatory Memorandum provide that a visitor "may" be excluded if he falls within one of the enumerated categories, is misplaced. The word "may" in this context simply means that prison authorities possess the discretion to allow visits from persons who fall within one of the enumerated categories.***

III

The prisoners in this case do not seek a right to unfettered visitation. All they ask is that the Court recognize that visitation is sufficiently important to warrant procedural protections to ensure that visitors are not arbitrarily denied. The protections need not be extensive, but simply commensurate with the special "needs and exigencies of the institutional environment." In making the threshold determination that the denial of visits can never implicate a prisoner's liberty interest, the majority thus establishes that when visitors are turned away, no process, not even notice, is constitutionally due. I cannot accept such a parsimonious reading of the Due Process Clause, and therefore dissent.

PRISONERS' RIGHTS TO USE OF THE MAIL

PROCUNIER v. MARTINEZ

416 U.S. 396, 94 S. Ct. 1800, 40 L. Ed. 2d 224 (1974)

MR. JUSTICE POWELL delivered the opinion of the court.

I

First we consider the constitutionality of the Director's Rules restricting the personal correspondence of prison inmates. Under these regulations, correspondence between inmates of California penal institutions and persons other than licensed attorneys and holders of public office was censored for nonconformity to certain standards. Rule 2401 stated the Department's general premise that personal correspondence by prisoners is "a privilege, not a right ° ° °." More detailed regulations implemented the Department's policy. Rule 1201 directed inmates not to write letters in which they "unduly complain" or "magnify grievances." Rule 1205 (d) defined as contraband writings "expressing inflammatory political, racial, religious or other views or beliefs ° ° °." Finally, Rule 2402 (8) provided that inmates "may not send or receive letters that pertain to criminal activity; are lewd, obscene, or defamatory, contain foreign matter, or are otherwise inappropriate."

Prison employees screened both incoming and outgoing personal mail for violations of these regulations. No further criteria were provided to help members of the mailroom staff decide whether a particular letter contravened any prison rule or policy. When a prison employee found a letter objectionable, he could take one or more of the following actions: (1) refuse to mail or deliver the letter and return it to the author; (2) submit a disciplinary report, which could lead to suspension of mail privileges or other sanctions; or (3) place a copy of the letter or a summary of its contents in the prisoner's file, where it might be a factor in determining the inmate's work and housing assignments and in setting a date for parole eligibility.

The District Court held that the regulations relating to prisoner mail authorized censorship of protected expression without adequate justification in violation of the First Amendment and that they were void for vagueness. The court also noted that the regulations failed to provide minimum procedural safeguards against error and arbitrariness in the censorship of inmate correspondence. Consequently, it enjoined their continued enforcement.

* * *

A

Traditionally, federal courts have adopted a broad hands-off attitude toward problems of prison administration. In part this policy is the product of various limitations on the scope of federal review of conditions in state penal institutions. More fundamentally, this attitude springs from complementary perceptions about the nature of the problems and the efficacy of judicial intervention. Prison administrators are responsible for maintaining internal order and discipline, for securing their institutions against unauthorized access or escape, and for rehabilitation, to the extent that human nature and inadequate resources allow, the inmates placed in their custody. The Herculean obstacles to effective discharge of these duties are too apparent to warrant explication. Suffice it to say that the problems of prisons in America are complex and intractable, and, more to the point, they are not readily susceptible of resolution by decree. Most require expertise, comprehensive planning, and the commitment of resources, all of which are peculiarly within the province of the legislative and executive branches of government. For all of those reasons, courts are ill-equipped to deal with the increasingly urgent problems of prison administration and reform.[9] Judicial recognition or that

fact reflects no more than a healthy sense of realism.

Moreover, where state penal institutions are involved, federal courts have a further reason for deference to the appropriate prison authorities. But a policy of judicial restraint cannot encompass any failure to take cognizance of valid constitutional claims whether arising in a federal or state institution. When a prison regulation or practice offends a fundamental constitutional guarantee, federal courts will discharge their duty to protect constitutional rights. Johnson v. Avery, 393 U.S. 483, 486 (1969). This is such a case. Although the District Court found the regulations relating to prisoner mail deficient in several respects, the first and principal basis for its decision was the constitutional command of the First Amendment, as applied to the States by the Fourteenth Amendment.[10]

---

9 They are also ill-suited to act as the front-line agencies for the consideration and resolution of the infinite variety of prisoner complaints. Moreover, the capacity of our criminal justice system to deal fairly and fully with legitimate claims will be impaired by a burgeoning increase of frivolous prisoner complaints. As one means of alleviating this problem, THE CHIEF JUSTICE has suggested that federal and state authorities explore the possibility of instituting internal administrative procedures for disposition of inmate grievances. 59 A.B.A.J. 1125, 1128 (1973). At the Third Circuit Judicial Conference meeting of October 15, 1973, at which the problem was addressed, suggestions also included (i) abstention where appropriate to avoid needless consideration of federal constitutional issues; and (ii) the use of federal magistrates who could be sent into penal institutions to conduct hearings and make findings of fact. We emphasize that we express no view as to the merit or validity of any particular proposal, but we do think it appropriate to indicate the necessity of prompt and thoughtful consideration by responsible federal and state authorities of this worsening situation.

10 Specifically, the District Court held that the regulations authorized restraint of lawful expression in violation of the First and Fourteenth Amendments, that they were fatally vague, and that they failed to provide minimum procedural safeguards against arbitrary or erroneous censorship of protected speech.

The issue before us is the appropriate standard of review for prison regulations restricting freedom of speech. This Court has not previously addressed this question, and the tension between the traditional policy of judicial restraint regarding prisoner complaints and the need to protect constitutional rights has led the federal courts to adopt a variety of widely inconsistent approaches to the problem. Some have maintained a hands-off posture in the face of constitutional challenges to censorship of prisoner mail. *E.g.*, McCloskey v. Maryland, 337 F.2d 72 (CA 4 1964); Lee v. Tahash, 352 F.2d 970 (CA 8 1965) (except insofar as mail censorship rules are applied to discriminate against a particular racial or religious group); Krupnick v. Crouse, 366 F.2d 851 (CA 10 1966); Pope v. Daggett, 350 F.2d 296 (CA 10 1965). Another has required only that censorship of personal correspondence not lack support "in any rational and constitutionally acceptable concept of a prison system." Sostre v. McGinnis, 442 F.2d 178, 199 (CA 2 1971), cert. denied, *sub nom.* Oswald v. Sostre, 405 U.S. 978 (1972). At the other extreme some courts have been willing to require demonstration of a "compelling state interest" to justify censorship of prisoner mail. *E.g.*, Jackson v. Godwin, 400 F.2d 529 (CA 5 1968) (decided on both equal protection and First Amendment grounds); Morales v. Schmidt, 340 F. Supp. 544 (W.D. Wis. 1972); Fortune Society v. McGinnis, 319 F.Supp. 901 (S.D. N.Y. 1970). Other courts phrase the standard in similarly demanding terms of "clear and present danger." Wilkinson v. Skinner, 462 F.2d 670, 672-673 (CA 2 1972). And there are various intermediate positions, most notably the view that a "regulation or practice which restricts the right of

free expression that a prisoner would have enjoyed, if he had not been imprisoned, must be related both reasonably and necessarily to the advancement of some justifiable purpose." Carothers v. Follette, 314 F.Supp. 1014, 1024 (S.D. N.Y. 1970) (citations omitted). See also Gates v. Collier, 349 F.Supp. 881, 896 (N.D. Miss. 1972); LeMon v. Zelker, 358 F.Supp. 554 (S.D. N.Y. 1973).

This array of disparate approaches and the absence of any generally accepted standard for testing the constitutionality of prisoner mail censorship regulations disserve both the competing interests at stake. On the one hand, the First Amendment interests implicated by censorship of inmate correspondence are given only haphazard and inconsistent protection. On the other, the uncertainty of the constitutional standard makes it impossible for correctional officials to anticipate what is required of them and invites repetitive, piecemeal litigation on behalf of inmates. The result has been unnecessarily to perpetuate the involvement of the federal courts in affairs of prison administration. Our task is to formulate a standard of review for prisoner mail censorship that will be responsive to these concerns.

B

We begin our analysis of the proper standard of review for constitutional challenges to censorship of prisoner mail with a somewhat different premise than that taken by the other federal courts that have considered the question. For the most part, these courts have dealt with challenges to censorship of prisoner mail as involving broad questions of "prisoners' rights." This case is no exception. The District Court stated the issue in general terms as "the applicability of First Amendment rights to prison inmates * * *." 354 F.Supp., at 1096, and the arguments of the parties reflect the assumption that the resolution of this case requires an assessment of the extent to which prisoners may claim First Amendment freedoms. In our view this inquiry is unnecessary. In determining the proper standard of review for prison restrictions on inmate correspondence, we have no occasion to consider the extent to which an individual's right to free speech survives incarceration, for a narrower basis of decision is at hand. In the case of direct personal correspondence between inmates and those who have a particularized interest in communicating with them,[11] mail censorship implicates more than the right of prisoners.

Communication by letter is not accomplished by the act of writing words on paper. Rather, it is effected only when the letter is read by the addressee. Both parties to the correspondence have an interest in securing that result, and censorship of the communication between them necessarily impinges on the interest of each. Whatever the status of a prisoner's claim to uncensored correspondence with an outsider, it is plain that the latter's interest is grounded in the First Amendment's guarantee of freedom of speech. And this does not depend on whether the nonprisoner correspondent is the author or intended recipient of a particular letter, for the addressee as well as the sender of direct personal correspondence derives from the First and Fourteenth Amendments a protection against unjustified governmental inter-

[11] Different considerations may come into play in the case of mass mailings. No such issue is raised on these facts, and we intimate no view as to its proper resolution.

ference with the intended communication. Lamont v. Postmaster General, 381 U.S. 301 (1965). Accord Kleindienst v. Mandel, 408 U.S. 752, 762-765 (1972); Martin v. City of Struthers, 319 U.S. 141, 143 (1943). We do not deal here with difficult questions of the so-called "right to hear" and third-party standing but with a particular means of communication in which the interests of both parties are inextricably meshed. The wife of a prison inmate who is not permitted to read all that her husband wanted to say to her has suffered an abridgement of her interest in communicating with him as plain as that which results from censorship of her letter to him. In either event, censorship of prisoner mail works a consequential restriction on the First and Fourteenth Amendments rights of those who are not prisoners.

Accordingly, we reject any attempt to justify censorship of inmate correspondence merely by reference to certain assumptions about the legal status of prisoners. Into this category of argument falls appellants' contention that "an inmate's rights with reference to social correspondence are something fundamentally different than those enjoyed by his free brother." Brief for Appellants 19. This line of argument and the undemanding standard of review it is intended to support fail to recognize that the First Amendment liberties of free citizens are implicated in censorship of prisoner mail. We therefore turn for guidance not to cases involving questions of "prisoners' rights" but to decisions of this Court dealing with the general problem of incidental restrictions on First Amendment liberties imposed in furtherance of legitimate governmental activities.

As the Court noted in Tinker v. Des Moines School District, 393 U.S. 503,

506, 49 Ohio Op.2d 222 (1969), First Amendment guarantees must be "applied in light of the special characteristics of the * * * environment." Tinker concerned the interplay between the right to freedom of speech of public high school students and "the need for affirming the comprehensive authority of the States and of school officials, consistent with fundamental constitutional safeguards, to prescribe and control the conduct in schools." Id., at 507. In overruling a school regulation prohibiting the wearing of anti-war armbands, the Court undertook a careful analysis of the legitimate requirements of orderly school administration in order to ensure that the students were afforded maximum freedom of speech consistent with those requirements. The same approach was followed in Healy v. James, 408 U.S. 169 (1972), where the Court considered the refusal of a state college to grant official recognition to a group of students who wished to organize a local chapter of the Students for a Democratic Society (SDS), a national student organization noted for political activism and campus disruption. The Court found that neither the identification of the local student group with the national SDS nor the purportedly dangerous political philosophy of the local group nor the college administration's fear of future, unspecified disruptive activities by the students could justify the incursion on the right of free association. The Court also found, however, that this right could be limited if necessary to prevent campus disruption, id., at n. 20, and remanded the case for determination of whether the students had in fact refused to accept reasonable regulations governing student conduct.

In United States v. O'Brien, 391 U.S. 367 (1968), the Court dealt with inci-dental restrictions on free speech occasioned by the exercise of the governmental power to conscript men for military service. O'Brien had burned his Selective Service registration certificate on the steps of a courthouse in order to dramatize his opposition to the draft and to our country's involvement in Vietnam. He was convicted of violating a provision of the Selective Service law that had recently been amended to prohibit knowing destruction or mutilation of registration certificates. O'Brien argued that the purpose and effect of the amendment were to abridge free expression and that the statutory provision was therefore unconstitutional, both as enacted and as applied to him. Although O'Brien's activity involved "conduct" rather than pure "speech," the Court did not define away the First Amendment concern, and neither did it rule that the presence of a communicative intent necessarily rendered O'Brien's actions immune to governmental regulation. Instead, it enunciated the following four-part test:

"[A] government regulation is sufficiently justified if it is within the constitutional power of the Government; if it furthers an important or substantial governmental interest; if the governmental interest is unrelated to the suppression of expression; and if the incidental restriction on alleged First Amendment freedoms is no greater than is essential to the furtherance of that interest." 391 U.S., at 377."

Of course, none of these precedents directly controls the instant case. In O'Brien the Court considered a federal statute which on its face prohibited certain conduct having no necessary connection with freedom of speech. This led the Court to differentiate between "speech" and "non-speech" elements of a single course of conduct, a distinction that has little relevance here. Both Tinker and Healy concerned First and Fourteenth Amendment liberties in the context of state educational institutions, a circumstance involving rather different governmental interests than are at stake here. In broader terms, however, these precedents involved incidental restrictions on First Amendment liberties by government action in furtherance of legitimate and substantial state interest other than suppression of expression. In this sense these cases are generally analogous to our present inquiry.

The case at hand arises in the context of prisons. One of the primary functions of government is the preservation of societal order through enforcement of the criminal law, and the maintenance of penal institutions is an essential part of that task. The identifiable governmental interests at stake in this task are the preservation of internal order and discipline, the maintenance of institutional security against escape or unauthorized entry, and the rehabilitation of the prisoners. While the weight of professional opinion seems to be that inmate freedom to correspond with outsiders advances rather than retards the goal of rehabilitation, the legitimate governmental interest in the order and security of penal institutions justifies the imposition of certain restraints on inmate correspondence. Perhaps the most obvious example of justifiable censorship of prisoner mail would be refusal to send or deliver letters concerning escape plans or containing other information concerning proposed criminal activity, whether within or without the prison. Similarly, prison officials may properly refuse to transmit encoded messages. Other less

obvious possibilities come to mind, but it is not our purpose to survey the range of circumstances in which particular restrictions on prisoner mail might be warranted by the legitimate demands of prison administration as they exist from time to time in the various kinds of penal institutions found in this country. Our task is to determine the proper standard for deciding whether a particular regulation or practice relating to inmate correspondence constitutes an impermissible restraint of First Amendment liberties.

Applying the teachings of our prior decisions to the instant context, we hold that censorship of prison mail is justified if the following criteria are met. First, the regulation or practice in question must further an important or substantial governmental interest unrelated to the suppression of expression. Prison officials may not censor inmate correspondence simply to eliminate unflattering or unwelcome opinions or factually inaccurate statements. Rather, they must show that a regulation authorizing mail censorship furthers one or more of the substantial governmental interests of security, order, and rehabilitation. Second, the limitation of First Amendment freedoms must be no greater than is necessary or essential to the protection of the particular governmental interest involved. Thus a restriction on inmate correspondence that furthers an important or substantial interest of penal administration will nevertheless be invalid if its sweep is unnecessarily broad. This does not mean, of course, that prison administrators may be required to show with certainty that adverse consequences would flow from the failure to censor a particular letter. Some latitude in anticipating the probable consequences of allowing certain speech in a prison environment is essential to the proper discharge of an administrator's duty. But any regulation or practice that restricts inmate correspondence must be generally necessary to protect one or more of the legitimate governmental interests identified above.

C

On the basis of this standard, we affirm the judgment of the District Court. The regulations invalidated by that court authorized, *inter alia*, censorship of statements that "unduly complain" or "magnify grievances," expression of "inflammatory political, racial, or religious, or other views," and matter deemed "defamatory" or "otherwise inappropriate." These regulations fairly invited prison officials and employees to apply their own personal prejudices and opinions as standards for prisoner mail censorship. Not surprisingly, some prison officials used the extraordinary latitude for discretion authorized by the regulations to suppress unwelcome criticism. For example, at one institution under the Department's jurisdiction, the checklist used by the mailroom staff authorized rejection of letters "criticizing policy, rules or officials," and the mailroom sergeant stated in a deposition that he would reject as "defamatory" letters "belittling staff or our judicial system or anything connected with the Department of Corrections." Correspondence was also censored for "disrespectful comments," "derogatory remarks," and the like.

Appellants have failed to show that these broad restrictions on prisoner mail were in any way necessary to the furtherance of a governmental interest unrelated to the suppression of expression. Indeed the heart of appellants' position is not that the regulations are justified by a legitimate governmental interest but that they do not need to be. This misconception is not only stated affirmatively; it also underlies appellants' discussion of the particular regulations under attack. For example, appellants' sole defense of the prohibition against matter that is "defamatory" or "otherwise inappropriate" is that it is "within the discretion of prison administrators." Brief for Appellants 21. Appellants contend that statements that "magnify grievances" or "unduly complain" are censored "as a precaution against flash riots and in the furtherance of inmate rehabilitation." Brief for Appellants 22. But they do not suggest how the magnification of grievances or undue complaining, which presumably occur in outgoing letters, could possibly lead to flash riots, nor do they specify what contribution the suppression of complaints makes to the rehabilitation of criminals. And, appellants defend the ban against "inflammatory political, racial, or religious or other views" on the ground that "[s]uch matter clearly presents a danger to prison security * * *." Brief for Appellants 21. The regulation, however, is not narrowly drawn to reach only material that might be thought to encourage violence nor is its application limited to incoming letters. In short, the Department's regulations authorized censorship of prisoner mail far broader than any legitimate interest of penal administration demands and were properly found invalid by the District Court.

D

We also agree with the District Court that the decision to censor or withhold delivery of a particular letter must be accompanied by minimum procedural safeguards. The interests of prisoners and their correspondents in uncensored communication by letter, grounded as it is in the First Amendment, is plainly a "liberty" interest within the meaning of the Fourteenth Amendment even though qualified of necessity by the circumstance of imprisonment. As such, it is protected from arbitrary governmental invasion. See Board of Regents v. Roth, 408 U.S. 564 (1972); Perry v. Sindermann, 408 U.S. 593 (1972). The District Court required that an inmate be notified of the rejection of a letter written by or addressed to him, that the author of that letter be given a reasonable opportunity to protest that decision, and that complaints be referred to a prison official other than the person who originally disapproved the correspondence. These requirements do not appear to be unduly burdensome, nor do appellants so contend. Accordingly, we affirm the judgment of the District Court with respect to the Department's regulations relating to prisoner mail.

WOLFF v. MCDONNELL
418 U.S. 539, 94 S. Ct. 2963, 41 L. Ed. 2d 65 (1987)

MR. JUSTICE WHITE delivered the opinion of the Court.

❋ ❋ ❋

VII

The issue of the extent to which prison authorities can open and inspect incoming mail from attorneys to inmates, has been considerably narrowed in the course of this litigation. The prison regulation under challenge provided that "all incoming and outgoing mail will be read and inspected," and no exception was made for attorney-prisoner mail. The District Court held that incoming mail from attorneys might be opened if normal contraband detection techniques failed to disclose contraband, and if there was a reasonable possibility that contraband would be included in the mail. It further held that if an incoming letter was marked "privileged," thus identifying it as from an attorney, the letter could not be opened except in the presence of the inmate. Prison authorities were not to read the mail from attorneys. The Court of Appeals affirmed the District Court order but placed additional restrictions on prison authorities. If there was doubt that a letter was actually from an attorney, "a simple telephone call should be enough to settle the matter," 483 F.2d at 1067, the court thus implying that officials might have to go beyond the face of the envelope, and the "privileged," label in ascertaining what kind of communication was involved. The court further stated that "the danger that a letter from an attorney, an officer of the court, will contain contraband is ordinarily too remote and too speculative to justify the [petitioners'] regulation permitting opening and inspection of all legal mail." While methods to detect contraband could be employed, a letter was to be opened only "in the appropriate circumstances" in the presence of the inmate.

The State now concedes that it cannot open and *read* mail from attorneys to inmates, but contends that it may open all letters from attorneys as long as it is done in the presence of the prisoners. The narrow issue thus presented is whether letters determined or found to be from attorneys may be opened by prison authorities in the presence of the inmate or whether such mail must be delivered unopened if normal detection techniques fail to indicate contraband.

Respondent asserts that his First, Sixth, and Fourteenth Amendment rights are infringed, under a procedure whereby the State may open mail from his attorney, even though in his presence and even though it may not be read. To begin with, the constitutional status of the rights asserted, as applied in this situation, is far from clear. While First Amendment rights of correspondents with prisoners may protect against the censoring of inmate mail, when not necessary to protect legitimate governmental interests, see Procunier v. Martinez, 416 U.S. 396, 71 Ohio Op.2d 139 (1974), this Court has not yet recognized First Amendment rights of prisoners in the context, cf. Cruz v. Beto, *supra*, Cooper v. Pate, *supra*. Furthermore, freedom from censorship is not equivalent to freedom from inspection or perusal. As to the Sixth Amendment, its reach is only to protect the attorney-client relationship from intrusion in the criminal setting, see Black v. United States, 385 U.S. 26 (1966); O'Brien v. United States, 386 U.S. 345 (1967); see also Coplon v. United States, 89 U.S.App. D.C. 103, 191 F.2d 749 (1951), while the claim here would insulate all mail from inspection, whether related to civil or criminal matters. Finally, the Fourteenth Amendment Due Process claim based on access to the courts, *Ex parte* Hill, *supra*, Johnson v. Avery, *supra*, Younger v. Gilmore, *supra*, has not been extended by this Court to apply further than protecting the ability of an inmate to prepare a petition or complaint. Moreover, even if one were to accept the argument that inspection of incoming mail from an attorney placed an obstacle to access to the court, it is far from clear that this burden is a substantial one. We need not decide, however, which, if any, of the asserted rights are operative here, for the question is whether, assuming some constitutional right is implicated, it is infringed by the procedure now found acceptable by the State.

In our view, the approach of the Court of Appeals is unworkable and none of the above rights is infringed by the procedures the state now accepts. If prison officials had to check in each case whether a communication was from an attorney, before opening it for inspection, a near impossible task of administration would be imposed. We think it entirely appropriate that the State require any such communications to be specially marked as originating from an attorney, with his name and address being given, if they are to receive special treatment. It would also certainly be permissible that prison authorities require that a lawyer desiring to correspond with a prisoner, *first* identify himself and his client to the prison officials, to assure the letters marked privileged are actually from members of the bar. As to the ability to open the mail in the presence of inmates, this could in no way constitute censorship, since the mail would not be read. Neither could it chill such communications since the inmate's presence insures that prison officials will not read the mail. The possibility that contraband will be enclosed in letters, even those from apparent attorneys, surely warrants prison officials in opening the letters. We disagree with the Court of Appeals that this should only be done in "appropriate circumstances." Since a flexible test, besides being unworkable, serves no arguable purpose in protecting any of the possible constitutional rights enumerated by respondent, we think the State, by acceding to a rule whereby the inmate is present when mail from attorneys is inspected, has done all, and perhaps even more, than the Constitution requires.

TURNER v. SAFLEY

482 U.S. 78, 107 S.Ct. 2254, 96 L. Ed. 2d 65 (1987)

[Citations and Footnotes Omitted]

JUSTICE O'CONNOR delivered the opinion of the Court.

This case requires us to determine the constitutionality of regulations promulgated by the Missouri Division of Corrections relating to *** inmate-to-inmate correspondence. The Court of Appeals for the Eighth Circuit, applying a strict scrutiny analysis, concluded that the regulations violate respondents' constitutional rights. We hold that a lesser standard of scrutiny is appropriate in determining the constitutionality of the prison rules. Applying that standard, we uphold the validity of the correspondence regulation....

I

Respondents brought this class action for injunctive relief and damages in the United States District Court for the Western District of Missouri. The regulations challenged in the complaint were in effect at all prisons within the jurisdiction of the Division of Corrections. This litigation focused, however, on practices at the Renz Correctional Institution (Renz), located in Cedar City, Missouri. The Renz prison population includes both male and female prisoners of varying security levels. Most of the female prisoners at Renz are classified as medium or maximum security inmates, while most of the male prisoners are classified as minimum security offenders. Renz is used on occasion to provide protective custody for inmates from other prisons in the Missouri system. The facility originally was built as a minimum security prison farm, and it still has a minimum security perimeter without guard towers or walls.

***

The first of the challenged regulations relates to correspondence between inmates at different institutions. It permits such correspondence "with immediate family members who are inmates in other correctional institutions," and it permits correspondence between inmates "concerning legal matters." Other correspondence between inmates, however, is permitted only if "the classification/treatment team of each inmate deems it in the best interest of the parties involved." Trial testimony indicated that as a matter of practice, the determination whether to permit inmates to correspond was based on team members' familiarity with the progress reports, conduct violations, and psychological reports in the inmates' files rather than on individual review of each piece of mail. At Renz, the District Court found that the rule "as practiced is that inmates may not write non-family inmates."

The District Court issued a memorandum opinion and order finding ... the correspondence ... regulations unconstitutional. The court, relying on *Procunier v. Martinez*, applied a strict scrutiny standard. The correspondence regulation also was unnecessarily broad, the court concluded, because prison officials could effectively cope with the security problems raised by inmate-to-inmate correspondence through less restrictive means, such as scanning the mail of potentially troublesome inmates. The District Court also held that the correspondence regulation had been applied in an arbitrary and capricious manner.

***

III

***

A

*** (T)he Missouri correspondence provision was promulgated primarily for security reasons. Prison officials testified that mail between institutions can be used to communicate escape plans and to arrange assaults and other violent acts. Witnesses stated that the Missouri Division of Corrections had a growing problem with prison gangs, and that restricting communications among gang members, both by transferring gang members to different institutions and by restricting their correspondence, was an important element in combating this problem. Officials also testified that the use of Renz as a facility to provide protective custody for certain inmates could be compromised by permitting correspondence between inmates at Renz and inmates at other correctional institutions.

The prohibition on correspondence between institutions is logically connected to these legitimate security concerns. Undoubtedly, communication with other felons is a potential spur to criminal behavior: this sort of contact frequently is prohibited even after an inmate has been released on parole. In Missouri prisons, the danger of such coordinated criminal activity is exacerbated by the presence of prison gangs. The Missouri policy of separating and isolating gang members—a strategy that has been frequently used to control gang activity,—logically is furthered by the restriction on prisoner-to-prisoner correspondence. Moreover, the correspondence regulation does not deprive prisoners of all means of expression. Rather, it bars communication only with a limited class of other people with whom prison officials have particular cause to be concerned—inmates at other institutions within the Missouri prison system.

*** Prison officials have stated that in their expert opinion, correspondence between prison institutions facilitates the development of informal organizations that threaten the core functions of prison administration, maintaining safety and internal security. As a result, the correspondence rights asserted by respondents, like the organizational activities at issue in *Jones v. North Carolina Prisoners' Union* can be exercised only at the cost of significantly less liberty and safety for everyone else, guards and other prisoners alike. Indeed, the potential "ripple effect" is even broader here than in Jones, because exercise of the right affects the inmates and staff of more than one institution. Where exercise of a right requires this kind of tradeoff, we think that the choice made by corrections officials—which is, after all, a judgment "peculiarly within [their] province and professional expertise," should not be lightly set aside by the courts.

Finally, there are no obvious, easy alternatives to the policy adopted by petitioners. Other well-run prison systems, including the Federal Bureau of Prisons, have concluded that substantially similar restrictions on inmate correspondence were necessary to protect institutional order and security. As petitioners have shown, the only alternative proffered by the claimant prisoners, the monitoring of inmate correspondence, clearly would impose more than a de minimis cost on the pursuit of legitimate corrections goals. Prison officials testified that it would be impossible to read every piece of inmate-to-inmate correspondence, and consequently there would be an appreciable risk of missing dangerous messages. In any event, prisoners could easily write in jargon or codes to prevent detection of their real messages. The risk of missing dangerous communications, taken together with the sheer burden on staff resources required to conduct item-by-item censorship, supports the judgment of prison officials that this alternative is not an adequate alternative to restricting correspondence.

The prohibition on correspondence is reasonably related to valid corrections goals. The rule is content neutral, it logically advances the goals of institutional security and safety identified by Missouri prison officials, and it is not an exaggerated response to those objectives. On that basis, we conclude that the regulation does not unconstitutionally abridge the First Amendment rights of prison inmates.

THORNBURGH v. ABBOTT

___ U.S. ___, 109 S.Ct. 1874, 104 S. Ct. 459 (1989)

[Citations and Footnotes Omitted]

JUSTICE BLACKMUN delivered the opinion of the Court.

I

Regulations promulgated by the Federal Bureau of Prisons broadly permit federal prisoners to receive publications from the "outside," but authorize prison officials to reject incoming publications found to be detrimental to institutional security. For 15 years, respondents, a class of inmates and certain publishers, have claimed that these regulations violate their First Amendment rights under the standard of review enunciated in *Procunier v. Martinez*. They mount a facial challenge to the regulations as well as a challenge to the regulations as applied to 46 specific publications excluded by the Bureau.

After a 10-day bench trial, the District Court refrained from adopting the *Martinez* standard. Instead, it favored an approach more deferential to the judgment of prison authorities, and upheld the regulations without addressing the propriety of the 46 specific exclusions. The Court of Appeals, on the other hand, utilized the *Martinez* standard, found the regulations wanting, and remanded the case to the District Court for an individualized determination of the constitutionality of the 46 exclusions.

***

We now hold that the District Court correctly anticipated that the proper inquiry in this case is whether the regulations are "reasonably related to legitimate penological interests," and we conclude that under this standard the regulations are facially valid. We therefore disagree with the Court of Appeals on the issue of facial validity, but we agree with that court's remand of the case to the District Court for a determination of the validity of the regulations as applied to each of the 46 publications.

II

We are concerned primarily with the regulations set forth at 28 C.F.R. §§ 540.70 and 540.71 (1988), first promulgated in 1979. These generally permit an inmate to subscribe to or to receive a publication without prior approval, but authorize the warden to reject a publication in certain circumstances. The warden may reject it "only if it is determined detrimental to the security, good order, or discipline of the institution or if it might facilitate criminal activity." The warden, however, may not reject a publication "solely because its content is religious, philosophical, political, social or sexual, or because its content is unpopular or repugnant." The regulations contain a nonexhaustive list of criteria which may support rejection of a publication. The warden is prohibited from establishing an excluded list of publications: each issue of a subscription publication is to be reviewed separately. The regulatory criteria for rejecting publications have been supplemented by Program Statement No. 5266.5, which provides further guidance on the subject of sexually explicit material.

The regulations provide procedural safeguards for both the recipient and the sender. The warden may designate staff to screen and, where appropriate, to approve incoming publications, but only the Warden may reject a publication. The warden must advise the inmate promptly in writing of the reasons for the rejection, and must provide the publisher or sender with a copy of the rejection letter. The notice must refer to "the specific article(s) or material(s) considered objectionable." The publisher or sender may obtain an independent review of the warden's rejection decision by a timely writing to the Regional Director of the Bureau. An inmate may appeal through the Bureau's Administrative Remedy Procedure. The warden is instructed to permit the inmate to review the rejected material for the purpose of filing an appeal "unless such review may provide the inmate with information of a nature which is deemed to pose a threat or detriment to the security, good order or discipline of the institution or to encourage or instruct in criminal activity."

III

There is little doubt that the kind of censorship just described would raise grave First Amendment concerns outside the prison context. It is equally certain that "[p]rison walls do not form a barrier separating prison inmates from the protections of the Constitution," nor do they bar free citizens from exercising their own constitutional rights by reaching out to those on the "inside." We have recognized, however, that these rights must be exercised with due regard for the "inordinately difficult undertaking that is modern prison administration.

In particular, we have been sensitive to the delicate balance that prison administrators must strike between the order and security of the internal prison environment and the legitimate demands of those on the "outside" who seek to enter that environment, in person or through the written word. Many categories of noninmates seek access to prisons. Access is essential to lawyers and legal assistants representing prisoner clients, to journalists seeking information about prison conditions, and to families and friends of prisoners who seek to sustain relationships with them. All these claims to prison access undoubtedly are legitimate; yet prison officials may well conclude that certain proposed interactions, though seemingly innocuous to laymen, have potentially significant implications for the order and security of the prison. Acknowledging the expertise of these officials and that the judiciary is "ill equipped" to deal with the difficult and delicate problems of prison management, this Court has afforded considerable deference to the determinations of prison administrators who, in the interest of security, regulate the relations between prisoners and the outside world.

In this case, there is no question that publishers who wish to communicate with those who, through subscription, willingly seek their point of view have a legitimate First Amendment interest in access to prisoners. The question here, as it has been in our previous First Amendment cases in this area, is what standard of review this Court should apply to prison regulations limiting that access.

Martinez was our first significant decision regarding First Amendment rights in the prison context. There, the Court struck down California regulations concerning personal correspondence between inmates and noninmates, regulations that provided for censorship of letters that "unduly complain," "magnify grievances," or "expres[s] inflammatory political, racial, religious or other views or beliefs." We reviewed these regulations under the following standard: "First, the regulation or practice in question must further an important or substantial governmental interest unrelated to the suppression of expression. Prison officials ... must show that a regulation authorizing mail censorship furthers one or more of the substantial governmental interests of security, order, and rehabilitation. Second, the limitation of First

Amendment freedoms must be no greater than is necessary or essential to the protection of the particular governmental interest involved. Thus a restriction on inmate correspondence that furthers an important or substantial interest of penal administration will nevertheless be invalid if its sweep is unnecessarily broad."

It is clear from this language, however, that we did not deprive prison officials of the degree of discretion necessary to vindicate "the particular governmental interest involved." Accordingly, we said: "Some latitude in anticipating the probable consequences of allowing certain speech in a prison environment is essential to the proper discharge of an administrator's duty. But any regulation or practice that restricts inmate correspondence must be generally necessary to protect one or more ... legitimate governmental interests."

The Court's subsequent decisions regarding First Amendment rights in the prison context, however, laid down a different standard of review from that articulated in *Martinez*. As recently explained in Turner, these later revisions, which we characterized as involving "prisoners' rights," adopted a standard of review that focuses on the reasonableness of prison regulations: the relevant inquiry is whether the actions of prison officials were "reasonably related to legitimate penological interests." The Court ruled that "such a standard is necessary if 'prison administrators ... and not the courts, [are] to made the difficult judgments concerning institutional operations.'" The Court set forth in *Turner* the development of this reasonableness standard in the respective decisions in *Pell* and *Jones* and in *Block v. Rutherford*, and we need not repeat that discussion here.

The Court's decision to apply a reasonableness standard in these cases rather than *Martinez*' less deferential approach stemmed from its concern that language in *Martinez* might be too readily understood as establishing a standard of "strict" or "heightened" scrutiny, and that such a strict standard simply was not appropriate for consideration of regulations that are centrally concerned with the maintenance of order and security within prisons. Specifically, the Court declined to apply the *Martinez* standard in "prisoners' rights" cases because, as was noted in *Turner*, *Martinez* could be (and has been) read to require a strict "least restrictive alternative" analysis, without sufficient sensitivity to the need for discretion in meeting legitimate prison needs. The Court expressed concern that "every administrative judgment would be subject to the possibility that some court somewhere would conclude that it had a less restrictive way of solving the problem at hand," and rejected the costs of a "least restrictive alternative" rule as too high.

Pell involved the right of representatives of the news media to conduct interviews in the prisons in order to inform the public about prison conditions. The asserted right at issue in *Jones* was the right of a prisoners' union to send its literature into the prison. In *Wolfish*, publishers sought to send hardback books into the prison. In all these cases, regulations worked a "consequential restriction on the ... rights of those who are not prisoners." But the Court in *Turner* observed: "In none of these ... cases did the Court apply a standard of heightened scrutiny, but instead inquired whether a prison regulation that burdens fundamental rights is 'reasonably related' to legitimate penological objectives, or whether it represents an 'exaggerated response' to those concerns." We do not believe that *Martinez* should, or need, be read as subjecting the decisions of prison officials to a strict "least restrictive means" test. As noted, *Martinez* required no more than that a challenged regulation be "generally necessary" to a legitimate governmental interest. Certainly, *Martinez* required a close fit between the challenged regulation and the interest it purported to serve. But a careful reading of *Martinez* suggests that our rejection of the regulation at issue resulted not from a least restrictive means requirement, but from our recognition that the regulated activity centrally at issue in that case—outgoing personal correspondence from prisoners—did not, by its very nature, pose a serious threat to prison order and security." We pointed out in *Martinez* that outgoing correspondence that magnifies grievances or contains inflammatory racial views cannot reasonably be expected to present a danger to the community inside the prison. In addition, the implications for security are far more predictable. Dangerous outgoing correspondence is more likely to fall within readily identifiable categories: examples noted in *Martinez* include escape plans, plans relating to ongoing criminal activity, and threats of blackmail or extortion. Although we were careful in *Martinez* not to limit unduly the discretion of prison officials to reject even outgoing letters, we concluded that the regulations at issue were broader than "generally necessary" to protect the interests at stake.

In light of these considerations, it is understandable that the Court in *Martinez* concluded that the regulations there at issue swept too broadly. Where, as in *Martinez*, the nature of the asserted governmental interest is such as to require a lesser degree of case-by-case discretion, a closer fit between the regulation and the purpose it serves may safely be required. Categorically different considerations—considerations far more typical of the problems of prison administration—apply to the case presently before this Court.

We deal here with incoming publications, material requested by an individual inmate but targeted to a general audience. Once in the prison, material of this kind reasonably may be expected to circulate among prisoners, with the concomitant potential for coordinated disruptive conduct. Furthermore, prisoners may observe particular material in the possession of a fellow prisoner, draw inferences

about their fellow's beliefs, sexual orientation, or gang affiliations from that material, and cause disorder by acting accordingly. As the Deputy Solicitor General noted at oral argument, "[t]he problem is not ... in the individual reading the materials in most cases. The problem is in the material getting into the prison." In the volatile prison environment, it is essential that prison officials be given broad discretion to prevent such disorder.

In *Turner*, we dealt with incoming personal correspondence from prisoners; the impact of the correspondence on the internal environment of the prison was of great concern. There, we recognized that *Martinez* was too readily understood as failing to afford prison officials sufficient discretion to protect prison security. In light of these same concerns, we now hold that regulations affecting the sending of a "publication" to a prisoner must be analyzed under the *Turner* reasonableness standard. Such regulations are "valid if [they are} reasonably related to legitimate penological interests."

Furthermore, we acknowledge today that the logic of our analyses in *Martinez* and *Turner* requires that *Martinez* be limited to regulations concerning outgoing correspondence. As we have observed, outgoing correspondence was the central focus of our opinion in *Martinez*. The implications of outgoing correspondence for prison security are of a categorically lesser magnitude than the implications of incoming materials.

Any attempt to justify a similar categorical distinction between incoming correspondence from prisoners (to which we applied a reasonableness standard in *Turner*) and incoming correspondence from nonprisoners would likely prove futile, and we do not invite it. To the extent that *Martinez* itself suggests such a distinction, we today overrule that case; the Court accomplished much of this step when it decided *Turner*.

In so doing, we recognize that it might have been possible to apply a reasonableness standard to all incoming materials without overruling *Martinez*: we instead could have made clear that *Martinez* does not uniformly require the application of a "least restrictive alternative" analysis. We choose not to go that route, however, for we prefer the express flexibility of the *Turner* reasonableness standard. We adopt the *Turner* standard in this case with confidence that, as petitioners here have asserted, "a reasonableness standard is not toothless."

IV

The Court in *Turner* identified several factors that are relevant to, and that serve to channel, the reasonableness inquiry.

The first *Turner* factor is multifold: we must determine whether the governmental objective underlying the regulations at issue is legitimate and neutral, and that the regulations are rationally related to that objective.

We agree with the District Court that this requirement has been met.

As to neutrality, "[w]e have found it important to inquire whether prison regulations restricting inmates' First Amendment rights operated in a neutral fashion, without regard to the content of the expression." The ban on all correspondence between certain classes of inmates at issue in *Turner* clearly met this "neutrality" criterion, as did the restrictions at issue in *Pell* and *Wolfish*. The issue, however, in this case is closer.

On their face, the regulations distinguish between rejection of a publication "solely because its content is religious, philosophical, political, social or sexual, or because its content is unpopular or repugnant" (prohibited) and rejection because the publication is detrimental to security (permitted). Both determinations turn, to some extent, on content. But the Court's reference to "neutrality" in *Turner* was intended to go no further than its requirement in *Martinez* that "the regulation or practice in question must further an important or substantial governmental interest unrelated to the suppression of expression." Where, as here, prison administrators withdraw distinctions between publications solely on the basis of their potential implications for prison security, the regulations are "neutral" in the technical sense in which we meant and used that term in *Turner*.

We also conclude that the broad discretion accorded prison wardens by the regulations here at issue is rationally related to security interests.

We reach this conclusion for two reasons. The first has to do with the kind of security risk presented by incoming publication. This has been explored above in Part III. The District Court properly found that publications can present a security threat, and that a more closely tailored standard "could result in admission of publications which, even if they did not lead directly to violence, would exacerbate tensions and lead indirectly to disorder." Where the regulations at issue concern the entry of materials into the prison, We agree with the District Court that a regulation which gives prison authorities broad discretion is appropriate.

Second, we are comforted by the individualized nature of the determinations required by the regulation. Under the regulations, no publication may be excluded unless the warden himself makes the determination that it is "detrimental to the security, good order, or discipline of the institution or ... might facilitate criminal activity." This is the controlling standard. A publication which fits within one of the "criteria" for exclusion may be rejected, but only if it is determined to meet that standard under the conditions prevailing at the institution at the time. Indeed, the regulations expressly reject certain shortcuts that would lead to needless exclusions. We agree that it is rational for the Bureau to exclude materials that, although not necessarily "likely" to lead to violence, are determined by the warden to create an intolerable risk of disorder under the conditions

of a particular prison at a particular time.

Respondents have argued that the record does not support the conclusion that exclusions are in fact based on particular events or conditions at a particular prison; they contend that variability in enforcement of the regulations stems solely from the censors' subjective views. These contentions go to the adequacy of the regulations as applied, and will be considered on remand. A second factor the Court in *Turner* held to be "relevant in determining the reasonableness of a prison restriction ... is whether there are alternative means of exercising the right that remain open to prison inmates. As has already been made clear in *Turner* and *O'Lone*, "the right in question must be viewed sensibly and expansively. The Court in *Turner* did not require that prisoners be afforded other means of communicating with inmates at other institutions, nor did it in *O'Lone* require that there be alternative means of attending the Jumu'ah religious ceremony. Rather, it held in *Turner* that it was sufficient if other means of expression not necessarily other means of communicating with inmates in other prisons remained available, and in *O'Lone* if prisoners were permitted to participate in other Muslim religious ceremonies. As the regulations at issue in the present case permit a broad range of publications to be sent, received, and read, this factor is clearly satisfied.

The third factor to be addressed under the *Turner* analysis is the impact that accommodation of the asserted constitutional right will have on others (guards and inmates) in the prison. Here, the class of publications to be excluded is limited to those found potentially detrimental to order and security; the likelihood that such material will circulate within the prison raises the prospect of precisely the kind of "ripple effect" with which the Court in *Turner* was concerned. Where, as here, the right in question "can be exercised only at the cost of significantly less liberty and safety for everyone else, guards and other prisoners alike," the courts should defer to the "informed discretion of corrections officials."

Finally, *Turner* held that "the existence of obvious, easy alternatives may be evidence that the regulation is not reasonable, but is an 'exaggerated response' to prison concerns.... But if an inmate claimant can point to an alternative that fully accommodates the prisoner's rights at de minimis cost to valid penological interests, a court may consider that as evidence that the regulation does not satisfy the reasonable relationship standard." We agree with the District Court that these regulations, on their face, are not an "exaggerated response" to the problem at hand; no obvious, easy alternative has been established.

***

V

In sum, we hold that *Turner's* reasonableness standard is to be applied to the regulations at issue in this case, and that those regulations are facially valid under that standard. We agree with the remand for an examination of the validity of the regulations as applied to any of the 46 publications introduced at trial as to which there remains a live controversy.

The judgment of the Court of Appeals is vacated and the case is remanded for further proceedings consistent with this opinion.

JUSTICE STEVENS, with whom JUSTICE BRENNAN and JUSTICE MARSHALL join, concurring in part and dissenting in part.

An article in Labyrinth, a magazine published by the Committee for Prisoner Humanity & Justice, began as follows:

"In January 1975, William Lowe, a black prisoner at the United States Penitentiary at Terre Haute, Indiana died of asthma.... In August 1975, Joseph (Yusef) Jones, Jr., a black prisoner at the U. S. Penitentiary, Terre Haute, IN. died of asthma.

"... The prison infirmary at that time had only one respirator[,] known to be inoperative in January 1975 when William Lowe died. It was still broken in August 1975 when Joseph Jones needed it.

"On the day of his death Jones was suffering an acute asthma attack; he was gasping for breath in the stale, hot, humid air in the cell. He requested medical aid of the guards. After several hours of unheeded pleading, accompanied by complaints to the guards from fellow prisoners in the cell block, Jones became frantic. Each breath was painful; each breath brought him closer to suffocation. Finally, guards called the PA (physician's assistant) ..., who brought with him the broken respirator. Finding the equipment unusable, the PA gave Jones an injection of the tranquilizer, thorazine, to calm him. Treatment with a tranquilizer was unquestionably contraindicated by Jones' medical condition. Twenty minutes later, Jones was dead.

. . .

"Conclusion: Jones, who was convicted of bank robbery and sentenced to 10 years in prison, was in fact, sentenced to death and was murdered by neglect."

The incident described above eventually came to the attention of this Court, which allowed Jones' mother to pursue her civil rights action against prison officials. Clearly the Labyrinth article's report of inadequate medical treatment of federal prisoners raised "a matter that is both newsworthy and of great public importance." As the Court concedes, both publishers and recipients of such criticism ordinarily enjoy the fullest First Amendment protections.

Yet Labyrinth's efforts to disseminate the article to its subscribers at Marion Federal Penitentiary met government resistance. Marion officials, acting within Federal Bureau of Prisons (Bureau) regulations, returned the magazine on the ground that "the article entitled 'Medical Murder' would be detrimental to the

good order and discipline of this institution .... [T]his type of philosophy could guide inmates in this institution into situations which could cause themselves and other inmates problems with the Medical Staff." Two years after publication a Marion official testified that he believed the article had posed no threat. Nonetheless, the District Court below found the suppression of this and 45 other publications "reasonable," and thus sustained the rejections wholesale. This Court holds today that such carte blanche deference was improper and remands for case-by-case review. I agree with this aspect of the Court's decision. I cannot agree, however, with either its holding that another finding of "reasonableness" will justify censorship or its premature approval of the Bureau's regulations. These latter determinations upset precedent in a headlong rush to strip inmates of all but a vestige of free communication with the world beyond the prison gate.

I

This Court first addressed the First Amendment in the prison context in *Procunier v. Martinez*. Prior lower court treatments had varied: some courts had maintained "a hands-off posture," while others had required "demonstration of a 'compelling state interest' to justify censorship of prisoner mail." With characteristic wisdom Justice Powell, in his opinion for the Court, rejected both extremes. The difficulties of prison administration, he perceived, make the strict scrutiny that the First Amendment demands in other contexts inappropriate. Focusing not on the rights of prisoners but on the "inextricably meshed" rights of non-prisoners "who have a particularized interest in communicating with them," he wrote that an "undemanding standard of review" could not be squared with the fact "that the First Amendment liberties of free citizens are implicated in censorship of prisoner mail." Thus he chose an "intermediate" means of evaluating speech restrictions, allowing censorship if it "further[ed] an important or substantial governmental interest unrelated to the suppression of expression," and "the limitation of First Amendment freedoms [was] no greater than [was] necessary or essential." "Prison officials may not censor inmate correspondence simply to eliminate unflattering or unwelcome opinions or factually inaccurate statements," Justice Powell stressed. Censorship might be permitted, however, to ensure "the preservation of internal order and discipline, the maintenance of institutional security against escape or unauthorized entry, and the rehabilitation of the prisoners." Prison administrators did not have "to show with certainty that adverse consequences would flow from the failure to censor a particular letter," but "any regulation or practice that restricts inmate correspondence must be generally necessary to protect one or more of the legitimate governmental interests identified above."

In the 15 years since *Martinez* was decided, lower courts routinely have applied its standard to review limitations not only on correspondence between inmates and private citizens, but also on communications—such as the newsletters, magazines, and books at issue—between inmates and publishers. Carefully examining free speech rights and countervailing governmental interests, these courts approved some restrictions and invalidated others. This Court thus correctly recognizes that *Martinez*' standard of review does not deprive prison officials of the discretion necessary to perform their difficult tasks. Inexplicably, it then partially overrules *Martinez* by limiting its scope to outgoing mail; letters and publications sent to prisoners now are subject only to review for "reasonableness."

This peculiar bifurcation of the constitutional standard governing communications between inmates and outsiders is unjustified. The decision in *Martinez* was based on a distinction between prisoners' constitutional rights and the protection the First Amendment affords those who are not prisoners—not between nonprisoners who are senders and those who are receivers. As Justice Powell explained:

"Whatever the status of a prisoner's claim to uncensored correspondence with an outsider, it is plain that the latter's interest is grounded in the First Amendment's guarantee of freedom of speech. And this does not depend on whether the nonprisoner correspondent is the author or intended recipient of a particular letter, for the addressee as well as the sender of direct personal correspondence derives from the First and Fourteenth Amendments a protection against unjustified governmental interference with the intended communication.... The wife of a prison inmate who is not permitted to read all that her husband wanted to say to her has suffered an abridgement of her interest in communicating with him as plain as that which results from censorship of her letter to him." The Court today abandons *Martinez'* fundamental premise. In my opinion its suggestion that three later opinions applying reasonableness standards warrant this departure, is disingenuous. Those cases did involve communications between inmates and outsiders; however, as I shall demonstrate, their legal and factual foundations differed critically from those in *Martinez* or in this case.

In *Pell v. Procunier*, inmates and reporters challenged regulations prohibiting face-to-face media interviews with specific prisoners. The infringement on prisoners' rights, the Court held, was reasonable because prisoners could write letters to the media—a means of communication less disruptive than the physical entry of reporters into the prison. The reporters' assertion of a special right of access could not prevail, the Court explained, because the First Amendment does not give the media greater access to public events or institutions—including prisons—than it

gives ordinary citizens. *Pell* in no way diluted the basic distinction articulated in *Martinez*.

Inmates in *Jones v. North Carolina Prisoners' Union*, had maintained that First Amendment associational rights protected their efforts to form a union. The Court concluded that the administrators' grounds for preventing union organizing within the prison an activity occurring largely among inmates—were reasonable. It also approved the officials' refusal to deliver bulk packets of union literature to specific inmates for distribution to others. Applying Equal Protection Clause as well as First Amendment standards, the Court held that the restriction was reasonable because it was limited in scope and because the union retained "other avenues of outside informational flow ...."

In the third case, *Bell v. Wolfish*, the Court upheld a regulation that allowed only publishers, bookstores, and book clubs to mail hardbound books to pretrial detainees. Hardbacks might serve as containers for contraband, jail administrators argued. Since the risk of improper use by publishers and similar sources was low, the jail delivered books from them but not from other outsiders. The Court found this explanation acceptable and held that the rule did not violate the detainees' First Amendment rights. Although the Court did not expressly address the rights of nonprisoners, the fact that softcover publications were delivered without restriction, minimized the abridgment of outsiders' rights. The approval in Wolfish of greater protection for publishers than for individual citizens reinforces Martinez' view that the First Amendment rights of nonprisoners must be carefully weighed, and undermines the Court's approach today.

Most recently, Turner v. Safley, confirmed the vitality of Martinez for evaluating encroachments on the First Amendment rights of nonprisoners. The Court relied on the three interim "prisoners' rights" cases to establish a reasonableness standard for reviewing inmate-to-inmate correspondence. But in its unanimous invalidation of a restriction on inmate marriages, the Court acknowledged that "because the regulation may entail a 'consequential restriction on the [constitutional] rights of those who are not prisoners,'" Martinez might posit the correct level of review. It did not "reach this question, however, because even under the reasonable relationship test, the marriage regulation does not withstand scrutiny."

The Turner opinion cited and quoted from Martinez more than 20 times; not once did it disapprove Martinez' holding, its standard, or its recognition of a special interest in protecting the First Amendment rights of those who are not prisoners. Notwithstanding, today the Court abandons the premise on which Martinez was grounded. This casual discarding of " 'the secure foundation' " of considered precedent ill serves the orderly development of the law.

II

In lieu of Martinez' rationale, which properly takes into consideration the effects that prison regulations have on the First Amendment rights of nonprisoners, the Court applies a manipulable "reasonableness" standard to a set of regulations that too easily may be interpreted to authorize arbitrary rejections of literature addressed to inmates. As I pointed out in my partial dissent in Turner, an "open-ended 'reasonableness' standard makes it much too easy to uphold restrictions on prisoners' First Amendment rights on the basis of administrative concerns and speculation about possible security risks rather than on the basis of evidence that the restrictions are needed to further an important governmental interest."

To be sure, courts must give prison administrators some berth to combat the "Herculean obstacles" blocking their efforts to maintain security and prevent escapes or other criminal conduct, and I do not object to those regulations clearly targeted at such interests. Nevertheless, I agree with the Court of Appeals that provisions allowing prison officials to reject a publication if they find its contents are "detrimental" to "security, good order, or discipline" or "might facilitate criminal activity" are impermissibly ambiguous. The term "detrimental" invites so many interpretations that it scarcely checks administrators' actions. Similarly, "might facilitate"—in contrast with "encourage" or "advocate"—so attenuates the causal connection between expression and proscribed conduct that the warden has virtually free rein to censor incoming publications.

Despite this vagueness, the Court accepts petitioners' assertion that they need "broad discretion" to prevent internal disorder, and thus holds that all the regulations are facially valid. This premature leap of faith creates a presumption that rejections pursuant to these regulations are "reasonable"—a presumption that makes likely far less judicial protection of publishers' rights than I believe the First Amendment requires. *** I am concerned that the Court today too readily "substitute[s] the rhetoric of judicial deference for meaningful scrutiny of constitutional claims in the prison setting."

The feeble protection provided by a "reasonableness" standard applied within the framework of these regulations is apparent in this record. Like the Labyrinth issue, many of the 46 rejected publications criticized prison conditions or otherwise presented viewpoints that prison administrators likely would not welcome. Testimony by one mail clerk and the rote explanations for decisions suggest that rejections were based on personal prejudices or categorical assumptions rather than individual assessments of risk. These circumstances belie the Court's interpretation of these regulations as "content-neutral" and its assertion that rejection decisions are made individually. Some of the rejected publications may represent the sole medium for

conveying and receiving a particular unconventional message; thus it is irrelevant that the regulations permit many other publications to be delivered to prisoners. No evidence supports the Court's assumption that, unlike personal letters, these publications will circulate within the prison and cause ripples of disruption. Nor is there any evidence that an incoming publication ever caused a disciplinary or security problem; indeed, some of the rejected publications were delivered to inmates in other prisons without incident. In sum, the record convinces me that under either the *Martinez* standard or the more deferential "reasonableness" standard these regulations are an impermissibly exaggerated response to security concerns.

III

If a prison official deems part of a publication's content—even just one page of a book—to present an intolerable security risk, the Bureau's regulations authorize the official to return the entire issue to the publisher. In their challenge to this all-or-nothing rule, respondents argue that First Amendment interests easily could be accommodated if administrators omitted the objectionable material and forwarded the rest of the publication to the inmate. The District Court, however, found that "defendant's fears" that "such censorship would create more discontent than the current practice" were "reasonable founded." To the contrary, the Court of Appeals applied the *Martinez* standard and held that "rejection of the balance is not 'generally necessary' to protect the legitimate government interest involved in the portion properly rejected."

In this Court petitioners argue that on remand the Court of Appeals should conduct "a detailed analysis of the evidence in this case" to determine if the all-or-nothing rule is "reasonable." "The validity of that policy," they continue, "will depend, among other things, on the security and administrative justifications for that policy, the availability of alternative courses of action, and the costs and risks associated with employing those alternatives." It is remarkable that after 16 years of litigation petitioners have failed to develop an argument that tells us anything about the assumed security or administrative justification for this rule. Even more remarkable is the Court's conclusion that since it does not apply the *Martinez* standard, it need not examine the appropriateness of the District Court's finding that the rule was reasonable. A review of the record reveals that the Court thus defers to "findings" of a security threat that even prison officials admitted to be nonexistent.

There is no evidence that delivery of only part of a publication would endanger prison security.

Rather, the primary justification advanced for the all-or-nothing rule was administrative convenience. The Bureau has objected that a contrary rule "would mean defacing the material and laboriously going over each article in each publication ..." But general speculation that some administrative burden might ensue should not be sufficient to justify a meat-ax abridgment of the First Amendment rights of either a free citizen or a prison inmate. It is difficult even to imagine such a burden in this instance: if, as the regulations' text seems to require, prison officials actually read an article before rejecting it, the incremental burden associated with clipping out the offending matter could not be constitutional significance. The Bureau's administrative convenience justification thus is insufficient as a matter of law under either the *Martinez* standard or a "reasonableness" standard. The District Court's contradictory finding simply highlights the likelihood that an attitude of broad judicial deference, coupled with a "reasonableness" standard, will provide inadequate protection for the rights at stake.

For these reasons, I would affirm the judgment of the Court of Appeals.

Cases relating to **Chapter 5**

ISOLATED CONFINEMENT—"THE HOLE"

JORDAN v. FITZHARRIS
257 F.Supp. 674 (N.D. Cal. 1966)

MEMORANDUM OPINION AND ORDER

GEORGE B. HARRIS, Chief Judge.

This is a civil rights action in which the plaintiff claims to have been unconstitutionally subjected to cruel and unusual punishment. The action is brought under 42 U.S.C.A. §§ 1981, 1983, 1985(3) and 1986; the Court's jurisdiction is had under 28 U.S.C.A. §§ 1331 and 1343. Plaintiff prays for injunctive and monetary relief.

Plaintiff Robert Charles Jordan, Jr., is an inmate of the California Correctional Training Facility at Soledad. Named as defendants are the State of California, the Correctional Training Facility at Soledad, the Director of Corrections of the State of Califor-

nia, the Superintendent of the facility at Soledad, and various subordinate officials at Soledad.

The action was initially begun by the plaintiff acting on his own behalf and proceeding in *forma pauperis.* Thereafter, the court appointed [counsel] to represent Mr. Jordan in all further proceedings. . . .

Plaintiff's cruel and unusual punishment contention arises out of his confinement from July 9 until July 20, 1965, in a so-called "strip cell" at Soledad. The strip cells (6 in number) form part of the isolation section of the prison's maximum-security Adjustment Center. Each strip cell measures approximately 6'-0" by 8'-4". The side and rear walls are solid concrete, as is the floor. The front wall is constructed of steel bars covered by a metal screen. Access is gained through a sliding barred door. A second front wall is located 2'-10" from the barred wall, thus forming a kind of vestibule between the cell proper and the corridor. Set into this otherwise solid wall are a 24" x 36" barred and screened window opening and a hinged steel door with a 12" x 18" barred and screened window opening. The window openings in this outer wall and outer door can be closed off by means of a metal flap which is hinged at the bottom of each window and can be swung up and latched at the top of the window opening. Immediately outside of this outer wall is an 8'-7½" wide corridor which runs past the six strip cells, through a barred barrier with a locked door, past the eighteen isolation cells, through a "sally port" (a small rectangular, barred enclosure having two locked doors) and into another corridor where it terminates. In this latter corridor is located the officers' area. Thus the strip cells are placed at the opposite end of the wing from the officers' area and an officer must pass through three locked doors to get from his area to the strip cells. Across the corridor from the strip cells is the outer wall of the wing. This wall has barred windows which formerly contained glass but now are partially covered by sheet metal.

The interiors of the strip cells are entirely devoid of furnishings except as follows: Four of the strip cells have an ordinary commode toilet encased in concrete. The remaining two strip cells have a so-called "Ori-

ental" toilet, i. e., a hole in the floor.[3] None of the toilets can be flushed by the occupant of the cell, but must be flushed from outside the cell by an officer or an inmate porter. The flushing mechanism is located in a tunnel immediately behind the row of strip cells.

Heat and ventilation are supplied to the strip cells through two ducts located high on the rear walls of the cells. The cells have no interior source of light. When the flaps on the outer wall are closed the cells are totally dark except for such light as may seep in through the cracks around the flaps and the outer door.

The strip cells, as described above, are the most secure and have the least facilities of any cells in the facility at Soledad. They represent the most extreme form of confinement the institution has to offer.

Plaintiff testified, and the records indicate, that he was placed in a strip cell on the evening of Friday, July 9, 1965. He remained continuously in the cell until the morning of Tuesday, July 20, 1965, except for a brief period on Tuesday, July 13, when he was removed from the cell, taken to a hearing before the Disciplinary Committee, and returned to the cell.

The amended complaint filed by Jordan, through his appointed counsel, particularized his grievances and charged substantially as follows:

On or about July 9, 1965, plaintiff was placed in a special punishment unit at the Correctional Training Facility, known as a "strip cell"

---

[3] The cell in which plaintiff was confined during the period of time which forms the basis of this action was one of the four strip cells having a commode toilet.

(hereinafter referred to as "strip cell"). Plaintiff was continuously confined in solitary confinement in said strip cell for twelve consecutive days.

During plaintiff's confinement in said strip cell, plaintiff was forced to remain in said strip cell with said flaps and door of the second wall closed. As a result, plaintiff was deprived of light and ventilation for twelve days, except that twice a day the door of the second wall was opened for approximately fifteen minutes.

The interior of said strip cell is without any facilities, except that there is a raised concrete platform at the rear of the cell containing a hole to receive bodily wastes. There is no mechanism within the cell for "flushing" bodily wastes from this hole. "Flushing" is controlled by personnel of the Correctional Training Facility from the exterior of said strip cell. The hole was only "flushed" at approximately 8:30 a. m. and 9:00 p. m. on some of the twelve days plaintiff was confined in said strip cell.

During plaintiff's confinement in said strip cell, the strip cell was never cleaned. As a result of the continuous state of filth to which plaintiff was subjected, plaintiff was often nauseous and vomited, and the vomit was never cleaned from the plaintiff's cell. When plaintiff was first brought to the strip cell, the floor and walls of the strip cell were covered with the bodily wastes of previous inhabitants of the strip cell. Plaintiff is informed and believes and on that basis alleges that said strip cell had not been cleaned for at least thirty days before plaintiff was confined therein.

Plaintiff was forced to remain in said strip cell for twelve days without any means of cleaning his hands, body or teeth. No means was provided which could enable plaintiff to clean any part of his body at any time. Plaintiff was forced to handle and eat his food without even the semblance of cleanliness or any provision for sanitary conditions.

For the first eight days of plaintiff's confinement in said strip cell, plaintiff was not permitted clothing of any nature and was forced to remain in said strip cell absolutely naked. Thereafter, plaintiff was given a pair of rough overalls only.

Plaintiff was forced to remain in said strip cell with no place to sleep but upon the cold concrete floor of the strip cell, except that a stiff canvas mat approximately 4½ feet by 5½ feet was provided. Said mat was so stiff that it could not be folded to cover plaintiff without such conscious exertion by plaintiff that sleep was impossible. Plaintiff is six feet and one inch tall and could not be adequately covered by said stiff canvas mat even when holding said mat over himself. The strip cell was not heated during the time that plaintiff was forced to remain there.

Plaintiff is informed and believes and on that basis alleges that plaintiff has been and may be subjected to confinement in said strip cell without the authorization of the Superintendent, the Deputy Superintendent, the Associate Superintendent, or anyone of comparable administrative rank; that lower-rank personnel of the Correctional Training Facility purport to have exercised and intend to exercise in the future broad discretion in confining plaintiff in said strip cell; that said lower-rank personnel purport to have the discretion to confine plaintiff in said strip cell for 60 consecutive days; and that there are no standards for the proper exercise of such discretion.

On many occasions prior to July 9, 1965, plaintiff has been confined in said strip cell, plaintiff is continually living under the threat of repeated confinement in said strip cell, and plaintiff is constantly subject to confinement in said strip cell pursuant to purported disciplinary procedures as they presently exist and will continue to exist unless enjoined by this Court.

Plaintiff has been denied adequate medical care prior to, during, and subsequent to said confinement in said strip cell, despite repeated oral and written requests for same made in good faith by or on behalf of plaintiff.

Prior to and subsequent to said confinement in said strip cell, plaintiff has been forced to endure confinement in "O Wing" of the Correctional Training Facility without adequate protection from the raw outdoor elements, in that plaintiff's cell front offers no protection from the elements, being only bars, there are no window panes for the large window openings in the outside wall of the corridor which is directly outside plaintiff's cell, and there is insufficient artificial heat, if any, to combat the outdoor climatic conditions which prevail in plaintiff's cell.

Jordan, called as a witness on his own behalf, gave testimony which fortified the foregoing allegations. He testified categorically concerning the practices engaged in by the defendants. He was subjected to a lengthy and searching cross-examination by the two attorneys representing the defendants. His testimony is clear and convincing.

More particularly, Jordan discharged the burden cast upon him with respect to the period of time he was confined in the strip cell; the fact that he was deprived of clothing for the period of time, at least for seven days; that he was required to sleep on a strong blanket ill adapted to the uses for which it was put; that the flaps were closed practically all of the time thus depriving him of both light and adequate ventilation in the cell; that the elements of cleanliness were likewise deprived him, to-wit, water, soap, towel, tooth brush, toothpaste, implements for cleaning the cell, and shower.

It is evident from the foregoing narrative of Jordan's testimony that he was required to eat the meager prison fare in the stench and filth that surrounded him, together with the accompanying odors that ordinarily permeated the cell. Absent the ordinary means of cleansing his hands preparatory to eating, it was suggested by the prison consulting psychiatrist, Dr. Hack, that he might very well use toilet paper for this purpose plus his small ration of water, being two cups a day.

Regarding medical care: Jordan requested from time to time medical assistance through the medical officer, Dr. Kunkel. As evidence of the limited medical care provided, the official records demonstrate that Dr. Kunkel came into the wing where the strip cells are located and spent eight minutes on one occasion and ten minutes on another occasion, thus servicing the one hundred and eight inmates.[5]

. . . .

It is to be observed that the inmates [testifying for plaintiff] and their testimony were subjected to vigorous and searching cross-examination. Notwithstanding such scrutiny, the narratives contain the essentials of truth and are credible and convincing.

. . . .

The trial itself, represented an intensely human drama of some precedential value. It may be noted that this is the first occasion that the United States District Court in this Circuit has undertaken to inquire into the procedures and practices of a State penal institution in a proceeding of this kind.

The legal principles applicable are not in serious dispute. The Cruel and Unusual Punishment clause of the Eighth Amendment is applicable to the states through the Due Process clause of the Fourteenth Amendment. Robinson v. State of California, 370 U.S. 660 (1962). The Civil Rights Act, 42 U.S.C. § 1983, creates a cause of action for deprivations, by persons acting under color of state law, of rights secured by the Constitution. See Monroe v. Pape, 365 U.S. 167 (1961). Persons confined in state prisons are within the protection of 42 U.S.C. § 1983. See Cooper v. Pate, 378 U.S. 546, 84 S.Ct. 1733, 12 L.Ed. 2d 1030 (1964). The right to be

free from cruel and unusual punishment is one of the rights that a state prisoner may, in a proper case, enforce under § 1983. [Citations omitted.]

"What constitutes a cruel and unusual punishment has not been exactly decided." Weems v. United States, 217 U.S. 349, 368 (1910). This statement is as true today as it was in 1910. It is possible, however, to identify three general approaches to the question. See Rudolph v. Alabama, 375 U.S. 889, 890-891 (1963), (dissenting opinion of Goldberg, J.). The first approach is to ask whether under all the circumstances the punishment in question is "of such character * * * as to shock general conscience or to be intolerable to fundamental fairness." Lee v. Tahash, supra, 352 F.2d at page 972. Such a judgment must be made in the light of developing concepts of elemental decency. Weems v. United States, supra, 217 U.S. at 378; Trop v. Dulles, 356 U.S. 86, 100-101 (1958) (opinion of Warren, C. J.); Rudolph v. Alabama, supra, 375 U.S. at 890 (dissenting opinion of Goldberg, J.). Secondly, a punishment may be cruel and unusual if greatly disproportionate to the offense for which it is imposed. Weems v. United States, supra; Robinson v. State of California, supra, at 676 (concurring opinion of Douglas, J.); Rudolph v. Alabama, supra, 375 U.S. at 891 (dissenting opinion of Goldberg, J.). Finally, a punishment may be cruel and unusual when, although applied in pursuit of a legitimate penal aim, it goes beyond what is necessary to achieve that aim; that is, when a punishment is unnecessarily cruel in view of the purpose for which it is used. Weems v. United

---

[5] It may be observed parenthetically that Esparza and Wells were subjected to 58 days in the strip cell with continuity, save four days' removal over the Thanksgiving holiday.

Esparza refused to turn over his coveralls. He testified that as a result he was shot in the face with a tear gas gun.

State, *supra,* 217 U.S. at 370; Robinson v. California, *supra,* 370 U.S. at 677 (concurring opinion of Douglas, J.); Rudolph v. Alabama, *supra,* at 891 (dissenting opinion of Goldberg, J.).

Defendants contend that the use of the "strip" or "quiet" cell is warranted in eliminating so-called "incorrigible" inmates from the rest of the inmates in the institution; that fighting, physical violence, throwing objects, vile, abusive and threatening language and epithets, some times coupled with overt conduct, call for stringent, strong and protective measures.

It is further contended by the defendants that the strip cells are used both as a preventive and punitive device. In some instances, it is pointed out, inmates with suicidal tendencies are incarcerated in such cells in order to prevent them from doing physical harm, either to themselves or to others. It may be noted that several inmates in the said strip cells were able to accomplish and consummate the suicide.

It appears that the cells in question were used to house those who are assertedly beyond the reach of ordinary controls and prison directives.

Usually the administrative responsibility of correctional institutions rests peculiarly within the province of the officials themselves, without attempted intrusion or intervention on the part of the courts. *[Citations omitted.]*

However, when, as it appears in the case at bar, the responsible prison authorities in the use of the strip cells have abandoned elemental concepts of decency by permitting conditions to prevail of a shocking and debased nature, then the courts must intervene—and intervene promptly—to restore the primal rules of a civilized community in accord with the mandate of the Constitution of the United States. *[Citations omitted.]*

In the opinion of the court, the type of confinement depicted in the foregoing summary of the inmates' testimony results in a slow-burning fire of resentment on the part of the inmates until it finally explodes in open revolt, coupled with their violent and bizarre conduct. Requiring man or beast to live, eat and sleep under the degrading conditions pointed out in the testimony creates a condition that inevitably does violence to elemental concepts of decency.

The testimony further reflects that the security officers made no effort to remedy the situation, notwithstanding persistent and violent complaints on the inmates' part.

. . . .

It is perfectly apparent to this court that whether a man is confined in a strip cell, or in solitary confinement, he is entitled to receive the essentials for survival. The essentials for survival necessarily include the elements of water and food and requirements for basic sanitation.

The defendants themselves have given recognition to these basic requirements under the apparent compulsion of their directors and superior officers. It appears from the testimony that an inmate so incarcerated now receives a basin, pitcher of water, towel, tooth brush and toothpaste, toilet tissue, and is permitted to shower once a week.

. . . .

Plaintiff requests that defendants be enjoined permanently from subjecting plaintiff to violations of 42 U.S.C.A. §§ 1981, 1983, 1985 and 1986.

This relief should be granted, save and except as to Sections 1985 and 1986, for, as it appears in the case at bar, there has been no evidence that plaintiff has been denied equal protection of the laws such as is required by Sections 1985 and 1986, *supra*.[1]

If the defendants intend to continue with the use of the so-called "strip" or "quiet" cell as a device in the general plan of solitary confinement, then its use must be accompanied by supplying the basic requirements which are essential to life, and by providing such essential requirements as may be necessary to maintain a degree of cleanliness compatible with elemental decency in accord with the standards of a civilized community.

While the court will not undertake to specify the precise procedures which the officials must adopt if they are to meet the demands of the Constitution, the practices set out in the [American Correctional Association's *A Manual of Corrections*] relied upon by defendants would, if adopted and followed, meet the minimum standards required by the Eighth Amendment.

The following excerpts are illustrative:

c) *Punitive segregation in a special punishment section or building.* This section is usually not a part of the regular living quarters. Inmates confined in this area usually receive a restricted diet and a loss of privileges. They should be in a punishment status and kept there for com-

paratively brief periods. Ordinarily no inmate should be retained in punitive segregation on restrictive diet more than fifteen days, and normally a shorter period is sufficient. Those who fail to make an adjustment under such conditions can often be treated more effectively in special administrative segregation facilities. The punitive segregation section should not be utilized for indefinite or permanent segregation. The not uncommon practice of confining insane inmates there is indefensible, all insane inmates should be transferred to a mental hospital or medical-psychiatric treatment facility.

The punitive segregation section and all the cells in it should be evenly heated and adequately lighted and ventilated. Artificial ventilation is usually necessary. High sanitary standards should be maintained, bathing facilities should be provided in the section and inmates permitted to bathe frequently. Most of the cells should contain a washbowl and toilet. It is necessary to omit this equipment from a few cells and assign them to inmates who persist in misusing the plumbing facilities. A few cells may have toilets that can be flushed only by the officer from outside the cell; these are either ordinary seat toilets or "Oriental type" toilets, which are openings level with the floor. Toilets which the occupant of the cell cannot flush need constant supervision by the officer. Wholly dark cells should not be used and if there is a solid door on the cell, it should be so designed that it does not exclude all light. Natural or artificial lighting should be pro-

[1] Collins v. Hardyman, 341 U.S. 651, 661 (1951); Joyce v. Ferrazzi, 323 F.2d 931, 932-933 (1st Cir. 1963).

vided during normal hours of the day or evening in keeping with standards for regular living quarters. (Italics ours)

Punitive segregation cells should be so constructed that all parts are visible to the patrolling officer from the corridor. Such cells or at least some of them should be sound-proofed for obvious reasons. Doors may be hollow with insulation in the hollow spaces. All efforts possible should be made to prevent the transmission of sound to the outside through ventilating shafts, ducts, etc.

Normally, inmates are not confined in cells with solid doors or placed on restricted diet unless they have created a disturbance while confined in standard cells in the segregation section. Occasionally they are put in cells of this type to prevent communication with other prisoners or to minimize noise from disturbances. Some institutions have solid fronts on all punishment cells, using wire glass or glass brick to admit some natural light and providing ample mechanical ventilation. The use of double doors with open grill gates supplemented by solid front doors, makes it possible to maintain better observation by leaving solid doors open except when necessary to control the noise of a disturbed or unruly inmate for temporary periods. View ports or windows of tempered glass should be provided in such cells to permit good supervision and to prevent mutilation or suicide.

The same housekeeping proce-dures will apply to the Adjustment Center as obtain in the general institution, except for disturbed and destructive inmates who will be handled as the situation indicates. This includes regular change of bedding, clothing, bathing and feeding.

Defendants, of recent date, have undertaken to install certain basic essentials, i. e., a basin, pitcher of water, towel, tooth brush, toothpaste, toilet tissue, and automatic toilet flushes.

The injunctive relief contemplated should embrace at least the foregoing revisions in practice, and such others as may be compatible with the constitutional mandate proscribing against cruel and unusual punishment with particular reference to the foregoing excerpts from the rules and regulations.

The Court has considered plaintiff's request that damages be assessed against the defendants. Such request is denied.

The Court has concluded that the ends of justice will be served by the issuance of injunctive relief, as prayed, together with any and all costs laid out and expended on behalf of the above named plaintiff Jordan by his appointed counsel, Charles B. Cohler.

In view of the court's foregoing disposition granting injunctive relief, the petition for the writ of habeas corpus (No. 44309) will be dismissed coincident with the filing of the within memorandum opinion and order.

Findings, decree and injunctive relief may be prepared consistent with the foregoing.

HANCOCK v. AVERY

301 F.Supp. 786 (M.D. Tenn. 1969)

WILLIAM E. MILLER, Chief Judge.

This action is before the Court for a temporary restraining order on the plaintiff's allegation that he has been subjected to cruel and unusual punishment. The action is before the Court on the amended complaint of Don Lee Hancock, an inmate of the Tennessee State Penitentiary at Nashville. Named as defendants in the original complaint are the former Commissioner of the Tennessee Department of Corrections, the former Warden of the Tennessee State Penitentiary at Nashville, and in the amended complaint their respective successors.

Plaintiff seeks injunctive relief from cruel and unusual punishment pursuant to 28 U.S.C.A. § 2281 et seq. More specifically, he prays that the Court grant injunctive relief restraining the enforcement, operation, or execution of T.C.A. § 41-707 which provides as follows:

> Solitary confinement for violation of rules:—If any convict neglects or refuses to perform the labor assigned him or willfully injures any of the materials, implements, or tools, or engages in conversation with another convict, or in any other manner violates any of the regulations of the penitentiary, he may be punished by solitary confinement for a period not exceeding thirty (30) days for each offense, at the discretion of the warden, or person acting in his place.

In support of plaintiff's allegations of cruel and unusual punishment, the record reveals the following facts. On June 3, 1969, plaintiff was placed in a so-called "dry cell" by prison officials for purposes of solitary confinement pursuant to the authority granted them by T.C.A. § 41-707 as set out above. The dry cell in which petitioner is confined measures approximately five by eight feet, is of concrete construction, and has a single steel door. The cell is unlighted save for dim artificial light which seeps into the cell from the outside corridor through two small slit screens in the cell door. Plaintiff alleges that he is thus being deprived of adequate light and ventilation for the entire duration of his stay in the cell.

The interior of the cell is devoid of furnishings except that there is at the rear of the cell a hole constructed to receive bodily wastes. There is, however, no mechanism within the cell to allow an occupant to flush waste material from the hole. Rather, the flushing operation is controlled by a guard operating a flushing device located outside of the cell. This operation is carried out only five times every twenty-four hours, three times during daylight hours and twice at night. As a result of this infrequent flushing, objectionable odors often permeate the cell.

While there is a factual dispute as to whether or not the dry cell had been cleaned when plaintiff was placed in it there is no dispute as to the fact that it is not normally cleaned during the duration of a prisoner's stay in the cell.

Plaintiff has been forced to remain in the dry cell without any means of cleaning his hands, body or teeth. He is denied the use of soap, towel, toilet paper, and other hygienic materials. No means have been provided which would enable him to clean any part of his body at anytime. He is fed three times a day, a slice of bread at breakfast and supper, and a regular meal at noon. The noon meal is folded into a paper container and given to plaintiff by sliding it through a small crack in the cell door. It is apparent from the foregoing facts that plaintiff is thus forced to handle and eat his food without any provision for cleanliness or even minimal sanitary conditions.

During the term of his confinement in the dry cell, plaintiff has not been permitted to wear clothing of any kind and is being forced to remain in the cell entirely nude. As a result, he is forced to sleep completely nude on the bare concrete floor. Even though he has requested a blanket, its use has been denied him.

Countering the contentions of plaintiff that he is being subjected to cruel and unusual punishment, defendants argue that plaintiff's confinement in the dry cell was necessary to protect the safety of prison personnel and plaintiff's own safety. They contend that confinement of plaintiff without clothing in the totally barren cell was necessary to prevent his access to any material from which a weapon could be fashioned for use against himself or prison personnel. They further contend that articles of clothing, plumbing fixtures and furnishings could all provide raw material for such a weap-

on and thus must be denied to the plaintiff. Defendants argue that plaintiff's health was not seriously endangered by such practices because he had daily opportunity to make medical complaints to prison medical personnel. Defendants' concern with these matters arises out of the fact that plaintiff has twice attempted suicide and is suspected of involvement in the serious stabbing of a prison guard. Furthermore, plaintiff has twice attempted to escape from cells less secure than the dry cell. It is defendants' contention that dry cells are employed only for the housing of those inmates who are so incorrigible as to be beyond the reach of normal methods of confinement. Finally, it is defendants' basic position that the determination as to the methods of dealing with such incorrigible persons is a matter of internal management of state prisons and should be left to the discretion of prison administrators.

. . . .

Turning to the merits of the claim with respect to cruel and unusual punishment in contravention of the Eighth Amendment, it appears that the legal principles involved have been judicially declared with a fair degree of certainty. The Cruel and Unusual Punishment Clause of the Eighth Amendment has been held applicable to the states through its incorporation into the Due Process Clause of the Fourteenth Amendment. Robinson v. State of California, 370 U.S. 660 (1962). Furthermore, it is clear that 42 U.S.C.A. § 1983 creates a cause of action for deprivation of constitutional rights against persons acting under color of state law. Monroe v. Pape, 365 U.S. 167 (1961). Of equal clarity is the rule that persons confined in state prisons may invoke the protection of 42 U.S.C.A. § 1983. *[Citations omitted.]* The Court is aware of the fact that until quite recently federal courts generally declined to entertain charges based on 42 U.S.C.A. § 1983 which arose out of disciplinary procedures in state prisons. This was due to a reluctance on the part of the federal courts to interfere in the internal administration of state prisons and the belief that a prisoner first had to exhaust all available state remedies before turning to the federal courts. As to the matter of exhaustion of state remedies, it is presently the rule that where an action is appropriately brought under provisions of the Civil Rights Act, the exhaustion of state remedies is not a condition precedent to federal jurisdiction. State and federal courts have concurrent jurisdiction in such cases. McNeese v. Board of Education, 373 U.S. 668 (1963); Monroe v. Pape, *supra.* It is important to note here, however, that the Civil Rights Act cannot be used in a situation appropriate to habeas corpus relief, as an alternative to the habeas corpus statutes, so as to circumvent the requirement of those statutes that state remedies be exhausted before federal relief is sought. Smartt v. Avery, 411 F.2d 408 (6th Cir. 1969); Johnson v. Walker, 317 F.2d 418 (6th Cir., 1963). The instant case, however, does not present a habeas corpus situation since plaintiff is not challenging the validity of his sentence with the ultimate object of obtaining release from the penitentiary. Instead, he is challenging the validity of punishments administered which are incidental to his sentence. Clearly, therefore, the instant case does not fall within the rule of Smartt v. Avery, *supra,* though it does present a cause of action under the Civil Rights Act appropriate for determination by this Court.

As to the traditional preference for leaving matters of internal prison management to state officials, an analysis of recent cases indicates that while federal courts are still sensitive to the problems created by interference of the federal judiciary in matters involving the internal discipline of state prisons, they will not hesitate to intervene in appropriate cases. That this intervention may extend to an examination of maximum security procedures in state prisons in order to insure the protection of constitutional rights is amply supported by precedent. *[Citations omitted.]* While the rule remains that matters of state prison discipline are not ordinarily subject to examination in federal court, the rule is otherwise if the treatment of prisoners is of such a nature that their constitutional rights are violated.

Federal courts have been particularly concerned in recent years with protecting the prisoner's Eighth Amendment right to be free from cruel and unusual punishment. It is evident that among the many rights secured to state prisoners under the Civil Rights Act, 42 U.S.C.A. § 1983, one of the most important is the right to seek relief from cruel and unusual punishment of a sort that contravenes the Eighth Amendment. Beard v. Lee, 396 F.2d 749 (5th Cir. 1968); Wright v. McMann, *supra;* Jordan v. Fitzharris, *supra.* Just what constitutes cruel and unusual punishment in the constitutional sense is a matter which defies concrete definition. However, it has long been understood that the concept of cruel and unusual punishment is one of wide application capable of acquiring new depths of meaning to conform to more enlightened concepts of criminal justice. Weems v. United States, 217 U.S. 349, 368 (1910). There appear to be several useful tests for the determination of whether or not cruel and unusual punishment is present in a given case. One such test is to ask whether under all the circumstances the punishment in question is "of such a character * * * as to shock general conscience or to be intolerable to fundamental fairness." Lee v. Tahash, 352 F.2d 970, 972 (8th Cir., 1965). Such a judgment should be made in light of "developing concepts of elemental decency. Weems v. United States, supra, 217 U.S. at 378;" Jordan v. Fitzharris, supra, 257 F.Supp. at 679. Also, "a punishment may be considered cruel and unusual when, although applied in pursuit of a legitimate penal aim, it goes beyond what is necessary to achieve that aim; that is, when a punishment is unnecessarily cruel in view of the purpose for which it is used. Weems v. United States, supra, 217 U.S., at 370, 30 S.Ct. at 544;" Jordan v. Fitzharris, supra, 257 F.Supp. at 679.

Applying both of these tests to the instant case, the Court finds that the effect of confining plaintiff in the dry cell under the conditions shown to have existed was to subject him to cruel and unusual punishment in violation of the Eighth Amendment. The conditions of his dry cell confinement are such as to make it evident that fundamental concepts of decency did not prevail. Particularly barbaric are the facts that plaintiff is forced to

sleep in the nude on a bare concrete floor without even the comfort of a blanket and that he is deprived at all times of adequate light and ventilation. Equally offensive is the fact that he is provided with no means by which he can maintain his personal cleanliness, with the result that he is forced to live and eat under animal-like conditions. The debasing conditions to which plaintiff is subjected offend more than some mere "fastidious squeamishness or private sentimentalism." Rochin v. People of California, 342 U.S. 165, 172 (1952). It is clear that requiring a prisoner to live, eat and sleep in such degrading circumstances does violence to civilized standards of human decency. Wright v. McMann, supra; Jordan v. Fitzharris, supra.

It is also apparent that the dry cell punishment, as administered in the instant case, is unnecessarily cruel in view of the purpose for which it is used. The stated aims in confining plaintiff in the dry cell were to protect him from self-inflicted injury,[1] to protect the general prison population and personnel from violent acts on his part, and to prevent his escape. Solitary confinement for the purpose of achieving such goals is not per se an unconstitutional form of punishment. Graham v. Willingham, supra. However, the Court is of the opinion that such goals can be attained without requiring a prisoner to live in the exacerbated conditions of filth and discomfort demonstrated in the instant case. Where prison officials impose such deplorable living conditions

---

[1] Where an inmate is intent on suicide, even such extreme measures as dry cell confinement have not prevented it. See Jordan v. Fitzharris, 257 F.Supp. 674 at 680. (N.D.Calif.1966).

in conjunction with solitary confine-ment, the Court is compelled to find that cruel and unusual punishment has been imposed in violation of the Constitution.

While it is true, as the defendants assert, that all imprisonment is to an extent inhumane, this fact does not excuse the imposition of forms of pun-ishment so harsh as to violate basic standards of human decency.

The conclusion here reached[2] is not

___

[2] Two earlier cases reaching the same re-sult on practically identical facts are Wright v. McMann, 387 F.2d 519 (2d Cir., 1967), and Jordan v. Fitzharris, 257 F.Supp. 674 (N.D.Calif.1966). Even where relief has been denied to petitioners claiming cruel and unusual punishment, courts have noted in dicta that dry cell conditions such as prevail in the instant case are of such a nature as to consti-tute forbidden cruel and unusual punish-ment. See, e. g., Board v. Lee, 396 F.2d 749, 751 at n: 1 (5th Cir. 1965); Cul-lum v. California Dept. of Corrections, 276 F.Supp. 524 (1967).

altered because the dry cell confine-ment under prison regulations could not exceed 15 days (15 days less than the maximum allowed by the state statute). Confinement under the con-ditions of harshness and cruelty re-flected by the present record should not be tolerated for any length of time, however brief.

This opinion constitutes the Court's findings of fact and conclusions of law in support of the temporary re-straining order heretofore issued.

Counsel for the respective parties are requested to confer to determine whether agreement may be reached that no further hearing is required and that on the basis of the Court's opinion a permanent injunction may issue to enjoin confinement in the dry cell under the circumstances of this case. Rulings on other issues in the case will be reserved.

FORD v. BOARD OF MANAGERS OF NEW JERSEY STATE PRISON
407 F.2d 937 (3d Cir. 1969)

PER CURIAM.

The appellant, Russell Ford, at the time an inmate of the New Jersey State Prison at Trenton brought this action under the authority of 42 U.S.C. §§ 1981 and 1983 alleging that the named defendants, the Board of Managers of the New Jersey State Prison, Lloyd McCorkle, Commis-sioner of Institutions & Agencies of the State of New Jersey and Howard Yeager, Principal Keeper of the New Jersey State Prison at Trenton, were subjecting him and other state pris-oners to cruel and unusual punish-ment in violation of the Eighth and

Fourteenth Amendments to the United States Constitution.

The suit was denominated in the complaint as a class action brought on behalf of all New Jersey prisoners similarly situated, presumably on the theory that they are exposed to like deprivations associated with solitary confinement. The complaint sought declaratory and injunctive relief as well as certain reforms in the prac-tices attendant upon the administra-tion of solitary confinement.

More particularly, appellant Ford alleged that he had been confined in solitary confinement from August 26 to August 31, 1967, as well as on previous occasions, in Wing 1-Left of the New Jersey State Prison at Trenton. While so situated, he was allegedly compelled to exist under the conditions set forth in paragraphs 9 and 10 of the complaint:

"9. None of the solitary confinement cells have wash bowls or running water nor is water for sanitary purposes provided so that plaintiff, during his recent confinement ° ° ° was unable to wash before eating or to maintain himself hygenically [sic] in any way. Since a shower is permitted only every fifth day, at the caprice of the officer in charge who being poorly supervised is often too lazy to attend to these matters, plaintiff did not receive a shower. Neither was the cell itself cleaned and at all times there is a pervasive stench. An old mattress with a clean cover on a cement shelf is provided for bedding.

"10. While confined solitarily ° ° ° plaintiff was permitted 4 slices of bread and a pint of water 3 times daily and *one* 'full' meal every third day. The so-called full meal may be scanty depending upon the menu for the day. Therefore, deprivation of food to the detriment of the prisoner's health is employed as a punitive measure."

Additionally, it is contended in a rather conclusory fashion that appellant was placed in solitary confinement as a punitive measure for threatening to bring suit if conditions in solitary were not changed.[4] Although

other purported abuses are set forth in the complaint, it appears that neither the appellant Ford nor the other appellants to be mentioned herein have been exposed to same.[5]

. . . .

[T]he Attorney General of New Jersey, on behalf of all of the defendants, moved to dismiss the complaint or for the entry of summary judgment in favor of the defendants. The District Court considered the motion on the basis of the pleadings and voluminous affidavits filed on behalf of the respective parties. In a thorough, well-reasoned opinion,[7] it concluded that although "[t]he right to be free from cruel and unusual punishment is one of the rights that a state prisoner may, in a proper case, enforce under Section 1983 of the Civil Rights Act," the appellants in this case had not shown that they had been "subjected to such punishment as the Eighth Amendment forbids." Appellees' motion for summary judgment was thus granted. In also holding that a class action was not the proper vehicle for challenging disciplinary action where the circumstances surrounding the imposition of punishment varied according to the individual case, the District Court denied as futile the motions for intervention. Thereupon [appellants] took this appeal.

. . .

---

[4] It is to be noted, however, that Ford does not deny that he had threatened to "blow up the Institution" and had made certain derogatory remarks about an officer, and that these were at least the ostensible reasons for his being placed in solitary.

[5] Included are allegations that the "4 wing" of the prison has been condemned on several occasions as being "unfit for human habitation," that mentally disturbed prisoners are placed in isolation to undergo "observation," and that none of the prisoner complaints with respect to these matters had been given any consideration by the responsible officials.

[7] Ford v. Board of Managers of the New Jersey State Prison, Civil No. 946-67, D.N.J., April 30, 1968.

Appellants argue that the District Court erred in granting appellees' motion for summary judgment, in holding that the instant suit was not a proper class action and in denying the motions for intervention. Disregarding any implications of mootness of the issues raised by Ford's complaint by reason of his transfer to Connecticut, and accepting as true all of the factual allegations in the complaint, excluding those which are merely conclusory, suffice it to say that no cause of action is stated under the Civil Rights Act or the Eighth and Fourteenth Amendments. As was stated in Gurczynski v. Yeager:

"Discipline reasonably maintained in those [New Jersey] prisons is not under the supervisory direction of the federal courts. * * * There is nothing in the circumstances related to indicate any reasonable basis for interference with the state authority, even though appellant's claim is under the guise of violation of his constitutional rights."[9]

9 Gurczynski v. Yeager, 339 F.2d 884, 884-885 (3 Cir. 1964). See Negrich v. Hohn, 379 F.2d 213 (3 Cir. 1967); United States ex rel. Knight v. Ragen, 337 F.2d 425 (7 Cir. 1964), cert. denied, 380 U.S. 985, 85 S.Ct. 1355, 14 L.Ed.2d 277 (1965); Kostal v. Tinsley, 337 F.2d 845 (10 Cir. 1964), cert.

None of the circumstances here revealed even remotely approximate the barbaric conditions found to constitute cruel and unusual punishment in Wright v. McMann[10] and Jordan v. Fitzharris.[11] Solitary confinement in and of itself does not violate Eighth Amendment prohibitions,[12] and the temporary inconveniences and discomforts incident thereto cannot be regarded as a basis for judicial relief. In light of this disposition of the case, appellants' other arguments, such as the right to intervention, the propriety of the suit as a class action and summary judgment, fall of their own weight.

The order of the United States District Court for the District of New Jersey of April 30, 1968, entering judgment in favor of the appellees will be affirmed.

denied, 380 U.S. 985, 85 S.Ct. 1354, 14 L.Ed.2d 277 (1965); Childs v. Pegelow, 321 F.2d 487 (4 Cir. 1963), cert. denied, 376 U.S. 932, 84 S.Ct. 702, 11 L.Ed.2d 652 (1964).
10 Wright v. McMann, 387 F.2d 519 (2 Cir. 1967).
11 Jordan v. Fitzharris, 257 F.Supp. 674 (N.D. Cal. 1966).
12 E.g., Graham v. Willingham, 265 F.Supp. 763 (D. Kan.) aff'd, 384 F.2d 367 (10 Cir. 1967); Roberts v. Barbosa, 227 F.Supp. 20 (S.D. Cal. 1964).

KNUCKLES v. PRASSE

302 F.Supp. 1036 (E.D. Pa, 1969)
aff'd, 435 F.2d 1255 (3d Cir. 1970)

HIGGINBOTHAM, District Judge.

I.

INTRODUCTION

These two consolidated actions under the Civil Rights Act, 42 U.S.C.A. § 1983, lead us into the difficult area where the exigencies of effective prison administration threaten to collide with those constitutionally protected freedoms assured all persons not in prison. Plaintiffs are five prisoners in the Pennsylvania State Correctional System. Knuckles, McKee, Green and

Tillery were inmates at the State Correctional Institution at Graterford, Pennsylvania (hereinafter referred to as "Graterford") during most of the time relevant hereto. Washington was an inmate at the State Correctional Institution at Philadelphia, Pennsylvania (hereinafter referred to as "Philadelphia)" during most of the time relevant hereto.

The plaintiffs allege that they were:

(1) Denied the right to practice their religion in violation of the First Amendment and the Fourteenth Amendment; and

(2) Denied the privilege of religious practice available to members of other faiths in violation of the Fourteenth Amendment; and

(3) Harassed and punished with particular harshness because of their religious beliefs in violation of the First Amendment and the Fourteenth Amendment; and

(4) Subjected to cruel and unusual punishment in violation of the Eighth Amendment.

A six day hearing produced some 928 pages of testimony and ninety exhibits. Extensive briefs and proposed findings of fact and conclusions of law were submitted, and there was subsequent oral argument.

. . .

Two sets of facts and their legal consequences call for attention here. There are questions about plaintiffs' constitutional rights and privileges to practice the Muslim religion while in prison. There are also questions about the treatment directed against four of the plaintiffs after they took part in the Graterford incident of May 23, 1966. For reasons to be elaborated below, I find that while certain of the restrictions placed on plaintiffs' practice of the Muslim religion were constitutionally valid, other restrictions were constitutionally invalid. Accordingly, plaintiffs must be given somewhat expanded rights to practice the Muslim religion. At the same time, it must be clearly understood that prison authorities continue to have the right to subject the practices of the followers of the Muslim religion or the followers of any other religion to "reasonable regulations, necessary for the protection and welfare of the community involved." Long v. Parker, 390 F.2d 816 at 820 (3rd Cir., 1968).

I further find that after the Graterford incident, plaintiffs were subjected to cruel and unusual punishment from the morning of May 23, 1966, until the afternoon of May 25, 1966 in violation of the Eighth Amendment, but since it does not appear that this unfortunate two and one-half day practice has been or will be continued, injunctive relief is DENIED.

A final decree is held in abeyance for thirty (30) days so that counsel may explore, and hopefully stipulate to, specific methods for affording relief to plaintiffs consistent with this opinion.

II.

FINDINGS OF FACT

. . . .

8. From before May, 1966, to the present, all of the plaintiffs have been and are followers of the teachings of the Honorable Elijah Muhammad.

9. The followers of the Honorable Elijah Muhammad, often called Muslims or Black Muslims, are a sect of the Islamic Religion, and for purposes of the issues before the court are rec-

ognized as members of a bona fide religion. In their brief, defendants stated:

"For the purposes of these actions, it is admitted that Black Muslimism is a 'religion' as that term is used in the United States Constitution."

. . . .

44. On May 23, 1966, at 10:00 or 10:30 A. M., about 120 inmates of a total prison population of 1500 were in the general recreation yard. About fourteen of the inmates, all followers of the Honorable Elijah Muhammad, were gathered together in the yard. When a non-Muslim inmate tried either to join or pass through the area occupied by the group or ran into one of the group, the Muslims turned on him, struck him and kicked him numerous times. They also struck and kicked another inmate.

45. When guards tried to break up the fight, some of the Muslims, including perhaps one or more of the plaintiffs, physically attacked them.

46. A few minutes after the guards arrived the Muslim group stopped fighting and formed a small circle.

47. The fourteen Muslims were taken into the main corridor of the prison and "strip searched". They were then told to dress, were handcuffed together in pairs and marched to the maximum security cell block (hereinafter referred to as "maximum security").

48. A "strip search" consists of the following:

(a) The person to be searched is made to disrobe completely;

(b) He is made to expose to inspection the palms of his hands and the soles of his feet;

(c) He is made to open his mouth for inspection;

(d) He is made to bend over from the waist and spread his buttocks for inspection; and

(e) Finally, his hair is examined.

49. In a maximum security prison the "strip search" is necessary to prevent the transportation of contraband.

50. When the Muslims arrived in maximum security, they were stripped, searched, and placed two inmates to a cell, in cells numbered 1 through 5, and one inmate per cell in cell 6 and cell 7 as follows:

Cell No. 1—William Knuckles and Isaiah Green.

Cell No. 2—Edwin Walker and Leon Hard.

Cell No. 3—John Hosendorf and Wendel Green.

Cell No. 4—Alex Howard and Joseph Tillery.

Cell No. 5—Arthur McKee and Willie Haywood.

Cell No. 6—Ronald Foster.

Cell No. 7—Harold Brooks.

51. Prior to the placement of these inmates in maximum security, there were 13 vacant cells, not including those reserved for inmates under sentence of death.

52. After their placement in maximum security there were six vacant cells, not including those reserved for inmates under sentence of death.

53. None of the occupied cells in maximum security contained more than one inmate except cells 1 through 5.

54. At the time the inmates were admitted to maximum security, prison

officials feared that further outbreaks might occur that day.

55. The inmates were placed two to a cell to segregate them as much as possible, to seal off their disturbing influence, and to leave a few cells vacant in the event further outbreaks necessitated the rapid segregation of offending prisoners.

56. The inmates listed in paragraph 50 above were placed in the cells in maximum security without any clothes, bedding, or toilet articles, including soap, towels and tissue paper.

57. The maximum security cells measured six feet by nine feet, eleven inches. The following were their physical characteristics on May 23, 1966. Each cell contained a concrete single piece commode with a water pipe extending from the wall and located about two and one-half feet above its top. The water pipe and commode were operated by two pedals located on the floor at the base of the commode. Each cell contained a steel bed attached to the wall with steel slats serving in place of springs. A smaller rectangular drain was located in one corner of the floor at the rear of each cell. In no cell were there any windows or artificial lights.

58. When the plaintiffs were placed in the cells on May 23, 1966, there were no mattresses, sheets, blankets, towels, soap or toilet paper there.

59. Because maximum security draws on a separate stock of supplies, it is routine and accepted practice to place inmates in maximum security cells without clothing, bedding, or toilet articles. These items are issued to all inmates placed there from the general prison population or from other prisons on transfer as soon as possible.

60. Approximately one hour after the plaintiffs were placed in their cells they were issued two blankets each by the guards.

61. There is no evidence that prison officials feared that the plaintiffs would commit suicide or intentionally damage clothing, bedding or toilet articles issued to them.

62. Contrary to applicable prison regulations and to any reasonable practice, the prisoners placed in maximum security on the morning of May 23, 1966, did not receive clothing, bedding, or toilet articles until the afternoon of May 25, 1966.

63. Because of the age of the facilities, the mechanisms which ran the water pipe and the toilet often did not work. This meant that the toilet or water pipe often could not be turned on or off.

64. When the water was turned on, it often splashed on the floor because there was no way to cover the toilet. The cells became damp and chilly despite the prison officials' practice of keeping the heat slightly above normal.

65. The prisoners had to use the blankets issued to them to wipe up the water and cover the commode so that one inmate in each of cells 1 through 5 could sleep on the floor. Each prisoner was thus left with one blanket to use as bedding and cover.

66. The Graterford incident of May 23, 1966, was one of the most serious in the last fifteen years and could have become a general riot if not quickly contained. It was one of the

few incidents which prompted prison officials to send a riot alert to state police.

Following the incident, prison officials and the Pennsylvania State Police conducted an investigation and lodged criminal charges against Knuckles, Green, Tillery and McKee for riot, assault, and conspiracy.

67. On May 25, 1966, the prisoners appeared for a hearing before Deputy Superintendent Wolfe at the Graterford Behavior Clinic.

68. As a result of the hearing, the prisoners were remanded to maximum security to await trial.

69. On May 26, 1966, the prisoners were arraigned in Montgomery County Court and were then returned to maximum security at Graterford.

70. At the time of the Graterford incident, the defendant prison officials knew that the plaintiffs referred to themselves and were referred to by others as Muslims or Black Muslims.

71. Responsible prison officials, including the prison doctor, visited maximum security between the time plaintiffs were placed in their cells there and the time they were first issued clothing and bedding.

72. When inmates are charged with assault, it is the routine and accepted practice in Pennsylvania prisons to keep them segregated until their trials are completed.

73. At Graterford, the same facility is used for administrative and punitive segregation. The only difference between the two is that the prisoner in administrative segregation gets more privileges, such as visitation rights and pencil and paper.

74. At Philadelphia there are separate cell blocks for administrative and punitive segregation.

75. During their first three days in segregation, plaintiffs were not permitted to exercise outside of their cells and were on "reduced diets."

76. With a "reduced diet" the inmate gets slightly less food than is normally given to inmates in the general prison population and no dessert.

77. At Graterford and Philadelphia, prisoners in maximum security who wish to participate in outside exercise must undergo a "strip search" before leaving and again before re-entering their cells.

78. It is a general and accepted prison practice to require maximum security prisoners to undergo a "strip search" each time they go out and return from exercise.

79. While in maximum security and prior to the time they began to accumulate misconducts, plaintiffs were not denied the opportunity to exercise. They were allowed to exercise for one hour per day.

80. Tillery refused to exercise because he felt that the "strip search" was too degrading and did not wish to undergo it.

81. Knuckles and McKee also refused the opportunity to exercise, although their reasons do not appear.

82. The periods and places of confinement of the plaintiffs from and after May 23, 1966, until August 11, 1967, was as follows:

	Knuckles	Green	Tillery	McKee
Total days in segregation	455 days	410 days	420 days	410 days
Total days in punitive or maximum security segregation	222 days	222 days	337 days	337 days
Total days separate administrative segregation unit	223 days	188 days	73 days	73 days
Longest consecutive periods in punitive or maximum security	189 and 31 days	189 and 31 days	189 and 31 days	189 and 31 days
Number of days in general population	0 days	35 days	25 days	35 days

83. During this 445 day period reviews of the cases or misconduct reports concerning Knuckles, Green, Tillery and McKee were held on the following dates:

(a) On May 25, 1966, at Graterford;

(b) On or about June 24, 1966, at Philadelphia; and

(c) In November, 1967, at Philadelphia.

84. It is the general practice and policy at Graterford to review the cases of prisoners held in maximum security at least once every thirty (30) days.

. . . .

103. The plaintiffs were not permitted to receive any visitors during the entire time that they were in maximum security or punitive segregation.

104. From the time of their incarceration in maximum security at Philadelphia—on or about June 24, 1966, the plaintiffs were never told precisely how long they would be kept in maximum security.

III.

DISCUSSION

The conflict here is between plaintiffs' desire to practice their religion while in the custody of the Pennsylvania State Correctional System and defendants' refusal to allow many aspects of that practice. Plaintiffs claim that they were discriminated against in that they were denied the privileges or "equal protection" accorded to inmates practicing other religions. Plaintiffs further claim that because of their religious beliefs, they were punished more severely for alleged infractions of prison rules than were other inmates of other faiths. Finally, plaintiffs claim that certain punishments to which they were subjected were of such a nature and severity as to violate the Eighth Amendment's prohibition against "cruel and unusual punishment."

. . . .

E. *The Cruel and Unusual Punishment and Equal Protection Issues.*

I turn now to plaintiffs' claim that after the Graterford incident they were subjected to discriminatory punishment and harassment contrary to the treatment accorded non-Muslims and in violation of their Fourteenth Amendment rights. Such treatment, plaintiffs further assert, was so unusual and so severe as to amount to cruel and unusual punishment. The following three circumstances allegedly existed and, plaintiffs maintain, support their requested conclusions of law:

(1) They were segregated, mostly in maximum security without privileges, for an overly long period during which time

(a) they were denied adequate exercise;

(b) they were repeatedly subjected to strip searches; and

(c) their cases were seldom reviewed by prison authorities.

(2) The guards in maximum security at Graterford mixed pork and pork products with other foods on plaintiffs' plates. This was done with the knowledge that plaintiffs' religion forbade their eating pork or pork products.

(3) They were kept two men to a cell six feet by nine feet, eleven inches for two and one-half days without any clothing, bedding (except for two blankets), or sanitary articles. The cells contained only a single bed and were damp and foul smelling because of a malfunctioning toilet.

That the plaintiffs were incarcerated in the maximum security punitive cell block at Graterford for an extended period of time is unfortunately due to the fact that the prison has only a single maximum security cell block which must be used for both punitive and administrative segregation. This is a matter beyond any question of discrimination. All prisoners assigned to segregation at Graterford—for whatever reason—must be housed in the prison's single maximum security cell block.

Certain privileges such as visitation rights and access to pencil and paper are permitted to prisoners in administrative segregation but denied to prisoners in punitive segregation. However, on the record before me, there is no basis for concluding that plaintiffs were denied the privileges of administrative segregation in a discriminatory manner.

At Philadelphia there are separate facilities for punitive and administrative segregation. However, prisoners charged with assault, as was the case here, are routinely kept in punitive segregation until their trials are completed. I find nothing unreasonable about this administrative decision, which is routine and accepted practice in Pennsylvania prisons.

After being interviewed at Philadelphia, plaintiffs were assigned to punitive segregation, where they remained without further review of their cases for about five months. During this time plaintiffs were cooperative and were charged with no misconducts. While as a matter of administrative discretion, some prison authorities would perhaps not have held plaintiffs in punitive segregation for the full five month period, I cannot as a matter of law find this to be an abuse of that discretion. Moreover, there is no evidence to indicate that other prisoners are treated otherwise on transfer from one penal institution to another, and thus no basis for a finding of discriminatory treatment.

Because of repeated misconducts, plaintiffs were given almost no opportunity to exercise during their first 29 days in maximum security at Graterford. In view of the seriousness of the May 23rd incident, the prison authorities acted well within permissible discretion in determining that it was too dangerous to allow the prisoners to exercise outside of their cells. Later, the prisoners were afforded the chance to exercise for one hour every day, but refused because they objected to having to undergo a strip search before and after each exercise period.

The testimony of expert witnesses regarding the ingenious methods devised by prisoners for secreting contraband, including weaponry, on their persons has convinced me that the regulations governing strip searches are neither arbitrary nor lacking in reasonable justification. There has been no showing that plaintiffs were treated any differently than other prisoners with regard to strip searches.

Food was served to maximum security inmates at Graterford on paper plates. As often as not, these plates did not have dividers and had to be bent somewhat to be passed through the opening at the base of the cell door. This might have caused food to run together on occasion. Of course, the prisoners were never required to eat pork or pork products, and, as there was no evidence that the guards maliciously or purposely mixed pork with the prisoners' food, there can be no finding of discrimination.

The circumstances discussed above have been found not to violate plaintiffs' Fourteenth Amendment due process and/or equal protection rights. The same facts are resubmitted by plaintiffs along with the two and one-half day incident of denuded incarceration to support their allegations of cruel and unusual punishment.

The major focus in deciding whether plaintiffs' Eighth Amendment rights have been violated must be on

the long period of maximum security segregation and the two and one-half days plaintiffs were forced to spend without clothing or bedding in cramped quarters. Such matters as reduced exercise opportunities, strip searches, and the serving of food mixed with pork do not rise to the level or severity associated with cruel and unusual punishment, and what has previously been said about these alleged Fourteenth Amendment violations warrants a similar denial of plaintiffs' Eighth Amendment claims as well.

Knuckles, Green, Tillery and McKee each spent more than 400 days in segregation, including one period of 189 consecutive days in maximum security. That period of time spent in segregation prior to trial does not enter into my consideration of the length of time plaintiffs were in segregation, because I find the policy of segregating inmates pending trial on charges of assaults *which took place in prison* to be well within the discretion of the prison authorities. For all save a small part of that time plaintiffs had the option of exercising for one hour each day. While in segregation plaintiffs were guilty of numerous and continuing misconducts. Penology experts testified that misconducts have a legitimate bearing on how long a prisoner is to be kept in segregation. Prison authorities are responsible for the security and stability of the entire institution, and when individual prisoners pose a threat to security or stability, when by their conduct prisoners demonstrate that they are not ready or able to adjust to congregated prison life, it seems well within the discretion of prison administrators to keep such prisoners for long periods—some experts were willing to say indefinite periods—of time in segregation. In view of the extremely serious nature of the Graterford incident of May 23, 1966, it was not unreasonable to segregate the prisoners for the periods of time stated.

In Graham v. Willingham, 10 Cir., 384 F.2d 367, a prisoner convicted of second degree murder alleged cruel and unusual punishment because of "prolonged and unreasonable segregated confinement in the maximum security facilities at Leavenworth". The facts of that Tenth Circuit case do not exactly match the cases at bar in that the petitioner there had participated in extreme violence, including murders, while he was at large among the prison population. For his conduct he was segregated continuously for more than two years. While petitioners here are not guilty of as severe misconduct, their periods of segregated confinement are far shorter. I agree with the Graham v. Willingham court which found the policy of segregation to be "perfectly proper and lawful." As the Court said, "its administration requires the highest degree of expertise in the discretionary function of balancing the security of the prison with fairness to the individuals confined." Here, as there, the prisoners' confinement in segregation was "the result of the considered judgment of the prison authorities and was not arbitrary." 384 F.2d 368.

Finally, there is the question of the two and one-half days spent by the plaintiffs, two to a cell—six feet by nine feet, eleven inches. The cells had no windows and no artificial light. Each cell had only a single bed and the cells were damp and foul smelling from water splashing on the floor as a result of malfunctioning toilets. The men were given no clothing or bedding, save two blankets, which had to be used to absorb water from the overflowing toilet and further as a mattress. The men were given no soap, no towels, no toilet tissue, no toilet articles.

The conditions were somewhat less severe but still quite similar to those described by the court in Wright v. McMann, 2 Cir., 387 F.2d 519. There the solitary confinement cell was described as "dirty, filthy and unsanitary, without adequate heat and virtually barren; the toilet and sink were encrusted with slime, dirt and human excremental residue * * *". The plaintiff was kept completely nude for eleven days and was denied all hygienic implements and utensils.

While petitioners here were faced with a damp cell and not a freezing one, and while there were no physical beatings and the period of confinement in question was two and one-half days and not eleven days, still I fully concur with the view of Judge Kaufman in the Wright v. McMann case and adopt it here:

"Civilized standards of humane decency simply do not permit a man for a substantial period of time to be denuded * * * and to be deprived of the basic elements of hygiene such as soap and toilet paper. The subhuman conditions * * * could only serve to destroy completely the spirit and undermine the sanity of the prisoner. The Eighth Amendment forbids treatment so foul, so inhuman and so violative of basic concepts of decency."

CONCLUSIONS OF LAW

1. The Court has jurisdiction of the consolidated actions under the Civil Rights Act, 42 U.S.C. § 1983.

. . . .

7. Plaintiffs were subjected to cruel and unusual punishment, but since it does not appear that this practice has been or will be continued, injunctive relief is DENIED.

8. Except as noted in Conclusions of Law (2) and (7), plaintiffs were not subjected to discriminatory punishment and harassment contrary to the treatment afforded non-Muslims and in violation of their Fourteenth Amendment rights.

9. No monetary damages are awarded.

ORDER

AND NOW, this 31st day of July, 1969, it is hereby ORDERED that counsel for the parties explore and stipulate to specific methods for affording relief to the plaintiffs consistent with this Opinion.

Counsel are directed to devise and submit to the Court within thirty (30) days a system for accrediting Muslim ministers to permit them to have collective worship services in Pennsylvania prisons in a manner which is substantially similar to that granted to ministers of other religious faiths.

The parties are FURTHER ORDERED to submit a proposed form of Order consistent with this Opinion.

SOSTRE v. McGINNIS
442 F.2d 178 (2d Cir. 1971)

IRVING R. KAUFMAN, Circuit Judge:

We voted to hear the initial argument of this appeal *en banc*, a procedure we reserve for extraordinary circumstances, so that we might give plenary review to a complex of urgent social and political conflicts persistently seeking solution in the courts as legal problems, a phenomenon de Tocqueville commented upon many years ago. Democracy in America, vol. I at 290 (Vintage ed. 1945). The elaborate opinion and order below raise important questions concerning the federal constitutional rights of state prisoners which neither Supreme Court precedent nor our own past decisions have answered. The sparse authority from other courts is for the most part either inconclusive or conflicting.

I.

PROCEEDINGS BELOW AND JURISDICTION

This is an appeal from an order entered May 14, 1970, by Judge Motley, sitting in the Southern District of New York, 312 F.Supp. 863, which granted plaintiff Martin Sostre punitive and compensatory damages against defendants Follette and McGinnis as well as a wide variety of injunctive relief in his action pursuant to the Civil Rights Act of 1871, 42 U.S.C.A. § 1983, and 28 U.S.C.A. §§ 1331, 1343(3). At the time Sostre filed his handwritten complaint, he was incarcerated in New York's Green Haven Prison (now called Green Haven Correctional Facility), serving a sentence of thirty to forty years for selling narcotics, followed by thirty days further imprisonment for contempt of court, imposed on him March 18, 1968. The original defendants included the Governor of New York as well as the State Commissioner of Correction, appellant McGinnis; the Warden of Green Haven, Harold W. Follette, who died shortly before the opinion below was entered and the Warden of Attica Prison (now called Attica Correctional Facility), appellant Vincent Mancusi. Sostre had been confined for one night in Attica immediately after sentencing, then transferred the following day to Green Haven.

Sostre does not appeal from the dismissal by the district court of his action against the Governor, in which Sostre had asserted the Governor's complicity in racial discrimination in the administration of New York's prison system.

. . . .

II.

FACTS

A. *Circumstances of Sostre's Commitment to Punitive Segregation*

On June 25, 1968, Warden Follette ordered that Sostre be committed pursuant to Section 140 of the New York Correction Law, McKinney's Consol. Laws, c. 43,[3] to "solitary confinement" (the words in the statute) or "puni-

---

[3] Section 140 was repealed and replaced with a new Section 137, effective July 8, 1970 (McKinney Supp. 1970). Section 137, subd. 6 of the new statute vests the Superintendent of each correctional facility (formerly called the Warden) with discretion to "keep any inmate confined in a cell or room apart from the accommodations provided for inmates who are participating in programs of the facility, for such period as may be necessary for maintenance of order and discipline. • • •"

tive segregation" (the term adopted by Judge Motley and by the parties on appeal, which we will use for that reason and also because he was not as isolated in his segregation as "solitary" would imply). The parties vigorously disagree as to the considerations that motivated Follette to inflict this punishment.

On June 25, 1968, the day he put Sostre in segregation, Follette called Sostre to his office. At this meeting, Follette questioned Sostre about his attempt that morning to mail to an attorney, Miss Joan Franklin of the National Association for the Advancement of Colored People, a letter with handwritten legal papers attached, including a motion for use in the trial of Mrs. Geraldine Robinson. Mrs. Robinson is described by Judge Motley and the parties on appeal as Sostre's "codefendant." Although she was joined with Sostre in the indictment which resulted in Sostre's imprisonment, they were not tried together. Follette told Sostre "he must confine his legal activities to his own incarceration" and accordingly that the motion would not be mailed. Follette explained that he objected to Sostre's attempt to "practice law" without a license. Sostre believed that he had a right to mail legal papers in behalf of Mrs. Robinson and refused to assure Follette, as Follette requested, that he would discontinue attempting to mail such documents through normal prison channels.

During the same interview, Follette questioned Sostre about a reference to an organization known as "R.N.A.," mentioned by Sostre in his letter to Miss Franklin and to which Sostre had referred in earlier correspondence. "R.N.A." in fact referred to the

Republic of New Africa, which Sostre identified at the trial before Judge Motley as a black liberation or black separatist organization. Sostre disputed Follette's testimony that Sostre had lied about R.N.A. at the June 25 interview by persistently claiming at that time that it was a "federal agency * * * 'Recovery National Administration' or something like this." Sostre did admit, as Follette asserted at trial, that after responding to a few questions Sostre refused to discuss R.N.A. further. The plaintiff's justification for his silence was that Follette had persisted in labelling R.N.A. a "subversive organization." Sostre "clammed up," as he testified, to avoid antagonizing Follette by further explaining or defending R.N.A.

Follette testified without contradiction that the organization known as the Republic of New Africa was of sufficient concern to him to have been the object of an investigation before the interview with Sostre. Follette feared that "this organization was a cloak for an attempt to organize prison inmates for riot and insurrection," based on information obtained from the F.B.I. and the New York State and Buffalo City Police. "[T]he possibility of insurrection at Green Haven" was a "major fear" to Follette at all times, but particularly so in June, 1968. Security at the prison had been weakened, in Follette's view, by an exceptionally high turnover of correction officers, approaching a rate of about fifty percent each year. An influx of new officers had not yet been cleared through the New York State Identification and Intelligence System. Moreover, Sostre had exacerbated Follette's concern with the possibility of major disorder

because of a statement in a letter that Sostre had written to his sister, dated May 19, 1968:

> As for me, there is no doubt in my mind whatsoever that I will be out soon, either by having my appeal reversed in the courts or by being liberated by the Universal Forces of Liberation.

This sentence is included in a broad indictment of militarism and oppression in this country and a prediction that "the power structure" would soon be overthrown.

Follette insists that his decision to commit Sostre to segregation reflected (1) Sostre's declared intent to defy Follette's order by preparing legal papers for his co-defendant; (2) his intransigence about R.N.A.; (3) the allusion in the letter to his sister to his impending liberation. Rule 54 of the "Inmate's Rule Book," a publication of the New York Department of Correction issued to each prisoner when he arrives at Green Haven, limits inmate correspondence to "their own personal matters." Follette interpreted this as proscribing the sending of legal papers in behalf of a co-defendant. Sostre's refusal to discuss R.N.A. and his persistence about Mrs. Robinson's legal papers both violated Rule 5 of the Inmate Rule Book which requires that an inmate obey orders "promptly and fully," pending whatever appeal he may wish to take to higher authority. In addition, his silence violated Rule 12, enjoining inmates to answer "fully and truthfully" all questions put by prison officials. In sum, Follette assigned as his motive for Sostre's punishment the fact that Sostre's "whole attitude was one of defiance, of flatly refusing * * * to conduct himself as a proper inmate within the rules, regulations and laws set down by the State of New York and the Department of Correction." Section 140 of the New York Correction Law authorized Follette, by its terms in his unfettered discretion, to commit Sostre to segregation when "necessary * * * to produce [his] entire submission and obedience" and to keep him there "until he shall be reduced to submission and obedience."

Judge Motley disbelieved each of Follette's asserted motives for punishing Sostre, crediting instead Sostre's testimony that Follette was motivated by Sostre's threat to sue Follette over his withholding the motion papers intended for Mrs. Robinson. Additionally, Judge Motley attributed to Follette an intent to punish Sostre because of his earlier activism in bringing litigation related to the practice of the Black Muslim religion in New York prisons and "because he is, unquestionably, a black militant who persists in writing and expressing his militant and radical ideas in prison." Judge Motley held that the summary meeting with Warden Follette which resulted in Sostre's commitment to segregation did not afford due process of law to Sostre before his "liberty" was taken.

Apart from the events of the June 25 interview, Judge Motley also dismissed as one of Follette's reasons for continuing Sostre's incarceration in segregated confinement several items of "contraband" which Follette claimed were the fruit of a search of Sostre's cell conducted immediately after he entered segregation. These items consisted of (1) two small (3 inches by 5 inches) pieces of heavy black emery paper covered with an abrasive material like sand which, according to Follette, could be flaked off and in some manner attached to a string to fashion an instrument capable of sawing through cell bars; (2) six tables of contents torn from issues of the *Harvard Law Review* and stamped by prison officials to indicate that the books, Sostre's personal property, were not to circulate to other prisoners; (3) a letter dated June 10, 1968, from the Appellate Division of the Supreme Court of New York addressed to a fellow-prisoner of Sostre's, Juan Moline, a Puerto Rican, which Sostre later explained he was translating for Moline from English into Spanish. Judge Motley believed Sostre's testimony that he had never seen the pieces of emery paper before they were introduced by defendants at trial. 312 F.Supp. at 869. The other contraband indicated that Sostre had violated prison rules by circulating his law periodicals to other prisoners and by giving a fellow-prisoner legal assistance without first securing the Warden's permission. The Court below not only declined to find that these activities motivated the punishment of Sostre, but held in addition, that Sostre's activities were protected by the Fourteenth Amendment.[4]

---

[4] On July 11, 1968, Deputy Warden Sawner called Sostre before a "disciplinary court," conducted by Sawner alone, and charged Sostre with sending letters covertly to unauthorized correspondents under the guise of writing to his sister, Letitia. Sostre admitted the infraction, which Follette claimed to have been under investigation as early as June 25, the day he committed Sostre to segregation. For this violation, Sostre was penalized with the loss of 90 days of "good behavior time" credit. In addition, Letitia was removed from the list of Sostre's approved correspondents.

B. *Conditions of Punitive Segregation*

Sostre remained confined in punitive segregation for twelve months and eight days, until Judge Motley restrained his continued punishment *pendente lite* on July 2, 1969. By regulation, Sostre lost the opportunity to earn 124 1/3 days of good behavior credit while he was segregated. We cannot avoid setting forth the precise conditions of Sostre's long confinement with some particularity because Judge Motley found as a matter of law, that (1) in view of those conditions, Sostre's punishment—or any confinement in segregation under similar conditions for longer than 15 days—was "cruel and unusual" under the Eighth Amendment; (2) this absolute rule aside, Judge Motley held that the penalty inflicted upon Sostre was so disproportionate to the offenses charged against him that his segregation would have been cruel and unusual even crediting each of Follette's assigned justifications for it. We cannot approve these conclusions. Our reasons for refusing to do so are based in part on undisputed facts in the record which do not appear in Judge Motley's otherwise entirely accurate description of Sostre's segregated environment. The following account draws upon those undisputed facts which do not appear in the opinion below, as well as those which do, in an effort to present the whole fabric.

1. *Isolation from Human Contact*

Although for four months only one other prisoner was confined with Sostre in his small "segment" of five cells, the entire punitive segregation unit at Green Haven housed on the average about 15 prisoners at any one time. During the period between June 28, 1967, and September 18, 1968, 179 prisoners were held in segregation for a total of 8,960 days. From September 19, 1968 to July 3, 1969, when Sostre was there, a total of 79 inmates were segregated at Green Haven. Of these, about ten percent were held in "protective" segregation. This term is used to describe those who are segregated from the general population to protect them from harm rather than as punishment. These prisoners were incarcerated in cells entirely separated from Sostre's cell in the punitive segregation unit. The other prisoners were confined in cells near Sostre's, so that he would have been able to communicate with them, albeit with some difficulty depending on the distance between Sostre and the other prisoners. We are informed of an incident where one prisoner brought to solitary and placed in another group of cells committed suicide. Sostre was able to communicate with this inmate and indeed was able to dictate a legal document to him.

Finally, although we do not doubt that "the crux of the matter is human isolation," as Judge Motley observed, Sostre aggravated his isolation by refusing to participate in a "group therapy" program offered each inmate in segregation beginning October or November 1968. "Therapy" sessions were conducted in groups of about eight per class, generally one each week or ten days, under the guidance of a "recreation supervisor," Sergeant Louis Profera. Profera had been trained in group counseling in a six month, 40-hour course by a psychiatrist at the New York State Vocational Institution. Special rules for punitive segregation posted in the segregation unit provided that inmates in punitive segregation would be "returned to the general population after demonstrating their willingness to accept and adhere to the institutional rules and regulations as shown by their participation in group counselling sessions. ° ° ° Refusal to participate in group counselling is indicative of the inmate's unwillingness to accept and abide by the rules and regulations of the institution." Profera's favorable recommendation generally resulted in a prisoner's release from segregation. Although one prisoner who testified at trial returned to the general population without participating in group therapy, there is no doubt that there was significant pressure to participate. Expert witnesses at trial disagreed as to whether coercion would increase or decrease the efficacy of group therapy.[5]

2. Other Conditions of Sostre's Segregated Confinement

Judge Motley heard extensive testimony describing such important details as Sostre's diet, his opportunity for exercise, the hygienic conditions of his cell, and the possibility for intellectual stimulation. It can hardly be questioned that his life in segregation was harsher than it would have been in the general population, but neither was it clearly unendurable or subhuman or cruel and inhuman in a constitutional sense.

Thus, Sostre would not be served seconds of the main course upon his demand; but there was no testimony that he would have had that privilege in the general population. He was denied the dessert that would have been available to the general population; but apart from the dessert his diet still consisted of 2800 to 3300 calories a day.[7] Sostre remained in his cell at all times except for a brief period once each week to shave and shower. An hour of exercise with four or five other prisoners in a small, enclosed yard, open to the sky was a daily routine. But the record reveals that Sostre refused this privilege because he would not submit to a "strip search." Officials testified that it was necessary to subject prisoners to such an examination each time they entered the exercise yard to prevent them from concealing on their bodies small bits of wire or other material suitable for use as a weapon.

Hygienic conditions were at least minimally adequate to permit Sostre to remain clean and healthy. Thus,

---

[5] New York State prisoners may earn a maximum of ten days "good behavior time" credit each month, thereby advancing both the date the prisoner will be eligible for parole and the date he is entitled as of right to be "conditionally released" (that is, released from custody subject to parole conditions). Prison authorities may restore good behavior time withheld or revoked. See N.Y.Penal Law §§ 70.30, subd. 4, 70.40, subd. 1 (McKinney's Consol.Law, c. 40 1967); N.Y. Correction Law §§ 230, 803 (McKinney 1968). The repeal of Section 230, as of July 8, 1970 (McKinney Supp.1970), does not affect allowances for good behavior permitted prior to that date. Forfeiture of the chance to earn "good time" credit during punitive segregation is prescribed by regulation. 7 N.Y.Codes, Rules & Regulations, Correction § 60.6(c).

[7] Several prisoners who had served time in Green Haven's punitive segregation unit testified that more punishing than the deprivation of desserts was the loss of the opportunities available to the general population to receive food packages from the outside, to borrow snacks from other prisoners, and to earn pay with which to buy extra food from the prison commissary.

Sostre was allowed to shave and shower with hot water once each week. The furnishings of his normal-sized (6 ft. x 8 ft.) cell included a toilet and a face bowl with running cold water, and he was provided with soap and a towel.

The strictures on Sostre's intellectual fare were severe. He could not buy or receive books, magazines or newspapers, and his access to the prison's library collection was limited to a selection among approximately thirty-five volumes, mostly "shoot-em-ups" as Sostre described them, chosen by the prison guards. Still, light from a single bulb, controlled by the guards and usually turned on early in the morning and off at 10 p.m., was adequate for reading. And although he could not attend school or watch television, as could the inmates in the general population, any material related to the law requested by him would be brought to his cell.

3. Length of Segregated Confinement

Pursuant to the usual practice at Green Haven, Sostre was sentenced to "solitary" confinement for an indefinite period. According to New York Correction Law Section 140, "submissiveness" was to be the touchstone for his release. Follette testified that Sostre could have returned to the general population either by successful participation in group therapy or by agreeing to live by the rules of the prison. Sostre's contention is that he refused to agree to obey rules that he considered an infringement of his constitutional rights.

. . . .

III.

THE DISTRICT COURT'S ORDER

Upon these findings which we have necessarily sketched, Judge Motley on May 14, 1970, entered the following order, which because of its complexity and importance to the questions we must decide, we reproduce in full. The district court subsequently granted a stay of its order pending appeal as to the bracketed portions. A stay as to the remainder of the order was denied.

It is now ordered, that defendants Follette, McGinnis and Mancusi, their employees, agents, successors, and all persons in active concert and participation with them be, and they are hereby, perpetually enjoined and restrained from:

1) Returning plaintiff to punitive segregation for charges previously preferred against him;

2) Placing plaintiff in punitive segregation or subjecting him to any other punishment as a result of which he loses accrued good time credit or is unable to earn good time credit, without:

a. giving him, in advance of a hearing, a written copy of any charges made against him, citing the written rule or regulation which it is charged he has violated;

b. granting him a recorded hearing before a disinterested official where he will be entitled to cross-examine his accusers and to call witnesses on his own behalf;

c. granting him the right to retain counsel or to appoint a counsel substitute;

d. giving him, in writing, the decision of the hearing officer in which is briefly set forth the evidence upon which it is based, the reasons for the decision, and the legal basis for the punishment imposed.[9]

[3] Censoring, refusing to mail or refusing to give to Sostre: 1) Any communication between Sostre and the following—(a) any court; (b) any public official or agency; (c) any lawyer; (d) his co-defendant in the criminal matter pending against him; and, 2) Any letter relating to any legal matter to or from any other inmate who requests the assistance of Sostre in translating that letter into English.]

4) Punishing Sostre for sharing with other inmates his law books, law reviews, and other legal materials, and from refusing to permit Sostre to assist any other inmate in any legal matter as long as defendants have not provided any court approved alternative means of legal assistance for such inmates.

[5] Punishing Sostre for having in his possession political literature and for setting forth his political views orally or in writing, except for violation of reasonable rules approved by the court regulating freedom of speech.]

[It is further ordered that the above named defendants submit, within 90 days from the date of this order, for approval by this court, proposed rules and regulations governing the following:

1) the receipt, distribution, discussion and writing of political literature;

2) all future disciplinary charges and hearings with respect thereto where the possible punishments include solitary confinement, punitive segregation or any other segregation, and any other punishment in connection with which there is loss of, or inability to earn, good time credit.]

It is further ordered that the above named defendants and their agents credit plaintiff with the 124 1/3 days of good time credit which he was unable to earn while wrongfully incarcerated in punitive segregation from June 25, 1968 to July 2, 1969.

[It is further ordered that the plaintiff, Martin Sostre, recover of the defendants, Warden Follette, and Commissioner McGinnis the sum of $13,020.00.]

IV.

PUNISHMENT FOR POLITICAL BELIEFS AND LEGAL ACTIVITIES

The question as to the propriety of withdrawing from incarcerated individuals constitutional privileges enjoyed by citizens of the community, although troublesome, is not new to the courts. It is clear that in many respects the constitutionally protected freedoms enjoyed by citizens-at-large may be withdrawn or constricted as to state prisoners, so far as "justified by the considerations underlying our penal system," Price v. Johnston, 334 U.S. 266, 285 (1948). Federal courts have been reluctant to intrude themselves into the complex and delicate

---

[9] A panel of this court on July 10, 1970, expedited the appeal and granted a further stay of subparagraph 2 to the extent that it was limited to placing Sostre in punitive segregation for more than three days at any one time or a total of more than ten days, pending the hearing of this appeal.

problems of prison administration. E.g., United States ex rel. Knight v. Ragen, 337 F.2d 425 (7th Cir.), *cert. denied*, 380 U.S. 985 (1964); Hatfield v. Bailleaux, 290 F.2d 632, 640 (9th Cir. 1961); Childs v. Pegelow, 321 F.2d 487 (4th Cir. 1963). The time is long since past, however, when a court might describe a prisoner as temporarily "a slave of the state," Ruffin v. Commonwealth, 62 Va. (21 Gratt.) 790, 796, or treat him as such. Among those rights *not* taken from Sostre when he entered Attica, either "expressly or by necessary implication," Coffin v. Reichard, 143 F.2d 443, 445 (6th Cir. 1944), is freedom from discriminatory punishment inflicted solely because of his beliefs, whether religious or secular. Cooper v. Pate, 378 U.S. 546 (1964) (per curiam) (unlawful to withdraw prison privileges because of inmate's religious faith); see Lee v. Washington, 390 U.S. 333 (1968) (per curiam) (racial segregation); Fulwood v. Clemmer, 206 F.Supp. 370, 373-374 (D.C.D.C.1962) (religious discrimination). Moreover, the Constitution protects with special solicitude, a prisoner's access to the courts. Ex parte Hull, 312 U.S. 546 (1941); Johnson v. Avery, 393 U.S. 483 (1969). Accordingly, Sostre's lengthy confinement to segregation violated due process of law if, as the district court found, Warden Follette inflicted the punishment either because of Sostre's militant political ideas or his litigation, past or threatened, against Follette or other state officials.

Sostre does not shrink from characterizing himself as a "jailhouse lawyer" and the record before us does justice to this label, as does the history of Sostre's earlier period of confinement in New York prisons from 1952-64 following his first conviction for selling narcotics. It is not unreasonable to suppose, as the district court apparently did, that Warden Follette was aware of Sostre's Black Muslim activities during that period; of his solitary confinement in Attica Prison for four years, resulting from his religious activism; and of his success in securing through earlier litigation before this court the recognition of certain constitutional liberties for state prisoners. See Pierce v. LaVallee, 293 F.2d 233 (2d Cir. 1961); Sostre v. McGinnis, 334 F.2d 906 (2d Cir.), *cert. denied*, 379 U.S. 892 (1964). Sostre's version of his June 25, 1968, interview with Follette, if believed, was a proper basis for Judge Motley's conclusion that Follette committed Sostre to segregation, if not in retaliation for his black militancy or past litigation, then at least to squelch Sostre's threat to take Follette to court over his censorship of Sostre's correspondence. Some substantiation for Sostre's account might be inferred from Follette's summary commitment of Sostre, without following the practice described in the New York Department of Correction's Employees' Rule Book (Rule 8.4), requiring trial by a "disciplinary officer or court."

On this evidence, we cannot conclude that the district judge was "clearly erroneous" in attributing improper motives to Follette, affording as we must "due regard * * * to the opportunity of the trial court to judge of the credibility" of Sostre and Follette, F.R.Civ.P. 52(a). See Zenith Radio Corp. v. Hazeltine Research, Inc., 395 U.S. 100 (1969) (reviewing court may overturn finding if on the entire evidence it is left with the definite and firm conviction that a mistake has been made). On the other hand, McGinnis was not privy to Follette's interview with Sostre. The record is barren of any justification for attributing to him, in sanctioning Sostre's continued confinement, any more sinister motive than appropriate deference to the judgment of Warden Follette. McGinnis on the record before us, had no reason to suspect Follette of other than proper motivation.

V.
CRUEL AND UNUSUAL PUNISHMENT

A reflection of maturing sensitivity in this country to the condition of some of our prisons may be seen in the district court's finding that deprivations such as Sostre endured for a year may not again be inflicted on New York State prisoners for longer than fifteen days, and only then for serious violations of prison rules. Otherwise, Judge Motley held, such punishment would run ashoal of the Eighth Amendment prohibition of cruel and unusual punishment, as applied to the states through the due process guarantee of the Fourteenth Amendment, Robinson v. California, 370 U.S. 660 (1962).

We respect the outrage, given form and content by scholarly research and reflection, that underlay the expert testimony at trial of Sol Rubin, for many years Counsel for the National Council on Crime and Delinquency, and Dr. Seymour Halleck, a psychiatrist at the University of Wisconsin with long experience in state correctional practices. Mr. Rubin testified that Sostre's segregated environment was degrading, dehumanizing, conducive to mental derangement, and

for these reasons "a gross departure" from enlightened and progressive contemporary standards for the proper treatment of prison inmates. Dr. Halleck feared that the isolation from human contact in punitive segregation might cause prisoners to hallucinate and to distort reality. Long-term isolation might have so serious an impact, in fact, as to "destroy" a person's "mentality." Dr. Halleck singled out for particular censure Green Haven's "group therapy" program, whose compulsory aspects he found repugnant to effective treatment of participants and indeed inconsistent with minimal standards of professionalism among trained group counsellors.[11]

Nor would candor permit us to dismiss these opinions as aberrational among those views revealed in relevant sources referred to us by counsel or known to us through our own research. To the contrary, it would not be misleading to characterize many of the opinions of plaintiff's experts as fairly representative of the perspective of adherents to the "new penology," see Knuckles v. Prasse, 302 F.Supp. 1036, 1047-1048 (E.D.Pa. 1969), the thrust of whose doctrine may be gauged by the preference for the adjective "correctional" rather than "penal" as more accurately indicating the proper function of a prison

---

[11] Dr. William C. Johnston, a psychiatrist and Director of Mattawan State Hospital for the criminally insane, with extensive experience in dealing with mentally disturbed prisoners, rejected Dr. Halleck's assessment. Dr. Johnston reported that he had in fact supervised a successful compulsory group counseling program while Director of Dannemora State Hospital. Dr. Johnston also did not agree with plaintiff's experts that segregated confinement would likely endanger prisoners' sanity.

system. The rapidly rising standards in the field of penology and corrections that Mr. Rubin referred to in his testimony are reflected in a growing preoccupation with institutional strictures and techniques designed to "reintegrate" prisoners with society or, in the jargon of the experts, to "provide ° ° ° motivation for acquiring a conventional role in a non-delinquent setting."[13] Conjugal visiting, daytime work or educational-release programs, vocational training, halfway houses, and inmate publication of prison newspapers are some of the vanguard weapons in the "modern" approach to prison administration. The key concepts are access and involvement of prisoners with the free society "on the outside."[14] Anathema to this perspective are perhaps more traditional practices which subject prisoners to deprivation, degradation, subservience, and isolation, in an attempt to "break" them and make them see the error of their ways.[15] It is

suggested by many observers that such techniques are counter-productive, tending only to instill in most prisoners attitudes hostile to rehabilitation, summarized by one author as "doubt, guilt, inadequacy, diffusion, self-absorption, apathy [and] despair."[16]

We do not question, either, the relevance to an inquiry under the Eighth Amendment of opinions which may represent a progressing sense of humaneness as well as a new calculation as to the efficacy of penal practices. See Trop v. Dulles, 356 U.S. 86, 101 (1958) (Eighth Amendment invokes "the evolving standards of decency that mark the progress of a maturing society").

For a federal court, however, to place a punishment beyond the power of a state to impose on an inmate is a drastic interference with the state's free political and administrative processes. It is not only that we, trained as judges, lack expertise in prison administration. Even a lifetime of study in prison administration and several advanced degrees in the field would not qualify us *as a federal court* to

---

[13] See U. S. Bureau of Prisons. The Residential Center: Corrections in the Community (1970).

[14] *See, e. g.,* Garabedian, Challenges for Contemporary Corrections, 33 Fed.Prob. No. 1, at 3 (Mar. 1969); Rachin, The Message Corrections Must Get Across, 34 Fed.Prob. No. 2, at 3 (June 1970); Summary of The Report of the President's Task Force on Prisoner Rehabilitation (1970), 34 Fed.Prob. No. 3, at 3 (Sept. 1970). We do not ignore New York's active participation in this reform movement. See N.Y.Correction Law Art. 26 (McKinney Supp.1970) (work release program).

[15] "Traditional prisons, jails, and juvenile institutions are highly impersonal and authoritarian. Mass handling, countless ways of humiliating the inmate in order to make him subservient to rules and orders, special rules of behavior designed to maintain social distance between keepers and inmates, frisking of inmates, regimented movement to work, eat, and play, drab prison clothing, and

similar aspects of daily life—all tend to depersonalize the inmate and reinforce his belief that authority is to be opposed, not co-operated with ° ° ° Such an attitude is, of course, antithetical to successful reintegration."
President's Commission on Law Enforcement and Administration of Justice, Task Force Report: Corrections 11 (1967) (hereinafter cited as "Corrections").

[16] Chief Justice Burger, a persistent critic of our system of criminal justice which places every protection around an accused but seems to abandon him when he is sentenced to prison, recently observed that "a man in a cage needs incentive, motivation, and something to look forward to." U. S. News and World Report 32 (Dec. 14, 1970).

command state officials to shun a policy that they have decided is suitable because to us the choice may seem unsound or *personally* repugnant. As judges we are obliged to school ourselves in such objective sources as historical usage, see Wilkerson v. Utah, 99 U.S. 130, 25 L.Ed. 345 (1870), practices in other jurisdictions, see Weems v. United States, 217 U.S. 349, 30 S.Ct. 544, 54 L.Ed. 793 (1910), and public opinion, see Robinson v. California, 370 U.S. 660, 666, 82 S.Ct. 1417, 8 L.Ed.2d 758 (1962), before we may responsibly exercise the power of judicial review to declare a punishment unconstitutional under the Eighth Amendment.

Accordingly, we have in the past declined to find an Eighth Amendment violation unless the punishment can properly be termed "barbarous" or "shocking to the conscience." See Church v. Hegstrom, 416 F.2d 449, 451 (2d Cir. 1969). Although the conditions Sostre endured were severe, we cannot agree with the district court that they were "so foul, so inhuman, and so violative of basic concepts of decency," Wright v. Mc-Mann, 387 F.2d 519 (2d Cir. 1967),[17] as to require that similar punishments be limited in the future to any particular length of time. Nor can we agree that Sostre's own long confinement—however contrary such prolonged segregation may be to the views of some experts—would have been "cruel and unusual" had Sostre in fact been confined for the reasons asserted by Warden Follette, rather than on account of his beliefs and litigiousness.

It is undisputed on this appeal that segregated confinement does not itself violate the Constitution. *[Citations omitted.]* Indeed, we learn that a similar form of confinement is probably used in almost every jurisdiction in this country and has been described as one of "the main traditional disciplinary tools" of our prison systems. President's Commission on Law Enforcement and Administration of Justice, Task Force Report: Corrections 50-51 (1967); S. Rubin, et al., The Law of Criminal Corrections 293 (1963).[18] Plaintiff has directed our attention to currently operative rules in other jurisdictions which limit the duration of segregated confinement, and to several commentaries recommending or approving such rules. In several states, however, incarceration in segregated cells seems to be for an indefinite period, as it is in New York.

---

[17] Cf. Burns v. Swenson, 430 F.2d 771 (8th Cir. Aug. 31, 1970) ("base, inhuman, and barbaric"); Hancock v. Avery, 301 F.Supp. 786, 791-792 (M.D.Tenn. 1969) ("barbaric," "debasing," "violates basic standards of human decency"); Holt v. Sarver, 309 F.Supp. 362, 380 (E.D.Ark.1970) ("grossly excessive," "shocking or disgusting"); Jordan v. Fitzharris, 257 F.Supp. 674 (N.D.Cal. 1966) ("shocking and debased" conditions justify court's intervention to "restore the primal rule of a civilized community").

[18] Indeed, the first prisons in this country, widely imitated in Europe, were intended "to serve as place[s] for reflection in solitude leading to repentance and redemption." The Eastern State Penitentiary in Pennsylvania (1829), where inmates lived, worked, and exercised without being permitted to talk with fellow prisoners "was copied abroad perhaps more than any other American invention." Corrections 3. See American Correctional Ass'n, Manual of Correctional Standards 13 (3d ed. 1966) [hereinafter cited as "Manual"]. All forms of prison punishment in this country pale by comparison with those endured by Henri Charriere in the dungeons and French Penal Colony described in his book *Papillon* (Morrow 1970).

The federal practice appears to be that prisoners shall be retained in solitary "for as long as necessary to achieve the purposes intended," sometimes "indefinitely." Furthermore, "willful refusal to obey an order or demonstrated defiance of personnel acting in line of duty may constitute sufficient basis for placing an inmate in segregation." Such analogous practices[22] do not impel us to the conclusion that the Eighth Amendment forbids indefinite confinement under the conditions endured by Sostre for all the reasons asserted by Warden Follette until such time as the prisoner agrees to abide by prison rules—however counter-productive as a correctional measure or however personally abhorrent the practice may seem to some of us.

In arriving at this conclusion, we have considered Sostre's diet, the availability in his cell of at least rudimentary implements of personal hygiene, the opportunity for exercise[25] and for participation in group therapy, the provision of at least some general reading matter from the prison library and of unlimited numbers of law books, and the constant possibility of communication with other

segregated prisoners. These factors in combination raised the quality of Sostre's segregated environment several notches above those truly barbarous and inhumane conditions heretofore condemned by ourselves and by other courts as "cruel and unusual."[27] See Ford v. Board of Managers, 407 F.2d 937 (3rd Cir. 1969) (no running water or wash bowl; bread and water diet except one regular meal each third day; held constitutional); Landman v. Peyton, 370 F.2d 135 (4th Cir. 1966), cert. denied, 388 U.S. 920, 87 S.Ct. 2142, 18 L.Ed. 2d 1367 (1967); Knuckles v. Prasse, 302 F.Supp. 1036 (E.D.Pa.1969) (400 days segregation held constitutional).

Finally, we cannot agree with Judge Motley that even if New York might in an appropriate case subject a pris-

---

[22] The Supreme Court has struck down a choice of punishments only when the penalty was authorized in almost no other civilized jurisdiction. Trop v. Dulles, 356 U.S. 86 (1958); Weems v. United States, 217 U.S. 349 (1910), or conflicted with moral precepts "universally held," Robinson v. California, 370 U.S. 660 (1962). See also Jackson v. Bishop, 404 F.2d 571, 580 (8 Cir. 1968) (use of strap permitted in only two states, outlawed in several).

[25] This element distinguishes the instant case from Krist v. Smith, 309 F.Supp. 497, 501 (S.D.Ga.1970), where the court found no constitutionally acceptable justification for denying segregated prisoners a chance to exercise.

[27] E. g., Wright v. McMann, 387 F.2d 519, 521 (2d Cir. 1967) (complaint alleged cell encrusted with excrement; plaintiff entirely naked 11 days, then clad only in thin underwear; windows open throughout subfreezing night; prisoner slept on concrete floor; no soap, towel, or toilet paper); Hancock v. Avery, 301 F.Supp. 786 (M.D.Tenn.1969) (virtually no light or ventilation; hole for wastes flushed irregularly by guards; no soap, towel, or toilet paper; two meals of bread, one full meal); Jordan v. Fitzharris, 257 F. Supp. 674 (N.D.Calif.1966) (conditions similar to Hancock and in addition prisoner slept naked on concrete floor).

Sostre does not allege that he was arbitrarily or discriminatorily punished or abused by prison authorities while he was segregated. See Fulwood v. Clemmer, 206 F.Supp. 370 (D.C.D.C.1962) (plaintiff, among other things, unlawfully denied exercise of his religion while segregated and improperly transferred from prison to a jail because of his religion); Holt v. Sarver, 309 F.Supp. 362, 380 (E.D.Ark.1970) (prisoners subjected to arbitrary power of other prisoners). Cf. Jackson v. Bishop, 404 F.2d 571, 579 (8th Cir. 1968) (impossible for prison authorities or courts to supervise administration of corporal punishment so as to prevent excesses).

oner to the conditions of Sostre's segregated confinement, had Follette's motives been as he described them, the punishment would in any event have been unconstitutionally disproportionate to the offense. Were we to rule otherwise, we would deny to prison authorities the power to use an entirely constitutional means of discipline in response not only to a credible threat to the security of the prison, but in response to a prisoner's refusal to answer appropriate questions put by prison authorities and to obey valid prison regulations.[28]

. . . .

It is appropriate, lest our action today be misunderstood, that we disclaim any intent by this decision to condone, ignore, or discount the deplorable and counter-productive conditions of many of this country's jails and prisons. We strongly suspect that many traditional and still widespread penal practices, including some which we have touched on in this case, take an enormous toll, not just of the prisoner who must tolerate them at whatever price to his humanity and prospects for a normal future life, but also of the society where prisoners return angry and resentful. Nevertheless, we would forget at our peril and at the peril of our free governmental process, that we are federal judges reviewing decisions made in due

course by officers of a sovereign state. We have interpreted and applied the law as it appears to us in light of circumstance and principle. We do not doubt the magnitude of the task ahead before our correctional systems become acceptable and effective from a correctional, social and humane viewpoint, but the proper tools for the job do not lie with a remote federal court. The sensitivity to local nuance, opportunity for daily perseverance, and the human and monetary resources required lie rather with legislators, executives, and citizens in their communities. See, Amsterdam, The Supreme Court and the Rights of Suspects in Criminal Cases, 45 N.Y.U. L.Rev. 785, 810 (1970).

LUMBARD, Chief Judge concurring.

WATERMAN, Circuit Judge concurring.

J. JOSEPH SMITH, Circuit Judge (concurring in part and dissenting in part):

I agree with most of Judge Kaufman's thoughtful and thorough opinion but disagree in two respects and therefore dissent in part.

I agree with Judge Feinberg that the district court's finding that Sostre's segregation for more than one year was cruel and unusual punishment is supported by the record. Punishment of a nature found likely to bring about an inmate's insanity should be proscribed whether or not it is shown to have succeeded in doing so in the particular case, and whether or not it could be alleviated by "submission."

. . . .

FEINBERG, Circuit Judge (dissenting and concurring):

---

[28] We stress the seriousness of the multiple offenses charged against Sostre by Warden Follette, see pp. 183-185, *supra*, and express no view as to the constitutionality of such segregated confinement as Sostre experienced if it were imposed for lesser offenses. Specifically, we express no view as to the constitutionality of such segregated confinement if it had been imposed on account of any one or any combination of the offenses charged against Sostre other than all of them.

Because I agree with most of the exhaustive majority opinion, I regret that I find it necessary to dissent from the treatment of the cruel and unusual punishment point . . . [a]s the majority opinion reaches three results, from each of which I dissent. The most important of these is the refusal to hold that there must be a definite limit on how long a prisoner may be kept in punitive segregation, or solitary confinement. The majority holds that for "serious" offenses, the Constitution requires no limits so long as the prisoner has the option of submitting to prison discipline. Second, the majority holds that Sostre's alleged offenses considered together would have been "serious," if Warden Follette had acted for proper motives. Third, even though the warden's motives were "improper," the majority refuses to rule that Sostre's punishment was cruel and unusual.

Before considering these three aspects of the majority opinion, it must be emphasized that Sostre was segregated for over a year and, as Judge Motley noted, would in all likelihood still be effectively isolated but for the intervention of the district court. There is an intimation in the majority opinion that Sostre was not effectively cut off from usual day to day contact with other human beings, but the district judge's opinion makes clear that he was. The district judge and the majority both agree that "the crux of the matter is human isolation," and the district court opinion sets forth in melancholy detail the conditions that were imposed upon Sostre and the reasons why. I will not repeat them here except to note that the full vindictive flavor of defendants' treatment of Sostre is indicated by one incident,

relegated to a footnote in the majority opinion. The day after Judge Motley ordered Sostre's release from over a year of segregation, he was again disciplined for having "dust on his cell bars." This caused him to miss the regular July 4th celebration, which would have brought him in contact with prisoners from another part of the prison, such contact being permitted only once a year on July 4. Judge Motley found that the punishment was imposed upon Sostre in retaliation for his legal success before her.

The district judge found that the isolation imposed on Sostre was "dangerous to the maintenance of sanity" and "could only serve to destroy completely the spirit and undermine the sanity of the prisoner." 312 F. Supp. 863, 868, 871 (S.D.N.Y.1970), quoting Wright v. McMann, 387 F.2d 519, 526 (2d Cir. 1967). This was a finding of fact. The judge also concluded as a matter of law that "subjecting a prisoner to the demonstrated risk of the loss of his sanity as punishment for any offense in prison is plainly cruel and unusual punishment as judged by the present standards of decency." Id. at 871. The majority opinion does not make explicit whether it overrules the judge's finding of fact, although it hints that it does. But in order to reverse the district court on this issue the majority must hold either that Judge Motley's finding of fact is clearly erroneous or that, even if true, the punishment imposed on Sostre did not amount to cruel and unusual punishment as a matter of law. Neither holding would be justified.

As to the first, it is difficult to see how Judge Motley's factual finding that Sostre's isolation threatened sanity could be characterized as clearly erroneous. Testimony at trial from experts with impressive credentials clearly supported that finding. Dr. Halleck, in response to a hypothetical question outlining the conditions of Sostre's punishment, stated that they could undermine the prisoner's sanity. Sol Rubin supported that view. It is true that Dr. Johnston, testifying for the State, disagreed. But while the district judge, as trier of fact, was free to believe the experts for plaintiff or for defendants, we may do neither. The trial judge chose to believe the former, and I do not see how her finding on this evidence can be characterized as clearly erroneous.

On the second assumption, what the majority does is to hold that Sostre's lengthy, unlimited isolation, which was "dangerous" to his sanity, does not violate the Eighth Amendment. With deference, I disagree. The standard for determining "cruel and unusual punishment" has been expressed in a number of ways, all imprecise; e. g., "the wanton infliction of pain," Louisiana ex rel. Francis v. Resweber, 329 U.S. 459, 463 (1947); conduct which "shocks the most fundamental instincts of civilized man," *id.* at 473 (dissenting opinion); a method of punishment which violates the "evolving standards of decency that mark the progress of a maturing society," Trop v. Dulles, 356 U.S. 86, 101 (1958). These notions are, of course, subjective to some extent. What may be safely said is that the amendment prohibits "a hard core of inhuman conduct," see 84 Harv.L.Rev. 456, 457 (1970). There is no doubt, as the majority concedes, that a prisoner is not a constitutional pariah. Were that

not the case, there would be no basis for the holding that the first amendment was violated here. But the eighth amendment, no less than the first, protects Sostre.[4] Its command is both spacious and changing.

The fact that solitary confinement for an indefinite period has historically been accepted as a viable instrument of prison discipline does not prevent us from finding that it violates the Eighth Amendment. What might once have been acceptable does not necessarily determine what is "cruel and unusual" today. Recently, the Eighth Circuit has held that whipping by strap is proscribed, although it had once been a familiar practice. Jackson v. Bishop, 404 F.2d 571 (8th Cir. 1968). Indeed, this court emphasized only a few years ago that the Eighth Amendment "is not fastened to the obsolete." See Wright v. McMann, *supra,* 387 F.2d at 525, quoting Weems v. United States, 217 U.S. 349, 378 (1910). In this Orwellian age, punishment that endangers sanity, no less than physical injury by the strap, is prohibited by the Constitution. Indeed, we have learned to our sorrow in the last few decades that true inhumanity seeks to destroy the psyche rather than merely the body. The majority opinion emphasizes that after all Sostre could have obtained release from isolation at any time by agreeing to abide by the rules and to cooperate. Perhaps that is so, but that does not change the case. That response could be made were a prisoner kept in solitary for two years instead of one, or for five years, or for ten, or

_____

[4] Through the due process clause of the Fourteenth Amendment. See Robinson v. California, 370 U.S. 660, 82 S.Ct. 1417, 8 L.Ed.2d 758 (1961).

more. The possibility of endless solitary confinement is still there, unless the prisoner "gives in." The same observation could be made if Sostre were tortured until he so agreed, but no one would argue that torture is therefore permitted. The point is that the means used to exact submission must be constitutionally acceptable, and the threat of virtually endless isolation that endangers sanity is not.

The crucial holding of the majority opinion is the refusal to put any limit upon the period of solitary confinement. It is the unusual duration and the open-ended nature of the isolation that the district court and the experts regarded as inflicting the worst psychological harm. Accordingly, as we did in Wright v. McMann, *supra*, 387 F.2d at 526, I would hold that the punishment here, "which could only serve to destroy completely the spirit and undermine the sanity of the prisoner," runs afoul of the eighth amendment.

The second fundamental reason why I differ with the majority opinion stems from the contrast between what it finds necessary to decide and what it refuses to decide. As indicated above, the majority states in an extended dictum that if the warden's motives had been proper, the combined effect of Sostre's alleged violations would have been "serious" enough to justify the harsh punishment he received. Thus, the majority stresses "the seriousness of the multiple offenses charged against Sostre" and expresses "no view as to the constitutionality of such segregated confinement if it had been imposed on account of any one or any combination of the offenses charged against Sostre other than all of them." But

the fact is that two of the allegedly serious "multiple offenses" were Sostre's refusal to desist from preparing legal papers for a codefendant and his possession of six tables of contents torn from issues of the Harvard Law Review. I would not hold unconstitutional the isolation of an adult prisoner for a sharply limited period as punishment for a serious breach of prison discipline, e. g., what the majority calls "a credible threat to the security of the prison," see p. 194, *supra*. But these two offenses were simply not grave enough to justify the extremely severe punishment visited upon Sostre. Accordingly, the excessiveness of the penalty for these two alleged transgressions would alone violate the Eighth Amendment's proscription of cruel and unusual punishment, and I would say so.

Finally, while the majority reaches out to decide that Sostre's confinement would have been constitutional under a hypothetical set of facts, it refuses to rule that his punishment was cruel and unusual even though it was actually meted out for improper reasons. It is true that the majority also leaves open the constitutionality of such "confinement as Sostre experienced," if imposed for "lesser offenses." The inconsistency of this approach is apparent since if such confinement, in the majority's view, could ever be so excessive a penalty as to be unconstitutional, it should be declared so when there was no basis for the confinement at all.

In sum, keeping Sostre in solitary for over a year was "cruel and unusual punishment" because (1) the length and open-ended nature of his confinement threatened sanity; (2)

two of the alleged offenses were so minor as to make the penalty constitutionally disproportionate; and (3) the ostensible reasons were a pretext for vindictive action. For the reasons and to the extent set forth above, I dissent.

HAYS, Circuit Judge, dissenting (with whom MOORE, Circuit Judge, concurs).

NOVAK v. BETO
453 F.2d 661 (5th Cir. 1971), *reh. denied,*
453 F.2d 661 (5th Cir. Mar. 8, 1972)

THORNBERRY, Circuit Judge.

Appellants are inmates in custody of the Texas Department of Corrections. In this class action brought under 42 U.S.C. § 1983 they challenge the constitutionality of various aspects of the treatment accorded them by the Texas prison system. . . . [A]ppellants attack the conditions of solitary confinement as administered in Texas as constituting "cruel and unusual punishment" in violation of the Eighth and Fourteenth Amendments.

The district court, 320 F.Supp. 1206, found against appellants on all of these issues. . . . We affirm the district court holding that solitary confinement as administered in Texas is not unconstitutional.

[The Court's opinion concerning the regulation of jailhouse lawyers in Texas is found in section 6, Legal Services.]

Solitary Confinement

In view of recent tragic incidents in this Nation's prisons and of the frequent assertion of the inadequacy of our penal systems, the burden of judging weighs upon us more than usual as we turn to appellants' contention that solitary confinement as administered by the TDC is cruel and unusual punishment. Just as our dissenting brother, we are deeply troubled by the lightless cell, the limited bedding, and the minimal food provided prisoners in solitary confinement in Texas. Nevertheless, we do not find that the imposition of these conditions constitutes cruel and unusual punishment as forbidden by the Eighth Amendment. As judges, we must look to the extant law and the general practices of our society. Otherwise, we run the risk of imposing our own personal moral code on a perhaps unready society.[1]

We begin by turning to the long line of cases, to which we have found no exception, holding that solitary confinement *per se* is not "cruel and unusual." *[Citations omitted.]* Our inquiry does not, however, end here since appellants challenge solitary confinement as implemented by the TDC.

---

[1] On this point, we share the views of Judge Kaufman of the Second Circuit, writing for the majority of that Court *en banc*, in Sostre v. McGinnis, 2d Cir. 1971, 442 F.2d 178, at 191, who stated:

> [e]ven a lifetime of study in prison administration and several advanced degrees in the field would not qualify us *as a federal court* to command state officials to shun a policy that they have decided is suitable because to us the choice may seem unsound or *personally* repugnant. As judges, we are obliged to school ourselves in such objective sources as historical usage . . . , practices in other jurisdictions . . . and public opinion, . . . before we may responsibly exercise the power of judicial review to declare a punishment unconstitutional under the Eighth Amendment. (Emphasis in original)

We must, therefore, examine the particular conditions that existed in each system previously scrutinized by the courts. Holt v. Sarver, E.D.Ark.1969, 300 F.Supp. 825. On the question of particular conditions, there are several cases that have concluded that certain prison conditions were so "base, inhuman and barbaric" that they violate the Eighth Amendment. We have studied these cases and the conditions depicted therein rather carefully, and find in none of them support for condemnation of solitary confinement in this case. In the first place, there is a common thread that runs through all these cases and that is not present in our case. That thread is the deprivation of basic elements of hygiene. *See, e. g.,* Wright v. McMann, 2d Cir. 1967, 387 F.2d 519 [complaint alleged cell encrusted with excrement, plaintiff entirely naked, forced to sleep on concrete floor, windows open throughout subfreezing weather, no soap, towel or toilet paper]; Hancock v. Avery, M.D.Tenn. 1969, 301 F.Supp. 786 [hole for waste, flushed irregularly by guard, no soap, towel or toilet paper, prisoner slept naked on floor]; Holt v. Sarver, *supra* [isolation cells dirty and unsanitary, pervaded with bad odors, plain cotton mattress uncovered and dirty; conducive to spreading, and did spread, infectious diseases]; Jordan v. Fitzharris, N.D.Cal.1966, 257 F.Supp. 674 [cells not cleaned regularly, prisoner had no means to clean himself, a hole for receiving bodily wastes, no flushing mechanism]. By contrast with these cases, the prisoners in the TDC solitary confinement cells are deprived of none of the basic elements of hygiene. It is uncontradicted that solitary cells are scrubbed by the guards each time the prisoner leaves to bathe, which occurs at least three times a week. The cells are identical to the regular cells of the TDC in size and facilities; they contain flush toilets, a drinking fountain, and a bunk. The prisoner is supplied with toilet paper, a toothbrush and toothpaste. Although the bunk is stripped in the sense that it has no mattress or pillow, the prisoner is given two blankets and is clothed in a gown or other garb, so that there is nothing to compare with the reports of prisoners sleeping naked on concrete floors in the above-cited cases. In addition, solitary cells in the TDC have the same temperature controls that regular cells in the prison have. We think it is correct to say, therefore, that no case has found conditions comparable to those in the TDC unconstitutional.

More important, most of the conditions challenged by appellants have withstood scrutiny by other courts,[2]

and are to be found in differing variations in almost every jurisdiction in the country. See Sostre v. McGinnis, *supra*, 442 F.2d at 193.

Finally, the TDC has been ranked second or third among the Nation's prisons for its progressiveness in prison administration and reform. This, to us, should be a weighty fact in any evaluation of the TDC under the cruel and unusual punishment clause.[3]

We would not put so much stock in the TDC's fine reputation if we did not find that reputation borne out by the record in this case. The impression we have of the TDC from this record is that it has progressed rapidly under Dr. Beto's administration, and that it engages in constant efforts to reform and to police itself. We think this may be demonstrated by a description of the TDC's policy with respect to solitary confinement. This policy is set out in a TDC memorandum of "Disciplinary Procedures" directed to all wardens from the

---

[2] In Ford v. Board of Managers, 3d Cir. 1969, 407 F.2d 937, for example, a bread and water diet supplemented by a regular meal each third day withstood the scrutiny of a federal court. See *also* the conditions described in Krist v. Smith, S.D. Ga.1970, 309 F.Supp. 497, *aff'd*, 5th Cir. 1971, 439 F.2d 146. The dissent has cited conditions in federal solitary confinement as favorable by comparison. We would point out, however, that the federal practice is to leave prisoners in solitary confinement *indefinitely*. See Sostre v. McGinnis, 2d Cir. 1971, 442 F.2d at 193. Moreover, while federal prisoners in solitary have light in their cells and a mattress on their bunks at night, their cells are stripped during the day and they have only a floor toilet. Moreover, as we understand the testimony in this case (there is some confusion between administrative segregation and punitive confinement throughout the record), the federal prisoners in solitary received a "bland loaf." Dr. Beto testified that the prisoners in the TDC had expressed a preference

for bread and water as opposed to the federal loaf. In short, while it seems that no two systems are alike, they all use variations of the same theme.

In addition, there is testimony that the main reason for the differences between the federal and state facilities is that federal prisons contain fewer persons who are in on assault and murder charges. The state prisons have more need to adopt measures designed to cope with inmates prone to violence. This appears to be the reason inmates in the TDC are usually given a thin gown rather than a full prison uniform when they go to solitary. Apparently, there was reason to believe that the inmates in solitary would use the heavier clothing to attack the guards or to stuff the toilet, causing it to flood.

[3] We find this fact particularly persuasive in light of the Supreme Court's tendency to strike down a choice of punishments "only when the penalty is authorized in almost no other civilized jurisdiction." See Sostre v. McGinnis, *supra*, at 193, note 22.

TDC's Assistant Director for Treatment. . . . As we understand the testimony in this case, this memorandum is modeled after, and complies substantially with, the American Correctional Association's Manual on Correctional Standards. The most effective way to reveal the thrust of the memorandum, which is 23 pages long, is to quote certain passages from it:
. . . .

"Punitive segregation is ordinarily used as punishment when reprimands, loss of privileges, suspended sentences, and similar measures have been tried without satisfactory results. Punitive segregation is a major disciplinary measure and should be used judiciously when all other forms of action prove inadequate, where the safety of others is concerned, or when the serious nature of the offense makes it necessary."

Then, after describing the more lenient forms of Punitive Segregation (which include restriction to one's cell with loss of privileges and a limited diet), the Memorandum sets out procedures to be followed in administering solitary confinement.

"*Solitary Confinement:*
Confined inmates in a punishment status, placed on a restricted diet, with loss of privileges and placed in special facilities for a comparatively brief period. Ordinarily no inmate should be retained in punishment segregation on restrictive diet more than 15 days, *and normally a shorter period is sufficient.* Punitive segregation is not for indefinite or permanent segregation.

A.   Punitive segregation procedures
(1) Period of confinement:
Fifteen days should be the maximum time spent in solitary.
Recalcitrant inmates at the end of this period should be taken out of solitary, placed in a cell or if dormitory residents, left in cell with door open. After two or three days, depending upon physical condition, he may be returned to solitary and the procedure continued.

(2) Diet
A.   Inmates in solitary are to be fed one slice of bread twice a day and are to be given unlimited drinking water.
B.   Each 72 hours inmates are to be fed a full meal. The meal shall be identical to the meal on the steam table at that time for the working inmates, i. e., seasoned foods, salad, meat, dessert, drink.
C.   If an inmate remains recalcitrant at the end of a 15-day period and is handled as defined above, he should be fed the regular full ration (three full meals) for a minimum of two days. The number of days he is fed full ration in his cell should be determined by physical condition and rapidity of strength renewal. When returned to solitary, restricted diet procedure will be in force.
(a) Written records should be made regarding date and time of feeding, and menu fed.

(3) Medical Care and Procedure
A.   Inmates who are to be placed in solitary should be

checked by a physician or medical officer prior to confinement. In the event neither is available, the medical classification should be carefully checked on the travel card, if medical classification is such that life will not be jeopardized, the inmate may be placed in solitary and checked by medical personnel at first available period. When there is doubt regarding health, the inmate should be placed in administrative segregation until evaluated by medical personnel. Diabetics, Epileptics, heart cases, cases of high blood pressure, ulcers, generally debilitated conditions should not be placed in solitary but all privileges may be denied to them and they may be confined in a hospital or clinic cell.

B. Inmates should be weighed at least once a week and more often if possible by medical personnel, written record reflecting weight should be kept either on solitary cell door, treatment card, or in a book reserved for this purpose.

C. All inmates in solitary must be checked by a physician or medical officer at least once a day. Written record of visit should be kept on treatment card or in a book reserved for this purpose.

D. Personal hygiene should be encouraged. Inmates should be given a bath at least three times a week. Inmates should be allowed to brush their teeth daily. Male inmates should be shaved twice a week.

(4) Clothing

Inmates in solitary confinement should be given coveralls, a gown or some other form of clothing, i. e., tee shirt and undershorts, tee shirt and regulation trousers. Changes of clothing shall be effected at least two times per week.

   *   *   *   *   *   *

(5) Bedding

   *   *   *   *   *   *

Inmates in punitive segregation, solitary, should be furnished with the necessary number of blankets to keep them warm.

   *   *   *   *   *   *

(6) Visits to Segregation

Prisoners in punitive segregation will be visited, observed, or evaluated a minimum of:

A. Two times each shift by a correctional officer.

B. Daily by both the officer in charge of the day shift and the officer in charge of the night shift.

C. Daily by medical personnel.

D. As frequently as necessary by Disciplinary Committee members to assure inmate's welfare is properly provided for and to determine time and method of release.

E. Daily by either warden or assistant warden.

(7) Release from Punitive Segregation

Disciplinary Committee members will frequently review the case of each inmate in punitive segregation, determine the inmate's attitude, and return the inmate to the regular inmate population when, in the Committee's opinion, he may reasonably be expected to adequately adjust and conform to the rules and regulations. *Segregation for punishment should always be for the shortest period of time that will accomplish the desired results of favorable adjustment.*

(8) Return to Work

After a man has been in solitary over an extended period, he will become weak and in no condition to do a hard day's work. He should be treated as a 'new inmate' and given a light but productive work assignment until his strength returns, this will vary according to the individual and his work assignment.

EXERCISE CAUTION SO THAT HEALTH IS NOT JEOPARDIZED.

After studying this record in its entirety, we have found ample evidence to establish that the TDC complies with virtually all of these guidelines in its administration of solitary confinement. First, there are statistics in the record to show that the ratio of the average number of male inmates confined to solitary on a given day to the average total inmate population over a period of one year runs around 2.1%, indicating that solitary is indeed used sparingly. Secondly, there are computerized reports kept on all inmates who are confined to solitary. These reports record, among other things, the duration of the inmate's stay in solitary. They reveal that of the 132 prisoners confined in

solitary at the time the reports were compiled, one had been in for a 14-day period, and 35 had been in for 7 days or more. The remaining 96 had been in for 6 days or less. Of the 11 who were let out on the day this report was compiled, 2 had been in for a full fifteen-day period, one had been in for one day only, 4 had been in for 6 days or less, and the remaining 4 had been in for 8-14 days. In addition, another yearly report showing the history of solitary confinement in the TDC revealed that most of those who had been confined were confined only once (in other words, the treatment was not repeated), while no more than 10% were returned after a second treatment for further periods of confinement. These reports convince us that solitary confinement is used sparingly in the TDC, that the period of confinement seldom equals the maximum fifteen-day period and is frequently well under that period, and that comparatively few of the prisoners in the TDC who are confined to solitary once have the punishment repeated a second time, and many fewer have it repeated a third time.

We turn now to the named prisoners who instituted this suit and who testified to their complaints about solitary confinement in the TDC. We think it should first be pointed out that each of the prisoners who testified came from the Ellis Unit, which is the TDC's maximum security unit where prisoners considered to be high security risks are housed. Each of them had compiled rather long records of non-conformity with prison rules. A brief sampling follows: The Appellant Brown had on his record two attempted escapes, two charges of possessing contraband [a knife in both instances], numerous charges of agitation, fighting, creating a disturbance, disobeying a direct order, not working properly, and stealing. Appellant Brassell had compiled an offense record which also included an attempt to escape, refusal to work and insolence. Appellant Cruz' record contains such offenses as refusal to work, insubordination, threatening the life of another inmate, impudence, possession of a prohibited weapon and agitation.

The confinement of each of these prisoners for violation of the prison regulation against inmate legal assistance should be viewed in the context of their entire records, and not as though this was the only offense they ever committed. It seems fair to say that the prison authorities might have concluded that these were prisoners *upon whom all lesser forms of discipline had failed.*

We have set out the above information in detail because it is important to view the use of solitary confinement in the TDC in the context of the whole prison system. We cannot view such conditions as a bread and water diet supplemented every 72 hours by a full meal in a vacuum. We must also take into account the fact that the prison authorities as a matter of policy are careful to limit use of the diet to avoid damage to the prisoner's health. Thus, as we consider each of the conditions in solitary, we must keep in mind that solitary is imposed as a last resort to obtain obedience from recalcitrant prisoners, that it is imposed for a limited amount of time [indeed, as we understand the testimony in this case, a prisoner will be released from soli-

tary any time he asks to be released and agrees that he will abide by the prison rules], and that precautionary measures are taken to protect the prisoner from an overdose of solitary.

Used in this manner, solitary confinement serves a legitimate purpose in the prison community as a deterrent and a punitive force. Both the testimony of the prisoners in this case and the statistics revealing the low rate of returns to solitary support the conclusion that solitary is an effective deterrent of nonconforming prison conduct. On this point, we differ with the dissent, which concludes that solitary "has a totally negative impact on any hope for rehabilitation." First, we would point out that while there is testimony by one psychologist that solitary confinement has no rehabilitative value, this testimony was contradicted by a psychiatrist who stated that often belligerent prisoners need to be segregated temporarily for their own good, as well as for the protection of others. In fact, the experts testified that there is an ongoing debate in their field over the harmful vis-a-vis the helpful effects of solitary confinement. See Sostre v. McGinnis, *supra*, 442 F.2d at 193, n. 25. There is also, of course, a vigorous debate over the comparative roles of punishment and rehabilitation in the correctional stage of our criminal justice system. It is not our place, however to resolve that debate. We think it is enough simply to say that, as of now, deterrence and punishment still have an active place in our prisons. It is beyond dispute, of course, that order must be maintained in the prisons. And when a prisoner continues to break prison rules even after losing such privileges as going to the movies and being assigned extra work, the authorities must have some harsher measure to induce compliance with prison regulations.

Our role as judges is not to determine which of these treatments is more rehabilitative than another, or which is more effective than another. The Constitution does not answer such questions. The scope of our review is very limited under the cruel and unusual punishment clause. And there are good reasons for the limitations on the scope of that review. In the first place we simply are not qualified to answer the many difficult medical, psychological, sociological, and correctional questions when it comes to choosing between one form of treatment and another. It is for this reason, we think, that courts have traditionally confined their review of prison regulations to such standards as "barbarous" and "shocking to the conscience." See Church v. Hegstrom, 2d Cir. 1969, 416 F.2d 449. See also Royal v. Clark, 5th Cir. 1971, 447 F. 2d 501 ("Federal courts will not interfere in the administration of prisons absent an abuse of the wide discretion allowed prison officials in maintaining order and discipline, . . ."). More important, however, we think it is apparent from our experience with this case, if it had not been apparent before, that courts simply are not equipped to police the prisons.[6]

There was testimony in this record, for example, that the prison medical officers did not always check on the prisoners in solitary. We cannot, however, condemn the whole system because the prison personnel deviate occasionally from the prison policy. Obviously, we cannot follow the medical officers on the rounds each day to see that they comply with their assigned duties. While we are not so naive as to believe that every prison employee obeys prison regulations to the letter, we believe that, absent a showing of bad faith on the part of prison officials, we must rely on the prison admininstrators to enforce the policies they adopt. . . .

Viewing the record as a whole, therefore, we have concluded that solitary confinement as it is used in the Texas Department of Corrections does not violate the cruel and unusual punishment clause. In reaching this conclusion, we have compared the TDC's practices with those of other prison systems. We have considered that solitary is used sparingly and only as a last resort to inducing compliance with prison regulation. We have considered the fact that the authorities as a matter of prison policy take many precautionary steps to see that the use of solitary does not result in harm to the prisoners. On this record we cannot conclude that the TDC's system is cruel and unusual, much less barbarous or shocking to the conscience.

---

[6] The limits of our ability to police the prisons manifests itself in various ways. One, of course, is the fact that prison reform is primarily a task for legislators and administrators. We cannot express this point better than did Judge Kaufman in Sostre v. McGinnis, supra, 442 F.2d at 205:

We do not doubt the magnitude of the task ahead before our correctional systems become acceptable and effective from a correctional, social and humane viewpoint, but the proper tools for the job do not lie with a remote federal court. The sensitivity to local nuance, opportunity for daily perseverance, and the human and monetary resources required lie rather with the legislators, executives, and citizens in their communities.

Affirmed in part, reversed in part.

TUTTLE, Circuit Judge (concurring in part and dissenting in part):

Although I agree with the majority, in so far as it holds that TDC's ban against inmate assistance cannot stand, I do so because I am convinced that this record *affirmatively shows* that the TDC has not supplied a reasonable alternative rather than because of the failure of the TDC to make a sufficient showing.

. . . .

Moreover, and more importantly, I am compelled to dissent from the portion of the opinion dealing with solitary confinement. I would hold that solitary confinement as actually carried out by the TDC, not as described in regulations, clearly constitutes a violation of the Eighth Amendment. I am quite reluctant to disagree with my brothers of the majority on an issue which, I think, necessarily, involves the application of a moral code to one of society's most difficult problems.[1] However, there is no indication that the majority and I differ as to our concept of what the moral code should be. The difference lies in our concept of the extent to which judges can "risk" permitting their "own personal moral code" in such an area as this to be "impose[d] . . . on a perhaps unready society." For myself, I do not hesitate to assert the proposition that the only way the law has progressed from the days of the rack, the screw and the wheel is the development of moral concepts, or, as stated by the Supreme Court in Trop v. Dulles, the application of "evolving

standards of decency" 356 U.S. 86, 78 S.Ct. 590, 2 L.Ed.2d 630 (1957).

This, therefore, poses a further difference between the members of the court. If, as is stated by the majority, they "are deeply troubled by the lightless cell, the limited bedding, [a blanket, according to the findings of the trial court] and the minimal food provided prisoners in solitary confinement in Texas," then I do not agree with them that we are limited by what has been done by other courts or by the "general practices of our society."

As to the limiting effect of the "extant law," which I shall undertake to analyze below, we must remember that in each of the cases referred to in the opinion in which cruel and unusual punishment was found to exist, *some* court had to take at least a short step beyond what had previously been decided. This, in fact, is the genius of the common law. I think it is the duty of the court whose members are "deeply troubled" by these conditions to seek a means of removing them that may offer more promise than merely saying that "prison reform is primarily a task for legislators and administrators."

I feel that it is permissible for us to take judicial notice, as the majority apparently did, of the current spate of criticisms of our penal systems. It would be utterly unrealistic to ignore the fact that penal reform comes more slowly than progress in other activities of our society which seem to have much higher priorities. To leave the prisoners to the tender mercies of the legislatures and thereafter to the administrators who are denied the means to accomplish the reforms, seems to me to hold out slight, if any,

---

[1] Note that the majority opinion commences with a reference to "tragic incidents in the Nation's prisons and of the frequent assertions of the inadequacy of our penal systems."

hope that these "deeply troubling" conditions will be outlawed.

For this court to tell the prisoner to look to the legislature and an administrator who has condoned, and still excuses them, would seem to me but an empty gesture, and calls to mind an answer right out of Aeschylus: "Hollow words, I deem are worst of ills." *Prometheus Bound.*

In sum, I think this is an area in which the court should move. Such action by us is not only justified, it is called for if the Anglo-Saxon system of justice is to remain living and vigorous. The Supreme Court, in Bartkus v. Illinois, 359 U.S. 121 at pg. 128, 79 S.Ct. 676, at pg. 680, 3 L.Ed. 2d 684 speaking through Mr. Justice Frankfurter, stated:

> "The Anglo-American system of law is based not on transcendental revelation but *upon the conscience of society* ascertained as best it may be by a tribunal disciplined for the task and environed by the best safeguards for disinterestedness and detachment." (emphasis supplied)

The duty of a court like ours to act in such a matter has, I think, been expressed with his usual great felicity by Judge Learned Hand:

> "[The common law] must be content to lag behind the best inspiration of its time until it feels behind it the weight of such general acceptance as will give sanction to its pretension to unquestioned dictation. Yet with this piety must go a taste for courageous experiment, by which alone the law has been built as we have it, an indubitable structure, organic and living. It is in this aspect that the profession of the law is in danger of failing in times

like our own when deep changes are taking place in the convictions of men. It is not as the priests of a completed revelation that the living successors of past law makers can most truly show their reverence or continue the traditions which they affect to regard. If they forget their pragmatic origin, they omit the most pregnant element of the faith they profess and of which they would henceforth become only the spurious and egregious descendants. Only as an articulate organ of the half-understood aspirations of living men, constantly recasting and adapting existing forms, bringing to the high light of expression the dumb impulses of the present, can they continue in the course of the ancestors whom they revere." "The Art and Craft of Judging—The Decisions of Judge Learned Hand", Hershel Shanks, page 17.

Now, what are these "deeply moving" conditions of solitary confinement?

A person sentenced to solitary is kept in a bare, pitch black cell on a bread and water diet. The cell has a barred iron gate backed up by a wooden door to keep out all light and prevent contact with those in the hall. He is fed only two slices of bread and water each day and one full meal every 72 hours.[2] This treatment can

---

[2] Although regulations provide for a full meal as served off the steam table upon the expiration of 72 hours (it may be breakfast, lunch or dinner) every inmate witness testified that in point of fact such meal *never* equaled the full meal—that there was no meat, no sweets and no drink, regardless when served. There was no specific rebuttal of this testimony, other than by persons who were not active observers of the service.

continue for up to fifteen days, at which point he is kept in the *same* cell,[3] but with the solid door open to let in the light and is fed regular meals for two days. This process may then be repeated again. As the record reveals, inmate Bobby Brown was kept in solitary for a period of about seven weeks. Another prisoner spent nine weeks in solitary within an eleven month period.

In addition to the bread and water diet, the cell is barren of furnishings except for a combination toilet-washbasin and a steel bunk. The bunk, however, has no mattresses, sheets or pillow. Though the prisoner is provided with a blanket, the inmate has no clothes, no shoes, only a cloth gown and, except when taken to the shower, he spends all of his time in the cell. While there he has no access to hot water; he is not allowed to have a comb or eyeglasses and, upon release from solitary, the inmate's head is shaved bald.

The regulations of the TDC require that an inmate be weighed and that the weight be recorded upon admittance and upon release. A study of the individual records indicates that frequently no weights were entered on release. Moreover, while one might assume that solitary is usually reserved for the most recalcitrant of prisoners, it is apparent from this record that such confinement may be meted out at any time for any offense,

regardless of its gravity, with no objective standards, and often summarily without a hearing.[4]

Except as noted these facts and conditions stand without dispute.

And indeed, there is one fact which I feel must be emphasized. While no evidence was introduced to show the calorie content of two slices of bread, it is of such common knowledge that

---

[3] The regulation clearly states that at the end of 15 days the prisoner "*should be taken out* of solitary, placed in a cell or if dormitory residence, left in cell with door open. After 2 or 3 days, depending upon physical condition, he may be returned to solitary and the procedure continued." (emphasis added) It is unrefuted that all those in solitary for more than 15 days never left the same cell.

[4] Records of inmates show that they have been sent to solitary for having called a guard a Klansman, for "impudence", for "insolence", or "insubordination", for "laziness", for "unsatisfactory work," for having a law book in a cell; for letting another inmate *look* at a law book; for "possession of an unauthorized writ, carrying it to Sunday School"; and for failing to "shell peanuts". (This is itself a punishment—inmates are required to shell enough peanuts to make a gallon of *shelled* peanuts, a task which, according to the record may take several hours.) We have noted that on one occasion Cruz was sentenced to shell three gallons—all after the day's work, of course.

Moreover, there is no categorical denial of the testimony as to specific repeated instances of *summary* punishment by any witness who was in a position to know the precise facts. The trial court made no finding of fact as to this.

Further, it is by no means clear that the regulations, even if followed, require a hearing prior to solitary confinement. They simply state:

"When a correctional employee witnesses or has knowledge of an act by an inmate which is in violation of the rules and regulations or good order, and if the infraction cannot be properly handled by the observing employee, he will take the action necessary to bring the inmate before the supervising officer on duty. *If the supervising officer is not able to properly dispose of the infraction, the report of the infraction will be processed* as follows for action by the *Unit Disciplinary Committee*." (Emphasis added).

The Unit Disciplinary Committee holds hearings only on those cases which have been referred to it. Thus, it is entirely possible that the regulations themselves allow what many prisoners have testified to—namely, commitment to solitary by a supervisory officer *with no opportunity for a hearing*.

it need not be documented, it seems to me, that a slice of bread normally contains from 70 to 90 calories, and the very maximum for enriched bread would be 125 calories. This would mean a maximum of 250 calories a day. *This is simply a starvation diet.* Dr. Beto's testimony that the prisoners in other kinds of segregation in TDC were given a 2100 calorie diet because they were not engaged in active work rules out any justification for furnishing a diet of 250 calories a day to prisoners in solitary except as a matter of physical punishment.[4A]

It must be noted at the outset that the TDC does not challenge the jurisdiction of the Federal Court to pass judgment on these conditions if questioned as cruel and unusual. It does not argue that such prison matters should not be interfered with because the state now has a program gradually aimed at eliminating the excesses described above and is at least moving toward what various commentators have described as the "rehabilitative ideal." It simply says these conditions should be acceptable as a part of the prison's disciplinary scheme. It argues that, despite the fact, as the trial court found, "that certain aspects of the Texas approach are below the standards of some other states . . . especially with respect to food, lighting and recreation," the

---

[4A] It is evident that during the testimony given on this point, there was a good deal of confusion as to whether a 2100 or a 2500 calorie diet was recommended as a bare minimum for prisoners confined in segregation. The fact that those in solitary, by receiving only two pieces of bread, in effect received roughly one/tenth of the calories of those in segregation was not specifically stated. This point can, I think, easily be inferred from this record.

conditions described above are not *as bad as those* in which courts have, in the past, found Eighth Amendment violations, and furthermore, such an ultimate sanction is absolutely necessary to preserve prison discipline.
. . . .

I would conclude that the *combination of circumstances* in this case not only raises serious Eighth Amendment questions, but is sharply out of line with the "evolving standards of decency," the standard set forth by the Supreme Court in Trop v. Dulles, 356 U.S. 86, 78 S.Ct. 590, 2 L.Ed.2d 630 (1957). Further, I find such treatment to be a startling example of overkill, which, on the basis of this record, has a totally negative impact on any hope for rehabilitation. In short, I would find the solitary confinement as implemented by TDC to be a violation of the cruel and unusual punishment clause of the Eighth Amendment.

A finding of cruel and unusual punishment does not depend upon the use of physical violence like the strap, the rack or the wheel of old. In Trop v. Dulles, *supra*, the Supreme Court held that deprivation of citizenship as a punishment for wartime desertion was cruel and unusual. In so doing the Court stated that denationalization was "a form of punishment more primitive than torture, for it destroys for the individual the political existence that was centuries in the development." The "dignity of man" was said to be the overriding value to be preserved by the prohibition, and the court clearly recognized that the standard for determining whether a method of punishment was cruel and unusual must be based upon "evolving standards of decency that mark the progress of a maturing society."

The majority, however, though recognizing the recent tragic incidents in this Nation's prisons, and "the lightless cell, the limited bedding, and the minimal food" provided the prisoners in this case, nevertheless states:

"As judges, we must look to the extant law and the general practices of our society. Otherwise, we run the risk of imposing our own personal moral code on a *perhaps unready society.*" (emphasis added)

Surely, our society has evolved to the point where a diet of two pieces of bread and a quantity of water, total darkness, scanty clothing, little or no exercise and the shaving of one's head (a final act of humiliation) is beyond such "standards of decency" that can be tolerated, whatever the alleged benefit to prison discipline such treatment may yield. Not only do these conditions demean the human dignity of the inmate involved, but as they reflect the extent to which society will go in punishing its prisoners, they affect us all. For it is implicit in the Court's opinion in *Trop* that imbedded in this society are certain standards of human decency that put a limit on the *kind* of punishment we will inflict on *anyone*, regardless of his offense. Though we may be dealing here with some of the most incorrigible members of our society (although not solely), how we treat these particular individuals determines, to a large extent, the moral fibre of our society as a whole and if we trespass beyond the bounds of decency, such excesses become an affront to the sensibility of each of us.

The majority also implies that were

we to find an Eighth Amendment violation in this case, we would be taking an unprecedented step.[5] A look to the distant past as well as to a recent line of cases requires, I feel, a different conclusion.

Indeed, the idea that certain kinds of solitary confinement constitute cruel and unusual punishment is not new. As long ago as 1890 the United States Supreme Court clearly saw and clearly articulated the vice of solitary confinement even for a relatively short period of time under conditions less onerous than those here under attack. In *Medley*, Petitioner, 134 U.S. 160, 10 S.Ct. 384, 33 L.Ed. 835, an original application for habeas corpus in the Supreme Court, the Court considered whether the sentence of solitary confinement as a prelude to execution of the death sentence (to be accomplished within four weeks) violated the prohibition of Section 10 article 1 of the Constitution forbidding the passage of any *ex post facto* law. At the time of commission of the crime of first degree murder for which Medley was convicted and sentenced, there was no provision for solitary confinement in the state penitentiary while awaiting execution; the law formerly in force provided that such convicted murderer remain in the county jail until executed. In considering whether this change was "such invasion(s) of his rights as to properly be called (an) *ex post facto* law(s)" the court said:

---

[5] Even if this were true, it would be merely the slightest step in a direction which I believe the majority agrees would be the right direction. The fact that it would be unprecedented for want of an identical prior decision is not, as I have already stated, an answer to the petitions here.

"This matter of solitary confinement is not, as seems to be supposed by counsel, and as is suggested in an able opinion on this statute, furnished us by the brief of the counsel for the State, by Judge Hayt, (in the case of Henry Tyson,) *a mere unimportant regulation as to the safe-keeping of the prisoner*, and is not relieved of its objectionable features by the qualifying language, that no person shall be allowed access to said convict except his attendants, counsel, physician, a spiritual adviser of his own selection, and members of his family, and then only in accordance with prison regulations.

Solitary confinement as a punishment for crime has a very interesting history of its own, in almost all countries where imprisonment is one of the means of punishment. In a very exhaustive article on this subject in the American Cyclopaedia, Volume XIII, under the word "Prison" this history is given.

In that article it is said that the first plan adopted when public attention was called to the evils of congregating persons in masses without employment, was the solitary prison connected with the Hospital San Michele at Rome, in 1703, but little known prior to the experiment in Walnut Street Penitentiary in Philadelphia in 1787. The peculiarities of this system were the complete isolation of the prisoner from all human society, and his confinement in a cell of considerable size, so arranged that he had no direct intercourse with or sight of any human being, and no employment or instruction. Other prisons on the same plan, which were less liberal in the size of their cells and the perfection of their appliances, were erected in Massachusetts, New Jersey, Maryland and some of the other States. But experience demonstrated that there were serious objections to it. *A considerable number of prisoners fell, after even a short confinement, into a semi-fatuous condition, from which it was next to impossible to arouse them, and others became violently insane; others, still, committed suicide; while those who stood the ordeal better were not generally reformed, and in most cases did not recover sufficient mental activity to be of any subsequent service to the community.* It became evident that some changes must be made in the system, and the separate system was originated by the Philadelphia Society for Ameliorating the Miseries of Public Prisons, founded in 1787.

⁕   ⁕   ⁕   ⁕   ⁕   ⁕

The brief of counsel for the prisoner furnishes us with the statutory history of solitary confinement in the English law. The act 25 George II, c. 37, entitled 'An act for the better preventing the horrid crime of murder,' is preceded by the following preamble: 'Whereas, the horrid crime of murder has of late been more frequently perpetrated than formerly; and whereas it is thereby become necessary that some further terror and peculiar mark of infamy be added to the punishment of death now by law upon such as shall be guilty of the said offense'—then follow certain enactments, the sixth section of which reads as follows: '*Be it further enacted,* That from and after such conviction and judgment given thereupon, the jailor or keeper to whom such criminal shall be delivered for safe custody shall confine such prisoner to some cell separate and apart from the other prisoners, and that no person or persons whatsoever, except the jailor or keeper, or his servants, shall have access to any such prisoner, without license being first obtained.'

This statute is very pertinent to the case before us, as showing, first, what was understood by solitary confinement at that day, and second, that *it was considered as an additional punishment of such a severe kind that it is spoken of in the preamble as 'a further terror and peculiar mark of infamy'* to be added to the punishment of death. In Great Britain, as in other countries, public sentiment revolted against this severity, and by the statute of 6 and 7 William IV, c. 30, *the additional punishment of solitary confinement was repealed."* (emphasis added)

The court concluded that this additional "infamous" punishment could not be meted out to the condemned murderer and since this was part of his sentence held to be void, and the law had repealed the old statute fixing punishment, the court was required to discharge the petitioner from his death sentence.

We recognize that the solitary confinement in Medley's case was while he was on death row, and this made more poignant, if not more punitive, the solitary confinement part of the sentence. However, we also note that there were not present several of the harshest features of solitary as it was

suffered by the plaintiffs here. There was no bread and water diet; there was no total darkness, and for all that appears there was no complete lack of visitation. Moreover, in its discussion of the effect on the prisoners— "A considerable number of the prisoners fell, *even after a short* confinement, into a semi-fatuous condition, from which it was next to impossible to arouse them, and others became violently insane; others, still, committed suicide; while those who stood the ordeal better *were not generally* reformed, and, in most cases did *not recover* sufficient mental activity *to be of any subsequent service* to *the community"* (emphasis added)— the court spoke directly to the use of solitary confinement unrelated to the circumstances of an impending death sentence.

The majority, however, notes that the recent cases which have held that certain conditions of solitary confinement have violated the cruel and unusual punishment clause have all involved unconscionably unsanitary conditions in the cells. Since the proof here is that the cells involved in this case are clean and the prisoners are provided with the basic implements of personal hygiene, no violation, they argue, has occurred.

I reject such a narrow reading of these cases. Indeed, as one commentator has pointed out:

". . . the courts have not rested their decisions simply on that ground (sanitation). Rather, they have considered the totality of the dehumanizing circumstances and have condemned that totality as unconstitutional. Turner, 23 Stan.L. Rev. 473 at — (1971)."

An examination of some of these cases reveals that unsanitary conditions were but one of many factors that led to the court's decision. The fact they are lacking in the case at bar does not make this case unprecedented. It simply means that I rely on a *different combination* of dehumanizing factors that compel me to conclude that the Eighth Amendment has been violated.

In Wright v. McMann, 387 F.2d 519 (2nd Cir. 1967), the solitary cell was encrusted with excrement. There was no soap, towels or toilet paper. Further, petitioner was placed in the cell entirely naked and, since there was only a toilet and a sink in the cell, he was forced to sleep on the concrete floor with the windows open, even during subfreezing weather. Petitioner also claimed that he received no advance notice from the prison authorities of the charges against him, was not permitted to call witnesses, confront his accusers or defend himself in any manner.

As shocking as these facts are, it must be noted that Wright was not, as here, subject to complete sensory deprivation. His cell was lighted. Further, he was not placed on a starvation diet, but continued to receive the regular institution diet. Finally, it should be noted that as in *Wright*, there is considerable testimony to suggest that this punishment is often given out in a manner devoid of any procedural protections.

In Hancock v. Avery, 301 F.Supp. 786 (M.D.Tenn.1969), the dry cell was unlighted, save for dim artificial light which was able to seep from the outside corridor through two small slit screens in the cell door, and the interior was devoid of furnishings ex-

cept for a hole in the rear of the cell constructed to receive bodily wastes. There was no mechanism in the cell to flush waste from this hole. This was controlled by a guard on the outside. As a result of infrequent flushing, objectionable odors often permeated the cell. Further, the cell was not cleaned while the prisoners occupied it and they were given no hygienic materials. Finally, they were forced to remain entirely nude. The trial court thus concluded that these conditions made "it evident that fundamental concepts of decency did not prevail."

By comparison, we note that in the case at bar the cell is pitch black. Further, the diet in *Hancock* was significantly better. Prisoners received *three* meals each day—bread at breakfast and supper, but a *full meal each noon*. Finally, the prisoners in this case, though clad in a prison gown and in possession of a blanket, also were forced to sleep on a steel bunk without a mattress.

In Holt v. Sarver, 300 F.Supp. 825 (E.D.Ark.1969), the solitary cells were in a heated, well ventilated building. There were no windows, but there were electric light bulbs. Each cell had a drinking fountain and a toilet, though it could be flushed only from the outside. The occupants were regularly fed a wholesome and sufficient food called "grue" which the court described as consisting "of meat, potatoes, vegetables, eggs, oleo, syrup and seasoning baked all together in a pan and served in four inch squares." Id. at 832. They were also given plain cotton mattresses. The cells, however, were dirty and the mattresses were unsanitary. There was evidence that infectious diseases were spread by the indiscriminate use of these mattresses. Further, these cells were often overcrowded with as many as four per cell. This greatly added to the unsanitary conditions then prevailing.

However, by comparison we again note that these cells were lighted. Their occupants were regularly fed a wholesome meal. Further, the court in that case specifically found that the punishment was not meted out "unjustly, arbitrarily, or discriminatorily." There was also at least an attempt to provide some kind of bedding.

. . . .

Surely, the combination of factors we deal with in the case at bar is not so out of line with the fact situations outlined above as to be offensive only due to "some fastidious squeamishness or private sentimentalism" (Rochin v. California, 342 U.S. 165, 172, 72 S.Ct. 205, 209, 96 L.Ed. 183 (1952) on my part. In no case cited above was there such complete sensory deprivation coupled with a starvation diet. Indeed, if there is a common thread running throughout all these cases, including the one at bar, it is not the presence or absence of unsanitary conditions, but the deprivation of what should be the minimal comforts and institutional privileges that make prison life tolerable. For those in solitary confinement, at the very least, there ought to be regular meals, light and bedding.

Finally, the majority states that the conditions we face in this case have withstood the scrutiny of other courts. Krist v. Smith, 309 F.Supp. 497 (S.D. Ga.1970), aff'd, 439 F.2d 146 (5th Cir. 1971) and Ford v. Board of Managers, 407 F.2d 937 (3rd Cir. 1969)

are cited. Each, I feel, is easily distinguishable.

The conditions of solitary confinement in Krist consisted of a cell in which there was a bed, a table, basin, shelf and a commode. The complaint, concerning the food, alleged that the diet was unbalanced in that there were no vegetables, no fruit and far too much turnip greens. The right kind of shampoo was not available. Petitioner could not get books from the prison library without considerable trouble. He complained that there was no television or movies and that the medical care he received was shoddy. The trial court held that such allegations were matters of internal prison administration. The Fifth Circuit agreed, adding that "federal courts will not interfere except where paramount federal constitutional or statutory rights intervene." Surely, there is little to compare in Krist with the conditions in our case. Such circumstances as found here clearly involve the protection afforded by the Eighth Amendment.

In Ford, the complaint alleged that none of the solitary confinement cells had wash bowls or running water, that the inmates' shower was not given every fifth day as required, that his cell was unsanitary, and that his diet consisted of four slices of bread and a pint of water three times daily with a full meal every third day.

While these are not the best of circumstances, the diet these inmates received was six times as much as the prisoners in this case. Further, the cell was lighted and "an old mattress with a clean cover on a cement shelf [was] provided for bedding." Further, it should be noted that this case never went to trial and thus, expert testimony regarding the effect of such treatment was not in the record.

Finally, Sostre v. McGinnis, 2 Cir., 442 F.2d 193 (1971) is cited as an example of an appropriate judicial response to such Eighth Amendment questions. Indeed, the court then invoked the traditional "hands off" doctrine in dealing with the problems it faced, but in that case this was not at all inappropriate. The prisoners' diet was, except for desserts, the same as that of the general population; rudimentary implements of personal hygiene were available; there was an opportunity for daily exercise in the open air; though the period of confinement was indefinite, an inmate could release himself from solitary by agreeing to participate in group therapy; reading matter from the prison library was available as well as unlimited access to legal materials. Further, the cell was lighted and there was the constant possibility of direct communication with other prisoners. Finally, the court noted the absence of any testimony that solitary threatened the mental or physical health of the prisoner. Surely, the Court in the Second Circuit was wise in not intervening in such a situation. Needless to say, with the exception of personal hygiene, every factor listed above is absent in this case.

Having concluded that the conditions of this case do not constitute cruel and unusual punishment, the majority undertakes to bolster its position by showing the context within which this punishment occurs. They find solace in TDC's regulations regarding disciplinary proceedings concluding that "after studying this record in its entirety, we have found ample evidence to establish that TDC complies with virtually all of these guidelines in its administration of solitary confinement."

I, too, have examined this record. I not only find it to be replete with evidence of violations of TDC's own regulations, but, to a large extent, I find that the kinds of guidelines and practices pointed out by the majority, though perhaps showing good faith on the part of TDC, are nonetheless irrelevant to the issues presented by this case.

One thing that stands out starkly—like the incandescent lamp that is lacking in these cells—is the fact that there is no word or suggestion in the regulations that the solitary cells are to be absolutely without lights. It speaks, somewhat euphoniously, about prisoners in punitive solitary confinement being placed in "special facilities." It is obvious that this makes much better reading than if the regulations expressly prescribed a "pitch black cell." Thus, it is plain that punishment as administered is much more harsh in one important detail than called for by the published regulations.

Also, as stated above, the full meal that should be granted is seldom a full meal; inmates are sent to solitary for a variety of offenses many of which are insignificant; their punishment is often handed out summarily, without a hearing; though the regulations say that the inmate should be weighed before, during and after solitary, such weights were rarely recorded. Indeed, in addition to the conditions of solitary, virtually every prisoner who testified complained of the blatant disregard of the regulations by TDC. This testimony was not refuted by anyone who was in a position to know the facts (by the guards, for example) and the trial court made no findings of fact.

Further, the majority finds comfort in the fact that there are statistics in this record which show that the ratio of the average number of male inmates confined to solitary on a given day to the average total inmate population over a period of one year runs around 2.1%. This, it is said, indicates that solitary is used sparingly. Moreover, the majority also points to a report which stated that *on the particular day* that it was compiled, few of the inmates confined were subjected to a full fifteen day detention.

I find such figures to be totally beside the issue in this case. Whether certain conditions constitute cruel and unusual punishment does not depend upon whether 1% or 99% of the prison population was forced to endure them. Suppose TDC used the strap, as did Arkansas until forbidden as cruel and unusual punishment, would its infrequent use make it any less of a violation of the Eighth Amendment? In a case of this sort, a decision must be based on the conditions themselves, not the number of inmates that must endure them.

Similarly, the fact that many prisoners do not spend a full fifteen days in solitary is also irrelevant. Indeed, the majority ignores the undisputed fact that inmate Bobby Brown was kept in solitary for a period of about seven weeks in 1968. Even if it were relevant to look to *the particular day* the majority takes its figures from, two inmates had been in for a full fifteen day period and 35 were in for a full

week or more.[8] In short, what is at issue here is the constitutionality of a regulation that submits prisoners to a particular form of punishment which *can* and *often is* imposed for 15 days or more. One must focus on the conditions themselves, not the frequency with which inmates must endure them for the full 15 day period, or more.

Nevertheless, even if it is conceded that these figures are relevant, my examination of the record conveys a completely different impression. Contained in this record is a computer print out entitled: "History of Solitary Confinement Since November, 1968". It covers the period of November 1968 to September 1969. It reveals that during this time span 2816 inmates were subjected to solitary confinement. This is roughly 22.5% of the entire prison population. Put another way, during a nine month period nearly one of every four prisoners at TDC can expect to be subjected to solitary confinement. Further, if one adds to this figure the number of times some of these same inmates repeated during this time span, the total grows to 4164. This is not what I would characterize as a sparing use of this form of punishment. And indeed, over the course of a full year the figure of 2816 could be expected to reach approximately 3500 without correcting for repeats.

The majority also points to the records of *some* of the inmates involved. They conclude that:

---

[8] The figure of 132 prisoners which was broken down, of course, shows only how long those 132 had been in solitary *up to that day.* This proves nothing. So far as the record shows all of the rest of the 132 may have remained in solitary for a week or ten days thereafter.

"It seems fair to say that the prison authorities *might have concluded* that these were prisoners upon whom all lesser forms of discipline had failed." (emphasis added)

Again I ask, would this fact justify the use of the strap or the rack or the wheel? A consideration such as this adds nothing to a decision concerning the constitutionality of the conditions TDC can subject *any* inmate to, be he a first offender or the most recalcitrant prisoner in the entire system. And indeed, the majority's reference to the fact that appellant Cruz is no stranger to this court seems to me to be wholly irrelevant. We all know that we are dealing with persons who have been tried and convicted and are serving time.

I would, in short, hold that the conditions of solitary confinement as implemented by TDC are totally out of line with the standard set forth in *Trop*. In addition, I would also hold that the punishment as applied is overbroad, and clearly goes much further than is necessary in carrying out the legitimate state interest in maintaining prison discipline. Even if I were to conclude that the treatment in this case did not constitute cruel and unusual punishment, its application because of violating for example, the ban on inmate assistance seems to me to be a striking example of overkill.[9] As the court in Jordan v. Fitzharris, 257 F.Supp. at 679, stated:

_____
[9] There may be some reason other than simple whimsicality or vindictiveness that would cause the "committee" to send one of the prisoners to solitary for 10 days for committing the felony of sodomy, while sending him to solitary for *two successive* 15 days sentences for having a law book or paper in his cell, but none occurs to us. Such a grotesquerie is shown by this record.

"A punishment may be [considered] cruel and unusual when, although applied in pursuit of a legitimate penal aim, it goes beyond what is necessary to achieve that aim; that is, when a punishment is unnecessarily cruel in view of the purpose for which it is used." Weems v. United States, 217 U.S. at [349] 370, 30 S.Ct. 544 [54 L.Ed. 793]

There is no doubt that there is a need to isolate certain prisoners. Indeed, I agree with appellees that a crucial question that must be answered is:

What can be done with the inmate who refuses to conform with prison rules—who refuses to change his attitude in response to either counseling or to a gradual withdrawal of prison incentive programs—and who is a constant source of trouble to authorities to the extent of disrupting their efforts at rehabilitation of other inmates?

Removing such a prisoner from the general population may, of course, be necessary. However, nothing in the record proves that such extreme treatment as here present *in connection with* segregation has either a deterrent effect upon him or the inmates or is at all necessary in maintaining order in the prison.

The majority, however, feels that the form of punishment in this case has a deterrent effect. They state:

Both the testimony of the prisoners in this case and the statistics revealing the low rate of returns to solitary support the conclusion that solitary is an effective deterrent of nonconforming prison conduct.

An examination of these statistics and a sample of testimony that is illustrative of this record refutes, I feel, this conclusion.

Of the 2816 inmates who were sentenced to solitary in a nine month period, 833 or 29.51% had the treatment repeated at least once within this relatively *short* span of time. 555 were confined twice; 170 were confined three times; 51 were confined four times; 27 were confined five times; 16 were confined 6 times; 6 were confined 7 times; 6 were confined 8 times; 1 was confined 9 times and 1 was confined *10 times*. Indeed, since this covers only a nine-month period, it can readily be assumed that the percentage of repeaters over a one or two year period is substantially higher. I would not characterize such figures as illustrative of any significant deterrent effect such treatment allegedly has.

. . . .

In addition to the overbreadth aspects of the treatment, it may be determined to be cruel and unusual on yet another ground. This record supports the proposition that TDC's treatment has a totally negative impact on any hope for rehabilitation. Indeed, the psychological effects of such confinement have long been considered most destructive. The record, for example, reveals that certain objects such as comb or eyeglasses are kept from one in solitary because he may be considering suicide. (See quotation from Medley, *supra*.) Surely, putting any man in a situation in which he contemplates suicide as a way out cannot be justified by any state interest in maintaining discipline. One does not have to be a trained psychologist to conclude that such treatment, intended to "break the spirit"

of an unruly inmate will, if successful destroy all except the very strongest personality.

The majority, however, notes that experts disagree on the use of solitary and it is not the place of this court to resolve such a matter. Suffice it to say, the debate that is going on does not deal with solitary confinement accompanied by a starvation diet, no light, scanty clothing, the shaving of a man's head, etc. Totally isolating a man in a humane environment may or may not be helpful. We are *not* deciding that question. The question before this court concerns a particular kind of solitary confinement. We would be resolving no psychological debates in holding that this *form* of solitary violates the Eighth Amendment.

In addition, I cannot help but note that James V. Bennet, former Director of the Federal Bureau of Prisons and a person cited favorably by both sides, has recently testified:

"(t)hat the use of the bread and water diet 'is an archaic and discredited' system which has 'no effect' except that it complicates the man's health problem.'" Hirschkop and Millemann, The Unconstitutionality of Prison Life, 55 Va.L. Rev. 795, 838 (1969).

I feel that this record supports this observation. Clearly, this ought never be the inevitable results of prison discipline even if it is aimed at maintaining order.[11]

-----

[11] Though federal guidelines do not necessarily have a bearing in determining whether state prison authorities have exceeded the bounds of the Eighth Amendment, it is interesting to note that federal prisoners put in solitary confinement continue to be fed the same as the gen-

Finally, the majority states that the judicial scope of our review is very limited under the cruel and unusual punishment clause. However, it must be kept in mind that the law of this Circuit has long been that once a prisoner is incarcerated

"Any further restraints or deprivations in excess of that inherent in the sentence and in the normal structure of prison life should be subject to judicial scrutiny." Jackson v. Godwin, 5 Cir., 400 F.2d 529 at 535.

Surely, the case before us and any like it is well within our scope of inquiry. Moreover, with a record replete with violations of TDC's own regulations, I cannot agree with the majority's willingness to give prison administrators the benefit of the doubt. As in other areas of the law, arbitrary thoughtlessness and administrative incompetence is every bit as offensive as the perversity of a willful scheme. See generally, Norwalk CORE v. Norwalk Redevelopment

_____

eral population, have adequate lighting and get at least some exercise. Further, they are provided with a mattress to sleep on as well as reading material, and some correspondence and visiting privileges.

The majority in footnote 2 of its opinion states that as they understand the testimony of this case, federal prisoners in solitary received a bland loaf. Our reading of the federal prison regulations does not support this statement.

This relevant regulation states:

"4. *Food.* As prescribed in existing Bureau regulations, segregated inmates shall be fed three times a day on the standard ration and menu of the day for the institution. Disposable utensils may be used when necessary."

Prior portions of the regulations made plain the fact that "segregated inmates" as used here refers to those in *punitive* segregation, the harshest kind in the federal system.

Agency, 395 F.2d 920, 929 (2d Cir. 1968).

In conclusion, I note one more excerpt from this record.

"The Court: Would you fear if they tied you to a stockade and beat you with a whip?

The Witness: That wouldn't make me no fear. I am sure it would abuse me.

The Court: Would it keep you from breaking the regulations?

The Witness: As severe punishment will not stop it. Even these severe sentences don't stop us. It even makes people commit the same crime over and over."

This answer, I feel, eloquently as well as logically sums up the entire gambit of what is in issue in this case: complaints that punishment is meted out without a fair hearing; that the punishment is not in proportion to the offense; that it is punishment that is cruel and unusual under any circumstances; and, finally, that it is not a deterrent and does nothing for rehabilitation.

This statement by a semi-literate prisoner witness is more eloquently and effectively elaborated in a recent volume written by two highly qualified students of penology, Norval Morris, Professor of Law and Criminology and Director of the Center for Studies in Criminal Justice, University of Chicago, and Gordon Hawkins, Senior Lecturer in Criminology, University of Sydney. They hold to the thesis that experience proves it to be possible to remove cruelties and infliction of physical or psychological suffering such as causes us here to be deeply troubled without harm to the end sought in deterring crime.

"(p)erhaps a more precise analysis of the relationship between mind and heart in penal reform is that our uniform experience, critically analyzed, seems to be that we can indulge our sense of decency, of reducing suffering even of criminals, without any adverse effect on the incidence of criminality. The history of penal reform thus becomes the history of the diminution of gratuitous suffering . . .

The diminution of gratuitous human suffering, gratuitous in the sense that no social good whatsoever flows from it, that it in no wise diminishes the incidence or seriousness of crime and delinquency, remains an important purpose of penal reform. One does not have to travel far anywhere in America to find thousands of convicted persons, adult and juvenile, subjected to needless suffering and for grossly protracted periods. And not only is such suffering useless; it is harmful to us. It tends to increase the social alienation of those we punish

beyond our social needs, and it is highly probable that we pay the penalty of increased recidivism and increased severity of the crimes committed by those who do return from such punishment to crime." *The Honest Politician's Guide to Crime Control,* Morris and Hawkins, pp. 246, 247.

I again express my reluctance to differ with my brothers on a matter involving moral standards, be they those of our society or of us as judges. I am especially conscious of the inordinate length of this dissenting opinion. However, this is an area of the law which will present close and perplexing questions for future decisions. I feel, therefore, that this fully tried clear-cut issue deserves the most careful consideration the court can give it.

I would reserve the judgment of the trial court and remand for the entry of an order requiring regular meals, light and bedding.

RHODES v. CHAPMAN
452 U.S. 337, 101 S. Ct. 2392, 69 L. Ed. 2d 59 (1981)

[footnotes and citations omitted]

Justice Powell delivered the opinion of the Court.

The question presented is whether the housing of two inmates in a single cell at the Southern Ohio Correctional Facility is cruel and unusual punishment prohibited by the Eighth and Fourteenth Amendments.

I

Respondents Kelly Chapman and Richard Jaworski are inmates at the Southern Ohio Correctional Facility (SOCF), a maximum-security state prison in Lucasville, Ohio. They were

housed in the same cell when they brought this action in the District Court for the Southern District of Ohio on behalf of themselves and all inmates similarly situated at SOCF. Asserting a cause of action under 42 U.S.C. § 1983, they contended that "double celling" at SOCF violated the Constitution. The gravamen of their complaint was that double celling confined cellmates too closely. It also was blamed for overcrowding at SOCF, said to have overwhelmed the prison's facilities and staff. As relief, respondents sought an injunction barring petitioners, who are Ohio officials responsible for the administration of SOCF, from housing more than one inmate in a cell, except as a temporary measure.

The District Court made extensive findings of fact about SOCF on the basis of evidence presented at trial and the court's own observations during an inspection that it conducted without advance notice. These findings describe the physical plant, inmate population, and effects of double celling. Neither party contends that these findings are erroneous.

SOCF was built in the early 1970's. In addition to 1620 cells, it has gymnasiums, workshops, school rooms, "day rooms," two chapels, a hospital ward, commissary, barber shop, and library. Outdoors, SOCF has a recreation field, visitation area, and garden. The District Court described this physical plant as "unquestionably a top-flight, first-class facility."

Each cell at SOCF measures approximately 63 square feet. Each contains a bed measuring 36 by 80 inches, a cabinet-type night stand, a wall-mounted sink with hot and cold running water, and a toilet that the inmate can flush from inside the cell. Cells housing two inmates have a two-tiered bunk bed. Every cell has a heating and air circulation vent near the ceiling, and 960 of the cells have a window that inmates can open and close. All of the cells have a cabinet, shelf, and radio built into one of the walls, and in all of the cells one wall consists of bars through which the inmates can be seen.

The "day rooms" are located adjacent to the cell blocks and are open to inmates between 6:30 a.m. and 9:30 p.m. According to the District Court, "[t]he day rooms are in a sense part of the cells and they are designed to fur-

nish that type of recreation or occupation which an ordinary citizen would seek in his living room or den." Each day room contains a wall-mounted television, card tables, and chairs. Inmates can pass between their cells and the day rooms during a 10-minute period each hour, on the hour, when the doors to the day rooms and cells are opened.

As to the inmate population, the District Court found that SOCF began receiving inmates in late 1972 and double celling them in 1975 because of an increase in Ohio's statewide prison population. At the time of trial, SOCF housed 2,300 inmates, 67% of whom were serving life or other long-term sentences for first-degree felonies. Approximately 1,400 inmates were double celled. Of these, about 75% had the choice of spending much of their waking hours outside their cells, in the day rooms, school, workshops, library, visits, meals, or showers. The other double celled inmates spent more time locked in their cells because of a restrictive classification.

The remaining findings by the District Court addressed respondents' allegation that overcrowding created by double celling overwhelmed SOCF's facilities and staff. The food was "adequate in every respect," and respondents adduced no evidence "whatsoever that prisoners have been underfed or that food facilities have been taxed by the prison population." The air ventilation system was adequate, the cells were substantially free of offensive odor, the temperature in the cell blocks was well controlled, and the noise in the cell blocks was not excessive. Double celling had not reduced significantly the availability of space in the day rooms or visitation facilities, nor had it rendered inadequate the resources of the library or school rooms. Although there were isolated incidents of failure to provide medical or dental care, there was no evidence of indifference by the SOCF staff to inmates' medical or dental needs. As to violence, the court found that the number of acts of violence at SOCF had increased with the prison population, but only in proportion to the increase in population. Respondents failed to produce evidence establishing that double celling itself caused greater violence, and the ratio of guards to inmates at SOCF satisfied the standard of acceptability offered by respondents' expert witness. Finally, the court did find that the SOCF administration, faced with more inmates than jobs, had "water[ed] down" jobs by assigning more inmates to each job than necessary and by reducing the number of hours that each inmate worked, *id.*, at 1015; it also found that SOCF had not increased its staff of psychiatrists and social workers since double celling had begun.

Despite these generally favorable findings, the District Court concluded that double celling at SOCF was cruel and unusual punishment. The court rested its conclusion on five considerations. One, inmates at SOCF are serving long terms of imprisonment. In the court's view, that fact "can only accent[uate] the problems of close confinement and overcrowding." Two, SOCF housed 38% more inmates at the time of trial than its "design capacity." In reference to this the court asserted, "Overcrowding necessarily involves excess limitation of general movement as well as physical and mental injury from long exposure." Three, the court accepted as contemporary standards of decency several studies recommending that

each person in an institution have at least 50-55 square feet of living quarters. In contrast, double celled inmates at SOCF share 63 square feet. Four, the court asserted that "[a]t best a prisoner who is double celled will spend most of his time in the cell with his cellmate." Five, SOCF has made double celling a practice; it is not a temporary condition.

On appeal to the Court of Appeals for the Sixth Circuit, petitioners argued that the District Court's conclusion must be read, in light of its finding, as holding that double celling is *per se* unconstitutional. The Court of Appeals disagreed; it viewed the District Court's opinion as holding only that double celling is cruel and unusual punishment under the circumstances at SOCF. It affirmed, without further opinion, on the ground that the District Court's findings were not clearly erroneous, its conclusions of law were "permissible from the findings," and its remedy was a reasonable response to the violations found.

***

We now reverse.

II

We consider here for the first time the limitation that the Eighth Amendment, which is applicable to the States through the Fourteenth Amendment, imposes upon the conditions in which a State may confine those convicted of crimes. It is unquestioned that "[c]onfinement in a prison. . .is a form of punishment subject to scrutiny under the Eighth Amendment standards." But until this case, we have not considered a disputed contention that the conditions of confinement at a particular prison constituted cruel and unusual punishment. Nor have we had an occasion to consider specifically the principles relevant to assessing claims that conditions of confinement violate the Eighth Amendment. We look, first, to the Eighth Amendment precedents for the general principles that are relevant to a State's authority to impose punishment for criminal conduct.

A

The Eighth Amendment, in only three words, imposes the constitutional limitation upon punishments: they cannot be "cruel and unusual." The Court has interpreted these words "in a flexible and dynamic manner," and has extended the Amendment's reach beyond the barbarous physical punishments at issue in the Court's earliest cases. Today the Eighth Amendment prohibits punishments which, although not physically barbarous, "involve the unnecessary and wanton infliction of pain," or are grossly disproportionate to the severity of the crime. Among "unnecessary and wanton" inflictions of pain are those that are "totally without penological justification."

No static "test" can exist by which courts determine whether conditions of confinement are cruel and unusual, for the Eighth Amendment "must draw its meaning from the evolving standards of decency that mark the progress of a maturing society." The Court has held, however, that "Eighth Amendment judgments should neither be nor appear to be merely the subjective views" of judges. To be sure, "the Constitution contemplates that in the end [a court's] own judgment will be brought to bear on the question of the acceptability" of a given punishment. But such " 'judgment[s] should be informed by objective factors to the maximum extent possible.' " For example, when the question was whether capital punishment for cer-

tain crimes violated contemporary values, the Court looked for "objective indicia" derived from history, the action of state legislatures, and the sentencing by juries. Our conclusion in *Estelle* v. *Gamble*, that deliberate indifference to an inmate's medical needs is cruel and unusual punishment rested on the fact, recognized by the common law and state legislatures, that "[a]n inmate must rely on prison authorities to treat his medical needs; if the authorities fail to do so, those needs will not be met."

These principles apply when the conditions of confinement compose the punishment at issue. Conditions must not involve the wanton and unnecessary infliction of pain, nor may they be grossly disproportionate to the severity of the crime warranting imprisonment. In *Estelle* v. *Gamble*, we held that the denial of medical care is cruel and unusual because, in the worst case, it can result in physical torture, and, even in less serious cases, it can result in pain without any penological purpose. In *Hutto*, the conditions of confinement in two Arkansas prisons constituted cruel and unusual punishment because they resulted in unquestioned and serious deprivations of basic human needs. Conditions other than those in *Gamble* and *Hutto*, alone or in combination, may deprive inmates of the minimal civilized measure of life's necessities. Such conditions could be cruel and unusual under the contemporary standard of decency that we recognized in *Gamble*. But conditions that cannot be said to be cruel and unusual under contemporary standards are not unconstitutional. To the extent that such conditions are restrictive and even harsh, they are part of the penalty that criminal offenders pay for their offenses against society.

B

In view of the District Court's findings of fact, its conclusion that double celling at SOCF constitutes cruel and unusual punishment is insupportable. Virtually every one of the court's findings tends to *refute* respondents' claim. The double celling made necessary by the unanticipated increase in prison population did not lead to deprivations of essential food, medical care, or sanitation. Nor did it increase violence among inmates or *create* other conditions intolerable for prison confinement. Although job and educational opportunities diminished marginally as a result of double celling, limited work hours and delay before receiving education do not inflict pain, much less unnecessary and wanton pain; deprivations of this kind simply are not punishments. We would have to wrench the Eighth Amendment from its language and history to hold that delay of these desirable aids to rehabilitation violates the Constitution.

The five considerations on which the District Court relied also are insufficient to support its constitutional conclusion. The court relied on the long terms of imprisonment served by inmates at SOCF; the fact that SOCF housed 38% more inmates than its "design capacity"; the recommendation of several studies that each inmate have at least 50-55 square feet of living quarters; the suggestion that double celled inmates spend most of their time in their cells with their cellmates; and the fact that double celling at SOCF was not a temporary condition. These general considerations fall far short in themselves of proving cruel and unusual punishment, for there is no evidence that double celling under these circumstances either inflicts unnecessary or wanton pain or is grossly disproportionate to the severity of crimes warranting imprisonment. At most, these considerations amount to a theory that double celling inflicts pain. Perhaps they reflect an aspiration toward an ideal environment for long-term confinement. But the Constitution does not mandate comfortable prisons, and prisons of SOCF's type, which house persons convicted of serious crimes, cannot be free of discomfort. Thus, these considerations properly are weighed by the legislature and prison administration rather than a court. There being no constitutional violation, the District Court had no authority to consider whether double celling in light of these considerations was the best response to the increase in Ohio's state-wide prison population.

III

This court must proceed cautiously in making an Eighth Amendment judgment because, unless we reverse it, "[a] decision that a given punishment is impermissible under the Eighth Amendment cannot be reversed short of a constitutional amendment," and thus "[r]evisions cannot be made in the light of further experience." In assessing claims that conditions of confinement are cruel and unusual, courts must bear in mind that their inquiries "spring from constitutional requirements and that judicial answers to them must reflect that fact rather than a court's idea of how best to operate a detention facility." *Bell* v. *Wolfish*, 441 U.S. at 539.

Courts certainly have a responsibility to scrutinize claims of cruel and unusual confinement, and conditions in a number of prisons, especially older ones, have justly been described as "deplorable" and "sordid." When conditions of confinement amount to cruel and unusual punishment, "federal courts will discharge their duty to protect constitutional rights." In discharging this oversight responsibility, however, courts cannot assume that state legislatures and prison officials are insensitive to the requirements of the Constitution or to the perplexing sociological problems of how best to achieve the goals of the penal function in the criminal justice system: to punish justly, to deter future crime, and to return imprisoned persons to society with an improved chance of being useful, law-abiding citizens.

In this case, the question before us is whether the conditions of confinement at SOCF are cruel and unusual. As we find that they are not, the judgment of the Court of Appeals is reversed.

It is so ordered.

DONALD G. BOAG, Petitioner

v.

ELLIS MacDOUGALL, Director, Arizona Department of Corrections

454 US 364, 70 L.Ed.2d 551, 102 S.Ct. 700 (1982)

PER CURIAM.

Petitioner, who was then an inmate of the Arizona Department of Corrections Reception and Treatment Center, filed a crudely written complaint in the United States District Court for the District of Arizona, in which he alleged, inter alia, that he had been placed in solitary confinement, without any notice of charges or any hearing, that he was threatened with violence when he asked what the charges were, and that he was still in "the hole" a week later. The District Court dismissed the complaint on the ground that the case was moot because petitioner had been transferred to another facility.

On appeal, the Court of Appeals did not endorse the District Court's mootness rationale, and rightfully so, since the transfer did not moot the damages claim. Nevertheless, the Court of Appeals affirmed, concluding that petitioner's action is frivolous because it does not state a claim upon which relief can be granted. [I]ts conclusion is erroneous as a matter of law. Construing petitioner's inartful pleading liberally, as Haines v. Kerner, 404 US 519, 30 L Ed 2d 652, 92 S Ct 594 (1972), instructs the federal courts to do in pro se actions, it states a cause of action. On the basis of the record before us, we cannot find a sufficient ground for affirming the dismissal of the complaint.

The motion of petitioner for leave to proceed in forma pauperis and the petition for certiorari are granted, the judgment of the Court of Appeals is reversed, and the case is remanded for further proceedings consistent with this opinion.

It is so ordered.

JUSTICE O'CONNOR, concurring.

I join in the per curiam, but write separately to emphasize nothing in the Court's opinion prevents the District Court on remand from dismissing this suit under 28 USC § 1915(d) [28 USCS § 1915(d)] if it finds grounds to believe that the complaint is "malicious or frivolous."

LOWELL D. HEWITT et al., Petitioners

v.

AARON HELMS

459 U.S. 460, 103 S. Ct. 864, 74 L. Ed. 2d 675 (1983)

JUSTICE REHNQUIST delivered the opinion of the Court.

Respondent Aaron Helms was serving a term in the State Correctional Institution at Huntingdon, Pennsylvania, (SCIH) which was administered by petitioners. He sued in the United States District Court for the Middle District of Pennsylvania, claiming that petitioners' actions confining him to administrative segregation within the prison violated his rights under the Due Process Clause of the Fourteenth Amendment to the United States Constitution. The District Court granted petitioners' motion for summary judgment, but the Court of Appeals for the Third Circuit reversed. We granted certiorari, to consider what limits the Due Process Clause of the Fourteenth Amendment places on the authority of prison administrators to remove inmates from the general prison population and confine them to a less desirable regimen for administrative reasons.

In the early evening of December 3, 1978, a prisoner in the state penitentiary at Huntingdon, assaulted two guards. The prisoner was subdued with the assistance of other guards. Later in the evening, the violence erupted into a riot during which a group of prisoners attempted to seize the institution's "control center."

This uprising was eventually quelled. Several hours after the riot ended, respondent Helms was removed from his cell and the general prison population for questioning by the state police. Following the interview, he was placed in restrictive confinement, and the state police and prison authorities began an investigation into his role in the riot.

On December 4, 1978, Helms was given a "Misconduct Report" charging him with "Assaulting Officers and Conspiracy to Disrupt Normal Institution Routine by Forcefully Taking Over the Control Center." The report briefly described the factual basis for the charge and contained a lengthy recitation of the procedures governing the institution's disciplinary hearing. On December 8, 1978, a "Hearing Committee," consisting of three prison officials charged with adjudicating alleged instances of misconduct by inmates, was convened to dispose of the charges against Helms. Following a review of the misconduct report, the panel summarized its decision as "No finding as to guilt reached at this time, due to insufficient information," and ordered that Helms' confinement in restricted housing be continued.

While as a matter of probabilities it seems likely that Helms appeared personally before the December 8 hearing committee, we agree with the Court of Appeals that the record does not allow definitive resolution of the issue on summary judgment. Helms signed a copy of the misconduct report stating that "[t]he circumstance of the charge has been read and fully explained to me," and that "I have had the opportunity to have my version reported as part of the record." Likewise, he admitted in an affidavit filed during this litigation that he was "informed by an institutional hearing committee" of the disposition of the misconduct charge against him. The same affidavit, however, asserted that no "hearing" was conducted on December 8, suggesting that respondent did not appear before the committee. The state did not file any affidavit controverting Helms' contention.

On December 11, 1978, the Commonwealth of Pennsylvania filed state criminal charges against Helms, charging him with assault and with riot. On January 2, 1979, SCIH's Program Review Committee, which consisted of three prison officials, was convened. The Committee met to review the status of respondent's confinement in administrative segregation and to make recommendations as to his future confinement. The Committee unanimously concluded that Helms should remain in administrative segregation; affidavits of the Committee members said that the decision was based on several related concerns. Helms was seen as "a danger to staff and to other inmates if released back into general population", he was to be arraigned the following day on state criminal charges, and the Committee was awaiting information regarding his role in the riot. The Superintendent of SCIH personally reviewed the Program Review Committee's determination and concurred in its recommendation.

The preliminary hearing on the state criminal charges against Helms was postponed on January 10, 1979, apparently due to a lack of evidence. On January 19, 1979, a second Misconduct Report was given to respondent; the report charged Helms with assaulting a second officer during the December 3 riot. On January 22 a Hearing Committee composed of three prison officials heard testimony from one guard and Helms. Based on this, the Committee found Helms guilty of the second misconduct charge and ordered that he be confined to disciplinary segregation for six months, effective December 3, 1978. The Committee also decided to drop the earlier misconduct charge against respondent, without determining guilt. On February 6, 1979, the State dropped criminal charges relating to the prison riot against Helms.

The Court of Appeals, reviewing these facts, concluded that Helms had a protected liberty interest in continuing to reside in the general prison population. While the court seemed to doubt that this interest could be found in the Constitution, it held that Pennsylvania regulations governing the administration of state prisons created such an interest. It then said that Helms could not be deprived of this interest without a hearing, governed by the procedures mandated in Wolff v. McDonnell, 418 US 539, 41 L Ed 2d 935, 94 S Ct 2963, 71 Ohio Ops 2d 336 (1974), to determine whether such confinement was proper. Being uncertain whether the hearing conducted on December 8th satisfied the Wolff requirements, the Court of Appeals remanded the case to the District Court for an evidentiary hearing regarding the character of that proceeding. On these same facts, we agree with the Court of Appeals that the Pennsylvania statutory framework governing the administration of state prisons gave rise to a liberty interest in respondent, but we conclude that the procedures afforded respondent were "due process" under the Fourteenth Amendment.

While no State may "deprive any person of life, liberty, or property, without due process of law," it is well-settled that only a limited range of interests fall within this provision. Liberty interests protected by the Fourteenth Amendment may arise from two sources—the Due Process Clause itself and the laws of the States. Meachum v. Fano, 427 US 215, 223-227, (1976). Respondent argues, that the Due Process Clause implicitly creates an interest in being confined to a general population cell, rather than the more austere and restrictive administrative segregation quarters. While there is little question on the record before us that respondent's confinement added to the restraints on his freedom, we think his argument seeks to draw from the Due Process Clause more than it can provide.

We have repeatedly said both that prison officials have broad administrative and discretionary authority over the institutions they manage and that lawfully incarcerated persons retain only a narrow range of protected liberty interests. As to the first point, we have recognized that broad discretionary authority is necessary because the administration of a prison is "at best an extraordinarily difficult undertaking," Wolff v. McDonnell, and have concluded that "to hold ... that *any* substantial deprivation imposed by prison authorities triggers the procedural protections of the Due Process Clause would subject to judicial review a wide spectrum of discretionary actions that traditionally have been the business of prison administrators rather than of the federal courts." Meachum v. Fano. As to the second point, our decisions have consistently refused to recognize more than the most basic liberty interests in prisoners. "Lawful incarceration brings about the necessary withdrawal or limitation of many privileges and rights, a retrac-

tion justified by the considerations underlying our penal system." Price v. Johnston, 334 US 266, 285, (1948).

[I]n Meachum v. Fano, the transfer of a prisoner from one institution to another was found unprotected by "the Due Process Clause in and of itself," even though the change of facilities involved a significant modification in conditions of confinement, later characterized by the Court as a "grievous loss." Moody v. Daggett, 429 US 78 (1976). As we have held previously, these decisions require that "[a]s long as the conditions or degree of confinement to which the prisoner is subjected is within the sentence imposed upon him and is not otherwise violative of the Constitution, the Due Process Clause does not in itself subject an inmate's treatment by prison authorities to judicial oversight." Montanye v. Haymes, 427 US 236, (1976). See also Vitek v. Jones, 445 US 480, (1980).

It is plain that the transfer of an inmate to less amenable and more restrictive quarters for nonpunitive reasons is well within the terms of confinement ordinarily contemplated by a prison sentence. The phrase "administrative segregation," as used by the state authorities here, appears to be something of a catch-all: it may be used to protect the prisoner's safety, to protect other inmates from a particular prisoner, to break up potentially disruptive groups of inmates, or simply to await later classification or transfer. Accordingly, administrative segregation is the sort of confinement that inmates should reasonably anticipate receiving at some point in their incarceration.

Despite this, respondent points out that the Court has held that a State may create a liberty interest protected by the Due Process Clause through its enactment of certain statutory or regulatory measures. [I]n Wolff, we found that Nebraska had created a right to such good credits. 418 US 556. See also Greenholtz v. Nebraska Penal Inmates, 442 US 1, (1979) (parole); Vitek v. Jones, 445 US 480, (1980) (transfer to mental institution). Likewise, and more relevant here, was our summary affirmance in Wright v. Enomoto, 462 F Supp 397 (ND Calif 1976), aff'd, 434 US 1052, (1978), where the district court had concluded that state law created a liberty interest in confinement to any sort of segregated housing within a prison.

Respondent argues that Pennsylvania, in its enactment of regulations governing the administration of state prisons, has created a liberty interest in remaining free from the restraints accompanying confinement in administrative segregation. Except to the extent that our summary affirmance in Wright v. Enomoto, supra, may be to the contrary, we have never held that statutes and regulations governing daily operation of a prison system conferred any liberty interest in and of themselves.

There are persuasive reasons why we should be loath to transpose all of the reasoning in the cases just cited to the situation where the statute and regulations govern the day to day administration of a prison system. The deprivations imposed in the course of the daily operations of an institution are likely to be minor when compared to the release from custody at issue in parole decisions and good time credits. Moreover, the safe and efficient operation of a prison on a day to day basis has traditionally been entrusted to the expertise of prison officials, see Meachum v. Fano, supra, 427 US, at 225.

Nonetheless, we conclude in the light of the Pennsylvania statutes and regulations here in question, that respondent did acquire a protected liberty interest in remaining in the general prison population.

Respondent seems to suggest that the mere fact that Pennsylvania has created a careful procedural structure to regulate the use of administrative segregation indicates the existence of a protected liberty interest. We cannot agree. The creation of procedural guidelines to channel the decision-making of prison officials is, in the view of many experts in the field, a salutary development. It would be ironic to hold that when a State embarks on such desirable experimentation it thereby opens the door to scrutiny by the federal courts, while States that choose not to adopt such procedural provisions entirely avoid the strictures of the Due Process Clause.

Nonetheless, in this case the Commonwealth has gone beyond simple procedural guidelines. It has used language of an unmistakably mandatory character, requiring that certain procedures "shall," "will," or "must" be employed, and that administrative segregation will not occur absent specified substantive predicates—viz., "the need for control," or "the threat of a serious disturbance."

[W]e are persuaded that the repeated use of explicitly mandatory language in connection with requiring specific substantive predicates demands a conclusion that the State has created a protected liberty interest.

That being the case, we must then decide whether the process afforded respondent satisfied the minimum requirements of the Due Process Clause. We think that it did. The requirements imposed by the Clause are, of course, flexible and variable dependent upon the particular situation being examined.

In determining what is "due process" in the prison context, we are reminded that "one cannot automatically apply procedural rules designed for free citizens in an open society . . . to the very different situation presented by a disciplinary proceeding in a state prison." Wolff v. McDonnell, supra, 418 US, at 560. "Prison administrators . . . should be accorded wide-ranging deference in the adoption and execution of policies and practices that in their judgment are needed to preserve internal order and discipline and to maintain institutional security." Bell v. Wolfish, 441 US 520, (1979). These considerations convince us that petitioners were obligated to engage only in an informal, nonadversary review of the information supporting respondent's administrative confinement, including whatever statement respondent wished to submit, within a reasonable time after confining him to administrative segregation.

Under Mathews v. Eldridge, 424 US 319, (1976), we consider the private interests at stake in a governmental decision, the governmental interests involved, and the value of procedural requirements in determining what process is due under the Fourteenth Amendment. Respondent's private interest is not one of great consequence. He was merely transferred from one extremely restricted environment to an even more confined situation. Unlike disciplinary confinement the stigma of wrongdoing or misconduct does not attach to administrative segregation under Pennsylvania's prison regulations. Finally, there is no indication that administrative segregation will have any significant effect on parole opportunities.

Petitioners had two closely related reasons for confining Helms to administrative segregation prior to conducting a hearing on the disciplinary charges against him. First, they concluded that if housed in the general population, Helms would pose a threat to the safety of other inmates and prison officials and to the security of the institution. Second, the prison officials believed that it was wiser to separate respondent from the general population until completion of state and institutional investigations of his role in the December 3 riot and the hearing on the charges against him. Plainly, these governmental interests are of great importance. The safety of the institution's guards and inmates is perhaps the most fundamental responsibility of the prison administration.

Neither of these grounds for confining Helms to administrative segregation involved decisions or judgments that would have been materially assisted by a detailed adversary proceeding. As we said in Rhodes v. Chapman, 452 US 337, (1981), "a prison's internal security is peculiarly a matter normally left to the discretion of prison administrators." In assessing the seriousness of a threat to institutional security, prison administrators necessarily draw on more than the specific facts surrounding a particular incident; instead, they must consider the character of the inmates confined in the institution, recent and longstanding relations between prisoners and guards, prisoners inter se, and the like. In the volatile atmosphere of a prison, an inmate easily may constitute an unacceptable threat to the safety of other prisoners and guards even if he himself has committed no misconduct; rumor, reputation, and even more imponderable factors may suffice to spark potentially disastrous incidents. The judgment of prison officials in this context, like that of those making parole decisions, turns largely on "purely subjective evaluations and on predictions of future behavior," Connecticut Board of Pardons v. Dumschat, 452 US 458, (1981); indeed, the administrators must predict not just one inmate's future actions, as in parole, but those of an entire institution. Owing to the central role of these types of intuitive judgments, a decision that an inmate or group of inmates represents a threat to the institution's security would not be appreciably fostered by the trial-type procedural safeguards suggested by respondent. This, and the balance of public and private interests, leads us to conclude that the Due Process Clause requires only an informal nonadversary review of evidence, discussed more fully below, in order to confine an inmate feared to be a threat to institutional security to administrative segregation.

Likewise, confining respondent to administrative segregation pending completion of the investigation of the disciplinary charges against him is not based on an inquiry requiring any elaborate procedural safeguards.

We think an informal, nonadversary evidentiary review sufficient both for the decision that an inmate represents a security threat and the decision to confine an inmate to ad-ministrative segregation pending completion of an investigation into misconduct charges against him. An inmate must merely receive some notice of the charges against him and an opportunity to present his views to the prison official charged with deciding whether to transfer him to administrative segregation. Ordinarily a written statement by the inmate will accomplish this purpose, although prison administrators may find it more useful to permit oral presentations in cases where they believe a written statement would be ineffective. So long as this occurs, and the decisionmaker reviews the charges and then-available evidence against the prisoner, the Due Process Clause is satisfied. This informal procedure permits a reasonably accurate assessment of probable cause to believe that misconduct occurred, and the "value [of additional "formalities and safeguards"] would be too slight to justify holding, as a matter of constitutional principle" that they must be adopted, Gerstein v. Pugh, supra, 420 US, at 122, 43 L Ed 2d 54, 95 S Ct 854.

Measured against these standards we are satisfied that respondent received all the process that was due after being confined to administrative segregation.

Accordingly, the judgment of the Court of Appeals is reversed.

RELIGION IN PRISON

THERIAULT v. CARLSON
339 F.Supp. 375 (N.D. Ga., 1972)

EDENFIELD, District Judge.

Harry William Theriault, self-styled Bishop of Tellus[1] and self-proclaimed leader of a group designated by petitioners as the Church of the New Song,[2] is also a federal prisoner in-

carcerated presently in the Atlanta federal penitentiary on "holdover" status from the Marion (Illinois) federal penitentiary. For a year and a half he has sought to compel prison officials in Atlanta and Marion to grant him the right to hold religious services in prison for those who shared his belief in the Eclatarian faith,[3] a faith of which he is the supreme exponent. The prison author-

---

[1] Theriault testified that he derives his authority to be "Bishop of Tellus" (Bishop of the Earth) from the Book of Revelations of the New Testament. Chapter 3, Verse 3 of the Book of Revelations states:
   "Remember then what you received and heard; keep that, and repent. If you will not awake, *I will come like a thief,* and you will not know at what hour I will come upon you." (Emphasis added.)
Theriault, who is incarcerated for robbery, claims that he is that "thief."

[2] Theriault testified that the name of the Church is derived from the "new song" that the younger generation is now sing-

ing as well as from the "new song" of the new era described in the Book of Revelations, 5:9 and 14:3 (". . . and they sang a new song.").

[3] According to Theriault, Eclat is the "new name" of the divinity referred to in the Book of Revelations, 3:12. The Eclatarian faithful, aside from one secretary, are to be found only in the federal penitentiaries of Atlanta and Marion.

381

ities denied his requests and his appeals to respondent Silber, Director of Chaplaincy Services for the Bureau of Prisons, and respondent Carlson, Director of the Bureau of Prisons, were unsuccessful. Petitioners then filed this class action here and the court, predicating its jurisdiction upon 28 U.S.C. § 1361 (1970), held four full days of hearings on the matter. Walker v. Blackwell, 360 F.2d 66 (5th Cir. 1966). ("Walker I".) The court has concluded that petitioners and the class they represent have been denied First Amendment rights, and it will order relief.

A full recitation of the history of this case is unnecessary. Briefly, Theriault and co-petitioner Dorrough founded the Church of the New Song and the Fountainhead Seminary in 1970 while incarcerated in Atlanta. They had obtained "doctor of divinity" certificates from a mail-order organization and, as a "game," they decided to challenge the chaplaincy program in the federal prisons and, at the same time, to develop a new religion of their own. The petition filed in this court alleged that the Government had established religion in the Atlanta penitentiary and was also prohibiting its free exercise by those prisoners who belonged to the Church of the New Song. Petitioners claimed that a "pall of establishment orthodoxy" had been cast over their lives because respondents Hanberry and Beane, the Protestant and Catholic chaplains, respectively, who were members of the prison staff and federal employees, regularly submitted reports on the religious activities of the prisoners which had a direct bearing on the grant or denial of parole. They also contended that the chap-

lains were promoting the majority faiths at the expense of minority faiths by failing to grant religious standing to the Church of the New Song. The petition was supported by the signatures of 165 prisoners.

Immediately after the petition was allowed filed in this court, Theriault was transferred to Marion which houses the most severe security risks in the federal system. Theriault now began to take his own religious claims seriously and attempted to explain them to the prisoners and staff at Marion. The Chief of Classification and Parole at Marion testified in this court that, at this point, Theriault's activities were truly religious in nature. Theriault approached the Protestant chaplain at Marion for permission to hold religious services for himself and his followers, but the request was denied because the chaplain felt the Church of the New Song was not "recognized." Theriault attempted to meet this objection by assuring the chaplain he would obtain an official church charter from the Universal Life Church, Inc., the mail-order organization which supplied Theriault with his "doctor of divinity" degree. The chaplain brought the matter to the attention of respondent Silber,[4] and Rev. Sil-

---

[4] The text of the chaplain's letter to Rev. Silber is as follows:

"FREDERICK SILBER,   25 Sept 70
DIRECTOR OF CH. SERV.
BUREAU OF PRISONS,
WASHINGTON, D. C.

WILLIAM G. EZELL,
PROTESTANT CHAPLAIN,
U. S. PENITENTIARY,
MARION, ILLINOIS
RECOGNITION OF CHURCH
GROUPS

ber testified in court that he upheld the decision of the Marion chaplain because the Church of the New Song and the Eclatarian faith were not "recognized." Theriault also wrote to respondent Carlson but received only a form response directing him to the institutional staff.

As Theriault continued his activities among the Marion prisoners, the staff began to suspect that he was actually organizing a radical political movement. One staff member filed a memorandum on the subject and urged that something be done to con-

---

As you know, Harry Theriault, #90987, was transferred to Marion from the Atlanta penitentiary. He represents himself as a Bishop in the Church of the New Song.

His initial moves to have use of the chapel, distribute literature and hold study classes have been denied. The reason for such denial is that he is not recognized as a church. He now comes with a letter addressed to a Universal Life Church in Modesto, California requesting a church charter, etc. It is reported that he has this kind of charter for the church he had in the penitentiary in Atlanta. There are no doubt 'diploma mills,' etc., who for fees or favors would send him the necessary papers and documents. We will have a check by a probation officer in this area made on this particular man and church.

When Theriault is denied one place, he goes another. He has some of our staff involved now in his requests for recognition. There is little question that if we deny his efforts to secure documents that there will be writs, etc. Therefore, if you have previous experience in similar cases or could advise us it would be appreciated. Also, we want to advise you of this case so you would not be unaware.

The move with him has been made with diplomacy and while it is not an emergency, it could develop. Any help in this matter would be appreciated.

WGE: kw"

trol Theriault's activities.[5] Three days after the memorandum was filed, Theriault was placed in punitive segregation ("H-Unit") for failing to

---

[5] The text of the memorandum is as follows:

"SUBJECT: Theriault's activities and organization of inmates. (90987-131)

During the past quarter in 'F' unit, I have observed Theriault's activities, both in and out of the unit. Following is a listing of incidents and observations that has led me to believe he has formulated a strong, radical power structure in this institution and others. Also, it would not be hard to believe, he may have some followers on the outside.

Theriault has organized a group called 'The New Church of World Song' or something similar to this. He is the leader and members address him as the Bishop. Others have been ordained as ministers by him. I have no idea, as to how large this organization might be. Some investigation would reveal this.

Kessler 1707-135, E-B-10, attempted to assist Theriault in his duties as F orderly, a few weeks ago. Both were warned and Kessler sent out of the unit. This time I was informed Kessler was one of his ministers and as such should be allowed to assist him.

Theriault was greatly upset, when Gomez F-C-18, was taken to H unit the first time and became very inquisitive after informing me this was another of his ministers and seemed to convey to me that he should be given this information because he was Gomez's Bishop.

He has constantly kept occupied, writing writs and other legal papers for the inmate population. This seems to be a very big business, that occupies most of his time.

Arnold from I unit recently made an attempt to assist in the orderly work and again both were warned. Minshew F-A-9 has assisted Theriault on a few occasions, before being assigned to the Food Service detail.

Mr. Tremper returned some papers to him recently, advising them they could not be sent out. He immediately asked me to call Mr. Keohane. I complied and was advised that Mr. Edmonds was in charge that day. Mr. Edmonds would not give Theriault permission to send

obey the order of a security officer to move. He was subsequently released and later cited for a minor violation and for threatening a security officer.

---

the papers out. Theriault became very upset and proceeded to say this was a conspiracy to prevent him from mailing this material. He proceeded to use several colorful adjectives to describe Mr. Edmonds to Welty F-A-8. I advised him to be careful in using these terms in relation to staff members. His comment was 'Freedom of speech, man.' During the discussion, Welty advised him, the matter should be taken to the Warden and not mess with these people.

Theriault became quiet frustrated after not being allowed to visit Alderisio 85719-132 in the hospital (12-10-70). He seemed to think regulations does not apply to him as one befitting his position.

I was told he held a meeting in the V.T. building (12/11/70), with several members of his group. This can be verified by the Supervisor of the evening watch and the V.T. officer. He left the unit 12/12/70 with a Bible. I believe he conducted a meeting somewhere on this date. This would need some checking. Gomez attempted to attend Mr. Sumners group on this date but suddenly changed his mind. He seemed to have some purpose in checking the group.

I have observed Cappola 1642-135, Heard, Kolburg 27388-138 and several other inmates, either contacting or being contacted by Theriault.

Considering these incidents and other information gathered during these past days, I feel Theriault has shown great disregard for the institutional authority and regulations and has went about setting up this organization, with him as the central power figure, utilizing the talents of several key figures as ministers. This group has members of all races and has the characteristics of an extremist group on the far left, completely against the system (whatever it may consist of) and will let nothing stop or stand in its way.

It is my opinion, that if something is not done to control the activities of Theriault, we will have an incident in the near future causing damage to the institution proper or injuries to personnel to compel agreement to the groups demands."

On April 1, 1971 Theriault approached Mr. J. Culley, a correctional supervisor, and demanded a place to hold religious services. Culley discussed the matter with Theriault but refused to accede to his demand. Then, "as a preventive measure," Culley had Theriault placed in punitive segregation ("H-Unit").[6] Theriault remained in

---

[6] The text of the report prepared by Culley on the incident is as follows:

"At approximately 5:30 p. m. this evening Theriault approached Mr. J. White C/S and myself in the east corridor and demanded a place to hold a religious service. I explained to him that to hold a meeting of a religious nature he would have to obtain approval of the Administration by working through the Chaplain. He would not accept this as an answer to his question or demand. At this time he appeared to be getting emotional, so I asked him to step into the office and we would discuss the matter.

"To take away the opportunity of Theriault creating an incident, if he so desired, I kept him in the office until the evening yard was closed and we had began to count.

"During our talk in the office, Theriault still demanded to be permitted to worship his lord in a place where other inmates could come if they so desired.

"He stated he would hold his services and if I attempted to break it up, I would have to resort to violence because no one would leave if I instructed them to leave. As Theriault left the office for count he commented, I will do what I feel I have to.

"As a preventive measure toward any type of incident taking place as he indicated, I placed him in H-Unit immediately after count before the general population was released for evening activities.

"Theriault offered no resistance during the move. He asked if this was my decision or had I called someone. I told him it was mine. He then stated, 'Can't we come to an understanding, I didn't say I was going to do it tonight.' He further stated that he would do as I instructed.

"In H-Unit Theriault refused to remove his clothing for a shakedown. It

H-Unit from that night until he was transferred to Atlanta for the hearings before this court.[7] The day Theriault was received back in Atlanta he was immediately placed in the segregation unit and he is still there today.[8] The court finds as fact that the sole basis for the punitive segregation of Theriault was his demand to hold religious services.

A. The "Establishment" Claim

The "establishment" claim raised by petitioners is, for the most part, without merit. The Bureau of Prisons is statutorily charged with the responsibility of providing for the care, subsistence, protection, instruction and discipline of federal prisoners. 18

---

was very clear that he wanted the staff to man-handle him. His pockets were emptied, belt removed and he was given a very thorough frisk shakedown. To assure the chance of contraband not being introduced into the unit, Theriault was placed in a closed front cell. NOTE: At approximately 9:00 p. m. I visited with Theriault in H-Unit. I asked if he was willing to submit to a strip shakedown. He stated, 'I am not playing your silly games and if you try something there will be violence.' I advised him again why he was in the closed front cell and if he submitted to the shake-down I would move him to the front at this time. He would not have anything to do with the request. /s/ JC"

[7] That night Theriault destroyed part of his H-Unit cell and the next day both kicked and threatened a security officer.

[8] On October 28, 1971, prior to Theriault's transfer to Atlanta, the Special Intelligence Supervisor at the Atlanta penitentiary circulated a memorandum advising all staff that Theriault was to be placed in segregation upon his reception at Atlanta and was not to be removed from segregation without the approval of the Associate Warden—Controls. When Theriault was received back at Atlanta on November 6, 1971, he was placed in the Segregation Unit in accordance with the October 28th memorandum.

U.S.C. § 4042 (1970). The Bureau has carried out this responsibility by creating programs to meet the needs of the inmates—be they physical, mental, or spiritual needs. In order to effectuate these programs the Bureau, of course, must hire professional staff—doctors, social workers, teachers, and clergymen. The Bureau cannot maintain a full complement of medical, educational, or religious professionals on the prison staffs, and a representative selection must necessarily suffice. The ordained clergymen on the federal payroll who serve as chaplains in the federal prison system are hired to provide for the spiritual needs of all prisoners, whatever their religious denomination, and they are not merely the emissaries of their respective churches. As Mr. Justice Brennan has written:

"There are certain practices, conceivably violative of the Establishment Clause, the striking down of which might seriously interfere with certain religious liberties also protected by the First Amendment. Provisions for churches and chaplains at military establishments for those in the armed services may afford one such example. The like provision by state and federal governments for chaplains in penal institutions may afford another example. It is argued that such provisions may be assumed to contravene the Establishment Clause, yet be sustained on constitutional grounds as necessary to secure to the members of the Armed Forces and prisoners those rights of worship guaranteed under the Free Exercise Clause. Since government has deprived such persons of the opportunity to practice their faith at places of their choice, the argument runs, government may, in order to avoid infringing the free exercise guarantees, provide substitutes where it requires such persons to be. . . .

"Such activities and practices seem distinguishable from the sponsorship of daily Bible reading and prayer recital. For one thing, there is no element of coercion present in the appointment of military or prison chaplains; the soldier or convict who declines the opportunities for worship would not ordinarily subject himself to the suspicion or obloquy of his peers. Of special significance to this distinction is the fact that we are here usually dealing with adults, not with impressionable children as in the public schools. Moreover, the school exercises are not designed to provide the pupils with general opportunities for worship denied them by the legal obligation to attend school. The student's compelled presence in school for five days a week in no way renders the regular religious facilities of the community less accessible to him than they are to others. The situation of the school child is therefore plainly unlike that of the isolated soldier or the prisoner.

"The State must be steadfastly neutral in all matters of faith, and neither favor nor inhibit religion. In my view, government cannot sponsor religious exercises in the public schools without jeopardizing that neutrality. On the other hand, hostility, not neutrality, would characterize the refusal to provide chaplains and places of worship for prisoners and soldiers cut off by the State from all civilian opportunities for public communion, the withholding of draft exemptions for ministers and conscientious objectors, or the denial of the temporary use of an empty public building to a congregation whose place of worship has been destroyed by fire or flood. . . ." Abington School District v. Schempp, 374 U.S. 203, 296-299, 83 S.Ct. 1560, 1610, 10 L.Ed.2d 844 (1963) (concurring opinion).

The court concludes that the maintenance by the Bureau of Prisons of chaplains at the Atlanta federal penitentiary is not unconstitutional. * * *

Notwithstanding this conclusion, the court does find merit in petitioners' claims about the filing of religious reports by respondents Hanberry and Beane. The testimony before this court established that Rev. Hanberry and Fr. Beane regularly submit reports to the caseworkers at the Atlanta penitentiary in which they comment on the inmates' participation or lack of participation in their respective religious activities. These reports, together with reports from other staff members, are culled by the caseworkers and form part of the inmates' profiles which are presented to the Board of Parole when the inmates are being considered for release on parole. It is not inconceivable that the grant or denial of parole is based, to some degree, on the religious reports submitted by the chaplains.

In the court's view, the submission of religious reports by respondents Hanberry and Beane involves the Government in a violation of the neutrality it must maintain with respect to religion. There can be no doubt that an inmate whose file contains a positive religious report stands a better chance of being released on parole than an inmate with a neutral or negative religious report. Indeed, it is likely that the inmates' very knowledge of the existence of these religious reports may compel some to participate in religious activities. The Government, by allowing these religious reports to be submitted, is in effect promoting religion among inmates and indirectly punishing the atheist, agnostic, or Eclatarian who declines to participate in these religious programs. This is unconstitutional. As the Supreme Court has declared:

"Government in our democracy, state and national, must be neutral in matters of religious theory, doctrine, and practice. It may not be hostile to any religion or to the advocacy of no-religion; and it may not aid, foster, or promote one religion or religious theory against another or even against the militant opposite. The First Amendment mandates governmental neutrality between religion and religion, and between religion and nonreligion." Epperson v. Arkansas, 393 U.S. 97, 103-104, 89 S.Ct. 266, 270, 21 L.Ed. 2d 228 (1968).

The court will accordingly enjoin the submission of these religious reports by respondents Hanberry and Beane.

B. *The "Free Exercise" Claim*

The chaplains at Atlanta and Marion, as well as Rev. Silber, denied Theriault's requests to hold religious services because they felt the Church of the New Song and the Eclatarian faith were not "recognized." The in-

sistence by these federal employees that Theriault and his followers meet this "recognition" standard before they might freely exercise their religious beliefs runs squarely afoul of the First Amendment.[9] One of the purposes of the First Amendment was to prohibit the imposition by government of *any* standard as a prerequisite to the free exercise of religion. As the Supreme Court has noted:

"By the time of the adoption of the Constitution, our history shows that there was a widespread awareness among many Americans of the dangers of a union of Church and States. These people knew, some of them from bitter personal experience, that one of the greatest dangers to the freedom of the individual to worship in his own way lay in the Government's placing its official stamp of approval upon one particular kind of prayer or one particular form of religious services. They knew the anguish, hardship, and bitter strife that could come when zealous religious groups struggled with one another to obtain the Government's stamp of approval from each King, Queen, or Protector that came to temporary power." Engel v. Vitale, 370 U.S. 421, 429, 20 Ohio Op.2d 328, 82 S.Ct. 1261, 1266, 8 L.Ed.2d 601 (1962).

But respondents go further. They argue that Theriault's "religion" is not

---

[9] It appears also to run afoul of Policy Statement 7300.43A of the Bureau of Prisons which was issued by respondent Carlson. That Statement commits the Bureau to extending the greatest amount of religious freedom possible within a prison context to committed offenders, and assisting them in the practice of "the religion of their choice." Nowhere in that Statement is there an indication that only "recognized" religions can be practiced.

a religion at all but merely a random amalgamation of pseudo-political notions; that his "church" is nothing but a collection of some of the worst prisoners in the federal system. Similar arguments were offered by prison officials when so-called Black Muslim prisoners began suing in federal court for religious freedom. One of the first courts to deal with these arguments responded as follows:

"Under freedom of religion in this country a person has an absolute right to embrace the religious belief of his choice. The Constitution does not define 'religion' and reference to standard sources of the meaning of words indicates that there is not complete agreement on even a definition of the term. Nor is it the function of the court to consider the merits or fallacies of a religion or to praise or condemn it, however excellent or fanatical or preposterous it may be. Whether one is right about his religion is not a subject of knowledge but only a matter of opinion.

"It is sufficient here to say that one concept of religion calls for a belief in the existence of a supreme being controlling the destiny of man. That concept of religion is met by the Muslims in that they believe in Allah, as a supreme being and as the one true god. It follows, therefore, that the Muslim faith is a religion." Fulwood v. Clemmer, 206 F.Supp. 370, 373 (D.D.C.1962).

The record in this case amply reflects the tenets, such as they are, of the Church of the New Song and the Eclatarian faith. The Eclatarian faithful worship a divine and universal spirit which they identify as "Eclat"

and which they believe manifests itself in all animate and inanimate objects. Since each person is thought to possess some of this universal spirit, the Eclatarians believe that loneliness may be overcome and true brotherhood achieved if people became more conscious of Eclat. Petitioners have their own Eclatarian Bible, their own Eclatarian newsletter ("The Leaves"), their own religious nomenclature, and various other religious paraphernalia. A number of inmates testified before this court that Theriault and his teachings have had a positive, rehabilitative effect upon their lives and have inspired them religiously. This court is not unmindful of the very real possibility that petitioners are still engaging in a "game" and attempting to perpetuate a colossal fraud upon both this court and the federal prison system. Nevertheless, with all due respect to respondents, the court cannot declare petitioners' religion illegitimate.

Respondents contend, however, that even if the Eclatarian faith is not illegitimate, they need not permit its free exercise in prison because Theriault and his followers are violent and threaten the security of the prison. Certainly if respondents could show that a compelling and substantial public interest required the subjugation of petitioners' First Amendment rights, they would prevail. Walker v. Blackwell, 411 F.2d 23 (5th Cir. 1969) ("Walker II").[10] But the burden

---

[10] This same standard has been applied in cases dealing with state institutions. E. g., Brown v. Peyton, 437 F.2d 1228 (4th Cir. 1971). In Long v. Parker, 390 F.2d 816 (3d Cir. 1968), and Banks v. Havener, 234 F.Supp. 27 (E.D.Va.1964), however, a "clear and present danger" test was enunciated. In a thoughtful

upon respondents is heavy, and a cursory review of the Black Muslim cases reveals how very heavy that burden is.

In Cooper v. Pate, 324 F.2d 165 (7th Cir. 1963), a state prisoner had filed a civil rights claim alleging that he was confined in punitive segregation and deprived of religious rights because he was a Black Muslim, and the district court had dismissed the prisoner's petition. On appeal the Attorney General of the State of Illinois asked the Seventh Circuit to take judicial notice of certain social studies purporting to show that, "despite its pretext of a religious facade," the Black Muslim Movement was an organization dedicated to the overthrow of the white race and to the incitement of riots and violence inside prison walls. The Attorney General also asked the court to take judicial notice of an official police study which documented numerous acts of violence committed by members of the Black Muslim Movement in a variety of state and federal prisons, including the Atlanta federal penitentiary. The

note, Judge Higginbotham has suggested that the "clear and present danger" test might be inapplicable in the context of a prison community and that a less rigorous "clear and *probable* danger" test might be more appropriate so that prison officials need not suffer a catastrophic riot in order to create a factual record sufficient to justify the imposition of restraints. Knuckles v. Prasse, 302 F.Supp. 1036, 1048-1049 (E.D.Pa. 1969), *aff'd*, 435 F.2d 1255 (3d Cir. 1970), *cert. denied*, 403 U.S. 936, 91 S.Ct. 2262, 29 L.Ed.2d 717 (1971).

Judge Higginbotham's observations have much appeal. However, in the instant case, this court concludes that respondents have not even shown a clear and *probable* danger emanating from Theriault or the Church of the New Song.

Seventh Circuit agreed to take judicial notice of these studies and affirmed the lower court's dismissal of the petition. The Supreme Court reversed and held that the petition stated a valid cause of action. Cooper v. Pate, 378 U.S. 546, 84 S.Ct. 1733, 12 L.Ed.2d 1030 (1964). On remand, the district court enjoined prison officials from denying the petitioner and other Black Muslim prisoners the right to communicate with and visit ministers of their faith and the right to attend religious services conducted by them. The Seventh Circuit affirmed. Cooper v. Pate, 382 F.2d 518 (7th Cir. 1967).

Similarly, in Long v. Parker, 384 U.S. 32, 86 S.Ct. 1285, 16 L.Ed.2d 333 (1966), the Supreme Court vacated the judgment of a district court, which had been affirmed by the Third Circuit, dismissing the petition of a Black Muslim prisoner at the federal penitentiary in Lewisburg, Pennsylvania who complained of the deprivation of religious rights. On remand, the district court denied relief and relied on its decision in Desmond v. Blackwell, 235 F.Supp. 246 (M.D.Pa.1964). In *Desmond* the district court found that Black Muslim meetings were devoted to the doctrine of hate, that those attending such meetings referred to staff as "monsters of inferior intelligence," "devils," and "skunks," that the supervision of such meetings caused a depletion in the staff force and made it less available for other duties, that military-trained prisoners known as the Fruit of the Islam stood guard at the entrance to the meetings, that some Black Muslims assaulted and stabbed another prisoner in order to induce him to join their faith, and that when disciplinary action had to be taken against one member of the group the entire membership approached the control center of the institution and demanded his release from administrative segregation. On appeal, however, the Third Circuit vacated the judgment of the district court and remanded the case for further proceedings. Long v. Parker, 390 F.2d 816 (3d Cir. 1968). The court found that the district court's reliance on *Desmond* was misplaced and that:

> "Mere antipathy caused by statements derogatory of, and offensive to the white race is not sufficient to justify the suppression of religious literature even in a prison. Nor does the mere speculation that such statements may ignite racial or religious riots in a penal institution warrant their proscription." At 822.

No one has testified that the Church of the New Song preaches hate. There was evidence that Theriault kicked a prison official, destroyed government property, threatened security officers,[11] and sent vile letters to a federal district judge in Illinois.[12] However, in view of the

---

[11] Prison officials from Marion testified that Theriault's threats caused them to fear he and his group might engage in violent and disruptive actions, and they characterized Theriault as a serious security risk. However, in response to questions from the bench, these officials admitted that they would characterize *all* the inmates at Marion as serious security risks, and that regular worship services are held at Marion for these inmates.

[12] It is a federal offense to send any mail which threatens to injure the person of the addressee. 18 U.S.C. § 876 (1970). A person who commits this offense is liable to a $10,000 fine or up to five years in prison. The vile letters which Theriault sent to the judge were brought to the attention of the warden at Marion

Black Muslim cases, this court cannot say on the basis of this evidence that Theriault or his group are so menacing that they should not be allowed to freely exercise their religion.

The court finds that respondents have failed to show a sufficiently compelling public interest requiring the subjugation of petitioners' First Amendment rights.[13] *Walker II, supra.* Accordingly, it must grant petitioners appropriate relief so they may freely exercise their rights within the context of a prison community.

1. *Religious activities*

This court interprets the First Amendment as guaranteeing the right of federal prisoners who share a common religion to gather for devotional meetings and to study the teachings

---

and respondent Carlson. Nevertheless, the letters were apparently not deemed sufficiently threatening to warrant criminal prosecution.

[13] The issues involved in this case might also be cast in an "equal protection" setting. Although the instant case involves a federal penal institution and the actions of federal employees so that the Equal Protection Clause of the Fourteenth Amendment is inapplicable, the Supreme Court has read "equal protection" notions into the Due Process Clause of the Fifth Amendment (which does apply to the federal government) and has held that federal action may be so discriminatory as to be violative of due process. Shapiro v. Thompson, 394 U.S. 618, 89 S.Ct. 1322, 22 L.Ed.2d 600 (1969); Schneider v. Rusk, 377 U.S. 163, 84 S.Ct. 1187, 12 L.Ed.2d 218 (1964); Bolling v. Sharpe, 347 U.S. 497, 74 S.Ct. 693, 98 L.Ed. 884 (1954).

Nevertheless, since this court finds ample room within the Free Exercise Clause to cover the issue in this case (see Brown v. Peyton, *supra*) and since the Supreme Court itself has warned that the "equal protection" and "due process" concepts may not be always interchangeable (Bolling v. Sharpe, *supra* at 499, 74 S.Ct. 693), the court will rest its conclusions on the First Amendment.

of that religion. This right cannot be denied the members of the Church of the New Song. Since respondent Carlson has already promulgated a detailed policy statement—Bureau of Prisons Policy Statement 7300.43A—concerning the religious rights of federal prisoners, the court need only order him to direct prison authorities to apply that policy to petitioners.

Policy Statement 7300.43A authorizes the scheduling of worship services, religious activities, and meetings of a religious nature "with reasonable frequency" for all committed offenders under supervisory procedures established by the warden. It also directs the prison chaplains to allocate a proportionate share of the funds they receive to meet the religious needs of interested faith groups. Thus, for example, the Black Muslims at the Atlanta penitentiary are given meeting space and permitted to meet twice weekly. Respondent Beane, who serves as their advisor in religious matters, reproduces religious material for the Muslims on institutional equipment, permits them the use of a tape recorder, and coordinates the purchase of various religious books from the funds of the institution. Bethea v. Daggett, 329 F.Supp. 796 (N.D.Ga.1970), aff'd. 444 F.2d 112 (5th Cir. 1971). This is not to say, of course, that respondents must pay for all the printing petitioners seek or that the members of the Church of the New Song may collect "tithes" to fund their own activities. As in other areas, prison officials should wisely use their discretion in the handling of these matters.

Since there are no ministers of the Eclatarian faith outside prison walls, prison authorities may not disqualify Theriault from leading religious services for his Church. See Bethea v. Daggett, supra. This does not mean Theriault is to be treated as a privileged person; he has no more "right" to a beard than any other inmate. Brooks v. Wainwright, 428 F.2d 652 (5th Cir. 1970); Brown v. Wainwright, 419 F.2d 1376 (5th Cir. 1970). And while Theriault may preach the doctrines of his faith—including the "Eclatarian Demandate of Natural Rights"—at his religious gatherings, any proclamations by him urging violence, riots, or insurrection, may be suppressed by prison authorities and may afford the authorities with a sufficient reason to discontinue the activities of the Church of the New Song. Knuckles v. Prasse, 302 F.Supp. 1036 (E.D.Pa.1969), aff'd. 435 F.2d 1255 (3d Cir. 1970), cert. denied, 403 U.S. 936, 91 S.Ct. 2262, 29 L.Ed.2d 717 (1971).

2. Religious Correspondence

The Fifth Circuit has held that Black Muslims and other federal prisoners may correspond with their religious leaders for spiritual guidance and advice. Walker II, supra. It follows that members of the Church of the New Song may correspond with their religious leader—Theriault—for spiritual guidance and spiritual advice.

Of course, prison authorities may ascertain the contents of such correspondence to make certain that what is sought is spiritual guidance and spiritual advice. However, they may not simply characterize all correspondence of the members of the Church of the New Song as "nonreligious" because of their subjective evaluations of the Eclatarian faith.

Theriault has no "right" to correspond with famous personalities to solicit funds for his Church. Such correspondence falls outside the scope of First Amendment protection and may be controlled by prison officials in the customary manner. Shack v. Wainwright, 391 F.2d 608 (5th Cir.), cert. denied, 392 U.S. 915, 88 S.Ct. 2078, 20 L.Ed.2d 1375 (1968).

3. Punishment for Religious Activities

This court has found as fact that Theriault was placed in punitive segregation at Marion on April 1, 1971 solely to prevent him from holding religious services for himself and his followers. He remained in punitive segregation thereafter and upon his transfer to Atlanta for the hearings before this court he was summarily placed in punitive segregation, where he is today.

Since the Marion authorities unconstitutionally denied Theriault his First Amendment rights and confined him in punitive segregation solely because he sought to exercise those rights, his present confinement in punitive segregation is unlawful and he must be restored to the general prison population. Cooper v. Pate, 382 F.2d 518 (7th Cir. 1967); Howard v. Smyth, 365 F.2d 428 (4th Cir. 1966), cert. denied, 385 U.S. 988, 87 S.Ct. 599, 17 L.Ed.2d 449 (1966).[14] *The court reiterates that authorities may take whatever disciplinary measures are necessary—including the imposition of*

---

[14] There is no basis in the record to support Theriault's claim that he was transferred to Marion in 1970 solely because he filed his petition in this court. Had there been such a basis, the court might have branded the transfer an abuse of administrative discretion. Cf., Lawrence v. Willingham, 373 F.2d 731 (10th Cir. 1967).

punitive segregation—if Theriault or his group begin to preach insurrection or violence or if they violate institutional rules and regulations requiring punishment subsequent to the date of this opinion and order.

4. Other Matters

Petitioners have raised four other issues which the court finds are unrelated to the central claim. They pray for:

(1) The right to give legal advice to all members of their faith:

(2) The right, at disciplinary hearings, to:
    (a) a written copy of the charge,
    (b) a hearing before an impartial official,
    (c) cross-examine accusers, call witnesses, and have legal counsel or counsel substitute, and
    (d) written decisions with specific findings and supporting conclusions;

(3) The right to subscribe to and receive an Atlanta weekly publication called "The Great Speckled Bird"; and

(4) The right to freely communicate with the press and the publishing media.

There has been no showing that respondents have prevented inmates—whether they be members of the Church of the New Song or not—from furnishing legal assistance to other inmates in contravention of Johnson v. Avery, 393 U.S. 483, 89 S.Ct. 747, 21 L.Ed.2d 718 (1969), and Wainwright v. Coonts, 409 F.2d 1337 (5th Cir. 1969). Of course, prison officials may regulate the legal activities of inmates and petitioners have not shown that respondents have arbitrarily or capriciously regulated their legal activities. *See* Arey v. Peyton, 378 F.2d 930 (4th Cir. 1967).

This court is aware that some recent decisions dealing with state prisons have granted the procedural due process rights sought by petitioners. *E. g.*, Landman v. Royster, 333 F. Supp. 621 (E.D.Va.1971); Clutchette v. Procunier, 328 F.Supp. 767 (N.D. Cal.1971). Nevertheless, the court finds itself in agreement with the observation of the Second Circuit that the federal prisons already afford inmates due process in disciplinary hearings (*see* Bureau of Prisons Policy Statements 7400.6A) and that those procedural rights which are not afforded are not constitutionally mandated. *See* Sostre v. McGinnis, 442 F.2d 178 (2d Cir. 1971), petition for cert. filed, 40 U.S.L.W. 3170 (U.S. Aug. 18, 1971) (No. 71-246).

No evidence was adduced at the hearings that petitioners ever requested "The Great Speckled Bird" or that such requests, if made, were denied. Petitioners do not contend that this publication is a religious newsletter of the Church of the New Song and no "free exercise" issue is involved. *Cf.* Jackson v. Godwin, 400 F.2d 529 (5th Cir. 1968). Prison officials may make reasonable regulations as to the circulation of magazines and newspapers and this court will not interfere with such administrative matters. Royal v. Clark, 447 F.2d 501 (5th Cir. 1971).

Finally, the court notes that Bureau of Prisons Policy Statement 1220.1A (February 11, 1972) now permits federal prisoners full access to the news media through the Prisoners Mail Box. The court also notes that under Bureau of Prisons Policy Statement 7300.46 federal prisoners may submit manuscripts for publication so long as they do not deal with the details of the author's life, other inmates, criminal careers, and matters currently in litigation, and so long as they do not jeopardize the security and discipline of federal prisons. The court does not find the limitations in Policy Statement 7300.46 unconstitutional and will not interfere with it. Royal v. Clark, *supra.*

ORDER

For the foregoing reasons petitioners' petition for injunctive and other relief is granted in part and denied in part. It is granted in part as follows:

(1) Respondents Hanberry and Beane are enjoined from preparing or submitting oral or written reports to other staff members of the Atlanta federal penitentiary concerning the religious activities of individual inmates at that penitentiary;

(2) Respondent Carlson and respondent Silber are ordered to direct prison authorities under their jurisdiction to grant petitioners the right to freely exercise their religion, including the right to correspond with petitioner Theriault for the purpose of seeking spiritual guidance, as regulated by Bureau of Prisons Policy Statement 7300.-43A and in accordance with the opinion of this court;

(3) Respondent Henderson is hereby ordered to immediately release petitioner Theriault from confinement in punitive segre-

gation and restore him to the general prison population; and

(4) Respondent Carlson is hereby ordered to instruct prison authorities under his jurisdiction that they may not re-impose confinement in punitive segregation upon petitioner Theriault unless Theriault violates an institutional rule or regulation

requiring such confinement subsequent to the date of this opinion and order or incites riot or insurrection during the conduct of his religious activities subsequent to the date of the opinion and order.

In all other respects it is denied. It is so ordered.

THERIAULT v. CARLSON
495 F.2d 390 (5th Cir. 1974)

* * *

AINSWORTH, Circuit Judge:

These three cases, consolidated for appeal, have as their central theme the alleged deprivation by certain federal prison authorities of the constitutional rights of prison inmates to practice their religious faith, known as the "Church of the New Song" or the "Eclatarian" faith. Harry W. Theriault, a federal prison inmate now serving sentences at LaTuna, Texas for various convictions, is the self-proclaimed founder, organizer, bishop, prophet and spiritual leader of the Eclatarians, a group of prison inmates which progressively continues to increase in size as Theriault's various incarcerations increase geographically. His prison sojourns at the federal penitentiaries at Atlanta, Georgia and LaTuna, Texas generated incidents which form the basis of these three appeals which will be referred to herein as Theriault I, Theriault II and Theriault III.[1]

[1] We find it unnecessary for purposes of this appeal to give a detailed account of the origin and tenets of Theriault's newly created religion. The Eclatarian faith, or Church of the New Song, was originally founded by Theriault and Jerry M. Dorrough at the fed-

THERIAULT—No. 72-2592

On June 18, 1970, "Dr. Harry W. Theriault" and a fellow inmate, "Reverend Jerry M. Dorrough," while incarcerated at the Atlanta, Georgia penitentiary, filed this "First Amendment Action" against the Catholic and Protestant chaplains at Atlanta, alleging various deprivations of their constitutional rights freely to practice their religion, seeking injunctive and other relief.[2] The complainants alleged that

eral penitentiary at Atlanta, Georgia, allegedly as the result of visions experienced by Theriault at the Marion, Illinois federal penitentiary in which he received prophetic messages from "Eclat" informing him that he was the "Eclatarian Nazarite" and directing him to establish the Church of the New Song.

[2] Theriault acquired his Doctor of Divinity certificate through a mail order application. Theriault then, as self-appointed "Bishop of Tellus" ordained Dorrough First Revelation Minister of the Church of the New Song, conferring upon him on the day of the trial at the courtroom the degrees of Doctor of Divinity, Doctor of Philosophy and Bachelor of Philosophy.

The complaint as amended includes 164 additional fellow inmates as plaintiffs and was treated by the district judge as a class action.

the Federal Government's use of taxpayers' money to compensate the chaplains for their services was violative of the Establishment Clause of the Constitution. They further alleged that members of their faith were being unconstitutionally denied the right freely to exercise their religion and that the actions of the chaplains in filing reports with the Parole Board relative to prisoners' participation or lack of participation in religious activities were violative of their First Amendment rights. Their complaint requested generally a recognition of their religion and the granting to them of the same prison religious privileges as those enjoyed by the Catholic and Protestant inmates.

Subsequent to the filing of this petition, Theriault was transferred to the federal penitentiary at Marion, Illinois, where because of his alleged threats to a correctional supervisor of violence upon being denied a place to hold religious serivces, he was placed in solitary confinement until he was returned to Atlanta in August 1971 for hearings on his June 18, 1970 petition. Extensive hearings were conducted in Atlanta in district court on three separate days during the latter part of 1971 and the early part of 1972 at which Theriault was both lead counsel and principal witness. "Bishop" Theriault and "Pope" Dorrough testified at length in regard to the source, history and tenets of the Eclatarian faith, acknowledging that Theriault had started it off as a game.[3]

Nevertheless, the district judge refused to allow the Government to present expert testimony relative to the validity of the Eclatarian faith as a religion. At the trial much of the testimony pertained to attempts by Theriault and his fellow inmates to hold secret religious services. There was likewise testimony of violence and threats of violence by Theriault which allegedly caused prison officials to refuse him access to assembly rooms. At the conclusion of these hearings the district judge scheduled another hearing for additional testimony concerning the Government's representations of Theriault's tendency to violence, announcing, however, the court's intention to give Theriault a "trial run" on holding his religious services. At the final hearing at Atlanta, held in January 1972, several correctional officers and other prison officials from the Marion, Illinois penitentiary testified about various threats by Theriault of mass violence, veiled threats of murder, actual physical assault and battery of prison officials, and destruction by Theriault of prison property. One such incident occurred on April 1, 1971, following a request by Theriault to use the chapel or auditorium for the purpose of honoring the birthday of St. Blanche, an Eclatarian saint. Theriault, an escape artist by his own admission, having several times broken away from federal custody, was considered by prison officials to be a high escape risk. Moreover, he and his followers were known troublemakers. Theriault was told of the prison policy requiring permission from the chaplain to secure a meeting place, as it was the chaplain's duty to coordinate religious activities. Theriault declined to follow instructions and announced his intention to hold the meeting, warning the prison authorities that if they used violence to

---

3 Later, according to Theriault, when he realized he was affecting other people's feelings he started to get more sincere. When he and Dorrough decided to file this complaint they needed the proper caption. Dorrough came forward with this suggestion which they adopted: "You put yourself down, you be the head of the church, that's the Bishop, you put yours, and put me down as the First Minister."

break it up there would be bloodshed. Because of his threats, Theriault was placed in solitary confinement, to which he reacted by kicking the correctional supervisor. He later broke the bed from the cell wall, destroyed the toilet with a piece of angle iron, shoved the bed against the cell door and warned that he would kill anyone who attempted to enter.

The district court (Judge Edenfield) granted in part the relief requested by Theriault and issued the following order directed to respondents Hanberry and Beane, Protestant and Catholic chaplains, respectively; Carlson, Director, Bureau of Prisons; Silber, Director of Chaplaincy Services, Bureau of Prisons; and Henderson, Warden, Atlanta Penitentiary.

"(1) Respondents Hanberry and Beane are enjoined from preparing or submitting oral or written reports to other staff members of the Atlanta federal penitentiary concerning the religious activities of individual inmates at that penitentiary;

"(2) Respondent Carlson and respondent Silber are ordered to direct prison authorities under their jurisdiction to grant petitioners the right to freely exercise their religion, including the right to correspond with petitioner Theriault for the purpose of seeking spiritual guidance . . . ;

"(3) Respondent Henderson is hereby ordered to immediately release petitioner Theriault from confinement in punitive segregation and restore him to the general prison population; and

"(4) Respondent Carlson is hereby ordered to instruct prison authorities under his jurisdiction that they may not re-impose confinement in punitive segregation upon petitioner Theriault unless Theriault violates

an institutional rule or regulation requiring such confinement subsequent to the date of this opinion and order or incites riot or insurrection during the conduct of his religious activities subsequent to the date of this opinion and order."[4]

Both the Government and Theriault appealed.

THERIAULT II—No. 73-1182

Subsequent to the Atlanta hearings Theriault was transferred to the federal penitentiary at LaTuna, Texas, on March 3, 1972, where he was again subjected to intermittent segregated confinement allegedly because of his disregard for prison security regulations and his renewed insistence, accompanied by physical violence, that he be allowed use of the prison chapel for religious services without prior approval of the prison chaplain. From LaTuna Theriault filed a petition in the United States District Court for the Western District of Texas seeking an evidentiary hearing in connection with allegations that his segregated confinement was punitive in nature, violative of Judge Edenfield's order (see Theriault I), that the prison chaplains at LaTuna were illegally reporting on his religious activities, and that the authorities at LaTuna were generally denying him religious privileges such as the rights to correspond with fellow members of the Eclatarian faith, to circulate among the prisoners, to obtain bibles peculiar to his sect, and to use the prison chapel. Theriault's petition was dismissed forthwith by the district court (Judge Guinn) on the day it was filed. Theriault appealed.

4 *See* Theriault v. Carlson, N.D. Ga., 1972, 339 F.Supp. 375.

THERIAULT III—No. 73-2183

Shortly after the filing of the petition with the Western District of Texas, Theriault, while still incarcerated at LaTuna, filed a motion with the district court at Atlanta alleging failure of respondents to comply with Judge Edenfield's previous order. A four-day evidentiary hearing was held resulting in a finding by the district judge that Directors Carlson and Silber were in contempt of his order in Theriault I.

The basis of the motion purportedly grew out of the failure of a prisoner incarcerated at Elgin, Florida, to receive a letter sent by Theriault in response to an inquiry about the Eclatarian faith. A four-day hearing was held. The Government admitted that Theriault's letter had not been delivered inasmuch as Elgin prison officials had not been informed of the court's order. The failure to so inform Elgin was based on the Government's belief that the court order applied only to the 166 petitioners to the original action, which petitioners were incarcerated at either LaTuna or Atlanta. A four-day hearing was held at Atlanta resulting in a finding of contempt against Directors Carlson and Silber. See Theriault v. Carlson, N.D. Ga., 1973, 353 F.Supp. 1061. The Government appealed.

Disposition of THERIAULT I

The Government contends that Theriault I should be remanded in order that it may present evidence that the Eclatarian faith is nothing more than a disruptive, anti-authoritarian political movement and therefore not a bona fide religion entitled to the protection of the Constitution. The Government's attempt to present this proof through expert witnesses was rejected by the district court in both Theriault I and Theriault III. We find the unwill-

ingness of the district court to hear evidence in this regard inexplicable considering the doubt entertained by it that the religion was nothing more than a game and since the proof adduced strongly suggests that petitioners are indeed so engaged. The testimony of Dorrough, co-founder of the faith, may explain why some of the original followers, all incarcerated convicts, find the freedom-seeking sect attractive. He explained on direct examination:

"In our Free Exercise Seminars, our revelation ministry is basically to destroy the Nicolaitans which we believe are the repressive rulers and the powercrats of the system. That means—meaning the prison system, the people in the prison system, the people in the parole system, the people in government in general, the judiciary, et cetera. And we believe in destroying them or changing their minds with the power of our mouth."

First Amendment freedoms are not absolute. They are properly restricted when a sufficiently important governmental interest appears. United States v. O'Brien, 391 U.S. 367, 376, 88 S.Ct. 1673, 1679, 20 L.Ed.2d 672 (1968). The long list of court actions to which Theriault is a party, some of which are still pending, as well as the lengthy prison record which he has established over the years,[5] is strongly suggestive of the necessity of employing sharp and care-

[5] See Theriault v. United States, 8 Cir., 1968, 401 F.2d 79; Theriault v. United States, 5 Cir., 1968, 402 F.2d 792; Theriault v. United States, 5 Cir., 1969, 409 F.2d 1313; Theriault v. United States, 5 Cir., 1970, 434 F.2d 212; United States v. Theriault, 5 Cir., 1971, 440 F.2d 713; United States v. Theriault, 5 Cir., 1972, 467 F.2d 486; United States v. Theriault, 5 Cir., 1973, 474 F.2d 359; Theriault v. United States, 5 Cir., 1973, 481 F.2d 1193; United States v. Theriault, No. EP73-173 (W.D., Texas).

ful scrutiny of his activities, including his claim of religious sincerity. One of the tasks of the court "is to decide whether the beliefs professed by [petitioners] . . . are sincerely held and whether they are, in [their] own scheme of things, religious." See United States v. Seeger, 380 U.S. 163, 185, 85 S.Ct. 850, 863, 13 L.Ed.2d 733 (1965).[6] While it is difficult for the courts to establish precise standards by which the bona fides of a religion may be judged,[7] such difficulties have proved to be no hindrance to denials of First Amendment protection to so-called religions which tend to mock established institutions and are obviously shams and absurdities and whose members are patently devoid of religious sincerity. See, e.g., United States v. Kuch, D.C., D.C., 1968, 288 F.Supp. 439.

This matter is therefore remanded and the district court is directed to re-open these proceedings and permit the Government to present additional evidence in the fullest possible manner. On remand the court should allow the greatest liberality of proof and examine every aspect of the case. The court must also determine if this is in truth

and in fact a class action in accordance with the rules pertaining thereto.

Disposition of THERIAULT II

The Government concedes in its brief, at page 14, "that the decision of the United States District Court for the Western District of Texas (Theriault II) requires remand in order for that court to enter a full factual explanation of its rejection of Theriault's contentions." We agree that remand is proper under the circumstances and therefore vacate the order of dismissal entered by the district court and remand for a full evidentiary hearing.

Disposition of THERIAULT III

The district court's holding that respondents Carlson and Silber are guilty of a civil contempt is clearly erroneous and unsupported by the evidence. The record shows that Carlson and Silber attempted to comply with an order that was susceptible of misinterpretation.[8] Upon determining what was intended by the order they complied forthwith. We are convinced of their complete sincerity and good faith. The contempt

---

6 The suggestion that we attempt now to establish precise standards is neither feasible nor practical.

7 In Wisconsin v. Yoder, 406 U.S. 205, 215-216, 92 S.Ct. 1526, 1533, 32 L.Ed.2d 15 (1972), in determining that the claims of the Old Order Amish religion for refusing to send their children to school after eighth grade rested on a religious basis, had this to say:

"Although a determination of what is a 'religious' belief or practice entitled to constitutional protection may present a most delicate question, the very concept of ordered liberty precludes allowing every person to make his own standards on matters of conduct in which society as a whole has important interests."

8 Although the district court directed Carlson and Silber to order prison authorities *under their jurisdiction* to grant petitioners the right to correspond with petitioner Theriault, the opinion also shows that the "Eclatarian faithful, aside from one secretary, are to be found only in the federal penitentiaries of Atlanta and Marion." See Theriault v. Carlson, N.D. Ga., 1972, 339 F.Supp. 375, 377 n. 3. Under these circumstances the failure of respondents to inform prison authorities other than those at Altanta and Marion was clearly an honest mistake. Apparently Judge Edenfield himself found his order wanting in clarity when in Theriault III, in rewriting parts of his order, he found it necessary to insert the word "all" before the term "prison authorities." See Theriault v. Carlson, N.D. Ga., 1973, 353 F.Supp. 1061, 1068.

finding by the district court was an abuse of discretion and must be reversed, annulled and set aside.

The district court's decision in Theriault I, No. 72-2592, is vacated and the cause is remanded for a full evidentiary hearing. In Theriault II, No. 73-1182, the district court's order is vacated and the cause is remanded for a full evidentiary hearing. In Theriault III, No. 73-2183, the district court's order is reversed, annulled and set aside.

KAHANE v. CARLSON
527 F.2d 492 (2d Cir. 1975)

* * *

J. JOSEPH SMITH, Circuit Judge:

In 1971, appellant Kahane, an orthodox Jewish rabbi, was sentenced in the Eastern District of New York to imprisonment and fine for conspiracy to violate the federal Firearms Act. 18 U.S.C. § 371. However, the sentence of imprisonment was suspended by the court, and Kahane was placed on probation. Kahane and his family had made their home in the Eastern District for many years prior to his conviction. While Kahane was on probation, they had removed to Israel with the permission of the court and Kahane had become a candidate for election to the Knesset, the Israeli Parliament. Kahane subsequently admitted to violating the terms of his probation. His probation was accordingly revoked, but his sentence of imprisonment was reduced to a term of one year. Kahane then sought, by several forms of action in the Eastern District of New York, orders requiring the prison administrators to conform the conditions of his incarceration to his religious beliefs concerning diet and prayer. The court, Jack B. Weinstein, *Judge,* found jurisdiction and venue in the Eastern District of New York and granted Kahane relief in the nature of mandamus.

We conclude that jurisdiction and venue were properly found by the district court in the instant action, that a need for relief was shown, but that the relief granted by the court was somewhat broader than required. We therefore modify the order and, as modified, affirm.

Jurisdiction in the court below was founded upon the mandamus power provided by 28 U.S.C. § 1361:

The district courts shall have original jurisdiction of any action in the nature of mandamus to compel an officer or employee of the United States or any agency thereof to perform a duty owed to the plaintiff.

The United States contends however that, even though mandamus jurisdiction exists generally in the district courts, venue does not properly lie in the Eastern District of New York for this particular mandamus action. 28 U.S.C. § 1391(e) governs venue in mandamus cases.[2] According to the

---

[2] 28 U.S.C. § 1391(e) provides:

A civil action in which each defendant is an officer or employee of the United States or any agency thereof acting in his official capacity or under color of legal authority, or an agency of the United States, may, except as otherwise provided by law, be brought in any judicial district in which: (1) a defendant in the action resides, or (2) the cause of action arose, or (3) any real property involved in the action is sit-

government, neither the prisoner's present or contemplated place of incarceration, nor the residence of any respondent was in the Eastern District. No real property is involved in the instant action nor could the cause of action regarding deprivation of kosher diet be said to have arisen in the Eastern District. Finally, the government maintains, plaintiff's residence is not in the Eastern District of New York. With this last assertion, we disagree.

The parties agree that the case does not qualify under subdivisions (1) and (3) of § 1391(e). We need not pass upon Kahane's contention that venue can be sustained under subdivision (2) since the circumstances do qualify the case under § 1391(e)(4), which establishes mandamus venue in the district of the plaintiff's residence. To be sure, residence for the purposes of § 1391 is often interpreted as equivalent to domicile, and there are some indications that Kahane has changed his domicile from the Eastern District of New York.

After his sentencing, Kahane moved to Israel with his family and ran for office there. Under ordinary circumstances that would be strong support for a finding of Israeli domicile. At the time of his conviction and sentence, however, he was a long-time resident of the Eastern District and was under active probation supervision there, a probation which he violated. Under these circumstances we hold that, until he had successfully completed probation and had been released from supervision, Kahane should have been considered a resident of the Eastern District for the purpose of venue, entitled to turn to the court for that district.

uated, or (4) the plaintiff resides if no real property is involed in the action.

Venue is a doctrine of convenience of the forum. Domicile is usually the best measure of that convenience since removal, with intent to relinquish personal ties to the old home and remain indefinitely at the new, is the handiest dividing line in measuring relative convenience of the forum. Here, however, continuing probation obligations to the court of the Eastern District made it more sensible to consider that district as Kahane's residence for the purposes of the venue statute. Because of the unusual circumstances here—Kahane's long-time residence in the Eastern District combined with his probation obligations to the court of that district—we conclude that venue was properly laid in the Eastern District of New York.[3]

We therefore reach the merits of the matter.

It is by now quite well established that, while prisoners in penal institutions are subject to restrictions on their freedoms,[4] the restrictions are not without limit. Procunier v. Martinez, 416 U.S. 396, 71 Ohio Op.2d 139, 94 S.Ct.

[3] Venue was broadened generally in mandamus actions against federal agencies to end concentration of actions in the District of Columbia and inconvenience to petitioners in the many distant districts in which the agencies operate. The Congress might well, however, consider narrowing the provisions for cases such as this which seek to affect the conduct of fixed institutions to the districts in which the institutions lie. See Coleman, J., dissenting in Ellingburg v. Connett, 457 F.2d 240 (5th Cir. 1972).

[4] We start with the familiar proposition that "[l]awful incarceration brings about the necessary withdrawal or limitation of many privileges and rights, a retraction justified by the considerations underlying our penal system." Price v. Johnston, 334 U.S. 266, 285, 68 S.Ct. 1049, 1060, 92 L. Ed. 1356 (1948). See also Cruz v. Beto, 405 U.S. 319, 321, 92 S.Ct. 1079, 1081, 3 L.Ed.2d 263 (1972). In the First Amendment context a corollary of this principle

1800, 40 L.Ed.2d 224 (1974). Where they operate on fundamental rights such as the freedom of worship, the degree of restriction must be only that which can be justified by an "important or substantial government interest" in the restriction by the penal institution.[5] *Id.* at 413, 94 S.Ct. 1800.[6]

The courts have properly recognized that prison authorities must accommodate the right of prisoners to receive diets consistent with their religious scruples.

is that a prison inmate retains those First Amendment rights that are not inconsistent with his status as a prisoner or with the legitimate penological objectives of the corrections system.
Pell v. Procunier, 417 U.S. 817, 822, 71 Ohio Op.2d 195, 94 S.Ct. 2800, 2804, 41 L.Ed.2d 495 (1974).

[5] When a prison regulation or practice offends a fundamental constitutional guarantee, federal courts will discharge their duty to protect constitutional rights. Johnson v. Avery, 393 U.S. 483, 486, 89 S.Ct. 747, 749, 21 L.Ed.2d 718 (1969).
Procunier v. Martinez, *supra*, 416 U.S. at 405-06, 94 S.Ct. at 1807.

[6] Because we hold that the denial of kosher food is not justified by any "important or substantial government interest," we need not decide whether restrictions on prisoners' First Amendment rights need be justified by an "important or substantial government interest" or by the more stringent demands of a "compelling government interest." This court expressly adopted the "compelling interest" formula in Goodwin v. Oswald, 462 F.2d 1237, 1244 (2 Cir. 1972). However, subsequent Supreme Court decisions, see Procunier v. Martinez, *supra*, use the language of an "important or substantial interest." Under that latter test, the government must presumably sustain a lesser burden in justifying restrictions on prisoners' rights. Because we hold that the denial of kosher food is unconsitutional using the standard more favorable to the government, we need not decide whether the more stringent "compelling interest" test is the one which is ultimately controlling.

Their [Muslims'] request for "one full-course pork-free diet once a day and coffee three times daily" is essentially a plea for a modest degree of official deference to their religious obligations. Certainly if this concession is feasible from the standpoint of prison management, it represents the bare minimum that jail authorities, with or without specific request, are constitutionally required to do, not only for Muslims but indeed for any group of inmates with religious restrictions on diet.

Barnett v. Rodgers, *supra* at 1001.

The evidence in this case justifies the court's finding of the deep religious significance to a practising orthodox Jew (which this prisoner concededly is) of the laws of Kashruth. The dietary laws are an important, integral part of the covenant between the Jewish people and the God of Israel.

The district court on the evidence before it was thoroughly justified in its finding of the religious importance to the prisoner of the Jewish dietary rules. We agree with the court below that the prison authorities are proscribed by the constitutional status of religious freedom from managing the institution in a manner which unnecessarily prevents Kahane's observance of his dietary obligations. The difficulties for the prisons inherent in this rule would seem surmountable in view of the small number of practising orthodox Jews in federal prisons (which the evidence indicated would not exceed approximately twelve), and in view of the fact that state and city prisons provide kosher food, that federal institutions do so on high holidays and that medical diets are not unknown in the federal system.

The order under review indicates

that there are severel means within the reach of the respondents by which Kahane's rights may be respected. Some of these means, such as methods for self-preparation of vegetables and fruits, are suggested by respondents themselves. Provision of tinned fish, boiled eggs and cheese may be made from regular institution supplies. The language of the opinion incorporated in the order[7] may be interpreted to require hot kosher TV dinners. If these are merely suggested methods, we find no fault with them. If, however, the order requires implementation of each and every one of these methods, it would go further than necessary to reach the required result. Such details are best left to the prison's management which can provide from the food supplies available within budgetary limitations. Prison authorities have reasonable discretion in selecting the means by which prisoners' rights are effectuated. See Pell v. Procunier, 417 U.S. 817.

The use of frozen, prepared foods, while perhaps helpful, is not constitutionally required if another acceptable means of keeping kosher is provided. We therefore modify the order to require the provision of a diet sufficient to sustain the prisoner in good health without violating the Jewish dietary laws, without otherwise mandating

[7] The relevant portion of Judge Weinstein's order reads as follows:
Under the precedents established by the Muslim dietary cases, at a minimum federal prisons must provide dietary alternatives to Jewish prisoners observing dietary laws that would not violate kosher requirements—for example, certain fruits, acceptable breads, cheeses, tinned fish, boiled eggs and vegetables, supplemented by hot kosher pre-cooked frozen meals.
App. at 198-99.

specific items of diet. As so modified, the order is affirmed.

Mandate may issue forthwith.

FRIENDLY, Circuit Judge (concurring):

Judge Weinstein's initial opinion in this case, dated May 7, 1975, predicated jurisdiction on 28 U.S.C. § 2255, or, alternatively, on 28 U.S.C. § 1361, although the only named defendant was the "United States of America." Following this court's decision in United States v. Huss, 520 F.2d 598 (1975), which held that § 2255 was unavailable for "matters of internal prison administration," id. at 603-04, and that § 1361 does not lie "against unknown federal respondents," id. 520 F.2d at 604-05, we returned this case to the district court for reconsideration. Kahane then filed a complaint under § 1361, and a petition for a writ of habeas corpus under 28 U.S.C. § 2241, each with named respondents. Judge Weinstein treated these complaints as amendments to the original case, and dismissed them insofar as they were separate actions. In an opinion dated August 21, 1975, the district court, in light of the amended pleadings, concluding "that it accordingly has jurisdiction over the subject matter and parties and that venue in this district is proper," denied "the defendants-respondents' motion for a transfer of this cause to a judicial district wherein the plaintiff-petitioner is or will be incarcerated." As to the merits, it reaffirmed the conclusions reached in the previous opinion.

On appeal, the Government, in regard to § 1361, possibly, although I think erroneously, feeling bound by the statement in United States v. Huss, supra, 520 F.2d at 604, quoted in the margin,[1] contests only the venue.

I agree that if this action was properly brought under § 1361, the district court was justified in sustaining venue on the ground of Kahane's residence in the Eastern District of New York, § 1391(e)(4). Thus I concur in affirmance. However, for reasons set forth below, I do not believe that the action was within § 1361 and consider that the Government is free to raise this important question on another occasion if so advised.

The spectacle of the warden of a large federal prison being answerable for prison conditions under § 1361 to district judges scattered from Maine to Hawaii and Florida to Alaska—an inevitable consequence if § 1361 and the concomitant venue provision entitling a plaintiff to sue in the district of his residence are applicable—is not a heartening one. The tortuous legislative history of § 1361 has been reviewed in Byse and Fiocca, Section 1361 of the Mandamus and Venue Act of 1962 and "Nonstatutory" Judicial Review of Federal Administrative Action, 81 Harv.L.Rev. 308 (1967), and by this court in Liberation News Service v. Eastland, 426 F.2d 1379, 1383-84 (2 Cir. 1970). Suffice it here to say that the primary purpose of Congress was to make the traditional remedy of mandamus more readily available by a broad venue provision, § 1391(e), not to expand the nature of mandamus. As I recently wrote, concurring in Economic Opportunity Comm'n of Nassau

County v. Weinberger, 524 F.2d 393, 407 (2 Cir. 1975):

The words "in the nature of mandamus" in § 1361 do mean something, very likely what the Supreme Court had said only four years before the statute was passed, Panama Canal Co. v. Grace Line Co., Inc., 356 U.S. 309, 317-18, 78 S.Ct. 752, 2 L.Ed.2d 788 (1958). The Senate Report stated that "The purpose of the amendment is to provide specifically that the jurisdiction conferred on the district courts by the bill is limited to compelling a Government official or agency to perform a duty owed to the plaintiff or to make a decision, but not to direct or influence the exercise of discretion of the officer or agency in the making of the decision." U.S. Code Cong. & Admin. News 2784 (87th Cong., 2d Sess. 1962).

While the distinction thus made is easier to state than to apply, there is a recognizable difference, as Mr. Justice Douglas said in Panama Canal Co. v. Grace Line Co., Inc., supra, 356 U.S. at 318, 78 S.Ct. at 757, between cases "[w]here the matter is peradventure clear, where the agency is clearly derelict in failing to act, where the inaction or action turns on a mistake of law," on the one hand, and, on the other, those "where the duty to act turns on matters of doubtful or highly debatable inferences from large or loose statutory terms"—here constitutional terms, and "the very construction of the statute is a distinct and profound exercise of discretion."

If the Bureau of Prisons had ruled that no attention whatever would be given to the Kosher food requirements of Orthodox Jews, that would have been such a blatant disregard of the First Amendment that § 1361 would be

---

[1] It has been held that § 1361 affords a district court with proper venue the jurisdiction to consider a claim that actions of federal prison officials violate first amendment rights. E.g., Barnett v. Rodgers, 133 App.D.C. 296, 410 F.2d 995 (1969); Long v. Parker, 390 F.2d 816, 819 (3d Cir. 1968).

available to such a defendant sentenced to a federal prison term. But the Bureau had taken no such position. It had been made clear by the testimony and findings in United States v. Huss, 394 F. Supp. 752 (S.D. N.Y. 1975), of which the district court took judicial notice and of which the parties were well aware, that the Bureau would go to considerable lengths to accommodate religious beliefs concerning diets. In the words of Bureau of Prisons Policy Statement 7300.43A,

> A committed offender may abstain from eating those food items, served to the general population, which are prohibited by the religion of the resident. The committed offender may receive added portions of non-rationed food items, from the main serving line, which in no way cause a violation of the restrictions of the faith professed by the committed offender. Ordinarily, the practical problems of institutional administration must be primary in arranging for the observance of religious holidays, sacraments, celebrations, diets, and the like.

An even stronger commitment was given by the Government in this case. In the argument after remand, while urging "the Court to decline to entertain the suit at this juncture and to, at the very least, transfer it," the Government's attorney said:

> I represent to the Court that [the prisoner] would be provided with a nutritionally adequate diet that would be acceptable, according to his religious tenets and with sufficient vitamin, mineral supplements so his health would not be placed in jeopardy.

Thus, the sole question to be litigated in the § 1361 action was whether the Bureau had gone far enough to satisfy its obligation to make an appropriate reconciliation of Rabbi Kahane's First Amendment right to free exercise of religion "with his status as a prisoner or with the legitimate penological objectives of the corrections system," Pell v. Procunier, 417 U.S. 817, 822, 825-26, 94 S.Ct. 2800, 2804, 41 L.Ed.2d 495 (1974). This falls in Mr. Justice Douglas' second category not his first.

It is doubtless true that, in an effort to avoid a jurisdictional amount requirement which seems senseless in suits against federal officers, see Wechsler, Federal Jurisdiction and the Revision of the Judicial Code, 13 Law & Comtemp. Prob. 216, 220 (1948); ALI, Study of the Division of Judisdiction between State and Federal Courts § 1311 and pp. 172-76 (1968) (original jurisdiction in all federal question cases); 1 Recommendations and Reports of the Administrative Conference of the United States 169 (1970); Friendly, Federal Jurisdiction: A General View 121-22 (1973), federal judges have sometimes indulged in a construction of § 1361 unwarranted by its words or history, as the writer did in Cortright v. Resor, 447 F.2d 245, 250-51 (2 Cir. 1971), cert. denied, 405 U.S. 965, 92 S. Ct. 1172, 31 L.Ed.2d 240 (1972), where the Government did not challenge § 1361 jurisdiction. Cf. Hart & Wechsler, The Federal Courts and the Federal System 1158-60 (2d ed. 1973). Whatever may be said about such latitudinarianism in other situations, there is no justification for it when habeas corpus under 28 U.S.C. § 2241 furnishes a wholly adequate remedy for federal prisoners in the best possible venue—the district in which the prisoner is confined.[2] Preiser v. Rodriguez, 411

---

2 The appropriateness and convenience of that forum are manifest. If Rabbi Kahane ever is

U.S. 475, 93 S.Ct. 1827, 36 L.Ed.2d 439 (1973), in no way decided that habeas corpus would not lie to challenge conditions of confinement; it decided only that a state prisoner who was seeking to challenge the length of confinement could not utilize 42 U.S.C. § 1983 and its jurisdictional counterpart, 28 U.S.C. § 1343(3), to avoid the exhaustion requirements of § 2254(b) and (c). Although Mr. Justice Stewart said only that the availability of habeas to challenge prison conditions was "arguable," 411 U.S. at 499, 93 S.Ct. 1827, the earlier cases cited by him, Johnson v. Avery, 393 U.S. 483, 89 S.Ct. 747, 21 L.Ed.2d 718 (1969), and Wilwording v. Swenson, 404 U.S. 249, 251, 92 S.Ct. 407, 30 L.Ed.2d 418 (1971), betrayed no uncertainty on the point. See also Developments in the Law—Federal Habeas Corpus, 84 Harv.L.Rev. 1038, 1083-84 (1970). The very inaptness of the

sent to a federal prison after the eight months of delay he has already obtained through proceedings in the sentencing court and in this court on appeal, one may safely guess that the present complaint will not be his last. When a new controversy arises, much will turn on the facts and the warden and other prison officials should not have to go to Brooklyn, or allow Rabbi Kahane to go there, in order to testify. The special consideration existing in Braden v. 30th Judicial Court of Kentucky, 410 U.S. 484, 93 S.Ct. 1123, 35 L.Ed.2d 443 (1973), would not be at all applicable in such a case. On the other side, if allowing Rabbi Kahane the privileges here decreed should cause disturbances on the part of other prisoners, as the Bureau of Prisons predicts, there ought to be an opportunity for the warden to seek speedy modification from a federal court near the prison; habeas corpus under § 2241 affords this whereas application of §§ 1361 and 1391(e) might require a warden in, for example, Atlanta, Ga., to seek modification of an order made by a district court in Alaska or Hawaii in a § 1361 action if the prisoner had obtained an order there on the basis of his residence.

venue provisions of § 1391(e) and the availability of § 2241 argue powerfully that Congress did not intend § 1361 to be utilized to challenge prison administration.

It is true, as we said in United States v. Huss, see footnote 1, that several circuit court decisions have held § 1361 to be an appropriate basis of jurisdiction for considering claims challenging the legality of prison conditions. However, most of these cases were brought in the district of confinement, with the warden of the prison named as a defendant. Since federal jurisdiction and venue would exist under § 2241, the approach I am suggesting would yield an identical result; indeed, several of these cases explicitly recognized that habeas corpus relief was also available —e.g., Mead v. Parker, supra.[3]

As far as I have been able to ascertain, only two circuits have assumed jurisdiction over a prisoner's grievance over the conditions of confinement under § 1361 when § 2241 would not also have been available. With respect to the decision of a divided panel utilizing the Fifth Circuit's summary calendar procedure, Ellingburg v. Connett, 457 F.2d 240 (1972), I find Judge Coleman's dissent, 457 F.2d at 242, much more persuasive than the majority opinion. Even in petitions not directed, at least in form, against the prisoner's immediate warden, the circuit has found it necessary to attempt to curb the enthusiasm of district judges by

[3] Insofar as the decisions which have advocated a broad reach for § 1361 have been based on the assumption that habeas corpus relief was unavailable to prisoners challenging the conditions of their confinement—see Long v. Parker, supra; Byse & Fiocca, supra, at 349-50; cf. Ashe v. McNamara, 355 F.2d 277 (1 Cir. 1965)—their force is vitiated by the invalidity of the assumption.

ruling that "absent extraordinary circumstances which we need not today delineate, such actions should ordinarily be transferred [to the district of confinement under 28 U.S.C. § 1404(a)] as a matter of course." Young v. Director, *supra*, 367 F.2d at 332. Enforcing that rule, and filling out the term "extraordinary circumstances," required the court of appeals to develop a complicated list of rules to govern the disposition of what is normally considered a matter for the trial court's discretion. See Starnes v. McGuire, *supra*, 512 F. 2d at 929-33. Included in that list is the consideration that, for cases which "should properly be brought" under § 2241, the district court "must be free to transfer the case" since "we believe that there is no reason in these cases for the court to deviate from the traditional rule that the residence of the immediate custodian (and thus the place of confinement) is the correct forum." 512 F.2d at 931-32.[4] How much more satisfactory it would be to rule that, except in extraordinary circumstances, § 1361 is not available and § 2241 is the exclusive remedy.[5]

[4] The Government has not argued on this appeal that the denial of its transfer motion was an abuse of discretion—much less the "clear-cut abuse of discretion" necessary under our decision in A. Olinick & Sons v. Dempster Brothers, Inc., 365 F.2d 439, 445 (2 Cir. 1966), to render such a denial appealable if it stood alone.

[5] The availability of transfer under 28 U.S.C. § 1404(a) is no answer, in view of the frequent reluctance of district judges to grant this and the limited availability of appellate review, see note 4 *supra*, not to speak of the time required.

I find further support for my view in the interrelation of § 2241 and § 2255. Section 2255, added to the Judicial Code in 1948, was enacted largely to cure problems of venue arising under the general habeas corpus statute: the inordinate case load in districts where federal prisons were located, and, more particularly, the unavailability in the district of confinement of witnesses who had testimony relevant to the legality of the sentence. As was said in United States v. Hayman, 342 U.S. 205, 220-21, 72 S.Ct. 263, 273, 96 L.Ed. 232 (1952), "[t]he very purpose of Section 2255 is to hold any required hearing in the sentencing court because of the inconvenience of transporting court officials and other necessary witnesses to the district of confinement." Since a prisoner who brings a § 2255 action must claim "the right to be released," it is clear that the section is not available to a prisoner attacking only the conditions of his confinement, as we held in United States v. Huss, *supra;* see also Mead v. Parker, *supra,* 464 F.2d at 1111. With § 2255 relief thus "inadequate or ineffective," a prisoner attacking the conditions of confinement may bring his claim under § 2241, in the district where he is confined—a forum as convenient for airing such claims as the sentencing district is for passing on claims of illegality. This rational decision of Congress with respect to the venue of federal prisoner applications is imperiled if a prisoner can invoke § 1361 in the district of his residence to review discretionary determinations of the warden or the Bureau of Prisons.

O'LONE v. SHABAZZ

482 U.S. 342, 107 S. Ct. 2400 (1987)

[Citations and Footnotes Omitted]

CHIEF JUSTICE REHNQUIST delivered the opinion of the Court.

This case requires us to consider once again the standard of review for prison regulations claimed to inhibit the exercise of constitutional rights. Respondents, members of the Islamic faith, were prisoners in New Jersey's Leesburg State Prison. They challenged policies adopted by prison officials which resulted in their inability to attend Jumu'ah, a weekly Muslim congregational service regularly held in the main prison building and in a separate facility known as "the Farm." Jumu'ah is commanded by the Koran and must be held every Friday after the sun reaches its zenith and before the Asr, or afternoon prayer. There is no question that respondents' sincerely held religious beliefs compelled attendance at Jumu'ah. We hold that the prison regulations here challenged did not violate respondents' rights under the Free Exercise Clause of the First Amendment to the United States Constitution.

Inmates at Leesburg are placed in one of three custody classifications. Maximum security and "gang minimum" security inmates are housed in the main prison building,

and those with the lowest classification—full minimum—live in "the Farm." Both respondents were classified as gang minimum security prisoners when this suit was filed, and respondent Mateen was later classified as full minimum.

Several changes in prison policy prompted this litigation. In April 1983, the New Jersey Department of Corrections issued Standard 853, which provided that inmates could no longer move directly from maximum security to full minimum status, but were instead required to first spend a period of time in the intermediate gang minimum status. This change was designed to redress problems that had arisen when inmates were transferred directly from the restrictive maximum security status to full minimum status, with its markedly higher level of freedom. Because of serious overcrowding in the main building, Standard 853 further mandated that gang minimum inmates ordinarily be assigned jobs outside the main building. These inmates work in details of 8 to 15 persons, supervised by one guard. Standard 853 also required that full minimum inmates work outside the main institution, whether on or off prison grounds, or in a satellite building such as the Farm.

Corrections officials at Leesburg implemented these policies gradually and ... with some difficulty. In the initial stages of outside work details for gang minimum prisoners, officials apparently allowed some Muslim inmates to work inside the main building on Fridays so that they could attend Jumu'ah. This alternative was eventually eliminated in March 1984, in light of the directive of Standard 853 that all gang minimum inmates work outside the main building.

Significant problems arose with those inmates assigned to outside work details. Some avoided reporting for their assignments, while others found reasons for returning to the main building during the course of the workday (including their desire to attend religious services). Evidence showed that the return of prisoners during the day resulted in security risks and administrative burdens that prison officials found unacceptable. Because details of inmates were supervised by only one guard, the whole detail was forced to return to the main gate when one prisoner desired to return to the facility. The gate was the site of all incoming foot and vehicle traffic during the day, and prison officials viewed it as a high security risk area. When an inmate returned, vehicle traffic was delayed while the inmate was logged in and searched.

In response to these burdens, Leesburg officials took steps to ensure that those assigned to outside

details remained there for the whole day. Thus, arrangements were made to have lunch and required medications brought out to the prisoners, and appointments with doctors and social workers were scheduled for the late afternoon. These changes proved insufficient, however, and prison officials began to study alternatives. After consulting with the director of social services, the director of professional services, and the prison's imam and chaplain, prison officials in March 1984 issued a policy memorandum which prohibited inmates assigned to outside work details from returning to the prison during the day except in the case of emergency.

The prohibition of returns prevented Muslims assigned to outside work details from attending Jumu'ah. Respondents filed suit under 42 U.S.C. § 1983, alleging that the prison policies unconstitutionally denied them their Free Exercise rights under the First Amendment, as applied to the States through the Fourteenth Amendment. The District Court, applying the standards announced in an earlier decision of the Court of Appeals for the Third Circuit, concluded that no constitutional violation had occurred. The District Court decided that Standard 853 and the March 1984 prohibition on returns "plausible advance" the goals of security, order, and rehabilitation. It rejected alternative arrangements suggested by respondents, finding that "no less restrictive alternative could be adopted without potentially compromising a legitimate institutional objective.

The Court of Appeals, sua sponte hearing the case en banc, decided that its earlier decision relied upon by the District Court was not sufficiently protective of prisoners' free exercise rights, and went on to state that prison policies could be sustained only if:

"the state ... show[s] that the challenged regulations were intended to serve, and do serve, the important penological goal of security, and that no reasonable method exists by which [prisoners'] religious rights can be accommodated without creating bona fide security problems. The expert testimony of prison officials should be given due weight, but such testimony is not dispositive of the issue whether no reasonable adjustment is possible.... Where it is found that reasonable methods of accommodation can be adopted without sacrificing either the state's interest in security or the prisoners' interest in freely exercising their religious rights, the state's refusal to allow the observance of a central religious practice cannot be justified and violates the prisoner's first amendment rights."

In considering whether a potential method of accommodation is reasonable, the court added, relevant factors include cost, the effects of overcrowding, understaffing, and inmates' demonstrated proclivity to unruly conduct. The case was remanded to the District Court for reconsideration under the standards enumerated in the opinion. We granted certiorari

to consider the important federal constitutional issues presented by the Court of Appeals' decision, and to resolve apparent confusion among the Courts of Appeals on the proper standards to be applied in considering prisoners' free exercise claims.

Several general principles guide our consideration of the issues presented here. First, "convicted prisoners do not forfeit all constitutional protections by reason of their conviction and confinement in prison." *Bell v. Wolfish.* Inmates clearly retain protections afforded by the First Amendment, *Pell v. Procunier.* including its directive that no law shall prohibit the free exercise of religion. See *Cruz v. Beto.* Second, "[l]awful incarceration brings about the necessary withdrawal or limitation of many privileges and rights, a retraction justified by the considerations underlying our penal system." *Price v. Johnston.* The limitations on the exercise of constitutional rights arise both from the fact of incarceration and from valid penological objectives-including deterrence of crime, rehabilitation of prisoners. and institutional security. *Pell v. Procunier; Procunier v. Martinez.*

In considering the appropriate balance of these factors, we have often said that evaluation of penological objectives is committed to the considered judgment of prison administrators, "who are actually charged with and trained in the running of the particular institution under examination." To ensure that courts afford appropriate deference to prison officials, we have determined that prison regulations alleged to infringe constitutional rights are judged under a "reasonableness" test less restrictive than that ordinarily applied to alleged infringements of fundamental constitutional rights. are recently restated the proper standard: "[W]hen a prison regulation impinges on inmates' constitutional rights, the regulation is valid if it is reasonably related to legitimate penological interests." This approach ensures the ability of corrections officials "to anticipate security problems and to adopt innovative solutions to the intractable problems of prison administration," and avoids unnecessary intrusion of the judiciary into problems particularly ill-suited to "resolution by decree."

We think the Court of Appeals decision in this case was wrong when it established a separate burden on prison officials to prove "that no reasonable method exists by which [prisoners'] religious rights can be accommodated without creating bona fide security problems." Though the availability of accommodations is relevant to the reasonableness inquiry, we have rejected the notion that "prison officials ... have to set up and then shoot down every conceivable alternative method of accommodating the claimant's constitutional complaint." By placing the burden on prison officials to disprove the availability of alternatives, the approach articulated by the Court of Appeals fails to reflect the respect and deference that the United States Constitu-

tion allows for the judgment of prison administrators.

Turning to consideration of the policies challenged in this case, we think the findings of the District Court establish clearly that prison officials have acted in a reasonable manner. *Turner v. Safley* drew upon our previous decisions to identify several factors relevant to this reasonableness determination. First, a regulation must have a logical connection to legitimate governmental interests invoked to justify it. The policies at issue here clearly meet that standard. The requirement that full minimum and gang minimum prisoners work outside the main facility was justified by concerns of institutional order and security, for the District Court found that it was "at least in part a response to a critical overcrowding in the state's prisons, and ... at least in part designed to ease tension and drain on the facilities during that part of the day when the inmates were outside the confines of the main buildings." We think it beyond doubt that the standard is related to this legitimate concern.

The subsequent policy prohibiting returns to the institution during the day also passes muster under this standard. Prison officials testified that the returns from outside work details generated congestion and delays at the main gate, a high risk area in any event. Return requests also placed pressure on guards supervising outside details, who previously were required to "evaluate each reason possibly justifying a return to the facilities and either accept or reject that reason." Rehabilitative concerns further supported the policy; corrections officials sought a simulation of working conditions and responsibilities in society. Chief Deputy Ucci testified: "One of the things that society demands or expects is that when you have a job, you show up on time, you put in your eight hours, or whatever hours you are supposed to put in, and you don't get off... . If we can show inmates that they're supposed to show up for work and work a full day, then when they get out at least we've done something." These legitimate goals were advanced by the prohibition on returns: it cannot seriously be maintained that "the logical connection between the regulation and the asserted goal is so remote as to render the policy arbitrary or irrational."

Our decision in Turner also found it relevant that "alternative means of exercising the right ... remain open to prison inmates." There are, of course, no alternative means of attending Jumu'ah; respondents' religious beliefs insist that it occur at a particular time. But the very stringent requirements as to the time at which Jumu'ah may be held may make it extraordinarily difficult for prison officials to assure that every Muslim prisoner is able to attend that service. While we in no way minimize the central importance of Jumu'ah to respondents, we are unwilling to hold that prison officials are required by the Constitution to sacrifice legitimate penological ob-

jectives to that end. In *Turner*, we did not look to see whether prisoners had other means of communicating with fellow inmates, but instead examined whether the inmates were deprived of "all means of expression." Here, similarly, we think it appropriate to see whether under these regulations respondents retain the ability to participate in other Muslim religious ceremonies. The record establishes that respondents are not deprived of all forms of religious exercise, but instead freely observe a number of their religious obligations. The right to congregate for prayer or discussion is "virtually unlimited except during working hours," and the state-provided imam has free access to the prison. Muslim prisoners are given different meals whenever pork is served in the prison cafeteria. Special arrangements are also made during the month-long observance of Ramadan, a period of fasting and prayer. During Ramadan, Muslim prisoners are awakened at 4 a.m. for an early breakfast, and receive dinner at 8:30 p.m. each evening. We think this ability on the part of respondents to participate in other religious observances of their faith supports the conclusion that the restrictions at issue here were reasonable.

Finally, the case for the validity of these regulations is strengthened by examination of the impact that accommodation of respondents' asserted right would have on other inmates, on prison personnel, and on allocation of prison resources generally. Respondents suggest several accommodations of their practices, including placing all Muslim inmates in one or two inside work details or providing weekend labor for Muslim inmates. As noted by the District Court, however, each of respondents' suggested accommodations would, in the judgment of prison officials, have adverse effects on the institution. Inside work details for gang minimum inmates would be inconsistent with the legitimate concerns underlying Standard 853, and the District Court found that the extra supervision necessary to establish weekend details for Muslim prisoners "would be a drain on scarce human resources" at the prison. Prison officials determined that the alternatives would also threaten prison security by allowing "affinity groups" in the prison to flourish. Administrator O'Lone testified that "we have found out and think almost every prison administrator knows that any time you put a group of individuals together with one particular affinity interest ... you wind up with ... a leadership role and an organizational structure that will almost invariably challenge the institutional authority." Finally, the officials determined that special arrangements for one group could create problems as "other inmates [see] that a certain segment is escaping a rigorous work detail" and perceive favoritism. These concerns of prison administrators provide adequate support for the conclusion that accommodations of respondents' request to attend Jumu'ah would have undesirable results in the institution. These

difficulties also make clear that there are no "obvious, easy alternatives to the policy adopted by petitioners."

We take this opportunity to reaffirm our refusal, even where claims are made under the First Amendment, to "substitute our judgment on ... difficult and sensitive matters of institutional administration," for the determinations of those charged with the formidable task of running a prison. Here the District Court decided that the regulations alleged to infringe constitutional rights were reasonably related to legitimate penological objectives. We agree with the District Court, and it necessarily follows that the regulations in question do not offend the Free Exercise Clause of the First Amendment to the United States Constitution. The judgment of the Court of Appeals is therefore

Reversed.

JUSTICE BRENNAN, with whom JUSTICE MARSHALL, JUSTICE BLACKMUN, and JUSTICE STEVENS join, dissenting.

The religious ceremony that these respondents seek to attend is not presumptively dangerous. and the prison has completely foreclosed respondents' participation in it. I therefore would require prison officials to demonstrate that the restrictions they have imposed are necessary to further an important government interest, and that these restrictions are no greater than necessary to achieve prison objectives. As a result, I would affirm the Court of Appeals' order to remand the case to the District Court, and would require prison officials to make this showing. Even were I to accept the Court's standard of review, however, I would remand the case to the District Court, since that court has not had the opportunity to review respondents' claim under the new standard established by this Court in *Turner*. As the record now stands, the reasonableness of foreclosing respondents' participation in Jumu'ah has not been established.

I

Prisoners are persons whom most of us would rather not think about. Banished from everyday sight, they exist in a shadow world that only dimly enters our awareness. They are members of a "total institution" that controls their daily existence in a way that few of us can imagine:

"[P]rison is a complex of physical arrangements and of measures, all wholly governmental, all wholly performed by agents of government, which determine the total existence of certain human beings (except perhaps in the realm of the spirit, and inevitably there as well) from sundown to sundown, sleeping, waking, speaking, silent, working, playing, viewing, eating, voiding, reading, alone, with others. It is not so, with members of the general adult population. State governments have not undertaken to require members of the general adult population to rise at a certain hour, retire at a certain hour, eat at certain hours, live for periods with no companionship whatever, wear certain clothing, or submit to oral and anal searches after visiting hours, nor have state governments undertaken to prohibit members of the general adult population from speaking to one another, wearing beards, embracing their spouses, or corresponding with their lovers." *Morales v. Schmidt*, 340 F. Supp. 544, 550 (W.D. Wis. 1972).

It is thus easy to think of prisoners as members of a separate netherworld, driven by its own demands, ordered by its own customs, ruled by those whose claim to power rests on raw necessity. Nothing can change the fact, however, that the society that these prisoners inhabit is our own. Prisons may exist on the margins of that society, but no act of will can sever them from the body politic. When prisoners emerge from the shadows to press a constitutional claim, they invoke no alien set of principles drawn from a distant culture. Rather, they speak the language of the charter upon which all of us rely to hold official power accountable. They ask us to acknowledge that power exercised in the shadows must be restrained at least as diligently as power that acts in the sunlight.

In reviewing a prisoner's claim of the infringement of a constitutional right, we must therefore begin from the premise that, as members of this society, prisoners retain constitutional rights that limit the exercise of official authority against them. At the same time, we must acknowledge that incarceration by its nature changes an individual's status in society. Prison officials have the difficult and often thankless job of preserving security in a potentially explosive setting, as well as of attempting to provide rehabilitation that prepares some inmates for re-entry into the social mainstream. Both these demands require the curtailment and elimination of certain rights.

The challenge for this Court is to determine how best to protect those prisoners' rights that remain. Our objective in selecting a standard of review is therefore not, as the Court declares, "[t]o ensure that courts afford appropriate deference to prison officials." The Constitution was not adopted as a means of enhancing the efficiency with which government officials conduct their affairs, nor as a blueprint for ensuring sufficient reliance on administrative expertise. Rather, it was meant to provide a bulwark against infringements that might otherwise be justified as necessary expedients of governing. The practice of Europe, wrote James Madison, was "charters of liberty ... granted by power"; of America, "charters of power granted by liberty." While we must give due consideration to the needs of those in power, this Court's role is to ensure that fundamental restraints on that power are enforced.

In my view, adoption of "reasonableness" as a standard of review for all constitutional challenges by inmates is inadequate to this task. Such a standard is categorically deferential, and does not discriminate among degrees of deprivation. From this perspective, restricting use of the prison library to certain hours warrants the same level of scrutiny as preventing inmates from reading at all. Various "factors" may be weighed differently in each situation, but the message to prison officials is clear: merely act "reasonably" and your actions will be upheld. If a directive that officials act "reasonably" were deemed sufficient to check all exercises of power, the Constitution would hardly be necessary. Yet the Court deems this single standard adequate to restrain any type of conduct in which prison officials might engage. It is true that the degree of deprivation is one of the factors in the Court's reasonableness determination. This by itself does not make the standard of review appropriate, however. If it did, we would need but a single standard for evaluating all constitutional claims, as long as every relevant factor were considered under its rubric. Clearly, we have never followed such an approach. A standard of review frames the terms in which justification may be offered, and thus delineates the boundaries within which argument may take place. The use of differing levels of scrutiny proclaims that on some occasions official power must justify itself in a way that otherwise it need not. A relatively strict standard of review is a signal that a decree prohibiting a political demonstration on the basis of the participants' political beliefs is of more serious concern, and therefore will be scrutinized more closely, than a rule limiting the number of demonstrations that may take place downtown at noon.

Thus, even if the absolute nature of the deprivation may be taken into account in the Court's formulation, it makes a difference that this is merely one factor in determining if official conduct is "reasonable." Once we provide such an elastic and deferential principle of justification, [t]he principle ... lies about like a loaded weapon ready for the hand of any authority that can bring forth a plausible claim of an urgent need. Every repetition imbeds that principle more deeply in our law and thinking and expands it to new purposes." Mere assertions of exigency have a way of providing a colorable defense for governmental deprivation, and we should be especially wary of expansive delegations of power to those who wield it on the margins of society. Prisons are too often shielded from public view; there is no need to make them virtually invisible.

An approach better suited to the sensitive task of protecting the constitutional rights of inmates is laid out by Judge Kaufman in *Abdul Wali v. Coughlin*, 754 F. 2d 1015 (CA2 1985). That approach maintains that the degree of scrutiny of prison regulations should depend on "the nature of the right being asserted by prisoners, the type of activity in which they seek to engage, and whether the challenged restriction works a total deprivation (as opposed to a mere limitation) on the exercise of that right." Essentially, if the activity in which inmates seek to engage is pre-

sumptively dangerous, or if a regulation merely restricts the time, place, or manner in which prisoners may exercise a right, a prison regulation will be invalidated only if there is no reasonable justification for official action. Where exercise of the asserted right is not presumptively dangerous, however, and where the prison has completely deprived an inmate of that right, then prison officials must show that "a particular restriction is necessary to further an important governmental interest, and that the limitations on freedoms occasioned by the restrictions are no greater than necessary to effectuate the governmental objective involved."

The court's analytical framework in Abdul Wali recognizes that in many instances it is inappropriate for courts "to substitute our judgments for those of trained professionals with years of firsthand experience." It would thus apply a standard of review identical to the Court's "reasonableness" standard in a significant percentage of cases. At the same time, the *Abdul Wali* approach takes seriously the Constitution's function of requiring that official power be called to account when it completely deprives a person of a right that society regards as basic. In this limited number of cases, it would require more than a demonstration of "reasonableness" to justify such infringement. To the extent that prison is meant to inculcate a respect for social and legal norms, a requirement that prison officials persuasively demonstrate the need for the absolute deprivation of inmate rights is consistent with that end. Furthermore, prison officials are in control of the evidence that is essential to establish the superiority of such deprivation over other alternatives. It is thus only fair for these officials to be held to a stringent standard of review in such extreme cases.

The prison in this case has completely prevented respondent inmates from attending the central religious service of their Muslim faith. I would therefore hold prison officials to the standard articulated in *Abdul Wali*, and would find their proffered justifications wanting. The State has neither demonstrated that the restriction is necessary to further an important objective nor proved that less extreme measures may not serve its purpose. Even if I accepted the Court's standard of review, however, I could not conclude on this record that prison officials have proved that it is reasonable to preclude respondents from attending Jumu'ah. Petitioners have provided mere unsubstantiated assertions that the plausible alternatives proposed by respondents are infeasible.

II

In *Turner*, the Court set forth a framework for reviewing allegations that a constitutional right has been infringed by prison officials. The Court found relevant to that review "whether there are alternative means of exercising the right that remain open to prison inmates." The Court in this case acknowledges that "respondents' sincerely held religious beliefs compe[l] attendance at Jumu'ah," and concedes that there are "no alternative means of attending Jumu'ah." Nonetheless, the Court finds that prison policy does not work a complete deprivation of respondents' asserted religious right, because respondents have the opportunity to participate in other religious activities. This analysis ignores the fact that, as the District Court found, Jumu'ah is the central religious ceremony of Muslims, "comparable to the Saturday service of the Jewish faith and the Sunday service of the various Christian sects." As with other faiths, this ceremony provides a special time in which Muslims "assert their identity as a community covenanted to God." As a result:

"unlike other Muslim prayers which are performed individually and can be made up if missed, the Jumu'ah is obligatory, cannot be made up, and must be performed in congregation. The Jumu'ah is therefore regarded as the central service of the Muslim religion, and the obligation to attend is commanded by the Qur'an, the central book of the Muslim religion."

Jumu'ah therefore cannot be regarded as one of several essentially fungible religious practices. The ability to engage in other religious activities cannot obscure the fact that the denial at issue in this case is absolute: respondents are completely foreclosed from participating in the core ceremony that reflects their membership in a particular religious community. If a Catholic prisoner were prevented from attending Mass on Sunday, few would regard that deprivation as anything but absolute, even if the prisoner were afforded other opportunities to pray, to discuss the Catholic faith with others, and even to avoid eating meat on Friday if that were a preference. Prison officials in this case therefore cannot show that `other avenues' remain available for the exercise of the asserted right."

Under the Court's approach, as enunciated in *Turner*, the availability of other means of exercising the right in question counsels considerable deference to prison officials. By the same token, the infliction of an absolute deprivation should require more than mere assertion that such a deprivation is necessary. In particular, "the existence of obvious, easy alternatives may be evidence that the regulation is not reasonable, but is an 'exaggerated response' to prison concerns." In this case, petitioners have not established the reasonableness of their policy, because they have provided only bare assertions that the proposals for accommodation offered by respondents are infeasible. As discussed below, the federal policy of permitting inmates in federal prisons to participate in Jumu'ah, as well as Leesburg's own policy of permitting participation for several years, lends plausibility to respondents' suggestion that their religious practice can be accommodated.

In *Turner*, the Court found that the practices of the Federal Bureau of Prisons were relevant to the availability of reasonable alternatives to the policy under challenge. In upholding a ban on inmate-to-inmate mail, the Court noted that the Bureau had adopted "substantially similar restrictions." In finding that there were alternatives to a stringent restriction on the ability to marry, the Court observed that marriages by inmates in federal prisons were generally permitted absent a threat to security or public safety. In the present case, it is therefore worth noting that Federal Bureau of Prisons regulations require the adjustment of work assignments to permit inmate participation in religious ceremonies, absent a threat to "security, safety, and good order." The Bureau's Directive implementing the regulations on Religious Beliefs and Practices of Committed Offenders, states that, with respect to scheduling religious observances. "[t]he more central the religious activity is to the tenets of the inmate's religious faith, the greater the presumption is for relieving the inmate from the institution program or assignment." Furthermore, the Chaplain Director of the Bureau has spoken directly to the issue of participation of Muslim inmates in Ju mu'ah:

"Provision is made, by policy, in all Bureau facilities for the observance of Jumu-ah by all inmates in general population who wish to keep this faith practice. The service is held each Friday afternoon in the general time frame that corresponds to the requirements of Islamic jurisprudence....

"Subject only to restraints of security and good order in the institution all routine and normal work assignments are suspended for the Islamic inmates to ensure freedom to attend such services....

"In those institutions where the outside work details contain Islamic inmates, they are permitted access to the inside of the institution to attend the Jumu-ah."

That Muslim inmates are able to participate in Jumu'ah throughout the entire federal prison system suggests that the practice is, under normal circumstances, compatible with the demands of prison administration. Indeed, the Leesburg State Prison permitted participation in this ceremony for five years, and experienced no threats to security or safety as a result. In light of both standard federal prison practice and Leesburg's own past practice, a reasonableness test in this case demands at Least minimal substantiation by prison officials that alternatives that would permit participation in Jumu'ah are infeasible. Under the standard articulated by the Court in *Turner*, this does not mean that petitioners are responsible for identifying and discrediting these alternatives; "prison officials do not have to set up and then shoot down every conceivable alternative method of accommodating the claimant's constitutional complaint." When prisoners themselves present alternatives, however, and when they fairly call into question official claims that these alternatives are infeasible, we must demand at least some evidence be-

yond mere assertion that the religious practice at issue cannot be accommodated. Examination of the alternatives proposed in this case indicates that prison officials have not provided such substantiation.

III

Respondents' first proposal is that gang minimum prisoners be assigned to an alternative inside work detail on Friday, as they had been before the recent change in policy. Prison officials testified that the alternative work detail is now restricted to maximum security prisoners, and that they did not wish maximum and minimum security prisoners to mingle. Even the District Court had difficulty with this assertion, as it commented that "[t]he defendants did not explain why inmates of different security levels are not mixed on work assignments when otherwise they are mixed." The court found, nonetheless, that this alternative would be inconsistent with Standard 853's mandate to move gang minimum inmates to outside work details. This conclusion, however, neglects the fact that the very issue is whether the prison's policy, of which Standard 853 is a part, should be administered so as to accommodate Muslim inmates. The policy itself cannot serve as a justification for its failure to provide reasonable accommodation. The record as it now stands thus does not establish that the Friday alternative work detail would create a problem for the institution.

Respondents' second proposal is that gang minimum inmates be assigned to work details inside the main building on a regular basis. While admitting that the prison used inside details in the kitchen, bakery, and tailor shop, officials stated that these jobs are reserved for the riskiest gang minimum inmates, for whom an outside job might be unwise. Thus, concluded officials, it would be a bad idea to move these inmates outside to make room for Muslim gang minimum inmates. Respondents contend, however, that the prison's own records indicate that there are a significant number of jobs inside the institution that could be performed by inmates posing a lesser security risk. This suggests that it might not be necessary for the riskier gang minimum inmates to be moved outside to make room for the less risky inmates. Officials provided no data on the number of inside jobs available, the number of high-risk gang minimum inmates performing them, the number of Muslim inmates that might seek inside positions, or the number of staff that would be necessary to monitor such an arrangement. Given the plausibility of respondents' claim, prison officials should present at least this information in substantiating their contention that inside assignments are infeasible.

Third, respondents suggested that gang minimum inmates be assigned to Saturday or Sunday work details, which would allow them to make up any time lost by attending Jumu'ah on Friday. While prison officials admitted the existence of weekend work details, they stated that "[s]ince prison personnel are needed for other programs on weekends, the creation of additional weekend details would be a drain on scarce human resources." The record provides no indication, however, of the number of Muslims that would seek such a work detail, the current number of weekend details, or why it would be infeasible simply to reassign current Saturday or Sunday workers to Friday, rather than create additional details. The prison is able to arrange work schedules so that Jewish inmates may attend services on Saturday and Christian inmates may attend services on Sunday. Despite the fact that virtually all inmates are housed in the main building over the weekend, so that the demand on the facility is greater than at any other time, the prison is able to provide sufficient staff coverage to permit Jewish and Christian inmates to participate in their central religious ceremonies. Given the prison's duty to provide Muslims a "reasonable opportunity of pursuing [their] faith comparable to the opportunity afforded fellow prisoners who adhere to conventional religious precepts," prison officials should be required to provide more than mere assertions of the infeasibility of weekend details for Muslim inmates.

Finally, respondents proposed that minimum security inmates living at the Farm be assigned to jobs either in the Farm building or in its immediate vicinity. Since Standard 853 permits such assignments for full minimum inmates, and since such inmates need not return to prison facilities through the main entrance, this would interfere neither with Standard 853 nor the concern underlying the no-return policy. Nonetheless, prison officials stated that such an arrangement might create an "affinity group" of Muslims representing a threat to prison authority. Officials pointed to no such problem in the five years in which Muslim inmates were permitted to assemble for Jumu'ah, and in which the alternative Friday work detail was in existence. Nor could they identify any threat resulting from the fact that during the month of Ramadan all Muslim prisoners participate in both breakfast and dinner at special times. Furthermore, there was no testimony that the concentration of Jewish or Christian inmates on work details or in religious services posed any type of "affinity group" threat. As the record now stands, prison officials have declared that a security risk is created by a grouping of Muslim inmates in the least dangerous security classification, but not by a grouping of maximum security inmates who are concentrated in a work detail inside the main building, and who are the only Muslims assured of participating in Jumu'ah. Surely, prison officials should be required to provide at least some substantiation for this facially implausible contention.

Petitioners also maintained that the assignment of full minimum Muslim inmates to the Farm or its near vicinity might provoke resent-

ment because of other inmates' perception that Muslims were receiving special treatment. Officials pointed to no such perception during the period in which the alternative Friday detail was in existence, nor to any resentment of the fact that Muslims' dietary preferences are accommodated and that Muslims are permitted to operate on a special schedule during the month of Ramadan. Nor do they identify any such problems created by the accommodation of the religious preferences of inmates of other faiths. Once again, prison officials should be required at a minimum to identify the basis for their assertions.

Despite the plausibility of the alternatives proposed by respondents in light of federal practice and the prison's own past practice, officials have essentially provided mere pronouncements that such alternatives are not workable. If this Court is to take seriously its commitment to the principle that "[p]rison walls do not form a barrier separating prison inmates from the protections of the Constitution," it must demand more than this record provides to justify a Muslim inmate's complete foreclosure from participation in the central religious service of the Muslim faith.

IV

That the record in this case contains little more than assertions is not surprising in light of the fact that the District Court proceeded on the basis of the approach set forth in *St. Claire v. Cuyler*, 634 F. 2d 109 (CA3 1980). That case held that mere "sincer[e]" and "arguably correct" testimony by prison officials is sufficient to demonstrate the need to limit prisoners' exercise of constitutional rights. This Court in *Turner*, however, set forth a more systematic framework for analyzing challenges to prison regulations. *Turner* directed attention to two factors of particular relevance to this case: the degree of constitutional deprivation and the availability of reasonable alternatives. The respondents in this case have been absolutely foreclosed from participating in the central religious ceremony of their Muslim faith. At least a colorable claim that such a drastic policy is not necessary can be made in light of the ability of federal prisons to accommodate Muslim inmates, Leesburg's own past practice of doing so, and the plausibility of the alternatives proposed by respondents. If the Court's standard of review is to repre

sent anything more than reflexive deference to prison officials, any finding of reasonableness must rest on firmer ground than the record now presents.

Incarceration by its nature denies a prisoner participation in the larger human community. To deny the opportunity to affirm membership in a spiritual community, however, may extinguish an inmate's last source of hope for dignity and redemption. Such a denial requires more justification than mere assertion that any other course of action is infeasible. While I would prefer that this case be analyzed under the approach set out in Part I, supra, I would at a minimum remand to the District Court for an analysis of respondents' claims in accordance with the standard enunciated by the Court in Turner and in this case. I therefore dissent.

LEGAL SERVICES

JOHNSON v. AVERY

393 U.S. 483, 89 S. Ct. 747, 21 L. Ed. 2d 718 (1969)

Mr. Justice Fortas delivered the opinion of the Court.

I.

Petitioner is serving a life sentence in the Tennessee State Penitentiary. In February, 1965, he was transferred to the maximum security building in the prison for violation of a prison regulation which provides:

"No inmate will advise, assist or otherwise contract to aid another, either with or without a fee, to prepare Writs or other legal matters. It is not intended that an innocent man be punished. When a man believes he is unlawfully held or illegally convicted, he should prepare a brief or state his complaint in letter form and address it to his lawyer or a judge. A formal Writ is not necessary to receive a hearing. False charges or untrue complaints may be punished. Inmates are forbidden to set themselves up as prac-

titioners for the purpose of promoting a business of writing Writs."

In July, 1965, petitioner filed in the United States District Court for the Middle District of Tennessee a "motion for law books and a typewriter," in which he sought relief from his confinement in the maximum security building. The District Court treated this motion as a petition for a writ of habeas corpus and, after hearing, ordered him released from disciplinary confinement and restored to the status of an ordinary prisoner. The District Court held that the regulation was void because it, in effect, barred illiterate prisoners from access to federal habeas corpus and conflicted with 28 U.S.C. § 2242. 252 F.Supp. 783.

By the time the District Court order was entered, petitioner had been transferred from the maximum security building, but he had been put in a disciplinary cell block in which he was entitled to fewer privileges than were given ordinary prisoners. Only when he promised to refrain from assistance to other inmates was he restored to regular prison conditions and privileges. At a second hearing, held in March, 1966, the District Court explored these issues concerning the compliance of the prison officials with its initial order. After the hearing, it reaffirmed its earlier order.

The State appealed. The Court of Appeals for the Sixth Circuit reversed, concluding that the regulation did not unlawfully conflict with the federal right of habeas corpus. According to the Sixth Circuit, the interest of the State in preserving prison discipline and in limiting the practice of law to licensed attorneys justified whatever burden the regulation might place on access to federal habeas corpus. 382 F. 2d 353.

II.

This Court has constantly emphasized the fundamental importance of the writ of habeas corpus in our constitutional scheme, and the Congress has demonstrated its solicitude for the vigor of the Great Writ. The Court has steadfastly insisted that "there is no higher duty than to maintain it unimpaired." *Bowen* v. *Johnston*, 306 U.S. 19, 26 (1939).

Since the basic purpose of the writ is to enable those unlawfully incarcerated to obtain their freedom, it is fundamental that access of prisoners to the courts for the purpose of presenting their complaints may not be denied or obstructed. For example, the Court has held that a State may not validly make the writ available only to prisoners who could pay a $4 filing fee. *Smith* v. *Bennett*, 365 U.S. 708 (1961). And it has insisted that, for the indigent as well as for the

affluent prisoner, post-conviction proceedings must be more than a formality. For instance, the State is obligated to furnish prisoners not otherwise able to obtain it, with a transcript or equivalent recordation of prior habeas corpus hearings for use in further proceedings. *Long* v. *District Court*, 385 U.S. 192 (1966). Cf. *Griffin* v. *Illinois*, 351 U.S. 12 (1956).

Tennessee urges, however, that the contested regulation in this case is justified as a part of the State's disciplinary administration of the prisons. There is no doubt that discipline and administration of state detention facilities are state functions. They are subject to federal authority only where paramount federal constitutional or statutory rights supervene. It is clear, however, that in instances where state regulations applicable to inmates of prison facilities conflict with such rights, the regulations may be invalidated.

For example, in *Lee* v. *Washington*, 390 U.S. 333 (1968), the practice of racial segregation of prisoners was justified by the State as necessary to maintain good order and discipline. We held, however, that the practice was constitutionally prohibited, although we were careful to point out that the order of the District Court, which we affirmed, made allowance for "the necessities of prison security and discipline." *Id.*, at 334. And in *Ex parte Hull*, 312 U.S. 546 (1941), this Court invalidated a state regulation which required that habeas corpus petitions first be submitted to prison authorities and then approved by the "legal investigator" to the parole board as "properly drawn" before being transmitted to the court

Here again, the State urged that the requirement was necessary to maintain prison discipline. But this Court held that the regulation violated the principle that "the state and its officers may not abridge or impair petitioner's right to apply to a federal court for a writ of habeas corpus." 312 U.S., at 549. Cf. *Cochran* v. *Kansas,* 316 U.S. 255, 257 (1942).

There can be no doubt that Tennessee could not constitutionally adopt and enforce a rule forbidding illiterate or poorly educated prisoners to file habeas corpus petitions. Here Tennessee has adopted a rule which, in the absence of any other source of assistance for such prisoners, effectively does just that. The District Court concluded that "[f]or all practical purposes, if such prisoners cannot have the assistance of a 'jail-house lawyer,' their possibly valid constitutional claims will never be heard in any court." 252 F.Supp., at 784. The record supports this conclusion.

Jails and penitentiaries include among their inmates a high percentage of persons who are totally or functionally illiterate, whose educational attainments are slight, and whose intelligence is limited. This appears to be equally true of Tennessee's prison facilities.

In most federal courts, it is the practice to appoint counsel in post-conviction proceedings only after a petition for post-conviction relief passes initial judicial evaluation and the court has determined that issues are presented calling for an evidentiary hearing. E. g., *Taylor* v. *Pegelow,* 335 F.2d 147 (C.A. 4th Cir. 1964); *United States ex rel. Marshall* v. *Wilkins,* 338 F. 2d 404 (C.A. 2d Cir. 1964). See 28 U.S.C. § 1915 (d);

R. Sokol, A Handbook of Federal Habeas Corpus 71-73 (1965).

It has not been held that there is any general obligation of the courts, state or federal, to appoint counsel for prisoners who indicate, without more, that they wish to seek post-conviction relief. See, e. g., *Barker* v. *Ohio,* 330 F. 2d 594 (C.A. 6th Cir. 1964). Accordingly, the initial burden of presenting a claim to post-conviction relief usually rests upon the indigent prisoner himself with such help as he can obtain within the prison walls or the prison system. In the case of all except those who are able to help themselves—usually a few old hands or exceptionally gifted prisoners—the prisoner is, in effect, denied access to the courts unless such help is available.

It is indisputable that prison "writ writers" like petitioner are sometimes a menace to prison discipline and that their petitions are often so unskillful as to be a burden on the courts which receive them. But, as this Court held in *Ex parte Hull, supra,* in declaring invalid a state prison regulation which required that prisoners' legal pleadings be screened by state officials:

"The considerations that prompted [the regulation's] formulation are not without merit, but the state and its officers may not abridge or impair petitioner's right to apply to a federal court for a writ of habeas corpus." 312 U.S., at 549.

Tennessee does not provide an available alternative to the assistance provided by other inmates. The warden of the prison in which petitioner was confined stated that the prison provided free notarization of prisoners' petitions. That obviously meets only a formal requirement. He also indicated that he sometimes allowed prisoners to examine the listing of attorneys in the Nashville telephone directory so they could select one to write to in an effort to interest him in taking the case, and that "on several occasions" he had contacted the public defender at the request of an inmate. There is no contention, however, that there is any regular system of assistance by public defenders. In its brief, the State contends that "[t]here is absolutely no reason to believe that prison officials would fail to notify the court should an inmate advise them of a complete inability, either mental or physical, to prepare a habeas application on his own behalf," but there is no contention that they have in fact ever done so.

This is obviously far short of the showing required to demonstrate that, in depriving prisoners of the assistance of fellow inmates, Tennessee has not, in substance, deprived those unable themselves, with reasonable adequacy, to prepare their petitions, of access to the constitutionally and statutorily protected availability of the writ of habeas corpus. By contrast, in several States, the public defender system supplies trained attorneys, paid from public funds, who are available to consult with prisoners regarding their habeas corpus petitions. At least one State employs senior law students to interview and advise inmates in state prisons. An-

other State has a voluntary program whereby members of the local bar association make periodic visits to the prison to consult with prisoners concerning their cases. We express no judgment concerning these plans, but their existence indicates that techniques are available to provide alternatives if the State elects to prohibit mutual assistance among inmates.

Even in the absence of such alternatives, the State may impose reasonable restrictions and restraints upon the acknowledged propensity of prisoners to abuse both the giving and the seeking of assistance in the preparation of applications for relief: for example, by limitations on the time and location of such activities and the imposition of punishment for the giving or receipt of consideration in connection with such activities. Cf. *Hatfield* v. *Bailleaux*, 290 F. 2d 632 (C.A. 9th Cir. 1961) (sustaining as reasonable regulations on the time and location of prisoner work on their own petitions). But unless and until the State provides some reasonable alternative to assist inmates in the preparation of petitions for post-conviction relief, it may not validly enforce a regulation such as that here in issue, barring inmates from furnishing such assistance to other prisoners.

The judgment of the Court of Appeals is reversed and the case is remanded for further proceedings consistent with this opinion.

Reversed and remanded.

IN RE HARRELL
3 Cal.3d 683 (1970)

SULLIVAN, Associate Justice.

. . . .

We first consider the contentions made concerning certain present limitations upon mutual prisoner assistance. Our starting point for this purpose is the decision of the United States Supreme Court in Johnson v. Avery, *supra*, 393 U.S. 483, 89 S.Ct. 747, 21 L.Ed.2d 718.

In *Johnson*, a Tennessee prisoner who had been disciplined for violation of a prison regulation prohibiting the rendering of legal assistance to other inmates sought relief by way of habeas corpus. The high court held that under the circumstances, the effect of the regulation was to forbid illiterate or poorly educated prisoners to file habeas corpus petitions. It was pointed out that Tennessee did not provide any alternative means whereby such prisoners could gain access to the courts and that, therefore, the expedient of mutual prisoner assistance was constitutionally necessary and could not be forbidden. It was emphasized, however, that although mutual prisoner assistance must be allowed in the absence of suitable alternatives, there could be reasonable regulation of the practice in light of institutional circumstances. "Even in the absence of such [alternative means of allowing illiterate and uneducated prisoners access to the courts], the State may impose reasonable restrictions and restraint upon the acknowledged propensity of prisoners to abuse both the giving and the seeking of assistance in the preparation of applications for relief: for example, by limitations on the time and location of such activities and the imposition of punishment for the giving or receipt of consideration in connection with such activities. Cf. Hatfield v. Bailleaux, 290 F. 2d 632 (C.A. 9th Cir. 1961) (sustaining as reasonable regulations on the time and location of prisoner work on their own petitions). But unless and until the State provides some reasonable alternative to assist inmates in the preparation of petitions for post-conviction relief, it may not validly enforce a regulation such as that here at issue, barring inmates from furnishing such assistance to other prisoners." (393 U.S. at p. 490, 89 S.Ct. at p. 751.)

At the date of the *Johnson* decision (February 24, 1969) the Rules of the Director of Corrections (hereafter Director's Rules) specifically forbade mutual legal assistance among prisoners. . . . Director's Rule D 2602 then provided in relevant part: "No inmate shall assist or receive assistance from another in the preparation of legal documents. Any brief or petition not pertaining to his own case found in the possession of an inmate shall be confiscated." The imposition of discipline for violation of this rule was also provided for in the Director's Rules.

However, on March 19, 1969, less than a month after the *Johnson* decision was rendered, the Director's Rules were altered in an effort to conform to the constitutional requirements there enunciated. Inserted at the beginning of that portion of the rules which deal with legal documents was a statement of policy providing as follows: "It is the policy of the Department to allow inmates every legal access to the courts. The Department, however, is neither equipped nor authorized to assist inmates in their legal efforts except to provide staff assistance to inmates, who are illiterate or otherwise physically incapable, in the preparation of forms adopted under rules of the United States Courts and by the Judicial Council of California for petitions for Habeas Corpus or Modification of Custody. There will be a suitable place in each institution where inmates, with the permission of the designated employee, may have access to study such institution law books as are available to them. Law books are defined to include constitutions, codes, court reports, texts, and dictionaries."

At the same time, Director's Rule D 2602 was wholly revised. It now provides: "One inmate may assist another inmate in the preparation of legal documents, but may not receive remuneration therefor. Remuneration is not limited to present benefits, but includes future as well as past benefits. A room or rooms may be designated by the Warden or Superintendent for this purpose. *All briefs, petitions and other legal papers must be and remain in the possession of the inmate to whom they pertain.*" (Italics added.)

A major question before us in this case is whether these amendments to the Director's Rules, and particularly the revised version of Rule D 2602, contain limitations upon the right of mutual assistance which are incon-sistent with the principles enunciated in Johnson v. Avery.

It is clear at the outset that the March 19, 1969, amendments to the Director's Rules reflect a sincere effort to provide for the legal assistance of less literate inmates in a way which both complies with the *Johnson* decision and is consistent with the realities of prison life. Thus, the statement of policy which now precedes the body of rules dealing with inmate legal work indicates that staff assistance will be provided to illiterate inmates and others who are "physically incapable" of preparing their own petitions. More significantly from the standpoint of *Johnson,* the amended version of Rule D 2602 expressly provides for the assistance of such inmates by other inmates and contemplates that space will be made available to facilitate consultation. The rule's prohibition against remuneration, of course, is expressly sanctioned by *Johnson.* (393 U.S. at p. 490, 89 S.Ct. 747.)

A difficult problem is presented, however, by the fact that Rule D 2602 continues to prohibit the possession of legal papers belonging to another inmate. Petitioners, on the one hand, argue that this prohibition violates the principles of *Johnson* because it has the effect of preventing any meaningful legal assistance of one prisoner by another. Such assistance can be provided, it is urged, only if the advising inmate can have more or less extended access to the papers pertaining to the case in order to permit the legal research and drafting necessary to the preparation of a petition.

The Director, on the other hand, points out that the possession of one

of abuses which can be dealt with by other effective means. We therefore hold that that portion of Rule D 2602 which provides "All briefs, petitions and other legal papers must be and remain in the possession of the inmate to whom they pertain" constitutes an unreasonable restriction upon the right of access to the courts and is invalid.

Petitioner McKinney also challenges several other restrictions which, he asserts, have a similarly extreme effect upon the right of access to the courts. In essence, his contention is that the restrictions cited have prevented him from operating effectively as legal counsel for the many inmates in several penal institutions whom he assists and purports to "represent." Thus, he complains that he has been prevented from filing legal documents on behalf of such "client" inmates; that he has been prevented from corresponding with inmates confined at institutions other than that in which he himself is confined; that he has not been allowed to interview an inmate confined in isolation; and that he has been denied access to the disciplinary records of prisoners whom he is assisting. Moreover, McKinney inveighs against the actions of prison officials which, in accordance with regulations applicable at Folsom Prison, have prevented him from possessing a library of personally owned law books in his cell.

We first place these complaints in the context required by the principles enunciated in Johnson v. Avery. As we have suggested above (see fn. 5, ante), it is the rights of illiterate and uneducated prisoners which are protected by Johnson—not the assumed prerogatives of those inmates who have, for one reason or another, set themselves up as legal consultants. Only when, as in Johnson itself, a prison regulation or restriction affecting those who offer legal assistance has the additional effect of preventing or tending to prevent disadvantaged inmates from receiving aid in the preparation of applications for relief can it be said that that regulation or restriction effectively impedes or discourages mutual prisoner assistance within the meaning of Johnson. Moreover, it must be emphasized that Johnson contemplates the giving of *assistance* by one inmate to another—not the legal *representation* of one inmate by another. Thus, any prison restriction which forbids representation rather than assistance involves no conflict with Johnson.

With these principles in mind we turn to the first of petitioner McKinney's specific complaints—i. e., that prison authorities have prevented him from filing an application for relief on behalf of another prisoner. In general, an application for relief, although it may be prepared by another, should be signed, verified and filed by the inmate or inmates seeking relief. As we have indicated, the principle of Johnson seeks to insure that a disadvantaged prisoner will receive aid in his personal efforts to apply to the courts for relief—not that such a prisoner will be represented by another inmate before the courts—and the courts will, generally speaking, refuse to entertain an application made by a prisoner other than him for whom relief is sought. Only in very exceptional circumstances will a "next friend" application (see Pen.Code, § 1474) be entertained. "[T]he complaint must set forth some reason or explanation satisfactory to the court showing why the detained person does not sign and verify the complaint and who 'the next friend' is. It was not intended that the writ of habeas corpus should be availed of, as a matter of course, by intruders or uninvited meddlers, styling themselves next friends. Gusman v. Marrero, 180 U.S. 81, 21 S.Ct. 293, 45 L.Ed. 436." [*Citations omitted*].

It should be emphasized, however, that these limitations do not imply a right on the part of prison authorities to determine when an application for relief is or is not properly filed. As the United States Supreme Court has stated with regard to such applications within the federal court system, "Whether a petition for writ of habeas corpus addressed to a federal court is properly drawn and what allegations it must contain are questions for that court alone to determine." (Ex parte Hull (1941) 312 U.S. 546, 549, 61 S.Ct. 640, 641, 85 L.Ed. 1034.) Similarly, we think that a state court to which an application for relief is directed has the exclusive power to determine whether that application is properly filed or states legal grounds for relief. Prison authorities may not refuse to forward a document addressed to a court on the ground that it is improperly filed.

As for petitioner McKinney's complaint concerning the refusal of prison authorities to allow him to correspond with inmates at other institutions, it is clear that the restriction in question has no significant effect upon the rights guaranteed in *Johnson*. Again it is the rights of the prisoner needing, rather than those of the prisoner giving, legal assistance which concerns us. *Johnson* certainly offers no

support for the proposition that illiterate and uneducated inmates have a constitutional right to the assistance of *a particular inmate* in the preparation of applications for relief; rather the right there enunciated is the right *to be assisted*. No infringement upon that right necessarily results from restrictions upon the activities of a particular inmate "lawyer." Thus, those inmates at institutions other than Folsom who are prevented from corresponding with petitioner McKinney by valid regulations limiting the number and identity of correspondents may seek legal assistance from inmates at their own institutions.

Similarly, restrictions upon the number of books which an inmate may have in his cell[2] impinge upon the rights enunciated in *Johnson* only to the extent it is shown that the ability of other inmates seeking legal assistance to gain such assistance is affected. Unless and until it is demonstrated that other sources of legal assistance—e. g., other inmates who use the prison library—cannot provide assistance to disadvantaged inmates, the state of any inmate's personal library is of no significance.

Petitioner McKinney's contention that he must be allowed to interview inmates in isolation is without merit. Granting that the status of isolation—which by its very nature forbids con-

---

[2] Director's Rule D 2601 provides in relevant part: "Personally-owned law books shall be limited by local regulations to the availability of space for personal property in the inmate's quarters. Law books in excess of this limitation may be donated to the library, sent home or destroyed, whichever the inmate prefers." Regulations applicable at Folsom provide that prisoners in the general population may have no more than 16 hard-cover books at any one time.

tact with other inmates—results in a significant curtailment of the extent to which the affected prisoner may avail himself of assistance by other prisoners,[3] we believe that such curtailment is justified by valid institutional considerations. Isolation is the extreme institutional sanction that is available to prison authorities for disciplinary purposes, and its importance in this regard warrants the limitations on prisoner legal assistance which are necessarily imposed thereby.[4]

Finally, we reject petitioner McKinney's contention that the principles of *Johnson* require that he be provided with prison disciplinary records concerning inmates to whom he is rendering legal assistance. Such records are not relevant to applications for relief from an invalid judgment of conviction. As for applications sought to vindicate rights in confinement (see In re Riddle (1962) 57 Cal.2d 848, 851, 22 Cal.Rptr. 472, 372 P.2d 304), relevant disciplinary reports will be brought before the court if the facts stated in the application are deemed sufficient to justify the issuance of an order to show cause. The institutional interest in having confidential disciplinary files is significant and warrants the restriction in question.

For the reasons stated we have concluded that the March 19, 1969, revision of Director's Rule D 2602, while in the main consistent with the principles enunciated in Johnson v. Avery, *supra*, 393 U.S. 488, 89 S.Ct. 750, 21 L.Ed.2d 718, is violative of those principles and therefore invalid insofar as it requires that "All briefs, petitions and other legal papers must be and remain in the possession of the inmate to whom they pertain." We have also examined several other present restrictions and limitations urged to be violative of *Johnson*. We now proceed to consider the contention concerning past disciplinary action taken by prison authorities on account of conduct which, in light of *Johnson* and the instant case, was consistent with the right of mutual prisoner assistance.

It is urged that an inmate's disciplinary record should be purged of any reference to past infractions of rules—notably of the rule forbidding the possession of legal papers belonging to another inmate—which have been held invalid under the principles enunciated in *Johnson*. It is also

---

[3] We do not consider that confinement in isolation wholly prevents an inmate from receiving the benefits of legal assistance by other prisoners. A prisoner who has been given access to the papers of an inmate subsequently placed in isolation may continue to prepare an application in that inmate's behalf during the period of isolation. In cases wherein the filing of an application during the period of isolation is thought necessary—e. g., where the legality of the imposition of isolation itself is sought to be challenged—a "next friend" application may be filed by an assisting inmate. As we have indicated, however, such a petition will not be considered on its merits in the absence of a strong showing of necessity.

[4] As we have indicated above (fn. 8, *ante*), the Director's Rules permit an inmate in isolation to prepare and file his own legal documents and correspond with an attorney. This rule, we believe, should be applied also to permit an inmate to correspond with another inmate in his institution for the purpose of preparing an application for relief. We presume that illiterate prisoners in isolation are provided with the clerical assistance necessary to their preparation of an application for relief or a letter to an attorney or assisting inmate. [Par.] It should also be noted that the normal maximum term of confinement in isolation is 30 days, and that a longer term may be imposed only with the approval of the Director himself. (Director's Rule D 4511.)

urged that custodial and parole authorities should be instructed to disregard infractions in their future actions and deliberations. We do not agree.

Assuming that disciplinary sentences for violations of rules contrary to *Johnson* have been served, the sole effects of entries in prison records reflecting such violations would be (1) their possible use in determining appropriate custodial classification and institutional placement, and (2) their possible use in deliberations of the Adult Authority. We do not believe that any beneficial purpose would be served by ordering that the public authorities concerned in each of these areas remove from their consideration all past rule infractions of the type here in question. Even upon the extravagantly optimistic assumption that it would be possible to determine whether any given past infraction actually involved conduct protected by *Johnson,* and putting to one side the vast administrative effort which even an attempt at that determination would entail, it is apparent that little practical benefit would result in view of the considerable discretionary powers of the subject authorities. (See In re Schoengarth (1967) 66 Cal.2d 295, 300, 57 Cal. Rptr. 600, 425 P.2d 200.) Moreover, although we believe that *future* consideration by custodial and parole authorities of *past* infractions should proceed in light of the *Johnson* decision, we are also of the view that authorities concerned with the assessment of conduct in the context of rehabilitation should not be required to wholly disregard conduct which manifests a disinclination to be governed by legal authority. The fact that such

conduct might be later declared to be a valid exercise of constitutional rights, while not to be excluded from consideration, does not operate to render the infraction an irrelevancy.

Although the constitutional rights of persons committed to prison must be accorded the same zealous protection that all constitutional rights enjoy, that axiom cannot be allowed to obscure the fundamental distinction between free citizens and those who have been subjected to imprisonment as a result of legal processes. Whereas the dynamics of a free society may accommodate challenge to invalid rules by violation thereof and subsequent judicial vindication, (See In re Berry (1968) 68 Cal.2d 137, 148-149, 65 Cal.Rptr. 273, 436 P.2d 273, and cases there cited), the purposes and functions of penal institutions—fundamental among which is the rehabilitation of prisoners through rendering them amenable to governance by rules—cannot permit the existence of such procedures. If we were to hold, as urged, that past infractions of prison rules found to be unconstitutional under present standards must be disregarded by prison and parole authorities, we would thereby encourage the flouting of rules thought to be constitutionally defective by individual inmates and severely impair the rehabilitative capabilities of penal institutions. This we decline to do.

We do not suggest that future disregard of the principles set forth in Johnson v. Avery and the cases filed here today will be insulated from judicial redress in all cases except those in which invalid disciplinary sentences are outstanding at the time of the application for relief. Indeed, if it should be made to appear that such disregard is occurring this court has ample power to prevent its continuance. We hold only that discipline imposed for past violations of rules subsequently held to be in violation of the principles announced in Johnson v. Avery will not be withheld from the future consideration of custodial and parole authorities.

Personal Access to the Courts

Petitioner Harrell contends that his right of access to the courts has been unreasonably restricted by the application to him of certain regulations governing the use of the prison library. Thus, he points out that at various times he has been limited to one visit per week to the prison library, that he has been disciplined for talking with other inmates while in the legal section of the library, and that he has experienced difficulty in obtaining books which he has ordered from the state library.

Prison records attached as exhibits to the return to the order to show cause reveal that petitioner has indeed been disciplined on numerous occasions for persistent infractions of rules relating to use of the prison library. Among the activities for which such discipline has been imposed are: use of the library more frequently than regulations permit; loud, boisterous, and defiant conduct while in the library causing disturbance and agitation of other inmates; failure to return overdue books; and an attempt to check out books when his privilege card had been suspended because of prior infractions.

In In re Allison, *supra,* 66 Cal.2d 282, 57 Cal.Rptr. 593, 425 P.2d 193 and In re Schoengarth, *supra,* 66 Cal.2d 295, 57 Cal.Rptr. 600, 425 P.2d

200, we held that prison rules promulgated pursuant to constitutional and statutory authority (see Cal.Const. art. X, § 1; Pen.Code, §§ 5054, 5058) may properly regulate the use of prison legal facilities by inmates in a manner which does not unreasonably impede access to the courts by such inmates. The rules involved in this case whose application has allegedly impaired petitioner Harrell's access to the courts are manifestly reasonable. Moreover, "they are responsive to the practical limitations of space, materials, and staff available, and to the necessity of maintaining control over a large number of prisoners confined within narrow bounds." (In re Allison, *supra,* 66 Cal.2d 282, 291, 57 Cal. Rptr. 593, 598, 425 P.2d 193, 198.) It does not appear that such rules have been applied to petitioner Harrell in a discriminatory manner or with a view to silencing his voice in the courts; rather, it appears that sanctions and limitations have been visited upon petitioner Harrell only because of his apparently adamant refusal to abide by reasonable regulations for the library applicable to the entire prison population. His access to the courts has not been unreasonably impeded.

Petitioners McKinney and Harrell contend that their right of access to the courts has been unreasonably restricted because the legal materials contained in the prison libraries at their respective institutions (Folsom and San Quentin) are inadequate to permit effective research.

Several decisions of this court, as well as one frequently cited decision of the United States Court of Appeals for the Ninth Circuit, have indicated in positive terms that inmates in the state prison system have no legally enforceable rights to engage in legal research except insofar as such research is necessary to insure access to the courts. [*Citations omitted*]. That standard, which conceptually begs the question asked of it, has nevertheless been applied to sustain former Director's Rule D 2602 forbidding mutual prisoner assistance (*Schoengarth*) and has operated to repel constitutional attack against various regulations effectively limiting prisoner access to legal materials (*Allison; Hatfield*).

We cannot fail to recognize, however, that the decision of the United States Supreme Court in Johnson v. Avery heralds the advent of new principles governing the question of prisoner access to legal materials. Our recognition of this fact is concretized in preceding pages of this opinion wherein we have attempted to develop a flexible standard governing restrictions upon the right of mutual prisoner assistance. Moreover, we are cognizant that the principles of *Johnson* may, in a proper case, require a judicial assessment of the adequacy of prison libraries to permit legal research of a certain minimum degree of effectiveness. This court has itself recognized that some kind of access to legal materials is necessary to the preparation of any effective application for relief "[A]lthough [an application] should ordinarily be predicated on a full and honest statement of the *facts* which the inmate believes give rise to a remedy (In re Chessman (1955) 44 Cal.2d 1, 10, 279 P.2d 24; In re Swain (1949) 34 Cal.2d 300, 302, 304, 209 P.2d 793), the relevance of certain facts may not be apparent to him un-

til he has done some legal research on the point." (In re Schoengarth, *supra*, 66 Cal.2d 295, 305, 57 Cal.Rptr. 600, 607, 425 P.2d 200, 207.)

We do not believe, however, that the records in the proceedings before us raise and expose the issue to the extent necessary for us to reach it. Petitioners are content to allege that the libraries at their institutions are insufficient to their needs; they make no effort to indicate the deficiencies which are the basis of their claim of constitutional insufficiency. Nothing has been presented as to the actual contents of the libraries in question. In these circumstances we think it wise to defer decision on the issue sought to be raised until a fuller record is before us.[5]

Right to Purchase and Receive Reading Materials

Petitioners Ingram and McKinney complain of various restrictions that

---

[5] We note that very recently a three-judge panel of the United States District Court for the Northern District of California—apparently with the benefit of a record more adequate to the task than that now before us—addressed itself to the problem of constitutional sufficiency of state prison libraries and issued an order granting relief to the prisoner plaintiffs. Specifically, the defendant state authorities were enjoined from enforcing a present regulation of the Department of Corrections specifying the contents of prison libraries and were ordered to file on or before September 1 new or amended regulations in accord with the principles announced by the court in its opinion—the court to render "such further decision as it deems appropriate" on the basis of such proposed regulations and further argument concerning the same. (Gilmore v. Lynch (N.D.Cal.1970).) In addition to the reasons which we have above stated, we think it appropriate at this time to refrain from considering the issue in question until the federal proceedings in *Gilmore* are completed.

have been placed upon their right to purchase and receive reading materials pursuant to section 2600 of the Penal Code.

We summarize the complaints of petitioners relative to restrictions which they claim are inconsistent with their rights under section 2600. (1) Petitioner McKinney complains of an institution rule at Folsom Prison which limits him to 16 hard-bound books in his cell at any one time and effectively prevents him from having sets of law books purchased by him. (2) Petitioner Ingram complains of an institution order at San Quentin which requires that books and other literature be purchased from a vendor approved by the institution. . . .

We turn first to the matter raised by petitioner McKinney. It appears that in September of 1969 petitioner McKinney requested and obtained permission to receive a number of legal publications which included "Lawyer's Edition Supreme Court Reporter 2d" and "Supreme Court Digest." Petitioner proceeded to make arrangements to purchase these items through approved correspondents, but prior to delivery prison authorities revoked the authorization. As the associate warden explained in a letter to petitioner's mother, prison authorities were unaware at the time of authorization that the material in question consisted of 42 volumes, and as soon as they were made aware of that fact the authorization was withdrawn because possession of 42 hard-bound books would be in violation of prison rules. The letter further explained to the mother that the two sets in question would be sent to her and that petitioner "may request through my office a varying number of the vol-

umes (so as not to exceed the 16-book limit) as he may need same."

It is clear, of course, that a limitation of the type here in question is expressly contemplated by Penal Code, section 2600. ("Nothing in this section shall be construed as limiting the right of prison authorities * * * (ii) to establish reasonable restrictions as to the number of newspapers, magazines, and books that the inmate may have in his cell or elsewhere in the prison at one time.") Moreover, we are of the view that the restriction placed by Folsom Warden's Rule F 2402 and Director's Rule D 2601 is reasonable in light of applicable custodial circumstances. The prison authorities have indicated a willingness to allow petitioner to use his personal "library" within the limits of the 16-book rule by means of mail requests to his mother. If petitioner wishes to have more convenient access to the whole of his "library" he may do so within the terms of Director's Rule D 2601 by donating it to the prison library.

We next consider the matter of approved vendors. San Quentin Institution Order No. 408 provides in substance that, whereas certain items not available at the prison canteen may be received from approved correspondents (typewriters, drafting equipment, musical instruments and equipment, and hobby tools), books may be received only from "Cottage Book Store [San Rafael] * * * or other suitable vendors." Petitioner Ingram contends that this restriction is unreasonable and irrational—and that it is not authorized by Penal Code, section 2600. It is urged that the institutional rationale for the rule—to

wit, the prevention of smuggled contraband—is much more applicable to
items such as musical instruments
than it is to books because the former
would provide a more convenient vehicle for smuggling contraband.

The Director, however, points out
a tenable basis for the distinction.
The number of items such as typewriters and musical instruments which
are sent to the inmates is relatively
small, so that authorities have the
time to make a thorough search of
them before delivery to the inmate.
On the other hand, the volume of
printed material coming to the inmates is great, and the institution is
not adequately staffed to permit mi-
nute inspection of all of this material.
Thus it has been determined that the
best way of preventing the smuggling
of contraband in books and other
printed material is to control the
source from which it is sent. Newspapers and magazines must come directly from the publisher. (Director's
Rule D 2402, subd. 12.) Books must
come from vendors who can be
counted upon to refrain from coop-
erating in schemes for smuggling contraband.

We believe that this arrangement,
although not expressly sanctioned by
Penal Code, section 2600, is reasonable and proper. Section 2600 cannot
be construed as a straitjacket limiting the ability of prison authorities
to deal with institutional realities.
Rather it is to be viewed as a prison
"bill of rights" setting forth certain
fundamental guarantees which are to
be protected against arbitrary infringement. The guarantee which
here concerns us—that of receiving
and reading "any and all" printed
matter other than that in prohibited
subject-matter categories—is not automatically infringed by a requirement
as to the source from which that material must come. Only if it should
be made to appear that certain non-
prohibited reading matter cannot be
obtained from authorized sources
would an infringement of the basic
guarantee be involved. No such
showing has been made in the instant
case.

. . . .

NOVAK v. BETO
320 F.Supp. 1206 (S.D. Tex. 1970)

SEALS, District Judge.

. . . .

I.

Inmate Legal Assistance—in General

The Supreme Court confronted the
problem of inmate legal assistance in
Johnson v. Avery, *supra*. The Court
held there that, unless the State provides a reasonable alternative to assist inmates in the preparation of petitions for post-conviction relief, it
may not validly enforce a regulation
prohibiting any form of legal assistance by one inmate to another. The
Court was dealing with a Tennessee
procedure that went no further than
the warden's sometimes allowing prisoners to examine the listing of attorneys in the telephone directory, and
occasionally contacting the public defender at the request of an inmate.
The Court did not specify the mini-

mum standards which a "reasonable alternative" must meet, but it was clear in condemning the Tennessee practice as "far short" of the constitutional requisite. *Id.*, at 489, 89 S.Ct. 747.

The Court's reluctance to structure in precise terms the requirements of inmate legal assistance indicates something more than the Court's common inclination to confine its opinions to narrowly framed issues. There is little doubt that the Court meant to approve a wide variety of legal assistance plans, and to allow each State much freedom in devising a plan that best suits its particular needs and temperament:

" * * * in several States, the public defender system supplies trained attorneys, paid from public funds, who are available to consult with prisoners regarding their habeas corpus petitions. At least one State employs senior law students to interview and advise inmates in state prisons. Another State has a voluntary program whereby members of the local bar association make periodic visits to the prison to consult with prisoners concerning their cases. We express no judgment concerning these plans, but their existence indicates that techniques are available to provide alternatives if the State elects to prohibit mutual assistance among inmates."
Id., at 489-490, 89 S.Ct., at 751.

Far from formulating exact standards, the Court held only that the Tennessee procedure failed to comply with minimum constitutional requirements.

The Fifth Circuit subsequently cast a pale light on the *Johnson* decision. By dictum in Beard v. Alabama Board

of Corrections, 413 F.2d 455 (5th Cir. 1969), that tribunal held that a regulation prohibiting inmate legal assistance altogether might be sustained only if the State were to make available a

"sufficient number of qualified attorneys or other persons capable and willing to render voluntary assistance in the preparation of petitions for habeas corpus." *Id.*, at 457.

It is in the dim light of *Beard* that we must test the validity of the inmate legal assistance program constructed by the Texas Department of Corrections.

The Department provides at each of its units a "writ room," available each week during specified hours and in which an inmate must perform all his legal work. A small "library" is available there and respondents have recently directed that prisoners be allowed to utilize the law books of fellow inmates as well as those maintained by the State. An extensive legal manual, composed in layman's language, will soon be available in the writ rooms and prison libraries to assist inmates in the preparation of petitions. In addition, prisoners may freely correspond with legal service organizations. Respondents prohibit, however, any other kind of legal assistance among inmates, including one prisoner's advising another or in any way aiding a fellow inmate in preparation of a writ.

But the major step undertaken by the Department to comply with the *Johnson* ruling indicates that Texas is not offering mere token compliance. In September, 1969, the prison system employed an attorney, Mr. Harry

Walsh, whose sole responsibility is the provision of legal assistance to inmates. Mr. Walsh testified that another full time attorney is now on the prison staff; that three senior law students were employed at the prison during the summer of 1970; and that law students may soon be available for inmate assistance throughout the year.

Mr. Walsh reported that, in less than a year as the inmate attorney, he has worked with 1371 prisoners. He is authorized even to represent an inmate in a judicial hearing for post-conviction relief and has done so on one occasion. Although he is not permitted to represent inmates in actions against prison officials, he refers complainants to the American Civil Liberties Union.

Mr. Walsh was most impressive in response to questions from the court about how he viewed his role as inmate attorney. He testified that he did not believe it his responsibility to advise prisoners to "take their punishment." Rather, his duty is to furnish legal counsel whenever desired:

"Q. [by the court]: What if you determine a man has no case and he says I want to file it anyway and he has no case?

"A. [by Mr. Walsh]: We will tell him where to file it. We will assist him in completing the forms. We will do all that we can under the circumstances. We will see that it does go to the right people. Of course, we can't make a good case out of a bad one."

Plaintiffs have asserted that one or a few attorneys cannot meet the needs of more than 13,000 inmates.

But as respondent correctly points out, not all inmates will wish to take advantage of Mr. Walsh's services, and certainly, not all will want them at the same time. Furthermore, since most courts appoint attorneys to represent indigent habeas corpus petitioners, Mr. Walsh's role is generally limited to giving advice and assisting prisoners in filing complaints.

When this suit was filed, many of those services which respondent now provides were not available to inmates. In view of the State's subsequent efforts to comply with the constitutional mandate, however, we adjudge as moot the question of past failures. There has been no showing that respondents will not continue diligently to conform to the spirit of Johnson v. Avery. Until presented with evidence to the contrary, we cannot assume that any party, especially an agency of the State, will choose deliberately to ignore the United States Constitution.

The record shows clearly that the petitioners in this action seek to protect their asserted right to *render* legal assistance, not to receive it. Dr. George Beto, Director of the Texas Department of Corrections, explained the probable motivation of the inmates:

"Q. [by the court]: Is there any particular reason why you do not want Fred Cruz assisting other prisoners in the preparation of writs?

"A. [by Dr. Beto]: He could develop an unconscionable control over other inmates by setting himself up as a lawyer. I would like to amplify, your honor. I live in mortal fear of a convict-run prison.

Earlier some attention was called to the article in the *New York Times* which described a classic example of a convict-run operation. "Q. [by the court]: Is that the one in reference to the Kansas penitentiary?

"A. [by Dr. Beto]: Yes, sir. We constantly strive against permitting that to happen. One way in which inmates can develop control of an institution is by aiding other inmates in the writing of writs."

It is the "prisoner client's rights, not the jailhouse lawyer's, which are most in need of protection." Johnson v. Avery, *supra,* 393 U.S. at 501, 89 S.Ct. at 757 (White, J., dissenting). The Constitution confers no right upon the non-lawyer to practice law. And the fact of his incarceration cannot augment this non-existent right. Courts are under no duty to protect " * * * the assumed prerogatives of those inmates who have, for one reason or another, set themselves up as legal consultants." In re Harrell, 2 Cal.3d 675, at 688, 87 Cal. Rptr. 504, at 512, 470 P.2d 640, at 648. (June 18, 1970).

Finally, we must take note of the great increase in recent years in applications for post-conviction relief as evidence that the Texas "alternative" is "reasonable." State prisoners in 1969 filed 616 petitions in federal district courts in Texas, an increase of 57.6 per cent from 1965. Dr. Beto has testified to the tremendous increase in petitions filed during his regime. And unless we would play the ostrich, we cannot ignore the devastating impact of the habeas corpus applications that have flooded this court in recent years. Since the advent of Mr.

Walsh, numerous of these petitions have been typed, and most of them have demonstrated a great increase in comprehensibility. Furthermore, petitioners have failed to cite a single specific instance in which an inmate has been prevented, or even inordinately delayed, in presenting his petition to a court.

In his dissenting opinion in Johnson v. Avery, Mr. Justice White suggests that the State be required to provide "reasonably adequate assistance" *Id.,* at 502, 89 S.Ct. 747 without resort to the jailhouse lawyer system. Whatever the merits of this proposal, this court is not required to express an opinion on the desirability of the "reasonable alternative" provided by Texas. We judge only its constitutionality. Within the bounds prescribed by Johnson v. Avery, and amplified upon in Beard v. Alabama Board of Corrections, Texas is free to devise its own plan of inmate assistance without the counsel and consent of the federal court. We find that the Texas alternative falls within the required limits.

II.

Inmate Legal Assistance—Death Row

Because the problem of legal assistance to Death Row inmates was considered by the court in a separate hearing, and because it presents special difficulties, it will be dealt with separately here. Both the State and the plaintiffs agree that the legal needs of Death Row inmates are generally more urgent than those of other prisoners. But many of the same considerations remain valid. For example, Dr. Beto has expressed concern that Death Row inmates with some knowledge of the law, were they allowed to furnish legal assistance, might be able to exercise undue control over their fellows. Furthermore, the same factors which impel our characterization of the general Texas practice as a "reasonable alternative" operate to justify by constitutional standards the Texas preference for legal assistance to Death Row inmates.

Mr. Walsh and his staff are available for counsel with Death Row prisoners and he testified that he has worked with two of them. Dr. Beto has instructed both the Death Row warden and the prison chaplain to insure that these inmates are provided with legal assistance sufficient to enable them to obtain stays of execution. Furthermore, a legal library,

identical to that in the writ room, is available for the exclusive use of those incarcerated on Death Row. And unlike the regular prison population, Death Row inmates may use the law books in their cells.

Texas has considered both the peculiar difficulties of Death Row incarceration and the often compelling need there for swift and certain action. The State has thus allowed Death Row inmates special privileges such as the use of law books in cells, in addition to granting them access to the assistance program devised by Mr. Walsh. It appears to the court that respondents have constructed a "reasonable alternative" for Death Row inmates that is fully in accord with the spirit of Johnson v. Avery.

NOVAK v. BETO
453 F.2d 661 (5th Cir. 1971)

THORNBERRY, Circuit Judge.

. . . .

Inmate Assistance

In Johnson v. Avery the Supreme Court held that Tennessee could not constitutionally ban fellow-prisoner assistance in the preparation of habeas corpus petitions so long as the state provided prisoners with no alternative assistance, since such a regulation effectively denied indigent, illiterate prisoners any access to the courts. . . .

The Court went on to notice that many states had alternative programs to supply legal assistance to prison inmates although it did not express its judgment concerning these plans. The Court did note their existence

and indicated that "techniques are available to provide alternatives if the State elects to prohibit mutual assistance among inmates." Johnson v. Avery, 393 U.S. at 490, 89 S.Ct. at 751.

It is undisputed that Texas prison officials prohibit any form of legal assistance by one inmate to another. Appellees argue, however, that they have provided appellants within reasonable alternatives to inmate assistance and thus are in compliance with Johnson v. Avery. Clearly, the TDC has been making progress toward complying with the dictates of Johnson v. Avery and Beard v. Alabama Bd. of Corrections, supra, in which this Court said:

A regulation prohibiting the granting of assistance altogether might well be sustained if the state were to make available a sufficient number of qualified attorneys or other persons capable and willing to render voluntary assistance in the preparation of petitions for habeas corpus relief. *Beard,* 413 F. 2d at 457.

Nevertheless, after studying the record carefully, we are unable to conclude as the district court did, that the State carried the burden of proving that it provided at the time of trial a reasonable alternative to inmate legal assistance. The State has failed to convince us that its effort was sufficient.

Many questions were left unanswered by the State that would have been relevant to our inquiry into the adequacy of the State's alternatives to inmate assistance. For instance, we would have been interested to know how many of the approximately 12,000 prisoners in the TDC expressed a need for legal assistance in seeking post-conviction relief. There is vague testimony that only a small number of the total prison population actually are interested in seeking post-conviction relief, but that testimony was insufficient to present any clear picture of the magnitude of the problem. Additionally, we would have been interested to know how much time is required to handle each prisoner's file. It might be, for example, that many of the complaints concern rather routine matters that could be handled adequately in an hour's time. If this were the case, the fact that a single attorney handled 1300 files his first year might be less striking. Moreover, the hiring of a

second attorney and three summertime law students should have relieved the situation considerably, but we were given very little specific information as to what degree, if any, the situation was relieved. Finally, we were told nothing specific about what amount of outside legal assistance in the form of legal aid and public defender programs might be available to prisoners. Johnson v. Avery appears to invite states to utilize such outside help in providing alternatives to inmate legal assistance.

What we have concluded, in short, is that although we cannot be certain from this record that the TDC has *not* provided a reasonable alternative to inmate legal assistance, neither can we be certain that the TDC *has* provided the requisite alternative. And since we think Johnson v. Avery places the burden of justifying its regulation against inmate legal assistance on the State, we must conclude that the State so far has failed in carrying that burden.

Having found that the State has failed to prove that it has provided a reasonable alternative to inmate assistance, we feel we should offer some guidance for future State action. We would require the State to carry the burden of justifying its regulation against inmate assistance by producing evidence that establishes *in specific terms* what the need is for legal assistance on habeas corpus matters in the TDC, and by demonstrating that it is reasonably satisfying that need. In defining the need for assistance and in responding to the need, TDC should give special consideration to the high illiteracy rate of the inmates, to the fact that a substantial number are Mexican-Americans who speak little English, and to the great geographical dispersion of the Texas correctional facilities. We would permit the state to draw upon any source of assistance available, whether it be voluntary or remunerated, and whether it be licensed or unlicensed to practice law, as long as that service could be systematically relied upon. We think the record in this case demonstrates that TDC has been making a substantial effort since Johnson v. Avery to provide a reasonable alternative to inmate legal assistance. The TDC could not, of course, develop a complete legal assistance program overnight. As soon, however, as the TDC has developed an alternative to inmate assistance that it feels would be acceptable to this Court, it will of course be free to return to court to seek approval of that alternative.

Because we are not convinced that Johnson v. Avery has been complied with in this case, we hold that the loss of good time suffered as a result of violating the regulation against inmate assistance must be restored to appellants.

Appellants also set forth the peculiar difficulties of Death Row prisoners in obtaining legal assistance. Some of the services performed by the "writ writers" include assisting Death Row prisoners obtain stays of execution. Because what we have decided regarding prisoners in general is applicable to those on Death Row, it is not necessary to examine their arguments separately.

CRUZ v. BETO
Civil No. 71-H-1371 (S.D. Tex., filed Mar. 18, 1976)

I. FINDINGS OF FACT

A. INTRODUCTION

Plaintiffs are an attorney, Mrs. Frances T. Jalet Cruz ("Mrs. Cruz"), and 12 prisoners ("prisoner-plaintiffs") who in 1971 were in the custody of the Texas Department of Corrections ("TDC"). Mrs. Cruz is a citizen of the United States and an attorney admitted to practice in the State of Texas and other states, as well as in the federal courts. All of the prisoner-plaintiffs are citizens of the United States.

Defendant George J. Beto is the former Director of the TDC and was serving as Director during 1971 and 1972. Defendant W. J. Estelle, Jr., is the present Director of the TDC, having succeeded defendant Beto on September 1, 1972. All the actions of both defendants involved in this case were taken under color of state law.

This controversy has arisen in part because of actions taken by defendant Beto against Mrs. Cruz for acts she allegedly committed while representing inmates at the TDC.

B. BACKGROUND OF MRS. CRUZ; RELATIONSHIP OF MRS. CRUZ WITH THE PRISONER-PLAINTIFFS

Prior to 1971 when the salient events of this lawsuit commenced, Mrs. Cruz had served for several years as an attorney working for legal aid organizations, the Office of Economic Opportunity, or Volunteers in Service to America ("VISTA"), at offices in Texas. Her extensive legal background and experience in poverty law as well as her initial participation as an inmates' attorney have been described previously by this Court. See Dreyer v. Jalet, 349 F.Supp. 453, 468-70 (S.D. Tex. 1972), aff'd per curiam, 479 F.2d 1044 (5th Cir. 1973).

Pursuing a career in poverty law and related areas in 1971, Mrs. Cruz was employed as a VISTA attorney. She provided prisoners with advice and representation in suits seeking post-conviction relief as well as in suits challenging the constitutionality of various prison practices and conditions. During the latter half of 1971, Mrs.

Cruz was providing advice and representation to all of the prisoner-plaintiffs. She assisted them in prosecuting their habeas corpus petitions and/or their "prison" suits under 42 U.S.C. § 1983. She was representing each of the prisoner-plaintiffs as clients in her capacity as an attorney. There is no persuasive evidence in this case, although defendants contend otherwise, that she did not have a proper attorney-client relationship with each of the prisoner-plaintiffs.

In representing these prisoner-plaintiffs or responding to other prisoners who sought her advice or assistance during the years in question, Mrs. Cruz devoted much of her time to prisoners and regularly visited and corresponded with many TDC inmates. The credible evidence in this case supports plaintiffs' position that these many visits were in keeping with Mrs. Cruz's views of her professional responsibility to her clients and the practice of her profession. At all material times, Mrs. Cruz was required to observe, and did observe, all visiting and correspondence regulations promulgated by the TDC. During the years before the occurrence of the events in question, Mrs. Cruz never knowingly violated any rules of the TDC and never was charged with any such violations by TDC authorities.

C. EXCLUSION OF MRS. CRUZ FROM TDC; SEGREGATION OF THE PRISONER-PLAINTIFFS

On October 14, 1971, defendant Beto as Director of the TDC wrote to Mrs. Cruz informing her as follows:

"Your continued and frequent visits to the Department of Corrections as well as your correspondence with inmates make it impossible for me to guarantee tranquility within the institutions and the protection of the inmates.

"Accordingly, effective this date, I am requesting all wardens of the Texas Department of Corrections to deny your admission to the institutions under my general supervision and to terminate correspondence between you and any inmate in the Texas Department of Corrections."

The communiqué from defendant Beto to Mrs. Cruz reflected his position that Mrs. Cruz had taken certain actions in coordination with some of the prisoner-plaintiffs to arouse the animosity of the TDC inmate population and to spur the filing of federal civil rights lawsuits by inmates. However, defendant Beto and later defendant Estelle and TDC subordinates never complained to any law enforcement agency that Mrs. Cruz had committed any illegal or improper act or participated in any unethical behavior. Also, defendants never complained of such conduct to the State Bar of Texas or any coordinate grievance committee.

The evidence conclusively demonstrates that Mrs. Cruz did not interfere with the "tranquility" of TDC institutions. Her contact with the TDC was solely initiated in the course of proper and professional representation of TDC prisoners whereby she advised inmates of their federal constitutional rights and represented them in lawsuits as described above.

The October 14, 1971, telegram from defendant Beto to Mrs. Cruz, provoked stringent efforts by several members of the State Bar of Texas and other out-of-state attorneys to object to the exclusion of Mrs. Cruz from the TDC. These letters of protest were accompanied by efforts at negotiation between counsel for Mrs. Cruz and defendant Beto. As a result of these negotiations, defendant Beto sent a telegram to Mrs. Cruz on November 5, 1971, which stated that he was restoring the communication between Mrs. Cruz and 27 inmates named in the telegram. These included the prisoner-plaintiffs, who had been represented by her and who thus had been deprived of access to any counsel between October 14 and November 5, 1971.

All of the inmates named in the telegram who wished to remain clients of Mrs. Cruz were then transferred by defendant Beto, without notice or any hearing, to one wing of the Wynne Unit of the TDC in November, 1971. They were segregated from other prisoners and deprived of many of the privileges they had formerly enjoyed as members of the general prison population. This wing of the Wynne Unit became known as the "Eight Hoe" Squad.

The segregation policy imposed in November, 1971, lasted for a period of approximately eleven (11) months, until October 25, 1972. With the exception of inmate Cruz, who was discharged from the TDC on March 8, 1972, after 125 days on the Eight Hoe Squad, each prisoner-plaintiff remained on Eight Hoe Squad a total of 356 days, until October 25, 1972. Certain other inmates who were at first assigned to the Eight Hoe Squad were later reclassified and removed to other less restrictive units only when they expressed their intention to relinquish Mrs. Cruz as their attorney. Inmates such as Gomez, Perry and Mills, upon relinquishment of Mrs. Cruz's representation, were transferred immediately from the Wynne Unit. They later were assigned to desirable positions, such as trusty, and had no difficulty in maintaining creditable ratings as prisoners.

The preponderance of the credible evidence demonstrates that during the prisoner-plaintiffs' period of segregation on the Eight Hoe Squad, lower echelon TDC officials under defendant Beto's direction regularly pressured such prisoners to abandon Mrs. Cruz's legal representation. As TDC officials expressed it to the prisoner-plaintiffs, such action would result promptly in their release from the Eight Hoe Squad and a corresponding improvement in their status as prisoners.

D. DEPRIVATIONS IMPOSED UPON THE PRISONER-PLAINTIFFS

The Point Incentive Program (PIP) is utilized by TDC officials as an equivalent to a "merit/demerit" rating system for prisoners. All privileges and parole consideration are keyed to attaining a certain number of PIP "points", or merits, which are awarded on a quarterly basis under this program. A level of 80-90 points must be earned by an inmate during each quarter for that quarter to be considered in determining parole eligibility.

At the time the segregation policy was imposed, each prisoner-plaintiff's PIP point total was altered uniformly to reflect a total of only 40 PIP points for the fourth quarter of 1971, well below a satisfactory level. No prisoner-plaintiff ever was able to attain a satisfactory level during the existence of the segregation policy. Thus, no remaining prisoner-plaintiff (inmate Cruz having been discharged from TDC on March 8, 1972), could maintain a high rating and remain eligible for privileges and time credited towards parole.

Certain prisoner-plaintiffs were not permitted to pursue the attainment of academic certificates. That is, as members of the Eight Hoe Squad, they were prohibited from enrolling or remaining in courses required in the respective educational programs in which they were enrolled. When the segregation policy was imposed, prisoner-plaintiffs Cruz, Mauricio and Baker were enrolled in college degree programs, and prisoner-plaintiffs Bilton and Barbosa were participating in the "G.E.D." program, a program offering secondary education level courses.

While on Eight Hoe, most of the prisoner-plaintiffs were required regularly to perform manual field labor. This work schedule was imposed on several Eight Hoe residents despite the fact that they had medical ratings of "Fourth Class". Such a rating denotes a poor medical condition and normally renders an inmate ineligible for any prison work assignment requiring rigorous physical exertion. Prisoner-plaintiffs Montana, Bilton, Zilka, Barbosa and Soto all had medical ratings of Fourth Class.

The segregation policy worked additional deprivations on the prisoner-plaintiffs as set out in the margin.[1]

---

[1] Additional deprivations to prisoner-plaintiffs as a result of the segregation in the Eight Hoe Squad fall within the category of "humiliation" and include: (a) denial of mailing privileges to their counsel, Mrs. Cruz; (b) elimination of recreation and time for an exercise period in the gym; (c) separation from all other inmates especially during meal times; (d) minimal availability of hot water for coffee and other amenities; (e) sharp reduction in time available for writ room privileges; (f) reduced available time for recreational television viewing to one television set for two-three hours at night with location of the lone television set in the writ room so as to interfere with use of the room for either writ writing or television recreation; (g) subjection to repeated "shakedowns" disproportionate to those imposed upon the general inmate population; and (h) subjection to repeated disciplinary actions and penalties disproportionate to those imposed on the general inmate population.

E. IMPACT OF INTERFERENCE WITH PLAINTIFFS' ATTORNEY-CLIENT RELATIONSHIP

Mrs. Cruz continued to be barred by defendants from communicating with any TDC inmates except those listed in the telegram of November 5, 1971, who remained assigned to the Eight Hoe Squad. There is no evidence that any other attorney has ever been barred from the TDC or so restricted in the exercise of rights conferred by the law license granted by the State Bar of Texas. Inmates represented by other Texas attorneys have not been denied the right to communicate with them. Mrs. Cruz thus could not fulfill her professional obligations to her clients because the prohibition against her prevented her from responding to numerous requests for legal assistance from other TDC inmates.

Inmates who attempted to write to Mrs. Cruz for assistance were prevented from doing so by defendants' agents at the direction of defendant Beto. Such actions impeded inmates' access to the courts in pending cases.

The prisoner-plaintiffs were without funds and unable to pay fees in order to retain another attorney to represent them. Because they were deprived of or penalized for accepting Mrs. Cruz's pro bono legal assistance and being generally poorly educated, they were unable to obtain adequate legal assistance. Yet they were in need of such assistance on various legal problems affecting both their convictions and sentences and their claims of violations of federal constitutional rights as prisoners.

F. ACTION OF DEFENDANT ESTELLE

Defendant Estelle assumed the Directorship of the TDC on September 1, 1972, and continued the enforcement of the policy of defendant Beto, alleging that it was necessary for the protection of the prisoner-plaintiffs. Having concluded that their safety was no longer in doubt, he terminated the policy on October 25, 1972, and returned the prisoner-plaintiffs to the general prison population.

G. DEFENDANTS' JUSTIFICATIONS FOR BARRING MRS. CRUZ AND FOR SEGREGATING THE PRISONER-PLAINTIFFS BETWEEN NOVEMBER, 1971, AND OCTOBER 25, 1972

Defendants seek to justify the actions which defendant Beto took against Mrs. Cruz and the prisoner-plaintiffs by asserting that these actions were prompted by the alleged existence of inflammatory prison conditions at the TDC in 1971; suggesting that the prisoner-plaintiffs operated a plan of group action designed to endanger other inmates or overturn the prison administration; and alleging that Mrs. Cruz conspired to contribute to unrest by attempting to incite inmate insurrection and stir up prisoner litigation.

However, defendants have failed to demonstrate in any persuasive fashion the existence during the subject period of time of any inflammatory prison situation that would require the caliber of action taken in this case. Defendants also have failed to demonstrate by any persuasive, objective evidence in this trial that either Mrs. Cruz or the prisoner-plaintiffs presented any real threat to prison security or inmate security under the circumstances. The evidence conclusively points to the fact that the prisoner-plaintiffs were segregated not because they were violence-prone but because they wished to have Mrs. Cruz represent them.

H. CONSISTENCY OF THE FINDING OF LACK OF JUSTIFICATION IN THE INSTANT CASE WITH THE FINDINGS

IN DREYER V. JALET

In view of the nature of this case, this Court has scrutinized the record with extreme care for some legally justifiable basis for defendant Beto's actions during the period in question. No such basis is evident, and this finding is re-enforced when the credibility of the evidence is evaluated. Indeed, the findings in this case are wholly consistent with those made by this Court some four years ago in Dreyer v. Jalet, *supra,* 349 F.Supp. 452,[2] in which no conspiracy was found to exist between Mrs. Cruz (then Mrs. Jalet) and TDC inmates.

In the instant case, which lasted but

---

2 In the Dreyer case, a consolidated action, three inmates of the TDC filed suits in this Court against Mrs. Cruz (then Mrs. Jalet) seeking injunctive relief to bar her from providing legal assistance to inmates of the TDC. The Dreyer suits were premised fundamentally on the theory that Mrs. Jalet was attempting to organize prisoners incarcerated at the TDC for the purpose of instigating an inmate uprising to the detriment of plaintiffs who would not join in the alleged conspiracy and who wished to serve their time without intimidation or deprivation of inmate privileges. 349 F.Supp. at 456-57.

Trial on the merits in this highly unusual case lasted approximately six weeks. In ruling on the merits, the Court recited preliminarily the antagonisms which previously had characterized the relationship between Mrs. Jalet and defendant Beto; the Court then proceeded to relate the events which culminated in the exclusionary and segregation policies of October and November, 1971, imposed by defendant Beto on Mrs. Jalet and her clients. 349 F.Supp. at 470-71.

The Court thereafter evaluated the Dreyer plaintiffs' allegations regarding the existence of a conspiracy between Mrs. Jalet and TDC inmates and concluded that there was no merit to the allegations. 349 F.Supp. at 472-74. The evidence presented at length in Dreyer demonstrated no illegal activity on the part of Mrs. Jalet and certainly no proof of any conduct on her part that rose to the level of a conspiracy. *Id.* at 474.

three days, the evidence forthcoming on conspiracy was even more attenuated.

I. THE REASONABLENESS AND GOOD FAITH OF DEFENDANT BETO'S ACTIONS

Defendants have failed to demonstrate in this record that defendant Beto acted reasonably and in good faith and solely for the purpose of preserving and protecting prison security. There is simply no persuasive evidence which reflects that defendant Beto had any reasonable or good faith grounds on which to base his actions.

The evidence conclusively demonstrates that: Mrs. Cruz engaged in no efforts to disrupt prison security and violated no prison regulations; the prisoner-plaintiffs operated no plan of group action, such as a communications network, designed to endanger other inmates or overturn the prison administration; defendant Beto's actions were prompted by his long-standing antagonism towards Mrs. Cruz's contact with TDC inmates; and they were taken primarily to discourage the prisoner-plaintiffs from exercising certain constitutional rights and to prevent Mrs. Cruz from representing TDC inmates in civil rights litigation. Under the circumstances such actions must be found to have been taken unjustifiably and in bad faith.

II. CONCLUSIONS OF LAW

A. APPLICABLE LEGAL PRINCIPLES

Jurisdiction is proper in this Court pursuant to 42 U.S.C. § 1983 and 28 U.S.C. § 1343.

Access to the courts must be provided to prisoners so that they may challenge unlawful convictions and seek redress for violations of their constitutional rights. Inmates must have a reasonable opportunity to seek and receive the assistance of counsel. Any regulation or practice which unjustifiably obstructs the availability of professional representation or other aspects of the right of access to the courts is invalid. Procunier v. Martinez, 416 U.S. 396, 419 (1974). This principle of federal constitutional guarantee has long and frequently been espoused by the federal courts. See Younger v. Gilmore, 404 U.S. 15 (1971) (per curiam), aff'g, Gilmore v. Lynch, 319 F.Supp. 105 (N.D. Cal. 1970).

A prisoner attempting to gain access to the courts cannot be disciplined in any manner. Andrade v. Hauck, 452 F.2d 1071, 1072 (5th Cir. 1971). Transferring a prisoner and causing him to lose privileges for using the courts is a very serious allegation. Wolff v. McDonnell, 418 U.S. 539 (1974); Hooks v. Kelley, 463 F.2d 1210, 1211 (5th Cir. 1972).

The segregation of these prisoner-plaintiffs under the circumstances in this case was therefore punitive in nature, not merely administrative, compare Carlo v. Gunter, 520 F.2d 1293 (1st Cir. 1975) with Shields v. Hopper, 519 F.2d 1131 (5th Cir. 1975), and presents the extreme circumstances alluded to by the United States Court of Appeals for the Fifth Circuit, see Young v. Wainwright, 449 F.2d 338, 339 (5th Cir. 1971) and cases cited therein, which justify the interference by this Court with prison administration and a finding of liability against defendant Beto. Cf. Woolsey v. Beto, 450 F.2d 321 (5th Cir. 1971).

A prisoner has the right to be represented by an attorney of his choice if the attorney indicates a willingness to represent him. This right is protected by the First and Fourteenth Amendments and may not be limited unreasonably by state officials. Sanders v. Russell, 401 F.2d 241, 245-47 (5th Cir.

1968).

The combination of a prisoner's impoverished financial condition and a prison official's interference with his right to legal representation translates into a denial of the prisoner-litigant's right to equal protection of the laws. *See* Weintraub v. Adair, 331 F.Supp. 148 (S.D. Fla. 1971).

As the Supreme Court has made clear in Procunier v. Martinez, the exchange of written communications between an attorney and his inmate client calls into play the inmate's First Amendment rights and the First Amendment rights of the attorney, who has a significant interest in receiving or sending such communications. 416 U.S. at 408. The attorney's First Amendment interest is enhanced by his obligation, as an officer of the court, to represent his client's interests adequately and to assist a court in which a client's suit is pending to adjudicate such a suit promptly and justly.

Impeding the access of an attorney to his prisoner clients may be necessary in certain cases based on the reasonable, good faith belief of prison officials that such action is required under the circumstances. *E.g.,* Elie v. Henderson, 340 F.Supp. 958 (E.D. La. 1972). The facts of Elie v. Henderson demonstrate an attorney's overt attempt, under the guise of representing inmate clients, to incite a riot at a prison as well as to participate in other activities which clearly have nothing to do with appropriate legal representation.

However, Elie v. Henderson should be the exception, not the rule, for First Amendment reasons. A prison official may not, by his own actions or through orders to subordinates, *see* Carter v. Estelle, 519 F.2d 1136 (5th Cir. 1975), impede communication between attorney and client by mail or in person

where no immediate threat of disorder exists. *Cf.* Glasson v. City of Louisville, 518 F.2d 899 (6th Cir. 1975).

Under the Fourteenth Amendment, the arbitrary barring of an attorney from communicating with his proper clients is impermissible because it contravenes the attorney's right to procedural due process. *In re* Ruffalo, 390 U.S. 544, 43 Ohio Op.2d 459 (1968). Legal aid attorneys have a right to represent prisoner clients. *Cf.* Weintraub v. Adair, *supra,* 331 F.Supp. 148.

Thus, when a prison official impedes "attorney access", his actions must be subjected to rigorous scrutiny to afford proper protection to the First Amendment rights of communication of the attorney and his clients.

B. VIOLATION OF PLAINTIFFS' RIGHTS

Defendant Beto's actions, including the blanket exclusion of Mrs. Cruz on October 14, 1971, and the segregation thereafter imposed upon her prisoner clients do not survive such rigorous scrutiny on the facts of this case.

Defendant Beto's actions denied the prisoner-plaintiff's their right of access to the courts during the period in question and their right to receive effective legal assistance from the attorney of their choice. Defendant Beto's actions further denied the prisoner-plaintiffs the right to equal protection of the laws and to due process of law by subjecting them to discriminatory treatment and deprivation of normal prison privileges as a consequence of their remaining clients of Mrs. Cruz.

Defendant Beto by his actions denied Mrs. Cruz the right to practice her profession. He also violated her First and Fourteenth Amendment rights by denying her access to her clients and by then attempting thereafter to punish her and her clients for maintaining an appropriate attorney-client relationship.

The segregation policy fashioned and enforced by defendant Beto in the instant case in 1971 denied the prisoner-plaintiffs their right of access to the courts by unjustifiably obstructing such right of access. The implementation of this policy by defendant Beto's subordinates, at his direction, by means of threats, intimidation, coercion or punishment also violates this principle. Campbell v. Beto, 460 F.2d 765, 768 (5th Cir. 1972). Conditioning release from Eight Hoe Squad upon the relinquishment of Mrs. Cruz's representation illustrates the violation by means of unlawful intimidation. Depriving the prisoner-plaintiffs of opportunities to educate and rehabilitate themselves for failure to relinquish Mrs. Cruz's representation illustrates the violation by means of the unlawful punishment exacted in this case.

Defendant Beto's actions in restricting Mrs. Cruz's representation and in making costly the prisoner-plaintiffs' exercise of their choice of her as counsel impeded and infringed unjustifiably her exercise of her First Amendment rights. Plaintiffs have demonstrated that Mrs. Cruz's conduct in no way justified the sanctions imposed upon her by defendants.

On the other hand, defendants have failed to demonstrate: that Mrs. Cruz presented a threat to TDC administration of the prisons; that Mrs. Cruz organized or participated in a conspiracy among inmates to challenge TDC administration, cf. Dreyer v. Jalet, 349 F.Supp. 452 (S.D. Tex. 1972); or that the actions of defendant Beto were motivated in good faith or by a genuine concern for prisoner safety or prison security.

Rather, the evidence demonstrates that defendant Beto instituted reprisals against Mrs. Cruz and, by association, those prisoners including the prisoner-plaintiffs who were her clients, for reasons totally unrelated to considerations of proper prison administration. Such actions were taken in violation of Mrs. Cruz's constitutional rights. Defendant Beto did not act with good purpose and with a belief that he was doing right. Wood v. Strickland, 420 U.S. 308, 321 (1975).

C. RELIEF

Defendant Beto is liable in damages to the prisoner-plaintiffs in the total amount of $9,291.00. Findings of Fact, supra. Additionally, defendant Beto is liable in damages to Mrs. Cruz in the amount of $1,000.00. Defendant Estelle is not liable in damages for any amount.

The plaintiffs are entitled to declaratory and injunctive relief. Defendants are hereby enjoined from arbitrarily restricting the access of inmates to the courts; from restricting the access of any inmate to Mrs. Cruz as an attorney in person or by mail; from restricting Mrs. Cruz's visitation privileges at the TDC in any manner when she journeys to a prison unit to consult with a client in a lawful way; and from arbitrarily imposing upon any prisoner or group of prisoners a policy of segregation prompted solely as a means to punish their choice of legal representative.

In view of the arbitrary reduction by defendant Beto of the PIP point rating of each prisoner-plaintiff during the period in which the segregation policy was imposed, defendants hereafter shall not evaluate any prisoner-plaintiff's PIP record so as to penalize him during such period when evaluating his present and future eligibility for parole. Cf. Novak v. Beto, 453 F.2d 661, 664 (5th Cir. 1971) (restoring lost "good time").

The Court has canvassed available case authority in the Fifth Circuit and the Texas federal courts and concludes that this is the first case in which defendant Beto has ever been held liable in money damages for actions taken as Director of the TDC which violated the constitutional rights of inmates or an attorney. *Cf.* McManis, *Personal Liability of State Officials Under State and Federal Law,* 9 Ga.L.Rev. 821, 846 (1975) ("cases in which prisoners [in the Fifth Circuit] have recovered damages have been few"). This situation is no doubt due in large part to defendant Beto's outstanding record as Director of the TDC, a tenure recognized for its

high quality by the Court of Appeals. Novak v. Beto, *supra,* 453 F.2d at 666.

The plaintiffs have prevailed here because of the extraordinary nature of the facts and circumstances of this case. This Court has noted earlier in this opinion the highly unusual nature of this lawsuit and its counterpart, Dreyer v. Jalet. Together these cases represent an unparalleled, indeed aberrant, episode in the administration of the TDC. Against this background, the unique circumstances which prompt the awarding of money damages in this case should also operate to isolate it sufficiently so as to deprive it of significant precedential value.

FRED A. CRUZ, Petitioner
v.
GEORGE J. BETO, Corrections Director
405 US 319, 31 L.Ed.2d 263, 92 S.Ct. 1079 (1972)

OPINION OF THE COURT
PER CURIAM.

The complaint, alleging a cause of action under 42 USC § 1983, states that Cruz is a Buddhist, who is in a Texas prison. While prisoners who are members of other religious sects are allowed to use the prison chapel, Cruz is not. He shared his Buddhist religious material with other prisoners and, according to the allegations, in retaliation was placed in solitary confinement on a diet of bread and water for two weeks, without access to newspapers, magazines, or other sources of news. He also alleged that

he was prohibited from corresponding with his religious advisor in the Buddhist sect. Those in the isolation unit spend 22 hours a day in total idleness.

Again, according to the allegations, Texas encourages inmates to participate in other religious programs, providing at state expense chaplains of the Catholic, Jewish, and Protestant faiths; providing also at state expense copies of the Jewish and Christian Bibles, and conducting weekly Sunday school classes and religious services. According to the allegations, points of good merit are given prisoners as a reward for attending orthodox religious services, those points enhancing a prisoner's eligibility for desirable job assignments and early parole consideration. Respondent answered, denying the allegations and moving to dismiss.

The Federal District Court denied relief without a hearing or any findings, saying the complaint was in an area that should be left "to the sound discretion of prison administration." It went on to say, "Valid disciplinary and security reasons not known to this court may prevent the 'equality' of exercise of religious practices in prison." The Court of Appeals affirmed.

Federal courts sit not to supervise prisons but to enforce the constitutional rights of all "persons", including prisoners. We are not unmindful that prison officials must be accorded latitude in the administration of prison affairs, and that prisoners necessarily are subject to appropriate rules and regulations. But persons in prison, like other individuals, have the right to petition the Government for redress of grievances which, of course, includes "access of prisoners to the courts for the purpose of presenting their complaints." Johnson v. Avery, 393 US 483. Moreover, racial segregation, which is unconstitutional outside prisons, is unconstitutional within prisons, save for "the necessities of prison security and discipline." Lee v. Washington, 390 US 333. Even more closely in point is Cooper v. Pate, 378 US 546, where we reversed a dismissal of a complaint brought under 42 USC § 1983. We said: "Taking as true the allegations of the complaint, as they must be on a motion to dismiss, the complaint stated a cause of action. Ibid. The allegation made by that petitioner was that solely because of

his religious beliefs he was denied permission to purchase certain religious publications and denied other privileges enjoyed by other prisoners.

If Cruz was a Buddhist and if he was denied a reasonable opportunity of pursuing his faith comparable to the opportunity afforded fellow prisoners who adhere to conventional religious precepts, then there was palpable discrimination by the State against the Buddhist religion, established 600 B.C., long before the Christian era.[1] The First Amendment applicable to the States by reason of the Fourteenth Amendment, Torcaso v. Watkins, 367 US 488, prohibits government from making a law "prohibiting the free exercise" of religion. If the allegations of this complaint are assumed to be true, as they must be on the motion to dismiss, Texas has violated the First and Fourteenth Amendments.

The motion for leave to proceed in forma pauperis is granted. The petition for certiorari is granted, the judgment is vacated, and the cause remanded for a hearing and appropriate findings.

So ordered.

MR. JUSTICE REHNQUIST, dissenting.

Unlike the Court, I am not persuaded that petitioner's complaint states a claim under the First Amendment.

---

[1] We do not suggest, of course, that every religious sect or group within a prison—however few in number—must have identical facilities or personnel. A special chapel or place of worship need not be provided for every faith regardless of size; nor must a chaplain, priest or minister be provided without regard to the extent of the demand. But reasonable opportunities must be afforded to all prisoners to exercise the religious freedom guaranteed by the First and Fourteenth Amendments without fear of penalty.

Under the First Amendment, of course, Texas may neither "establish a religion" nor may it "impair the free exercise" thereof. Petitoner alleges that voluntary services are made available at prison facilities so that Protestants, Catholics, and Jews may attend church services of their choice. None of our prior holdings indicates that such a program on the part of prison officials amounts to the establishment of a religion.

None of our holdings under the First Amendment requires that, in addition to being allowed freedom of religious belief, prisoners be allowed freely to evangelize their views among other prisoners. There is no indication in petitioner's complaint that the prison officials have dealt more strictly with his efforts to convert other convicts to Buddhism than with efforts of communicants of other faiths to make similar conversions.

By reason of his status, petitioner is obviously limited in the extent to which he may *practice* his religion. He is assuredly not free to attend the church of his choice outside the prison walls. But the fact that the Texas prison system offers no Buddhist services at this particular prison does not, under the circumstances pleaded in his complaint, demonstrate that his religious freedom is being impaired. Presumably prison officials are not obligated to provide facilities for any particular denominational services within a prison, although once they undertake to provide them for some they must make only such reasonable distinctions as may survive analysis under the Equal Protection Clause.

What petitioner's basic claim amounts to is that because prison facilities are provided for denominational services for religions with more numerous followers, the failure to provide prison facilities for Buddhist services amounts to a denial of the equal protection of the laws. There is no indication from petitioner's complaint how many practicing Buddhists, there are in the particular prison facility in which he is incarcerated, nor is there any indication of the demand upon available facilities for other prisoner activities. Neither the decisions of this Court after full argument, nor those summarily reversing the dismissal of a prisoner's civil rights complaint have ever given full consideration to the proper balance to be struck between prisoners' rights and the extensive administrative discretion that must rest with correction officials. I would apply the rule of deference to administrative discretion that has been overwhelmingly accepted in the courts of appeals.

A long line of decisions by this Court has recognized that the "equal protection of the laws" guaranteed by the Fourteenth Amendment is not to be applied in a precisely equivalent way in the multitudinous fact situations that may confront the courts. On the one hand, we have held that racial classifications are "invidious" and "suspect." I think it quite consistent with the intent of the framers of the Fourteenth Amendment, many of whom would doubtless be surprised to know that convicts came within its ambit, to treat prisoner claims at the other end of the spectrum from claims of racial discrimination. Absent a complaint alleging facts showing that the difference in treatment between petitioner and his fellow Buddhists and practitioners of denominations with more numerous adherents could not reasonably be justified under any rational hypothesis, I would leave the matter in the hands of the prison officials.

VERNON LEE BOUNDS, etc., et al., Petitioners

v.

ROBERT (BOBBY) SMITH et al.

430 U.S. 817, 52 L.Ed.2d 72, 97 S.Ct. 1491 (1977)

OPINION OF THE COURT

MR. JUSTICE MARSHALL delivered the opinion of the Court.

The issue in this case is whether States must protect the right of prisoners to access to the courts by providing them with law libraries or alternative sources of legal knowledge. In Younger v. Gilmore, 404 US 15, (1971), we held per curiam that such services are constitutionally mandated. Petitioners, officials of the State of North Carolina, ask us to overrule that recent case, but for reasons explained below, we decline the invitation and reaffirm our previous decision.

I

Respondents are inmates incarcerated in correctional facilities of the Division of Prisons of the North Carolina Department of Correction. They filed three separate actions under 42 USC § 1983 [42 USCS § 1983], all eventually consolidated in the District Court for the Eastern District of North Carolina. Respondents alleged, in pertinent part, that they were denied access to the courts in violation of their Fourteenth Amendment rights by the State's failure to provide legal research facilities.

The District Court granted respondents' motion for summary judgment on this claim, finding that the sole prison library in the State was "severely inadequate" and that there was no other legal assistance available to inmates. The court recognized, however, that determining the "ap-

propriate relief to be ordered ...
presents a difficult problem." Rather
than attempting "to dictate precisely
what course the State should follow,"
the court "charge[d] the Department
of Correction with the task of devising
a Constitutionally sound program" to
assure inmate access to the courts. It
left to the State the choice of what
alternative would "most easily and
economically" fulfill this duty, suggesting that a program to make available lawyers, law students, or public
defenders might serve the purpose at
least as well as the provision of law
libraries.

The State responded by proposing
the establishment of seven libraries in
institutions located across the State
chosen so as to serve best all prison
units. In addition, the State planned
to set up smaller libraries in the Central Prison segregation unit and the
Women's Prison. Under the plan, inmates desiring to use a library would
request appointments. They would be
given transportation and housing, if
necessary, for a full day's library
work. In addition to its collection of
lawbooks, each library would stock
legal forms and writing paper and
have typewriters and use of copying
machines. The State proposed to train
inmates as research assistants and
typists to aid fellow prisoners. It was
estimated that ultimately some 350 inmates per week could use the libraries, although inmates not facing
court deadlines might have to wait
three or four weeks for their turn at a
library.

The District Court [found] the
State's plan "both economically feasible and practicable," and one that,
fairly and efficiently run, would "insure each inmate the time to prepare
his petitions."

Both sides appealed from those por-

tions of the District Court orders
adverse to them. The Court of Appeals for the Fourth Circuit affirmed
in all respects save one. It found that
the library plan denied women prisoners the same access rights as men to
research facilities.

We affirm.

II

It is now established beyond doubt
that prisoners have a constitutional
right of access to the courts. This
Court recognized that right more than
35 years ago when it struck down a
regulation prohibiting state prisoners
from filing petitions for habeas corpus
unless they were found " 'properly
drawn' " by the " 'legal investigator' "
for the parole board. Ex parte Hull,
312 US 546, (1941).

More recent decisions have struck
down restrictions and required
remedial measures to insure that inmate access to the courts is adequate,
effective, and meaningful. Thus, in
order to prevent "effectively foreclosed access," indigent prisoners
must be allowed to file appeals and
habeas corpus petitions without payment of docket fees. Burns v. Ohio,
360 US 252, 257, (1959); Smith v.
Bennett, 365 US 708, (1961). Because
we recognized that "adequate and effective appellate review" is impossible
without a trial transcript or adequate
substitute, we held that States must
provide trial records to inmates unable to buy them. Griffin v. Illinois,
351 US 12, (1956). Similarly, counsel
must be appointed to give indigent inmates "a meaningful appeal" from
their convictions. Douglas v. California, 372 US 353, 358, (1963).

Johnson v. Avery, 393 US 483,
(1969), struck down a regulation prohibiting prisoners from assisting each
other with habeas corpus applications

and other legal matters. And even as it rejected a claim that indigent defendants have a constitutional right to appointed counsel for discretionary appeals, the Court reaffirmed that States must "assure the indigent defendant an adequate opportunity to present his claims fairly." Ross v. Moffitt, 417 US, at 616, "[M]eaningful access" to the courts is the touchstone.

Petitioners contend, however, that this constitutional duty merely obliges States to allow inmate "writ writers" to function. They argue that under Johnson v. Avery, supra, as long as inmate communications on legal problems are not restricted, there is no further obligation to expend state funds to implement affirmatively the right of access. This argument misreads the cases.

[O]ur decisions have consistently required States to shoulder affirmative obligations to assure all prisoners meaningful access to the courts. The inquiry is rather whether law libraries or other forms of legal assistance are needed to give prisoners a reasonably adequate opportunity to present claimed violations of fundamental constitutional rights to the courts.

We reject the State's claim that inmates are "ill-equipped to use" "the tools of the trade of the legal profession," making libraries useless in assuring meaningful access. [T]his Court's experience indicates that pro se petitioners are capable of using lawbooks to file cases raising claims that are serious and legitimate even if ultimately unsuccessful.

We hold, therefore, that the fundamental constitutional right of access to the courts requires prison authorities to assist inmates in the preparation and filing of meaningful legal papers by providing prisoners with adequate law libraries or adequate assistance from persons trained in the law.

It should be noted that while adequate law libraries are one constitutionally acceptable method to assure meaningful access to the courts, our decision here, does not foreclose alternative means to achieve that goal. Nearly half the States and the District of Columbia provide some degree of professional or quasi-professional legal assistance to prisoners. Such programs take many imaginative forms and may have a number of advantages over libraries alone. Among the alternatives are the training of inmates as paralegal assistants to work under lawyers' supervision, the use of paraprofessionals and law students, either as volunteers or in formal clinical programs, the organization of volunteer attorneys through bar associations or other groups, the hiring of lawyers on a part-time consultant basis, and the use of full-time staff attorneys, working either in new prison legal assistance organizations or as part of public defender or legal services offices. Legal services plans not only result in more efficient and skillful handling of prisoner cases, but also avoid the disciplinary problems associated with writ writers.

[A] legal access program need not include any particular element we have discussed, and we encourage local experimentation. Any plan, however, must be evaluated as a whole to ascertain its compliance with constitutional standards.

The judgment is affirmed.

MURRAY v. GIARRATANO

___ U.S. ___, 109 S. Ct. 2765, 106 L. Ed. 2d 1 (1989)

(Citations and Footnotes Omitted)

CHIEF JUSTICE REHNQUIST announced the judgment of the Court and delivered an opinion, in which JUSTICE WHITE, JUSTICE O'CONNOR, and JUSTICE SCALIA join.

Virginia death row inmates brought a civil rights suit against various officials of the Commonwealth of Virginia. The prisoners claimed, based on several theories, that the Constitution required that they be provided with counsel at the State's expense for the purpose of pursuing collateral proceedings related to their convictions and sentences. The courts below ruled that appointment of counsel upon request was necessary for the prisoners to enjoy their constitutional right to access to the courts in pursuit of state habeas corpus relief. We think this holding is inconsistent with our decision two Terms ago in *Pennsylvania v. Finley*, and rests on a misreading of our decision in *Bounds v. Smith*.

In *Finley* we ruled that neither the Due Process Clause of the Fourteenth Amendment nor the equal protection guarantee of "meaningful access" required the State to appoint counsel for indigent prisoners seeking state postconviction relief. The Sixth and Fourteenth Amendments to the Constitution assure the right of an indigent defendant to counsel at the trial stage of a criminal proceeding and an indigent defendant is similarly entitled as a matter of right to counsel for an initial appeal from the judgment and sentence of the trial court. But we held in *Ross v. Moffitt*, that the right to counsel at these earlier stages of a criminal procedure did not carry over to a discretionary appeal provided by North Carolina law from the intermediate appellate court to the Supreme Court of North Carolina. We contrasted the trial stage of a criminal proceeding where the State by presenting witnesses and arguing to a jury attempts to strip from the defendant the presumption of innocence and convict him of a crime, with the appellate stage of such a proceeding, where the defendant needs an attorney "not as a shield to protect him against being 'haled into court' by the State and stripped of his presumption of innocence, but rather as a sword to upset the prior determination of guilt."

We held in *Finley* that the logic of *Ross v. Moffit* required the conclusion that there was no federal constitutional right to counsel for the indigent prisoners seeking state postconviction relief: "Postconviction relief is even further removed from the criminal trial than is discretionary direct review. It is not part of the criminal proceeding itself, and it is in fact considered to be civil in nature. States have no obligation to provide this avenue of relief, and when they do, the fundamental fairness mandated by the due Process Clause does not require that the state supply a lawyer as well.

The Court of Appeals ... relied on what was perceived as a tension between the rule in *Finley* and the implication of our decisions in *Bounds v. Smith*; we find no such tension. Whether the right of access at issue in *Bounds* is primarily one of due process or equal protection, in either case it rests on a constitutional theory considered in *Finley*. The Court held in *Bounds* that a prisoner's "right to access" to the courts required a state to furnish access to adequate law libraries in order that the prisoners might prepare petitions for judicial relief. But it would be a strange jurisprudence that permitted the extension of that holding to partially overrule a subsequently decided case such as *Finley* which held that prisoners seeking judicial relief from their sentence in state proceedings were not entitled to counsel.

It would be an even stranger jurisprudence to allow, as the dissent would, the "right of access" involved in *Bounds v. Smith*, to partially overrule *Pennsylvania v. Finley* based on "factual" findings of a particular District Court regarding matters such as the perceived difficulty of capital

sentencing law and the general psychology of death-row inmates. Treating such matters as "factual findings," presumably subject only to review under the "clearly erroneous" standard, would permit a different constitutional rule to apply in a different State if the district judge hearing that claim reached different conclusions. Our cases involving the right to counsel have never taken this tack; they have been categorical holdings as to what Constitution requires with respect to a particular stage of a criminal proceeding in general. Indeed, as the dissent itself points out, it was the Court's dissatisfaction with the case-by-case approach of *Betts v. Brady*, that led to the adoption of the categorical rule requiring appointed counsel for indigent felony defendants in *Gideon*.

There is no inconsistency whatever between the holding of *Bounds* and the holding in *Finley*; the holding of neither case squarely decides the question presented in this case. For the reasons previously stated in this opinion, we now hold that *Finley* applies to those inmates under sentence of death as well as to other inmates, and that holding necessarily imposes limits on *Bounds*.

The judgment of the Court of Appeals is
Reversed.

JUSTICE O'CONNOR concurring.

I join in THE CHIEF JUSTICE's opinion. As his opinion demonstrates, there is nothing in the Constitution or the precedents of this Court which requires that a State provide counsel in

postconviction proceedings is not part of the criminal process itself, but is instead a civil action designed to overturn a presumptively valid criminal judgment. Nothing in the Constitution requires the States to provide such proceedings, nor does it seem to me that the Constitution requires the States to follow any particular federal model in those proceedings. I also join in JUSTICE KENNEDY's opinion concurring in the judgment, since I do not view it as inconsistent with the principles expressed above. As JUSTICE KENNEDY observes, our decision in *Bounds v. Smith*, allows the States considerable discretion in assuring that those imprisoned in its jails obtain meaningful access to the judicial process. Beyond the requirements of *Bounds*, the matter is one of legislative choice based on difficult policy considerations and the allocation of scarce legal resources. Our decision today rightly leaves these issues to resolution by Congress and the state legislatures.

JUSTICE KENNEDY, with whom JUSTICE O'CONNOR joins, concurring in the judgment.

It cannot be denied that collateral relief proceedings are a central part of the review process for prisoners sentenced to death. As JUSTICE STEVENS observes, a substantial proportion of these prisoners succeed in having their death sentences vacated in habeas corpus proceedings, the complexity of our jurisprudence in this area, moreover, makes it unlikely that capital defendants will be able to file successful petitions for collateral relief without the assistance of persons learned in the law.

The requirement of meaningful access can be satisfied in various ways, however. This was made explicit in our decision in *Bounds v. Smith*. The intricacies and range of options are of sufficient complexity that state legislatures and prison administrators must be given "wide discretion" to select appropriate solutions. Indeed, judicial imposition of a categorical remedy such as that adopted by the court below might pretermit other responsible solutions being considered in Congress and state legislatures. Assessments of the difficulties presented by collateral litigation in capital cases are now being conducted by committees of the American Bar Association and the Judicial Conference, and Congress has stated its intention to give the matter serious consideration.

Unlike Congress, this Court lacks the capacity to undertake the searching and comprehensive review called for in this area, for we can decide only the case before us. While Virginia has not adopted procedures for securing representation that are as far reaching and effective as those available in other States, no prisoner on death row in Virginia has been unable to obtain counsel to represent him in postconviction proceedings, and Virginia's prison system is staffed with institutional lawyers to assist in preparing petitions for postconviction relief. I am not prepared to say that this scheme violates the Constitution.

On the facts and record of this case, I concur in the judgment of the Court.

JUSTICE STEVENS, with whom JUSTICE BRENNAN, JUSTICE MARSHALL, and JUSTICE BLACKMUN join in, dissenting.

Two Terms ago this Court reaffirmed that the Fourteenth Amendment to the Federal Constitution obligates a State "to assure the indigent defendant an adequate opportunity to present his claims fairly in the context of the State's appellate process." *Pennsylvania v. Finley.* The narrow question presented is whether that obligation includes appointment of counsel for indigent death row inmates who wish to pursue state postconviction relief. Viewing the facts in light of our precedents, we should answer that question in the affirmative.

I

The parties before us, like the Court of Appeals en banc and the District Court below, have accorded controlling importance to our deci

sion in *Bounds v. Smith.* In that case, inmates had alleged that North Carolina violated the Fourteenth Amendment by failing to provide research facilities to help them prepare habeas corpus petitions and federal civil rights complaints. Stressing "meaningful" access to the courts as a "touchstone," we held: "[T]he fundamental constitutional right of access to the courts requires prison authorities to assist inmates in the preparation and filing of meaningful legal papers by providing prisoners with adequate law libraries or adequate assistance from persons trained in the law." Far from creating a discrete constitutional right, *Bounds* constitutes one part of a jurisprudence that encompasses "right-to-counsel" as well as "access-to-courts" cases. Although each case is shaped by its facts, all share a concern, based upon the Fourteenth Amendment, that accused and convicted persons be permitted to seek legal remedies without arbitrary governmental interference.

***

I respectfully dissent.

PRISON DISCIPLINARY PROCEEDINGS

BAXTER v. PALMIGIANO

425 U.S. 308, 96 S. Ct. 1551, 47 L. Ed. 2d 810 (1976)

[Citations and Footnotes omitted]

[In *Baxter v. Palmigiano*, a state prison inmate was charged with inciting a prison disturbance and was informed that he might be prosecuted for a violation of state law. At a Prison hearing on the charge, he was told that he had a right to remain silent during the hearing, but that if he did so his silence would be held against him. The inmate remained silent, and on the basis of the hearing he was placed in "primitive segregation" for 30 days. He filed an action for damages and injunctive relief, which the District Court denied, but the Court of Appeals reversed. It held that an inmate must be advised of his right to remain silent and that he must not be questioned further once he exercises that right. It held that such silence could never be used against the inmate and that where the inmate was subject to outside criminal prosecution, the prison officials should consider whether defense counsel, if requested by the inmate, should be permitted at the disciplinary proceeding.

The Supreme Court reversed the decisions of both the Courts of Appeals, holding that the requirements they set down were inconsistent with the approach taken in *Wolff v. McDonnell*, which left many areas to the discretion of prison officials. Reiterating *Wolff*, the Court said that inmate have no right to either retained or appointed counsel in disciplinary proceedings. It validated the use of the adverse inference which was drawn from the inmate's silence in *Enomoto*. It said that the requirement of explaining the denial of confrontation and cross-examination infringed on the discretion which Wolff left to prison officials. Lastly, the Court said that there was no basis in the record for requiring the minimal due process procedures when only a loss of privileges was at stake.]

MR. JUSTICE WHITE delivered the opinion of the Court.

In *Wolff v. McDonnell*, drawing comparisons to *Gagnon v. Scarpelli*, we said

461

"The insertion of counsel into the [prison] disciplinary process would inevitably give the proceedings a more adversary cast and tend to reduce their utility as a means to further correctional goals. There would also be delay and very practical problems in providing counsel in sufficient numbers at the time and place where hearings are to be held. At this stage of the development of these procedures we are not prepared to hold that inmates have a right to either retained or appointed counsel in disciplinary proceedings."

Relying on *Miranda v. Arizona*, and *Mathis v. United States*, both Courts of Appeals in these cases held that prison inmates are entitled to representation at prison disciplinary hearings where the charges involved conduct punishable as a crime under state law, not because of the services that counsel might render in connection with the disciplinary proceedings themselves, but because statements inmates might make at the hearings would perhaps be used in later state-court prosecutions for the same conduct.

Neither *Miranda*, nor *Mathis*, has any substantial bearing on the question whether counsel must be provided at "[p]rison disciplinary hearings [which] are not part of a criminal prosecution." The Court has never held, and we decline to do so now, that the requirements of those cases must be met to render pretrial statements admissible in other criminal cases.

We see no reason to alter our conclusion so recently made in *Wolff* that inmates do not "have a right to either retained or appointed counsel in disciplinary hearings." Plainly, therefore, state authorities were not in error in failing to advise Palmigiano to the contrary, i.e., that he was entitled to counsel at the hearing and that the State would furnish counsel if he did not have one of his own.

III

Palmigiano was advised that he was not required to testify at his disciplinary hearing and that he could remain silent but that his silence could be used against him. ... As the Court has often held, the Fifth Amendment "not only protects the individual against being involuntarily called as a witness against himself in a criminal prosecution but also privileges him not to answer official questions put to him in any other proceeding, civil or criminal, formal or informal, where the answers might incriminate him in future criminal proceedings." Prison disciplinary hearings are not criminal proceedings; but if inmates are compelled in those proceedings to furnish testimonial evidence that might incriminate them in later criminal proceedings, they must be offered "whatever immunity is required to supplant the privilege" and may not be required to "waive such immunity." In this line of cases from *Garrity* to *Lefkowitz*, the States, pursuant to statute, sought to interrogate individuals about their job performance or about their contractual relations with the State; insisted upon waiver of the Fifth Amendment privilege not to respond or to object to later use of the incriminating statements in criminal prosecutions, and, upon refusal to waive, automatically terminated employment or eligibility to contract with the State. Holding that the State could not constitutionally seek to compel testimony that had not been immunized by threats of serious economic reprisal, we invalidated the challenged statutes.

***

The Rhode Island prison rules do not transgress the foregoing principles. No criminal proceedings are or were pending against Palmigiano. The State has not, contrary to Griffin, sought to make evidentiary use of his silence at the disciplinary hearing in any criminal proceeding. Neither has Rhode Island insisted or asked that Palmigiano waive his Fifth Amendment privilege. He was notified that he was privileged to remain silent if he chose. He was also advised that his silence could be used against him, but a prison inmate in Rhode Island electing to remain silent during his disciplinary hearing, as respondent Palmigiano did here, is not in consequence of his silence automatically found guilty of the infraction with which he has been charged. Under Rhode Island law, disciplinary decisions "must be based on substantial evidence manifested in the record of the disciplinary proceeding." It is thus undisputed that an inmate's silence in and of itself is insufficient to support an adverse decision by the Disciplinary Board ... Here, Palmigiano remained silent at the hearing in the face of evidence that incriminated him; and, as far as this record reveals, his silence was given no more evidentiary value than was warranted by the facts surrounding his case. This does not smack of an invalid attempt by the State to compel testimony without granting immunity or to penalize the exercise of the privilege. The advice given inmates by the decisionmakers is merely a realistic reflection of the evidentiary significance of the choice to remain silent.

Had the State desired Palmigiano's testimony over his Fifth Amendment objection, we can but assume that it would have been extended whatever use immunity is required by the Federal Constitution. Had this occurred and had Palmigiano nevertheless refused to answer, it surely would not have violated the Fifth Amendment to draw whatever inference from his silence that the circumstances warranted. Insofar as the privilege is concerned, the situation is little different where the State advises the inmate of his right to silence but also plainly notifies him that his silence will be weighed in the balance.

Our conclusion is consistent with the prevailing rule that the Fifth Amendment does not forbid adverse inferences against parties to civil actions when they refuse to testify in response to probative evidence offered against them: the Amendment "does not preclude the inference where the privilege is claimed by a party to a civil cause." In criminal cases, where the stakes are higher and the State's sole interest is to convict, Griffin prohibits the judge and prosecutor from suggesting to the jury that it may treat the defendant's silence as substantive evidence of guilt. Disciplinary proceedings in state prisons, however, involve the correctional process and important state interests other than conviction for crime. We decline to extend the Griffin rule to this context.

***

Although acknowledging the strictures of Wolff with respect to confrontation and cross-examination, the Court of Appeals for the Ninth Circuit ... went on to require prison authorities to provide reasons in writing to inmates denied the privilege to cross-examine or confront witnesses against them in disciplinary proceedings; absent explanation, failure to set forth reasons related to the prevention of one or more of the four concerns expressly mentioned in Wolff would be deemed prima facie abuse of discretion.

This conclusion is inconsistent with Wolff. We characterized as "useful," but did not require, written reasons for denying inmates the limited right to call witnesses in their de

fense. We made no such suggestion with respect to the confrontation and cross-examination which, as was there pointed out, stand on a different footing because of their inherent danger and the availability of adequate bases of decision without them. Mandating confrontation and cross-examination, except where prison officials can justify their denial on one or more grounds that appeal to judges, effectively preempts the area that Wolff left to the sound discretion of prison officials.

***

We said in Wolff v. McDonnell: "As the nature of the prison disciplinary process changes in future years, circumstances may then exist which will require further consideration and reflection of this Court. It is our view, however, that the procedures we have now required in prison disciplinary proceedings represent a reasonable accommodation between the interests of the inmates and the needs of the institution." We do not retreat from that view. However, the procedures required by the Courts of Appeals ... are either inconsistent with the "reasonable accommodation" reached in Wolff, or premature on the bases of the records before us. The judgments ... accordingly are

Reversed.

WOLFF v. McDONNELL

418 U.S. 539, 94 S.Ct. 2963, 41 L.Ed.2d. 935 (1974)

[Footnotes and citations omitted]

[Prison discipline in Nebraska resulted in forfeiture or withholding of statutory "good-time" credits, confinement in a disciplinary cell for serious misconduct, and deprivation of privileges for less serious misconduct. The procedure for imposing these sanctions involved a preliminary conference between a supervisor, the charging party, and the inmate charged with a violation. A conduct report was then prepared and the inmate appeared before a disciplinary board composed of three prison officials. The inmate could ask questions of the charging party.

An inmate filed a complaint for damages and injunctive relief alleging that this procedure violated due process. The District Court rejected the inmate's due process claim. The Court of Appeals reversed and held that the procedures required for revocation of parole were required in prison disciplinary proceedings, and that the specific application of the procedures was to be determined by the District Court.

The Supreme Court held that the full range of procedures required for the revocation of parole did not apply, but that certain minimal due process requirements were applicable, taking into account both the interests of the inmates and the unique institutional environment. The Court specifically required that the inmate receive written notice of the charges no less than 24 hours before an appearance before the disciplinary hearing, that the board must make a written statement of the evidence relied on and the reasons for the disciplinary action, and that the inmate should be allowed to call witnesses and present documentary evidence, unless this would jeopardize institutional safety or correctional goals. The Court held that there was no right to confrontation and cross-examination, but that this was left to the discretion of prison officials. Further, it held that inmates have no right to retained or appointed counsel at such proceedings, but that in certain situations an inmate may have a staff member or inmate act as "counsel substitute." The Court held that the disciplinary board in this case was sufficiently impartial to satisfy due process requirements.]

Mr. Justice White delivered the opinion of the Court.

***

[The State of Nebraska] assert that the procedure for disciplining prison inmates for serious misconduct is a matter of policy raising no constitutional issue. If the position implies that prisoners in state institutions are wholly without the protections of the Constitution and the Due Process Clause, it is plainly untenable. Lawful imprisonment necessarily makes unavailable many rights and privileges of the ordinary citizen, a "retraction justified by the considerations underlying our penal system." Though his rights may be diminished by the needs and exigencies of the institutional environment, a prisoner is not wholly stripped of constitutional protections when he is imprisoned for crime. There is no iron curtain drawn between the Constitution and the prisons of this country. Prisoners have been held to enjoy substantial religious freedom under the First and Fourteenth Amendments. They retain right of access to the courts. Prisoners are protected under the Equal Protection Clause of the Fourteenth Amendment from invidious discrimination based on race. Prisoners may also claim the protections of the Due Process Clause. They may not be deprived of life, liberty, or property without due process of law.

Of course, as we have indicated, the fact that prisoners retain rights under the Due Process Clause in no way implies that these rights are not subjected to restrictions imposed by the nature of the regime to which they have been lawfully committed. Prison disciplinary proceedings are not part of a criminal prosecution, and the full panoply of rights due a defendant in such proceedings does not apply. In sum, there must be mutual accommodation between institutional needs and objectives and the provisions of the Constitution that are of general application.

We also reject the assertion of the State that whatever may be true of the Due Process Clause in general or of other rights protected by that Clause against state infringement, the interest of prisoners in disciplinary procedures is not included in that "liberty" protected by the Fourteenth Amendment. It is true that the Constitution itself does not guarantee good-time credit for satisfactory behavior while in prison. But here the State itself has not only provided a statutory right to good time but also specifies that is to be forfeited only for serious misbehavior. Nebraska may have the authority to create, or not, a right to a shortened prison sentence though the accumulation of credits for good behavior, and it is true that the Due Process Clause does not require a hearing "in every conceivable case of government impairment of private interest." But the State having created the right to good time and itself recognizing that its deprivation is a sanction authorized for major misconduct, the prisoner's interest has real substance and is sufficiently embraced within Fourteenth Amendment "liberty" to entitle him to those minimum procedures appropriate under the circumstances and required by the Due Process Clause to insure that the state-created right is not arbitrarily abrogated. This is the thrust of recent cases in the prison disciplinary context. In *Haines v. Kerner*, the state prisoner asserted a "denial of due process in the steps leading to [disciplinary] confinement." We reversed the dismissal of the Sec. 1983 complaint for failure to state a claim. In *Preiser v. Rodriguez*, the prisoner complained that he had been deprived of good-time credits without notice or hearing and without due process of law. We considered the claim a proper subject for a federal habeas corpus proceeding.

This analysis as to liberty parallels the accepted due process analysis as to property. The Court has consistently held that some kind of hearing is required at some time before a person is finally deprived of his property interests. The requirement for some kind of a hearing applies to the taking of private property, the revocation of licenses, the operation of state dispute-settlement mechanisms, when one person seeks to take property from another, or to government-created jobs held, absent "cause" for termination.

We think a person's liberty is equally protected, even when the liberty itself is a statutory creation of the State. The touchstone of due process is protection of the individual against arbitrary action of government. Since prisoners in Nebraska can only lose good-time credits if they are guilty of serious misconduct, the determination of whether such behavior has occurred becomes critical, and the minimum requirements of procedural

due process appropriate for the circumstances must be observed.

IV
***

Morrissey held that due process imposed certain minimum procedural requirements which must be satisfied before parole could finally be revoked. These procedures were: "(a) written notice of the claimed violations of parole; (b) disclosure to the parolee of evidence against him; (c) opportunity to be heard in person and to present witnesses and documentary evidence; (d) the right to confront and cross-examine adverse witnesses (unless the hearing officer specifically finds good cause for not allowing confrontation); (e) a 'neutral and detached' hearing body such as traditional parole board, members of which need not be judicial officers or lawyers; and (f) a written statement by the factfinders as to the evidence relied on and reasons for revoking parole."

***

We have often repeated that "[t]he very nature of due process negates any concept of inflexible procedures universally applicable to every imaginable situation." "[C]onsideration of what procedures due process may require under any given set of circumstances must begin with a determination of the precise nature of the government function involved as well as of the private interest that has been affected by governmental action." Viewed in this light it is immediately apparent that one cannot automatically apply procedural rules designed for free citizens in an open society, or for parolees or probationers under only limited restraints, to the very different situation presented by a disciplinary proceeding in a state prison.

Revocation of parole may deprive the parolee of only conditional liberty, but it nonetheless "inflicts a 'grievous loss' on the parolee and often on others." Simply put, revocation proceedings determine whether the parolee will be free or in prison, a matter of obvious great moment to him. For the prison inmate, the deprivation of good time is not the same immediate disaster that the revocation of parole is for the parolee. The deprivation, very likely, does not then and there work any change in the conditions of his liberty. It can postpone the date of eligibility for parole and extend the maximum term to be served, but it is not certain to do so, for good time may be restored. Even if not restored, it cannot be said with certainty that the actual date of parole will be affected; and if parole occurs, the extension of the maximum term resulting from loss of good time may affect only the termination of parole, and it may not even do that. The deprivation of good time is unquestionably a matter of considerable importance. The State reserves it as a sanction for serious misconduct, and we should not unrealistically discount its significance. But it is qualitatively and quantitatively different from the revocation of parole or probation.

In striking the balance that the Due Process Clause demands, however, we think the major consideration militating against adopting the full range of procedures suggested by Morrissey for alleged parole violators is the very different stake the State has in the structure and content of the prison disciplinary hearing. That the revocation of parole be justified and based to an accurate assessment of the facts is a critical matter to the State as well as the parolee; but the procedures by which it is determined whether the conditions of parole have been breached do not themselves threaten other important state interests, parole officers, police, or witnesses—at least no more so than in the case of the ordinary criminal trial. Prison disciplinary proceedings, on the other hand, take place in a closed, tightly controlled environment peopled by those who have chosen to violate the criminal law and who have been lawfully incarcerated for doing so. Some are first offenders, but many are recidivists who have repeatedly employed illegal and often very violent means to attain their ends. They may have little regard for the safety of others or their property or for the rules designed to provide an orderly and reasonably safe prison life. Although there are very many varieties of prisons with different degrees of security, we must realize that in many of them the inmates are closely supervised and their activities controlled around the clock. Guards and inmates co-exist in direct and intimate contact. Tension between them is unremitting. Frustration, resentment, and despair are commonplace. Relationships among the inmates are varied and complex and perhaps subject to the unwritten code that exhorts inmates not to inform on a fellow prisoner.

It is against this background that disciplinary proceedings must be structured by prison authorities; and it is against this background that we must make our constitutional judgments, realizing that we are dealing with the maximum security institution as well as those where security considerations are not paramount. The reality is that disciplinary hearings and the imposition of disagreeable sanctions necessarily involve confrontations between inmates and authority and between inmates who are being disciplined and those who would charge or furnish evidence against them. Retaliation is much more than a theoretical possibility; and the basic and unavoidable task of providing reasonable personal safety for guards and inmates may be at stake, to say nothing of the impact of disciplinary confrontations and the resulting escalation of personal antagonisms on the important aims of the correctional process.

Indeed, it is pressed upon us that the proceedings to ascertain and sanction misconduct themselves play a major role in furthering the institutional goal of modifying the behavior and value systems of prison inmates sufficient to permit them to live within the law when they are released. Inevitably there is a great range of personality and character among those who have transgressed the criminal law. Some are more amenable to suggestion and persuasion than others. Some may be incorrigible and would merely disrupt and exploit the disciplinary process for their own ends. With some, rehabilitation may be best achieved by simulating procedures of a free society to the maximum possible extent; but with others, it may be essential that discipline be swift and sure. In any event, it is argued, there would be great unwisdom in encasing the disciplinary procedures in an inflexible constitutional straitjacket that would necessarily call for adversary proceedings typical of the criminal trial, very likely raise the level of confrontation between staff and inmate, and make more difficult the utilization of the disciplinary process as a tool to advance the rehabilitative goals of the institution. This consideration, along with the necessity to maintain an acceptable level of personal security in the institution, must be taken into account as we now examine in more detail the Nebraska procedures that the Court of Appeals found wanting.

V

Two of the procedures that the Court held should be extended to parolees facing revocation proceedings are not, but must be, provided to prisoners in the Nebraska Complex if the minimum requirements of procedural due process are to be satisfied. These are advance written notice of the claimed violation and a written statement of the factfinders as to the evidence relied upon and the reasons for the disciplinary action taken. As described by the Warden in his oral testimony, on the basis of which the District Court made its findings, the inmate is now given oral notice of the charges against him at least as soon as the conference with the Chief Corrections Supervisor and charging party. A written record is there compiled and the report read to the inmate at the hearing before the Adjustment Committee where the charges are discussed and pursued. There is no indication that the inmate is ever given a written statement by the Committee as to the evidence or informed in writing or otherwise as to the reasons for the disciplinary action taken.

Part of the function of notice is to give the charged party a chance to marshal the facts in his defense and to clarify what the charges are, in fact. Neither of these functions was performed by the notice described by the Warden. Although the charges are discussed orally with the inmate somewhat in advance of the hearing, the inmate is sometimes brought before the Adjustment Committee shortly after he is orally informed of the charges. Other times, after this initial discussion, further investigation takes place which may reshape the nature of the charges or the evidence relied upon. In those instances, under procedures in effect at the time of the trial, it would appear that the inmate first receives notice of the actual charges at the time of the

hearing before the Adjustment Committee. We hold that written notice of the charges must be given to the disciplinary-action defendant in order to inform him of the charges and to enable him to marshal the facts and prepare a defense. At least a brief period of time after the notice, no less than 24 hours, should be allowed to the inmate to prepare for the appearance before the Adjustment Committee.

We also hold that there must be a "written statement by the factfinders as to the evidence relied on and reasons" for the disciplinary action. Although Nebraska does not seem to provide administrative review of the action taken by the Adjustment Committee, the actions taken at such proceedings may involve review by other bodies. They might furnish the basis of a decision by the Director of Corrections to transfer an inmate to another institution because he is considered "to be incorrigible by reason of frequent intentional breaches of discipline," and are certainly likely to be considered by the state parole authorities in making parole decisions. Written records of proceedings will thus protect the inmate against collateral consequences based on a misunderstanding of the nature of the original proceeding. Further, as to the disciplinary action itself, the provision for a written record helps to insure that administrators, faced with possible scrutiny by state officials and the public, and perhaps even the courts, where fundamental constitutional rights may have been abridged, will act fairly. Without written records, the inmate will be at a severe disadvantage in propounding his own cause to or defending himself from others. It may be that there will be occasions where personal or institutional safety is so implicated that the statement may properly exclude certain items of evidence, but in that event the statement should indicate the fact of the omission. Otherwise, we perceive no conceivable rehabilitative objective or prospect of prison disruption that can flow from the requirement of these statements.

We are also of the opinion that the inmate facing disciplinary proceedings should be allowed to call witnesses and present documentary evidence in his defense when permitting him to do so will not be unduly hazardous to institutional safety or correctional goals. Ordinarily, the right to present evidence is basic to a fair hearing; but the unrestricted right to call witnesses from the prison population carries obvious potential for disruption and for interference with the swift punishment that in individual cases may be essential to carrying out the correctional program of the institution. We should not be too ready to exercise oversight and put aside the judgment of prison administrators. It may be that an individual threatened with serious sanctions would normally be entitled to present witnesses and relevant documentary evidence; but here we must balance the inmate's interest in avoiding loss of good time against the needs of the prison, and some amount of flexibility and accommodation is required.

Prison officials must have the necessary discretion to keep the hearing within reasonable limits and to refuse to call witnesses that may create a risk of reprisal or undermine authority, as well as to limit access to other inmates to collect statements or to compile other documentary evidence. Although we do not prescribe it, it would be useful for the Committee to state its reason for refusing to call a witnesses, whether it be for irrelevance, lack of necessity, or the hazards presented in individual cases. Any less flexible rule appears untenable as a constitutional matter, at least on the record made in this case. The operation of a correctional institution is at best an extraordinarily difficult undertaking. Many prison officials, on the spot and with the responsibility for the safety of inmates and staff, are reluctant to extend the unqualified right to call witnesses; and in our view, they must have the necessary discretion without being subject to unduly crippling constitutional impediments. There is this much play in the joints of the Due Process Clause, and we stop short of imposing a more demanding rule with respect to witnesses and documents.

Confrontation and cross-examination present greater hazards to institutional interests. If confrontation and cross-examination of those furnishing evidence against the inmate were to be allowed as a matter of course, as in criminal trials, there would be considerable potential for havoc inside the prison walls. Proceedings would inevitably be longer and tend to unmanageability. These procedures are essential in criminal trials where the accused, if found guilty, may be subjected to the most serious deprivations, or where a person may lose his job in society. But they are not rights universally applicable to all hearings. Rules of procedure may be shaped by consideration of the risks of error, and should also be shaped by the consequences which will follow their adoption. Although some States do seem to allow cross-examination in disciplinary hearings, we are not apprised of the conditions under which the procedure may be curtailed; and it does not appear that confrontation and cross-examination are generally required in this context. We think that the Constitution should not be read to impose the procedure at the present time and that adequate bases for decision in prison disciplinary cases can be arrived at without cross-examination.

Perhaps as the problems of penal institutions change and correctional goals are reshaped, the balance of interests involved will require otherwise. But in the current environment, where prison disruption remains a serious concern to administrators, we cannot ignore the desire and effort of many States, including Nebraska, and the Federal Government to avoid situations that may trigger deep emotions and that may scuttle the disciplinary process as a rehabilitation vehicle. To some extent, the American adversary trial presumes contestants who are able to cope with the pressures and aftermath of the battle, and such may not generally be the case of those in the prisons of this country. At least, the constitution, as we interpret it today, does not require the contrary assumption. Within the limits set forth in this opinion we are content for now to leave the continuing development of measures to review adverse actions affecting inmates to the sound discretion of corrections officials administering the scope of such inquiries.

We recognize that the problems of potential disruption may differ depending on whom the inmate proposes to cross-examine. If he proposes to examine an unknown fellow inmate, the danger may be the greatest, since the disclosure of the identity of the accuser, and the cross-examination which will follow, may pose a high risk of reprisal within the institution. Conversely, the inmate accuser, who might freely tell his story privately to prison officials, may refuse to testify or admit any knowledge of the situation in question. Although the dangers posed by cross-examination of known inmate accusers, or guards, may be less, the resentment which may persist after confrontation may still be substantial. Also, even where the accuser or adverse witness is known, the disclosure of third parties may pose a problem. There may be a class of cases where the facts are closely disputed, and the character of the parties minimizes the dangers involved. However, any constitutional rule tailored to meet these situations would undoubtedly produce great litigation and attendant costs in a much wider range of cases. Further, in the last analysis, even within the narrow range of cases where interest balancing may well dictate cross-examination, courts will be faced with the assessment of prison officials as to the dangers involved, and there would be a limited basis for upsetting such judgments. The better course at this time, in a period where prison practices are diverse and somewhat experimental, is to leave these matters to the sound discretion of the officials of state prisons.

As to the right to counsel, ... [t]he insertion of counsel into the disciplinary process would inevitably give the proceedings a more adversary cast and tend to reduce their utility as a means to further correctional goals. There would also be delay and very practical problems in providing counsel in sufficient numbers at the time and place where hearings are to be held. At this stage of the development of these procedures we are not prepared to hold that inmates have a right to either retained or appointed counsel in disciplinary proceedings.

Where an illiterate inmate is involved, however, or where the complexity of the issue makes it unlikely that the inmate will be able to collect and present the evidence necessary for an adequate comprehension of the case, he should be free to seek the aid of a fellow inmate, or if that is forbidden, to have adequate substitute aid in the form of help from the staff or from a sufficiently competent in-

mate designated by the staff. We need not pursue the matter further here, however, for there is no claim that respondent, McDonnell, is within the class of inmates entitled to advice or help from others in the course of a prison disciplinary hearing.

Finally, we decline to rule that the Adjustment Committee which conducts the required hearings at the Nebraska Prison Complex and determines whether to revoke good time is not sufficiently impartial to satisfy the Due Process Clause. The Committee is made up of the Associate Warden Custody as chairman, the Correctional Industries Superintendent, and the Reception Center Director. The Chief Corrections Supervisor refers cases to the Committee after investigation and an initial interview with the inmate involved. The Committee is not left at large with unlimited discretion. It is directed to meet daily and to operate within the principles stated in the controlling regulations, among which is the command that "[f]ull consideration must be given to the causes for the adverse behavior, the setting and circumstances in which it occurred, the man's accountability, and the correctional treatment goals," as well as the direction that "disciplinary measures will be taken only at such times and to such degrees as are necessary to regulate and control a man's behavior within acceptable limits and will never be rendered capriciously or in the nature of retaliation or revenge." We find no warrant in the record presented here for concluding that the

Adjustment Committee presents such a hazard of arbitrary decisionmaking that it should be held violative of due process of law.

Our conclusion that some, but not all, of the procedures specified in *Morrissey* and *Scarpelli* must accompany the deprivation of good time by state prison authorities not graven in stone. As the nature of the prison dis ciplinary process changes in future years, circumstances may then exist which will require further consideration and reflection of this Court. It is our view, however, that the procedures we have not required in prison disciplinary proceedings present a reasonable accommodation between the interests of the inmates and the needs of the institution. ***

PAROLE

MORRISSEY v. BREWER

408 U.S. 471, 92 S. Ct. 2593, 33 L. Ed. 2d 484 (1972)

Mr. Chief Justice Burger delivered the opinion of the Court.

We granted certiorari in this case to determine whether the Due Process Clause of the Fourteenth Amendment requires that a State afford an individual some opportunity to be heard prior to revoking his parole.

Petitioner Morrissey was convicted of false drawing or uttering of checks in 1967 pursuant to his guilty plea, and was sentenced to not more than seven years' confinement. He was paroled from the Iowa State Penitentiary in June 1968. Seven months later, at the direction of his parole officer, he was arrested in his home town as a parole violator and incarcerated in the county jail. One week later, after review of the parole officer's written report, the Iowa Board of Parole revoked Morrissey's parole, and he was returned to the penitentiary located about 100 miles from his home. Petitioner asserts he received no hearing prior to revocation of his parole.

The parole officer's report on which the Board of Parole acted shows that petitioner's parole was revoked on the basis of information that he had violated the conditions of parole by buying a car under an assumed name and operating it without permission, giving false statements to police concerning his address and insurance company after a minor accident, obtaining credit under an assumed name, and failing to report his place of residence to his parole officer. The report states that the officer interviewed Morrissey, and that he could not explain why he did not contact his parole officer despite his effort to excuse this on the ground that he had been sick. Further, the report asserts that Morrissey admitted buying the car and obtaining credit under an assumed name, and also admitted being involved in the accident. The parole officer recommended that his parole be revoked because of "his continual violating of his parole rules."

The situation as to petitioner Booher is much the same. Pursuant to his guilty plea, Booher was convicted of forgery in 1966 and sentenced to a maximum term of 10 years. He was paroled November 14, 1968. In August 1969, at his parole officer's direction, he was arrested in his home town for a violation of his parole and confined in the county jail several miles away. On September 13, 1969, on the basis of a written report by his parole officer, the Iowa Board of Parole revoked Booher's parole and Booher was recommitted to the state penitentiary, located about 250 miles from his home, to complete service of his sentence. Petitioner asserts he received no hearing prior to revocation of his parole.

The parole officer's report with respect to Booher recommended that his parole be revoked because he had violated the territorial restrictions of his parole without consent, had obtained a driver's license under an assumed name, operated a motor vehicle without permission, and had violated the employment condition of his parole by failing to keep himself in gainful employment. The report stated that the officer had interviewed Booher and that he had acknowledged to the parole officer that he had left the specified territorial limits and had operated the car and had obtained a license under an assumed name "knowing that it was wrong." The report further noted that Booher had stated that he had not found employment because he could not find work that would pay him what he wanted—he stated he would not work for $2.25 to $2.75 per hour—and that he had left the area to get work in another city.

After exhausting state remedies, both petitioners filed habeas corpus petitions in the United States District Court for the Southern District of Iowa alleging that they had been denied due process because their paroles had been revoked without a hearing. The State responded by arguing that no hearing was re-

quired. The District Court held on the basis of controlling authority that the State's failure to accord a hearing prior to parole revocation did not violate due process. On appeal, the two cases were consolidated.

The Court of Appeals, dividing 4 to 3, held that due process does not require a hearing. The majority recognized that the traditional view of parole as a privilege rather than a vested right is no longer dispositive as to whether due process is applicable; however, on a balancing of the competing interests involved, it concluded that no hearing is required. The court reasoned that parole is only "a correctional device authorizing service of sentence outside the penitentiary," 443 F.2d 942, 947; the parolee is still "in custody." Accordingly, the Court of Appeals was of the view that prison officials must have large discretion in making revocation determinations, and that courts should retain their traditional reluctance to interfere with disciplinary matters properly under the control of state prison authorities. The majority expressed the view that "non-legal, non-adversary considerations" were often the determinative factors in making a parole revocation decision. It expressed concern that if adversary hearings were required for parole revocation, "with the full panoply of rights accorded in criminal proceedings," the function of the parole board as "an administrative body acting in the role of *parens patriae* would be aborted," *id.*, at 949, and the board would be more reluctant to grant parole in the first instance—an apprehension that would not be without some basis if the choice were between a full-scale adversary proceeding or no hearing at all. Additionally, the majority reasoned that the parolee has no statutory right to remain on parole.

Iowa law provides that a parolee may be returned to the institution at any time. Our holding in Mempa v. Rhay, 389 U.S. 128 (1967), was distinguished on the ground that it involved deferred sentencing upon probation revocation, and thus involved a stage of the criminal proceeding, whereas parole revocation was not a stage in the criminal proceeding. The Court of Appeals' decision was consistent with many other decisions on parole revocations.

In their brief in this Court, respondents assert for the first time that petitioners were in fact granted hearings after they were returned to the penitentiary. More generally, respondents say that within two months after the Board revokes an individual's parole and orders him returned to the penitentiary, on the basis of the parole officer's written report it grants the individual a hearing before the Board. At that time, the Board goes over "each of the alleged parole violations with the returnee, and he is given an opportunity to orally present his side of the story to the Board." If the returnee denies the report, it is the practice of the Board to conduct a further investigation before making a final determination either affirming the initial revocation, modifying it, or reversing it.[1] Respondents assert that Morrissey, whose parole was revoked on January 31, 1969, was granted a hearing before the Board on February 12, 1969. Booher's parole was revoked on Sep-

tember 13, 1969, and he was granted a hearing on October 14, 1969. At these hearings, respondents tell us—in the briefs—both Morrissey and Booher admitted the violations alleged in the parole violation reports.

Nothing in the record supplied to this Court indicates that respondent claimed, either in the District Court or the Court of Appeals, that petitioners had received hearings promptly after their paroles were revoked, or that in such hearing they admitted the violations; that information comes to us only in the respondents' brief here. Further, even the assertions that respondents make here are not based on any public record but on interviews with two of the members of the parole board. In the interview relied on to show that petitioners admitted their violations, the board member did not assert he could remember that both Morrissey and Booher admitted the parole violations with which they were charged. He stated only that, according to his memory, in the previous several years all but three returnees had admitted commission of the parole infractions alledged and that neither of the petitioners was among the three who denied them.

We must therefore treat this case in the posture and on the record respondents elected to rely on in the District Court and the Court of Appeals. If the facts are otherwise, respondents may make a showing in the District Court that petitioners in fact have admitted the violations charged before a neutral officer.

I

Before reaching the issue of whether due process applies to the parole system, it is important to recall the function of parole in the correctional process.

---

[1] The hearing required by due process, as defined herein, must be accorded *before* the effective decision. See Armstrong v. Manzo, 380 U.S. 545 (1965). Petitioners assert here that only one of the 540 revocations ordered most recently by the Iowa Parole Board was reversed after hearing, Petitioners' Reply Brief 7, suggesting that the hearing may not objectively evaluate the revocation decision.

During the past 60 years, the practice of releasing prisoners on parole before the end of their sentences has become an integral part of the penological system. Note, Parole Revocation in the Federal System, 56 Geo. L. J. 705 (1968). Rather than being an *ad hoc* exercise of clemency, parole is an established variation on imprisonment of convicted criminals. Its purpose is to help individuals reintegrate into society as constructive individuals as soon as they are able, without being confined for the full term of the sentence imposed. It also serves to alleviate the costs to society of keeping an individual in prison.[2] The essence of parole is release from prison, before the completion of sentence, on the condition that the prisoner abide by certain rules during the balance of the sentence. Under some systems, parole is granted automatically after the service of a certain portion of a prison term. Under others, parole is granted by the discretionary action of a board, which evaluates an array of information about a prisoner and makes a prediction whether he is ready to reintegrate into society.

To accomplish the purpose of parole, those who are allowed to leave prison early are subjected to specified conditions for the duration of their terms. These conditions restrict their activities substantially beyond the ordinary restrictions imposed by law on an individual citizen. Typically, parolees are forbidden to use liquor or to have associations or correspondence with certain categories of undesirable persons. Typically, also they must seek permission from their parole officers before engaging in specified activities, such as changing employment or living quarters, marrying, acquiring or operating a motor vehicle, traveling outside the community, and incurring substantial indebtedness. Additionally, parolees must regularly report to the parole officer to whom they are assigned and sometimes they must make periodic written reports of their activities. Arluke, A Summary of Parole Rules—Thirteen Years Later, 15 Crime & Delin. 267, 272-273 (1969).

The parole officers are part of the administrative system designed to assist parolees and to offer them guidance. The conditions of parole serve a dual purpose; they prohibit, either absolutely or conditionally, behavior that is deemed dangerous to the restoration of the individual into normal society. And through the requirement of reporting to the parole officer and seeking guidance and permission before doing many things, the officer is provided with information about the parolee and an opportunity to advise him. The combination puts the parole officer into the position in which he can try to guide the parolee into constructive development.[3]

The enforcement leverage that supports the parole conditions derives from the authority to return the parolee to prison to serve out the balance of his sentence if he fails to abide by the rules. In practice, not every violation of parole conditions automatically leads to revocation. Typically, a parolee will be counseled to abide by the conditions of parole, and the parole officer ordinarily

---

2 See Warren, Probation in the Federal System of Criminal Justice, 19 Fed. Prob. 3 (Sept. 1955); Annual Report, Ohio Adult Parole Authority 1964/65, pp. 13-14; Note, Parole: A Critique of Its Legal Foundations and Conditions, 38 N.Y.U.L.Rev. 702, 705-707 (1963).

3 Note, Observations on the Administration of Parole, 79 Yale L. J. 698, 699-700 (1970).

does not take steps to have parole revoked unless he thinks that the violations are serious and continuing so as to indicate that the parolee is not adjusting properly and cannot be counted on to avoid antisocial activity.[4] The broad discretion accorded the parole officer is also inherent in some of the quite vague conditions, such as the typical requirement that the parolee avoid "undesirable" associations or correspondence. Cf. Arciniega v. Freeman, 404 U.S. 4 (1971). Yet revocation of parole is not an unusual phenomenon, affecting only a few parolees. It has been estimated that 35%-45% of all parolees are subjected to revocation and returned to prison.[5] Sometimes revocation occurs when the parolee is accused of another crime; it is often preferred to a new prosecution because of the procedural ease of recommitting the individual on the basis of a lesser showing by the State.[6]

Implicit in the system's concern with parole violations is the notion that the parolee is entitled to retain his liberty as long as he substantially abides by the conditions of his parole. The first step in a revocation decision thus involves a wholly retrospective factual question: whether the parolee has in fact acted in violation of one or more conditions of his parole. Only if it is determined that the parolee did violate the conditions does the second question arise: should the parolee be recommitted to prison or should other steps be taken to protect society and improve chances of rehabilitation? The first step is relatively simple; the second is more complex. The second question involves the application of expertise by the parole authority in making a prediction as to the ability of the individual to live in society without committing antisocial acts. This part of the decision, too, depends on facts, and therefore it is important for the board to know not only that some violation was committed but also to know accurately how many and how serious the violations were. Yet this second step, deciding what to do about the violation once it is identified, is not purely factual but also predictive and discretionary.

If a parolee is returned to prison, he usually receives no credit for the time "served" on parole.[7] Thus, the returnee may force a potential term of substantial imprisonment.

II

We begin with the proposition that the revocation of parole is not part of a criminal prosecution and thus the full panoply of rights due a defendant in such a proceeding does not apply to parole revocations. Cf. Mempa v. Rhay, 389 U.S. 128 (1967). Parole arises after the end of the criminal prosecution, including imposition of sentence. Supervision is not directly by the court but by an administrative agency, which is sometimes an arm of the court and sometimes of the executive. Revocation

---

4 Ibid.

5 President's Commission on Law Enforcement and Administration of Justice, Task Force Report: Corrections 62 (1967). The substantial revocation rate indicates that parole administrators often deliberately err on the side of granting parole in borderline cases.

6 See Morrissey v. Brewer, 443 F.2d 942, at 953-954, n. 5 (CA8 1971) (Lay, J., dissenting); Rose v. Haskins, 45 Ohio Op.2d 395, 388 F.2d 91, 104 (CA6 1968) (Celebrezze, J., dissenting).

7 Arluke, A Summary of Parole Rules—Thirteen Years Later, 15 Crime and Delinquency 267, 271 (1969); Note, Parole Revocation in the Federal System, 56 Geo. L. J. 705, 733 (1968).

deprives an individual, not of the absolute liberty to which every citizen is entitled, but only of the conditional liberty properly dependent on observance of special parole restrictions.

We turn, therefore, to the question whether the requirements of due process in general apply to parole revocations. As MR. JUSTICE BLACKMUN has written recently, "this Court now has rejected the concept that constitutional rights turn upon whether a governmental benefit is characterized as a 'right' or as a 'privilege.'" Graham v. Richardson, 403 U.S. 365, 374 (1971). Whether any procedural protections are due depends on the extent to which an individual will be "condemned to suffer grievous loss." Joint Anti-Fascist Refugee Committee v. McGrath, 341 U.S. 123, 168 (1951) (Frankfurter, J., concurring), quoted in Goldberg v. Kelly, 397 U.S. 254, 263 (1970). The question is not merely the "weight" of the individual's interest, but whether the nature of the interest is one within the contemplation of the "liberty or property" language of the Fourteenth Amendment. Fuentes v. Shevin, 407 U.S. 67 (1972). Once it is determined that due process applies, the question remains what process is due. It has been said so often by this Court and others as not to require citation of authority that due process is flexible and calls for such procedural protections as the particular situation demands. "[C]onsideration of what procedures due process may require under any given set of circumstances must begin with a determination of the precise nature of the government function involved as well as of the private interest that has been affected by governmental action." Cafeteria & Restaurant Workers Union v. McElroy, 367 U.S. 886, 895 (1961). To say that the concept of due process is flexible does not mean that judges are at large to apply it to any and all relationships. Its flexibility is in its scope once it has been determined that some process is due; it is a recognition that not all situations calling for procedural safeguards call for the same kind of procedure.

We turn to an examination of the nature of the interest of the parolee in his continued liberty. The liberty of a parolee enables him to do a wide range of things open to persons who have never been convicted of any crime. The parolee has been released from prison based on an evaluation that he shows reasonable promise of being able to return to society and function as a responsible, self-reliant person. Subject to the conditions of his parole, he can be gainfully employed and is free to be with family and friends and to form the other enduring attachments of normal life. Though the State properly subjects him to many restrictions not applicable to other citizens, his condition is very different from that of confinement in a prison.[8] He may have been on parole for a number of years and may be living a relatively normal life at the time he is faced with revocation.[9] The parolee has relied on at least an implicit promise that parole will be revoked only if he fails to live up to the parole conditions. In many cases, the parolee faces

---

[8] "It is not sophistic to attach greater importance to a person's justifiable reliance in maintaining his conditional freedom so long as he abides by the conditions of his release, than to his mere anticipation or hope of freedom." United States ex rel. Bey v. Connecticut Board of Parole, 443 F.2d 1079, 1086 (CA2 1971).

[9] See, e.g., Murray v. Page, 429 F.2d 1359 (CA10 1970) (parole revoked after eight years; 15 years remaining on original term).

lengthy incarceration if his parole is revoked.

We see, therefore, that the liberty of a parolee, although indeterminate, includes many of the core values of unqualified liberty and its termination inflicts a "grievous loss" on the parolee and often on others. It is hardly useful any longer to try to deal with this problem in terms of whether the parolee's liberty is a "right" or a "privilege." By whatever name, the liberty is valuable and must be seen as within the protection of the Fourteenth Amendment. Its termination calls for some orderly process, however informal.

Turning to the question what process is due, we find that the State's interests are several. The State has found the parolee guilty of a crime against the people. That finding justifies imposing extensive restrictions on the individual's liberty. Release of the parolee before the end of his prison sentence is made with the recognition that with many prisoners there is a risk that they will not be able to live in society without committing additional antisocial acts. Given the previous conviction and the proper imposition of conditions, the State has an overwhelming interest in being able to return the individual to imprisonment without the burden of a new adversary criminal trial if in fact he has failed to abide by the conditions of his parole.

Yet, the State has no interest in revoking parole without some informal procedural guarantees. Although the parolee is often formally described as being "in custody," the argument cannot even be made here that summary treatment is necessary as it may be with respect to controlling a large group of potentially disruptive prisoners in actual custody. Nor are we persuaded by the argument that revocation is so

totally a discretionary matter that some form of hearing would be administratively intolerable. A simple factual hearing will not interfere with the exercise of discretion. Serious studies have suggested that fair treatment on parole revocation will not result in fewer grants of parole.[10]

This discretionary aspect of the revocation decision need not be reached unless there is first an appropriate determination that the individual has in fact breached the conditions of parole. The parolee is not the only one who has a stake in his conditional liberty. Society has a stake in whatever may be the chance of restoring him to normal and useful life within the law. Society thus has an interest in not having parole revoked because of erroneous information or because of an erroneous evaluation of the need to revoke parole, given the breach of parole conditions. See People ex rel. Menechino v. Warden, 27 N.Y.2d 376, 379 and n. 2, 267 N.E.2d 238, 239, and n. 2 (1971) (parole board had less than full picture of facts). And society has a further interest in treating the parolee with basic fairness: fair treatment in parole revocations will enhance the chance of rehabilitation by avoiding reactions to arbitrariness.[11]

---

10 Sklar, Law and Practice in Probation and Parole Revocation Hearings, 55 J. Crim. L. C. & P. S. 175, 194 (1964) (no decrease in Michigan, which grants extensive rights); Rose v. Haskins, 45 Ohio Op.2d 395, 388 F.2d 91, 102 n. 16 (CA6 1968) (Celebrezze, J., dissenting) (cost of imprisonment so much greater than parole system that procedural requirements will not change economic motivation).

11 See President's Commission on Law Enforcement and Administration of Justice, Task Force Report: Corrections 83, 88 (1967).

Given these factors, most States have recognized that there is no interest on the part of the State in revoking parole without any procedural guarantees at all.[12] What is needed is an informal hearing structured to assure that the finding of a parole violation will be based on verified facts and that the exercise of discretion will be informed by an accurate knowledge of the parolee's behavior.

III

We now turn to the nature of the process that is due, bearing in mind that the interest of both State and parolee will be furthered by an effective but informal hearing. In analyzing what is due, we see two important stages in the typical process of parole revocation.

(a) Arrest of Parolee and Preliminary Hearing. The first stage occurs when the parolee is arrested and detained, usually at the direction of his parole officer. The second occurs when parole is formally revoked. There is typically a substantial time lag between the arrest and the eventual determination by the parole board whether parole should be revoked. Additionally, it may be that the parolee is arrested at a place distant from the state institution, to which he may be returned before the final decision is made concerning revocation. Given these factors, due process would

seem to require that some minimal inquiry be conducted at or reasonably near the place of the alleged parole violation or arrest and as promptly as convenient after arrest while information is fresh and sources are available. Cf. Hyser v. Reed, 115 U.S. App. D.C. 254, 318 F.2d 225 (1963). Such an inquiry should be seen as in the nature of a "preliminary hearing" to determine whether there is probable cause or reasonable ground to believe that the arrested parolee has committed acts that would constitute a violation of parole conditions. Cf. Goldberg v. Kelly, 397 U.S., at 267-271.

In our view, due process requires that after the arrest, the determination that reasonable ground exists for revocation of parole should be made by someone not directly involved in the case. It would be unfair to assume that the supervising parole officer does not conduct an interview with the parolee to confront him with the reasons for revocation before he recommends an arrest. It would also be unfair to assume that the parole officer bears hostility against the parolee that destroys his neutrality; realistically the failure of the parolee is in a sense a failure for his supervising officer.[13] However, we need make no assumptions one way or the other to conclude that there should be an uninvolved person to make this preliminary evaluation of the basis for believing the conditions of parole have been violated. The officer directly involved in making recommendations cannot always have complete objec-

---

12 See n. 15, *infra.* As one state court has written, "Before such a determination or finding can be made it appears that the principles of fundamental justice and fairness would afford the parolee a reasonable opportunity to explain away the accusation of a parole violation. [The parolee] . . . is entitled to a conditional liberty and possessed of a right which can be forfeited only by reason of a breach of the conditions of the grant." Chase v. Page, 456 P.2d 590, 594 (Okla. Crim. App. 1969).

13 Note, Observations on the Administration of Parole, 79 Yale L. J. 698, 704-706 (1970) (parole officers in Connecticut adopt role model of social worker rather than an adjunct of police, and exhibit a lack of punitive orientation).

tivity in evaluating them.[14] Goldberg v. Kelly found it unnecessary to impugn the motives of the caseworker to find a need for an independent decisionmaker to examine the initial decision.

This independent officer need not be a judicial officer. The granting and revocation of parole are matters traditionally handled by administrative officers. In Goldberg, the Court pointedly did not require that the hearing on termination of benefits be conducted by a judicial officer or even before the traditional "neutral and detached" officer; it required only that the hearing be conducted by some person *other* than one initially dealing with the case. It will be sufficient, therefore, in the parole revocation context, if an evaluation of whether reasonable cause exists to believe that conditions of parole have been violated is made by someone such as a parole officer other than the one who has made the report of parole violations or has recommended revocation. A State could certainly choose some other independent decisionmaker to perform this preliminary function.

With respect to the preliminary hearing before this officer, the parolee should be given notice that the hearing will take place and that its purpose is to determine whether there is probable cause to believe he has committed a parole violation. The notice should state what parole violations have been alleged. At the hearing the parolee may appear and speak in his own behalf; he may bring letters, documents, or individuals who can give relevant information to the hearing officer. On request

of the parolee, a person who has given adverse information on which parole revocation is to be based is to be made available for questioning in his presence. However, if the hearing officer determines that an informant would be subjected to risk of harm if his identity were disclosed, he need not be subjected to confrontation and cross-examination.

The hearing officer shall have the duty of making a summary, or digest, of what occurs at the hearing in terms of the responses of the parolee and the substance of the documents or evidence given in support of parole revocation and of the parolee's position. Based on the information before him, the officer should determine whether there is probable cause to hold the parolee for the final decision of the parole board on revocation. Such a determination would be sufficient to warrant the parolee's continued detention and return to the state correctional institution pending the final decision. As in Goldberg, "the decision maker should state the reasons for his determination and indicate the evidence he relied on . . ." but it should be remembered that this is not a final determination calling for "formal findings of fact and conclusions of law." 397 U.S., at 271. No interest would be served by formalism in this process; informality will not lessen the utility of this inquiry in reducing the risk of error.

(b) The Revocation Hearing. There must also be an opportunity for a hearing, if it is desired by the parolee, prior to the final decision on revocation by the parole authority. This hearing must be the basis for more than determining probable cause; it must lead to a final evaluation of any contested relevant facts and consideration of whether the facts as determined warrant revocation.

---

14 This is not an issue limited to bad motivation. "Parole agents are human, and it is possible that friction between the agent and parolee may have influenced the agent's judgment." 4 Attorney General's Survey on Release Procedures: Parole 246 (1939).

The parolee must have an opportunity to be heard and to show, if he can, that he did not violate the conditions, or, if he did, that circumstances in mitigation suggest that the violation does not warrant revocation. The revocation hearing must be tendered within a reasonable time after the parolee is taken into custody. A lapse of two months, as respondents suggest occurs in some cases, would not appear to be unreasonable.

We cannot write a code of procedure; that is the responsibility of each State. Most States have done so by legislation, others by judicial decision usually on due process grounds.[15] Our

task is limited to deciding the minimum requirements of due process. They include (a) written notice of the claimed violations of parole; (b) disclosure to the parolee of evidence against him; (c) opportunity to be heard in person and to present witnesses and documentary evidence; (d) the right to confront and cross-examine adverse witnesses (unless the hearing officer specifically finds good cause for not allowing confrontation); (e) a "neutral and detached" hearing body such as a traditional parole board, members of which need not be judicial officers or lawyers; and (f) a written statement by the factfinders as to the evidence relied on and reasons for revoking parole. We emphasize there is no thought to equate this second stage of parole revocation to a criminal prosecution in any sense. It is a narrow inquiry; the process should be flexible enough to consider evidence including letters, affidavits, and other material that would not be admissible in an adversary criminal trial.

We do not reach or decide the question whether the parolee is entitled to the assistance of retained counsel or to

---

15 Very few States provide no hearing at all in parole revocations. Thirty States provide in their statutes that a parolee shall receive some type of hearing. See Ala. Code, Tit. 42, § 12 (1959); Alaska Stat. § 33.15.220 (1962); Ariz. Rev. Stat. Ann. § 31-417 (1956); Ark. Stat. Ann. § 43-2810 (Supp. 1971); Del. Code Ann., Tit. 11, § 4352 (Supp. 1970); Fla. Stat. Ann. § 947.23(1) (Supp. 1972); Ga. Code Ann. § 77-519 (Supp. 1971); Haw. Rev. Stat. § 353-66 (1968); Idaho Code §§ 20-229, 20-229A (Supp. 1971); Ill. Ann. Stat., c. 108, §§ 204(e), 207 (Supp. 1972); Ind. Ann. Stat. § 13-1611 (Supp. 1972); Kan. Stat. Ann. § 22-3721 (1971); Ky. Rev. Stat. Ann. § 439.330(1)(e) (1962); La. Rev. Stat. Ann. § 15:574.9 (Supp. 1972); Me. Rev. Stat. Ann., Tit. 34, § 1675 (Supp. 1970-1971); Md. Ann. Code, Art. 41, § 117 (1971); Mich. Comp. Laws § 791.240a, Mich. Stat. Ann. § 28.2310(1) (Supp. 1972); Miss. Code Ann. § 4004-13 (1956); Mo. Ann. Stat. § 549.265 (Supp. 1971); Mont. Rev. Codes Ann. §§ 94-9838, 94-9835 (1969); N. H. Rev. Stat. Ann. § 607:46 (1955); N. M. Stat. Ann. § 41-17-28 (1972); N. Y. Correc. Law § 212 subd. 7 (Supp. 1971); N. D. Cent. Code § 12-59-15 (Supp. 1971); Pa. Stat. Ann., Tit. 61, § 331.21a(b) (1964) Tenn. Code Ann. § 40-3619 (1955); Tex. Code Crim. Proc., Art. 42.12, § 22 (1966); Vt. Stat. Ann., Tit. 28, § 1081(b) (1970); Wash. Rev. Code §§ 9.95.120 through 9.95.126 (Supp. 1971); W. Va. Code Ann.

§ 62-12-19 (1966). Decisions of state and federal courts have required a number of other States to provide hearings. See Hutchison v. Patterson, 267 F.Supp. 433 (Colo. 1967) (approving parole board regulations); United States ex rel. Bey v. Connecticut State Board of Parole, 443 F.2d 1079 (CA 2 1971) (requiring counsel to be appointed for revocation hearings); State v. Holmes, 109 N.J. Super. 180, 262 A.2d 725 (1970); Chase v. Page, 456 P.2d 590 (Okla. Crim. App. 1969); Bearden v. South Carolina, 443 F.2d 1090 (CA4 1971); Baine v. Beckstead, 10 Utah 2d 4, 347 P.2d 554 (1959); Goolsby v. Gagnon, 322 F.Supp. 460 (ED Wis. 1971). A number of States are affected by no legal requirement to grant any kind of hearing.

appointed counsel if he is indigent.[16]

We have no thought to create an inflexible structure for parole revocation procedures. The few basic requirements set out above, which are applicable to future revocations of parole, should not impose a great burden on any State's parole system. Control over the required proceedings by the hearing officers can assure that delaying tactics and other abuses sometimes present in the traditional adversary trial situation do not occur. Obviously a parolee cannot relitigate issues determined against him in other forums, as in the situation presented when the revocation is based on conviction of another crime.

In the peculiar posture of this case, given the absence of an adequate record, we conclude the ends of justice will be best served by remanding the case to the Court of Appeals for its return of the two consolidated cases to the District Court with directions to make findings on the procedures actually followed by the Parole Board in these two revocations. If it is determined that petitioners admitted parole violations to the Parole Board, as respondents contend, and if those violations are found to be reasonable grounds for revoking parole under state standards, that would end the matter. If the procedures followed by the Parole Board are found to meet the standards laid down in this opinion that, too, would dispose of the due process claims for these cases.

We reverse and remand to the Court of Appeals for further proceedings consistent with this opinion.

Reversed and remanded.

MR. JUSTICE BRENNAN, with whom MR. JUSTICE MARSHALL joins, concurring in the result.

I agree that a parole may not be revoked, consistently with the Due Process Clause, unless the parolee is afforded, first, a preliminary hearing at the time of arrest to determine whether there is probable cause to believe that he has violated his parole conditions and, second, a final hearing within a reasonable time to determine whether he has, in fact, violated those conditions and whether his parole should be revoked. For each hearing the parolee is entitled to notice of the violations alleged and the evidence against him, opportunity to be heard in person and to present witnesses and documentary evidence, and the right to confront and cross-examine adverse witnesses, unless it is specifically found that a witness would thereby be exposed to a significant risk of harm. Moreover, in each case the decisionmaker must be impartial, there must be some record of the proceedings, and the decisionmaker's conclusions must be set forth in written form indicating both the evidence and the reasons relied upon. Because the Due Process Clause requires these procedures, I agree that the case must be remanded as the Court orders.

The Court, however, states that it does not now decide whether the parolee is also entitled at each hearing to the assistance of retained counsel or of appointed counsel if he is indigent. Goldberg v. Kelly, 397 U.S. 254 (1970), nonetheless plainly dictates that he at least "must be allowed to retain an attorney if he so desires." *Id.*, at 270. As the Court said there, "Counsel can help

---

16 The Model Penal Code § 305.15(1) (Proposed Official Draft 1962) provides that "[t]he institutional parole staff shall render reasonable aid to the parolee in preparation for the hearing and he shall be permitted to advise with his own legal counsel."

delineate the issues, present the factual contentions in an orderly manner, conduct cross-examination, and generally safeguard the interests of" his client. *Id.*, at 270-271. The only question open under our precedents is whether counsel must be furnished the parolee if he is indigent.

Mr. Justice Douglas, dissenting in part.

Each petitioner was sentenced for a term in an Iowa penitentiary for forgery. Somewhat over a year later each was released on parole. About six months later, each was arrested for a parole violation and confined in a local jail. In about a week, the Iowa Board of Parole revoked their paroles and each was returned to the penitentiary. At no time during any of the proceedings which led to the parole revocations were they granted a hearing or the opportunity to know, question, or challenge any of the facts which formed the basis of their alleged parole violations. Nor were they given an opportunity to present evidence on their own behalf or to confront and cross-examine those on whose testimony their paroles were revoked.

Each challenged the revocation in the state courts and, obtaining no relief, filed the present petitions in the Federal District Court, which denied relief. Their appeals were consolidated in the Court of Appeals which, sitting en banc, in each case affirmed the District Court by a four-to-three vote, 443 F.2d 942. The cases are here on a petition for a writ of certiorari, 404 U.S. 999, which we granted because there is a conflict between the decision below and Hahn v. Burke, 430 F.2d 100, decided by the Court of Appeals for the Seventh Circuit.

Iowa has a board of parole[1] which determines who shall be paroled. Once paroled, a person is under the supervision of the director of the division of corrections of the Department of Social Services, who, in turn, supervises parole agents. Parole agents do not revoke the parole of any person but only recommend that the board of parole revoke it. The Iowa Act provides that each parolee "shall be subject, at any time, to be taken into custody and returned to the institution" from which he was paroled.[2] Thus, Iowa requires no notice or hearing to put a parolee back in prison, Curtis v. Bennett, 256 Iowa 1164, 131 N.W.2d 1; and it is urged that since parole, like probation, is only a privilege it may be summarily revoked.[3] See Escoe v. Zerbst,

---

1 Iowa Code § 247.5 (1971) provides in part:

"The board of parole shall determine which of the inmates of the state penal institutions qualify and thereafter shall be placed upon parole. Once an inmate is placed on parole he shall be under the supervision of the director of the division of corrections of the department of social services. There shall be a sufficient number of parole agents to insure proper supervision of all persons placed on parole. Parole agents shall not revoke the parole of any person but may recommend that the board of parole revoke such parole."

2 *Id.*, § 247.9 provides in part:

"All paroled prisoners shall remain, while on parole, in the legal custody of the warden or superintendent and under the control of the chief parole officer, and shall be subject, at any time, to be taken into custody and returned to the institution from which they were paroled."

3 "A fundamental problem with [the right-privilege] theory is that probation is now the most frequent penal disposition just as release on parole is the most frequent form of release from an institution. They bear little resemblance to episodic acts of mercy by a forgiving sovereign. A more accurate view of supervised release is that it is now an integral part of the criminal justice

295 U.S. 490, 492-493; Ughbanks v. Armstrong, 208 U.S. 481. But we have long discarded the right-privilege distinction. See, *e.g.*, Graham v. Richardson, 403 U.S. 365, 374; Bell v. Burson, 402 U.S. 535, 539; Pickering v. Board of Education, 391 U.S. 563, 568; cf. Van Alstyne, The Demise of the Right-Privilege Distinction in Constitutional Law, 81 Harv. L. Rev. 1439 (1968).

The Court said in United States v. Wilson, 7 Pet. 150, 161, that a "pardon is a deed." The same can be said of a parole, which when conferred gives the parolee a degree of liberty which is often associated with property interests.

We held in Goldberg v. Kelly, 397 U.S. 254, that the termination by a State of public assistance payments to a recipient without a prior evidentiary hearing denies him procedural due process in violation of the Fourteenth Amendment. Speaking of the termination of welfare benefits we said:

"Their termination involves state action that adjudicates important rights. The constitutional challenge cannot be answered by an argument that public assistance benefits are 'a "privilege" and not a "right."' Shapiro v. Thompson, 394 U.S. 618, 627 n. 6 (1969). Relevant constitutional restraints apply as much to the with-

drawal of public assistance benefits as to disqualification for unemployment compensation, Sherbert v. Verner, 374 U.S. 398 (1963); or to denial of a tax exemption, Speiser v. Randall, 357 U.S. 513 (1958); or to discharge from public employment, Slochower v. Board of Higher Education, 350 U.S. 551 (1956). The extent to which procedural due process must be afforded the recipient is influenced by the extent to which he may be 'condemned to suffer grievous loss,' Joint Anti-Fascist Refugee Committee v. McGrath, 341 U.S. 123, 168 (1951) (Frankfurter, J., concurring), and depends upon whether the recipient's interest in avoiding that loss outweighs the governmental interest in summary adjudication. Accordingly, as we said in Cafeteria & Restaurant Workers Union v. McElroy, 367 U.S. 886, 895 (1961), 'consideration of what procedures due process may require under any given set of circumstances must begin with a determination of the precise nature of the government function involved as well as of the private interest that has been affected by governmental action.' See also Hannah v. Larche, 363 U.S. 420, 440, 442 (1960)." 397 U.S., at 262-263.

Under modern concepts of penology, paroling prisoners is part of the rehabilitative aim of the correctional philosophy. The objective is to return a prisoner to a full family and community life. See generally Note, Parole Revocation in the Federal System, 56 Geo. L. J. 705 (1968); Note, Parole: A Critique of Its Legal Foundations and Conditions, 38 N.Y. U. L. Rev. 702 (1963); Comment, 72 Yale L. J. 368 (1962); and see Baine v. Beckstead, 10 Utah 2d 4, 347 P.2d 554 (1959). The status he enjoys as a parolee is as important a right

---

process and shows every sign of increasing popularity. Seen in this light, the question becomes whether legal safeguards should be provided for hundreds of thousands of individuals who daily are processed and regulated by governmental agencies. The system has come to depend on probation and parole as much as do those who are enmeshed in the system. Thus, in dealing with claims raised by offenders, we should make decisions based not on an outworn cliche but on the basis of present-day realities." F. Cohen, The Legal Challenge to Corrections: Implications for Manpower and Training 32 (Joint Commission on Correctional Manpower and Training 1969).

as those we reviewed in Goldberg v. Kelly. That status is conditioned upon not engaging in certain activities and perhaps in not leaving a certain area or locality. Violations of conditions of parole may be technical, they may be done unknowingly, they may be fleeting and of no consequence.[4] See, e.g., Arciniega v. Freeman, 404 U.S. 4; Cohen, Due Process, Equal Protection and State Parole Revocation Proceedings, 42 U. Colo. L. Rev. 197, 229 (1970). The parolee should, in the concept of fairness implicit in due process, have a chance to explain. Rather, under Iowa's rule revocation proceeds on the *ipse dixit* of the parole agent; and on his word alone each of these petitioners has already served three additional years in prison.[5] The charges may or may not be true. Words of explanation may be adequate to transform into trivia what looms large in the mind of the parole officer.

"[T]here is no place in our system of law for reaching a result of such tremendous consequences without ceremony—without hearing, without effective assistance of counsel, without a statement of reasons." Kent v. United States, 383 U.S. 541, 554 (1966).

---

[4] The violations alleged in these cases on which revocation was based are listed by the Court of Appeals, 443 F.2d 942, 943-944, nn. 1 and 2.

For a discussion of the British system that dispenses with precise conditions usually employed here see 120 U. Pa. L. Rev. 282, 311-312 (1971). As to conditions limiting constitutional rights see *id.*, at 313-324, 326-339.

[5] As to summary deprivations of individual liberty in Communist nations, see, e.g., Shao-chuan Leng, Justice In Communist China 34 (1967); 1 P. Tang, Communist China Today 271 (2d ed. 1961); J. Hazard, Communists and Their Law 121-126 (1969).

Parole,[6] while originally conceived as a judicial function, has become largely an administrative matter. The parole boards have broad discretion in formulating and imposing parole conditions. "Often vague and moralistic, parole conditions may seem oppressive and unfair to the parolee." R. Dawson, Sentencing 306 (1969). They are drawn "to cover any contingency that might occur," *id.*, at 307, and are designed to maximize "control over the parolee by his parole officer." *Ibid.*

Parole is commonly revoked on mere suspicion that the parolee may have committed a crime. *Id.*, at 366-367. Such great control over the parolee vests in a parole officer a broad discretion in revoking parole and also in counseling the parolee—referring him for psychiatric treatment or obtaining the use of specialized therapy for narcotic addicts or alcoholics. *Id.*, at 321. Treatment of the parolee, rather than revocation of his parole, is a common course. *Id.*, at 322-323. Counseling may include extending help to a parolee in finding a job. *Id.*, at 324 *et seq.*

A parolee, like a prisoner, is a person entitled to constitutional protection, including procedural due process.[7] At the federal level, the construction of regulations of the Federal Parole Board presents federal questions of which we have taken cognizance. See Arciniega

---

[6] "Parole is used after a sentence has been imposed while probation is usually granted in lieu of a prison term." R. Clegg, Probation and Parole 22 (1964). See Baine v. Beckstead, 10 Utah 2d 4, 9, 347 P.2d 554, 558; People ex rel. Combs v. LaVallee, 29 App. Div. 2d 128, 131, 286 N.Y.S. 2d 600, 603.

[7] See President's Commission on Law Enforcement and Administration of Justice, Task Force Report: Corrections 83, 84 (1967); 120 U. Pa. L. Rev. 282, 348-358 (1971).

v. Freeman, 404 U.S. 4. At the state level, the construction of parole statutes and regulations is for the States alone, save as they implicate the Federal Constitution in which event the Supremacy Clause controls.

It is only procedural due process, required by the Fourteenth Amendment, that concerns us in the present cases. Procedural due process requires the following.

If a violation of a condition of parole is involved, rather than the commission of a new offense, there should not be an arrest of the parolee and his return to the prison or to a local jail.[8] Rather, notice of the alleged violation should be given to the parolee and a time set for a hearing.[9] The hearing should not be before the parole officer, as he is the one who is making the charge and "there is inherent danger in combining the functions of judge and advocate." Jones v. Rivers, 338 F.2d 862, 877 (CA4 1964) (Sobeloff, J., concurring). Moreover, the parolee should

be entitled to counsel.[10] See Hewett v. North Carolina, 415 F.2d 1316, 1322-

findings, the evidence used to prove the Government's case must be disclosed to the individual so that he has an opportunity to show that it is untrue. While this is important in the case of documentary evidence, it is even more important where the evidence consists of the testimony of individuals whose memory might be faulty or who, in fact, might be perjurers or persons motivated by malice, vindictiveness, intolerance, prejudice, or jealousy. We have formalized these protections in the requirements of confrontation and cross-examination. They have ancient roots. They find expression in the Sixth Amendment which provides that in all criminal cases the accused shall enjoy the right 'to be confronted with the witnesses against him.' This Court has been zealous to protect these rights from erosion. It has spoken out not only in criminal cases, but also in all types of cases where administrative and regulatory actions were under scrutiny." (Citations omitted).

---

[8] As Judge Skelly Wright said in Hyser v. Reed, 115 U.S. App. D.C. 254, 291, 318 F.2d 225, 262 (1963) (concurring in part and dissenting in part):

"Where serious violations of parole have been committed, the parolee will have been arrested by local or federal authorities on charges stemming from those violations. Where the violation of parole is not serious, no reason appears why he should be incarcerated before hearing. If, of course, the parolee willfully fails to appear for his hearing, this in itself would justify issuance of the warrant." Accord, In re Tucker, 5 Cal. 3d 171, 199-200, 486 P.2d 657, 676 (1971) (Tobriner, J., concurring and dissenting).

[9] As we said in another connection in Greene v. McElroy, 360 U.S. 474, 496-497:

"Certain principles have remained relatively immutable in our jurisprudence. One of these is that where governmental action seriously injures an individual, and the reasonableness of the action depends on fact

[10] American Bar Association Project on Standards for Criminal Justice, Providing Defense Services 43 (Approved Draft 1968); Model Penal Code § 301.4, § 305.15 (1) (Proposed Official Draft 1962); R. Dawson, Sentencing (1969). For the experience of Michigan in giving hearings to parolees see id., at 355. In Michigan, it is estimated that only one out of six parole violators retains counsel. One who cannot afford counsel is said to be protected by the hearing members of the board. Id., at 354. The number who ask for public hearings are typically five or six a year, the largest in a single year being 10. Michigan has had this law since 1937. Id., at 355. But the Michigan experience may not be typical, for a parole violator is picked up and returned at once to the institution from which he was paroled. Id., at 352-353.

By way of contrast, parole revocation hearings in California are secretive affairs conducted behind closed doors and with no written record of the proceedings and in which the parolee is denied the assistance of counsel and the opportunity to present witnesses on his behalf. Van Dyke, Parole Hearings in California: The Right to Counsel, 59 Calif. L. Rev. 1215 (1971). See also Note, 56 Geo. L. J. 705 (1968) (federal parole revocation procedures).

1325 (CA4 1969); People ex rel. Combs v. LaVallee, 29 App. Div. 2d 128, 286 N.Y.S. 2d 600 (1968); Perry v. Williard, 247 Ore. 145, 427 P.2d 1020 (1967). As the Supreme Court of Oregon said in Perry v. Williard, "A hearing in which counsel is absent or is present only on behalf of one side is inherently unsatisfactory if not unfair. Counsel can see that relevant facts are brought out, vague and insubstantial allegations discounted, and irrelevancies eliminated." Id., at 148, 427 P.2d at 1022. Cf. Mempa v. Rhay, 389 U.S. 128, 135.

The hearing required is not a grant of the full panoply of rights applicable to a criminal trial. But confrontation with the informer may, as Roviaro v. United States, 353 U.S. 53, illustrates, be necessary for a fair hearing and the ascertainment of the truth. The hearing is to determine the fact of parole violation. The results of the hearing would go to the parole board—or other authorized state agency—for final action, as would cases which involved voluntary admission of violations.

The rule of law is important in the stability of society. Arbitrary actions in the revocation of paroles can only impede and impair the rehabilitative aspects of modern penology. "Notice and opportunity for hearing appropriate to the nature of the case," Boddie v. Connecticut, 401 U.S. 371, 378, are the rudiments of due process which restore faith that our society is run for the many, not the few, and that fair dealing rather than caprice will govern the affairs of men.[11]

I would not prescribe the precise formula for the management of the parole problems. We do not sit as an ombudsman, telling the States the precise procedures they must follow. I would hold that so far as the due process requirements of parole revocation are concerned:[12]

(1) the parole officer—whatever may be his duties under various state statutes—in Iowa appears to be an agent having some of the functions of a prosecutor and of the police: the parole officer is therefore not qualified as a hearing officer;

(2) the parolee is entitled to a due process notice and a due process hearing of the alleged parole violations including, for example, the opportunity to be confronted by his accusers and to present evidence and argument on his own behalf; and

(3) the parolee is entitled to the freedom granted a parolee until the results of the hearing are known and the parole board—or other authorized state agency—acts.[13]

---

11 The Brief of the American Civil Liberties Union, amicus curiae, contains in Appendix A the States that by statute or decision require some form of hearing before parole is revoked and those that do not. All but nine States now hold hearings on revocation of probation and parole, some with trial-type rights including representation by counsel.

12 We except of course the commission of another offense which from the initial step to the end is governed by the normal rules of criminal procedure.

13 The American Correctional Association states in its Manual of Correctional Standards 279 (3d ed. 1966) that:

"To an even greater extent than in the case of imprisonment, probation and parole practice is determined by an administrative discretion that is largely uncontrolled by legal standards, protections, or remedies. Until statutory and case law are more fully developed, it is vitally important within all of the correctional fields that there should be established and maintained reasonable norms and remedies against the sorts of abuses that are likely to develop where men have great power over their fellows and where relationships may become both mechanical and arbitrary."

And it provides for parole revocation hearings:

"As soon as practicable after causing an

I would reverse the judgments and remand for further consideration in light of this opinion.

alleged violator [to be] taken into custody on the basis of a parole board warrant, the prisoner should be given an opportunity to appear before the board or its representative. The prisoner should be made fully aware of the reasons for the warrant, and given ample opportunity to refute the charges placed against him or to comment as to extenuating circumstances. The hearing should be the basis for consideration of possible reinstatement to parole supervision on the basis of the findings of fact or of reparole where it appears that further incarceration would serve no useful purpose." *Id.,* at 130.

The American Bar Association states at p. 10 of its brief *amicus* in the present cases that it is "in full agreement with the American Correctional Association in this instance. The position that a hearing is to be afforded on parole revocation is consistent with several sets of criminal justice standards formally approved by the Association through its House of Delegates."

GAGNON v. SCARPELLI
411 U.S. 778, 93 S. Ct. 1756, 36 L. Ed. 2d 656 (1973)

MR. JUSTICE POWELL delivered the opinion of the Court.

This case presents the related questions whether a previously sentenced probationer is entitled to a hearing when his probation is revoked and, if so, whether he is entitled to be represented by appointed counsel at such a hearing.

I

Respondent, Gerald Scarpelli, pleaded guilty in July, 1965, to a charge of armed robbery in Wisconsin. The trial judge sentenced him to 15 years' imprisonment, but suspended the sentence and placed him on probation for seven years in the custody of the Wisconsin Department of Public Welfare ("the Department"). At that time, he signed an agreement specifying the terms of his probation and a "Travel Permit and Agreement to Return" allowing him to reside in Illinois, with supervision there under an interstate compact. On August 5, 1965, he was accepted for supervision by the Adult Probation Department of Cook County, Illinois.

On August 6, respondent was apprehended by Illinois police, who had surprised him and one Fred Kleckner, Jr., in the course of the burglary of a house. After being apprised of his constitutional rights, respondent admitted that he and Kleckner had broken into the house for the purpose of stealing merchandise or money, although he now asserts that his statement was made under duress and is false. Probation was revoked by the Wisconsin Department on September 1, without a hearing. The stated grounds for revocation were that:

"1. [Scarpelli] has associated with known criminals, in direct violation of his probation regulations and his supervising agent's instructions;

"2. [Scarpelli] while associating with a known criminal, namely Fred Kleckner, Jr., was involved in, and arrested for, a burglary * * * in Deerfield, Illinois." App., p. 20.

On September 4, 1965, he was incarcerated in the Wisconsin State Reformatory at Green Bay to begin serving the 15 years to which he had been sentenced by the trial judge. At no time was he afforded a hearing.

Some three years later, on December

16, 1968, respondent applied for a writ of habeas corpus. After the petition had been filed, but before it had been acted upon, the Department placed respondent on parole.[2] The District Court found that his status as parolee was sufficient custody to confer jurisdiction on the court and that the petition was not moot because the revocation carried "collateral consequences," presumably including the restraints imposed by his parole. On the merits, the District Court held that revocation without a hearing and counsel was a denial of due process. 317 F.Supp. 72 (ED Wis. 1970). The Court of Appeals affirmed, *sub nom.* Gunsolus v. Gagnon, 454 F.2d 416 (CA7 1971), and we granted certiorari. 408 U.S. 921 (1972).

II

Two prior decisions set the bounds of our present inquiry. In Mempha v. Rhay, 389 U.S. 128 (1967), the Court held that a probationer is entitled to be represented by appointed counsel at a combined revocation and sentencing hearing. Reasoning that counsel is required "at every stage of a criminal proceeding where substantial rights of a criminal accused may be affected," 389 U.S., at 134, and that sentencing is one such stage, the Court concluded that counsel must be provided an indigent at sentencing even when it is accomplished as part of a subsequent, probation revocation proceeding. But this line of reasoning does not require a hearing or counsel at the time of probation revocation in a case such as the present one, where the probationer was

sentenced at the time of trial.

Of greater relevance is our decision last Term in Morrissey v. Brewer, 408 U.S. 471 (1972). There we held that the revocation of parole is not a part of a criminal prosecution.

"Parole arises after the end of the criminal prosecution, including imposition of sentence. ° ° ° Revocation deprives an individual, not of the absolute liberty to which every citizen is entitled, but only of the conditional liberty properly dependent on observance of special parole restrictions." 408 U.S., at 480.

Even though the revocation of parole is not a part of the criminal prosecution, we held that the loss of liberty entailed is a serious deprivation requiring that the parolee be accorded due process. Specifically, we held that a parolee is entitled to two hearings, one a preliminary hearing at the time of his arrest and detention to determine whether there is probable cause to believe that he has committed a violation of his parole and the other a somewhat more comprehensive hearing prior to the making of the final revocation decision.

Petitioner does not contend that there is any difference relevant to the guarantee of due process between the revocation of parole and the revocation of probation, nor do we perceive one.[3] Probation revocation, like parole revocation, is not a stage of a criminal prosecution, but does result in a loss of

---

[2] Respondent was initially paroled to a federal detainer to serve a previously imposed federal sentence arising from another conviction. He was subsequently released from federal custody, but remains a parolee under the supervision of the Department.

[3] Despite the undoubted minor difference between probation and parole, the commentators have agreed that revocation of probation where sentence has been imposed previously is constitutionally indistinguishable from the revocation of parole.

• • •

liberty.[4] Accordingly, we hold that a probationer, like a parolee, is entitled to a preliminary and a final revocation hearing, under the conditions specified in Morrissey v. Brewer, *supra*.[5]

III

The second, and more difficult, ques-

[4] It is clear at least after MORRISSEY v. BREWER, *supra*, that a probationer can no longer be denied due process, in reliance on the dictum in ESCOE v. ZERBST, 295 U.S. 490, 492 (1935), that probation is an "act of grace."

[5] Petitioner argues in addition that the MORRISSEY hearing requirements impose serious practical problems in cases such as the present one in which a probationer or parolee is allowed to leave the convicting State for supervision in another State. Such arrangements are made pursuant to an interstate compact adopted by all of the States, including Wisconsin. Wis. Stat. Ann. § 57.13. Petitioner's brief asserts that as of June 30, 1972, Wisconsin had a total of 642 parolees and probationers under supervision in other States and that incomplete statistics as of June 30, 1971, indicated a national total of 24, 693 persons under out-of-state supervision. Petitioner's Brief, pp. 21-22.

Some amount of disruption inevitably attends any new constitutional ruling. We are confident, however, that modification of the interstate compact can remove without undue strain the more serious technical hurdles to compliance with MORRISSEY. An additional comment is warranted with respect to the rights to present witnesses and to confront and cross-examine adverse witnesses. Petitioner's greatest concern is with the difficulty and expenses of procuring witnesses from perhaps thousands of miles away. While in some cases there is simply no adequate alternative to live testimony, we emphasize that we did not in MORRISSEY intend to prohibit use where appropriate of the conventional substitutes for live testimony, including affidavits, depositions, and documentary evidence. Nor did we intend to foreclose the States from holding both the preliminary and the final hearings at the place of violation or from developing other creative solutions to the practical difficulties of the MORRISSEY requirements.

tion posed by this case is whether an indigent probationer or parolee has a due process right to be represented by appointed counsel at these hearings.[6] In answering that question, we draw heavily on the opinion in Morrissey. Our first point of reference is the character of probation or parole. As noted in Morrissey regarding parole, the "purpose is to help individuals reintegrate into society as constructive individuals as soon as they are able * * *" 408 U.S., at 477. The duty and attitude of the probation or parole officer reflect this purpose:

> "While the parole or probation officer recognizes his double duty to the welfare of his clients and to the safety of the general community, by and large concern for the client dominates his professional attitude. The parole agent ordinarily defines his role as representing his client's best interests as long as these do not constitute a threat to public safety."

Because the probation or parole officer's function is not so much to compel conformance to a strict code of behavior as to supervise a course of rehabilitation, he has been entrusted traditionally with broad discretion to judge the progress of rehabilitation in individual cases, and has been armed with the power to recommend or even to declare revocation.

[6] In MORRISSEY v. BREWER, *supra*, we left open the question "whether the parolee is entitled to the assistance of retained counsel or to appointed counsel if he is indigent." 408 U.S., at 489. Since respondent did not attempt to retain counsel but asked only for appointed counsel, we have no occasion to decide in this case whether a probationer or parolee has a right to be represented at a revocation hearing by retained counsel in situations other than those where the State would be obliged to furnish counsel for an indigent.

In Morrissey, we recognized that the revocation decision has two analytically distinct components:

"The first step in a revocation decision involves a wholly retrospective factual question: whether the parolee has in fact acted in violation of one or more conditions of his parole. Only if it is determined that the parolee did violate the conditions does the second question arise: should the parolee be recommitted to prison or should other steps be taken to protect society and improve chances of rehabilitation?" Morrissey v. Brewer, *supra*, 408 U.S., at 479-480.[8]

The parole officer's attitude toward these decisions reflects the rehabilitative rather than punitive focus of the probation/parole system:

"Revocation * * * is, if anything, commonly treated as a failure of supervision. While presumably it

---

8 The factors entering into these decisions relate in major part to a professional evaluation, by trained probation or parole officers, as to the overall social readjustment of the offender in the community, and include consideration of such variables as the offender's relationship toward his family, his attitude toward the fulfillment of financial obligations, the extent of his cooperation with the probation officer assigned to his case, his personal associations, and—of course—whether there have been specific and significant violations of the conditions of the probation. The importance of these considerations, some factual and others entirely judgmental, is illustrated by a Wisconsin empirical study which disclosed that, in the sample studied, probation or parole was revoked in only 34.5% of the cases in which the probationer or parolee violated the terms of his release. S. Hunt, The Revocation Decision: A Study of Probation and Parole Agent's discretion 10 (unpublished thesis on file at the library of the University of Wisconsin) (1964), cited in Petitioner's Brief, Addendum, p. 106.

would be inappropriate for a field agent *never* to revoke, the whole thrust of the probation-parole movement is to keep men in the community, working with adjustment problems there, and using revocation only as a last resort when treatment has failed or is about to fail."

But an exclusive focus on the benevolent attitudes of those who administer the probation/parole system when it is working successfully obscures the modification in attitude which is likely to take place once the officer has decided to recommend revocation. Even though the officer is not by this recommendation converted into a prosecutor committed to convict, his role as counsellor to the probationer or parolee is then surely compromised.

When the officer's view of the probationer's or parolee's conduct differs in this fundamental way from the latter's own view, due process requires that the difference be resolved before revocation becomes final. Both the probationer or parolee and the State have interests in the accurate finding of fact and the informed use of discretion, the probationer or parolee to insure that his liberty is not unjustifiably taken away and the State to make certain that it is neither unnecessarily interrupting a successful effort to rehabilitation nor imprudently prejudicing the safety of the community.

It was to serve all of these interests that Morrissey mandated preliminary and final revocation hearings. At the preliminary hearing, a probationer or parolee is entitled to notice of the alleged violations of probation or parole, an opportunity to appear and to present evidence in his own behalf, a conditional right to confront adverse witnesses, an independent decisionmaker, and a written report of the hearing. Morrissey v. Brewer, *supra,* 408 U.S., at 487. The final hearing is a less summary one because the decision under consideration is the ultimate decision to revoke rather than a mere determination of probable cause, but the "minimum requirements of due process" include very similar elements:

"(a) written notice of the claimed violations of [probation or] parole; (b) disclosure to the [probationer or] parolee of evidence against him; (c) opportunity to be heard in person and to present witnesses and documentary evidence; (d) the right to confront and cross-examine adverse witnesses (unless the hearing officer specifically finds good cause for not allowing confrontation); (e) a 'neutral and detached' hearing body such as a traditional parole board, members of which need not be judicial officers or lawyers; and (f) a written statement by the fact-finders as to the evidence relied on and reasons for revoking [probation or] parole." Morrissey v. Brewer, *supra,* 408 U.S., at 489.

These requirements in themselves serve as substantial protection against ill-considered revocation, and petitioner argues that counsel need never be supplied. What this argument overlooks is that the effectiveness of the right guaranteed by Morrissey may in some circumstances depend on the use of skills which the probationer or parolee is unlikely to possess. Despite the informal nature of the proceedings and the absence of technical rules of procedure or evidence, the unskilled or uneducated probationer or parolee may well have difficulty in presenting his version of a disputed set of facts where the presentation requires the examining or cross-examining of witnesses or the offering or dissecting of complex documentary evidence.

By the same token, we think that the Court of Appeals erred in accepting respondent's contention that the State is under a constitutional duty to provide counsel for indigents in all probation or parole revocation cases. While such a rule has the appeal of simplicity, it would impose direct costs and serious collateral disadvantages without regard to the need or the likelihood in a particular case for a constructive contribution by counsel. In most cases, the probationer or parolee has been convicted of committing another crime or has admitted the charges against him. And while in some cases he may have a justifiable excuse for the violation or a convincing reason why revocation is not the appropriate disposition, mitigating evidence of this kind is often not susceptible of proof or is so simple as not to require either investigation or exposition by counsel.

The introduction of counsel into a revocation proceeding will alter significantly the nature of the proceeding. If counsel is provided for the probationer or parolee, the State in turn will normally provide its own counsel; lawyers, by training and disposition, are advocates and bound by professional duty to present all available evidence and arguments in support of their clients' positions and to contest with vigor all adverse evidence and views. The role of the hearing body itself, aptly described in Morrissey as being "predictive and discretionary" as well as factfinding, may become more akin to that of a judge at a trial, and less attuned to the rehabilitative needs of the individual probationer or parolee. In the greater self-consciousness of its quasi-judicial role, the hearing body may be less tolerant of marginal deviant behavior and feel more pressure to reincarcerate rather than continue nonpunitive rehabilitation. Certainly, the decisionmaking process will be prolonged, and the financial cost to the State—for appointed counsel, counsel for the State, a longer record, and the possibility of judicial review—will not be insubstantial.

In some cases, these modifications in the nature of the revocation hearing must be endured and the costs borne because, as we have indicated above, the probationer's or parolee's version of a disputed issue can fairly be represented only by a trained advocate. But due process is not so rigid as to require that the significant interests in informality, flexibility, and economy must always be sacrificed.

In so concluding, we are of course aware that the case-by-case approach to the right to counsel in felony prosecutions adopted in Betts v. Brady, 316 U.S. 455 (1942), was later rejected in favor of a *per se* rule in Gideon v. Wainwright, 372 U.S. 335, 23 Ohio Op. 2d 258 (1963). See also Argersinger v. Hamlin, 407 U.S. 25 (1972). We do not, however, draw from Gideon and Argersinger the conclusion that a case-by-case approach to furnishing counsel is necessarily inadequate to protect constitutional rights asserted in varying types of proceedings; there are critical differences between criminal trials and probation or parole revocation hearings, and both society and the probationer or parolee have stakes in preserving these differences.

In a criminal trial, the State is represented by a prosecutor; formal rules of evidence are in force; a defendant enjoys a number of procedural rights which may be lost if not timely raised; and, in a jury trial, a defendant must make a presentation understandable

to untrained jurors. In short, a criminal trial under our system is an adversary proceeding with its own unique characteristics. In a revocation hearing, on the other hand, the State is represented not by a prosecutor but by a parole officer with the orientation described above; formal procedures and rules of evidence are not employed; and the members of the hearing body are familiar with the problems and practice of probation or parole. The need for counsel at revocation hearings derives not from the invariable attributes of those hearings but rather from the peculiarities of particular cases.

The differences between a criminal trial and a revocation hearing do not dispose altogether of the argument that under a case-by-case approach there may be cases in which a lawyer would be useful but in which none would be appointed because an arguable defense would be uncovered only by a lawyer. Without denying that there is some force in this argument, we think it a sufficient answer that we deal here not with the right of an accused to counsel in a criminal prosecution, but with the more limited due process right of one who is a probationer or parolee only because he has been convicted of a crime.

We thus find no justification for a new inflexible constitutional rule with respect to the requirement of counsel. We think, rather, that the decision as to the need for counsel must be made on a case-by-case basis in the exercise of a sound discretion by the state authority charged with responsibility for administering the probation and parole system. Although the presence and participation of counsel will probably be both undesirable and constitutionally unnecessary in most revocation hearings, there will remain certain cases in which fundamental fairness—the touchstone of due process—will require that the State provide at its expense counsel for indigent probationers or parolees.

It is neither possible nor prudent to attempt to formulate a precise and detailed set of guidelines to be followed in determining when the providing of counsel is neccessary to meet the applicable due process requirements. The facts and circumstances in preliminary and final hearings are susceptible of almost infinite variation, and a considerable discretion must be allowed the responsible agency in making the decision. Presumptively, it may be said that counsel should be provided in cases where, after being informed of his right to request counsel, the probationer or parolee makes such a request, based on a timely and colorable claim (i) that he has not committed the alleged violation of the conditions upon which he is at liberty; or (ii) that, even if the violation is a matter of public record or is uncontested, there are substantial reasons which justified or mitigated the violation and make revocation inappropriate and that the reasons are complex or otherwise difficult to develop or present. In passing on a request for the appointment of counsel, the responsible agency also should consider, especially in doubtful cases, whether the probationer appears to be capable of speaking effectively for himself. In every case in which a request for counsel at a preliminary or final hearing is refused, the grounds for refusal should be stated succinctly in the record.

IV

We return to the facts of the present case. Because respondent was not afforded either a preliminary hearing or a final hearing, the revocation of his probation did not meet the standards of due process prescribed in Morrissey, which we have here held applicable to probation revocations. Accordingly, respondent was entitled to a writ of habeas corpus. On remand, the District Court should allow the State an opportunity to conduct such a hearing. As to whether the State must provide counsel, respondent's admission to having committed another serious crime creates the very sort of situation in which counsel need not ordinarily be provided. But because of respondent's subsequent assertions regarding that admission, see p. 2, *ante*, we conclude that the failure of the Department to provide respondent with the assistance of counsel should be re-examined in light of this opinion. The general guidelines outlined above should be applied in the first instance by those charged with conducting the revocation hearing.

Affirmed in part, reversed in part, and remanded.

GREENHOLTZ v NEBRASKA PENAL INMATES
442 U.S. 1, 60 L.Ed.2d 668, 99 S.Ct. 2100 (1979)

[footnotes and citations omitted]

Mr. Chief Justice Burger delivered the opinion of the Court.

We granted certiorari to decide whether the Due Process Clause of the Fourteenth Amendment applies to discretionary parole release determinations made by the Nebraska Board of Parole, and, if so, whether the procedures the Board currently provides meet constitutional requirements.

I

Inmates of the Nebraska Penal and Correctional Complex brought a class action under 42 USC § 1983 claiming that they had been unconstitutionally denied parole by the Board of Parole. The suit was filed against the individual members of the Board. One of the claims of the inmates was that the statutes and the Board's procedures denied them procedural due process.

The statutes provide for both mandatory and discretionary parole. Parole is automatic when an inmate has served his maximum term, less good-time credits. An inmate becomes eligible for discretionary parole when the minimum term, less good-time credits has been served. Only discretionary parole is involved in this case.

The procedures used by the Board to determine whether to grant or deny discretionary parole arise partly from statutory provisions and partly from the Board's practices. Two types of hearings are conducted; initial parole review hearings and final parole hearings. At least once each year initial review hearings must be held for every inmate, regardless of parole eligibility. At the initial review hearing, the Board examines the inmate's entire preconfinement and postconfinement record. Following that examination it provides an informal hearing; no evidence as such is introduced, but the Board interviews the inmate and considers any letters or statements that he wishes to present in support of a claim for release.

If the Board determines from its examination of the entire record and the personal interview that he is not yet a good risk for release, it denies parole, informs the inmate why release was deferred and makes recommendations designed to help correct any deficiencies observed. It also schedules another initial review hearing to take place within one year.

If the Board determines from the file and the initial review hearing that the inmate is a likely candidate for release, a final hearing is scheduled. The Board then notifies the inmate of the month in which the final hearing will be held; the exact day and time is posted on a bulletin board that is accessible to all inmates on the day of the hearing. At the final parole hearing, the inmate may present evidence, call witnesses and be represented by private counsel of his choice. It is not a traditional adversary hearing since the inmate is not permitted to hear adverse testimony or to cross-examine witnesses who present such evidence. However, a complete tape recording of the hearing is preserved. If parole is denied, the Board furnishes a written statement of the reasons for the denial within 30 days.

II

The District Court held that the procedures used by the Parole Board did not satisfy due process. It concluded that the inmate had the same kind of constitutionally protected "conditional liberty" interest, recognized by this Court in Morrissey v. Brewer, held that some of the procedures used by the Parole Board fell short of constitutional guarantees, and prescribed several specific requirements.

On appeal, the Court of Appeals for the Eighth Circuit agreed with the District Court that the inmate had a Morrissey-type, conditional liberty interest at stake and also found a statutorily defined, protectible interest in Neb.Rev.Stat. § 83-1.114. The Court of Appeals, however, modified the procedures required by the District Court as follows:

(a) When eligible for parole each inmate must receive a full formal hearing;

(b) the inmate is to receive written notice of the precise time of the hearing reasonably in advance of the hearing, setting forth the factors which may be considered by the Board in reaching its decision;

(c) subject only to security considerations, the inmate may appear in person before the Board and present documentary evidence in his own behalf. Except in unusual circumstances, however, the inmate has no right to call witnesses in his own behalf;

(d) a record of the proceedings, capable of being reduced to writing, must be maintained; and

(e) within a reasonable time after the hearing, the Board must submit a full explanation, in writing, of the facts relied upon and reasons for the Board's action denying parole.

* * *

III

The Due Process Clause applies when government action deprives a person of liberty or property; accordingly, when there is a claimed denial of due process we have inquired into the nature of the individual's claimed interest.

"[T]o determine whether due process requirements apply in the first place, we must look not to the 'weight' but to the nature of the interest at stake. . . ."

This has meant that to obtain a protectible right

"a person clearly must have more than an abstract need or desire for it. He must have more than a unilateral expectation of it. He must, instead, have a legitimate claim of entitlement to it."

There is no constitutional or inherent right of a convicted person to be conditionally released before the expiration of a valid sentence. The natural desire of an individual to be released is indistinguishable from the initial resistance to being confined. But the conviction, with all its procedural safeguards, has extinguished that liberty right: "[G]iven a valid conviction, the criminal defendant has been constitutionally deprived of his liberty."

Decisions of the Executive Branch, however serious their impact, do not automatically invoke due process protection; there simply is no constitutional guarantee that all executive decision-making must comply with standards that assure error-free determinations. This is especially true with respect to the sensitive choices presented by the administrative decision to grant parole release.

A state may, as Nebraska has, establish a parole system, but it has no duty to do so. Moreover, to insure that the state-created parole system serves the public interest purposes of rehabilitation and deterrence, the state may be specific or general in defining the conditions for release and the factors that should be considered by the parole authority. It is thus not surprising that there is no prescribed or defined combination of facts which, if shown, would mandate release on parole. Indeed the very institution of parole is still in an experimental stage. In parole releases, like its siblings probation release and institutional rehabilitation, few certainties exist. In each case, the decision differs from the traditional mold of judicial decision-making in that the choice involves a synthesis of record facts and personal observation filtered through the experience of the decisionmaker and leading to a predictive judgment as to what is best both for the individual inmate and for the community. This latter conclusion requires the Board to assess whether, in light of the nature of the crime, the inmate's release will minimize the gravity of the offense, weaken the deterrent impact on others and undermine respect for the administration of justice.

The entire inquiry is, in a sense, an "equity" type judgment that cannot always be articulated in traditional findings.

IV

Respondents suggest two theories to support their view that they have a constitutionally protected interest in a parole determination which calls for the process mandated by the Court of Appeals. First, they claim that a reasonable entitlement is created whenever a state provides for the *possibility* of parole. Alternatively, they claim that the language in Nebraska's statute creates a legitimate expectation of parole, invoking due process protections.

A

In support of their first theory, respondents rely heavily on Morrissey v. Brewer, supra, where we held that a parole revocation determination must meet certain due process standards. They argue that the ultimate interest at stake both in a parole revocation decision and in a parole determination is conditional liberty and that since the underlying interest is the same the two situations should be accorded the same constitutional protection.

The fallacy in respondents' position is that parole *release* and parole *revocation* are quite different. There is a crucial distinction between being deprived of a liberty one has, as in parole and being denied a conditional liberty that one desires. The parolees in Morrissey (and probationers in Gagnon) were at liberty and as such could "be gainfully employed and [were] free to be with family and friends and to form the enduring attachments of normal life." The inmates here, on the other hand, are confined and thus subject to all of the necessary restraints that inhere in a prison.

A second important difference between discretionary parole *release* from confinement and *termination* of parole lies in the nature of the decision that must be made in each case. As we recognized in Morrissey, the parole revocation determination actually requires two decisions: whether the parolee in fact acted in violation of one or more conditions of parole and whether the parolee should be recommitted either for his or society's benefit. "The first step in a revocation decision thus involves a wholly retrospective factual question."

The parole release decision, however, is more subtle and depends on an amalgam of elements, some of which are factual but many of which are purely subjective appraisals by the Board members based upon their experience with the difficult and sensitive task of evaluating the advisability of parole release. Unlike the revocation decision, there is no set of facts which, if shown, mandate a decision favorable to the individual. The parole determination, like a prisoner transfer decision, may be made

"for a variety of reasons and often involve no more than informed predictions as to what would best serve [correctional purposes] or the safety and welfare of the inmate."

The decision turns on a "discretionary assessment of a multiplicity of imponderables, entailing primarily what a man is and what he may become rather than simply what he has done."

The differences between an initial grant of parole and the revocation of the conditional liberty of the parolee are well recognized. In United States ex rel. Bey v. Connecticut Board of Parole, the Second Circuit took note of this critical distinction:

> "It is not sophistic to attach greater importance to a person's justifiable reliance in maintaining his conditional freedom so long as he abides by the conditions of his release, than to his mere anticipation or hope of freedom."

Judge Henry Friendly cogently noted that: "[T]here is a human difference between losing what one has and not getting what one wants."

That the state holds out the *possibility* of parole provides no more than a mere hope that the benefit will be obtained. To that extent the general interest asserted here is no more substantial than the inmate's hope that he will not be transferred to another prison, a hope which is not protected by due process.

B

Respondents' second argument is that the Nebraska statutory language itself creates a protectible expectation of parole. They rely on the section which provides in part:

> "Whenever the Board of Parole considers the release of a committed offender who is eligible for release on parole, it shall order his release unless it is of the opinion that his release should be deferred because:
>
> "(a) There is a substantial risk that he will not conform to the conditions of parole;
>
> "(b) His release would depreciate the seriousness of his crime or promote disrespect for law;
>
> "(c) His release would have a substantially adverse effect on institutional discipline; or

> "(d) His continued correctional treatment, medical care, or vocational or other training in the facility will substantially enhance his capacity to lead a law-abiding life when released at a later date."

Respondents emphasize that the structure of the provision together with the use of the word "shall" binds the Board of Parole to release an inmate unless any one of the four specifically designated reasons are found. In their view the statute creates a presumption that parole release will be granted, and that this in turn creates a legitimate expectation of release absent the requisite finding that one of the justifications for deferral exists.

It is argued that the Nebraska parole determination provision is similar to the Nebraska statute involved in Wolff v. McDonnell that granted good-time credits to inmates. There we held that due process protected the inmates from the arbitrary loss of the statutory right to credits because they were provided subject only to good behavior. We held that the statute created a liberty interest protected by due process guarantees. The Board argues in response that a presumption would be created only if the statutory conditions for deferral were essentially factual, as in Wolff and Morrissey, rather than predictive.

Since respondents elected to litigate their due process claim in federal court, we are denied the benefit of the Nebraska courts' interpretation of the scope of the interest, if any, its statute was intended to afford to inmates. We can accept respondent's view that the expectancy of release provided in this statute is entitled to some measure of constitutional protection. However, we emphasize that this statute has unique structure and language and thus whether any other state statute provides a protectible entitlement must be decided on a case-by-case basis. We therefore turn to an examination of the statutory procedures to determine whether they provide the process that is due in these circumstances.

It is axiomatic that due process "is flexible and calls for such procedural protections as the particular situation demands." The function of legal process, as that concept is embodied in the Constitution, and in the realm of factfinding, is to minimize the risk of erroneous decisions. Because of the broad spectrum of concerns to which the term must apply, flexibility is necessary to gear the process to the particular need; the quantum and quality of the process due in a particular situation depends upon the need to serve the purpose of minimizing the risk of error.

Here, as we noted previously, the Parole Board's decision as defined by Nebraska's statute is necessarily subjective in part and predictive in part. Like most parole statutes, it vests very broad discretion in the Board. No ideal, error-free way to make parole release decisions has been developed; the whole question has been and will continue to be the subject of experimentation involving analysis of psychological factors combined with fact evaluation guided by the practical experience of the actual parole decisionmakers in predicting future behavior. Our system of federalism encourages this state experimentation. If parole determinations are encumbered by procedures that states regard as burdensome and unwarranted, they may abandon or curtail parole.

It is important that we not overlook the ultimate purpose of parole which is a component of the long-range objective of rehabilitation. The fact that anticipations and hopes for rehabilitation programs have fallen far short of expectations of a generation ago need not lead States to abandon hopes for those objectives; states may adopt a balanced approach in making parole determinations, as in all problems of administering the correctional systems. The objective of rehabilitating convicted persons to be useful, law-abiding members of society can remain a goal no matter how disappointing the progress. But it will not contribute to these desirable objectives to invite or encourage a continuing state of adversary relations between society and the inmate.

Procedures designed to elicit specific facts, such as those required in Morrissey, Gagnon, and Wolff, are not necessarily appropriate to a Nebraska parole determination. Merely because a statutory expectation exists cannot mean that in addition to the full panoply of due process required to convict and confine there must also be repeated, adversary hearings in order to continue the confinement. However, since the Nebraska Parole Board provides at least one and often two hearings every year to each eligible inmate, we need only consider whether the additional procedures mandated by the Court of Appeals are required under the standards set out in Mathews v. Eldridge. ***

Two procedures mandated by the Court of Appeals are particularly challenged by the Board; the requirement that a formal hearing be held for every inmate, and the requirement that every adverse parole decision include a statement of the evidence relied upon by the Board.

The requirement of a hearing as

prescribed by the Court of Appeals in all cases would provide at best a negligible decrease in the risk of error. When the Board defers parole after the initial review hearing, it does so because examination of the inmate's file and the personal interview satisfies it that the inmate is not yet ready for conditional release. The parole determination therefore must include consideration of what the entire record shows up to the time of the sentence, including the gravity of the offense in the particular case. The behavior record of an inmate during confinement is critical in the sense that it reflects the degree to which the inmate is prepared to adjust to parole release. At the Board's initial interview hearing, the inmate is permitted to appear before the Board and present letters and statements on his own behalf. He is thereby provided with an effective opportunity to insure, first, that the records before the Board are in fact the records relating to his case; and second, to present any special considerations demonstrating why he is an appropriate candidate for parole. Since the decision is one that must be made largely on the basis of the inmate's files, this procedure adequately safeguards against serious risks of error and thus satisfies due process.

Next, we find nothing in the due process concepts as they have thus far evolved that requires the Parole Board to specify the particular "evidence" in the inmate's file or at his interview on which it rests the discretionary determination that an inmate is not ready for conditional release. The Board communicates the reason for its denial as a guide to the inmate for his future behavior. To require the parole authority to provide a summary of the evidence would tend to convert the process into an adversary proceeding and to equate the Board's parole release determination with a guilt determination. The Nebraska statute contemplates, and experience has shown, that the parole release decision is, as we noted earlier, essentially an experienced prediction based on a host of variables. The Board's decision is much like a sentencing judge's choice—provided by many states—to grant or deny probation following a judgment of guilt, a choice never thought to require more than what Nebraska now provides for the parole release determination. The Nebraska procedure affords an opportunity to be heard and when parole is denied it informs the inmate in what respects he falls short of qualifying for parole; this affords the process that is due under these circumstances. The Constitution does not require more.

Accordingly the judgment of the Court of Appeals is reversed and the case is remanded for further proceedings consistent with this opinion.

Reversed.

* * *

CONNECTICUT BD. OF PARDONS v. DUMSCHAT
452 U.S. 458, 29 Cr.L. 3077 (1981)

[footnotes and citations omitted]

Chief Justice Burger delivered the opinion of the Court.

The question presented is whether the fact that the Connecticut Board of Pardons has granted approximately three-fourths of the applications for commutation of life sentences creates a constitutional "liberty interest" or "entitlement" in life-term inmates so as to require that Board to explain its reasons for denial of an application for commutation.

I

In 1964, respondent Dumschat was sentenced to life imprisonment for murder. Under state law, he was not eligible for parole until December 1983. The Connecticut Board of Pardons is empowered to commute the sentences of life inmates by reducing the minimum prison term, and such a commutation accelerates eligibility for parole. The authority of the Board of Pardons derives from Conn. Gen. Stat. Ann. § 18-26 (1981 Supp.), which provides in pertinent part:

"(a) Jurisdiction over the granting of, and the authority to grant, commutations of punishment or releases, conditioned or absolute, in the case of any person convicted of any offense against the state and commutations from the penalty of death shall be vested in the board of pardons.

"(b) Said board shall have authority to grant pardons, conditioned or absolute, for any offense against the state at any time after the imposition and before or after the service of any sentence."

On several occasions prior to the filing of this suit in February 1976, Dumschat applied for a commutation of his sentence. The Board rejected each application without explanation. Dumschat then sued the Board under 42 U.S.C. § 1983, seeking a declaratory judgment that the Board's failure to provide him with a written statement of reasons for denying commutation violated his rights guaranteed by the Due Process Clause of the Fourteenth Amendment.

After hearing testimony from officials of the Board of Pardons and the Board of Parole, the District Court concluded (a) that Dumschat had a constitutionally protected liberty entitlement in the pardon process, and (b) that his due process rights had been violated when the Board failed to give "a written statement of reasons and facts relied upon" in denying commutation. The court relied chiefly on a showing that "at least 75 percent of all lifers [*sic*] received some favorable action from the pardon board prior to completing their minimum sentences" and that virtually all of the pardoned inmates were promptly paroled. In response to post-judgment motions, the District Court allowed other life inmates to intervene, certified the suit as a class action, and heard additional evidence. The court held that all prisoners serving life sentences in Connecticut state prisons have a constitutionally protected expectancy of commutation and therefore that they have a right to a statement of reasons when commutation is not granted. The Court of Appeals affirmed. A petition for a writ of certiorari was filed, and we vacated and remanded for reconsideration in light of *Greenholtz* v. *Inmates of the Nebraska Penal and Correctional Complex*, 442 U.S. 1 (1979).

On remand, the Court of Appeals reaffirmed its original decision, 618 F.2d 216 (CA2 1980), stating:

"In marked contrast [to the Nebraska statute considered in *Greenholtz*], Connecticut's pardons statute contains neither a presumption in favor of pardon nor a list of factors to be considered by the Board of Pardons. Instead, the statute grants the board unfettered discretion in the exercise of its power. The statute offers only the 'mere hope' of pardon; it does not create a legitimate expectation of freedom and therefore does not implicate due process."

The Court of Appeals also noted that the District Court's holding that the mere possibility of a pardon creates a constitutionally cognizable liberty interest or entitlement was "no longer tenable" in light of *Greenholtz*. However, the Court of Appeals then proceeded to conclude that "[t]he overwhelming likelihood that Connecticut life inmates will be pardoned and released before they complete their minimum terms gives them a constitutionally protected liberty interest in pardon proceedings." The Court of Appeals also understood our opinion in *Greenholtz* to hold that under the Due Process Clause, a brief statement of reasons is "not only constitutionally sufficient but also constitutionally *necessary*." On that reading of *Greenholtz*, the case was remanded to the District Court for a determination of "how many years life inmates must serve before the probability of pardon becomes so sig-

nificant as to give rise to a protected liberty interest."

II

A

A State-created right can, in some circumstances, beget yet other rights to procedures essential to the realization of the parent right. See *Meachum* v. *Fano*, 427 U.S. 215, 226 (1976); *Wolff* v. *McDonnell*, 418 U.S. 539, 557 (1974). Plainly, however, the underlying right must have come into existence before it can trigger due process protection.

In *Greenholtz*, far from spelling out any judicially divined "entitlement," we did no more than apply the unique Nebraska statute. We rejected the claim that a constitutional entitlement to release from a valid prison sentence exists independently of a right explicitly conferred by the State. Our language in *Greenholtz* leaves no room for doubt:

"There is *no constitutional or inherent right* of a convicted person to be conditionally released before the expiration of a valid sentence. The natural desire of an individual to be released is indistinguishable from the initial resistance to being confined. But the conviction, with all its procedural safeguards, has extinguished that liberty right: '[G]iven a valid conviction, the criminal defendant has been constitutionally deprived of his liberty.' "

Greenholtz pointedly distinguished parole revocation and probation revocation cases, noting that there is a "critical" difference between denial of a prisoner's request for initial release on parole and revocation of a parolee's conditional liberty. Unlike probation, pardon and commutation decisions have not traditionally been the business of courts; as such, they are rarely, if ever, appropriate subjects for judicial review.

A decision whether to commute a long-term sentence generally depends not simply on objective factfinding, but also on purely subjective evaluations and on predictions of future behavior by those entrusted with the decision. A commutation decision therefore shares some of the characteristics of a decision whether to grant parole. Far from supporting an "entitlement," *Greenholtz* therefore compels the conclusion that an inmate has "no constitutional or inherent right" to commutation of his sentence.

Respondents nevertheless contend that the Board's consistent practice of granting commutations to most life inmates is sufficient to create a protectible liberty interest. They argue that:

"[T]he State Board has created an unwritten common law of sentence commutation and parole acceleration for Connecticut life inmates. . . .

"In effect, there is an unspoken understanding between the State Board [of Pardons] and inmates. The terms are simple: If the inmate cooperates with the State, the State will exercise its parole [*sic*] power on the inmate's behalf. Both the State and the inmate recognize those terms. Each expects the other to abide by them."

This case does not involve parole, and respondents' argument wholly misconceives the nature of a decision by a state to commute the sentence of a convicted felon. The petition in each case is nothing more than an appeal for clemency. In terms of the Due Process Clause, a Connecticut felon's expectation that a lawfully imposed sentence will be commuted or pardoned

is no more substantial than an inmate's expectation, for example, that he will not be transferred to another prison; it is simply a unilateral hope. A constitutional entitlement cannot "be created—as if by estoppel—merely because a wholly and *expressly* discretionary state privilege has been granted generously in the past." No matter how frequently a particular form of clemency has been granted, the statistical probabilities standing alone generate no constitutional protections; a contrary conclusion would trivialize the Constitution. The ground for a constitutional claim, if any, must be found in statutes or other rules defining the obligations of the authority charged with exercising clemency.

B

The Court of Appeals correctly recognized that Connecticut has conferred "unfettered discretion" on its Board of Pardons, but—paradoxically—then proceeded to fetter the Board with a halter of constitutional "entitlement." The statute imposes no limit on what procedure is to be followed, what evidence may be considered, or what criteria are to be applied by the Board. Respondents challenge the Board's procedure precisely because of "the absence of any apparent standards." We agree that there are no explicit standards by way of statute, regulation, or otherwise.

This contrasts dramatically with the Nebraska statutory procedures in *Greenholtz*, which expressly mandated that the Nebraska Board of Parole "shall" order the inmate's release "unless" it decided that one of four specified reasons for denial was applicable. The Connecticut commutation statute, having no definitions, no criteria, and no mandated "shalls," creates no analogous duty or constitutional entitlement.

It is clear that the requirement for articulating reasons for denial of parole in *Greenholtz* derived from unique mandates of the Nebraska statutes. Thus, although we noted that under the terms of the Nebraska statute, the inmates' expectancy of parole release "is entitled to some measure of constitutional protection," we emphasized that

> "[T]his statute has unique structure and language and thus whether any other state statute provides a protectible entitlement must be decided on a case-by-case basis."

Moreover, from the standpoint of a reasons requirement, there is a vast difference between a denial of parole—particularly on the facts of *Greenholtz*—and a State's refusal to commute a lawful sentence. When Nebraska statutes directed that inmates who are eligible for parole "shall" be released "unless" a certain finding has been made, the statutes created a right. By contrast, the mere existence of a power to commute a lawfully imposed sentence, and the granting of commutations to many petitioners, creates no right or "entitlement." A State cannot be required to explain its reasons for a decision when it is not required to act on prescribed grounds.

We hold that the power vested in the Connecticut Board of Pardons to commute sentences conferred no rights on respondents beyond the right to seek commutation.

Reversed.

MINOR MOODY, Petitioner

v.

LOREN DAGGETT, Warden

429 U.S. 78, 50 L.Ed.2d 236, 97 S.Ct. 274 (1976)

OPINION OF THE COURT

MR. CHIEF JUSTICE BURGER delivered the opinion of the Court.

We granted certiorari in this case to decide whether a federal parolee imprisoned for a crime committed while on parole is constitutionally entitled to a prompt parole revocation hearing when a parole violator warrant is issued and lodged with the institution of his confinement but not served on him.

(1)

In 1962 petitioner was convicted in the United States District Court for the District of Arizona of the crime of rape on an Indian reservation, and petitioner received a 10-year prison sentence. He was paroled in 1966 with almost six years remaining to be served. While on parole, petitioner shot and killed two persons on the Fort Apache Indian Reservation. He was convicted on a guilty plea of manslaughter as to one victim and second-degree murder as to the other, he received concurrent 10-year sentences for these two offenses. These crimes constituted obvious violations of the terms of petitioner's 1966 parole. Soon after petitioner's incarceration for the two homicides, the United States Board of Parole issued but did not execute a parole violator warrant; this was lodged with prison officials as a "detainer."[1] Petitioner requested the Board to execute the warrant immediately so that any imprisonment imposed for violation of his earlier parole under the rape conviction could run concurrently with his 1971 homicide sentences. The Board replied that it intended to execute the warrant only upon petitioner's release from his second sentence.

Relying on Morrissey v. Brewer, 408 US 471, (1972), petitioner began this federal habeas corpus action in January 1975, seeking dismissal of the parole violator warrant on the ground that he had been denied a prompt hearing at which the pending parole revocation issues could be aired.

The District Court dismissed the petition without awaiting a responsive pleading, stating:

"[A] parole revocation hearing is not required until the parole violator warrant has been executed. The parole board is under no obligation to execute the warrant inasmuch as petitioner has been in custody on his 1971 manslaughter [and murder] sentence[s] since the time the warrant was issued and filed as a detainer against him."

The Court of Appeals affirmed, relying on its earlier holding in Small v.

Britton, 500 F2d 299 (CA10 1974), in which that court had held that an incarcerated parolee is deprived of no liberty interest by the lodging of a detainer against him, and is thus entitled to no due process safeguards unless and until the parole violator warrant is actually executed.

(2)

The Parole Commission and Reorganization Act, Pub L 94-233, 90 Stat 219 et seq., was enacted shortly after we granted certiorari.

Throughout the progress of this case below, however, parole revocation procedures were controlled by the former statutes, 18 USC §§ 4205 and 4207. Under them, and the Board's own regulations, 28 CFR § 2.53 (1975), it was the Board's practice to issue a parole violator warrant as a matter of course whenever a federal parolee was convicted of a new offense. Under the former statute and regulations, if the subsequent sentence called for incarceration the warrant was lodged at the institution of confinement as a detainer, for possible later service. A parolee so confined was then notified of the issuance of the unserved warrant and given the opportunity to make a written response. Upon receipt of the response the Board was authorized, in its discretion, to conduct a dispositional interview designed to get the facts relevant to its revocation decision. The parolee could retain counsel for the interview and call witnesses. In lieu of an interview, the Board in its discretion could review the parolee's case based on the record and the written response.

After review—or interview—the Board had three options for disposing of its parole violator warrant:

(a) It could execute the warrant im-

---

[1] A detainer in this context is an internal administrative mechanism to assure that an inmate subject to an unexpired term of confinement will not be released from custody until the jurisdiction asserting a parole violation has had an opportunity to act—in this case by taking the inmate into custody or by making a parole revocation determination. When two autonomous jurisdictions are involved, as for example when a federal detainer is placed against an inmate of a state institution, a detainer is a matter of comity.

mediately and take the parolee into custody. If parole was revoked at that stage, the remainder of the parolee's original federal sentence, reinstated by the parole revocation, would run concurrently with the subsequent sentence from the time of execution of the warrant.

(b) The Board's second option was to dismiss the warrant and detainer altogether, which operated as a decision not to revoke parole, and under which the parolee retained both his good-time credit and credit for the time spent on parole.

(c) Third, the Board was free to defer a final decision on parole revocation until expiration of the subsequent sentence, as it elected to do in this case; under this third option, the Board was authorized to execute the warrant, take the parolee into custody immediately upon his release, and then conduct a revocation hearing. Deferral of decision while permitting the warrant to stand unexecuted would operate to allow the original sentence to remain in the status it occupied at the time of the asserted parole violation.

Previously it was general practice to defer execution of the warrant to completion of the subsequent sentence. It is now firm Commission policy that unless "substantial mitigating circumstances" are shown, the parole violator term of a parolee convicted of crime is to run consecutively to the sentence imposed for the subsequent offense. 28 CFR § 2.47(c) (1976).

Petitioner asserts protected liberty interests in both the length and conditions of his confinement. Those interests, he argues, are disregarded in several respects by issuance against him of an unexecuted parole violator warrant, which bars him from serving his 1962 rape conviction sentence con-

currently with his 1971 homicide sentences, retards his parole eligibility on the later convictions, and adversely affects his prison classification status. He argues that lack of a prompt hearing risks the loss of evidence in mitigation which might induce the Board not to revoke his parole. Respondent's position is that whatever process may eventually be due petitioner, the mere issuance of a parole violator warrant works no present deprivation of protected liberty sufficient to invoke due process protection.

(3)

In Morrissey, we held that the conditional freedom of a parolee generated by statute is a liberty interest protected by the Due Process Clause of the Fourteenth Amendment which may not be terminated absent appropriate due process safeguards.

The revocation hearing mandated by Morrissey[2] is bottomed on the parallel interests of society and the parolee in establishing whether a parole violation has occurred and, if so, whether under all the circumstances the quality of that violation calls for parole revocation. The issue before us here, however, is not

[2] In the present case, where petitioner has already been convicted of and incarcerated on a subsequent offense, there is no need for the preliminary hearing which Morrissey requires upon arrest for a parole violation. This is so both because the subsequent conviction obviously gives the parole authority "probable cause or reasonable ground to believe that the . . . parolee has committed acts that would constitute a violation of parole conditions," 408 US at 485, 33 L Ed 2d 484, 92 S Ct 2593, and because issuance of the warrant does not immediately deprive the parolee of liberty. The 1976 Act calls for no preliminary hearing in such cases. 18 USCA § 4214(b)(1) (June 1976 Supp) [18 USCS § 4214(b)(1)]; see 28 CFR § 2.48(f) (1976).

whether a Morrissey-type hearing will ever be constitutionally required in the present case, but whether a hearing must be held at the present time, before the parolee is taken into custody as a parole violator. We hold that there is no requirement for an immediate hearing.

Petitioner's present confinement and consequent liberty loss derive not in any sense from the outstanding parole violator warrant, but from his two 1971 homicide convictions. Issuance of the warrant and notice of that fact to the institution of confinement did no more than express the Board's intent to defer consideration of parole revocation to a later time.

Though the gravity of petitioner's subsequent crimes places him under a cloud, issuance of the warrant was not a determination that petitioner's parole under his 1962 rape conviction will be revoked; the time at which the Commission must make that decision has not yet arrived. With only a prospect of future incarceration which is far from certain, we cannot say that the parole violator warrant has any present or inevitable effect upon the liberty interests which Morrissey sought to protect. Indeed, in holding that "[t]he revocation hearing must be tendered within a reasonable time after the parolee is taken into custody," Morrissey, 408 US, at 488, we established execution of the warrant and custody under that warrant as the operative event triggering any loss of liberty attendant upon parole revocation. This is a functional designation, for the loss of liberty as a parole violator does not occur until the parolee is taken into custody under the warrant.

The other injuries petitioner claims to suffer either do not involve a loss of protected liberty or have not occurred by reason of the warrant and detainer. His real complaint is that he desires to serve his sentence for the 1962 rape conviction concurrently with his sentences for two 1971 homicides. But, as we have noted, even after completion of the homicide sentences the Commission retains full discretion to dismiss the warrant or decide, after hearing, that petitioner's parole need not be revoked. If revocation is chosen, the Commission has power to grant, retroactively, the equivalent of concurrent sentences and to provide for unconditional or conditional release upon completion of the subsequent sentence.

Thus, deferral of the revocation decision does not deprive petitioner of any such opportunity; nothing in the statute or regulations gives him any "right" to force the decision of the Commission at this time.

Accordingly, and without regard to what process may be due petitioner before his parole may be finally revoked, we hold that he has been deprived of no constitutionally protected rights simply by issuance of a parole violator warrant. The Commission therefore has no constitutional duty to provide petitioner an adversary parole hearing until he is taken into custody as a parole violator by execution of the warrant.

Affirmed.

MR. JUSTICE STEVENS, with whom MR. JUSTICE BRENNAN joins, dissenting.

The Court holds that the lodging of a detainer with an institution in which a parolee is confined does not have the kind of impact on his custodial status that requires a due process hearing. That holding does not answer the question which I regard as critical in this case. For it is clear that sooner or later a parole revocation hearing will be held; the question is whether the timing of that hearing is an element of the procedural fairness to which the parolee is constitutionally entitled. I am persuaded that it is.

I start from the premise that parole revocation is a deprivation of liberty within the meaning of the Fifth and Fourteenth Amendments and therefore must be preceded by due process. [R]evocation affects the length of confinement and therefore may result in a "grievous loss" of liberty. Accordingly, it is clear that the parolee's constitutional right to have the revocation hearing conducted fairly is not affected by his custodial status. Moreover, since the parole revocation process begins when the Parole Commission issues the revocation warrant, it plainly follows that the constitutional protections afforded the parolee attach at that time. The question, then, is whether the parolee's right to a fair hearing includes any right to have the hearing conducted with reasonable dispatch.

It is apparently the position of the Parole Commission that it has no obligation to go forward with the revocation hearing until after the parolee has completed the service of his sentence for the second offense. It may therefore wait as long as 10 or 20 years after commencing the revocation process by issuing a warrant. This position, I submit, can be tenable only if one assumes that the constitutional right to a fair hearing includes no right whatsoever to a prompt hearing. Precedent, tradition, and reason require rejection of that assumption.

This Court has already held that present incarceration for one offense does not deprive an inmate of his right to a prompt trial on a second charge. Smith v. Hooey, 393 US 374, Strunk v. United States, 412 US 434. Moreover, the Court has made it clear that the constitutional protection applies not only to the determination of guilt but also to the discretionary decision on what disposition should be made of the defendant. This point was squarely decided with respect to parole revocation in Morrissey v. Brewer. And in Pollard v. United States, 352 US 354, the Court, recognized that a defendant's right to a speedy trial included a right to a prompt sentencing determination. The entire Court subscribed to the view that delay in regard to disposition "must not be purposeful or oppressive." Id., at 361. That view contrasts sharply with the Parole Commission's conscious policy of delaying parole revocation decisions under these circumstances.

Those holdings recognize the defendant's legitimate interest in changing the uncertainty associated with a pending charge into the greater certainty associated with its disposition.

Petitioner argues that the detainer itself is the source of his grievous loss which mandates a hearing. That is not my view. In my judgment the detainer is comparable to an arrest or an indictment which identifies a time when it is clear that the government has a basis for going forward with appropriate proceedings and from which the right to a speedy determination accrues. Since I believe the right to orderly procedure leading to a reasonably prompt decision is a fundamental attribute of due process, I cannot accept the conclusion that the right is vindicated by simply lodging a detainer and letting it remain outstanding for year after year while the prisoner's interest in knowing where he stands may be entirely ignored.

I therefore respectfully dissent.

A.R. JAGO, Former Superintendent, Southern Ohio Correctional Facility, et al., Petitioners

v.

GEORGE D. VAN CUREN

454 U.S. 14, 70 L.Ed.2d 13, 102 S.Ct. 31 (1981)

OPINION OF THE COURT
PER CURIAM.

After pleading guilty to embezzlement and related crimes, respondent was sentenced by an Ohio court to not less than 6 nor more than 100 years in prison. Under existing law respondent would have become eligible for parole in March 1976. On January 1, 1974, however, Ohio enacted a "shock parole" statute which provided for the early parole of first offenders who had served more than six months in prison for nonviolent crimes.

Pursuant to this statute, respondent was interviewed on April 17, 1974, by a panel representing the Ohio Adult Parole Authority (OAPA). The panel recommended that respondent be paroled "on or after April 23, 1974," and OAPA subsequently approved the panel's recommendation. Respondent was notified of the decision by a parole agreement which stated:

"The Members of the Parole Board have agreed that you have earned the opportunity of parole and eventually a final release from your present conviction. The Parole Board is therefore ordering a Parole Release in your case."

Respondent attended and completed prison prerelease classes and was measured for civilian clothes.

At a meeting six days after the panel's interview with respondent, OAPA was informed that respondent had not been entirely truthful in the interview or in the parole plan that he had submitted to his parole officers.

Specifically, respondent had told the panel that he had embezzled $1 million when in fact he had embezzled $6 million, and had reported in his parole plan that he would live with his half brother if paroled when in fact he intended to live with his homosexual lover. As a result of these revelations, OAPA rescinded its earlier decision to grant respondent "shock parole" and continued his case to a June 1974 meeting at which parole was formally denied. Neither at this meeting nor at any other time was respondent granted a hearing to explain the false statements he had made during the April interview and in the parole plan which he had submitted.

After denial of his parole, respondent brought a mandamus action against OAPA. The Supreme Court of Ohio held that OAPA was not required to grant respondent a hearing and that it could not be commanded to recall its decision rescinding parole. We denied respondent's petition for certiorari to review the decision of the Supreme Court of Ohio. 429 US 959, (1976).

Respondent then filed a petition for a writ of habeas corpus in the Federal District Court for the Southern District of Ohio, claiming that the rescission without hearing violated his right to due process of law under the United States Constitution. The District Court denied the writ and the United States Court of Appeals for the Sixth Circuit summarily affirmed the denial. We granted certiorari, vacated the judgment of the Court of Appeals, and remanded for further consideration in light of our decision in Greenholtz v. Nebraska Penal Inmates, 442 US 1.

On remand the Court of Appeals in turn remanded to the District Court for further consideration. Applying Greenholtz, the District Court determined that "early release in Ohio is a matter of grace" and that Ohio law "is fairly unambiguous that no protectable interest in early release arises until actual release." Accordingly, the District Court held that the rescission of respondent's parole without a hearing did not violate due process.

[T]he Court of Appeals reversed the decision of the District Court. Relying upon language from our decision in Perry v. Sindermann, 408 US 593, (1972), the Court of Appeals concluded that a liberty interest such as that asserted by respondent can arise from "mutually explicit understandings." Thus, it held:

> "Having been notified that he 'ha[d] been paroled' and that 'the Board is ordering a Parole Release in your case,' [respondent] had a legitimate expectation that his early release would be effected. This expectation was a liberty interest, the deprivation of which would indeed constitute a grievous loss. It was an interest which could not be taken from him without according [respondent] procedural due process." 641 F2d, at 416.

We do not doubt that respondent suffered "grievous loss" upon OAPA's rescission of his parole. But we have previously "reject[ed] . . . the notion that *any* grievous loss visited upon a person by the State is sufficient to invoke the procedural protections of the Due Process Clause." Meachum v. Fano, 427 US 215, (1976). In this case, as in our previous cases, "[t]he question is not merely the 'weight' of the individual's interest, but whether the nature of the interest is one within the contemplation of the 'liberty or property language of the Fourteenth Amendment.' " Morrissey v. Brewer, 408 US 471, 481, (1972). We hold that the Court of Appeals erred in finding a constitutionally protected liberty interest by reliance upon the "mutually explicit understandings" language of Perry v. Sindermann, supra.

Our decision in Sindermann was concerned only with the Fourteenth Amendment's protection of "property" interests and its language, relied upon by the Court of Appeals, was expressly so limited.

To illustrate the way in which "mutually explicit understandings" operate to create "property" interests, we relied in Sindermann upon two analogous doctrines. First, we compared such understandings to implied contracts. That the implied-contract aspect of Sindermann "understandings" has been limited to the creation of property interests is illustrated by Bishop v. Wood, 426 US 341, (1976), another property interest case in which we relied upon the "understandings" language of Sindermann to conclude that "[a] property interest in employment can, of course, be created by ordinance, or by an implied contract." 426 US, at 344.

Principles of contract law naturally serve as useful guides in determining whether or not a constitutionally protected property interest exists. Such principles do not, however, so readily lend themselves to determining the existence of constitutionally protected liberty interests in the setting of prisoner parole. In Meachum v. Fano, we recognized that the administrators of our penal systems need considerable latitude in operating those systems, and that the protected interests of prisoners are necessarily limited.

We would severely restrict the necessary flexibility of prison administrators and parole authorities were we to hold that any one of their myriad decisions with respect to individual inmates may, as under the general law of contracts, give rise to protected "liberty" interests which could not thereafter be impaired without a constitutionally mandated hearing under the Due Process Clause.

The second analogy relied upon in Sindermann to give content to the notion of "mutually explicit understandings" was the labor law principle that the tradition and history of an industry or plant may add substance to collective-bargaining agreements. See 408 US, at 602. [H]owever, we rejected an argument that a sort of "industrial common law" could give rise to a liberty interest in the prisoner parole setting in Connecticut Board of Pardons v. Dumschat, 452 US 458, (1981).

Thus, this Court has recognized that the "mutually explicit understandings" of Sindermann have a far more useful place in determining protected property interests than in determining those liberty interests protected by the Due Process Clause of the Fourteenth Amendment.

[T]he majority opinion in the Court of Appeals for the Sixth Circuit observed: "Parole for Ohio prisoners lies wholly within the discretion of the OAPA. The statutes which provide for parole do not create a protected liberty interest for due process purposes." 641 F2d, at 414.

Notwithstanding its conclusion that the granting of parole was a purely discretionary matter, the majority of the Court of Appeals in this case concluded that, once the recommendation for "shock parole" had been made, respondent was entitled to a hearing for the purpose of explaining his false statements and representations because the initial recommendation for "shock parole" gave rise to a "mutually explicit understanding." As we have previously stated, however, we deal here not with "property" interests but with "liberty" interests protected by the Fourteenth Amendment. We think that the reasoning of Greenholtz v. Nebraska Penal Inmates, 442 US 1, (1979), Dumschat, supra, and the Court of Appeals' own concession that Ohio law creates no protected "liberty" interest, require reversal of the holding of the Court of Appeals that respondent was entitled to a hearing prior to denial of his parole in June.

The petition for certiorari is granted, the respondent's motion to proceed in forma pauperis is granted, and the judgment of the Court of Appeals for the Sixth Circuit is reversed.

JUSTICE STEVENS, with whom JUSTICE BRENNAN and JUSTICE MARSHALL join, dissenting.

The Court has fashioned a constitutional distinction between the decision to revoke parole and the decision to grant or to deny parole. Arbitrary revocation is prohibited by Morrissey v. Brewer, 408 US 471, whereas arbitrary denial is permitted by Greenholtz v. Nebraska Penal Inmates, 442 US 1. Even if one accepts the validity of that dubious distinction, I believe the Court misapplies it in this case.

In the Court's view, the grant of parole creates a constitutionally protected interest in liberty that previously did not exist. Under that view, a profound change in the status of an individual occurs when he is paroled; he has greater legal rights after parole than before. The question is what event triggers this change in legal status, the act of walking through the exit gates or the State's formal decision, conveyed to the prisoner, to grant him his conditional freedom.

For the ordinary litigant, the entry of judgment by the decisionmaker —not the execution of that judgment by the sheriff—determines his legal rights. In my opinion, the interests in orderly decisionmaking that are protected by the Due Process Clause of the Fourteenth Amendment dictate a similar answer in the context of this case.

When the Ohio Adult Parole Authority revoked its decision to grant respondent parole, it acted on the basis of ex parte information which respondent had no opportunity to deny or to explain. Even if that information was entirely accurate in this case, and even if it was sufficiently important to justify the changed decision, the effect of the Court's holding today is to allow such decision to stand even if wrong and wholly arbitrary. I am persuaded that such a holding is erroneous.

DANNY R. BEARDEN, Petitioner

v.

GEORGIA

461 U.S. 660, 103 S. Ct. 2064, 76 L. Ed. 2d 221 (1983)

OPINION OF THE COURT

JUSTICE O'CONNOR delivered the opinion of the Court.

The question in this case is whether the Fourteenth Amendment prohibits a State from revoking an indigent defendant's probation for failure to pay a fine and restitution. Its resolution involves a delicate balance between the acceptability, and indeed wisdom, of considering all relevant factors when determining an appropriate sentence for an individual and the impermissibility of imprisoning a defendant solely because of his lack of financial resources. We conclude that the trial court erred in automatically revoking probation because petitioner could not pay his fine, without determining that petitioner had not made sufficient bona fide efforts to pay or that adequate alternative forms of punishment did not exist. We therefore reverse the judgment of the Georgia Court of Appeals upholding the revocation of probation, and remand for a new sentencing determination.

I

In September 1980, petitioner was indicted for the felonies of burglary and theft by receiving stolen property. He pleaded guilty, and was sentenced on October 8, 1980. Pursuant to the Georgia First Offender's Act, the trial court did not enter a judgment of guilt, but deferred further proceedings and sentenced petitioner to three years on probation for the burglary charge and a concurrent one year on probation for the theft harge. As a condition of probation, he trial court ordered petitioner to ay a $500 fine and $250 in restitu- ion. Petitioner was to pay $100 that lay, $100 the next day, and the $550 alance within four months.

Petitioner borrowed money from his parents and paid the first $200. About a month later, however, peti- ioner was laid off from his job. Peti- ioner, who has only a ninth grade education and cannot read, tried repeatedly to find other work but was unable to do so. The record indicates that petitioner had no income or assets during this period.

Shortly before the balance of the fine and restitution came due in February 1981, petitioner notified the probation office he was going to be late with his payment because he could not find a job. In May 1981, the State filed a petition in the trial court to revoke petitioner's probation because he had not paid the balance. After an evidentiary hearing, the trial court revoked probation for failure to pay the balance of the fine and restitution, entered a conviction and sentenced petitioner to serve the re- maining portion of the probationary period in prison. The Georgia Court of Appeals, relying on earlier Georgia Supreme Court cases, rejected peti- tioner's claim that imprisoning him for inability to pay the fine violated the Equal Protection Clause of the Fourteenth Amendment. The Georgia Supreme Court denied review. Since other courts have held that revoking the probation of indigents for failure to pay fines does violate the Equal Protection Clause, we granted cer- tiorari to resolve this important issue in the administration of criminal justice.

II

This Court has long been sensitive to the treatment of indigents in our criminal justice system. Over a quarter-century ago, Justice Black declared that "there can be no equal justice where the kind of trial a man gets depends on the amount of money he has." Griffin v. Illinois, 351 US 12, (1956). Griffin's principle of "equal justice," which the Court applied there to strike down a state practice of granting appellate review only to per- sons able to afford a trial transcript, has been applied in numerous other contexts.

Most relevant to the issue here is the holding in Williams v. Illinois, 399 US 235, (1970), that a State cannot sub- ject a certain class of convicted defen- dants to a period of imprisonment beyond the statutory maximum solely because they are too poor to pay the fine. Williams was followed and ex- tended in Tate v. Short, 401 US 395, (1971), which held that a State cannot convert a fine imposed under a fine- only statute into a jail term solely because the defendant is indigent and cannot immediately pay the fine in full. But the Court has also recognized limits on the principle of protecting indigents in the criminal justice system. For example, in Ross v. Mof- fitt, 417 US 600, (1974), we held that indigents had no constitutional right to appointed counsel for a discre- tionary appeal. In United States v. MacCollum, 426 US 317, (1976) (plurality opinion), we rejected an equal protection challenge to a federal statute which permits a district court to provide an indigent with a free trial transcript only if the court certifies that the challenge to his conviction is not frivolous and the transcript is necessary to prepare his petition.

Due process and equal protection principles converge in the Court's analysis in these cases. Most decisions in this area have rested on an equal protection framework.

As we recognized in Ross v. Moffitt, we generally analyze the fairness of relations between the criminal defendant and the State under the Due Process Clause, while we approach the question whether the State has invidiously denied one class of defendants a substantial benefit available to another class of defendants under the Equal Protection Clause.

The question presented here is whether a sentencing court can revoke a defendant's probation for failure to pay the imposed fine and restitution, absent evidence and findings that the defendant was somehow responsible for the failure or that alternative forms of punishment were inadequate.

Whether analyzed in terms of equal protection or due process, the issue cannot be resolved by resort to easy slogans or pigeonhole analysis, but rather requires a careful inquiry into such factors as "the nature of the individual interest affected, the extent to which it is affected, the rationality of the connection between legislative means and purpose, [and] the existence of alternative means for effectuating the purpose. . . ." Williams v. Illinois, 399 US 235 (1970).

In analyzing this issue, both Williams and Tate [must be] analyzed. The reach and limits of their holdings are vital to a proper resolution of the issue here. In Williams, a defendant was sentenced to the maximum prison term and fine authorized under the statute. Because of his indigency he could not pay the fine.

Pursuant to another statute equating a $5 fine with a day in jail, the defendant was kept in jail for 101 days beyond the maximum prison sentence to "work out" the fine. The Court struck down the practice, holding that "[o]nce the State had defined the outer limits of incarceration necessary to satisfy its penological interests and policies, it may not then subject a certain class of convicted defendants to a period of imprisonment beyond the statutory maximum solely by reason of their indigency." 399 US, at 233-234. In Tate v. Short, 401 US 395, (1971), we faced a similar situation, except that the statutory penalty there permitted only a fine. Quoting from a concurring opinion in Morris v. Schoonfield, 399 US 508, (1970), we reasoned that "the same constitutional defect condemned in Williams also inheres in jailing an indigent for failing to make immediate payment of any fine, whether or not the fine is accompanied by a jail term and whether or not the jail term of the indigent extends beyond the maximum term that may be imposed on a person willing and able to pay a fine." 401 US, at 398.

The rule of Williams and Tate, then, is that the State cannot "impos[e] a fine as a sentence and then automatically conver[t] it into a jail term solely because the defendant is indigent and cannot forthwith pay the fine in full."

In other words, if the State determines a fine or restitution to be the appropriate and adequate penalty for the crime, it may not thereafter imprison a person solely because he lacked the resources to pay it. Both Williams and Tate carefully distinguished this substantive limitation on the imprisonment of indigents from the situation where a defendant was at fault in failing to pay the fine.

This distinction, based on the reasons for non-payment, is of critical importance here. If the probationer has willfully refused to pay the fine or restitution when he has the means to pay, the State is perfectly justified in using imprisonment as a sanction to enforce collection.

But if the probationer has made all reasonable efforts to pay the fine or restitution, and yet cannot do so through no fault of his own, it is fundamentally unfair to revoke probation automatically without considering whether adequate alternative methods of punishing the defendant are available.

The decision to place the defendant on probation, however, reflects a determination by the sentencing court that the State's penological interests do not require imprisonment. The State nevertheless asserts three reasons why imprisonment is required to further its penal goals.

First, the State argues that revoking probation furthers its interest in ensuring that restitution be paid to the victims of crime. A rule that imprisonment may befall the probationer who fails to make sufficient bona fide efforts to pay restitution may indeed spur probationers to try hard to pay, thereby increasing the number of probationers who make restitution. Such a goal is fully served, however, by revoking probation only for persons who have not made sufficient bona fide efforts to pay.

Second, the State asserts that its interest in rehabilitating the probationer and protecting society requires it to remove him from the temptation of committing other crimes. This is no more than a naked assertion that a probationer's poverty by itself indicates he may commit crimes in the future and thus that society needs for him to be incapacitated. This would be little more than punishing a person for his poverty.

Third, and most plausibly, the State argues that its interests in punishing the lawbreaker and deterring others from criminal behavior require it to revoke probation for failure to pay a fine or restitutiton. The State clearly has an interest in punishment and deterrence, but this interest can often be served fully by alternative means. As we said in Williams, and reiterated in Tate, "[t]he State is not powerless to enforce judgments against those financially unable to pay a fine." For example, the sentencing court could extend the time for making payments, or reduce the fine, or direct that the probationer perform some form of labor or public service in lieu of the fine.

[A] sentencing court can often establish a reduced fine or alternate public service in lieu of a fine that adequately serves the State's goals of punishment and deterrence, given the defendant's diminished financial resources. Only if the sentencing court determines that alternatives to imprisonment are not adequate in a particular situation to meet the State's interest in punishment and deterrence may the State imprison a probationer who has made sufficient bona fide efforts to pay.

We hold, therefore, that in revocation proceedings for failure to pay a fine or restitution, a sentencing court must inquire into the reasons for the failure to pay. If the probationer willfully refused to pay or failed to make sufficient bona fide efforts legally to acquire the resources to pay, the court may revoke probation and sentence the defendant to imprisonment within the authorized range of its sentencing authority. If the probationer could not pay despite sufficient bona fide efforts to acquire the resources to do so, the court must consider alternate measures of punishment other than imprisonment. Only if alternate measures are not adequate to meet the State's interests in punishment and deterrence may the court imprison a probationer who has made sufficient bona fide efforts to pay. To do otherwise would deprive the probationer of his conditional freedom simply because, through no fault of his own, he cannot pay the fine. Such a deprivation would be contrary to the fundamental fairness required by the Fourteenth Amendment.

We do not suggest by our analysis of the present record that the State may not place the petitioner in prison. If,

upon remand, the Georgia courts determine that petitioner did not make sufficient bona fide efforts to pay his fine, or determine that alternate punishment is not adequate to meet the State's interests in punishment and deterrence, imprisonment would be a permissible sentence. Unless such determinations are made, however, fundamental fairness requires that the petitioner remain on probation.

IV

The judgment is reversed, and the case remanded for further proceedings not inconsistent with this opinion.

It is so ordered.

MARTINEZ v CALIFORNIA
444 U.S. 277, 62 L.Ed.2d 481, 100 S.Ct. 553 (1980)

[*footnotes and citations omitted*]

Mr. Justice Stevens delivered the opinion of the Court.

The two federal questions that appellants ask us to decide are (1) whether the Fourteenth Amendment invalidates a California statute granting absolute immunity to public employees who make parole-release determinations, and (2) whether such officials are absolutely immune from liability in an action brought under the federal Civil Rights Act of 1871, 42 U.S.C. § 1983. We agree with the California Court of Appeal that the state statute is valid when applied to claims arising under state law, and we conclude that appellants have not alleged a claim for relief under federal law.

The case arises out of the murder of a 15-year-old girl by a parolee. Her survivors brought this action in a California court claiming that the state officials responsible for the parole-release decision are liable n damages for the harm caused by the parolee.

The complaint alleged that the parolee, one Thomas, was convicted of attempted rape in December 1969. He was first committed to a state mental hospital as a "Mentally Disordered Sex Offender not amenable to treatment" and thereafter sentenced to a term of imprisonment of 1 to 20 years, with a recommendation that he not be paroled. Nevertheless, five years later, appellees decided to parole

Thomas to the care of his mother. They were fully informed about his history, his propensities, and the likelihood that he would commit another violent crime. Moreover, in making their release determination they failed to observe certain "requisite formalities." Five months after his release Thomas tortured and killed appellants' decedent. We assume, as the complaint alleges, that appellees knew, or should have known, that the release of Thomas created a clear and present danger that such an incident would occur. Their action is characterized not only as negligent, but also as reckless, willful, wanton and malicious. Appellants prayed for actual and punitive damages of $2 million.

The trial judge sustained a demurrer to the complaint and his order was upheld on appeal. After the California Supreme Court denied appellants' petition for a hearing, we noted probable jurisdiction.

I

Section 845.8(a) of the Cal Gov't Code Ann provides:

"Neither a public entity nor a public employee is liable for:

"(a) Any injury resulting from determining whether to parole or release a prisoner or from determining the terms and conditions of his parole or release or from determining whether to revoke his parole or release."

The California courts held that this statute provided appellees with a complete defense to appellants' state-law claims. They considered and rejected the contention that the immunity statutes as so construed violates the Due Process Clause of the Fourteenth Amendment to the Federal Constitution.

Like the California courts, we cannot accept the contention that this statute deprived Thomas' victim of her life without due process of law because it condoned a parole decision that led indirectly to her death. The statute neither authorized nor immunized the deliberate killing of any human being. It is not the equivalent of a death penalty statute which expressly authorizes state agents to take a person's life after prescribed procedures have been observed. This statute merely provides a defense to potential state tort-law liability. At most, the availability of such a defense may have encouraged members of the parole board to take somewhat greater risks of recidivism in exercising their authority to release prisoners than they otherwise might. But the basic risk that repeat offenses may occur is always present in any parole system. A legislative decision that has an incremental impact on the probability that death will result in any given situation—such as setting the speed limit at 55-miles-per-hour instead of 45—cannot be characterized as state action depriving a person of life just because it may set in motion a chain of events that ultimately leads to the random death of an innocent bystander.

Nor can the statute be characterized as an invalid deprivation of property. Arguably, the cause of action for wrongful death that the State has created is a species of "property" protected by the Due Process Clause. On that hypothesis, the immunity statute could be viewed as depriving the plaintiffs of that property interest insofar as they seek to assert a claim against parole officials. But even if one characterizes the immunity defense as a statutory deprivation, it would remain true that the State's interest in fashioning its own rules of tort law is paramount to any discernible federal interest, except perhaps an interest in protecting the individual citizen from state action that is wholly arbitrary or irrational.

We have no difficulty in accepting California's conclusion that there "is a rational relationship between the state's purposes and the statute." In fashioning state policy in a "practical and troublesome area" like this, the California Legislature could reasonably conclude that judicial review of a parole officer's decisions "would inevitably inhibit the exercise of discretion." That inhibiting effect could impair the State's ability to implement a parole program designed to promote rehabilitation of inmates as well as security within prison walls by holding out a promise of potential rewards. Whether one agrees or disagrees with California's decision to provide absolute immunity for parole officials in a case of this kind, one cannot deny that it rationally furthers a policy that reasonable lawmakers may favor. As federal judges, we have no authority to pass judgment on the wisdom of the underlying policy determination. We therefore find no merit in the contention that the State's immunity statute is unconstitutional when applied to defeat a tort claim arising under state law.

II

We turn then to appellants' § 1983 claim that appellees, by their action in releasing Thomas, subjected appellants' decedent to a deprivation of her life without due process of law.

It is clear that the California immunity statute does not control this claim even though the federal cause of action is being asserted in the state courts. We also conclude that it is not necessary for us to decide any question concerning the immunity of state parole officials as a matter of federal law because, as we recently held in Baker v. McCollan, 443 U.S. 137, 61 L.Ed.2d 433, 99 S.Ct. 2689, "[t]he first inquiry in any § 1983 suit...is whether the plaintiff has been deprived of a right 'secured by the Constitution and laws' " of the United States. The answer to that inquiry disposes of this case.

Appellants contend that the decedent's right to life is protected by the Fourteenth Amendment to the Constitution. But the Fourteenth Amendment protected her only from deprivation by the "State...of life... without due process of law." Although the decision to release Thomas from prison was action by the State, the action of Thomas five months later cannot be fairly characterized as state action. Regardless of whether, as a matter of state tort law, the parole board could be said either to have had a "duty" to avoid harm to his victim or to have proximately caused her death, we hold that, taking these particular allegations as true, appellees did not "deprive" appellants' decedent of life within the meaning of the Fourteenth Amendment.

Her life was taken by the parolee five months after his release. He was in no sense an agent of the parole board. Cf. Scheuer v. Rhodes, 416 U.S. 232, 40 L.Ed.2d 90, 94 S.Ct. 1683, 71 Ohio Op2d 474. Further, the parole board was not aware that appellants' decedent, as distinguished from the public at large, faced any special danger. We need not and do not decide that a parole officer could never be deemed to "deprive" someone of life by action taken in connection with the release of a prisoner on parole.[11] But we do hold that at least under the particular circumstances of this parole decision, appellants' dece-

_____

11. We reserve the question of what immunity, if any, a state parole officer has in a § 1983 action where a constitutional violation is made out by the allegations.

dent's death is too remote a consequence of the parole officers' action to hold them responsible under the federal civil rights law. Although a § 1983 claim has been described as "a species of tort liability," it is perfectly clear that not every injury in which a state official has played some part is actionable under that statute.

The judgment is affirmed.

So ordered.

GRIFFIN v. WISCONSIN

483 U.S. 868, 107 S. Ct. 3164, 97 L. Ed. 2d 709 (1987)

[Citations and Footnotes Omitted]

JUSTICE SCALIA delivered the opinion of the Court.

Petitioner Joseph Griffin, who was on probation, had his home searched by probation officers acting without a warrant. The officers found a gun that later served as the basis of Griffin's conviction of a state-law weapons offense. We granted certiorari, to consider whether this search violated the Fourth Amendment.

I

On September 4, Griffin, who had previously been convicted of a felony, was convicted in Wisconsin state court of resisting arrest, disorderly conduct, and obstructing an officer. He was placed on probation.

Wisconsin law puts probationers in the legal custody of the State Department of Health and Social Ser-

vices and renders them "subject ... to ... conditions set by the court and rules and regulations established by the department." One of the Department's regulations permits any probation officer to search a probationer's home without a warrant as long as his supervisor approves and as long as there are "reasonable grounds" to believe the presence of contraband—including any item that the probationer cannot possess under the probation conditions. The rule provides than an officer should consider a variety of factors in determining whether "reasonable grounds" exist, among which are information provided by an informant, the reliability and specificity of that information, the reliability of the informant (including whether the informant has any incentive to supply inaccurate information), the officer's own experience with the probationer, and the "need to verify compliance with rules of supervision and state and federal law." Another regulation makes it a violation of the terms of probation to refuse to consent a home search. And still another forbids a probationer to possess a firearm without advance approval from a probation officer.

On April 5, 1983, while Griffin was still on probation, Michael Lew, the supervisor of Griffin's probation officer, received information from a detective on the Beloit Department that there were or might be guns in Griffin's apartment. Unable to secure the assistance of Griffin's own probation officer, Lew, accompanied by another probation officer and three plainclothes policemen, went to the apartment. When Griffin answered the door, Lew told him who they were and informed him that they were going to search his home. During the subsequent search—carried out entirely by the probation officers under the authority of Wisconsin's probation regulation—they found a handgun.

Griffin was charged with possession of a firearm by a convicted felon, which is itself a felony. He moved to suppress the evidence seized during the search. The trial court denied the motion, concluding that no warrant was necessary and that the search was reasonable. A jury convicted Griffin of the firearms violation, and he was sentenced to two years' imprisonment.

***

We think the Wisconsin Supreme Court correctly concluded that this warrantless search did not violate the Fourth Amendment. To reach that result, however, we find it unnecessary to embrace a new principle of law, as the Wisconsin court evidently did, that any search of a probationer's home by a probation officer satisfies the Fourth Amendment as long as the information possessed by the officer satisfies a federal "reasonable grounds" standard. As his sentence for the commission of a crime, Griffin was committed to the legal custody of the Wisconsin State Department of Health and Social Services, and thereby made subject to that Department's rules and regulations. The search of Griffin's home satisfied the demands of the Fourth Amendment because it was carried out pursuant to a regulation that itself satisfies the Fourth Amendment's reasonableness requirement under well-established principles.

A

A probationer's home, like anyone else's, is protected by the Fourth Amendment's requirement that searches be "reasonable." Although we usually require that a search be undertaken only pursuant to a warrant (and thus supported by probable cause, as the Constitution says warrants must be), we have permitted exceptions when "special needs, beyond the normal need for law enforcement, make the warrant and probable-cause requirement impracticable." Thus, we have held that government employers and supervisors may conduct warrantless, work-related searches of employees' desks and offices without probable cause, and that school officials may conduct warrantless searches of some student property, also without probable cause. We have also held, for similar reasons, that in certain circumstances government investigators conducting searches pursuant to a regulatory scheme need not adhere to the usual warrant or probable-cause requirements as their searches meet "reasonable legislative or administrative standards."

A State's operation of a probation system, like its operation of a school, government office or prison, or its supervision of a regulated industry, likewise presents "special needs" beyond normal law enforcement that may justify departures from the usual warrant and probable-cause requirements. Probation, like incarceration, is a "form of criminal sanction imposed by a court upon a offender after verdict, finding, or plea of guilty." G. Killinger, H. Kerper, & P. Cromwell, Probation and Parole in the Criminal Justice System 14 (1976). Probation is simply one point (or, more accurately, one set of points) on a continuum of possible punishments ranging from solitary confinement in a maximum-security facility to a few hours of mandatory community service. A number of different options lie between those extremes, including confinement in a medium- or minimum-security facility, work-release programs, "halfway houses," and probation—which can

itself be more or less confining depending upon the number and severity of restrictions imposed.

These restrictions are meant to assure that the probation serves as a period of genuine rehabilitation and that the community is not harmed by the probationer's being at large. These same goals require and justify the exercise of supervision to assure that the restrictions are in fact observed. Recent research suggests that more intensive supervision can reduce recidivism, see Petersilia, Probation and Felony Offenders, 49 Fed. Probation 9 (June 1985), and the importance of supervision has grown as probation has become an increasingly common sentence for those convicted of serious crimes. Supervision, then, is a "special need" of the State permitting a degree of impingement upon privacy that would not be constitutional if applied to the public at large. That permissible degree is not unlimited, however, so we next turn to whether it has been exceeded here.

B

In determining whether the "special needs" of its probation system justify Wisconsin's search regulations, we must take that regulation as it has been interpreted by state corrections officials and state courts. As already noted, the Wisconsin Supreme Court—the ultimate authority on issues of Wisconsin law—has held that a tip from a police detective that Griffin "had" or "may have had" an illegal weapon at his home constituted the requisite "reasonable grounds." Whether or not we would choose to interpret a similarly worded federal regulation in that fashion, we are bound by the state court's interpretation, which is relevant to our constitutional analysis only insofar as it fixes the meaning of the regulation. We think it clear that the special needs of Wisconsin's probation system make the warrant requirement impracticable and justify replacement of the standard or probable cause by "reasonable grounds," as defined by the Wisconsin Supreme Court.

A warrant requirement would interfere to an appreciable degree with the probation system, setting up a magistrate rather than the probation officer as the judge of how close a supervision the probationer requires. Moreover, the delay inherent in obtaining a warrant would make it more difficult for probation officials to respond quickly to evidence of misconduct, and would reduce the deterrent effect that the possibility of expeditious searches would otherwise create. By way of analogy, one might contemplate how parental custodial authority would be impaired by requiring judicial approval for search of a minor child's room. And on the other side of the equation—the effect of dispensing with a warrant upon the probationer: Although a probation officer is not an impartial magistrate, neither is he the police officer who normally conducts searches against the ordinary citizen. He is an employee of the State Department of Health and Social Services who, while assuredly charged with pro-

tecting the public interest, is also supposed to have in mind the welfare of the probationer (who in the regulations is called a "client.") The applicable regulations require him, for example, to [p]rovid[e] individualized counseling designed to foster growth and development of the client as necessary," "[m]onito[r] the client's progress where services are provided by another agency and evaluat[e] the need for continuation of the services." In such a setting, we think it reasonable to dispense with the warrant requirement.

JUSTICE BLACKMUN'S dissent would retain a judicial warrant requirement, though agreeing with our subsequent conclusion that reasonableness of the search does not require probable cause. This, however, is a combination that neither the text of the Constitution nor any of our prior decisions permits. While it is possible to say that Fourth Amendment reasonableness demands probable cause without a judicial warrant, the reverse runs up against the constitutional provision that "no Warrants shall issue, but upon probable cause." The Constitution prescribes, in other words, that where the matter is of such a nature as to require a judicial warrant, it is also of such a nature as to require probable cause. Although we have arguably come to permit an exception to that prescription for administrative search warrants, which may but do not necessarily have to be issued by courts, we have never done so for constitutionally mandated judicial warrants.

There it remains true that "[i]f a search warrant be constitutionally required, the requirement cannot be flexibly interpreted to dispense with the rigorous constitutional restrictions for its issue." JUSTICE BLACKMUN neither gives a justification for departure from that principle nor considers its implications for the body of Fourth Amendment law.

We think that the probation regime would also be unduly disrupted by a requirement of probable cause. To take the facts of the present case, it is most unlikely that the unauthenticated tip of a police officer—bearing, as far as the record shows, no indication whether its basis was firsthand knowledge or, if not, whether the firsthand source was reliable, and merely stating that Griffin "had or might have" guns in his residence, not that he certainly had them—would meet the ordinary requirement of probable cause. But this is different from the ordinary case in two related respects: First, even more than the requirement of a warrant, a probable-cause requirement would reduce the deterrent effect of the supervisory arrangement. The probationer would be assured that so long as his illegal (and perhaps socially dangerous) activities were sufficiently concealed as to give rise to no more than reasonable suspicion, they would go undetected and uncorrected. The second difference is well reflected in the regulation specifying what is to be considered "[i]n deciding whether there are reasonable grounds to believe ... a client's living

quarters or property contained contraband," The factors include not only the usual elements that a police officer or magistrate would consider, such as the detail and consistency of the information suggesting the presence of contraband and the reliability and motivation to dissemble of the informant, but also "[i]nformation provided by the client which is relevant to whether the client possesses contraband," and "[t]he experience of a staff member with that client or in a similar circumstance." As was true, then, in *O'Connor v. Ortega*, and *New Jersey v. T.L.O.*, we deal with a situation in which there is an ongoing supervisory relationship—and one that is not, or at least not entirely, adversarial—between the object of the search and the decisionmaker.

In such circumstances it is both unrealistic and destructive of the whole object of the continuing probation relationship to insist upon the same degree of demonstrable reliability of particular items of supporting data, and upon the same degree of certainty of violation, as is required in other contexts. In some case—especially those involving drugs or illegal weapons—the probation agency must be able to act based upon a lesser degree of certainty than the Fourth Amendment would otherwise require in order to intervene before a probationer does damage to himself or society. The agency, moreover, must be able to proceed on the basis of its entire experience with the probationer, and to assess probabilities in the light of its knowledge of his life, character, and circumstances.

To allow adequate play for such factors, we think it reasonable to permit information provided by a police officer, whether or not on the basis of firsthand knowledge, to support a probationer search. The same conclusion is suggested by the fact that the police may be unwilling to disclose their confidential sources to probation personnel. For the same reason, and also because it is the very assumption of the institution of probation that the probationer is in need of rehabilitation and is more likely than the ordinary citizen to violate the law, we think it enough if the information provided indicates, as it did here, only the likelihood ("had or might have guns") of facts justifying the search.

The search of Griffin's residence was "reasonable" within the meaning of the Fourth Amendment because it was conducted pursuant to a valid regulation governing probationers. This conclusion makes its unnecessary to consider whether, as the court below held and the State urges, any search of a probationer's home by a probation officer is lawful when there are "reasonable grounds" to believe contraband is present. For the foregoing reasons, the judgment of the Wisconsin Supreme Court is

Affirmed.

JUSTICE BLACKMUN, with whom JUSTICE MARSHALL joins and, as to Parts I-B and I-C, JUSTICE BRENNAN joins and, as to Part I-C, JUSTICE STEVENS joins, dissenting.

In ruling that the home of a probationer may be searched by a probation officer without a warrant, the Court today takes another step that diminishes the protection given by the Fourth Amendment to the "right of the people to be secure in their persons, houses, papers, and effects, against unreasonable searches and seizures." In my view, petitioner's probationary status provides no reason to abandon the warrant requirement. The probation system's special law enforcement needs may justify a search by a probation officer on the basis of "reasonable suspicion," but even that standard was not met in this case.

I

The needs for supervision in probation presents one of the "exceptional circumstances in which special needs, beyond the normal need for law enforcement," justify an application of the Court's balancing test and an examination of the practicality of the warrant and probable cause requirements. The Court, however, fails to recognize that this is a threshold determination of special law enforcement needs. The warrant and probable-cause requirements provide the normal standard for "reasonable" searches. "[O]nly when the practical realities of a particular situation suggest that a government official cannot obtain a warrant based upon probable cause without sacrificing the ultimate goals to which a search would contribute, does the Court turn to a 'balancing' test to formulate a standard of reasonableness for this context." The presence of special law enforcement needs justifies resort to the balancing test, but it does not preordain the necessity of recognizing exceptions to the warrant and probable-cause requirements.

My application of the balancing test leads me to conclude that special law enforcement needs justify a search by a probation agent of the home of a probationer on the basis of a reduced level of suspicion. The acknowledged need for supervision, however, does not also justify an exception to the warrant requirement, and I would retain this means of protecting a probationer's privacy. Moreover, the necessity for the neutral check provided by the warrant's requirement is demonstrated by this case, in which the search was conducted on the basis of information that did not begin to approach the level of "reasonable grounds."

A

The probation officer is not dealing with an average citizen, but with a person who has been convicted of a crime. This presence of an offender in the community creates the need for special supervision. I therefore agree that a probation agent must have latitude in observing a probationer if the agent is to carry out his supervisory responsibilities effectively. Recidivism among probationers is a major problem, and supervi-

sion is one means of combating that threat. Supervision also provides a crucial means of advancing rehabilitation by allowing a probation agent to intervene at the first sign of trouble.

One important aspect of supervision is the monitoring of a probationer's compliance with the conditions of his probation. In order to ensure compliance with those conditions, a probation agent may need to search a probationer's home to check for violations. While extensive inquiry may be required to gather the information necessary to establish probable cause that a violation has occurred, a "reasonable grounds" stand allows a probation agent to avoid this delay and to intervene at an earlier stage of suspicion. This standard is thus consistent with the level of supervision necessary to protect the public and to aid rehabilitation. At the same time, if properly applied, the standard of reasonable suspicion will protect a probationer from unwarranted intrusions into his privacy.

B

I do not think, however, that special law enforcement needs justify a modification of the protection afforded a probationer's privacy by the warrant requirement. The search in this case was conducted in petitioner's home, the place that traditionally has been regarded as the center of a person's private life, the bastion in which one has a legitimate expectation of privacy protected by the Fourth Amendment.

...

A probationer usually lives at home, and often, as in this case, with a family. He retains a legitimate privacy interest in the home that must be respected to the degree that it is not incompatible with substantial governmental needs. The Court in *New Jersey v. T.L.O.* acknowledged that the Fourth Amendment issue needs to resolved in such a way as to "ensure that the [privacy] interests of students will be invaded no more than is necessary to achieve the legitimate end of preserving order in the schools." The privacy interests of probationers should be protected by a similar standard, and invaded no more than is necessary to satisfy probation's dual goals of protecting the public safety and encouraging the rehabilitation of the probationer.

The search in this case was not the result of an ordinary home visit by petitioner's probation agent for which no warrant is required. It was a search pursuant to a tip, ostensibly from the police, for the purpose of uncovering evidence of a criminal violation. There is nothing about the status of probation that justifies a special exception to the warrant requirement under these circumstances. If in a particular case there is a compelling need to search the home of a probationer without delay, then it is possible for a search to be conducted immediately under the established exception for exigent circumstances. There is no need to create a separate warrant exception for probationers. The existing exception provides a

probation agent with all the flexibility the agent needs.

The circumstances of this case illustrate the fact that the warrant requirement does not create any special impediment to the achievement of the goals of probation. The probation supervisor, Michael T. Lew, waited "[t]wo or three hours" after receiving the telephone tip before he proceeded to petitioner's home to conduct the search. He testified that he was waiting for the return of petitioner's official agent who was attending a legal proceeding, and that eventually he requested another probation agent to initiate the search. Mr. Lew thus had plenty of time to obtain a search warrant. If the police themselves had investigated the report of a gun at petitioner's residence, they would have been required to obtain a warrant. There simply was no compelling reason to abandon the safeguards provided by neutral review.

The Court appears to hold the curious assumption that the probationer will benefit by dispensing with the warrant requirement. It notes that a probation officer does not normally conduct searches, as does a police officer, and, moreover, the officer is "supposed to have in mind the welfare of the probationer." The implication is that a probation agent will be less likely to initiate an inappropriate search than a law-enforcement officer, and is thus less in need of neutral review. Even if there were data to support this notion, a reduced need for review does not justify a complete removal of the warrant requirement.

Furthermore, the benefit that a probationer is supposed to gain from probation is rehabilitation. I fail to see how the role of the probation agent in " 'foster[ing] growth and development of the client,' " is enhanced the slightest bit by the ability to conduct a search without the checks provided by prior neutral review. If anything, the power to decide to search will prove a barrier to establishing any degree of trust between agent and "client."

The Court also justifies the exception to the warrant requirement that it would find in the Wisconsin regulations by stressing the need to have a probation agent, rather than a judge, decide how closely supervised a particular probationer should be. This argument mistakes the nature of the search at issue. The probation agent retains discretion over the terms of a probationer's supervision—the warrant requirement introduces a judge or a magistrate into the decision only when a full-blown search for evidence of a criminal violation is at stake. The Court's justification for the conclusion that the warrant requirement would interfere with the probation system by way of an analogy to the authority possessed by parents over their children is completely unfounded. The difference between the two situations is too obvious to belabor. Unlike the private nature of a parent's interaction with his or her child, the probation system is a governmental operation, with explicit standards. Experience has shown that a neutral judge can best determine if

those standards are met and a search is justified. This case provides an excellent illustration of the need for neutral review of a probation officer's decision to conduct a search, for it is obvious that the search was not justified even by a reduced standard of reasonable suspicion.

C

The Court concludes that the search of petitioner's home satisfied the requirements of the Fourth Amendment "because it was carried out pursuant to a regulation that itself satisfies the Fourth Amendment's reasonableness requirement under well-established principles." In the Court's view, it seems that only the single regulation requiring "reasonable grounds" for a search is relevant to its decision. When faced with the patent failure of the probation agents to comply with the Wisconsin regulations, the Court concludes that it "is irrelevant to the case before us" that the probation agents "may have violated Wisconsin state regulations." All of these other regulations, which happen to define the steps necessary to ensure that reasonable grounds are present, can be ignored. This conclusion that the existence of a facial requirement for "reasonable grounds" automatically satisfies the constitutional protection that a search be reasonable can only be termed tautological. The content of a standard is found in its application and, in this case, I cannot discern the application of any standard whatsoever.

The suspicion in this case was based on an unverified tip from an unknown source. With or without the Wisconsin regulation, such information cannot constitutionally justify a search. Mr. Lew testified that he could not recall which police officer called him with the information about the gun, although he thought it "probably" was Officer Pittner. Officer Pittner, however, did not remember making any such telephone call. From all that the record reveals, the call could have been placed by anyone. It is even plausible that the information did not come from the police at all, but from someone impersonating an officer.

Even assuming that a police officer spoke to Mr. Lew, there was little to demonstrate the reliability of the information he received from that unknown officer. The record does not reveal even the precise content of the tip. The unknown officer actually may have reported that petitioner "had" contraband in his possession, or he merely may have suggested that petitioner "may have had guns in his apartment." Mr. Lew testified to both at different stages of the proceedings. Nor do we know anything about the ultimate source of the information. The unknown officer's belief may have been founded on a hunch, a rumor, or an informant's tip. Without knowing more about the basis of the tip, it is impossible to form a conclusion, let alone a reasonable conclusion, that there were "reasonable grounds" to justify a search.

Mr. Lew failed completely to make the most rudimentary effort to confirm the information he had received or to evaluate whether reasonable suspicion justified a search. Conspicuously absent was any attempt to comply with the Wisconsin regulations that governed the content of the "reasonable grounds" standard. No observations of a staff member could have been considered, as required by subsection (7) (a), for Mr. Lew did not consult the agent who had personal knowledge of petitioner's case. When information was provided by an informant, subsections (7) (c) and (d) required evaluation of the reliability of the information relied upon and the reliability of the informant. Mr. Lew proceeded in violation of these basic requirements. Subsection (7) (f) referred to "information provided by the client" and the explanatory notes stated that "the client should be talked to before the search. Sometimes, this will elicit information helpful in determining whether a search should be made. " This requirement, too, was ignored. Nor do any of the other considerations support a finding of reasonable grounds to conduct the search. There is no indication that there had been prior seizures of contraband from petitioner, or that his case presented any special need to verify compliance with the law.

The majority acknowledges that it is "most unlikely" that the suspicion in this case would have met the normal "probable cause" standard. It concludes, however, that this is not an "ordinary" case because of the need for supervision and the continuing relationship between the probationer and the probation agency. In view of this continuing relationship, the regulations mandated consideration of factors that go beyond those normally considered in determining probable cause to include information provided by the probationer and the experience of the staff member with the probationer. But unless the agency adheres to the regulations, it is sophistic to rely on them as a justification for conducting a search on a lesser degree of suspicion. Mr. Lew drew on no special knowledge of petitioner in deciding to search his house. He had no contact with the agent familiar with petitioner's case before commencing the search. Nor, as discussed above, was there the slightest attempt to obtain information from petitioner. In this case, the continuing relationship between petitioner and the agency did not supply support for any suspicion, reasonable or otherwise, that would justify a search of petitioner's home.

II

There are many probationers in this country, and they have committed crimes that range widely in seriousness. The Court has determined that all of them may be subjected to such searches in the absence of a warrant. Moreover, in authorizing these searches on the basis of a reduced level of suspicion, the Court overlooks the feeble justification for the search in this case.

I respectfully dissent.

JUSTICE STEVENS, with whom JUSTICE MARSHALL joins, dissenting.

Mere speculation by a police officer that a probationer "may have had" contraband in his possession is not a constitutionally sufficient basis for a warrantless, nonconsensual search of a private home. I simply do not understand how five Members of this court can reach a contrary conclusion. Accordingly, I respectfully dissent.

RIGHT TO TREATMENT, RIGHT TO MEDICAL AID, AND RIGHT TO LIFE

EHRLICH ANTHONY COKER, Petitioner

v.

STATE OF GEORGIA

433 U.S. 584, 53 L.Ed.2d 982, 97 S.Ct. 2861 (1977)

Mr. Justice White announced the judgment of the Court and filed an opinion in which Mr. Justice Stewart, Mr. Justice Blackmun, and Mr. Justice Stevens, joined.

Georgia Code Ann § 26-2001 (1972) provides that "[a] person convicted of rape shall be punished by death or by imprisonment for life, or by imprisonment for not less than one nor more than 20 years." Punishment is determined by a jury in a separate sentencing proceeding in which at least one of the statutory aggravating circumstances must be found before the death penalty may be imposed. Petitioner Coker was convicted of rape and sentenced to death. Both convic-

tion and sentence were affirmed by the Georgia Supreme Court. Coker was granted a writ of certiorari, limited to the single claim, rejected by the Georgia court, that the punishment of death for rape violates the Eighth Amendment, which proscribes "cruel and unusual punishments" and which must be observed by the States as well as the Federal Government.

I

While serving various sentences for murder, rape, kidnapping, and aggravated assault, petitioner escaped from the Ware Correctional Institution near Waycross, Ga. [P]etitioner entered the house of Allen and Elnita Carver through an unlocked kitchen door. Threatening the couple with a "board," he obtained a knife from the kitchen, and took Mr. Carver's money and the keys to the family car. Brandishing the knife and saying "you know what's going to happen to you if you try anything, don't you," Coker then raped Mrs. Carver. Soon thereafter, petitioner drove away in the Carver car, taking Mrs. Carver with him. [N]ot long thereafter petitioner was apprehended. Mrs. Carver was unharmed.

Petitioner was charged with escape, armed robbery, motor vehicle theft, kidnapping, and rape. The jury returned a verdict of guilty, rejecting his general plea of insanity. A sentencing hearing was then conducted. The jury was instructed that it could consider as aggravating circumstances whether the rape had been committed by a person with a prior record of conviction for a capital felony and whether the rape had been committed in the course of committing another capital felony, namely, the armed robbery of Allen Carver. The court also instructed, pursuant to statute, that even if aggravating circumstances were present, the death penalty need not be imposed if the jury found they were outweighed by mitigating circumstances, that is, circumstances not constituting justification or excuse for the offense in question, "but which, in fairness and mercy, may be considered as extenuating or reducing the degree" of moral culpability or punishment. The jury's verdict on the rape count was death by electrocution. Both aggravating circumstances on which the court instructed were found to be present by the jury.

II

It is now settled that the death penalty is not invariably cruel and unusual punishment within the meaning of the Eighth Amendment; it is not inherently barbaric or an unacceptable mode of punishment for crime; neither is it always disproportionate to the crime for which it is imposed. It is also established that imposing capital punishment, at least for murder, in accordance with the procedures provided under the Georgia statutes saves the sentence from the infirmities which led the Court to invalidate the prior Georgia capital punishment statute in Furman v. Georgia. 428 U.S. 153 (1976).

In sustaining the imposition of the death penalty in Gregg, however, the Court firmly embraced the holdings and dicta from prior cases, Furman v. Georgia, to the effect that the Eighth Amendment bars not only those punishments that are "barbaric" but also those that are "excessive" in relation to the crime committed. Under Gregg, a punishment is "excessive" and unconstitutional if it (1) makes no measurable contribution to acceptable goals of punishment and hence is nothing more than the purposeless and needless imposition of pain and suffering; or (2) is grossly out of proportion to the severity of the crime. A punishment might fail the test on either ground. Furthermore, these Eighth Amendment judgments should not be, or appear to be, merely the subjective views of individual Justices; judgment should be informed by objective factors to the maximum possible extent. To this end, attention must be given to the public attitudes concerning a particular sentence—history and precedent, legislative attitudes, and the response of juries reflected in their sentencing decisions are to be consulted. In Gregg, after giving due regard to such sources, the Court's judgment was that the death penalty for deliberate murder was neither the purposeless imposition of severe punishment nor a punishment grossly disproportionate to the crime. But the Court reserved the question of the constitutionality of the death penalty when imposed for other crimes. 428 US, at 187.

III

That question, with respect to rape of an adult woman, is now before us. We have concluded that a sentence of death is grossly disproportionate and excessive punishment for the crime of rape and is therefore forbidden by the Eighth Amendment as cruel and unusual punishment.

A

As advised by recent cases, we seek guidance in history and from the objective evidence of the country's present judgment concerning the acceptability of death as a penalty for rape of an adult woman. At no time in the last 50 years has a majority of the States authorized death as a punishment for rape. In 1925, 18 States, the District of Columbia, and the Federal Government authorized capital punishment for the rape of an adult female. By 1971 just prior to the decision in Furman v. Georgia, that number had declined, but not substantially, to 16 States plus the Federal Government. Furman then invalidated most of the capital punishment statutes in this country, including the rape statutes, because, among other reasons, of the manner in which the death penalty was imposed and utilized under those laws.

With their death penalty statutes for the most part invalidated, the States were faced with the choice of enacting modified capital punishment laws in an attempt to satisfy the requirements of Furman or of being satisfied with life imprisonment as the ultimate punishment for *any* offense. Thirty-five States immediately reinstituted the death penalty for at least limited kinds of crime. This public judgment as to the acceptability of capital punishment, evidenced by the immediate, post-Furman legislative reaction in a large majority of the States, heavily influenced the Court to sustain the death penalty for murder in Gregg v. Georgia.

But if the most marked indication of society's endorsement of the death penalty for murder is the legislative response to Furman v. Georgia, it should also be telling datum that the public judgment with respect to rape, as reflected in the statutes providing the punishment for that crime, has been dramatically different.

The current judgment with respect to the death penalty for rape is not wholly unanimous among state legislatures, but it obviously weighs very heavily on the side of rejecting capital punishment as a suitable penalty for raping an adult woman.

B

[T]he legislative rejection of capital punishment for rape strongly confirms our own judgment, which is that death is indeed a disproportionate penalty for the crime of raping an adult woman.

We do not discount the seriousness of rape as a crime. It is highly reprehensible, both in a moral sense and in its almost total contempt for the personal integrity and autonomy of the female victim and for the latter's privilege of choosing those with whom intimate relationships are to be established. Short of homicide, it is the "ultimate violation of self." It is also a violent crime because it normally involves force, or the threat of force or intimidation, to overcome the will and the capacity of the victim to resist. Rape is very often accompanied by physical injury to the female and can also inflict mental and psychological damage. Because it undermines the community's sense of security, there is public injury as well.

Rape is without doubt deserving of serious punishment; but in terms of moral depravity and of the injury to the person and to the public, it does not compare with murder, which does involve the unjustified taking of human life. Although it may be accompanied by another crime, rape by definition does not include the death of or even the serious injury to another person. The murderer kills; the rapist, if no more than that, does not. Life is over for the victim of the murderer; for the rape victim, life may not be nearly so happy as it was, but it is not over and normally is not beyond repair. We have the abiding conviction that the death penalty, which "is unique in its severity and irrevocability," Gregg v. Georgia, is an excessive penalty for the rapist who, as such, does not take human life.

The judgment of the Georgia Supreme Court upholding the death sentence is reversed, and the case is remanded to that court for further proceedings not inconsistent with this opinion.

So ordered.

MR. JUSTICE POWELL, concurring in the judgment in part and dissenting in part.

[T]he plurality draws a bright line between murder and all rapes—regardless of the degree of brutality of the rape or the effect upon the victim. I dissent because I am not persuaded that such a bright line is appropriate. As noted in Snider v. Peyton, 356 F2d 626, 627 (CA4 1966), "[t]here is extreme variation in the degree of culpability of rapists." The deliberate viciousness of the rapist may be greater than that of the murderer. Rape is never an act committed accidentally. Rarely can it be said to be unpremeditated. There also is wide variation in the effect on the victim. The plurality opinion says that "[l]ife is over for the victim of the murderer; for the rape victim, life may not be nearly so happy as it was, but it is not over and normally is not beyond repair." Ante, at 598, 53 L Ed 2d 993. But there is indeed "extreme variation" in the crime of rape. Some victims are so grievously injured physically or psychologically that life *is* beyond repair.

Thus, it may be that the death penalty is not disproportionate punishment for the crime of aggravated rape. Final resolution of the question must await careful inquiry into objective indicators of society's "evolving standards of decency," particularly legislative enactments and the responses of juries in capital cases. The plurality properly examines these indicia, which do support the conclusion that society finds the death penalty unacceptable for the crime of rape in the absence of excessive brutality or severe injury. But it has not been shown that society finds the penalty disproportionate for all rapists. In a proper case a more discriminating inquiry than the plurality undertakes well might discover that both juries and legislatures have reserved the ultimate penalty for the case of an outrageous rape resulting in serious, lasting harm to the victim. I would not prejudge the issue. To this extent, I respectfully dissent.

MR. CHIEF JUSTICE BURGER, with whom MR. JUSTICE REHNQUIST joins, dissenting.

I accept that the Eighth Amendment's concept of disproportionality bars the death penalty for minor crimes. But rape is not a minor crime; hence the Cruel and Unusual Punishments Clause does not give the Members of this Court license to engraft their conceptions of proper public policy onto the considered legislative judgments of the States. Since I cannot agree that Georgia lacked the constitutional power to impose the penalty of death for rape, I dissent from the Court's judgment.

A rapist not only violates a victim's privacy and personal integrity, but inevitably causes serious psychological as well as physical harm in the process. The long-range effect upon the victim's life and health is likely to be irreparable; it is impossible to measure the harm which results.

Rape is not a mere physical attack—it is destructive of the human personality. The remainder of the victim's life may be gravely affected, and this in turn may have serious detrimental effect upon her husband and any children she may have.

Victims may recover from the physical damage of knife or bullet wounds, or a beating with fists or a club, but recovery from such a gross assault on the human personality is not healed by medicine or surgery. To speak blandly, as the plurality does, of rape victims who are "unharmed," or to classify the human outrage of rape, as does Mr. Justice Powell, in terms of "excessive[ly] brutal," versus "moderately brutal," takes too little account of the profound suffering the crime imposed upon the victims and their loved ones.

The subjective judgment that the death penalty is simply disproportionate for the crime of rape is disturbing. The plurality's conclusion on this point is based upon the bare fact that murder necessarily results in the physical death of the victim, while rape does not. However, no Member of the Court explains why this distinction has relevance, much less constitutional significance. It is, after all, not irrational—nor constitutionally impermissible—for a legislature to make the penalty more severe than the criminal act it punishes in the hope it would deter wrongdoing.

Rape thus is not a crime "light years" removed from murder in the degree of its heinousness; it certainly poses a serious potential danger to the life and safety of innocent victims—apart from the devastating psychic consequences. It would seem to follow therefore that, affording the States proper leeway under the broad standard of the Eighth Amendment, murder is properly punishable by death, rape should be also, if that is the considered judgment of the legislators.

[I] cannot agree that it is constitutionally impermissible for a state legislature to make the "solemn judgment" to impose such penalty for the crime of rape. Accordingly, I would leave to the States the task of legislating in this area of the law.

SANDRA LOCKETT, Petitioner
v.
STATE OF OHIO
438 U.S. 586, 57 L.Ed.2d 973, 98 S.Ct. 2954 (1978)

OPINION OF THE COURT

MR. CHIEF JUSTICE BURGER delivered the opinion of the Court with respect to the constitutionality of the statute under which petitioner was sentenced to death, and announced the judgment of the Court.

We granted certiorari in this case to consider, among other questions, whether Ohio violated the Eighth and Fourteenth Amendments by sentencing Sandra Lockett to death pursuant to a statute that narrowly limits the sentencer's discretion to consider the circumstances of the crime and the record and character of the offender as mitigating factors.

I

Lockett was charged with aggravated murder with the aggravating specifications (1) that the murder was "committed for the purpose of escaping detection, apprehension, trial, or punishment" for aggravated robbery, and (2) that the murder was "committed while . . . committing, attempting to commit, or fleeing immediately after committing or attempting to commit . . . aggravated robbery." That offense was punishable by death in Ohio. See Ohio Rev Code Ann §§ 2929.03, 2929.04 (1975). She was also charged with aggravated robbery.

(facts are summarized as follows [])

[The record indicated that Lockett, petitioner in the case *sub judice*, and three companions carried out a plan to commit a robbery of a pawnshop. The plan included the

decision to use a gun in the robbery. Once at the scene, Lockett remained in the automobile and served as the driver in the subsequent flight from the scene. The robbery proceeded according to plan, until the pawnbroker grabbed the gun and was fatally shot in the process.

Pursuant to the flight from the crime scene, Lockett took possession of the gun. Subsequently, the participant who brandished the gun during the robbery pleaded guilty to murder and testified against the remaining three. In addition to Lockett, the petitioner herein, the other two participants similarly were convicted of aggravated murder.

The State's case consisted primarily of testimony from the coparticipant who had pleaded guilty to murder. Lockett did not take the stand. The remaining coparticipants were called as defense witnesses, but both refused to testify, choosing instead to invoke their Fifth Amendment Rights. Thus, the defense introduced no evidence to rebut the prosecutor's case.]

The court instructed the jury that, before it could find Lockett guilty, it had to find that she purposely had killed the pawnbroker while committing or attempting to commit aggravated robbery. The jury was further charged that one who

"purposely aids, helps, associates himself or herself with another for the purpose of committing a crime is regarded as if he or she were the principal offender and is just as guilty as if the person performed every act constituting the offense...."

Regarding the intent requirement, the court instructed:

"A person engaged in a common design with others to rob by force and violence an individual or individuals of their property is presumed to acquiesce in whatever may reasonably be necessary to accomplish the object of their enterprise....

"If the conspired robbery and the manner of its accomplishment would be reasonably likely to produce death, each plotter is equally guilty with the principal offender as an aider and abettor in the homicide.... An intent to kill by an aider and abettor may be found to exist beyond a reasonable doubt under such circumstances."

The jury found Lockett guilty as charged.

Once a verdict of aggravated murder with specifications had been returned, the Ohio death penalty statute required the trial judge to impose a death sentence unless, after "considering the nature and circumstances of the offense" and Lockett's "history, character, and condition," he found by a preponderance of the evidence that (1) the victim had induced or facilitated the offense, (2) it was unlikely that Lockett would have committed the offense but for the fact that she "was under duress, coercion, or strong provocation," or (3) the offense was "primarily the product of [Lockett's] psychosis or mental deficiency." Ohio Rev Code §§ 2929.03-2929.04(B) (1975).

In accord with the Ohio statute, the trial judge requested a presentence report as well as psychiatric and psychological reports. The reports contained detailed information about Lockett's intelligence, character, and background.

After considering the reports and hearing argument on the penalty issue, the trial judge concluded that the offense had not been primarily the product of psychosis or mental deficiency. Without specifically addressing the other two statutory mitigating factors, the judge said that he had "no alternative, whether [he] like[d] the law or not" but to impose the death penalty. He then sentenced Lockett to death.

* * * *

III

Lockett challenges the constitutionality of Ohio's death penalty statute on a number of grounds. We find it necessary to consider only her contention that her death sentence is invalid because the statute under which it was imposed did not permit the sentencing judge to consider, as mitigating factors, her character, prior record, age, lack of specific intent to cause death, and her relatively minor part in the crime. To address her contention from the proper perspective, it is helpful to review the developments in our recent cases where we have applied the Eighth and Fourteenth Amendments to death penalty statutes. We do not write on a "clean slate."

A

Prior to Furman v. Georgia, 408 US 238 (1972), every State that authorized capital punishment had abandoned mandatory death penalties, and instead permitted the jury unguided and unrestrained discretion regarding the imposition of the death penalty in a particular capital case. Mandatory death penalties had proved unsatisfactory, as the plurality noted in Woodson v. North Carolina, 428 US 280 (1976), in part because juries, "with some regularity, disregarded their oaths and refused to convict defendants where a death sentence was the automatic consequence of a guilty verdict."

This Court had never intimated prior to Furman that discretion in sentencing offended the Constitution. As recently as McGautha v. California, 402 US 183 (1971), the Court had specifically rejected the contention that discretion in imposing the death penalty violated the fundamental standards of fairness embodied in Fourteenth Amendment due process.

The constitutional status of discretionary sentencing in capital cases changed abruptly, however, as a result of the separate opinions supporting the judgment in Furman. The question in Furman was whether "the imposition and carrying out of the death penalty [in the cases before the Court] constitute[d] cruel and unusual punishment in violation of the Eighth and Fourteenth Amendments." 408 US, at 239. Two Justices concluded that the Eighth Amendment prohibited the death penalty altogether and on that ground voted to reverse the judgments sustaining the death penalties. Three Justices were unwilling to hold the death penalty per se unconstitutional under the Eighth and Fourteenth Amendments, but voted to reverse the judgments on other grounds. In separate opinions, the three concluded that discretionary sentencing, unguided by legislatively defined standards, violated the Eighth Amendment because it was "pregnant with discrimination," because it permitted the death penalty to be "wantonly" and "freakishly" imposed and because it imposed the

death penalty with "great infrequency" and afforded "no meaningful basis for distinguishing the few cases in which it [was] imposed from the many cases in which it [was] not," id., at 313. Thus, what had been approved under the Due Process Clause of the Fourteenth Amendment in McGautha became impermissible under the Eighth and Fourteenth Amendments by virtue of the judgment in Furman. See, Gregg v. Georgia, 428 US 153, 195-196 (1976) (opinion of Stewart, Powell, and Stevens, JJ.).

Predictably, the variety of opinions supporting the judgment in Furman engendered confusion as to what was required in order to impose the death penalty in accord with the Eighth Amendment. Some States responded to what was thought to be the command of Furman by adopting mandatory death penalties for a limited category of specific crimes thus eliminating all discretion from the sentencing process in capital cases. Other States attempted to continue the practice of individually assessing the culpability of each individual defendant convicted of a capital offense and, at the same time, to comply with Furman, by providing standards to guide the sentencing decision.

Four years after Furman, we considered Eighth Amendment issues posed by five of the post-Furman death penalty statutes.[1] Four Justices took the position that all five statutes complied with the Constitution; two

---

[1] Gregg v. Georgia, 428 U.S. 153, 49 L.Ed.2d 859, 96 S.Ct. 2909 (1976); Proffitt v. Florida, 428 U.S. 242, 49 L.Ed.2d 913, 96 S.Ct. 2960 (1976); Jurek v. Texas, 428 U.S. 262, 49 L.Ed.2d 929, 96 S.Ct. 2950 (1976); Woodson v. North Carolina, supra; and Roberts (Stanislaus) v. Louisiana, 428 U.S. 325, 49 L.Ed.2d 974, 96 S.Ct. 3001 (1976).

Justices took the position that none of them complied. Hence, the disposition of each case varied according to the votes of three Justices who delivered a joint opinion in each of the five cases upholding the constitutionality of the statutes of Georgia, Florida, and Texas, and holding those of North Carolina and Louisiana unconstitutional.

The joint opinion reasoned that to comply with Furman, sentencing procedures should not create "a substantial risk that the death penalty [will] be inflicted in an arbitrary and capricious manner." Gregg v. Georgia, supra, at 188. In the view of the three Justices, however, Furman did not require that all sentencing discretion be eliminated, but only that it be "directed and limited," 428 US, at 189, so that the death penalty would be imposed in a more consistent and rational manner and so that there would be a "meaningful basis for distinguishing the . . . cases in which it is imposed from . . . the many cases in which it is not." Id., at 188. The plurality concluded, in the course of invalidating North Carolina's mandatory death penalty statute, that the sentencing process must permit consideration of the "character and record of the individual offender and the circumstances of the particular offense as a constitutionally indispensable part of the process of inflicting the penalty of death." Woodson v. North Carolina, 428 US, at 304, in order to ensure the reliability, under Eighth Amendment standards, of the determination that "death is the appropriate punishment in a specific case." Id., at 305.

In the last decade many of the States have been obliged to revise their death penalty statutes in response to the various opinions supporting the judgments in Furman and Gregg and its companion cases. The signals from this Court have not, however, always been easy to decipher. The States now deserve the clearest guidance that the Court can provide; we have an obligation to reconcile previously differing views in order to provide that guidance.

B

With that obligation in mind we turn to Lockett's attack on the Ohio statute. Essentially she contends that the Eighth and Fourteenth Amendments require that the sentencer be given a full opportunity to consider mitigating circumstances in capital cases and that the Ohio statute does not comply with that requirement. She relies, in large part, on the plurality opinions in Woodson, and Roberts, and the joint opinion in Jurek, but she goes beyond them.

We begin by recognizing that the concept of individualized sentencing in criminal cases generally, although not constitutionally required, has long been accepted in this country.

Consistent with that concept, sentencing judges traditionally have taken a wide range of factors into account. That States have authority to make aiders and abettors equally responsible, as a matter of law, with principals, or to enact felony-murder statutes is beyond constitutional challenge. But the definition of crimes generally has not been thought automatically to dictate what should be the proper penalty. And where sentencing discretion is granted, it generally has been agreed that the sentencing judge's "possession of the fullest information possible concerning the defendant's life and characteristics" is "[h]ighly relevant—*if not essential*—[to the] selection of an appropriate sentence...." Williams v. New York. (Emphasis added.)

The opinions of this Court going back many years in dealing with sentencing in capital cases have noted the strength of the basis for individualized sentencing. Most would agree that "the 19th century movement away from mandatory death sentences marked an enlightened introduction of flexibility into the sentencing process." Furman v. Georgia. (Burger, C.J., dissenting).

Although legislatures remain free to decide how much discretion in sentencing should be reposed in the judge or jury in noncapital cases, the plurality opinion in Woodson, after reviewing the historical repudiation of mandatory sentencing in capital cases, concluded that

"in capital cases the fundamental respect for humanity underlying the Eighth Amendment ... requires consideration of the character and record of the individual offender and the circumstances of the particular offense as a constitutionally indispensable part of the process of inflicting the penalty of death." Id., at 304.

That declaration rested "on the predicate that the penalty of death is qualitatively different" from any other sentence. Id., at 305. We are satisfied that this qualitative difference between death and other penalties calls for a greater degree of reliability when the death sentence is imposed. The mandatory death penalty statute in Woodson was held invalid because it permitted *no* consideration of "relevant facets of the character and record of the individual offender or the circumstances of the

particular offense." Id., at 304. The plurality did not attempt to indicate, however, which facets of an offender or his offense it deemed "relevant" in capital sentencing or what degree of consideration of "relevant facets" it would require.

We are now faced with those questions and we conclude that the Eighth and Fourteenth Amendments require that the sentencer, in all but the rarest kind of capital case, not be precluded from considering *as a mitigating factor,* any aspect of a defendant's character or record and any of the circumstances of the offense that the defendant proffers as a basis for a sentence less than death. We recognize that, in noncapital cases, the established practice of individualized sentences rests not on constitutional commands, but on public policy enacted into statutes. The considerations that account for the wide acceptance of individualization of sentences in noncapital cases surely cannot be thought less important in capital cases. Given that the imposition of death by public authority is so profoundly different from all other penalties, we cannot avoid the conclusion that an individualized decision is essential in capital cases. The need for treating each defendant in a capital case with that degree of respect due the uniqueness of the individual is far more important than in noncapital cases. A variety of flexible techniques—probation, parole, work furloughs, to name a few—and various postconviction remedies, may be available to modify an initial sentence of confinement in noncapital cases. The nonavailability of corrective or modifying mechanisms with respect to an executed capital sentence underscores the need for individualized consideration as a constitutional requirement in imposing the death sentence.

There is no perfect procedure for deciding in which cases governmental authority should be used to impose death. But a statute that prevents the sentencer in all capital cases from giving independent mitigating weight to aspects of the defendant's character and record and to circumstances of the offense proffered in mitigation creates the risk that the death penalty will be imposed in spite of factors which may call for a less severe penalty. When the choice is between life and death, that risk is unacceptable and incompatible with the commands of the Eighth and Fourteenth Amendments.

C

The Ohio death penalty statute does not permit the type of individualized consideration of mitigating factors we now hold to be required by the Eighth and Fourteenth Amendments in capital cases. Its constitutional infirmities can best be understood by comparing it with the statutes upheld in Gregg, Proffitt, and Jurek.

In upholding the Georgia statute in Gregg, Justices Stewart, Powell, and Stevens noted that the statute permitted the jury "to consider any aggravating or mitigating circumstances," 428 US, at 206, and that the Georgia Supreme Court had approved "open and far-ranging argument" in presentence hearings, id., at 203. Although the Florida statute approved in Proffitt contained a list of mitigating factors, six Members of this Court assumed, in approving the statute, that the range of mitigating factors listed in the statute was not exclusive. Jurek involved a Texas statute which made no explicit reference to

mitigating factors. 428 US, at 272. Rather, the jury was required to answer three questions in the sentencing process, the second of which was "whether there is a probability that the defendant would commit criminal acts of violence that would constitute a continuing threat to society." Tex Code Crim Proc Art 37.071(b). The statute survived the petitioner's Eighth and Fourteenth Amendment attack because three Justices concluded that the Texas Court of Criminal Appeals had broadly interpreted the second question—despite its facial narrowness—so as to permit the sentencer to consider "whatever mitigating circumstances" the defendant might be able to show. Id., at 272-273, citing and quoting, Jurek v. State, 522 SW2d 934, 939-940 (Tex Crim App 1975). None of the statutes we sustained in Gregg and the companion cases clearly operated at that time to prevent the sentencer from considering any aspect of the defendant's character and record or any circumstances of his offense as an independently mitigating factor.

In this regard the statute now before us is significantly different. Once a defendant is found guilty of aggravated murder with at least one of seven specified aggravating circumstances, the death penalty must be imposed unless, considering "the nature and circumstances of the offense and the history, character, and condition of the offender," the sentencing judge determines that at least one of the following mitigating circumstances is established by a preponderance of the evidence:

"(1) The victim of the offense induced or facilitated it.

"(2) It is unlikely that the offense would have been committed, but for the fact that the offender was under duress, coercion, or strong provocation.

"(3) The offense was primarily the product of the offender's psychosis or mental deficiency, though such condition is insufficient to establish the defense of insanity." Ohio Rev Code Ann § 2929.04(B) (1975).

The Ohio Supreme Court has concluded that there is no constitutional distinction between the statute approved in Proffitt, and Ohio's statute, because the mitigating circumstances in Ohio's statute are "liberally construed in favor of the accused." State v. Bell, 48 Ohio St 2d 270, 281, 358 NE2d 556, 564 (1976); see State v. Bayless, supra, at 86, 357 NE2d, at 1046, and because the sentencing judge or judges may consider factors such as the age and criminal record of the defendant in determining whether any of the mitigating circumstances is established. State v. Bell, supra, at 281, 358 NE2d, at 564. But even under the Ohio court's construction of the statute, only the three factors specified in the statute can be considered in mitigation of the defendant's sentence. We see, therefore, that once it is determined that the victim did not induce or facilitate the offense, that the defendant did not act under duress or coercion, and that the offense was not primarily the product of the defendant's mental deficiency, the Ohio statute mandates the sentence of death. The absence of direct proof that the defendant intended to cause the death of the victim is relevant for mitigating purposes only if it is determined that it sheds some light on one of the three statutory mitigating factors. Similarly, consideration of a defendant's comparatively minor role in the offense, or age, would generally not be permitted, as such, to affect the sentencing decision.

The limited range of mitigating circumstances which may be considered by the sentencer under the Ohio statute is incompatible with the Eighth and Fourteenth Amendments. To meet constitutional requirements, a death penalty statute must not preclude consideration of relevant mitigating factors.

Accordingly, the judgment under review is reversed to the extent that it sustains the imposition of the death penalty, and the case is remanded for further proceedings.

So ordered.

BUSH v. REID
516 P.2d 1215 (Alas.Sup.Ct. 1973)

OPINION

BOOCHEVER, Justice.

James F. Bush originally filed this lawsuit in superior court to recover damages for injuries received in an automobile accident. At the time of the accident and the filing of the suit, appellant Bush was a felon on parole. The Reids, as defendants below, filed, and the superior court subsequently granted, a motion to dismiss the complaint on the ground that AS 11.05.070[1] suspends the civil rights of a person sentenced to imprisonment in the penitentiary for a term less than life. Bush here appeals on the grounds that the superior court erred in interpreting the statute, or, alternatively, that the statute if interpeted to bar appellant from access to the courts, violates the Alaska and United States constitutions. AS 11.05.070 and AS 33.15.190[2] when

read together clearly indicate that a parolee's civil rights, similarly to those of a prisoner, remain suspended during the time he is in the custody of the parole board. The first question presented to this court is whether the right to bring and maintain a civil suit is among the civil rights suspended by AS 11.05.070.

The general rule has been that in a jurisdiction where a convict loses his civil rights, he cannot sue while under such disability.[3] This rule has recently

---

[1] AS 11.05.070 provides:
A judgment of imprisonment in the penitentiary for a term less than for life suspends the civil rights of the person sentenced, and forfeits all public offices and all private trusts, authority, or power during the term or duration if imprisonment.

[2] AS 33.15.190 provides:
The board may permit a parolee to return to his home if it is in the state, or to go elsewhere in the state, upon such terms and conditions, including personal reports from the paroled person as the board prescribes. The board may permit the parolee to go into another state upon terms and conditions as the board pre-

scribes, and subject to the provisions of any compact executed under the authority of ch. 10 of this title and amendments to it. A prisoner released on parole remains in the legal custody of the board until the expiration of the maximum term or terms to which he was sentenced, less good time allowances provided by law. While in the custody of the board, a person is subject to the disabilities imposed by AS 11.05.070.

[3] Quick v. Western Ry. of Alabama, 207 Ala. 376, 92 So. 608, 609 (1922); Sullivan v. Prudential Ins. Co. of America, 131 Me. 228, 160 A. 777, 779 (1932); McLaughlin v. McLaughlin, 228 Mo. 635, 129 S.W. 21, 23 (1910); Avery v. Everett, 110 N.Y. 317, 18 N.E. 148, 154 (1888); Miller v. Turner, 64 N.D. 463, 253 N.W. 437, 439 (1934).
The supporting rationale for this suspension of civil rights of prisoners is explained in Tabor v. Hardwick, 224 F.2d 526, 529 (5th Cir. 1955), cert. denied, 350 U.S. 971, 76 S.Ct. 445, 100 L.Ed. 843 (1956):
We do not question the wisdom of the rule recognized by such decisions as Ex parte Hull [, 312 U.S. 546, 61 S.Ct. 640, 85 L.Ed. 1034] and White v. Ragen [, 324 U.S. 760, 65 S.Ct. 978, 89 L.Ed. 1348], supra, that penitentiary inmates

been applied and upheld in Kansas and Oregon. New York courts consistently have held that Penal Code Sec. 510, which suspends all rights of a prisoner while incarcerated comprises the right to file a civil lawsuit. Cases which allow convicts the right to initiate civil actions have been decided in the absence of statutes suspending civil rights such as the one in point here.

Bush argues, however, that this court should consider the use of "*the* civil rights" instead of "*all* civil rights" in As 11.05.070 (Kansas, Oregon, and New York provisions use "all civil rights"), and liberally construe the provision so as not to extend denial of civil access to the courts. The substitution of "the" for "all", while seemingly minor, does allow the possibility that certain civil rights might not be denied. We have been given no authority for such distinction however, and find no indication that this was the intent of the legislature. In light of this absence of indications of such legislative intent,

---

ought to have their right to inquire into the validity of their restraint of personal liberty and freedom zealously safeguarded by the courts, but we think that the principle of the cases so holding should not be extended to give them an absolute and unrestricted right to file any civil action they might desire. Otherwise, pentitentiary wardens and the courts might be swamped with an endless number of unnecessary and even spurious law suits filed by inmates in remote jurisdictions in the hope of obtaining leave to appear at the hearing of any such case, with the consequent disruption of prison routine and concomitant hazard of escape from custody. As a matter of necessity, however regrettable the rule may be, it is well settled that, "Lawful incarceration brings about the necessary withdrawal or limitation of many privileges and rights, a retraction justified by the considerations underlying our penal system." [citations omitted].

and the strong common-law authority holding that convicts are denied civil access to the courts, we hold that AS 11.05.070 and AS 33.15.190 combine to deny parolees the right to initiate civil suit.

Such finding, however, does not conclude our inquiry. We must also consider Bush's contention that these statutes, if read to bar him from access to the courts, are contrary to the Alaska and United States constitutions. Bush argues that AS 11.05.070 provides for "cruel and unusual punishment" and violates the due process clauses of the Alaska and United States constitutions. While we do not find the punishment provided to be so severe as to constitute "cruel and unusual punishment", nor the statute void for vagueness, we do hold that AS 33.15.190 violates the due process and equal protection clauses of the Alaska and United States constitutions insofar as it prohibits parolees from having access to the civil courts.

Both art. I, sec. 7 of the Alaska Constitution and sec. 1 of the fourteenth amendment of the United States Constitution prohibit the state from depriving any person of "life, liberty, or property, without due process of law." Bush contends that the right to bring a civil action for damages is property, and that therefore, the suspension of such right is a deprivation of property without due process of law.

Any suggestion that a parolee was deprived by his custodial status of standing to assert a denial of due process was dissolved by the United States Supreme Court in Morrissey v. Brewer. The nature of protection due "depends on the extent to which an individual will be 'condemned to suffer grievous loss.'" The loss suffered must have some relationship to a "liberty or property" interest within the ambit of the fourteenth amendment.

Because Bush seeks to overcome a statutory denial of access to the courts as a plaintiff, the starting point of our analysis must be Boddie v. Connecticut,[4] in which the United States Supreme Court held that a state could not deprive indigents of access to divorce tribunals by imposing a prohibitive filing fee.

Justice Harlan, writing for the Court in Boddie, recognized the centrality of the concept of due process in maintaining both order and justice in the resolution of the disputes which inevitably arise from human interaction. Upon that jurisprudential foundation he built the holding that where the state commands a monopoly over the only available legitimate means of dispute settlement and the relationship underlying the dispute is warp and woof of the fabric of society, the state may not deny access to the forum of settlement on account of poverty.[5]

We note superficial distinctions between the social context of the instant dispute and that in Boddie, but upon reflection we conclude that the denial of access to the civil courts rends the fabric of justice as surely here as in Boddie.

Although the collision of automobiles results in a dispute at first subject to private resolution, often the reconciliation of competing interests may be accomplished only by resort to the formal judicial process. The state exercises a monopoly over that paramount process where the "private structuring of individual relationships and repair of their breach" has failed.[6] No "recognized, effective alternatives for the adjustment of differences remain." Thus the initial element of the Boddie analysis exists here.

The second aspect of Boddie dealt with the importance of the marital relationship. Based on the hierarchy of social values the resolution of personal injury lawsuits might not be considered of such grave importance so as to justify invalidating this statute, although in the instance of a gravely-injured plaintiff, the very quality of his future existence may be dependent upon the outcome. In Boddie, Justice Harlan sought the fundamental human relationship doctrine to satisfy the due process clause only because denial of access to a divorce court does not impair a simpler "liberty or property" interest. Here we must apply the test of Morrissey: whether the individual is "condemned to suffer grievous loss" in conjunction with an interest "within the contemplation of the 'liberty or property' language of the Fourteenth Amendment."

We begin with the understanding that a chose in action, such as Bush's claim for personal injuries, is a form of property. The judicial process exists to reduce such claims to money judgment where private settlement is unavailing (or to extinguish them as non-meritorious). Judgments may be executed or assigned for substantially their face value, presuming solvency of the debtor. Unlitigated claims for personal injury have slight market value. Deprivation of access to the courts thus denies both the ability to reduce the claim to a money judgment and the ability to collect the claim or otherwise convert it into property of an appreciable value

---

[4] Boddie v. Connecticut, 401 U.S. 371, 91 S.Ct. 780, 28 L.Ed.2d 113 (1971).

[5] Id. at 374-376, 383, 91 S.Ct. at 784-785, 28 L.Ed.2d at 117, 122.

[6] Id. at 375-376, 91 S.Ct. at 785, 28 L.Ed.2d at 117.

and liquid nature during the parole status. Because the only reasonable use of the "property" represented by an unlitigated claim is reduction to judgment followed by collection or assignment, deprivation of that use deprives the claimant of the whole value of his property so long as he remains *non sui juris* (not his own master). The deprivation is no less severe than the taking of disputed wages or property during the pendency of litigation. Additionally, the denial of access to the courts creates an unfair leverage in the potential defendant who may avoid or reduce a meritorious claim because the ordinarily penurious state of the parolee dictates an early settlement on whatever terms are available. Finally, the risk of loss of the entire property due to staleness of evidence, loss of witnesses and similar complications constitutes an unreasonable burden. We note that the tolling of the statute of limitations during disability prevents the baldest of takings; nevertheless, the disability robs the parolee of the opportunity to be heard at a meaningful time and in a meaningful manner.

We conclude that a parolee denied access to the judicial process by reason of his custodial status is thereby condemned to suffer a grievous loss of property rights protected by the due process clause of the fourteenth amendment of the United States Constitution. We further declare that we would reach an identical result in interpreting the due process provisions of the Alaska Constitution alone, finding as we do that Justice Harlan's insightful analysis of the social compact applies with equal force to our constitution. We have several times held that "we are free, and we are under a duty, to develop additional constitutional rights and privileges under our Alaska Constitution."

Finding as we do that "civil death" of parolees violates the spirit and intention of the Alaska Constitution, we would not be impeded in our constitutional progress by a narrower holding of the United States Supreme Court.

The finding of a deprivation of a property right does not conclude a due process analysis; the assessment of what process is due requires a balancing of the individual's interest against the state's justification for its enactment. Denial of incarcerated felons' access to the civil judicial process has been justified by fears of disruption of prison routine, spurious litigation commenced in the hope of spending a few hours beyond the bars of prison and increased risks of escape by prisoners en route to hearings. Where the litigant is a parolee, to state these arguments is to reveal their absurdity. No argument has been pressed that engaging in civil litigation will encourage recidivism or otherwise interfere with the rehabilitation of an offender. If one may anticipate any effect, it is that active participation in the system of justice will develop added respect for the system and a sense of belonging in the mainstream of society.

Given this utter vacancy of rationale for the continued deprivation of access to the judicial process, we hold that AS 33.15.190, insofar as it suspends, in conjunction with AS 11.05.070, the access of parolees to civil courts, violates the due process clauses of the Alaska and United States constitutions.

Additionally, we find that AS 33.15.190 denies parolees "the equal protection of the laws", in violation of the fourteenth amendment to the United States Constitution, and art. I, sec. 1 of the Alaska Constitution. The state, by AS 33.15.190 and 11.05.070, denies parolees the right of access to the civil courts possessed by other persons. We find that the state interest in denying parolees this right satisfies neither the "compelling state interest" test applied when a "fundamental right" is at stake, nor the traditional, more lenient "rational basis" test otherwise applicable.

The state may have a reasonable basis for denying convicts while imprisoned access to civil courts, but the administration of a parole system differs so substantially from the administration of a prison that these reasons cannot logically support the "civil death" of parolees. Thus, although the state has a legitimate interest in restricting some activities of parolees, prohibiting a parolee from initiating civil actions has no logical connection with such an interest. The only interest here pertinent is preventing behavior which is detrimental to the restoration of a parolee into normal society. Since the parolee is no longer incarcerated, there is no justification based on the furthering of smooth penal administration. The parolee's ability to avail himself of the civil judicial process in order to vindicate his rights and protect his property interests in fact furthers, rather than restricts, the parolee's constructive development and restoration into normal society.

Failing to find either a "compelling state interest" or a "rational basis" for the state's denial to parolees of the right to initiate civil actions, we therefore hold that AS 33.15.190 denies parolees the "equal protection of the laws", in violation of the Alaska and United States constitutions.

For the reasons expressed above, we reverse the judgment of the superior court and remand the case for proceedings in accordance with this opinion.

Reversed and remanded.

. . . .

GREGG v. GEORGIA
428 U.S. 153, 96 S. Ct. 2909, 49 L. Ed. 2d 859 (1976)

MR. JUSTICE STEWART, MR. JUSTICE POWELL, and MR. JUSTICE STEVENS announced the judgment of the Court and filed an opinion delivered by MR. JUSTICE STEWART.

The issue in this case is whether the imposition of the sentence of death for the crime of murder under the law of Georgia violates the Eighth and Fourteenth Amendments.

I

The petitioner, Troy Gregg, was charged with committing armed robbery and murder. In accordance with Georgia procedure in capital cases, the trial was in two stages, a guilt stage and a sentencing stage. The evidence at the guilt trial established that on November 21, 1973, the petitioner and a traveling companion, Floyd Allen, while hitchhiking north in Florida were picked up by Fred Simmons and Bob Moore. While still in Florida, they picked up another hitchhiker, Dennis Weaver, who rode with them to Atlanta, where he was let out about 11 p.m. A short time later the four men interrupted their journey for a rest stop along the highway. The next morning the bodies of Simmons and Moore were discovered in a ditch nearby.

On November 23, after reading about the shootings in an Atlanta newspaper, Weaver communicated with the Gwinnett County police and related information concerning the journey with the victims, including a description of the car. The next afternoon, the petitioner and Allen, while in Simmons' car, were arrested in Asheville, N.C. In the search incident to the arrest a .25-caliber pistol, later shown to be that used to kill Simmons and Moore, was found in the petitioner's pocket. After receiving the warnings required by Miranda v. Arizona, 384 U.S. 436, 36 Ohio Op.2d 237 (1966), and signing a written waiver of his rights, the petitioner signed a statement in which he admitted shooting, then robbing Simmons and Moore. He justified the slayings on grounds of self-defense. The next day, while being transferred to Lawrenceville, Ga., the petitioner and Allen were taken to the scene of the shootings. Upon arriving there, Allen recounted the events leading to the slayings. His version of these events was as follows: After Simmons and Moore left the car, the petitioner stated that he intended to rob them. The petitioner then took his pistol in hand and positioned himself on the car to improve his aim. As Simmons and Moore came up an embankment towards the car, the petitioner fired three shots and the two men fell near a ditch. The petitioner, at close range, then fired a shot into the head of each. He robbed them of valuables and drove away with Allen.

Although Allen did not testify, a police detective recounted the substance of Allen's statements about the slayings and indicated that directly after Allen had made these statements the petitioner had admitted that Allen's account was accurate. The petitioner testified in his own defense. He confirmed that Allen had made the statements described by the detective, but denied their truth or ever having admitted to their accuracy. He indicated

that he had shot Simmons and Moore because of fear and in self-defense, testifying they had attacked Allen and him, one wielding a pipe and the other a knife.

The trial judge submitted the murder charges to the jury on both felony-murder and nonfelony-murder theories. He also instructed on the issue of self-defense but declined to instruct on manslaughter. He submitted the robbery case to the jury on both an armed-robbery theory and on the lesser included offense of robbery by intimidation. The jury found the petitioner guilty of two counts of armed robbery and two counts of murder.

At the penalty stage, which took place before the same jury, neither the prosecutor nor the petitioner's lawyer offered any additional evidence. Both counsel, however, made lengthy arguments dealing generally with the propriety of capital punishment under the circumstances and with the weight of the evidence of guilt. The trial judge instructed the jury that it could recommend either a death sentence or a life prison sentence on each count. The judge further charged the jury that in determining what sentence was appropriate the jury was free to consider the facts and circumstances presented by the parties, if any, in mitigation or aggravation.

Finally, the judge instructed the jury that it "would not be authorized to consider [imposing] the sentence of death" unless it first found beyond a reasonable doubt one of these aggravating circumstances:

"One—That the offense of murder was committed while the offender was engaged in the commission o[f] two other capit[a]l felonies, to-wit the armed ro[b]bery of [Simmons and Moore].

"Two—That the offender committed the offense of murder for the purpose of receiving money and the automobile described in the indictment.

"Three—The offense of murder was outrageously and wantonly vile, horrible and inhuman, in that they [sic] involved the depravity of the mind of the defendant."

Finding the first and second of these circumstances, the jury returned verdicts of death on each count.

The Supreme Court of Georgia affirmed the convictions and the imposition of the death sentences for murder. 233 Ga. 117, 210 S.E.2d 659 (1974). After reviewing the trial transcript and the record, including the evidence, and comparing the evidence and sentence in similar cases in accordance with the requirements of Georgia law, the court concluded that, considering the nature of the crime and the defendant, the sentences of death had not resulted from prejudice or any other arbitrary factor and were not excessive or disproportionate to the penalty applied in similar cases. The death sentences imposed for armed robbery, however, were vacated on the grounds that the death penalty had rarely been imposed in Georgia for that offense and that the jury improperly considered the murders as aggravating circumstances for the robberies after having considered the armed robberies as aggravating circumstances for the murders. 233 Ga., at 127, 210 S.E.2d, at 667.

We granted the petitioner's application for a writ of certiorari challenging the imposition of the death sentences in this case as "cruel and unusual" punishment in violation of the Eighth and the Fourteenth Amendments. ___ U.S. ___ (1976).

II

Before considering the issues presented it is necessary to understand the Georgia statutory scheme for the imposition of the death penalty. The Georgia statute, as amended after our decision in Furman v. Georgia, 408 U.S. 238 (1972), retains the death penalty for six categories of crime: murder,[4] kidnapping for ransom or where the victim is harmed, armed robbery,[5] rape, treason, and aircraft hijacking.[6]

---

[4] Section 26-1101 (1972) provides:

"(a) A person commits murder when he unlawfully and with malice aforethought, either express or implied, causes the death of another human being. Express malice is that deliberate intention unlawfully to take away the life of a fellow creature, which is manifested by external circumstances capable of proof. Malice shall be implied where no considerable provocation appears, and where all the circumstances of the killing show an abandoned and malignant heart.

"(b) A person also commits the crime of murder when in the commission of a felony he causes the death of another human being, irrespective of malice.

"(c) A person convicted of murder shall be punished by death or by imprisonment for life."

[5] Section 26-1902 (1972) provides:

"A person commits armed robbery when, with intent to commit theft, he takes property of another from the person or the immediate presence of another by use of an offensive weapon. The offense robbery by intimidation shall be a lesser included offense in the offense of armed robbery. A person convicted of armed robbery shall be punished by death or imprisonment for life, or by imprisonment for not less than one nor more than 20 years."

[6] These capital felonies currently are defined as they were when Furman was decided. The 1973 amendments to the Georgia statute, however, narrowed the class of crimes potentially punishable by death by eliminating capital perjury. Compare § 26-2401 (Supp. 1975) with § 26-2401 (1972).

The capital defendant's guilt or innocence is determined in the traditional manner, either by a trial judge or a jury, in the first stage of a bifurcated trial.

If trial is by jury, the trial judge is required to charge lesser included offenses when they are supported by any view of the evidence. After a verdict, finding, or plea of guilty to a capital crime, a presentence hearing is conducted before whomever made the determination of guilt. The sentencing procedures are essentially the same in both bench and jury trials. At the hearing,

"the judge [or jury] shall hear additional evidence in extenuation, mitigation, and aggravation of punishment, including the record of any prior criminal convictions and pleas of guilty or pleas of nolo contendere of the defendant, or the absence of any prior conviction and pleas: Provided, however, that only such evidence in aggravation as the State has made known to the defendant prior to his trial shall be admissible. The judge [or jury] shall also hear argument by defendant or his counsel and the prosecuting attorney . . . regarding the punishment to be imposed." § 27-2503. (Supp. 1975.)

The defendant is accorded substantial latitude as to the types of evidence that he may introduce. Evidence considered during the guilt stage may be considered during the sentencing stage without being resubmitted.

In the assessment of the appropriate sentence to be imposed the judge is also required to consider or to include in his instructions to the jury "any mitigating circumstances or aggravating circumstances otherwise authorized by law and any of [10] statutory aggravating circumstances which may be sup-

ported by the evidence. . . ." The scope of the non-statutory aggravating or mitigating circumstances is not delineated in the statute. Before a convicted defendant may be sentenced to death, however, except in cases of treason or aircraft hijacking, the jury, or the trial judge in cases tried without a jury, must find beyond a reasonable doubt one of the 10 aggravating circumstances specified in the statute. The sentence of death may be imposed only if the jury (or judge) finds one of the statutory aggravating circumstances and then elects to impose that sentence. If the verdict is death the jury or judge must specify the aggravating circumstance(s) found. In jury cases, the trial judge is bound by the jury's recommended sentence.

In addition to the conventional appellate process available in all criminal cases, provision is made for special expedited direct review by the Supreme Court of Georgia of the appropriateness of imposing the sentence of death in the particular case. The court is directed to consider "the punishment as well as any errors enumerated by way of appeal," and to determine:

"(1) Whether the sentence of death was imposed under the influence of passion, prejudice, or any other arbitrary factor, and

"(2) Whether, in cases other than treason or aircraft hijacking, the evidence supports the jury's or judge's finding of a statutory aggravating circumstance as enumerated in section 27.2534.1(b), and

"(3) Whether the sentence of death is excessive or disproportionate to the penalty imposed in similar cases, considering both the crime and the defendant."

If the court affirms a death sentence, it is required to include in its decision reference to similar cases that it has taken into consideration.

A transcript and complete record of the trial, as well as a separate report by the trial judge, are transmitted to the court for its use in reviewing the sentence. The report is in the form of a six and one-half page questionnaire, designed to elicit information about the defendant, the crime, and the circumstances of the trial. It requires the trial judge to characterize the trial in several ways designed to test for arbitrariness and disproportionality of sentence. Included in the report are responses to detailed questions concerning the quality of the defendant's representation, whether race played a role in the trial, and, whether, in the trial court's judgment, there was any doubt about the defendant's guilt or the appropriateness of the sentence. A copy of the report is served upon defense counsel. Under its special review authority, the court may either affirm the death sentence or remand the case for resentencing. In cases in which the death sentence is affirmed there remains the possibility of executive clemency.[11]

III

We address initially the basic contention that the punishment of death for the crime of murder is, under all circumstances, "cruel and unusual" in violation of the Eighth and Fourteenth Amendments of the Constitution. In Part IV of this opinion, we will consider the sentence of death imposed under the Georgia statutes at issue in this case.

---

[11] See Ga. Const. Ann. § 2-3011 (1972); Ga. Code Ann. §§ 77-501, 77-511, 77-513 (Board of Pardons and Paroles is authorized to commute sentence of death except in cases where Governor refuses to suspend that sentence).

The Court on a number of occasions has both assumed and asserted the constitutionality of capital punishment. In several cases that assumption provided a necessary foundation for the decision, as the Court was asked to decide whether a particular method of carrying out a capital sentence would be allowed to stand under the Eighth Amendment. But until Furman v. Georgia, 408 U.S. 238 (1972), the Court never confronted squarely the fundamental claim that the punishment of death always, regardless of the enormity of the offense or the procedure followed in imposing the sentence, is cruel and unusual punishment in violation of the Constitution. Although this issue was presented and addressed in Furman, it was not resolved by the Court. Four Justices would have held that capital punishment is not unconstitutional *per se;* two Justices would have reached the opposite conclusion; and three Justices, while agreeing that the statutes then before the Court were invalid as applied, left open the question whether such punishment may ever be imposed. We now hold that the punishment of death does not invariably violate the Constitution.

A

The history of the prohibition of "cruel and unusual" punishment already has been reviewed by this Court at length. The phrase first appeared in the English Bill of Rights of 1689, which was drafted by Parliament at the accession of William and Mary. See Granucci, "Nor Cruel and Unusual Punishments Inflicted:" The Original Meaning, 57 Cal.L.Rev. 839, 852-853 (1969). The English version appears to have been directed against punishments unauthorized by statute and beyond the jurisdiction of the sentencing court, as well as those disproportionate to the offense involved. The American draftsmen, who adopted the English phrasing in drafting the Eighth Amendment, were primarily concerned, however, with proscribing "tortures" and other "barbarous" methods of punishment."

In the earliest cases raising Eighth Amendment claims, the Court focused on particular methods of execution to determine whether they were too cruel to pass constitutional muster. The constitutionality of the sentence of death itself was not at issue, and the criterion used to evaluate the mode of execution was its similarity to "torture" and other "barbarous" methods.

But the Court has not confined the prohibition embodied in the Eighth Amendment to "barbarous" methods that were generally outlawed in the 18th century. Instead, the Amendment has been interpreted in a flexible and dynamic manner. The Court early recognized that "a principle to be vital must be capable of wider application than the mischief which gave it birth." Weems v. United States, 217 U.S. 349, 373 (1910). Thus the clause forbidding "cruel and unusual" punishments "is not fastened to the obsolete but may acquire meaning as public opinion becomes enlightened by a humane justice." See also Furman v. Georgia, 408 U.S., at 429-430 (POWELL, J., dissenting); Trop v. Dulles, 356 U.S., at 100-101 (plurality opinion).

In Weems the Court addressed the constitutionality of the Philippine punishment of *cadena temporal* for the crime of falsifying an official document. That punishment included imprisonment for at least 12 years and one day, in chains, at hard and painful labor; the loss of many basic civil rights; and subjection to lifetime surveillance. Al-

though the Court acknowledged the possibility that "the cruelty of pain" may be present in the challenged punishment, 217 U.S., at 366, it did not rely on that factor, for it rejected the proposition that the Eighth Amendment reaches only punishments that are "inhuman and barbarous, torture and the like." Rather, the Court focused on the lack of proportion between the crime and the offense:

"Such penalties for such offenses amaze those who have formed their conception of the relation of a state to even its offending citizens from the practice of the American commonwealths, and believe that it is a precept of justice that punishment for crime should be graduated and proportioned to offense."

Later, in Trop v. Dulles, 356 U.S. 86 (1958), the Court reviewed the constitutionality of the punishment of denationalization imposed upon a soldier who escaped from an Army stockade and became a deserter for one day. Although the concept of proportionality was not the basis of the holding, the plurality observed in dicta that "[f]ines, imprisonment and even execution may be imposed depending upon the enormity of the crime."

The substantive limits imposed by the Eighth Amendment on what can be made criminal and punished were discussed in Robinson v. California, 370 U.S. 660 (1962). The Court found unconstitutional a state statute that made the status of being addicted to a narcotic drug a criminal offense. It held, in effect, that it is "cruel and unusual" to impose any punishment at all for the mere status of addiction. The cruelty in the abstract of the actual sentence imposed was irrelevant: "Even one day in prison would be cruel and unusual punishment for the 'crime' of having a common cold." Most recently, in Furman v. Georgia, 408 U.S. 238 (1972), three Justices in separate concurring opinions found the Eighth Amendment applicable to procedures employed to select convicted defendants for the sentence of death.

It is clear from the foregoing precedents that the Eighth Amendment has not been regarded as a static concept. As Chief Justice Warren said, in an oft-quoted phrase, "[t]he Amendment must draw its meaning from the evolving standards of decency that mark the progress of a maturing society." Thus, an assessment of contemporary values concerning the infliction of a challenged sanction is relevant to the application of the Eighth Amendment. As we develop below more fully, *infra,* this assessment does not call for a subjective judgment. It requires rather, that we look to objective indicia that reflect the public attitude toward a given sanction.

But our cases also make clear that public perceptions of standards of decency with respect to criminal sanctions are not conclusive. A penalty also must accord with "the dignity of man," which is the "basic concept underlying the Eighth Amendment." This means, at least, that the punishment not be "excessive." When a form of punishment in the abstract (in this case, whether capital punishment may ever be imposed as a sanction for murder) rather than in the particular (the propriety of death as a penalty to be applied to a specific defendant for a specific crime) is under consideration, the inquiry into "excessiveness" has two aspects. First, the punishment must not involve the unnecessary and wanton infliction of pain. Second, the punishment must not be grossly out of proportion to the severity of the crime.

B

Of course, the requirements of the Eighth Amendment must be applied with an awareness of the limited role to be played by the courts. This does not mean that judges have no role to play, for the Eighth Amendment is a restraint upon the exercise of legislative power.

"Judicial review, by definition, often involves a conflict between judicial and legislative judgment as to what the Constitution means or requires. In this respect, Eighth Amendment cases come to us in no different posture. It seems conceded by all that the Amendment imposes some obligations on the judiciary to judge the constitutionality of punishment and that there are punishments that the Amendment would bar whether legislatively approved or not."

But, while we have an obligation to insure that constitutional bounds are not overreached, we may not act as judges as we might as legislators.

"Courts are not representative bodies. They are not designed to be a good reflex of a democratic society. Their judgment is best informed, and therefore most dependable, within narrow limits. Their essential quality is detachment, founded on independence. History teaches that the independence of the judiciary is jeopardized when courts become embroiled in the passions of the day and assume primary responsibility in choosing between competing political, economic and social pressures."

Therefore, in assessing a punishment selected by a democratically elected legislature against the constitutional measure, we presume its validity. We may not require the legislature to select the least severe penalty possible so long as the penalty selected is not cruelly inhumane or disproportionate to the crime involved. And a heavy burden rests on those who would attack the judgment of the representatives of the people.

This is true in part because the constitutional test is intertwined with an assessment of contemporary standards and the legislative judgment weighs heavily in ascertaining such standards. "[I]n a democratic society legislatures, not courts, are constituted to respond to the will and consequently the moral values of the people." The deference we owe to the decisions of the state legislatures under our federal system, *id.*, at 465-470 (REHNQUIST, J., dissenting), is enhanced where the specification of punishments is concerned, for "these are peculiarly questions of legislative policy." Caution is necessary lest this Court become, "under the aegis of the Cruel and Unusual Punishment Clause, the ultimate arbiter of the standards of criminal responsibility . . . throughout the country." A decision that a given punishment is impermissible under the Eighth Amendment cannot be reversed short of a constitutional amendment. The ability of the people to express their preference through the normal democratic processes, as well as through ballot referenda, is shut off. Revisions cannot be made in the light of further experience.

C

In the discussion to this point we have sought to identify the principles and considerations that guide a court in addressing an Eighth Amendment claim. We now consider specifically whether the sentence of death for the crime of murder is a *per se* violation of the Eighth and Fourteenth Amendments to the Constitution. We note first that history and precedent strongly support a negative answer to this question.

1

The imposition of the death penalty for the crime of murder has a long history of acceptance both in the United States and in England. The common-law rule imposed a mandatory death sentence on all convicted murderers. And the penalty continued to be used into the 20th century by most American States, although the breadth of the common-law rule was diminished, initially by narrowing the class of murders to be punished by death and subsequently by widespread adoption of laws expressly granting juries the discretion to recommend mercy.

It is apparent from the text of the Constitution itself that the existence of capital punishment was accepted by the Framers. At the time the Eighth Amendment was ratified, capital punishment was a common sanction in every State. Indeed, the First Congress of the United States enacted legislation providing death as the penalty for specified crimes. The Fifth Amendment, adopted at the same time as the Eighth, contemplated the continued existence of the capital sanction by imposing certain limits on the prosecution of capital cases:

"No person shall be held to answer for a capital, or otherwise infamous crime, unless on a presentment or indictment of a Grand Jury . . . ; nor shall any person be subject for the same offense to be twice put in jeopardy of life or limb; . . . nor be deprived of life, liberty, or property, without due process of law. . . ."

And the Fourteenth Amendment, adopted over three-quarters of a century later, similarly contemplates the existence of the capital sanction in providing that no State shall deprive any person of "life, liberty, or property" without due process of law.

For nearly two centuries, this Court, repeatedly and often expressly, has recognized that capital punishment is not invalid *per se.* In Wilkerson v. Utah, 99 U.S., at 134-135, where the Court found no constitutional violation in inflicting death by public shooting, it said:

"Cruel and unusual punishments are forbidden by the Constitution, but the authorities referred to are quite sufficient to show that the punishment of shooting as a mode of executing the death penalty for the crime of murder in the first degree is not included in that category, within the meaning of the eighth amendment."

Rejecting the contention that death by electrocution was "cruel and unusual," the Court in *In re* Kemmler, 136 U.S., at 447, reiterated:

". . . the punishment of death is not cruel, within the meaning of that word as used in the Constitution. It implies there [is] something inhuman and barbarous, something more than the mere extinguishment of life."

Again, in Louisiana ex rel. Francis v. Resweber, 329 U.S., at 464, the Court remarked: "The cruelty against which the Constitution protects a convicted man is cruelty inherent in the method of punishment, not the necessary suffering involved in any method employed to extinguish life humanely." And in Trop v. Dulles, 356 U.S., at 99, Chief Justice Warren, for four Justices, wrote:

"Whatever the arguments may be against capital punishment, both on moral grounds and in terms of accomplishing the purposes of punishment . . . the death penalty has been employed throughout our history, and, in a day when it is still widely

accepted, it cannot be said to violate the constitutional concept of cruelty."

Four years ago, the petitioners in Furman and its companion cases predicated their argument primarily upon the asserted proposition that standards of decency had evolved to the point where capital punishment no longer could be tolerated. The petitioners in those cases said, in effect, that the evolutionary process had come to an end, and that standards of decency required that the Eighth Amendment be construed finally as prohibiting capital punishment for any crime regardless of its depravity and impact on society. This view was accepted by two Justices. Three other Justices were unwilling to go so far; focusing on the procedures by which convicted defendants were selected for the death penalty rather than on the actual punishment inflicted, they joined in the conclusion that the statutes before the Court were constitutionally invalid.

The petitioners in the capital cases before the Court today renew the "standards of decency" argument, but developments during the four years since Furman have undercut substantially the assumptions upon which their argument rested. Despite the continuing debate, dating back to the 19th century, over the morality and utility of capital punishment, it is now evident that a large proportion of American society continues to regard it as an appropriate and necessary criminal sanction.

The most marked indication of society's endorsement of the death penalty for murder is the legislative response to Furman. The legislatures of at least 35 States have enacted new statutes that provide for the death penalty for at least some crimes that result in the death of another person.

And the Congress of the United States, in 1974, enacted a statute providing the death penalty for aircraft piracy that results in death. These recently adopted statutes have attempted to address the concerns expressed by the Court in Furman primarily (i) by specifying the factors to be weighed and the procedures to be followed in deciding when to impose a capital sentence, or (ii) by making the death penalty mandatory for specified crimes. But all of the post-Furman statutes make clear that capital punishment itself has not been rejected by the elected representatives of the people.

In the only statewide referendum occurring since Furman and brought to our attention, the people of California adopted a constitutional amendment that authorized capital punishment, in effect negating a prior ruling by the Supreme Court of California in People v. Anderson, 6 Cal. 3d 628, 493 P.2d 880, cert. denied, 406 U.S. 958 (1972), that the death penalty violated the California Constitution.

The jury also is a significant and reliable objective index of contemporary values because it is so directly involved. The Court has said that "one of the most important functions any jury can perform in making . . . a selection [between life imprisonment and death for a defendant convicted in a capital case] is to maintain a link between contemporary community values and the penal system." It may be true that evolving standards have influenced juries in recent decades to be more discriminating in imposing the sentence of death. But the relative infrequency of jury verdicts imposing the death sentence does not indicate rejection of capital punishment per se. Rather, the reluctance of juries in many cases to impose the sentence may well reflect

the humane feeling that this most irrevocable of sanctions should be reserved for a small number of extreme cases. Indeed, the actions of juries in many States since Furman is fully compatible with the legislative judgments, reflected in the new statutes, as to the continued utility and necessity of capital punishment in appropriate cases. At the close of 1974 at least 254 persons had been sentenced to death since Furman, and by the end of March, 1976, more than 460 persons were subject to death sentences.

As we have seen, however, the Eighth Amendment demands more than that a challenged punishment be acceptable to contemporary society. The Court also must ask whether it comports with the basic concept of human dignity at the core of the Amendment. Although we cannot "invalidate a category of penalties because we deem less severe penalties adequate to serve the ends of penology," the sanction imposed cannot be so totally without penological justification that it results in the gratuitous infliction of suffering.

The death penalty is said to serve two principal social purposes: retribution and deterrence of capital crimes by prospective offenders.

In part, capital punishment is an expression of society's moral outrage at particularly offensive conduct. This function may be unappealing to many, but it is essential in an ordered society that asks its citizens to rely on legal processes rather than self-help to vindicate their wrongs.

"The instinct for retribution is part of the nature of man, and channeling that instinct in the administration of criminal justice serves an important purpose in promoting the stability of a society governed by law. When people begin to believe that organized society is unwilling or unable to impose upon criminal offenders the punishment they 'deserve,' then there are sown the seeds of anarchy —of self-help, vigilante justice, and lynch law."

Retribution is no longer the dominant objective of the criminal law," but neither is it a forbidden objective nor one inconsistent with our respect for the dignity of men. Indeed, the decision that capital punishment may be the appropriate sanction in extreme cases is an expression of the community's belief that certain crimes are themselves so grievous an affront to humanity that the only adequate response may be the penalty of death.

Statistical attempts to evaluate the worth of the death penalty as a deterrent to crimes by potential offenders have occasioned a great deal of debate. The results simply have been inconclusive. As one opponent of capital punishment has said:

". . . after all possible inquiry, including the probing of all possible methods of inquiry, we do not know, and for systematic and easily visible reasons cannot know, what the truth about this 'deterrent' effect may be....

The inescapable flaw is . . . that social conditions in any state are not constant through time, and that social conditions are not the same in any two states. If an effect were observed (and the observed effects, one way or another, are not large) then one could not at all tell whether any of this effect is attributable to the presence or absence of capital punishment. A 'scientific'—that is to say, a soundly based—conclusion is simply impossible, and no methodological path out of this tangle suggests itself."

Although some of the studies suggest that the death penalty may not function as a significantly greater deterrent than lesser penalties, there is no convincing empirical evidence either supporting or refuting this view. We may nevertheless assume safely that there are murderers, such as those who act in passion, for whom the threat of death has little or no deterrent effect. But for many others, the death penalty undoubtedly is a significant deterrent. There are carefully contemplated murders, such as murder for hire, where the possible penalty of death may well enter into the cold calculus that precedes the decision to act. And there are some categories of murder, such as murder by a life prisoner, where other sanctions may not be adequate.

The value of capital punishment as a deterrent of crime is a complex factual issue the resolution of which properly rests with the legislatures, which can evaluate the results of statistical studies in terms of their own local conditions and with a flexibility of approach that is not available to the courts. Indeed, many of the post-Furman statutes reflect just such a responsible effort to define those crimes and those criminals for which capital punishment is most probably an effective deterrent.

In sum, we cannot say that the judgment of the Georgia legislature that capital punishment may be necessary in some cases is clearly wrong. Considerations of federalism, as well as respect for the ability of a legislature to evaluate, in terms of its particular state the moral consensus concerning the death penalty and its social utility as a sanction, require us to conclude, in the absence of more convincing evidence, that the infliction of death as a punishment for murder is not without justification and thus is not unconstitutionally severe.

Finally, we must consider whether the punishment of death is disproportionate in relation to the crime for which it is imposed. There is no question that death as a punishment is unique in its severity and irrevocability. When a defendant's life is at stake, the Court has been particularly sensitive to insure that every safeguard is observed. But we are concerned here only with the imposition of capital punishment for the crime of murder, and when a life has been taken deliberately by the offender, we cannot say that the punishment is invariably disproportionate to the crime. It is an extreme sanction, suitable to the most extreme of crimes.

We hold that the death penalty is not a form of punishment that may never be imposed, regardless of the circumstances of the offense, regardless of the character of the offender, and regardless of the procedure followed in reaching the decision to impose it.

IV

We now consider whether Georgia may impose the death penalty on the petitioner in this case.

A

While Furman did not hold that the infliction of the death penalty *per se* violates the Constitution's ban on cruel and unusual punishments, it did recognize that the penalty of death is different in kind from any other punishment imposed under our system of criminal justice. Because of the uniqueness of the death penalty, Furman held that it could not be imposed under sentencing procedures that created a substantial risk that it would be inflicted in an arbitrary and capricious manner. Mr. Justice White concluded that "the

death penalty is exacted with great infrequency even for the most atrocious crimes and . . . there is no meaningful basis for distinguishing the few cases in which it is imposed from the many cases in which it is not." Indeed, the death sentences examined by the Court in Furman were "cruel and unusual in the same way that being struck by lightning is cruel and unusual. For, of all the people convicted of [capital crimes], many just as reprehensible as these, the petitioners [in Furman were] among a capriciously selected random handful upon which the sentence of death has in fact been imposed. . . . [T]he Eighth and Fourteenth Amendments cannot tolerate the infliction of a sentence of death under legal systems that permit this unique penalty to be so wantonly and so freakishly imposed."

Furman mandates that where discretion is afforded a sentencing body on a matter so grave as the determination of whether a human life should be taken or spared, that discretion must be suitably directed and limited so as to minimize the risk of wholly arbitrary and capricious action.

It is certainly not a novel proposition that discretion in the area of sentencing be exercised in an informed manner. We have long recognized that "[f]or the determination of sentences, justice generally requires . . . that there be taken into account the circumstances of the offense together with the character and propensities of the offender." Otherwise, "the system cannot function in a consistent and rational manner."

The cited studies assumed that the trial judge would be the sentencing authority. If an experienced trial judge, who daily faces the difficult task of imposing sentences, has a vital need for accurate information about a defendant and the crime he committed in order to be able to impose a rational sentence in the typical criminal case, then accurate sentencing information is an indispensable prerequisite to a reasoned determination of whether a defendant shall live or die by a jury of people who may never before have made a sentencing decision.

Jury sentencing has been considered desirable in capital cases in order "to maintain a link between contemporary community values and the penal system—a link without which the determination of punishment could hardly reflect 'the evolving standards of decency that mark the progress of a maturing society.'" But it creates special problems. Much of the information that is relevant to the sentencing decision may have no relevance to the question of guilt, or may even be extremely prejudicial to a fair determination of that question. This problem, however, is scarcely insurmountable. Those who have studied the question suggest that a bifurcated procedure—one in which the question of sentence is not considered until the determination of guilt has been made—is the best answer. The drafters of the Model Penal Code concluded that if a unitary proceeding is used

"the determination of punishment must be based on less than all the evidence that has a bearing on that issue, such for example as a previous criminal record of the accused, or evidence must be admitted on the ground that it is relevant to sentence, though it would be excluded as irrelevant or prejudicial with respect to guilt or innocence alone. Trial lawyers understandably have little confidence in a solution that admits the evidence and trusts to an instruction to the jury that it should be considered only in determining the

penalty and disregarded in assessing guilt.

". . . The obvious solution . . . is to bifurcate the proceeding, abiding strictly by the rules of evidence until and unless there is a conviction, but once guilt has been determined opening the record to further information that is relevant to sentence. This is the analogue of the procedure in the ordinary case when capital punishment is not in issue; the court conducts a separate inquiry before imposing sentence."

When a human life is at stake and when the jury must have information prejudicial to the question of guilt but relevant to the question of penalty in order to impose a rational sentence, a bifurcated system is more likely to ensure elimination of the constitutional deficiencies identified in Furman.

But the provision of relevant information under fair procedural rules is not alone sufficient to guarantee that the information will be properly used in the imposition of punishment, especially if sentencing is performed by a jury. Since the members of a jury will have had little, if any, previous experience in sentencing, they are unlikely to be skilled in dealing with the information they are given. To the extent that this problem is inherent in jury sentencing, it may not be totally correctible. It seems clear, however, that the problem will be alleviated if the jury is given guidance regarding the factors about the crime and the defendant that the State, representing organized society, deems particularly relevant to the sentencing decision.

The idea that a jury should be given guidance in its decisionmaking is also hardly a novel proposition. Juries are invariably given careful instructions on the law and how to apply it before they are authorized to decide the merits of a lawsuit. It would be virtually unthinkable to follow any other course in a legal system that has traditionally operated by following prior precedents and fixed rules of law. When erroneous instructions are given, retrial is often required. It is quite simply a hallmark of our legal system that juries be carefully and adequately guided in their deliberations.

While some have suggested that standards to guide a capital jury's sentencing deliberations are impossible to formulate, the fact is that such standards have been developed. When the drafters of the Model Penal Code faced this problem, they concluded "that it is within the realm of possibility to point to the main circumstances of aggravation and of mitigation that should be weighed, *and weighed against each other,* when they are presented in a concrete case." While such standards are by necessity somewhat general, they do provide guidance to the sentencing authority and thereby reduce the likelihood that it will impose a sentence that fairly can be called capricious or arbitrary. Where the sentencing authority is required to specify the factors it relied upon in reaching its decision, the further safeguard of meaningful appellate review, is available to ensure that death sentences are not imposed capriciously or in a freakish manner.

In summary, the concerns expressed in Furman that the penalty of death not be imposed in an arbitrary or capricious manner can be met by a carefully drafted statute that ensures that the sentencing authority is given adequate information and guidance. As a general proposition these concerns are best met by a system that provides for a bifurcated proceeding at which

the sentencing authority is apprised of the information relevant to the imposition of sentence and provided with standards to guide its use of the information.

We do not intend to suggest that only the above-described procedures would be permissible under Furman or that any sentencing system constructed along these general lines would inevitably satisfy the concerns of Furman, for each distinct system must be examined on an individual basis. Rather, we have embarked upon this general exposition to make clear that it is possible to construct capital-sentencing systems capable of meeting Furman's constitutional concerns.

B

We now turn to consideration of the constitutionality of Georgia's capital-sentencing procedures. In the wake of Furman, Georgia amended its capital punishment statute, but chose not to narrow the scope of its murder provisions. See Part II, *supra.* Thus, now as before Furman, in Georgia "[a] person commits murder when he unlawfully and with malice aforethought, either express or implied, causes the death of another human being." All persons convicted of murder "shall be punished by death or by imprisonment for life."

Georgia did act, however, to narrow the class of murderers subject to capital punishment by specifying 10 statutory aggravating circumstances, one of which must be found by the jury to exist beyond a reasonable doubt before a death sentence can ever be imposed. In addition, the jury is authorized to consider any other appropriate aggravating or mitigating circumstances. The jury is not required to find any mitigating circumstance in order to make a recommendation of mercy that is binding on the trial court, but it must find a *statutory* aggravating circumstance before recommending a sentence of death.

These procedures require the jury to consider the circumstances of the crime and the criminal before it recommends sentence. No longer can a Georgia jury do as Furman's jury did: reach a finding of the defendant's guilt and then, without guidance or direction, decide whether he should live or die. Instead, the jury's attention is directed to the specific circumstances of the crime: Was it committed in the course of another capital felony? Was it committed for money? Was it committed upon a peace officer or judicial officer? Was it committed in a particularly heinous way or in a manner that endangered the lives of many persons? In addition, the jury's attention is focused on the characteristics of the person who committed the crime: Does he have a record of prior convictions for capital offenses? Are there any special facts about this defendant that mitigate against imposing capital punishment (*e.g.*, his youth, the extent of his cooperation with the police, his emotional state at the time of the crime). As a result, while some jury discretion still exists, "the discretion to be exercised is controlled by clear and objective standards so as to produce nondiscriminatory application."

As an important additional safeguard against arbitrariness and caprice, the Georgia statutory scheme provides for automatic appeal of all death sentences to the State's supreme court. That court is required by statute to review each sentence of death and determine whether it was imposed under the influence of passion or prejudice, whether the evidence supports the jury's finding of a statutory aggravating circum-

stance, and whether the sentence is disproportionate compared to those sentences imposed in similar cases.

In short, Georgia's new sentencing procedures require as a prerequisite to the imposition of the death penalty, specific jury findings as to the circumstances of the crime or the character of the defendant. Moreover to guard further against a situation comparable to that presented in Furman, the Supreme Court of Georgia compares each death sentence with the sentences imposed on similarly situated defendants to ensure that the sentence of death in a particular case is not disproportionate. On their face these procedures seem to satisfy the concerns of Furman. No longer should there be "no meaningful basis for distinguishing the few cases in which [the death penalty] is imposed from the many cases in which it is not."

The petitioner contends, however, that the changes in the Georgia sentencing procedures are only cosmetic, that the arbitrariness and capriciousness condemned by Furman continue to exist in Georgia—both in traditional practices that still remain and in the new sentencing procedures adopted in response to Furman.

1

First, the petitioner focuses on the opportunities for discretionary action that are inherent in the processing of any murder case under Georgia law. He notes that the state prosecutor has unfettered authority to select those persons whom he wishes to prosecute for a capital offense and to plea bargain with them. Further, at the trial the jury may choose to convict a defendant of a lesser included offense rather than find him guilty of a crime punishable by death, even if the evidence would support a capital verdict. And finally, a defendant who is convicted and sentenced to die may have his sentence commuted by the Governor of the State and the Georgia Board of Pardons and Paroles.

The existence of these discretionary stages is not determinative of the issues before us. At each of these stages an actor in the criminal justice system makes a decision which may remove a defendant from consideration as a candidate for the death penalty. Furman, in contrast, dealt with the decision to impose the death sentence on a specific individual who had been convicted of a capital offense. Nothing in any of our cases suggests that the decision to afford an individual defendant mercy violates the Constitution. Furman held only that, in order to minimize the risk that the death penalty would be imposed on a capriciously selected group of offenders, the decision to impose it had to be guided by standards so that the sentencing authority would focus on the particularized circumstances of the crime and the defendant.

2

The petitioner further contends that the capital-sentencing procedures adopted by Georgia in response to Furman do not eliminate the dangers of arbitrariness and caprice in jury sentencing that were held in Furman to be violative of the Eighth and Fourteenth Amendments. He claims that the statute is so broad and vague as to leave juries free to act as arbitrarily and capriciously as they wish in deciding whether to impose the death penalty. While there is no claim that the jury in this case relied upon a vague or overbroad provision to establish the existence of a statutory aggravating circumstance, the petitioner looks to the sentencing

system as a whole (as the Court did in Furman and we do today) and argues that it fails to reduce sufficiently the risk of arbitrary infliction of death sentences. Specifically, Gregg urges that the statutory aggravating circumstances are too broad and too vague, that the sentencing procedure allows for arbitrary grants of mercy, and that the scope of the evidence and argument that can be considered at the presentence hearing is too wide.

The petitioner attacks the seventh statutory aggravating circumstance, which authorizes imposition of the death penalty if the murder was "outrageously or wantonly vile, horrible or inhuman in that it involved torture, depravity of mind, or an aggravated battery to the victim," contending that it is so broad that capital punishment could be imposed in any murder case. It is, of course, arguable that any murder involves depravity of mind or an aggravated battery. But this language need not be construed in this way, and there is no reason to assume that the Supreme Court of Georgia will adopt such an open-ended construction. In only one case has it upheld a jury's decision to sentence a defendant to death when the only statutory aggravating circumstance found was that of § 7, and that homicide was a horrifying torture-murder.

The petitioner also argues that two of the statutory aggravating circumstances are vague and therefore susceptible to widely differing interpretations, thus creating a substantial risk that the death penalty will be arbitrarily inflicted by Georgia juries. In light of the decisions of the Supreme Court of Georgia we must disagree. First, the petitioner attacks that part of § 1 that authorizes a jury to consider whether a defendant has a "substantial history of serious assaultive criminal convictions." The Supreme Court of Georgia, however, has demonstrated a concern that the new sentencing procedures provide guidance to juries. It held this provision to be impermissibly vague in Arnold v. State, 236 Ga. 534, 540; S.E.2d (1976), because it did not provide the jury with "sufficiently 'clear and objective standards.'" Second, the petitioner points to § 3 which speaks of creating a "great risk of death to more than one person." While such a phrase might be susceptible to an overly broad interpretation, the Supreme Court of Georgia has not so construed it. The only case in which the court upheld a conviction in reliance on this aggravating circumstance involved a man who stood up in a church and fired a gun indiscriminately into the audience. On the other hand, the court expressly reversed a finding of great risk when the victim was simply kidnapped in a parking lot.

The petitioner next argues that the requirements of Furman are not met here because the jury has the power to decline to impose the death penalty even if it finds that one or more statutory aggravating circumstances is present in the case. This contention misinterprets Furman. Moreover, it ignores the role of the Supreme Court of Georgia which reviews each death sentence to determine whether it is proportional to other sentences imposed for similar crimes. Since the proportionality requirement on review is intended to prevent caprice in the decision to inflict the penalty, the isolated decision of a jury to afford mercy does not render unconstitutional death sentences imposed on defendants who were sentenced under a system that does not create a substantial risk of arbitrariness or caprice.

The petitioner objects, finally, to the wide scope of evidence and argument allowed at presentence hearings. We think that the Georgia court wisely has chosen not to impose unnecessary restrictions on the evidence that can be offered at such a hearing and to approve open and far-ranging argument. So long as the evidence introduced and the arguments made at the presentence hearing do not prejudice a defendant, it is preferable not to impose restrictions. We think it desirable for the jury to have as much information before it as possible when it makes the sentencing decision.

3

Finally, the Georgia statute has an additional provision designed to assure that the death penalty will not be imposed on a capriciously selected group of convicted defendants. The new sentencing procedures require that the state supreme court review every death sentence to determine whether it was imposed under the influence of passion, prejudice, or any other arbitrary factor, whether the evidence supports the findings of a statutory aggravating circumstance, and "[w]hether the sentence of death is excessive or disproportionate to the penalty imposed in similar cases, considering both the crime and the defendant." In performing its sentence review function, the Georgia court has held that "if the death penalty is only rarely imposed for an act or it is substantially out of line with sentences imposed for other acts it will be set aside as excessive." The court on another occasion stated that "we view it to be our duty under the similarity standard to assure that no death sentence is affirmed unless in similar cases throughout the state the death penalty has been imposed generally...."

It is apparent that the Supreme Court of Georgia has taken its review responsibilities seriously. In Coley, it held that "[t]he prior cases indicate that the past practice among juries faced with similar factual situations and like aggravating circumstances has been to impose only the sentence of life imprisonment for the offense of rape, rather than death." It thereupon reduced Coley's sentence from death to life imprisonment. Similarly, although armed robbery is a capital offense under Georgia law, the Georgia court concluded that the death sentences imposed in this case for that crime were "unusual in that they are rarely imposed for [armed robbery]. Thus, under the test provided by statute, . . . they must be considered to be excessive or disproportionate to the penalties imposed in similar cases." The court therefore vacated Gregg's death sentences for armed robbery and has followed a similar course in every other armed robbery death penalty case to come before it.

The provision for appellate review in the Georgia capital-sentencing system serves as a check against the random or arbitrary imposition of the death penalty. In particular, the proportionality review substantially eliminates the possibility that a person will be sentenced to die by the action of an aberrant jury. If a time comes when juries generally do not impose the death sentence in a certain kind of murder case, the appellate review procedures assures that no defendant convicted under such circumstances will suffer a sentence of death.

V

The basic concern of Furman centered on those defendants who were being condemned to death capriciously and arbitrarily. Under the procedures before the Court in that case, sentencing authorities were not directed to give attention to the nature or circumstances of the crime committed or to the character or record of the defendant. Left unguided, juries imposed the death sentence in a way that could only be called freakish. The new Georgia sentencing procedures, by contrast, focus the jury's attention on the particularized nature of the crime and the particularized characteristics of the individual defendant. While the jury is permitted to consider any aggravating or mitigating circumstances, it must find and identify at least one statutory aggravating factor before it may impose a penalty of death. In this way the jury's discretion is channeled. No longer can a jury wantonly and freakishly impose the death sentence; it is always circumscribed by the legislative guidelines. In addition, the review function of the Supreme Court of Georgia affords additional assurance that the concerns that prompted our decision in Furman are not present to any significant degree in the Georgia procedure applied here.

For the reasons expressed in this opinion, we hold that the statutory system under which Gregg was sentenced to death does not violate the Constitution. Accordingly, the judgment of the Georgia Supreme Court is affirmed.

It is so ordered.

MR. JUSTICE WHITE, with whom THE CHIEF JUSTICE and MR. JUSTICE REHNQUIST join, concurring in the judgment.

In Furman v. Georgia, 408 U.S. 238 (1972), this Court held the death penalty as then administered in Georgia to be unconstitutional. That same year

circumstances. . . ." Unless the jury unanimously determines that the death penalty should be imposed, the defendant will be sentenced to life imprisonment. In the event that the jury does imposed the death penalty, it must designate in writing the aggravating circumstance which it found to exist beyond a reasonable doubt.

An important aspect of the new Georgia legislative scheme, however, is its provision for appellate review. Prompt review by the Georgia Supreme Court is provided for in every case in which the death penalty is imposed. To assist it in deciding whether to sustain the death penalty, the Georgia Supreme Court is supplied, in every case, with a report from the trial judge in the form of a standard questionnaire. The questionnaire contains, *inter alia,* six questions designed to disclose whether race played a role in the case and one question asking the trial judge whether the evidence forecloses "all doubt respecting the defendant's guilt." In deciding whether the death penalty is to be sustained in any given case, the court shall determine:

"(1) Whether the sentence of death was imposed under the influence of passion, prejudice, or any other arbitrary factor, and

"(2) Whether in cases other than treason or aircraft hijacking, the evidence supports the jury's or judge's finding of a statutory aggravating circumstance as enumerated in Code section 27-2534.1(b), and

"(3) Whether the sentence of death is excessive or disproportionate to the penalty imposed in similar cases, considering both the crime and the defendant. . . ."

In order that information regarding "similar cases" may be before the court, the post of Assistant to the Supreme Court was created. The Assistant must "accumulate the records of all capital cases in which sentence was imposed after January 1, 1970, or such earlier date as the court may deem appropriate." The court is required to include in its decision a reference to "those similar cases which it took into consideration."

II

Petitioner Troy Gregg and a 16-year-old companion, Sam Allen, were hitchhiking from Florida to Asheville, N. C., on November 21, 1973. They were picked up in an automobile driven by Fred Simmons and Bob Moore, both of whom were drunk. The car broke down and Simmons purchased a new one—a 1960 Pontiac—using part of a large roll of cash which he had with him. After picking up another hitchhiker in Georgia and dropping him off in Atlanta, the car proceeded north to Gwinnett County, Ga., where it stopped so that Moore and Simmons could urinate. While they were out of the car Simmons was shot in the eye and Moore was shot in the right cheek and in the back of the head. Both died as a result.

On November 24, 1973, at 3 p.m., on the basis of information supplied by the hitchhiker, petitioner and Allen were arrested in Asheville, N. C. They were then in possession of the car which Simmons had purchased; petitioner was in possession of the gun which had killed Simmons and Moore and $107 which had been taken from them; and in the motel room in which petitioner was staying was a new stereo and a car stereo player.

At about 11 p.m., after the Gwinnett County police had arrived, petitioner made a statement to them admitting that he had killed Moore and Simmons, but asserting that he had killed them

the Georgia Legislature enacted a new statutory scheme under which the death penalty may be imposed for several offenses, including murder. The issue in this case is whether the death penalty imposed for murder on petitioner Gregg under the new Georgia statutory scheme may constitutionally be carried out. I agree that it may.

I

Under the new Georgia statutory scheme a person convicted of murder may receive a sentence either of death or of life imprisonment. Under Georgia Code Ann § 26-3102 (1975 Supp.), the sentence will be life imprisonment unless the jury at a separate evidentiary proceeding immediately following the verdict finds unanimously and beyond a reasonable doubt at least one statutorily defined "aggravating circumstance." The aggravating circumstances are,

"(1) The offense of murder, rape, armed robbery, or kidnapping was committed by a person with a prior record of conviction for a capital felony, or the offense of murder was committed by a person who has a substantial history of serious assaultive criminal convictions.

"(2) The offense of murder, rape, armed robbery, or kidnapping was committed while the offender was engaged in the commission of another capital felony or aggravated battery, or the offense of murder was committed while the offender was engaged in the commission of burglary or arson in the first degree.

"(3) The offender by his act of murder, armed robbery, or kidnapping knowingly created a great risk of death to more than one person in a public place by means of a weapon or device which would normally be hazardous to the lives of more than one person.

"(4) The offender committed the offense of murder for himself or another, for the purpose of receiving money or any other thing of monetary value.

"(5) The murder of a judicial officer, former judicial officer, district attorney or solicitor or former district attorney or solicitor during or because of the exercise of his official duty.

"(6) The offender caused or directed another to commit murder or committed murder as an agent or employee of another person.

"(7) The offense of murder, rape, armed robbery, or kidnapping was outrageously or wantonly vile, horrible or inhuman in that it involved torture, depravity of the mind, or an aggravated battery to the victim.

"(8) The offense of murder was committed against any peace officer, corrections employee or fireman while engaged in the performance of his official duties.

"(9) The offense of murder was committed by a person in, or who has escaped from, the lawful custody of a peace officer or place of lawful confinement.

"(10) The murder was committed for the purpose of avoiding, interfering with, or preventing a lawful arrest or custody in a place of lawful confinement, of himself or another." Having found an aggravating circumstance, however, the jury is not required to impose the death penalty. Instead, it is merely authorized to impose it after considering evidence of "any mitigating circumstances or aggravating circumstances otherwise authorized by law and any of the [enumerated] statutory aggravating

in self-defense and in defense of Allen. He also admitted robbing them of $400 and taking their car. A few moments later petitioner was asked why he had shot Moore and Simmons and responded, "By God, I wanted them dead."

At about 1 a.m. the next morning, petitioner and Allen were released to the custody of the Gwinnett County police and were transported in two cars back to Gwinnett County. On the way, at about 5 a.m., the car stopped at the place where Moore and Simmons had been killed. Everyone got out of the car. Allen was asked, in petitioner's presence, how the killing occurred. He said that he had been sitting in the back seat of the 1960 Pontiac and was about half asleep. He woke up when the car stopped. Simmons and Moore got out, and as soon as they did petitioner turned around and told Allen, "get out, we're going to rob them." Allen said that he got out and walked toward the back of the car, looked around and could see petitioner, with a gun in his hand, leaning up against the car so he could get a good aim. Simmons and Moore had gone down the bank and had relieved themselves and as they were coming up the bank petitioner fired three shots. One of the men fell, the other staggered. Petitioner then circled around the back and approached the two men, both of whom were now lying in the ditch, from behind. He placed the gun to the head of one of them and pulled the trigger. Then he went quickly to the other one and placed the gun to his head and pulled the trigger again. He then took the money, whatever was in their pockets. He told Allen to get in the car and they drove away.

When Allen had finished telling his story, one of the officers asked petitioner if this was the way it had happened. Petitioner hung his head and said that it was. The officer then said, "You mean you shot these men in cold blooded murder just to rob them," and petitioner said yes. The officer then asked him why and petitioner said he didn't know. Petitioner was indicted in two counts for murder and in two counts for robbery.

At trial, petitioner's defense was that he had killed in self-defense. He testified in his own behalf and told a version of the events similar to that which he had originally told to the Gwinnett County police. On cross-examination, he was confronted with a letter to Allen recounting a version of the events similar to that to which he had just testified and instructing Allen to memorize and burn the letter. Petitioner conceded writing the version of the events, but denied writing the portion of the letter which instructed Allen to memorize and burn it. In rebuttal, the State called a handwriting expert who testified that the entire letter was written by the same person.

The jury was instructed on the elements of murder and robbery. The trial judge gave an instruction on self-defense, but refused to submit the lesser included offense of manslaughter to the jury. It returned vedicts of guilty on all counts.

No new evidence was presented at the sentencing proceeding. However, the prosecutor and the attorney for petitioner each made arguments to the jury on the issue of punishment. The prosecutor emphasized the strength of the case against petitioner and the fact that he had murdered in order to eliminate the witnesses to the robbery. The defense attorney emphasized the possibility that a mistake had been made and that petitioner was not guilty. The trial judge instructed the jury on their sentencing function and in so doing submitted to them three statutory aggravating circumstances. He stated:

"Now, as to counts one and three, wherein the defendant is charged with the murders of—has been found guilty of the murders of Fred Edward Simmons and Bob Edward Moore, the following aggravating circumstances are some that you can consider, as I say, you must find that these existed beyond a reasonable doubt before the death penalty can be imposed.

"One—That the offense of murder was committed while the offender was engaged in the commission of two other capital felonies, to-wit the armed robbery of Fred Edward Simmons and Bob Edward Moore.

"Two—That the offender committed the offense of murder for the purpose of receiving money and the automobile described in the indictment.

"Three—The offense of murder was outrageously and wantonly vile, horrible and inhuman, in that they involved the depravity of mind of the defendant.

"Now, so far as the counts two and four, that is the counts of armed robbery, of which you have found the defendant guilty, then you may find—inquire into these aggravating circumstances.

"That the offense of armed robbery was committed while the offender was engaged in the commission of two capital felonies, to-wit the murders of Fred Edward Simmons and Bob Edward Moore or that the offender committed the offense of armed robbery for the purpose of receiving money and the automobile set forth in the indictment, or three,

that the offense of armed robbery was outrageously and wantonly vile, horrible and inhuman in that they involved the depravity of the mind of the defendant.

"Now, if you find that there was [sic] one or more of these aggravating circumstances existed beyond a reasonable doubt, then and I refer to each individual count, then you would be authorized to consider imposing the sentence of death.

"If you do not find that one of these aggravating circumstances existed beyond a reasonable doubt, in either of these counts, then you would not be authorized to consider the penalty of death. In that event, the sentence as to counts one and three, those are the counts wherein the defendant was found guilty of murder, the sentence could be imprisonment for life. . . ."

The jury returned the death penalty on all four counts finding all the aggravating circumstances submitted to it, except that it did not find the crimes to have been "outrageously or wantonly vile," etc.

On appeal the Georgia Supreme Court affirmed the death sentences on the murder counts and vacated the death sentences on the robbery counts Gregg v. State, 233 Ga. 117, 210 S.E.2d 659 (1974). It concluded that the murder sentences were not imposed under the influence of passion, prejudice, or any other arbitrary factor, that the evidence supported the finding of a statutory aggravating factor with respect to the murders; and, citing several cases in which the death penalty had been imposed previously for murders of persons who had witnessed a robbery, held that

"After considering both the crimes and the defendant and after comparing the evidence and the sentences in this case with those of previous murder cases, we are also of the opinion that these two sentences of death are not excessive or disproportionate to the penalties imposed in similar cases which are hereto attached."

However, it held with respect to the robbery sentences:

"Although there is no indication that these two sentences were imposed under the influence of passion, prejudice or any other arbitrary factor, the sentences imposed here are unusual in that they are rarely imposed for this offense. Thus, under the test provided by statute for comparison (Code Ann. § 27-1537(b),(3)), they must be considered to be excessive or disproportionate to the penalties imposed in similar cases."

Accordingly, the sentences on the robbery counts were vacated.

III

The threshold question in this case is whether the death penalty may be carried out for murder under the Georgia legislative scheme consistent with the decision in Furman v. Georgia, *supra.* In Furman, this Court's judgment operated to preclude the practice of giving the sentencer unguided discretion to impose or not to impose the death penalty for murder had resulted in Georgia and other States, in that the penalty was being imposed discriminatorily, wantonly and freakishly and so infrequently that any given death sentence was cruel and unusual. Petitioner argues that, as in Furman, the jury is still the sentencer; that the statutory criteria to be considered by the jury on the issue of sentence under Georgia's new statutory scheme are vague and do not purport to be all inclusive; and that, in any event, there are *no* circum-

stances under which the jury is required to impose the death penalty. Consequently, the petitioner argues that the death penalty will inexorably be imposed in as discriminatory, standardless, and rare a manner as it was imposed under the scheme declared invalid in Furman.

The argument is considerably overstated. The Georgia Legislature has made an effort to identify those aggravating factors which it considers necessary and relevant to the question whether a defendant convicted of capital murder should be sentenced to death. The jury which imposes sentence is instructed on all statutory aggravating factors which are supported by the evidence, and is told that it may not impose the death penalty unless it unanimously finds at least one of those factors to have been established beyond a reasonable doubt. The Georgia Legislature has plainly made an effort to guide the jury in the exercise of its discretion, while at the same time permitting the jury to dispense mercy on the basis of factors too intangible to write into a statute and I cannot accept the naked assertion that the effort is bound to fail. As the types of murders for which the death penalty may be imposed become more narrowly defined and are limited to those which are particularly serious or for which the death penalty is peculiarly appropriate as they are in Georgia by reason of the aggravating circumstance requirement, it becomes reasonable to expect that juries—even given discretion *not* to impose the death penalty—will impose the death penalty in a substantial portion of the cases so defined. If they do, it can no longer be said that the penalty is being imposed wantonly and freakishly or so infrequently that it loses its usefulness as a sentencing device.

There is, therefore, reason to expect that Georgia's current system would escape the infirmities which invalidated its previous system under Furman. However, the Georgia Legislature was not satisfied with a system which might but might not turn out in practice to result in death sentences being imposed with reasonable consistency for certain serious murders. Instead, it gave the Georgia Supreme Court the power and the obligation to perform precisely the task which three Justices of this Court, whose opinions were necessary to the result, performed in Furman: namely the task of deciding whether *in fact* the death penalty was being administered for any given class of crime in a discriminatory, standardless, or rare fashion.

In considering any given death sentence on appeal, the Georgia Supreme Court is to determine whether the sentence imposed was consistent with the relevant statutes—*i.e.*, whether there was sufficient evidence to support the finding of an aggravating circumstance. However, it must do much more than determine whether the penalty was lawfully imposed. It must go on to decide—after reviewing the penalties imposed in "similar cases"—whether the penalty is "excessive or disproportionate" considering both the crime and the defendant. The new Assistant to the Supreme Court is to assist the court in collecting the records of "all capital cases" in the State of Georgia in which sentence was imposed after January 1, 1970. The court also has the obligation of determining whether the penalty was "imposed under the influence of passion, prejudice, or any other arbitrary factor." The Georgia Supreme Court has interpreted the appellate review statute to require it to set aside the death sentence whenever juries

across the State impose it only rarely for the type of crime in question; but to require it to affirm death sentences whenever juries across the State generally impose it for the crime in question. Thus, in this case the Georgia Supreme Court concluded that the death penalty was so rarely imposed for the crime of robbery that it set aside the sentences on the robbery counts, and effectively foreclosed that penalty from being imposed for that crime in the future under the legislative scheme now in existence. Similarly, the Georgia Supreme Court has determined that juries impose the death sentence too rarely with respect to certain classes of rape. However, it concluded that juries "generally throughout the State" have imposed the death penalty for those who murder witnesses to armed robberies. Consequently, it affirmed the sentences in this case on the murder counts. If the Georgia Supreme Court is correct with respect to this factual judgment, imposition of the death penalty in this and similar cases is consistent with Furman. Indeed, if the Georgia Supreme Court properly performs the task assigned to it under the Georgia statutes, death sentences imposed for discriminatory reasons or wantonly or freakishly for any given category of crime will be set aside. Petitioner has wholly failed to establish, or even attempted to establish, that the Georgia Supreme Court failed properly to perform its task in this case or that it is incapable of performing its task adequately in all cases; and this Court should not assume that it did not do so.

Petitioner also argues that decisions made by the prosecutor—either in negotiating a plea to some offense lesser than capital murder or in simply declining to charge capital murder—are standardless and will inexorably result in the wanton and freakish imposition of the penalty condemned by the judgment in Furman. I address this point separately because the cases in which no capital offense is charged escape the view of the Georgia Supreme Court and are not considered by it in determining whether a particular sentence is excessive or disproportionate.

Petitioner's argument that prosecutors behave in a standardless fashion in deciding which cases to try as capital felonies is unsupported by any facts. Petitioner simply asserts that since prosecutors have the power not to charge capital felonies they will exercise that power in a standardless fashion. This is untenable. Absent facts to the contrary, it cannot be assumed that prosecutors will be motivated in their charging decision by factors other than the strength of their case and the likelihood that a jury would impose the death penalty if it convicts. Unless prosecutors are incompetent in their judgments, the standards by which they decide whether to charge a capital felony will be the same as those by which the jury will decide the questions of guilt and sentence. Thus defendants will escape the death penalty through prosecutorial charging decisions only because the offense is not sufficiently serious; or because the proof is insufficiently strong. This does not cause the system to be standardless any more than the jury's decision to impose life imprisonment on a defendant whose crime is deemed insufficiently serious or its decision to acquit someone who is probably guilty but whose guilt is not established beyond a reasonable doubt. Thus the prosecutor's charging decisions are unlikely to have removed from the sample of cases considered by the Georgia Supreme Court any which are truly "similar." If the

cases really were "similar" in relevant respects, it is unlikely that prosecutors would fail to prosecute them as capital cases; and I am unwilling to assume the contrary.

Petitioner's argument that there is an unconstitutional amount of discretion in the system which separates those suspects who receive the death penalty from those who receive life imprisonment, a lesser penalty, or are acquitted or never charged, seems to be in final analysis an indictment of our entire system of justice. Petitioner has argued, in effect, that no matter how effective the death penalty may be as a punishment, government, created and run as it must be by humans, is inevitably incompetent to administer it. This cannot be accepted as a proposition of constitutional law. Imposition of the death penalty is surely an awesome responsibility for any system of justice and those who participate in it. Mistakes will be made and discriminations will occur which will be difficult to explain. However, one of society's most basic tasks is that of protecting the lives of its citizens and one of the most basic ways in which it achieves the task is through criminal laws against murder. I decline to interfere with the manner in which Georgia has chosen to enforce such laws on what is simply an assertion of lack of faith in the ability of the system of justice to operate in a fundamentally fair manner.

IV

For the reasons stated in dissent in Roberts v. Louisiana, *post*, neither can I agree with the petitioner's other basic argument that the death penalty, however imposed and for whatever crime, is cruel and unusual punishment.

I therefore concur in the judgment of affirmance.

Statement of THE CHIEF JUSTICE and MR. JUSTICE REHNQUIST:

We join the opinion of MR. JUSTICE WHITE, agreeing with its analysis that Georgia's system of capital punishment comports with the Court's holding in Furman v. Georgia, 408 U.S. 238 (1972).

MR. JUSTICE BLACKMUN, concurring in the judgment.

I concur in the judgment. See Furman v. Georgia, 408 U.S. 238, 405-414 (1972) (BLACKMUN, J., dissenting), and id., at 375, 414, and 465.

MR. JUSTICE BRENNAN, dissenting.

The Cruel and Unusual Punishments Clause "must draw its meaning from the evolving standards of decency that mark the progress of a maturing society." The opinions of MR. JUSTICE STEWART, MR. JUSTICE POWELL, and MR. JUSTICE STEVENS today hold that "evolving standards of decency" require focus not on the essence of the death penalty itself but primarily upon the procedures employed by the State to single out persons to suffer the penalty of death. Those opinions hold further that, so viewed, the Clause invalidates the mandatory infliction of the death penalty but not its infliction under sentencing procedures that MR. JUSTICE STEWART, MR. JUSTICE POWELL, and MR. JUSTICE STEVENS conclude adequately safeguard against the risk that the death penalty was imposed in an arbitrary and capricious manner.

In Furman v. Georgia, 408 U.S. 238, 257 (1972), I read "evolving standards of decency" as requiring focus upon the essence of the death penalty itself and not primarily or solely upon the procedures under which the determination to inflict the penalty upon a particular person was made. I there said:

"From the beginning of our Nation, the punishment of death has stirred acute public controversy. Although pragmatic arguments for and against the punishment have been frequently advanced, this longstanding and heated controversy cannot be explained solely as the result of differences over the practical wisdom of a particular government policy. At bottom, the battle has been waged on moral grounds. The country has debated whether a society for which the dignity of the individual is the supreme value can, without a fundamental inconsistency, follow the practice of deliberately putting some of its members to death. In the United States, as in other nations of the western world, 'the struggle about this punishment has been one between ancient and deeply rooted beliefs in retribution, atonement or vengeance on the one hand, and, on the other, beliefs in the personal value and dignity of the common man that were born of the democratic movement of the eighteenth century, as well as beliefs in the scientific approach to an understanding of the motive forces of human conduct, which are the result of the growth of the sciences of behavior during the nineteenth and twentieth centuries.' It is this essentially moral conflict that forms the backdrop for the past changes in and the present operation of our system of imposing death as a punishment for crime."

That continues to be my view. For the Clause forbidding cruel and unusual punishments under our constitutional system of government embodies in unique degree moral principles restraining the punishments that our civilized society may impose on those persons who transgress its laws. Thus, I too say: "For myself, I do not hesitate to assert the proposition that the only way the law has progressed from the days of the rack, the screw and the wheel is the development of moral concepts, or, as stated by the Supreme Court . . . the application of 'evolving standards of decency'. . . ."

This Court inescapably has the duty, as the ultimate arbiter of the meaning of our Constitution, to say whether, when individuals condemned to death stand before our Bar, "moral concepts" require us to hold that the law has progressed to the point where we should declare that the punishment of death, like punishments on the rack, the screw and the wheel, is no longer morally tolerable in our civilized society. My opinion in Furman v. Georgia concluded that our civilization and the law had progressed to this point and that therefore the punishment of death, for whatever crime and under all circumstances, is "cruel and unusual" in violation of the Eighth and Fourteenth Amendments of the Constitution. I shall not again canvass the reasons that led to that conclusion. I emphasize only that foremost among the "moral concepts" recognized in our cases and inherent in the Clause is the primary moral principle that the State, even as it punishes, must treat its citizens in a manner consistent with their intrinsic worth as human beings—a punishment must not be so severe as to be degrading to human dignity. A judicial determination whether the punishment of death comports with human dignity is therefore not only permitted but compelled by the Clause.

I do not understand that the Court disagrees that "[i]n comparison to all other punishments today . . . the deliberate extinguishment of human life by the State is uniquely degrading to human dignity." For three of my Brethren

hold today that mandatory infliction of the death penalty constitutes the penalty cruel and unusual punishment. I perceive no principled basis for this limitation. Death for whatever crime and under all circumstances "is truly an awesome punishment. The calculated killing of a human being by the State involves, by its very nature, a denial of the executed person's humanity. . . . An executed person has indeed 'lost the right to have rights.' " Death is not only an unusually severe punishment, unusual in its pain, in its finality, and in its enormity, but it serves no penal purpose more effectively than a less severe punishment; therefore the principle inherent in the Clause that prohibits pointless infliction of excessive punishment when less severe punishment can adequately achieve the same purposes invalidates the punishment.

The fatal constitutional infirmity in the punishment of death is that it treats "members of the human race as nonhumans, as objects to be toyed with and discarded. [It is] thus inconsistent with the fundamental premise of the Clause that even the vilest criminal remains a human being possessed of common human dignity." As such it is a penalty that "subjects the individual to a fate forbidden by the principle of civilized treatment guaranteed by the [Clause]." I therefore would hold, on that ground alone, that death is today a cruel and unusual punishment prohibited by the Clause. "Justice of this kind is obviously no less shocking than the crime itself, and the new 'official' murder, far from offering redress for the offense committed against society, adds instead a second defilement to the first."

I concur in the judgments in No. 75-5491, Woodson v. North Carolina, and No. 75-5844, Roberts v. Louisiana, that set aside the death sentences imposed under the North Carolina and Louisiana death sentence statutes as violative of the Eighth and Fourteenth Amendments.

I dissent, however, from the judgments in No. 74-6257, Gregg v. Georgia, No. 75-5706, Proffitt v. Florida, and No. 75-5394, Jurek v. Texas, insofar as each upholds the death sentences challenged in those cases. I would set aside the death sentences imposed in those cases as violative of the Eighth and Fourteenth Amendments.

MR. JUSTICE MARSHALL, dissenting.

In Furman v. Georgia, 408 U.S. 238, 314 (1972), I set forth at some length my views on the basic issue presented to the Court in these cases. The death penalty, I concluded, is a cruel and unusual punishment prohibited by the Eighth and Fourteenth Amendments. That continues to be my view.

I have no intention of retracing the "long and tedious journey," that led to my conclusion in Furman. My sole purposes here are to consider the suggestion that my conclusion in Furman has been undercut by developments since then, and briefly to evaluate the basis for my Brethren's holding that the extinction of life is a permissible form of punishment under the Cruel and Unusual Punishments Clause.

In Furman I concluded that the death penalty is constitutionally invalid for two reasons. First, the death penalty is excessive. And second, the American people, fully informed as to the purposes of the death penalty and its liabilities, would in my view reject it as morally unacceptable.

Since the decision in Furman, the legislatures of 35 States have enacted new statutes authorizing the imposition of the death sentence for certain crimes,

and Congress has enacted a law providing the death penalty for air piracy resulting in death. I would be less than candid if I did not acknowledge that these developments have a significant bearing on a realistic assessment of the moral acceptability of the death penalty to the American people. But if the constitutionality of the death penalty turns, as I have urged, on the opinion of an *informed* citizenry, then even the enactment of new death statutes cannot be viewed as conclusive. In Furman, I observed that the American people are largely unaware of the information critical to a judgment on the morality of the death penalty, and concluded that if they were better informed, they would consider it shocking, unjust, and unacceptable. A recent study, conducted after the enactment of the post-Furman statutes, has confirmed that the American people know little about the death penalty, and that the opinions of an informed public would differ significantly from those of a public unaware of the consequences and effects of the death penalty.

Even assuming, however, that the post-Furman enactment of statutes authorizing the death penalty renders the prediction of the views of an informed citizenry an uncertain basis for a constitutional decision, the enactment of those statutes has no bearing whatsoever on the conclusion that the death penalty is unconstitutional because it is excessive. An excessive penalty is invalid under the Cruel and Unusual Punishments Clause "even though popular sentiment may favor" it. The inquiry here, then, is simply whether the death penalty is necessary to accomplish the legitimate legislative purposes in punishment, or whether a less severe penalty—life imprisonment—would do as well.

The two purposes that sustain the death penalty as nonexcessive in the Court's view are general deterrence and retribution. In Furman, I canvassed the relevant data on the deterrent effect of capital punishment. The state of knowledge at that point, after literally centuries of debate, was summarized as follows by a United Nations Committee:

"It is generally agreed between the retentionists and abolitionists, whatever their opinions about the validity of comparative studies of deterrence, that the data which now exists show no correlation between the existence of capital punishment and lower rates of capital crime."

The available evidence, I concluded in Furman, was convincing that "capital punishment is not necessary as a deterrent to crime in our society."

The Solicitor General in his *amicus* brief in these cases relies heavily on a study by Isaac Ehrlich, reported a year after Furman, to support the contention that the death penalty does deter murder. Since the Ehrlich study was not available at the time of Furman and since it is the first scientific study to suggest that the death penalty may have a deterrent effect, I will briefly consider its import.

The Ehrlich study focused on the relationship in the Nation as a whole between the homicide rate and "execution risk"—the fraction of persons convicted of murder who were actually executed. Comparing the differences in homicide rate and execution risk for the years 1933 to 1969, Ehrlich found that increases in execution risk were associated with increases in the homicide rate. But when he employed the statistical technique of multiple regression analysis to control for the influence of other variables posited to have an impact on the homicide rate, Ehrlich found a negative correlation between changes in the homicide rate and changes in execution risk. His tentative conclusion was that for the period from 1933 to 1967 each additional execution in the United States might have saved eight lives.

The methods and conclusions of the Ehrlich study have been severely criticized on a number of grounds. It has been suggested, for example, that the study is defective because it compares execution and homicide rates on a nationwide, rather than a State-by-State basis. The aggregation of data from all States—including those that have abolished the death penalty—obscures the relationship between murder and execution rates. Under Ehrlich's methodology, a decrease in the execution risk in one State combined with an increase in the murder rate in another State would, all other things being equal, suggest a deterrent effect that quite obviously would not exist. Indeed, a deterrent effect would be suggested if, once again all other things being equal, one State abolished the death penalty and experienced no change in the murder rate, while another State experienced an increase in the murder rate.

The most compelling criticism of the Ehrlich study is that its conclusions are extremely sensitive to the choice of the time period included in the regression analysis. Analysis of Ehrlich's data reveals that all empirical support for the deterrent effect of capital punishment disappears when the five most recent years are removed from his time series —that is to say, whether a decrease in the execution risk corresponds to an increase or decrease in the murder rate depends on the ending point of the sample period. This finding has cast severe doubts on the reliability of Ehrlich's tentative conclusions. Indeed, a recent regression study, based on Ehrlich's theoretical model but using cross-section state data for the years 1950 and 1960, found no support for the conclusion that executions act as a deterrent.

The Ehrlich study, in short, is of little, if any, assistance in assessing the deterrent impact of the death penalty. The evidence I reviewed in Furman remains convincing, in my view, that "capital punishment is not necessary as a deterrent to crime in our society." The justification for the death penalty must be found elsewhere.

The other principal purpose said to be served by the death penalty is retribution. The notion that retribution can serve as a moral justification for the sanction of death finds credence in the opinion of my Brothers STEWART, POWELL, and STEVENS, and that of my Brother WHITE in Roberts v. Louisiana, post. It is this notion that I find to be the most disturbing aspect of today's unfortunate decision.

The concept of retribution is a multifaceted one, and any discussion of its role in the criminal law must be undertaken with caution. On one level, it can be said that the notion of retribution or reprobation is the basis of our insistence that only those who have broken the law be punished, and in this sense the notion is quite obviously central to a just system of criminal sanctions. But our recognition that retribution plays a crucial role in determining who may be punished by no means requires approval of retribution as a general justification for punishment. It is the question whether retribution can provide a moral justification for punishment—in particular, capital punishment—that we must consider.

My Brothers, STEWART, POWELL, and STEVENS offer the following explanation of the retributive justification for capital punishments:

"'The instinct for retribution is part of the nature of man, and channeling that instinct in the administration of criminal justice serves an important purpose in promoting the stability of a society governed by law. When people begin to believe that organized society is unwilling or unable to impose upon criminal offenders the punishment they 'deserve,' then there are sown the seeds of anarchy —of self-help, vigilante justice, and lynch law.'"

This statement is wholly inadequate to justify the death penalty. As my Brother BRENNAN stated in Furman, "[t]here is no evidence whatever that utilization of imprisonment rather than death encourages private blood feuds and other disorders." It simply defies belief to suggest that the death penalty is necessary to prevent the American people from taking the law into their own hands.

In a related vein, it may be suggested that the expression of moral outrage through the imposition of the death penalty serves to reinforce basic moral values—that it marks some crimes as particularly offensive and therefore to be avoided. The argument is akin to a deterrence argument, but differs in that it contemplates the individual's shrinking from anti-social conduct not because he fears punishment, but because he has been told in the strongest possible way that the conduct is wrong. This contention, like the previous one, provides no support for the death penalty. It is inconceivable that any individual concerned about conforming his conduct to what society says is "right" would fail to realize that murder is "wrong" if the penalty were simply life imprisonment.

The foregoing contentions—that society's expression of moral outrage through the imposition of the death penalty pre-empts the citizenry from taking the law into its own hands and reinforces moral values—are not retributive in the purest sense. They are essentially utilitarian in that they portray the death penalty as valuable because of its beneficial results. These justifications for the death penalty are inadequate because the penalty is, quite clearly I think, not necessary to the accomplishment of those results.

There remains for consideration, however, what might be termed the purely retributive justification for the death penalty—that the death penalty is appropriate, not because of its beneficial effect on society, but because the taking of the murderer's life is itself morally good. Some of the language of the plurality's opinion appears positively to embrace this notion of retribution for its own sake as a justification for capital punishment. My Brothers STEWART, POWELL, and STEVENS state:

"[T]he decision that capital punishment may be the appropriate sanction in extreme cases is an expression of the community's belief that certain crimes are themselves so grievous an affront to humanity that the only adequate response may be the penalty of death."

The plurality then quotes with approval from Lord Justice Denning's remarks before the British Royal Commission on Capital Punishment:

"The truth is that some crimes are so outrageous that society insists on adequate punishment, because the wrong-doer deserves it, irrespective of whether it is a deterrent or not."

Of course it may be that these statements are intended as no more than observations as to the popular demands that it is thought must be responded to in order to prevent anarchy. But the implication of the statements appears to me to be quite different—namely, that society's judgment that the murderer "deserves" death must be respected not simply because the preservation of order requires it, but because it is appropriate that society make the judgment and carry it out. It is this latter notion, in particular, that I consider to be fundamentally at odds with the Eighth Amendment. The mere fact that the community demands the murderer's life in return for the evil he has done cannot sustain the death penalty, for as the plurality reminds us, "the Eighth Amendment demands more than that a challenged punishment be acceptable to contemporary society." To be sustained under the Eighth Amendment, the death penalty must "[comport] with the basic concept of human dignity at the core of the Amendment," (opinion of STEWART, POWELL, and STEVENS, JJ.); the objective in imposing it must be "[consistent] with our respect for the dignity of other men." Under these standards, the taking of life "because the wrong-doer deserves it" surely must fall, for such a punishment has as its very basis the total denial of the wrong-doer's dignity and worth.

The death penalty, unnecessary to promote the goal of deterrence or to further any legitimate notion of retribution, is an excessive penalty forbidden by the Eighth and Fourteenth Amendments. I respectfully dissent from the Court's judgment upholding the sentences of death imposed upon the petitioners in these cases.

❊ ❊ ❊

PROFFITT v. FLORIDA
428 U.S. 242, 96 S. Ct. 2960, 49 L. Ed. 2d 913 (1976)

Mr. Justice Stewart, Mr. Justice Powell, and Mr. Justice Stevens announced the judgment of the Court and filed an opinion delivered by Mr. Justice Powell.

The issue presented by this case is whether the imposition of the sentence of death for the crime of murder under the law of Florida violates the Eighth and Fourteenth Amendments.

I

The petitioner, Charles William Proffitt, was tried, found guilty, and sentenced to death for the first-degree murder of Joel Medgebow. The circumstances surrounding the murder were testified to by the decedent's wife, who was present at the time it was committed. On July 10, 1973, Mrs. Medgebow awakened around 5 a.m. in the bedroom of her apartment to find her husband sitting up in bed, moaning. He was holding what she took to be a ruler. Just then a third person jumped up, hit her several times with his fist, knocked her to the floor, and ran out of the house. It soon appeared that Medgebow had been fatally stabbed with a butcher knife. Mrs. Medgebow was not able to identify the attacker, although she was able to give a description of him.

The petitioner's wife testified that on the night before the murder the petitioner had gone to work dressed in a white shirt and gray pants, and that he had returned at about 5:15 a.m. dressed in the same clothing but without shoes. She said that after a short conversation the petitioner had packed his clothes and departed. A young woman boarder, who overheard parts

of the petitioner's conversation with his wife, testified that the petitioner had told his wife that he had stabbed and killed a man with a butcher knife while he was burglarizing a place, and that he had beaten a woman. One of the petitioner's coworkers testified that they had been drinking together until 3:30 or 3:45 a.m. on the morning of the murder and that the petitioner had then driven him home. He said that the petitioner at this time was wearing gray pants and a white shirt.

The jury found the defendant guilty as charged. Subsequently, as provided by Florida law, a separate hearing was held to determine whether the petitioner should be sentenced to death or to life imprisonment. Under the state law that decision turned on whether certain statutory aggravating circumstances surrounding the crime outweighed any statutory mitigating circumstances found to exist. At that hearing it was shown that the petitioner had one prior conviction, a 1967 charge of breaking and entering. The State also introduced the testimony of the physician at the jail where the petitioner had been held pending trial, Dr. Crumbley. He testified that the petitioner had come to him as a physician and told him that he was concerned that he would harm other people in the future, that he had had an uncontrollable desire to kill that had already resulted in his killing one man, that this desire was building up again, and that he wanted psychiatric help so he would not kill again. Dr. Crumbley also testified that, in his opinion, the petitioner was dangerous and would be a danger to his fellow inmates if imprisoned but that his condition could be treated successfully.

The jury returned an advisory verdict recommending the sentence of death. The trial judge ordered an independent psychiatric evaluation of the petitioner, the results of which indicated that the petitioner was not, then or at the time of the murder, mentally impaired. The judge then sentenced the petitioner to death. In his written findings supporting the sentence, the judge found as aggravating circumstances that (1) the murder was premeditated and occurred in the course of a felony (burglary); (2) the petitioner has the propensity to commit murder; (3) the murder was especially heinous, atrocious, and cruel; and (4) the petitioner knowingly, through his intentional act, created a great risk of serious bodily harm and death to many persons. The judge also found specifically that none of the statutory mitigating circumstances existed. The Supreme Court of Florida affirmed. We granted certiorari to consider whether the imposition of the death sentence in this case constitutes cruel and unusual punishment in violation of the Eighth and Fourteenth Amendments.

II

The petitioner argues that the imposition of the death penalty under any circumstances is cruel and unusual punishment in violation of the Eighth and Fourteenth Amendments. We reject this argument for the reasons stated today in Gregg v. Georgia.

III

A

In response to Furman v. Georgia, 408 U.S. 238 (1972), the Florida Legislature adopted new statutes that authorize the imposition of the death penalty on those convicted of first-degree mur-

der. At the same time Florida adopted a new capital-sentencing procedure, patterned in large part on the Model Penal Code. Under the new statute, if a defendant is found guilty of a capital offense, a separate evidentiary hearing is held before the trial judge and jury to determine his sentence. Evidence may be presented on any matter the judge deems relevant to sentencing and must include matters relating to certain legislatively specified aggravating and mitigating circumstances. Both the prosecution and the defense may present argument on whether the death penalty shall be imposed.

At the conclusion of the hearing the jury is directed to consider "[w]hether sufficient mitigating circumstances exist . . . which outweigh aggravating circumstances found to exist; and . . . [b]ased on those considerations, whether the defendant should be sentenced to life [imprisonment] or death." The jury's verdict is determined by majority vote. It is only advisory; the actual sentence is determined by the trial judge. The Florida Supreme Court has stated, however, that "[i]n order to sustain a sentence of death following a jury recommendation of life, the facts suggesting a sentence of death should be so clear and convincing that virtually no reasonable person could differ."

The trial judge is also directed to weigh the statutory aggravating and mitigating circumstances when he determines the sentence to be imposed on a defendant. The statute requires that if the trial court imposes a sentence of death, "it shall set forth in writing its findings upon which the sentence of death is based as to the facts: (a) [t]hat sufficient [statutory] aggravating circumstances exist . . . and (b) [t]hat there are insufficient [statutory] mitigating circumstances . . . to outweigh the aggravating circumstances."

The statute provides for automatic review by the Supreme Court of Florida of all cases in which a death sentence has been imposed. The law differs from that of Georgia in that it does not require the court to conduct any specific form of review. Since, however, the trial judge must justify the imposition of death sentence with written findings, meaningful appellate review of each such sentence is made possible, and the Supreme Court of Florida, like its Georgia counterpart, considers its function to be "guarantee . . . that the [aggravating and mitigating] reasons present in one case will reach a similar result to that reached under similar circumstances in another case. . . . If a defendant is sentenced to die, this Court can review that case in light of the other decisions and determine whether or not the punishment is too great."

On their face these procedures, like those used in Georgia, appear to meet the constitutional deficiencies identified in Furman. The sentencing authority in Florida, the trial judge, is directed to weigh eight aggravating factors against seven mitigating factors to determine whether the death penalty shall be imposed. This determination requires the trial judge to focus on the circumstances of the crime and the character of the individual defendant. He must, consider whether the defendant has a prior criminal record, whether the defendant acted under duress or under the influence of extreme mental or emotional disturbance, whether the defendant's role in the crime was that of a minor accomplice, and whether the defendant's youth argues in favor of a more lenient sentence than might otherwise be imposed. The trial judge must also determine whether the crime was committed in the course of one of several enumerated felonies, whether it was committed for pecuniary gain, whether it was committed to assist in an escape from custody or to prevent a lawful arrest, and whether the crime was especially heinous, atrocious, or cruel. To answer these questions, which are not unlike those considered by a Georgia sentencing jury, compare Gregg v. State, the sentencing judge must focus on the individual circumstances of each homicide and each defendant.

The basic difference between the Florida system and the Georgia system is that in Florida the sentence is determined by the trial judge rather than by the jury. This Court has pointed out that jury sentencing in a capital case can perform an important societal function, but it has never suggested that jury sentencing is constitutionally required. And it would appear that judicial sentencing should lead, if anything, to even greater consistency in the imposition at the trial court level of capital punishment, since a trial judge is more experienced in sentencing than a jury, and therefore is better able to impose sentences similar to those imposed in analogous cases.

The Florida capital-sentencing procedures thus seek to assure that the death penalty will not be imposed in an arbitrary or capricious manner. Moreover, to the extent that any risk to the contrary exists, it is minimized by Florida's appellate review system, under which the evidence of the aggravating and mitigating circumstances is reviewed and reweighed by the Supreme Court of Florida "to determine independently whether the imposition of the ultimate penalty is warranted."

The Supreme Court of Florida, like that of Georgia, has not hesitated to vacate a death sentence when it has determined that the sentence should not have been imposed. Indeed, it has vacated eight of the 21 death sentences that it has reviewed to date.

Under Florida's capital-sentencing procedures, in sum, trial judges are given specific and detailed guidance to assist them in deciding whether to impose a death penalty or imprisonment for life. Moreover, their decisions are reviewed to ensure that they are consistent with other sentences imposed in similar circumstances. Thus, in Florida, as in Georgia, it is no longer true that there is " 'no meaningful basis for distinguishing the few cases in which [the death penalty] is imposed from the many cases where it is not.' " On its face the Florida system thus satisfies the constitutional deficiencies identified in Furman.

B

As in Gregg, the petitioner contends, however, that, while perhaps facially acceptable, the new sentencing procedures in actual effect are merely cosmetic, and that arbitrariness and caprice still pervade the system under which Florida imposes the death penalty.

(1)

The petitioner first argues that arbitrariness is inherent in the Florida criminal justice system because it allows discretion to be exercised at each stage of a criminal proceeding—the prosecutor's decision whether to charge a capital offense in the first place, his decision whether to accept a plea to a lesser offense, the jury's consideration of lesser included offenses, and, after conviction and unsuccessful appeal, the

Executive's decision whether to commute a death sentence. As we noted in Gregg, this argument is based on a fundamental misinterpretation of Furman, and we reject it for the reasons expressed in Gregg.

(2)

The petitioner next argues that the new Florida sentencing procedures in reality do not eliminate the arbitrary infliction of death that was condemned in Furman. Basically he contends that the statutory aggravating and mitigating circumstances are vague and overbroad, and that the statute gives no guidance as to how the mitigating and aggravating circumstances should be weighed in any specific case.

(a)

Initially the petitioner asserts that the enumerated aggravating and mitigating circumstances are so vague and so broad that "virtually any first degree murder convict [is] a candidate for a death sentence." In particular, the petitioner attacks the eighth and third statutory aggravating circumstances, which authorize the death penalty to be imposed if the crime is "especially heinous, atrocious, or cruel," or if "[t]he defendant knowingly created a great risk of death to many persons." These provisions must be considered as they have been construed by the Supreme Court of Florida.

That Court has recognized that while it is arguable "that all killings are atrocious, . . . [s]till we believe that the Legislature intended something 'especially' heinous, atrocious, or cruel when it authorized the death penalty for first degree murder." As a consequence, the Court has indicated that the eighth statutory provision is directed only at "the conscienceless or pitiless crime which is unnecessarily torturous to the victim." We cannot say that the provision, as so construed, provides inadequate guidance to those charged with the duty of recommending or imposing sentences in capital cases.

In the only case, except for the instant case, in which the third aggravating factor—"the defendant knowingly created a great risk of death to many persons"—was found, Alvord v. State, 322 So.2d 533 (1975), the State Supreme Court held that the defendant created a great risk of death because he "obviously murdered two of the victims in order to avoid a surviving witness to the [first] murder." As construed by the Supreme Court of Florida these provisions are not impermissibly vague.

(b)

The petitioner next attacks the imprecision of the mitigating circumstances. He argues that whether a defendant acted "under the influence of extreme mental or emotional disturbance," whether a defendant's capacity "to conform his conduct to the requirements of law was substantially impaired," or whether a defendant's participation as an accomplice in a capital felony was "relatively minor," are questions beyond the capacity of a jury, or judge to determine.

He also argues that neither a jury nor a judge is capable of deciding how to weigh a defendant's age or determining whether he had a "significant history of prior criminal activity." In a similar vein the petitioner argues that it is not possible to make a rational determination whether there are "sufficient" aggravating circumstances that are not outweighed by the mitigating circumstances, since the state law assigns no specific weight to any of the various circumstances to be considered.

While these questions and decisions may be hard, they require no more line-drawing than is commonly required of a fact finder in a lawsuit. For example, juries have traditionally evaluated the validity of defenses such as insanity or reduced capacity, both of which involve the same considerations as some of the above-mentioned mitigating circumstances. While the various factors to be considered by the sentencing authorities do not have numerical weights assigned to them, the requirements of Furman are satisfied when the sentencing authority's discretion is guided and channeled by requiring examination of specific factors that argue in favor of or against imposition of the death penalty, thus eliminating total arbitrariness and capriciousness in its imposition.

The directions given to judge and jury by the Florida statute are sufficiently clear and precise to enable the various aggravating circumstances to be weighed against the mitigating ones. As a result, the trial court's sentencing discretion is guided and channeled by a system that focuses on the circumstances of each individual homicide and individual defendant in deciding whether the death penalty is to be imposed.

(c)

Finally, the Florida statute has a provision designed to assure that the death penalty will not be imposed on a capriciously selected group of convicted defendants. The Supreme Court of Florida reviews each death sentence to ensure that similar results are reached in similar cases.

Nonetheless the petitioner attacks the Florida appellate review process because the role of the Supreme Court of Florida in reviewing death sentences is necessarily subjective and unpredictable. While it may be true that that Court has not chosen to formulate a rigid objective test as its standard of review for all cases, it does not follow that the appellate review process is ineffective or arbitrary. In fact, it is apparent that the Florida Court has undertaken responsibly to perform its function of death sentence review with a maximum of rationality and consistency. For example, it has several times compared the circumstances of a case under review with those of previous cases in which it has assessed the imposition of death sentences. By following this procedure the Florida Court has in effect adopted the type of proportionality review mandated by the Georgia statute. And any suggestion that the Florida Court engages in only cursory or rubber stamp review of death penalty cases is totally controverted by the fact that it has vacated over one-third of the death sentences that have come before it.

IV

Florida, like Georgia, has responded to Furman by enacting legislation that passes constitutional muster. That legislation provides that after a person is convicted of first-degree murder, there shall be an informed, focused, guided, and objective inquiry into the question whether he should be sentenced to death. If a death sentence is imposed, the sentencing authority articulates in writing the statutory reasons that led to its decision. Those reasons, and the evidence supporting them, are conscientiously reviewed by a court which, because of its statewide jurisdiction, can assure consistency, fairness, and rationality in the evenhanded operation of the state law. As in Georgia, this system serves to assure that sentences

of death will not be "wantonly" or "freakishly" imposed. Accordingly, the judgment before us is affirmed.

It is so ordered.

MR. JUSTICE WHITE, with whom THE CHIEF JUSTICE and MR. JUSTICE REHNQUIST join, concurring in the judgment.

There is no need to repeat the statement of the facts of this case and of the statutory procedure under which the death penalty was imposed, both of which are described in detail in the opinion of MR. JUSTICE STEWART, MR. JUSTICE POWELL, and MR. JUSTICE STEVENS (hereinafter the plurality). I agree with the plurality, see Part III-B (2)(a) and (b), that although the statutory aggravating and mitigating circumstances are not susceptible to mechanical application as they are by no means so vague and overbroad as to leave the discretion of the sentencing authority unfettered. Under Florida law, the sentencing judge is *required* to impose the death penalty on all first-degree murders as to whom the statutory aggravating factors outweigh the mitigating factors. There is good reason to anticipate, then, that as to certain categories of murderers, the penalty will not be imposed freakishly or rarely but will be imposed with regularity; and consequently it cannot be said that the death penalty in Florida as to those categories has ceased "to be a credible deterrent or measurably to contribute to any other end of punishment in the criminal justice system." Accordingly, the Florida statutory scheme for imposing the death penalty does not run afoul of this Court's holding in Furman v. Georgia, *supra*.

For the reasons set forth in my concurring opinion in Gregg v. Georgia, and my dissenting opinion in Roberts

v. Louisiana, this conclusion is not undercut by the possibility that some murderers may escape the death penalty solely through exercise of prosecutorial discretion or executive clemency. For the reasons set forth in my dissenting opinion in Roberts v. Louisiana, I also reject petitioner's argument that under the Eighth Amendment the death penalty may never be imposed under any circumstances.

I concur in the judgment of affirmance.

MR. JUSTICE BLACKMUN, concurring in the judgment.

I concur in the judgment.

* * *

MARK J. MILLS et al., Petitioners

v.

RUBIE ROGERS et al.

457 US 291, 73 L.Ed.2d 16, 102 S.Ct. 2442 (1982)

OPINION OF THE COURT

JUSTICE POWELL delivered the opinion of the Court.

The Court granted certiorari in this case to determine whether involuntarily committed mental patients have a constitutional right to refuse treatment with antipsychotic drugs.

I

This litigation began on April 27, 1975, when respondent Rubie Rogers and six other persons filed suit against various officials and staff of the May and Austin Units of the Boston State Hospital. The plaintiffs all were present or former mental patients at the institution. During their period of institutionalization all had been forced to accept unwanted treatment with antipsychotic drugs. Alleging that forcible administration of these drugs violated rights protected by the Constitution of the United States, the plaintiffs—respondents here—sought compensatory and punitive damages and injunctive relief.

The District Court certified the case as a class action. Although denying relief in damages, the court held that mental patients enjoy constitutionally protected liberty and privacy interests in deciding for themselves whether to submit to drug therapy.

The Court of Appeals for the First Circuit affirmed in part and reversed in part. It agreed that mental patients have a constitutionally protected interest in deciding for themselves whether to undergo treatment with antipsychotic drugs.

Because the judgment of the Court of Appeals involved constitutional issues of potentially broad significance, we granted certiorari.

II

A

The principal question on which we granted certiorari is whether an involuntarily committed mental patient has a constitutional right to refuse treatment with antipsychotic drugs. This question has both substantive and procedural aspects. The parties agree that the Constitution recognizes a liberty interest in avoiding the unwanted administration of antipsychotic drugs. Assuming that they are correct in this respect, the substantive issue involves a definition of that protected constitutional interest, as well as identification of the conditions under which competing state interests might outweigh it.

The procedural issue concerns the minimum procedures required by the Constitution for determining that the individual's liberty interest actually is outweighed in a particular instance.

As a practical matter both the substantive and procedural issues are intertwined with questions of state law.

For purposes of determining actual rights and obligations, however, questions of state law cannot be avoided. Within our federal system the substantive rights provided by the Federal Constitution define only a minimum. State law may recognize liberty interests more extensive than those independently protected by the

Federal Constitution. If so, the broader state protections would define the actual substantive rights possessed by a person living within that State.

Where a State creates liberty interests broader than those protected directly by the Federal Constitution, the procedures mandated to protect the federal substantive interests also might fail to determine the actual procedural rights and duties of persons within the State. Because state-created liberty interests are entitled to the protection of the federal Due Process Clause, full scope of a patient's due process rights may depend in part on the substantive liberty interests created by state as well as federal law. Moreover, a State may confer *procedural* protections of liberty interests that extend beyond those minimally required by the Constitution of the United States. If a State does so, the minimal requirements of the Federal Constitution would not be controlling, and would not need to be identified in order to determine the legal rights and duties of persons within that State.

B

Roughly five months after the Court of Appeals decided this case, and shortly after this Court granted certiorari, the Supreme Judicial Court of Massachusetts announced its decision in Guardianship of Roe, 383 Mass ____, 421 NE2d 40 (1981).

Expressly resting its decision on the common law of Massachusetts as well as on the Federal Constitution, Massachusetts' highest court held in Roe that a person has a protected liberty interest in " 'decid[ing] for himself whether to submit to the serious and potentially harmful medical treatment that is represented by the administration of antipsychotic drugs.' " Id., at ____, 421 NE2d, at 51. The court found—again apparently on the basis of the common law of Massachusetts as well as the Constitution of the United States—that this interest of the individual is of such importance that it can be overcome only by "an overwhelming State interest." Id., at ____, 421 NE2d, at 51. Roe further held that a person does not forfeit his protected liberty interest by virtue of becoming incompetent, but rather remains entitled to have his "substituted judgment" exercised on his behalf. Ibid. Defining this "substituted judgment" as one for which "[n]o medical expertise is required," id., at ____, 421 NE2d, at 52, the Massachusetts Supreme Judicial Court required a *judicial* determination of substituted judgment before drugs could be administered in a particular instance, except possibly in cases of medical emergency.

C

[R]espondents have argued in this Court that Roe may influence the correct disposition of the case at hand. We agree.

Especially in the wake of Roe, it is distinctly possible that Massachusetts recognizes liberty interests of persons adjudged incompetent that are broader than those protected directly by the Constitution of the United States.

If the state interest is broader, the *substantive* protection that the Constitution affords against the involuntary administration of antipsychotic drugs would not determine the actual substantive rights and duties of persons in the State of Massachusetts.

Procedurally, it also is quite possible that a Massachusetts court, as a matter of state law, would require greater protection of relevant liberty interests than the minimum adequate to survive scrutiny under the Due Process Clause.

Again on this hypothesis state law would be dispositive of the procedural rights and duties of the parties to this case.

Finally, even if state procedural law itself remains unchanged by Roe, the federally mandated procedures will depend on the nature and weight of the *state* interests, as well as the individual interests, that are asserted. To identify the nature and scope of state interests that are to be balanced against an individual's liberty interests, this Court may look to state law.

Here we view the underlying state-law predicate for weighing asserted state interests as being put into doubt, if not altered, by Roe.

D

Until certain questions have been answered, we think it would be inappropriate for us to attempt to weigh or even to identify relevant liberty interests that might be derived directly from the Constitution, independently of state law. It is this Court's settled policy to avoid unnecessary decisions of constitutional issues. This policy is supported, although not always required, by the prohibition against advisory opinions.

In applying this policy of restraint, we are uncertain here which if any constitutional issues now must be decided to resolve the controversy between the parties. In the wake of Roe, we cannot say with confidence that adjudication based solely on identification of federal constitutional interests would determine the actual rights and duties of the parties before us.

Because of its greater familiarity both with the record and with Massachusetts law, the Court of Appeals is better situated than we to determine how Roe may have changed the law of Massachusetts and how any changes may affect this case. Accordingly, we think it appropriate for the Court of Appeals to determine in the first instance whether Roe requires revision of its holdings or whether it may call for the certification of potentially dispositive state-law questions to the Supreme Judicial Court of Massachusetts.

The judgment of the Court of Appeals is therefore vacated, and the case is remanded for further proceedings consistent with this opinion.

So ordered.

DUANE YOUNGBERG, etc., et al., Petitioners

v.

NICHOLAS ROMEO, an incompetent, by his mother and next friend, PAULA ROMEO

457 US 307, 73 L.Ed.2d 28, 102 S.Ct. 2452 (1982)

OPINION OF THE COURT

JUSTICE POWELL delivered the opinion of the Court.

The question presented is whether respondent, involuntarily committed to a state institution for the mentally retarded, has substantive rights under the Due Process Clause of the Fourteenth Amendment to (i) safe conditions of confinement; (ii) freedom from bodily restraints; and (iii) training or "habilitation." Respondent sued under 42 USC § 1983 [42 USCS § 1983] three administrators of the institution, claiming damages for the alleged breach of his constitutional rights.

I

Respondent Nicholas Romeo is profoundly retarded. Although 33 years old, he has the mental capacity of an 18-month-old child, with an I.Q. between 8 and 10. He cannot talk and lacks the most basic self-care skills. Until he was 26, respondent lived with his parents in Philadelphia. But after the death of his father in May 1974, his mother was unable to care for him. Within two weeks of the father's death, respondent's mother sought his temporary admission to a nearby Pennsylvania hospital.

Shortly thereafter, she asked the Philadelphia County Court of Common Pleas to admit Romeo to a state facility on a permanent basis. Her petition to the court explained that she was unable to care for Romeo or control his violence. As part of the commitment process, Romeo was examined by a physician and a psychologist. They both certified that respondent was severely retarded and unable to care for himself. On June 11, 1974, the Court of Common Pleas committed respondent to the Pennhurst State School and Hospital, pursuant to the applicable involuntary commitment provision of the Pennsylvania Mental Health and Mental Retardation Act.

At Pennhurst, Romeo was injured on numerous occasions, both by his own violence and by the reactions of other residents to him. Respondent's mother became concerned about these injuries. After objecting to respondent's treatment several times, she filed this complaint on November 4, 1976, in the United States District Court for the Eastern District of Pennsylvania as his next friend. The complaint alleged that "[d]uring the period July, 1974 to the present, plaintiff has suffered injuries on at least sixty-three occasions." The complaint originally sought damages and injunctive relief from Pennhurst's director and two supervisors; it alleged that these officials knew, or should have known, that Romeo was suffering injuries and that they failed to institute appropriate preventive procedures, thus violating his rights under the Eighth and Fourteenth Amendments.

Thereafter, in late 1976, Romeo was transferred from his ward to the hospital for treatment of a broken arm. While in the infirmary, and by order of a doctor, he was physically restrained during portions of each day. These restraints were ordered by Dr. Gabroy, not a defendant here, to protect Romeo and others in the hospital, some of whom were in traction or were being treated intravenously. Although respondent normally would have returned to his ward when his arm healed, the parties to this litigation agreed that he should remain in the hospital due to the pending lawsuit. Nevertheless, in December 1977, a second amended complaint was filed alleging that the defendants were restraining respondent for prolonged periods on a routine basis. The second amended complaint also added a claim for damages to compensate Romeo for the defendants' failure to provide him with appropriate "treatment or programs for his mental retardation." All claims for injunctive relief were dropped prior to trial because respondent is a member of the class seeking such relief in another action.

An 8-day jury trial was held in April 1978. Petitioners introduced evidence that respondent participated in several programs teaching basic self-care skills. A comprehensive behavior-modification program was designed by staff members to reduce Romeo's aggressive behavior, but that program was never implemented because of his mother's objections.

Respondent introduced evidence of his injuries and of conditions in his unit.

At the close of the trial, the court instructed the jury that "if any or all of the defendants were aware of and failed to take all reasonable steps to prevent repeated attacks upon Nicholas Romeo," such failure deprived him of constitutional rights. The jury also was instructed that if the defendants shackled Romeo or denied him treatment "as a punishment for filing this lawsuit," his constitutional rights were violated under the Eighth Amendment. Finally, the jury was instructed that only if they found the defendants "deliberate[ly] indifferen[t] to the serious medical [and psychological] needs" of Romeo could they find that his Eighth and Fourteenth Amendment rights had been violated.

The jury returned a verdict for the defendants, on which judgment was entered.

The Court of Appeals for the Third Circuit, sitting en banc, reversed and remanded for a new trial. The court held that the Eighth Amendment, prohibiting cruel and unusual punishment of those convicted of crimes, was not an appropriate source for determining rights of the involuntarily committed. Rather, the Fourteenth Amendment and the liberty interest protected by that Amendment provided the proper constitutional basis for these rights. In applying the Fourteenth Amendment, the court found that the involuntarily committed retain liberty interest in freedom of movement and in personal security. These were "fundamental liberties" that can be limited only by an "overriding, nonpunitive" state interest. It further found that the involuntarily committed have a liberty interest in habilitation designed to "treat" their mental retardation.

We granted the petition for certiorari because of the importance of the question presented to the administration of state institutions for the mentally retarded.

II

We consider here for the first time the substantive rights of involuntarily committed mentally retarded persons under the Fourteenth Amendment to the Constitution.[1] In this case, respondent has been committed under the laws of Pennsylvania, and he does not challenge the commitment. Rather, he argues that he has a constitutionally protected liberty interest in safety, freedom of movement, and training within the institution; and that petitioners infringed these rights by failing to provide constitutionally required conditions of confinement.

The mere fact that Romeo has been committed under proper procedures

---

[1] In pertinent part, that Amendment provides that a State cannot deprive "any person of life, liberty, or property, without due process of law...." U.S. Const, Amdt 14, § 1.

Respondent no longer relies on the Eighth Amendment as a direct source of constitutional rights.

does not deprive him of all substantive liberty interests under the Fourteenth Amendment.

We must decide whether liberty interests exist in safety, freedom of movement, and training. If such interests do exist, we must further decide whether they have been infringed in this case.

A

Respondent's first two claims involve liberty interests recognized by prior decisions of this Court, interests that involuntary commitment proceedings do not extinguish. The first is a claim to safe conditions. In the past, this Court has noted that the right to personal security constitutes a "historic liberty interest" protected substantively by the Due Process Clause.

If it is cruel and unusual punishment to hold convicted criminals in unsafe conditions, it must be unconstitutional to confine the involuntarily committed—who may not be punished at all—in unsafe conditions.

Next, respondent claims a right to freedom from bodily restraint. In other contexts, the existence of such an interest is clear in the prior decisions of this Court.

This interest survives criminal conviction and incarceration. Similarly, it must also survive involuntary commitment.

B

Respondent's remaining claim is more troubling. In his words, he asserts a "constitutional right to minimally adequate habilitation." This is a substantive due process claim that is said to be grounded in the liberty component of the Due Process Clause of the Fourteenth Amendment. Respondent emphasizes that

the right he asserts is for "minimal" training, and he would leave the type and extent of training to be determined on a case-by-case basis "in light of present medical or other scientific knowledge."

In addressing the asserted right to training, we start from established principles. As a general matter, a State is under no constitutional duty to provide substantive services for those within its border. When a person is institutionalized—and wholly dependent on the State—it is conceded by petitioners that a duty to provide certain services and care does exist, although even then a State necessarily has considerable discretion in determining the nature and scope of its responsibilities.

Respondent, in light of the severe character of his retardation, concedes that no amount of training will make possible his release. And he does not argue that if he were still at home, the State would have an obligation to provide training at its expense. The record reveals that respondent's primary needs are bodily safety and a minimum of physical restraint, and respondent clearly claims training related to these needs. As we have recognized that there is a constitutionally protected liberty interest in safety and freedom from restraint, training may be necessary to avoid unconstitutional infringement of those rights. On the basis of the record before us, it is quite uncertain whether respondent seeks any "habilitation" or training unrelated to safety and freedom from bodily restraints.

If, as seems the case, respondent seeks only training related to safety and freedom from restraints, this case does not present the difficult question whether a mentally retarded person, involuntarily committed to a state institution, has some general constitutional right to training per se, even when no type or amount of training would lead to freedom.

[W]e conclude that respondent's liberty interests require the State to provide minimally adequate or reasonable training to ensure safety and freedom from undue restraint. In view of the kinds of treatment sought by respondent and the evidence of record, we need go no further in this case.

III

A

We have established that Romeo retains liberty interests in safety and freedom from bodily restraint. Yet these interests are not absolute; indeed to some extent they are in conflict. In operating an institution such as Pennhurst, there are occasions in which it is necessary for the State to restrain the movement of residents—for example, to protect them as well as others from violence. Similar restraints may also be appropriate in a training program. And an institution cannot protect its residents from all danger of violence if it is to permit them to have any freedom of movement. The question then is not simply whether a liberty interest has been infringed but whether the extent or nature of the restraint or lack of absolute safety is such as to violate due process.

In determining whether a substantive right protected by the Due Process Clause has been violated, it is necessary to balance "the liberty of the individual" and "the demands of an organized society." Poe v. Ullman, 367 US 497, 542 (1961) (Harlan, J., dissenting). In seeking this balance in other cases, the Court has weighed the

individual's interest in liberty against the State's asserted reasons for restraining individual liberty. In Bell v. Wolfish, 441 US 520 (1979), for example, we considered a challenge to pretrial detainees' confinement conditions. We agreed that the detainees, not yet convicted of the crime charged, could not be punished. But we upheld those restrictions on liberty that were reasonably related to legitimate government objectives and not tantamount to punishment. We have taken a similar approach in deciding procedural due process challenges to civil commitment proceedings. In Parham v. J.R., 442 US 584 (1979), for example, we considered a challenge to state procedures for commitment of a minor with parental consent. In determining that *procedural* due process did not mandate an adversarial hearing, we weighed the liberty interest of the individual against the legitimate interests of the State, including the fiscal and administrative burdens additional procedures would entail.

Accordingly, whether respondent's constitutional rights have been violated must be determined by balancing his liberty interests against the relevant state interests. If there is to be any uniformity in protecting these interests, this balancing cannot be left to the unguided discretion of a judge or jury. We therefore turn to consider the proper standard for determining whether a State adequately has protected the rights of the involuntarily committed mentally retarded.

B

We think the standard articulated by [the Court of Appeals in the instant case] affords the necessary guidance and reflects the proper balance between the legitimate interests of the

State and the rights of the involuntarily committed to reasonable conditions of safety and freedom from unreasonable restraints. [The Court of Appeals] would have held that "the Constitution only requires that the courts make certain that professional judgment in fact was exercised. It is not appropriate for the courts to specify which of several professionally acceptable choices should have been made." 644 F2d, at 178. Persons who have been involuntarily committed are entitled to more considerate treatment and conditions of confinement than criminals whose conditions of confinement are designed to punish. At the same time, this standard is lower than the "compelling" or "substantial" necessity tests the Court of Appeals would require a State to meet to justify use of restraints or conditions of less than absolute safety. We think this requirement would place an undue burden on the administration of institutions such as Pennhurst and also would restrict unnecessarily the exercise of professional judgment as to the needs of residents.

Moreover, we agree that respondent is entitled to minimally adequate training. In this case, the minimally adequate training required by the Constitution is such training as may be reasonable in light of respondent's liberty interests in safety and freedom from unreasonable restraints. In determining what is "reasonable"— in this and in any case presenting a claim for training by a State—we emphasize that courts must show deference to the judgment exercised by a qualified professional. By so limiting judicial review of challenges to conditions in state institutions, interference by the federal judiciary with the internal operations of these institutions should be minimized.

Moreover, there certainly is not reason to think judges or juries are better qualified than appropriate professionals in making such decisions. For these reasons, the decision, if made by a professional, is presumptively valid; liability may be imposed only when the decision by the professional is such a substantial departure from accepted professional judgment, practice, or standards as to demonstrate that the person responsible actually did not base the decision on such a judgment. In an action for damages against a professional in his individual capacity, however, the professional will not be liable if he was unable to satisfy his normal professional standards because of budgetary constraints; in such a situation, good-faith immunity would bar liability.

IV

In deciding this case, we have weighted those post-commitment interests cognizable as liberty interests under the Due Process Clause of the Fourteenth Amendment against legitimate state interests and in light of the constraints under which most state institutions necessarily operate. We repeat that the State concedes a duty to provide adequate food, shelter, clothing, and medical care. These are the essentials of the care that the State must provide. The State also has the unquestioned duty to provide reasonable safety for all residents and personnel within the institution. And it may not restrain residents except when and to the extent professional judgment deems this necessary to assure such safety or to provide needed training. In this case, therefore, the State is under a duty to provide respondent with such training as an appropriate professional would consider reasonable to ensure his safety and to facilitate his ability to function free from bodily restraints. It may well be unreasonable not to provide training when training could significantly reduce the need for restraints or the likelihood of violence.

Respondent thus enjoys constitutionally protected interests in conditions of reasonable care and safety, reasonably nonrestrictive confinement conditions, and such training as may be required by these interests. Such conditions of confinement would comport fully with the purpose of respondent's commitment. In determining whether the State has met its obligations in these respects, decisions made by the appropriate professional are entitled to a presumption of correctness. Such a presumption is necessary to enable institutions of this type—often, unfortunately, overcrowded and understaffed—to continue to function. A single professional may have to make decisions with respect to a number of residents with widely varying needs and problems in the course of a normal day. The administrators, and particularly professional personnel, should not be required to make each decision in the shadow of an action for damages.

In this case, we conclude that the jury was erroneously instructed on the assumption that the proper standard of liability was that of the Eighth Amendment. We vacate the decision of the Court of Appeals and remand for further proceedings consistent with this decision.

So ordered.

TURNER v. SAFLEY

482 U.S. 78, 107 S. Ct. 2254, 96 L. Ed. 2d 65 (1987)

[Citations and Footnotes Omitted]

JUSTICE O'CONNOR delivered the opinion of the Court.

This case requires us to determine the constitutionality of regulations promulgated by the Missouri Division of Corrections relating to inmate marriages ... The Court of Appeals for the Eighth Circuit, applying a strict scrutiny analysis, concluded that the regulations violate respondents' constitutional rights. We hold that a lesser standard of scrutiny is appropriate in determining the constitutionality of the prison rules. Applying that standard, we ... conclude that the marriage restriction cannot be sustained.

I

Respondents brought this class action for injunctive relief and damages in the United States District Court for the Western District of

Missouri. The regulations challenged in the complaint were in effect at all prisons within the jurisdiction of the Missouri Division of Corrections. This litigation focused, however, on practices at the Renz Correctional Institution (Renz), located in Cedar City, Missouri. The Renz prison population includes both male and female prisoners of varying security levels. Most of the female prisoners at Renz are classified as medium or maximum security inmates, while most of the male prisoners are classified as minimum security offenders. Renz is used on occasion to provide protective custody for inmates from other prisons in the Missouri system. The facility originally was built as a minimum security prison farm, and it still has a minimum security perimeter without guard towers or walls.

... The challenged marriage regulation, which was promulgated while this litigation was pending, permits an inmate to marry only with the permission of the superintendent of the prison, and provides that such approval should be given only "when there are compelling reasons to do so." The term "compelling" is not defined, but prison officials testified at trial that generally only a pregnancy or the birth of an illegitimate child would be considered a compelling reason. Prior to the promulgation of this rule, the applicable regulation did not obligate Missouri Division of Corrections officials to assist an inmate who wanted to get married, but it also did not specifically authorize the superintendent of an institution to

prohibit inmates from getting married. ...

The District Court issued a memorandum opinion and order finding ... the marriage regulations unconstitutional. The court, relying on *Procunier v. Martinez*, applied a strict scrutiny standard. It held the marriage regulation to be an unconstitutional infringement upon the fundamental right to marry because it was far more restrictive than was either reasonable or essential for the protection of the State' interests in security and rehabilitation....

...

B

In support of the marriage regulation, petitioners first suggest that the rule does not deprive prisoners of a constitutionally protected right. They concede that the decision to marry is a fundamental right under *Zablocki v. Redhail*, and *Loving v. Virginia*, but they imply that a different rule should obtain "in ... a prison forum." Petitioners then argue that even if the regulation burdens inmates' constitutional rights, the restriction should be tested under a reasonableness standard. They urge that the restriction is reasonably related to legitimate security and rehabilitation concerns.

We disagree with petitioners that *Zablocki* does not apply to prison inmates. It is settled that a prison inmate "retains those [constitutional] rights that are not inconsistent with his status as a prisoner or with the legitimate penological objectives of the corrections system." The right to marry, like many other rights, is subject to substantial restrictions as a result of incarceration. Many important attributes of marriage remain, however, after taking into account the limitations imposed by prison life. First, inmate marriages, like others, are expressions of emotional support and public commitment. These elements are an important and significant aspect of the marital relationship. In addition, many religions recognize marriage as having spiritual significance, for some inmates and their spouses, therefore, the commitment of marriage may be an exercise of religious faith as well as an expression of personal dedication. Third, most inmates eventually will be released by parole or commutation, and therefore most inmate marriages are formed in the expectation that they ultimately will be fully consummated. Finally, marital status often is a precondition to the receipt of government benefits (e.g., Social Security benefits), property rights(e.g., tenancy by the entirety, inheritance rights), and other, less tangible benefits (e.g., legitimation of children born out of wedlock). These incidents of marriage, like the religious and personal aspects of the marriage commitment, are unaffected by the fact of confinement or the pursuit of legitimate corrections goals.

Taken together, we conclude that these remaining elements are sufficient to form a constitutionally protected marital relationship in the prison context. Our decision in *Butler*

v. Wilson ... is not to the contrary. That case involved a prohibition on marriage only for inmates sentenced to life imprisonment; and, importantly, denial of the right was part of the punishment for the crime.

The Missouri marriage regulation prohibits inmates from marrying unless the prison superintendent has approved the marriage after finding that there are compelling reasons for doing so. As noted previously, generally only pregnancy or birth of a child is considered a "compelling reason" to approve a marriage. In determining whether this regulation impermissibly burdens the right to marry, we note initially that the regulation prohibits marriages between inmates and civilians, as well as marriages between inmates. Although not urged by respondents, this implication of the interests of nonprisoners may support application of the *Martinez* standard, because the regulation may entail a "consequential restriction of the [constitutional] rights of those who are not prisoners." We need not reach this question, however, because even under the reasonable relationship test, the marriage regulation does not withstand scrutiny.

Petitioners have identified both security and rehabilitation concerns in support of the marriage prohibition. The security concern emphasized by petitioners is that "love triangles" might lead to violent confrontations between inmates. With respect to rehabilitation, prison officials testified that female prisoners often were subject to abuse at home or were overly dependent on male figures, and that this dependence or abuse was connected to the crimes they had committed. The superintendent at Renz, petitioner William Turner, testified that in his view, these women prisoners needed to concentrate on developing skills of self-reliance, and that the prohibition on marriage furthered this rehabilitative goal. Petitioners emphasize that the prohibition on marriage should be understood in the light of Superintendent Turner's experience with several ill-advised marriage requests from female inmates.

We conclude that on this record, the Missouri prison regulation, as written, is not reasonably related to these penological interests. No doubt legitimate security concerns may require placing reasonable restrictions upon an inmate's right to marry, and may justify requiring approval of the superintendent. The Missouri regulation, however, represents an exaggerated response to such security objectives. There are obvious, easy alternatives to the Missouri regulation that accommodate the right to marry while imposing a de minimis burden on the pursuit of security objectives. We are aware of no place in the record where prison officials testified that such ready alternatives would not fully satisfy their security concerns. Moreover, with respect to the security concern emphasized in petitioners' brief—the creation of "love triangles"—petitioners have pointed to nothing in the record suggesting that the marriage regulation was viewed

as preventing such entanglements. Common sense likewise suggests that there is no logical connection between the marriage restriction and the formation of love triangles: surely in prisons housing both male and female prisoners, inmate rivalries are as likely to develop without a formal marriage ceremony as with one. Finally, this is not an instance where the "ripple effect" on the security of fellow inmates and prison staff justifies a broad restriction on inmates' rights—indeed, where the inmate wishes to marry a civilian, the decision to marry (apart from the logistics of the wedding ceremony) is a completely private one.

Nor, on this record, is the marriage restriction reasonably related to the articulated rehabilitation goal. First, in requiring refusal of permission absent a finding of compelling reason to allow the marriage, the rule sweeps much more broadly than can be explained by petitioners' penological objectives. Missouri prison officials testified that generally they had experienced no problem with the marriage of male inmates, and the District Court found that such marriages had routinely been allowed as a matter of practice at Missouri correctional institutions prior to adoption of the rule. The proffered justification thus does not explain the adoption of a rule banning marriages by these inmates. Nor does it account for the prohibition on inmate marriages to civilians. Missouri prison officials testified that generally they had no objection to inmate-civilian marriages, and Superintendent Turner testified that he usually did not object to the marriage of either male or female prisoners to civilians. The rehabilitation concern appears from the record to have been centered almost exclusively on female inmates marrying other inmates or ex-felons; it does not account for the ban on inmate-civilian marriages.

Moreover, although not necessary to the disposition of this case, we note that on this record the rehabilitative objective asserted to support the regulation itself is suspect. Of the several female inmates whose marriage requests were discussed by prison officials at trial, only one was refused on the basis of fostering excessive dependency. The District Court found that the Missouri prison operated on the basis of excessive paternalism in that the proposed mar

riages of all female inmates were scrutinized carefully even before the adoption of the current regulation—only one was approved at Renz in the period from 1979-1983—whereas the marriages of male inmates during the same period were routinely approved. That kind of lopsided rehabilitation concern cannot provide a justification for the broad Missouri marriage rule.

It is undisputed that Missouri prison officials may regulate the time and circumstances under which marriage ceremony itself takes place. On this record, however, the almost complete ban on the decision to marry is not reasonably related to legitimate penological objectives. We conclude, therefore, that the Missouri marriage regulation is facially invalid.

W.J. ESTELLE, JR. v. J.W. GAMBLE
429 U.S. 97, 97 S. Ct. 285, 50 L. Ed. 2d 251 (1976)

Argued October 5, 1976. Decided November 30, 1976

OPINION OF THE COURT

Mr. Justice Marshall delivered the opinion of the Court.

Respondent J. W. Gamble, an inmate of the Texas Department of Corrections, was injured on November 9, 1973, while performing a prison work assignment. On February 11, 1974, he instituted this civil rights action under 42 U.S.C. § 1983 [42 U.S.C.S. § 1983], complaining of the treatment he received after the injury. Named as defendants were the petitioners, W. J. Estelle, Jr., Director of the Department of Corrections, H. H. Husbands, warden of the prison, and Dr. Ralph Gray, medical director of the Department and chief medical officer of the prison hospital. The District Court, sua sponte, dismissed the complaint for failure to state a claim upon which relief could be granted. The Court of Appeals reversed and remanded with instructions to reinstate the complaint. 516 F.2d 937 (CA5 1975). We granted certiorari, 424 U.S. 907, 47 L.Ed.2d 311, 96 S.Ct. 1101 (1976).

I

Because the complaint was dismissed for failure to state a claim, we must take as true its handwritten, pro se allegations. Cooper v. Pate, 378 U.S. 546, 12 L.Ed.2d 1030, 84 S.Ct. 1733 (1964). According to the complaint, Gamble was injured on November 9, 1973, when a bale of cotton fell on him while he was unloading a truck. He continued to work but after four hours he became stiff and was granted a pass to the unit hospital. At the hospital a medical assistant, "Captain" Blunt, checked him for a hernia and sent him back to his cell. Within two hours the pain became so intense that Gamble returned to the hospital where he was given pain pills by an inmate nurse and then was examined by a doctor. The following day, Gamble saw a Dr. Astone who diagnosed the injury as a lower back strain, prescribed Zactirin (a pain reliever) and Robaxin (a muscle relaxant), and placed respondent on "cell-pass, cell-feed" status for two days, allowing him to remain in his cell at all times except for showers. On November 12, Gamble again saw Dr. Astone who continued the medication and cell-pass, cell-feed for another seven days. He also ordered that respondent be moved from an upper to a lower bunk for one week, but the prison authorities did not comply with that directive. The following week, Gamble returned to Dr. Astone. The doctor continued the muscle relaxant but prescribed a new pain reliever, Febridyne, and placed respondent on cell-pass for seven days, permitting him to remain in his cell except for meals and showers. On November 26, respondent again saw Dr. Astone, who put respondent back on the original pain reliever for five days and continued the cell-pass for another week.

On December 3, despite Gamble's statement that his back hurt as much as it had the first day, Dr. Astone took him off cell-pass, thereby certifying him to be capable of light work. At the same time, Dr. Astone prescribed Febridyne for seven days. Gamble then went to a Major Muddox and told him that he was in too much pain to work. Muddox had respondent moved to "administrative segregation." On December 5, Gamble was taken before the prison disciplinary committee, apparently because of his refusal to work. When the committee heard his complaint of back pain and high blood pressure, it directed that he be seen by another doctor.

On December 6, respondent saw petitioner Gray, who performed a urinalysis, blood test, and blood pressure measurement. Dr. Gray prescribed the drug Ser-Ap-Es for the high blood pressure and more Febridyne for the back pain. The following week respondent again saw Dr. Gray, who continued the Ser-Ap-Es for an additional 30 days. The prescription was not filled for four days, however, because the staff lost it. Respondent went to the unit hospital twice more in December; both times he was seen by Captain Blunt, who prescribed tiognolos (described as a muscle relaxant). For all of December, respondent remained in administrative segregation.

In early January, Gamble was told on two occasions that he would be sent to the "farm" if he did not return to work. He refused, nonetheless, claiming to be in too much pain. On January 7, 1974, he requested to go on sick call for his back pain and migraine headaches. After an initial refusal, he saw Captain Blunt who prescribed sodium salicylate (a pain reliever) for seven days and Ser-Ap-Es for 30 days. Respondent returned to Captain Blunt on January 17 and January 25, and received renewals of the pain reliever prescription both times. Throughout the month, respondent was kept in administrative segregation.

On January 31, Gamble was brought before the prison disciplinary committee for his refusal to work in early January. He told the committee that he could not work because of his severe back pain and his high blood pressure. Captain Blunt testified that Gamble was in "first class" medical condition. The committee, with no further medical examination or testimony, placed respondent in solitary confinement.

Five days later, on February 4, at 8 a.m., respondent asked to see a doctor for chest pains and "blank outs." It was not until 7:30 that night that a medical assistant examined him and ordered him hospitalized. The following day a Dr. Heaton performed an electrocardiogram; one day later respondent was placed on quinidine for treatment of irregular cardiac rhythm and moved to administrative segregation. On February 7, respondent again experienced pain in his chest, left arm, and back and asked to see a doctor. The guards refused. He asked again the next day. The guards again refused. Finally, on February 9, he was allowed to see Dr. Heaton, who ordered the quinidine continued for three more days. On February 11, he swore out his complaint.

II

The gravamen of respondent's § 1983 complaint is that petitioners have subjected him to cruel and unusual punishment in violation of the Eighth Amendment, made applicable to the States by the Fourteenth. See Robinson v. California, 370 U.S. 660, 8 L.Ed. 2d 758, 82 S.Ct. 1417 (1962). We therefore base our evaluation of respondent's complaint on those amendments and our decisions interpreting them.

The history of the constitutional prohibition of "cruel and unusual punishments" has been recounted at length in prior opinions of the Court and need not be repeated here. See, e.g., Gregg v. Georgia, 428 U.S. 153, 49 L.Ed.2d 859, 96 S.Ct. 2909 (1976) (plurality opinion); see also Granucci, Nor Cruel and Unusual Punishment Inflicted: The Original Meaning, 57 Cal. L. Rev. 839 (1969). It suffices to note that the primary concern of the drafters was to proscribe "tortures" and other "barbarous" methods of punishment. Id., at 842. Accordingly, this Court first applied the Eighth Amendment by comparing challenged methods of execution to concededly inhuman techniques of punishment. See Wilkerson v. Utah, 99 U.S. 130, 136, 25 L.Ed. 345 (1879) ("[I]t is safe to affirm that punishments of torture . . . and all others in the same line of unnecessary cruelty, are forbidden by that amendment. . . ."); In re Kemmler, 136 U.S. 436, 447, 34 L. Ed. 519, 10 S.Ct. 930 (1890) ("Punishments are cruel when they involve torture or a lingering death. . . .")

Our more recent cases, however, have held that the Amendment proscribes more than physically barbarous punishments. See, e.g., Gregg v. Georgia, supra, at 49 L.Ed.2d 859, 96 S.Ct. 2909 (plurality opinion); Trop v. Dulles, 356 U.S. 86, 100-101, 2 L.Ed.2d 630, 78 S.Ct. 590 (1958); Weems v. United States, 217 U.S. 349, 373, 54 L.Ed. 793, 30 S.Ct. 544 (1910). The Amendment embodies "broad and idealistic concepts of dignity, civilized standards, humanity, and decency . . . ," Jackson v. Bishop, 404 F.2d 571, 579 (CA8 1968), against which we must evaluate penal measures. Thus, we have held repugnant to the Eighth Amendment punishments which are incompatible with "the evolving standards of decency that mark the progress of a maturing society," Trop v. Dulles, supra, at 101, 2 L.Ed.2d 630, 78 S.Ct. 590; see

also Gregg v. Georgia, supra, 49 L.Ed. 2d 859, 96 S.Ct. 2909 (plurality opinion); Weems v. United States, supra, at 378, 54 L.Ed. 793, 30 S.Ct. 544, or which "involve the unnecessary and wanton infliction of pain," Gregg v. Georgia, supra, at 49 L.Ed.2d 859, 96 S.Ct. 2909 (plurality opinion); see also Louisiana ex rel. Francis v. Resweber, 329 U.S. 459, 463, 91 L.Ed. 422, 67 S.Ct. 374 (1947); Wilkerson v. Utah, supra, at 136, 25 L.Ed. 345.

These elementary principles establish the government's obligation to provide medical care for those whom it is punishing by incarceration. An inmate must rely on prison authorities to treat his medical needs; if the authorities fail to do so, those needs will not be met. In the worst cases, such a failure may actually produce physical "torture or a lingering death," In re Kemmler, supra, the evils of most immediate concern to the drafters of the Amendment. In less serious cases, denial of medical care may result in pain and suffering which no one suggests would serve any penological purpose. Cf. Gregg v. Georgia, supra, at 49 L.Ed.2d 859, 96 S.Ct. 2909 (plurality opinion). The infliction of such unnecessary suffering is inconsistent with contemporary standards of decency as manifested in modern legislation codifying the common-law view that "[i]t is but just that the public be required to care for the prisoner, who cannot, by reason of the deprivation of his liberty, care for himself."

We therefore conclude that deliberate indifference to serious medical needs of prisoners constitutes the "unnecessary and wanton infliction of pain," Gregg v. Georgia, supra, at 49 L.Ed.2d 859, 96 S.Ct. 2909, proscribed by the Eighth Amendment. This is true whether the indifference is manifested by prison doctors in their response to the prisoner's needs[10] or by prison guards in intentionally denying or delaying access to medical care or intentionally interfering with the treatment once prescribed. Regardless of how evidenced, deliberate indifference to a prisoner's serious illness or injury states a cause of action under § 1983.

This conclusion does not mean, however, that every claim by a prisoner that he has not received adequate medical treatment states a violation of the Eighth Amendment. An accident, although it may produce added anguish, is not on that basis alone to be characterized as a wanton infliction of unnecessary pain. In Louisiana ex rel. Francis v. Resweber, 329 U.S. 459, 91 L.Ed. 422, 67 S.Ct. 374 (1947), for example, the Court concluded that it was not unconstitutional to force a prisoner to undergo a second effort to electrocute him after a mechanical malfunction had thwarted the first attempt. Writing for the plurality, Justice Reed

reasoned that the second execution would not violate the Eighth Amendment because the first attempt was an "unforeseeable accident." *Id.*, at 464, 91 L.Ed. 422, 67 S.Ct. 374. Justice Frankfurter's concurrence, based solely on the Due Process Clause of the Fourteenth Amendment, concluded that since the first attempt had failed because of "an innocent misadventure," *id.*, at 470, 91 L.Ed. 422, 67 S.Ct. 374, the second would not be " 'repugnant to the conscience of mankind,' " *id.*, at 471, 91 L.Ed. 422, 67 S.Ct. 374, quoting Palko v. Connecticut, 302 U.S. 319, 323, 82 L.Ed. 288, 58 S.Ct. 149 (1937).

Similarly, in the medical context, an inadvertent failure to provide adequate medical care cannot be said to constitute a "wanton infliction of unnecessary pain" or to be "repugnant to the conscience of mankind." Thus, a complaint that a physician has been negligent in diagnosing or treating a medical condition does not state a valid claim of medical mistreatment under the Eighth Amendment. Medical malpractice does not become a constitutional violation merely because the victim is a prisoner. In order to state a cognizable claim, a prisoner must allege acts or omissions sufficiently harmful to evidence deliberate indifference to serious medical needs. It is only such indifference that can offend "evolving standards of decency" in violation of the Eighth Amendment.[14]

---

10 See, e.g., Williams v. Vincent, 508 F.2d 541 (CA2 1974) (doctor's choosing the "easier and less efficacious treatment" of throwing away the prisoner's ear and stitching the stump may be attributable to "deliberate indifference . . . rather than an exercise of professional judgment"); Thomas v. Pate, 493 F.2d 151, 158 (CA7), cert. denied sub nom. Thomas v. Cannon, 419 U.S. 879, 42 L.Ed.2d 119, 95 S.Ct. 143 (1974) (injection of penicillin with knowledge that prisoner was allergic, and refusal of doctor to treat allergic reaction); Jones v. Lockhart, 484 F.2d 1192 (CA8 1973) (refusal of paramedic to provide treatment); Martinez v. Mancusi, 443 F.2d 921 (CA2 1970), cert. denied, 401 U.S. 983, 28 L.Ed.2d 335, 91 S.Ct. 1202 (1971) (prison physician refuses to administer prescribed pain killer and renders leg surgery unsuccessful by requiring prisoner to stand despite contrary instructions of surgeon).

14 The Courts of Appeals are in essential agreement with this standard. All agree that mere allegations of malpractice do not state a claim, and, while their terminology regarding what is sufficient varies, their results are not inconsistent with the standard of deliberate indifference. See Page v. Sharpe, 487 F.2d 567, 569 (CA1 1973); Williams v. Vincent, 508 F.2d 541, 544 (CA2 1974) (uses the phrase "deliberate

III

Against this backdrop, we now consider whether respondent's complaint states a cognizable § 1983 claim. The handwritten pro se document is to be liberally construed. As the Court unanimously held in Haines v. Kerner, 404 U.S. 519, 30 L.Ed.2d 652, 92 S.Ct. 594 (1972), a pro se complaint, "however inartfully pleaded," must be held to "less stringent standards than formal pleadings drafted by lawyers" and can only be dismissed for failure to state a claim if it appears "beyond doubt that the plaintiff can prove no set of facts in support of his claim which would entitle him to relief." Id., at 520-521, 30 L.Ed.2d 652, 92 S.Ct. 594, quoting Conley v. Gibson, 355 U.S. 41, 45-46, 2 L.Ed.2d 80, 78 S.Ct. 99 (1957).

Even applying these liberal standards, however, Gamble's claims against Dr. Gray, both in his capacity as treating physician and as medical director of the Corrections Department, are not cognizable under § 1983. Gamble was seen by medical personnel on 17 occasions spanning a three-month period: by Dr. Astone five times; by Dr. Gray twice; by Dr. Heaton three times; by an unidentified doctor and inmate nurse on the day of the injury; and by

indifference"); Gittlemacker v. Prasse, 428 F.2d 1, 6 (CA3 1970); Russell v. Sheffer, 528 F.2d 319 (CA4 1975); Newman v. Alabama, 503 F.2d 1320, 1330 n 14 (CA5 1974), cert. denied, 421 U.S. 948, 44 L.Ed. 2d 102, 95 S.Ct. 1680 (1975) ("callous indifference"); Westlake v. Lucas, 537 F.2d 857, 860 (CA6 1976) ("deliberate indifference"); Thomas v. Pate, 493 F.2d 151, 158 (CA7), cert. denied sub nom. Thomas v. Cannon, 419 U.S. 879, 42 L.Ed. 119, 95 S.Ct. 143 (1974); Wilbron v. Hutto, 509 F.2d 621, 622 (CA8 1975) ("deliberate indifference"); Tolbert v. Eyman, 434 F.2d 625, 626 (CA9 1970); Dewell v. Lawson, 489 F.2d 877, 881-882 (CA10 1974).

medical assistant Blunt six times. They treated his back injury, high blood pressure, and heart problems. Gamble has disclaimed any objection to the treatment provided for his high blood pressure and his heart problem; his complaint is "based solely on the lack of diagnosis and inadequate treatment of his back injury." Response to Petition for Certiorari, at 4; see also Brief for Respondent, at 19. The doctors diagnosed his injury as a lower back strain and treated it with bed rest, muscle relaxants and pain relievers. Respondent contends that more should have been done by way of diagnosis and treatment, and suggests a number of options that were not pursued. Id., at 17, 19. The Court of Appeals agreed, stating that "Certainly an x-ray of [Gamble's] lower back might have been in order and other tests conducted that would have led to appropriate diagnosis and treatment for the daily pain and suffering he was experiencing." 516 F.2d, at 941. But the question whether an X-ray—or additional diagnostic techniques or forms of treatment —is indicated is a classic example of a matter for medical judgment. A medical decision not to order an X-ray, or like measures, does not represent cruel and unusual punishment. At most it is medical malpractice, and as such the proper forum is state court under the Texas Tort Claims Act. The Court of Appeals was in error in holding that the alleged insufficiency of the medical treatment required reversal and remand. That portion of the judgment of the District Court should have been affirmed.

The Court of Appeals focused primarily on the alleged actions of the doctors, and did not separately consider whether the allegations against the Director of the Department of Corrections, Estelle, and the warden of the prison, Husbands, stated a cause of action. Although we reverse the judgment as to the doctors, we remand the case to the Court of Appeals to allow it an opportunity to consider, in conformity with this opinion, whether a cause of action has been stated against the other prison officials.

It is so ordered.

Cases relating to **Chapter 11**

CIVIL AND CRIMINAL LIABILITIES OF PRISON OFFICIALS

SCHEUER v. RHODES

416 U.S. 232, 94 S. Ct. 1683, 40 L. Ed. 2d 90 (1974)

* * *

Mr. Chief Justice Burger delivered the opinion of the Court.

We granted certiorari[1] in these cases to resolve whether the District Court correctly dismissed civil damage actions, brought under 42 U.S.C. § 1983, on the ground that these actions were, as a matter of law, against the State of Ohio, and hence barred by the Eleventh Amendment to the Constitution and, alternatively, that the actions were against state officials who were immune from liability for the acts alleged in the complaints. These cases arise out of the same period of alleged civil disorders on the campus of Kent State University in Ohio during May 1970 which was before us, in another context, in Gilligan v. Morgan, 413 U.S. 1, 66 Ohio Op.2d 19 (1973).

In these cases the personal representatives of the estates of three students who died in that episode seek damages against the Governor, the Adjutant General, and his assistant, various named and unnamed officers and enlisted members of the Ohio National Guard, and the president of Kent State

University. The complaints in both cases allege a cause of action under the Civil Rights Act of 1871, 17 Stat. 13, now 42 U.S.C. § 1983. Petitioner Scheuer also alleges a cause of action under Ohio law on the theory of pendent jurisdiction. Petitioners Krause and Miller make a similar claim, asserting jurisdiction on the basis of diversity of citizenship.[2]

The District Court dismissed the complaints for lack of jurisdiction over the subject matter on the theory that these actions, although in form against the named individuals, were, in substance and effect, against the State of Ohio and thus barred by the Eleventh Amendment. The Court of Appeals affirmed the action of the District Court, agreeing that the suit was in legal effect

---

[2] The Krause complaint states that the plaintiff is a citizen of Pennsylvania and expressly invokes federal diversity jurisdiction under 28 U.S.C. § 1332. The Miller complaint states that the plaintiff is a citizen of New York. While the complaint does not specifically refer to jurisdiction under 28 U.S.C. § 1332, it alleges facts which clearly support diversity jurisdiction. App. in No. 72-1318, p. 85. See Fed. Rule Civ. Proc. 8(a)(1).

---

[1] 413 U.S. 919 (1973).

one against the State of Ohio, and, alternatively, that the common-law doctrine of executive immunity barred action against the state officials who are respondents here. 471 F.2d 430 (1972). We are confronted with the narrow threshold question whether the District Court properly dismissed the complaints. We hold that dismissal was inappropriate at this stage of the litigation and accordingly reverse the judgments and remand for further proceedings. We intimate no view on the merits of the allegations since there is no evidence before us at this stage.

I

The complaints in these cases are not identical but their thrust is essentially the same. In essence, the defendants are alleged to have "intentionally, recklessly, willfully and wantonly" caused an unnecessary deployment of the Ohio National Guard on the Kent State campus and, in the same manner, ordered the Guard members to perform allegedly illegal actions which resulted in the death of plaintiffs' decedents. Both complaints allege that the action was taken "under color of state law" and that it deprived the decedents of their lives and rights without due process of law. Fairly read, the complaints allege that each of the named defendants, in undertaking such actions, acted either outside the scope of his respective office or, if within the scope, acted in an arbitrary manner, grossly abusing the lawful powers of office.

* * *

II

The Eleventh Amendment to the Constitution of the United States provides: "The Judicial power of the United States shall not be construed to extend to any suit in law or equity,

commenced or prosecuted against one of the United States by Citizens of another State. . . ." It is well established that the Amendment bars suits not only against the State when it is the named party but also when it is the party in fact. Edelman v. Jordan, 415 U.S. 651 (1974); Poindexter v. Greenhow, 114 U.S. 270, 287 (1885); Cunningham v. Macon & Brunswick R. Co., 109 U.S. 446 (1883). Its applicability "is to be determined not by the mere names of the titular parties but by the essential nature and effect of the proceeding, as it appears from the entire record." *Ex parte* New York, 256 U.S. 490, 500 (1921).

However, since *Ex parte* Young, 209 U.S. 123 (1908), it has been settled that the Eleventh Amendment provides no shield for a state official confronted by a claim that he had deprived another of a federal right under the color of state law. *Ex parte* Young teaches that when a state officer acts under a state law in a manner violative of the Federal Constitution, he

"comes into conflict with the superior authority of that Constitution, and he is in that case stripped of his official or representative character and is subjected *in his person* to the consequences of his individual conduct. The State has no power to impart to him any immunity from responsibility to the supreme authority of the United States." *Id.*, at 159-160. (Emphasis supplied.)

Ex parte Young, like Sterling v. Constantin, 287 U.S. 378 (1932), involved a question of the federal courts' injunctive power, not, as here, a claim for monetary damages. While it is clear that the doctrine of *Ex parte* Young is of no aid to a plaintiff seeking damages from the public treasury, Edelman v. Jordan, *supra;* Kennecott Copper Corp.

v. State Tax Comm'n, 327 U.S. 573 (1946); Ford Motor Co. v. Dept. of Treasury, 323 U.S. 459 (1945); Great Northern Life Insurance Co. v. Read, 322 U.S. 47 (1944), damages against individual defendants are a permissible remedy in some circumstances notwithstanding the fact that they hold public office. Myers v. Anderson, 238 U.S. 368 (1915). See generally Monroe v. Pape, 365 U.S. 167 (1961); Moor v. County of Alameda, 411 U.S. 693 (1973). In some situations a damage remedy can be as effective a redress for the infringement of a constitutional right as injunctive relief might be in another.

Analyzing the complaints in light of these precedents, we see that petitioners allege facts that demonstrate they are seeking to impose individual and personal liability on the *named defendants* for what they claim—but have not yet established by proof—was a deprivation of federal rights by these defendants under color of state law. Whatever the plaintiffs may or may not be able to establish as to the merits of their allegations, their claims, as stated in the complaints, given the favorable reading required by the Federal Rules of Civil Procedure, are not barred by the Eleventh Amendment. Consequently, the District Court erred in dismissing the complaints for lack of jurisdiction.

III

The Court of Appeals relied upon the existence of an absolute "executive immunity" as an alternative ground for sustaining the dismissal of the complaints by the District Court. If the immunity of a member of the executive branch is absolute and comprehensive as to all acts allegedly performed within the scope of official duty, the Court of Appeals was correct; if, on the other

hand, the immunity is not absolute but rather one that is qualified or limited, an executive officer may or may not be subject to liability depending on all the circumstances that may be revealed by evidence. The concept of the immunity of government officers from personal liability springs from the same root considerations that generated the doctrine of sovereign immunity. While the latter doctrine—that the "King can do no wrong"—did not protect all government officers from personal liability, the common law soon recognized the necessity of permitting officials to perform their official functions free from the threat of suits for personal lability.[4]

---

[4] In England legislative immunity was secured after a long struggle, by the Bill of Rights of 1689: "That the Freedom of Speech, and Debates or Proceedings in Parliament, ought not to be impeached or questioned in any Court or Place out of Parliament," 1 W. & M. Sess. 2, c. 2. See Stockdale v. Hansard, 9 Ad. & E. 1, 113-114, 112 Eng. Rep. 1112, 1155-1156 (Q. B. 1839). The English experience, of course, guided the drafters of our "Speech or Debate" Clause. See Tenney v. Brandhove, 341 U.S. 367, 372-375 (1951); United States v. Johnson, 383 U.S. 169, 177-178, 181 (1966); United States v. Brewster, 408 U.S. 501 (1972).

In regard to judicial immunity, Holdsworth notes: "In the case of courts of record ... it was held, certainly as early as Edward III's reign, that a litigant could not go behind the record, in order to make a judge civilly or criminally liable for an abuse of his jurisdiction." 6 W. Holdsworth, A History of English Law 235 (1927). The modern concept owes much to the elaboration and restatement of Coke and other judges of the sixteenth and early seventeenth centuries. *Id.,* at 234 *et seq.* See Floyd v. Barker, 12 Co. Rep. 23, 77 Eng. Rep. 1305 (K. B. 1607). The immunity of the Crown has traditionally been of a more limited nature. Officers of the Crown were at first insulated from responsibility since the King could claim the act as his own. This absolute insulation was gradually eroded. Statute of Westminster I, 3 Edw. 1, c. 24 (1275) (repealed); Statute of Westminster II, 13 Edw. 1, c. 13 (1285)

This official immunity apparently rested, in its genesis, on two mutually dependent rationales:[5] (1) the injustice, particularly in the absence of bad faith, of subjecting to liability an officer who is required, by the legal obligations of his position, to exercise discretion; (2) the danger that the threat of such liability would deter his willingness to execute his office with the decisiveness and the judgment required by the public good.

In this country, the development of the law of immunity for public officials has been the product of constitutional provision as well as legislative and judicial processes. The Federal Constitution grants absolute immunity to Members of both Houses of the Congress with respect to any speech, debate, vote, report, or action done in session. Art. I, § 6. See Gravel v. United States, 408 U.S. 606 (1972); United States v. Brewster, 408 U.S. 501 (1972); and Kilbourn v. Thompson, 103 U.S.

(repealed). The development of liability, especially during the times of the Tudors and Stuarts, was slow; see, e.g., Public Officers Protection Act, 7 Jac. 1, c. 5 (1609) (repealed). With the accession of William and Mary, the liability of officers saw what Jaffe has termed "a most remarkable and significant extension" in Ashby v. White, 1 Bro. P. C. 62, 1 Eng. Rep. 417 (H. L. 1704), reversing 6 Mod. 45, 87 Eng. Rep. 808 (Q. B. 1703). Jaffe, Suits Against Governments and Officers: Sovereign Immunity, 77 Harv. L.Rev. 1, 14 (1963); A. Dicey, The Law of the Constitution 193-194 (10th ed. 1959) (footnotes omitted). See generally Barr v. Matteo, 360 U.S. 564 (1959). Good-faith performance of a discretionary duty has remained, it seems, a defense. See Jaffe, Suits Against Governments and Officers: Damage Actions, 77 Harv.L.Rev. 209, 216 (1963). See also Spalding v. Vilas, 161 U.S. 483, 493 et seq. (1896).

5 Jaffe, Suits Against Governments and Officers: Damage Actions, 77 Harv.L.Rev., at 223.

168 (1881). This provision was intended to secure for the Legislative Branch of the Government the freedom from executive and judicial encroachment which had been secured in England in the Bills of Rights of 1689 and carried to the original Colonies.[6] In United States v. Johnson, 383 U.S. 169, 182 (1966), Mr. Justice Harlan noted:

"There is little doubt that the instigation of criminal charges against critical or disfavored legislators by the executive in a judicial forum was the chief fear prompting the long struggle for parliamentary privilege in England and, in the context of the American system of separation of powers, is the predominate thrust of the Speech or Debate Clause."

Immunity for the other two branches—long a creature of the common law—remained committed to the common law. See, e.g., Spalding v. Vilas, 161 U.S. 483, 498-499 (1896).

Although the development of the general concept of immunity, and the mutations which the underlying rationale has undergone in its application to various positions are not matters of immediate concern here, it is important to note, even at the outset, that one policy consideration seems to pervade the analysis: the public interest requires decisions and action to enforce laws for the protection of the public. Mr. Justice Jackson expressed this general proposition succinctly, stating "it is not a tort for government to govern."

6 Mr. Justice Frankfurter noted in Tenney v. Brandhove, 341 U.S., at 373: "The provision in the United States Constitution was a reflection of political principles already firmly established in the States. Three State Constitutions adopted before the Federal Constitution specifically protected the privilege." See Coffin v. Coffin, 4 Mass. 1, 27 (1808). See also Kilbourn v. Thompson, 103 U.S. 168, 202 (1881).

Dalehite v. United States, 346 U.S. 15, 57 (1953) (dissenting opinion). Public officials, whether governors, mayors or police, legislators or judges, who fail to make decisions when they are needed or who do not act to implement decisions when they are made do not fully and faithfully perform the duties of their offices.[7] Implicit in the idea that officials have some immunity—absolute or qualified—for their acts, is a recognition that they may err. The concept of immunity assumes this and goes on to assume that it is better to risk some error and possible injury from such error than not to decide or act at all. In Barr v. Matteo, 360 U.S. 564, 572-573 (1959), the Court observed, in the somewhat parallel context of the privilege of public officers from defamation actions: "The privilege is not a badge or emolument of exalted office, but an expression of a policy designed to aid in the effective functioning of government." See also Spalding v. Vilas, 161 U.S., at 498-499.

---

[7] For example, in Floyd v. Barker, *supra*, Coke emphasized that judges "are only to make an account to God and the King" since a contrary rule "would tend to the scandal and subversion of all justice. And those who are the most sincere, would not be free from continual calumniations. . . ." 12 Co. Rep., at 25, 77 Eng. Rep., at 1307. See also Yaselli v. Goff, 12 F.2d 396, 399 (CA2 1926), *aff'd per curiam*, 275 U.S. 503 (1927). In Spalding v. Vilas, 161 U.S., at 498, the Court noted:

"In exercising the functions of his office, the head of an Executive Department, keeping within the limits of his authority, should not be under an apprehension that the motives that control his official conduct may, at any time, become the subject of inquiry in a civil suit for damages. It would seriously cripple the proper and effective administration of public affairs as entrusted to the executive branch of the government, if he were subjected to any such restraint."

For present purposes we need determine only whether there is an absolute immunity, as the Court of Appeals determined, governing the specific allegations of the complaint against the chief executive officer of a State, the senior and subordinate officers and enlisted personnel of that State's National Guard, and the president of a state-controlled university. If the immunity is qualified, not absolute, the scope of that immunity will necessarily be related to facts as yet not established either by affidavits, admissions, or a trial record. Final resolution of this question must take into account the functions and responsibilities of these particular defendants in their capacities as officers of the state government, as well as the purposes of 42 U.S.C. § 1983. In neither of these inquiries do we write on a clean slate. It can hardly be argued, at this late date, that under no circumstances can the officers of state government be subject to liability under this statute. In Monroe v. Pape, *supra*, MR. JUSTICE DOUGLAS, writing for the Court, held that the section in question was meant "to give a remedy to parties deprived of constitutional rights, privileges and immunities by an official's abuse of his position." 365 U.S., at 172. Through the Civil Rights statutes, Congress intended "to enforce provisions of the Fourteenth Amendment against those who carry a badge of authority of a State and represent it in some capacity, whether they act in accordance with their authority or misuse it." *Id.*, at 171-172.

Since the statute relied on thus included within its scope the " '[m]isuse of power, possessed by virtue of state law and made possible only because the wrongdoer is clothed with the authority of state law,' " *id.*, at 184 (quoting United States v. Classic, 313

U.S. 299, 326 (1941)), government officials, as a class, could not be totally exempt, by virtue of some absolute immunity, from liability under its terms. Indeed, as the Court also indicated in Monroe v. Pape, *supra*, the legislative history indicates that there is no absolute immunity. Soon after Monroe v. Pape, Mr. Chief Justice Warren noted in Pierson v. Ray, 386 U.S. 547 (1967), that the "legislative record [of § 1983] gives no clear indication that Congress meant to abolish wholesale all common-law immunities," *id.*, at 554. The Court had previously recognized that the Civil Rights Act of 1871 does not create civil liability for legislative acts by legislators "in a field where legislators traditionally have power to act." Tenney v. Brandhove, 341 U.S. 367, 379 (1951). Noting that "[t]he privilege of legislators to be free from arrest or civil process for what they do or say in legislative proceedings has taproots in the Parliamentary struggles of the Sixteenth and Seventeenth Centuries," *id.*, at 372, the Court concluded that it was highly improbable that "Congress—itself a staunch advocate of legislative freedom—would impinge on a tradition so well grounded in history and reason by covert inclusion in the general language ..." of this statute. *Id.*, at 376.

In similar fashion, Pierson v. Ray, *supra*, examined the scope of judicial immunity under this statute. Noting that the record contained no "proof or specific allegation," 386 U.S., at 553, that the trial judge had "played any role in these arrests and convictions other than to adjudge petitioners guilty when their cases came before his court," *ibid.*, the Court concluded that, had the Congress intended to abolish the common-law "immunity of judges for acts within the judicial role," *id.*, at 554, it would have done so specifically.

A judge's

"errors may be corrected on appeal, but he should not have to fear that unsatisfied litigants may hound him with litigation charging malice or corruption. Imposing such a burden on judges would contribute not to principled and fearless decision-making but to intimidation." *Ibid.*

The Pierson Court was also confronted with whether immunity was available to that segment of the executive branch of a state government that is most frequently and intimately involved in day-to-day contacts with the citizenry and, hence, most frequently exposed to situations which can give rise to claims under § 1983—the local police officer. Mr. Chief Justice Warren, speaking for the Court, noted that the police officers

"did not defend on the theory that they believed in good faith that it was constitutional to arrest the ministers solely for using the ['white only'] waiting room. Rather, they claimed and attempted to prove that ... [they arrested them] solely for the purpose of preventing violence. They testified, in contradiction to the ministers, that a crowd gathered and that imminent violence was likely. If the jury believed the testimony of the officers and disbelieved that of the ministers, and if the jury found that the officers reasonably believed in good faith that the arrest was constitutional, then a verdict for the officers would follow even though the arrest was in fact [without probable cause and] unconstitutional." *Id.*, at 557.

The Court noted that the "common law has never granted police officers an absolute and unqualified immunity," *id.*, at 555, but that "the prevailing view in this country [is that] a peace officer who arrests someone with probable cause is not liable for false arrest simply because the innocence of the suspect is later proved," *ibid.*; the Court went on to observe that a "policeman's lot is not so unhappy that he must choose between being charged with dereliction of duty if he does not arrest when he has probable cause, and being mulcted in damages if he does." *Ibid.* The Court then held that

"the defense of good faith and probable cause, which the Court of Appeals found available to the officers in the common-law action for false arrest and imprisonment, is also available to them in the action under § 1983." *Id.,* at 557.

When a court evaluates police conduct relating to an arrest its guideline is "good faith and probable cause." *Ibid.* In the case of higher officers of the executive branch, however, the inquiry is far more complex since the range of decisions and choices— whether the formulation of policy, of legislation, of budgets, or of day-to-day decisions—is virtually infinite. In common with police officers, however, officials with a broad range of duties and authority must often act swiftly and firmly at the risk that action deferred will be futile or constitute virtual abdication of office. Like legislators and judges, these officers are entitled to rely on traditional sources for the factual information on which they decide and act.[8] When a condition of civil

disorder in fact exists, there is obvious need for prompt action, and decisions must be made in reliance on factual information supplied by others. While both federal and state laws plainly contemplate the use of force when the necessity arises, the decision to invoke military power has traditionally been viewed with suspicion and skepticism since it often involves the temporary suspension of some of our most cherished rights—government by elected civilian leaders, freedom of expression, of assembly, and of association. Decisions in such situations are more likely than not to arise in an atmosphere of confusion, ambiguity, and swiftly moving events and when, by the very existence of some degree of civil disorder, there is often no consensus as to the appropriate remedy. In short, since the options which a chief executive and his principal subordinates must consider are far broader and far more subtle than those made by officials with less responsibility, the range of discretion must be comparably broad. In a context other than a § 1983 suit, Mr. Justice Harlan articulated these considerations in Barr v. Matteo, *supra:*

"To be sure, the occasions upon which the acts of the head of an executive department will be protected by the privilege are doubtless far broader than in the case of an

---

8 In Spalding v. Vilas, 161 U.S., at 498, the Court, after discussing the early principles of judicial immunity in the country, cf. Randall v. Brigham, 7 Wall. 523, 535 (1869), Bradley v. Fisher, 13 Wall. 335 (1872), and Yates v. Lansing, 5 Johns. 282 (N.Y. 1810), noted the similarity in the controlling policy considerations in the case of high-echelon executive officers and judges:

"We are of opinion that the same general considerations of public policy and convenience which demand for judges of courts of superior jurisdiction immunity from civil suits for damages arising from acts done by them in the course of the performance of their judicial functions, apply to a large extent to official communications made by heads of Executive Departments when engaged in the discharge of duties imposed upon them by law. The interests of the people require that due protection be accorded to them in respect of their official acts."

officer with less sweeping functions. But that is because the higher the post, the broader the range of responsibilities and duties, and the wider the scope of discretion, it entails. It is not the title of his office but the duties with which the particular officer sought to be made to respond in damages is entrusted—the relation of the act complained of to 'matters committed by law to his control or supervision,' Spalding v. Vilas, *supra*, at 498—which must provide the guide in delineating the scope of the rule which clothes the official acts of the executive officer with immunity from civil defamation suits." 360 U.S., at 573-574.

These considerations suggest that, in varying scope, a qualified immunity is available to officers of the executive branch of government, the variation being dependent upon the scope of discretion and responsibilities of the office and all the circumstances as they reasonably appeared at the time of the action on which liability is sought to be based. It is the existence of reasonable grounds for the belief formed at the time and in light of all the circumstances, coupled with good-faith belief, that affords a basis for qualified immunity of executive officers for acts performed in the course of official conduct. Mr. Justice Holmes spoke of this, stating:

"No doubt there are cases where the expert on the spot may be called upon to justify his conduct later in court, notwithstanding the fact that he had sole command at the time and acted to the best of his knowledge. That is the position of the captain of a ship. But even in that case great weight is given to his determination and the matter is to be judged on the facts as they appeared then and not

merely in the light of the event." Moyer v. Peabody, 212 U.S. 78, 85 (1909). (Citations omitted.)

Under the criteria developed by precedents of this Court, § 1983 would be drained of meaning were we to hold that the acts of a governor or other high executive officer have "the quality of a supreme and unchangeable edict, overriding all conflicting rights of property and unreviewable through the judicial power of the Federal Government." Sterling v. Constantin, 287 U.S., at 397. In Sterling, Mr. Chief Justice Hughes put it in these terms:

"If this extreme position could be deemed to be well taken, it is manifest that the fiat of a state Governor, and not the Constitution of the United States, would be the supreme law of the land; that the restrictions of the Federal Constitution upon the exercise of state power would be but impotent phrases, the futility of which the State may at any time disclose by the simple process of transferring powers of legislation to the Governor to be exercised by him, beyond control, upon his assertion of necessity. Under our system of government, such a conclusion is obviously untenable. There is no such avenue of escape from the paramount authority of the Federal Constitution. When there is a substantial showing that the exertion of state power has overridden private rights secured by that Constitution, the subject is necessarily one for judicial inquiry in an appropriate proceeding directed against the individuals charged with the transgression." *Id.*, at 397-398.

Gilligan v. Morgan, by no means indicates a contrary result. Indeed, there we specifically noted that we neither held nor implied "that the conduct of the National Guard is always beyond judicial review or that there may not be accountability in a judicial forum for violations of law or for specific unlawful conduct by military personnel, whether by way of damages or injunctive relief." 413 U.S., at 11-12. (Footnote omitted.) See generally Laird v. Tatum, 408 U.S. 1, 15-16 (1972); Duncan v. Kahanamoku, 327 U.S. 304 (1946).

IV

These cases, in their present posture, present no occasion for a definitive exploration of the scope of immunity available to state executive officials nor, because of the absence of a factual record, do they permit a determination as to the applicability of the foregoing principles to the respondents here. The District Court acted before answers were filed and without any evidence other than the copies of the proclamations issued by respondent Rhodes and brief affidavits of the Adjutant General and his assistant. In dismissing the complaints, the District Court and the Court of Appeals erroneously accepted as a fact the good faith of the Governor, and took judicial notice that "mob rule existed at Kent State University." There was no opportunity afforded petitioners to contest the facts assumed in that conclusion. There was no evidence before the courts from which such a finding of good faith could be properly made and, in the circumstances of these cases, such a dispositive conclusion could not be judicially noticed. We can readily grant that a declaration of emergency by the chief executive of a State is entitled to great weight but it

is not conclusive. Sterling v. Constantin, *supra.*

The documents properly before the District Court at this early pleading stage specifically placed in issue whether the Governor and his subordinate officers were acting within the scope of their duties under the Constitution and laws of Ohio; whether they acted within the range of discretion permitted the holders of such office under Ohio law and whether they acted in good faith both in proclaiming an emergency and as to the actions taken to cope with the emergency so declared. Similarly, the complaints place directly in issue whether the lesser officers and enlisted personnel of the Guard acted in good-faith obedience to the orders of their superiors. Further proceedings, either by way of summary judgment or by trial on the merits, are required. The complaining parties are entitled to be heard more fully than is possible on a motion to dismiss a complaint.

We intimate no evaluation whatever as to the merits of the petitioners' claims or as to whether it will be possible to support them by proof. We hold only that, on the allegations of their respective complaints, they were entitled to have them judicially resolved.

The judgments of the Court of Appeals are reversed and the cases are remanded for further proceedings consistent with this opinion.

It is so ordered.

MR. JUSTICE DOUGLAS took no part in the decision of these cases.

WOOD v. STRICKLAND
420 U.S. 308, 95 S. Ct. 992, 43 L. Ed. 2d 214 (1975)

*   *   *

MR. JUSTICE WHITE delivered the opinion of the Court.

Respondents Peggy Strickland and Virginia Crain brought this lawsuit against petitioners, who were members of the school board at the time in question, two school administrators, and the Special School District of Mena, Arkansas, purporting to assert a cause of action under 42 U.S.C. § 1983, and claiming that their federal constitutional rights to due process were infringed under color of state law by their expulsion from the Mena Public High School on the grounds of their violation of a school regulation prohibiting the use or possession of intoxicating beverages at school or school activities. The complaint as amended prayed for compensatory and punitive damages against all petitioners, injunctive relief allowing respondents to resume attendance, preventing petitioners from imposing any sanctions as a result of the expulsion, and restraining enforcement of the challenged regulation, declaratory relief as to the constitutional invalidity of the regulation, and expunction of any record of their expulsion. After the declaration of a mistrial arising from the jury's failure to reach a verdict, the District Court directed verdicts in favor of petitioners on the ground that petitioners were immune from damages suits absent proof of malice in the sense of ill will toward respondents. 348 F.Supp. 244 (WD Ark. 1972). The Court of Appeals, finding that the facts showed a violation of respondents' rights to "substantive due process," reversed and remanded for appropriate

injunctive relief[2] and a new trial on the question of damages. 485 F.2d 186 (CA8 1973). A petition for rehearing en banc was denied, with three judges dissenting. See *id.*, at 191. Certiorari was granted to consider whether this application of due process by the Court of Appeals was warranted and whether that court's expression of a standard governing immunity for school board members from liability for compensatory damages under 42 U.S.C. § 1983 was the correct one. 416 U.S. 935 (1974).

I

The violation of the school regulation[3] prohibiting the use or possession of intoxicating beverages at school or school activities with which respondents were charged concerned their "spiking" of the punch served at a meeting of an extracurricular school organization attended by parents and students. At the time in question, respondents were 16 years old and were in the 10th grade. The relevant facts begin with their discovery that the

---

2 The Court of Appeals noted that reinstatement was no longer possible since the term of expulsion had ended, but that the respondents were entitled to have the records of the expulsions expunged and to be relieved of any other continuing punishment, if any. *Id.*, at 190.

3 "3. Suspension

"b. Valid causes for suspension from school on first offense: Pupils found to be guilty of any of the following shall be suspended from school on the first offense for the balance of the semester and such suspension will be noted on the permanent record of the student along with reason for suspension.

"(4) The use of intoxicating beverage or possession of same at school or at a school sponsored activity." App. 102.

punch had not been prepared for the meeting as previously planned. The girls then agreed to "spike" it. Since the county in which the school is located is "dry," respondents and a third girl drove across the state border into Oklahoma and purchased two 12-ounce bottles of "Right Time," a malt liquor. They then bought six 10-ounce bottles of a soft drink, and, after having mixed the contents of the eight bottles in an empty milk carton, returned to school. Prior to the meeting, the girls experienced second thoughts about the wisdom of their prank, but by then they were caught up in the force of events and the intervention of other girls prevented them from disposing of the illicit punch. The punch was served at the meeting, without apparent effect.

Ten days later, the teacher in charge of the extracurricular group and meeting, Mrs. Curtis Powell, having heard something about the "spiking," questioned the girls about it. Although first denying any knowledge, the girls admitted their involvement after the teacher said that she would handle the punishment herself. The next day, however, she told the girls that the incident was becoming increasingly the subject of talk in the school and that the principal, P. T. Waller, would probably hear about it. She told them that her job was in jeopardy but that she would not force them to admit to Waller what they had done. If they did not go to him then, however, she would not be able to help them if the incident became "distorted." The three girls then went to Waller and admitted their role in the affair. He suspended them from school for a maximum two-week period, subject to the decision of the school board. Waller also told them that the board would meet that night, that the girls could tell their parents

about the meeting, but that the parents should not contact any members of the board.

Neither the girls nor their parents attended the school board meeting that night. Both Mrs. Powell and Waller, after making their reports concerning the incident, recommended leniency. At this point, a telephone call was received by S. L. Inlow, then the superintendent of schools, from Mrs. Powell's husband, also a teacher at the high school, who reported that he had heard that the third girl involved had been in a fight that evening at a basketball game. Inlow informed the meeting of the news, although he did not mention the name of the girl involved. Mrs. Powell and Waller then withdrew their recommendations of leniency, and the board voted to expel the girls from school for the remainder of the semester, a period of approximately three months.

The board subsequently agreed to hold another meeting on the matter, and one was held approximately two weeks after the first meeting. The girls, their parents, and their counsel attended this session. The board began with a reading of a written statement of facts as it had found them.[4] The girls

---

4 "FACTS FOUND BY SCHOOL BOARD

"1. That Virginia Crain, Peggy Strickland and Jo Wall are students of Mena High School and subject to the governing rules and policies of Mena High School.

"2. That on or about February 7, 1972 these three girls were charged with the responsibility of providing refreshments for a school function, being a gathering of students of the Home Economic class and some of their parents, on school premises, being the auditorium building of Mena High School, and being under the direction of Mrs. Curtis Powell.

"3. That the three girls in question traveled to Oklahoma, purchased a number of bottles of malt liquor, a beer type bever-

admitted mixing the malt liquor into the punch with the intent of "spiking" it, but asked the board to forego its rule punishing such violations by such substantial suspensions. Neither Mrs. Powell nor Waller was present at this meeting. The board voted not to change its policy and, as before, to expel the girls for the remainder of the semester.[5]

II

The District Court instructed the jury that a decision for respondents had to be premised upon a finding that petitioners acted with malice in expelling them and defined "malice" as meaning "ill will against a person—a wrongful act done intentionally without just cause or excuse." 348 F.Supp., at 248. In ruling for petitioners after the jury had been unable to agree, the District Court found "as a matter of law" that there was no evidence from which malice could be inferred. Id., at 253.

The Court of Appeals, however, viewed both the instruction and the decision of the District Court as being erroneous. Specific intent to harm wrongfully, it held, was not a requirement for the recovery of damages. Instead, "[i]t need only be established

---

age, and later went onto school premises with the alcoholic beverage and put two or more of the bottles of the drink into the punch or liquid refreshment which was to be served to members of the class and parents." App. 137.

The Court of Appeals in its statement of the facts observed that the malt liquor and soft drinks were mixed by the girls prior to their return to school, 485 F.2d, at 187, and petitioners in their brief recite the facts in this manner. Brief for Petitioners 5. This discrepancy in the board's findings of fact is not material to any issue now before the Court.

[5] By taking a correspondence course and an extra course later, the girls were able to graduate with their class. Tr. of Oral Arg. 38-39.

that the defendants did not, in the light of all the circumstances, act in good faith. The test is an objective, rather than a subjective, one." 485 F.2d, at 191 (footnote omitted).

Petitioners as members of the school board assert here, as they did below, an absolute immunity from liability under § 1983 and at the very least seek to reinstate the judgment of the District Court. If they are correct and the District Court's dismissal should be sustained, we need go no further in this case. Moreover, the immunity question involves the construction of a federal statute, and our practice is to deal with possibly dispositive statutory issues before reaching questions turning on the construction of the Constitution. Cf. Hagans v. Lavine, 415 U.S. 528, 549 (1974).[6] We essentially sustain the posi-

[6] In their original complaint, respondents sought only injunctive and declaratory relief. App. 11-12. In their amendment complaint, they added a prayer for compensatory and punitive damages. Id., at 92. Trial was to a jury; and the District Court in ruling on motions after declaring a mistrial appears to have treated the case as having developed into one for damages only since it entered judgment for petitioners and dismissed the complaint on the basis of their good-faith defense. In a joint motion for a new trial, respondents specifically argued that the District Court had erred in treating the case as one for the recovery of damages only and in failing to give them a trial and ruling on their claims for injunctive and declaratory relief Id., at 131. The District Court denied the motion. Id., at 133. Upon appeal, respondents renewed these contentions, and the Court of Appeals, after finding a substantive due process violation, directed the District Court to give respondents an injunction requiring expunction of the expulsion records and restraining any further continuing punishment. 485 F.2d, at 190. In their brief in this Court petitioners urge that we reverse the Court of Appeals and order the complaint dismissed. Brief for Petitioners 48. Respondents, however, again stress that the relief they sought included

tion of the Court of Appeals with respect to the immunity issue.

The nature of the immunity from awards of damages under § 1983 available to school administrators and school board members is not a question which the lower federal courts have answered with a single voice. There is general agreement on the existence of a "good faith" immunity, but the courts have either emphasized different factors as elements of good faith or have not given specific content to the good-faith standard.[7]

This Court has decided three cases dealing with the scope of the immunity

equitable relief. Brief for Respondents 47-48, 50.

In light of the record in this case, we are uncertain as to the basis for the District Court's judgment, for immunity from damages does not ordinarily bar equitable relief as well. The opinion of the Court of Appeals does not entirely dispel this uncertainty. With the case in this posture, it is the better course to proceed directly to the question of the immunity of school board members under § 1983.

[7] In McLaughlin v. Tilendis, 398 F.2d 287, 290-291 (CA7 1968), a case relied upon by the Court of Appeals below, the immunity was extended to school board members and the superintendent of schools only to the extent that they could establish that their decisions were founded on "justifiable grounds." Cf. Scoville v. Board of Ed. of Joliet Township, 425 F.2d 10, 15 (CA7), cert. denied, 400 U.S. 826 (1970). In Smith v. Losee, 485 F.2d 334, 344 (CA10 1973) (en banc), cert. denied, 417 U.S. 908 (1974), the immunity protecting university officials was described as one of good faith and the absence of malice where the facts before the officials "showed a good and valid reason for the decision although another reason or reasons advanced for nonrenewal or discharge may have been constitutionally impermissible." The District Court in Kirstein v. Rector and Visitors of University of Virginia, 309 F. Supp. 184, 189 (ED Va. 1970), extended the immunity to action taken in good faith and in accordance with "long standing legal principle."

protecting various types of governmental officials from liability for damages under § 1983. In Tenney v. Brandhove, 341 U.S. 367 (1951), the question was found to be one essentially of statutory construction.[8] Noting that the language of § 1983 is silent with respect to immunities, the Court concluded that there was no basis for believing that Congress intended to eliminate the traditional immunity of legislators from civil liability for acts done wthin their sphere of legislative action. That immunity, "so well grounded in history and reason. . . ," id., at 376, was absolute and consequently did not depend upon the motivations of the legislators. In Pierson v. Ray, 386 U.S. 547, 554 (1967), finding that "[t]he legislative record gives no clear indication that Congress meant to abolish wholesale all common-law immunities" in enacting § 1983, we concluded that the common-law doctrine of absolute judicial immunity survived. Similarly, § 1983 did not preclude ap-

[8] "Did Congress by the general language of its 1871 statute mean to overturn the tradition of legislative freedom achieved in England by Civil War and carefully preserved in the formation of State and National Governments here? Did it mean to subject legislators to civil liability for acts done within the sphere of legislative activity? Let us assume, merely for the moment, that Congress has constitutional power to limit the freedom of State legislators acting within their traditional sphere. That would be a big assumption. But we would have to make an even rasher assumption to find that Congress thought it had exercised the power. These are difficulties we cannot hurdle. The limits of §§ 1 and 2 of the 1871 statute . . . were not spelled out in debate. We cannot believe that Congress—itself a staunch advocate of legislative freedom—would impinge on a tradition so well grounded in history and reason by covert inclusion in the general language before us." Tenney v. Brandhove, 341 U.S. 367, 376 (1951).

plication of the traditional rule that a policeman, making an arrest in good faith and with probable cause, is not liable for damages, although the person arrested proves innocent. Consequently the Court said: "Although the matter is not entirely free from doubt, the same consideration would seem to require excusing him from liability for acting under a statute that he reasonably believed to be valid but that was later held unconstitutional, on its face or as applied." *Id.*, at 555 (footnote omitted). Finally, last Term we held that the chief executive officer of a State, the senior and subordinate officers of the State's National Guard, and the president of a state-controlled university were not absolutely immune from liability under § 1983, but instead were entitled to immunity, under prior precedent and in light of the obvious need to avoid discouraging effective official action by public officers charged with a considerable range of responsibility and discretion, only if they acted in good faith as defined by the Court:

"[I]n varying scope, a qualified immunity is available to officers of the executive branch of government, the variation being dependent upon the scope of discretion and responsibilities of the office and all the circumstances as they reasonably appeared at the time of the action on which liability is sought to be based. It is the existence of reasonable grounds for the belief formed at the time and in light of all the circumstances, coupled with good-faith belief, that affords a basis for qualified immunity of executive officers for acts performed in the course of official conduct." Scheuer v. Rhodes, 416 U.S. 232, 247-248 (1974).

Common-law tradition, recognized in our prior decisions, and strong public-policy reasons also lead to a construction of § 1983 extending a qualified good-faith immunity to school board members from liability for damages under that section. Although there have been differing emphases and formulations of the common-law immunity of public school officials in cases of student expulsion or suspension, state courts have generally recognized that such officers should be protected from tort liability under state law for all good-faith, nonmalicious action taken to fulfill their official duties.

As the facts of this case reveal, school board members function at different times in the nature of legislators and adjudicators in the school disciplinary process. Each of these functions necessarily involves the exercise of discretion, the weighing of many factors, and the formulation of long-term policy. "Like legislators and judges, these officers are entitled to rely on traditional sources for the factual information on which they decide and act." Scheuer v. Rhodes, *supra*, at 246 (footnote omitted). As with executive officers faced with instances of civil disorder, school officials, confronted with student behavior causing or threatening disruption, also have an "obvious need for prompt action, and decisions must be made in reliance on factual information supplied by others." *Ibid.*

Liability for damages for every action which is found subsequently to have been violative of a student's constitutional rights and to have caused compensable injury would unfairly impose upon the school decisionmaker the burden of mistakes made in good faith in the course of exercising his discretion within the scope of his official duties. School board members, among other duties, must judge whether there have been violations of school regulations and, if so, the appropriate sanctions for the violations. Denying any measure of immunity in these circumstances "would contribute not to principled and fearless decision-making but to intimidation." Pierson v. Ray, *supra*, at 554. The imposition of monetary costs for mistakes which were not unreasonable in the light of all the circumstances would undoubtedly deter even the most conscientious school decisionmaker from exercising his judgment independently, forcefully, and in a manner best serving the long-term interest of the school and the students. The most capable candidates for school board positions might be deterred from seeking office if heavy burdens upon their private resources from monetary liability were a likely prospect during their tenure.[11]

These considerations have undoubtedly played a prime role in the development by state courts of a qualified immunity protecting school officials from liability for damages in lawsuits claiming improper suspensions or expulsions.[12] But at the same time, the

judgment implicit in this common-law development is that absolute immunity would not be justified since it would not sufficiently increase the ability of school officials to exercise their discretion in a forthright manner to warrant the absence of a remedy for students subjected to intentional or otherwise inexcusable deprivations.

Tenney v. Brandhove, Pierson v. Ray, and Scheuer v. Rhodes drew upon a very similar background and were animated by a very similar judgment in construing § 1983. Absent legislative guidance, we now rely on those same sources in determining whether and to what extent school officials are immune from damage suits under § 1983. We think there must be a degree of immunity if the work of the schools is to go forward; and, however worded, the immunity must be such that public school officials understand that action taken in the good-faith fulfillment of their responsibilities and within the bounds of reason under all the circumstances will not be punished and that they need not exercise their discretion with undue timidity.

"Public officials, whether governors, mayors or police, legislators or judges, who fail to make decisions when they are needed or who do not act to implement decisions when they are made do not fully and faithfully perform the duties of their offices. Implicit in the idea that officials have some immunity—absolute or qualified—for their acts, is a recognition that they may err. The concept of immunity assumes this and goes-

---

11 The overwhelming majority of school board members are elected to office. See A. White, Local School Boards: Organization and Practices 8 (U.S. Office of Education, OE-23023, Bulletin No. 8, 1962); National School Boards Association, Survey of Public Education in the Member Cities of the Council of Big City Boards of Education 3 (Nov. 1968); Campbell, Cunningham, & McPhee, *supra*, n. 10, at 164-170. Most of the school board members across the country receive little or no monetary compensation for their service. White, *supra*, at 67-79; National School Boards Association, *supra*, at 3, 15-21; Campbell, Cunningham, & McPhee, *supra*, at 172.

12 "[School directors] are authorized, and it is their duty to adopt reasonable rules for the government and management of the school, and it would deter responsible and suitable men from accepting the position,

if held liable for damages to a pupil expelled under a rule adopted by them, under the impression that the welfare of the school demanded it, if the courts should deem it improper." Dritt v. Snodgrass, 66 Mo., at 293.

on to assume that it is better to risk some error and possible injury from such error than not to decide or act at all." Scheuer v. Rhodes, 416 U.S., at 241-242 (footnote omitted).

The disagreement between the Court of Appeals and the District Court over the immunity standard in this case has been put in terms of an "objective" versus a "subjective" test of good faith. As we see it, the appropriate standard necessarily contains elements of both. The official himself must be acting sincerely and with a belief that he is doing right, but an act violating a student's constitutional rights can be no more justified by ignorance or disregard of settled, indisputable law on the part of one entrusted with supervision of students' daily lives than by the presence of actual malice. To be entitled to a special exemption from the categorical remedial language of § 1983 in a case in which his action violated a student's constitutional rights, a school board member, who has voluntarily undertaken the task of supervising the operation of the school and the activities of the students, must be held to a standard of conduct based not only on permissible intentions, but also on knowledge of the basic, unquestioned constitutional rights of his charges. Such a standard neither imposes an unfair burden upon a person assuming a responsible public office requiring a high degree of intelligence and judgment for the proper fulfillment of its duties, nor an unwarranted burden in light of the value which civil rights have in our legal system. Any lesser standard would deny much of the promise of § 1983. Therefore, in the specific context of school discipline, we hold that a school board member is not immune from liability for damages under § 1983 if he knew or reasonably should have known

that the action he took within his sphere of official responsibility would violate the constitutional rights of the student affected, or if he took the action with the malicious intention to cause a deprivation of constitutional rights or other injury to the student. That is not to say that school board members are "charged with predicting the future course of constitutional law." Pierson v. Ray, 386 U.S., at 557. A compensatory award will be appropriate only if the school board member has acted with such an impermissible motivation or with such disregard of the student's clearly established constitutional rights that his action cannot reasonably be characterized as being in good faith.

III

The Court of Appeals, based upon its review of the facts but without the benefit of the transcript of the testimony given at the four-day trial to the jury in the District Court,[13] found that the board had made its decision to expel the girls on the basis of no evidence that the school regulation had been violated:

"To justify the suspension, it was necessary for the Board to establish that the students possessed or used an 'intoxicating' beverage at a school-sponsored activity. No evidence was presented at either meeting to establish the alcoholic content of the liquid brought to the campus. Moreover, the Board made no finding that the liquid was intoxicating. The only evidence as to the nature of the drink was that supplied by the girls, and

[13] At the time of the Court of Appeals decision, the testimony at the trial to the jury had not been transcribed because of counsel's concern with limiting litigation costs. Tr. of Oral Arg. 23, The transcript was filed in the District Court after certiorari was granted. App. 120 n. 2.

it is clear that they did not know whether the beverage was intoxicating or not." 485 F.2d, at 190.

Although it did not cite the case as authority, the Court of Appeals was apparently applying the due process rationale of Thompson v. City of Louisville, 362 U.S. 199, 206 (1960),[14] to the public school disciplinary process. The applicability of Thompson in this setting, however, is an issue that need not be reached in this case.[15] The record reveals that the decision of the Court of Appeals was based upon an erroneous construction of the school regulation in question. Once that regulation is properly construed, the Thompson issue disappears.

The Court of Appeals interpreted the school regulation prohibiting the use or possession of intoxicating beverages as being linked to the definition of "intoxicating liquor" under Arkansas statutes[16] which restrict the term to beverages with an alcoholic content exceeding 5% by weight.[17] Testimony at

the trial, however, established convincingly that the term "intoxicating beverage" in the school regulation was not intended at the time of its adoption in 1967 to be linked to the definition in the state statutes or to any other technical definition of "intoxicating."[18] The adoption of the regulation was at a time when the school board was concerned with a previous beer-drinking episode.[19] It was applied prior to respondents' case to another student charged with possession of beer.[20] In its statement of facts issued prior to the onset of this litigation, the school board expressed its construction of the regulation by finding that the girls had

---

[14] [Footnote omitted].

[15] That is not to say that the requirements of procedural due process do not attach to expulsions. Over the past 13 years the courts of appeals have without exception held that procedural due process requirements must be satisfied if a student is to be expelled. See Goss v. Lopez, 419 U.S. 565, 576-578, n. 8 (1975).

[16] See Ark. Stat. Ann. §§ 48-107, 48-503 (1964).

[17] The Court of Appeals referred to comments which seemed also to adopt this construction made by the District Court in its findings of fact when it denied respondents' motion for a preliminary injunction. 485 F.2d, at 190; App. 80. After noting the District Court's initial view that petitioners would find it difficult to prove the requisite alcoholic content, the Court of Appeals expressed puzzlement at the failure of the lower court to discuss the absence of such evidence in its final opinion. The District Court, however, indicated in its instructions

that the question of the proper construction of the regulation would not be revelant if the jury found that the school officials in good faith considered the malt liquor and punch to fall within the regulation. 348 F. Supp., at 248. The District Court's ultimate conclusion apparently made unnecessary a final decision on the coverage of the regulation.

Despite its construction of the present regulation, the Court of Appeals indicated that the school board had the authority to prohibit the use and possession of *alcoholic* beverages or to continue its policy of proscribing only *intoxicating* beverages. 485 F.2d, at 191.

[18] Two members of the school board at the time that the regulation was adopted testified that there had been no discussion of tying the regulation to the State Alcohol Control Act and that the intent of the board members when the regulation was adopted was to cover beer. Tr. 466-467 (testimony of petitioner Wood); id., at 589-590 (testimony of Mrs. Gerald Goforth).

[19] See the minutes of the board meeting at which the regulation was adopted in App. 103-104. See also Tr. 431-432 (testimony of Mrs. Mary L. Spencer, also a board member when the regulation was adopted); id., at 587-588 (Mrs. Goforth).

[20] The student was suspended in October 1971 for the possession of beer at a school activity. There is no indication in the record of the alcoholic content of the beer. See Tr. 258-259, 268-269 (testimony of former Superintendent Inlow).

brought an "alcoholic beverage" onto school premises.[21] The girls themselves admitted knowing at the time of the incident that they were doing something wrong [for] which [they] might be punished.[22] In light of this evidence, the Court of Appeals was ill advised to supplant the interpretation of the regulation of those officers who adopted it and are entrusted with its enforcement. Cf. Grayned v. City of Rockford, 408 U.S. 104, 110 (1972).

When the regulation is construed to prohibit the use and possession of beverages containing alcohol, there was no absence of evidence before the school board to prove the charge against respondents. The girls had admitted that they intended to "spike" the punch and that they had mixed malt liquor into the punch that was served. The third girl estimated at the time of their admissions to Waller that the malt liquor had an alcohol content of 20%. After the expulsion decision had been made and this litigation had begun, it was conclusively determined that the malt liquor in fact had an alcohol content not exceeding 3.2% by weight.[23] Testimony at trial put the alcohol content of the punch served at 0.91%.[24]

Given the fact that there *was* evidence supporting the charge against respondents, the contrary judgment of the Court of Appeals is improvident. It is not the role of the federal courts to

21 See n. 4, *supra*. Soon after this litigation had begun, the board issued a statement which said that the regulation "prohibits the use and possession of alcoholic beverage on school premises. . . ." App. 139.

22 See Tr. 75 (Strickland); *id.*, at 119, 121 (Crain).

23 This percentage content was established through the deposition of an officer of the company that produces "Right Time" malt liquor. App. 93-94.

24 Tr. 205 (testimony of Dr. W. F. Turner).

set aside decisions of school administrators which the court may view as lacking a basis in wisdom or compassion. Public high school students do have substantive and procedural rights while at school. See Tinker v. Des Moines Independent Community School District, 393 U.S. 503, 49 Ohio Op.2d 222 (1969); West Virginia State Board of Education v. Barnette, 319 U.S. 624 (1943); Goss v. Lopez, 419 U.S. 565 (1975). But § 1983 does not extend the right to relitigate in federal court evidentiary questions arising in school disciplinary proceedings or the proper construction of school regulations. The system of public education that has evolved in this Nation relies necessarily upon the discretion and judgment of school administrators and school board members, and § 1983 was not intended to be a vehicle for federal court correction of errors in the exercise of that discretion which do not rise to the level of violations of specific constitutional guarantees. See Epperson v. Arkansas, 393 U.S. 97, 104 (1968); Tinker, *supra*, at 507, 49 Ohio Op.2d 222 at 224.

IV

Respondents' complaint alleged that their procedural due process rights were violated by the action taken by petitioners. App. 9. The District Court did not discuss this claim in its final opinion, but the Court of Appeals viewed it as presenting a substantial question. It concluded that the girls were denied procedural due process at the first school board meeting, but also intimated that the second meeting may have cured the initial procedural deficiencies. Having found a substantive due process violation, however, the court did not reach a conclusion on this procedural issue. 485 F.2d, at 190.

Respondents have argued here that there was a procedural due process violation which also supports the result reached by the Court of Appeals. Brief for Respondents 27-28, 36. But because the District Court did not discuss it, and the Court of Appeals did not decide it, it would be preferable to have the Court of Appeals consider the issue in the first instance.

The judgment of the Court of Appeals is vacated and the case remanded for further proceedings consistent with this opinion.

So ordered.

o   o   o

DANIEL v. WILLIAMS

474 U.S. 327, 106 S. Ct. 662, 88 L. Ed. 2d 662 (1985)

[Footnotes and Citations Omitted]

JUSTICE REHNQUIST delivered the opinion of the Court

In *Parratt v. Taylor*, a state prisoner sued under 42 U.S.C. § 1983, claiming that prison officials had negligently deprived him of his property without due process of law. After deciding that § 1983 contains no independent state-of-mind requirement, we concluded that although petitioner had been "deprived" of property within the meaning of the Due Process Clause of the Fourteenth Amendment, the State's postdeprivation tort remedy provided the process that was due. Petitioner's claim in this case, which also rests on an alleged Fourteenth Amendment "deprivation" caused by the negligent conduct of a prison official, leads us to reconsider our statement in Parratt that "the alleged loss, even though negligently caused, amounted to a deprivation." We conclude that the Due Process Clause is simply not implicated by a negligent act of an official causing intended loss of or injury to life, liberty, or property.

In this § 1983 action, petitioner seeks to recover damages for back and ankle injuries allegedly sustained when he fell on a prison stairway. He claims that, while an inmate at the city jail in Richmond, Virginia, he slipped on a pillow negligently left on the stairs by respondent, a correctional deputy stationed at the jail. Respondent's negligence, the argument runs, "deprived" petitioner of his "liberty" interest in freedom from bodily injury, because respondent maintains that he is entitled to the defense of sovereign immunity in a state tort suit, petitioner is without an "adequate" state remedy. Accordingly, the deprivation of liberty was without "due process of law."

***

Because of the inconsistent approaches taken by lower courts in determining when tortious conduct by state officials rises to the level of a constitutional tort, and the apparent lack of adequate guidance from this Court, we granted certiorari. We now affirm.

In *Parratt v. Taylor*, we granted certiorari, as we had twice before, "to decide whether mere negligence will support a claim for relief under § 1983." After examining the language, legislative history, and prior interpretations of the statute, we concluded that § 1983, unlike its criminal counterpart, 18 U.S.C. § 242, contains no state-of-mind requirement independent of that necessary to state a violation of the underlying constitutional right. We adhere to that conclusion. But in any given § 1983 suit, the plaintiff must still prove a violation of the underlying constitutional right; and depending on the right, merely negligent conduct may not be enough to state a claim.

In *Parratt*, before concluding that Nebraska's tort remedy provided all the process that was due, we said that the loss of the prisoner's hobby kit, "even though negligently caused, amounted to a deprivation [under the Due Process Clause]." JUSTICE POWELL, concurring in the result, criticized the majority for "pass[ing] over" this important question of the state of mind required to constitute a "deprivation" of property. He argued that negligent acts by state officials, though causing loss of property, are not actionable under the Due Process Clause. To JUSTICE POWELL, mere negligence could not "wor[k] a deprivation in the constitutional sense."

Not only does the word "deprive" in the Due Process Clause connote more than a negligent act, but we should not "open the federal courts to lawsuits where there has been no affirmative abuse of power." Upon reflection, we agree and overrule *Parratt* to the extent that it states that mere lack of due care by a state official may "deprive" an individual of life, liberty, or property under the Fourteenth Amendment.

The Due Process Clause of the Fourteenth Amendment provides: "[N]or shall any state deprive any person of life, liberty, or property, without due process of law." Historically, this guarantee of due process has been applied to deliberate decisions of government officials to deprive a person of life, liberty, or property. No decision of this court before *Parratt* supported the view that negligent conduct by a state official, even though causing injury, constitutes a deprivation under the Due Process Clause. This history reflects the traditional and commonsense notion that the Due Process Clause, like its forebear in the Magna Carta, was " 'intended to secure the individual from the arbitrary exercise of the powers of government.' " By requiring the government to follow appropriate procedures when its agents decide to "deprive any person of life, liberty, or property," the Due Process Clause promotes fairness in such decisions. And by barring certain government actions regardless of the fairness of the procedures used to implement them, it serves to prevent governmental power from being "used for purposes of oppression."

We think that the actions of prison custodians in leaving a pillow on the prison stairs, or mislaying an inmate's property, are quite remote from the concerns just discussed. Far from an abuse of power, lack of due care suggests no more than a failure to measure up to the conduct of a reasonable person. To hold that injury caused by such conduct is a deprivation within the meaning of the Fourteenth Amendment would trivialize the centuries-old principle of due process of law.

The Fourteenth Amendment is part of a Constitution generally designed to allocate governing authority among the Branches of the Federal Government and between that Government and the States, and to secure certain individual rights against both State and Federal Government. When dealing with a claim that such a document creates a right in prisoners to sue a government official because he negligently created an unsafe condition in the prison, we bear in mind Chief Justice Marshall's admonition that "we must never forget, that it is a constitution we are expounding," Our Constitution deals with the large concerns of the governors and the governed, but it does not purport to supplant traditional tort law in laying down rules of conduct to regulate liability for injuries that attend living together in society. We have previously rejected reasoning that " 'would make of the Fourteenth Amendment a font of tort law to be superimposed upon whatever systems may already be administered by the States.' "

The only tie between the facts of this case and anything governmental in nature is the fact that respondent was a sheriff's deputy at the Richmond city jail and petitioner was an inmate confined in that jail. But while the Due Process Clause of the Fourteenth Amendment obviously speaks to some facets of this relationship, we do not believe its protections are triggered by lack of due care by prison officials.

***

That injuries inflicted by governmental negligence are not addressed by the United States Constitution is not to say that they may not raise significant legal concerns and lead to the creation of protectible legal interests. The enactment of tort claim statutes, for example, reflects the view that injuries caused by such negligence should generally be redressed. It is no reflection on either the breadth of the United States Constitution or the importance of traditional tort law to say that they do not address the same concerns.

In support of his claim that negligent conduct can give rise to a due process "deprivation," petitioner makes several arguments, none of which we find persuasive. He states, for example, that "it is almost certain that some negligence claims are within § 1983," and cites as an example the failure of a State to comply with the procedural requirements of *Wolff v. McDonnell*, before depriving an inmate of good-time credit. We think the relevant action of the prison officials in that situation is their deliberate decision to deprive the inmate of good-time credit, not their hypothetically negligent failure to accord him the procedural protections of the Due Process Clause. But we need not rule out the possibility that there are other constitutional provisions that would be violated by mere lack of care in order to hold, as we do, that such conduct does not implicate the Due Process Clause of the Fourteenth Amendment.

Petitioner also suggests that artful litigants, undeterred by a requirement that they plead more than mere negligence, will often be able to allege sufficient facts to support a claim of intentional deprivation. In the instant case, for example, petitioner notes that he could have alleged that the pillow was left on the stairs with the intention of harming him. This invitation to "artful" pleading, petitioner contends, would engender sticky (and needless) disputes over what is fairly pleaded. What's more, requiring complainants to allege something more than negligence would raise serious questions about what "more" than negligence—intent, recklessness, or "gross negligence"—is required, and indeed about what these exclusive terms mean. But even if accurate, petitioner's observations do not carry the day. In the first place, many branches of the law abound in nice distinctions that may be troublesome but have been thought nonetheless necessary:

"I do not think we need trouble ourselves with the thought that my view depends on differences of degree. The whole law does so as soon as it is civilized."

More important, the difference between one end of the spectrum—negligence—and the other—intent—is abundantly clear. In any event, we decline to trivialize the Due Process Clause in an effort to simplify constitutional litigation.

Finally, citing *South v. Maryland*, petitioner argues that respondent's conduct, even if merely negligent, breached a sheriff's "special duty of care" for those in his custody. The Due Process Clause, petitioner notes, "was intended to give Americans at least the protection against governmental power that they had enjoyed as Englishmen against the power of the crown." And *South v. Maryland* suggests that one such protection was the right to recover against a sheriff for breach of his ministerial duty to provide for the safety of prisoners in his custody. Due process demands that the State protect those whom it incarcerates by exercising reasonable care to assure their safety and by compensating them for negligently inflicted injury.

We disagree. We read *South v. Maryland*, supra, an action brought under federal diversity jurisdiction on a Maryland sheriff's bond, as stating no more than what this Court thought to be the principles of common law and Maryland law applicable to that case; it is not cast at all in terms of constitutional law, and indeed could not have been, since at the time it was rendered there was no due process clause applicable to the States. Petitioner's citation to *Ingraham v. Wright* does not support the notion that all common-law duties owed by government actors were somehow constitutionalized by the Fourteenth Amendment. Jailers may owe a special duty of care to those in their custody under state tort law, but for the reasons previously stated we reject the contention that the Due Pro

cess Clause of the Fourteenth Amendment embraces such a tort law concept. Petitioner alleges that he was injured by the negligence of respondent, a custodial official at the city jail. Whether other provisions of state law or general jurisprudence he may rightly invoke, the Fourteenth Amendment to the United States Constitution does not afford him a remedy.

Affirmed.

CARLSON v GREEN
446 U.S. 14, 64 L.Ed.2d 15, 100 S.Ct. 1468 (1980)

[footnotes and citations omitted]

Respondent brought this suit in the District Court for the Southern District of Indiana on behalf of the estate of her deceased son, Joseph Jones, Jr., alleging that he suffered personal injuries from which he died because the petitioners, federal prison officials, violated his due process, equal protection, and Eighth Amendment rights. [S]he claimed compensatory and punitive damages for the constitutional violations. Two questions are presented for decision: (1) Is a remedy available directly under the Constitution, given that respondent's allegations could also support a suit against the United States under the Federal Tort Claims Act? and (2) If so, is survival of the cause of action

governed by federal common law or by state statutes?

I

The District Court held that under Estelle v. Gamble, 429 U.S. 97 (1976), the allegations set out in note 1, supra, pleaded a violation of the Eighth Amendment's proscription against infliction of cruel and unusual punishment giving rise to a cause of action for damages under Bivens v. Six Unknown Fed. Narcotics Agents, 403 U.S. 388 (1971).

II

Bivens established that the victims of a constitutional violation by a federal agent have a right to recover damages against the official in federal court despite the absence of any statute conferring such a right. Such a cause of action may be defeated in a particular case, however, in two situations. The first is when defendants demonstrate "special factors counselling hesitation in the absence of affirmative action by Congress." The second is when defendants show that Congress has provided an alternative remedy which it explicitly declared to be a substitute for recovery directly under the Constitution and viewed as equally effective.

Neither situation obtains in this case. First, the case involves no special factors counselling hesitation in the absence of affirmative action by Congress. Petitioners do not enjoy such independent status in our constitutional scheme as to suggest that judicially created remedies against them might be inappropriate. Moreover, even if requiring them to defend respondent's suit might inhibit their efforts to perform their official duties, the qualified immunity accorded them under Butz v. Economou, 438 U.S. 478 (1978), provides adequate protection.

Second, we have here no explicit congressional declaration that persons injured by federal officers' violations of the Eighth Amendment may not recover money damages from the agents but must be remitted to another remedy, equally effective in the view of Congress. Petitioners point to nothing in the Federal Tort Claims Act (FTCA) or its legislative history to show that Congress meant to pre-empt a Bivens remedy or to create an equally effective remedy for constitutional violations. FTCA was enacted long before Bivens was decided, but when Congress amended

FTCA in 1974 to create a cause of action against the United States for intentional torts committed by federal law enforcement officers, the congressional comments accompanying that amendment made it crystal clear that Congress views FTCA and Bivens as parallel, complementary causes of action:

> "[A]fter the date of enactment of this measure, innocent individuals who are subjected to raids [like that in Bivens] will have a cause of action against the individual Federal agents *and* the Federal Government. Furthermore, this provision should be viewed as a *counterpart* to the Bivens case and its progeny [sic], in that it waives the defense of sovereign immunity so as to make the Government independently liable in damages for the same type of conduct that is alleged to have occurred in Bivens (and for which that case imposes liability upon the individual Government officials involved.)"

In the absence of a contrary expression from Congress, § 2680(h) thus contemplates that victims of the kind of intentional wrongdoing alleged in this complaint shall have an action under FTCA against the United States as well as a Bivens action against the individual officials alleged to have infringed their constitutional rights.

This conclusion is buttressed by the significant fact that Congress follows the practice of explicitly stating when it means to make FTCA an exclusive remedy. Furthermore, Congress has not taken action on other bills that would expand the exclusivity of FTCA.

Four additional factors, each suggesting that the Bivens remedy is more effective than the FTCA remedy, also support our conclusion that Congress did not intend to limit respondent to an FTCA action. First, the Bivens remedy, in addition to compensating victims, serves a deterrent purpose. Because the Bivens remedy is recoverable against individuals, it is a more effective deterrent than the FTCA remedy against the United States. It is almost axiomatic that the threat of damages has a deterrent effect,[7] Imbler v. Pachtman, 424 U.S. 409, 442 (1976) (White, J., concurring in judgment), surely particularly so when the individual official faces personal financial liability.

Petitioners argue that FTCA liability is a more effective deterrent because the individual employees responsible for the Government's liability would risk loss of employment and because the Government would be forced to promulgate corrective policies. That argument suggests, however, that the superiors would not take the same actions when an employee is found personally liable for violation of a citizen's constitutional rights. The more reasonable assumption is that responsible superiors are motivated not only by concern for the public fisc but also by concern for the Government's integrity.

Second, our decisions, although not expressly addressing and deciding the question, indicate that punitive damages may be awarded in a Bivens suit. Punitive damages are "a par-

ticular remedial mechanism normally available in the federal courts," and are especially appropriate to redress the violation by a Government official of a citizen's constitutional rights. Moreover, punitive damages are available in "a proper" § 1983 action, Carey v. Piphus, 435 U.S. 247 (1978) (punitive damages not awarded because District Court found defendants "did not act with a malicious intention to deprive respondents of their rights or to do them other injury"),[9] and Butz v. Economou, suggests that the "constitutional design" would be stood on its head if federal officials did not face at least the same liability as state officials guilty of the same constitutional transgression. But punitive damages in an FTCA suit are statutorily prohibited. Thus FTCA is that much less effective than a Bivens action as a deterrent to unconstitutional acts.

Third, a plaintiff cannot opt for a jury in an FTCA action, as he may in a Bivens suit. Petitioners argue that this is an irrelevant difference because juries have been biased against Bivens claimants. Significantly, however, they do not assert that judges trying the claims as FTCA actions would have been more receptive, and they cannot explain why the plaintiff should not retain the choice.

Fourth, an action under FTCA exists only if the State in which the alleged misconduct occurred would permit a cause of action for that misconduct to go forward. 28 U.S.C. § 1346(b) (United States liable "in ac-

7. Indeed, underlying the qualified immunity which public officials enjoy for actions taken in good faith is the fear that exposure to personal liability would otherwise deter them from acting at all. See Butz v. Economou, 438 U.S. 478, 497 (1978); Scheuer v. Rhodes, 416 U.S. 232 (1974).

9. Moreover, after Carey, punitive damages may be the only significant remedy available in some § 1983 actions where constitutional rights are maliciously violated but the victim cannot prove compensable injury.

cordance with the law of the place where the act or omission occurred"). Yet it is obvious that the liability of federal officials for violations of citizens' constitutional rights should be governed by uniform rules. See Part III, infra. The question whether respondent's action for violations by federal officials of federal constitutional rights should be left to the vagaries of the laws of the several States admits of only a negative answer in the absence of a contrary congressional resolution.

Plainly FTCA is not a sufficient protector of the citizens' constitutional rights, and without a clear congressional mandate we cannot hold that Congress relegated respondent exclusively to the FTCA remedy.

III

Bivens actions are a creation of federal law and, therefore, the question whether respondent's action survived Jones' death is a question of federal law. Petitioners, however, would have us fashion a federal rule of survivorship that incorporates the survivorship laws of the forum State, at least where the state law is not inconsistent with federal law. Respondent argues, on the other hand, that only a uniform federal rule of survivorship is compatible with the goal of deterring federal officials from infringing federal constitutional rights in the manner alleged in respondent's complaint. We agree with respondent. Whatever difficulty we might have resolving the question were the federal involvement less clear, we hold that only a uniform federal rule of survivorship will suffice to redress the constitutional deprivation here alleged and to protect against repetition of such conduct.

In short, we agree with and adopt the reasoning of the Court of Appeals:

"The essentiality of the survival of civil rights claims for complete vindication of constitutional rights is buttressed by the need for uniform treatment of those claims, at least when they are against federal officials. As this very case illustrates, uniformity cannot be achieved if courts are limited to applicable state law. Here the relevant Indiana statute would not permit survival of the claim, while in Beard [v. Robinson, 563 F.2d 331 (CA7 1977),] the Illinois statute permitted survival of the Bivens action. The liability of federal agents for violation of constitutional rights should not depend upon where the violation occurred. ... In sum, we hold that whenever the relevant state survival statute would abate a Bivens-type action brought against defendants whose conduct results in death, the federal common law allows survival of the action."

Robertson v. Wegmann, 436 U.S. 584 (1978), holding that a § 1983 action would abate in accordance with Louisiana survivorship law is not to the contrary. There the plaintiff's death was not caused by the acts of the defendants upon which the suit was based. Moreover, Robertson expressly recognized that to prevent frustration of the deterrence goals of § 1983 (which in part also underlie Bivens actions, see Part II, supra) "[a] state official contemplating illegal activity must always be prepared to face the prospect of a § 1983 action being filed against him." A federal official contemplating unconstitutional conduct similarly must be prepared to face the prospect of a Bivens action. A uniform rule that claims such as respondent's survive the decedent's death is essential if we are not to "frustrate in [an] important way the achievement" of the goals of Bivens actions.

Affirmed.

GEORGIA PATSY, Petitioner

v.

BOARD OF REGENTS OF THE STATE OF FLORIDA, etc.

457 US 496, 73 L.Ed.2d 172, 102 S.Ct. 2557 (1982)

OPINION OF THE COURT

JUSTICE MARSHALL delivered the opinion of the Court.

This case presents the question whether exhaustion of state administrative remedies is a prerequisite to an action under 42 USC § 1983. Petitioner Georgia Patsy filed this action, alleging that her employer, Florida International University (FIU), had denied her employment opportunities solely on the basis of her race and sex. By a divided vote, the United States Court of Appeals for the Fifth Circuit found that petitioner was required to exhaust "adequate and appropriate" administrative remedies, and remanded the case to the District Court to consider the adequacy of the administrative procedures. We granted certiorari, and reverse the decision of the Court of Appeals.

I

Petitioner alleges that even though she is well qualified and has received uniformly excellent performance evaluations from her supervisors, she has been rejected for more than 13 positions at FIU.[1] She further claims that

---

[1] Because this case is here on a motion to dismiss, we accept as true the factual allegations in petitioner's amended complaint. The

FIU has unlawfully filled positions through intentional discrimination on the basis of race and sex. She seeks declaratory and injunctive relief or, in the alternative, damages.

The United States District Court for the Southern District of Florida granted respondent Board of Regents' motion to dismiss because petitioner had not exhausted available administrative remedies. On appeal, a panel of the Court of Appeals reversed, and remanded the case for further proceedings. The full court then granted respondent's petition for rehearing and vacated the panel decision.

The Court of Appeals reviewed numerous opinions of this Court holding that exhaustion of administrative remedies was not required, and concluded that these cases did not preclude the application of a "flexible" exhaustion rule. After canvassing the policy arguments in favor of an exhaustion requirement, the Court of Appeals decided that a § 1983 plaintiff could be required to exhaust administrative remedies if the following minimum conditions are met: (1) an orderly system of review or appeal is provided by statute or agency rule; (2) the agency can grant relief more or less commensurate with the claim; (3) relief is available within a reasonable period of time; (4) the procedures are fair, are not unduly burdensome, and are not used to harass or discourage those with legitimate claims; and (5) interim relief is available, in appropriate cases, to prevent irreparable injury and to preserve the plaintiff's rights during the administrative process. Where

District Court granted petition leave to amend, and she amended her complaint to name the Board of Regents "on behalf of" FIU.

these minimum standards are met, a court must further consider the particular administrative scheme, the nature of the plaintiff's interest, and the values served by the exhaustion doctrine in order to determine whether exhaustion should be required. The Court of Appeals remanded the case to the District Court to determine whether exhaustion would be appropriate in this case.

II

The question whether exhaustion of administrative remedies should ever be required in a § 1983 action has prompted vigorous debate and disagreement. See, e.g., Turner, When Prisoners Sue: A Study of Prisoner Section 1983 Cases in the Federal Courts, 92 Harv L Rev 610 (1979); Note, 8 Ind L Rev 565 (1975); Comment, 41 U Chi L Rev 537 (1974). Our resolution of this issue, however, is made much easier because we are not writing on a clean slate. This Court has addressed this issue, as well as related issues, on several prior occasions.

Respondent suggests that our prior precedents do not control our decision today, arguing that these cases can be distinguished on their facts or that this Court did not "fully" consider the question whether exhaustion should be required. This contention need not detain us long. Beginning with McNeese v. Board of Education, 373 US 668 (1963), we have on numerous occasions rejected the argument that a § 1983 action should be dismissed where the plaintiff has not exhausted state administrative remedies. Respondent may be correct in arguing that several of these decisions could have been based on traditional exceptions to the exhaustion doctrine. Nevertheless, this Court has stated categorically that exhaustion is not a prerequisite to an action under § 1983, and we have not deviated from that position in the 19 years since McNeese. Therefore, we do not address the question presented in this case as one of first impression.

III

Respondent argues that we should reconsider these decisions and adopt the Court of Appeals' exhaustion rule. This Court has never announced a definitive formula for determining whether prior decisions should be overruled or reconsidered. However, in Monell v. New York City Dept. of Social Services, 436 US 658 (1978), we articulated four factors that should be considered. Two of these factors—whether the decisions in question misconstrued the meaning of the statute as revealed in its legislative history and whether overruling these decisions would be inconsistent with more recent expressions of congressional intent—are particularly relevant to our decision today. Both concern legislative purpose, which is of paramount importance in the exhaustion context because Congress is vested with the power to prescribe the basic procedural scheme under which claims may be heard in federal courts. Of course, courts play an important role in determining the limits of an exhaustion requirement even where Congress has not expressly so provided. However, the initial question whether exhaustion is required should be answered by reference to congressional intent; and a court should not defer the exercise of jurisdiction under a federal statute unless it is consistent with that intent.[2] Therefore, in

deciding whether we should reconsider our prior decisions and require exhaustion of state administrative remedies, we look to congressional intent as reflected in the legislative history of the predecessor to § 1983 and in recent congressional activity in this area.

A

In determining whether our prior decisions misconstrued the meaning of § 1983, we begin with a review of the legislative history to § 1 of the Civil Rights Act of 1871, 17 Stat 13, the precursor to § 1983. Although we recognize that the 1871 Congress did not expressly contemplate the exhaustion question, we believe that the tenor of the debates over § 1 supports our conclusion that exhaustion of administrative remedies in § 1983 actions should not be judicially imposed. The Civil Rights Act of 1871, along with the Fourteenth Amendment it

---

[2] Congressional intent is important in determining the application of the exhaustion doctrine to cases in which federal administrative remedies are available, as well as to those in which state remedies are available. Of course, exhaustion is required where Congress provides that certain administrative remedies shall be exclusive. See Myers v. Bethlehem Shipbuilding Corp., 303 US 41, 82 L Ed 638, 58 S Ct 459 (1938). Even where the statutory requirement of exhaustion is not explicit, courts are guided by congressional intent in determining whether application of the doctrine would be consistent with the statutory scheme. In determining whether exhaustion of federal administrative remedies is required, courts generally focus on the role Congress has assigned to the relevant federal agency, and tailor the exhaustion rule to fit the particular administrative scheme created by Congress. See McKart v. United States, 395 US 185, 193-195, 23 L Ed 2d 194, 89 S Ct 1657 (1969). With state administrative remedies, the focus is not so much on the role assigned to the state agency, but the role of the state agency becomes important once a court finds that deferring its exercise of jurisdiction is consistent with statutory intent.

was enacted to enforce, were crucial ingredients in the basic alteration of our federal system accomplished during the Reconstruction Era. During that time, the Federal Government was clearly established as a guarantor of the basic federal rights of individuals against incursions by state power. As we recognized in Mitchum v. Foster, 407 US 225 (1972) "[t]he very purpose of § 1983 was to interpose the federal courts between the States and the people, as guardians of the people's federal rights—to protect the people from unconstitutional action under color of state law, 'whether that action be executive, legislative, or judicial.' "

At least three recurring themes in the debates over § 1 cast serious doubt on the suggestion that requiring exhaustion of state administrative remedies would be consistent with the intent of the 1871 Congress. First, in passing § 1, Congress assigned to the federal courts a paramount role in protecting constitutional rights.

The 1871 Congress intended § 1 to "throw open the doors of the United States courts" to individuals who were threatened with, or who had suffered, the deprivation of constitutional rights and to provide these individuals immediate access to the federal courts notwithstanding any provision of state law to the contrary.

A second theme in the debates further suggests that the 1871 Congress would not have wanted to impose an exhaustion requirement. A major factor motivating the expansion of federal jurisdiction through §§ 1 and 2 of the bill was the belief of the 1871 Congress that the state authorities had been unable or unwilling to protect the constitutional rights of individuals or to punish those who violated these rights. Of primary importance to the

exhaustion question was the mistrust that the 1871 Congress held for the factfinding processes of state institutions. This Congress believed that federal courts would be less susceptible to local prejudice and to the existing defects in the factfinding processes of the state courts. This perceived defect in the States' factfinding processes is particularly relevant to the question of exhaustion of administrative remedies: exhaustion rules are often applied in deference to the superior factfinding ability of the relevant administrative agency. See, e.g., McKart v. United States.

A third feature of the debates relevant to the exhaustion question is the fact that many legislators interpreted the bill to provide dual or concurrent forums in the state and federal system, enabling the plaintiff to choose the forum in which to seek relief. Cf. Monroe v. Pape, 365 US 167, 183 (1961) ("[T]he federal remedy is supplementary to the state remedy, and the latter need not be first sought and refused before the federal one is invoked").

This legislative history supports the conclusion that our prior decisions, holding that exhaustion of state administrative remedies is not a prerequisite to an action under § 1983, did not misperceive the statutory intent: it seems fair to infer that the 1871 Congress did not intend that an individual be compelled in every case to exhaust state administrative remedies before filing an action under § 1 of the Civil Rights Act. We recognize, however, that drawing such a conclusion from this history alone is somewhat precarious: the 1871 Congress was not presented with the question of exhaustion of administrative remedies, nor was it aware of the potential role of state administrative agencies. Therefore, we do not rely exclusively on this legislative history in deciding the question presented here. Congress addressed the question of exhaustion under § 1983 when it recently enacted 42 USC § 1997e (1976 ed, Supp IV) [42 USCS § 1997e]. The legislative history of § 1997e provides strong evidence of congressional intent on this issue.

B

The Civil Rights of Institutionalized Persons Act, 42 USC §§ 1997 et seq. (1976 ed, Supp IV) [42 USCS §§ 1997 et seq.], was enacted primarily to ensure that the United States Attorney General has "legal standing to enforce existing constitutional rights and Federal statutory rights of institutionalized persons." In § 1997e, Congress also created a specific, limited exhaustion requirement for adult prisoners bringing actions pursuant to § 1983. Section 1997e and its legislative history demonstrate that Congress understood that exhaustion is not generally required in § 1983 actions, and that it decided to carve out only a narrow exception to this rule. A judicially imposed exhaustion requirement would be inconsistent with Congress' decision to adopt § 1997e and would usurp policy judgments that Congress has reserved for itself.

In considering whether an exhaustion requirement should be incorporated into the bill, Congress clearly expressed its belief that a decision to require exhaustion for certain § 1983 actions would work a change in the law. Witnesses testifying before the Subcommittee that drafted the bill discussed the decisions of this Court holding that exhaustion was not required.

The debates over adopting an exhaustion requirement also reflect this understanding. With the understanding that exhaustion generally is not required, Congress decided to adopt the limited exhaustion requirement of § 1997e in order to relieve the burden on the federal courts by diverting certain prisoner petitions back through state and local institutions, and also to encourage the States to develop appropriate grievance procedures. Implicit in this decision is Congress' conclusion that the no-exhaustion rule should be left standing with respect to other § 1983 suits.

A judicially imposed exhaustion requirement would also be inconsistent with the extraordinarily detailed exhaustion scheme embodied in § 1997e. Section 1997e carves out a narrow exception to the general no-exhaustion rule to govern certain prisoner claims, and establishes a procedure to ensure that the administrative remedies are adequate and effective. The exhaustion requirement is expressly limited to § 1983 actions brought by an adult convicted of a crime. 42 USC § 1997e(a)(1) (1976 ed, Supp IV) [42 USCS § 1997e(a)(1)]. Section 1997e(b)(1) instructs the Attorney General to "promulgate minimum standards for the development and implementation of a plain, speedy, and effective system" of administrative remedies, and § 1997e(b)(2) specifies certain minimum standards that must be included. A court may require exhaustion of administrative remedies only if "the Attorney General has certified or the court has determined that such administrative remedies are in substantial compliance with the minimum acceptable standards promulgated under subsection (b)." § 1997e(a)(2). Before exhaustion may be required, the court must further conclude that it "would be appropriate and in the interests of justice." § 1997e(a)(1). Finally, in those § 1983 actions meeting all the statutory requirements for exhaustion, the district court may not dismiss the case, but may only "continue such case for a period of not to exceed ninety days in order to require exhaustion." Ibid. This detailed scheme is inconsistent with discretion to impose, on an ad hoc basis, a judicially developed exhaustion rule in other cases.

Congress hoped that § 1997e would improve prison conditions by stimulating the development of successful grievance mechanisms. To further this purpose, Congress provided for the deferral of the exercise of federal jurisdiction over certain § 1983 claims only on the condition that the state prisons develop adequate procedures. This purpose would be frustrated by judicial discretion to impose exhaustion generally: the States would have no incentive to adopt grievance procedures capable of certification, because prisoner § 1983 cases could be diverted to state administrative remedies in any event.

In sum, the exhaustion provisions of the Act make sense, and are not superfluous, only if exhaustion could not be required before its enactment and if Congress intended to carve out a narrow exception to this no-exhaustion rule. The legislative history of § 1997e demonstrates that Congress has taken the approach of carving out specific exceptions to the general rule that federal courts cannot require exhaustion under § 1983. It is not our province to alter the balance struck by Congress in establishing the procedural framework for bringing actions under § 1983.

C

Respondent and the Court of Ap-peals argue that exhaustion of administrative remedies should be required because it would further various policies. They argue that an exhaustion requirement would lessen the perceived burden that § 1983 actions impose on federal courts, would further the goal of comity and improve federal-state relations by postponing federal-court review until after the state administrative agency had passed on the issue; and would enable the agency, which presumably has expertise in the area at issue, to enlighten the federal court's ultimate decision.

As we noted earlier, policy considerations alone cannot justify judicially imposed exhaustion unless exhaustion is consistent with congressional intent. Furthermore, as the debates over incorporating the exhaustion requirement in § 1997e demonstrate, the relevant policy considerations do not invariably point in one direction, and there is vehement disagreement over the validity of the assumptions underlying many of them. The very difficulty of these policy considerations, and Congress' superior institutional competence to pursue this debate, suggest that legislative not judicial solutions are preferable. 447 U.S. 303, 317, 65 L Ed2d 144, 100 S Ct 2204 (1980); Steelworkers v. Bouligny, Inc., 382 US 145, 150, 153, 15 L Ed 2d 217, 86 S Ct 272 (1965).

Beyond the policy issues that must be resolved in deciding *whether* to require exhaustion, there are equally difficult questions concerning the design and scope of an exhaustion requirement. These questions include how to define those categories of § 1983 claims in which exhaustion might be desirable; how to unify and centralize the standards for judging the kinds of administrative procedures that should be exhausted;[3] what tolling requirements and time limitations should be adopted; what is the res judicata and collateral estoppel effect of particular administrative determinations; what consequences should attach to the failure to comply with procedural requirements of administrative proceedings; and whether federal courts could grant necessary interim injunctive relief and hold the action pending exhaustion, or proceed to judgment without requiring exhaustion even though exhaustion might otherwise be required, where the relevant administrative agency is either powerless or not inclined to grant such interim relief. These and similar questions might be answered swiftly and surely by legislation, but would create costly, remedy-delaying, and court-burdening litigation if answered incrementally by the judiciary in the context of diverse constitutional claims relating to thousands of different state agencies. The very variety of claims, claimants, and state agencies involved in § 1983 cases

argues for congressional considerations of the myriad of policy considerations, and may explain why Congress, in deciding whether to require exhaustion in certain § 1983 actions brought by adult prisoners, carved out such a narrow, detailed exception to the no-exhaustion rule. After full debate and consideration of the various policy arguments, Congress adopted § 1997, taking the largest class of § 1983 actions and constructing an exhaustion requirement that differs substantially from the McKart-type standard urged by respondent and adopted by the Court of Appeals. It is not for us to say whether Congress will or should create a similar scheme for other categories of § 1983 claims or whether Congress will or should adopt an altogether different exhaustion requirement for nonprisoner § 1983 claims.

IV

Based on the legislative histories of both § 1983 and § 1997e, we conclude that exhaustion of state administrative remedies should not be required as a prerequisite to bringing an action pursuant to § 1983. We decline to overturn our prior decisions holding that such exhaustion is not required. The decision of the Court of Appeals is reversed, and the case is remanded for proceedings consistent with this opinion.

It is so ordered.

---

[3] Section 1997e resolved this problem by directing the Attorney General to promulgate minimum standards and to establish a procedure by which prison administrative remedies could be reviewed and certified. §§ 1997e(b) and (c). If a procedure has not been certified, the court is directed to compare the procedure with the Attorney General's standards and to continue the case pending exhaustion only if the procedure is in substantial compliance with the standards of the Attorney General. § 1997e(a)(2).

BRYCE N. HARLOW and ALEXANDER P. BUTTERFIELD, Petitioners
v.
A. ERNEST FITZGERALD
457 US 800, 73 L.Ed.2d 396, 102 S.Ct. 2727 (1982)

OPINION OF THE COURT
JUSTICE POWELL delivered the opinion of the Court.

The issue in this case is the scope of the immunity available to the senior aides and advisers of the President of the United States in a suit for damages based upon their official acts.

I

In this suit for civil damages petitioners Bryce Harlow and Alexander Butterfield are alleged to have participated in a conspiracy to violate the constitutional and statutory rights of the respondent A. Ernest Fitzgerald. Respondent avers that petitioners entered the conspiracy in their capacities as senior White House aides of former President Richard M. Nixon.

Respondent claims that Harlow joined the conspiracy in his role as the Presidential aide principally responsible for congressional relations. At the conclusion of discovery the supporting evidence remained inferential.

Together with their codefendant Richard Nixon, petitioners Harlow and Butterfield moved for summary judgment on February 12, 1980. In denying the motion the District Court upheld the legal sufficiency of Fitzgerald's Bivens (Bivens v. Six Unknown Fed. Narcotics Agents, 403 US 388 (1971)) claim under the First Amendment and his "inferred" statutory causes of action under 5 USC § 7211 (1976 ed, Supp IV) [5 USCS § 7211] and 18 USC § 1505 [18 USCS § 1505]. The court found that genuine issues of disputed fact remained for resolution at trial. It also ruled that petitioners were not entitled to absolute immunity.

Independently of former President Nixon, petitioners invoked the collateral order doctrine and appealed the denial of their immunity defense to the Court of Appeals for the District of Columbia Circuit. The Court of Appeals dismissed the appeal without opinion. Never having determined the immunity available to the senior aides and advisers of the President of the United States, we granted certiorari.

II

[O]ur decisions consistently have held that Government officials are entitled to some form of immunity from suits for damages. As recognized at common law, public officers require this protection to shield them from undue interference with their duties and from potentially disabling threats of liability.

Our decisions have recognized immunity defenses of two kinds. For officials whose special functions or constitutional status requires complete protection from suit, we have recognized the defense of "absolute immunity." The absolute immunity of legislators, in their legislative functions, see, e.g., Eastland v. United States Servicemen's Fund, 421 US 491 (1975), and of judges, in their judicial functions, see, e.g., Stump v. Sparkman, 435 US 349 (1978), now is well settled. Our decisions also have extended absolute immunity to certain officials of the Executive Branch. These include prosecutors and similar officials, see Butz v. Economou, 438 US -478 (1978), executive officers engaged in adjudicative functions, id., at 513-517, and the President of the United States, see Nixon v. Fitzgerald, 457 US 731 (1982).

For executive officials in general, however, our cases make plain that qualified immunity represents the norm. In Scheuer v. Rhodes, 416 US 232 (1974), we acknowledged that high officials require greater protection than those with less complex discretionary responsibilities. Nonetheless, we held that a governor and his aides could receive the requisite protection from qualified or good-faith immunity. In Butz v. Economou, supra, we extended the approach of Scheuer to high federal officials of the Executive Branch. [T]he recognition of a qualified immunity defense for high executives reflected an attempt to balance competing values: not only the importance of a damages remedy to protect the rights of citizens, 438 US, at 504-505, but also "the need to protect officials who are required to exercise their discretion and the related public interest in encouraging the vigorous exercise of official authority." Id., at 506. Butz acknowledge[d] that the special functions of some officials might require absolute immunity. But the Court held that "federal officials who seek absolute exemption from personal liability for unconstitutional conduct must bear the burden of showing that public policy requires an exemption of that scope." Id., at 506. This we reaffirmed in Nixon v. Fitzgerald.

III

A

Petitioners argue that they are en-titled to a blanket protection of absolute immunity as an incident of their offices as Presidential aides. Having decided in Butz that Members of the Cabinet ordinarily enjoy only qualified immunity from suit, we conclude today that it would be equally untenable to hold absolute immunity an incident of the office of every Presidential subordinate based in the White House. Members of the Cabinet are direct subordinates of the President, frequently with greater responsibilities, both to the President and to the Nation, than White House staff. The considerations that supported our decision in Butz apply with equal force to this case. It is no disparagement of the offices held by petitioners to hold that Presidential aides, like Members of the Cabinet, generally are entitled only to a qualified immunity.

B

In disputing the controlling authority of Butz, petitioners rely on the principles developed in Gravel v. United States, 408 US 606 (1972). [In Gravel] we held the Speech and Debate Clause derivatively applicable to the "legislative acts" of a Senator's aide that would have been privileged if performed by the Senator himself.

Petitioners contend that the rationale of Gravel mandates a similar "derivative" immunity for the chief aides of the President of the United States. Emphasizing that the President must delegate a large measure of authority to execute the duties of his office, they argue that recognition of derivative absolute immunity is made essential by all the considerations that support absolute immunity for the President himself.

[I]n general our cases have followed a "functional" approach to immunity law. We have recognized that the judicial, prosecutorial, and legislative functions require absolute immunity. But this protection has extended no further than its justification would warrant. In Gravel, for example, we emphasized that Senators and their aides were absolutely immune only when performing "acts legislative in nature," and not when taking other acts even "in their official capacity." 408 US, at 625. Our cases involving judges and prosecutors have followed a similar line. The undifferentiated extension of absolute "derivative" immunity to the President's aides therefore could not be reconciled with the "functional" approach that has characterized the immunity decisions of this Court, indeed including Gravel itself.

IV

[P]etitioners assert that public policy at least mandates an application of the qualified immunity standard that would permit the defeat of insubstantial claims without resort to trial. We agree.

A

The resolution of immunity questions inherently requires a balance between the evils inevitable in any available alternative. In situations of abuse of office, an action for damages may offer the only realistic avenue for vindication of constitutional guarantees. It is this recognition that has required the denial of absolute immunity to most public officers. At the same time, however, it cannot be disputed seriously that claims frequently run against the innocent as well as the guilty—at a cost not only to the defendant officials, but to the society as a whole. These social costs include the expenses of litigation, the

diversion of official energy from pressing public issues, and the deterrence of able citizens from acceptance of public office.

B

Qualified or "good faith" immunity is an affirmative defense that must be pleaded by a defendant official. Gomez v. Toledo, 446 US 635 (1980). Decisions of this Court have established that the "good faith" defense has both an "objective" and a "subjective" aspect. The objective element involves a presumptive knowledge of and respect for "basic, unquestioned constitutional rights." Wood v. Strickland, 420 US 308, 322 (1975). The subjective component refers to "permissible intentions." Ibid. Characteristically the Court has defined these elements by identifying the circumstances in which qualified immunity would *not* be available. Referring both to the objective and subjective elements, we have held that qualified immunity would be defeated if an official *"knew or reasonably should have known* that the action he took within his sphere of official responsibility would violate the constitutional rights of the [plaintiff], or if he took the action *with the malicious intention* to cause a deprivation of constitutional rights or other injury...." Ibid. (Emphasis added.)

The subjective element of the good-faith defense frequently has proved incompatible with our admonition in Butz that insubstantial claims should not proceed to trial. Rule 56 of the Federal Rules of Civil Procedure provides that disputed questions of fact ordinarily may not be decided on motions for summary judgment. And an official's subjective good faith has been considered to be a question of fact that some courts have regarded as inherently requiring resolution by a jury.

In the context of Butz's attempted balancing of competing values, it now is clear that substantial costs attend the litigation of the subjective good faith of government officials. Not only are there the general costs of subjecting officials to the risks of trial—distraction of officials from their governmental duties, inhibition of discretionary action, and deterrence of able people from public service. There are special costs to "subjective" inquiries of this kind. Immunity generally is available only to officials performing discretionary functions. In contrast with the thought processes accompanying "ministerial" tasks, the judgments surrounding discretionary action almost inevitably are influenced by the decisionmaker's experiences, values, and emotions. These variables explain in part why questions of subjective intent so rarely can be decided by summary judgment. Yet they also frame a background in which there often is no clear end to the relevant evidence. Judicial inquiry into subjective motivation therefore may entail broad-ranging discovery and the deposing of numerous persons, including an official's professional colleagues. Inquiries of this kind can be peculiarly disruptive of effective government. Consistently with the balance at which we aimed in Butz, we conclude today that bare allegations of malice should not suffice to subject government officials either to the costs of trial or to the burdens of broad-reaching discovery. We therefore hold that government officials performing discretionary functions generally are shielded from liability for civil damages insofar as their conduct does not violate clearly established statutory or constitutional rights of which a rea-

sonable person would have known. Reliance on the objective reasonableness of an official's conduct, as measured by reference to clearly established law, should avoid excessive disruption of government and permit the resolution of many insubstantial claims on summary judgment. On summary judgment, the judge appropriately may determine, not only the currently applicable law, but whether that law was clearly established at the time an action occurred. If the law at that time was not clearly established, an official could not reasonably be expected to anticipate subsequent legal developments, nor could he fairly be said to "know" that the law forbade conduct not previously identified as unlawful. Until this threshold immunity question is resolved, discovery should not be allowed. If the law was clearly established, the immunity defense ordinarily should fail, since a reasonably competent public official should know the law governing his conduct. Nevertheless, if the official pleading the defense claims extraordinary circumstances and can prove that he neither knew nor should have known of the relevant legal standard, the defense should be sustained. But again, the defense would turn primarily on objective factors.

C

In this case petitioners have asked us to hold that the respondent's pretrial showings were insufficient to survive their motion for summary judgment. We think it appropriate, however, to remand the case to the District Court for its reconsideration of this issue in light of this opinion.

V

The judgment of the Court of Appeals is vacated, and the case is remanded for further action consistent with this opinion.

So ordered.

WILLIAM H. SMITH, Petitioner

v.

DANIEL R. WADE

461 U.S. 30, 103 S. Ct. 1625, 75 L. Ed. 2d 632 (1983)

OPINION OF THE COURT

JUSTICE BRENNAN delivered the opinion of the Court.

We granted certiorari in this case, to decide whether the District Court for the Western District of Missouri applied the correct legal standard in instructing the jury that it might award punitive damages under 42 USC § 1983 [42 USCS § 1983].[1] The Court of Appeals for the Eighth Circuit sustained the award of punitive damages. We affirm.

I

The petitioner, William H. Smith, is a guard at Algoa Reformatory, a unit of the Missouri Division of Corrections for youthful first offenders. The respondent, Daniel R. Wade, was assigned to Algoa as an inmate in 1976. In the summer of 1976 Wade voluntarily checked into Algoa's pro-

tective custody unit. Because of disciplinary violations during his stay in protective custody, Wade was given a short term in punitive segregation and then transferred to administrative segregation. On the evening of Wade's first day in administrative segregation, he was placed in a cell with another inmate. Later, when Smith came on duty in Wade's dormitory, he placed a third inmate in Wade's cell. According to Wade's testimony, his cellmates harassed, beat, and sexually assaulted him.

Wade brought suit under 42 USC § 1983 [42 USCS § 1983] against Smith and four other guards and correctional officials, alleging that his Eighth Amendment rights had been violated. At trial his evidence showed that he had placed himself in protective custody because of prior incidents of violence against him by other inmates. The third prisoner whom Smith added to the cell had been placed in administrative segregation for fighting. Smith had made no effort to find out whether another cell was available; in fact there was another cell in the same dormitory with only one occupant. Further, only a few weeks earlier, another inmate had been beaten to death in the same dormitory during the same shift, while Smith had been on duty. Wade asserted that Smith and the other defendants knew or should have

---

[1] Rev Stat § 1979, amended, 93 Stat 1284. Section 1983 reads in relevant part:

Every person who, under color of any statute, ordinance, regulation, custom, or usage, of any State or Territory or the District of Columbia, subjects, or causes to be subjected, any citizen of the United States or other person within the jurisdiction thereof to the deprivation of any rights, privileges, or immunities secured by the Constitution and laws, shall be liable to the party injured in an action at law, suit in equity, or other proper proceeding for redress.

known that an assault against him was likely under the circumstances.

During trial, the district judge entered a directed verdict for two of the defendants. He instructed the jury that Wade could make out an Eighth Amendment violation only by showing "physical abuse of such base, inhumane and barbaric proportions as to shock the sensibilities." Further, because of Smith's qualified immunity as a prison guard, see Procunier v. Navarette, 434 US 555, 55 L Ed 2d 24, 98 SCt 855 (1978), the judge instructed the jury that Wade could recover only if the defendants were guilty of "gross negligence" (defined as "a callous indifference or a thoughtless disregard for the consequences of one's act or failure to act") or "egregious failure to protect" Wade (defined as "a flagrant or remarkably bad failure to protect"). He reiterated that Wade could not recover on a showing of simple negligence.

The district judge also charged the jury that it could award punitive damages on a proper showing:

"In addition to actual damages, the law permits the jury, under certain circumstances, to award the injured person punitive and exemplary damages, in order to punish the wrongdoer for some extraordinary misconduct, and to serve as an example or warning to others not to engage in such conduct.

"If you find the issues in favor of the plaintiff, and if the conduct of one or more of the defendants is shown to be *a reckless or callous disregard of, or indifference to, the rights or safety of others*, then you may assess punitive or exemplary damages in addition to any award of actual damages.

". . . The amount of punitive or

exemplary damages assessed against any defendant may be such sum as you believe will serve to punish that defendant and to deter him and others from like conduct." (Emphasis added.)

The jury returned verdicts for two of the three remaining defendants. It found Smith liable, however, and awarded $25,000 in compensatory damages and $5,000 in punitive damages. The District Court entered judgment on the verdict, and the Court of Appeals affirmed.

In this Court, Smith attacks only the award of punitive damages. He does not challenge the correctness of the instructions on liability or qualified immunity, nor does he question the adequacy of the evidence to support the verdict of liability for compensatory damages.

II

Section 1983 is derived from § 1 of the Civil Rights Act of 1871, 17 Stat 13. It was intended to create "a species of tort liability" in favor of persons deprived of federally secured rights. Carey v. Piphus, 435 US 247, 253, 55 LEd2d 252, 98 SCt 1042 (1978). We noted in Carey that there was little in the section's legislative history concerning the damages recoverable for this tort liability. In the absence of more specific guidance, we looked first to the common law of torts (both modern and as of 1871), with such modification or adaptation as might be necessary to carry out the purpose and policy of the statute. We have done the same in other contexts arising under § 1983, especially the recurring problem of common-law immunities.

Smith correctly concedes that "punitive damages are available in a 'proper' § 1983 action. . . ." Carlson v. Green, 446 US 14, 22, 64 LEd2d 15, 100 SCt 1468 (1980). Although there was debate about the theoretical correctness of the punitive damages doctrine in the latter part of the last century, the doctrine was accepted as settled law by nearly all state and federal courts, including this Court. It was likewise generally established that individual public officers were liable for punitive damages for their misconduct on the same basis as other individual defendants. See also Scott v. Donald, 165 US 58, 77-89, 41 LEd 632, 17 SCt 265 (1897) (punitive damages for constitutional tort). Further, although the precise issue of the availability of punitive damages under § 1983 has never come squarely before us, we have had occasion more than once to make clear our view that they are available; indeed, we have rested decisions on related questions on the premise of such availability.[2]

Smith argues, nonetheless, that this was not a "proper" case in which to award punitive damages. More particularly, he attacks the instruction that punitive damages could be awarded on a finding of reckless or callous disregard of or indifference to Wade's rights of safety. Instead, he contends that the proper test is one of actual malicious intent—"ill will, spite, or intent to injure." He offers two arguments for this position: first, that actual intent is the proper standard for punitive damages in all cases

[2] In Newport v. Fact Concerts, Inc., 453 US 247, 69 LEd2d 616, 101 SCt 2748 (1981), for example, we held that a municipality (as opposed to an individual defendant) is immune from liability for punitive damages under § 1983. A significant part of our reasoning was that deterrence of constitutional violations would be adequately accomplished by allowing punitive damage awards directly against the responsible individuals.

under § 1983; and second, that even if intent is not always required, it should be required here because the threshold for punitive damages should always be higher than that for liability in the first instance. We address these in turn.

III

Smith does not argue that the common law, either in 1871 or now, required or requires a showing of actual malicious intent for recovery of punitive damages.

Perhaps not surprisingly, there was significant variation (both terminological and substantive) among American jurisdictions in the latter nineteenth century on the precise standard to be applied in awarding punitive damages—variation that was exacerbated by the ambiguity and slipperiness of such common terms as "malice" and "gross negligence." Most of the confusion, however, seems to have been over the degree of negligence, recklessness, carelessness, or culpable indifference that should be required—not over whether actual intent was essential. On the contrary, the rule in a large majority of jurisdictions was that punitive damages (also called exemplary damages, vindictive damages, or smart money) could be awarded without a showing of actual ill will, spite, or intent to injure.

The large majority of state and lower federal courts were in agreement that punitive damage awards did not require a showing of actual malicious intent; they permitted punitive awards on variously stated standards of negligence, recklessness, or other culpable conduct short of actual malicious intent.

The same rule applies today. The Restatement (Second) of Torts (1977), for example, states: "Punitive damages may be awarded for conduct that is outrageous, because of the defendant's evil motive or *his reckless indifference to the rights of others.*" Id., § 908(2) (emphasis added); see also id., Comment *b*. Most cases under state common law, although varying in their precise terminology, have adopted more or less the same rule, recognizing that punitive damages in tort cases may be awarded not only for actual intent to injure or evil motive, but also for recklessness, serious indifference to or disregard for the rights of others, or even gross negligence.

The remaining question is whether the policies and purposes of § 1983 itself require a departure from the rules of tort common law. As a general matter, we discern no reason why a person whose federally guaranteed rights have been violated should be granted a more restrictive remedy than a person asserting an ordinary tort cause of action. Smith offers us no persuasive reason to the contrary.

Smith's argument, which he offers in several forms, is that an actual intent standard is preferable to a recklessness standard because it is less vague. He points out that punitive damages, by their very nature, are not awarded to compensate the injured party. He concedes, of course, that deterrence of future egregious conduct is a primary purpose of both § 1983, see Newport, 453 US 247, 69 LEd2d 616, 101 SCt 2748 (1981); Owen v. City of Independence, 445 US 622, 651, 63 LEd2d 673, 100 SCt 1398 (1980); Robertson v. Wegmann, 436 US 584, 591, 56 LEd2d 554, 98 SCt 1991 (1978), and of punitive damages, see Newport; Restatement (Second) of Torts § 908(1) (1977). But deterrence, he contends, cannot be achieved unless the standard of con-

duct sought to be deterred is stated with sufficient clarity to enable potential defendants to conform to the law and to avoid the proposed sanction. Recklessness or callous indifference, he argues, is too uncertain a standard to achieve deterrence rationally and fairly. A prison guard, for example, can be expected to know whether he is acting with actual ill will or intent to injure, but not whether he is being reckless or callously indifferent.

Smith's argument, if valid, would apply to ordinary tort cases as easily as to § 1983 suits; hence, it hardly presents an argument for adopting a different rule under § 1983. In any event, the argument is unpersuasive. While, arguendo, an intent standard may be easier to understand and apply to particular situations than a recklessness standard, we are not persuaded that a recklessness standard is too vague to be fair or useful.

More fundamentally, Smith's argument for certainty in the interest of deterrence overlooks the distinction between a standard for punitive damages and a standard of liability in the first instance. Smith seems to assume that prison guards and other state officials look mainly to the standard for punitive damages in shaping their conduct. We question the premise; we assume, and hope, that most officials are guided primarily by the underlying standards of federal substantive law—both out of devotion to duty, and in the interest of avoiding liability for compensatory damages. At any rate, the conscientious officer who desires clear guidance on how to do his job and avoid lawsuits can and should look to the standard for actionability in the first instance. The need for exceptional clarity in the standard for punitive damages arises only if one assumes that there are substantial numbers of officers who will not be deterred by compensatory damages; only such officers will seek to guide their conduct by the punitive damages standard. The presence of such officers constitutes a powerful argument *against* raising the threshold for punitive damages.

In this case, the jury was instructed to apply a high standard of constitutional right ("physical abuse of such base, inhumane and barbaric proportions as to shock the sensibilities"). It was also instructed, under the principle of qualified immunity, that Smith could not be held liable at all unless he was guilty of "a callous indifference or a thoughtless disregard for the consequences of [his] act or failure to act," or of "a flagrant or remarkably bad failure to protect" Wade. These instructions are not challenged in this Court, nor were they challenged on grounds of vagueness in the lower courts. Smith's contention that this recklessness standard is too vague to provide clear guidance and reasonable deterrence might more properly be reserved for a challenge seeking different standards of liability in the first instance. As for punitive damages, however, in the absence of any persuasive argument to the contrary based on the policies of § 1983, we are content to adopt the policy judgment of the common law—that reckless or callous disregard for the plaintiff's rights, as well as intentional violations of federal law, should be sufficient to trigger a jury's consideration of the appropriateness of punitive damages.

IV

Smith contends that even if § 1983 does not ordinarily require a showing of actual malicious intent for an award of punitive damages, such a

showing should be required in this case. He argues that the deterrent and punitive purposes of punitive damages are served only if the threshold for punitive damages is higher in every case than the underlying standard for liability in the first instance. In this case, while the district judge did not use the same precise terms to explain the standards of liability for compensatory and punitive damages, the parties agree that there is no substantial difference between the showings required by the two instructions; both apply a standard of reckless or callous indifference to Wade's rights. Hence, Smith argues, the district judge erred in not requiring a higher standard for punitive damages, namely, actual malicious intent.

This argument incorrectly assumes that, simply because the instructions specified the same *threshold* of liability for punitive and compensatory damages, the two forms of damages were equally available to the plaintiff. The argument overlooks a key feature of punitive damages—that they are never awarded as of right, no matter how egregious the defendant's conduct. "If the plaintiff proves sufficiently serious misconduct on the defendant's part, the question whether to award punitive damages is left to the jury, which may or may not make such an award." D. Dobbs, Handbook on the Law of Remedies 204 (1973) (footnote omitted).[3] Compensatory damages, by contrast, are

[3] See also, e.g., Restatement (Second) of Torts § 908, comment *d* (1977); J. Ghiardi & J. Kircher, Punitive Damages Law and Practice § 5.38 (1981); C. McCormick, Handbook on the Law of Damages 296 (1935); W. Prosser, Handbook on the Law of Torts 13 (4th ed 1971); K. Redden, Punitive Damages § 3.4(A) (1980); Chuy v. Philadelphia Eagles Football Club, 595 F2d 1265, 1277-1278, n. 15 (CA3 1979) (en banc).

mandatory; once liability is found, the jury is required to award compensatory damages in an amount appropriate to compensate the plaintiff for his loss. Hence, it is not entirely accurate that punitive and compensatory damages were awarded in this case on the same standard. To make its punitive award, the jury was required to find not only that Smith's conduct met the recklessness threshold (a question of ultimate fact), but *also* that his conduct merited a punitive award of $5,000 in addition to the compensatory award (a discretionary moral judgment).

This common-law rule makes sense in terms of the purposes of punitive damages. Punitive damages are awarded in the jury's discretion "to punish [the defendant] for his outrageous conduct and to deter him and others like him from similar conduct in the future." Restatement (Second) of Torts § 908(1) (1977). The focus is on the character of the tortfeasor's conduct—whether it is of the sort that calls for deterrence and punishment over and above that provided by compensatory awards. If it is of such a character, then it is appropriate to allow a jury to assess punitive damages; and that assessment does not become less appropriate simply because the plaintiff in the case faces a more demanding standard of actionability. To put it differently, society has an interest in deterring and punishing *all* intentional or reckless invasions of the rights of others, even though it sometimes chooses not to impose any liability for lesser degrees of fault.

As with his first argument, Smith gives us no good reason to depart from the common-law rule in the context of § 1983. He argues that too low a standard of exposure to punitive damages

in cases such as this threatens to undermine the policies of his qualified immunity as a prison guard. The same reasoning would apply with at least as much force to, for example, the First Amendment and common-law immunities involved in the defamation cases described above. In any case, Smith overstates the extent of his immunity. Smith is protected from liability for mere negligence because of the need to protect his use of discretion in his day-to-day decisions in the running of a correctional facility. See generally Procunier v. Navarette, 434 US 555, 55 LEd2d 24, 98 SCt 855 (1978); Wood v. Strickland, 420 US 308, 43 LEd2d 214, 95 SCt 992 (1975). But the immunity on which Smith relies is coextensive with the interest it protects. The very fact that the privilege is qualified reflects a recognition there is no societal interest in protecting those uses of a prison guard's discretion that amount to reckless or callous indifference to the rights and safety of the prisoners in his charge. Once the protected sphere of privilege is exceeded, we see no reason why state officers should not be liable for their reckless misconduct on the same basis as private tortfeasors.

V

We hold that a jury may be permitted to assess punitive damages in an action under § 1983 when the defendant's conduct is shown to be motivated by evil motive or intent, or when it involves reckless or callous indifference to the federally protected rights of others. We further hold that this threshold applies even when the underlying standard of liability for compensatory damages is one of recklessness. Because the jury instructions in this case are in accord with this rule, the judgment of the Court of Appeals is affirmed.

ADDITIONAL LITIGATION

MONTANYE v. HAYMES
427 U.S. 236, 96 S. Ct. 2543, 43 L. Ed. 2d 466 (1976)

* * *

MR. JUSTICE WHITE delivered the opinion of the Court.

On June 7, 1972, respondent Haymes was removed from his assignment as inmate clerk in the law library at the Attica Correctional Facility in the State of New York. That afternoon Haymes was observed circulating among other inmates a document prepared by him and at the time signed by 82 other prisoners. Among other things, each signatory complained that he had been deprived of legal assistance as the result of the removal of Haymes and another inmate from the prison law library. The document, which was addressed to a federal judge but sought no relief, was seized and held by prison authorities. On June 8, Haymes was advised that he would be transferred to Clinton Correctional Facility, which, like Attica, was a maximum-security institution. The transfer was effected the next day. No loss of good time, segregated confinement, loss of privileges or any other disciplinary measures accompanied the transfer. On August 3, Haymes filed a petition with the United States District Court which was construed by the judge to be an application under 42 U.S.C. § 1983 and 28 U.S.C.

§ 1343 seeking relief against petitioner Montanye, the then superintendent at Attica. The petition complained that the seizure and retention of the document, despite requests for its return, not only violated Administrative Bulletin No. 20, which allegedly made any communication to a court privileged and confidential, but also infringed Haymes' federally guaranteed right to petition the court for redress of grievances. It further asserted that Haymes' removal to Clinton was to prevent him from pursuing his remedies and also was in reprisal for his having rendered legal assistance to various prisoners as well as having, along with others, sought to petition the court for redress.

In response to a show-cause order issued by the court, petitioner Brady, the correctional officer at Attica in charge of the law library, stated in an affidavit that Haymes had been relieved from his assignment as an inmate clerk in the law library "because of his continual disregard for the rules governing inmates and the use of the law library" and that only one of the inmates who had signed the petition being circulated by Haymes had ever made an official request for legal assistance. The affidavit of Harold Smith,

653

Deputy Superintendent of Attica, furnished the court with Paragraph 21 of the Inmate's Rule Book, which prohibited an inmate from furnishing legal assistance to another inmate without official permission and with a copy of a bulletin board notice directing inmates with legal problems to present them to Officer Brady—inmates were in no circumstances to set themselves up as legal counsellors and receive pay for their services. The affidavit asserted that the petition taken from Haymes was being circulated "in direct disregard of the above rule forbidding legal assistance without the approval of the Superintendent" and that Haymes had been cautioned on several occasions about assisting other inmates without the required approval.

Haymes responded by a motion to join Brady as a defendant, which was granted, and with a counteraffidavit denying that there was a rule book at Attica, reasserting that the document seized was merely a letter to the court not within the scope of the claimed rule and alleging that his removal from the law library, the seizure of his petition and his transfer to Clinton were acts of reprisal for his having attempted to furnish legal assistance to the other prisoners rather than merely hand out library books to them.

After retained counsel had submitted a memorandum on behalf of Haymes, the District Court dismissed the action. It held that the rule against giving legal assistance without consent was reasonable and that the seizure of Haymes' document was not in violation of the Constitution. The court also ruled that the transfer to Clinton did not violate Haymes' rights: "Although a general allegation is made that punishment was the motive for the transfer, there is no allegation that the facilities at Green Haven are harsher or substantially different from those afforded petitioner at Attica . . . petitioner's transfer was consistent with the discretion given to prison officials in exercising proper custody of inmates." App. 26a.

The Court of Appeals for the Second Circuit reversed. Because the District Court had considered affidavits outside the pleadings, the dismissal was deemed to have been a summary judgment under Rule 56, Federal Rules of Civil Procedure. The judgment was ruled erroneous because there were two unresolved issues of material fact: whether Haymes' removal to Clinton was punishment for a disobedience of prison rules and if so whether the effects of the transfer were sufficiently burdensome to require a hearing under the Due Process Clause of the Fourteenth Amendment.

The court's legal theory was that Haymes should no more be punished by a transfer having harsh consequences than he should suffer other deprivations which under prison rules could not be imposed without following specified procedures. Disciplinary transfers, the Court of Appeals thought, were in a different category from "administrative" transfers. "When harsh treatment is meted out to reprimand, deter or reform an individual, elementary fairness demands that the one punished be given a satisfactory opportunity to establish that he is not deserving of such handling . . . the specific facts upon which decision to punish are predicated can most suitably be ascertained at an impartial hearing to review the evidence of the alleged misbehavior, and to assess the effect which the transfer will have on the inmate's future incarceration." The Court of Appeals found it difficult "to look upon the circumstances of transfer as a mere coincidence;" it was also convinced that Haymes might be able to demonstrate sufficiently burdensome consequences attending the transfer to trigger the protections of the Due Process Clause, even though Attica and Clinton were both maximum-security prisons. The case was therefore remanded for further proceedings to the District Court. We granted certiorari and heard the case with Meachum v. Fano. We reverse the judgment of the Court of Appeals.

The Court of Appeals did not hold, as did the Court of Appeals in Meachum v. Fano, that every disadvantageous transfer must be accompanied by appropriate hearings. Administrative transfers, although perhaps having very similar consequences for the prisoner, were exempt from the Court of Appeals ruling. Only disciplinary transfers having substantial adverse impact on the prisoner were to call for procedural formalities. Even so, our decision in Meachum requires a reversal in this case. We held in Meachum v. Fano, that no Due Process Clause liberty interest of a duly convicted prison inmate is infringed when he is transferred from one prison to another within the State, whether with or without a hearing, absent some right or justifiable expectation rooted in state law that he will not be transferred except for misbehavior or upon the occurrence of other specified events. We therefore disagree with the Court of Appeals' general proposition that the Due Process Clause by its own force requires hearings whenever prison authorities transfer a prisoner to another institution because of his breach of prison rules, at least where the transfer may be said to involve substantially burdensome consequences. As long as the conditions or degree of confinement

to which the prisoner is subjected are within the sentence imposed upon him and are not otherwise violative of the Constitution, the Due Process Clause does not in itself subject an inmate's treatment by prison authorities to judicial oversight. The Clause does not require hearings in connection with transfers whether or not they are the result of the inmate's misbehavior or may be labeled as disciplinary or punitive.

We also agree with the State of New York that under the law of that State Haymes had no right to remain at any particular prison facility and no justifiable expectation that he would not be transferred unless found guilty of misconduct. Under New York law, adult persons sentenced to imprisonment are not sentenced to particular institutions but are committed to the custody of the Commissioner of Corrections. He receives adult, male felons at a maximum-security reception center for initial evaluation and then transfers them to specified institutions. Thereafter, the Commissioner is empowered by statute to "transfer inmates from one correctional facility to another." The Court of Appeals reasoned that because under the applicable state statutes and regulations, various specified punishments were reserved as sanctions for breach of prison rules and could not therefore be imposed without appropriate hearings, neither could the harsh consequences of a transfer be imposed as punishment for misconduct absent appropriate due process procedures. But under the New York law, the transfer of inmates is not conditional upon or limited to the occurrence of misconduct. The statute imposes no conditions on the discretionary power to transfer and we are advised by the State that no such requirements have been promulgated. Transfers are not among the punishments which may be imposed only after a prison disciplinary hearing. Whatever part an inmate's behavior may play in decision to transfer, there is no more basis in New York law for invoking the protections of the Due Process Clause than we found to be the case under the Massachusetts law in the Meachum case.

The judgment of the Court of Appeals is reversed and the case is remanded to that court for further proceedings consistent with this opinion.

So ordered.

* * *

MR. JUSTICE STEVENS, with whom MR. JUSTICE BRENNAN and MR. JUSTICE MARSHALL join, dissenting.

Respondent's complaint, fairly read, alleges two quite different theories of recovery: First, that he was entitled to a hearing before he could be transferred from one facility to another because the transfer deprived him of an interest in liberty; second, that the transfer was a form of punishment for circulating a petition, for communicating with a court, and for rendering legal assistance to other inmates. Since respondent has not alleged a material difference between the two facilities, I agree with the Court that the transfer did not cause him a grievous loss entitling him to a hearing. In my opinion this conclusion is unaffected by the motivation for the transfer, because I think it is the seriousness of its impact on the inmate's residuum of protected liberty that determines whether a deprivation has occurred.

I am persuaded, however, that the allegations of his complaint are sufficient to require a trial of his claim that the transfer was made in retribution for his exercise of protected rights. On this claim, the reason for the defendants' action is critical and the procedure followed is almost irrelevant. I do not understand the Court to disagreed with this analysis, and assume that the Court of Appeals, consistently with this Court's mandate, may direct the District Court to conduct a trial.

The reason for my dissent is that the same result would follow from a simple affirmance. Thus, although the Court has explained why it believes the *opinion* of the Court of Appeals should be "reversed," it has not explained why that Court's *judgment* was not correct. I would affirm that judgment.

* * *

MEACHUM v. FANO
427 U.S. 215, 96 S. Ct. 2532, 49 L. Ed. 2d 451 (1976)

* * *

MR. JUSTICE WHITE delivered the opinion of the Court.

The question here is whether the Due Process Clause of the Fourteenth Amendment entitles a state prisoner to a hearing when he is transferred to a prison the conditions of which are substantially less favorable to the prisoner, absent a state law or practice conditioning such transfers on proof of serious misconduct or the occurrence of other events. We hold that it does not.

I

During a two and one-half month period in 1974, there were nine serious fires at the Massachusetts Correctional Institution at Norfolk—a medium security institution. Based primarily on reports from informants, the six respondent inmates were removed from the general prison population and placed in the Receiving Building, an administrative detention area used to process new inmates. Proceedings were then had before the Norfolk prison classification board with respect to whether respondents were to be transferred to another institution—possibly a maximum-security institution, the living conditions at which are substantially less favorable than those at Norfolk. Each respondent was notified of the classification hearing and was informed that the authorities had information indicating that he had engaged in criminal conduct.

Individual classification hearings were held, each respondent being represented by counsel. Each hearing began by the reading of a prepared statement by the classification board. The board then heard, *in camera* and out of the respondents' presence, the testimony of petitioner Meachum, the Norfolk prison superintendent, who repeated the information that had been received from informants. The respondent was then told that the evidence supported the allegations contained in the notice but was not then—or ever—given transcripts or summaries of Meachum's testimony before the Board. Each respondent was allowed to present evidence in his own behalf; and each denied involvement in the particular infraction being investigated. Some respondents submitted supportive testimony or written statements from correction officers. A social worker also testified in the presence of each respondent, furnishing the respondent's criminal and custodial record, including prior rule infractions, if any, and other aspects of his performance and "general adjustment" at Norfolk.

The Board recommended that Royce be placed in administrative segregation for 30 days; that Fano, Dussault, and MacPhearson be transferred to Walpole, a maximum-security institution where the living conditions are substantially less favorable to the prisoners than those at Norfolk, and that DeBrosky and Hathaway be transferred to Bridgewater which has both maximum- and medium-security facilities. The reasons for its actions were stated in the Board's reports, which, however, were not then available to respondents. Although respondents were aware of the general import of the informant's allegations and were told that the recommendations drew upon informant sources, the details of this information were not revealed to respondents and are not included in the Board's reports which are part of the record before us.

The Board's recommendations were reviewed by the Acting Deputy Commissioner for Classification and Treatment and by the Commissioner of Corrections on the basis of the written report prepared by the Board. They accepted the recommendations of the Board with respect to Fano, Dussault, Hathaway, and MacPhearson. DeBrosky and Royce were ordered transferred to Walpole. The transfers were carried out, with two exceptions. No respondent was subjected to disciplinary punishment upon arrival at the transfer prison. None of the transfers ordered entailed loss of good time, or disciplinary confinement.

Meanwhile respondents had brought this action under 42 U.S.C. § 1983 against petitioners Meachum, the prison superintendent; Hall, the State Commissioner of Corrections; and Dawber, the Acting Deputy for Classification and Treatment, alleging that respondents were being deprived of liberty without due process of law in that petitioners had ordered them transferred to a less favorable institution without an adequate factfinding hearing. They sought an injunction setting aside the ordered transfer, declaratory relief and damages.

The District Court understood Wolff v. McDonnell, 418 U.S. 539, 71 Ohio Op.2d 336 (1974), to entitle respondents to notice and hearing and held both constitutionally inadequate in this case. Respondents were ordered returned to the general prison population at Norfolk until transferred after proper notice and hearing. Petitioners were also ordered to promulgate regulations to establish procedures governing future transfer hearings involving informant testimony. A divided panel of the Court of Appeals affirmed, holding that the transfers from Norfolk to maximum-security institutions involved "a significant modification of the overall conditions of confinement" and that this change in circumstances was "serious enough to trigger the application of due process protections."

We granted the prison officials' petition for writ of certiorari in order to determine whether the Constitution required petitioners to conduct a factfinding hearing in connection with the transfers in this case where state law does not condition the authority to transfer on the occurrence of specific acts of misconduct or other events and, if so, whether the hearings granted in this case were adequate. In light of our resolution of the first issue, we do not reach the second.

II

The Fourteenth Amendment prohibits any State from depriving a person of life, liberty, or property without due process of law. The initial inquiry is whether the transfer of respondents from Norfolk to Walpole and Bridgewater infringed or implicated a "liberty" interest of respondents within the meaning of the Due Process Clause. Contrary to the Court of Appeals, we hold that it did not. We reject at the outset the notion that *any* grievous loss visited upon a person by the State is sufficient to invoke the procedural protections of the Due Process Clause. In Board of Regents v. Roth, 408 U.S. 564 (1972), a university professor was deprived of his job, a loss which was surely a matter of great substance, but because the professor had no property interest in his position, due process procedures were not required in connection with his dismissal. We there held that the determining factor is the nature of the interest involved rather than its weight.

Similarly, we cannot agree that *any* change in the conditions of confinement having a substantial adverse impact on the prisoner involved is sufficient to invoke the protections of the Due Process Clause. The Due Process Clause by its own force forbids the State from convicting any person of crime and depriving him of his liberty without complying fully with the requirements of the Clause. But given a valid conviction, the criminal defendant has been constitutionally deprived of his liberty to the extent that the State may confine him and to subject him to the rules of its prison system so long as the conditions of confinement do not otherwise violate the Constitution. The Constitution does not require that the State have more than one prison for convicted felons; nor does it guarantee that the convicted prisoner will be placed in any particular prison if, as is likely, the State has more than one correctional institution. The initial decision to assign the convict to a particular institution is not subject to audit under the Due Process Clause, although the degree of confinement in one prison may be quite different from that in another. The conviction has sufficiently extinguished the defendant's liberty interest to empower the State to confine him in *any* of its prisons.

Neither, in our view, does the Due Process Clause in and of itself protect a duly convicted prisoner against transfer from one institution to another within the state prison system. Confinement in any of the State's institutions is within the normal limits or range of custody which the conviction has authorized the State to impose. That life in one prison is much more disagreeable than in another does not in itself signify that a Fourteenth Amendment liberty interest is implicated when a prisoner is transferred to the institution with the more severe rules.

Our cases hold that the convicted felon does not forfeit all constitutional protections by reason of his conviction and confinement in prison. He retains a variety of important rights that the courts must be alert to protect. See Wolff v. McDonnell, 418 U.S. 539, 556, 71 Ohio Op.2d 336, 342 (1974), and cases there cited. But none of these cases reaches this one; and to hold as we are urged to do that *any* substantial deprivation imposed by prison authorities triggers the procedural protections of the Due Process Clause would subject to judicial review a wide spectrum of discretionary actions that traditionally have been the business of prison administrators rather than of the federal courts.

Transfers between institutions, for example, are made for a variety of rea-sons and often involve no more than informed predictions as to what would best serve institutional security or the safety and welfare of the inmate. Yet under the approach urged here, any transfer, for whatever reason, would require a hearing as long as it could be said that the transfer would place the prisoner in substantially more burdensome conditions that he had been experiencing. We are unwilling to go so far.

Wolff v. McDonnell, on which the Court of Appeals heavily relied, is not to the contrary. Under that case, the Due Process Clause entitles a state prisoner to certain procedural protections when he is deprived of good-time credits because of serious misconduct. But the liberty interest there identified did not originate in the Constitution, which "itself does not guarantee good-time credit for satisfactory behavior while in prison." The State itself, not the Constitution, had "not only provided a statutory right to good time but also specifies that it is to be forfeited only for serious misbehavior." We concluded that:

"A person's liberty is equally protected, even when the liberty itself is a statutory creation of the State. The touchstone of due process is protection of the individual against arbitrary action of the Government, Dent v. West Virginia, 129 U.S. 114, 123 (1889). Since prisoners in Nebraska only lose good time credit if they are guilty of serious misconduct, the determination of whether such behavior has occurred becomes critical, and the minimum requirements of procedural due process appropriate for the States must be observed."

The liberty interest protected in Wolff had its roots in state law, and the minimum procedures appropriate under the circumstances were held required by the Due Process Clause "to insure that the state-created right is not arbitrarily abrogated." This is consistent with our approach in other due process cases such as Goss v. Lopez, 419 U.S. 565 (1975); Board of Regents v. Roth, 408 U.S. 564 (1972); Perry v. Sindermann, 408 U.S. 593 (1972); Goldberg v. Kelly, 397 U.S. 254 (1970).

Here, Massachusetts law conferred no right on the prisoner to remain in the prison to which he was initially assigned, defeasible only upon proof of specific acts of misconduct. Insofar as we are advised, transfers between Massachusetts prisons are not conditioned upon the occurrence of specified events. On the contrary, transfer in a wide variety of circumstances is vested in prison officials. The predicate for invoking the protection of the Fourteenth Amendment as construed and applied in Wolff v. McDonnell is totally nonexistent in this case.

Even if Massachusetts has not represented that transfers will occur only on the occurrence of certain events, it is argued that charges of serious misbehavior, as in this case, often initiate and heavily influence the transfer decision and that because allegations of misconduct may be erroneous, hearings should be held before transfer to a more confining institution is to be suffered by the prisoner. That an inmate's conduct, in general or in specific instances, may often be a major factor in the decision of prison officials to transfer him is to be expected unless it be assumed that transfers are mindless events. A prisoner's past and anticipated future behavior will very likely be taken into account in selecting a prison in which he will be initially incarcerated or to which he will be transferred to best serve the State's penological goals.

A prisoner's behavior may precipitate a transfer; and absent such behavior, perhaps transfer would not take place at all. But, as we have said, Massachusetts prison officials have the discretion to transfer prisoners for any number of reasons. Their discretion is not limited to instances of serious misconduct. As we understand it no legal interest or right of these respondents under Massachusetts law would have been violated by their transfer whether or not their misconduct had been proved in accordance with procedures that might be required by the Due Process Clause in other circumstances. Whatever expectation the prisoner may have in remaining at a particular prison so long as he behaves himself, it is too ephemeral and insubstantial to trigger procedural due process protections as long as prison officials have discretion to transfer him for whatever reason or for no reason at all.

Holding that arrangements like this are within reach of the procedural protections of the Due Process Clause would place the Clause astride the day-to-day functioning of state prisons and involve the judiciary in issues and discretionary decisions that are not the business of federal judges. We decline to so interpret and apply the Due Process Clause. The federal courts do not sit to supervise state prisons, the administration of which is of acute interest to the States. The individual States, of course, are free to follow another course, whether by statute, by rule or regulation or by interpretation of their own constitutions. They may thus decide that prudent prison administration requires pretransfer hearings. Our holding is that the Due Process Clause does not impose a nationwide rule mandating transfer hearings.

The judgment of the Court of Appeals accordingly is

Reversed.

* * *

MR. JUSTICE STEVENS, with whom MR. JUSTICE BRENNAN and MR. JUSTICE MARSHALL join, dissenting.

The Court's rationale is more disturbing than its narrow holding. If the Court had merely held "that the transfer of a prisoner from one penal institution to another does not cause a sufficiently grievous loss to amount to a deprivation of liberty within the meaning of the Due Process Clause of the Fourteenth Amendment, I would disagree with the conclusion but not with the constitutional analysis. The Court's holding today, however, appears to rest on a conception of "liberty" which I consider fundamentally incorrect.

The Court indicates that a "liberty interest" may have either of two sources. According to the Court, a liberty interest may "originate in the Constitution," or it may have "its roots in state law." Apart from those two possible origins, the Court is unable to find that a person has a constitutionally protected interest in liberty.

If a man were a creature of the State, the analysis would be correct. But neither the Bill of Rights nor the laws of sovereign States create the liberty which the Due Process Clause protects. The relevant constitutional provisions are limitations on the power of the sovereign to infringe on the liberty of the citizen. The relevant state laws either create property rights, or they curtail the freedom of the citizen who must live in an ordered society. Of course, law is essential to the exercise and enjoyment of individual liberty in a complex society. But it is not the source of liberty, and surely not the exclusive source.

I had though it self-evident that all men were endowed by their Creator with liberty as one of the cardinal unalienable rights. It is that basic freedom which the Due Process Clause protects, rather than the particular rights or privileges conferred by specific laws or regulations.

A correct description of the source of the liberty protected by the Constitution does not, of course, decide this case. For, by hypothesis, we are dealing with persons who may be deprived of their liberty because they have been convicted of criminal conduct after a fair trial. We should therefore first ask whether the deprivation of liberty which follows conviction is total or partial.

At one time the prevailing view was that deprivation was essentially total. The penitentiary inmate was considered "the slave of the State." Although the wording of the Thirteenth Amendment provided some support for that point of view, "courts in recent years have moderated the harsh implications of the Thirteenth Amendment."

The moderating trend culminated in this Court's landmark holding that notwithstanding the continuation of legal custody pursuant to a criminal conviction, a parolee has a measure of liberty that is entitled to constitutional protection.

"We see, therefore, that the liberty of a parolee, although indeterminate, includes many of the core values of unqualified liberty and its termination inflicts a 'grievous loss' on the parolee and often on others. It is hardly useful any longer to try to deal with this problem in terms of whether the parolee's liberty is a 'right' or a 'privilege.' By whatever name, the liberty is valuable and must be seen as within the protection of the Fourteenth Amendment. Its termination calls for some orderly process, however informal." Morrissey v. Brewer, 408 U.S. 471, 482.

Although the Court's opinion was narrowly written with careful emphasis on the permission given to the parolee to live outside the prison walls, the Court necessarily held that the individual possesses a residuum of constitutionally protected liberty while in legal custody pursuant to a valid conviction. For release on parole is merely conditional, and it does not interrupt the State's legal custody. I remain convinced that the Court of Appeals for the Seventh Circuit correctly analyzed the true significance of the Morrissey holding, when I wrote for that Court in 1973:

"In view of the fact that physical confinement is merely one species of legal custody, we are persuaded that Morrissey actually portends a more basic conceptual holding: liberty protected by the due process clause may—indeed must to some extent—coexist with legal custody pursuant to conviction. The deprivation of liberty following an adjudication of guilt is partial, not total. A residuum of constitutionally protected rights remains.

"As we noted in Morales v. Schmidt, the view once held that an inmate is a mere slave is now totally rejected. The restraints and the punishment which a criminal conviction entails do not place the citizen beyond the ethical tradition that accords respect to the dignity and intrinsic worth of every individual. 'Liberty' and 'custody' are not mutually exclusive concepts.

"If the Morrissey decision is not narrowly limited by the distinction between physical confinement and conditional liberty to live at large in society, it requires that due process precede any substantial deprivation of the liberty of persons in custody. We believe a due regard for the interests of the individual inmate, as well as the interests of that substantial segment of our total society represented by inmates, requires that Morrissey be so read." U.S. ex rel. Miller v. Twomey, 479 F.2d 701, 712-713

It demeans the holding in Morrissey—more importantly it demeans the concept of liberty itself—to ascribe to that holding nothing more than a protection of an interest that the State has created through its own prison regulations. For if the inmate's protected liberty interests are no greater than the State chooses to allow, he is really little more than the slave described in the 19th century cases. I think it clear that even the inmate retains an unalienable interest in liberty—at the very minimum the right to be treated with dignity—which the Constitution may never ignore.

This basic premise is not inconsistent with recognition of the obvious fact that the State must have wide latitude in determining the conditions of confinement that will be imposed following conviction of crime. To supervise and control its prison population, the State must retain the power to change the conditions for individuals, or for groups of prisoners, quickly and without judicial review. In may respects the State's problems in governing its inmate population are comparable to those encountered in governing a military force. Prompt and unquestioning obedience by the individual, even to commands he does not understand, may be essential to the preservation of order and discipline. Nevertheless, within the limits imposed by the basic restraints governing the controlled population, each individual retains his dignity and, in time, acquires a status that is entitled to respect.

Imprisonment is intended to accomplish more than the temporary removal of the offender from society in order to prevent him from committing like offenses during the period of his incarceration. While custody denies the inmate the opportunity to offend, it also gives him an opportunity to improve himself and to acquire skills and habits that will help him to participate in an open society after his release. Within the prison community, if any basic hypothesis is correct, he has a protected right to pursue his limited rehabilitative goals, or at the minimum, to maintain whatever attributes of dignity are associated with his status in a tightly controlled society. It is unquestionably within the power of the State to change that status, abruptly and adversely; but if the change is sufficiently grievous, it may not be imposed arbitrarily. In such case due process must be afforded.

That does not mean, of course, that every adversity amounts to a deprivation within the meaning of the Fourteenth Amendment. There must be grievous loss, and that term itself is somewhat flexible. I would certainly not consider every transfer within a prison system, even to more onerous conditions of confinement, such a loss. On the other hand, I am unable to identify a principle basis for differentiating between a transfer from the general prison population to solitary confinement and a transfer involving equally disparate conditions between one physical facility and another.

In view of the Court's basic holding, I merely note that I agree with the Court of Appeals that the transfer involved in this case was sufficiently serious to invoke the protection of the Constitution.

I respectfully dissent.

BELL v WOLFISH
441 U.S. 520, 60 L.Ed. 2d 447, 99 S.Ct. 1861 (1979)

[footnotes and citations omitted]

Mr. Justice Rehnquist delivered the opinion of the Court.

Over the past five Terms, this Court has in several decisions considered constitutional challenges to prison conditions or practices by convicted prisoners. This case requires us to examine the constitutional rights of pretrial detainees—those persons who have been charged with a crime but who have not yet been tried on the charge. The parties concede that to ensure their presence at trial, these persons legitimately may be incarcerated by the Government prior to a determination of their guilt or innocence, *** and it is the scope of their rights during this period of confinement prior to trial that is the primary focus of this case.

This lawsuit was brought as a class action in the United States District Court for the Southern District of New York to challenge numerous conditions of confinement and practices at the Metropolitan Correctional Center (MCC), a federally operated short term custodial facility in New

York City designed primarily to house pretrial detainees. The District Court, in the words of the Court of Appeals for the Second Circuit, "intervened broadly into almost every facet of the institution" and enjoined no fewer than 20 MCC practices on constitutional and statutory grounds. The Court of Appeals largely affirmed the District Court's constitutional rulings and in the process held that under the Due Process Clause of the Fifth Amendment, pretrial detainees may "be subjected to only those 'restrictions and privations' which 'inhere in their confinement itself or which are justified by compelling necessities of jail administration.' " *** We granted certiorari to consider the important constitutional questions raised by these decisions and to resolve an apparent conflict among the circuits. We now reverse.

I

The MCC was constructed in 1975 to replace the converted waterfront garage on West Street that had served as New York City's federal jail since 1928. It is located adjacent to the Foley Square federal courthouse and has as its primary objective the housing of persons who are being detained in custody prior to trial for federal criminal offenses in the United States District Courts for the Southern and Eastern Districts of New York and for the District of New Jersey. Under the Bail Reform Act a person in the federal system is committed to a detention facility only because no other less drastic means can reasonably ensure his presence at trial. In addition to pretrial detainees, the MCC also houses some convicted inmates who are awaiting sentencing or transportation to federal prison or

who are serving generally relatively short sentences in a service capacity at the MCC, convicted prisoners who have been lodged at the facility under writs of habeas corpus ad prosequendum or ad testificandum issued to ensure their presence at upcoming trials, witnesses in protective custody and persons incarcerated for contempt.

The MCC differs markedly from the familiar image of a jail; there are no barred cells, dank, colorless corridors, or clanging steel gates. It was intended to include the most advanced and innovative features of modern design of detention facilities. As the Court of Appeals stated: "[I]t represented the architectural embodiment of the best and most progressive penological planning." The key design element of the 12-story structure is the "modular" or "unit" concept, whereby each floor designed to house inmates has one or two largely self-contained residential units that replace the traditional cellblock jail construction. Each unit in turn has several clusters or corridors of private rooms or dormitories radiating from a central 2-story "multipurpose" or common room, to which each inmate has free access approximately 16 hours a day.

When the MCC opened in August 1975, the planned capacity was 449 inmates, an increase of 50% over the former West Street facility. Despite some dormitory accommodations, the MCC was designed primarily to house these inmates in 389 rooms, which originally were intended for single occupancy. While the MCC was under construction, however, the number of persons committed to pretrial detention began to rise at an "unprecedented rate." The Bureau of Prisons took several steps to accommodate this unexpected flow of persons assigned to the facility, but despite these efforts, the inmate population at the MCC rose above its planned capacity within a short time after its opening. To provide sleeping space for this increased population, the MCC replaced the single bunks in many of the individual rooms and dormitories with double bunks. Also, each week some newly arrived inmates had to sleep on cots in the common areas until they could be transferred to residential rooms as space became available.

On November 28, 1975, less than four months after the MCC had opened, the named respondents initiated this action by filing in the District Court a petition for a writ of habeas corpus. The District Court certified the case as a class action on behalf of all persons confined at the MCC, pretrial detainees and sentenced prisoners alike. The petition served up a veritable potpourri of complaints that implicated virtually every facet of the institution's conditions and practices. Respondents charged, inter alia, that they had been deprived of their statutory and constitutional rights because of overcrowded conditions, undue length of confinement, improper searches, inadequate recreational, educational and employment opportunities, insufficient staff and objectionable restrictions on the purchase and receipt of personal items and books.

In two opinions and a series of orders, the District Court enjoined numerous MCC practices and conditions. With respect to pretrial detainees, the court held that because they are "presumed to be innocent and held only to ensure their presence at trial, 'any deprivation or restriction of . . . rights beyond those which are necessary for confinement alone, must be justified by a compelling necessity.' " And while acknowledging that the rights of sentenced inmates are to be measured by the different standard of the Eighth Amendment, the court declared that to house "an inferior minority of persons . . . in ways found unconstitutional for the rest" would amount to cruel and unusual punishment.

Applying these standards on cross-motions for partial summary judgment, the District Court enjoined the practice of housing two inmates in the individual rooms and prohibited enforcement of the so-called "publisher-only" rule, which at the time of the court's ruling prohibited the receipt of all books and magazines mailed from outside the MCC except those sent directly from a publisher or a book club. After a trial on the remaining issues, the District Court enjoined, inter alia, the doubling of capacity in the dormitory areas, the use of the common rooms to provide temporary sleeping accommodations, the prohibition against inmates' receipt of packages containing food and items of personal property, and the practice of requiring inmates to expose their body cavities for visual inspection following contact visits. The court also granted relief in favor of pretrial detainees, but not convicted inmates, with respect to the requirement that detainees remain outside their rooms during routine inspections by MCC officials.

The Court of Appeals largely affirmed the District Court's rulings, although it rejected that court's Eighth Amendment analysis of conditions of confinement for convicted prisoners because the "parameters of judicial intervention into . . . conditions . . . for sentenced prisoners are more restrictive than in the case of pretrial detainees." Accordingly, the court remanded the matter to the District Court for it to determine whether the housing for sentenced inmates at the MCC was constitutionally "adequate." But the Court of Appeals approved the due process standard employed by the District Court in enjoining the conditions of pretrial confinement. It therefore held that the MCC had failed to make a showing of "compelling necessity" sufficient to justify housing two pretrial detainees in the individual rooms. And for purposes of our review (since petitioners challenge only some of the Court of Appeals' rulings), the court affirmed the District Court's granting of relief against the "publisher-only" rule, the practice of conducting body cavity searches after contact visits, the prohibition against receipt of packages of food and personal items from outside the institution, and the requirement that detainees remain outside their rooms during routine searches of the rooms by MCC officials.

II

As a first step in our decision, we shall address "double-bunking" as it is referred to by the parties, since it is a condition of confinement that is alleged only to deprive pretrial detainees of their liberty without due process of law in contravention of the Fifth Amendment.

***

A

The Court of Appeals did not dispute that the Government may permissibly incarcerate a person charged with a crime but not yet convicted to ensure his presence at trial. However, reasoning from the "premise that an individual is to be treated as innocent until proven guilty," the court concluded that pretrial detainees retain the "rights afforded unincarcerated individuals," and that therefore it is not sufficient that the conditions of confinement for pretrial detainees "merely comport with contemporary standards of decency prescribed by the cruel and unusual punishment clause of the eighth amendment." Rather, the court held, the Due Process Clause requires that pretrial detainees "be subjected to only those 'restrictions and privations' which 'inhere in their confinement itself or which are justified by compelling necessities of jail administration.' " Under the Court of Appeals' "compelling necessity" standard, "deprivation of the rights of detainees cannot be justified by the cries of fiscal necessity, . . . administrative convenience, . . . or by the cold comfort that conditions in other jails are worse." The court acknowledged, however, that it could not "ignore" our admonition in Procunier v Martinez, 416 US 396, 405, that "courts are ill-equipped to deal with the increasingly urgent problems of prison administration," and concluded that it would "not [be] wise for [it] to second-guess the expert administrators on matters on which they are better informed."

Our fundamental disagreement with the Court of Appeals is that we fail to find a source in the Constitution for its compelling necessity standard. Both the Court of Appeals and the District Court seem to have relied on the "presumption of innocence" as the source of the detainee's substantive right to be free from conditions of confinement that are not justified by compelling necessity. But the presumption of innocence provides no support for such a rule.

The presumption of innocence is a doctrine that allocates the burden of proof in criminal trials; it also may serve as an admonishment to the jury to judge an accused's guilt or innocence solely on the evidence adduced at trial and not on the basis of suspicions that may arise from the fact of his arrest, indictment or custody or from other matters not introduced as proof at trial. It is "an inaccurate, short-hand description of the right of the accused to 'remain inactive and secure, until the prosecution has taken up its burden and produced evidence and effected persuasion . . .' [; an] 'assumption' that is indulged in the absence of contrary evidence." Without question, the presumption of innocence plays an important role in our criminal justice system. "The principle that there is a presumption of innocence in favor of the accused is the undoubted law, axiomatic and elementary, and its enforcement lies at the foundation of the administration of our criminal law." But it has no application to a determination of the rights of a pretrial detainee during confinement before his trial has even begun.

The Court of Appeals also relied on what it termed the "indisputable rudiments of due process" in fashioning its compelling necessity test. We do not doubt that the Due Process Clause protects a detainee from certain conditions and restrictions of pretrial detainment. Nonetheless, that clause provides no basis for application of a compelling necessity standard to conditions of pretrial confinement that are not alleged to infringe

any other, more specific guarantee of the Constitution.

It is important to focus on what is at issue here. We are not concerned with the initial decision to detain an accused and the curtailment of liberty that such a decision necessarily entails. Neither respondents nor the courts below question that the Government may permissibly detain a person suspected of committing a crime prior to a formal adjudication of guilt. Nor do they doubt that the Government has a substantial interest in ensuring that persons accused of crimes are available for trials and, ultimately, for service of their sentences, or that confinement of such persons pending trial is a legitimate means of furthering that interest. Instead, what is at issue when an aspect of pretrial detention that is not alleged to violate any express guarantee of the Constitution is challenged, is the detainee's right to be free from punishment, and his understandable desire to be as comfortable as possible during his confinement, both of which may conceivably coalesce at some point. It seems clear that the Court of Appeals did not rely on the detainee's right to be free from punishment, but even if it had that right does not warrant adoption of that court's compelling necessity test. And to the extent the court relied on the detainee's desire to be free from discomfort, it suffices to say that this desire simply does not rise to the level of those fundamental liberty interests.***

B

In evaluating the constitutionality of conditions or restrictions of pretrial detention that implicate only the protection against deprivation of liberty without due process of law, we think that the proper inquiry is whether those conditions amount to punishment of the detainee. For under the Due Process Clause, a detainee may not be punished prior to an adjudication of guilt in accordance with due process of law. A person lawfully committed to pretrial detention has not been adjudged guilty of any crime. He has had only a "judicial determination of probable cause as a prerequisite to [the] extended restraint of [his] liberty following arrest." And, if he is detained for a suspected violation of a federal law, he also has had a bail hearing. Under such circumstances, the Government concededly may detain him to ensure his presence at trial and may subject him to the restrictions and conditions of the detention facility so long as those conditions and restrictions do not amount to punishment, or otherwise violate the Constitution.

Not every disability imposed during pretrial detention amounts to "punishment" in the constitutional sense, however. Once the Government has exercised its conceded authority to detain a person pending trial, it obviously is entitled to employ devices that are calculated to effectuate this detention. Traditionally, this has meant confinement in a facility which, no matter how modern or how antiquated, results in restricting the movement of a detainee in a manner in which he would not be restricted if he simply were free to walk the streets pending trial. Whether it be called a jail, a prison, or custodial center, the purpose of the facility is to detain. Loss of freedom of choice and privacy are inherent incidents of confinement in such a facility. And the fact that such detention interferes with the detainee's understandable desire to live as comfortably as possible and with as little restraint as possible during confinement does not convert the conditions or restrictions of detention into "punishment."

This Court has recognized a distinction between punitive measures that may not constitutionally be imposed prior to a determination of guilt and regulatory restraints that may. ***

The factors identified in *Mendoza-Martinez* [372 US 144] provide useful guideposts in determining whether particular restrictions and conditions accompanying pretrial detention amount to punishment in the constitutional sense of that word. A court must decide whether the disability is imposed for the purpose of punishment or whether it is but an incident of some other legitimate governmental purpose. Absent a showing of an expressed intent to punish on the part of detention facility officials, that determination generally will turn on "[w]hether an alternative purpose to which [the restriction] may rationally be connected is assignable for it, and whether it appears excessive in relation to the alternative purpose assigned [to it]." Thus, if a particular condition or restriction of pretrial detention is reasonably related to a legitimate governmental objective, it does not, without more, amount to "punishment." Conversely, if a restriction or condition is not reasonably related to a legitimate goal—if it is arbitrary or purposeless—a court permissibly may infer that the purpose of the governmental action is punishment that may not constitutionally be inflicted upon detainees qua detainees. Courts must be mindful that these inquiries spring from constitutional requirements and that judicial answers to them must reflect that fact rather than a court's idea of how best to operate a detention facility.

One further point requires discussion. The Government asserts, and respondents concede, that the "essential objective of pretrial confinement is to insure the detainees' presence at trial." While this interest undoubtedly justifies the original decision to confine an individual in some manner, we do not accept respondent's argument that the Government's interest in ensuring a detainee's presence at trial is the *only* objective that may justify restraints and conditions once the decision is lawfully made to confine a person. "If the government could confine or otherwise infringe the liberty of detainees only to the extent necessary to ensure their presence at trial, house arrest would in the end be the only constitutionally justified form of detention." The Government also has legitimate interests that stem from its need to manage the facility in which the individual is detained. These legitimate operational concerns may require administrative measures that go beyond those that are, strictly speaking, necessary to ensure that the detainee shows up at trial. For example, the Government must be able to take steps to maintain security and order at the institution and make certain no weapons or illicit drugs reach detainees. Restraints that are reasonably related to the institution's interest in maintaining jail security do not, without more, constitute unconstitutional punishment, even if they are discomforting and are restrictions that the detainee would not have experienced had he been released while awaiting trial. We need not here attempt to detail the precise ex-

tent of the legitimate governmental interests that may justify conditions or restrictions of pretrial detention. It is enough simply to recognize that in addition to ensuring the detainees' presence at trial, the effective management of the detention facility once the individual is confined is a valid objective that may justify imposition of conditions and restrictions of pretrial detention and dispel any inference that such restrictions are intended as punishment.

C

Judged by this analysis, respondents' claim that double-bunking violated their due process rights fails. Neither the District Court nor the Court of Appeals intimated that it considered double-bunking to constitute punishment; instead, they found that it contravened the compelling necessity test, which today we reject. On this record, we are convinced as a matter of law that double-bunking as practiced at the MCC did not amount to punishment and did not, therefore, violate respondents' rights under the Due Process Clause of the Fifth Amendment.

The rooms at the MCC that house pretrial detainees have a total floor space of approximately 75 square feet. Each of them designated for double-bunking contains a double bunkbed, certain other items of furniture, a wash basin and an uncovered toilet. Inmates generally are locked into their rooms from 11 p.m. to 6:30 a.m. and for brief periods during the afternoon and evening head counts. During the rest of the day, they may move about freely between their rooms and the common areas.

Based on affidavits and a personal visit to the facility, the District Court concluded that the practice of double-bunking was unconstitutional. The court relied on two factors for its conclusion: (1) the fact that the rooms were designed to house only one inmate, and (2) its judgment that confining two persons in one room or cell of this size constituted a "fundamental denial of decency, privacy, personal security, and, simply, civilized humanity...." The Court of Appeals agreed with the District Court. In response to petitioners' arguments that the rooms at the MCC were larger and more pleasant than the cells involved in the cases relied on by the District Court, the Court of Appeals stated:

"[W]e find the lack of privacy inherent in double-celling in rooms intended for one individual a far more compelling consideration than a comparison of square footage or the substitution of doors for bars, carpet for concrete, or windows for walls. The Government has simply failed to show any substantial justification for double-celling."

We disagree with both the District Court and the Court of Appeals that there is some sort of "one man, one cell" principle lurking in the Due Process Clause of the Fifth Amendment. While confining a given number of people in a given amount of space in such a manner as to cause them to endure genuine privations and hardship over an extended period of time might raise serious questions under the Due Process Clause as to whether those conditions amounted to punishment, nothing even approaching such hardship is shown by this record.

Detainees are required to spend only seven or eight hours each day in their rooms, during most or all of which they presumably are sleeping. The rooms provide more than adequate space for sleeping. During the remainder of the time, the detainees are free to move between their rooms and the common area. While double-bunking may have taxed some of the equipment or particular facilities in certain of the common areas, this does not mean that the conditions at the MCC failed to meet the standards required by the Constitution. Our conclusion in this regard is further buttressed by the detainees' length of stay at the MCC. Nearly all of the detainees are released within 60 days. We simply do not believe that requiring a detainee to share toilet facilities and this admittedly rather small sleeping place with another person for generally a maximum period of 60 days violates the Constitution.

III

Respondents also challenged certain MCC restrictions and practices that were designed to promote security and order at the facility on the ground that these restrictions violated the Due Process Clause of the Fifth Amendment, and certain other constitutional guarantees, such as the First and Fourth Amendments. The Court of Appeals seemed to approach the challenges to security restrictions in a fashion different from the other contested conditions and restrictions. It stated that "once it has been determined that the mere fact of confinement of the detainee justifies the restrictions, the institution must be permitted to use reasonable means to insure that its legitimate interests in security are safeguarded." The court might disagree with the choice of means to effectuate those interests, but it should not "second-guess the expert administrators on matters on which they are better informed.... Concern with minutiae of prison administration can only distract the court from detached consideration of the one overriding question presented to it: does the practice or condition violate the Constitution?" Nonetheless, the court affirmed the District Court's injunction against several security restrictions. The Court rejected the arguments of petitioners that these practices served the MCC's interest in security and order and held that the practices were unjustified interferences with the retained constitutional rights of *both* detainees and convicted inmates. In our view, the Court of Appeals failed to heed its own admonition not to "second-guess" prison administrators.

Our cases have established several general principles that inform our evaluation of the constitutionality of the restrictions at issue. First, we have held that convicted prisoners do not forfeit all constitutional protections by reason of their conviction and confinement in prison. "There is no iron curtain drawn between the Constitution and the prisons of this country." So, for example, our cases have held that sentenced prisoners enjoy freedom of speech and religion under the First and Fourteenth Amendments, that they are protected against invidious discrimination on the basis of race under the Equal Protection Clause of the Fourteenth Amendment, and that they may claim the protection of the Due Process Clause to prevent additional deprivation of life, liberty or property without due process of law,***. A fortiori, pretrial detainees, who have not been convicted of any crimes, retain at least those constitutional rights that we

have held are enjoyed by convicted prisoners.

But our cases also have insisted on a second proposition: simply because prison inmates retain certain constitutional rights does not mean that these rights are not subject to restrictions and limitations. "Lawful incarceration brings about the necessary withdrawal or limitation of many privileges and rights, a retraction justified by the considerations underlying our penal system." The fact of confinement as well as the legitimate goals and policies of the penal institution limit these retained constitutional rights. There must be a "mutual accommodation between institutional needs and objectives and the provisions of the Constitution that are of general application." This principle applies equally to pretrial detainees and convicted prisoners. A detainee simply does not possess the full range of freedoms of an unincarcerated individual.

Third, maintaining institutional security and preserving internal order and discipline are essential goals that may require limitation or retraction of the retained constitutional rights of both convicted prisoners and pretrial detainees. "Central to all other corrections goals is the institutional consideration of internal security within the corrections facilities themselves." Prison officials must be free to take appropriate action to ensure the safety of inmates and corrections personnel and to prevent escape or unauthorized entry. Accordingly, we have held that even when an institutional restriction infringes a specific constitutional guarantee, such as the First Amendment, the practice must be evaluated in the light of the central objective of prison administration, safeguarding institutional security.

Finally, as the Court of Appeals correctly acknowledged, the problems that arise in the day-to-day operation of a corrections facility are not susceptible of easy solutions. Prison administrators therefore should be accorded wide-ranging deference in the adoption and execution of policies and practices that in their judgment are needed to preserve internal order and discipline and to maintain institutional security. "Such considerations are peculiarly within the province and professional expertise of corrections officials, and, in the absence of substantial evidence in the record to indicate that the officials have exaggerated their response to these considerations, courts should ordinarily defer to their expert judgment in such matters." We further observe that on occasion, prison administrators may be "experts" only by Act of Congress or of a state legislature. But judicial deference is accorded not merely because the administrator ordinarily will, as a matter of fact in a particular case, have a better grasp of his domain than the reviewing judge, but also because the operation of our correctional facilities is peculiarly the province of the Legislative and Executive Branches of our Government, not the Judicial. With these teachings of our cases in mind, we turn to an examination of the MCC security practices that are alleged to violate the Constitution.

A

At the time of the lower courts' decisions, the Bureau of Prisons' "publisher-only" rule, which applies to all Bureau facilities, permitted inmates to receive books and magazines from outside the institution only if the materials were mailed directly from the publisher or a book club. The warden of the MCC stated in an affidavit that "serious" security and administrative problems were caused when bound items were received by inmates from unidentified sources outside the facility. He noted that in order to make a "proper and thorough" inspection of such items, prison officials would have to remove the covers of hardback books and to leaf through every page of all books and magazines to ensure that drugs, money, weapons or other contraband were not secreted in the material. "This search process would take a substantial and inordinate amount of available staff time." However, "there is relatively little risk that material received directly from the publisher or book club would contain contraband, and therefore, the security problems are significantly reduced without a drastic drain on staff resources."

The Court of Appeals rejected these security and administrative justifications and affirmed the District Court's order enjoining enforcement of the "publisher-only" rule at the MCC. The Court of Appeals held that the rule "severely and impermissibly restricts the reading material available to inmates" and therefore violates their First Amendment and due process rights.

It is desirable at this point to place in focus the precise question that now is before this Court. Subsequent to the decision of the Court of Appeals, the Bureau of Prisons amended its "publisher-only" rule to permit the receipt of books and magazines from bookstores as well as publishers and book clubs. In addition, petitioners have informed the Court that the Bureau proposes to amend the rule further to allow receipt of paperback books, magazines and other soft-covered materials from any source. The Bureau regards hardback books as the "more dangerous source of risk to institutional security," however, and intends to retain the prohibition against receipt of hardback books unless they are mailed directly from publishers, book clubs or bookstores. Accordingly, petitioners request this Court to review the District Court's injunction only to the extent it enjoins petitioners from prohibiting receipt of hardcover books that are not mailed directly from publishers, book clubs or bookstores.

We conclude that a prohibition against receipt of hardback books unless mailed directly from publishers, book clubs or bookstores does not violate the First Amendment rights of MCC inmates. That limited restriction is a rational response by prison officials to an obvious security problem. It hardly needs to be emphasized that hardback books are especially serviceable for smuggling contraband into an institution; money, drugs and weapons easily may be secreted in the bindings. They also are difficult to search effectively. There is simply no evidence in the record to indicate that MCC officials have exaggerated their response to this security problem and to the administrative difficulties posed by the necessity of carefully inspecting each book mailed from unidentified sources. Therefore, the considered judgment of these experts must control in the absence of prohibitions far more sweeping than those involved here.

Our conclusion that this limited restriction on receipt of hardback books does not infringe the First Amendment rights of MCC inmates is influenced by several other factors. The rule operates in a neutral fashion, without regard to the content of the expression. And there are alternative means of obtaining reading material that have not been shown to be burdensome or insufficient. "We regard the available 'alternative means of [communication as] a relevant factor' in a case such as this where 'we [are] called upon to balance First Amendment rights against [legitimate] governmental ... interests.' " The restriction, as it is now before us, allows soft bound books and magazines to be received from any source and hardback books to be received from publishers, bookstores and book clubs. In addition, the MCC has a "relatively large" library for use by inmates. To the limited extent the rule might possibly increase the cost of obtaining published materials, this Court has held that where "other avenues" remain available for the receipt of materials by inmates, the loss of "cost advantages does not fundamentally implicate *free speech* values." We are also influenced in our decision by the fact that the rule's impact on pretrial detainees is limited to a maximum period of approximately 60 days. In sum, considering all the circumstances, we view the rule, as we now find it, to be a "reasonable 'time, place and manner' regulation ... [that is] necessary to further significant governmental interests...."

B

Inmates at the MCC were not permitted to receive packages from outside the facility containing items of food or personal property, except for one package of food at Christmas. This rule was justified by MCC officials on three grounds. First, officials testified to "serious" security problems that arise from the introduction of such packages into the institution, the "traditional file in the cake kind of situation" as well as the concealment of drugs "in heels of shoes [and] seams of clothing." As in the case of the "publisher-only" rule, the warden testified that if such packages were allowed, the inspection process necessary to ensure the security of the institution would require a "substantial and inordinate amount of available staff time." Second, officials were concerned that the introduction of personal property into the facility would increase the risk of thefts, gambling and inmate conflicts, the "age-old problem of you have it and I don't." Finally, they noted storage and sanitary problems that would result from inmates' receipt of food packages. Inmates are permitted, however, to purchase certain items of food and personal property from the MCC commissary.

The District Court dismissed these justifications as "dire predictions." It was unconvinced by the asserted security problems because other institutions allow greater ownership of personal property and receipt of packages than does the MCC. And because the MCC permitted inmates to purchase items in the commissary, the court could not accept official fears of increased theft, gambling or conflicts if packages were allowed. Finally, it believed that sanitation could be assured by proper housekeeping regulations. Accordingly, it ordered the MCC to promulgate regulations to permit receipt of at least items of the

kind that are available in the commissary. The Court of Appeals accepted the District Court's analysis and affirmed, although it noted that the MCC could place a ceiling on the permissible dollar value of goods received and restrict the number of packages.

Neither the District Court nor the Court of Appeals identified which provision of the Constitution was violated by this MCC restriction. We assume, for present purposes, that their decisions were based on the Due Process Clause of the Fifth Amendment, which provides protection for convicted prisoners and pretrial detainees alike against the deprivation of their property without due process of law. But as we have stated, these due process rights of prisoners and pretrial detainees are not absolute; they are subject to reasonable limitation or retraction in light of the legitimate security concerns of the institution.

We think the District Court and the Court of Appeals have trenched too cavalierly into areas that are properly the concern of MCC officials. It is plain from their opinion, that the lower courts simply disagreed with the judgment of MCC officials about the extent of the security interests affected and the means required to further those interests. But our decisions have time and again emphasized that this sort of unguided substitution of judicial judgment for that of the expert prison administrators on matters such as this is inappropriate. We do not doubt that the rule devised by the District Court and modified by the Court of Appeals may be a reasonable way of coping with the problems of security, order and sanitation. It simply is not, however, the only constitutionally permissible approach to these problems. Certainly, the Due Process Clause does not mandate a "lowest common denominator" security standard, whereby a practice permitted at one penal institution must be permitted at all institutions.

Corrections officials concluded that permitting the introduction of packages of personal property and food would increase the risks of gambling, theft and inmate fights over that which the institution already experienced by permitting certain items to be purchased from its commissary. "It is enough to say that they have not been conclusively shown to be wrong in this view." It is also all too obvious that such packages are handy devices for the smuggling of contraband. There simply is no basis in this record for concluding that MCC officials have exaggerated their response to these serious problems or that this restriction is irrational. It does not therefore deprive the convicted inmates or pretrial detainees of the MCC of their property without due process of law in contravention of the Fifth Amendment.

C

The MCC staff conducts unannounced searches of inmate living areas at irregular intervals. These searches generally are formal unit "shakedowns" during which all inmates are cleared of the residential units, and a team of guards searches each room. Prior to the District Courts' order, inmates were not permitted to watch the searches. Officials testified that permitting inmates to observe room inspections would lead to friction between the inmates and security guards and would allow the inmates to attempt to frustrate the

search by distracting personnel and moving contraband from one room to another ahead of the search team.

The District Court held that this procedure could not stand as applied to pretrial detainees because MCC officials had not shown that the restriction was justified by "compelling necessity." The court stated that "[a]t least until or unless [petitioners] can show a pattern of violence or other disruptions taxing the powers of control—a kind of showing not remotely approached by the Warden's expressions—the security argument for banishing inmates while their rooms are searched must be rejected." It also noted that in many instances inmates suspected guards of thievery. The Court of Appeals agreed with the District Court. It saw "no reason whatsoever not to permit a detainee to observe the search of his room and belongings from a reasonable distance," although the court permitted the removal of any detainee who became "obstructive."

The Court of Appeals did not identify the constitutional provision on which it relied in invalidating the room search rule. The District Court stated that the rule infringed the detainee's interest in privacy and indicated that this interest in privacy was founded on the Fourth Amendment. It may well be argued that a person confined in a detention facility has no reasonable expectation of privacy with respect to his room or cell and that therefore the Fourth Amendment provides no protection for such a person. In any case, given the realities of institutional confinement, any reasonable expectation of privacy that a detainee retained necessarily would be of a diminished scope. Assuming, arguendo, that a pretrial detainee retains such a diminished expectation of privacy after commitment to a custodial facility, we nonetheless find that the room search rule does not violate the Fourth Amendment.

It is difficult to see how the detainee's interest in privacy is infringed by the room search rule. No one can rationally doubt that room searches represent an appropriate security measure and neither the District Court nor the Court of Appeals prohibited such searches. And even the most zealous advocate of prisoners' rights would not suggest that a warrant is required to conduct such a search. Detainees' drawers and beds and personal items may be searched, even after the lower courts' rulings. Permitting detainees to observe the searches does not lessen the invasion of their privacy; its only conceivable beneficial effect would be to prevent theft or misuse by those conducting the search. The room search rule simply facilitates the safe and effective performance of the search which all concede may be conducted. The rule itself, then, does not render the searches "unreasonable" within the meaning of the Fourth Amendment.

D

Inmates at all Bureau of Prisons facilities, including the MCC, are required to expose their body cavities for visual inspection as a part of a strip search conducted after every contact visit with a person from outside the institution. Corrections officials testified that visual cavity searches were necessary not only to discover but also to deter the smuggling of weapons, drugs and other contraband into the institution. The District Court upheld the strip search

procedure but prohibited the body cavity searches, absent probable cause to believe that the inmate is concealing contraband. Because petitioners proved only one instance in the MCC's short history where contraband was found during a body cavity search, the Court of Appeals affirmed. In its view, the "gross violation of personal privacy inherent in such a search cannot be outweighed by the government's security interest in maintaining a practice of so little actual utility."

Admittedly, this practice instinctively gives us the most pause. However, assuming for present purposes that inmates, both convicted prisoners and pretrial detainees, retain some Fourth Amendment rights upon commitment to a corrections facility, we nonetheless conclude that these searches do not violate that Amendment. The Fourth Amendment prohibits only unreasonable searches, and under the circumstances, we do not believe that these searches are unreasonable.

The test of reasonableness under the Fourth Amendment is not capable of precise definition or mechanical application. In each case it requires a balancing of the need for the particular search against the invasion of personal rights that the search entails. Courts must consider the scope of the particular intrusion, the manner in which it is conducted, the justification for initiating it and the place in which it is conducted. A detention facility is a unique place fraught with serious security dangers. Smuggling of money, drugs, weapons and other contraband is all too common an occurrence. And inmate attempts to secrete these items into the facility by concealing them in body cavities are documented in this record, ... That there has been only one instance where an MCC inmate was discovered attempting to smuggle contraband into the institution on his person may be more a testament to the effectiveness of this search technique as a deterrent than to any lack of interest on the part of the inmates to secrete and import such items when the opportunity arises.

We do not underestimate the degree to which these searches may invade the personal privacy of inmates. Nor do we doubt, as the District Court noted, that on occasion a security guard may conduct the search in an abusive fashion. Such abuse cannot be condoned. The searches must be conducted in a reasonable manner. But we deal here with the question whether visual body cavity inspections as contemplated by the MCC rules can *ever* be conducted on less than probable cause. Balancing the significant and legitimate security interests of the institution against the privacy interests of the inmates, we conclude that they can.

IV

Nor do we think that the four MCC security restrictions and practices described in Part III, supra, constitute "punishment" in violation of the rights of pretrial detainees under the Due Process Clause of the Fifth Amendment. Neither the District Court nor the Court of Appeals suggested that these restrictions and practices were employed by MCC officials with an intent to punish the pretrial detainees housed there. Respondents do not even make such a suggestion; they simply argue that the restrictions were greater than necessary to satisfy

petitioners' legitimate interest in maintaining security. Therefore, the determination whether these restrictions and practices constitute punishment in the constitutional sense depends on whether they are rationally related to a legitimate nonpunitive governmental purpose and whether they appear excessive in relation to that purpose. Ensuring security and order at the institution is a permissible nonpunitive objective, whether the facility houses pretrial detainees, convicted inmates, or both. For the reasons set forth in Part III, supra, we think that these particular restrictions and practices were reasonable responses by MCC officials to legitimate security concerns. Respondents simply have not met their heavy burden of showing that these officials have exaggerated their response to the genuine security considerations that actuated these restrictions and practices. And as might be expected of restrictions applicable to pretrial detainees, these restrictions were of only limited duration so far as the MCC pretrial detainees were concerned.

V

There was a time not too long ago when the federal judiciary took a completely "hands-off" approach to the problem of prison administration. In recent years, however, these courts largely have discarded this "hands-off" attitude and have waded into this complex arena. The deplorable conditions and draconian restrictions of some of our Nation's prisons are too well known to require recounting here, and the federal courts rightly have condemned these sordid aspects of our prison systems. But many of these same courts have, in the name of the Constitution, become increasingly enmeshed in the minutiae of prison operations. Judges, after all, are human. They, no less than others in our society, have a natural tendency to believe that their individual solutions to often intractable problems are better and more workable than those of the persons who are actually charged with and trained in the running of the particular institution under examination. But under the Constitution, the first question to be answered is not whose plan is best, but in what branch of the Government is lodged the authority to initially devise the plan. This does not mean that constitutional rights are not to be scrupulously observed. It does mean, however, that the inquiry of federal courts into prison management must be limited to the issue of whether a particular system violates any prohibition of the Constitution, or in the case of a federal prison, a statute. The wide range of "judgment calls" that meet constitutional and statutory requirements are confided to officials outside of the Judicial Branch of Government.

The judgment of the Court of Appeals is, accordingly, reversed and the case is remanded for proceedings consistent with this opinion.

It is so ordered.

SEPARATE OPINIONS

Mr. Justice **Powell**, concurring in part and dissenting in part.

I join the opinion of the Court except the discussion and holding with respect to body cavity searches. In view of the serious intrusion on one's privacy occasioned by such a search, I think at least some level of cause, such as a reasonable suspicion, should be

required to justify the anal and genital searches described in this case. I therefore dissent on this issue.

Mr. Justice **Marshall**, dissenting.

***

III

D

In my view, the body cavity searches of MCC inmates represent one of the most grievous offenses against personal dignity and common decency. After every contact visit with someone from outside the facility, including defense attorneys, an inmate must remove all of his or her clothing, bend over, spread the buttocks, and display the anal cavity for inspection by a correctional officer. Women inmates must assume a suitable posture for vaginal inspection, while men must raise their genitals. And, as the Court neglects to note, because of time pressures, this humiliating spectacle is frequently conducted in the presence of other inmates.

The District Court found that the stripping was "unpleasant, embarrassing, and humiliating." A psychiatrist testified that the practice placed inmates in the most degrading position possible, a conclusion amply corroborated by the testimony of the inmates themselves. There was evidence, moreover, that these searches engendered among detainees fears of sexual assault, were the occasion for actual threats of physical abuse by guards, and caused some inmates to forego personal visits.

Not surprisingly, the Government asserts a security justification for such inspections. These searches are necessary, it argues, to prevent inmates from smuggling contraband into the facility. In crediting this justification despite the contrary findings of the two courts below, the Court overlooks the critical facts. As respondents point out, inmates are required to wear one-piece jumpsuits with zippers in the front. To insert an object into the vaginal or anal cavity, an inmate would have to remove the jumpsuit at least from the upper torso. Since contact visits occur in a glass enclosed room and are continuously monitored by corrections officers, such a feat would seem extraordinarily difficult. There was medical testimony, moreover, that inserting an object into the rectum is painful and "would require time and opportunity which is not available in the visiting areas," and that visual inspection would probably not detect an object once inserted. Additionally, before entering the visiting room, visitors and their packages are searched thoroughly by a metal detector, fluoroscope, and by hand. Correction officers may require that visitors leave packages or handbags with guards until the visit is over. Only by blinding itself to the facts presented on this record can the Court accept the Government's security rationale.

Without question, these searches are an imposition of sufficient gravity to invoke the compelling necessity standard. It is equally indisputable that they cannot meet that standard. Indeed, the procedure is so unnecessarily degrading that it "shocks the conscience." Even in Rochin, the police had reason to believe that the petitioner had swallowed contraband. Here, the searches are employed absent any suspicion of wrongdoing. It was this aspect of the MCC practice that the Court of Appeals

redressed, requiring that searches be conducted only when there is probable cause to believe that the inmate is concealing contraband. The Due Process Clause, on any principled reading, dictates no less.

That the Court can uphold these indiscriminate searches highlights the bankruptcy of its basic analysis. Under the test adopted today, the rights of detainees apparently extend only so far as detention officials decide the cost and security will permit. Such unthinking deference to administrative convenience cannot be justified where the interests at stake are those of presumptively innocent individuals, many of whose only proven offense is the inability to afford bail. I dissent.

Mr. Justice **Stevens**, with whom Mr. Justice **Brennan** joins, dissenting.

This is not an equal protection case. An empirical judgment that most persons formally accused of criminal conduct are probably guilty would provide a rational basis for a set of rules that treat them like convicts until they establish their innocence. No matter how rational such an approach might be—no matter how acceptable in a community where equality of status is the dominant goal—it is obnoxious to the concept of individual freedom protected by the Due Process Clause. If ever accepted in this country, it would work a fundamental change in the character of our free society.

Nor is this an Eighth Amendment case. That provision of the Constitution protects individuals convicted of crimes from punishment that is cruel and unusual. The pretrial detainees whose rights are at stake in this case, however, are innocent men and women who have been convicted of no crimes. Their claim is not that they have been subjected to cruel and unusual punishment in violation of the Eighth Amendment, but that to subject them to any form of punishment at all is an unconstitutional deprivation of their liberty.

This is a due process case. The most significant—and I venture to suggest the most enduring—part of the Court's opinion today is its recognition of this initial constitutional premise. The Court squarely holds that "under the Due Process Clause, a detainee may not be punished prior to an adjudication of guilt in accordance with due process of law."

This right to be free of punishment is not expressly embodied in any provision in the Bill of Rights. Nor is the source of this right found in any statute. The source of this fundamental freedom is the word "liberty" itself as used in the Due Process Clause, and as informed by "history, reason, the past course of decisions," and the judgment and experience of "those whom the Constitution entrusted" with interpreting that word.

In my opinion, this latter proposition is obvious and indisputable. Nonetheless, it is worthy of emphasis because the Court has now accepted it in principle. In recent years, the Court has mistakenly implied that the concept of liberty encompasses only those rights that are either created by statute or regulation or are protected by an express provision of the Bill of Rights. Today, however, without the help of any statute, regulation, or express provision of the Constitution, the Court has derived the innocent person's right not to be punished from the Due Process Clause itself. It has accordingly abandoned its parsimonious definition of the "liberty" protected by the majestic words of the Clause. I concur in that abandonment. It is with regard to the scope of this fundamental right that we part company.

I

* * *

Prior to conviction every individual is entitled to the benefit of a presumption both that he is innocent of prior criminal conduct and that he has no present intention to commit any offense in the immediate future. That presumption does not imply that he may not be detained or otherwise subjected to restraints on the basis of an individual showing of probable cause that he poses relevant risks to the community. For our system of justice has always and quite properly functioned on the assumption that probable cause to believe (1) that a person has committed a crime, and (2) that absent the posting of bail he poses at least some risk of flight, justifies pretrial detention to ensure his presence at trial.

The fact that an individual may be unable to pay a bail bond, however, is an insufficient reason for subjecting him to indignities that would be appropriate punishment for convicted felons. Nor can he be subject on that basis to onerous restraints that might properly be considered regulatory with respect to particularly obstreperous or dangerous arrestees. An innocent man who has no propensity toward immediate violence, escape or subversion may not be dumped into a pool of second-class citizens and subjected to restraints designed to regulate others who have. For him, such treatment amounts to punishment. And because the due process guarantee is individual and personal, it mandates that an innocent person be treated as an individual human being and be free of treatment which, as to him, is punishment.

It is not always easy to determine whether a particular restraint serves the legitimate, regulatory goal of ensuring a detainee's presence at trial and his safety and security in the meantime, or the unlawful end of punishment. But the courts have performed that task in the past, and can and should continue to perform it in the future. Having recognized the constitutional right to be free of punishment the Court may not point to the difficulty of the task as a justification for confining the scope of the punishment concept so narrowly that it effectively abdicates to correction officials the judicial responsibility to enforce the guarantees of due process.

In addressing the constitutionality of the rules at issue in this case, the Court seems to say that as long as the correction officers are not motivated by "an expressed intent to punish" their wards, and as long as their rules are not "arbitrary or purposeless," these rules are an acceptable form of regulation and not punishment. Lest that test be too exacting, the Court abjectly defers to the prison administrator unless his conclusions are "conclusively shown to be wrong."

Applying this test, the Court concludes that enforcement of the challenged restrictions does not constitute punishment because there is no showing of a subjective intent to punish and there is a rational basis for each of the challenged rules. In my view, the Court has reached an untenable conclusion because its test for punishment is unduly permissive.

The requirement that restraints have a rational basis provides an individual with virtually no protection against punishment. Any restriction that may reduce the cost of the facility's warehousing function could not be characterized as "purposeless or arbitrary" and could not be "conclusively shown" to have no reasonable relation to the Government's mission. This is true even of a restraint so severe that it might be cruel and unusual.

Nor does the Court's intent test ensure the individual the protection that the Constitution guarantees. For the Court seems to use the term intent to mean the subjective intent of the jail administrator. This emphasis can only "encourage hypocrisy and unconscious self-deception." While a subjective intent may provide a sufficient reason for finding that punishment has been inflicted, such an intent is clearly not a necessary nor even the most common element of a punitive sanction.

In short, a careful reading of the Court's opinion reveals that it has attenuated the detainee's constitutional protection against punishment into nothing more than a prohibition against irrational classifications or barbaric treatment. Having recognized in theory that the source of that protection is the Due Process Clause, the Court has in practice defined its scope in the far more permissive terms of equal protection and Eighth Amendment analysis.

* * *

VITEK v. JONES
449 U.S. 433, 101 S. Ct. 703, 66 L. Ed. 2d 641 (1980)

[footnotes and citations omitted]

Mr. JUSTICE WHITE delivered the opinion of the court.

The question in this case is whether the Due Process Clause of the Fourteenth Amendment entitles a prisoner convicted and incarcerated in the State of Nebraska to certain procedural protections, including notice, an adversary hearing, and provision of counsel, before he is transferred involuntarily to a state mental hospital for treatment of a mental disease or defect.

I

Nebraska Rev Stat § 83-176(2) (1976) authorizes the Director of Correctional Services to designate any available, suitable, and appropriate residence facility or institution as a place of confinement for any state prisoner and to transfer a prisoner from one place of confinement to another. Section 83-180(1), however, provides that when a designated physician or psychologist finds that a prisoner "suffers from a mental disease or defect" and "cannot be given proper treatment in that facility," the director may transfer him for examination, study, and treatment to another institution within or without the Department of Corrections. Any prisoner so transferred to a mental hospital is to be returned to the Department if, prior to the expiration of his sentence, treatment is no longer necessary. Upon expiration of sentence, if the State desires to retain the prisoner in a mental hospital, civil commitment proceedings must be promptly commenced.

On May 31, 1974, Jones was convicted of robbery and sentenced to a term of three to nine years in state prison. He was transferred to the penitentiary hospital in January 1975. Two days later he was placed in solitary confinement, where he set his mattress on fire, burning himself severely. He was treated in the burn unit of a private hospital. Upon his release and based on findings required by § 83-180 that he was suffering from a mental illness or defect and could not receive proper treatment in the penal complex, he was transferred to the security unit of the Lincoln

Regional Center, a state mental hospital under the jurisdiction of the Department of Public Institutions.

Jones then intervened in this case, which was brought by other prisoners against the appropriate state officials (the State) challenging on procedural due process grounds the adequacy of the procedures by which the Nebraska statutes permit transfers from the prison complex to a mental hospital. On August 17, 1976, a three-judge District Court denied the State's motion for summary judgment and trial ensued. On September 12, 1977, the District Court declared § 83-180 unconstitutional as applied to Jones, holding that transferring Jones to a mental hospital without adequate notice and opportunity for a hearing deprived him of liberty without due process of law contrary to the Fourteenth Amendment and that such transfers must be accompanied by adequate notice, an adversary hearing before an independent decision-maker, a written statement by the factfinder of the evidence relied on and the reasons for the decision, and the availability of appointed counsel for indigent prisoners. *Miller* v. *Vitek.* Counsel was requested to suggest appropriate relief.

In response to this request, Jones revealed that on May 27, 1977, prior to the District Court's decision, he had been transferred from Lincoln Regional Center to the psychiatric ward of the penal complex but prayed for an injunction against further transfer to Lincoln Regional Center. The State conceded that an injunction should enter if the District Court was firm in its belief that the section was unconstitutional. The District Court then entered its judgment declaring § 83-180 unconstitutional as applied to Jones and permanently enjoining the

State from transferring Jones to Lincoln Regional Center without following the procedures prescribed in its judgment.

We noted probable jurisdiction 434 US 1060. Meanwhile, Jones had been paroled, but only on condition that he accept psychiatric treatment at the Veterans' Administration hospital. We vacated the judgment of the District Court and remanded the case to that court for consideration of the question of mootness. *Vitek v. Jones.* Both the State and Jones at this juncture insisted that the case was not moot. The State represented that because "Jones' history of mental illness indicates a serious threat to his own safety, as well as to that of others ... there is a very real expectation" that he would again be transferred if the injunction was removed. Jones insisted that he was receiving treatment for mental illness against his will and that he was continuing to suffer from the stigmatizing consequences of the previous determination that he was mentally ill. On these representations, the District Court found that the case was not moot because Jones "is subject to and is in fact under threat of being transferred to the state mental hospital under § 83-180." The District Court reinstated its original judgment. We postponed consideration of jurisdiction to a hearing on the merits. 441 US 922. Meanwhile, Jones had violated his parole, his parole had been revoked, and he had been reincarcerated in the penal complex.

II

We agree with the parties in this case that a live controversy exists and that the case is not moot, Jones was declared to be mentally ill pursuant to § 83-180 and was transferred to a mental hospital and treated. He was later paroled but only on condition that he accept mental treatment. He violated that parole and has been returned to the penal complex. On our remand to consider mootness, the District Court, relying on Jones' history of mental illness and the State's representation that he represented a serious threat to his own safety as well as to that of others, found that Jones "is in fact under threat of being transferred to the state mental hospital under § 83-180." We see no reason to disagree with the District Court's assessment at that time, and the reality of the controversy between Jones and the State has not been lessened by the cancellation of his parole and his return to the state prison, where he is protected from further transfer by the outstanding judgment and injunction of the District Court. The State, believing that the case is not moot, wants the injunction removed by the reversal of the District Court's judgment. Jones, on the other hand, insists that the judgment of the District Court be sustained and the protection against transfer to a mental hospital, except in accordance with the specified procedures, be retained.

Against this background, it is not "absolutely clear," absent the injunction, "that the allegedly wrongful behavior could not reasonably be expected to recur." Furthermore, as the matter now stands, the § 83-180 determination that Jones suffered from mental illness has been declared infirm by the District Court. Vacating the District Court's judgment as moot would not only vacate the injunction against transfer but also the declaration that the procedures employed by the State afforded an inadequate basis for declaring Jones to be mentally ill.

In the posture of the case, it is not moot.

III

On the merits, the threshold question in this case is whether the involuntary transfer of a Nebraska state prisoner to a mental hospital implicates a liberty interest that is protected by the Due Process Clause. The District Court held that it did and offered two related reasons for its conclusion. The District Court first identified a liberty interest rooted in § 83-180(1), under which a prisoner could reasonably expect that he would not be transferred to a mental hospital without a finding that he was suffering from a mental illness for which he could not secure adequate treatment in the correctional facility. Second, the District Court was convinced that characterizing Jones as a mentally ill patient and transferring him to the Lincoln Regional Center had "some stigmatizing" consequences which, together with the mandatory behavior modification treatment to which Jones would be subject at the Lincoln Center, constituted a major change in the conditions of confinement amounting to a "grievous loss" that should not be imposed without the opportunity for notice and an adequate hearing. We agree with the District Court in both respects.

A

We have repeatedly held that state statutes may create liberty interests that are entitled to the procedural protections of the Due Process Clause of the Fourteenth Amendment. There is no "constitutional or inherent right" to parole, Greenholtz v. Nebraska Penal Inmates, 442 U.S. 1, 7 (1979), but once a State grants a prisoner the conditional liberty properly dependent on the observance of special parole restrictions, due process protections attach to the decision to revoke parole. Morrissey v. Brewer, 408 U.S. 471 (1972). The same is true of the revocation of probation. Gagnon v. Scarpelli, 411 U.S. 778 (1973). In Wolff v. McDonnell, 418 U.S. 539 (1974), we held that a state-created right to good-time credits, which could be forfeited only for serious misbehavior, constituted a liberty interest protected by the Due Process Clause. We also noted that the same reasoning could justify extension of due process protections to a decision to impose "solitary" confinement because "[it] represents a major change in the conditions of confinement and is normally imposed only when it is claimed and proved that there has been a major act of misconduct." Once a State has granted prisoners a liberty interest, we held that due process protections are necessary "to insure that the state-created right is not arbitrarily abrogated."

In Meachum v. Fano, 427 U.S. 215 (1976), and Montanye v. Haymes, 427 U.S. 236 (1976), we held that the transfer of a prisoner from one prison to another does not infringe a protected liberty interest. But in those cases transfers were discretionary with the prison authorities, and in neither case did the prisoner possess any right or justifiable expectation that he would not be transferred except for misbehavior or upon the occurrence of other specified events. Hence, "the predicate for invoking the protection of the Fourteenth Amendment as construed and applied in Wolff v. McDonnell [was] totally nonexistent." Meachum v. Fano.

Following Meachum v. Fano and Montanye v. Haymes, we continued to recognize that state statutes may grant prisoners liberty interests that invoke due process protections when prisoners are transferred to solitary confinement for disciplinary or administrative reasons. Enomoto v. Wright, 434 U.S. 1052 (1978), summarily affg 462 F Supp 397 (ND Cal 1976). Similarly, in Greenholtz v. Nebraska Penal Inmates, supra, we held that state law granted petitioners a sufficient expectancy of parole to entitle them to some measure of constitutional protection with respect to parole decisions.

We think the District Court properly understood and applied these decisions. Section 83-180(1) provides that if a designated physician finds that a prisoner "suffers from a mental disease or defect" that "cannot be given proper treatment" in prison, the Director of Correctional Services may transfer a prisoner to a mental hospital. The District Court also found that in practice prisoners are transferred to a mental hospital only if it is determined that they suffer from a mental disease or defect that cannot adequately be treated within the penal complex. This "objective expectation, firmly fixed in state law and official Penal Complex practice," that a prisoner would not be transferred unless he suffered from a mental disease or defect that could not be adequately treated in the prison, gave Jones a liberty interest that entitled him to the benefits of appropriate procedures in connection with determining the conditions that warranted his transfer to a mental hospital. Under our cases, this conclusion of the District Court is unexceptionable.

Appellants maintain that any state-created liberty interest that Jones had was completely satisfied once a physi-

cian or psychologist designated by the director made the findings required by § 83-180(1) and that Jones was not entitled to any procedural protections. But if the State grants a prisoner a right or expectation that adverse action will not be taken against him except upon the occurrence of specified behavior, "the determination of whether such behavior has occurred becomes critical, and the minimum requirements of procedural due process appropriate for the circumstances must be observed." Wolff v. McDonnell. These minimum requirements being a matter of federal law, they are not diminished by the fact that the State may have specified its own procedures that it may deem adequate for determining the preconditions to adverse official action. In Morrissey, Gagnon, and Wolff, the States had adopted their own procedures for determining whether conditions warranting revocation of parole, probation, or good-time credits had occurred; yet we held that those procedures were constitutionally inadequate. In like manner, Nebraska's reliance on the opinion of a designated physician or psychologist for determining whether the conditions warranting a transfer exist neither removes the prisoner's interest from due process protection nor answers the question of what process is due under the Constitution.

B

The District Court was also correct in holding that independently of § 83-180(1), the transfer of a prisoner from a prison to a mental hospital must be accompanied by appropriate procedural protections. The issue is whether after a conviction for robbery, Jones retained a residuum of liberty that would be infringed by a transfer to a mental hospital without complying with minimum requirements of due process.

We have recognized that for the ordinary citizen, commitment to a mental hospital produces "a massive curtailment of liberty," Humphrey v. Cady, 405 U.S. 504 (1972), and in consequence "requires due process protection." Addington v. Texas, 441 U.S. 418 (1979); O'Connor v. Donaldson, 422 U.S. 563, 580 (1975) (Burger, C.J., concurring). The loss of liberty produced by an involuntary commitment is more than a loss of freedom from confinement. It is indisputable that commitment to a mental hospital "can engender adverse social consequences to the individual" and that "[w]hether we label this phenomena 'stigma' or choose to call it something else . . . we recognize that it can occur and that it can have a very significant impact on the individual." Also, "[a]mong the historic liberties" protected by the Due Process Clause is the "right to be free from, and to obtain judicial relief for, unjustified intrusions on personal security." Ingraham v. Wright, 430 U.S. 651 (1977). Compelled treatment in the form of mandatory behavior modification programs, to which the District Court found Jones was exposed in this case, was a proper factor to be weighed by the District Court.

The District Court, in its findings, was sensitive to these concerns:

"[T]he fact of greater limitations on freedom of action at the Lincoln Regional Center, the fact that a transfer to the Lincoln Regional Center has some stigmatizing consequences, and the fact that additional mandatory behavior modification systems are used at the Lincoln Regional Center combine to make the transfer a 'major change

in the conditions of confinement' amounting to a 'grievous loss' to the inmate." Miller v. Vitek, 437 F Supp, at 573.

Were an ordinary citizen to be subjected involuntarily to these consequences, it is undeniable that protected liberty interests would be unconstitutionally infringed absent compliance with the procedures required by the Due Process Clause. We conclude that a convicted felon also is entitled to the benefit of procedures appropriate in the circumstances before he is found to have a mental disease and transferred to a mental hospital.

Undoubtedly, a valid criminal conviction and prison sentence extinguish a defendant's right to freedom from confinement. Greenholtz v. Nebraska Penal Inmates. Such a conviction and sentence sufficiently extinguish a defendant's liberty "to empower the State to confine him in any of its prisons." Meachum v. Fano. It is also true that changes in the conditions of confinement having a substantial adverse impact on the prisoner are not alone sufficient to invoke the protections of the Due Process Clause "[a]s long as the conditions or degree of confinement to which the prisoner is subjected is within the sentence imposed upon him." Montanye v. Haymes.

Appellants maintain that the transfer of a prisoner to a mental hospital is within the range of confinement justified by imposition of a prison sentence, at least after certification by a qualified person that a prisoner suffers from a mental disease or defect. We cannot agree. None of our decisions holds that conviction for a crime entitles a State not only to confine the convicted person but also to determine that he has a mental illness and to subject him involuntarily to institutional care in a mental hospital. Such consequences visited on the prisoner are qualitatively different from the punishment characteristically suffered by a person convicted of crime. Our cases recognize as much and reflect an understanding that involuntary commitment to a mental hospital is not within the range of conditions of confinement to which a prison sentence subjects an individual. A criminal conviction and sentence of imprisonment extinguish an individual's right to freedom from confinement for the term of his sentence, but they do not authorize the State to classify him as mentally ill and to subject him to involuntary psychiatric treatment without affording him additional due process protections.

In light of the findings made by the District Court, Jones' involuntary transfer to the Lincoln Regional Center pursuant to § 83-180, for the purpose of psychiatric treatment, implicated a liberty interest protected by the Due Process Clause. Many of the restrictions on the prisoner's freedom of action at the Lincoln Regional Center by themselves might not constitute the deprivation of a liberty interest retained by a prisoner, see Wolff v. McDonnell; cf. Baxter v. Palmigiano, 425 U.S. 308, 323 (1976). But here, the stigmatizing consequences of a transfer to a mental hospital for involuntary psychiatric treatment, coupled with the subjection of the prisoner to mandatory behavior modification as a treatment for mental illness, constitute the kind of deprivations of liberty that requires procedural protections.

IV

The District Court held that to afford sufficient protection to the liberty interest it had identified, the State was required to observe the following minimum procedures before transferring a prisoner to a mental hospital:

"A. Written notice to the prisoner that a transfer to a mental hospital is being considered;

"B. A hearing, sufficiently after the notice to permit the prisoner to prepare, at which disclosure to the prisoner is made of the evidence being relied upon for the transfer and at which an opportunity to be heard in person and to present documentary evidence is given;

"C. An opportunity at the hearing to present testimony of witnesses by the defense and to confront and cross-examine witnesses called by the state, except upon a finding, not arbitrarily made, of good cause for not permitting such presentation, confrontation, or cross-examination;

"D. An independent decisionmaker;

"E. A written statement by the factfinder as to the evidence relied on and the reasons for transferring the inmate;

"F. Availability of legal counsel, furnished by the state, if the inmate is financially unable to furnish his own; and

"G. Effective and timely notice of all the foregoing rights." 437 F Supp, at 575.

A

We think the District Court properly identified and weighed the relevant factors in arriving at its judgment. Concededly the interest of the State in segregating and treating mentally ill patients is strong. The interest of the prisoner in not being arbitrarily classified as mentally ill and subjected to unwelcome treatment is also powerful, however; and as the District Court found, the risk of error in mak-

ing the determinations required by §
83-180 is substantial enough to warrant appropriate procedural safeguards against error.

We recognize that the inquiry involved in determining whether or not
to transfer an inmate to a mental
hospital for treatment involves a question that is essentially medical. The
question whether an individual is
mentally ill and cannot be treated in
prison "turns on the meaning of the
facts which must be interpreted by expert psychiatrists and psychologists."
Addington v. Texas. The medical
nature of the inquiry, however, does
not justify dispensing with due process
requirements. It is precisely "[t]he
subtleties and nuances of psychiatric
diagnoses" that justify the requirement of adversary hearings.

Because prisoners facing involuntary transfer to a mental hospital are
threatened with immediate deprivation of liberty interests they are currently enjoying and because of the inherent risk of a mistaken transfer, the
District Court properly determined
that procedures similar to those required by the Court in Morrissey v.
Brewer, were appropriate in the circumstances present here.

The notice requirement imposed by
the District Court no more than
recognizes that notice is essential to
afford the prisoner an opportunity to
challenge the contemplated action
and to understand the nature of what
is happening to him. Wolff v. McDonnell. Furthermore, in view of the
nature of the determinations that
must accompany the transfer to a
mental hospital, we think each of the
elements of the hearing specified by
the District Court was appropriate.
The interests of the State in avoiding
disruption was recognized by limiting
in appropriate circumstances the

prisoner's right to call witnesses, to
confront and cross examine. The
District Court also avoided unnecessary intrusion into either
medical or correctional judgments by
providing that the independent decisionmaker conducting the transfer
hearing need not come from outside
the prison or hospital administration.

B

The District Court did go beyond
the requirements imposed by prior
cases by holding that counsel must be
made available to inmates facing
transfer hearings if they are financially unable to furnish their own. We
have not required the automatic appointment of counsel for indigent
prisoners facing other deprivations of
liberty, Gagnon v. Scarpelli; Wolff v.
McDonnell; but we have recognized
that prisoners who are illiterate and
uneducated have a greater need for
assistance in exercising their rights.
Gagnon v. Scarpelli; Wolff v.
McDonnell. A prisoner thought to be
suffering from a mental disease or
defect requiring involuntary treatment probably has an even greater
need for legal assistance, for such a
prisoner is more likely to be unable to
understand or exercise his rights. In
these circumstances, it is appropriate
that counsel be provided to indigent
prisoners whom the State seeks to
treat as mentally ill.

Mr. Justice Powell, concurring in
part.

I join the opinion of the Court except for Part IV-B. I agree with Part
IV-B insofar as the Court holds that
qualified and independent assistance
must be provided to an inmate who is
threatened with involuntary transfer
to a state mental hospital. I do not
agree, however, that the requirement

of independent assistance that a licensed attorney be provided.

I

In Gagnon v. Scarpelli (1973), my opinion for the Court held that counsel is not necessarily required at a probation revocation hearing. In reaching this decision the Court recognized both the effects of providing counsel to each probationer and the likely benefits to be derived from the assistance of counsel. "The introduction of counsel into a revocation proceeding [would] alter significantly the nature of the proceeding," because the hearing would inevitably become more adversary. We noted that probationers would not always need counsel because in most hearings the essential facts are undisputed. In lieu of a per se rule we held that the necessity of providing counsel should be determined on a case-by-case basis. In particular, we stressed that factors governing the decision to provide counsel include (i) the existence of factual disputes or issues which are "complex or otherwise difficult to develop or present," and (ii) "whether the probationer appears to be capable of speaking effectively for himself."

Consideration of these factors, and particularly the capability of the inmate, persuades me that the Court is correct that independent assistance must be provided to an inmate before he may be transferred involuntarily to a mental hospital. The essence of the issue in an involuntary commitment proceeding will be the mental health of the inmate. The resolution of factual disputes will be less important than the ability to understand and analyze expert psychiatric testimony that is often expressed in language relatively incomprehensible to lay-

men. It is unlikely that an inmate threatened with involuntary transfer to mental hospitals will possess the competence or training to protect adequately his own interest in these state-initiated proceedings. And the circumstances of being imprisoned without normal access to others who may assist him places an additional handicap upon an inmate's ability to represent himself. I therefore agree that due process requires the provision of assistance to an inmate threatened with involuntary transfer to a mental hospital.

II

I do not believe, however, that an inmate must always be supplied with a licensed attorney. "[D]ue Process is flexible and calls for such procedural protections as the particular situation demands." Morrissey v. Brewer. Our decisions defining the necessary qualifications for an impartial decision-maker demonstrate the requirements of due process turn on the nature of the determination which must be made. "Due Process has never been thought to require that the neutral and detached trier of fact be law-trained or a judicial or administrative officer." Parham v. J.R. In that case, we held that due process is satisfied when a staff physician determines whether a child may be voluntarily committed to a state mental institution by his parents. That holding was based upon recognition that the issues of civil commitment "are essentially medical in nature," and that " 'neither judges nor administrative hearing officers are better qualified than psychiatrists to render psychiatric judgments.' " Parham v. J.R.

In my view, the principle that due process does not always require a law-trained decisionmaker supports the ancillary conclusion that due process may be satisfied by the provision of a qualified and independent adviser who is not a lawyer. As in Parham v. J.R., the issue here is essentially medical. Under state law, a prisoner may be transferred only if he "suffers from a mental disease or defect" and "cannot be given proper treatment" in the prison complex. Neb Rev Stat § 83-180(1) (1976). The opinion of the Court allows a nonlawyer to act as the impartial decisionmaker in the transfer proceeding.

The essence of procedural due process is a fair hearing. I do not think that the fairness of an informal hearing designed to determine a medical issue requires participation by lawyers. Due process merely requires that the State provide an inmate with qualified and independent assistance. Such assistance may be provided by a licensed psychiatrist or other mental health professional. Indeed, in view of the nature of the issue involved in the transfer hearing, a person possessing such professional qualifications normally would be preferred. As the Court notes, "[t]he question whether an individual is mentally ill and cannot be treated in prison 'turns on the meaning of the facts which must be interpreted by expert psychiatrists and psychologists.' " I would not exclude, however, the possibility that the required assistance may be rendered by competent laymen in some cases. The essential requirements are that the person provided by the State be competent and independent, and that he be free to act solely in the inmate's best interest.

In sum, although the State is free to appoint a licensed attorney to represent an inmate, it is not constitutionally required to do so. Due process will be satisfied so long as an inmate facing involuntary transfer to a mental hospital is provided qualified and independent assistance.

CUYLER v ADAMS
449 U.S. 433, 101 S. Ct. 703, 66 L. Ed. 2d 641 (1981)

[footnotes and citations omitted]

Justice Brennan delivered the opinion of the Court.

This case requires us to decide a recurring question concerning the relationship between the Interstate Agreement on Detainers and the Uniform Criminal Extradition Act. The specific issue presented is whether a prisoner incarcerated in a jurisdiction that has adopted the Extradition Act is entitled to the procedural protections of that Act—particularly the right to a pre-transfer hearing—before being transferred to another jurisdiction pursuant to Art. IV of the Detainer Agreement. The Court of Appeals for the Third Circuit held as a matter of statutory construction that a prisoner is entitled to such protections. The Courts of Appeals and State Courts are divided upon the question, and we granted certiorari to resolve the conflict.

I

In April 1976, respondent John Adams was convicted in Pennsylvania state court of robbery and was sentenced to 30 years in the State Correctional Institution at Graterford, Pa.

The Camden County (New Jersey) prosecutor's office subsequently lodged a detainer against respondent and in May 1977 filed a "Request for Temporary Custody" pursuant to Art. IV of the Detainer Agreement in order to bring him to Camden for trial on charges of armed robbery and other offenses.

In an effort to prevent his transfer, respondent filed a *pro se* class action complaint in June 1977 in the United States District Court for the Eastern District of Pennsylvania. He sought declaratory, injunctive and monetary relief under 42 U.S.C. §§ 1981 and 1983, alleging (1) that petitioners had violated the Due Process and Equal Protection Clauses by failing to grant him the pre-transfer hearing that would have been available had he been transferred pursuant to the Extradition Act; and (2) that petitioners had violated the Due Process Clause by failing to inform him of his right pursuant to Art. IV(a) of the Detainer Agreement to petition Pennsylvania's Governor to disapprove New Jersey's request for custody. Respondent contended *inter alia* that had he been granted a hearing or advised of his right to petition the Governor, he would have been able to convince Pennsylvania authorities to deny the custody request.

The District Court, without reaching the class certification issue, dismissed respondent's complaint in October 1977 for failure to state a claim upon which relief could be granted. Respondent was then transferred to New Jersey, where he was convicted, sentenced to a nine-and-one-half year prison term (to be served concurrently with his Pennsylvania sentence), and returned to Pennsylvania.

The Court of Appeals for the Third Circuit vacated the District Court

judgment and remanded for further proceedings. Finding no need to reach respondent's constitutional claims, it concluded as a matter of statutory construction that respondent had a right under Art. IV(d) of the Detainer Agreement to the procedural safeguards, including a pre-transfer "hearing," prescribed by § 10 of the Extradition Act. It made no finding with respect to respondent's argument that he was entitled to notification of his right to petition the Governor.

II

While this case was on appeal, a Pennsylvania state court held that state prisoners transferred under Art. IV of the Detainer Agreement have no constitutional right to a pre-transfer hearing. *Commonwealth ex rel. Coleman* v. *Cuyler*, 261 Pa. Super. 274, 396 A. 2d 394 (1978). Although the Court of Appeals did not reach this constitutional issue, it held that it was not bound by the state court's result because the Detainer Agreement is an interstate compact approved by Congress and is thus a federal law subject to federal rather than state construction. Before reaching the merits of the Third Circuit's decision, we must determine whether that conclusion was correct. We hold that it was.

The Compact Clause of the United States Constitution, Art. I, § 10, cl. 3, provides that "No State shall, without the consent of Congress...enter into any Agreement or Compact with another State...." Because congressional consent transforms an interstate compact within this Clause into a law of the United States, we have held that the construction of an interstate agreement sanctioned by Congress under the Compact Clause presents a federal question. It thus remains to be determined whether the Detainer

Agreement is a congressionally sanctioned interstate compact within Art. I, § 10, of the Constitution.

The requirement of congressional consent is at the heart of the Compact Clause. By vesting in Congress the power to grant or withhold consent, or to condition consent on the States' compliance with specified conditions, the Framers sought to ensure that Congress would maintain ultimate supervisory power over cooperative state action that might otherwise interfere with the full and free exercise of federal authority. See Frankfurter and Landis, The Compact Clause of the Constitution—A Study in Interstate Adjustments, 34 Yale L.J. 685, 694—695 (1925).

Congressional consent is not required for interstate agreements that fall outside the scope of the Compact Clause. Where an agreement is not "directed to the formation of any combination tending to the increase of political power in the States, which may encroach upon or interfere with the just supremacy of the United States," it does not fall within the scope of the Clause and will not be invalidated for lack of congressional consent. But where Congress has authorized the States to enter into a cooperative agreement, and where the subject matter of that agreement is an appropriate subject for congressional legislation, the consent of Congress transforms the States' agreement into federal law under the Compact Clause.

Congress may consent to an interstate compact by authorizing joint state action in advance or by giving expressed or implied approval to an agreement the States have already joined. In the case of the Detainer Agreement, Congress gave its consent in advance by enacting the Crime Control Consent Act of 1934. In pertinent part, this Act provides:

"The consent of Congress is hereby given to any two or more States to enter into agreements or compacts for cooperative effort and mutual assistance in the prevention of crime and in the enforcement of their respective criminal laws and policies...."

Because this Act was intended to be a grant of consent under the Compact Clause, and because the subject matter of the Act is an appropriate subject for congressional legislation, we conclude that the Detainer Agreement is a congressionally sanctioned interstate compact the interpretation of which presents a question of federal law. We therefore turn to the merits of the Court of Appeals' holding that as a matter of statutory construction Art. IV(d) of the Detainer Agreement is to be read as incorporating the procedural safeguards provided by § 10 of the Extradition Act.

III

The Detainer Agreement and the Extradition Act both establish procedures for the transfer of a prisoner in one jurisdiction to the temporary custody of another jurisdiction. A prisoner transferred under the Extradition Act is explicitly granted a right to a pre-transfer "hearing" at which he is informed of the receiving State's request for custody, his right to counsel, and his right to apply for a writ of habeas corpus challenging the custody request. He is also permitted "a reasonable time" in which to apply for the writ. However, no similar explicit provision is to be found in the Detainer Agreement.

The Detainer Agreement establishes two procedures under which the prisoner against whom a detainer has been lodged may be transferred to the temporary custody of the receiving State. One of these procedures may be invoked by the prisoner; the other by the prosecuting attorney of the receiving State.

Article III of the Agreement provides the prisoner-initiated procedure. It requires the warden to notify the prisoner of all outstanding detainers and then to inform him of his right to request final disposition of the criminal charges underlying those detainers. If the prisoner initiates the transfer by demanding disposition (which under the Agreement automatically extends to *all* pending charges in the receiving State), the authorities in the receiving State must bring him to trial within 180 days or the charges will be dismissed with prejudice, absent good cause shown.

Article IV of the Agreement provides the procedure by which the prosecutor in the receiving State may initiate the transfer. First, the prosecutor must file with the authorities in the sending State written notice of the custody request, approved by a court having jurisdiction to hear the underlying charges. For the next 30 days, the prisoner and prosecutor must wait while the Governor of the sending State, on his own motion or that of the prisoner, decides whether to disapprove the request. If the Governor does not disapprove, the prisoner is transferred to the temporary custody of the receiving State where he must be brought to trial on the charges underlying the detainer within 120 days of his arrival. Again, if the prisoner is not brought to trial within the time period, the charges will be dismissed with prejudice, absent good cause shown.

Although nothing in the Detainer Agreement explicitly provides for a pre-transfer hearing, respondent contends that prisoners who are involuntarily transferred under Art. IV are entitled to greater procedural protections than those who initiate the transfer procedure under Art. III. He argues that a prisoner who initiates his own transfer to the receiving State receives a significant benefit under the Agreement and may thus be required to waive any right he might have to contest his transfer; but that a prisoner transferred against his will to the receiving State under Art. IV does not benefit from the Agreement and is thus entitled to assert any right he might have had under the Extradition Act (or any other state law applicable to interstate transfer of prisoners) to challenge his transfer.

Respondent's argument has substantial support in the language of the Detainer Agreement. Article III provides that "[a]ny request for final disposition made by a prisoner [under this Article] *shall also be deemed to be a waiver of extradition* with respect to any charge or proceeding contemplated thereby...." (Emphasis added.) The reference to "waiver of extradition" can reasonably be interpreted to mean "waiver of those rights the sending state affords persons being extradited." Since Pennsylvania has adopted the Uniform Criminal Extradition Act, those rights would include the rights provided by § 10 of that Act.

The language of Art. IV supports respondent's further contention that a prisoner's extradition rights are meant to be preserved when the receiving State seeks disposition of an outstanding detainer. Article IV(d) provides:

"Nothing contained in this Article shall be construed to deprive any prisoner of any right which he may have to contest the legality of his delivery as provided in paragraph (a) hereof, but such delivery may not be opposed or denied on the ground that the executive authority of the sending state has not affirmatively consented to or ordered such delivery."

Petitioners argue that the phrase "as provided in paragraph (a) hereof" modifies "right," not "delivery," and that paragraph (d) does no more than protect the right paragraph (a) gives the prisoner to petition the Governor to disapprove the custody request. The Court of Appeals rejected this interpretation, concluding that the phrase "as provided in paragraph (a) hereof" modifies "delivery," not "right." Since the major thrust of paragraph (a) is to describe the means by which the receiving State may obtain temporary custody of the prisoner, the Court of Appeals held that paragraph (d) must have been intended as the vehicle for incorporating all rights a prisoner would have under State or other laws to contest his transfer, except that the prisoner must forfeit his right, otherwise available under § 7 of the Extradition Act, to oppose such transfer on the ground that the Governor had not explicitly approved the custody request.

There are three textual reasons why we find this interpretation convincing. First, if paragraph (d) protects only the right provided by paragraph (a) to petition the Governor, as petitioners claim, it is difficult to understand what purpose paragraph (d) serves in the Agreement. Why would the drafters add a second provision to protect a right already explicitly provided? Common sense requires paragraph (d) to be construed as securing something more.

Second, the one ground for contesting a transfer that paragraph (d) explicitly withholds from the prisoner—that the transfer has not been affirmatively approved by the Governor—is a ground that the Extradition Act expressly reserves to the prisoner. It is surely reasonable to conclude from the elimination of this ground in the Detainer Agreement that the drafters meant the Detainer Agreement to be read as not affecting any rights given prisoners by the Extradition Act that are not expressly withheld by the Detainer Agreement. As the Court of Appeals concluded, "the fact that Article IV(d) does specifically refer to one minor procedural feature of the extradition process which is to be affected suggests forcefully that the other aspects, particularly those furnishing safeguards to the prisoner, are to continue in effect."

Finally, paragraph (d) refers to "*any* right [the prisoner] may have" (emphasis added) to challenge the legality of his transfer. This suggests that more than one right is involved, a suggestion that is consistent with respondent's contention that *all* pre-existing rights are preserved. If petitioners' contention were correct—that the only right preserved is the right provided in paragraph (a) to petition the governor—it is much more likely that paragraph (d) would have referred narrowly to "*the* right the prisoner *does* have" to challenge the legality of his transfer.

The legislative history of the Detainer Agreement, contained in the comments on the draft Agreement made by the Council of State Governments at its 1956 conference and circulated to all the adopting States, further supports the Court of Appeals' reading. In discussing the different degrees of protection to which a prisoner is entitled under Arts. III and IV of the Agreement, the drafters stated:

"Article IV(d) safeguards certain of the prisoner's rights. Normally, the only way to get a prisoner from one jurisdiction to another for purposes of trial on an indictment, information or complaint is through resort to extradition or waiver thereof. If the prisoner waives, there is no problem. However, *if he does not waive extradition, it is not appropriate to attempt to force him to give up the safeguards of the extradition process, even if this could be done constitutionally."* Council of State Governments, Suggested State Legislation, Program for 1957, at 78-79 (1956) (emphasis added).

The suggestion, of course, is that a prisoner transferred against his will under Art. IV should be entitled to whatever "safeguards of the extradition process" he might otherwise have enjoyed. Those safeguards include the procedural protections of the Extradition Act (in those States that have adopted it), as well as any other procedural protections the sending State guarantees persons being extradited from within its borders.

That this is what the drafters intended is further suggested by the distinction they make between Art. III and Art. IV procedures:

"The situation contemplated by this portion of the agreement [Article IV] is different from that dealt with in Article III. [Article III] relates to proceedings initiated at the request of the prisoner. Accordingly, in such instances it is fitting that the prisoner be required to waive extradition. In Article IV the prosecutor initiates the proceeding. Consequently, it probably would be improper to require the prisoner to

waive those features of the extradition process which are designed for the protection of his rights."

These statements strongly support respondent's contention that prisoners were meant to be treated differently depending on which Article was being invoked, and that the general body of procedural rights available in the extradition context was meant to be preserved when the transfer was effected pursuant to Art. IV.

Article IX of the Detainer Agreement states that the Agreement "shall be liberally construed so as to effectuate its purpose." The legislative history of the Agreement, including the comments of the Council of State Governments and the congressional reports and debates preceding the adoption of the Agreement on behalf of the District of Columbia and the Federal Government, emphasizes that a primary purpose of the Agreement is to protect prisoners against whom detainers are outstanding. As stated in the House and Senate Reports:

"[A] prisoner who has had a detainer lodged against him is seriously disadvantaged by such action. He is in custody and therefore in no position to seek witnesses or to preserve his defense. He must often be kept in close custody and is ineligible for desirable work assignments. What is more, when detainers are filed against a prisoner he sometimes loses interest in institutional opportunities because he must serve his sentence without knowing what additional sentences may lie before him, or when, if ever, he will be in a position to employ the education and skills he may be developing."

The remedial purpose of the Agreement supports an interpretation that gives prisoners the right to a judicial hearing in which they can bring a limited challenge to the receiving State's custody request. In light of the purpose of the Detainer Agreement, as reflected in the structure of the Agreement, its language, and its legislative history, we conclude as a matter of federal law that prisoners transferred pursuant to the provisions of the Agreement are not required to forfeit any pre-existing rights they may have under state or federal law to challenge their transfer to the receiving State. Respondent Adams has therefore stated a claim for relief under 42 U.S.C. § 1983 for the asserted violation by state officials of the terms of the Detainer Agreement.

Affirmed.

HOWE v. SMITH
452 U.S. 473, 29 Cr.L 3081 (1981)

[footnotes and citations omitted]

Chief Justice Burger delivered the opinion of the Court.

The question presented by this case is whether a State may transfer a prisoner to federal custody pursuant to 18 U.S.C. § 5003 in the absence of a prior determination that the prisoner who is being transferred has a need for specialized treatment available in the federal prison system.

I

In December 1974, the Commissioner of Corrections for the State of Vermont announced that he would soon close the 187-year-old Windsor prison, the State's only maximum-security facility, because Windsor had become inadequate in several respects. In anticipation of that closing, the United States and Vermont entered into an agreement pursuant to 18 U.S.C. § 5003(a) by which the United States agreed to house in federal prisons up to 40 prisoners originally committed to the prisons of Vermont. The contract recited that the Director of the United States Bureau of Prisons had certified that facilities were available at federal institutions to accommodate 40 Vermont prisoners.

In 1975, when Windsor was finally closed, Vermont was left with several minimum-security community correctional centers and the Vermont Correction and Diagnostic Treatment Facility at St. Albans, Vt. St. Albans has the capacity for short-term incarceration of inmates with high security needs, but it is not designed for long-term incarceration of inmates classified as high security risks.

II

The petitioner, Robert Howe, was convicted in a Vermont court of first-degree murder arising out of the rape and strangulation of an elderly female neighbor. He was sentenced to life imprisonment and assigned to the St. Albans facility to begin serving his sentence. Because of the nature of his offense and the length of his term, however, the Classification Committee of the Vermont Department of Corrections determined that he should be kept in a maximum-security facility and recommended that he be transferred to a federal prison. Accordingly, the Vermont Department of Corrections held a hearing to decide whether he should be transferred to a federal institution. Howe was afforded advance notice of the hearing and the reasons for the proposed transfer; he was present at the hearing; and he was represented by a law adviser from the facility's staff, who submitted various items of evidence in opposition to the proposed transfer.

The hearing officer recommended that the petitioner be transferred to a federal institution on the ground that "no treatment programs exist in the

State of Vermont which could provide both treatment and long term maximum security supervision" for him. The hearing officer found that Howe was dangerous and could not be integrated into a community-based program. The State relied on a psychiatric report describing Howe as a "dangerous person who could well repeat the same pattern of assaultive behavior toward women at any time in the future." The hearing examiner also found that Howe would be "highly resistant to treatment" and that he was an escape risk. Indeed, Howe had escaped from the maximum-security wing of St. Albans while detained there prior to his trial.

On March 9, 1977, Vermont's Acting Commissioner of Corrections approved Howe's transfer to the federal prison system. Under the terms of the contract between the United States and Vermont, he was incarcerated initially in the federal pentitentiary at Atlanta, Ga. and later was transferred to the federal penitentiary at Terre Haute, Ind.

As an inmate in the federal maximum-security penitentiaries, Howe enjoyed the same complete freedom of movement within the institution as other prisoners. By contrast, at St. Albans, he had not been given his freedom of movement, but had been generally confined to the maximum-security wing. The programs at St. Albans were substantially the same as those at the federal prisons, although Howe had less opportunity to take advantage of them because of the restrictions on his mobility at the state facility. The only two programs in which he actually participated at St. Albans were psychiatric counseling and educational courses. At Terre Haute, he ran a sewing machine until he had a heart attack. His principal activities now are knitting and crocheting.

On December 5, 1978, the petitioner filed this civil action in the United States District Court for the District of Vermont, naming as defendants the Attorney General of the United States and the Director of the Federal Bureau of Prisons. Respondent William Ciuros, Vermont's Commissioner of Corrections, intervened. Relying on *Lono v. Fenton*, 581 F.2d 645 (CA7 1978) (en banc), the petitioner challenged his transfer to the federal prison system on the ground that the federal officials lacked statutory authority to accept custody. It was the petitioner's position that the sole statutory authority for transfers of state inmates, § 5003, requires federal authorities to make an individual determination that each state prisoner so transferred needs a particular specialized treatment program available in the federal prison system. The petitioner argued that no such individual determination had been made in his case, and that the transfer had not been effected for special treatment needs but for general penological reasons, that is, maximum-security incarceration.

Following a hearing, the District Court denied the petitioner's request for relief, holding:

"[T]he [A]ct plainly and unambiguously requires no showing of specialized treatment needs for facilities before a Vermont state prisoner may be transferred to the federal prison system in accordance with the contract under which [the petitioner] was so transferred...18 U.S.C. 5003(a) requires nothing more of the Director of the Bureau of Prisons than a certification that facilities exist within the federal system in which state prisoners may be accommodated. That requirement has been met in the case at hand."

The Court of Appeals for the Second Circuit affirmed. The court observed that 18 U.S.C. § 5003 authorizes States to contract not simply for "treatment" but for the "custody, care, subsistence, education, treatment, and training of persons convicted." It reasoned that nothing in the language of the statute gives "treatment" primacy or provides a basis for concluding that, whatever other services are provided, "treatment" must always be furnished to prisoners transferred under the statute. While acknowledging that there was a modicum of support in the legislative history for the petitioner's argument, the Court of Appeals rejected it because it "has no basis in the language of the statute."

III

The challenge here is not to the action of the State of Vermont in seeking to transfer the petitioner, but to the authority of the Federal Government, in the official person of the Attorney General, to receive and to hold him in a federal penitentiary. Under 18 U.S.C. § 4001(a) "no citizen shall be imprisoned or otherwise detained by the United States except pursuant to an Act of Congress." The petitioner avers that he is being held by the federal authorities illegally because neither § 5003 nor any other provision authorizes his detention. In particular, he argues that § 5003 has a narrow and limited thrust: that is, that a state prisoner may not be transferred to a federal institution except for an identified specialized

treatment and that, before any such transfer may be made, the Federal Government must conduct an inquiry and make an individualized determination that the transferee needs, and the federal facility can provide, that treatment. On the other hand, the respondents contend the § 5003 is not so limited, and that the petitioner's detention is clearly authorized by the plain language of that provision.

Because § 5003 obviously authorizes federal detention of state prisoners under *some* circumstances, our task is to determine the precise nature of those circumstances and whether appropriate circumstances are present in this case.

A

As in every case involving the interpretation of a statute, analysis must begin with the language employed by Congress. By its terms, § 5003(a) authorizes the Attorney General to contract with a State or Territory "for the custody, care, subsistence, education, treatment, and training of persons convicted of criminal offenses in the courts of [that] State or Territory." On its face, the authority furnished by this language encompasses much more than a limited authority to provide for the specialized treatment needs of state prisoners. "Treatment" is, after all, only one of several services catalogued; the focus of the statute is upon care, custody, subsistence, education and training as well as upon treatment. Nothing in the construction of the provision supports the view that "treatment" is more important than any of the other listed categories, and nothing in the passage can be fairly read as requiring that some kind of "treatment" must be furnished to every state prisoner transferred to a federal facility pursuant to a contract authorized by § 5003(a).

The petitioner does not contest the breadth of the charter granted by the language just quoted. Rather, he focuses on the requirement that the Director of the Federal Bureau of Prisons certify the availability of "proper and adequate treatment facilities and personnel." The petitioner reads this requirement as imposing a substantive limitation or restriction on the purposes for which prisoners may be transferred; to wit, a prisoner may be transferred only for treatment.

The petitioner's reading of the statute strains the plain meaning of its language. The act of certification by the Director is nothing more than the starting point in the process of contractual negotiation envisioned by § 5003(a). Absent surplus capacity in the federal system, discussions between federal and state authorities regarding the transfer of state prisoners to federal facilities would be pointless. Once the Director certifies that a surplus capacity exists—that is, that there is room for more inmates—the transfer becomes a possibility. The certification clause cannot be read as requiring any more than that federal facilities and personnel must be available to handle whatever prisoners are received.

There is no special significance to the fact that the Director certifies the existence of "*treatment* facilities," as opposed to prison facilities generally.[6] First, the term "treatment facilities" is an appropriate general reference to the existing federal prison facilities. It is true, of course, that other terms may be used—and, in fact, are used—to describe the federal prisons; that, however, does not belie the appropriateness of the term "treatment facilities" as a general reference to the federal penal system.

Second, if, as the petitioner advocates, the phrase "treatment facilities" is read as a substantive restriction upon the purposes for which a prisoner may be transferred, § 5003 is rendered internally inconsistent. According to the petititoner, by virtue of § 5003(a), a state prisoner may be transferred to a federal prison only if that facility affords him specialized treatment found to be needed. However, § 5003(c) provides, with certain exceptions not applicable to this case, that all state prisoners in federal custody are subject to the same statutory and regulatory scheme that governs federal prisoners. And that statutory and regulatory scheme contains provisions that would undermine § 5003(a) as that section is read by the petititoner. For example, by statute, federal prisoners may be transferred from one facility to another at the discretion of the Attorney General, 18 U.S.C. § 4082(b), and federal officials have discretion to decide which inmates have access to rehabilitation programs. It makes no sense to interpret § 5003 as forcing federal authorities to accept only a state prisoner who is in need of treatment at a particular facility when those same officials are free to transfer that same prisoner from the facility, thereby de-

---

6. The petitioner argues that the concept of "treatment" is limited to such things as medical treatment, psychiatric treatment, alcohol or drug rehabilitation programs, and special programs for juve- niles. In his view, the concept does not include secure incarceration for dangerous offenders.

nying him access to the treatment program.

In sum, the plain language of § 5003(a) authorizes contracts not simply for treatment, but also for the custody, care, subsistence, education, and training of state prisoners in federal facilities. The certification requirement is simply a housekeeping measure designed to ensure that the federal system has the capacity to absorb the state prisoners. Nothing in the language of § 5003(a) restricts or limits the use of federal prison facilities to those state prisoners who are in need of some particular treatment.

B

When the terms of a statute are unambiguous, our inquiry comes to an end, except "in 'rare and exceptional circumstances.' " No rare and exceptional circumstances are present here; our reading of the statute is fully supported by the legislative history of § 5003.

The petitioner disagrees. He notes that, when asked on the Senate floor to explain § 5003(a), Senator McCarran answered that, whereas 18 U.S.C. § 4002 allows the Federal Government to contract with state officials for the confinement of federal prisoners,

"[t]his bill would authorize a more or less reciprocal arrangement whereby, under certain conditions in a limited category of cases...the Attorney General may contract with State officials for the custody of persons convicted and sentenced under State laws."

The petitioner finds significance in the Senator's use of the words "under certain conditions" and "in a limited category of cases."

Read as a whole, the legislative

record reveals that § 5003 was enacted to provide a practical solution to a simple problem, that is, to permit the States to transfer their prisoners to federal custody in the same way that the Federal Government for years had been placing prisoners in state custody pursuant to 18 U.S.C. § 4002. Until this century, there was no federal prison system to speak of; instead, federal prisoners were housed in state prisons. By 1952, however, a sufficient number of federal prisons had been built that Congress could respond to requests from the States that the Federal Bureau of Prisons provide facilities in cases where state facilities were inadequate in some way. Section 5003 was the congressional response to this evolving situation.

A desire to help States with insufficient facilities, a sentiment that permeates the legislative history of § 5003, may be detected even in the remarks of Senator McCarran quoted by the petitioner. The Senator described the new section as a "reciprocal" of § 4002, one authorizing the Attorney General to extend *to* the States the same type of service he was authorized to receive *from* them under § 4002. Because federal officials exercise broad authority under § 4002, the "reciprocal" authority purportedly extended under § 5003(a) likely was understood by Congress to be equally broad.

In addition to Senator McCarran's remarks, the petitioner relies heavily upon a passage in the Report of the House Judiciary Committee on the bill that was to become § 5003. The Committee stated:

"The proposed legislation restricts or limits the use of Federal prison facilities to those convicted State offenders who are in need of treatment. The term "treatment" as used in this bill, in addition to its ordinary meaning of providing medical care, is also meant to include corrective and preventive guidance and training as defined in the Youth Corrections Act."

The petitioner's reliance upon this passage is understandable, but a single sentence—especially one taken from a report issued five months after one chamber, the Senate, had passed § 5003—cannot obscure the unmistakable intent of Congress to create by § 5003 broad authority in federal officials to accept custody of state prisoners in the federal prisons. Indeed, nowhere is this intent clearer than in another passage from the very same page:

"State prisons for many years housed and cared for Federal prisoners—until the Federal Government built its own institutions. Today, by [virtue of § 4002], the Attorney General is authorized to contract for the care and custody of our Federal prisoners.... The committee sees no reason why Federal facilities and personnel should not, in turn, be made available for State offenders, provided, of course, the Federal Government is reimbursed for any expenses involved."

The legislative history of § 5003 reveals that Congress perceived a need to respond to state requests for the federal prison system to undertake "custody, treatment and training" of state prisoners where the States lacked an institutional capacity to do so themselves. It is clear that § 5003 was a broad response to this perceived need. Nothing in the legislative history of § 5003 makes this case one of the "rare and exceptional cases" re-

quiring a departure from the plain language of the statute.

C

Because the Attorney General, and through him the Bureau of Prisons, are charged with the administration of § 5003, their view of the meaning of the statute is entitled to considerable deference. Moreover, in this case, the Bureau's interpretation of the statute merits greater-than-normal weight because it was the Bureau that drafted the legislation and steered it through Congress with little debate.

The contract between the United States and Vermont that served as the basis for the petitioner's transfer to federal custody is just one indication that the Federal Bureau of Prisons has construed § 5003 as broadly authorizing it to accept whatever prisoners are referred to it by state officials. In nearly 30 years of administering this statute, several Attorneys General have interpreted the statute consistently as a grant of plenary authority to contract with the States, limited only by certification that space and personnel were available.

Furthermore, Congress has had ample opportunity to express whatever dissatisfaction it might have regarding this administrative interpretation of § 5003. As early as 1952, in its Annual Report, the Bureau of Prisons advised Congress of its view of the statute:

"[Section 5003] authorizes the Attorney General, when adequate facilities and personnel are available, to contract with State officials for the care and custody of State prisoners....

"The confinement of Federal prisoners in State institutions has been authorized since 1776.... The present act affords an opportunity for reciprocity which had not hitherto existed. While it is not anticipated that the new statute will be used widely, States may on occasion wish to request Federal care for particular prisoners who need facilities available in the Federal prison system but not in their own. For example, *a State may wish to transfer a vicious intractable offender who cannot be handled readily in its own institutions*, or a female prisoner for whom appropriate facilities are not available, or a prisoner needing special medical or psychiatric care."

Congress indicated no reservation or objection to this interpretation of § 5003 in 1952, or in any year thereafter. Furthermore, in 1965, when Congress added § 5003(d) so as to include the Canal Zone within the purview of § 5003, the Senate Report expressly described § 5003(a) as broadly permitting the transfer of persons convicted in the Canal Zone to federal prisons.

The contemporaneous and uniform construction of § 5003(a) by the agency that proposed its enactment and is charged with its enforcement has been that the statute authorizes contracts based upon a broad range of purposes, including the transfer shown by this record. In the absence of any evidence of congressional objection, the agency's interpretation must be given great weight.

IV

The plain language, the legislative history, and the long-standing administrative interpretation of § 5003(a) clearly demonstrate that the provision is a broad charter authorizing the transfer of state prisoners to federal custody. There is no basis in § 5003(a) for the petitioner's challenge to his transfer to federal custody. Given our disposition of this issue, it is unnecessary to address the other arguments made by the petitioner.

Accordingly, the judgment of the Court of Appeals is

Affirmed.

ANTONE OLIM, et al., Petitioners

v.

DELBERT KAAHANUI WAKINEKONA

461 U.S. 238, 103 S. Ct. 1741, 75 L. Ed. 2d 813 (1983)

JUSTICE BLACKMUN delivered the opinion of the Court.

The issue in this case is whether the transfer of a prisoner from a state prison in Hawaii to one in California implicates a liberty interest within the meaning of the Due Process Clause of the Fourteenth Amendment.

I

A

Respondent Delbert Kaahanui Wakinekona is serving a sentence of life imprisonment without the possibility of parole as a result of his murder conviction in a Hawaii state court. He

also is serving sentences for various other crimes, including rape, robbery, and escape. At the Hawaii State Prison outside Honolulu, respondent was classified as a maximum security risk and placed in the maximum control unit.

Petitioner Antone Olim is the administrator of the Hawaii State Prison. The other petitioners constituted a prison "Program Committee." On August 2, 1976, the Committee held hearings to determine the reasons for a breakdown in discipline and the failure of certain programs within the prison's maximum control unit. Inmates of the unit appeared at these hearings. The Committee singled out respondent and another inmate as troublemakers. On August 5, respondent received notice that the Committee, at a hearing to be held on August 10, would review his correctional program to determine whether his classification within the system should be changed and whether he should be transferred to another Hawaii facility or to a mainland institution.

The August 10 hearing was conducted by the same persons who had presided over the hearings on August 2. Respondent retained counsel to represent him. The Committee recommended that respondent's classification as a maximum security risk be continued and that he be transferred to a prison on the mainland. Petitioner Olim, as administrator, accepted the Committee's recommendation, and a few days later respondent was transferred to Folsom State Prison in California.

B

Rule IV of the Supplementary Rules and Regulations of the Corrections Division, Department of Social Services and Housing, State of Hawaii, approved in June 1976, recites that the inmate classification process is not concerned with punishment. Rather, it is intended to promote the best interests of the inmate, the State, and the prison community. Paragraph 3 of Rule IV requires a hearing prior to a prison transfer involving "a grievous loss to the inmate," which the Rule defines "generally" as "a serious loss to a reasonable man." The administrator, under ¶2 of the Rule, is required to establish "an impartial Program Committee" to conduct such a hearing, the Committee to be "composed of at least three members who were not actively involved in the process by which the inmate . . . was brought before the Committee." Under ¶3, the Committee must give the inmate written notice of the hearing, permit him, with certain stated exceptions, to confront and cross-examine witnesses, af-

ford him an opportunity to be heard, and apprise him of the Committee's findings.

The Committee is directed to make a recommendation to the administrator, who then decides what action to take. The regulations contain no standards governing the administrator's exercise of his discretion.

C

Respondent filed suit under 42 U.S.C. § 1983 against petitioners as the state officials who caused his transfer. He alleged that he had been denied procedural due process because the Committee that recommended his transfer consisted of the same persons who had initiated the hearing, this being in specific violation of Rule IV, ¶2, and because the Committee was biased against him. The United States District Court for the District of Hawaii dismissed the complaint, holding that the Hawaii regulations governing prison transfers do not create a substantive liberty interest protected by the Due Process Clause. 459 F.Supp. 473 (1978).

The United States Court of Appeals for the Ninth Circuit, by a divided vote, reversed. It held that Hawaii had created a constitutionally protected liberty interest by promulgating Rule IV. In so doing, the court declined to follow cases from other Courts of Appeals holding that certain procedures mandated by prison transfer regulations do not create a liberty interest. See, e.g., Cofone v. Manson, 594 F.2d 934 (CA2 1979); Lombardo v. Meachum, 548 F.2d 13 (CA1 1977). The court reasoned that Rule IV gives Hawaii prisoners a justifiable expectation that they will not be transferred to the mainland absent a hearing, before an impartial committee, concerning the facts alleged in the pre-hearing notice. Because the Court of Appeals' decision created a conflict among the circuits, and because the case presents the further question whether the Due Process Clause in and of itself protects against interstate prison transfers, we granted certiorari.

II

In Meachum v. Fano, 427 U.S. 215, (1976), and Montanye v. Haymes, 427 U.S. 236, 96 S.Ct. 2543, 49 L.Ed.2d 466 (1976), this Court held that an intrastate prison transfer does not directly implicate the Due Process Clause of the Fourteenth Amendment. Just as an inmate has no justifiable expectation that he will be incarcerated in any particular prison within a State, he has no justifiable expectation that he will be incarcerated in any particular State. Often, confinement in the inmate's home State will not be possible. A person convicted of a federal crime in a State without a federal correctional facility usually will serve his sentence in another State. Overcrowding and the need to separate particular prisoners may necessitate interstate transfers. For any number of reasons, a State may lack prison facilities capable of providing appropriate correctional programs for all offenders.

Statutes and interstate agreements recognize that, from time to time, it is necessary to transfer inmates to prisons in other States. On the federal level, 18 U.S.C. § 5003(a) authorizes the Attorney General to contract with a State for the transfer of a state prisoner to a federal prison, whether in that State or another. Title 18 U.S.C. § 4002 (1976 ed. and Supp. V) permits the Attorney General to contract with any State for the placement of a federal prisoner in state custody for up to three years. Neither statute requires that the prisoner remain in the State in which he was convicted and sentenced.

On the state level, many States have statutes providing for the transfer of a state prisoner to a federal prison. Corrections compacts between States, implemented by statutes, authorize incarceration of a prisoner of one State in another State's prison. And prison regulations such as Hawaii's Rule IV anticipate that inmates sometimes will be transferred to prisons in other States.

In short, it is neither unreasonable nor unusual for an inmate to serve practically his entire sentence in a State other than the one in which he was convicted and sentenced, or to be transferred to an out-of-state prison after serving a portion of his sentence in his home State. Confinement in another State, unlike confinement in a mental institution, is "within the normal limits or range of custody which the conviction has authorized the State to impose." Meachum, 427 U.S., at 225.

Even when, as here, the transfer involves long distances and an ocean crossing, the confinement remains within constitutional limits. The difference between such a transfer and an intrastate or interstate transfer of shorter distance is a matter of degree, not of kind, and Meachum instructs that "the determining factor is the nature of the interest involved rather than its weight." 427 U.S., at 224.

The reasoning of Meachum and Montanye compels the conclusion that an interstate prison transfer, including one from Hawaii to California, does not deprive an inmate of any liberty interest protected by the Due Process Clause in and of itself.

III

The Court of Appeals held that Hawaii's prison regulations create a constitutionally protected liberty interest. In Meachum, however, the State had "conferred no right on the prisoner to remain in the prison to which he was initially assigned, defeasible only upon proof of specific acts of misconduct," 427 U.S., at 226, and "ha[d] not represented that transfers [would] occur only on the occurrence of certain events," id., at 228. Because the State had retained "discretion to transfer [the prisoner] for whatever reason or for no reason at all," ibid., the Court found that the State had not created a constitutionally protected liberty interest. Similarly, because the state law at issue in Montanye "impose[d] no conditions on the discretionary power to transfer," 427 U.S., at 243, there was no basis for invoking the protections of the Due Process Clause.

These cases demonstrate that a State creates a protected liberty interest by placing substantive limitations on official discretion. An inmate must show "that particularized standards or criteria guide the State's decisionmakers." Connecticut Board of Pardons v. Dumschat, 452 U.S. 458, 467 (1981). If the decisionmaker is not "required to base its decisions on objective and defined criteria," but instead "can deny the requested relief for any constitutionally permissible reason or for no reason at all," ibid., the State has not created a constitutionally protected liberty interest. See Id., at 466-467, see also Vitek v. Jones, 445 U.S., at 488-491, (summarizing cases).

Hawaii's prison regulations place no substantive limitations on official discretion and thus create no liberty interest entitled to protection under the Due Process Clause. As Rule IV itself makes clear, and as the Supreme Court of Hawaii has held in Lono v. Arivoshi, 63 Haw. 138, 621 P.2d 976 (1981), the prison administrator's discretion to transfer an inmate is completely unfettered. No standards govern or restrict the administrator's determination.

The Court of Appeals thus erred in attributing significance to the fact that the prison regulations require a particular kind of hearing before the administrator can exercise his unfettered discretion. As the United States Court of Appeals for the Seventh Circuit recently stated in Shango v. Jurich, 681 F.2d 1091, 1100-1101 (1982), "[a] liberty interest is of course a substantive interest of an individual; it cannot be the right to demand needless formality." Process is not an end in itself. Its constitutional purpose is to protect a substantive interest to which the individual has a legitimate claim of entitlement. The State may choose to require procedures for reasons other than protection against deprivation of substantive rights, of course, but in making that choice the State does not create an independent substantive right.

IV

In sum, we hold that the transfer of respondent from Hawaii to California did not implicate the Due Process Clause directly, and that Hawaii's prison regulations do not create a protected liberty interest. Accordingly, the judgment of the Court of Appeals is

Reversed.

HUDSON v. PALMER

468 U.S. 517, 104 S. Ct. 3194, 82 L. Ed. 2d 393 (1984)

[Footnotes and Citations Omitted]

CHIEF JUSTICE BURGER delivered the opinion of the Court.

We granted certiorari ... to decide whether a prison inmate has a reasonable expectation of privacy in his prison cell entitling him to the protection of the Fourth Amendment against unreasonable searches seizures.***

I

The facts underlying this dispute are relatively simple. Respondent

Palmer is an inmate at the Bland Correctional Center in Bland, Va., serving sentences for forgery, uttering, grand larceny, and bank robbery convictions. On September 16, 1981, petitioner Hudson, an officer at the Correctional Center, with a fellow officer, conducted a "shakedown," the officers discovered a ripped pillowcase in a trash can near respondent's cell bank. Charges against Palmer were instituted under the prison disciplinary procedures for destroying state property. After a hearing, Palmer was found guilty on the charge and was ordered to reimburse the State for the cost of the material destroyed; in addition, a reprimand was entered on his prison record.

Palmer subsequently brought this pro se action in United States District Court under 42 U.S.C. § 1983. Respondent claimed that Hudson had conducted the shakedown search of his cell and had brought a false charge against him solely to harass him, and that, in violation of his Fourteenth Amendment right not to be deprived of property without due process of law, Hudson had intentionally destroyed certain of his noncontraband personal property during the September 16 search. Hudson denied each allegation; he moved for and was granted summary judgment. The District Court accepted respondent's allegations as true but held nonetheless, relying on *Parratt v. Taylor*, that the alleged destruction of respondent's property, even if intentional, did not violate the Fourteenth Amendment because were for state

tort remedies available to redress the deprivation, and that the alleged harassment did not "rise to the level of a constitutional deprivation." The Court of Appeals affirmed in part, reversed in part, and remanded for further proceedings. The court affirmed the District Court's holding that respondent was not deprived of his property without due process. The court acknowledged that we considered only a claim of negligent property deprivation in *Parratt v. Taylor*, It agreed with the District Court, however, that the logic of *Parratt* applies equally to unauthorized intentional deprivations of property by state officials: "[O]nce it is assumed that a postdeprivation remedy can cure an unintentional but negligent act causing injury, inflicted by a state agent which is unamendable to prior review, then that principle applies as well to random and unauthorized intentional acts." ***

The Court of Appeals reversed the summary judgment on respondent's claim that the shakedown search was unreasonable. The court recognized that *Bell v. Wolfish*, authorized irregular unannounced shakedown searches of prison cells. But the court held that an individual prisoner has a "limited privacy right" in his cell entitling him to protection against searches conducted solely to harass or to humiliate. The shakedown of a single prisoner's property, said the court, is permissible only if "done pursuant to an established program of conducting random searches of single cells or groups of cells reasonably designed to deter or discover the possession of contraband" or upon reasonable belief that the particular prisoner possessed contraband. Because the Court of Appeals concluded that the record reflected a factual dispute over whether the search of respondent's cell was routine or conducted to harass respondent, it held that summary judgment was inappropriate, and that a remand was necessary to determine the purpose of the cell search.

***

We affirm in part and reverse in part.

II

A

The first question we address is whether respondent has a right of privacy in his prison cell entitling him to the protection of the Fourth Amendment against unreasonable searches. As we have noted, the Court of Appeals held that the District Court's summary judgment in petitioner's favor was premature because respondent had a "limited privacy right" in his cell that might have been breached. The court concluded that, to protect this privacy right, shakedown searches of an individual's cell should be performed only "pursuant to an established program of conducting random searches ... reasonably designed to deter or discover the possession of contraband" or upon reasonable belief that the prisoner possesses contraband. Petitioner contends that the Court of Appeals erred in holding that respondent had even a limited privacy right in his cell, and urges that we adopt the "bright line" rule that prisoners have no legitimate expectation of privacy in their individual cells that would entitle them to Fourth Amendment protection.

... (W)hile persons imprisoned for crime enjoy many protections of the Constitution, it is also clear that imprisonment carries with it the circumscription or loss of many significant rights. These constraints on inmates, and in some cases the complete withdrawal of certain rights, are "justified by the considerations underlying our penal system." The curtailment of certain rights is necessary, as a practical matter, to accommodate a myriad of "institutional needs and objectives" of prison facilities, chief among which is internal security. Of course, these restrictions or retractions also serve, incidentally, as reminders that, under our system of justice, deterrence and retribution are factors in addition to correction.

We have not before been called upon to decide the specific question whether the Fourth Amendment applies within a prison cell, but the nature of our inquiry is well defined. We must determine here, as in other Fourth Amendment contexts, if a "justifiable" expectation of privacy is at stake. The applicability of the Fourth Amendment turns on whether "the person invoking its protection can claim a 'justifiable,' a 'reasonable,' or a 'legitimate expectation of privacy' that has been invaded by government action." We must decide, in Justice Harlan's words, whether a prisoner's expectation of privacy in his prison cell is the kind of expectation that "society is prepared to recognize it as 'reasonable.' "

Notwithstanding our caution in approaching claims that the Fourth Amendment is inapplicable in a given context, we hold that society is not prepared to recognize as legitimate any subjective expectation of privacy that a prisoner might have in his prison cell and that, accordingly, the Fourth Amendment proscription against unreasonable searches does not apply within the confines of the prison cell. The recognition of privacy rights for prisoners in their individual cells simply cannot be reconciled with the concept of incarceration and the needs and objectives of penal institutions.

Prisons, by definition, are places of involuntary confinement of persons who have a demonstrated proclivity for anti-social criminal, and often violent, conduct. Inmates have necessarily shown a lapse in ability to control and conform their behavior to the legitimate standards of society by the normal impulses of self-restraint; they have shown an inability to regulate their conduct in a way that reflects either a respect for law or an appreciation of the rights of others. Even a partial survey of the statistics on violent crime in our Nation's prisons illustrates the magnitude of the problem. During 1981 and first half of 1982, there were over 120 prisoners murdered by fellow inmates in state and federal prisons. A number of prison personnel were murdered by prisoners during this period. Over 29

riots or similar disturbances were reported in these facilities for the same time frame. And there were over 125 suicides in these institutions. Additionally, informal statistics from the United States Bureau of Prisons show that in the federal system during 1983, there were 11 inmate homicides, 359 inmate assaults on other inmates, 227 inmate assaults on prison staff, and 10 suicides. There were in the same system in 1981 and 1982 over 750 inmate assaults on other inmates and over 570 inmate assaults on prison personnel.

Within this volatile "community" prison administrators are to take all necessary steps to ensure the safety of not only the prison staffs and administrative personnel, but also visitors. They are under an obligation to the reasonable measures to guarantee the safety of the inmates themselves. They must be ever alert to attempts to introduce drugs and other contraband into the premises which, we can judicially notice, is one of the most perplexing problems of prisons today; they must prevent, so far as possible, the flow of illicit weapons into the prison; they must be vigilant to detect escape plots, in which drugs or weapons may be involved, before the schemes materialize. In addition to these monumental tasks, it is incumbent upon these officials at the same time to maintain as sanitary an environment for the inmates as feasible, given the difficulties of the circumstances.

The administration of a prison, we have said, is "at best an extraordinary difficult undertaking." But it would be literally impossible to accomplish the prison objectives identified above if inmates retained a right of privacy in their cells. Virtually the only place inmates can conceal weapons, drugs, and other contraband is in their cells. Unfettered access to these cells by prison officials, thus, is imperative if drugs and contraband are to be ferreted out and sanitary surroundings are to be maintained.

Determining whether an expectation of privacy is "legitimate" or "reasonable" necessarily entails a balancing of interests. The two interests here are the interest of society in the security of its penal institutions and the interest of the prisoner in privacy within his cell. The latter interest, of course, is already limited by the exigencies of the circumstances: A prison "shares none of the attributes of privacy of a home, an automobile, an office, or a hotel room." We strike the balance in favor of institutional security, which we have noted is "central to all other corrections goals." A right of privacy in traditional Fourth Amendment terms is fundamentally incompatible with the close and continual surveillance of inmates and their cells required to ensure institutional security and internal order. We are satisfied that society would insist that the prisoner's expectation of privacy always yield to what must be considered the paramount interest in institutional security. We believe that it is accepted by our society that "[l]oss of freedom

and choice and privacy are inherent incidents of confinement."

The Court of Appeals was troubled by the possibility of searches conducted solely to harass inmates; it reasoned that a requirement that searches be conducted only pursuant to an established policy or upon reasonable suspicion would prevent such searches to the maximum extent possible. Of course, there is a risk of maliciously motivated searches, and of course, intentional harassment of even the most hardened criminals cannot be tolerated by a civilized society. However, we disagree with the court's proposed solution. The uncertainty that attends random searches of cells renders these searches perhaps the most effective weapon of the prison administrator in the constant fight against the proliferation of knives and guns, illicit drugs, and other contraband. The Court of Appeals candidly acknowledged that "the device [of random cell searches] is of ... obvious utility in achieving the goal of prison security."

A requirement that even random searches be conducted pursuant to an established plan would seriously undermine the effectiveness of this weapon. It is simply naive to believe that prisoners would not eventually decipher any plan officials might devise for "planned random searches," and thus be able routinely to anticipate searches. The Supreme Court of Virginia identified the shortcomings of an approach such as that adopted by the Court of Appeals and the necessity of allowing prison administrators flexibility:

"For one to advocate that prison searches must be conducted only pursuant to an enunciated general policy or when suspicion is directed at a particular inmate is to ignore the realities of prison operation. Random searches of inmates, individually or collectively, and their cells and lockers are valid and necessary to ensure the security of the institution and the safety of inmates and all others within its boundaries. This type of search allows prison officers flexibility and prevents inmates from anticipating, and thereby thwarting, a search for contraband."

We share the concerns so well expressed by the Supreme Court and its view that wholly random searches are essential to the effective security of penal institutions. We, therefore, cannot accept even the concededly limited holding of the Court of Appeals.

Respondent acknowledges that routine shakedowns of prison cells are essential to the effective administration of prisons. He contends, however, that he is constitutionally entitled not to be subjected to searches conducted only to harass. The crux of his claim is that "because searches and seizures to harass are unreason

able, a prisoner has a reasonable expectation of privacy not to have his cell, locker, personal effects, person invaded for such a purpose." This argument, which assumes the answer to the predicate question whether a prisoner has a legitimate expectation of privacy in his prison cell at all, is merely a challenge to the reasonableness of the particular search of respondent's cell. Because we conclude that prisoners have no legitimate expectation of privacy and that the Fourth Amendment's prohibition on unreasonable searches does not apply in prison cells, we need not address this issue.

Our holding that respondent does not have a reasonable expectation of privacy enabling him to invoke the protections of the Fourth Amendment does not mean that he is without a remedy for calculated harassment unrelated to prison needs. Nor does it mean that prison attendants can ride roughshod over inmates' property rights with impunity. The Eighth Amendment always stands as a protection against "cruel and unusual punishments." By the same token, there are adequate state tort and common-law remedies available to respondent to redress the alleged destruction of his personal property.

**

APPENDIX I

PAROLE COMMISSION AND REORGANIZATION ACT

[The Parole Commission and Reorganization Act is repealed as of 1992 by the Sentencing Reform Act of 1984, 28 U.S.C. Secs. 991, 994, and 995(a)(1) which, inter alia, created the United States Sentencing Commission, 18 U.S.C. Sec. @ 3551 et seq. (1982 ed., Supp. IV), and 28 U.S.C. Secs. 991-998 (1982 ed., Supp IV).]

"§ 4206. *Parole determination criteria* (18 U.S.C. 4206)

"(a) If an eligible prisoner has substantially observed the rules of the institution or institutions to which he has been confined, and if the Commission, upon consideration of the nature and circumstances of the offense and the history and characteristics of the prisoner, determines:

"(1) that release would not depreciate the seriousness of his offense or promote disrespect for the law; and

"(2) that release would not jeopardize the public welfare; subject to the provisions of subsections (b) and (c) of this section, and pursuant to guidelines promulgated by the Commission pursuant to section 4203(a) (1), such prisoner shall be released,

"(b) The Commission shall furnish the eligible prisoner with a written notice of its determination not later than twenty-one days, excluding holidays, after the date of the parole determination proceeding. If parole is denied such notice shall state with particularity the reasons for such denial.

"(c) The Commission may grant or deny release on parole notwithstanding the guidelines referred to in subsection (a) of this section if it determines there is good cause for so doing: *Provided,* That the prisoner is furnished written notice stating with particularity the reasons for its determination, including a summary of the information relied upon.

"(d) Any prisoner, serving a sentence of five years or longer, who is not earlier released under this section or any other applicable provision of law, shall be released on parole after having served two-thirds of each consecutive term or terms, or after serving thirty years of each consecutive term or terms of more than forty-five years including any life term, whichever is earlier: *Provided, however,* That the Commission shall not release such prisoner if it determines that he has seriously or frequently violated institution rules and regulations or that there is a reasonable probability that he will commit any Federal, State, or local crime.

"§ 4207. *Information considered (18 U.S.C. 4207)*

"In making a determination under this chapter (relating to release on parole) the Commission shall consider, if available and relevant:

"(1) reports and recommendations which the staff of the facility in which such prisoner is confined may make;

"(2) official reports of the prisoner's prior criminal record, including a report or record of earlier probation and parole experiences;

"(3) presentence investigation reports;

"(4) recommendations regarding the prisoner's parole made at the time of sentencing by the sentencing judge; and

"(5) reports of physical, mental, or psychiatric examination of the offender.

There shall also be taken into consideration such additional relevant information concerning the prisoner (including information submitted by the prisoner) as may be reasonably available.

"§ 4208. *Parole determination proceeding; time (18 U.S.C. 4208)*

"(a) In making a determination under this chapter (relating to parole) the Commission shall conduct a parole determination proceeding unless it determines on the basis of the prisoner's record that the prisoner will be released on parole. Whenever feasible, the initial parole determination proceeding for a prisoner eligible for parole pursuant to subsections (a) and (b)(1) of section 4205 shall be held not later than thirty days before the date of such eligibility for parole. Whenever feasible, the initial parole determination proceeding for a prisoner eligible for parole pursuant to subsection (b)(2) of section 4205 or released on parole and whose parole has been revoked shall be held not later than one hundred and twenty days following such prisoner's imprisonment or reimprisonment in a Federal institution, as the case may be. An eligible prisoner may knowingly and intelligently waive any proceeding.

"(b) At least thirty days prior to any parole determination proceeding, the prisoner shall be provided with (1) written notice of the time and place of the proceeding, and (2) reasonable access to a report or other document to be used by the Commission in making its determination. A prisoner may waive such notice, except that if notice is not waived the proceeding shall be held during the next regularly scheduled proceedings by the Commission at the institution in which the prisoner is confined.

"(c) Subparagraph (2) of subsection (b) shall not apply to—

"(1) diagnostic opinions which, if made known to the eligible prisoner, could lead to a serious disruption of his institutional program;

"(2) any document which reveals sources of information obtained upon a promise of confidentiality; or

"(3) any other information which, if disclosed, might result in harm, physical or otherwise, to any person. If any document is deemed by either the Commission, the Bureau of Prisons, or any other agency to fall within the exclusionary provisions of subparagraphs (1), (2), or (3) of this subsection, then it shall become the duty of the Commission, the Bureau, or such other agency, as the case may be, to summarize the basic contents of the material withheld, bearing in mind the need for confidentiality or the impact on the inmate, or both, and furnish such summary to the inmate.

"(d)(1) During the period prior to the parole determination proceeding as provided in subsection (b) of this section, a prisoner may consult, as provided by the director, with a representative as referred to in subparagraph (2) of this subsection, and by mail or otherwise with any person concerning such proceeding.

"(2) The prisoner shall, if he chooses, be represented at the parole determination proceeding by a representative who qualifies under rules and regulations promulgated by the Commission. Such rules shall not exclude attorneys as a class.

"(e) The prisoner shall be allowed to appear and testify on his own behalf at the parole determination proceeding.

"(f) A full and complete record of every proceeding shall be retained by the Commission. Upon request, the

Commission shall make available to any eligible prisoner such record as the Commission may retain of the proceeding.

"(g) If parole is denied, a personal conference to explain the reasons for such denial shall be held, if feasible, between the prisoner and the Commissioners or examiners conducting the proceeding at the conclusion of the proceeding. When feasible, the conference shall include advice to the prisoner as to what steps may be taken to enhance his chance of being released at a subsequent proceeding.

"(h) In any case in which release on parole is not granted, subsequent parole determination proceedings shall be held not less frequently than:

"(1) eighteen months in the case of a prisoner with a term or terms of more than one year but less than seven years; and

"(2) twenty-four months in the case of a prisoner with a term or terms of seven years or longer.

"§ 4213. *Summons to appear or warrant for retaking of parolee (18 U.S.C. 4213)*

"(a) If any parolee is alleged to have violated his parole, the Commission may—

"(1) summon such parolee to appear at a hearing conducted pursuant to section 4214; or

"(2) issue a warrant and retake the parolee as provided in this section.

"(b) Any summons or warrant issued under this section shall be issued by the Commission as soon as practicable after discovery of the alleged violation, except when delay is deemed necessary. Imprisonment in an institution shall not be deemed grounds for delay of such issuance, except that, in the case of any parolee charged with a criminal offense, issuance of a summons or warrant may be suspended pending disposition of the charge.

"(c) Any summons or warrant issued pursuant to this section shall provide the parolee with written notice of—

"(1) the conditions of parole he is alleged to have violated as provided under section 4209;

"(2) his rights under this chapter; and

"(3) the possible action which may be taken by the Commission.

"(d) Any officer of any Federal penal or correctional institution, or any Federal officer authorized to serve criminal process within the United States, to whom a warrant issued under this section is delivered, shall execute such warrant by taking such parolee and returning him to the custody of the regional commissioner, or to the custody of the Attorney General, if the Commission shall so direct.

"§ 4214. *Revocation of parole (18 U.S.C. 4214)*

"(a)(1) Except as provided in subsections (b) and (c), any alleged parole violator summoned or retaken under section 4213 shall be accorded the opportunity to have—

"(A) a preliminary hearing at or reasonably near the place of the alleged parole violation or arrest, without unnecessary delay, to determine if there is probable cause to believe that he has violated a condition of his parole; and upon a finding of probable cause a digest shall be prepared by the Commission setting forth in writing the factors considered and the reasons for the decision, a copy of which shall be given to the parolee within a reasonable period of time; except that after a finding of probable cause the Commission may restore any parolee to parole supervision if:

"(i) continuation of revocation proceedings is not warranted; or

"(ii) incarceration of the parolee pending further revocation proceedings is not warranted by the alleged frequency or seriousness of such violation or violations;

"(iii) the parolee is not likely to fail to appear for further proceedings; and

"(iv) the parolee does not constitute a danger to himself or others.

"(B) upon a finding of probable cause under subparagraph (1)(A), a revocation hearing at or reasonably near the place of the alleged parole violation or arrest within sixty days of such determination of probable cause except that a revocation hearing may be held at the same time and place set for the preliminary hearing.

"(2) Hearings held pursuant to subparagraph (1) of this subsection shall be conducted by the Commission in accordance with the following procedures:

"(A) notice to the parolee of the conditions of parole alleged to have been violated, and the time, place, and purposes of the scheduled hearing;

"(B) opportunity for the parolee to be represented by an attorney (retained by the parolee, or if he is financially unable to retain counsel, counsel shall be provided pursuant to section 3006A) or, if he so chooses, a representative as provided by rules and regulations, unless the parolee knowingly and intelligently waives such representation.

"(C) opportunity for the parolee to appear and testify, and present witnesses and relevant evidence on his own behalf; and

"(D) opportunity for the parolee to be apprised of the evidence against him and, if he so requests, to confront and cross-examine adverse witnesses, unless the Commission specifically finds substantial reason for not so allowing.

For the purposes of subparagraph (1) of this subsection, the Commission may subpena witnesses and evidence, and pay witness fees as established for the courts of the United States. If a person refuses to obey such a subpena, the Commission may petition a court of the United States for the judicial district in which such parole proceeding is being conducted, or in which such person may be found, to request such person to attend, testify, and produce evidence. The court may issue an order requiring such person to appear before the Commission, when the court finds such information, thing, or testimony directly related to a matter with respect to which the Commission is empowered to make a determination under this section. Failure to obey such an order is punishable by such court as a contempt. All process in such a case may be served in the judicial district in which such a parole proceeding is being conducted, or in which such person may be found.

"(b)(1) Conviction for a Federal, State, or local crime committed subsequent to release on parole shall constitute probable cause for purposes of subsection (a) of this section. In cases in which a parolee has been convicted of such a crime and is serving a new sentence in an institution, a parole revocation warrant or summons issued pursuant to section 4213 may be placed against him as a detainer. Such detainer shall be reviewed by the Commission within one hundred and eighty days of notification to the Commission of placement. The parolee shall receive notice of the pending review, have an opportunity to submit a written application containing information relative to the disposition of the detainer, and, unless waived, shall have counsel as provided in subsection (a)(2)(B) of this section to assist him in the preparation of such application.

"(2) If the Commission determines that additional information is needed to review a detainer, a dispositional hearing may be held at the institution where the parolee is confined. The parolee shall have notice of such hearing, be allowed to appear and testify on his own behalf, and, unless waived, shall have counsel as provided in subsection (a)(2)(B) of this section.

"(3) Following the disposition review, the Commission may:

"(A) let the detainer stand; or

"(B) withdraw the detainer.

"(c) Any alleged parole violator who is summoned or retaken by warrant under section 4213 who knowingly and intelligently waives his right to a hearing under subsection (a) of this section, or who knowingly and intelligently admits violation at a preliminary hearing held pursuant to subsection (a)(1)(A) of the section, or who is retaken pursuant to subsection (b) of this section, shall receive a revocation hearing within ninety days of the date of retaking. The Commission may conduct such hearing at the institution to which he has been returned, and the alleged parole violator shall have notice of such hearing, be allowed to appear and testify on his own behalf, and, unless waived, shall have counsel or another representative as provided in subsection (a)(2)(B) of this section.

"(d) Whenever a parolee is summoned or retaken pursuant to section 4213, and the Commission finds pursuant to the procedures of this section and by a preponderance of the evidence that the parolee has violated a condition of his parole the Commission may take any of the following actions:

"(1) restore the parolee to supervision;

"(2) reprimand the parolee;

"(3) modify the parolee's conditions of the parole;

"(4) refer the parolee to a residential community treatment center for all or part of the remainder of his original sentence; or

"(5) formally revoke parole or release as if on parole pursuant to this title.

The Commission may take any such action provided it has taken into consideration whether or not the parolee has been convicted of any Federal, State, or local crime subsequent to his release on parole, and the seriousness thereof, or whether such action is warranted by the frequency or seriousness of the parolee's violation of any other condition or conditions of his parole.

"(e) The Commission shall furnish the parolee with a written notice of its determination not later than twenty-one days, excluding holidays, after the date of the revocation hearing. If parole is revoked, a digest shall be prepared by the Commission setting forth in writing the factors considered and reasons for such action, a copy of which shall be given to the parolee.

"§ 4218. Applicability of Administrative Procedure Act (18 U.S.C. 4218)

"(a) For purposes of the provisions of chapter 5 of title 5, United States Code, other than sections 554, 555, 556, and 557, the Commission is an 'agency' as defined in such chapter.

"(b) For purposes of subsection (a) of this section, section 553(b)(3)(A) of title 5, United States Code, relating to rulemaking, shall be deemed not to include the phrase 'general statements of policy'.

"(c) To the extent that actions of the Commission pursuant to section 4203 (a)(1) are not in accord with the provisions of section 553 of title 5, United States Code, they shall be reviewable in accordance with the provisions of sections 701 through 706 of title 5, United States Code.

"(d) Actions of the Commission pursuant to paragraphs (1), (2), and (3) of section 4203(b) shall be considered actions committed to agency discretion for purposes of section 701(a)(2) of title 5, United States Code."

APPENDIX II

ARTICLES IN ADDITION TO, AND AMENDMENT OF THE CONSTITUTION OF THE UNITED STATES OF AMERICA, PROPOSED BY CONGRESS, AND RATIFIED BY THE LEGISLATURES OF THE SEVERAL STATES, PURSUANT TO THE FIFTH ARTICLE OF THE ORIGINAL CONSTITUTION

ARTICLE [I.]

Congress shall make no law respecting an establishment of religion, or prohibiting the free exercise thereof; or abridging the freedom of speech, or of the press; or the right of the people peaceably to assemble, and to petition the Government for a redress of grievances.

ARTICLE [II.]

A well regulated militia, being necessary to the security of a free State, the right of the people to keep and bear arms, shall not be infringed.

ARTICLE [III.]

No Soldier shall, in time of peace be quartered in any house, without the consent of the owner, nor in time of war, but in a manner to be prescribed by law.

ARTICLE [IV.]

The right of the people to be secure in their persons, houses, papers, and effects, against unreasonable searches and seizures, shall not be violated, and no warrants shall issue, but upon probable cause, supported by oath or affirmation, and particularly describing the place to be searched, and the persons or things to be seized.

ARTICLE [V.]

No person shall be held to answer for a capital, or otherwise infamous crime, unless on a presentment or indictment of a Grand Jury, except in cases arising in the land or naval forces, or in the militia, when in actual service in time of war or public danger; nor shall any person be subject for the same offence to be twice put in jeopardy of life or limb; nor shall be compelled in any criminal case to be a witness against himself, nor be deprived of life, liberty, or property, without due process of law; nor shall private property be taken for public use, without just compensation.

ARTICLE [VI.]

In all criminal prosecutions, the accused shall enjoy the right to a speedy and public trial, by an impartial jury of the State and district wherein the crime shall have been committed, which district shall have been previously ascertained by law, and to be informed of the nature and cause of the accusation; to be confronted with the witnesses against him; to have compulsory process for obtaining witnesses in his favor, and to have the assistance of counsel for his defence.

ARTICLE [VII.]

In Suits at common law, where the value in controversy shall exceed twenty dollars, the right of trial by jury shall be preserved, and no fact tried by

717

a jury, shall be otherwise reexamined in any Court of the United States, than according to the rules of the common law.

Article [VIII.]

Excessive bail shall not be required, nor excessive fines imposed, nor cruel and unusual punishments inflicted.

Article [IX.]

The enumeration in the Constitution, of certain rights, shall not be construed to deny or disparage others retained by the people.

Article [X.]

The powers not delegated to the United States by the Constitution, nor prohibited by it to the States, are reserved to the States respectively, or to the people.

Article [XI.]

The Judicial power of the United United States shall not be construed to extend to any suit in law or equity, commenced or prosecuted against one of the United States by Citizens of another State, or by Citizens or Subjects of any Foreign State.

The eleventh amendment of the Constitution of the United States was proposed to the legislatures of the several States by the Third Congress, on the 4th of March 1794; and was declared in a message from the President to Congress, dated the 8th of January, 1798, to have been ratified by the legislatures of three-fourths of the States.

Article [XII.]

The Electors shall meet in their respective states and vote by ballot for President and Vice President, one of whom, at least, shall not be an inhabitant of the same state with themselves; they shall name in their ballots the person voted for as President, and in distinct ballots the person voted for as Vice President, and they shall make distinct lists of all persons voted for as President, and of all persons voted for as Vice President, and of the number of votes for each, which lists they shall sign and certify, and transmit sealed to the seat of the government of the United States, directed to the President of the Senate;— The President of the Senate shall, in the presence of the Senate and House of Representatives; open all the certificates and the votes shall then be counted; —The person having the greatest number of votes for President, shall be the President, if such number be a majority of the whole number of Electors appointed; and if no person have such majority, then from the persons having the highest numbers not exceeding three on the list of those voted for as President, the House of Representatives shall choose immediately, by ballot, the President. But in choosing the President, the votes shall be taken by states, the representation from each state having one vote; a quorum for this purpose shall consist of a member or members from two-thirds of the states, and a majority of all the states shall be necessary to a choice. And if the House of Representatives shall not choose a President whenever the right of choice shall devolve upon them, before the fourth day of March next following, then the Vice President shall act as President, as in the case of the death or other constitutional disability of the President.— The person having the greatest number of votes as Vice President, shall be the Vice President, if such number be a majority of the whole number of Electors appointed, and if no person have a majority, then from the two highest numbers on the list, the Senate shall choose the Vice President; a quorum for the purpose shall consist of two-thirds of the whole number of Senators, and a majority of the whole number shall be necessary to a choice. But no person constitutionally ineligible to the office of President shall be eligible to that of Vice President of the United States.

ARTICLE [XIII.]

SECTION 1. Neither the slavery nor involuntary servitude, except as a punishment for crime whereof the party shall have been duly convicted, shall exist within the United States, or any place subject to their jurisdiction.

SECTION 2. Congress shall have power to enforce this article by appropriate legislation.

ARTICLE [XIV.]

SECTION 1. All persons born or naturalized in the United States, and subject to the jurisdiction thereof, are citizens of the United States and of the State wherein they reside. No State shall make or enforce any law which shall abridge the privileges or immunities of citizens of the United States; nor shall any State deprive any person of life, liberty, or property, without due process of law; nor deny to any person within its jurisdiction the equal protection of the laws.

SECTION 2. Representatives shall be apportioned among the several States according to their respective numbers, counting the whole number of persons in each State, excluding Indians not taxed. But when the right to vote at any election for the choice of electors for President and Vice President of the United States, Representatives in Congress, the Executive and Judicial officers of a State, or the members of the Legislature thereof, is denied to any of the male inhabitants of such State, being twenty-one years of age, and citizens of the United States, or in any way

abridged, except for participation in rebellion, or other crime, the basis of representation therein shall be reduced in the proportion which the number of such male citizens shall bear to the whole number of male citizens twenty-one years of age in such State.

SECTION 3. No person shall be a Senator or Representative in Congress, or elector of President and Vice President, or hold any office, civil or military, under the United States, or under any State, who, having previously taken an oath, as a member of Congress, or as an officer of the United States, or as a member of any State legislature, or as an executive or judicial officer of any State, to support the Constitution of the United States, shall have engaged in insurrection or rebellion against the same, or given aid or comfort to the enemies thereof. But Congress may by a vote of two-thirds of each House remove such disability.

SECTION 4. The validity of the public debt of the United States, authorized by law, including debts incurred for payment of pensions and bounties for services in suppressing insurrection or rebellion, shall not be questioned. But neither the United States nor any State shall assume or pay any debt or obligation incurred in aid of insurrection or rebellion against the United States, or any claim for the loss or emancipation of any slave; but all such debts, obligations and claims shall be held illegal and void.

SECTION 5. The Congress shall have power to enforce, by appropriate legislation, the provisions of this article.

ARTICLE [XV.]

SECTION 1. The right of citizens of the United States to vote shall not be denied or abridged by the United States or by any State on account of race, color, or previous condition of servitude.

SECTION 2. The Congress shall have power to enforce this article by appropriate legislation.

ARTICLE [XVI.]

The Congress shall have power to lay and collect taxes on incomes, from whatever source derived, without apportionment among the several States, and without regard to any census or enumeration.

ARTICLE [XVII.]

The Senate of the United States shall be composed of two Senators from each State, elected by the people thereof, for six years; and each Senator shall have one vote. The electors in each State shall have the qualifications requisite for electors of the most numerous branch of the State legislatures.

When vacancies happen in the representation of any State in the Senate, the executive authority of such State shall issue writs of election to fill such vacancies: *Provided*, That the legislature of any State may empower the executive thereof to make temporary appointments until the people fill the vacancies by election as the legislature may direct.

This amendment shall not be so construed as to affect the election or term of any Senator chosen before it becomes valid as part of the Constitution.

ARTICLE [XVIII.]

SECTION 1. After one year from the ratification of this article the manufacture, sale, or transportation of intoxicating liquors within, the importation thereof into, or the exportation thereof from the United States and all territory subject to the jurisdiction thereof for beverage purposes is hereby prohibited.

SECTION 2. The Congress and the several States shall have concurrent power to enforce this article by appropriate legislation.

SECTION 3. This article shall be inoperative unless it shall have been ratified as an amendment to the Constitution by the legislatures of the several States, as provided in the Constitution, within seven years from the date of the submission hereof to the States by the Congress.

ARTICLE [XIX.]

The right of citizens of the United States to vote shall not be denied or abridged by the United States or by any State on account of sex.

Congress shall have power to enforce this article by appropriate legislation.

ARTICLE [XX.]

SECTION 1. The terms of the President and Vice President shall end at noon on the 20th day of January, and the terms of Senators and Representatives at noon on the 3d day of January, of the years in which such terms would have ended if this article had not been ratified; and the terms of their successors shall then begin.

SECTION 2. The Congress shall assemble at least once in every year, and such meeting shall begin at noon on the 3d day of January, unless they shall by law appoint a different day.

SECTION 3. If, at the time fixed for the beginning of the term of the President, the President elect shall have died, the Vice President elect shall become President. If a President shall not have been chosen before the time fixed for the beginning of his term, or if the President elect shall have failed to qualify, then the Vice President elect shall act as President until a President shall have qualified; and the Congress may by law provide for the case wherein neither a President elect nor a Vice President elect shall have qualified, declaring who shall then act as President, or the manner in which one who is to act shall be selected, and such person shall act accordingly until a President or Vice President shall have qualified.

Section 4. The Congress may by law provide for the case of the death of any of the persons from whom the House of Representatives may choose a President whenever the right of choice shall have devolved upon them, and for the case of the death of any of the persons from whom the Senate may choose a Vice President whenever the right of choice shall have devolved upon them.

Section 5. Sections 1 and 2 shall take effect on the 15th day of October following the ratification of this article.

Section 6. This article shall be inoperative unless it shall have been ratified as an amendment to the Constitution by the legislatures of three-fourths of the several States within seven years from the date of its submission.

Article [XXI.]

Section 1. The eighteenth article of amendment to the Constitution of the United States is hereby repealed.

Section 2. The transportation or importation into any State, Territory, or possession of the United States for delivery or use therein of intoxicating liquors, in violation of the laws thereof, is hereby prohibited.

Section 3. This article shall be inoperative unless it shall have been ratified as an amendment to the Constitution by conventions in the several States, as provided in the Constitution, within seven years from the date of the submission hereof to the States by the Congress.

Article [XXII.]

Section 1. No person shall be elected to the office of the President more than twice, and no person who has held the office of President, or acted as President, for more than two years of a term to which some other person was elected President shall be elected to the office of the President more than once. But this Article shall not apply to any person holding the office of President when this Article was proposed by the Congress, and shall not prevent any person who may be holding the office of the President, or acting as President, during the term within which this Article becomes operative from holding the office of President or acting as President during the remainder of such term.

Section 2. This article shall be inoperative unless it shall have been ratified as an amendment to the Constitution by the legislatures of three-fourths of the several States within seven years from the date of its submission to the States by the Congress.

Article [XXIII.]

Section 1. The District constituting the seat of Government of the United States shall appoint in such manner as the Congress may direct:

A number of electors of President and Vice President equal to the whole number of Senators and Representatives in Congress to which the District would be entitled if it were a State, but in no event more than the least populous State; they shall be in addition to those appointed by the States, but they shall be considered, for the purposes of the election of President and Vice President, to be electors appointed by a State; and they shall meet in the District and perform such duties as provided by the twelfth article of amendment.

SECTION 2. The Congress shall have power to enforce this article by appropriate legislation.

ARTICLE [XXIV.]

SECTION 1. The right of citizens of the United States to vote in any primary or other election for President or Vice President, for electors for President or Vice President, or for Senator or Representative in Congress, shall not be denied or abridged by the United States or any State by reasons of failure to pay any poll tax or other tax.

SECTION 2. The Congress shall have power to enforce this article by appropriate legislation.

ARTICLE [XXV.]

SECTION 1. In case of the removal of the President from office or of his death or resignation, the Vice President shall become President.

SECTION 2. Whenever there is a vacancy in the office of the Vice President, the President shall nominate a Vice President who shall take office upon confirmation by a majority vote of both Houses of Congress.

SECTION 3. Whenever the President transmits to the President pro tempore of the Senate and the Speaker of the House of Representatives his written declaration that he is unable to discharge the powers and duties of his office, and until he transmits to them a written declaration to the contrary, such powers and duties shall be discharged by the Vice President as Acting President.

SECTION 4. Whenever the Vice President and a majority of either the principal officers of the executive departments or of such other body as Congress may by law provide, transmit to the President pro tempore of the Senate and the Speaker of the House of Representatives their written declaration that the President is unable to discharge the powers and duties of his office, the Vice President shall immediately assume the powers and duties of the office as Acting President.

Thereafter, when the President transmits to the President pro tempore of the Senate and the Speaker of the House of Representatives his written declaration that no inability exists, he shall resume the powers and duties of his office unless the Vice President and a majority of either the principal officers of the executive department or of such other body as Congress may by law provide, transmit within four days to the President pro tempore of the Senate and the Speaker of the House of Representatives their written declaration that the President is unable to discharge the powers and duties of his office. Thereupon Congress shall decide the issue, assembling within forty-eight hours for that purpose if not in session. If the Congress, within twenty-one days after receipt of the latter written declaration, or, if Congress is required to assemble, determines by two-thirds vote of both Houses that the President is unable to discharge the powers and duties of his office, the Vice President shall continue to discharge the same as Acting President; otherwise, the President shall resume the powers and duties of his office.

ARTICLE [XXVI.]

SECTION 1. The right of citizens of

the United States, who are eighteen years of age or older, to vote shall not be denied or abridged by the United States or by any State on account of age.

SECTION 2. The Congress shall have power to enforce this article by appropriate legislation.

APPENDIX III

§ 1983. CIVIL ACTION FOR DEPRIVATION OF RIGHTS

Every person who, under color of any statute, ordinance, regulation, custom, or usage, of any State or Territory, subjects, or causes to be subjected, any citizen of the United States or other person within the jurisdiction thereof to the deprivation of any rights privileges, or immunities secured by the Constitution and laws, shall be liable to the party injured in an action at law, suit in equity, or other proper proceeding for redress.

R.S. § 1979.

APPENDIX IV

RIGHTS OF OFFENDERS

"Report on Corrections," 1973, pp. 17-72. Prepared by the National Advisory Commission on Criminal Justice Standards and Goals.

Increased assertion and recognition of the rights of persons under correctional control has been an insistent force for change and accountability in correctional systems and practices. Traditional methods of doing things have been reexamined; myths about both institutionalized offenders and those under community supervision have been attacked and often proved to be without foundation. The public has become increasingly aware of both prisons and prisoners.

Although the process by which the courts are applying constitutional standards to corrections is far from complete, the magnitude and pace of change within corrections as the result of judicial decrees is remarkable. The correctional system is being subjected not only to law but also to public scrutiny. The courts have thus provided not only redress for offenders but also an opportunity for meaningful correctional reform.

In theory, the corrections profession has accepted the premise that persons are sent to prison *as* punishment, not *for* punishment. The American Prison Association in its famous "Declaration of Principles" in 1870 recognized that correctional programs should reflect the fact that offenders were human beings with the need for dignity as well as reformation. The following selec-

tion of principles is instructive:

V. The prisoner's destiny should be placed measurably in his own hands; he must be put into circumstances where he will be able, through his own exertions, to continually better his own condition. . . .

XI. A system of prison discipline, to be truly reformatory, must gain the will of the prisoner. He is to be amended; but how is this possible with his mind in a state of hostility?

XIV. The prisoner's self-respect should be cultivated to the utmost, and every effort made to give back to him his manhood. There is no greater mistake in the whole compass of penal discipline, than its studied imposition of degradation as a part of punishment. . . .

More recently, the American Correctional Association and the President's Commission on Law Enforcement and Administration of Justice issued warnings about respect for offenders' rights.

In 1966, The American Correctional Association's *Manual of Correctional Standards* declared:

The administrator should always be certain that he is not acting capriciously or unreasonably but that established procedures are reasonable and not calculated to infringe upon the legal rights of the prisoners. . . .

Until statutory and case law are more fully developed, it is vitally important within all of the correctional fields that there should be established and maintained reasonable norms and remedies against the sorts of abuses that are likely to develop where men have great power over their fellows and where relationships may become both mechanical and arbitrary. Minimum standards should become more uniform, and correctional administrators should play an important role in the eventual formulation and enactment of legal standards that are sound and fair.[1]

In 1967, the President's Commission on Law Enforcement and Administration of Justice emphasized the importance of administrative action.

Correctional administrators should develop guidelines defining prisoners' rights with respect to such issues as access to legal materials, correspondence, visitors, religious practice, medical care, and disciplinary sanctions. Many correctional systems have taken important steps in this direction, but there is a long way to go.

Such actions on the part of correctional administrators will enable the courts to act in a reviewing rather than a directly supervisory capacity. Where administrative procedures are adequate, courts are not likely to intervene in the merits of correctional decisions. And where well thoughtout policies regarding prisoners' procedural and substantive rights have been established, courts are likely to defer to administrative expertise.[2]

Despite the recognition of the need for reform, abuse of offenders' rights continued. It remained for the judiciary to implement as a matter of constitutional law what the corrections profession had long accepted in theory as appropriate correctional practice.

EVOLVING JUDICIAL REGARD FOR OFFENDERS' RIGHTS

Until recently, an offender as a matter of law was deemed to have forfeited virtually all rights upon conviction and to have retained only such rights as were expressly granted to him by statute or correctional authority. The belief was common that virtually anything could be done with an offender in the name of "correction," or in some instances "punishment," short of extreme physical abuse. He was protected only by the restraint and responsibility of correctional administrators and their staff. Whatever comforts, services, or privileges the offender received were a matter of grace—in the law's view a privilege to be granted or withheld by the state. Inhumane conditions and practices were permitted to develop and continue in many systems.

The courts refused for the most part to intervene. Judges felt that correctional administration was a technical matter to be left to experts rather than to courts, which were deemed ill-equipped to make appropriate evaluations. And, to the extent that courts believed the offenders' complaints involved privileges rather than rights, there was no special necessity to confront correctional practices, even when

---

1 American Correctional Association, *Manual of Correctional Standards* (Washington: ACC, 1966), pp. 266, 279.

2 President's Commission on Law Enforcement and Administration of Justice, *Task Force Report: Corrections* (Washington: Government Printing Office, 1967), p. 85.

they infringed on basic notions of human rights and dignity protected for other groups by constitutional doctrine.

This legal view of corrections was possible only because society at large did not care about corrections. Few wanted to associate with offenders or even to know about them. The new public consciousness (and the accompanying legal scrutiny) did not single out corrections alone as an object of reform. Rather, it was part of a sweeping concern for individual rights and administrative accountability which began with the civil rights movement and subsequently was reflected in areas such as student rights, public welfare, mental institutions, juvenile court systems, and military justice. It was reinforced by vastly increased contact of middle-class groups with correctional agencies as byproducts of other national problems (juvenile delinquency, drug abuse, and political and social dissent). The net result was a climate conducive to serious reexamination of the legal rights of offenders.

Applying criminal sanctions is the most dramatic exercise of the power of the state over individual liberties. Although necessary for maintaining social order, administering sanctions does not require general suspension of the freedom to exercise basic rights. Since criminal sanctions impinge on the most basic right—liberty—it is imperative that other restrictions be used sparingly, fairly, and only for some socially useful purpose.

Eventually the questionable effectiveness of correctional systems as rehabilitative instruments, combined with harsh and cruel conditions in institutions, could no longer be ignored by courts. They began to redefine the legal framework of corrections and place restrictions on previously unfettered discretion of correctional administrators. Strangely, correctional administrators, charged with rehabilitating and caring for offenders, persistently fought the recognition of offenders' rights throughout the judicial process. This stance, combined with the general inability of correctional administrators to demonstrate that correctional programs correct, shook public and judicial confidence in corrections.

The past few years have witnessed an explosion of requests by offenders for judicial relief from the conditions of their confinement or correctional program. More dramatic is the increased willingness of the courts to respond. Reflective of the new judicial attitude toward sentenced offenders is the fact that in the 1971-72 term, the U.S. Supreme Court decided eight cases directly affecting convicted offenders and at least two others which have implications for correctional practices. In all eight cases directly involving corrections, the offender's contention prevailed, five of them by unanimous vote of the Court.

The Court unanimously ruled that formal procedures were required in order to revoke a person's parole,[3] that the United States Parole Board must follow its own rules in revoking parole,[4] that institutionalized offenders are entitled to access to legal materials,[5] and that offenders committed under special provisions relating to defective delinquents[6] or sexually related offenses[7] are entitled to formal procedures if their sentences are to be extended.

[3] Morrissey v. Brewer, 408 U.S. 471 (1972).
[4] Arciniega v. Freeman, 404 U.S. 4 (1971).
[5] Younger v. Gilmore, 404 U.S. 15 (1971) affirming Gilmore v. Lynch, 319 F.Supp. 105 (N.D. Cal. 1970).
[6] McNeil v. Director, Patuxent Institution, 407 U.S. 245 (1971).
[7] Wilwording v. Swenson, 404 U.S. 249 (1971).

With one dissent, the Court also ruled that prison officials are required to provide reasonable opportunities to all prisoners for religious worship,[8] and that prisoners need not exhaust all possible State remedies before pursuing Federal causes of action challenging the conditions of their confinement.[9] The Court also held that a sentencing judge could not use unconstitutionally obtained convictions as the basis for sentencing an offender.[10]

Two additional cases have potential ramifications for the rights of offenders. In Argersinger v. Hamlin, 407 U.S. 25 (1972), the Court held that the State must provide counsel in criminal trials for indigent defendants regardless of the seriousness of the offense charged where a person's liberty is at stake. Throughout the correctional process various officials may make decisions which increase the time spent in confinement. This effect on the offender's liberty may require appointment of counsel and other procedural formalities.

In Jackson v. Indiana, 406 U.S. 715 (1972), the Court held that indefinite commitment of a person who is not mentally competent to stand trial for a criminal offense violates due process of law. The Court noted that the State had the right to confine such an individual for a reasonable time to determine if he could be restored to competency by treatment but, if he could not, he must be released. In the course of his opinion, agreed to by the six other justices hearing the case, Justice Blackmun commented: "At the least, due process requires that the nature and duration of commitment bear some reasonable relation to the purpose for

which the individual is committed." The effect of such a rule if applied to correctional confinement is yet to be determined.

These cases demonstrate the distance the law has come from the older view that courts ought not intervene in correctional activities. However, the real ferment for judicial intervention has come in the lower courts, particularly in the Federal district courts. Broadening interpretations of the Federal civil rights acts, the writ of habeas corpus, and other doctrines providing for Federal court jurisdiction have facilitated the application of constitutional principles to corrections. And it is in these courts that the "hands off" doctrine has been either modified or abandoned altogether.

Contemporaneously with the increased willingness of the courts to consider offenders' complaints came a new attitude toward offenders' rights. As first enunciated in Coffin v. Reichard, 143 F.2d 443 (6th Cir. 1944), courts are more readily accepting the premise that "[a] prisoner retains all the rights of an ordinary citizen except those expressly or by necessary implication taken from him by law." To implement such a rule, courts have found that where necessity is claimed as justification for limiting some right, the burden of proof (of the necessity) should be borne by the correctional authority. Administrative convenience is no longer to be accepted as sufficient justification for deprivation of rights. Additionally, correctional administrators are subjected to due process standards which require that agencies and programs be administered with clearly enunciated policies and established, fair procedures for the resolution of grievances.

A concomitant doctrine now emerg-

8 Cruz v. Beto, 405 U.S. 319 (1972).
9 Humphrey v. Cady, 405 U.S. 504 (1972).
10 U.S. v. Tucker, 404 U.S. 443 (1972).

ing is that of the "least restrictive alternative" or "least drastic means." This tenet simply holds that, once the corrections administrator has demonstrated that some restriction on an offender's rights is necessary, he must select the least restrictive alternative to satisfy the state's interests.

This change of perspective has worked major changes in the law governing correctional control over sentenced offenders. By agreeing to hear offenders' complaints, the courts were forced to evaluate correctional practices against three fundamental constitutional commands: (1) State action may not deprive citizens of life, liberty, or property without due process of law; (2) State action may not deprive citizens of their right to equal protection of the law; and (3) the State may not inflict cruel and unusual punishment. Courts have found traditional correctional practices in violation of all three commands. The standards in this chapter examine the various issues which have been—or in the future no doubt will be—the subject of litigation.

IMPLEMENTATION OF OFFENDERS' RIGHTS

Courts

The courts perform two functions within the criminal justice system. They are participants in the process of trying and sentencing those accused of crime; and at the same time they act as guardian of the requirements of the Constitution and statutory law. In the latter role, they oversee the criminal justice system at work. It was this function which inevitably forced the courts to evaluate correctional practices a decade before they subjected the police to constitutional scrutiny. Thus the courts have not only the authority but also the responsibility to continue to judge corrections against constitutional dictates.

It should be recognized, however, that the Constitution requires only minimal standards. The prohibition against cruel and unusual punishment has not to date required affirmative treatment programs. If courts view their role as limited to constitutional requirements, litigation will merely turn filthy and degrading institutions into clean but unproductive institutions. Courts, however, have a broader role. A criminal sentence is a court order and like any court order should be subject to continuing judicial supervision. Courts should specify the purpose for which an offender is given a particular sentence and should exercise control to insure that the treatment of the offender is consistent with that purpose. A sentence for purposes of rehabilitation is hardly advanced by practices which degrade and humiliate the offender.

On the other hand, litigation alone cannot solve the problems of corrections or of offenders' rights. The process of case-by-case adjudication of offenders' grievances inevitably results in uncertainties and less-than-comprehensive rulemaking. Courts decide the issue before them. They are ill-equipped to enter broad mandates for change. Similarly the sanctions available to courts in enforcing their decrees are limited. While some courts have been forced to appoint masters to oversee the operation of a prison, full implementation of constitutional and correctional practices which aid rather than degrade offenders requires the commitment of funds and public support. Courts alone cannot implement offenders' rights.

Correctional Agencies

Implementation of offenders' rights is consistent with good correctional practice. Corrections has moved from a punitive system to one which recognizes that 99 percent of those persons sentenced to confinement will one day return to the free society. This fact alone requires that offenders be prepared for reintegration into the community. An important precedent to successful reintegration is the establishment of personal rights prior to release. Thus the judicial philosophy which provides that offenders retain all rights of free citizens unless there are compelling reasons for restrictions is compatible with and supportive of the correctional philosophy of the reintegration of offenders into the community. And therefore correctional administrators have a professional interest in completing the implementation of the rights of the offender that is begun by the judiciary.

Additionally, correctional administrators are responsible for the welfare of offenders committed to their charge. Judicial decisions which improve the conditions under which an offender labors should b e welcomed, rather than resisted, by correctional officers. Maurice Sigler noted in his address as retiring president of the American Correctional Association in 1972:

> In committing offenders to us, the courts have assigned us the responsibility for their care and welfare. All of us have acknowledged that responsibility. It is inconsistent and ill-advised for us to fight every case that comes along involving the rights of our clients. After all, who is supposed to be most concerned about their welfare?

The corrections profession has a critical role to play in implementing the rights of offenders. No statutory mandate or judicial declaration of rights can be effectively realized and broadly obtained without the understanding, cooperation, and commitment of correctional personnel. Corrections will have to adopt new procedures and approaches in such areas as discipline, inmate grievances, censorship, and access to legal assistance. Traditions, schedules, and administrative techniques will have to be reevaluated and in many instances modified or abandoned. Line personnel will have to be trained to understand the substance of offenders' rights and the reasons for enforcing them.

Corrections, at the same time, is provided with an opportunity for meaningful progress. Most prisons are degrading, not because corrections wants them to be but because resources for improvement have not been available. Judicial decrees requiring change should make available additional resources. In the last analysis, the Constitution may require either an acceptable correctional system or none at all.

Legislatures

Full implementation of offenders' rights will require participation by the legislature. The inefficiencies and uncertainties of case-by-case litigation in the courts over definition of offenders' rights can be minimized if legislatures enact a comprehensive code which recognizes the new philosophy regarding offenders. Legislatures have generally been slow in modernizing correctional legislation, but pressure from the courts should stimulate badly needed reform.

Legislatures may well discover that in the short run a constitutionally permissible system of corrections is more costly than the traditional model. Legislatures can insure that only the minimal dictates of judicial decrees are met, or they can utilize the opportunity provided to commit the resources necessary to provide an effective correctional system.

The Public

While the Constitution prescribes conduct by government rather than by private persons, the public has not only a stake in implementing offenders' rights but also a responsibility to help realize them. Most people think of corrections as a system that deals with violent individuals—murderers, rapists, robbers, and muggers. To them the philosophy of "eye for eye" seems correctionally sound. This attitude may account for public tolerance of deplorable conditions in correctional facilities and the rigid disabilities imposed upon released offenders. But even a philosophy of retribution does not require blanket suspension of constitutional rights.

On the other hand, many people believe minor criminal incidents should be dealt with compassionately, especially where youthful offenders are involved. They realize that most offenders are involved in crimes against property rather than against persons and thus present a smaller risk to community safety than those perceived as being violent.

To the extent that the community continues to discriminate on the basis of prior criminality, efforts toward reintegration will be frustrated. There must be recognition that society does not benefit in the long run from attempts to banish, ignore, or degrade offenders. In part such a response is a self-fulfilling prophecy: if an offender is considered a social outcast, he will act like one. Removing legal obstacles is of little benefit if individual employers will not hire ex-offenders. Statutory provisions for community-based programs are for naught if no one wants a halfway house in his neighborhood. Efforts to improve the offender's ability to relate to others mean little if family and friends do not wish to associate with him.

Affirmative and organized efforts must be made by community leaders, corrections officials, legislators, and judges to influence public opinion. Acceptance can be fostered by improving the public's understanding of offenders' problems and of correctional processes. This chapter's standards on visiting and media access aim at improving such understanding as well as removing limitations on the exercise of basic rights. Correctional institutions and programs should be opened to citizens' groups and individuals, not for amusement but so that citizens may interact on a one-to-one basis with offenders.

In the final analysis, the offender's social status may be the most important determinant of reintegration. Any person will respond with outrage, hostility, and nonconformity to a community that continually rejects, labels, and otherwise treats him as an outlaw.

STANDARDS FOR OFFENDERS' RIGHTS— AN EXPLANATION

The standards in this chapter are expressed in terms of the legal norm needed to protect the substantive rights under discussion. This norm may be implemented by statute, judicial decision, or administrative regulation. Case law and precedent are relied on heavily. Where they are lacking, the intent is to set standards that should withstand judicial review. The emphasis is on a framework to define the rights of offenders subject to correctional control, consistent with concepts of fundamental legal rights, sound correctional practice, and humane treatment of offenders.

The standards presented are meant to cover adults, juveniles, males, females, probation, parole, institutions, pretrial and post-trial detention, and all community programs. Unless specifically qualified, general statements or rights cover all offenders in these categories.

An attempt has been made to achieve maximum breadth and universality in defining standards. Nevertheless, distinctions between adult and juvenile offenders, between pretrial and post-conviction prisoners, and between offenders in institutions and those under community supervision have been necessary in several cases. In some instances the differences stem from the nature of correctional contact. For example, it is unnecessary to define rights concerning institutional safety or censorship of offenders living in the community. In other cases distinctions are based on the type of offender, such as special protection to keep juveniles separate from adults or limitations on controls for pretrial detainees as opposed to prisoners serving sentences.

The standards can be divided into five categories. The first three govern the right of offenders to seek the protection of the law within the judicial system. Access to the courts, and the corollary rights of access to legal services and materials are set forth. These three are fundamental if the remainder of the standards are to be implemented. And not unexpectedly, these methods of ensuring the right of access to the courts were among the first to be recognized as constitutionally mandated.

Standards 2.4 through 2.10 relate to the conditions under which a sentenced offender lives. Since the greater the level of confinement the more dependent the offender is on the state for basic needs, these standards have special force for institutionalized offenders. Whenever the state exercises control over an individual, it should retain some responsibility for his welfare. The standards are directed toward that end.

Standards 2.11 through 2.14 speak to the discretionary power which correctional agencies exercise over offenders and how that power is to be regulated and controlled. No system of individualized treatment can avoid discretionary power over those to be treated, but such power must be controlled in order to avoid arbitrary and capricious action.

Standards 2.15 through 2.17 are directed toward implementing the basic first amendment rights of offenders. Courts have been slow in responding to offenders' insistence that they retain such rights. Freedom to speak and to associate in the context of a correctional institution are particularly controversial subjects. Communication with the public at large directly and through the media not only are important personal rights but have public significance. The correctional system of the past, and too often of the present, has isolated itself from the public. To enlist public support for correctional reform, that isolation must be abandoned. Full implementation of the offender's rights to communicate not only supports the notion that he is an individual but likewise assists in bringing the needs of corrections to the public's attention.

Standard 2.18 addresses the question of remedies for violations of rights already declared. It is directed primarily at judicial enforcement.

STANDARD 2.1

ACCESS TO COURTS

Each correctional agency should immediately develop and implement policies and procedures to fulfill the right of persons under correctional supervision to have access to courts to present any issue cognizable therein, including (1) challenging the legality of their conviction or confinement; (2) seeking redress for illegal conditions or treatment while incarcerated or under correctional control; (3) pursuing remedies in connection with civil legal problems; and (4) asserting against correctional or other governmental authority any other rights protected by constitutional or statutory provision or common law.

1. The State should make available to persons under correctional authority for each of the purposes enumerated herein adequate remedies that permit, and are administered to provide, prompt resolution of suits, claims, and petitions. Where adequate remedies already exist, they should be available to offenders, including pretrial detainees, on the same basis as to citizens generally.

2. There should be no necessity for an inmate to wait until termination of confinement for access to the courts.

3. Where complaints are filed against conditions of correctional control or against the administrative actions or treatment by correctional or other governmental authorities, offenders may be required first to seek recourse under established administrative procedures and appeals and to exhaust their administrative remedies. Administrative remedies should be operative within 30 days and not in a way that would unduly delay or hamper their use by aggrieved offenders. Where no reasonable administrative means are available for presenting and resolving disputes or where past practice demonstrates the futility of such means, the doctrine of exhaustion should not apply.

4. Offenders should not be prevented by correctional authority administrative policies or actions from filing timely appeals of convictions or other judgments; from transmitting pleadings and engaging in correspondence with judges, other court officials, and attorneys; or from instituting suits and actions. Nor should they be penalized for so doing.

5. Transportation to and attendance at court proceedings may be subject to reasonable requirements of correctional security and scheduling. Courts dealing with offender matters and suits should cooperate in formulating arrangements to accommodate both offenders and correctional management.

6. Access to legal services and materials appropriate to the kind of action or remedy being pursued should be provided as an integral element of the offender's right to access to the courts. The right of offenders to have access to legal materials was affirmed in Younger v. Gilmore, 404 U.S. 15 (1971), which is discussed in Standard 2.3.

Commentary

The law clearly acknowledges and protects the right of prisoners and offenders to reasonable access to the courts. The doctrine has been affirmed by the Supreme Court, *Ex parte* Hall, 312 U.S. 546 (1941) and is adhered to by State courts as well. The guarantee is visibly evident, at least in the area of postconviction remedies, by the dramatic increase in the volume of prisoner petitions now filed annually, in the Federal courts (from 2,150 in 1960 to more than 16,000 in 1970, when they constituted 15.3 percent of all civil filings in the Federal courts). Access is less evident in assertions of claims related to civil problems of prisoners or their treatment while under confinement or correctional supervision.

The chief problem relates not to the general principle as much as to implementation. The standard is framed to address major problems of implementation other than those of contact with counsel and access to the legal materials, which are treated in other standards.

First, the problem of adequate remedies is addressed by calling for their creation, where non-existent, or for reasonable access by offenders when available. Many States, for example, have complex and unwieldy remedies for challenging conviction or confinement and could benefit by comprehensive, simplified systems for postconviction review such as proposed by the American Bar Association's *Standards Relating to Post-Conviction Remedies* (Project on Minimum Standards for Criminal Justice—1968).

In the area of civil actions, the standard takes a position contrary to the practice in many States (in some cases judicially approved) preventing offenders while confined from filing civil suits unrelated to their personal liberty. When offenders must wait years to commence actions, they are placed under great disadvantage in garnering witnesses and preserving evidence. The practice is a considerable burden to the effective provision of civil legal services to prisoners. Similarly, the pre-

vailing situation in most States that precludes prisoners from attacking indictments brought under detainer also is disapproved.

The principle that, in asserting right of access to courts, offenders must first use and exhaust administrative remedies is incorporated in the standard. This requirement is necessary for assuring use of less costly, more speedy, and possibly more responsive administrative grievance or negotiation machinery such as that suggested in these standards. It is seen as a legitimate qualification to the right of access to courts and an important protection to maintain the integrity of correctional authority or other nonjudicial apparatus for remedying abuses and legitimate grievances. Where no such reasonable administrative mechanism exists, the exhaustion principle should not apply.

Finally, the standard affirms the impropriety, established in numerous cases, of restrictions on the right of access through administrative policy or procedure. This would include such practices as prior staff screening of petitions for regularity or objectionable content, delay in parole hearings for prisoners who seek postconviction writs, and delay in transmitting petitions or failure to do so for inmates in disciplinary segregation.

References

1. Almond v. Kent, 459 F.2d 200 (4th Cir. 1972) (Prisoners may not be forced to sue through a State-appointed committee rather than individually in presenting a claim for mistreatment under the Civil Rights Act.)

2. American Bar Association. *Standards Relating to Post-Conviction Remedies.* New York: Office of the

Criminal Justice Project, 1968.

3. Campbell v. Beto, 460 F.2d 765 (5th Cir. 1972) (Reversed lower court's refusal to docket an impoverished offender as defined by the Federal Civil Rights Act, which, if true, stated a good cause of action on its face.)

4. Cohen, Fred. *The Legal Challenge to Corrections.* Washington: Joint Commission on Correctional Manpower and Training, 1969, pp. 67-69.

5. Dowd v. U.S. ex rel. Cook, 340 U.S. 206 (1951) (Prison regulations may not keep inmate from filing timely appeal.)

6. *Ex parte* Hull, 312 U.S. 546 (1941) (Invalidated regulation that all habeas corpus petitions be approved by parole board lawyers as "proper drawn.")

7. Goldfarb, Ronald, and Singer, Linda. "Redressing Prisoners' Grievances," *George Washington Law Review,* 39 (1970), 231-234.

8. National Council on Crime and Delinquency. *Model Act for the Protection of Rights of Prisoners.* New York: NCCD, 1972, Sec. 6.

9. Note, *Washington University Law Quarterly,* 417 (1966).

10. Smartt v. Avery, 370 F.2d 788 (6th Cir. 1967) (Invalidated parole board rule delaying parole hearings one year for prisoners unsuccessfully seeking writ of habeas corpus.)

Related Standards

The following standards may be applicable in implementing Standard 2.1.

2.2 Access to Legal Services.

2.3 Access to Legal Materials.

5.9 Continuing Jurisdiction of Sentencing Court.

16.2 Administrative Justice.

16.3 Code of Offenders' Rights.

STANDARD 2.2

ACCESS TO LEGAL SERVICES

Each correctional agency should immediately develop and implement policies and procedures to fulfill the right of offenders to have access to legal assistance, through counsel or counsel substitute, with problems or proceedings relating to their custody, control, management, or legal affairs while under correctional authority. Correctional authorities should facilitate access to such assistance and assist offenders affirmatively in pursuing their legal rights. Governmental authority should furnish adequate attorney representation and, where appropriate, lay representation to meet the needs of offenders without the financial resources to retain such assistance privately.

The proceedings or matters to which this standard applies include the following:

1. Postconviction proceedings testing the legality of conviction or confinement.

2. Proceedings challenging conditions or treatment under confinement or other correctional supervision.

3. Probation revocation and parole grant and revocation proceedings.

4. Disciplinary proceedings in a correctional facility that impose major penalties and deprivations.

5. Proceedings or consultation in

connection with civil legal problems relating to debts, marital status, property, or other personal affairs of the offender.

In the exercise of the foregoing rights:

1. Attorney representation should be required for all proceedings or matters related to the foregoing items 1 to 3, except that law students, if approved by rule of court or other proper authority, may provide consultation, advice, and initial representation to offenders in presentation of *pro se* postconviction petitions.

2. In all proceedings or matters described herein, counsel substitutes (law students, correctional staff, inmate paraprofessionals, or other trained paralegal persons) may be used to provide assistance to attorneys of record or supervising attorneys.

3. Counsel substitutes may provide representation in proceedings or matters described in foregoing items 4 and 5, provided the counsel substitute has been oriented and trained by qualified attorneys or educational institutions and receives continuing supervision from qualified attorneys.

4. Major deprivations or penalties should include loss of "good time," assignment to isolation status, transfer to another institution, transfer to higher security or custody status, and fine or forfeiture of inmate earnings. Such proceedings should be deemed to include administrative classification or reclassification actions essentially disciplinary in nature; that is, in response to specific acts of misconduct by the offender.

5. Assistance from other inmates should be prohibited only if legal counsel is reasonably available in the institution.

6. The access to legal services pro-

vided for herein should apply to all juveniles under correctional control.

7. Correctional authorities should assist inmates in making confidential contact with attorneys and lay counsel. This assistance includes visits during normal institutional hours, uncensored correspondence, telephone communication, and special consideration for after-hour visits where requested on the basis of special circumstances.

Commentary

Right to and availability of counsel, both in court litigation and critical phases of administrative decisionmaking on offender status, has been a major trend in the current expansion of prisoners' rights. The presence of counsel assures that the complicated adversary proceeding is carried out properly and that the factual bases for decisionmaking are accurate. This standard seeks to address virtually all issues now the subject of debate and does so without distinction between the indigent and nonindigent offender.

The emphasis on a full range of legal services is consistent with the opinion of today's correctional administrators. When Boston University's Center for Criminal Justice conducted a national survey in 1971 among correctional leaders (system administrators, institutional wardens, and treatment directors), majorities in each category expressed the view that legal service programs should be expanded. Corrections officials stated this expansion would provide a safety valve for grievances and help reduce inmate tension and power structures. They also said it would not have adverse effects on prison security and would provide a positive experience contributing to rehabilitation.

Representation of offenders in post-conviction status always has lagged considerably behind that of the criminally accused. Although indigent defendants constitutionally are entitled to appointed counsel at their trial or appeal, lawyers have not generally been available to represent offenders seeking postconviction relief or challenging prison or supervision conditions through civil suits or administrative procedures. Where the right is asserted as part of administrative procedure (for example, parole revocation and forfeiture of good time), counsel often is flatly denied, even when the offender has the means to retain his own lawyer.

Access to representation for those confronted by private legal problems such as divorce, debt, or social security claims is virtually nonexistent except for a few experimental legal aid, law school, or bar association programs. The offender must take his place at the bottom of the ladder of the still modest but growing national commitment to provision of legal services for the poor. In summary, prisoners generally must represent themselves, even though many are poorly educated and functionally illiterate.

The standard asserts a new right to representation for major disciplinary proceedings within correctional systems and to civil legal assistance. Here the principle of "counsel substitute" or "lay representation" is accepted, consistent with those court decisions that have examined the issue, the realities of effective correctional administration, and limited attorney resources for such services. The Supreme Court indirectly sanctioned lay representation, even in court actions, when it held in Johnson v. Avery, 393 U.S. 483 (1969), that States not providing reasonable legal service alternatives could not bar assistance to other prisoners by "jailhouse lawyers."

Recognizing the large and probably unmanageable burden on existing attorney resources, the standard validates supplemental use of lay assistance (law students, trained correctional staff, "jailhouse lawyers," or other paraprofessionals) even in matters requiring formal attorney representation. In this regard, a recent judicial observation in a California case dealing with right to counsel in parole revocation is instructive. The ruling, In re Tucker, 5 Cal.3d 171, 486 P.2d 657, 95 Cal.Rptr. 761 (1971) stated:

Formal hearings, with counsel hired or provided, for the more than 4,000 parole suspensions annually would alone require an undertaking of heroic proportions. But that is only the beginning. For if there is a right to counsel at parole revocation or suspension proceedings, no reason in law or logic can be advanced why a prisoner, appearing before the Adult Authority as an applicant for parole and seeking to have his indeterminate sentence made determinate, should not also have legal representation. The conclusion is inescapable that my dissenting brethren are in effect insisting upon counsel for a potential of 32,000 appearances annually: 28,000 parole applicants and 4,000 parole revokees. This monumental requirement would stagger the imagination.

This standard rejects that view. If the criminal justice system must provide legal counsel in every instance where a man's liberty may be jeopardized, a clear reading of Argersinger v. Hamlin, 407 U.S. 25 (1972), would indicate that its duty should not end there. The system must and can find ways to meet the cost involved. In other situations where liberty is not directly at stake, those serving as counsel substitutes would be required to receive reasonable training and continuing supervision by attorneys. The opportunity this presents for broadening of perspectives on the part of correctional staff and a new legitimacy and vocational path for the trained "jailhouse lawyer" may prove to be valuable by-products. In addition, full cooperation with correctional authorities by public defender programs, civil legal aid systems, law schools, bar groups, and federally supported legal service offices for the poor will be necessary to put the standard into practice.

Careful definition of those major disciplinary penalties involving the right to representation has been undertaken. There is general agreement on the substance of these penalties, including solitary confinement, loss of good time, and institutional transfer. Reasonable minimums have been established that would permit handling limited penalties in these categories by less formal procedure and without counsel or counsel substitute. The Federal system and several State systems already are making provision for representation while considering major disciplinary sanctions.

It will be noted that "classification proceedings" cannot be used under the standard to avoid disciplinary sanctions where the basic issue involved is offender misconduct. A preferred status also has been established for use of attorneys rather than counsel substitute, wherever possible.

In the juvenile area, the standard makes clear that right to counsel applies to the "person in need of supervision" category or other juveniles under correctional custody for non-criminal conduct.

Finally, the right to free and confi-

dential access between offenders and attorneys through visits, correspondence, and, where feasible, telephonic communication is made clear. Beyond that, a policy of special accommodation is suggested where the circumstances of the legal assistance being rendered reasonably support such a preference, as in afterhour visits and special telephone calls. Past interference in some jurisdiction with confidential and free inmate-attorney access is documented in recent case law—for example, *In re Ferguson*, 55 Cal.2d 663, 361 P.2d 417, 12 Cal.Rptr. 753 (1961) (State supreme court forbids authority to censor or screen letters to attorneys) and *Stark v. Cory*, 382 P.2d 1019 (1963) (Electronic eavesdropping of attorney interviews banned)—and thus warrants that this critical facet of the attorney-client relationship be emphasized.

References

1. American Bar Association. *Standards Relating to Probation.* New York: Office of the Criminal Justice Project, 1968, Sec. 5.4.

2. American Bar Association. *Standards Relating to Providing Defense Services.* New York: Office of the Criminal Justice Project, 1968, Sec. 412 on "Collateral Proceedings" and Appendix B on "Standards for Defender Systems."

3. Argersinger v. Hamlin, 407 U.S. 25 (1972).

4. Boston University Center for Criminal Justice. "Perspectives on Prison Legal Services." Unpublished paper, 1971.

5. Comment, "The Emerging Right to Counsel at Parole Revocation Hearings," *Houston Law Review,* 9 (1971), 290.

6. Jacob, Bruce R., and Sharma, K. M. "Justice after Trial: Prisoner's

Need For Legal Services in the Criminal Correctional Process," *University of Kansas Law Review*, 18 (1970), 505.

7. Johnson v. Avery, 393 U.S. 483 (1969) (Where State provided no reasonable alternative, it could not prohibit the operations of the "jailhouse lawyer.")

8. Mempa v. Rhay, 389 U.S. 128 (1967) (Right to counsel affirmed in deferred sentencing/probation revocation proceedings conducted by State courts.)

9. Note, *Duke Law Journal* (1968), 343.

10. Note, *Stanford Law Review*, 19 (1967), 887.

11. Note, *Wisconsin Law Review* (1967), 514.

Related Standards

The following standards may be applicable in implementing Standard 2.2.

2.1 Access to Courts.

2.3 Access to Legal Materials.

5.9 Continuing Jurisdiction of Sentencing Court.

6.2 Classification for Inmate Management.

12.3 The Parole Grant Hearing.

12.4 Revocation Hearings.

16.2 Administrative Justice.

16.3 Code of Offenders' Rights.

STANDARD 2.3

ACCESS TO LEGAL MATERIALS

Each correctional agency, as part of its responsibility to facilitate access to courts for each person under its custody, should immediately establish policies and procedures to fulfill the right of offenders to have reasonable access to legal materials, as follows:

1. An appropriate law library should be established and maintained at each facility with a design capacity of 100 or more. A plan should be developed and implemented for other residential facilities to assure reasonable access to an adequate law library.

2. The library should include:

    a. The State constitutional and State statutes, State decisions, State procedural rules and decisions thereon, and legal works discussing the foregoing.

    b. Federal case law materials.

    c. Court rules and practice treatises.

    d. One or more legal periodicals to facilitate current research.

    e. Appropriate digests and indexes for the above.

3. The correctional authority should make arrangements to insure that persons under its supervision but not confined also have access to legal materials.

Commentary

In 1971 the Supreme Court unanimously affirmed a lower court ruling that California's failure to provide an adequate law library in State institutions was a denial of the equal protection of the laws guaranteed by the fourteenth amendment, since only wealthy inmates could exercise their right of access to courts. The court thus settled the legal principle, although it did not resolve the administrative problem of what constitutes an adequate law library.

The standard, in providing for an actual law library only at those correctional facilities which can or do house 100 or more persons, recognizes a major dilemma. As stated, the standard would include all of the prisons now in operation and one-eighth (500) of the county and municipal jails. Thus, the total number of complete law libraries would approach 1,000. Establishment of this number of law libraries will be a major and costly undertaking, but the right to such access is undeniable.

In Younger v. Gilmore, 404 U.S. 15 (1971), a library containing the following list of titles was deemed an inadequate collection:

1. The California Penal Code.
2. The California Welfare and Institutions Code.
3. The California Health and Safety Code.
4. The California Vehicle Code.
5. The United States and California Constitutions.
6. A recognized law dictionary.
7. Witkin's California Criminal Procedures.
8. Subscription to California Weekly Digest.
9. California Rules of Court.
10. Rules of United States Court of Appeals (Ninth Circuit).
11. Rules of United States Supreme Court.
12. In addition, offenders had access to other sets of legal materials from the State Law Library although many of the sets available for offender use were incomplete.

Correctional authorities should consult with law librarians as well as with the appropriate State law official to determine the contents of an appropriate law library. It is clear that a single prescription as to what would constitute a standard law library will not suffice for all States. At a minimum, copies of State and Federal criminal codes, State and Federal procedure and pleading treatises, and recent State and Federal decisions or reporters containing such decisions would be necessary components. In the case of juveniles or women, modified or augmented collections may be required to assure that materials relevant to the individuals concerned are available.

A leading law book publisher has estimated the cost of an adequate institution law library at $6,000 to $10,000. It must be recognized that maintenance of law libraries is required to sustain their usefulness, and that annual new acquisitions could total from 10 to 12 percent of the initial cost. Librarians and supervisory personnel represent other ongoing cost factors.

The standard suggests that the interests of those incarcerated in relatively small institutions can be met by development and implementation of a plan for securing legal materials on an as-needed basis. Such a plan could involve transporting inmates, when necessary, to an existing law library (county bar association, district judge's office, law school, etc.) in the vicinity of the facility in which they are incarcerated. These ideas do not exhaust the list of possibilities. For example, mobile library facilities and master libraries with full and prompt delivery of materials to smaller institutions also may be considered. The adopted plan should have the potential to meet the inmates' needs and the correctional authority should be committed to its implementation.

References

1. American Correctional Association. *Guidelines for Legal Reference*

Service in Correctional Institutions: A Tool for Correctional Administrators. Washington: ACA, 1972.

2. American Correctional Association. *Manual of Correctional Standards.* 3d ed. Washington: ACA, 1966.

3. Goldberg, Nancy E. "Younger v. Gilmore: The Constitutional Implications of Prison Libraries," *Clearinghouse Review,* 5 (1972) 645.

4. National Sheriffs' Association. *Manual on Jail Administration.* Washington: NSA, 1970.

5. Special Committee on Law Library Services to Prisoners, American' Association of Law Libraries. *Rec-*

ommended Minimum Collection for Prison Law Libraries. Chicago: AALL, 1972.

6. Younger v. Gilmore, 404 U.S. 15 (1971), affirming Gilmore v. Lynch, 319 F.Supp. 105 (N.D. Cal. 1970).

Related Standards

The following standards may be applicable in implementing Standard 2.3.

2.1 Access to Courts.

2.2 Access to Legal Services.

5.9 Continuing Jurisdiction of Sentencing Court.

16.3 Code of Offenders' Rights.

STANDARD 2.4

PROTECTION AGAINST PERSONAL ABUSE

Each correctional agency should establish immediately policies and procedures to fulfill the right of offenders to be free from personal abuse by correctional staff or other offenders. The following should be prohibited:

1. Corporal punishment.

2. The use of physical force by correctional staff except as necessary for self-defense, protection of another person from imminent physical attack, or prevention of riot or escape.

3. Solitary or segregated confinement as a disciplinary or punitive measure except as a last resort and then not extending beyond 10 days' duration.

4. Any deprivation of clothing, bed and bedding, light, ventilation, heat, exercise, balanced diet, or hygienic necessities.

5. Any act or lack of care, whether by wilful act or neglect, that injures or significantly impairs the health of any offender.

6. Infliction of mental distress, degradation, or humiliation.

Correctional authorities should:

1. Evaluate their staff periodically to identify persons who may constitute a threat to offenders and where such individuals are identified, reassign or discharge them.

2. Develop institution classification procedures that will identify violence-prone offenders and where such offenders are identified, insure greater supervision.

3. Implement supervision procedures and other techniques that will provide a reasonable measure of safety for offenders from the attacks of other offenders. Technological devices such as closed circuit television should not be exclusively relied upon for such purposes.

Correctional agencies should compensate offenders for injuries suffered because of the intentional or negligent acts or omissions of correctional staff.

Commentary

The courts recently have recognized a number of situations in which individual conditions of correctional confinement (for example, use of the strip cell and beatings) or a multiplicity of conditions under which prisoners are housed and handled can amount to the infliction of "cruel and unusual punishments" prohibited by the eighth amendment.

In this area particularly, standards should be more prohibitive than judicial interpretation of the eighth amendment, because they give credence to the new philosophy of corrections as a reintegrative force, rather than a punitive one. This standard enumerates a variety of punitive activities which, at least on an individual basis, may fall short of the eighth amendment ban but which should be included in the legal protections available to the offender.

The list of prohibited activities in the standard commences with the basic ban on imposition of corporal punishment (now recognized by the statutes and regulations of most jurisdictions) and proceeds to disapprove the use of any physical force beyond that necessary for self-defense; to prevent imminent physical attack on staff, inmates, or other persons; or to prevent riot or escape. In these instances, utilization of the least drastic means necessary to secure order or control should be the rule.

The standard would fix a firm maximum limit on the use of solitary or segregated confinement (10 days) somewhat less than the general norm recommended in the 1966 standards of the American Correctional Association. This refers to "solitary" as a disciplinary or punitive imposition now utilized in all State correctional systems, rather than "separation" used as an emergency measure to protect the offender from self-destructive acts, from present danger of acts of violence to staff or other inmates, or voluntary reasons related to fear of subjection to physical harm by other inmates. Action of this emergency nature should be sanctioned only with proper determinations of key institutional administrators and, when appropriate, continuing medical and psychiatric reviews. In all cases, solitary confinement should be the least preferred alternative.

Adoption of the standard would go far toward curtailment of excessive use of the most widespread, controversial, and inhumane of current penal practices—extended solitary confinement. One recent model act—NCCD's 1972 Model Act for the Protection of Rights of Prisoners—has refused to recognize any disciplinary use whatsoever of solitary confinement. Courts as yet have failed to classify solitary confinement as "cruel and unusual punishment," except when conjoined with other inhumane conditions, although several decisions have viewed extended periods of isolation with disapproval and some court orders have fixed maximum periods for such punishment. The standard recognizes, in setting its relatively modest maximum, that most cases require much shorter use of punitive segregation as a disciplinary measure and enjoins correctional authorities to minimize use of the technique.

The Commission recognizes that the field of corrections cannot yet be persuaded to give up the practice of solitary confinement as a disciplinary measure. But the Commission wishes to record its view that the practice is inhumane and in the long run brutalizes those who impose it as it brutalizes those upon whom it is imposed.

Two further prohibitions would assure offenders against deprivation of the basic amenities of humane institutional life. Under one, all offenders, even those in disciplinary status, would be accorded the right to basic clothing, bedding, sanitation, light, ventilation, adequate heat, exercise, and diet as applicable to the general confined population. Under the other prohibition, affirmative action or willful neglect that impairs the physical or mental health of any offender would be banned. Extreme abuse in these areas prompted the court decisions declaring that "strip cell" practices or shocking isolation, sanitary, or nutritional regimes as a punitive denial could amount to "cruel and unusual punishment."

The last prohibition recognizes that mental abuse can be as damaging to an offender as physical abuse. The infliction of mental distress, degradation, or humiliation as a disciplinary measure or as a correctional technique should be prohibited.

The standard requires correctional authorities to take affirmative steps to diminish the level of violence and abuse within correctional institutions. To minimize the problem of staff-caused violence, the correctional authority should institute screening procedures to detect staff members with potential personality problems. Staff with such problems should not be assigned to duties where they would interact with offenders in situations that might trigger an aggressive response.

Protecting offenders from the violent acts of other offenders is more difficult. A variety of measures undoubtedly is necessary, including physical changes in some institutions (converting to single rooms or cells) and changes in staff scheduling (extra night duty staff). A precise program taking into account the situation in each institution should be developed. A more "normalized" institutional environment with positive inmate-staff relationships probably is the best safeguard against frequent violence. In any event, a person convicted of crime and placed under the authority of the state should not be forced to fear personal violence and abuse.

Existing law does not clearly establish that the correctional authority is responsible for protecting persons sentenced to incarceration. Most law in this area has been developed in the context of a civil suit in which an injured prisoner is seeking to recover damages from the correctional authority. In many cases, the prisoner has been able to recover where negligence or intent on the part of correctional authorities is shown. Correctional agencies should be required to respond in damages to compensate offenders for injuries suffered by the lack of appropriate care.

Only the correctional authority is in a position to protect inmates, and the need to do so is clear. Observers of correctional institutions agree that inmate attacks on one another—often sexually motivated—are commonplace and facilitated by lack of personal supervision or lack of concern on the part of supervisory personnel. In many cases the tort law standard of a foreseeable risk of harm involving specific individuals has not been properly applied in the face of the pervasive and constant threat apparently existing today.

References

1. American Correctional Association. *Manual of Correctional Standards*. 3rd ed. Washington: ACA, 1966.

Chapter 24.

2. Annotation, "Liability of Prison Authorities for Injury to Prisoners Directly Caused by Assualt by Other Prisoners," 41 ALR 3rd 1021 (1972).

3. Davis, John. "Sexual Assaults in the Philadelphia Prison System and Sheriff's Vans," *Trans-Action*, 6 (1968), p. 8.

4. Comment, "Prisoners' Rights: Personal Security," *University of Colorado Law Review*, 42 (1970), 305.

5. Goldfarb, Ronald, and Singer, Linda. "Redressing Prisoners' Grievances," *George Washington Law Review*, 39 (1970), 186-208.

6. Hirschkop, Philip J., and Milleman, Michael A. "The Unconstitutionality of Prison Life," *Virginia Law Review*, 55 (1969), 795.

7. Holt v. Sarver, 309 F.Supp. 362 (E.D. Ark. 1970), *aff'd.*, 442 F.2d 304 (8th Cir. 1971) (Totality of poor personal safety, physical, and rehabilitative conditions deemed to render whole State prison systems as unconstitutional imposition of cruel and unusual punishment.)

8. Jackson v. Bishop, 404 F.2d 571 (8th Cir. 1968) (Use of strap as punitive device banned.)

9. Jackson v. Hendrick, 40 Law Week 2710 (Ct. Common Pleas, Pa. 1972.) (Total living, health, overcrowding, and program deficiencies render Philadelphia's entire 3-facility penal system cruel, inhumane, and unconstitutional.)

10. Jordan v. Fitzharris, 257 F.Supp. 674 (N.D. Cal. 1966.) (Strip cell confinement without clothing, bedding, medical care and adequate heat, light, ventilation, or means for keeping clean deemed cruel and unusual punishment.)

11. National Council on Crime and Delinquency. *Model Act for the Protection of Rights of Prisoners.* New York: NCCD, 1972. Secs. 2 and 3.

12. Ratliff v. Stanley, 224 Ky. 819, 7 S.W.2d 230 (1928).

13. Riggs v. German, 81 Wash. 128, 142 P. 479 (1914).

14. Singer, Richard G. "Bringing the Constitution to Prison: Substantive Due Process and the Eighth Amendment," *University of Cincinnati Law Review*, 39 (1970), 650.

15. Tolbert v. Bragan, 451 F.2d 1020 (5th Cir. 1971) (Severe physical abuse of prisoners by their keepers without cause or provocation is actionable under Federal Civil Rights Act.)

16. Valvano v. McGrath, 325 F.Supp. 408 (E.D. N.Y. 1971) (Correctional authority ordered to present plan for impartial investigation and prosecution of charges against correctional officers and supervisors *re* the mistreatment of inmates.)

17. Weems v. United States, 217 U.S. 349 (1910) (Condemned chaining of prisoners and "hard and painful" labor for making false entries in a public record.)

18. Wright v. McMann, 387 F.2d 519 (2d Cir. 1967) (1 month confinement in strip cell under conditions similar to Fitzharris case held cruel and unusual if proved.) See also Wright v. McMann, 460 F.2d 126 (2d Cir. 1972), where the conditions alleged were proved.

Related Standards

The following standards may be applicable in implementing Standard 2.4.

2.1 Access to Courts.

6.2 Classification for Inmate Management.

9.3 State Inspection of Local Facilities.

14.11 Staff Development.

16.3 Code of Offenders' Rights.

STANDARD 2.5

HEALTHFUL SURROUNDINGS

Each correctional agency should immediately examine and take action to fulfill the right of each person in its custody to a healthful place in which to live. After a reasonable time to make changes, a residential facility that does not meet the requirements set forth in State health and sanitation laws should be deemed a nuisance and abated.

The facility should provide each inmate with:

1. His own room or cell of adequate size.

2. Heat or cooling as appropriate to the season to maintain temperature in the comfort range.

3. Natural and artificial light.

4. Clean and decent installations for the maintenance of personal cleanliness.

5. Recreational opportunities and equipment; when climatic conditions permit, recreation or exercise in the open air.

Healthful surroundings, appropriate to the purpose of the area, also should be provided in all other areas of the facility. Cleanliness and occupational health and safety rules should be complied with.

Independent comprehensive safety and sanitation inspections should be performed annually by qualified personnel: State or local inspectors of food, medical, housing, and industrial safety who are independent of the correctional agency. Correctional facilities should be subject to applicable State and local statutes or ordinances.

Commentary

Custody means more than possession; it means care. When a judge grants custody over an offender to the correctional authority, he is at once declaring that the correctional authority has power over the offender and that this power must be used to promote the health of the offender. The obligation of the correctional authority to a pretrial detainee—convicted of no crime—can be no less. Yet correctional facilities are remarkably health-endangering. In a 1972 study, "The Contemporary Jails of the United States: An Unknown and Neglected Area of Justice," Hans Mattick states:

Perhaps the most pervasive characteristic of jails, and a direct consequence of their general physical condition, is their state of sanitation and cleanliness. Some old jails can be kept tolerably clean and some new jails are filthy to the point of human degradation but, in general, the sanitary condition of jails leaves much to be desired. The general low level of cleanliness in jails has an immediate impact, not only on the health and morale of the inmates and staff who are confined together in the jail, but has the most serious and widespread effects on the surrounding community.

Especially in facilities for juvenile confinement, failure to implement the highest standards may have lifelong impact for the inmates, who are in formative years of life.

Correctional authorities are not unmindful of their obligation to avoid endangering the health of those they supervise. Principles and standards of the American Correctional Association, the National Council on Crime and Delinquency, and the National Sheriffs'

Association leave no doubt about what constitutes good practice. Given the general level of sanitation and health in the United States, the current tolerance of deficient conditions, particularly in local jails and detention facilities, is inexplicable.

Overcrowding, which the standard implicitly prohibits, is especially harmful. It exacerbates health hazards and also contributes to tensions in the institutional context. It is recognized that the requirement of the standard for each inmate to have his own room or cell cannot be achieved immediately. But as the use of facilities for pretrial confinement and service of sentence declines (as recommended throughout this report), the goal should become achievable. All new construction, of course, should incorporate the requirement of this standard.

Medical literature indicates that recreation is essential to good health. All standard correctional literature recognizes the value of a well-designed and comprehensive recreation program for incarcerated offenders. Nevertheless, what most often stands out about correctional institutions—especially jails—is the amount of time when no program is being conducted and no organized recreation program is available. Courts have included recreation programs in evaluating the adequacy of institutions particularly access of persons in solitary confinement to physical exercise.

The nonliving area of the correctional facility also should be designed and maintained with health and safety in mind. Kitchens, especially, must be operated in accordance with the highest standards. Vocational education, shop, and industrial areas of the correctional facility should be operated in accordance with Federal and State occupational safety laws.

The standard recognizes that the States usually legislate comprehensively in the health area; therefore, specifics are minimized in favor of a general statement of essential factors. The standard does state a remedy that should be available in the case of any unhealthful institution. Courts of equity have power to take control of, or close, buildings that constitute a threat to the health or morals of the community.

References

1. American Correctional Association. *Manual of Correctional Standards.* 3d ed. Washington: ACA, 1966. Principle XVI and chs. 26, 32.
2. *Matter of Savoy,* Doc. No. 70-4804 (D.C. Juv. Court, 1970) (Court finds lack of "big muscle" recreation facilities for indoor physical activity unacceptable for juveniles in prehearing detention.)
3. Mattick, Hans. "The Contemporary Jails of the United States: An Unknown and Neglected Area of Justice" in Daniel Glaser, ed., *Handbook of Corrections* (Rand McNally, forthcoming), draft page 63.
4. National Council on Crime and Delinquency. *A Model Act for the Protection of Rights of Prisoners.* New York: NCCD, 1972, Sec. 1.
5. National Sheriffs' Association. *Manual on Jail Administration.* Washington: NSA, 1970. Ch. XX.
6. Sinclair v. Henderson, 331 F.Supp. 1123 (E.D. La. 1971) (Federal Court condemns lack of outdoor exercise for death-row prisoners in extended confinement as "cruel and inhuman" punishment.)
7. United States Department of Economic and Social Affairs. *Standard Minimum Rules for the Treatment of Prisoners and Related Recommenda-*

tions. New York: United Nations, 1958. "Accommodation."

Related Standards

The following standards may be applicable in implementing Standard 2.5.

2.1 Access to Courts.

5.9 Continuing Jurisdiction of Sentencing Court.

8.3 Juvenile Detention Center Planning.

9.3 State Inspection of Local Facilities.

9.10 Local Facility Evaluation and Planning.

11.1 Planning New Correctional Institutions.

11.2 Modification of Existing Institutions.

16.3 Code of Offenders' Rights.

STANDARD 2.6

MEDICAL CARE

Each correctional agency should take immediate steps to fulfill the right of offenders to medical care. This should include services guaranteeing physical, mental, and social well-being as well as treatment for specific diseases or infirmities. Such medical care should be comparable in quality and availability to that obtainable by the general public and should include at least the following:

1. A prompt examination by a physician upon commitment to a correctional facility.

2. Medical services performed by persons with appropriate training under the supervision of a licensed physician.

3. Emergency medical treatment on a 24-hour basis.

4. Access to an accredited hospital.

Medical problems requiring special diagnosis, services, or equipment should be met by medical furloughs or purchased services.

A particular offender's need for medical care should be determined by a licensed physician or other appropriately trained person. Correctional personnel should not be authorized or allowed to inhibit an offender's access to medical personnel or to interfere with medical treatment.

Complete and accurate records documenting all medical examinations, medical findings, and medical treatment should be maintained under the supervision of the physician in charge.

The prescription, dispensing, and administration of medication should be under strict medical supervision.

Coverage of any governmental medical or health program should include offenders to the same extent as the general public.

Commentary

One of the most fundamental responsibilities of a correctional agency is to care for offenders committed to it. Adequate medical care is basic, as food and shelter are basic. Withholding medical treatment is not unlike the infliction of physical abuse. Offenders do not give up their rights to bodily integrity whether from human or natural forces because they were convicted of a crime.

With medical resources in short supply for the free community, it is not surprising that the level of medical services available to committed offenders is in many instances far below acceptable levels.

A 1970 survey conducted for the Law Enforcement Assistance Administration showed that nearly half of all jails in cities of 25,000 or more population have no medical facilities.

A recent Alabama decision, Newman v. State, 12 Crim. L. Rptr. 2113 (M.D. Ala. 1972) documented conditions which the court found "barbarous" as well as unconstitutional. Medical services were withheld by prison staff for disciplinary purposes; medical treatment, including minor surgery, was provided by unsupervised prisoners without appropriate training; medical supplies were in short supply; and few if any trained medical personnel were available.

Medical care is of course a basic human necessity. It also contributes to the success of any correctional program. Physical disabilities or abnormalities may contribute to an individual's socially deviant behavior or restrict his employment. In these cases, medical or dental treatment is an integral part of the overall rehabilitation program. Most incarcerated offenders are from lower socioeconomic classes, which have a worse health status generally than more affluent persons. Thus, there is a greater need for medical and dental services than in the population at large. Since "care" is implicitly or explicitly part of correctional agencies' enabling legislation, medical services at least comparable to those available to the general population should be provided. The standard should not be "what the individual was accustomed to." Finally, unlike persons in the free community, those who are institutionalized cannot seek out needed care. By denying normal access to such services, the state assumes the burden of assuring access to quality medical care for those it so restricts.

A clear affirmative responsibility is imposed on the correctional authority. It extends beyond treatment of injuries and disease to include preventive medicine and dentistry, corrective or restorative medicine, and mental as well as physical health.

Medical services should be part of the intake procedure at all correctional facilities. Regardless of the hour, trained practitioners should be available to investigate any suspicious conditions. Even relatively brief delays in securing medical care can have and often do have fatal consequences.

The specific provisions of the standard should be read against the requirement that correctional medical services should be comparable to service obtainable by the general public. The medical program of each institution should accommodate private consultations and privileged communications between medical staff and inmates. In view of the usual limitations on the range of staff medical specialists, the correctional authority should be able to purchase the services of other medical practitioners. Contracts should be considered for prepayment for all services provided over a specified period with various practitioners or medical groups to maximize the individual's options for care and minimize problems of billing. Access to nonstaff physicians should be available to all inmates, regardless of ability to pay.

While the use of nurses and paraprofessionals is contemplated by the standard, they should be under the supervision of a licensed physician. He should also supervise the collection, retention, and dissemination of medical records and the dispensing and prescription of medicines. Infirmaries in many institutions serve as sources for illicit drugs, and strict procedures should be adopted to avoid this possibility. This may require the elimination, or reducton in the use, of offenders as staff in medical programs.

Offenders should not be discriminated against in governmental health programs. Legislation providing for government assistance should be applicable to those convicted of crime.

References

1. Alexander, Susan. "The Captive Patient: The Treatment of Health Problems in American Prisons." *Clearinghouse Review*, 6 (1972), 16. (Contains citations to numerous judicial opinions upholding offenders' rights to medical care.)
2. American Correctional Association. *Manual of Correctional Standards.* 3d ed. Washington: ACA, 1966. Ch. 26.
3. McCollum v. Mayfield, 130 F. Supp. 112 (N.D. Cal. 1955) (Refusal of prison authorities to provide inmate with needed medical care actionable under Federal Civil Rights Act.)
4. National Sheriffs' Association. *Manual on Jail Administration.* Washington: NSA, 1970. Ch. XX.
5. Newman v. State, 12 Crim. L. Rptr. 2113 (M.D. Ala. 1972).
6. Sneidman, Barney. "Prisoners and Medical Treatment: Their Rights and Remedies," *Colorado Bulletin*, 4 (1968), 450.
7. South Carolina Department of Corrections. *The Emerging Rights of the Confined.* Columbia: 1972. Ch. 16.
8. Talley v. Stephens, 247 F.Supp. 683 (E.D. Ark. 1965) (Arkansas prison official ordered to provide inmates with reasonable medical conditions and not work those in poor physical condition beyond their capacity.)

Related Standards

The following standards may be applicable in implementing Standard 2.6.
2.1 Access to Courts.
5.9 Continuing Jurisdiction of Sentencing Court.
8.3 Juvenile Detention Center Planning.
9.3 State Inspection of Local Facilities.
9.10 Local Facility Evaluation and Planning.
11.1 Planning New Correctional Institutions.
11.2 Modification of Existing Institutions.
16.3 Code of Offenders' Rights.

STANDARD 2.7

SEARCHES

Each correctional agency should immediately develop and implement policies and procedures governing searches and seizures to insure that the rights of persons under their authority are observed.

1. Unless specifically authorized by the court as a condition of release, persons supervised by correctional authorities in the community should be subject to the same rules governing searches and seizures that are applicable to the

general public.

2. Correctional agencies operating institutions should develop and present to the appropriate judicial authority or the officer charged with providing legal advice to the corrections department for approval a plan for making regular administrative searches of facilities and persons confined in correctional institutions.

a. The plan should provide for:

(1) Avoiding undue or unnecessary force, embarrassment, or indignity to the individual.

(2) Using non-intensive sensors and other technological advances instead of body searches wherever feasible.

(3) Conducting searches no more frequently than reasonably necessary to control contraband in the institution or to recover missing or stolen property.

(4) Respecting an inmate's rights in property owned or under his control, as such property is authorized by institutional regulations.

(5) Publication of the plan.

Any search for a specific law enforcement purpose or one not otherwise provided for in the plan should be conducted in accordance with specific regulations which detail the officers authorized to order and conduct such a search and the manner in which the search is to be conducted. Only top management officials should be authorized to order such searches.

Commentary

Three stituations should be distinguished when discussing searches of persons under correctional supervision:

• When a person is under community supervision.

• When a person is an inmate of a correctional institution and the pro-

posed search is of the general type, routinely conducted to prevent accumulation of contraband (administrative search).

• When a person is an inmate and the proposed search relates to a particular crime, incident, or item of contraband (law enforcement search).

Since the respective interests of the correctional authority and the person to be searched are different in each of these situations, different rules are necessary in each case.

By all accounts, even in programs with small caseloads, the amount of direct interaction between a correctional worker and probationer, parolee, or participant in another community correctional program is small. The paucity of these contacts eliminates security as a justification for any special search power in the correctional authority. Having few or no contacts with the offender means that searches of a supervised offender in the community are for law enforcement rather than administrative purposes. An entire body of law regulates the conditions under which government may invade an individual's privacy. The standard states that in the case of these offenders, except where periodic searches (in the case of former addicts, for example) are specifically authorized by the court or paroling authority as a condition of release, the correctional authority must comply with the requirements of the fourth amendment regarding searches.

In correctional institutions, the acquisition of contraband by an inmate is power. The limitation of contraband facilitates maintenance of control and safety. Some contraband is inherently dangerous to institutional security. All weapons fall into this category. In other instances, possession of contraband may be a source of power to manipulate other inmates.

Establishing this need, however, does not justify carte blanche searches of inmates and their property. Indeed, since the threat is predictable and ongoing, the correctional authority has ample opportunity to evaluate the security requirements of the institution and plan and implement countermeasures.

In view of the constitutional issues possibly involved, the standard recommends that the corrections department seek judicial review or consult the officer charged with providing legal advice to the department. At the State level, the officer should be a member of the attorney general's staff. At the local level, the appropriate person would be the district attorney or the corporation counsel.

The recommendation of a judicially approved plan for administrative searches is not unlike the rules governing such searches in the free community. In Camara v. Municipal Court of the City and County of San Francisco, 387 U.S. 523 (1967), and See v. City of Seattle, 387 U.S. 541 (1967), the Supreme Court held that general regulatory searches such as housing inspections must be conducted pursuant to a judicial warrant, which can authorize area searches if the governmental interest "reasonably justifies" the search. The court stated: "If a valid public interest justifies the intrusion contemplated, then there is probable cause to issue a suitably restricted search warrant."

There is no doubt that weapons and contraband are valid interest justifying administrative searches. The recommendation for prior approval of an overall plan for such searches is intended to assure that such searches are "suitably restricted." Too frequent or too intrusive searches are unrelated to contraband; they are more often used as harassment.

Requiring judicial approval of the plan for administrative searches in advance may at first blush run counter to the general reluctance of courts to give advisory opinions. However, the Camara and See cases support the notion that a warrant for administrative searches may extend over a wide geographic area rather than being confined to a specific site to be searched. Judicial approval of the correctional search plan is analogous to a warrant procedure extending not the geographic area but the time in which the search may take place. It is also consistent with the Commission's recommendations that the courts maintain continuing jurisdiction over sentenced offenders to have a detached judicial determination of whether the frequency and manner of administrative searches is reasonable.

Rapid progress has been made in recent years in the development of sensors and detectors for a variety of law enforcement purposes. Those associated with prevention of "skyjacking" and sale or possession of narcotics are perhaps the most heralded. These various devices generally have not been integrated into institutional security systems. As a result, correctional authorities continue to rely on physical searches.

In addition to the apparently legitimate bases for many searches, correctional authorities sometimes have other purposes, including harassment. The balance between proper and improper motives, between disruptive searches and less intrusive ones, is unknown. The correctional administrator in the past has exercised unreviewed discretion.

As a condition for approval of the

plan, the reviewing authority could require periodic reviews, outside monitoring, and incorporation of advanced technology. It might require further that the search plan include a means for controlling excessive zeal on the part of employees conducting the search.

Requirements for conducting specific law enforcement searches of confined offenders raise more complicated issues. These searches, directed at solving a particular crime, involve not only correctional interest but also the interest in a fair trial. The offender may, as a result of a specific search, face further criminal charges, and for persons in the free society the fourth amendment would not only govern such searches but also prohibit the introduction of evidence at the trial which was illegally obtained. Serious constitutional questions thus arise where specific law enforcement searches are conducted within correctional institutions without compliance with the fourth amendment requirements.

The Commission does not make a recommendation as to the extent to which the fourth amendment applies to these searches within institutions. The Commission does recommend that in light of the seriousness of the issues involved, only specific top management correctional officials be authorized to order such searches and that middle managers and line officers not be allowed to conduct such searches on their own initiative. The correctional agency should also adopt specific regulations detailing the manner in which such searches are to be conducted and under what circumstances.

References

1. Camara v. Municipal Court of the City and County of San Francisco, 387 U.S. 523 (1967).
2. U.S. v. Hill, 447 F.2d 817 (7th Cir. 1971) (Recognizing propriety of fourth amendment protection for probationer but rejecting application of exclusionary rule.)
3. National Sheriffs' Association. *Manual on Jail Administration.* Washington: NSA, 1970. Ch. XV.
4. See v. City of Seattle, 387 U.S. 541 (1967).
5. Singer, Richard G. "Privacy, Autonomy, and Dignity in the Prison: A Preliminary Inquiry Concerning Constitutional Aspects of the Degradation Process in Our Prisons," *Buffalo Law Review,* 21 (1972), 669.
6. U.S. ex rel. Sperling v. Fitzpatrick, 426 F.2d 1161 (2nd Cir. 1970).

Related Standards

The following standards may be applicable in implementing Standard 2.7.
2.1 Access to Courts.
2.4 Protection Against Personal Abuse.
5.9 Continuing Jurisdiction of Sentencing Court.
12.7 Measures of Control (Parole).
16.3 Code of Offenders' Rights.

STANDARD 2.8

NONDISCRIMINATORY TREATMENT

Each correctional agency should immediately develop and implement policies and procedures assuring the right of offenders not to be subjected to discriminatory treatment based on race, religion, nationality, sex, or political beliefs. The policies and procedures should assure:

1. An essential equality of opportunity in being considered for various program options, work assignments, and decisions concerning offender status.

2. An absence of bias in the decision process, either by intent or in results.

3. All remedies available to noninstitutionalized citizens open to prisoners in case of discriminatory treatment.

This standard would not prohibit segregation of juvenile or youthful offenders from mature offenders or male from female offenders in offender management and programming, except where separation of the sexes results in an adverse and discriminatory effect in program availability or institutional conditions.

Commentary

Perhaps the most sensitive problems in the "equal treatment" arena, at least in recent years, have revolved around the issue of racial discrimination and segregation. Generally, the courts have proceeded vigorously to disapprove correctional policies clearly discriminating against racial minorities. With the demise of the "separate but equal" doctrine in the field of public education (Brown v. Board of Education), it was inevitable that segregated programs in correctional institutions soon would be challenged.

Early cases dealing with juvenile training schools, in which the analogy to education was most obvious, brought an end to the practice. Subsequent cases attacked the overall operation of segregated prisons and jails. Here, also, the judicial response was to require integration. Soon the Supreme Court confirmed this constitutional interpretation in a case that invalidated State legislation requiring the segregation of the races in correctional institutions, Lee v. Washington, 390 U.S. 333 (1968).

The courts have made it clear that practices which on the surface seem unobjectionable but prove to be discriminatory in effect also are vulnerable to the equal protection mandate of the fourteenth amendment (for example, limiting prisoner literature to "hometown" newspapers where there are no such periodicals for black inmates).

Factors such as racial tension, political hostility, and treatment services tied to religious belief or nationality may be considered when placing inmates in situations where adequate supervision cannot guarantee personal safety, but only when demonstrably relevant to institutional security. Until now, courts have recognized that correctional authorities, in seeking to maintain institutional order and discipline, cannot ignore the marked racial tensions and aggressiveness frequently found in prisons. The burden of demonstrating lack of bias when such factors are taken into account, however, would fall on the correctional authority.

Some adjustments in current separation of the sexes is required where an adverse and discriminatory effect is shown in program availability or institutional conditions. Such separation has long been considered an important custodial requirement, but in recent years less so, particularly for juvenile and youthful offenders. The "equal treatment" guarantees of the standard do not necessarily prohibit separation of juvenile or youthful offenders from mature offenders.

Discriminatory treatment based on political views has been discouraged in cases dealing with free speech rights and imposition of unreasonable parole conditions. The standard includes political belief within its broad reach. It recognizes, in particular, the more "politicized" character of present offender populations and the significant impact on correctional operations of those incarcerated for criminal conduct related to social and political dissent.

References

1. Goldfarb, Ronald, and Singer, Linda. "Redressing Prisoners' Grievances," *George Washington Law Review*, 39 (1970), 223-226.
2. Higgenbotham, Leon. "Is Yesterday's Racism Relevant to Today's Corrections?" in *Outside Looking In*. Washington: Law Enforcement Assistance Administration, 1970.
3. McClelland v. Sigler, 456 F.2d 1266 (8th Cir. 1972) (Potential hostility of some white inmates not adequate ground for racial segregation of State facility.)
4. National Council on Crime and Delinquency. *A Model Act for the Protection of Prisoners' Rights*. New York: NCCD, 1972, Sec. 2.

Related Standards

The following standards may be applicable in implementing Standard 2.8.

2.1 Access to Courts.
5.9 Continuing Jurisdiction of Sentencing Court.
6.1 Comprehensive Classification Systems.
16.2 Administrative Justice.
16.3 Code of Offenders' Rights.

STANDARD 2.9

REHABILITATION

Each correctional agency should immediately develop and implement policies, procedures, and practices to fulfill the right of offenders to rehabilitation programs. A rehabilitative purpose is or ought to be implicit in every sentence of an offender unless ordered otherwise by the sentencing court. A correctional authority should have the affirmative and enforceable duty to provide programs appropriate to the purpose for which a person was sentenced. Where such programs are absent, the correctional authority should (1) establish or provide access to such programs or (2) inform the sentencing court of its inability to comply with the purpose for which sentence was imposed. To further define this right to rehabilitative services:

1. The correctional authority and the governmental body of which it is a part should give first priority to implementation of statutory specifications or statements of purpose on rehabilitative services.

2. Each correctional agency providing parole, probation, or other community supervision, should supplement its rehabilitative services by referring offenders to social services and activities available to citizens generally. The correctional authority should, in planning its total range of rehabilitative programs, establish a presumption in favor of community-based programs to the maximum extent possible.

3. A correctional authority's rehabilitation program should include a mixture of educational, vocational, counseling, and other services appropriate to offender needs. Not every facility need offer the entire range of programs, except that:

a. Every system should provide opportunities for basic education up to high school equivalency, on a basis comparable to that available to citizens generally, for offenders capable and desirous of such programs;

b. Every system should have a selection of vocational training programs available to adult offenders; and

c. A work program involving offender labor on public maintenance, construction, or other projects should not be considered part of an offender's access to rehabilitative services when he requests (and diagnostic efforts indicate that he needs) educational, counseling, or training opportunities.

4. Correctional authorities regularly should advise courts and sentencing judges of the extent and availability of rehabilitative services and programs within the correctional system to permit proper sentencing decisions and realistic evaluation of treatment alternatives.

5. Governmental authorities should be held responsible by courts for meeting the requirements of this standard.

6. No offender should be required or coerced to participate in programs of rehabilitation or treatment nor should the failure or refusal to participate be used to penalize an inmate in any way in the institution.

Commentary

An enforceable right to "treatment" or rehabilitative services has not yet been established in the courts in any significant measure. Although much discussed in recent years, it remains the most elusive and ephemeral of the offender rights being asserted. This is so despite the firm commitment of the corrections profession for more than a century to a rehabilitation rather than a punishment goal ("Declaration of Principles of the American Prison Association." Cincinnati, Ohio—1870) and an expression of rehabilitative intent in most State correctional codes and virtually all juvenile court and corrections statutes. Perhaps the lack of an affirmative, legally enforceable responsibility to provide services accounts for the extreme inadequacy of rehabilitative resources that has plagued American corrections for decades. The resources found wanting include educational, vocational, psychiatric, and casework services.

Explicit judicial validation of a right to treatment has been limited to the criminally insane or mentally defective offender and, on a much narrower basis, to juvenile or youthful offenders. Even here, the concept has been established in only a few cases. It has involved few jurisdictions and has in some cases turned on interpretation of a statutory mandate rather than a constitutional right. Although the chief legal bulwark for an affirmative right to rehabilitative services will remain statutory, a substantial due process argument is increasingly being recognized. As Justice Blackmun noted in the Supreme Court opinion in Jackson v. Indiana, 406 U.S. 715 (1972): "At the least, due process requires that the nature and duration of commitment bear some reasonable relation to the purpose for which the individual is committed."

Initial suggestions of an affirmative right to rehabilitative services for criminal offenders seem to have stemmed from an emerging, judicially confirmed "right to treatment" in civil commitment of the mentally ill. The first crossover probably was a District of Columbia case concerning a statute requiring mandatory hospital treatment of defendants acquitted by reason of insanity. A Federal court, Rouse v. Cameron, 373 F.2d 451 (D.C. Cir. 1966), found that the statute created for the defendant an enforceable right to treatment while institutionalized. This ruling was followed by a Massachusetts decision, Nason v. Superintendent of Bridgewater State Hospital, 353 Mass. 604 (S.Ct. 1968), ordering a more adequate treatment program for an offender incompetent to stand trial who was receiving only custodial care.

Applicability to the juvenile justice system was suggested by two more District of Columbia cases: Creek v. Stone, 379 F.2d 106 (1967) and In re Elmore, 382 F.2d 125 (1967). One involved a juvenile in prehearing detention, the other an adjudicated offender in a juvenile institution. A right to treatment, or release if treatment could not be supplied, was enunciated here. Reliance was placed on the standard injunction in juvenile court acts that children removed from home shall receive care, custody, and discipline equivalent to that which should have been supplied by parents. As in the other right-to-treatment cases, the deficiencies at issue related to psychiatric and mental health care rather than general rehabilitative programs. However, a recent District of Columbia case, Matter of Savoy (Docket #70-4804 D.C. Juvenile Ct. 1970), enforced a more generalized program of rehabilitative services against a statutory standard, including compulsory education and recreation.

In two recent decisions, the tendency toward carving a right to treatment from enabling legislation was continued. In one case, McCray v. State, 10 Crim. L. Rptr. 2132 (Montgomery Cty., Md. Cir. Ct. 1971), involving an institution for legally sane but mentally or emotionally deficient offenders, the court stated that the statute "implicitly connoted treatment and rehabilitation." It found that a total rehabilitative effort was missing and treatment should be accelerated notwithstanding budgetary limitations imposed by the State and even for recalcitrant and noncooperative prisoners.

In the other case, U.S. v. Allsbrook, 10 Crim. L. Rptr. 2185 (D.Ct. D.C. 1971), the danger to public safety and recidivism was stressed. The court found that failure to provide the full rehabilitative services contemplated by the Federal Youth Corrections Act for District of Columbia offenders barred further commitments under the Act without a Justice Department certification of treatment availability. There was a further determination that this situation infringed on the court's constitutional sentencing authority and justified orders to the executive branch to provide adequate facilities as contemplated by the Act.

On the other hand, right to treatment claims in adult prisons concerning general rehabilitative programs have not as yet received recognition. In Georgia, Wilson v. Kelley, 294 F.Supp. 1005 (N.D. Ga. 1968), prisoners were unsuccessful in seeking a judicial declaration that sentencing convicts to county work camps where no effort was made to rehabilitate them was unconstitutional. And even in the landmark Arkansas case, Holt v. Sarver, 309 F.Supp. 362 (E.D. Ark. 1970), determining that conditions in the Arkansas prison system amounted to constitutionally prohibited "cruel and unusual punishment," the court refrained from ordering the implementation of rehabilitative plans and opportunities, although it did note that lack of proper rehabilitative programs was a factor in finding the prison unconstitutional.

The standard has been formulated in light of the limited but growing legal status of the right to treatment. The standard provides that offenders have the right to programs appropriate to the purpose for which they were sentenced. Where a court sentences a person for rehabilitation, rehabilitation programs should be available. Thus in the first instance the duty is placed on correctional agencies to respond to the sentencing order. If because of lack of resources or other reason the correctional agency cannot provide appropriate programs, it should then be required to report this fact to the sentencing court. Remedies for enforcing offenders' rights, provided in Standard 2.18, should then be utilized.

The standard recognizes that not every program can be available for every offender. The test to be applied should be whether the offender has access to some programs which are "appropriately related" to the purpose for which he was sentenced.

The right to rehabilitative services in the parole or probation context is defined. Because the offender is at liberty in the community, his situation is equated to that of citizens generally seeking access to social service or other community agencies. This, of course, does not ban special treatment programs for probationers or parolees but recognizes that it is equally valid to integrate them into general vocational, educational, and counseling programs in the community.

The standard requires that courts and sentencing judges be regularly advised of the true extent of rehabilitative services and programs available within their adult and juvenile correctional systems. This requirement is needed for sentencing officials to make proper choices among the sentencing alternatives available to them and to avoid mistaken ideas of what can be provided to sentenced offenders. This important corollary to the right to rehabilitative services has long been neglected in interaction between courts and correctional systems.

Endorsement of the right to treatment does not carry with it the right of correctional authorities to require or coerce offenders into participating in rehabilitative programs. Considerations of individual privacy, integrity, dignity, and personality suggest that coerced programs should not be permitted. In addition, a forced program of any nature is unlikely to produce constructive results. This principle, as applied to juveniles, must be qualified under the parens patriae concept, but nonetheless it would appear to have considerable validity here also.

References

1. Comment, "A Statutory Right to Treatment for Prisoners: Society's Right of Self-Defense," *Nebraska Law Review*, 50 (1971), 543.
2. Dawson, Robert. "Legal Norms and the Juvenile Correctional Process" in Cohen, Fred, *The Legal Challenge to Corrections*. Washington: Joint Commission on Correctional Manpower and Training, 1969.
3. Goldfarb, Ronald, and Singer, Linda. "Redressing Prisoners' Grievances," *George Washington Law Review*, 39 (1970), 208.
4. Note, *Southern California Law Review*, 45 (1972), 616.
5. Schwitzegebel, Ralph K. "Limitation on The Coercive Treatment of Offenders," *Criminal Law Bulletin*, 8 (1972), 267.

Related Standards

The following standards may be applicable in implementing Standard 2.9.

2.1 Access to Courts.

2.18 Remedies for Violation of an Offender's Rights.

5.9 Continuing Jurisdiction of Sentencing Court.

10.2 Services to Probationers.

12.6 Community Services for Parolees.

16.1 Comprehensive Correctional Legislation.

STANDARD 2.10

RETENTION AND RESTORATION OF RIGHTS

Each State should enact legislation immediately to assure that no person is deprived of any license, permit, employment, office, post of trust or confidence, or political or judicial rights based solely on an accusation of criminal behavior. Also, in the implementation of Standard 16.17, Collateral Consequences of a Criminal Conviction, legislation depriving convicted persons of civil rights should be repealed. This legislation should provide further that a convicted and incarcerated person should have restored to him on release all rights not otherwise retained.

The appropriate correctional authority should:

1. With the permission of an accused person, explain to employers, families, and others the limited meaning of an arrest as it relates to the above rights.

2. Work for the repeal of all laws and regulations depriving accused or convicted persons of civil rights.

3. Provide services to accused or convicted persons to help them retain or exercise their civil rights or to obtain restoration of their rights or any other limiting civil disability that may occur.

Commentary

Modern rhetoric aside, punishment of the accused begins long before conviction. According to the National Jail Census, on March 15, 1970 more than 83,000 unconvicted persons were held in jails. Two-thirds of the 7,800 detained juveniles were unadjudicated.

Pretrial detention imposes an immediate economic hardship on accused persons who have jobs. Not only is their immediate sources of income cut off but also an advantageous relationship with their employers is often terminated. An arrest record per se, although not proof of criminality, may forever reduce a person's employability.

The theory is that these persons are being held to assure their attendance at trial or another judicial proceeding. Again in theory, every reasonable effort should be made to avoid interfering with the lives of these people. The overwhelming majority of detention facilities lack any recreation or education facilities. Only half have medical facilities available, and what little is known of the quality of existing facilities makes even this half suspect. The theory is seldom recognized in practice.

The shameful fact is that these impositions fall with greater weight upon the poor than on any other group. Rarely is there any compensation—monetary or otherwise—for the losses suffered by pretrial detainees. When only one course of conduct or mode of operation can be followed, those who run the jails tend to treat each inmate as though he is dangerous.

In addition to loss of liberty and the direct concomitants set out herein—and others like them—events are set in train that seriously interfere with individuals' rights. The pretrial detainee retains the right to vote, but the right may be effectively lost unless a special effort is made to transport him to the polls or enroll him for absentee voting. Also, a license may lapse when renewal is due because no jail officer is empowered to notarize the inmate's signature.

The standard seeks to minimize the number and severity of disadvantages to which accused but unconvicted persons are subject by requiring the correctional authority to develop and implement an affirmative program to protect their rights.

Civil liabilities resulting from criminal conviction directly restrict offender reintegration. Some outright employment restrictions force releases into the least remunerative jobs. Prohibiting contracts makes property holding impossible. Being unable to vote or hold public office only further aggravates the individual's alienation and isolation.

Many individual judgments contribute to social stigmatization, and no standard can address those disabilities arising from personal choice. But a myriad of official governmental actions far too broad, counterproductive of rehabilitation and reintegration into the community, and no longer justifiable still operate in this field. Indeed, the very existence of governmental sanctions for these continuing punishments may produce, encourage, or buttress negative private actions.

The vision of an offender leaving a correctional institution, his debt to so-ciety paid, rejoining his community, and building a new life is a false image. In many ways, the punishment an ex-convict faces is more lasting, more insidious, and more demeaning than that punishment he undergoes while incarcerated. The scar of the "offender" label can be more vicious than the physical scars sometimes inflicted in confinement.

Most of the civil rights and privileges lost by those convicted of crimes are withdrawn by specific legislation. The content and effect of such statutory provisions differ among the various jurisdictions. Recommendations for repeal of most of these legislative disabilities are contained in Standard 16.17.

The standard would provide a broad, positive program to change the existing situation. First, it automatically would restore lost, forfeited, and suspended rights and privileges. This is meant to include licenses of all types and the right to vote.

The correctional authority has a major interest in seeing the offender fully integrated into the community and, where restoration is not automatic, the correctional authority is assigned the duty of helping the offender regain his rights. This assistance is analogous to the process of granting "gate money" to inmates being released from correctional institutions. Institutional training programs have no value if the individual cannot make use of the training. Even today, it is not uncommon to operate training programs for licensed occupations (barbering, for example) that exclude ex-offenders. Many probation, parole, and other community-based correctional workers already provide help of the type indicated.

Federal, State, and local governments should take the lead in removing all employment restrictions based solely on prior criminal conviction. Since public sector employment is about one-sixth of total employment in the United States, to bar the ex-offender from government jobs considerably reduces his options. Interestingly, correctional agencies will employ someone at substandard wages in prison industries but refuse to employ the same person on release.

Restrictive government practices are a bad example to private employers who can ask properly why they should hire ex-offenders who are not "safe bets" for governmental employment. Example and active leadership by government is required.

The standard calls on the correctional authority itself to lead the campaign to roll back restrictions that have developed over the years but are not consistent with and supportive of the current reintegration approach to corrections. This is a natural role, since the correctional authority has contributed to the rise of the problem and therefore must work to undo that which present views make unacceptable.

Limitations on political rights and those involving courts, such as the right to sue and the use of an ex-offender's record as grounds for impeaching his testimony, are among the most onerous restrictions. They involve, in essence, a statement by government that offenders and former offenders, as a class, are worth less than other men. This lessening of status on the outside reinforces the debasement so common in the institutional setting and hardens the resentment offenders commonly feel toward society in general.

Most importantly, the state is responsible for the welfare and rights of all citizens. To the extent that the state abridges or denies the free exercise of those rights, for whatever purpose, it bears a heavy burden to retain a deep interest in their full reinstatement and in minimizing their collateral effects, once that purpose has been fulfilled. Denial of liberty is so grave as to require greater attention and compensation to those so denied.

References

1. Advisory Commission on Intergovernmental Relations. *State-Local Relations in the Criminal Justice System*. Washington: Government Printing Office, 1971. Recommendation 36.

2. American Correctional Association. *Manual of Correctional Standards*. 3rd ed. Washington. ACA, 1966. Principle XXVII.

3. Carter v. Gallagher, 452 F.2d 315 (8th Cir. 1971) (Fire Department enjoined from rejecting applicant for arrest information.)

4. Griggs v. Duke Power Co., 401 U.S. 424 (1971).

5. Gregory v. Litton Systems, Inc., 316 F.Supp. 401 (C.D. Cal. 1970) (Finds Civil Rights Act, Title VII violation in employer denial of job to black applicant based on arrest record.)

6. Miller, Herbert S. "The Closed Door: The Effect of a Criminal Record on Employment with State and Local Public Agencies." Report prepared in 1972 for Manpower Administration, U.S. Dept. of Labor.

7. National Clearinghouse on Offender Employment Restrictions. *Removing Offender Employment Restrictions*. Washington: American Bar Association, 1972.

8. Note, *Cornell Law Review*, 55 (1970), 306.

9. President's Commission on Law Enforcement and Administration of

Justice. *Task Force Report: Corrections.* Washington: Government Printing Office, 1967, ch. 8.

10. Special Project, *Collateral Consequences of a Criminal Conviction,* Vanderbilt Law Review, 29 (1970), 929.

11. U.S. Children's Bureau, *Standards for Juvenile and Family Courts.* Washington: Department of Health, Education and Welfare, 1966. Ch. VI.

Related Standards

The following standards may be applicable in implementing Standard 2.10.

2.1 Access to Courts.
9.9 Jail Release Program.
14.4 Employment of Ex-Offenders.
16.17 Collateral Consequences of a Criminal Conviction.

STANDARD 2.11

RULES OF CONDUCT

Each correctional agency should immediately promulgate rules of conduct for offenders under its jurisdiction. Such rules should:

1. Be designed to effectuate or protect an important interest of the facility or program for which they are promulgated.

2. Be the least drastic means of achieving that interest.

3. Be specific enough to give offenders adequate notice of what is expected of them.

4. Be accompanied by a statement of the range of sanctions that can be imposed for violations. Such sanctions should be proportionate to the gravity of the rule and the severity of the violation.

5. Be promulgated after appropriate consultation with offenders and other interested parties consistent with procedures recommended in Standard 16.2, Administrative Justice.

Correctional agencies should provide offenders under their jurisdiction with an up-to-date written statement of rules of conduct applicable to them.

Correctional agencies in promulgating rules of conduct should not attempt generally to duplicate the criminal law. Where an act is covered by administrative rules and statutory law the following standards should govern:

1. Acts of violence or other serious misconduct should be prosecuted criminally and not be the subject of administrative sanction.

2. Where the State intends to prosecute, disciplinary action should be deferred.

3. Where the State prosecutes and the offender is found not guilty, the correctional authority should not take further punitive action.

Commentary

A source of severe dissatisfaction with the correctional systems is the belief widely held among offenders that the system charged with instilling respect for law punishes arbitrarily and unfairly.

Not only do such practices contribute to problems of managing offenders but they also violate one of the most basic concepts of due process. Advance notice of what behavior is expected must be given so that the person being controlled may avoid sanctions for misbehavior. Failure to be specific will result in legal challenge on grounds of vagueness.

Codes of offender conduct are notorious for their inclusiveness and ambiguity and as a source of dissatisfaction. Rules should not repeat the mistakes of existing criminal codes by attempting to include every sort of behavior that is considered morally reprehensible. "Feigning illness" and "being untidy," for example, are of dubious threat to institutional or public security, personal safety, or operational efficiency. Vague rules allow too much discretion and often are abused; rules trivial in their intent engender hostility and lack of respect for the correctional authority.

Codes of conduct should be limited to observable behavior that can be shown clearly to have a direct adverse effect on an individual or others. Rules prohibiting attitudinal predispositions, such as "insolence," should be avoided because their ambiguity permits undue interpretative discretion. What one person describes as "insolence" another may consider a display of independence indicating improved self-perception. Ambiguous or abstract prohibitions make individual culpability questionable because they are difficult to communicate.

As evidenced by decisions regarding the elements of a fair disciplinary proceeding, courts deem an advance notice procedure to be of compelling importance. Notice of the alleged violation always is required to prepare an adequate defense. Giving full notice of the rules before alleged misconduct may contribute to a reduction of disciplinary cases.

Correctional agencies' rules of conduct, no less than the criminal code itself, should be enforced with penalties related to the gravity of the offense. The concept of proportionality of punishment should be fully applicable; several courts have recognized that disciplinary punishments in many instances are far in excess of this standard.

Virtually all correctional literature recognizes the need for established codes of offender conduct. The trend in practice today is to maximize offender participation in rulemaking. Procedures recommended in Standard 16.2 for promulgation of administrative rules generally should be applicable here. They would assure participation by offenders and other interested parties.

The criminal code is applicable to those already convicted of crime. Inevitably—because of the breadth of criminal codes—disciplinary rules promulgated by correctional authorities will duplicate the criminal law, but correctional agencies should not attempt to promulgate parallel rules. Criminal action by offenders should be subject to trial as in any other case, with the potential sanction and the appropriate formal safeguards.

Where overlap occurs, correctional administrators should defer to prosecution wherever possible. And where prosecution is unsuccessful, justice requires that further administrative punitive measures be prohibited.

References

1. American Correctional Association. *Manual of Correctional Standards*. 3rd ed. Washington: ACA, 1966. P. 408.

2. Cluchette v. Procunier, 328 F. Supp. 767 (N.D. Cal. 1971).

3. Landman v. Peyton, 370 F.2d 135 (4th Cir. 1966), *cert. denied*, 388 U.S.

920 (1967).
4. National Council on Crime and Delinquency. *A Model Act for the Protection of Rights of Prisoners.* New York: NCCD, 1972, Sec. 4.

Related Standards

The following standards may be applicable in implementing Standard 2.11.

2.12 Disciplinary Procedures.
16.2 Administrative Justice.

STANDARD 2.12

DISCIPLINARY PROCEDURES

Each correctional agency immediately should adopt, consistent with Standard 16.2, disciplinary procedures for each type of residential facility it operates and for the persons residing therein.

Minor violations of rules of conduct are those punishable by no more than a reprimand, or loss of commissary, entertainment, or recreation privileges for not more than 24 hours. Rules governing minor violations should provide that:

1. Staff may impose the prescribed sanctions after informing the offender of the nature of his misconduct and giving him the chance to explain or deny it.

2. If a report of the violation is placed in the offender's file, the offender should be so notified.

3. The offender should be provided with the opportunity to request a review by an impartial officer or board of the appropriateness of the staff action.

4. Where the review indicates that the offender did not commit the violation or the staff's action was not appropriate, all reference to the incident should be removed from the offender's file.

Major violations of rules of conduct are those punishable by sanctions more stringent than those for minor viola-

tions, including but not limited to, loss of good time, transfer to segregation or solitary confinement, transfer to a higher level of institutional custody or any other change in status which may tend to affect adversely an offender's time of release or discharge.

Rules governing major violations should provide for the following prehearing procedures:

1. Someone other than the reporting officer should conduct a complete investigation into the facts of the alleged misconduct to determine if there is probable cause to believe the offender committed a violation. If probable cause exists, a hearing date should be set.

2. The offender should receive a copy of any disciplinary report or charges of the alleged violation and notice of the time and place of the hearing.

3. The offender, if he desires, should receive assistance in preparing for the hearing from a member of the correctional staff, another inmate, or other authorized person (including legal counsel if available.)

4. No sanction for the alleged violation should be imposed until after the hearing except that the offender may be segregated from the rest of the population if the head of the institution finds that he constitutes a threat to other in-

mates, staff members, or himself.

Rules governing major violations should provide for a hearing on the alleged violation which should be conducted as follows:

1. The hearing should be held as quickly as possible, generally not more than 72 hours after the charges are made.

2. The hearing should be before an impartial officer or board.

3. The offender should be allowed to present evidence or witnesses on his behalf.

4. The offender may be allowed to confront and cross-examine the witnesses against him.

5. The offender should be allowed to select someone, including legal counsel, to assist him at the hearing.

6. The hearing officer or board should be required to find substantial evidence of guilt before imposing a sanction.

7. The hearing officer or board should be required to render its decision in writing setting forth its findings as to controverted facts, its conclusion, and the sanction imposed. If the decision finds that the offender did not commit the violation, all reference to the charge should be removed from the offender's file.

Rules governing major violations should provide for internal review of the hearing officer's or board's decision. Such review should be automatic. The reviewing authority should be authorized to accept the decision, order further proceedings, or reduce the sanction imposed.

Commentary

The nature of prison discipline and the procedures utilized to impose it are very sensitive issues, both to correctional administrators and to committed offenders. The imposition of drastic disciplinary measures can have a direct impact on the length of time an offender serves in confinement. The history of inhumane and degrading forms of punishment, including institutional "holes" where offenders are confined without clothing, bedding, toilet facilities, and other decencies, has been adequately documented in the courts. These practices are still widespread.

The administration of some form of discipline is necessary to maintain order within a prison institution. However, when that discipline violates constitutional safeguards or inhibits or seriously undermines reformative efforts, it becomes counter-productive and indefensible.

The very nature of a closed, inaccessible prison makes safeguards against arbitrary disciplinary power difficult. The correctional administration has power to authorize or deny every aspect of living from food and clothing to access to toilet facilities. It is this power, more than perhaps any other within the correctional system, which must be brought under the "rule of law."

Court decisions such as Goldberg v. Kelley, 397 U.S. 254 (1970) and Morrissey v. Brewer, 408 U.S. 471 (1972) have established the hearing procedure as a basic due process requirement in significant administrative deprivations of life, liberty, or property. There has been considerably less clarity, especially in the correctional context, of what minimal requirements must attend such a hearing. Court decisions have varied in interpretation. At one end of the spectrum they have provided only adequate notice of charges, a reasonable investigation into relevant facts, and an opportunity for the prisoner to reply to charges. At the other they have upheld the right to written notice of charges, hearing before an impartial tribunal, reasonable time to prepare defense, right to confront and cross-examine witnesses, a decision based on evidence at the hearing, and assistance by lay counsel (staff or inmate) plus legal counsel where prosecutable crimes are involved.

Correctional systems on their own initiative have implemented detailed disciplinary procedures incorporating substantial portions of the recognized elements of administrative agency due process. The standard largely follows this trend, emanating from both courts and correctional systems, toward more formalized procedures with normal administrative due-process protections in the administration of correctional discipline.

Due process is a concept authorizing varying procedures in differing contexts of governmental action. It does not require in all cases the formal procedures associated with a criminal trial. On the other hand, due process does contain some fundamentals that should regulate all governmental action having a potentially harmful effect on an individual.

Basic to any system that respects fundamental fairness are three requirements: (1) that the individual understand what is expected of him so he may avoid the consequences of inappropriate behavior; (2) if he is charged with a violation, that he be informed of what he is accused; and (3) that he be given an opportunity to present evidence in contradiction or mitigation of the charge.

As the consequences to the individual increase, other procedural devices to assure the accuracy of information on which action will be based come into play. These include the right to confront the individual making the charge of violation with an opportunity to cross-examine him; the right to assistance in presenting one's case, including legal counsel; the right to a formal hearing before an impartial tribunal or officer; the right to have proceedings of the hearing recorded in writing; and the right to written findings of fact.

Prison discipline can range in degree from an oral reprimand to loss of good time or disciplinary segregation. Where the punishment to be imposed extends or potentially extends the period of incarceration, or substantially changes the status of the offender either by placing him in disciplinary segregation or removing him from advantageous work assignments, the wider range of procedural safeguards should be employed. These decisions are critical not only to the offender but to the public. Since these procedures are designed only to assure a proper factual basis for governmental action, both the public and the offender have an interest in their implementation.

References

1. Council on the Diagnosis and Evaluation of Criminal Defendants. *Illinois Unified Code of Corrections: Tentative Final Draft.* St. Paul: West, 1971, section 335-9 and section 340-7.

2. Hirschkop, Philip J., and Milleman, Michael A. "The Unconstitutionality of Prison Life," *Virginia Law Review*, 55 (1969), 795.

3. Landman v. Royster, 333 F.Supp. 621 (E.D. Va. 1971) (Virginia case on hearing and related procedures for imposition of solitary confinement, transfer to maximum security, padlock confinement over 10 days and loss of good time.)

4. McGee, Thomas A. "Minimum Standards for Disciplinary Decision

Making." Unpublished paper prepared for the California Department of Corrections, Sacramento, 1972.

5. Milleman, Michael A. "Prison Disciplinary Hearings and Procedural Due Process—The Requirement of a Full Administrative Hearing," *Maryland Law Review*, 31 (1971), 27.

6. Morris v. Travisono, 310 F.Supp. 857 (D.R.I. 1970) (Due process safeguards for discipline involving segregation.)

7. Sostre v. McGinnis, 442 F.2d 178 (2d Cir. 1971), *cert. denied*, 404 U.S. 1049 (1972). (Due process safeguards for cases of substantial discipline.)

8. South Carolina Department of Corrections. *The Emerging Rights of the Confined*. Columbia: 1972.

9. Turner, William B. "Establishing the Rule of Law in Prisons: A Manual for Prisoners' Rights Litigation," *Stanford Law Review*, 23 (1971), 473, and authorities cited therein.

Related Standards

The following standards may be applicable in implementing Standard 2.12.

2.2 Access to Legal Services.

2.11 Rules of Conduct.

5.9 Continuing Jurisdiction of Sentencing Court.

16.2 Administrative Justice.

16.3 Code of Offenders' Rights.

STANDARD 2.13

PROCEDURES FOR NONDISCIPLINARY CHANGES OF STATUS

Each correctional agency should immediately promulgate written rules and regulations to prescribe the procedures for determining and changing offender status, including classification, transfers, and major changes or decisions on participation in treatment, education, and work programs within the same facility.

1. The regulations should:

a. Specify criteria for the several classifications to which offenders may be assigned and the privileges and duties of persons in each class.

b. Specify frequency of status reviews or the nature of events that prompt such review.

c. Be made available to offenders who may be affected by them.

d. Provide for notice to the offender when his status is being reviewed.

e. Provide for participation of the offender in decisions affecting his program.

2. The offender should be permitted to make his views known regarding the classification, transfer, or program decision under consideration. The offender should have an opportunity to oppose or support proposed changes in status or to initiate a review of his status.

3. Where reviews involving substantially adverse changes in degree, type, location, or level of custody are conducted, an administrative hearing should be held, involving notice to the offender, an opportunity to be heard, and a written report by the correctional authority communicating the final outcome of the review. Where such actions, particularly transfers, must be made on an emergency basis, this procedure should be followed subsequent to the action. In the case of transfers

between correctional and mental institutions, whether or not maintained by the correctional authority, such procedures should include specified procedural safeguards available for new or initial commitments to the general population of such institutions.

4. Proceedings for nondisciplinary changes of status should not be used to impose disciplinary sanctions or otherwise punish offenders for violations of rules of conduct or other misbehavior.

Commentary

The area of nondisciplinary classification and status determinations long has been considered a proper subject for the diagnostic, evaluation, and decisional expertise of correctional administrators and specialists. Yet decisions of this kind can have a critical effect on the offender's degree of liberty, access to correctional services, basic conditions of existence within a correctional system, and eligibility for release. This is true especially in jurisdictions with indeterminate sentence structures and simple commitment of offenders to the correctional authority, without statutory or court specification of kinds of institutional or program treatment.

This standard seeks to strike an appropriate balance between the interests of the system and those of the offender, specifying some basic principles of offenders' rights in this area but with a specificity and degree of formality much less pervasive than the "due process" elements proposed for imposition of major disciplinary sanctions.

First, the standard requires written rules and regulations, available to the offender, which clearly establish the basis for classification and other status determinations. This helps the individual understand the personal implications of each alternative choice so he

can express an informed preference. In addition, specifying decision criteria communicates to the offender that decisions are not capricious or arbitrary.

The effectiveness of rehabilitation is related directly to the offender's understanding and acceptance of program objectives. An individual is more likely to accept and understand the reasons for a decision in which he participates. Therefore, the standard calls for notice to the offender when his status is under review and a maximum attempt to solicit his views in all of the wide range of decisionmaking that may be applied while he is under correctional control.

A formal hearing right is specified for reviews involving potential changes of a substantially adverse character in the offender's degree, type, or level of custody. Courts already have shown concern for such procedural protections in the case of transfers from prisons to hospitals for the criminally insane and from juvenile institutions to adult facilities.

References

1. American Correctional Association. *Manual of Correctional Standards.* 3d ed. Washington: ACA, 1966. Chs. 7, 26.

2. Baxstrom v. Herold, 383 U.S. 107 (1966) (Administrative commitment of prisoner to hospital for criminally insane at end of prison term without new judicial determination available to others so committed denies equal protection of laws.)

3. Cohen, Fred. *The Legal Challenge to Corrections.* Washington: Joint Commission on Correctional Manpower and Training, 1969.

4. Goldfarb, Ronald, and Singer, Linda. "Redressing Prisoners' Grievances," *George Washington Law Review,* 39 (1970), 298-301.

5. Morris v. Travisono, 310 F.Supp. 857 (D.R.I. 1970) (Responding to charge of discriminatory classification procedures in State prison, court order required (i) regular periodic review of classification, (ii) enumeration of privileges and restrictions of each classification, (iii) written record of classification proceedings and notification to inmate of contemplated changes with reasons.)

6. People ex rel. Goldfinger v. Johnston, 53 Misc. 2d 949, 280 N.Y.S. 2d 304 (Sup. Ct. 1967) (Court requires hearing before transferring juvenile from correctional school to institution for "defective delinquents.")

7. Shone v. Maine, 406 F.2d 844 (1st Cir. 1969) (Juvenile entitled to hearing and assistance of attorney in procedure to transfer from a juvenile institution to a men's prison as an "incorrigible.")

8. South Carolina Department of Corrections. *The Emerging Rights of the Confined.* Columbia: 1972.

9. U.S. ex rel. Schuster v. Herold, 410 F.2d 1071 (2d Cir. 1969). (Prisoner under life sentence could not be transferred to hospital for criminally insane without procedures, periodic review, and jury determination available for involuntary civil commitments.)

Related Standards

The following standards may be applicable in implementing Standard 2.13.

6.2 Classification for Inmate Management.

16.2 Administrative Justice.

16.4 Unifying Correctional Programs.

STANDARD 2.14

GRIEVANCE PROCEDURE

Each correctional agency immediately should develop and implement a grievance procedure. The procedure should have the following elements:

1. Each person being supervised by the correctional authority should be able to report a grievance.

2. The grievance should be transmitted without alteration, interference, or delay to the person or entity responsible for receiving and investigating grievances.

   a. Such person or entity preferably should be independent of the correctional authority. It should not, in any case, be concerned with the day-to-day administration of the corrections function that is the subject of the grievance.

   b. The person reporting the grievance should not be subject to any adverse action as a result of filing the report.

3. Promptly after receipt, each grievance not patently frivolous should be investigated. A written report should be prepared for the correctional authority and the complaining person. The report should set forth the findings of the investigation and the recommendations of the person or entity responsible for making the investigation.

4. The correctional authority should respond to each such report, indicating what disposition will be made of the recommendations received.

Commentary

Institutions, especially closed institutions, have a great capacity to produce unrest, dissatisfaction, and tension. By limiting a man's perspective and liberty, the institution focuses his attention inward and deprives him of the opportunity to avoid conditions or persons he finds unpleasant. Unresolved minor displeasures can grow to major grievances increasing hostility and institutional tension. Too frequently, grievances have multiplied until violence appeared to be the only means available to secure relief.

Open lines of communication between inmate and staff can do much to keep the correctional authority alert to developing problems. Unfortunately, a number of factors frequently limit the viability of such informal means. The following are among them:

• Staff and inmates may not communicate effectively because of age, racial, or other differences.

• Staff may discount offender views and complaints and fail or refuse to transmit them through channels for investigation.

• Investigators may be too close to conditions to perceive the validity of grievances or the existence of reasonable alternatives.

A formal procedure to insure that offenders' grievances are fairly resolved should alleviate much of the existing tension within institutions. The first amendment requirements protecting the right of persons to petition their government for redress speaks eloquently of the importance attached to a government responsive to the complaints of its citizenry. Peaceful avenues for redress of grievances are a prerequisite if violent means are to be avoided. Thus all correctional agencies have not only a responsibility but an institutional interest in maintaining procedures that are, and appear to offenders to be, designed to resolve their complaints fairly.

The standard is broadly drawn to include all correctional functions. While the noninstitutionalized correctional population has numerous opportunities to relieve tensions, there is no reason to exclude this group from access to grievance machinery. Moreover, persons on whom the system operates are in a unique position to contribute to its improvement.

The standard has three main features. To encourage use of the procedure, it must be open to all, and no reprisals should flow from its use. Second, all grievances with merit should be investigated. A natural outcome is a report of what was found and what is being done, with a copy to the originator of the grievance.

Finally, someone not directly connected with the function being investigated should be charged with the responsibility of evaluating the grievance. In addition to producing a balanced report, as free as possible of self-serving conclusions, this step is calculated to gain credibility for the mechanism. The standard encompasses use of an ombudsman, an independent grievance commission, or an internal review or inspection office.

References

1. American Correctional Association. *Riots and Disturbances in Correctional Institutions*. Washington: ACA, 1970. Chs. 1, 2.

2. Council on the Diagnosis and Evaluation of Criminal Defendants. *Illinois Unified Code of Corrections: Tentative Final Draft*. St. Paul: West, 1971. Sections 340-348.

3. Goldfarb, Ronald, and Singer, Linda. "Redressing Prisoners' Grievances," *George Washington Law Re-*

view, 39 (1970), 175, 304, 316.
4. National Sheriffs' Association. *Manual on Jail Administration.* Washington: NSA, 1970. Pp. 20, 24.
5. National Council on Crime and Delinquency. *A Model Act for the Protection of Rights of Prisoners.* New York: NCCD, 1972. Ch. 5.

Related Standards

The following standards may be applicable in implementing Standard 2.14.

5.9 Continuing Jurisdiction of Sentencing Court.

16.2 Administrative Justice.

STANDARD 2.15

FREE EXPRESSION AND ASSOCIATION

Each correctional agency should immediately develop policies and procedures to assure that individual offenders are able to exercise their constitutional rights of free expression and association to the same and subject to the same limitations as the public at large. Regulations limiting an offender's right of expression and association should be justified by a compelling state interest requiring such limitation. Where such justification exists, the agency should adopt regulations which effectuate the state interest with as little interference with an offender's rights as possible.

Rights of expression and association are involved in the following contexts:

1. Exercise of free speech.
2. Exercise of religious beliefs and practices. (See Standard 2.16).
3. Sending or receipt of mail. (See Standard 2.17).
4. Visitations. (See Standard 2.17).
5. Access to the public through the media. (See Standard 2.17).
6. Engaging in peaceful assemblies.
7. Belonging to and participating in organizations.
8. Preserving identity through distinguishing clothing, hairstyles, and other characteristics related to physical appearance.

Justification for limiting an offender's right of expression or association would include regulations necessary to maintain order or protect other offenders, correctional staff, or other persons from violence, or the clear threat of violence. The existence of a justification for limiting an offender's rights should be determined in light of all the circumstances, including the nature of the correctional program or institution to which he is assigned

Ordinarily, the following factors would not constitute sufficient justification for an interference with an offender's rights unless present in a situation which constituted a clear threat to personal or institutional security.

1. Protection of the correctional agency or its staff from criticism, whether or not justified.
2. Protection of other offenders from unpopular ideas.
3. Protection of offenders from views correctional officials deem not conducive to rehabilitation or other correctional treatment.
4. Administrative inconvenience.
5. Administrative cost except where unreasonable and disproportionate to that expended on other offenders for similar purposes.

Correctional authorities should encourage and facilitate the exercise of the right of expression and association by providing appropriate opportunities and facilities.

Commentary

Offenders' first amendment right of free expression and association has been one of the last to receive judicial review in the shift from the "hands off" doctrine. A number of older court decisions have upheld severe limitations on oral and written speech, particularly in the prison context, without consideration of the existence of any significant free-speech rights. Nevertheless, an impressive and continually increasing number of recent decisions have made it clear that the legal status of the offender (and the pretrial detainee) must incorporate the first amendment right to free expression that may not be limited without a credible showing of significant danger to institutional order, security, or other major societal interests. These decisions have been applied to offenders under parole or probation supervision and those in prisons and other institutions.

This standard recommends the applicability of the first amendment to all offenders and detainees. For offenders the exercise of the right and any imposed limitations should be on the same basis applicable to the general population. Recent decisions have invalidated parole conditions prohibiting expression of opinion critizing Federal laws limiting participation in peaceful political demonstrations.

In general, the first amendment as applied to ordinary citizens protects against two different forms of governmental regulation: (1) prior restraints, which include pre-speech censorship; and (2) punishments after the fact for speech or speech-related activities. In the correctional setting, prior restraints would include regulations prohibiting speech entirely on various subjects or censoring mail or other written matter. Disciplinary action for speech or speech-related activities also is common.

The justifications asserted for prior restraints include protection of the public safety or national security. In some instances, censorship of material deemed obscene has been authorized. All jurisdictions likewise have statutory crimes involving speech-related activities—many of which are of the type not protected by the first amendment. Acts providing criminal penalties for inciting riots or distributing obscene material are typical examples. In addition, in limited instances, persons injured by the spoken or written word may recover damages from the instigator through common law libel and slander doctrines. These principles encouraging or limiting the expression of ideas should be applicable to ciminal offenders as well as to the general public.

Rights of expression and association are involved in a number of differing contexts. This standard proposes general rules protecting such rights in any context. More specific standards dealing with specific problems involved in specific contexts follow. However, it is important to view the rights of expression and association as general rights. For example, in some cases offenders have been prohibited from wearing medallions. Some courts have focused on whether the medallion had religious connotation sufficient to raise a first amendment right. Even if the medallion is not of religious significance, however, it may still be protected as a right of general expression unrelated to religious freedom. An offender has the right to belong to a political organization as well as a religious organization, and the same rules should govern correctional interference with that right. While mail and visitation procedures often are singled out for specific procedures often are singled out for specific treatment and rules, they relate to forms of communication and association and should be governed by general standards protecting free speech.

The standard recommends two general rules that should govern the regulation of expression and association of offenders whether or not they are sentenced to total confinement. The first is that there must be a compelling state interest before interference with expression or association is justified. Second, where such a showing is made, the authorities should intrude on freedom of expression to the least degree possible while protecting the state interest. All alternative means to protect the state interest not involving interference with these rights should be explored.

Free speech is not an absolute right in the free community and thus would not be an absolute right within a correctional program. It has long been recognized that one is not free to yell "fire" in a crowded theatre, and an offender would not be free to yell "riot" within a prison. Correctional authorities would be justified in limiting speech and other related activities if it were necessary to protect institutional security or to protect persons from violence or the clear threat of violence. While the determination in a given case as to whether limitations are necessary is a difficult one, it can be made and should be made in light of all the surrounding circumstances. An offender on parole or probation or other community-based program would have

wider latitude than a confined offender. A speech permissible in the context of a small, minimum security institution might exacerbate the tensions in a large maximum security prison to an unacceptable level. Traditionally, agencies have applied a flat rule regardless of the circumstances and the standard seeks to correct this situation.

Various arguments have been advanced by correctional authorities to support infringement of offenders' right of expression. It has been claimed that certain ideas are disruptive influences on the prison population, tending to promote violence or other forms of attacks on institutional authority. It has been argued that offenders often lie about prison conditions, bringing undue and often unfair pressure on correctional administrators by persons in the free community. Administrators also fear that other offenders will become offended by the ideas or speeches of a few "troublemakers" and this will lead to tension within the prison. They also contend that certain expression is not conducive to rehabilitation.

The first of the four arguments can be considered worthy of support for regulations involving interferences with freedom of speech. In the confined atmosphere of a correctional facility, with its inevitable tensions and hostilities, speech inciting riots or violence cannot be tolerated.

Correctional administrators' fear of unjustified criticisms, real or imagined, does not alone represent a sufficient justification for abridgement of the offender's rights. A public dialogue, with its inevitable inaccuracies and misperceptions, is as useful to the correctional process as it is to the political process. Much of the current interest in corrections reform among the general public has been developed because of the complaints of offenders, generally transmitted through court proceedings. It is clear that many such complaints are frivolous or not supported in fact. But many are true. A democratic system requires a free flow of ideas—many of which will turn out to be false. Corrections has much to gain and little to lose by allowing and encouraging public discussion of correctional practices.

The first amendment does not authorize prohibiting speech because the audience finds what is said offensive. Protection for speech is unnecessary where there is universal acceptance of an idea. The purpose of protecting speech is to protect diversity, not accuracy. Offenders who eventually will find themselves back in the free community where diversity is tolerated should not be protected from views they find offensive while confined. It is not appropriate training for their eventual release. In the prison setting, however, unlike free society, an individual cannot always escape offensive views. The audience, as well as the speaker, is confined in a limited area. Where tensions are great and a threat of violence clear, correctional authorities can act. Speech not "conducive to rehabilitation" implies that "rehabilitation" contemplates forcing individual offenders into a preset mold. It does not.

Correctional authorities should seek to assure reasonable opportunities for dissemination of various points of view. Thus facilities for oral and written expression should be provided to offenders on a reasonable basis. Typewriters, pencil and paper, musical instruments, and other types of material should be accessible to those offenders who desire them. Leisure activities should allow for the exchange of ideas.

In a number of instances administrative inconvenience and expense have been asserted to justify interferences with the rights of expression and association. Society incurs responsibilities when it confines a person. Feeding offenders involves inconvenience and expense, but no one urges that offenders not be fed. Rights of expression and association cannot be withdrawn merely because they may require action on the part of correctional staff. In addition, facilitation of expression or association is effective correctional treatment and should not be considered "inconvenient" but a part of the staff's responsibility.

The extent to which administrative expense should justify prohibitions on free expression poses difficult issues. In all the rights proposed in this chapter there is a distinction between what the government must provide and what the government must allow. If the request of the offender is related to his rights of expression or association and he is willing to pay for the exercise of those rights, then the correctional authorities should not interfere. In some instances, however, the correctional agency should be obligated to provide facilities or opportunities at governmental expense.

Two concepts should govern determinations as to when expense justifies inaction. If the expense is reasonable in light of existing resources and in relationship to the benefit to be obtained, the expenditure should be made. Likewise, if the government expends funds to facilitate the rights of some offenders, it is obligated to expend proportionally for all offenders. For example, to allow Black Muslims to abide by their dietary restrictions on eating pork may require some nominal expenditure. Reasonable substitutes for pork do exist. However, if some religious faith required champagne and pheasant under glass for each meal, the cost would be disproportionate to the cost of providing meals generally and might be considered unreasonable.

The courts generally have not had the opportunity to decide questions regarding inmates' rights to organize or belong to various organizations and their right to peacefully assemble. In Roberts v. Pepersack, 256 F.Supp. 415 (D. Md. 1966), cert. denied, 389 U.S. 877 (1967), the court found no constitutional right to promote an organization that would advocate open defiance of authority within a prison. The court does not deal with the right to organize generally where the motive does not constitute a danger to prison security.

Implicit in the cases involving religious freedom is the ability to belong to various religious organizations. Organizations such as Alcoholics Anonymous and Junior Chambers of Commerce long have been utilized within institutions. The first amendment should similarly protect an offender's right to belong to political organizations as long as the organization does not present a clear and present danger to a compelling state interest. Reasonable regulations designed to provide correctional administrators with information concerning the aims, procedures, and membership of organizations within institutions may be justified, provided such regulations are applied equally to all organizations and are not used to harass individual offenders or unpopular organizations. Such regulations should relate to the legitimate objectives of the agency in allocating facilities for organization meetings, scheduling events, and maintaining institutional security.

The right to assemble is particularly sensitive within the context of a correctional institution. The tension bred by close confinement may be exacerbated by large gatherings of offenders. Thus the danger of violence may be more easily shown within the prison environment than in the free community. But the test of a clear and present danger should be applicable.

In addition to the expression of particular ideas or beliefs, the first amendment has been held in some circumstances to assure a person the right to maintain his identity. Some courts, while not relying on the first amendment, have found other constitutional provisions which protect an individual in his manner of dress or the style in which he wears his hair. These freedoms as applied to schoolchildren have caused conflict and controversy in the courts, with some courts accepting the view that school authorities have a substantial burden to justify regulations affecting appearance. Courts that have confronted similar claims by committed offenders have been reluctant to overturn prison regulations prohibiting facial hair.

Several studies of prisons have indicated that their most degrading feature is their dehumanizing influence on prisoners. The institution for purposes increasingly difficult to justify, withdraws from confined offenders all semblances of their separate identity. Offenders wear similar clothing. Each has his hair cut the same way. Each is given a number rather than retaining his name. The effect of this approach is becoming increasingly clear. Offenders lose whatever self-respect they have; their adjustment to free society upon release is made more difficult if not impossible. Prohibiting offenders from maintaining their identities defeats the purposes of corrections.

Correctional authorities undoubtedly have a compelling interest in being able to identify committed offenders. In some instances the ability of offenders to effectuate extreme alterations in appearance within a short period may constitute a justification for reasonable regulations. The recommendation thus contemplates that while offenders should be allowed to maintain individuality through clothing, hair styles, and other appearance-related characteristics, the correctional authorities should be authorized to promote reasonable regulations to maintain ease of identification. However, this justification should be subject to the same restraint that the least drastic regulaion be adopted.

There is no evidence that the requirements of sanitation—so often asserted by correctional authorities to justify rules prohibiting facial hair or long hair—require an absolute prohibition. Regulations assuring normal cleanliness should be sufficient.

References

1. Barnett v. Rodgers, 410 F.2d 995 (D.C. Cir. 1969) ("Treatment that degrades the inmate, invades his privacy, and frustrates the ability to choose pursuits through which he can manifest himself and gain self-respect erodes the very foundations upon which he can prepare for a socially useful life.")
2. Bishop v. Colaw, 450 F.2d 1069 (8th Cir. 1971) (Overturning dress code regulations for schoolchildren.)
3. Cohen, Fred. The Legal Challenge to Corrections. Washington: Joint Commission on Correctional Manpower and Training, 1969. Ch. III.
4. Goldfarb, Ronald, and Singer, Linda. "Redressing Prisoners' Griev-ances," George Washington Law Review, 39 (1970), 221-223. (Free expression generally.)
5. Nolan v. Fitzpatrick, 451 F.2d 545 (1st Cir. 1971) (First amendment protects prisoners in speech with news media and invalidates prison rule against correspondence with press.)
6. Palmigiano v. Travisono, 317 F. Supp. 776 (D.R.I. 1970) (Affirming freedom of publishers to circulate materials to prisoners except for hard core porongraphy.)
7. Porth v. Templar, 453 F.2d 330 (10th Cir. 1971) (Invalidating parole conditions barring expression of opinion as to constitutionality of Federal income tax law.)
8. Sobell v. Reed, 327 F.Supp. 1294 (S.D. N.Y. 1971) (Invalidating application of parole conditions to prevent parolee from peacefully participating in 1969 and 1970 Washington peace marches.)
9. Sostre v. McGinnis, 442 F.2d 178 (2d Cir. 1971) Cert. denied, 404 U.S. 1049 (1972) (Affirms lower court prohibiting punishment of offender for constitutionally protected speech in written and oral form.)
10. Sostre v. Otis, 330 F.Supp. 941 (S.D. N.Y. 1971) (Requiring notice to prisoner and opportunity to be heard before withholding access to radical literature and periodicals otherwise protected as part of first amendment speech.)
11. Turner, William B. "Establishing the Rule of Law in Prisons: A Manual for Prisoners' Rights Litigation," Stanford Law Review, 23 (1971), 473.
12. U.S. ex rel. Shakur v. McGrath, 303 F.Supp. 303 (S.D. N.Y. 1969) (Permits inmate members of Black Panther party to read party magazine subject to correctional authority's discretion on dissemination to

other inmates and when and how Panthers can read the periodical.)

Related Standards

The following standards may be applicable in implementing Standard 2.15.

2.1 Access to Courts.
5.9 Continuing Jurisdiction of Sentencing Court.
16.2 Administrative Justice.
16.3 Code of Offenders' Rights.

STANDARD 2.16

EXERCISE OF RELIGIOUS BELIEFS AND PRACTICES

Each correctional agency immediately should develop and implement policies and procedures that will fulfill the right of offenders to exercise their own religious beliefs. These policies and procedures should allow and facilitate the practice of these beliefs to the maximum extent possible, within reason, consistent with Standard 2.15, and reflect the responsibility of the correctional agency to:

1. Provide access to appropriate facilities for worship or meditation.

2. Enable offenders to adhere to the dietary laws of their faith.

3. Arrange the institution's schedule to the extent reasonably possible so that inmates may worship or meditate at the time prescribed by their faith.

4. Allow access to clergymen or spiritual advisers of all faiths represented in the institution's population.

5. Permit receipt of any religious literature and publications that can be transmitted legaly through the United States mails.

6. Allow religious medals and other symbols that are not unduly obtrusive.

Each correctional agency should give equal status and protection to all religions, traditional or unorthodox. In determining whether practices are religiously motivated, the following factors among others should be considered as supporting a religious foundation for the practice in question:

1. Whether there is substantial literature supporting the practice as related to religious principle.

2. Whether there is a formal, organized worship of shared belief by a recognizable and cohesive group supporting the practice.

3. Whether there is a loose and informal association of persons who share common ethical, moral, or intellectual views supporting the practice.

4. Whether the belief is deeply and sincerely held by the offender.

The following factors should not be considered as indicating a lack of religious support for the practice in question:

1. The belief is held by a small number of individuals.

2. The belief is of recent origin.

3. The belief is not based on the concept of a Supreme Being or its equivalent.

4. The belief is unpopular or controversial.

In determining whether practices are religiously motivated, the correctional agency should allow the offender to present evidence of religious foundations to the official making the determination.

The correctional agency should not

proselytize persons under its supervision or permit others to do so without the consent of the person concerned. Reasonable opportunity and access should be provided to offenders requesting information about the activities of any religion with which they may not be actively affiliated.

In making judgments regarding the adjustment or rehabilitation of an offender, the correctional agency may consider the attitudes and perceptions of the offender but should not:

1. Consider, in any manner prejudicial to determinations of offender release or status, whether or not such beliefs are religiously motivated.

2. Impose, as a condition of confinement, parole, probation, or release, adherence to the active practice of any religion or religious belief.

Commentary

Religious freedom has always been preferred and fundamental status in our concepts of individual liberty and expression. The first amendment both protects the free exercise of religion and prohibits the government from giving special consideration to a particular religion.

The criminal law reflects a number of moral judgments that have deep roots in religious doctrines. Corrections has a long history of gauging religious beliefs to determine whether an offender is ready to return to society. Religious instructions has been utilized extensively as a correctional tool. However, when offenders representing more diverse religious backgrounds increased and became more adamant in their demands for religious freedom within institutions, correctional authorities retreated. The Black Muslims, particularly seen as a threat to institutional order, were subjected to restraints on their religious practices.

The area of religious freedom was one of the first in which courts abandoned the hands-off attitude and examined the rules and restrictions of prison life and correctional control. Much of the litigation centered on the question of what restrictions on religious practices were reasonable in the prison setting. As in the general cases on freedom of religion, courts made a distinction between the prisoner's religious belief and his more qualified right to engage in specific religious practices. Beliefs are for the most part free from governmental intervention. But where those beliefs are reflected in actions, more difficult questions arise.

The first amendment as applied to the public at large authorizes some governmental interference with religious practices. One of the earlier cases, Reynolds v. U.S., 98 U.S. 145 (1878), held that the Mormon practice of polygamy, though religiously based, was subservient to the state's interest in the monoganous family relationship. On the other hand, two recent cases have indicated that the state's interest must be substantial before religious practices may be condemned. In Welsh v. U.S., 398 U.S. 333 (1970), the Supreme Court gave a broad interpretation to the statute authorizing conscientious objection based on religious training as an exemption from the Selective Service Act. The broad definition of religious training was developed to avoid the constitutional problems of discrimination between traditional religious beliefs and those with a more unorthodox foundation. Likewise, in Wisconsin v. Yoder, 406 U.S. 205 (1972), the Court found that the State's interest in compulsory school laws was not sufficient to compel Amish children to attend school beyond the eighth grade, a practice contrary to their religious beliefs.

The standard responds to these issues by: (1) encouraging the system to make the maximum possible accommodation to religious beliefs and practices, even in difficult areas such as dietary laws; (2) permitting reasonable limitations to meet the legitimate demands of correctional security and order but only when the burden of demonstration is met by the correctional authority; (3) requiring that new sects and smaller denominations receive equal treatment; (4) prohibiting consideration of religious belief or practice in reaching decisions concerning prisoner status or release; and (5) invalidating the coerced maintenance of religious practice as a condition of parole or probation status. These positions stem from a recognition that, while the nature of confinement restricts movement and free access to religious practice, such effects are unintended collateral consequences not related to the purposes of confinement. Therefore, the correctional authority assumes a special responsibility to permit freedom of religious practice for those it so restricts.

The most difficult issue arising in protecting religious freedom is the definition of what a religion is. Courts have struggled with the definition without satisfactory resolution. In the context of these standards, the determination of whether a given offender's request is religiously based may be important. While the standards provide for wide latitude in allowing offenders to express their own individuality, where actions of needs are of religious orientation, correctional agencies have a broader responsibility to provide adequate resources. Thus the correctional agency may be required to expend money to facilitate religious worship but not to support an individual's self-expression that is not founded on religious principle.

Practices asserted merely to harass correctional staff or to obtain privileges not otherwise available to offenders should not be protected. However, practices founded in religious belief, even though unorthodox, should be allowed. The standard attempts to list some factors which would tend to indicate a religious base and others that should not be considered relevant. The standard also recommends that, where difficult questions arise, correctional agencies should authorize the offender involved to present evidence regarding the religious motivation of the practice asserted.

In the last analysis, the issue of whether a particular practice is religiously motivated will be left to the courts. However, Standard 2.15 recognizes that offenders have a right to express themselves and to retain their identity as individuals. Thus correctional authorities should grant broad leeway toward practices involving merely the expression of individuality, whether or not based on religious belief.

The standard also recommends that correctional decisions involving the release or status of the offender not be made on the basis of whether he has adhered to a particular faith or is "religious." While release and status decisions will inevitably and properly be based on an offender's attitudes toward law, society, and his fellow man, the fact that they are or are not religiously based should be of no consequence.

References

1. American Correctional Associa-

tion. *Manual of Correctional Standards.* 3d ed. Washington: ACA, 1966. Ch. 29.

2. Barnett v. Rogers, 410 F.2d 995, 1001 (D.C. Cir. 1969) (Jail officials must make some effort to accommodate Muslim dietary restrictions.)

3. Brown, Dulcey A. "Black Muslims in Prisons and Religious Discrimination: The Developing Criteria for Judicial Review," *George Washington Law Review,* 32 (1964), 1124.

4. Frankino, Steven P. "Manacles and the Messenger: A Short Study in Religious Freedom in the Prison," *Catholic University Law Review,* 30 (1965).

5. Goldfarb, Ronald, and Singer, Linda. "Redressing Prisoners' Grievances," *George Washington Law Review,* 39 (1970), 216-221.

6. Howard v. Smyth, 365 F.2d 428 (4th Cir. 1966), *cert. denied,* 385 U.S. 988 (1967) (Inmate may not be punished for refusal to divulge names of Black Muslims in population.)

7. Long v. Parker, 390 2d 816 (3rd Cir. 1968) (If the other religions receive religious literature, Muslims may not be denied unles corrections authority shows "clear and present danger" to prison discipline.)

8. Note, *Rutgers Law Review,* 20 (1966), 528.

9. Walter v. Blackwell, 411 F.2d 23 (5th Cir. 1969) (Should religious newspaper later develop inflammatory effect on inmates, officials could act to avoid violence.)

10. Gittlemaker v. Prasse, 428 F.2d 1 (3rd Cir. 1970) (State need not provide full-time chaplain for every denomination.)

Related Standards

The following standards may be applicable in implementing Standard 2.16.

2.15 Free Expression and Association.

11.7 Religious Programs.

16.2 Administrative Justice.

16.3 Code of Offenders' Rights.

STANDARD 2.17

ACCESS TO THE PUBLIC

Each correctional agency should develop and implement immediately policies and procedures to fulfill the right of offenders to communicate with the public. Correctional regulations limiting such communication should be consistent with Standard 2.15. Questions of right of access to the public arise primarily in the context of regulations affecting mail, personal visitation, and the communications media.

MAIL. Offenders should have the right to communicate or correspond with persons or organizations and to send and receive letters, packages, books, periodicals, and any other material that can be lawfully mailed. The following additional guidelines should apply:

1. Correctional authorities should not limit the volume of mail to or from a person under supervision.

2. Correctional authorities should have the right to inspect incoming and outgoing mail, but neither incoming nor outgoing mail should be read or censored. Cash, checks, or money orders should be removed from incom-

ing mail and credited to offenders' accounts. If contraband is discovered in either incoming or outgoing mail, it may be removed. Only illegal items and items which threaten the security of the institution should be considered contraband.

3. Offenders should receive a reasonable postage allowance to maintain community ties.

VISITATION. Offenders should have the right to communicate in person with individuals of their own choosing. The following additional guidelines should apply:

1. Correctional authorities should not limit the number of visitors an offender may receive or the length of such visits except in accordance with regular institutional schedules and requirements.

2. Correctional authorities should facilitate and promote visitation of offenders by the following acts:

a. Providing transportation for visitors from terminal points of public transportation. In some instances, the correctional agency may wish to pay the entire transportation costs of family members where the offender and the family are indigent.

b. Providing appropriate rooms for visitation that allow ease and informality of communication in a natural environment as free from institutional or custodial attributes as possible.

c. Making provisions for family visits in private surroundings conducive to maintaining and strengthening family ties.

3. The correctional agency may supervise the visiting area in an unobtrusive manner but should not eavesdrop on conversations or otherwise interfere with the participants' privacy.

MEDIA. Except in emergencies such as institutional disorders, offenders should be allowed to present their views through the communications media. Correctional authorities should encourage and facilitate the flow of information between the media and offenders by authorizing offenders, among other things, to:

1. Grant confidential and uncensored interviews to representatives of the media. Such interviews should be scheduled not to disrupt regular institutional schedules unduly unless during a newsworthy event.

2. Send uncensored letters and other communications to the media.

3. Publish articles or books on any subject.

4. Display and sell original creative works.

As used in this standard, the term "media" encompasses any printed or electronic means of conveying information to the public including but not limited to newspapers, magazines, books, or other publications regardless of the size or nature of their circulation and licensed radio and television broadcasting. Representatives of the media should be allowed access to all correctional facilities for reporting items of public interest consistent with the preservation of offenders' privacy.

Offenders should be entitled to receive any lawful publication, or radio and television broadcast.

Commentary

The walls of correctional institutions have served not merely to restrain criminal offenders but to isolate them. They have been isolated from the public in general and from their families and friends. As a result, the public does not know what is happening in prisons, and in large part the offender does not know what is going on outside the prisons. While many restrictions on communications were imposed under theories of institutional security, they have resulted in making correctional programs more difficult. If corrections is to assure that an offender will readjust to the free society upon release, the adjustment process must begin long before the day of release. To accomplish this, the public must be concerned about what happens in corrections. Information is a prerequisite to concern. Likewise, the offender must retain his ties to the community and his knowledge of what the free community is like if he is to be able to live there satisfactorily upon release.

Isolation of correctional institutions also contains additional dangers. Judge Gesell commented in Washington Post Co. v. Kleindienst, 11 Crim. L. Rptr. 2045 (D.D.C. 1972):

> Whenever people are incarcerated, whether it be in a prison, an insane asylum, or an institution such as those for the senile and retarded, opportunity for human indignities and administrative insensitivity exists. Those thus deprived of freedom live out of the public's view. It is largely only through the media that a failure in a particular institution to adhere to minimum standards of human dignity can be exposed. Indeed, needed reforms in these areas have often been sparked by press attention. Conversely, secrecy is inconsistent with responsible official conduct of public institutions for it creates suspicion, rumor, indifference, if not distrust. Disinterest causes abuses to multiply.

The three major contexts in which the isolation of the offender from the public can be diminished are mail, visitation, and access to media. Involved in these three areas are the rights of an offender to express himself and associate with others. Thus the general rules justifying correctional regulations interfering with mail, visitation, and access to media should be the same as those regulating speech in general. The test of a clear and convincing evidence of a compelling state interest proposed in Standard 2.15 should be applicable to these regulations. Standard 2.17 addresses specific aspects of mail, visitation, and media access.

In discussing the rights of offenders to have access to the public, the rights of the public to know what occurs within correctional programs also should be considered.

Mail. In censoring and regulating mail, correctional authorities have not limited themselves to keeping out harmful or potentially dangerous objects or substances. The censorship of mail all too often has been utilized to exclude ideas deemed by the censor to be threatening or harmful to offenders or critical of the correctional agency. These efforts results in the diversion of manpower from other tasks and, to avoid excessive manpower drains, limitations on the volume of correspondence permitted. Censorship and limitations on correspondence directly generate inmate hostilities and serve to make correctional progress more difficult.

Courts began to look critically at this process when it came to their attention that correctional authorities were limiting access to courts. Instances of failure to mail complaints, invasion of privileged attorney-client communications, and reprisals against inmates for attempting to send out information about deficient conditions were documented. Limitations on access to religious material also were discovered and critized.

Contraband must be excluded from correctional institutions to preserve their security and good order by limiting the development of inmate power groups often resulting from acquisition of contraband. The standard authorizes the correctional administrator to inspect incoming and outgoing mail for contraband but not to read or censor the contents.

Correctional authorities have a duty to insure that offenders are able to correspond with members of the public. A reasonable postage allowance should be provided each offender as part of an affirmative program to help him retain community ties.

Visitation. Whether a person is confined across town in a jail or across the State in a prison, confinement totally disrupts his relationship with his community. The longer confinement persist, the more alienated the individual becomes. Strained ties with family and friends increase the difficulty of making the eventual transition back to the community.

The critical value for offenders of a program of visiting with relatives and friends long has been recognized. Nevertheless, a substantial number of jails have no visiting facilities. In many institutions the facilities are demeaning and degrading, as well as violative of privacy. This defeats the purpose of visiting. Screening or glass partitions between the offender and his visitor emphasize their separation rather than the retaining common bonds and interests.

Correctional authorities should not merely tolerate visiting but should encourage it. This extends to providing or paying for transportation when the cost of traveling to the facility would be a limiting factor. Such a provision is plainly needed to equalize the situation of rich and poor inmates. Expenses of this type can be minimized by incarcerating offenders in their own community or through expanded use of furlough programs.

Other steps to encourage visits are required. Family visits will overcome difficult and expensive babysitting problems. Seven-day visiting would permit visitors to come on days when they are not employed. Arbitrary time limits on the duration of visits discriminate against those who cannot make frequent visits. Expansion of visiting hours and facilities in institutions with consistently crowded visiting facilities would alleviate problems caused by inadequate space.

Visiting should not be barred under any but the most exceptional circumstances. Where the administrator can meet the test recommended in Standard 2.15 of clear and convincing evidence of a compelling state interest, visiting can be regulated and in unusual circumstances prohibited.

The standard recommends provisions for family visits in surroundings conducive to the maintenance and strengthening of family ties. The setting should provide privacy and a non-institutional atmosphere. In institutions where such facilities are not available, furloughs should be granted custodially qualified offenders in order to maintain family relationships. It is recognized that the so-called conjugal visit is controversial, partly because the concept seems to focus entirely on sexual activity.

The furlough system is far superior to the institutional arrangement. However, the recommendations of this report contemplate that, as institutional confinement ceases to be a common criminal sanction, prisons will increasingly house more dangerous offenders for whom furlough programs will not be appropriate. Provision of settings where an entire family can visit in private surroundings could add much to an offender's receptivity to correctional programs and strengthen his family relationships.

Media. While mail and visitation allow offenders contact with specific individuals, access to the communications media provides contact with the public generally. The public has a right to be informed of their government's activities through customary mass communications. Offenders have a right to have their story told as well as to be informed of events in the free society.

Several recent court decisions have recognized both the public's right to know and the offender's right to tell. In Washington Post Co. v. Kleindienst, 11 Crim. L. Rptr. 2045 (D.D.C. 1972), the court struck down the Federal Bureau of Prisons' total ban against press interviews with confined inmates. The court ordered that "the thrust of new press regulations should be to permit uncensored confidential interviews wherever possible and to withhold permission to interview on an individual basis only where demonstrable administrative or disciplinary considerations dominate." In Burnham v. Oswald, 333 F.Supp. 1128 (W.D. N.Y. 1971) the court required the correctional authorities to show a clear and present danger to prison order, security, or discipline, or prior abuse of an interview right by the inmate before press interviews could be prohibited.

Inmate interviews should be permitted when either party requests the interview, assuming media representatives show reasonable regard for the timing, duration, and location for interviews. Confidentiality should be respected.

When press contacts are not initiated by the inmate, his desires must be considered. The correctional authority should not release information about individuals without their permission, except in connection with a legitimate news story. In this instance only matters of public record should be divulged.

Incoming information from the press and other media should not be controlled. The laws governing printing, mailing, and electronic communications offer the needed protections to the correctional authority. In addition to meeting constitutional requirements, offenders' access to newspapers, magazines, periodicals, and other printed material is important in maintaining ties with the community.

References

1. American Correctional Association. *Manual of Correctional Standards.* 3d ed. Washington: ACA, 1966.

2. Burnham v. Oswald, 333 F.Supp. 1128 (W.D. N.Y. 1971).

3. Comment, "Prisoner Mail Censorship and the First Amendment." *Yale Law Journal,* 81 (1971), 87.

4. Fortune Society v. McGinnis, 319 F.Supp. 901 (S.D. N.Y. 1970) (Upholding right of inmate to receive newsletter published by society of former inmates.)

5. Glaser, Daniel. *The Effectiveness of a Prison and Parole System.* Indianapolis: Bobbs-Merrill, 1964.

6. Jackson v. Godwin, 400 F.2d 529 (5th Cir. 1968).

7. Nolan v. Fitzpatrick, 541 F.2d 545 (1st Cir. 1971) (Inmate right to correspond with news media upheld.)

8. Palmigiano v. Travisono, 317 F. Supp. 776 (D. R.I. 1970).

9. Rowan, Joseph R. *Public Relations and Citizen Action in the Delinquency and Crime Field—Our Greatest Need.* Undated monograph.

10. Singer, Richard G. "Censorship of Prisoners' Mail and the Constitution," *American Bar Association Journal*, 56 (1970), 1051.

11. South Carolina Department of Corrections. *Emerging Rights of the Confined.* Columbia: 1972. Ch. 7.

12. Washington Post Co. v. Kleindienst, 11 Crim. L. Rptr. 2045 (D.C. 1972).

13. Stollery, Peter. "Families Come to the Institution: A Five Day Experience in Rehabilitation," *Federal Probation*, 36 (1970), 346.

Related Standards

The following standards may be applicable in implementing Standard 2.17.

8.3 Juvenile Detention Center Planning.

9.10 Local Facility Evaluation and Planning.

11.1 Planning New Correctional Institutions.

11.2. Modification of Existing Institutions.

11.3 Social Environment of Institutions.

16.3 Code of Offenders' Rights.

STANDARD 2.18

REMEDIES FOR VIOLATION OF AN OFFENDER'S RIGHTS

Each correctional agency immediately should adopt policies and procedures, and where applicable should seek legislation, to insure proper redress where an offender's rights as enumerated in this chapter are abridged.

1. Administrative remedies, not requiring the intervention of a court, should include at least the following:

a. Procedures allowing an offender to seek redress where he believes his rights have been or are about to be violated. Such procedures should be consistent with Standard 2.14, Grievance Procedure.

b. Policies of inspection and supervision to assure periodic evaluation of institutional conditions and staff practices that may affect offenders' rights.

c. Policies which:

(1) Assure wide distribution and understanding of the rights of offenders among both offenders and correctional staff.

(2) Provide that the intentional or persistent violation of an offender's rights is justification for removal from office or employment of any correctional worker.

(3) Authorize the payment of claims to offenders as compensation for injury caused by a violation of any right.

2. Judicial remedies for violation of rights should include at least the following:

a. Authority for an injunction either prohibiting a practice violative of an offender's rights or requiring affirmative action on the part of governmental officials to assure compliance with offenders' rights.

b. Authority for an award of damages against either the correctional agency or, in appropriate circumstances, the staff member involved to compensate the offender for injury caused by a violation of his rights.

c. Authority for the court to exercise continuous supervision of a correctional facility or program including the power to appoint a special master responsible to the court to oversee implementation of offenders' rights.

d. Authority for the court to prohibit further commitments to an institution or program.

e. Authority for the court to shut down an institution or program and require either the transfer or release of confined or supervised offenders.

f. Criminal penalties for intentional violations of an offender's rights.

Commentary

Recognition that those convicted of criminal offenses retain substantial rights is a necessary step toward the alleviation of the misery and degradation evident in many of our jails and prisons. However, such recognition is ineffective unless mechanisms are designed to assure that the offender is able to enforce these rights against correctional authorities.

The pressure for recognition of rights for the offender has come through active judicial intervention into the correctional system, for the most part at the insistence of offenders. Thus, at first, traditional judicial relief was requested. It is not surprising that most prisoner rights cases arose through the use of the writ of habeas corpus, since that writ is designed primarily to test the legality of confinement and the offender's desired relief is, in most cases, release. Although courts accepted the responsibility to review correctional practices, release from the institution was considered impractical, and courts have attempted to fashion more flexible remedies.

Judicial action, while necessary in many instances to define the rights available, should not be considered the exclusive method of enforcing rights once defined. Correctional administrators also have a responsibility to insure the protection of offenders' rights. Administrative policies and procedures should be designed to provide an effective way of assuring that offenders are properly treated. The standard recommends that correctional authorities develop such mechanisms.

Certain rights, where they involve a conflict with agency policy established at the highest level, will not be directly amenable to administrative resolution. However, particularly where staff practices contravene announced policies, administrative remedies would be effective. A procedure available for handling offender grievances, as recommended elsewhere in this report, should be utilized for determination of these issues where appropriate. Also top management officials should assure through adequate inspection and supervision that offenders' rights are respected. Particularly in large agencies, administrative devices to assure review of intermediate and line staff practices are essential.

In addition, each correctional agency should assure wide-scale understanding of the rights of offenders. Inservice training programs for correctional staff should concentrate on the nature, as well as the justification, of the rights of offenders. The most effective assurance of respect for such rights in the long run is recognition by correctional personnel that protection of these rights not only is required by the Constitution but also is good correctional practice.

Agency policy should specify that respect for offenders' rights is a condition of employment with the agency. Personnel policies should insure that persons who intentionally or persistently violate offenders 'rights are discharged. Where civil service or other statutory provisions govern correctional employment practices and require "cause" for removal, "cause" should either be defined to include violation of offenders' rights or should be amended to provide such definition.

In many instances, violations of the rights of an offender result in injury that can be compensated in monetary terms. Offenders should be provided with a means of filing claims with the jurisdiction for such damages without the requirement of a lawsuit. In many jurisdictions, such procedures already exist for claims against other governmental agencies. These should be made applicable to violation of the rights of offenders.

Courts have been increasingly willing to fashion remedies appropriate to the right violated. Federal courts have available various remedies arising out of Federal statutes protecting civil rights, which are applicable to prisoner complaints. However, State courts may have some difficulty in devising flexible yet effective remedies. Where required, legislation should be enacted specifically authorizing the remedies recommended by the standard.

Courts should be authorized to grant injunctions to protect offenders' rights. This would include injunctions prohibiting conduct that violates offenders' rights as well as requiring affirmative acts to assure an offender's rights are preserved. Violation of such orders should be subjected to contempt charges as in other cases.

Civil liability for violating a person's rights is a particularly effective remedy and should be more widely utilized. In many instances, persons clothed with governmental authority have little incentive to comply with the rights of persons subject to their jurisdiction because they have no personal stake in compliance. Making governmental officials personally liable for money damages to the person whose rights are violated provides such an incentive. Where a governmental employee intentionally violates an offender's rights or the agency engages in tactics designed solely to make the attainment of offender's rights more difficult, civil liability is an appropriate remedy. Such liability is provided, but rarely utilized, in Federal civil rights statutes.

Some courts have taken more drastic steps. In some instances, further commitments to a particular institution have been prohibited because of intolerable conditions. Courts likewise should be able to close an institution or stop a program where other remedies are not effective.

Chapter 5 of this report recommends that sentencing courts exercise continuous jurisdiction over sentenced offenders to insure that the sentence imposed by the court is carried out. It may be necessary in assuring compliance with the rights of an offender that the court exercise similar supervisory powers over correctional officials. In exercising this power, courts should be authorized to appoint and pay a special master who would be responsible to the court. The master could engage in such inspection and supervision activities as is deemed appropriate to insure that offenders are properly treated.

Criminal penalties for most cases are ineffective and inappropriate. Making it a criminal offense to violate another person's rights is advisable only where there is intentional or willful conduct abridging the rights in question. It is unlikely that prosecutors would bring charges against correctional officials in any but the most unusual circumstances. Thus while criminal penalties should be available, they should not be considered effective remedies for the vast majority of cases arising to protect the rights of offenders.

References

1. Goldfarb, Ronald, and Singer, Linda. "Redressing Prisoners' Grievances." *George Washington Law Review*, 39 (1970), 175.
2. Jackson v. Hendrick, 40 Law Week 2710 (Ct. Comm. Pls. Pa. 1972) (Appointing special master to supervise the Philadelphia Prison System.)
3. National Council on Crime and Delinquency. *A Model Act for the Protection of Rights of Prisoners.*

New York: NCCD, 1972.
4. Sostre v. McGinnis, 442 F.2d 178 (2d Cir. 1971) (Awarding compensatory damages of $25 per day for each day spent in segregation under conditions constituting cruel and unusual punishment and also punitive damages of $9,300.)

Related Standards

The following standards may be applicable in implementing Standard 2.18.

2.1 Access to Courts.
2.14 Grievance Procedure.
5.9 Continuing Jurisdiction of Sentencing Court.
14.11 Staff Development.
16.2 Administrative Justice.
16.3 Code of Offenders' Rights.

APPENDIX V

A.B.A. STANDARDS FOR CRIMINAL JUSTICE: LEGAL STATUS OF PRISONERS

PART I. GENERAL PRINCIPLE

Standard 23-1.1. General principle

Prisoners retain the rights of free citizens except:

(a) as specifically provided to the contrary in these standards; or

(b) when restrictions are necessary to assure their orderly confinement and interaction; or

(c) when restrictions are necessary to provide reasonable protection for the rights and physical safety of all members of the prison system and the general public.

Related Standards

NAC, Corrections 2.10, 16.3
NCCUSL, Model Sentencing and Corrections Act art. 4, prefatory note

PART II. ACCESS TO THE JUDICIAL PROCESS, LEGAL SERVICES, AND LEGAL MATERIALS

Standard 23-2.1. Access to the judicial process

(a) Prisoners should have free and meaningful access to the judicial process; governmental authorities should assure such access. Regulations or actions should not unduly delay or adversely affect the outcome of a prisoner's claim for relief or discourage prisoners from seeking judicial consideration for their grievances. Interests of institutional security and scheduling may justify regulations that affect the manner in which access is provided.

(b) To implement the principles in paragraph (a), the following standards should apply:

(i) Access should not be restricted by the nature of the action or the relief sought. Prisoners should be entitled to present any judicially cognizable issue, including:

(A) challenges to the legality of their conviction or confinement;

(B) assertions against correctional or other governmental authorities of any rights protected by constitutional, statutory, or administrative provision or the common law;

(C) civil legal problems; and

(D) assertions of a defense to any action brought against them.

(ii) Judicial procedures should be available to facilitate the prompt resolution of disputes involving the legality, duration, or conditions of confinement. The doctrine of exhaustion of remedies should apply unless past practice or other facts have demonstrated the futility of the available process. An administrative process unable to reach a decision within [thirty]* working days is presumptively unreasonable.

(iii) When directed by a court, prisoners' attendance at legal proceedings directly involving their in-

---

*Bracketed materials in the standards are suggested guidelines for consideration by corrections officials.

Standard 23-2.2. Access to legal services

terests should be assured by correctional authorities.

(iv) Prisoners should be allowed to prepare and retain legal documents. The time, place, or manner of their preparation may be regulated for purposes of institutional security and scheduling. Retention of legal documents may be regulated only for purposes of health and safety. Regulations covering the preparation or retention of legal documents should be the least restrictive necessary.

(v) Legal documents should not be read, censored, or altered by correctional authorities, nor should their delivery be delayed.

(vi) Prisoners' decisions to seek judicial relief should not adversely affect their program, status within a correctional institution, or opportunity for release.

Related Standards

ACA, Standards for Adult Correctional Institutions 4017, 4210, 4210.01, 4211, 4280-4284, 4346

NAC, Corrections 2.1

NCCUSL, Model Sentencing and Corrections Act §4-109

NSA, Inmates' Legal Rights, pp. 35-36

(a) Prisoners should have access to legal advice and counseling, and, in appropriate instances, will have a right to counsel, in connection with all personal legal matters, including but not limited to:

(i) court proceedings challenging conditions of confinement, correctional treatment, or supervision;

(ii) parole grant and revocation proceedings;

(iii) hearings to determine the length of sentences to imprisonment;

(iv) civil matters, to the same extent as provided to members of the general public who are financially unable to obtain adequate representation; and

(v) institutional disciplinary, classification, grievance, and other administrative proceedings.

This standard does not limit existing rights to representation in parole revocation proceedings or in cases arising under subparagraph (a)(i) or (iv). Neither, however, does it require correctional and parole authorities to allow the representation by legal counsel of prisoners at parole grant and other institutional hearings except as provided by law.

(b) Legal assistance for postconviction proceedings challenging the legality of a prisoner's conviction or confinement should conform to the requirements of standard 22-3.1.

(c) Prisoners should be entitled to retain counsel of their choice when able to do so and, when financially unable to obtain adequate respresentation, to have legal assistance provided for them by responsible governmental authorities to the same extent that such assistance is made available to members of the general public with comparable legal needs. Governmental authorities should establish programs to assure that adequate legal services are reasonably available to prisoners.

(d) Legal assistance for prisoners should be rendered by persons authorized by law to give legal advice or provide representation. When legal assistance is rendered by a person who is not an attorney, such counsel substitute should be trained by an attorney or educational institution and should receive continuing supervision by an attorney. Prison regulations should not restrict a prisoner's attorney in the selection of those assisting him or her.

(e) The relationship between a person providing legal assistance under paragraph (d) and a prisoner should be protected by the attorney-client privilege. Correctional authorities should facilitate confidential contact and communication between prisoners and persons providing legal assistance to them.

(f) Correctional and parole authorities should regulate by rule the roles of all persons who participate in institutional hearings.

Related Standards

ACA, Standards for Adult Correctional Institutions 4211, 4212, 4281-4283, 4330, 4346, 4349, 4354

NAC, Corrections 2.2

NCCUSL, Model Sentencing and Corrections Act §4-108

NSA, Inmates' Legal Rights, pp. 18, 30, 33

Standard 23-2.3. Access to legal materials

(a) Correctional authorities should make available to prisoners educational services pertaining to their legal rights even when they have access to legal services. Printed materials outlining the recognized grounds for postconviction relief and the resources available to any person to pursue legal questions, specially prepared for prison inmates and written in terms understandable to them, are most desirable. Alternatively, an adequate collection of standard legal reference materials related to criminal law and procedures and cognate constitutional provisions should be part of a prison library.

(b) Prisoners should be entitled to acquire personal law books and other legal research material. Any regulation of the storage of legal material in personal quarters or other areas should not unreasonably interfere with access to or use of these materials. The retention of personal legal materials may be regulated and restricted in accordance with standard 23-1.1.

Related Standards

ABA Standards for Criminal Justice 22-3.1

ACA, Standards for Adult Correctional Institutions 4017, 4216, 4283, 4360.02, 4409-4413.01

NAC, Corrections 2.3

NCCUSL, Model Sentencing and Corrections Act §4-110

NSA, Inmates' Legal Rights, p.33

Part III. Institutional Decision Making

Standard 23-3.1. Rules of conduct

(a) Correctional authorities should promulgate clear written rules for prisoner conduct. These rules and implementing criteria should include:

(i) a specific definition of offenses, a statement that the least severe punishment appropriate to each offense should be imposed, and a schedule indicating the minimum and maximum possible punishment for each offense, proportionate to the offense; and

(ii) specific criteria and procedures for prison discipline and classification decisions, including decisions involving security status and work and housing assignments.

(b) A personal copy of the rules

should be provided to each prisoner upon entry to the institution. For the benefit of illiterate and foreign-language prisoners, a detailed oral explanation of the rules should be given. In addition, a written translation should be provided in any language spoken by a significant number of prisoners.

Related Standards

ACA, Standards for Adult Correctional Institutions 4310-4314, 4363, 4373, 4377, 4379.01

NAC, Corrections 2.11

NCCUSL, Model Sentencing and Corrections Act §4-501

NSA, Inmates' Legal Rights, pp. 22-23

Standard 23-3.2. Disciplinary hearing procedures

(a) At a hearing where a minor sanction is imposed, the prisoner should be entitled to:

(i) written notice of the charge, in a language the prisoner understands, within [seventy-two] hours of the time he or she is suspected of having committed an offense; within another [twenty-four] hours the prisoner should be given copies of any further written information the tribunal may consider;

(ii) a hearing within [three] working days of the time the written notice of the charge was received;

(iii) be present and speak on his or her own behalf;

(iv) a written decision based upon a preponderance of the evidence, with specified reasons for the decision. The decision should be rendered promptly and in all cases

within [five] days after conclusion of the hearing; and

(v) appeal, within [five] days, to the chief executive officer of the institution, and the right to a written decision by that officer within [thirty] days, based upon a written summary of the hearing, any documentary evidence considered at the hearing, and the prisoner's written reason for appealing. The chief executive officer should either affirm or reverse the determination of misconduct and decrease or approve the punishment imposed. Execution of the punishment should be suspended during the appeal unless individual safety or individual security will be adversely affected thereby.

(b) At a hearing where a major sanction is imposed, in addition to the requirements of paragraph (a), the prisoner should be entitled to have in attendance any person within the local prison community who has relevant information, and to examine or cross-examine such witnesses except when the hearing officer(s):

(i) exclude testimony as unduly cumulative; or

(ii) receive testimony outside the presence of the prisoner pursuant to a finding that the physical safety of a person would be endangered by the presence of a particular witness or by disclosure of his or her identity.

(c) Disciplinary hearings should be conducted by one or more impartial persons.

(d) Unless the prisoner is found guilty, no record relating to the charge should be retained in the prisoner's file or used against the prisoner in any way.

(e) Where necessary, in accordance with standard 23-1.1(b) or (c), pending the hearing required by paragraph (b), correctional authorities may confine separately a prisoner alleged to have committed a major violation. Such prehearing confinement should not extend more than [seven] days unless necessitated by the prisoner's request for a continuance or by the pendency of criminal investigation or prosecution as provided in standard 23-3.3(b).

(f) In the event of a situation requiring the chief executive officer to declare all, or a part, of an institution to be in a state of emergency, the rights provided in this standard may be temporarily suspended for up to [twenty-four] hours after the emergency has terminated.

Related Standards

ACA, Standards for Adult Correctional Institutions 4310-4319.02, 4323-4333

NAC, Corrections 2.12

NCCUSL, Model Sentencing and Corrections Act §4-507

NSA, Inmates' Legal Rights, pp. 24-26

NSA, Jail Security, Classification, and Discipline, pp. 59-70

Standard 23-3.3. Criminal misconduct

(a) Where a prisoner is alleged to have engaged in conduct that would be a criminal offense under state or federal law, the prosecutor should be notified and, in consultation with the chief executive officer, should determine promptly whether to charge the prisoner. Institutional proceedings arising from the same conduct need not be suspended while the decision to charge is being made or while resolution of the charge is pending. However, correctional authorities should exercise caution in conducting institutional proceedings so that the right of the public and of the prisoner to a fair criminal trial is not infringed.

(b) If required by institutional order and security, the prisoner to be charged criminally may be confined in his or her assigned quarters or in a more secure housing unit for no more than [ninety] days, unless during that time an indictment or information is brought against the prisoner. If a charge is made, the prisoner may be so confined until the criminal proceeding is resolved.

(c) After disposition of the criminal charge, the prisoner may be reclassified. The prisoner also may be subjected to disciplinary proceedings if they were suspended during the prosecution.

Related Standards

ACA, Standards for Adult Correctional Institutions 4320

NAC, Corrections 2.11

NCCUSL, Model Sentencing and Corrections Act §4-511

NSA, Inmates' Legal Rights, pp. 38-39

Standard 23-3.4. Classification

(a) The initial classification of a prisoner according to security risk status and job or other assignment should be accomplished informally within [thirty] days of the prisoner's arrival at the place of classification.

(b) The prisoner should meet with a properly trained representative of the classification committee. The committee representative should:

(i) explain the classification process, the options the prisoner may have, and the relevant criteria; and

(ii) seek to develop a classification consistent with the needs of the prisoner and the institution; and

(iii) submit such classification to the classification committee and the prisoner.

(c) The classification of a prisoner should be reviewed by the classification committee at least every [six] months based on the written record of the prisoner's conduct for the most recent [six]-month period.

(d) Each decision of the classification committee should explain the considerations and factors that led to the committee's decision. The prisoner should receive a copy of the committee's written decision.

(e) If the classification committee or the prisoner rejects a classification (or if the prisoner is dissatisfied with the committee's periodic review), the prisoner should be given a prompt hearing before the classification committee if a request is made within [five] days of receipt of the classification decision.

(f) At a classification hearing, the prisoner should be entitled to:

(i) timely discovery of any written information the committee may consider; and

(ii) be present and speak on his or her own behalf.

(g) In any classification decision, the presence of a detainer based on a charged, but as yet unproven, criminal offense or parole violation should not be considered if the detainer has been pending for more than [six] months without formal action by the responsible authority after demand by the prisoner. All other detainers may be considered by the committee, but the mere presence of any detainer should not be given conclusive weight in deciding the prisoner's security classification.

Related Standards

ACA, Standards for Adult Correctional Institutions 4364, 4372-4385

NAC, Corrections 2.13, 6.1-6.3

NCCUSL, Model Sentencing and Corrections Act §§4-401 to 4-408, 4-412 to 4-414

NSA, Jail Security, Classification, and Discipline, pp. 31-36

Part IV. Prisoner Employment
and Institutional Programs

Standard 23-4.1. Prisoner participation in housekeeping and maintenance programs

(a) All prisoners may be compelled to maintain the cleanliness and orderliness of their personal living quarters without compensation. Pretrial detainees should not be compelled to engage in other institutional programs or activities except as required to maintain institutional security and order.

(b) Prisoners other than detainees may be compelled to engage in work assignments essential to the overall housekeeping operation, including cleaning, sanitation procedures, food service, maintenance, and prison industries for the production of goods for government use. Compensation should be provided for well-performed work at least sufficient to enable the prisoner to make commissary purchases and to accumulate some funds for release.

Related Standards

ACA, Standards for Adult Correctional Institutions 4242, 4295, 4386, 4390

NCCUSL, Model Sentencing and Corrections Act §4-808

NSA, Jail Programs, pp. 30-32

Standard 23-4.2. Availability of remunerative employment

Prisoners should have access to remunerative employment while confined. To implement this principle, the following standards should apply:

(a) Prisons should seek the advice and cooperation of industry and labor, as well as the support of the public, in order to encourage the introduction of an appropriate variety of privately owned and operated industries, as well as public works, within or adjacent to prison facilities, which can provide a meaningful range of employment opportunities for prisoners, not only to help minimize prisoner idleness but also to provide opportunities for prisoners to acquire and enhance marketable skills to increase the likelihood of meaningful employment upon release from prison.

(b) Legal provisions that restrict the goods that can be produced by prisoners or the types of employment that can be offered to prisoners should be repealed.

(c) Legal provisions that restrict the marketing, sale, or transportation of goods produced in correctional institutions or by prisoners should be repealed.

(d) Availability of outside work release programs should be encouraged in order to provide employment opportunity for prisoners, giving due regard to institutional and community security.

Related Standards

ACA, Standards for Adult Correctional Institutions 4017, 4386, 4387, 4390, 4445.01, 4446

NAC, Corrections 11.10, 16.13, 16.14

NCCUSL, Model Sentencing and Corrections Act §§4-801 to 4-804

NSA, Jail Programs, pp. 30-38

Standard 23-4.3. Wages and hours of employment

For work performed for private employers, prisoners should receive compensation and benefits at the prevailing rate paid to nonprisoners for the same work. The following standards should apply to all such employment:

(a) Prisoners should be governed by provisions comparable to those of the Fair Labor Standards Act of 1938.

(b) Prisoners should receive the same wages and be required to work no more than the number of hours that prevail in free society for similar work by persons with like training and experience.

(c) Prisoners should receive the same fringe benefits that prevail in free society for similar employment.

(d) In order not to give prisoners any inequitable advantage over nonprisoners, they should be required to make payments and/or reimbursements as provided in standard 23-4.4.

Where existing legislation or established local custom provides a barrier to full implementation of this standard, efforts should be begun to remove these impediments.

Related Standards

ACA, Standards for Adult Correctional Institutions 4388-4392.04

NAC, Corrections 11.10, 16.13

NCCUSL, Model Sentencing and Corrections Act §§4-811 to 4-812

Standard 23-4.4. Prisoner payments

(a) Prisoners receiving wages comparable to or prevailing in free society should:

(i) reimburse the jurisdiction for a reasonable share of its costs in maintaining them;

(ii) pay any contributions or withholding required by law or normally paid by workers in private industry working at comparable employment at comparable wages; and

(iii) pay any costs associated with their employment, such as for transportation, tools, and uniforms, that normally would be borne by workers in private industry working at comparable employment at comparable wages.

(b) As required by law prisoners should pay:

(i) taxes; and

(ii) any other legal obligations, including family support and court-ordered restitution.

Related Standards

ACA, Standards for Adult Correctional Institutions 4392

NAC, Corrections 11.10, 16.13

NCCUSL, Model Sentencing and Corrections Act §4-812

Standard 23-4.5. Conditions of employment

Subject to standard 23-1.1, prisoners generally should work under the same conditions that prevail in similar types of employment in free society. Prisoners should not be excluded from otherwise applicable legislation concerning their employment. These standards are not intended to extend to prisoners the right to strike or take other concerted action to affect the wages, hours, benefits, terms, or other conditions of their employment within correctional institutions.

Related Standards

ACA, Standards for Adult Correctional Institutions 4229.03, 4238, 4246, 4391.01

NAC, Corrections 11.10, 16.13

NCCUSL, Model Sentencing and Corrections Act §§4-901 to 4-903

NSA, Jail Programs, pp. 30-32

Standard 23-4.6. Availability of rehabilitative programs

Correctional authorities, after consultation with the prisoners and consideration of their records, should determine the types of rehabilitation programs, including self-improvement and educational programs, that will be beneficial to them, and should thereafter seek to provide access to as many such programs as feasible, either by establishing such programs or by contracting with outside agencies or individuals for such services.

Related Standards

ACA, Standards for Adult Correctional Institutions 4007.02, 4017, 4050.01

NAC, Corrections 2.9

Part V. Medical Treatment

Standard 23-5.1. Care to be provided

(a) Prisoners should receive routine and emergency medical care, which includes the diagnosis and treatment of physical, dental, and mental health problems. A prisoner who requires care not available in the correctional institution should be transferred to a hospital or other appropriate place for care.

(b) Personnel providing medical care in the correctional institution should have qualifications equivalent to medical care personnel performing similar functions in the community.

(c) If an institution operates a hospital, it should meet the standards for a licensed general hospital in the community with respect to the services it offers.

Related Standards

ACA, Standards for Adult Correctional Institutions 4253.01-4258.13, 4288

NAC, Corrections 2.6

NCCUSL, Model Sentencing and Corrections Act §4-105

NSA, Inmates' Legal Rights, pp.14-15

NSA, Jail Administration, p. 45

NSA, Jail Programs, pp. 13-15

NSA, Jail Security, Classification, and Discipline, pp. 37-39

Standard 23-5.2. Prompt medical treatment

Each correctional institution should have adequate trained personnel to:

(a) provide needed emergency medical care in a timely manner consistent with accepted medical practice and standards; and

(b) be present or otherwise available on a daily basis to evaluate requests from prisoners for medical care and render necessary care in a timely manner.

No correctional official or officer should impede or unreasonably delay a prisoner's access to medical care.

Related Standards

ACA, Standards for Adult Correctional Institutions 4253.01-4279.10

NAC, Corrections 2.6

NCCUSL, Model Sentencing and Corrections Act §4-105

NSA, Jail Administration, p. 45

NSA, Jail Programs, pp. 14-15

Standard 23-5.3. Medical examinations

(a) Upon admission to a correctional institution a prisoner should receive an examination by a person trained to ascertain visible or common symptoms of communicable disease and conditions requiring immediate medical attention by a physician.

(b) A sentenced prisoner should receive a thorough physical (including an appropriate evaluation of apparent mental condition) and dental examination in accordance with accepted medical practice and standards:

(i) within [two] weeks of admission to the correctional institution;

(ii) not less than every [two] years thereafter; and

(iii) upon release from confinement if the most recent examination was given more than [one] year earlier.

(c) A person detained in a correctional institution who is not a sentenced prisoner should be afforded a thorough physical and dental examination upon request when the person is confined for more than [two] weeks.

Related Standards

ACA, Standards for Adult Correctional Institutions 4219.01, 4260.01-4261.06, 4261.11, 4263.02

NAC, Corrections 2.6

NCCUSL, Model Sentencing and Corrections Act §4-105

NSA, Inmates' Legal Rights, p. 14

NSA, Jail Programs, p. 14

NSA, Jail Security, Classification, and Discipline, pp. 37-38

Standard 23-5.4. Medical records

Prisoners' medical records should be:

(a) compiled and maintained in accordance with accepted medical practice and standards;

(b) maintained in a confidential and secure manner; and

(c) retained for at least [five] years after the prisoner's release.

Related Standards

ACA, Standards for Adult Correc-

tional Institutions 4265, 4279.05-4279.08
   NAC, Corrections 2.6
   NCCUSL, Model Sentencing and Corrections Act §4-105
   NSA, Jail Programs, p. 15
   NSA, Jail Security, Classification, and Discipline, pp. 37-38

Standard 23-5.5. Refusal of medical treatment

A prisoner should be permitted to decline medical examination or a course of medical treatment except:

(a) when required by order of a court;

(b) when reasonably believed by the responsible physician to be necessary to detect or treat communicable disease or otherwise to protect the health of other persons; or

(c) when reasonably believed to be necessary in an emergency to save the life of the person or to prevent permanent and serious damage to the person's health.

Related Standards

ACA, Standards for Adult Correctional Institutions 4268.03
NCCUSL, Model Sentencing and Corrections Act §4-126

Standard 23-5.6. Control of drugs

All drugs should be under the control and supervision of the physician in charge of the institution's medical care program. Normally, only medical care personnel should administer prescription drugs. In an emergency, correctional officials may administer such drugs at the direction of medical care personnel. In no instance should prisoners administer drugs.

Related Standards

ACA, Standards for Adult Correctional Institutions 4268.01, 4279.03, 4279.10

NSA, Jail Programs, p. 15
NSA, Jail Security, Classification, and Discipline, pp. 38-39

Standard 23-5.7. Services for women prisoners

Pending determination of child welfare and placement by courts having appropriate jurisdiction, correctional authorities should assure:

(a) that accommodations for all necessary prenatal and postnatal care and treatment are available for women prisoners. Arrangements should be made whenever practicable for children to be born in a hospital outside an institution. The fact that a child was born in a correctional institution should not be mentioned in the birth certificate; and

(b) that it is possible for women prisoners to keep their young children with them for a reasonable time, preferably on extended furlough or in an appropriate community facility or, if that is not feasible, that alternative care be promptly arranged. Where the young children remain with the mother in an institution, a nursery staffed by qualified persons should be provided.

Related Standards

ACA, Standards for Adult Correctional Institutions 4267.01
NAC, Corrections 11.6
NSA, Jail Programs, p. 20

Standard 23-5.8. Experimental programs

(a) Nontherapeutic experimentation, including but not limited to aversive behavior modification, psychosurgery, drug testing, electrical stimulation of the brain, and psychopharmacology, should not be allowed under any circumstances.

(b) Once an institution has substantially met the standards enunciated in this chapter, a prisoner should be allowed to participate in a therapeutic medical program deemed to be beneficial to him or her, provided that:

(i) the program has been approved as medically sound and in conformance with medically accepted standards;

(ii) the prisoner has given full voluntary and informed written consent; and

(iii) in the case of psychosurgery, electrical stimulation of the brain, and aversive conditioning, approval has been given by an appropriate court after an adversary hearing to determine that the program is sound and that the prisoner has given informed consent.

(c) A program should be considered medically sound and in conformance with medically accepted standards only after it has been reviewed by a committee established by law to evaluate its medical validity.

(d) A prisoner should be considered to have given informed consent only after that consent has been reviewed by an independent committee, including prisoners and ex-offenders, and the committee has personally interviewed the prisoner.

(e) As used in this standard, "informed consent" means that the prisoner is informed of:

(i) the likely effects, including possible side effects, of the procedure;

(ii) the likelihood and degree of improvement, remission, control, or cure resulting from the procedure;

(iii) the uncertainty of the benefits and hazards of the procedure;

(iv) the reasonable alternatives to the procedure; and

(v) the ability to withdraw at any time.

Related Standards
ACA, Standards for Adult Correctional Institutions 4127.01, 4268.04

PART VI. PERSONAL INTEGRITY AND SECURITY

Standard 23-6.1. Communication rights

(a) Any limitations on prisoners' communications should be the least restrictive necessary to serve the legitimate interests of institutional order and security and the protection of the public.

(b) An envelope, package, or container sent to or by a prisoner may be opened and inspected to determine if it contains contraband or other prohibited material.

(c) Correctional authorities may authorize the intentional reading of written communications and the intentional hearing of oral communications upon obtaining reliable information that a particular communication may jeopardize the safety of the public or the security or safety within a correctional institution, or is being used in furtherance of illegal activity.

(d) A communication not otherwise subject to reading or hearing should not be intercepted except pursuant to a court order, or unless authorized by law, when the communication is reasonably anticipated to be:

(i) between a prisoner and his or her attorney; or

(ii) between a prisoner and a member of a specified class of persons and organizations, including but not limited to courts, officials of the confining authority, state and local chief executive officers, legislators, administrators of grievance systems, and the paroling authority.

(e) Indigent prisoners should be afforded a reasonable amount of stationery and free postage for letters to attorneys, courts, and public officials, and to permit them to maintain contact with family and friends in the community.

(f) Indigent prisoners should be allowed reasonable use of a free telephone to communicate with their attorneys of record and court officials of courts in which their current litigation is pending, if correctional authorities determine that written communication would not be effective. Pay telephones should be available for other communications.

(g) Prisoners should be entitled to receive magazines, soft-cover books, newspapers, and other written materials that can be lawfully mailed, subject to the provisions of standard 23-1.1.

Related Standards

ACA, Standards for Adult Correctional Institutions 4210, 4282, 4291.06, 4340-4349

NAC, Corrections 2.15, 2.17

NCCUSL, Model Sentencing and Corrections Act §§4-114, 4-117

NSA, Inmates' Legal Rights, pp. 42-43

Standard 23-6.2. Visitation; general

(a) Home furlough programs should be established, giving due regard to institutional and community security, to enable prisoners to maintain and strengthen family and community ties.

(b) Subject to the provisions of standard 23-1.1, correctional authorities should accommodate and encourage visiting by establishing reasonable visiting hours, including time on weekends and holidays, suited to the convenience of visitors.

(c) Subject to the provisions of stan-

dard 23-1.1, institutional visiting facilities should promote informal communications and afford opportunities for physical contact. Extended visits between prisoners and their families in suitable accommodations should be allowed for prisoners who are not receiving home furloughs.

(d) Prisoners should be able to receive any visitor not excluded by correctional authorities for good cause. A prisoner may have the exclusion of a prospective visitor reconsidered through a grievance procedure. All visitors may be subjected to nonintrusive forms of personal search.

(e) Visitation periods should be at least [one] hour long, and prisoners should be able to cumulate visitation periods to permit extended visits. Visits with attorneys, clergy, and public officials should not be counted against visiting periods, and should be unlimited except as to time and duration.

(f) Where resources and facilities permit, correctional authorities are encouraged to facilitate and promote visitation by providing transportation or by providing guidance, directions, and assistance as to available travel to visitors arriving in local terminals.

Related Standards

ACA, Standards for Adult Correctional Institutions 4024, 4282, 4291.05, 4350-4355.01, 4450

NAC, Corrections 2.17

NCCUSL, Model Sentencing and Corrections Act §§4-115, 4-118

NSA, Inmates' Legal Rights, pp. 42-44

NSA, Jail Security, Classification, and Discipline, pp. 57-58

Standard 23-6.3. Visitation; prisoners undergoing discipline

Prisoners who have violated a

disciplinary rule should have the same opportunity to receive visitors as prisoners in the general population of the institution, subject to the provisions of standard 23-1.1.

Related Standards

ACA, Standards for Adult Correctional Institutions 4210.01

NCCUSL, Model Sentencing and Corrections Act §4-115(b)(3)

Standard 23-6.4. Group and media visits

Correctional authorities should accommodate groups and representatives of the media who request permission to visit a correctional institution. The time, place, and manner of such visits may be regulated to preserve the privacy and dignity of prisoners and the security and order of the institution. Authorized conversations should not be monitored except as provided in standard 23-6.1(c) and (d).

Related Standards

ACA, Standards for Adult Correctional Institutions 4291.07

NAC, Corrections 2.15, 2.17

NSA, Inmates' Legal Rights, p. 43

NSA, Jail Administration, pp. 50-52

Standard 23-6.5. Religious freedom

(a) Prisoners' religious beliefs should not be restricted or inhibited by correctional authorities in any way.

(b) Prisoners should be entitled to pursue any lawful religious practice consistent with their orderly confinement and the security of the institution.

(c) Correctional authorities should provide prisoners with diets or nutritious food consistent with their religious beliefs. Prisoners should be entitled to observe special religious rites, including fasting and special dining hours, on major holidays generally observed by their religion, subject to standard 23-1.1.

(d) Prisoners should not be required to engage in religious activities.

(e) Correctional authorities should not maintain any information (other than directory information) concerning a prisoner's religious activities.

(f) Modes of dress or appearance, including religious medals and other symbols, should be permitted to the extent they do not interfere with identification and security of prisoners.

(g) Even while being punished, prisoners should be allowed religious counseling.

(h) Resources and facilities made available for religious purposes should be equitably allocated according to the proportions of prisoners adhering to each faith.

Related Standards

ACA, Standards for Adult Correctional Institutions 4218, 4291.04, 4291.08, 4363.01, 4430-4436.02

NAC, Corrections 2.16

NCCUSL, Model Sentencing and Corrections Act §4-113

NSA, Inmates' Legal Rights, pp. 40-41

NSA, Jail Programs, pp. 39-40

Standard 23-6.6. Organizations and petitions

(a) Subject to the provisions of standard 23-1.1, prisoners should be permitted to form, join, or belong to organizations whose purposes are lawful. Correctional authorities should develop rules concerning organization formation, meetings, and activities which do not unfairly discriminate against organizations within the institution. When the safety of the public or the security or safety of persons within the prison community is not thereby jeopardized, correctional authorities should allow reasonable participation by members of the general public in the authorized meetings or activities of organizations.

(b) Individual prisoners, or prisoner organizations, should be permitted to circulate petitions for signature, or peacefully to distribute lawful materials, subject to reasonable time and place limitations, so long as no intimidation is practiced.

(c) This standard is not intended to extend to prisoners the right to strike or take other concerted action to affect institutional conditions, programs, or policies.

Related Standards

ACA, Standards for Adult Correctional Institutions 4291.06

NAC, Corrections 2.15

NCCUSL, Model Sentencing and Corrections Act §4-125

Standard 23-6.7. Prisoner communications media

(a) Where resources and facilities permit, prisoners should be allowed to establish and operate newspapers and other communications media for the dissemination of information, opinions, and other material of interest to prisoners.

(b) Correctional authorities may require that prior to publication or determination:

(i) material that might constitute an attack upon a person or group be furnished to that person or group so that a right of reply can be exercised contemporaneously; and

(ii) all material be submitted for review by a designated official. Correctional authorities may pro-

hibit the publication or dissemination of material that is obscene or that constitutes a substantial threat to institutional security or order. Material also may be censored if correctional authorities could censor it if it were contained in publications sent to prisoners through the mail.

(c) Any person or group aggrieved by a decision concerning the inclusion or exclusion of material in a medium of expression, including the prisoner responsible for the publication, should use available grievance procedures to secure review of the decision.

Related Standards

ACA, Standards for Adult Correctional Institutions 4427

NAC, Corrections 2.15

NCCUSL, Model Sentencing and Corrections Act §4-124

Standard 23-6.8. Personal grooming

Subject to the provisions of standard 23-1.1 and the need for maintenance of appropriate hygienic standards, prisoners should be allowed a reasonable choice in the selection of their own hair styles and personal grooming.

Related Standards

ACA, Standards for Adult Correctional Institutions 4245, 4249, 4252, 4291.03

NAC, Corrections 2.15

NSA, Inmates' Legal Rights, p. 15

NSA, Jail Security, Classification, and Discipline, p. 56

Standard 23-6.9. Physical security

Prisoners should be entitled to a healthful place in which to live and to protection from personal injury, disease, property damage, and personal abuse or harassment, including sexual assault or manipulation.

Related Standards

ACA, Standards for Adult Correctional Institutions 4098, 4140-4149.-06, 4178.04, 4205-4209.02, 4217.01, 4219.01, 4291.08, 4360.02

NAC, Corrections 2.4, 2.5

NCCUSL, Model Sentencing and Corrections Act §§4-104, 4-106, 4-107

NSA, Jail Security, Classification, and Discipline, p. 51

NSA, Inmates' Legal Rights, pp. 13-16, 27

Standard 23-6.10. Search of facilities and prisoners

(a) Any area of a correctional institution, except prisoners' living quarters, may be searched by any correctional employee without specific information or cause at any time.

(b) Routine visual inspections of prisoners' living quarters to determine whether they are being maintained in accordance with health, safety, and security regulations should be conducted periodically by any correctional employee without specific prior authorization.

(c) Without specific cause, the chief executive officer, or in his or her absence the acting chief executive officer, of a correctional institution may authorize a routine and random intrusive search of prisoners' living quarters and belongings.

(d) An intrusive search of a prisoner's living quarters and belongings, other than a routine and random search pursuant to paragraph (c), should:

(i) require the prior written authorization of a supervisor; and

(ii) be based upon a reasonable belief that contraband or other prohibited material will be found.

However, if the correctional officer who reasonably believes the search is necessary also reasonably believes that the material to be sought will be disposed of while authorization is being obtained, the officer may act without prior authorization.

(e) All searches of prisoner living quarters and belongings should be conducted so as to minimize harm to prisoner property and to minimize invasion of privacy.

(f) In conducting searches of a prisoner, correctional authorities should strive to preserve the privacy, dignity, and bodily integrity of the prisoner. In addition:

(i) correctional authorities should use nonintrusive sensors instead of body searches whenever possible;

(ii) a prisoner may be patted down to determine whether he or she is carrying contraband or other prohibited material;

(iii) a search requiring a prisoner to disrobe, including a visual inspection of body cavities, should be conducted only when based upon an articulable suspicion that the prisoner is carrying contraband or other prohibited material. It should be conducted by a supervisor in a private place, out of the sight of others, except that the prisoner may request the presence of another available officer of the institution; and

(iv) digital or instrumental inspection of the anal or vaginal cavities should require written authorization from the chief executive officer of the institution, and should be permitted only when that written authorization includes the factual basis leading to a reasonable belief that the prisoner is carrying contraband or other prohibited material there. All such searches should be conducted by a medically trained person other than another prisoner, in the prison hospital or another private place. The prisoner may request the presence of another available officer of the institution.

(g) Upon completion of any search for which written authorization is required or any search that results in the seizure of contraband or other prohibited material, a written report should be made as directed by the chief executive officer. The report should identify the circumstances of the search, the person(s) conducting the search, and any witnesses. When any property is taken from the living quarters or body of a prisoner, a copy of the report or a portion of it should be given to the prisoner as a receipt.

Related Standards

ACA, Standards for Adult Correctional Institutions 4173.01-4173.02a, 4292, 4293, 4317, 4360.01-4361

NAC, Corrections 2.7

NCCUSL, Model Sentencing and Corrections Act §§4-119, 4-120

NSA, Jail Security, Classification, and Discipline, pp. 45-46

Standard 23-6.11. Confidentiality of prisoner records

(a) Directory information, which includes routine identifying data or statistical information customarily usable in nonidentifying compilations, can be released from a prisoner's file without the prisoner's consent. All other information should be disclosed only upon the prisoner's written consent unless:

(i) the disclosure is to an agency involved with investigation, prosecution, disposition, or custody of criminal offenders and an agency official specifies in writing the par-

ticular information desired;

(ii) the material is sought only for statistical, research, or reporting purposes and is not in a form containing the prisoner's name, number, symbol, or other identifying particular; or

(iii) the disclosure is made pursuant to a valid court order.

(b) Prisoners should be entitled to examine and copy information in their files, challenge its accuracy, and request its amendment. Upon notice to the prisoner, correctional authorities may withhold:

(i) information that constitutes diagnostic opinion that might seriously disrupt a program of rehabilitation;

(ii) sources of information obtained upon a promise of confidentiality;

(iii) information that, if disclosed, might result in harm, physical or otherwise, to any person; or

(iv) any other information that might jeopardize prison security if disclosed.

(c) Information given by a prisoner to any employee of the correctional authority in a designated counseling relationship under a representation of confidentiality should be privileged, except where the information concerns a contemplated crime or disclosure is required by court order.

Related Standards

ACA, Standards for Adult Correctional Institutions 4068.03, 4130-4139.05, 4265, 4359

NCCUSL, Model Sentencing and Corrections Act §§4-121, 4-122

Standard 23-6.12. Compensation for injury or death

(a) Legislation should be enacted

which extends some form of compensation coverage to prisoners injured while working on the maintenance or operation of correctional institutions or in any business, commercial, industrial, or agricultural enterprise.

(b) Legislation should be enacted which extends the coverage of tort claims systems to prisoners in circumstances where members of the general public could recover from appropriate governmental authorities.

(c) For injury or death not compensable under a workers' compensation or tort claims system, prisoners should have the remedies available under law to the general public.

Related Standards

ACA, Standards for Adult Correctional Institutions 4052

NAC, Corrections 2.4

NCCUSL, Model Sentencing and Corrections Act §§4-901 to 4-905

NSA, Jail Administration, p. 46

Standard 23-6.13. Use of force or deadly force

(a) Imprisonment inherently requires involuntary physical confinement that must be enforced with meticulous attention to internal and external security coupled with maximum orderliness. Thus, all correctional officials who share direct responsibility for enforcing such security should be provided with a comprehensive set of officially approved written policies and thoroughly understandable, workable procedures based thereon to guide them in discharging this responsibility at all times and under every conceivable circumstance. Such policies and procedures should be periodically evaluated and revised as warranted in the light of actual experience, relevant case law, applicable legislative

developments, and professionally recognized research. A documented record of all such evaluations and revisions should be maintained by correctional authorities as part of the administrative files for reference purposes and afforded proper security.

(i) Included in such policies and procedures should be a specific emphasis on minimizing and eliminating where possible those circumstances when physical or deadly force need be invoked.

(ii) Physical or deadly force should be authorized when the correctional employee is confronted with a situation that would reasonably support an on-site judgment that physical or deadly force is immediately necessary to effectuate one of the purposes listed below, but then only to the extent necessary to effectuate such purposes as:

(A) preventing an escape. Deadly force may be authorized when necessary to prevent an escape from an institution used primarily for the custody of persons convicted of felonies unless the actor has reason to know:

(1) that the person escaping is not a person who has been charged with or convicted for having committed a felony involving violence; or

(2) that the person escaping is unlikely to endanger human life or to inflict serious bodily harm if not prevented from escaping.

Deadly force may be utilized when necessary to prevent an escape from an institution used primarily for the custody of persons convicted of misdemeanors or awaiting trial if the corrections employee has reason to believe there is a substantial risk that the person escaping will cause death or serious bodily harm unless prevented from escaping and when, in the employee's on-site professional judgment, lesser force would fail or would endanger other lives.

(B) maintaining control of an institution. When property is being destroyed or when a prisoner constitutes a threat to himself or herself or another, or threatens or disrupts the order of a living area, or threatens by his or her actions the security of the institution, force may be used to move or effectively restrain the prisoner. Deadly force should not be authorized unless otherwise justified by the law of the jurisdiction governing self-defense or the defense of others.

(iii) "Deadly force" includes force that the trained and authorized professional employee uses with the purpose of causing, or which he or she knows will create a substantial risk of causing, death or serious bodily harm.

(b) In order to assist responsible correctional personnel in discharging their enforcement duties, adequate security devices, including firearms, ammunition, chemical agents, riot control weapons, and restraining devices, should be supplied to them for their official and judicious use in accordance with applicable policies and procedures.

(c) Corrections personnel should not be assigned responsibilities potentially requiring the use of force, including deadly force, unless they are initially and periodically evaluated as being physically, mentally, and temperamentally fit for such hazardous and sensitive duties; and under no circumstances should any person so certified be assigned to such duty until he or she has successfully completed an adequate course of training in the safety, mechanical functioning, and effective use of all assigned security devices, including defensive tactics and the effective use of physical force. During the tenure of such duty assignments, all such personnel must participate fully in regularly scheduled training, and official contemporaneous records of continuing proficiency must be maintained and be available for spot check inspection.

(d) Correctional authorities should establish and implement effective procedures requiring responsible personnel to submit an adequate written report to the chief executive officer or his or her designee no later than the conclusion of the shift, which report will contain all pertinent details concerning any instance of the use of force or deadly force in facilities, including discharging firearms or using chemical agents or any other weapon to control prisoners. Upon receiving such reports, the chief executive officer should be responsible for promptly making certain that the report is self-sufficient, and if not, for seeing that adequate investigation is undertaken to obtain complete findings of fact, which can be the basis for evaluating the appropriateness of ensuing administrative actions, evaluating applicable policy and procedures, and formulating future training procedures.

Related Standards

ACA, Standards for Adult Correctional Institutions 4097-4098, 4150, 4154, 4165-4170, 4178.05-4182, 4184.01, 4189

NAC, Corrections 2.4

NCCUSL, Model Sentencing and

Corrections Act §§4-104, 4-510
  NSA, Jail Administration, p. 44
  NSA, Jail Security, Classification, and Discipline, p. 66

Standard 23-6.14. Maintenance of institutions

(a) Every correctional institution should:

(i) comply with health, sanitation, fire, and industrial safety codes applicable to private residential facilities or other public buildings such as schools and hospitals;

(ii) comply with applicable state standards for correctional institutions;

(iii) be inspected regularly, not less than [annually], by food, medical, housing, fire, and safety inspectors who are independent of the agency being inspected; and

(iv) be subject to enforcement penalties and procedures, including abatement procedures for noncompliance, applicable to other institutions subject to such codes.

(b) Prisoners in correctional institutions other than residential institutions utilized as part of a community release program should have the opportunity to have their own separate living quarters of adequate size. If such separate living quarters cannot be provided and dormitories and other multiple-prisoner living quarters are used, they should be staffed to ensure prisoner safety. All prisoner living quarters should be designed to allow prisoners substantial privacy consistent with their security classification.

(c) Correctional authorities should provide prisoners with:

(i) heating and ventilation systems to maintain humane comfort;

(ii) natural and artificial light in their living quarters sufficient to permit reading;

(iii) an adequate balanced diet;

(iv) adequate, clean, and functioning private toilet and other facilities for the maintenance of personal cleanliness;

(v) supplies for the maintenance of personal cleanliness;

(vi) freedom from excessive noise;

(vii) clean clothing and bedding appropriate to the season;

(viii) varied opportunities for daily physical exercise and recreation; and

(ix) medical care as provided in part V of this chapter.

(d) A prisoner restricted to his or her assigned living quarters or placed in a more secure housing unit pursuant to disciplinary or classsification action may be physically separated from other prisoners, but should not be deprived of those items necessary for the maintenance of psychological and physical well-being, such as books or other reading matter, mail, physical exercise, items of personal care or hygiene, medical care, light, ventilation, regular diet, and visiting or oral communication opportunities with other persons. A prisoner so confined should not be subjected to conditions that unnecessarily cause physical or mental deterioration.

Related Standards

ACA, Standards for Adult Correctional Institutions 4140-4149.19, 4205-4222, 4224-4232.02, 4238-4252

NAC, Corrections 2.5

NCCUSL, Model Sentencing and Corrections Act §4-106

NSA, Inmates' Legal Rights, pp. 13-16

NSA, Jail Administration, pp. 46-47

Standard 23-6.15. Nondiscriminatory treatment

Prisoners should not be subjected to discriminatory treatment based solely on race, sex, religion, or national origin. Appropriate facilities also should be provided for the physically handicapped. Prisoners of either sex may be assigned to the same facility. They may also be assigned to separate facilities if there is essential equality in living conditions, decision-making processes affecting the status and activities of prisoners, and the availability of community and institutional programs, including education, employment, and vocational training opportunities.

Related Standards

ACA, Standards for Adult Correctional Institutions 4149.01, 4291.01a, 4291.08, 4309

NAC, Corrections 2.8

NCCUSL, Model Sentencing and Corrections Act §4-111

NSA, Inmates' Legal Rights, p. 21

NSA, Jail Programs, pp. 9, 20

PART VII. IMPLEMENTING PRISONERS' RIGHTS: ADMINISTRATIVE, JUDICIAL, AND LEGISLATIVE OVERSIGHT

Standard 23-7.1. Resolving prisoner grievances

(a) Correctional authorities should authorize and encourage correctional employees to resolve prisoner grievances on an informal basis whenever possible.

(b) Every correctional institution should adopt a formal procedure to resolve specific prisoner grievances, including any complaint arising out of institutional policies, rules, practices, and procedures or the action of any correctional employee or official. Grievance procedures should not be used as a substitute appellate procedure for individual decisions reached by adjudicative bodies, for example, parole, classification, and disciplinary boards, although a complaint involving the procedures or general policies employed by any correctional adjudicative body should be subject to grievance procedures.

(c) Correctional authorities should make forms available so that a grievant may initiate review by describing briefly the nature of the grievance, the persons involved, and the remedy sought.

(d) The institution's grievance procedure should be designed to ensure the cooperation and confidence of prisoners and correctional officials and should include:

(i) provision for written responses to all grievances, including the reasons for the decision;

(ii) provision for response within a prescribed, reasonable time limit. A request that is not responded to or resolved within [thirty] working days should be deemed to have been denied;

(iii) special provision for responding to emergencies;

(iv) provision for advisory review of grievances;

(v) provision for participation by staff and prisoners in the design of the grievance procedure;

(vi) provision for access by all prisoners, with guarantees against reprisal;

(vii) applicability over a broad range of issues; and

(viii) means for resolving questions of jurisdiction.

Related Standards

ACA, Standards for Adult Correctional Institutions 4007.02, 4291.11

NAC, Corrections 2.14

NCCUSL, Model Sentencing and

Corrections Act §§1-104, 4-301 to 4-307

NSA, Inmates' Legal Rights, p. 37
NSA, Jail Security, Classification, and Discipline, p. 62

Standard 23-7.2. Regulation of correctional institutions

(a) The organization, procedures, policies, and practices of each correctional institution should be governed by rules adopted by procedures comparable to those of the Model State Administrative Procedure Act. "Rule" means the whole or any part of a statement of general applicability and future effect concerning such matters.

(b) Prisoners should be given notice of any rules adopted by correctional authorities and of any other statement adopted to govern prisoners.

Related Standards

ACA, Standards for Adult Correctional Institutions 4007.03, 4310, 4311

NAC, Corrections 2.11, 9.7, 16.2

NCCUSL, Model Sentencing and Corrections Act §1-103

NSA, Jail Administration, pp. 41-42

Standard 23-7.3. Administrative oversight

(a) The policies, practices, operations, and conditions of correctional institutions and the acts of correctional employees should be subject to inspection and investigation by an auditor-general or inspector-general responsible to the senior correctional authority of the jurisdiction.

(b) In any jurisdiction with an ombudsman or similar official, the jurisdiction of that person should extend to receiving and investigating complaints from prisoners.

Related Standards

NCCUSL, Model Sentencing and Corrections Act §§4-201 to 4-203

NSA, Jail Administration, pp. 46-47

Standard 23-7.4. Legislative responsibilities

Each state legislature should enact legislation to implement these standards and to provide sufficient resources to ensure implementation of the legal rights of prisoners.

Related Standards

ACA, Standards for Adult Correctional Institutions 4001, 4020, 4034

NAC, Corrections 16.1, 16.3

PART VIII. CIVIL DISABILITIES OF CONVICTED PERSONS

Standard 23-8.1. Repeal of mandatory civil disabilities

Laws or regulations which require that convicted persons be subjected to collateral disabilities or penalties, or be deprived of civil rights, should be repealed except for those specifically preserved in part VIII of these standards.

Related Standards

NAC, Corrections 16.1, 16.17

NCCUSL, Model Sentencing and Corrections Act §4-1001

NSA, Jail Administration, p. 49

Standard 23-8.2. Expungement of convictions

Each jurisdiction should have a judicial procedure for expunging criminal convictions, the effect of which would be to mitigate or avoid collateral disabilities.

Related Standards

NAC, Corrections 16.17

Standard 23-8.3. Procedure for imposing authorized disabilities

(a) When the imposition of collateral disabilities or penalties, or the deprivation of civil rights, is authorized as a consequence of a conviction, a procedure should be established to assure that there is a determination in each individual case that the disability or penalty is necessary to advance an important governmental or public interest.

(b) The procedure established should be comparable to that provided for agency adjudications in the Model State Administrative Procedure Act.

(c) A disability should be imposed for a stated period, after which the person subject to the disability should be entitled to have the appropriateness of the disability reconsidered. Within the stated period of the disability, if a person can present evidence that the disability imposed no longer effectuates an important governmental interest, the person should be entitled to a reconsideration.

(d) The burden of proving the appropriateness of the disability should be on those seeking to impose it, except a convicted person should bear the burden of proving an allegation that the fact of conviction has unfairly affected his or her application for or status in private employment.

Related Standards
None

Standard 23-8.4. Voting rights

Persons convicted of any offense should not be deprived of the right to vote either by law or by the action or inaction of government officials. Prisoners should be authorized to vote at their last place of residence prior to confinement unless they can establish some other residence in accordance with rules applicable to the general public. They should not, however, be authorized to establish voting residence or domicile in the jurisdiction where they are incarcerated solely because of that incarceration.

Related Standards
NCCUSL, Model Sentencing and Corrections Act §§4-112, 4-1003

Standard 23-8.5. Judicial rights

Persons convicted of any offense should be entitled to:

(a) initiate and defend suit in any court in their own name under procedures applicable to the general public;

(b) serve on juries except while actually confined or while on probation or parole;

(c) execute judicially enforceable documents and agreements; and

(d) serve as court-appointed fiduciaries except during actual confinement.

Related Standards
NAC, Corrections 2.1, 2.10, 16.17
NCCUSL, Model Sentencing and Corrections Act §§ 4-1001, 4-1002

Standard 23-8.6. Domestic rights

(a) The domestic relationships of convicted persons should be governed by rules applicable to the general public. Conviction or confinement alone should be insufficient to deprive a person of any of the following domestic rights:

(i) the right to contract or dissolve a marriage;

(ii) parental rights, including the right to direct the rearing of children;

(iii) the right to grant or withhold consent to the adoption of children; and

(iv) the right to adopt children.

(b) Conviction or confinement alone should not constitute neglect or abandonment of a spouse or child, and persons convicted or confined should be assisted in making appropriate arrangements for their spouse or children during periods of confinement.

Related Standards

NCCUSL, Model Sentencing and Corrections Act §4-1001

Standard 23-8.7. Property and financial rights

(a) Persons convicted of any offense should not be deprived of the right to acquire, inherit, sell, or otherwise dispose of real or personal property consistent with the rule that a person should not profit from his or her own wrong. Persons unable to manage or preserve their property by reason of confinement should be entitled to appoint someone of their own choosing to act on their behalf.

(b) Persons convicted of any offense or confined as a result of a conviction should not, for that reason alone, lose any otherwise vested pension rights or become ineligible to participate in any governmental program providing relief, medical care, and old age pension.

(c) State departments of insurance should require companies to offer insurance of all kinds to persons who have been convicted of any offense and should ensure that any rate differential based solely on a conviction is justified.

(d) Agencies that compile and report information used to determine a person's suitability for credit or employment should be prohibited from disclosing criminal convictions that from the date of parole or release antedate the report by more than [five] years.

Related Standards

NAC, Corrections 16.17

NCCUSL, Model Sentencing and Corrections Act §§4-127, 4-1001

Standard 23-8.8. Employment and licensing

(a) Barriers to employment of convicted persons based solely on a past conviction should be prohibited unless the offense committed bears a substantial relationship to the functions and responsibilities of the employment. Among the factors that should be considered in evaluating the relationship between the offense and the employment are the following:

(i) the likelihood the employment will enhance the opportunity for commission of similar offenses;

(ii) the time elapsed since conviction;

(iii) the person's conduct subsequent to conviction; and

(iv) the circumstances of the offense and of the person that led to the crime and the likelihood that such circumstances will recur.

(b) Each jurisdiction should enact legislation protecting persons convicted of criminal offenses from unreasonable barriers in private employment. Such legislation should govern:

(i) denying employment;

(ii) discharging persons from employment;

(iii) denying fair employment conditions, remuneration, or promotion;

(iv) denying membership in a labor union or other organization affecting employability; and

(v) denying or revoking a license necessary to engage in any occupation, profession, or employment. Jurisdictions should adopt appropriate mechanisms for the enforcement of prohibitions against barriers to private employment applicable to convicted persons.

(c) Past convictions should not bar a person from running for elected office, although jurisdictions may provide that conviction of specified offenses will result in the automatic forfeiture of elective office held at the time of conviction. A conviction should not bar a person from holding appointive public office, although the appointing entity may require forfeiture of an office held at the time of conviction.

(d) Public employment should be governed by the same standards proposed for private employment.

(e) For purposes of this standard, "appointive public office" includes policy-making positions. "Public employment" includes positions that generally are governed by civil service or personnel systems, or are considered career appointments.

(f) Licensing or other governmental regulations should not automatically exclude persons convicted of any offense from participation in regulated activities. Persons should not be barred from regulated activity on the basis of a conviction unless the offense committed bears a substantial relationship to participation in the activity. In determinations of whether such a relationship exists, the factors listed in paragraph (a) should be considered.

Related Standards

ACA, Standards for Adult Correctional Institutions 4055.06

NAC, Corrections 2.10

NCCUSL, Model Sentencing and Corrections Act §§4-1004, 4-1005

APPENDIX VI

UNITED NATIONS
STANDARD MINIMUM RULES FOR THE TREATMENT OF PRISONERS AND RELATED RECOMMENDATIONS

A. Standard Minimum Rules for the Treatment of Prisoners

Resolution adopted on 30 August 1955

The First United Nations Congress on the Prevention of Crime and the Treatment of Offenders,

Having adopted the Standard Minimum Rules for the Treatment of Prisoners annexed to the present Resolution,

1. *Requests* the Secretary-General, in accordance with paragraph (*d*) of the annex to resolution 415(V) of the General Assembly of the United Nations, to submit these rules to the Social Commission of the Economic and Social Council for approval;

2. *Expresses* the hope that these rules be approved by the Economic and Social Council and, if deemed appropriate by the Council, by the General Assembly, and that they be transmitted to governments with the recommendation (*a*) that favourable consideration be given to their adoption and application in the administration of penal institutions, and (*b*) that the Secretary-General be informed every three years of the progress made with regard to their application;

3. *Expresses* the wish that, in order to allow governments to keep themselves informed of the progress made in this respect, the Secretary-General be requested to publish in the International Review of Criminal Policy the information sent by governments in pursuance of paragraph 2, and that he be authorized to ask for supplementary information if necessary;

4. *Expresses* also the wish that the Secretary-General be requested to arrange that the widest possible publicity be given to these rules.

Annex

STANDARD MINIMUM RULES FOR THE TREATMENT OF PRISONERS

Preliminary observations

1. The following rules are not intended to describe in detail a model system of penal institutions. They seek only, on the basis of the general consensus of contemporary thought and the essential elements of the most adequate systems of today, to set out what is generally accepted as being good principle and practice in the treatment of prisoners and the management of institutions.

2. In view of the great variety of legal, social, economic and geographical conditions of the world, it is evident that not all of the rules are capable of application in all places and at all times. They should, however, serve to stimulate a constant endeavour to overcome practical difficulties in the way of their application, in the knowledge that they represent, as a whole, the minimum conditions which are accepted as suitable by the United Nations.

3. On the other hand, the rules cover a field in which thought is constantly developing. They are not intended to preclude experiment and practices, provided these are in harmony with the principles and seek to

815

further the purposes which derive from the text of the rules as a whole. It will always be justifiable for the central prison administration to authorize departures from the rules in this spirit.

4. (1) Part I of the rules covers the general management of institutions, and is applicable to all categories of prisoners, criminal or civil, untried or convicted, including prisoners subject to "security measures" or corrective measures ordered by the judge.

(2) Part II contains rules applicable only to the special categories dealt with in each section. Nevertheless, the rules under section A, applicable to prisoners under sentence, shall be equally applicable to categories of prisoners dealt with in sections B, C and D, provided they do not conflict with the rules governing those categories and are for their benefit.

5. (1) The rules do not seek to regulate the management of institutions set aside for young persons such as Borstal institutions or correctional schools, but in general, Part I would be equally applicable in such institutions.

(2) The category of young prisoners should include at least all young persons who come within the jurisdiction of juvenile courts. As a rule, such young persons should not be sentenced to imprisonment.

PART I. RULES OF GENERAL APPLICATION

Basic principle

6. (1) The following rules shall be applied impartially. There shall be no discrimination on grounds of race, colour, sex, language, religion, political or other opinion, national or social origin, property, birth or other status.

(2) On the other hand, it is necessary to respect the religious beliefs and moral precepts of the group to which a prisoner belongs.

Register

7. (1) In every place where persons are imprisoned there shall be kept a bound registration book with numbered pages in which shall be entered in respect of each prisoner received:

(a) Information concerning his identity;

(b) The reasons for his commitment and the authority therefor;

(c) The day and hour of his admission and release.

(2) No person shall be received in an institution without a valid commitment order of which the details shall have been previously entered in the register.

Separation of categories

8. The different categories of prisoners shall be kept in separate institutions or parts of institutions taking account of their sex, age, criminal record, the legal reason for their detention and the necessities of their treatment. Thus,

(a) Men and women shall so far as possible be detained in separate institutions; in an institution which receives both men and women the whole of the premises allocated to women shall be entirely separate;

(b) Untried prisoners shall be kept separate from convicted prisoners;

(c) Persons imprisoned for debt and other civil prisoners shall be kept separate from persons imprisoned by reason of a criminal offence;

(*d*) Young prisoners shall be kept separate from adults.

Accommodation

9. (1) Where sleeping accommodation is in individual cells or rooms, each prisoner shall occupy by night a cell or room by himself. If for special reasons, such as temporary overcrowding, it becomes necessary for the central prison administration to make an exception to this rule, it is not desirable to have two prisoners in a cell or room.

(2) Where dormitories are used, they shall be occupied by prisoners carefully selected as being suitable to associate with one another in those conditions. There shall be regular supervision by night, in keeping with the nature of the institution.

10. All accommodation provided for the use of prisoners and in particular all sleeping accommodation shall meet all requirements of health, due regard being paid to climatic conditions and particularly to cubic content of air, minimum floor space, lighting, heating and ventilation.

11. In all places where prisoners are required to live or work,

(*a*) The windows shall be large enough to enable the prisoners to read or work by natural light, and shall be so constructed that they can allow the entrance of fresh air whether or not there is artificial ventilation;

(*b*) Artificial light shall be provided sufficient for the prisoners to read or work without injury to eyesight.

12. The sanitary installations shall be adequate to enable every prisoner to comply with the needs of nature when necessary and in a clean and decent manner.

13. Adequate bathing and shower installations shall be provided so that every prisoner may be enabled and required to have a bath or shower, at a temperature suitable to the climate, as frequently as necessary for general hygiene according to season and geographical region, but at least once a week in a temperate climate.

14. All parts of an institution regularly used by prisoners shall be properly maintained and kept scrupulously clean at all times.

Personal hygiene

15. Prisoners shall be required to keep their persons clean, and to this end they shall be provided with water and with such toilet articles as are necessary for health and cleanliness.

16. In order that prisoners may maintain a good appearance compatible with their self-respect, facilities shall be provided for the proper care of the hair and beard, and men shall be enabled to shave regularly.

Clothing and bedding

17. (1) Every prisoner who is not allowed to wear his own clothing shall be provided with an outfit of clothing suitable for the climate and adequate to keep him in good health. Such clothing shall in no manner be degrading or humiliating.

(2) All clothing shall be clean and kept in proper condition. Underclothing shall be changed and washed as often as necessary for the maintenance of hygiene.

(3) In exceptional circumstances, whenever a prisoner is removed outside the institution for an authorized purpose, he shall be allowed to wear

his own clothing or other inconspicuous clothing.

18. If prisoners are allowed to wear their own clothing, arrangements shall be made on their admission to the institution to ensure that it shall be clean and fit for use.

19. Every prisoner shall, in accordance with local or national standards, be provided with a separate bed, and with separate and sufficient bedding which shall be clean when issued, kept in good order and changed often enough to ensure its cleanliness.

Food

20. (1) Every prisoner shall be provided by the administration at the usual hours with food of nutritional value adequate for health and strength, of wholesome quality and well prepared and served.

(2) Drinking water shall be available to every prisoner whenever he needs it.

Exercise and sport

21. (1) Every prisoner who is not employed in out-door work shall have at least one hour of suitable exercise in the open air daily if the weather permits.

(2) Young prisoners, and others of suitable age and physique, shall receive physical and recreational training during the period of exercise. To this end, space, installations and equipment should be provided.

Medical services

22. (1) At every institution there shall be available the services of at least one qualified medical officer who should have some knowledge of psychiatry. The medical services should be organized in close relationship to the general health administration of the community or nation. They shall include a psychiatric service for the diagnosis and, in proper cases, the treatment of states of mental abnormality.

(2) Sick prisoners who require specialist treatment shall be transferred to specialized institutions or to civil hospitals. Where hospital facilities are provided in an institution, their equipment, furnishings and pharmaceutical supplies shall be proper for the medical care and treatment of sick prisoners, and there shall be a staff of suitably trained officers.

(3) The services of a qualified dental officer shall be available to every prisoner.

23. (1) In women's institutions there shall be special accommodation for all necessary pre-natal and postnatal care and treatment. Arrangements shall be made wherever practicable for children to be born in a hospital outside the institution. If a child is born in prison, this fact shall not be mentioned in the birth certificate.

(2) Where nursing infants are allowed to remain in the institution with their mothers, provision shall be made for a nursery staffed by qualified persons, where the infants shall be placed when they are not in the care of their mothers.

24. The medical officer shall see and examine every prisoner as soon as possible after his admission and thereafter as necessary, with a view particularly to the discovery of physical or mental illness and the taking of all necessary measures; the segregation of prisoners suspected of infectious or contagious conditions; the

noting of physical or mental defects which might hamper rehabilitation, and the determination of the physical capacity of every prisoner for work.

25. (1) The medical officer shall have the care of the physical and mental health of the prisoners and should daily see all sick prisoners, all who complain of illness, and any prisoner to whom his attention is specially directed.

(2) The medical officer shall report to the director whenever he considers that a prisoner's physical or mental health has been or will be injuriously affected by continued imprisonment or by any condition of imprisonment.

26. (1) The medical officer shall regularly inspect and advise the director upon:

(a) The quantity, quality, preparation and service of food;

(b) The hygiene and cleanliness of the institution and the prisoners;

(c) The sanitation, heating, lighting and ventilation of the institution;

(d) The suitability and cleanliness of the prisoners' clothing and bedding;

(e) The observance of the rules concerning physical education and sports, in cases where there is no technical personnel in charge of these activities.

(2) The director shall take into consideration the reports and advice that the medical officer submits according to rules 25 (2) and 26 and, in case he concurs with the recommendations made, shall take immediate steps to give effect to those recommendations; if they are not within his competence or if he does not concur with them, he shall immediately submit his own report and the advice of the medical officer to higher authority.

Discipline and punishment

27. Discipline and order shall be maintained with firmness, but with no more restriction than is necessary for safe custody and well-ordered community life.

28. (1) No prisoner shall be employed, in the service of the institution, in any disciplinary capacity.

(2) This rule shall not, however, impede the proper functioning of systems based on self-government, under which specified social, educational or sports activities or responsibilities are entrusted, under supervision, to prisoners who are formed into groups for the purposes of treatment.

29. The following shall always be determined by the law or by the regulation of the competent administrative authority:

(a) Conduct constituting a disciplinary offence;

(b) The types and duration of punishment which may be inflicted;

(c) The authority competent to impose such punishment.

30. (1) No prisoner shall be punished except in accordance with the terms of such law or regulation, and never twice for the same offence.

(2) No prisoner shall be punished unless he has been informed of the offence alleged against him and given a proper opportunity of presenting his defence. The competent authority shall conduct a thorough examination of the case.

(3) Where necessary and practicable the prisoner shall be allowed to make his defence through an interpreter.

31. Corporal punishment, punishment by placing in a dark cell, and all cruel, inhuman or degrading punishments shall be completely prohibited as punishments for disciplinary offences.

32. (1) Punishment by close confinement or reduction of diet shall never be inflicted unless the medical officer has examined the prisoner and certified in writing that he is fit to sustain it.

(2) The same shall apply to any other punishment that may be prejudicial to the physical or mental health of a prisoner. In no case may such punishment be contrary to or depart from the principle stated in rule 31.

(3) The medical officer shall visit daily prisoners undergoing such punishments and shall advise the director if he considers the termination or alteration of the punishment necessary on grounds of physical or mental health.

Instruments of restraint

33. Instruments of restraint, such as handcuffs, chains, irons and straitjackets, shall never be applied as a punishment. Furthermore, chains or irons shall not be used as restraints. Other instruments of restraint shall not be used except in the following circumstances:

(a) As a precaution against escape during a transfer, provided that they shall be removed when the prisoner appears before a judicial or administrative authority;

(b) On medical grounds by direction of the medical officer;

(c) By order of the director, if other methods of control fail, in order to prevent a prisoner from injuring himself or others or from damaging property; in such instances the director shall at once consult the medical officer and report to the higher administrative authority.

34. The patterns and manner of use of instruments of restraint shall be decided by the central prison administration. Such instruments must not be applied for any longer time than is strictly necessary.

Information to and complaints by prisoners

35. (1) Every prisoner on admission shall be provided with written information about the regulations governing the treatment of prisoners of his category, the disciplinary requirements of the institution, the authorized methods of seeking information and making complaints, and all such other matters as are necessary to enable him to understand both his rights and his obligations and to adapt himself to the life of the institution.

(2) If a prisoner is illiterate, the aforesaid information shall be conveyed to him orally.

36. (1) Every prisoner shall have the opportunity each week day of making requests or complaints to the director of the institution or the officer authorized to represent him.

(2) It shall be possible to make requests or complaints to the inspector of prisons during his inspection. The prisoner shall have the opportunity to talk to the inspector or to any other inspecting officer without the director or other members of the staff being present.

(3) Every prisoner shall be allowed to make a request or complaint, without censorship as to substance but in proper form, to the central prison administration, the judicial au-

thority or other proper authorities through approved channels.

(4) Unless it is evidently frivolous or groundless, every request or complaint shall be promptly dealt with and replied to without undue delay.

Contact with the outside world

37. Prisoners shall be allowed under necessary supervision to communicate with their family and reputable friends at regular intervals, both by correspondence and by receiving visits.

38. (1) Prisoners who are foreign nationals shall be allowed reasonable facilities to communicate with the diplomatic and consular representatives of the State to which they belong.

(2) Prisoners who are nationals of States without diplomatic or consular representation in the country and refugees or stateless persons shall be allowed similar facilities to communicate with the diplomatic representative of the State which takes charge of their interests or any national or international authority whose task it is to protect such persons.

39. Prisoners shall be kept informed regularly of the more important items of news by the reading of newspapers, periodicals or special institutional publications, by hearing wireless transmissions, by lectures or by any similar means as authorized or controlled by the administration.

Books

40. Every institution shall have a library for the use of all categories of prisoners, adequately stocked with both recreational and instructional books, and prisoners shall be encouraged to make full use of it.

Religion

41. (1) If the institution contains a sufficient number of prisoners of the same religion, a qualified representative of that religion shall be appointed or approved. If the number of prisoners justifies it and conditions permit, the arrangement should be on a full-time basis.

(2) A qualified representative appointed or approved under paragraph (1) shall be allowed to hold regular services and to pay pastoral visits in private to prisoners of his religion at proper times.

(3) Access to a qualified representative of any religion shall not be refused to any prisoner. On the other hand, if any prisoner should object to a visit of any religious representative, his attitude shall be fully respected.

42. So far as practicable, every prisoner shall be allowed to satisfy the needs of his religious life by attending the services provided in the institution and having in his possession the books of religious observance and instruction of his denomination.

Retention of prisoners' property

43. (1) All money, valuables, clothing and other effects belonging to a prisoner which under the regulations of the institution he is not allowed to retain shall on his admission to the institution be placed in safe custody. An inventory thereof shall be signed by the prisoner. Steps shall be taken to keep them in good condition.

(2) On the release of the prisoner all such articles and money shall be returned to him except in so far as he has been authorized to spend money or send any such property out of the institution, or it has been found

necessary on hygienic grounds to destroy any article of clothing. The prisoner shall sign a receipt for the articles and money returned to him.

(3) Any money or effects received for a prisoner from outside shall be treated in the same way.

(4) If a prisoner brings in any drugs or medicine, the medical officer shall decide what use shall be made of them.

Notification of death, illness, transfer, etc.

44. (1) Upon the death or serious illness of, or serious injury to a prisoner, or his removal to an institution for the treatment of mental afflictions, the director shall at once inform the spouse, if the prisoner is married, or the nearest relative and shall in any event inform any other person previously designated by the prisoner.

(2) A prisoner shall be informed at once of the death or serious illness of any near relative. In case of the critical illness of a near relative, the prisoner should be authorized, whenever circumstances allow, to go to his bedside either under escort or alone.

(3) Every prisoner shall have the right to inform at once his family of his imprisonment or his transfer to another institution.

Removal of prisoners

45. (1) When prisoners are being removed to or from an institution, they shall be exposed to public view as little as possible, and proper safeguards shall be adopted to protect them from insult, curiosity and publicity in any form.

(2) The transport of prisoners in conveyances with inadequate ventilation or light, or in any way which would subject them to unnecessary physical hardship, shall be prohibited.

(3) The transport of prisoners shall be carried out at the expense of the administration and equal conditions shall obtain for all of them.

Institutional personnel

46. (1) The prison administration shall provide for the careful selection of every grade of the personnel, since it is on their integrity, humanity, professional capacity and personal suitability for the work that the proper administration of the institutions depends.

(2) The prison administration shall constantly seek to awaken and maintain in the minds both of the personnel and of the public the conviction that this work is a social service of great importance, and to this end all appropriate means of informing the public should be used.

(3) To secure the foregoing ends, personnel shall be appointed on a full-time basis as professional prison officers and have civil service status with security of tenure subject only to good conduct, efficiency and physical fitness. Salaries shall be adequate to attract and retain suitable men and women; employment benefits and conditions of service shall be favourable in view of the exacting nature of the work.

47. (1) The personnel shall possess an adequate standard of education and intelligence.

(2) Before entering on duty, the personnel shall be given a course of training in their general and specific duties and be required to pass theoretical and practical tests.

(3) After entering on duty and during their career, the personnel

shall maintain and improve their knowledge and professional capacity by attending courses of in-service training to be organized at suitable intervals.

48. All members of the personnel shall at all times so conduct themselves and perform their duties as to influence the prisoners for good by their examples and to command their respect.

49. (1) So far as possible, the personnel shall include a sufficient number of specialists such as psychiatrists, psychologists, social workers, teachers and trade instructors.

(2) The services of social workers, teachers and trade instructors shall be secured on a permanent basis, without thereby excluding part-time or voluntary workers.

50. (1) The director of an institution should be adequately qualified for his task by character, administrative ability, suitable training and experience.

(2) He shall devote his entire time to his official duties and shall not be appointed on a part-time basis.

(3) He shall reside on the premises of the institution or in its immediate vicinity.

(4) When two or more institutions are under the authority of one director, he shall visit each of them at frequent intervals. A responsible resident official shall be in charge of each of these institutions.

51. (1) The director, his deputy, and the majority of the other personnel of the institution shall be able to speak the language of the greatest number of prisoners, or a language understood by the greatest number of them.

(2) Whenever necessary, the services of an interpreter shall be used.

52. (1) In institutions which are large enough to require the services of one or more full-time medical officers, at least one of them shall reside on the premises of the institution or in its immediate vicinity.

(2) In other institutions the medical officer shall visit daily and shall reside near enough to be able to attend without delay in cases of urgency.

53. (1) In an institution for both men and women, the part of the institution set aside for women shall be under the authority of a responsible woman officer who shall have the custody of the keys of all that part of the institution.

(2) No male member of the staff shall enter the part of the institution set aside for women unless accompanied by a woman officer.

(3) Women prisoners shall be attended and supervised only by women officers. This does not, however, preclude male members of the staff, particularly doctors and teachers, from carrying out their professional duties in institutions or parts of institutions set aside for women.

54. (1) Officers of the institutions shall not, in their relations with the prisoners, use force except in self-defense or in cases of attempted escape, or active or passive physical resistance to an order based on law or regulations. Officers who have recourse to force must use no more than is strictly necessary and must report the incident immediately to the director of the institution.

(2) Prison officers shall be given special physical training to enable them to restrain aggressive prisoners.

(3) Except in special circumstances, staff performing duties which bring them into direct contact with

prisoners should not be armed. Furthermore, staff should in no circumstances be provided with arms unless they have been trained in their use.

Inspection

55. There shall be a regular inspection of penal institutions and services by qualified and experienced inspectors appointed by a competent authority. Their task shall be in particular to ensure that these institutions are administered in accordance with existing laws and regulations and with a view to bringing about the objeotives of penal and correctional services.

PART II. RULES APPLICABLE TO SPECIAL CATEGORIES

A. Prisoners under sentence
Guiding principles

56. The guiding principles hereafter are intended to show the spirit in which penal institutions should be administered and the purposes at which they should aim, in accordance with the declaration made under Preliminary Observation 1 of the present text.

57. Imprisonment and other measures which result in cutting off an offender from the outside world are afflictive by the very fact of taking from the person the right of self-determination by depriving him of his liberty. Therefore the prison system shall not, except as incidental to justifiable segregation or the maintenance of discipline, aggravate the suffering inherent in such a situation.

58. The purpose and justification of a sentence of imprisonment or a similar measure deprivative of liberty is ultimately to protect society against crime. This end can only be achieved if the period of imprisonment is used to ensure, so far as possible, that upon his return to society the offender is not only willing but able to lead a law-abiding and self-supporting life.

59. To this end, the institution should utilize all the remedial, educational, moral, spiritual and other forces and forms of assitance which are appropriate and available, and should seek to apply them according to the individual treatment needs of the prisoners.

60. (1) The régime of the institution should seek to minimize any differences between prison life and life at liberty which tend to lessen the responsibility of the prisoners or the respect due to their dignity as human beings.

(2) Before the completion of the sentence, it is desirable that the necessary steps be taken to ensure for the prisoner a gradual return to life in society. This aim may be achieved, depending on the case, by a pre-release régime organized in the same institution or in another appropriate institution, or by release on trial under some kind of supervision which must not be entrusted to the police but should be combined with effective social aid.

61. The treatment of prisoners should emphasize not their exclusion from the community, but their continuing part in it. Community agencies should, therefore, be enlisted wherever possible to assist the staff of the institution in the task of social rehabilitation of the prisoners. There should be in connexion with every institution social workers charged with the duty of maintaining and improving all desirable relations of a

prisoner with his family and with valuable social agencies. Steps should be taken to safeguard, to the maximum extent compatible with the law and the sentence, the rights relating to civil interests, social security rights and other social benefits of prisoners.

62. The medical services of the institution shall seek to detect and shall treat any physical or mental illnesses or defects which may hamper a prisoner's rehabilitation. All necessary medical, surgical and psychiatric services shall be provided to that end.

63. (1) The fulfilment of these principles requires individualization of treatment and for this purpose a flexible system of classifying prisoners in groups; it is therefore desirable that such groups should be distributed in separate institutions suitable for the treatment of each group.

(2) These institutions need not provide the same degree of security for every group. It is desirable to provide varying degrees of security according to the needs of different groups. Open institutions, by the very fact that they provide no physical security against escape but rely on the self-discipline of the inmates, provide the conditions most favourable to rehabilitation for carefully selected prisoners.

(3) It is desirable that the number of prisoners in closed institutions should not be so large that the individualization of treatment is hindered. In some countries it is considered that the population of such institutions should not exceed five hundred. In open institutions the population should be as small as possible.

(4) On the other hand, it is undesirable to maintain prisons which are so small that proper facilities cannot be provided.

64. The duty of society does not end with a prisoner's release. There should, therefore, be governmental or private agencies capable of lending the released prisoner efficient after-care directed towards the lessening of prejudice against him and towards his social rehabilitation.

Treatment

65. The treatment of persons sentenced to imprisonment or a similar measure shall have as its purpose, so far as the length of the sentence permits, to establish in them the will to lead law-abiding and self-supporting lives after their release and to fit them to do so. The treatment shall be such as will encourage their self-respect and develop their sense of responsibility.

66. (1) To these ends, all appropriate means shall be used, including religious care in the countries where this is possible, education, vocational guidance and training, social casework, employment counselling, physical development and strengthening of moral character, in accordance with the individual needs of each prisoner, taking account of his social and criminal history, his physical and mental capacities and aptitudes, his personal temperament, the length of his sentence and his prospects after release.

(2) For every prisoner with a sentence of suitable length, the director shall receive, as soon as possible after his admission, full reports on all the matters referred to in the foregoing paragraph. Such reports shall aways include a report by a medical officer, wherever possible qualified in psychiatry, on the physi-

cal and mental condition of the prisoner.

(3) The reports and other relevant documents shall be placed in an individual file. This file shall be kept up to date and classified in such a way that it can be consulted by the responsible personnel whenever the need arises.

Classification and individualization

67. The purposes of classification shall be:

(a) To separate from others those prisoners who, by reason of their criminal records or bad characters, are likely to exercise a bad influence;

(b) To divide the prisoners into classes in order to facilitate their treatment with a view to their social rehabilitation.

68. So far as possible separate institutions or separate sections of an institution shall be used for the treatment of the different classes of prisoners.

69. As soon as possible after admission and after a study of the personality of each prisoner with a sentence of suitable length, a programme of treatment shall be prepared for him in the light of the knowledge obtained about his individual needs, his capacities and dispositions.

Privileges

70. Systems of privileges appropriate for the different classes of prisoners and the different methods of treatment shall be established at every institution, in order to encourage good conduct, develop a sense of responsibility and secure the interest and cooperation of the prisoners in their treatment.

Work

71. (1) Prison labour must not be of an afflictive nature.

(2) All prisoners under sentence shall be required to work, subject to their physical and mental fitness as determined by the medical officer.

(3) Sufficient work of a useful nature shall be provided to keep prisoners actively employed for a normal working day.

(4) So far as possible the work provided shall be such as will maintain or increase the prisoners' ability to earn an honest living after release.

(5) Vocational training in useful trades shall be provided for prisoners able to profit thereby and especially for young prisoners.

(6) Within the limits compatible with proper vocational selection and with the requirements of institutional administration and discipline, the prisoners shall be able to choose the type of work they wish to perform.

72. (1) The organization and methods of work in the institutions shall resemble as closely as possible those of similar work outside institutions, so as to prepare prisoners for the conditions of normal occupational life.

(2) The interests of the prisoners and of their vocational training, however, must not be subordinated to the purpose of making a financial profit from an industry in the institution.

73. (1) Preferably institutional industries and farms should be operated directly by the administration and not by private contractors.

(2) Where prisoners are employed in work not controlled by the administration, they shall always be under the supervision of the institution's personnel. Unless the work is

for other departments of the government the full normal wages for such work shall be paid to the administration by the persons to whom the labour is supplied, account being taken of the output of the prisoners.

74. (1) The precautions laid down to protect the safety and health of free workmen shall be equally observed in institutions.

(2) Provision shall be made to indemnify prisoners against industrial injury, including occupational disease, on terms not less favourable than those extended by law to free workmen.

75. (1) The maximum daily and weekly working hours of the prisoners shall be fixed by law or by administrative regulation, taking into account local rules or custom in regard to the employment of free workmen.

(2) The hours so fixed shall leave one rest day a week and sufficient time for education and other activities required as part of the treatment and rehabilitation of the prisoners.

76. (1) There shall be a system of equitable remuneration of the work of prisoners.

(2) Under the system prisoners shall be allowed to spend at least a part of their earnings on approved articles for their own use and to send a part of their earnings to their family.

(3) The system should also provide that a part of the earnings should be set aside by the administration so as to constitute a savings fund to be handed over to the prisoner on his relase.

Education and recreation

77. (1) Provision shall be made for the further education of all prisoners capable of profiting thereby, including religious instruction in the countries where this is possible. The education of illiterates and young prisoners shall be compulsory and special attention shall be paid to it by the administration.

(2) So far as practicable, the education of prisoners shall be integrated with the educational system of the country so that after their release they may continue their education without difficulty.

78. Recreational and cultural activities shall be provided in all institutions for the benefit of the mental and physical health of prisoners.

Social relations and after-care

79. Special attention shall be paid to the maintenance and improvement of such relations between a prisoner and his family as are desirable in the best interests of both.

80. From the beginning of a prisoner's sentence consideration shall be given to his future after release and he shall be encouraged and assisted to maintain or establish such relations with persons or agencies outside the institution as may promote the best interests of his family and his own social rehabilitation.

81. (1) Services and agencies, governmental or otherwise, which assist released prisoners to re-establish themselves in society shall ensure, so far as is possible and necessary, that released prisoners be provided with appropriate documents and identification papers, have suitable homes and work to go to, are suitably and adequately clothed having regard to the climate and season, and have sufficient means to reach their destination and maintain themselves in the peri-

od immediately following their release.

(2) The approved representatives of such agencies shall have all necessary access to the institution and to prisoners and shall be taken into consultation as to the future of a prisoner from the beginning of his sentence.

(3) It is desirable that the activities of such agencies shall be centralized or co-ordinated as far as possible in order to secure the best use of their efforts.

B. INSANE AND MENTALLY ABNORMAL PRISONERS

82. (1) Persons who are found to be insane shall not be detained in prisons and arrangements shall be made to remove them to mental institutions as soon as possible.

(2) Prisoners who suffer from other mental diseases or abnormalities shall be observed and treated in specialized institutions under medical management.

(3) During their stay in a prison, such prisoners shall be placed under the special supervision of a medical officer.

(4) The medical or psychiatric service of the penal institutions shall provide for the psychiatric treatment of all other prisoners who are in need of such treatment.

83. It is desirable that steps should be taken, by arrangement with the appropriate agencies, to ensure if necessary the continuation of psychiatric treatment after release and the provision of social-psychiatric aftercare.

C. PRISONERS UNDER ARREST OR AWAITING TRIAL

84. (1) Persons arrested or imprisoned by reason of a criminal charge against them, who are detained either in police custody or in prison custody (jail) but have not yet been tried and sentenced, will be referred to as "untried prisoners" hereinafter in these rules.

(2) Unconvicted prisoners are presumed to be innocent and shall be treated as such.

(3) Without prejudice to legal rules for the protection of individual liberty or prescribing the procedure to be observed in respect of untried prisoners, these prisoners shall benefit by a special régime which is described in the following rules in its essential requirements only.

85. (1) Untried prisoners shall be kept separate from convicted prisoners.

(2) Young untried prisoners shall be kept separate from adults and shall in principle be detained in separate institutions.

86. Untried prisoners shall sleep singly in separate rooms, with the reservation of different local custom in respect of the climate.

87. Within the limits compatible with the good order of the institution, untried prisoners may, if they so desire, have their food procured at their own expense from the outside, either through the administration or through their family or friends. Otherwise, the administration shall provide their food.

88. (1) An untried prisoner shall be allowed to wear his own clothing if it is clean and suitable.

(2) If he wears prison dress, it shall be different from that supplied to convicted prisoners.

89. An untried prisoner shall always be offered opportunity to work, but shall not be required to work. If

he chooses to work, he shall be paid for it.

90. An untried prisoner shall be allowed to procure at his own expense or at the expense of a third party such books, newspapers, writing materials and other means of occupation as are compatible with the interests of the administration of justice and the security and good order of the institution.

91. An untried prisoner shall be allowed to be visited and treated by his own doctor or dentist if there is reasonable ground for his application and he is able to pay any expenses incurred.

92. An untried prisoner shall be allowed to inform immediately his family of his detention and shall be given all reasonable facilities for communicating with his family and friends, and for receiving visits from them, subject only to such restrictions and supervision as are necessary in the interests of the administration of justice and of the security and good order of the institution.

93. For the purposes of his defence, an untried prisoner shall be allowed to apply for free legal aid where such aid is available, and to receive visits from his legal adviser with a view to his defence and to prepare and hand to him confidential instructions. For these purposes, he shall if he so desires be supplied with writing material. Interviews between the prisoner and his legal adviser may be within sight but not within the hearing of a police or institution official.

D. CIVIL PRISONERS

94. In countries where the law permits imprisonment for debt or by order of a court under any other non-criminal process, persons so imprisoned shall not be subjected to any greater restriction or severity than is necessary to ensure safe custody and good order. Their treatment shall be not less favourable than that of untried prisoners, with the reservation, however, that they may possibly be required to work.

B. SELECTION AND TRAINING OF PERSONNEL FOR PENAL AND CORRECTIONAL INSTITUTIONS

Resolution adopted on 1 September 1955

The First United Nations Congress on the Prevention of Crime and the Treatment of Offenders,

Having adopted recommendations, annexed to the present resolution, on the question of the selection and training of personnel for penal and correctional institutions,

1. *Requests* the Secretary-General, in accordance with paragraph (*d*) of the annex to resolution 415(V) of the General Assembly of the United Nations, to submit these recommendations to the Social Commission of the Economic and Social Council for approval;

2. *Expresses* the hope that the Economic and Social Council will endorse these recommendations and draw them to the attention of governments, recommending that governments take them as fully as possible into account in their practice and when considering legislative and administrative reforms;

3. *Expresses* also the wish that the Economic and Social Council request the Secretary-General to give the widest publicity to these recommendations and authorize him to collect periodically information on the matter from the various countries, and to publish such information.

Annex

RECOMMENDATIONS ON THE SELECTION AND TRAINING OF PERSONNEL FOR PENAL AND CORRECTIONAL INSTITUTIONS

A. MODERN CONCEPTION OF PRISON SERVICE

I. *Prison service in the nature of a social service*

(1) Attention is drawn to the change in the nature of prison staffs which results from the development in the conception of their duty from that of guards to that of members of an important social service demanding ability, appropriate training and good team work on the part of every member.

(2) An effort should be made to arouse and keep alive in the minds both of the public and of the staff an understanding of the nature of modern prison service. For this purpose all appropriate means of informing the public should be used.

II. *Specialization of functions*

(1) This new conception is reflected in the tendency to add to the staff an increasing number of specialists, such as doctors, psychiatrists, psychologists, social workers, teachers, technical instructors.

(2) This is a healthy tendency and it is recommended that it should be favourably considered by govern-ments even though additional expense would be involved.

III. *Co-ordination*

(1) The increasing specialization may, however, hamper an integrated approach to the treatment of prisoners and present problems in the co-ordination of the work of the various types of specialized staff.

(2) Consequently, in the treatment of prisoners, it is necessary to ensure that all the specialists concerned work together as a team.

(3) It is also considered necessary to ensure, by the appointment of a co-ordinating committee or otherwise, that all the specialized services follow a uniform approach. In this way the members of the staff will also have the advantage of gaining a clear insight into the various aspects of the problems involved.

B. STATUS OF STAFF AND CONDITIONS OF SERVICE

IV. *Civil service status*

Full-time prison staff should have the status of civil servants, that is, they should:

(a) Be employed by the government of the country or State and hence be governed by civil service rules;

(b) Be recruited according to certain rules of selection such as competitive examination;

(c) Have security of tenure subject only to good conduct, efficiency and physical fitness;

(d) Have permanent status and be entitled to the advantages of a civil service career in such matters as promotion, social security, allowances, and retirement or pension benefits.

V. *Full-time employment*

(1) Prison staff, with the exception of certain professional and technical grades, should devote their entire time to their duties and therefore be appointed on a full-time basis.

(2) In particular, the post of director of an institution must not be a part-time appointment.

(3) The services of social workers, teachers and trade instructors should be secured on a permanent basis, without thereby excluding part-time workers.

VI. *Conditions of service in general*

(1) The conditions of service of institutional staff should be sufficient to attract and retain the best qualified persons.

(2) Salaries and other employment benefits should not be arbitrarily tied to those of other public servants but should be related to the work to be performed in a modern prison system, which is complex and arduous and is in the nature of an important social service.

(3) Sufficient and suitable living quarters should be provided for the prison staff in the vicinity of the institution.

VII. *Non-military organization of the staff*

(1) Prison staff should be organized on civilian lines with a division into ranks or grades as this type of administration requires.

(2) Custodial staff should be organized in accordance with the disciplinary rules of the penal institution in order to maintain the necessary grade distinctions and order.

(3) Staff should be specially recruited and not seconded from the armed forces or police or other public services.

VIII. *Carrying of arms*

(1) Except in special circumstances, staff performing duties which bring them into direct contact with prisoners should not be armed.

(2) Staff should in no circumstances be provided with arms unless they have been trained in their use.

(3) It is desirable that prison staff should be responsible for guarding the enclosure of the institution.

C. RECRUITMENT OF STAFF

IX. *Competent authority and general administrative methods*

(1) As far as possible recruitment should be centralized, in conformity with the structure of each State, and be under the direction of the superior or central prison administration.

(2) Where other State bodies such as a civil service commission are responsible for recruitment, the prison administration should not be required to accept a candidate whom they do not regard as suitable.

(3) Provision should be made to exclude political influence in appointments to the staff of the prison service.

X. *General conditions of recruitment*

(1) The prison administration should be particularly careful in the recruitment of staff, selecting only persons having the requisite qualities of integrity, humanitarian approach, competence and physical fitness.

(2) Members of the staff should be able to speak the language of the greatest number of prisoners or a language understood by the greatest number of them.

XI. *Custodial staff*

(1) The educational standards and intelligence of this staff should be sufficient to enable them to carry out their duties effectively and to profit by whatever in-service training courses are provided.

(2) Suitable intelligence, vocational and physical tests for the scientific evaluation of the candidates' capacities are recommended in addition to the relevant competitive examinations.

(3) Candidates who have been admitted should serve a probationary period to allow the competent authorities to form an opinion of their personality, character and ability.

XII. *Higher administration*

Special care should be taken in the appointment of persons who are to fill posts in the higher administration of the prison services; only persons who are suitably trained and have sufficient knowledge and experience should be considered.

XIII. *Directors or executive staff*

(1) The directors or assistant directors of institutions should be adequately qualified for their functions by reason of their character, administrative ability, training and experience.

(2) They should have a good educational background and a vocation for the work. The administration should endeavour to attract persons with specialized training which offers adequate preparation for prison service.

XIV. *Specialized and administrative staff*

(1) The staff performing specialized functions, including administrative functions, should possess the professional or technical qualifications required for each of the various functions in question.

(2) The recruitment of specialized staff should therefore be based on the professional training diplomas or university degrees evidencing their special training.

(3) It is recommended that preference should be given to candidates who, in addition to such professional qualifications, have a second degree or qualification, or specialized experience in prison work.

XV. *Staff of women's institutions*

The staff of women's institutions should consist of women. This does not, however, preclude male members of the staff, particularly doctors and teachers, from carrying out their professional duties in institutions or parts of institutions set aside for women. Female staff, whether lay or religious, should, as far as possible, possess the same qualifications as those required for appointment to institutions for men.

D. PROFESSIONAL TRAINING

XVI. *Training prior to final appointment*

Before entering on duty, staff should be given a course of training in their general duties, with a view particularly to social problems, and in the specific duties and be required to pass theoretical and practical examinations.

XVII. *Custodial staff*

(1) A programme of intensive professional training for custodial staff is recommended. The following might serve as an example for the or-

ganization of such training in three stages:

(2) The first stage should take place in a penal institution, its aim being to familiarize the candidate with the special problems of the profession and at the same time to ascertain whether he possesses the necessary qualities. During this initial phase the candidate should not be given any responsibility, and his work should be constantly supervised by a member of the regular staff. The director should arrange an elementary course in practical subjects for the candidates.

(3) During the second stage, the candidate should attend a school or course organized by the superior or central prison administration, which should be responsible for the theoretical and practical training of officers in professional subjects. Special attention should be paid to the technique of relations with the prisoners, based on the elementary principles of psychology and criminology. The training courses should moreover comprise lessons on the elements of penology, prison administration, penal law and related matters.

(4) It is desirable that during the first two stages candidates should be admitted and trained in groups, so as to obviate the possibility of their being prematurely employed in the service and to facilitate the organization of courses of training.

(5) The third stage, intended for candidates who have satisfactorily completed the first two and shown the greatest interest and a vocation for the service, should consist of actual service during which they will be expected to show that they possess all the requisite qualifications. They should also be offered an opportunity to attend more advanced training courses in psychology, criminology, penal law, penology and related subjects.

XVIII. *Directors or executive staff*

(1) As methods vary greatly from country to country at the present time, the necessity for adequate training, which directors and assistant directors should have received prior to their appointment in conformity with paragraph XIII above, should be recognized as a general rule.

(2) Where persons from the outside with no previous experience of the work but with proved experience in similar fields are recruited as directors or assistant directors, they should, before taking up their duties, receive theoretical training and gain practical experience of prison work for a reasonable period, it being understood that a diploma granted by a specialized vocational school or a university degree in a relevant subject may be considered as sufficient theoretical training.

XIX. *Specialized staff*

The initial training to be required from specialized staff is determined by the conditions of recruitment, as described in paragraph XIV above.

XX. *Regional training institutes for prison personnel*

The establishment of regional institutes for the training of the staff of penal and correctional institutions should be encouraged.

XXI. *Physical training and instruction in the use of arms*

(1) Prison officers shall be given special physical training to enable

them to restrain aggressive prisoners by the means prescribed by the authorities in accordance with the relevant rules and regulations.

(2) Officers who are provided with arms shall be trained in their use and instructed in the regulations governing their use.

XXII. *In-service training*

(1) After taking up their duties and during their career, staff should maintain and improve their knowledge and professional capacity by attending advanced courses of in-service training which are to be organized periodically.

(2) The in-service training of custodial staff should be concerned with questions of principle and technique rather than solely with rules and regulations.

(3) Whenever any type of special training is required it should be at the expense of the State and those undergoing training should receive the pay and allowances of their grade. Supplementary training to fit the officer for promotion may be at the expense of the officer and in his own time.

XXIII. *Discussion groups, visits to institutions, seminars for senior personnel*

(1) For senior staff, group discussions are recommended on matters of practical interest rather than on academic subjects, combined with visits to different types of institutions, including those outside the penal system. It would be desirable to invite specialists from other countries to participate in such meetings.

(2) It is also recommended that exchanges be organized between various countries in order to allow senior personnel to obtain practical experience in institutions of other countries.

XXIV. *Joint consultation, visits and meetings for all grades of staff*

(1) Methods of joint consultation should be established to enable all grades of prison personnel to express their opinion on the methods used in the treatment of prisoners. Moreover, lectures, visits to other institutions and, if possible, regular seminars should be organized for all categories of staff.

(2) It is also recommended that meetings should be arranged at which the staff may exchange information and discuss questions of professional interest.

C. OPEN PENAL AND CORRECTIONAL INSTITUTIONS

Resolution adopted on 29 August 1955

The First United Nations Congress on the Prevention of Crime and the Treatment of Offenders,

Having adopted recommendations, annexed to the present resolution on the question of open penal and correctional institutions,

1. *Requests* the Secretary-General, in accordance with paragraph (*d*) of the annex to resolution 415(V) of the General Assembly of the United Nations, to submit these recommendations to the Social Commission of the Economic and Social Council for approval;

2. *Expresses* the hope that the

Economic and Social Council will endorse these recommendations and draw them to the attention of governments, recommending that governments take them as fully as possible into account in their practice and when considering legislative and administrative reforms;

3. *Expresses* also the wish that the Economic and Social Council request the Secretary-General to give the widest publicity to these recommendations and authorize him to collect periodically information on the matter from the various countries, and to publish such information.

Annex
RECOMMENDATIONS ON OPEN PENAL AND CORRECTIONAL INSTITUTIONS

I. An open institution is characterized by the absence of material or physical precautions against escape (such as walls, locks, bars, armed or other special security guards), and by a system based on self-discipline and the inmate's sense of responsibility towards the group in which he lives. This system encourages the inmate to use the freedom accorded to him without abusing it. It is these characteristics which distinguish the open institution from other types of institutions, some of which are run on the same prnciples without, however, realizing them to the full.

II. The open institution ought, in principle, to be an independent establishment; it may, however, where necessary, form a separate annex to an institution of another type.

III. In accordance with each country's prison system, prisoners may be sent to such an institution either at the beginning of their sentence or after they have served part of it in an institution of a different type.

IV. The criterion governing the selection of prisoners for admission to an open institution should be, not the particular penal or correctional category to which the offender belongs, nor the length of his sentence, but his suitability for admission to an open institution and the fact that his social readjustment is more likely to be achieved by such a system than by treatment under other forms of detention. The selection should, as far as possible, be made on the basis of a medico-psychological examination and a social investigation.

V. Any inmate found incapable of adapting himself to treatment in an open institution or whose conduct is seriously detrimental to the proper control of the institution or has an unfortunate effect on the behaviour of other inmates should be transferred to an institution of a different type.

VI. The success of an open institution depends on the fulfilment of the following conditions in particular:

(*a*) If the institution is situated in the country, it should not be so isolated as to obstruct the purpose of the institution or to cause excessive inconvenience to the staff.

(*b*) With a view to their social rehabilitation, prisoners should be employed in work which will prepare them for useful and remunerative employment after release. While the provision of agricultural work is an advantage, it is desirable also to provide workshops in which the prisoners can receive vocational and industrial training.

(c) If the process of social re-adjustment is to take place in an atmosphere of trust, it is essential that the members of the staff should be acquainted with and understand the character and special needs of each prisoner and that they should be capable of exerting a wholesome moral influence. The selection of the staff should be governed by these considerations.

(d) For the same reason, the number of inmates should remain within such bounds as to enable the director and senior officers of the staff to become thoroughly acquainted with each prisoner.

(e) It is necessary to obtain the effective co-operation of the public in general and of the surrounding community in particular for the operation of open institutions. For this purpose it is therefore, among other things, necessary to inform the public of the aims and methods of each open institution, and also of the fact that the system applied in it requires a considerable moral effort on the part of the prisoner. In this connexion, local and national media of information may play a valuable part.

VII. In applying the system of open institutions each country, with due regard for its particular social, economic and cultural conditions, should be guided by the following observations:

(a) Countries which are experimenting with the open system for the first time should refrain from laying down rigid and detailed regulations in advance for the operation of open institutions;

(b) During the experimental stage they should be guided by the methods of organization and the pro-cedure already found to be effective in countries which are more advanced in this respect.

VIII. While in the open institution the risk of escape and the danger that the inmate may make improper use of his contacts with the outside world are admittedly greater than in other types of penal institutions, these disadvantages are amply outweighed by the following advantages, which make the open institution superior to the other types of institution:

(a) The open institution is more favourable to the social readjustment of the prisoners and at the same time more conductive to their physical and mental health.

(b) The flexibility inherent in the open system is expressed in a liberalization of the regulations; the tensions of prison life are relieved and discipline consequently improves. Moreover, the absence of material and physical constraint and the relations of greater confidence between prisoners and staff tend to create in the prisoners a genuine desire for social readjustment.

(c) The conditions of life in open institutions resemble more closely those of normal life. Consequently, desirable contacts can more easily be arranged with the outside world and the inmate can thus be brought to realize that he has not severed all links with society; in this connexion it might perhaps be possible to arrange, for instance, group walks, sporting competitions with outside teams, and even individual leave of absence, particularly for the purpose of preserving family ties.

(d) The same measure is less costly if applied in an open institu-

TABLE OF CASES

References are to section numbers

Entries appearing in **boldface** type also appear in Part II: Judicial Decisions Relating to Part I. See page 231 for the Table of Cases for Part II.

DISCIPLINE
Isolated Confinement, 5.1
Religion, restrictions on exercise of, 6.2, 6.2.1
Use of Force, 2.5, 2.8
Visitation restrictions, 3.1

DISCIPLINARY PROCEEDING
Administrative review, 8.3.5
Appeal, 8.3.5
Arbitrary action, 8.3.5
Attorney, 8.3, 8.3.3
Command influence, 8.3.7
Confrontation/cross-examination, 8.3, 8.3.4
Counsel, 8.3.3
Counsel substitute, 8.3, 8.3.3
Defenses, 8.3.10
Discretion
    Abuse of, 8.3.4, 8.3.6, 8.5
    Exercise of, 8.3, 8.3.6, 8.3.8
Double jeopardy, 8.3.9
Due process
    Procedural, 8.2, 8.3, 8.5
    Substantive, 8.2, 8.5
Emergencies, 8.3.8
Evidence, 8.3.4, 8.3.10
Expungement, 8.4
Grievous loss, 8.5
Impartial trier, 8.3, 8.3.7
Inference, adverse, 8.3.2
Legal remedies, 8.4
Notice, 8.3, 8.3.1
Opportunity to be heard, 8.3, 8.3.2
Polygraph, 8.3.10
Prehearing detention, 8.3.8
Procedure, 8.3
Reclassification, 8.3
Record, 8.3, 8.3.4, 8.3.6
Rules of conduct, 8.3.10
Self-defense, 8.3.10
Stay pending appeal, 8.3.5
Undue hazard, 8.3.4
Waiver of right, 8.3.1
Witnesses, 8.3, 8.3.4, 8.3.5